PENGUIN BOOKS

THE NEW PENGUIN GUIDE TO THE LAW

John Pritchard was in practice as a solicitor until 1990. Since then he has devoted himself full-time to his publishing activities, through his company Legalease.

John Pritchard is best known as editor in chief of *Legal 500*, described by *The Times* as 'the bible of the legal profession'. He is also editor in chief of *Legal Business* and *Legal Times*. In addition, he is in charge of other Legalease publications, including *Law Firms in Europe*, *Practical Lawyer*, *In-House Lawyer* and *European Corporate Lawyer*.

In 1994 John Pritchard launched *Link*, which has now grown to be the largest on-line system for lawyers outside North America. He also has, in the *International Center for Commercial Law*, one of the largest legal sites on the Internet.

THE NEW PENGUIN GUIDE
TO THE LAW

THIRD EDITION

JOHN PRITCHARD WITH HELEN GARLICK
AND RICHARD BARR, STUART BAKER,
PAUL ELMHIRST, CHRISTOPHER OSMAN,
EDITH RUDINGER, PETER WILDE,
JOHN WADHAM (AND LIBERTY)

PENGUIN BOOKS

PENGUIN BOOKS

Published by the Penguin Group
Penguin Books Ltd, 27 Wrights Lane, London W8 5TZ, England
Penguin Putnam Inc., 375 Hudson Street, New York, New York 10014, USA
Penguin Books Australia Ltd, Ringwood, Victoria, Australia
Penguin Books Canada Ltd, 10 Alcorn Avenue, Toronto, Ontario, Canada M4V 3B2
Penguin Books (NZ) Ltd, 182–190 Wairau Road, Auckland 10, New Zealand

Penguin Books Ltd, Registered Offices: Harmondsworth, Middlesex, England

First published by Penguin Books 1982
Reprinted with minor revisions 1983
Second edition 1986
Published simultaneously by Viking
Third edition published by Viking 1992
Published in Penguin Books 1993
10 9 8 7 6 5

The acknowledgements on page 1021 constitute an extension of this copyright page

Printed in England by Clays Ltd, St Ives plc

To Mary, who helped;
also to Tom, Sam, and Becky – who didn't

Contents

Contents

PART NINE   THE ENGLISH LEGAL SYSTEM   (*Richard Barr*)

APPENDICES

Acknowledgements

This is a 'thank you' page. As such, it is often skipped by the reader, but to the author it is perhaps the most important page of all. Without the help of the people mentioned below, this book would never have been completed.

My acknowledgements fall into two main categories: authors and readers. The following people have all written major sections of the book: Richard Barr (The English Legal System and Appendices); Stuart Baker (Motoring); Helen Garlick (The Family and Business); Paul Elmhirst (Death); Christopher Osman (Employment); Edith Rudinger (The Consumer); Peter Wilde (Tenants); Aileen Wong (Children and Crime); and John Wadham's team at Liberty – Simon Farrell, Tess Gill, Carl Hackman, Jane Hill, Malcolm Hurwitt, Vickie King, Andrew Nicol, Dennis Quinn, Michelle Strange, Victoria Teggin and Heather Williams (Civil Liberties). The other sections are my own.

A full list of the chapters contributed by each of these individuals is on the Contents page. Needless to say, I am extremely grateful to them for all the hard work – and expert knowledge – that they have put into the book, and especially to Helen Garlick, for her help in coordinating the team.

Then there are the readers. As author of *The New Penguin Guide to the Law*, I receive many letters from people who are unhappy with the law, or with lawyers. I am grateful to many of those correspondents for their helpful suggestions and comments. To date, *The New Penguin Guide to the Law* has sold about half a million copies, and it is important that people who buy the book should not be reluctant to write in with any comments or criticisms of the legal system. You are welcome to contact me c/o Penguin Books. If you have any grouses about the law in general, or ideas for law reform, please let me know.

As a general point, there are many other people I could thank. Perhaps one category that should be mentioned is 'clients'. Over the years, it is my clients who have taught me a lot about the law – and what is wrong with the law. Every solicitor should always remember that the law is there to serve the client, and not to serve the lawyer!

Introduction

This book cannot tell you all the law. No one knows all the law, not even the most eminent judge – and certainly not me!

The law is as huge as it is indefinable. Suffice to say that it is impossible to compress more than just a smattering of knowledge into a book of this size. All I can do is to try to extract those parts of the law that seem – to me – to be most relevant and useful to the general reader. So if you see this book as a substitute for the considered advice of a solicitor or barrister, think again.

What a guide of this sort can do is to introduce the reader to the complexities of the law, to remove some of the mysteries that shroud it, and to give an overall view of the law. I hope that information will be sufficient to enable readers to identify the legal element in a problem and to point them in the right direction towards solving that problem.

Overall, the aim has been to produce a book that concentrates on topics that directly affect private individuals. Primarily, it reflects my own experiences and practice as a solicitor in north-west London. Accordingly, topics such as housing and employment received far greater coverage than, for instance, bankruptcy, tax and other commercial matters. To a large extent, the book is one man's view of the law. However, it is important to recognize that the law is increasing in complexity every year. Indeed, the law is now far more complex and specialist than it was a decade ago. In producing this edition of *The New Penguin Guide to the Law*, I have enlisted the help of several leading experts who have contributed major sections to the book. All of us have, though, had the same aim – mainly, to produce a guide to the law that is readable, comprehensive and informative. It is by these criteria that the book should be judged.

Finally, two cautionary notes. First, the law changes quickly and any part of this book might be out of date when you read it, so do not treat what is written here as being gospel truth. Secondly, remember that 'a little knowledge can be a dangerous thing'. This book presents a condensed view of the law and it may be that the details which have been omitted are crucial in deciding the answer to your particular legal problem. If in doubt, take legal advice.

The law as described here is up-to-date to May 1992. It applies only to England and Wales, since Scotland and Northern Ireland have their own laws.

John Pritchard,   May 1992

PART ONE

THE FAMILY

Introduction

As we approach the twenty-first century, fewer households conform to what was once the family norm of two married parents, father working outside the home with mother looking after the children and home full-time. More women are in paid employment. More fathers are reversing old roles, either by choice or by necessity, to become primary carers of their children. And more children are being born outside marriage. One in four children born in 1987 was born outside marriage, most likely into a stable relationship: seven in ten non-marital births were registered by both parents living at the same address.

The law has been changing in line with the changing patterns of society. The Family Law Reform Act 1987 (effective since 1 April 1989) abolished the legal stigma of illegitimacy (although a few differences still remain in the legal treatment of children born within and outside marriage). The Children Act 1989 (which came into force on 14 October 1991) recognizes the important roles that both parents have to play in children's lives even after divorce.

It is worth noting that the law is an everchanging field and that this third edition was published in 1992.

1 Living Together

An increasing number of couples are living together without first going up the aisle. Their motives for so doing of course vary. Some do so as a form of trial marriage, intending to wed if the relationship withstands the test of intimate everyday domesticity; others make a positive long-term commitment to live and bring up children together free from the traditional marital bond. The law has thus far avoided coming to terms with the consequences of this alternative family form. Even if the couple live together for years, the law does not provide any special protection for a 'common-law' wife if the relationship later fails.

THERE'S NO SUCH THING AS A COMMON-LAW MARRIAGE

In England and Wales common-law marriages were legally abolished over 200 years ago, although the term continues to be popularly used. A woman whose common-law marriage ends is usually in a much worse position legally than her married sister on divorce. (This is not so north of the Border, where couples who live together for a long time are treated by the Scottish law as if they were married: 'Marriage by custom and repute'.)

There are three particular areas where the English common-law wife is seriously disadvantaged:

1 She cannot claim maintenance for herself (although she can of course claim maintenance for the children).
2 She has fewer rights over the family home:
   – unless she is the owner of the home (or joint owner) she can be evicted by her partner;
   – she can only exceptionally claim a share in the value of the home for herself if it is owned solely by the man. She may be able to claim a share in the home for the children, or for herself for the benefit of the children, by a claim under the Children Act 1989, but if the couple were married, she would be entitled to claim a share of the home's value in her own right.
3 Unless the man has made any provision for her in his will, she will receive nothing under the rules of intestacy and will be able to claim a share of his

estate only if she can prove she was dependent on him (a widow receives the first £75,000 of the estate and shares the remainder with her children).

On the other hand, unmarried fathers are automatically in a much weaker position than unmarried mothers *vis-à-vis* their children. Without any special agreement or court order, unmarried mothers have sole 'parental responsibility' for the child and thus the right to take decisions alone about how the child is brought up (although this does not relieve unmarried fathers of the duty to support their children financially).

The main differences in the law relating to married and unmarried couples are summarized on pages 17–19. The law's comparative non-interference for cohabitees may suit some couples, but they would be wise to consider whether they should take action to avoid some of the legal pitfalls that might otherwise catch them unawares.

THE FAMILY HOME

When the home is privately owned

The main legal and financial problems that cohabitees usually face are over ownership of the family home. If a couple are married, the law assumes that they are both entitled to a share in the value of the family home. The fact that the house or flat may be legally owned in the name of the husband only is usually irrelevant. The court will regard the home as a family asset to be divided up between husband and wife should the marriage end in divorce. Generally, the wife will receive up to half its value, plus the right to maintenance (see page 68).

But if the couple are unmarried the law does not take such a generous view, for it is primarily concerned with who is the strict legal owner of the property. Since there was no marriage, the courts will not presume that the home is family property to be divided up when the relationship ends. So, more often than not, the house or flat will go to the person whose name is on the title deeds. Thus, if the property is in the sole name of the man, it is likely that he alone will be entitled to it. By the same reasoning, if the property is in their joint names then they will probably be regarded as joint owners with both of them entitled to 50 per cent of its value.

So if the couple are unmarried the legal starting-point is to say that the house or flat should go to the person who owns it; the fact that it has been used as a family home is not important.

But this presumption is rebuttable. In other words, the person who is not on the title deeds can claim a share of the property if he or she can show that it is, in fact, jointly owned. Often, though, it will be difficult to prove this.

The sort of evidence that must be produced to show that the house is jointly owned would include:

- correspondence between the couple which supports the contention that the property was to be jointly owned even though it was to be put in the sole name of one of them;

• if the deposit for the property was provided by the person whose name is not on the title deeds;

• if the mortgage repayments were financed by the person whose name is not on the title deeds, even though the mortgage was taken out in the name of the 'owner';

• if the person whose name is not on the title deeds has done *a great deal* of work to the property and so increased its value.

If there is a dispute as to whether the house or flat is jointly owned the person whose name is not on the title deeds should take legal advice. If it seems that he or she is entitled to a share of the property, the solicitor will start proceedings under the Law of Property Act 1925, which allows the court to pronounce on the true ownership of property and give the applicant whatever percentage of the value of the property they are entitled to. These proceedings will be expensive (unless legal aid is available) and slow – probably taking about twelve months or so. In the meantime the 'owner' should be prevented from selling it. This can be done by the solicitor registering the non-owner's claim as a charge against the property and so making it virtually unsellable until the dispute has been resolved.

If the property is in the man's name: establishing a claim for the woman in her own right

The law has often been contradictory about what rights a woman has if the house is in the name of the man alone, but the 1990 case of Lloyds Bank plc v. Rosset helped clear up some of the uncertainty. The court said that there are three ways that a woman can show she has a claim on the ownership of the property:

• if there was an agreement between the couple to share;
• if there appeared to be a common intention to share;
• if the man promised her a permanent home.

The court also said that in addition to proving one of these, the woman must also show:

• that she believed she would have an interest in the property;
• that she acted to her detriment relying on that belief;
• that the legal owner knew she was acting to her detriment.

An agreement to share

The courts will declare that the woman has an interest in the property where the cohabitees clearly agreed to buy a house together but the legal title to the home was put in the man's name alone. Usually this arises where the man lied to the woman about why she could not be shown as a joint legal owner.

The man told the woman that the only reason why the property was in his name alone was that she was too young to be a legal owner. The woman carried out improvements to the property and was held to have a 25 per cent share in it. Eves v. Eves (1975)

A man told his cohabitee that her name should not go on the title deeds to avoid difficulties in her divorce proceedings. She contributed to expenses and was held to have a 50 per cent share in the property. Grant v. Edwards (1986)

A common intention to share

If the woman contributes money directly to the purchase or substantial improvement of the home (e.g. for an extension or for the cost of central heating), she will usually be held to have a share in it.

If she has not contributed hard cash, contributions by way of hard labour can give her an interest in the property, although this means more than just carrying out repairs or simple maintenance.

A woman carried out 'an unusual amount of work for a woman', wielding a sledge hammer and helping to build a bungalow. She was given a one-third share of the home. Cooke v. Head (1972)

Contributions towards furnishings, decoration or household expenses will not, however, count, even if by so helping out with the finances the man's income can be used to buy property for himself.

The man and woman lived together in a rented flat in the sole name of the man, who was a builder. He purchased a derelict building in his own name, using the building for storage – it was never habitable. The woman contributed to the outgoings of the flat. She argued that by doing so he had been freed to develop his business and so buy the building, so she should have a share of the building. Held: There was no common intention to share at the time of the purchase. The law had to be interpreted strictly and she had acquired no interest in his property. Howard v. Jones (1989)

Contributions to household expenditure by a woman reflected her natural concern with the well-being of a household and nothing more. They did not give her a share in the value of the family home. Burns v. Burns (1984)

The promise of a permanent home

The promise of a permanent home can occasionally give a woman an interest in the property.

In reliance on Mr Pascoe's promise that 'the house and everything in it are yours', Mrs Turner spent a quarter of her capital on the house, which was owned by Mr Pascoe alone. The court held that Mr Pascoe had intended to make a gift of the property and that he could not later renege on his promise. It ordered him to transfer the property to Mrs Turner. Pascoe v. Turner (1979)

But the courts look at such cases very strictly. The woman must show that the man unequivocally intended her to have the house or a share of it. So in a 1989 case a man's rather vaguer promise, 'Don't worry – I have told you I will always look after you', did not give the woman either an interest in the value of the home or even a licence to live there.

If the woman cannot cross the numerous legal hurdles to establish that she has a share in the land, all she has legally is a personal licence – permission – to live in the man's home, which he can bring to an end by giving her reasonable notice to leave. Twenty-eight days is generally regarded as the minimum period of notice that could be reasonable, and if she has children the court may extend that period to at least six months.

If the property is in the man's name: establishing a claim for the children or for the woman on behalf of the children

Since the implementation of the Children Act 1989 on 14 October 1991, the woman, if she is looking after the children, can make a claim against the man for a transfer of the home for herself for the benefit of the children or for the children direct. At the time of going to press, no case has yet come up before the courts to test this new right and it is difficult to predict how bullish the courts are going to be in interpreting the new law. The court must look at the needs and resources of both ex-partners and the child, any special needs of the child and the way in which the child was being or could have expected to be educated or trained. It is likely that the courts will consider making a transfer only where there are fairly substantial assets involved and if the man is able to rehouse himself adequately.

If the property is in joint names

Usually the proceeds of the sale will be divided fifty/fifty. If one of the parties thinks he or she is entitled to more than 50 per cent then they can apply to the court under the 1925 Act (see above).

It sometimes happens that only one of the joint owners wants to sell, whilst the other wants to keep the property. In these cases, the person who wants to sell can usually insist on a sale and, if necessary, obtain a court order against their reluctant co-owner. If the property has been a family home, then the court may occasionally decide that it should remain a family home until the youngest child reaches eighteen. Thus, a sale may be refused until that time – but note that this will apply only if the home was in joint names. If it is in one name only, then almost certainly the court will say that the other partner has no claim on it, and that it would be wrong to prevent the sale (see above).

Finally, note that the fact that both of the parties have their names on the title deeds does not *guarantee* that they will both have a share in the property. If the court decides that one of them put their name to the purchase only to help with the mortgage application (but did not, in fact, make any real financial contribution to the mortgage payments), then it may be the case that they are not entitled to a share in the property. But such cases are rare, and the general rule remains that a joint owner can expect a half-share in the property – for, usually, the court will find that there was some home-making contribution (e.g. bringing up the children) that should be taken into account, even if there was no financial contribution.

Avoiding disputes over ownership of the home

Cohabitees can avoid future arguments by clarifying in advance who owns what share of the home and what will happen about the home if the relationship ends, whether by death or by separation. This is usually done by way of a trust deed, which states clearly the proportion in which the couple own the property, whether fifty/fifty or in unequal shares. The trust deed can also cover other matters. For example:
- granting an option for one party to buy out the other's share;
- setting out the circumstances in which each party could insist on a sale or alternatively delaying a sale (e.g. until the children leave school);
- agreements as to how the cost of mortgage repayments, repairs, insurance payments and running costs will be divided;
- provisions as to whether cohabitees can assign their shares in the home to someone else.

Trust deeds settle once and for all the division of property between the couple. They are not usually open to challenge by the courts unless there are exceptional circumstances, like a cohabitee being forced to sign by fraud. The use of trust deeds is not just confined to cohabitees; they can be used by anyone wanting to purchase property together.

When the home is rented

When a marriage ends the courts can often transfer a tenancy from one spouse to another. Thus, it is usually irrelevant whose name is on the rent book or lease, for the court can simply override that and transfer the tenancy as it thinks fit (see page 90).

However, the courts do not have these powers when the relationship between an unmarried couple ends. The courts cannot simply transfer the tenancy as they think best, but must allow it to remain with the lawful tenant. Thus it is of crucial importance to see whose name is on the rent book or lease.

If one partner is the sole tenant

If one partner is the sole tenant he or she can evict the other party (after giving reasonable notice, of course). Alternatively, the tenancy can be surrendered to the landlord without being obliged to offer it to the ex-partner first.

Living Together

Only rarely can the person whose name is not on the rent book or lease claim to be a tenant. He or she would have to produce sufficient evidence to show that it was intended by the couple that they should both be tenants. Generally this is difficult to prove.

Sometimes the man is the tenant and he simply abandons the woman and children in the rented flat. Since the woman is not the tenant she has no right to stay on in the flat and so the landlord can apply to the court for an eviction order against her. (She might, however, be able to make a claim to stay on under the Children Act if there are children.) The abandoned common-law wife cannot remain in the rented home unless the landlord is prepared to agree to her staying there. The woman who is caught in this position is best advised to say nothing and just carry on paying the rent. Once the landlord has accepted her rent it will be difficult for him to deny that she is the lawful tenant, although the landlord can overcome this if he can prove that he thought the man was still living there and that the woman was merely acting as his agent in paying the rent.

If the man is the tenant of the family home and he dies, the woman can claim the tenancy as his 'survivor'. This is because the Rent Acts specifically allow a tenancy to be inherited by a 'member of the family' who was living with the deceased tenant. The courts have held that a mistress, or common-law wife, can be included as a 'member of the family' for this purpose. Similarly, if the woman is the tenant, the man can inherit the tenancy on her death (see page 312).

If the tenancy is in joint names

What happens if the tenancy is in joint names and one cohabitee wants to bring the tenancy to an end whilst the other wants to stay on in the home? The position of the second tenant depends on whether the tenancy is a *joint assured* or *secure periodic* tenancy on the one hand or any other tenancy (see also Chapter 17).

Joint assured or secure periodic tenancy. If one cohabitee of a joint assured or secure periodic tenancy serves a notice to quit on the other, that will bring the tenancy to an end with effect from the end of the notice period (Hammersmith and Fulham Borough Council v. Monk 1990). So one joint assured or secure periodic tenant can, by serving notice to quit, deprive the other of the right to occupy, and they will be forced to look for other accommodation.

This rule does not, however, apply to joint periodic tenancies under the Rent Act 1977 or to statutory tenancies. Here a notice to quit will formally bring the tenancy to an end, but because of the extra protection afforded by the law, the tenant who wants to stay on will be able to do so under a statutory tenancy which gives him or her a personal right to occupy. The law is complex and further legal advice should be sought about particular individual cases.

11

COHABITEES AND CHILDREN

If, when children are born, the parents are unmarried, then the mother has sole parental responsibility, giving her alone the right and duty to make decisions about the children's upbringing, such as what names they are given, where they will go to school, what religion they adopt and so on (see also page 121). This contrasts with married parents, who both are deemed to have parental responsibility.

Cohabiting parents who intend to live permanently together and share parental care of the children can agree to share parental responsibility. To do so they must sign a special court form, a parental responsibility agreement, available from most county courts, and then register it with the Principal Register of the Family Division (see opposite). Both parties should, however, seek legal advice, as the sharing of parental responsibility is a permanent step, effective until the child comes of age, even if the relationship does not survive that long.

Unmarried fathers can also acquire parental responsibility by successfully applying to court for a parental responsibility order or a residence order.

MAKING A WILL

Making a will is vitally important for cohabitees, as the rules of intestacy give the surviving partner no right to inherit: the estate will automatically be inherited by the deceased's family (see Rules on Intestacy, page 226).

If the surviving partner was financially dependent on the deceased, he or she may be able to make a claim against the estate (see Chapter 13), but the procedure is likely to be lengthy and costly. The Law Commission have recommended that this rule be changed to allow non-dependent cohabitees to claim. Change is long overdue but nothing yet has been done about it.

The only exception to this is an eccentric legal right called '*donatio mortis causa*' (DMC). Gifts made on the deceased's deathbed can be recognized by the law if they fulfil three requirements:

1 The gift must be made in contemplation of death.
2 The gift must be conditional on death.
3 The gifted object must be handed over in some way (e.g. by the delivery of car keys).

It is, however, far more sensible to make a will rather than rely on the deathbed bounty of a dying partner.

COHABITEES AND TAX

Sometimes the decision whether or not to marry can be influenced by whether or not a couple will have to pay more tax. Before 1 August 1988 there were tax

Parental Responsibility Agreement

Section 4 (1) (b)   The Children Act 1989

▶ Please use black ink.

▶ The making of this agreement will seriously affect the legal position of both parents.
   You should both seek legal advice before completing this form.

▶ If there is more than one child, you should fill in a separate form for each child.

—————————————— THE ▬▬ CHILDREN ▬▬ ACT ——————————————

This is a parental responsibility agreement between

| the child's mother | Name |
| | Address |

and

| the child's father | Name |
| | Address |

We agree that the father of the child named below should have parental responsibility for [him] [her] in addition to the mother.

Name	Boy / Girl	Date of birth	Date of 18th birthday

Ending of the agreement

Once a parental responsibility agreement has been made it can only end :

- by an order of the court made on application of any person who has parental responsibility for the child.
- by an order of the court made on the application of the child with leave of the court.
- when the child reaches the age of 18.

Signed (mother)		Date	
Signature of witness		Date	
Signed (father)		Date	
Signature of witness		Date	

This agreement will not take effect until this form has been filed with the Principal Registry of the Family Division. Once this form has been completed and signed please take or send it and two copies to :

> The Principal Registry of the Family Division
> Somerset House
> Strand
> London WC2R 1LP

—————————————— THE ▬▬ CHILDREN ▬▬ ACT ——————————————

advantages in living together, as opposed to marrying, the biggest one being double mortgage-interest relief. Towards the end of the 1980s tax treatment of cohabitees and married couples became increasingly similar as tax incentives for cohabitation were removed.

There are now pluses and minuses in comparing cohabitation and marriage taxwise. Below is a summary of some important tax differences, but as the whole area of tax is complex, further investigation and research will be needed to find out about how the tax laws affect individual couples.

Income tax

Each cohabitee has their own personal allowance (£3,445 if under sixty-five for the tax year 1992/3) but of course no married couple's allowance. Cohabitees are taxed separately and are separately responsible for their own tax affairs.

An unmarried parent has an additional personal allowance (£1,720 in 1992/3 – i.e. the same amount as the married couple's allowance) but an unmarried couple can only have one allowance (irrespective of how many children and which belong to whom) divided between them in the shares that they choose where both are parents.

Mortgage-interest relief

Where cohabitees purchased a home (or even just exchanged contracts) together before 1 August 1988, they are each entitled to relief on interest payments on a mortgage or loan used to buy the home (if it is their only or main residence) up to £30,000. Married couples never had this tax advantage; they always had to share the £30,000 relief. Nor does this relief apply to cohabitees who bought on or after 1 August 1988, when the law changed so that the limit applied to a residence rather than an individual borrower.

But the double tax relief can be kept only if the cohabitees put a freeze on future change: if they marry, sell the home or remortgage, the double relief will be lost.

In some circumstances the tax law provides a small (rarely usable) cushion. If they move and buy another main residence with the aid of a mortgage before selling the current home on which they are getting double tax relief, as long as they are still unmarried they can claim tax relief on both loans (and will still get the double tax relief on the old loan) for up to a year. Thereafter they will be treated like everyone else and have to share the £30,000 relief.

Capital gains tax (CGT)

Every individual, whether married or not, has an exemption allowance to set off against capital gains tax (£5,800 in the tax year 1992/3). But there are two important differences between married couples and cohabitees.

First, a gift from one spouse to another does not give rise to any CGT, but gifts from cohabitees to each other can (see example below).

A spouse who receives a gift from the other spouse will be treated as having acquired the gift at the same price which the donor paid for it and on the same date when he or she originally acquired it.

So, for example, if a husband bought a painting in 1960 for £500 and then gave it to his wife as a present in 1990 (by which time it was worth £8,000), she will not be liable for CGT when she receives the painting. If she later on sells it, she will be treated as having bought it in 1960 for £500, not having acquired it in 1990 for £8,000.

A gift to a cohabitee, however, will be treated as an immediate chargeable gain. So if the couple above were unmarried but the same circumstances applied, at the date of the gift the woman may be liable for CGT on £7,500 (although she will be able to set off her personal exemptions and relief for inflation over the period to reduce the amount of tax paid).

Secondly, a married couple have only one principal private residence exemption from CGT between them, whereas cohabitees each have their own principal private residence exemption if they each own (and usually occupy) separate homes. In practice this can be a considerable tax advantage for cohabitees.

Inheritance tax

Cohabitees are at a particular disadvantage for inheritance tax.

First, the spouse exemption (a spouse who benefits from the deceased partner's will does not have to pay any inheritance tax) does not apply. If inheritance tax is payable, the cohabitee is in no better position than anyone else.

Secondly, cohabitees (obviously) receive no exemptions for gifts made on their marriage.

COHABITATION CONTRACTS

Cohabitation contracts are by no means a guaranteed way of protecting the common-law wife's position. Historically, contracts between partners have been held to be unenforceable because they were found:

- to be contrary to public policy;
- to be for no consideration (and thus created no proper legal contract);
- to have no intention to create legal relations;
- to have tried to oust the courts' jurisdiction.

Cohabitation (and marriage) contracts are, however, popular in the United States and in Europe and pressure has been mounting for them to be accepted in this country. As yet no case has decided that cohabitation contracts are legally enforceable. Thus in law cohabitation contracts are useful for clarifying agreements between partners but they may well not be worth the paper they are written on in terms of their legal effectiveness.

See also Marriage Contracts, page 33.

MAINTENANCE

Ex-cohabitees cannot claim maintenance for themselves following a breakup, but they can claim maintenance for the children. This can often result in hardship for a woman ex-cohabitee who has spent all her time looking after the family and home and thus has limited work experience and skills to offer in a competitive job market. The law has sometimes implicitly recognized this unfairness by increasing maintenance payments to the children so that they indirectly provide a form of financial support for the woman too, but this approach has been taken only where the man is well off.

Of course, *both* parents are responsible for financially supporting the children, so claims can be made against the woman too for child support if she deserts the family.

Financial claims for the children are not just limited to income; claims can also be made for lump sums and even for transfers of property.

For claims for child maintenance and other financial relief, see page 75.

PERSONAL EFFECTS

The usual rule is that each partner keeps their own belongings (i.e. goods given to them or purchased by one or other individually). Goods bought by the couple intended by them to be jointly owned or out of joint funds should usually be divided fifty/fifty.

If an ex-cohabitee becomes bankrupt, the rule that the things required to satisfy basic domestic needs (e.g. clothes, bedding, furniture and household equipment) do not fall into the hands of the trustee in bankruptcy applies (see page 102).

HOMOSEXUAL COHABITEES

Homosexual cohabitees are dealt with in the same way by the law as their heterosexual counterparts. If male, they must both be over twenty-one (see page 133). But civil remedies for domestic violence are far more limited (see Chapter 6).

INJUNCTIONS AGAINST COHABITEES

See page 102.

A List of the Main Differences in the Legal Position of the Married and Unmarried Couple

	Married couple	*Unmarried couple*
Maintenance	Husband and wife have obligation to maintain one another during the marriage and perhaps afterwards as well.	Neither has a duty to maintain his or her partner, either when they are living together or after they have broken up.
Maintenance for children	Husband has obligation to maintain the children during the marriage and afterwards as well. He is assumed to be the father of all the children born during the marriage. After Child Support Act implemented, mother can ask Child Support Agency to assess and collect maintenance.	Before the Child Support Act comes into force, the mother must apply to court for child maintenance (there is no automatic duty on the father to pay). After, the Child Support Agency will assess and collect maintenance. But the mother must prove the father is the father.
Rights over the children	Both husband and wife have an equal say in the child's upbringing. The court can make an order for residence, contact etc. if it is in the child's best interests.	The father has no automatic rights, for the mother has sole parental responsibility, but the father can acquire parental responsibility by agreement with the mother or by court order. Only in an exceptional case will the court grant him a residence order.
Income tax	A married couple have an extra personal allowance, the married couple's allowance, which will reduce the husband's tax bill unless his income is insufficient to need it. They are taxed separately.	An unmarried couple can claim only their single person's allowances, and must always be separately assessed for tax purposes.
Capital transfer tax	Transfer of property between spouses is exempt.	Transfer between the couple may be taxable.
State pension	A married woman can earn a state pension in her own right, but if she has not made enough contributions she may well be able to claim a pension by virtue of her husband's contributions.	An unmarried woman can claim a state pension only by virtue of her own contributions; she cannot claim a pension by virtue of the man's contributions.
Other state benefits	1. Lump-sum maternity grant can be claimed on the basis of the woman's NI contributions	1. Lump-sum maternity grant and weekly maternity allowance can be claimed only on the basis

	Married couple	*Unmarried couple*
	or those of her husband. Weekly maternity allowance is only payable on the woman's own NI contributions.	of the woman's NI contributions – not on her lover's contributions.
	2. Other benefits: the married woman is eligible for widow's allowance, widowed mother's allowance and widow's pension.	2. The unmarried woman is not eligible for any of the widow's benefits.
	3. Legal aid: when one spouse applies for legal aid the finances of the other spouse will be taken into account, unless the couple are in dispute (e.g. divorce proceedings).	3. A cohabitee's finances are not taken into account when assessing financial eligibility.
Insurance	A married couple can take out insurance against each other's death.	An unmarried couple cannot take out insurance against each other's death; instead they have to insure their own lives and then legally assign the benefit of the insurance policy to their cohabitee.
Inheritance on death	1. If either makes a will that does not provide sufficiently for the other spouse (or the children) the court will alter the will.	1. If either makes a will that does not provide sufficiently for the other cohabitee (or the children) the court can alter the will.
	2. If either dies without a will, most of his/her property will go to the other spouse.	2. If either dies without making a will all his/her property will go to the family (see page 226) and not to the other cohabitee. However, it may be possible to get the court to order that part of the estate goes to the cohabitee or the children.
	3. Survivor will inherit funds in joint bank account.	3. Survivor will inherit funds in joint bank account.
Immigration	Either can usually join the spouse who is settled in UK.	Unmarried partner unlikely to be able to join partner who is settled in UK.

	Married couple	*Unmarried couple*
Right to occupy the home	Both spouses have equal rights to occupy the matrimonial home, until the marriage is ended by a decree absolute.	Only the owner of the flat/house has a right to occupy it. The other cohabitee can be evicted after due notice – unless he or she has obtained an injunction excluding the owner from the home because of, e.g., 'domestic violence' etc.
Rent/mortgage arrears	Other spouse can compel landlord/mortgagee to accept rent/mortgage payments from him or her.	Other partner cannot compel landlord/mortgagee to accept payments from him or her (unless is joint tenant or joint borrower).
Inheriting a tenancy of the family home	Will be inherited by surviving spouse (see page 312).	Will be inherited by the other partner (see page 312).
Right to a share of the family assets	On the breakup of the marriage the wife can claim a share of all the family assets even if they are in the husband's sole name (e.g. the house). Often she will be awarded one-half of the assets.	The woman can claim only what is legally hers – she cannot automatically claim a share of her cohabitee's assets (e.g. his house or car). Only if she can show that she helped pay for the property (e.g. by mortgage instalments) or perhaps if she increased its value (e.g. helped modernize it) can she claim a share of it. If the property is jointly owned it will usually be divided fifty/fifty.
Domestic violence	The wife can get her violent husband excluded from the home by applying to court. The question of whose name is on the title deeds or rent book is virtually irrelevant (see page 102).	The woman can get her violent cohabitee excluded from the home by applying to court. The question of whose name is on the title deeds or rent book whilst not a major factor, is more relevant than it would be if they were a married couple (see page 102).
Ending the relationship	A marriage can be ended only by a court order (i.e. divorce, nullity etc.). There can be no divorce in the first year of marriage.	The cohabitation arrangement can be ended without notice and without any legal formalities at any time either of the couple chooses to terminate it.

2 Change of Name

An adult can use whatever surname he or she chooses to use. It is the name by which he or she is commonly called that is the correct surname. Thus a person called Brown can simply decide to adopt the name Smith, and the change of name will be valid. The only restriction on this is that the change of name must not have a fraudulent intent (e.g. to use someone else's cheque book).

It also follows from this that a married woman need not take her husband's surname (see page 28). Her husband is free to take her name and indeed they can hyphenate the two original names if they so choose. An unmarried woman can also take her partner's name as her surname (even if he disagrees) or again they can add their surnames together and use the new hyphenated version (however pretentious).

From the law's point of view, anyone can simply change their name as and when they decide to, as long as they then use that name in everyday life.

However, other people may not be prepared to accept such an informal change of name; in particular, banks, the DSS, and other people who pay money to the person will want more formal proof of the new name. On marriage, a copy of the marriage certificate will generally be accepted as sufficient evidence, but otherwise the person may need to produce one of the three following documents.

1 *A note signed by a respected member of the community* (*e.g. solicitor, JP, doctor, clergyman*). The note should confirm that the new name is the name by which the person is commonly known; however, an unofficial document of this sort is unlikely to impress a bank or other institution (although the passport office will usually accept it).

2 *A statutory declaration.* This is an official way of formalizing the change of name. It is a sworn statement (similar to an affidavit) and a solicitor would probably charge £50 for preparing it. A typical statutory declaration is shown overleaf.

3 *A deed poll.* This is the most formal method of regularizing the change of name and, in practice, is the method most commonly used. A solicitor prepares a formal deed which is signed by the person (i.e. both the old and new names) in front of a solicitor (it must be a solicitor from a different firm

of solicitors). The deed might also need to be enrolled with the Supreme Court if the person is a member of one of the professions, so that the deed poll is kept as a permanent record of the change of name. A solicitor would probably charge £50 for preparing and stamping a deed poll.

Changing the name of children

The law does not prevent the change of name of a child unless a residence order is in force (see page 148). If a parent who has parental responsibility wants to change the child's name and the other objects, one parent should take the initiative and apply to court to resolve the dilemma by a specific issue order application (see also page 149).

It is not possible to alter the name on a birth certificate. The normal rule is that a birth certificate cannot be altered more than twelve months after registration.

How to change your name

Usually, a statutory declaration is the best method. Prepare a document along the lines of the one below, and then go to a solicitor and 'swear' it in front of him or her (you will be charged a £4.50 fee).

I . . . [*old* name, plus address and occupation] do solemnly and sincerely declare that:

1. I absolutely and entirely renounce, relinquish and abandon the use of my said former surname of . . . and assume, adopt and determine to take and use from the date hereof the surname of . . . in substitution for my former surname of . . .

2. I shall at all times hereafter in all records, deeds and other writings and in all actions and proceedings, as in all dealings and transactions and on all occasions whatsoever, use and subscribe the said name of . . . as my surname in substitution for my former surname of . . . so relinquished as aforesaid to the intent that I may hereafter be called, known or distinguished not by the former surname of . . . but by the surname of . . . only.

3. I authorize and require all persons at all times to designate, describe and address me by the adopted surname of . . .
AND I make this solemn declaration conscientiously believing the same to be true and by virtue of the provisions of the Statutory Declarations Act 1835.

Declared at . . .
this . . . day of . . . 199- . . . [signature] . . .
before me . . .
a solicitor
empowered to administer oaths

21

3 Getting Married

The law attaches little significance to engagement; it is only when the couple come to marry that the law lays down detailed requirements as to their status and age. Similarly, the legal effects of an engagement are few, whereas the legal effects of a marriage are many – ranging from the duty to cohabit to the obligation to maintain and provide for the spouse.

Engagement requires no legal formalities; no one's consent needs to be obtained and the couple do not even have to be over the age of sixteen. This is because the engagement has no legal effect and cannot be enforced by the courts.

Prior to 1970, a contract to marry (i.e. an engagement) was like any other contract, and if it was broken the rejected suitor could sue for breach of contract. But the right to sue has now been abolished and so an agreement to marry (i.e. an engagement) is no longer a legally binding contract. Further, the rejected suitor cannot even sue to recover any losses or expenses incurred in planning and preparing for the marriage. For example, the jilted groom may have booked hotel rooms, or the jilted bride may have spent money on a trousseau, dress, cake, and all the other costs of a reception; none of the expenses can be recovered from the other party unless it was specifically agreed beforehand that he or she would pay them. Similarly, if the father of the rejected bride booked a hall for the reception, he cannot sue the ex-fiancé or even demand that he pay half the booking fee.

Returning the gifts on cancellation

If the couple were sent presents before the wedding was cancelled, then generally those presents must be returned to the people who gave them. The law assumes that the gifts were given on the understanding that the couple were to be married, and so if the marriage is called off they are no longer entitled to the presents. If the people who gave the presents do not want them back, the law will usually allow the man to keep the gifts from his friends and relatives and the woman to keep the gifts from her friends and relatives.

The same applies to gifts made by the couple to each other. The law assumes that the gifts were conditional on the marriage taking place, and so should be returned if the marriage is called off. It makes no difference who is to blame for the cancellation of the marriage – the 'guilty' lover is still entitled to have his or her presents returned.

The only exception to this is the engagement ring; the woman can nearly always hold on to t̤ ͵ even if it is her fault that the marriage has been cancelled. Only in exceptional cases would a court order her to return the ring; for example, when the ɪing was a family heirloom, and the man had given it to her only on the clear understanding that if she did not become a member of his family then the ring was to be returned.

All these rules are based on a presumption that the gifts were conditional on the marriage taking place. So, if a present was not conditional on the marriage, it would not be returnable. Thus Christmas and birthday presents will not normally have to be returned.

Property bought jointly

Sometimes an engaged couple will buy a house together before their wedding day. If the wedding is cancelled what happens to the house?

If they cannot agree on what to do with the house or flat, the court will normally order that it be sold. After paying off the mortgage, and the estate agent's and solicitor's fees, the remaining money will be divided between them. The amount that each will receive will depend upon their percentage share in the house, which will partly depend upon how much each put into the purchase. Often, the money will be split fifty/fifty unless there is clear evidence for dividing it in some other way – for instance, they may have agreed on a one-third/two-thirds ownership when the property was bought.

Warning: complications can arise if the property was not bought in the couple's joint names. See page 10 for the principles that apply.

Similar rules apply to furniture and other possessions bought by the couple. If they cannot agree, either can ask the court to order the sale of the items concerned – although it is obviously best to do everything possible to avoid the expense of going to court.

MARRIAGE REQUIREMENTS

Generally, romantic love is the basis of marriage in this country, but this is a relatively recent development. In the past bride seizure, payment and parental arrangement were regarded as the normal methods for deciding on marriage partners.

To be legally valid, a marriage must be:

- voluntary
- between two single people

- who are over sixteen
- of the opposite sex
- and not closely related.

1. 'Voluntary'

Both man and woman must be acting voluntarily. Force, fear and duress will all invalidate the marriage. But it must be real duress: for instance, social pressure and the desire to please one's parents do not invalidate the marriage.

The marriage will also be invalid if one of the couple does not realize what he or she is doing (e.g. if drink or old age affects their awareness of what is happening).

Similarly, if there was a mistake as to the identity of the other partner the marriage would be invalid. But other mistakes will not invalidate it. For instance, if the man is mistaken as to the financial standing, social status or career prospects of his wife, he cannot argue that he would not otherwise have married her and so claim that the marriage is invalid. Duress and social pressure can also invalidate the marriage. This can be a particular problem with arranged marriages.

A nineteen-year-old Hindu girl was forced into an arranged marriage. Had she not agreed, her parents would have thrown her out of the house, leaving her homeless and penniless. The Court of Appeal granted a declaration that the marriage was a nullity – 'the crucial question in these cases . . . is whether the threats, pressure, or whatever it is, is such as to destroy the reality of the consent and overbear the will of the individual'. So, in many ways it was the threat of homelessness and social ostracism that were the key factors in this case, and not so much the mere parental and social pressure. Hirani (1983)

This case should not be taken as showing that all arranged marriages can be set aside, but it is clear evidence of a change of attitude by the courts in being prepared to tackle this difficult problem.

2. 'Between two single people'

Neither party can be already married. So they must both be either single, widowed or divorced. If one party is divorced, the final decree of divorce must have been obtained (the decree absolute). If either is married at the time of the ceremony the marriage will be void and the offence of bigamy will have been committed (but see Polygamy, page 26). In fact, bigamy prosecutions are relatively rare these days because the police do not prosecute if the sole purpose was to allow the couple to live respectably as man and wife. Only 20 per cent or so of bigamy cases are prosecuted. Obviously if the bigamist was acting maliciously or fraudulently then he or she would be prosecuted.

Problems arise when a married person separated from the other spouse many years ago and now wishes to remarry. To avoid the risk of a bigamy prosecution, the court should be asked to grant a decree of presumption of death and divorce, or to grant a divorce based on five years' separation (see page 49). Unless such an order is obtained there is always a risk that the second marriage will be bigamous, although there is a special defence for those who have not heard from their spouse for at least seven years and who have no reason to suppose that he or she is still alive. This defence, even if it reduces the risks of a bigamy conviction, may not be enough to save the second marriage. Almost certainly, the second, bigamous, marriage will be null and void, so the couple will be in the same position as if they had never been married.

3. 'Who are over sixteen'

Since 1929 the minimum age for marriage has been sixteen. Before then, it was fourteen for boys and twelve for girls.

If a boy or girl of under sixteen is married, the marriage will be null and void. In addition, the child will be committing a criminal offence.

A person under the age of eighteen needs to obtain parental, or other, consent to the marriage. If the consent is forged, or if the child states that he or she is over eighteen in order to make consent unnecessary, the marriage will remain valid, but the child will be committing a criminal offence. The marriage will only be invalid if the child is under sixteen.

Consents. A sixteen- or seventeen-year-old will need the signed consent of parents and anyone else with parental responsibility (see page 147), but see the table below.

Circumstances	Consent needed from
Married parents	
If the parents were married at the child's birth	Both parents
If the parents have divorced or separated	Both parents
If one of the parents has died	The surviving parent
If both parents have died	The guardian
Where the parents were not married	The mother alone (unless the father has parental responsibility, then he must give consent too)
If the mother has died	The guardian
If there is a residence order for the child	The person in whose favour the residence order was made
If the child is adopted	The adoptive parents
If the child is a ward of court	The court
If the child is in the care of the local authority	The local authority and parents with parental responsibility

If for some reason one of the parents cannot give consent (e.g. because he or she cannot be traced), then special consent will be needed; the registrar of marriages can provide details.

If the parents refuse their consent the child can apply to the court for its consent. Although the application can be to a Family Proceedings Court (a magistrates' court), a county court, or the High Court, it is usually most convenient to apply to the local Family Proceedings Court. The child should go to the court as though he or she wanted to issue an application and explain the position to the warrant officer.

4. 'Of the opposite sex'

Gay (i.e. homosexual or lesbian) marriages have no legal validity. Nor do sex-change marriages:

April Ashley was born a man. In 1960 he had undergone a sex-change operation involving removal of the testicles and most of the scrotum, and the formation of an artificial vagina. In September 1963 April Ashley married a man – who was aware of the sex change – and they lived together as man and wife. Three months later the man asked that the marriage be declared null and void because it was a marriage between two men. April Ashley disagreed, saying it was a marriage between a man and a woman. Held: It was not a valid marriage. April Ashley had been born a man and by all medical criteria he was a male, although psychologically he was trans-sexual. The sex change had not altered his biological (legal) sex and so the marriage was void. In addition, the marriage could be annulled on the grounds of non-consummation since the artificial vagina did not allow of true intercourse. Corbett (1970).

5. 'And not closely related'

Society disapproves of marriages between people from the same family. This is so even when one of the parties is adopted into the family or is now divorced out of the family. So, for example, whilst a man may marry his female cousin, he cannot marry his son's divorced wife or his brother's adopted daughter.

Polygamous marriages

No marriage that takes place in this country can be valid if one of the parties is already married. Such a marriage is void and also bigamous (see page 24). But some societies allow a man to have more than one wife and the question then arises of whether our courts will recognize all the marriages made by a polygamous foreigner or whether they will recognize only the first marriage and regard the others as bigamous. The position is complicated, but basically our courts will recognize all the marriages if:
1 The marriages complied with the laws of the country where they took place.

A Sikh marriage took place in India. The husband was abroad but was represented at the marriage ceremony by a photograph of himself. Held: This was a valid marriage in India and so it could be recognized in this country. Birang (1977)

2 The spouses must also have been capable of marrying (i.e. of age, not within the prohibited degrees etc.) according to the laws of their respective countries of domicile.

However, the law is complex and anyone in doubt should take legal advice.

'The Prohibited Degrees': When Marriage within a Family is Prohibited

A man cannot marry his:	*A woman cannot marry her*:
mother	father
daughter	son
grandmother	grandfather
granddaughter	grandson
sister	brother
mother-in-law	father-in-law
stepdaughter	stepson
stepmother	stepfather
daughter-in-law	son-in-law
grandfather's wife	grandmother's husband
wife's grandmother	husband's grandfather
wife's granddaughter	husband's grandson
grandson's wife	granddaughter's husband
aunt	uncle
niece	nephew

The formalities of marriage

The Marriage Act 1949 sets out the formalities for a valid marriage. But the Act largely repeats the law that has evolved over the centuries and so the result is a confusing muddle.

There are two basic methods of marrying: in a Church of England ceremony or in a civil ceremony.

Church of England marriages

Before the couple can be married they must comply with the formalities. There are four ways in which they can do this:

Banns. The names of the couple are read out in their parish churches on three Sundays. The marriage must then take place within three months of the last reading of the banns.

Common licence. This is a licence granted by a diocesan bishop and it is valid for three months. It will only be granted if one of the couple has lived for the preceding fifteen days in the parish where the marriage is to take place and an affidavit may be required confirming that there is nothing to prevent the marriage. Only one clear day's notice is required.

Special licence. This can only be granted by the Archbishop of Canterbury and it allows the marriage to take place anywhere and at any time. Only about 250 special licences are issued in any one year. They tend to be used for special and urgent reasons: for example, if a person who wishes to marry is too ill to leave hospital.

Superintendent registrar's certificate. Both bride and groom must give at least seven days' notice of their intention to marry to the civil registry office for the area in which they live. A certificate allowing the marriage to take place will be issued twenty-one days after notice was given.

Civil marriages

Unless the marriage is to be by Church of England ceremony, it can take place only if a superintendent registrar's certificate has been issued. There are two alternatives. The certificate can be issued 'with a licence' or 'without a licence'.

A certificate without a licence. Allows the marriage to take place twenty-one days after the notice was given to the registrars for the areas where both parties live. There is a seven-day residence requirement.

A certificate with a licence. Allows the marriage to take place one day after the notice was given. Notice need be given only to one registrar, but one of the parties must have been resident in that area for at least fifteen days beforehand.

In both instances the marriage ceremony must take place in the registrar's office, or in a church, chapel, synagogue or meeting-house appropriate to the couple's religion.

For all marriages

Before the service any necessary certificates or licences must be handed to the registering official. For a marriage to be solemnized, there must be two adult witnesses (who can be complete strangers to the couple) who will also sign their names on the Register.

THE LEGAL EFFECTS OF MARRIAGE

Getting married leads to the creation of new rights and new obligations between the couple. Amongst other things, they have a duty to maintain one another and to live together, and they impliedly agree to have sex with each other.

The legal consequences for the woman

A new name?

For a woman the most obvious change brought about by the marriage will usually be a change of name. However, there is no legal obligation on her to change her name and she can retain her maiden name if she wishes. She and her husband may also agree to hyphenate their surnames together.

If she chooses to adopt the husband's name on marriage, she is then entitled to keep her husband's name (and any title) even after he dies or after they divorce and remarry. Alternatively, she can revert to her maiden name if she prefers.

In English law, anybody can call themselves by whatever name they choose, and they can change their names as and when they wish (see page 20).

A new nationality?

No. Not automatically. Nationality is a political status of an individual and this is not affected by marriage. A British citizen who marries a foreigner can retain his or her citizenship – but may have dual citizenship (although this depends on the law of the other country involved). The UK law accepts dual citizenship but not every country does (e.g. the USA), so if a woman wants to claim US citizenship she may have to give up her British citizenship.

A new domicile?

A wife need not acquire her husband's domicile, although in practice she will often do so. Domicile should not be confused with nationality, citizenship or residence. *Domicile* is where a person has his or her permanent home or, if he or she is living abroad, where he or she intends to return to permanently. *Residence* is the place where a person happens to be living; a person can be resident in several countries at the same time but can have only one domicile.

How domicile is decided. At birth, a baby will normally acquire its father's domicile, or if the father is dead, its mother's domicile. This is called the 'domicile of origin'.

In practice it is very difficult to change that domicile until the child is sixteen, but thereafter the child can acquire a 'domicile of choice', depending on the place where he or she is now permanently resident or intends to reside permanently.

Although a wife need not acquire her husband's domicile on marriage, it will usually be the case that she will live with him and that she will plan to spend her life with him in his domicile. Thus, in practice, she will usually acquire that new domicile.

A new passport?

The newly married woman can, if she chooses, have a new passport in her married name. In practice, the bride-to-be who is planning a foreign honeymoon can obtain a passport in her married name before the wedding takes place, although she must agree to surrender it should the marriage be cancelled.

An existing passport can be altered to the woman's new name by sending the passport and the marriage certificate to the Passport Office. They will amend the passport to show her new name.

A newly married wife is not obliged to have a passport in her married name, for she can continue to use her existing passport until it expires. The new passport will then have to be in her married name – assuming, of course, that she has adopted her husband's name and has not retained her maiden name.

Another alternative is for the newly married wife to have her name included in a joint passport with her husband.

The Passport Office will accept the title 'Ms'.

A new bank account?

If a newly married woman adopts her husband's name she should ensure that her bank changes her account name.

The couple may also consider opening a joint bank account. Generally, this is a good idea but it should be realized that if the marriage breaks down it is quite likely that the money in the account will be divided equally between the couple. As a general guide it can be said that if the wife is dependent on the husband she ought to insist on a joint account; and if he is dependent on her, then he should insist on a joint account (see page 66).

A new will?

Marriage automatically revokes a will unless the will was specifically made in contemplation of that marriage. So both new spouses may have to make new wills.

The financial effects of marriage

Marriage may result in:

New tax arrangements

Not only is there an extra tax allowance for married people, but the date of the marriage may affect tax liability (see page 65).

New entitlement to DSS benefits

The wife will probably be eligible for national insurance widow's benefit and other benefits if her husband dies before her.

New inheritance rights

If a married person dies without having made a will, then most of his or her possessions will pass to the surviving spouse. If there is a will but it leaves little or nothing to the surviving spouse, then the court can intervene to award him or her a fair share of the estate (see Chapter 13).

New credit rights

A wife may be able to make her husband liable to pay some of the household bills she incurs (see page 67).

New property rights

Both husband and wife will be able to claim a share in their joint assets (see page 68).

Maintenance

Both husband and wife are liable to maintain one another (see page 68).

A new home?

When a couple marry they impliedly agree to live together; this is the 'duty to cohabit'. Married couples are obliged to live together and to give each other the benefit of their company and support; the legal term for this is 'consortium'.

But the courts will not enforce these obligations by making the parties live together or by preventing one spouse from leaving the other. The law regards either spouse as being free to leave if he or she wishes but, by doing so, that spouse will be in desertion and so may be liable to be divorced and be ordered to pay maintenance to the other. In practice, though, many women are not free to leave the marital home when they might otherwise choose to do so; their financial dependence on their husbands, and the need for a home for themselves and the children, prevent them from leaving.

Given that the couple are expected to live together, which one of them can choose where the home is to be? Obviously, the views of both husband and wife should be taken into account, but all things being equal, it is the need to be near the main breadwinner's place of work that often decides the issue. But all the circumstances must be considered, and so the health of the wife or the schooling of the children may be held as sufficient reasons to justify a wife's refusal to move home. Obviously, if both husband and wife are at work, the parties have equal say in the matter and the other circumstances may be decisive.

Sometimes the partners have to accept that, for a temporary period, their homes will be separate. But, overall, such questions are usually of academic interest only. If the couple cannot agree on where to live, it is likely that this is merely a symptom of a deeper problem in their relationship and that the argument over moving is merely a means of expressing their discontent.

A new bedfellow

Sex is part of the duty to cohabit, for by marrying the couple impliedly agree to have sexual intercourse with each other.

But, as with so many things legal, the concept of 'reasonableness' prevails and so marriage is taken as an implied consent to a reasonable amount of sex. So, excessive demands for sex or a virtual refusal to have sex will be unreasonable and may justify a petition for divorce on the grounds of 'unreasonable behaviour'. It all depends on the circumstances. For example, a refusal of sex by an invalid may be reasonable, but a refusal of sex by a healthy active person is probably unreasonable. So also will be an insistence on always using contraceptives so that the couple will never have any children.

Note also that if the marriage is never consummated (i.e. no sex), it may be annulled (see page 62).

For a Dark Ages period between 1736 and 1991, it was legally impossible for a man to rape his wife. But a House of Lords case on 23 October 1991 ended the exemption of husbands from rape and a man can no longer use marriage as a watertight defence to the charge of rape (although some cases still appear to show he might get a lesser sentence).

Finally, if the woman becomes pregnant the husband cannot stop her having an abortion to destroy the foetus.

A wife asked for an abortion and two doctors certified that continuing the pregnancy could injure her health. She had not consulted her husband, so he sought an injunction forbidding her to have the abortion. Held: No. A husband does not have a legal right to stop his wife having a legal abortion. Paton (1978)

It might be possible, though, for a husband to use his wife's insistence on an abortion as evidence of 'unreasonable behaviour' for a divorce petition.

Contractual obligations between man and wife

Marriage is a contract, but the courts will not enforce the contract between husband and wife. For instance, if the woman was persuaded to marry the man because he said he was wealthy, she cannot sue him for misrepresentation if he lied about his supposed wealth.

The courts will not interfere with a working marriage. So, if a husband arranges to meet his wife at twelve o'clock but she does not keep the appointment, he cannot hold her liable for the losses and expenses he has suffered. This is all part of the wear and tear of marriage. The courts will intervene only if the couple clearly intended a legal relationship to follow on from an agreement, such as when they are discussing a business matter.

Different considerations arise if the marriage is breaking down. If it is no longer a working marriage the courts will intervene in extreme situations. So, if the couple decided to separate and drew up a separation agreement, the courts would probably enforce it if one of the parties did not carry out his or her part of the bargain (although the court could override the terms of the agreement if it was unfair).

Marital confidences and secrets

Most married people tell one another things that they would not tell other people. If necessary, these marital confidences and secrets will be respected by the courts.

So, in a criminal trial the husband or wife of the accused cannot normally be called to give evidence for the prosecution; neither can he or she be forced to give evidence for the defence. Similarly, in a civil case, whilst the spouse can be called or subpoenaed to give evidence, the judge will excuse the spouse from answering questions if to do so would involve a breach of marital confidences.

If one of the spouses plans to publish the marital secrets the courts may grant an injunction to stop the publication.

The Duke of Argyll divorced the Duchess of Argyll because of her adultery. A year later, the Duke wrote an article for the People *in which he disclosed secrets of the Duchess's personal life and conduct, based on what she had told him when they were married. The Duchess applied for an injunction. Held: The injunction would be granted since the articles were a breach of marital confidences.* Argyll (1965)

But, the granting of an injunction is a discretionary remedy, and the court will refuse an injunction to someone who has previously been willing to publicize his private life. For instance:

John Lennon, the ex-Beatle, applied for an injunction to stop his former wife, Cynthia Lennon, from writing newspaper articles about their married life. Held: An injunction would be refused. Both John and Cynthia Lennon had previously made public – in return for payment – intimate details of their relationship. An injunction would not be appropriate. Lennon (1978)

Marriage contracts

Marriage contracts have attracted much media interest, not least because, in addition to those once bitten, they are more often entered into by stars than by the average man and woman in the street. A 1991 Law Society paper noted: 'Current interest in marriage contracts seems to be most marked amongst those who have already experienced the trauma of divorce and wish to protect themselves in the future, the very rich or those who have connections with foreign countries where the use of marriage contracts is common.'

The term *marriage contract* actually covers two different types of agreement:
• pre-nuptial agreements, made before a couple marry;

• contracts made during marriage, which can include arrangements for division of their property on separation or divorce.

The purpose behind both types is to clarify who will get what in the event of marriage breakdown (whether by separation, death or divorce), often by sidestepping or trying to override the court's powers. The formats can, however, be flexible enough to cover agreements about other areas of concern for a couple (e.g. when they want to start trying to conceive). For a suggested list of issues to be covered by a marriage contract see below.

Whether the purpose of circumventing the courts will be successful is in some doubt. Marriage contracts are by no means tried and tested, and in principle English courts are resistant to the notion that their powers can be overridden. The main case cited in support of the effectiveness of marriage contracts does not give a sure-fire answer and actually related to a marriage in Brazil.

A husband and wife had, as is usual in Brazil, entered into a marriage contract. Could the wife obtain a divorce and claim for financial relief in this country having already made a marriage contract? Held: Yes she could claim. The marriage contract would be included as one of the factors which the court would consider in accordance with section 25 of the Matrimonial Causes Act 1973. Sabbagh (1975)

So the position remains currently unclear and the law should be changed to give more certainty. Until that time, entering into a marriage contract is a gamble: it can make your intentions *vis-à-vis* each other as husband and wife clear, but whether the courts will uphold it is another matter.

What Marriage Contracts Can Cover *

The Family Law Committee of the Law Society recommend that Heads of Agreement would include:

• Ownership of income and assets acquired before the marriage and the possibility of making claims against that property whether on death or divorce.
• Ownership of income or assets acquired in contemplation of or since the marriage:
  – whether assets are to be owned as joint tenants or tenants in common and if so in what proportions;
  – whether assets below a certain value are to be excluded.
• Treatment of gifts or inheritances.
• Ownership of items of personal use: e.g. jewellery.
• Liability for tax and debts.
• Provisions relating to duration, variation, review.
• Which country's law will govern the agreement.
• Liabilities for costs and expenses in relation to drawing up the agreement and any ancillary documentation.
• Methods of resolution of any disputes arising from the document.
• Any other issues of importance to the individual couple concerned.

---

* Extracted from *Maintenance on Capital Provision on Divorce: Recommendations for Reform of the Law and Procedure made by the Family Law Committee*, May 1991.

4 Separation and Divorce

In this chapter we are concerned with marriages that are no longer working properly; for some reason the marriage has broken down and either, or both, of the parties now want to separate and perhaps put an end to the marriage.

These days the law does not look closely at the conduct of the parties when a marriage is failing. Blame will be relevant only in exceptional cases, for the courts are generally most concerned to safeguard the welfare of any children and to ensure that a dead marriage is not perpetuated as a sham.

When a marriage is in trouble, most people immediately think of divorce as the obvious legal remedy, but there are, in fact, six legal remedies that can be used (see below). With all six procedures the courts have wide powers to sort out the couple's financial affairs.

WHICH TO CHOOSE

Each of the six remedies has its uses, its advantages and disadvantages. But the basic decision is to choose between ending the marriage (usually by divorce) or simply separating and keeping the marriage legally alive. Which to choose will obviously depend on individual circumstances and individual emotions. If there is any prospect of a reconciliation then separation is the better choice, since divorce effectively terminates the marriage. If the couple want an amicable

Legal remedy	See page	Effect
1 Separation by informal agreement	36	These do not legally end the marriage – they just end the obligation to cohabit; the parties cannot remarry
2 Separation under a written deed or formal agreement	37	
	38	
3 Magistrates' court order	38	
4 Judicial separation (rare)		
5 Divorce	38	These legally end the marriage (i.e. the husband and wife are both single people again)
6 Annulment (rare)	62	

divorce, separating for a period beforehand can help reduce the bitterness and make the eventual divorce less emotionally charged.

WHEN A HUSBAND LEAVES HIS WIFE

Whichever long-term remedy the woman decides to pursue, she must ensure she immediately takes steps to protect herself in the short term.

Housing. She should check that her husband is still paying the rent or mortgage. If he is not, she should arrange to do so herself. A landlord or building society cannot refuse to accept payment from her just because the home is in his name. See page 90.

Financial. She should claim income support (or family credit) if she has little or no money. She should also consider applying for maintenance for herself and the children. If she has a joint bank account with her husband she should make sure he cannot draw out all the money – perhaps she should even draw it out before he does!

Violence. If her husband has been violent and there is danger of further violence, she should see a solicitor. It might be possible to have her husband excluded from the home (see page 102).

SEPARATION

If the marriage is in difficulty, the first step need not be divorce. A period of separation can give both parties time to consider whether an end to the marriage is really what they want. If later they do want to go ahead with the divorce, the time spent apart can often pave the way for less heated legal proceedings.

There are four ways of legally separating:

1 A simple agreement to live apart.
2 A formalized agreement to live apart, set out in a deed.
3 By magistrates' court order. This used to be called a non-cohabitation order but is now known as an exclusion order.
4 By judicial separation (relatively rare).

1. An informal separation agreement

The couple may simply decide to separate, and not reach any formal agreement about maintenance or who looks after the children. Alternatively, they may swap letters and accept those letters as binding. But the trouble is that the law might not regard the agreement as binding. First, the courts do not like to enforce contracts made between husband and wife (see page 33) and, secondly, they may have scant regard for an agreement that was made without the parties having had the benefit of legal advice. Accordingly, it is usually better to consult solicitors, obtain their advice and then have the terms of the agreement set out in a deed.

A couple married in 1954. The wife worked and managed the family finances although the house was bought with equal contributions of capital by both husband and wife, and they both contributed to the mortgage repayments. In 1973, the wife left the husband and went off with another man, taking one of the two children with her. The husband took legal advice and his solicitors drew up a document transferring the house from joint ownership to the husband. The wife did not take legal advice before she signed. In 1975 the wife applied for a share in the family assets. Held: The 1973 transfer should be overruled since it was made at a time of emotional stress. The wife should have a share in the value of the house, on the basis of its 1973 value. B (1977)

However, if the husband's solicitors had fully explained the effect of the transfer to the wife and urged her to take legal advice, it is likely that the transaction would have been allowed to stand.

2. A formal separation deed

The courts can vary and alter the terms of a formal separation deed, but they are much less likely to do so than if it was just an informal agreement. This is because a formal deed indicates an intention for the parties to be legally bound and it also shows that they took legal advice before signing the agreement. A well-thought-out and considered deed will also reduce the likelihood of future argument as to exactly what was agreed. Once there were tax advantages to be had in formalizing maintenance payments under a deed, but these have now disappeared.

The typical separation deed will contain a maintenance agreement, arrangements for the children and a mutual covenant releasing the other spouse from the marital duty to cohabit. It may also go on to divide up the family assets between the couple.

But the terms of the deed can never be totally binding. The court always has the power to alter and vary the terms if it thinks that would be just – for instance, if the husband's income had increased significantly, or if he had deliberately concealed the true size of his wealth and so 'conned' the wife into under-settling. One point to note is that a provision that the wife will accept a stated level of maintenance payment for the rest of her life will always be void.

From the wife's point of view it is important that the deed should entitle her to maintenance. It may be that at the moment she does not need maintenance from her husband but she can protect her position by inserting an obligation on the husband to pay her a nominal sum – even if it is only 5p a year. As long as a specific sum is stated she can always go to the courts and ask for it to be increased. If no sum is stated, she may find it difficult at a later date to persuade the court to order that she be paid any.

It is usually wise to specify the circumstances that will bring the agreement to an end. These could include the death of either spouse, the commencement of

divorce proceedings (in which case the court could make an order for maintenance etc.) or if the wife should permanently cohabit with another man.

If the agreement releases the spouses from their mutual duty to cohabit then
neither can later petition for divorce on the grounds of the other's desertion. If
there is no duty to cohabit there can be no desertion.

3. A magistrates' court order

A magistrates' court can order the couple to live apart. Usually this is only
done when there is a real danger of violence to the wife or children. These
exclusion, and personal protection, orders are discussed in Chapter 6 (page 102).
For maintenance orders in magistrates' courts see page 65.

4. Judicial separation

Judicial separation is a rarely used alternative to divorce proceedings. There are
generally only some 1,600 decrees each year, and of these over 90 per cent are
presented by women. Judicial separation does not end the marriage in the same
way that a divorce does. Accordingly, the parties are not free to remarry. But it
does end the parties' obligation to live together. If one of the spouses dies
intestate (i.e. without a will) the survivor will be able to claim the estate as the
surviving spouse.

To obtain a judicial separation, the petitioner has to prove one of the same
five grounds as is used to obtain a divorce (see page 41). However, there is no
need to show that the marriage has broken down irretrievably. The main
procedural difference is that there is no three-year rule and so the petitioner can
get a judicial separation when he or she would not be able to obtain a divorce.

Judicial separation is of limited use these days. It is mainly used by petitioners
who have religious scruples about divorcing, but it does not prevent the other
spouse from obtaining a divorce if he or she can – and don't forget that after
five years' separation he or she can get a divorce against the wishes of the other
spouse.

DIVORCE

The modern divorce laws

Originally, the church courts dealt with all matrimonial matters and those who
wanted a divorce had to obtain a special Act of Parliament. The Victorians
changed the law to allow a husband to obtain a divorce on the ground of his
wife's adultery; later, women were also permitted to obtain a divorce on the
ground of adultery. And that was the position until 1937. In that year, A. P.
Herbert sponsored an Act which allowed divorce if any one of several
'matrimonial offences' could be proved – such as adultery, desertion, and
cruelty. This was a radical reform and it made divorce more easily obtainable.

But its disadvantage was that it emphasized the 'matrimonial offence' and the need to find the other spouse guilty of misconduct. Thus 'conduct' became very important, for only the sinned-against could start divorce proceedings. The sinner could not initiate the divorce. The concept of the matrimonial offence as the basis of our divorce laws was removed in 1969 when Leo Abse piloted the Divorce Reform Act through Parliament, an Act which aroused bitter controversy and claims that it was a Casanova's charter.

Gone is the concept of the matrimonial offence; instead we have the overall question: 'Has the marriage broken down irretrievably?' If so (and this has to be proved by showing one of five facts, such as unreasonable behaviour) then the marriage will be ended, irrespective of who is to blame. The 'sinner' as well as the 'sinned-against' can now petition for divorce.

The modern divorce law requires the petitioner (the person asking for the divorce) to clear two hurdles before the divorce can be given:

1 Has the marriage lasted a year?
2 Has the marriage broken down irretrievably? This is shown by proving one of five sets of circumstances.

In addition, the petitioner must be resident or domiciled in this country (see page 51).

Divorce Hurdle No. 1. Has the marriage lasted a year?

No one can apply for a divorce unless they have been married for at least a year. This is an absolute rule – there are no exceptions. If a married person wants a divorce within the one-year period, all he or she can do is to leave the spouse and wait for the year to expire before filing a divorce petition. (See page 36 for separation.) In practical terms no one can obtain a divorce until about eighteen months after marriage. This is because the one-year rule prevents them starting the divorce proceedings for twelve months, and then it generally takes at least six months for the divorce to go through.

Divorce Hurdle No. 2. Has the marriage broken down irretrievably?

The court wants dead marriages to be ended gracefully. But the law insists that the marriage must be dead. The phrase used is 'that the marriage has irretrievably broken down'. If the marriage has not died – for instance, if it has just temporarily broken down – then divorce is not allowed.

Before the courts will be persuaded that a marriage has irretrievably broken down, the petitioner must first prove that one of five factors, or sets of circumstances, exists. If the petitioner cannot bring his or her case within one of these five grounds for divorce, then the court cannot say that the marriage has irretrievably broken down, and so no divorce can be granted.

In practice, once the petitioner can show that one of the five factors exists,

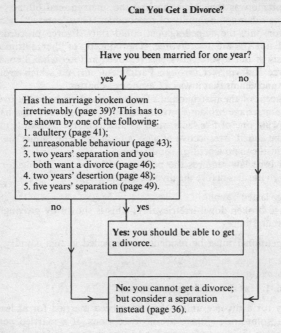

Can You Get a Divorce?

Have you been married for one year?

yes   no

Has the marriage broken down
irretrievably (page 39)? This has to
be shown by one of the following:
1. adultery (page 41);
2. unreasonable behaviour (page 43);
3. two years' separation and you
   both want a divorce (page 46);
4. two years' desertion (page 48);
5. five years' separation (page 49).

no   yes

Yes: you should be able to get
a divorce.

No: you cannot get a divorce;
but consider a separation
instead (page 36).

then the court will more or less presume that the marriage has irretrievably broken down. So, in effect, divorce is now automatically available on any one of these five grounds:

1 The other spouse has committed *adultery* and it is intolerable to live with him/her.
2 The other spouse has *behaved unreasonably*.
3 Husband and wife both want a divorce and have been *separated* (living apart) for at least two years.
4 The other spouse has been in *desertion* for at least two years.
5 Husband and wife have been *separated* (living apart) for at least five years.

Note, in particular, No. 2, 'the other spouse has behaved unreasonably' – this is a catch-all phrase that covers marital misconduct that does not come within any of the four other factors.

Generally, the courts are not very demanding in the standard of proof they require. In an undefended case the court will often give the petitioner the benefit of the doubt, even when the evidence is rather weak. The courts will not obstruct the dissolution of dead marriages. This is why it is usually unwise to defend a divorce petition; the mere fact that the couple have got to the divorce court will often be a clear indication that the marriage is not working, and both parties are likely to be advised that there is little point in defending the divorce. This does not, of course, prevent them from defending claims for maintenance, a share of the family assets, or applying for orders about the children. So, although the divorce may go through 'on the nod', there can still be a long and bitter argument about children and finances – those matters are distinct from the question of whether or not there should be a divorce. The divorce may be undefended, even though everything else is disputed.

GROUNDS FOR DIVORCE

1. The other spouse has committed adultery

More than mere adultery is needed. The law requires two things:

• that the other spouse has committed adultery;
• that the petitioner finds it intolerable to live with the other spouse, for whatever reason.

So, strictly speaking, proving adultery is not enough, for the petitioner must also convince the court that he or she finds it intolerable to live with his or her spouse. In practice, though, the courts will readily assume that if there has been adultery, the petitioner finds it intolerable to live with the other spouse.

What is adultery?

Everyone knows what adultery is: it is voluntary sex between two people of different sexes, either or both of them being married. The courts have decided that actual sexual intercourse, involving penetration, but not necessarily orgasm, is necessary for there to be adultery. Sexual familiarity, foreplay or masturbation is not enough. Since adultery must be a voluntary act, sex when drunk or when raped cannot count as adultery. Artificial insemination is not adultery – although it might be grounds for divorce based on 'unreasonable behaviour' if it took place without the consent of the other spouse.

Proving adultery

Fortunately, the courts do not require eyewitness evidence of adultery. They will look at the surrounding circumstances; usually, if the petitioner can show inclination and opportunity, then the court will assume that intercourse took place. Circumstantial evidence will usually suffice: for instance, that the couple have been seen holding hands, kissing, or in a parked car together late at night when they are supposed to be somewhere else; love letters or the contracting of venereal disease may also be sufficient evidence. Similarly, if a wife has a child when it was impossible for the husband to have been the father, that will be proof of her adultery.

41

Tests can also be used to show that the husband is not the father of his wife's child. Blood tests cannot prove who is the father, but newer and more accurate DNA tests can prove conclusively who the child's father is.

If the petitioner thinks his or her spouse is committing adultery but has no evidence, he or she may have to hire an inquiry agent to obtain evidence. He will watch the spouse and keep a record of when and where they met their lover. However, inquiry agents are expensive to hire and it would be unwise for a suspicious husband or wife to hire an agent without first taking advice from a solicitor.

Usually there will be no need for the adultery to be proved by an inquiry agent or by other circumstantial evidence. More often than not, the adulterous spouse will sign a 'confession statement', which is a simple admission setting out when and where the adultery took place and with whom. Before 14 October 1991, only rarely would the court allow the name of the other person (the 'co-respondent') to be kept secret. Since then the respondent has been able to conceal the identity of the co-respondent and can simply confess to an act of adultery taking place with an anonymous third party.

Under the old, pre-1969, divorce law, the courts were very concerned with which spouse was the 'guilty party', and in those days an admission of adultery might have seriously affected the rights of that spouse when the court came to decide custody of the children, the division of the family assets and the payment of maintenance. Now, 'guilt' is usually ignored (see page 158) and so the adulterous spouse can sign a confession statement knowing that it will probably make no difference to his or her position when the court decides about who should look after the children and how the money is to be divided.

Carrying on living with the adulterous spouse

At one time, a petitioner had to show that he or she had stopped living with his or her spouse as soon as they had learnt of the adultery. If they cohabited with him or her they would probably be held to have forgiven him or her and so lost the right to petition for divorce. That rule has now been changed so that the petitioner can live with the adulterer for up to six months without it being held against him or her. This is sometimes called the 'kiss-and-make-up rule' – so called, because it allows the couple a chance to try living together and working out their problems without prejudicing their divorce rights.

The six-month period need not be one single period, but can be the total of several short periods of cohabitation. For instance, a husband may commit adultery in January. If the wife continues living with him until March, but then moves out, and returns again in July, she has until September to decide whether to rely on the January adultery as a ground for a divorce. Once the six months is exceeded, that act of adultery cannot be used as a ground for divorce, except as evidence of the other spouse's 'unreasonable behaviour' if that is made the ground for divorce.

In October 1973 the wife obtained a decree nisi on the ground of her husband's adultery. In January 1974 they started living together again, and the wife told her solicitors not to apply for the decree nisi to be made a decree absolute. In December 1974 the relationship deteriorated and in June 1975 the wife applied for the decree nisi to be made absolute. Held: No. There had been more than six months' cohabitation and so there could be no decree absolute. Biggs (1976)

If a further act of adultery occurs, a new six-month period starts.

Is it intolerable to live with the adulterous spouse?

The law requires the petitioner to prove more than a simple act of adultery; he or she must also show that they find it intolerable to carry on living with their spouse. As explained above, the court will usually accept the act of adultery as being enough to make living together intolerable. The mere fact that the couple lived together for up to six months following the adultery cannot be used to suggest that it is not intolerable for the couple to live together.

The position of the co-respondent

Finally, what of the co-respondent – the person with whom the adultery was committed? The petitioning spouse can name the co-respondent in the divorce petition and ask that the legal costs be paid by the adulterous spouse and/or the co-respondent.

The co-respondent can defend the divorce even if the respondent does not. It sometimes happens that the court finds that the respondent did commit adultery but dismisses the case against the co-respondent for lack of evidence.

In practice, it is rare for the co-respondent to have to pay more than nominal costs. Years ago, petitioners used to be able to sue the co-respondent for having sex with the other spouse, but this is no longer possible.

2. The other spouse has behaved unreasonably

'Unreasonable behaviour' is a vague and imprecise phrase; deliberately so, for this is the 'catch-all' ground for divorce. Neither Parliament nor the courts have laid down a precise definition of 'unreasonable behaviour' because to do so might narrow the scope of this ground for divorce.

Instead, we have an overall test – is the behaviour such that this petitioner cannot reasonably be expected to carry on living with this husband or wife? So it all depends on the facts of the individual case: how serious is the misconduct and what is its effect on the petitioner?

If there is clear physical violence to the petitioner or the children that will undoubtedly be 'unreasonable behaviour'. But few cases are that straightforward – usually there is not one single incident but a succession of small, seemingly trivial events which together combine to make the behaviour unreasonable. So small incidents can together add up to unreasonable behaviour, whether the misbehaviour is aimed at the children or the petitioner.

Unreasonable behaviour is the most popular ground for divorce, followed by adultery, probably because both of these grounds allow for a divorce to be started straight away, without a waiting period. Both, however, can also lead to much greater friction. Agreeing the contents of the petition in advance with the respondent can pave the way for a less angry divorce.

What is unreasonable behaviour?

Examples are given of the sort of conduct that the courts will look at to see if there has been 'unreasonable behaviour' and, if so, whether the marriage has broken down. Remember that it is impossible to give a simple guide to behaviour that will be regarded as grounds for divorce; it always depends on the circumstances. But examples of conduct that have been held to be 'unreasonable behaviour' include:

• physical assault or ill-treatment, whether or not it causes personal injury, and whether it is aimed at the petitioner or at the children;

• verbal assault (i.e. ill-treatment of a non-physical kind) such as persistent nagging, insults, unkindness, or persistently ignoring the other spouse; threats of assault; boasting of sexual experiences with other people – whether true or not;

• sexual activity with another person which, while improper, is not adultery, such as a lesbian or homosexual relationship, bestiality or petting and kissing;

• adultery followed by over six months' cohabitation as husband and wife;

• unreasonable sexual activity, such as excessive sexual demands on the petitioner, or a complete refusal to have sex or to have sex without using contraceptives, or sodomy and other unnatural sexual activities forced on the petitioner;

• refusal to have children;

• obsessive tidiness; persistent nagging; dirty habits;

• frequent drunkenness – although much will depend upon the effect of the drunkenness; drug-taking;

• financial irresponsibility, such as failure to provide sufficient housekeeping money; failure to look after the home; irresponsible gambling; refusal to work when a reasonable job is available.

A few cases will illustrate how the courts decide whether or not there is 'unreasonable behaviour'.

Cases where the behaviour was unreasonable

A religious wife refused to allow her husband to smoke or drink, and she only allowed him to watch a strictly limited amount of TV. He was not allowed to entertain himself on Sundays, and in addition she would refuse to go to any social function with him – whatever the day of the week. Held: Unreasonable behaviour. Allen (1976)

The husband was retired and decided to renovate the house. He took up floorboards, mixed cement in the living room, and removed the lavatory door for six months. Held: Unreasonable behaviour. O'Neill (1975)

The wife suffered from fits and her physical and mental condition deteriorated as a result. She was an in-patient for eighteen months and then went home to see if her husband could cope with looking after her. He did everything for her for three weeks but became tense, nervous and irritable. The wife also threw things at the husband's mother, who lived with them. Held: Unreasonable behaviour, despite the fact that her behaviour was due to a mental condition. Thurlow (1975)

Cases where the behaviour was not unreasonable

Attitudes change. In a 1947 case a judge could say: 'It may no doubt be galling – or in some sense of the word humiliating – for the wife to find that the husband prefers the company of his men-friends, his club, his newspapers, his games, his hobbies, or indeed his own society, to association with her . . . But this may be called the reasonable wear and tear of married life.' Forty years later, these complaints would be sufficient to justify a divorce petition. Nowadays, the courts do not require serious misbehaviour.

The couple had been married for six years and had two children when the husband suddenly lost interest in his wife and was no longer sexually attracted by her. He went out a lot and became absorbed in sports. He refused to visit a marriage guidance counsellor, and eventually he left the home. Held: This was not unreasonable behaviour. (However, he was in desertion and so his wife would have been able to obtain a divorce on that ground after two years; see page 48.) Stringfellow (1976)

The husband left his wife because she did not show her affection openly. His nature was such that he required open, loving demonstration and reassurance. Held: The wife had not behaved unreasonably. Pheasant (1972)

The wife petitioned for divorce on the grounds of unreasonable behaviour because of her husband's low sex-drive. Held: Although intercourse was infrequent and unsatisfactory, despite the fact that this made the wife unhappy, this did not of itself amount to unreasonable behaviour. Dowder (1978)

The test for unreasonable behaviour

Most of the cases deciding what was and was not unreasonable behaviour came soon after the current divorce laws were introduced. The courts have latterly taken a common-sense, pragmatic approach, spelt out in this case:

The correct test for an unreasonable behaviour divorce petition was whether a right-thinking person, knowing the parties and all the circumstances, would consider it reasonable to expect the petitioner to live with the respondent. It was not necessary for the petitioner to prove that the marriage breakdown had actually been caused by the facts she included in her petition. Buffery (1989)

Proving the unreasonable behaviour

It can be desirable (although it is not necessary) to have evidence from other people to back up an allegation of unreasonable behaviour. For instance, if a wife has been assaulted by her husband and she received hospital treatment, she should obtain a certificate from the hospital confirming the date, time and nature of the treatment. Similarly, if her GP has been consulted in connection with the marital difficulties, he should write a letter confirming the attendance and his opinion as to the cause. Medical evidence showing that the marriage problems are getting on top of the petitioner can be invaluable.

Friends, neighbours and relatives may also be able to give evidence as to loss of weight, nervousness, tension, sleeplessness, depression, inability to concentrate at work, lack of interest in hobbies and also of weepiness.

The petitioner should also try to keep a record or diary of the husband's (or wife's) behaviour (i.e. noting, on the day, any way in which he abused or insulted her).

This evidence may be sufficient to prove the case, for the court will not expect to be presented with independent eyewitness evidence of assaults or other grave misbehaviour. Usually circumstantial evidence, and evidence of the effect of the misbehaviour, will be sufficient.

Carrying on living with the 'unreasonable' spouse

As with adultery, there is a six-month 'kiss-and-make-up' period for a petitioner relying on unreasonable behaviour. This means that he or she can live with the spouse, and have sexual relations, for a total of up to six months after the last act of misbehaviour. Cohabitation during this kiss-and-make-up period will not be held against him or her. However, once they have lived together for six months then the cohabitation during the kiss-and-make-up period can be taken into account by the court. So the misbehaviour can still be used as the basis of an 'unreasonable behaviour' claim – but their continued living together becomes more relevant.

3. The husband and wife both want a divorce and have been separated (living apart) for at least two years

This is the 'divorce by consent' provision that aroused such controversy when the 1969 reforms were introduced. In essence it allows a couple who have been living apart for two years to end the marriage mutually.

But if only one of them wants a divorce and the other will not consent, there can be no divorce until they have been living apart for five years (see page 49).

The main difficulties that arise concern the meaning of 'living apart', for with the housing shortage it is often unrealistic to expect one of the couple to be able to move out and obtain accommodation elsewhere. To meet this situation, the courts have held that a couple can be living in the same house and yet be living apart, if they have 'separate households'. So, although they may share the same kitchen and bathroom, they must not share the same bedroom or living-room, nor should they cook for one another, spend their evenings together or watch TV together. In other words, they should cease living as a couple and act as though they were two strangers sharing the same house.

If the couple have shared the same accommodation and yet claim that they have not been living together, they will need to produce evidence confirming the state of affairs and how they have ceased to cohabit.

When the two-year period starts

The two-year period of separation starts either from the date when the couple started living apart *or* from the date when they decided that the marriage was over – whichever is the later. Usually, of course, this will mean the date the couple started living apart, but this need not always be so.

Illustration. *A couple may be arguing and decide that a 'trial separation' would help them sort out their problems. They then separate but both have an intention of resuming cohabitation in the future. However, suppose that soon afterwards the wife decides that the marriage is dead and that there is no point in their resuming cohabitation together; in that case, the two-year period does not run from the date when they started living apart, but from the date when it was decided that the marriage was at an end.*

The effect of living together during the two-year period

As with adultery and unreasonable behaviour, there is a six-month 'kiss-and-make-up' period for the two-year separation. This allows the couple to resume cohabitation for up to six months without that ending their separation. If they decide to carry on living apart before the six months are up, then the two-year period of separation carries on as before.

Illustration. *Suppose a couple decide to separate and do so for twelve months. They then resume cohabitation for three months, live apart again for six months, and then cohabit again for two months. So far they have lived eighteen months apart and five months together. As long as they do not resume cohabitation for more than a month, they will be able to petition for divorce after a further six months of living apart.*

Changing your mind

Before the divorce is made either the husband or wife can change his or her mind and withdraw consent for the divorce. If the decree nisi has been granted, the husband or wife can still apply to the judge on financial grounds, and the judge will not make the decree absolute unless he is satisfied that:

- the petitioner has made reasonable provision for the other spouse or has promised to do so;
- or the other spouse does not need maintenance.

4. The other spouse has been in desertion for at least two years

Desertion is now rarely used as a ground for divorce. However, it was a popular ground before the 1969 reforms and it has evolved into a complex and technical subject. What follows is only an outline, and it is usually wise to take legal advice before petitioning for divorce on the ground of desertion.

There are four elements to desertion:
- living apart;
- with the intention of deserting;
- against the wishes of the other spouse;
- and without justifiable cause.

'Living apart'

This means that there must be two separate households. But it is possible for the couple to live in the same house and yet be living apart (see page 46).

'With the intention of deserting'

Desertion must be a voluntary act. So if a spouse is in prison or in hospital it will usually not be desertion.

'Against the wishes of the other spouse'

If they both agree to live apart it is 'separation', not desertion.

'Without justifiable cause'

Obviously if a wife is driven out of the family home by her husband's unreasonable behaviour, she will not be in desertion. But he will be – even though he remains in the family home. This is called 'constructive desertion' and arises where a spouse has behaved in such a way that he or she should have realized that the other spouse would be forced to leave. Constructive desertion cases are rare these days since such behaviour will usually be sufficient to justify a petition on the ground of 'unreasonable behaviour'.

Ending the desertion

The main ways of ending desertion are:
- by a separation agreement – if the couple agree to separate and draw up a

separation agreement (see page 37), then the living apart will no longer be against the wishes of one of them, so it will become separation, not desertion;
● by a judicial separation order – this ends the marital duty to cohabit and so there can no longer be desertion;
● if the deserter's offer to come home is rejected by the deserted husband or wife – if an honest and genuine offer too return is made, the deserted spouse will become the deserter if the offer is rejected.

The effect of living together again

As with the other grounds of divorce, there is a six-month 'kiss-and-make-up' period in desertion cases. This allows a deserted spouse to resume cohabiting with the other spouse and know that their living together will not end the desertion until they have cohabited for a total of six months. In effect it allows the two-year period to be interrupted for trial periods of reconciliation.

5. Husband and wife have been separated (living apart) for at least five years

This allows a blameless spouse to be divorced against his or her will. Subject only to the 'hardship' exception, explained below, there is virtually no way that the petitioner can be prevented from obtaining a divorce.

Living apart

The couple must be living in separate households throughout the five-year period. But it is possible for them to be living in the same house and yet be living in 'separate households' (see page 46).

The effect of living together during the five-year period

As with the other grounds for divorce, the six-month 'kiss-and-make-up' rule applies. So the five-year period can be interrupted by up to six months' resumption of cohabitation, but once they have lived together for more than six months, the five-year period has to start running again.

A couple separated in 1970, but the husband visited the wife regularly, spending weekends and sometimes several weekday nights with her. On three occasions he spent a whole week with her, and between January and March 1975 he lived there continuously. In September 1975 he petitioned for divorce but the wife disputed that they had been living apart for five years. Held: The couple had not been legally 'living together' since they had separated in 1970. They had been keeping separate households since then and his visits had not altered the nature of the relationship. Piper (1978)

However, this was a borderline decision.

The 'hardship' exception

There is a special defence available in separation cases. This allows the respondent (i.e. the defending spouse) to oppose the petition on the grounds that granting the divorce would cause him or her 'grave financial or other hardship, and that in all the circumstances it would be wrong (i.e. unjust) to dissolve the marriage'.

At first glance, this seems to be a defence that could be raised in many cases, especially those in which the respondent is a wife with several children who will be forced to accept a drastic reduction in her living standards. However, the courts have applied it very narrowly, for if the defence were of general application it would undermine the policy of the divorce laws – namely that dead marriages should be ended and not allowed to continue against the wishes of one of the parties.

In 1947, the husband, a Pole, had married his wife, a Sicilian, but the marriage had failed by the end of the year. The wife then went to live in Sicily with the new-born child. In 1972 the husband petitioned for divorce on the ground of five years' separation. The wife said divorce would cause her 'grave hardship' because (a) she was Roman Catholic and divorce was anathema to her, and (b) divorce would result in her and her son being socially ostracized in Sicily to such an extent that they would not be able to continue living there. Held: This was not sufficient hardship. Divorce granted. Rukat (1975)

Husband, aged sixty-seven, was divorcing wife aged sixty-three. She pleaded 'other grave hardship' because she was looking after their invalid son and a divorce would cause her great hardship. The trial judge held this was 'grave hardship' and refused the divorce. The husband appealed and, before the appeal was heard, the invalid son died. Held: The divorce would be granted. Lee (1973)

Wife opposed the divorce because she and her husband belonged to a backward Hindu caste, and divorce would result in a serious social stigma and reduce their daughter's marriage prospects. Held: The divorce would be granted. Balraj (1981)

In fact, the 'grave financial or other hardship' defence has only succeeded in a tiny number of cases. This was one of those exception:

H and W married in 1943. H was now sixty-one and W was fifty-five. The three children had left home. H had deserted some nine years ago. He was a policeman and if W survived him she would receive an index-linked pension of nearly £2,000 a year. H had no other financial resources and was too old to insure his life. So the divorce petition was refused because if it was granted W would suffer 'grave financial hardship'. Johnson (1982)

The courts have made it clear that the defence is more likely to protect women than men, and that it is intended to benefit older women, rather than those who are young and healthy and who might remarry. Even so, courts will usually expect such wives to make financial claims in the divorce proceedings to alleviate hardship rather than allow a sham of a marriage to continue.

Financial arrangements

The judge can grant a decree nisi but refuse to make it absolute until he is satisfied that adequate financial provision has been made for the other spouse. This is the same as with the two-year separation by mutual agreement but, in practice, it applies to only a few cases.

DIVORCE: DOMICILE AND RESIDENCE QUALIFICATIONS

Our courts can only grant a divorce if either husband or wife:
• has been resident in England or Wales for one year prior to filing the divorce petition;
• or is domiciled in England or Wales (i.e. England or Wales must be his or her home country). The domicile can be a domicile of choice or of origin (see page 29).

THE DEFENCES TO A DIVORCE PETITION

If you are served with a petition for divorce and you do not want to be divorced, are there any defences you can raise to stop the divorce? It will be clear from the above section on the five grounds for divorce that the only possible defences are:

1 That the facts set out in the petition are not true and so the petitioner is not entitled to a divorce (e.g. you have not behaved unreasonably or committed adultery).
2 Although the facts specified in the petition are true, you do not agree that the marriage has broken down irretrievably. It will be remembered that the five grounds for divorce are no more than the permitted ways of showing irretrievable breakdown and that, in theory, one of the grounds can exist without the marriage having broken down. But, in practice, if the petitioner says he or she regards the marriage as having irretrievably broken down, there is usually little that you can do to disprove it.
    The following was an unusual case:

The wife committed adultery and, despite telling her husband that she would end the affair, she continued to see the man involved. She then petitioned for divorce on the grounds of her husband's unreasonable behaviour. She complained that the husband was sulking because they had intercourse so rarely. The husband did not ask for a divorce. Held: The wife's petition was refused. The marital breakdown was not necessarily irretrievable. Welfare (1977)

3 There has been more than the six months' cohabitation allowed under the kiss-and-make-up rule. All the grounds for divorce allow trial reconciliation periods of up to six months without prejudicing the divorce petition (for instance, you can sleep together for up to six months after adultery; you can

cohabit for up to six months during a two-year separation period). If you want to argue that there has been more than six months' cohabitation you will have to produce supporting evidence, such as a diary or the evidence of friends.

4 If you are being divorced against your will under No. 5 (husband and wife have been separated at least five years), then you may be able to raise the special defence that the divorce will cause you 'grave financial or other hardship'. But it is virtually unknown for the defence to succeed and for all practical purposes it might just as well not exist, so limited is its application.

5 If you are being divorced under No. 3 (husband and wife both want a divorce and have been separated for at least two years) or No. 5 (husband and wife have been separated for at least five years) then you can object to the decree nisi being made absolute if the financial arrangements made for you are inadequate (see page 50). But in practice this defence is rarely used because the courts feel that financial matters are best dealt with separately, and kept distinct from the decision whether or not to grant the divorce.

These are the only defences that can be raised to a divorce petition. Generally, therefore, a well-grounded divorce petition cannot be defended. This is reflected in the fact that 99 per cent of petitions are undefended – although this does not mean that the parties are in agreement about the financial arrangements or the future of the children.

These matters – often referred to as 'ancillary relief' – are dealt with in a private hearing in the judge's chambers, and are separate from the question of whether or not there should be a divorce. The point to grasp is that a divorce can be 'undefended' even though the couple are at loggerheads about everything else. The divorce, being undefended, will be simple and straightforward even if there are then long and difficult negotiations (and court hearings) about the children and the finances.

If the divorce is defended – and only 1 per cent are – legal aid may be available, although the respondent will have to pass means and merit tests. It is not available for undefended divorces although the green-form scheme may provide some of the cost of legal advice and assistance (see page 53).

GETTING A DIVORCE

How much will it cost?

The cost will vary according to the complexity of the case. The more work involved, the more a solicitor will charge. The basic factor will be whether or not the divorce is defended by the other spouse. If it is defended then the costs will rise dramatically, but only a few divorces are in fact defended. In addition, the costs will increase if there are complicated financial disputes or if there is disagreement over the arrangements for the children.

The petitioner cannot be sure that the case will be undefended until the day of the court hearing, for either spouse can change his or her mind right up until the last moment. Usually, though, the petitioner will know when the respondent returns the divorce papers to the court, for amongst the questions is one asking whether or not it is intended to defend the case. If the answer is 'yes' the case is defended and is transferred from the county court to the High Court. If it is defended, legal advice will be necessary, and legal aid may be available to help with the cost.

How much? It all depends therefore on the extent of the disagreement between the husband and wife. In most cases, the divorce is undefended and one could think in terms of a solicitor charging between £300 and £400 (plus VAT), to which would have to be added court and swearing fees of approximately £60 in total. Generally, solicitors in the south charge more than those in the north! If there is a dispute, and so the case has to go to a trial, one must accept that the legal costs will be high. A defended divorce will probably cost each spouse over £1,500. A dispute over maintenance would probably cost anything from £800 upwards (costs have risen dramatically in recent years). Children applications probably start at about £800, but could go up to £3,000 or even more if several hearings were needed (although the involvement of 'experts', such as psychiatrists, can result in a bill running into several thousand pounds). In short, therefore, the size of the legal bill will depend upon the extent of the disagreement between the parties.

Remember that legal aid may be available, but a husband or wife on legal aid usually ends up paying their own legal fees (since the family assets will often be used towards repaying the legal-aid costs). This is a most important point that is often overlooked; see page 976 for how the rules work. The moral is that there are sound financial reasons for spouses to try to reach some sort of compromise rather than throw away their money on legal costs.

Will legal aid pay the costs?

The rules as to financial eligibility for legal aid are set out on page 967. Many middle-class wives who, when securely married, were outside the legal-aid limits may well be eligible when at loggerheads with their husbands and so deprived of their income.

Defended divorces can be very expensive. However, legal aid is available to help with all or part of the legal costs – assuming that the applicant comes within the current financial limits.

Legal aid is not available for undefended divorces, although it may be available to cover the costs of disputes over the children and/or money matters. This general denial of legal aid is, however, subject to two exceptions.

1. *Legal advice may be available under the green-form scheme*

The green-form scheme is technically different from legal aid (which covers court proceedings) in that it covers 'legal advice and assistance' – that is, everything except court proceedings. (See page 957 for how the green-form scheme works and the financial limits.)

So although a petitioner may not be entitled to full legal aid for an undefended divorce, he or she may be able to obtain legal advice and assistance under the green-form scheme, covering up to three hours of solicitor's fees (the solicitor can apply for extensions of this initial upper limit). This will usually be enough to allow the solicitor to draft the divorce petition, give general advice on the divorce and perhaps write a few letters. In short, they can do most of the work in the case, except take the actual steps in the proceedings. These must be done by the petitioner, since the green-form scheme does not cover a solicitor's costs in court proceedings, although it will cover the solicitor's fees in telling the petitioner what to do.

2. Legal aid may be granted in more complicated cases

If there are legal wrangles over the children or finances, the petitioner may be able to obtain legal aid, even though the divorce is undefended. If legal aid is granted it will cover the solicitor's fees in conducting the dispute for the petitioner – unlike the green-form scheme, which covers only advice and assistance from the solicitor.

Only exceptionally will legal aid be granted for an undefended divorce (e.g. if one of the parties does not speak English or is subnormal).

In an undefended case there is an alternative to paying a solicitor to handle the divorce. Both petitioner and respondent can act for themselves – a summary of the steps to be taken in a do-it-yourself divorce is set out on page 57.

Whilst a petitioner or respondent is entitled to act for himself or herself in a defended divorce case, this is usually unwise. The complexity of the procedures and the issues involved make it advisable to use a solicitor.

Consulting a solicitor

For how to find a solicitor, see Chapter 65. But remember that solicitors specialize, and the solicitor who handled a friend's conveyance may not be as efficient or knowledgeable when conducting a divorce. For a list of local solicitors who specialize in family law, send a stamped-addressed envelope to:

The Administrative Secretary, SFLA, PO Box 302, Keston, Kent BR2 6EZ. Tel: 0689 850227

All solicitor members have to sign a code of practice saying that they will promote a constructive and conciliatory rather than an aggressive or angry approach to resolving marriage breakdown problems.

Many people find it embarrassing to have to tell a complete stranger the full details of their marital affairs, including, perhaps, their sexual relationship. However, lawyers will treat their information as strictly confidential and will not tell anyone else about it. They will not be shocked or embarrassed by anything they may be told; in all probability, they will 'have heard it all before' and will treat the matter in as unemotional a manner as would a doctor. It is not for them to become emotionally involved in the case; they are paid to provide objective advice and cannot do that if their judgement is clouded by prejudice in favour of their client.

They will also test the strength of their client's case by asking the sort of questions that the other spouse's solicitor may, in time, ask. Some people are surprised when they are cross-examined by their own solicitor in this way; the reason is that solicitors need to find out the weaknesses in the case so that they can then take steps to strengthen them.

A client who is not happy with his or her choice of solicitor should consider changing to another firm. But this should be only a last resort.

In particular it is important not to blame the solicitor for the law. Just because a solicitor tells a client that the case is hopeless it does not follow that the solicitor is incompetent, or that he or she dislikes the client. If the law does not support the case then it will be pointless to go to another solicitor.

Preparing for the interview with the solicitor

A solicitor's time is money, so to reduce the time spent by the solicitor (and thus reduce costs) it is worthwhile preparing for the interview in advance by providing the solicitor with a summary of the facts of the case. The following is a useful checklist. Of course, not all the information may be readily accessible, but giving as much as you can helps the solicitor to concentrate on the main disputes.

Personal
- Full names and ages of both spouses.
- Telephone numbers (work and home) and addresses (including address where spouses last lived together as husband and wife).
- The date and place of the marriage.
- Both spouses' occupations.
- Details of any previous marriages and relevant court proceedings.

The Children
- Full names and dates of birth of natural children and children of the family (like stepchildren).
- Details of schools attended or other training and any special needs (e.g. if a child is disabled).
- Any agreements made about where the children will live, who will look after them and any arrangements for child support.

Finances
- Both spouses' income (if known).

- Debts both individual and joint.
- Details of the home:
  - if owned, whether in sole or joint names, its approximate value and the name and address of the mortgagee;
  - if rented, whether the tenancy is in sole or joint names and the name and address of the landlord or local authority.
- Details of bank, building society or other accounts and any savings.
- Other assets.

For the first interview it can be useful to take along (if available):
- the marriage certificate;
- copies of any previous relevant court orders;
- correspondence from solicitors;
- anything else relevant (e.g. letters from creditors).

Reconciliation

Divorce is only for dead marriages. If there is any possibility of a reconciliation then the divorce should not go through. There are numerous agencies that will give advice and help to a couple in difficulties: for instance, Relate (formerly Marriage Guidance Council), priests, doctors, therapists and, for more specialized problems, the Family Planning Association, the probation service, childcare officers etc.

Voluntary conciliation and mediation

Conciliation is often (and understandably) confused with reconciliation, but the two concepts are quite different. *Reconciliation* means couples getting back together as husband and wife. The purpose of *conciliation* is to get both parents together and assist them to work out decisions about how their children will be cared for in the future that are acceptable to both of them. Courts usually offer in-court conciliation appointments in disputes over children, but the service tends to be limited and a court setting is not an ideal forum for trying to deal with complex issues like the upbringing of children (see also page 146).

How much publicity for the divorce?

Generally, a divorce will receive no publicity; with over 150,000 divorces each year, the press are likely to be interested only if one of the parties is a public figure.

Undefended divorces are generally arranged by post so there is no court hearing. Defended cases are always heard in open court, however, and the press and public can attend if they wish. But discussion of money matters and of arrangements for the children (called 'ancillary matters') is heard in private, in what are called 'chambers', so these matters are always kept secret.

In addition, the press are subject to strict regulations as to what they can report, namely only:
- the names, addresses and occupations of those involved;
- any charges, defences and counter-charges that are supported by evidence – but not the evidence given;
- any submission on a point of law (and the court's decision);
- the court's judgement and any observations made by the judge when giving judgement and during his summing-up. So the judge can use this indirect route to allow the evidence to be reported.

Is court attendance necessary?

Since the Children Act came into force on 14 October 1991, court appearances in divorces involving children have become much less frequent. It is now possible to get a divorce where all matters are agreed without ever entering the portals of a court. But the broad rule of thumb remains that wherever there is a dispute – over a defended divorce, over the children or over finances – then you will end up in court unless the dispute is resolved by the solicitors or the parties themselves.

The divorce certificate

When the court grants a divorce it will first issue a decree nisi. The decree absolute is applied for six weeks later, and is usually a formality. It is the certificate of the decree absolute that is needed as a divorce certificate (e.g. if asked for by the tax authorities or by the local authority when applying for rehousing). Copies can be obtained either from the divorce registry or from the county court that granted the divorce.

DIY divorce: the undefended divorce petition

Two factors have made DIY divorce popular in recent years. First, legal aid is no longer available for undefended divorces and, secondly, the procedure involved has been considerably simplified.

It is not difficult to conduct your own undefended divorce case. But be sure that you are not making a false economy in saving on solicitor's fees. If there is a considerable amount of money to be argued over or if there are children involved, it is usually wiser to take legal advice than to risk making a mess of your case. Similarly, it is unwise to act for yourself if the case is defended. Defended cases are heard in the High Court, where the procedure is much more formal and legalistic than in a divorce county court, where undefended divorces are heard. If your spouse is likely to be obstructive in any way you would probably be advised to employ a solicitor.

When you start the divorce proceedings (see page 58) you may not know whether your spouse will defend the petition. It is not uncommon for the spouse to say initially that he or she will defend the petition when this is in fact no more than a bargaining tactic in the dispute over the children and/or money. Usually a compromise is worked out and the case ends up as undefended.

For instance, a wife may petition for divorce on the grounds of her husband's unreasonable behaviour. He denies this and cross-petitions (i.e. asks for a divorce from her) on the grounds of her adultery. She admits that she has committed adultery. Both sides want a divorce but are raising issues against the other in an attempt to secure more of the family assets or to improve their chances of gaining custody of the children. In the end, the husband proposes that the wife can have her divorce if she accepts only a reduced amount of the value of the matrimonial home, rather than the larger amount she might otherwise have received. If this should happen to you, consult a solicitor before agreeing to anything.

It must be appreciated that the tactics in a divorce case are these days really aimed at the negotiations over money matters and over the children. The divorce itself is usually regarded as of relatively minor importance, since it is probably a foregone conclusion that the divorce petition will succeed.

For how the courts deal with money matters and children, see Chapters 5, 7 and 8.

A summary of how to obtain your own undefended divorce

1 Obtain a certified copy of your marriage certificate (or the original if you still have it).
2 Draft the divorce papers.
   (a) Go to the local divorce county court (or legal stationers) and obtain:
      ● three copies (four if it is an adultery case and the co-respondent is named) of the standard divorce petition;
      ● if there are children, three copies of the standard Statement of Arrangements for the children (ask for form M4);
      ● a copy of the notes for guidance on filling in the forms (usually contained within the petition) and the free booklet on DIY divorce.
   (b) Fill in one copy of the Statement of Arrangements form and endeavour to agree the contents with the respondent if possible and get him/her to countersign the form. Also you may wish to try to agree the contents of the petition with the respondent too.

   If the respondent refuses to countersign the Statement of Arrangements and will not cooperate, you can still go ahead with filing the divorce papers (but it would be wise to seek legal advice).

   Use the notes for guidance and the free booklet and the books recommended below for advice on how to fill out the forms.
3 Start the divorce proceedings.
   Take or send to the divorce county court:

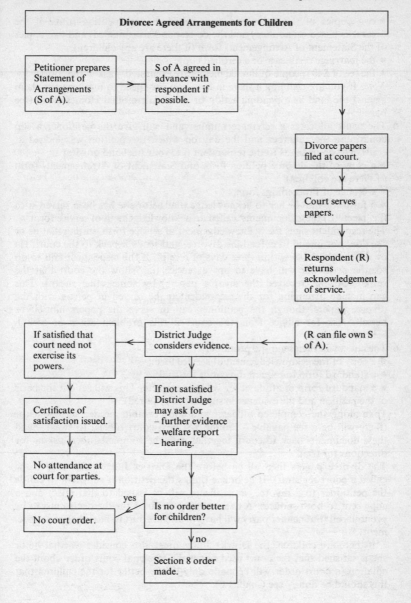

Divorce: Agreed Arrangements for Children

Petitioner prepares Statement of Arrangements (S of A). → S of A agreed in advance with respondent if possible. →

Divorce papers filed at court.

Court serves papers.

Respondent (R) returns acknowledgement of service.

(R can file own S of A). →

District Judge considers evidence. →

If satisfied that court need not exercise its powers.

Certificate of satisfaction issued.

No attendance at court for parties.

No court order.

If not satisfied District Judge may ask for
– further evidence
– welfare report
– hearing.

Is no order better for children? — yes →

no ↓

Section 8 order made.

- two copies of the completed and signed divorce petition (three if the divorce is based on adultery and the co-respondent is named) and two copies of the Statement of Arrangements form (if there are any children);
- the marriage certificate or a certified copy;
- the fee of £40 (people of limited means are exempted – ask at the court).

Note: If you are claiming a share in land you may need to register your claim against the land as a pending action or as a Matrimonial Homes claim (see page 95).

4 The court allocates a reference number and will give the petitioner a slip confirming that number and the day on which the petition was lodged at court. The court sends to the respondent (i.e. your husband or wife):
- a copy of the divorce petition form and Statement of Arrangements form (if there are children);
- a Notice of Proceedings form;
- a form for him or her to acknowledge that he or she has been served with (i.e. received) these documents, called an acknowledgement of service form.

5 The respondent signs the acknowledgement of service form, stating that he or she does not intend to defend the divorce, and sends it back to the court. He or she should do so within three days of receipt. If the respondent fails to do so, the petitioner will have to prove service (i.e. show the court that the respondent has received the divorce papers) by some other means. This can include arranging for the respondent to be served in person with the divorce papers, though the petitioner cannot serve the papers himself or herself. Ask for advice from the court if this problem arises or seek a solicitor's help.

6 The court will then send the petitioner:
- a copy of the acknowledgement of service form;
- a standard form to request directions for trial;
- a standard form of affidavit for you to complete. This will set out the basis of the petition and the evidence in support (if required).

7 Take along the completed affidavit and copy exhibits needed to a solicitor (there will be a fee payable – around £5) or a court official to swear. Send these documents back to court, together with the completed form asking for directions for trial.

8 The divorce papers then all go before the District Judge (who used to be called a court registrar). If he or she thinks the petition is sufficient to entitle the petitioner to a divorce, a certificate will be issued to that effect and a copy sent to both spouses. A date will also be fixed for the decree nisi to be pronounced (but neither party will have to attend court to hear the pronouncement).

If there are children, the District Judge must also consider whether he or she is satisfied that the court need not make a formal court order about the children (a court order will be made only if it is better for the children that this should be done – see Chapter 8).

If the District Judge is so satisfied, again a certificate will be issued to that effect and no court attendance will be required.

If the District Judge is not so satisfied, then the court can ask for:

- a welfare report;
- further evidence;
- a court hearing when the parties attend.

After that has been done, the court will again have to consider whether an order is better for the children and either make no order about the children at all or make a section 8 order (see page 147).

9 Once the decree nisi has been pronounced a copy is sent to both spouses, together with the District Judge's certificate or court order about the children.

10 Six weeks and one day after the decree nisi, the petitioner can apply for a decree absolute (the final stage of divorce.) Obtain a copy of the standard application form (ask for form M8) and send copy of the completed form to the divorce court with court fee – currently £15.

11 If the petitioner fails to do this the respondent will have to wait for an extra period of three calendar months (i.e. four and a half months since the date of the decree nisi) before making his or her own application for the decree absolute.

12 The District Judge makes the decree absolute and a certificate of decree absolute is sent to both petitioner and respondent.

And that's all there is to it! The whole process usually takes around four or five months, though it is possible to speed things up if there is a special reason (e.g. if the woman is pregnant and wants to get divorced to remarry the father of her unborn child) and if both parties cooperate.

Since the Children Act came into force in 1991, the vast majority of divorce cases, even those involving children, will be dealt with by paperwork only, under the inaptly named special procedure (there is nothing special about it at all). The odd old arrangement of 'section 41 appointments', when parents had to go in front of a judge for an average of four minutes to explain what was happening about the children, has now been scrapped. Now neither party will usually have to attend court about an undefended divorce or about agreed arrangements for the children (although they may have to if there is a problem over finances).

Further information

There are several DIY divorce books on the market. Recommended is *The Which? Guide to Divorce* (Helen Garlick, Hodder & Stoughton). Also there is a useful thirty-page booklet called *Undefended Divorce*, available from any divorce county court. In a completely straightforward case it will be a sufficient guide, as long as the parties are able to overcome the hurdles of struggling with legal forms.

ALTERNATIVES TO SEPARATION OR DIVORCE

A much less common alternative to separation or divorce is to have the marriage annulled.

ANNULMENT

Annulment is like divorce in that it ends a marriage. But, whereas divorce is granted because the marriage has now broken down irretrievably, an annulment is granted if the marriage was not valid in the first place or if it is defective in some way. It is, in one sense, as if the marriage never existed. Annulments are relatively rare these days for most eligible couples are able to obtain a divorce instead. Some couples still prefer an annulment, especially if they have religious objections to divorce (e.g. either 'spouse' could remarry in a Church of England church). There are about 1,000 applications each year – compared with some 150,000 divorce petitions. One advantage of an annulment claim is that there is no need for the marriage to have lasted a year before the proceedings can be started (cf. the rule in divorce cases, page 39). As with divorce, the court can also make orders concerning maintenance, money and the children.

The law distinguishes between two types of annulled marriages – those that are *void* and those that are *voidable*. The distinction is of little practical importance and basically amounts to the fact that (in theory) with the former there was never a marriage, whereas with the latter there was a marriage but it was defective. The children of a voidable marriage will always be legitimate; with a void marriage the children will be illegitimate only if at the time of the conception one of the parents knew that the marriage was probably invalid (which is, of course, extremely rare in practice).

The grounds for annulling a marriage

Void

1 The couple are too closely related.
2 Either was under sixteen at the time of marriage.
3 Certain marriage formalities were not followed.
4 The marriage is bigamous.
5 The couple are of the same sex.
6 Invalid polygamous marriage – because, although the marriage was valid abroad, one of the parties was domiciled here at the time of the marriage.

Voidable

7. No consummation of the marriage because one of the couple was incapable.
  Consummation is any one act of sexual intercourse involving full penetration

and a sustained erection; ejaculation is not necessary. Premarital sex does not count as consummation.*

8 Wilful refusal by the other spouse to consummate the marriage. 'Wilful refusal' means a determined refusal, persisted in over a period of time. It does not cover nervous first-night fears! Only one act of intercourse is necessary for the marriage to have been consummated, but if a spouse then refuses any further sexual advances, he or she is almost certainly guilty of 'unreasonable behaviour', justifying the other spouse in obtaining a divorce (see page 24).*

9 Lack of consent at the time of the marriage (e.g. the spouse was drunk, coerced etc.; see page 24); or 'mental disorder' as defined by the Mental Health Act.*†

10 At the time of the marriage the other spouse was suffering from communicable venereal disease.*†

11 At the time of the marriage the woman was pregnant by another man.*†

---

* The other spouse can defend the petition if he or she can show both (1) that the petitioner knew of the ground and yet led him/her into believing it would not be used against him/her and also (2) that it would be unjust to grant the decree. Generally this covers the situation where the petitioning spouse had accepted the position and treated the marriage as a proper one, but now wants an excuse to end it. Similarly, it would cover the case of a man who advertised for a housekeeper and then proposed marriage to her as a matter of convenience only. If it was clear that there was an implied no-sex agreement then nullity on the ground of wilful refusal to consummate would be refused.

† Proceedings must normally be started within three years of the marriage, otherwise the claim will not be allowed.

5 Money Matters

Married couples are not just legally united; they are also financially united. Both have an obligation to maintain the other and both can claim a share of the joint family assets if the marriage breaks down.

This chapter looks at how the law treats the finances of a married couple. For the law on the finances of an unmarried couple see Chapter 1.

TAX AND MARRIAGE

For over 180 years it was a fundamental feature of the UK tax system that the income of a wife was automatically combined with that of her husband. A husband was responsible for dealing with his wife's tax as well as his own and he could even find himself saddled with her tax bill. Wives were treated as tax nonentities.

Husbands and wives could elect for separate taxation but there were disadvantages, taxwise, in doing so unless both were earning fairly high incomes. Indeed, there were a considerable number of tax disadvantages in being married at all; continuing to cohabit or even to get divorced were sensible decisions from a tax viewpoint.

Those sexist anachronisms have finally been consigned to the past. Since 6 April 1990, wives have become fully responsible for their own tax affairs and for paying tax on their own income. Where husbands have to complete a tax return, they have to provide only details of their own income. Wives have separate tax returns to complete and sign. When corresponding with their tax office, the Inland Revenue will deal with wives in their own right and not (as so irritatingly happened in the past) send letters (or even tax refunds) to their husbands.

Husbands and wives, like everyone else, are now each entitled to their own tax-exempt single person's allowance (£3,445 in tax year 1992/3). In addition, there is the married couple's allowance (£1,720 in 1992/3). In the first instance, this is given to the husband as an extra allowance to set off against his income tax. It is possible to transfer it to the wife if the husband does not have enough income to absorb the allowance. Otherwise it is not transferable.

Tax in the year of marriage

A man will be able to claim one-twelfth of the married couple's allowance for each month or part of month he is married. Months for tax purposes run from the 6th of every month. So as long as the marriage is before 6 May, the full married couple's allowance for that year can be claimed. If the marriage is before 6 June, eleven-twelfths of the allowance can be claimed, and so on. So for the tax year 1992/3, the following approximate proportions would be claimable:

Date of marriage	Amount of allowance	Date of marriage	Amount of allowance
Before 6 May	£1,720	Before 6 November	£860
Before 6 June	£1,577	Before 6 December	£717
Before 6 July	£1,433	Before 6 January	£573
Before 6 August	£1,290	Before 6 February	£430
Before 6 September	£1,147	Before 6 March	£287
Before 6 October	£1,003	Before 6 April	£143

GIFTS BETWEEN SPOUSES

Usually it is obvious if a gift is intended. For instance, if a woman buys her husband a set of cuff-links they can be presumed to be a present.

But it is not always so straightforward. If an item is to be transferred from one spouse to the other then problems can arise. This is because the law is not satisfied with a simple statement, 'You can have my ... (e.g. car), dear.' The law demands that there should be not only an intention to hand over the item but also either a deed recording the transfer or, at the least, a physical delivery of the item from one spouse to the other. In fact, these rules apply to all gifts, whether they be to a spouse, child or friend. But with husband and wife there is more of a risk that the rules will not be complied with. Often, though, they are complied with – but more by luck than design.

For instance, if a husband decides to give his wife his car because he is buying another, it is more likely than not that they will tell the registration authority of the change of ownership, and in addition, he will obviously give her the keys to the car, so the legal requirements are met. Similarly with land, it is usual for the legal formalities to be met, because most people know that transferring land is complicated: the couple will probably instruct a solicitor to do the necessary work and so the legal formalities will be followed.

But these rules can cause hardship. Suppose a man owns valuable antique furniture which he decides to give to his wife. He tells her she can have the furniture but the gift is not recorded in writing and clearly there will be no physical transfer of the furniture; it simply stays where it is. Years later, if the husband should become bankrupt and have his assets seized, the wife would lose the furniture. She would be unable to show that it had been given to her by her husband and so it could be seized by the creditors. If the husband had known of the law he could have avoided this by making a signed deed, giving the furniture to his wife – although, obviously, it would have been invalid had it been done just to defraud his creditors.

Tax advantages under the new system

Income tax

One advantage of the new system is that wives can use their own single person's allowance to set off against investment income from savings or, for example, shares – unlike under the old rules, when they could use tax allowances only to set off against *earned* income. So if a couple have savings which earn interest, it is worthwhile considering transferring some of them to make sure that the tax allowances available to both of the couple are fully used.

Illustration. *Say the wife has no income or assets of her own, while the husband has a high income, paying higher-rate tax, and also has income-producing assets. By the husband giving some of his investments to his wife to use up fully her tax-free allowance, their combined annual tax bill could be reduced by up to £1,378 in 1992/3. The tax savings will increase in following years as the tax allowances are set higher.*

The catch is that the gift has to be free from any strings attached. Once the gift is made, the original owning spouse can have no control, influence or benefit from the assets. If both parties trust one another and intend remaining married to one another, there are considerable benefits. But if they later divorce or separate, the original owner cannot stop the other spouse from walking off with the gifted asset.

Capital gains tax

Since 6 April 1990, husband and wife are each entitled to a separate annual exemption from CGT (£5,800 in 1992/3). Transfers between spouses do not immediately attract CGT: the receiving spouse is treated as having first acquired the asset at the date when the donor spouse first acquired it. Spouses, then, can reduce CGT bills by transferring assets so that both of their CGT allowances are used to maximum advantage.

JOINT BANK ACCOUNTS

It is advisable for a couple to have a joint bank account, especially if one of the couple is dependent on the other.

If there is a joint account the court will assume that it is owned equally, unless the contrary can be proved. For instance, if one spouse made *all* the payments into the account and could prove there was no intention to share the money in the account, then he or she may be able to claim all the money in it. But the general rule is that if both husband and wife pay money into the account at various times, they will both be entitled to a half share, even if one spouse contributed more than the other.

Usually, though, if there is a dispute it is likely to be just part of a larger dispute over dividing up the family assets because the marriage has broken down. In that case, the court can make whatever order it thinks fair and the money in the joint account is likely to be dealt with as part of an overall financial settlement (for instance, the money in the joint account may go to the husband, while the wife receives a larger share in the matrimonial home).

SPOUSES' LIABILITIES FOR EACH OTHER'S DEBTS

Husbands and wives are not usually responsible for each other's individual debts. But they are jointly and severally responsible for debts from joint accounts or for joint responsibilities – like mortgage repayments or rent. They are also potentially liable for unpaid community charge (poll tax) bills and other outgoings on the home, even if those are not in their individual names.

What happens if a husband and wife separate and the husband leaves the home, pays the wife maintenance, but is worried that he will end up paying for household bills which are mounting without his having any control over them?

The old law says that it is a defence to a claim by a creditor to show that the husband did in fact pay his wife a reasonable amount of maintenance. If the bill arose simply as the result of the woman's bad management, then he should not be held liable. But he must show that the amount was sufficient to cover the expenses.

On the other hand, what happens if the man deserts the woman and fails to pay her anything and she is worried about paying for his old household debts? If she contacts the utility and telephone companies, she can ask them to read the meters as soon as possible – the date when they are read then becomes the cut-off date – and transfer the new bills into her own name. While she will be responsible for future bills, it will be up to the utility and telephone companies to chase the man for the old debts.

This applies to the community charge too. Spouses are jointly and severally liable for each other's community charge until the day that the marriage ends or the spouses stop living together. It thus makes good sense to notify the community charge registration officer of the day a spouse left home (CCROs will not initiate their own inquiries).

All debts are potential time-bombs if ignored, but the ones that require immediate action are those secured on the home, like mortgages. Mortgagees – banks or building societies – must accept payments from a spouse. Contact creditors as soon as possible rather than ignore them; they can agree reduced payments to help tide you over a crisis period.

When dealing with larger debts especially, it is important to look at the overall picture rather than rush frantically around, trying to pay off the creditors who shout loudest for payments. Many Citizens' Advice Bureaux offer a debt counselling service that can advise in greater depth about individuals' rights and responsibilities, and about planning for coping with debt problems.

MAINTENANCE PAYMENTS AND DIVISION OF THE FAMILY ASSETS WHEN THE MARRIAGE HAS COME TO AN END

There are two fundamental principles:

1 **Every wife has a right to be maintained by her husband and every husband has a right to be maintained by his wife.** This mutual obligation to maintain is one of the legal consequences of marriage and the duty to cohabit together. Even if the couple stop cohabiting, the wife (or husband) may still be able to obtain maintenance for herself and she will certainly be able to obtain maintenance for the children.

2 **When the marriage ends, the courts have a free hand in dividing up the family assets between the couple.** For instance, the house may be in the husband's name, yet the court can order that it be transferred to the wife. One of the most common misapprehensions is that when a marriage ends the husband and wife split everything fifty/fifty. This is not so. More likely the wife will be awarded maintenance and between one-third and a half of the family assets (such as the house), but she can receive the whole house if the court thinks it best.

But is a clean break possible?

Courts must now look at whether it will be possible to have a financial 'clean break' between the spouses – usually this is achieved by giving the wife the lion's share of the assets, in return for which she gives up her right to maintenance. But the courts will never order a clean break in respect of children: both parents remain liable financially for children until they are at least sixteen (and older if they continue their education).

How can you get maintenance?

If your husband/wife will voluntarily agree to pay you maintenance there will be no need to go to court. Usually, though, a court application is necessary. The procedure to be followed will depend upon whether or not you want a divorce:

● *if you do want a divorce*: once divorce proceedings have been begun you can apply to the divorce court (i.e. the divorce county court in an undefended divorce; the High Court in a defended case). The court can order maintenance even before the divorce is granted – this is called maintenance pending suit (see page 83).

• *if you don't want a divorce*: apply to the Family Proceedings Court (a magistrates' court), where the magistrates have been trained to deal with family cases; for maintenance – there is a simple, quick and cheap procedure (see page 77).

How can you get a share of the family assets?

Unless your spouse will voluntarily agree to transferring a fair share of the assets a court application will be necessary. The procedure to be followed will depend upon whether or not you want a divorce:

• *if you do want a divorce*: the divorce court can divide up the family assets and property as it thinks fit when the divorce is granted. Often the court will simply be rubber-stamping an agreement worked out beforehand by the couple and their lawyers.

• *if you don't want a divorce*: the court can divide up the family assets and order that they be sold. But the court will look only at the true ownership of the property. For instance, if the wife is not named on the title deeds she will not receive a share of the matrimonial home unless she contributed money towards its purchase. The court will not apply the one-third rule but will apply similar rules as with an unmarried couple who are in dispute over property (see page 6). Thus a wife will usually be better off if she petitions for a divorce or for judicial separation, for then the court has a wider discretion and will generally give her a larger share.

How much?

A set of guidelines has emerged over the years and all the courts apply them, although each court will vary slightly in the terms of the orders it will make. Remember that every case is unique, with its own particular facts and its own set of circumstances. So what follows can only be a guide – it does not claim to be a guarantee of what will happen in any particular case. See the warning on page 100!

For advice on how to apply to the different courts for the different orders see page 77.

There are no fixed rules, but . . .

The starting-point is to give the wife (approximately):
• one-third of the *family assets*, and
• *maintenance* so that her total income will be one-third of their combined gross incomes.

This is the so-called 'one-third' rule – but it isn't really a rule; it is just a starting-point. The courts have kept emphasizing how each case must be decided on its own individual facts, but it can be useful to start by seeing how a one-third division would work out. The figures will then have to be adjusted – either up or down – to reach the fairest result.

It is vital to realize that:

• there is no hard and fast rule which says how much each spouse is to get;

• no two cases are ever identical, so it is always impossible to be 100 per cent sure about what a court would order;

• in practice, there is rarely enough money to go around. What might have been a reasonable income for the maintenance of one household will often be totally inadequate for two households. So, usually, both husband and wife must resign themselves to a drop in their living standards;

• going to court to argue about 'who gets what' is expensive. Even a person on legal aid will probably have to put most of his/her share towards the legal costs (see page 99), so it is usually better to do everything possible to reach a compromise agreement by negotiation. The only people who benefit when a case goes to court are the lawyers!

• the new rules about payment of child support (see page 76 *et seq.*) can increase the amounts of maintenance paid to the children, so the wife gets proportionately less if there are dependent children of the family.

So, what follows is no more than a rough guide – each case has its own facts (and its own problems). See the warning on page 100!

What does the court look at?

Each case will be judged on its own merits, but there are a number of considerations which the court must take into account (set out in section 25 of the Matrimonial Causes Act 1973). So it will look at:

• the income, earning capacity, property and other financial resources of both spouses;

• both spouses' financial needs and obligations;

• the standard of living before the marriage broke down;

• both spouses' ages and the length of the marriage;

• any physical or mental disabilities;

• the contributions each has made to the welfare of the family (this includes, e.g., caring for the children);

• in some circumstances, spouses' conduct;

• the value of any benefit, like a pension, which either spouse would lose the chance of acquiring as a result of the divorce.

The approach the court takes is a pragmatic one (it would be foolish to try anything else), looking basically at each party's 'needs and resources'. In practice the wife usually receives somewhere between 25 and 35 per cent of the joint gross income for herself, and maintenance for the children (if there are any) will be added on top of that. However, no husband has ever been ordered to pay a maintenance bill of more than half of his income to his former wife and children, however great the size of the family.

Changes under the new Child Support Act

From 1993 there are new rules about how maintenance payments for children can be calculated. Instead of the old, somewhat rough-and-ready approach, which often produced inconsistencies in the amount of maintenance payments ordered to be paid, the Child Support Act sets out a formula to calculate child support payments. At the time of going to press it was expected that the new rules would result in higher maintenance payments for children, leaving less to go round for the couple themselves. Check first (with a solicitor or Citizens' Advice Bureau) whether the new rules have come into force before continuing with this section and see page 76 for more about the Child Support Act.

The aim of the court

The court will realize that it cannot hope to put the parties in the same financial position as if there had not been a divorce; there is unlikely to be enough money for that. The court will look at all the circumstances, but it places particular emphasis on the welfare of the children (making sure they have a roof over their heads if possible) and the desirability of the couple becoming financially independent.

Making an agreement with your spouse

What follows is some guidance on how the court will deal with financial disputes between ex-spouses. But that does not mean that ex-spouses have to go to court to work out a division of family money. Most – around 90 per cent – come to an agreement between themselves without ever having to go to the expense of a full court hearing – and thus save more to share between members of the family rather than lining lawyers' pockets.

If there are difficulties in negotiating with a spouse, solicitors can sometimes help not hinder, as long as the solicitors are specialists in family law (see page 54). Otherwise conciliation or mediation services are worth thinking about (see also page 153). Also see page 85 concerning out-of-court settlements. But before making an agreement, ensure that the terms are fair – this can usually only be done by checking with a solicitor.

1. MAINTENANCE

Wachtel (1973) was the case that first spelt out the one-third rule. But even then it was emphasized that it was no more than a starting-point. As Lord Denning said,

There may be cases where more than one-third is right. There are likely to be many others where less than one-third is the only practicable solution. But one-third as a flexible starting-point is in general more likely to lead to the correct final result than a starting-point of equality or one-quarter.

In *Wachtel*, both husband and wife were aged forty-six. The husband was earning £6,000 p.a. and the wife's earning capacity was £750 p.a. The only asset was the house, worth some £20,000. The wife received £1,500 p.a. maintenance:

husband's income (gross)	£6,000
add wife's income (gross)	£ 750
	£6,750
divide by 3	£2,250
deduct wife's income	£ 750
maintenance payable	£1,500

The wife also received a lump sum of £6,000 (one-third of the family assets would have been £6,666).

The calculation

The traditional starting-point is to take the combined gross (not net of tax) earnings of both spouses. National insurance and some other outgoings (but not tax) are deducted. The court then sees how much maintenance the wife would need to give her one-third of that total figure. For instance, at its simplest, this might be:

husband's earnings	£14,000
wife's earnings	£ 4,000
total gross earnings	£18,000
one third is	£ 6,000
deduct wife's earnings	£ 4,000
maintenance is therefore	£ 2,000

But this is no more than a starting-point. The next stage is to see how this would affect each of the parties. So the court might then work out the net income of both husband and wife (after tax) if such a one-third order was made; the total household budgets would therefore be calculated (in a fairly rough-and-ready way). The earnings of any new boyfriend or girlfriend might be taken into account; tax, NI, mortgage or rent payments, heating, gas, phone, electricity, HP payments, etc. would all be deducted. At the end of this one could see whether both spouses could afford to live on their respective incomes – and how much, if anything, would be left at the end of the week. If there was a wide disparity (e.g. the wife having £50 left to save at the end of each week and the husband having only £15) then the court would probably juggle the figures and partly redress the balance (e.g. by reducing the wife's maintenance by £10 per week, so that she would be left with £40 per week and the husband with £25).

In short, it is a case of juggling the figures to make the best of a bad job. Summarized, it is a two-step procedure:

1 Try to give the wife one-third of the combined gross incomes.
2 See how this would work in practice, after allowing for living expenses. Would the outcome be roughly fair? If not, then try adjusting the figures to see if a fairer outcome can be arranged.

When the wife earns more

Sometimes the wife will earn a wage that is more than one-third of the combined incomes. In such a case the one-third approach may be varied so that the wife still receives some maintenance – but not much.

Alternatively, the court may decide that the wife should not receive any maintenance – or just give her maintenance for a short period. This is because the modern trend is to end the financial interdependence of the couple (so that there is a 'clean break', enabling them to start again). Thus, if the wife can be financially independent (or could be working), then she may well be denied maintenance.

When there isn't enough money

Often the courts cannot apply the one-third rule because the husband's income cannot stretch to supporting two households. In such a case, all the court can do is to order the husband to pay as much as it thinks he can afford.

But the court will not order the husband to pay so much that he will end up with less than the current social-security subsistence levels. As an illustration, income support rates in 1992 were (approximately): couple over eighteen, £66.60; single householder over twenty-five, £42.45; dependent child (aged eleven to fifteen), £21.40; dependent child (under eleven), £14.55. (To this would be added normally full rent via housing benefit.)

The relevance of conduct

If the wife has been adulterous, can she still expect to receive one-third of the family assets and combined income? The answer is basically 'yes'. The same applies to other types of misconduct, such as cruelty, for the court is only supposed to take it into account if it is 'gross and obvious'. This is a hopelessly vague phrase but in practical terms it generally means that the courts will not ignore bad behaviour if it would be really unfair to do so. So, in a case where a husband attacked his wife with an axe, severely disfiguring her, that conduct was taken into account in her claims for financial relief. That was an extreme example: in practice the courts tend to overlook spousal behaviour towards each other.

Short marriages

If the marriage is short-lived the wife may not be entitled to anything. For instance:

A wife deserted the husband after a year of marriage. They were both in their twenties and the wife had a steady job as a nurse. A magistrates' court ordered the husband to pay her £8 p.w. He appealed. Held: When the marriage is short and the parties are young and capable of earning a living, only a nominal order should be made. She was entitled to 10p p.w. The judge said, 'In these days of women's lib, there is no reason why a wife whose marriage has not lasted long, and has no child, should have a bread ticket for life.' Graves (1973)

However, if the marriage lasts a few years, the wife will almost certainly be entitled to a third, although, in one case, a four-year marriage was regarded as 'short' (and so the wife got no share of the husband's assets). But there were no children in that case and it is best regarded as very much an exceptional decision. This is more typical:

H and W married when W was twenty-four and H was twenty-one. They parted two years later, there being no children. Both had jobs but he earned more than her (so he was left with about £25 p.w. after expenses, and she had only £5 p.w.). Held: She was only entitled to nominal maintenance (i.e. £1 a year). She should not receive normal maintenance despite the fact that H was much better off than she was. Frisby (1984)

If the husband drives the wife out she is more likely to receive one-third (but – as always – remember that one-third is only a rough-and-ready guide). Once there is a child of the marriage, the courts tend to pay little attention to the length of the marriage.

Clean breaks

Since 1984 the courts have had the power to impose a clean break financially, i.e. ending the wife's right to maintenance even if she adamantly opposes such a step (beforehand the wife always had to consent to a clean break order). The courts now potentially have the power to order a clean break whenever an application comes up before them – this can include a later application for a variation of maintenance payments. They will make a clean break order where to do otherwise would cause undue hardship to the husband.

The husband and wife divorced in 1971 and he was ordered to pay her periodical payments. She suffered from schizophrenia and was dependent on state benefits. He was a self-employed artist, had remarried and had two sons. His former wife made four applications for an increase in maintenance. He argued he could not even afford to pay the current order of £60 per month and that in any event the ex-wife would not be affected by an increase in the order as the maintenance was deducted pound for pound from her welfare benefits. Held: The courts had to bear in mind the policies both of not casting the burden of maintaining a spouse on the state and of achieving a clean break between spouses where it would not cause undue hardship. The husband was not devious but a genuine struggler. It was not right to continue to force him to pay so a clean break would be imposed. Ashley (1988)

The courts will also look at whether imposing a clean break order will cause undue hardship to the wife. Wherever there has been a short marriage with no children and the parties are still young and able to look after themselves financially, a clean break is probable. In other cases, if the husband wants a clean break from the wife he will have to compensate her properly for giving up her right to maintenance.

The husband was a partner in a successful decorating business and the wife was a director. When the marriage broke up, the wife was ordered to be given the house and contents and maintenance of £1,800 p.a. He then sold the business for £1.8 million. The wife applied for an increase in maintenance: the husband asked for maintenance to be stopped either immediately or at some future date on payment of £40,000. Held: The proper sum for maintenance for the wife was £16,000 p.a. She could not adjust without undue hardship to termination of the payments and if the husband wanted a clean break he had to provide her with a sum sufficient to give her a comparable income to the right amount of maintenance. £40,000 was inadequate. Boylan (1988)

Clean breaks are more often ordered where the husband and wife are richer (or poorer) than average. In the case of the average family with one main asset, the home, often there is not enough cash to buy out the wife's right to maintenance and there is no other option but for the husband to pay the wife maintenance until the children have left school or until she is able to earn a decent income in her own right. Once the Child Support Act is in force (see page 117) husbands may also be ordered to pay more maintenance for the children, so fewer may be able to afford a clean break.

Note: clean breaks are limited to maintenance for a wife; courts will never order a clean break in respect of maintenance payments to children.

The children's maintenance

In any divorce, the court's overriding concern will be with the welfare of the children. So, proper maintenance for the children will take precedence over the financial claims of the parents. The court will want to do what is best for the children. For example, it may allow the wife to continue living in the home because she will be looking after the children – and their need for a home will take precedence over the father's desire to realize his share of the property's value).

There are no longer any tax advantages in making maintenance payments directly to the children. See page 87, Tax on Maintenance Payments.

How much maintenance the wife receives for the children will depend on the financial circumstances. As a guide, many practising solicitors take the current income support allowance for children as a starting-point. Others take the amounts fixed every year by the National Foster Care Association for the cost of bringing up foster children (see examples on page 76). It has been calculated that, on average, the maintenance for each child is $7\frac{1}{2}$ per cent of the father's gross income, but obviously such an arithmetical calculation is no more than a rough guide to the likely figures.

DSS Income Support Rates for Dependent Children (1992)	
Aged under 11 years	£14.55
11–15	£21.40
16–17	£25.55
18	£33.60

Examples of National Foster Care Association's Minimum Fostering Allowances (April 1992)		
	Outside London	*London*
Aged 0–4 years	£47.46	£55.79
16–18	£94.99	£111.72

The NFCA publishes annually uprated recommended minimum fostering allowances. Their publication, *Foster Care Finance*, is available from Francis House, Francis Street, London SW1P 1DE, Tel: 071-828 6266.

A new formula for children's maintenance

The confusion about how much absent parents should pay for child support is soon to come to an end. In 1991 the government passed a new law, the Child Support Act, which makes it the responsibility of a new body, the Child Support Agency – not the courts – to calculate amounts of maintenance. The Child Support Agency will also collect and enforce child support payments from an absent parent.

The Act sets out a formula to calculate the amount of child support for each child, based on its age and the father's income and other financial responsibilities (see page 117).

The DSS are asking the courts to apply the new formula from early summer 1992 if they make an application for maintenance against a liable relative (this applies only if the caring parent is in receipt of welfare benefits). The new Child Support Agency itself will not be up and running until April 1993.

The effect of remarriage on maintenance payments

A wife will lose her right to maintenance payments as soon as she remarries. However, her former husband will still be liable to pay maintenance to his children; that liability will be unaffected by the mother's remarriage.

If the ex-wife decides to cohabit with another man, but not marry him, she may still forfeit her maintenance. The court always has the power to vary the amount of maintenance she should receive. However, it would be up to the husband to apply to the court to reduce the maintenance (see page 79). Mere sexual liaisons will not affect the wife's right to maintenance.

Property orders are not affected by a remarriage. So if a wife was given a third of the matrimonial home and then remarried, the husband could not ask the court to reverse its previous decision. So a wife who is negotiating financial arrangements with her husband should ask for a high property settlement, or lump sum, and a low maintenance payment, if she plans to remarry afterwards.

The man's remarriage does not bring his maintenance obligations to an end. However, his new commitments may be a ground for his asking that the amount of the maintenance payments be reduced.

HOW TO APPLY FOR MAINTENANCE

A wife or husband can apply for a maintenance order whether or not divorce proceedings have been started. If divorce proceedings have begun, the application is made to the divorce court (i.e. the divorce county court or the High Court). If divorce proceedings have not begun, the application is made to the local magistrates' court, or to the divorce county court.

Both the divorce courts and the magistrates' courts have wide powers that allow them to order one spouse to pay maintenance to the other, although in practice it will nearly always be the husband who is ordered to pay maintenance to the wife. In addition, the court can order maintenance to cover the needs of the children.

The principles used in the different courts are the same, although there are differences in the way in which the application to the court is made.

Although the different courts have similar powers to order maintenance payments, they have different powers when it comes to dividing up the family assets and property, such as the home and possessions. Basically, the magistrates' courts cannot make these orders, for it is only the divorce court that has these powers. So, if a wife (or husband) wants the court to divide up the family property in addition to ordering maintenance, then divorce or judicial separation proceedings must be begun.

Most maintenance applications are made by wives against husbands. However, it is possible for a man to apply for maintenance from his wife – for instance, if he is unable to work, or if the wife is wealthy, or if he gave up his job or home by marrying her, or if he is looking after the children.

Applying for maintenance in the magistrates' court

It is quite easy to apply for a maintenance order in the magistrates' court without the help of a solicitor. Only if the sums involved are large, or if there are any particular difficulties, is a solicitor advisable.

To start the proceedings the wife goes to the local magistrates' court; this can be any magistrates' court in the county where either her husband or she lives. Her application will be dealt with by the Family Proceedings Panel of the magistrates' court which deals with family and care matters only (and not criminal cases). If she is embarrassed about applying in a court near her home she can go to another court in the same county, although the proceedings could be transferred to her home town if that would be more convenient to everyone else. The wife should try to be at the court by 9.45 a.m.

At the court she should ask for the warrant officer and tell him that she wishes to apply for a maintenance order – and any other order she may be seeking, such as an exclusion order (see page 102). The wife will then have to fill in a form, which is her formal complaint. She then appears before a magistrate, who will probably ask her a few questions before he issues a summons against the husband. The summons is the court's order telling him to appear at the court on a particular day to defend the maintenance claim. The issuing of the summons does not mean that the wife has been, or will be, awarded maintenance; it just signifies the start of the legal proceedings. The court staff will arrange for the summons to be served on the husband.

It will probably be a week or so before the case is heard. In the meantime, the wife can apply to the DSS for income support.

Both the wife and her husband will have to attend the court hearing. Maintenance applications are 'domestic proceedings' and must, therefore, be heard in private. There must be either two or three magistrates, picked from the Family Proceedings Panel, hearing the application, and if possible they should include members of both sexes.

Both the wife and her husband will be asked about their family finances, where they are both living, the age of any children, their income, and so on. It is helpful if they have documentary evidence to put before the magistrates so there can be no dispute as to their financial commitments – for instance, wage slips, bank statements, mortgage agreement, rent books, savings books and hire-purchase agreements.

Having heard the evidence in a fairly informal manner, the magistrates will decide whether the wife should receive maintenance, and if so, how much. They will also decide whether maintenance should be paid in respect of the children (before the Child Support Act comes fully into force).

The court will order maintenance only if it is satisfied that the husband (or, exceptionally, the wife) has either

• failed to provide the wife, or the children, with a reasonable amount of maintenance, *or*

• behaved in such a way that the wife cannot reasonably be expected to live with him, *or*

• deserted the wife.

The amount of maintenance will depend on the facts of the individual case. Magistrates' courts are generally more cautious than divorce courts. A survey by the DSS in 1990 showed that whereas the average weekly maintenance orders for children were £20 in the county courts, they were £15 in the magistrates' court. Magistrates' courts can also be more influenced by the good or bad conduct of the parties than are the divorce courts.

It should not be forgotten that the magistrates are unlikely to order the husband to pay a sum of maintenance that will leave him (and his new family, if he has one) on less than income support subsistence levels. In practice, the magistrates will probably make sure that the husband is left with:

● one-quarter of his net (i.e. take-home) pay, *plus*
● his rent, *plus*
● income support rate sums for himself (and for his new family, if any).

So the maintenance for the ex-wife will be limited to whatever figure would ensure that he is not left with less than this amount. If this means that she is left with insufficient maintenance, then she will have to claim income support.

If the ex-wife is on income support, she can ask the court to 'make the maintenance order over to the DSS'. (See page 81 for more details.)

Changing the amount of the order

The ex-wife can go back to the court at any time if she wants the amount increased, either for herself or for the children. Similarly, the husband can go back to the court if he wants it reduced. But the court will only increase or decrease the amount if good grounds for doing so can be shown – for instance, if the husband has had a wage rise or become unemployed. This can cover the situation where the ex-wife has been prevented from working because she has had another child by another man:

Following a consent order whereby the wife and child received periodical payments, the wife had another child by another man. She applied to increase the amount. Held: The birth of the second child affected the wife's earning capacity. An increase in maintenance was ordered. Fisher (1989)

And also the situation where the ex-husband has additional financial commitments in the form of a new family:

The husband was ordered to pay £12 maintenance to the wife and their three children. He went to live with another woman and her son. The husband applied to vary the amount of the order but lost before the magistrates. He appealed. Held: These were circumstances where a man had responsibility for his cohabitee and her child. The court must take into account all the circumstances. Blower (1986)

The amount of the maintenance can be increased any time after the original order – even if it is decades later:

A couple married in 1942 and lived together for two years. In 1945 the wife obtained maintenance of £2 p.w., which was reduced to £1.50 p.w. in 1948. In 1953 she obtained a divorce because of her husband's desertion. She had a job until 1970, when she was forced to retire because of ill-health. In 1977 she was living on state benefits and the £1.50 p.w. maintenance. The husband was earning £110 p.w. She applied for increased maintenance. Held: She should receive £12 p. w. (which was approximately the value of £2 in 1945). She would have received more if the marriage had not been so short, and if it had not ended so long ago. McGrady (1977)

To prevent tedious repeated applications to court for an increase in maintenance payments to cover inflation, the amount of maintenance payments can be linked to, for example, the RPI. The wife can then ensure that the maintenance keeps pace with increasing living costs without having to shell out more legal costs for later court applications for a variation.

When does the maintenance end?

The wife's right to maintenance will automatically end if she remarries, or if she resumes cohabitation with her husband for a continuous period of six months. If the woman starts living permanently with another man, the ex-husband may be able to get the court to reduce (or even stop) the wife's maintenance – but not the children's – though only if the cohabitee is actually supporting the ex-wife. But the court will not force a woman indirectly to marry.

After divorce a consent order was made whereby the wife received periodical payments of £6,500. She began living with another man. She applied to increase the payments and the husband applied to stop them. Held: Cohabitation was not the same as marriage. A court order should not place pressure on a former wife to regularize her position with a cohabitee so that he would assume a husband's obligations. Hepburn (1989)

A child's maintenance order will usually continue until the first birthday after he reaches the minimum school-leaving age of sixteen. However, the court can order it to continue until he is eighteen (e.g. if he is still at school) and even beyond the age of eighteen if the child is undergoing further education, or if there is some other reason justifying such an order.

The wife's and the children's maintenance will also end if the man dies, although both wife and children can apply to the court for a share of his estate (see Chapter 13). The child's maintenance will also end if he is adopted, as the parents' duty to maintain him will then cease.

Making sure the husband pays

If the man has a steady job, an attachment of earnings order can be a good way of enforcing the maintenance order. It is a court order telling the man's employer to deduct the maintenance from the man's wage packet and pass it on to the court. Thus, the maintenance is deducted before the man receives his wages. This type of enforcement can be asked for right at the start, when the order for maintenance is made. Since 1991, the wife does not have to wait until arrears have built up. Obviously, such an order is of no use when the man is unemployed, self-employed, or flitting from job to job.

If the husband stops paying

The husband is supposed to pay the maintenance to the wife every week (or month). If he stops paying, she will have to go back to the court to enforce the order. She should go to the warrant officer and tell him she wishes to apply for 'an arrears of maintenance summons'. Some magistrates' clerks are reluctant to issue these summonses unless the arrears are considerable; however, they have no right to refuse to do so, even if there is only one week of arrears. So the wife should be prepared to insist on her rights. The summons will be issued and served on the husband by the court. When the date of the hearing arrives both husband and wife will have to attend court. The husband will have to explain why he has not paid the maintenance. If he can show good cause (e.g. he has become unemployed; he has moved in with another woman and so has additional financial responsibilities) then the magistrate may reduce the amount of the maintenance order. Generally, though, the husband is simply told to pay up.

He will probably be told to pay off the arrears of maintenance by instalments, but any arrears of more than twelve months will be written off. The magistrates may back up their order by threatening imprisonment.

If the magistrates are satisfied that the husband has not paid the maintenance because of 'wilful default or culpable neglect' (i.e. if he could have paid it, but didn't) then he can be sent to prison. But prison is the last resort and will be ordered only against a persistent offender and where an attachment of earnings order would not be appropriate. No more than six weeks' imprisonment will be imposed.

Often the magistrates will sentence the husband to prison but say that the sentence will be suspended if he pays the maintenance, plus the arrears, in instalments. Thus the man is given one more chance; if he does not keep up the payments, he will go to prison. Usually, these 'suspended orders' are successful, but in about 10 per cent of cases the husband still refuses to pay the money and so he ends up in prison.

Going to prison does not wipe out the arrears of maintenance. The husband will still be liable to pay them off when he comes out. But, in practice, the man will often avoid having to pay the arrears, because the court may decide to give him a fresh start by cancelling the debt ('remitting the arrears' is the term used), and, more important, he cannot be sent back to prison for a second time because of the same arrears. Thus the wife's chances of recovering these hard-core arrears are usually non-existent.

Signing the maintenance order over to the DSS

Often, a wife who is separated from her husband will be totally dependent on her maintenance; it will be her only income. If the husband stops paying she will have to apply to the DSS for income support. She may, therefore, be living from week to week; one week the maintenance arrives, but next week it does not and she will have to go down to the DSS office to queue for income support.

The solution is for the maintenance order to be made over to the DSS. If the husband pays the maintenance, then the DSS will receive it direct from the court; if he does not, then the DSS can try to enforce the maintenance order against him. But the wife will be relieved of worrying whether the maintenance will be paid. She will receive income support each week and although the amounts may not be large, at least they will be regular. She now has a guaranteed regular income which arrives on the same day each week, and she will no longer have to worry about whether he will pay up each week (and nor will she have the problem of having to go back to the court to try to enforce the maintenance order).

So the wife whose maintenance is less than the income support (IS) level should always ask the magistrates' court clerk if the order can be signed over to the DSS. If her maintenance is less, then the magistrates' court clerk should agree without too much difficulty. If it is more than the IS level, then an application to the court may well be necessary – and a signing-over order is unlikely to be made unless the husband has previously defaulted on his payments.

In practical terms, the importance of being able to sign over the maintenance to the DSS cannot be over-emphasized. It is estimated that as many as three-quarters of all maintenance orders are signed over in this way.

Applying for maintenance in the county court

If a wife does not want to commence divorce proceedings she has three methods of obtaining a maintenance order against her husband:

1 She can apply to the magistrates' court (see above).
2 She can apply to the county court on the basis of her husband's failure to maintain her or the children.
3 She can apply to the magistrates' court, a Family Hearing Centre (i.e. county court) or the High Court for an order for maintenance or other money benefit for the children.

But against this, the fact that magistrates' courts usually make lower orders should also be considered.

The county court can make a maintenance order if there has been a failure to provide 'reasonable maintenance' for the other spouse or for one of the children. Basically, the court will decide an application on the merits of the case, using similar principles to those used in the magistrates' court and in the High Court on a divorce. In practical terms, it is easier and simpler to apply in the magistrates' court. Also, legal aid is more readily obtainable for magistrates' court applications and so most women do, in fact, apply to the magistrates' and not to the county court.

Whilst it is usually possible to get a maintenance order in the magistrates' court within two or three weeks, it can take two or three months in the county courts. Another disadvantage of applying in the county court is that the county court cannot enforce its maintenance order if the husband defaults – to enforce a county court maintenance order, you generally go back to the magistrates' court (see page 80).

Applying for maintenance in the divorce court

When a wife (or a husband) files a petition for divorce, she can include a request for maintenance for herself and/or the children. The form, filled in when filing the divorce petition, contains a section for requesting maintenance. There is no need to wait for the divorce to be granted before asking for maintenance.

Maintenance can be awarded before the divorce petition is heard. This is called *maintenance pending suit* and will only be a temporary award until a proper, final award is made.

If the couple cannot reach an agreement about maintenance pending suit, the wife should file a notice in the divorce court, which is then served on her husband. He has fourteen days in which to file an answer setting out details of his income, capital and expenses. The court arranges a private hearing before the District Judge, who hears the evidence and then decides on how much maintenance pending suit should be paid. The order remains effective until the decree absolute.

There is no obligation on a wife (or indeed a husband) to apply for maintenance pending suit. If a temporary agreement can be worked out between the couple then no application is needed.

An application for maintenance proper should be made as soon as the divorce proceedings are started. The application must be supported by full details of the applicant's finances and an estimate of the other spouse's financial status. The husband (or wife) will also have to file details in his or her answer. Legal aid can cover maintenance disputes, even if the divorce itself is undefended.

When the maintenance application is heard by the District Judge, in his chambers, he will go through the evidence and probably question both husband and wife. If necessary, he can call for papers and other documents. Sometimes it is not easy to work out a man's income – if, for instance, he is self-employed in a cash business. In such a case the court might base its order on his apparent standard of living; it would not necessarily accept that the figures on his income-tax return were accurate. The wife's lawyers would, of course, arrange for his accounts to be carefully examined by an independent accountant.

The amount of maintenance awarded will usually be determined on the principles set out in the *Wachtel* case – i.e. around one-third of the combined-incomes (see page 71). Obviously, though, if the wife is receiving an unusually large share of the house or a lump-sum payment, then she will probably have to accept a smaller amount of maintenance.

The wife can always ask for the maintenance order to be registered in the magistrates' court – this will simplify matters if the husband stops paying (see page 80).

Divorce court: if the husband stops paying the maintenance

If the husband stops paying, he will have broken the court order. The wife's remedy is to go back to the court and ask it to enforce the order against him – either by giving him a warning, applying for a warrant of execution or even sending him to prison.

However, it is easier to apply to the magistrates' court than to the divorce court (i.e. High Court or county court). With a magistrates' court order the wife can simply go along to the court and a summons will be issued against her husband straight away; the case will probably be heard in a week or two. In the divorce court it is likely to be several weeks (or even months!) before the application is heard.

This difficulty can be overcome if the divorce court's maintenance order is registered with the magistrates' court – in other words, the divorce court makes the maintenance order but it then gives the magistrates' court the power to enforce it. If the husband stops paying, the wife can go along to the magistrates' court and issue an 'arrears of maintenance summons' in the usual way (see page 81). The procedure then is exactly as though the original maintenance order had been made by the magistrates' court and not the divorce court.

Another advantage of registering the maintenance order with the magistrates' court is that it allows it to be made over to the DSS in cases where the maintenance is less than income support (see page 81).

Is it worth applying for maintenance?

Many women have found that it is not worth applying for maintenance when they part from their husbands. Rather than go to the magistrates' court and ask for maintenance (see page 77) they wait until the divorce is granted. In the meantime the woman claims income support.

If she does claim income support, the DSS cannot force her to start maintenance proceedings against her husband. However, the DSS is under a statutory duty to recover money paid out to a claimant and her (or his) children from a liable relative – usually the father (see page 86).

If the woman is in full-time employment she will not be eligible for income support, however poor she may be. However, she might be able to claim family credit. If in receipt of family credit she might well decide that it would be better not to claim maintenance from her husband. This is because the maintenance would be treated as income and it might increase her income so as to make her ineligible for family credit. Apart from losing family credit, she would automatically lose other welfare benefits that are given to those on family credit (such as free prescriptions, glasses, dental treatment, school dinners for children and free legal advice under the green-form scheme). If she had maintenance she would be in danger of falling into the 'poverty trap', when a small increase in income results in a larger loss of welfare benefits.

So, the best order will often be for the wife to get the matrimonial home (which will not prevent her claiming benefit), with no order for her maintenance. If the couple do not own their own home, but pay rent, then a lump sum will probably be better than regular maintenance (although problems can arise when it is more than £6,000 since she will then be ineligible for income support). However, after the Child Support Act 1991 is fully implemented, this comparative freedom of choice no longer applies. If a parent claims income support or family credit, the Child Support Agency will automatically try to recover child support from the absent parent.

When the divorce is granted, the court can make maintenance orders and also property orders (for instance, giving the wife a lump sum or transferring the house to her). But, if resources are limited, the wife might be better advised to forgo maintenance for herself and negotiate instead for a lump sum and/or transfer of the home (or its tenancy) to her. This may be a more sensible course of action because:

1 The husband may not pay the maintenance.
2 Maintenance will affect her income support (or family credit) eligibility. A capital sum of up to £8,000 will not (although capital of between £3,000 and £8,000 will reduce benefit). An even larger amount will be ignored by the DSS if it is to be used by the wife to buy a home.
3 A lump sum can be used as a deposit for a house purchase.
4 If she remarries, her maintenance payments would end, but she would not have to refund any lump sum she received.
5 If the home is transferred to her, the mortgage interest though not the capital repayments can be met by income support.

An out-of-court agreement

Often the husband and wife will be able to work out a satisfactory financial arrangement between themselves. It is always advisable to have the terms of the agreement drawn up into a formal document which can then be placed before the divorce judge. He will then make a 'consent order' which confirms that both husband and wife agree to the terms and that it is now an order of the court.

There are dangers in not having a consent order drawn up by the court. Verbal agreements have a habit of unravelling over time as one or other spouse 'forgets' what was agreed. Even carelessly drafted orders can leave loopholes for a former spouse to exploit if the situation of the other improves in future.

Mr and Mrs Twiname were married in 1940 and divorced in 1971. Mr T remarri
did not. Mrs T's divorce petition included a claim for 'such sum
provision and/or such sums by way of maintenance and alimony

just'. At the time of the divorce one of Mr T's companies was wound up and divided, 51 per cent to Mr T and 49 per cent to Mrs T, with maintenance for her too. The consent order made no mention of the lump-sum claim (usually this would be dismissed). In 1989 Mrs T applied not only for increased maintenance but also for a lump sum as Mr T had just sold his business for £6 million. Mr T argued that the late application would cause him hardship and was 'vexatious'. The court disagreed and allowed Mrs T's claim to go ahead (at the time of going to press it had still not been decided). Twiname (1990)

If the court order does not entitle the wife to be paid any maintenance (for instance, she might be given the matrimonial home and in return agree to forgo maintenance), she cannot later change her mind and reapply to the court for maintenance. The courts say that when there is a clean break between the spouses in this way, the consent order should normally be binding. For instance:

Mr and Mrs Minton were divorced in 1972. In 1973 they reached an agreement about the family assets and it was agreed that Mrs Minton would be given the matrimonial home in return for £10,000 cash and for agreeing to forgo any maintenance. The agreement was made a consent order by the court. However, the bargain proved disastrous from Mrs Minton's point of view, for she soon found herself deep in debt, in poor health, and with the children to bring up. In 1976 she applied to the court for maintenance for herself. Held: She was not entitled to maintenance. By agreeing to the consent order she had forfeited her right to claim maintenance, and it was only fair on her husband that there should be a clean break between them. However, this did not, of course, prevent the court increasing the amount of maintenance for the children, their maintenance settlement being completely separate from that of their mother. Minton (1979)

When the DSS can claim the maintenance

A man is legally obliged to maintain his wife and children. If he does not maintain them, and they claim income support, then the DSS can take him to court to recover the IS payments they have paid out. These are called 'liable-relative proceedings' (i.e. because the man is sued for maintenance in respect of relatives for whom he is liable).

Prior to divorce, liable-relative proceedings can be brought by the DSS for money paid to both the wife and the children. After divorce, the husband is no longer obliged to maintain his ex-wife (unless a maintenance order was made in the divorce proceedings) and so liable-relative proceedings can only be brought in respect of the children – the obligation to maintain them is not ended by the divorce. This is an important point and should be remembered by a husband who is trying to negotiate a clean break with his wife and children. The wife may suggest that he gives her the house and that she have no maintenance: this will leave her free to claim IS (whereas if she had maintenance payments they would simply reduce her IS entitlement – see above). The attraction for the husband will be that he can make a fresh start and not be burdened by future maintenance payments. But, if the wife claims IS for the children, there is a risk that the DSS will claim from the ex-husband, and if necessary start liable-relative proceedings against him. So a husband should not negotiate a clean break from the children if the wife and children will have to claim IS.

Liable-relative proceedings

If the DSS do go to court, they will get reimbursement for payments made to the wife (if there has not been a divorce, assuming no maintenance order) or to the children. But they will make sure that the husband is left enough to live on. The court will not order the husband to reimburse the DSS if the result would be to leave him with less than his own financial needs.

The new Child Support Act 1991

Once this Act is implemented in 1993, the Child Support Agency must try to recover from the absent parent support payments made to the children (see also page 117).

TAX AND SEPARATION

How income tax personal allowances are treated

In the year in which the couple separate:
• *the man* has the married couple's allowance from the separation plus his single person's allowance;
• *the woman* has the single person's allowance and from the date of separation can claim the additional personal allowance if she has a child living with her.
   In the following tax years:
• *the man* receives a single person's allowance, unless he is looking after the children, when he can claim the additional personal allowance too;
• *the woman* receives a single person's allowance and can, as above, claim the additional personal allowance if she has a child living with her.

Tax on maintenance payments

There are no longer any tax advantages in making maintenance payments directly to the children. The only tax benefit available is that if the husband makes maintenance payments directly to the wife either for herself or for the children (whether or not under a court order), he can continue claiming the equivalent of the married couple's allowance as an additional allowance against tax.
   But this limited tax benefit is only available for a limited time. So:
• the ex-husband cannot claim the married couple's allowance after the couple separate if he is not maintaining her;
• if the ex-husband is paying maintenance either for his ex-wife or to her for the children, he can claim the married couple's allowance only until divorce.
   As soon as the divorce comes through (the stage of decree absolute) the ex-husband is left with only a single person's tax allowance to reduce his tax bill

and he has to pay maintenance for his ex-wife or for the children out of his already taxed income.

Maintenance payments are not taxable in the hands of the recipients so ex-wives do not have to pay tax on maintenance payments received for themselves or for the children. An ex-wife who looks after the children (or even the ex-husband, if he is the primary carer) and is working or has an income from savings can claim the additional relief for a single parent (£1,720 in 1992/3) as well as the single person's tax allowance.

Illustration. *Sam Selwyn and his wife Liz separate on 30 September 1992. They have two children who are both living with Liz. Sam's salary is £28,000 and Liz has a part-time job which pays £7,500. In return for Liz having a greater share of the home, Liz and Sam agree that he will make maintenance payments limited to £3,900 per annum, or £75 per week. For 1992/3 he will pay £2,025.*

Liz's income		
Salary		£7,500
Less		
Personal allowance	£3,445	
Additional personal	£1,720	
		£5,165
Taxable income		£2,335
Tax payable		
20% on £2,000		£400
25% on £335		£ 83.75
Total		£483.75

In addition to her after-tax income of £7,016.25 (£7,500 – tax of £483.75), Liz receives the maintenance of £2,025, making her total income for 1992/3 £9,041.25.

Sam's income		
Salary		£28,000
Less		
Personal allowance	£3,445	
Married couple's allowance	£1,720	
(he can currently claim this as long as the maintenance is expressed to be in favour of Liz)	£5,165	
Taxable income		£22,835
Tax payable		
20% on £2,000		£400
25% on £20,835		£5,208.75
Total		£5,608.75

Sam's after-tax salary will be £22,391.25 (£28,000 − tax of £5,608.75), from which he must also pay maintenance of £2,025, leaving his net income at £20,366.25.
Note: after the Child Support Act 1991 comes into force, it is likely that the maintenance bill will be much higher.

Old orders for maintenance

The new rules (as stated above) apply to:
● maintenance agreements made on or after 15 March 1988 (unless they alter or replace an arrangement to which the old rules apply);
● maintenance agreements made before 15 March 1988 but which were not notified to the Revenue in writing by 30 June 1988;
● court orders applied for after 15 March 1988.

The old rules still apply to old orders or agreements for child support made before the above dates.

If you pay maintenance under the old rules

Maintenance payers under the old rules get tax relief at their highest rate on maintenance paid to an ex-wife, ex-husband or children (although they cannot get any tax relief on maintenance payments made to an ex-cohabitee). Tax relief payments were frozen in 1988/9, so the amount of tax relief in any tax year will be the lower of:
● the payments actually made during the tax year, *or*
● the amount for which tax relief was given in 1988/9.

If the maintenance amounts have increased since 1988/9, the amount of tax relief will not go up proportionately (although maintenance payers under the old rules are treated more favourably than payers under the present system).

The payer should deduct tax at the basic rate from the sum ordered to be paid and give the payee a tax form (Form R185) to show the amount of tax deducted.

If you receive maintenance under the old rules

Maintenance payees under the old rules may have to pay tax on maintenance received. But they have to pay tax only if the amount of maintenance exceeds their own tax-exempt personal allowances (£3,445 in 1992/3). So the payee should calculate whether any repayment of tax is due and claim a refund from the Inland Revenue, usually at the end of the tax year.

If maintenance payments have increased since 1988/9, no tax is payable on the extra bit.

For child maintenance, there is no tax-free band, but tax is chargeable only on the amount of maintenance fixed in 1988/9.

Illustration. *John Sidney pays maintenance under the old rules. He pays £3,000 to his ex-wife Amy and £2,000 direct to each of their two children, payable under a court order made in 1988. The amount of maintenance has not increased since then.*

Although his maintenance payments for the children are actually £100 more than the sums paid by Sam, John will pay less than Sam overall. In the tax year 1988/9 he will be viewed as having paid £4,000 to the children (even though he will be deducting tax at source). Until the maintenance order ends, he will be able to pay £4,000 out of his gross rather than his net income.

If Amy has no income other than her maintenance payments, she will have to pay no tax in 1992/3, as the maintenance payments are less than her single person's allowance. Likewise, the children would not be liable for tax because their income falls within the tax-free bands. Although John has to pay more overall in maintenance, he pays a lot less tax.

If John also earns £28,000 his income will be as follows:

John's income

Salary		£28,000
Less		
1988/9 maintenance for Amy	£3,000	
1988/9 maintenance for the children	£4,000	
Personal allowance	£3,445	
		£10,445
Taxable income		£17,445
Tax payable		
20% on £2,000		£400
25% on £15,445		£3,861.25
Total		£4,261.25

John's net income after tax will be £23,738.75, from which he will have to pay maintenance of £7,000, leaving him a net income of £16,738.75.

2. DEALING WITH THE FAMILY HOME

In addition to maintenance, a wife may be entitled to a share of the family property and assets, such as the house and the car.

Such an order can be made only by the divorce court and so it will be necessary to start divorce (or judicial separation) proceedings. When granting the divorce, the court has complete discretion as to how it divides up the property. As always, the main concern will be with the welfare of the children – and who is to have the home will often depend on who is to have the children.

The court's order will depend upon whether the home is owned or rented.

1. Owner-occupiers

Often the only substantial asset will be the family home in which the children are living. This presents a grave problem because if the assets are to be divided up the house will have to be sold, and often the parent with primary care of the children will be unable to afford to buy another property. When that is the case, the courts insist that the financial entitlements of the two spouses should take second place to the needs of the children; the availability of the home for the children must be ensured.

In practical terms, there are usually three possibilities:

(a) Transfer the house to one of the spouses

For instance, if there are children – and they will be living with the woman – the court might give the house totally to the wife. In practice:

● the court will rarely make such an order of its own accord (although it has, exceptionally, been ordered);

● it is quite common, however, for it to be agreed to by the parties as the best arrangement. Usually, in return for her husband's agreement, the wife will agree to abandon any right to maintenance for herself. Thus, there is a clean break – the husband gives her the house, and knows that he will not have the burden of maintenance payments hanging over him for years to come;

● similarly, such an arrangement is often agreed if the wife has left the home to go and live with another man. The ex-husband may then buy out her share for a lumpsum payment.

(b) Sell the property and divide the money

This may well be the best solution if neither can afford to keep the house or flat. Often it is agreed to sell the house so that the proceeds can be used to enable the wife to buy a cheaper home, with the husband giving her a larger-than-normal share of the proceeds in return for a reduced (or nil) maintenance entitlement.

A practical problem can arise if one (or both) of the parties is on legal aid. This is because the Legal Aid Board (the body which covers the legal-aid costs) has the right to have legal costs paid straight away (rather than deferring payment until later) out of monies 'recovered or preserved' for a legally aided party. This is often called the 'statutory charge'. But there are some limits on how the statutory charge operates in family cases which can help families struggling to provide a home for the children.

If the family home is not sold but is transferred to or kept by one spouse (and/or the children), then the Legal Aid Board will not ask for the legal costs to be paid straight away but will wait until the home is eventually sold before claiming repayment. In the meantime the Legal Aid Board will register a charge against the home (like a mortgage).

If the home is sold, then the Legal Aid Board can ask for the money to be paid straight away, unless the proceeds of sale are used to buy a new home for the legally aided spouse (and/or the children) within a year of sale of the old home. The Legal Aid Board will then register a charge against the new home when it is bought and again the costs will have to be repaid once this new home is sold. But if the new home is bought later than a year after the sale of the old one, then the legal costs will have to be paid straight away (so it is usually not worthwhile hanging around to see if a better deal can be obtained).

In both cases, a special form of wording must be used in the court order which deals with the family home. It is not enough to have a simple agreement or even a court order which does not say specifically what the sale proceeds will be used for. The wording (adapted as necessary for particular cases) is:

And it is certified for the purpose of the Civil Legal Aid (General) Regulations 1989 that the lump sum of £x has been ordered to be paid to enable the petitioner/respondent to purchase a home for herself/himself (or her/his dependants) [that the property (state address) has been recovered/preserved for the petitioner/respondent for use as a home for herself/himself (or her/his dependants].

If this special wording is used, then payment of the costs will be put off until the home (present or new) is sold in future. The drawback is that interest (at 10.5 per cent) will continue running on the unpaid legal costs until they are eventually repaid in full, but the advantage is that the home can be kept on and the legally aided party (and children) will not be forced on to the streets.

If the property is sold, it is usually best to agree a percentage division rather than a fixed sum, especially in times of volatile house markets.

The wife was awarded a lump sum of £32,000 with an order that if the husband defaulted on paying this sum, the home should be sold. The husband's appeal was dismissed and the house was ordered to be sold – it was then worth £116,000. The husband kept on delaying and the house meanwhile increased in value to £200,000. The wife thus asked the court for an increased lump sum. Held: Supervening events had falsified the old order: the wife should receive 40 per cent of the sale proceeds. Hope-Smith (1989)

That case was decided when house prices were rocketing up, but its principle is just as important when house prices are falling or if houses take a long time to sell. Then the costs which must be deducted from the sale proceeds may increase and thus decrease the overall value of the home.

(c) Keep the house for the wife to live in

This is the order that is often made if there are young children – indeed it is often the only feasible solution. The typical order will then be for the wife to live in the house with the children, and for the house to be sold when the youngest child reaches eighteen. For instance:

A couple married in 1956. In 1970 the husband left the matrimonial home and the wife obtained a divorce and custody of their only child, a girl. The wife asked for the house to be transferred to her. Both husband and wife were planning new marriages; the husband had already bought a house with his cohabitee, and the wife's new partner had transferred his house to his ex-wife. Held: The husband should not lose all his share in the home. The property would be held jointly until the daughter was seventeen, when it could be sold. In the meantime, the wife should pay all the outgoings, including the mortgage. Mesher (1973)

That was a 1973 case, and since then the courts have refined the orders a bit. Now, generally, sale will also be ordered if the wife dies, remarries, or if she wishes to move home.

The problem with this sort of order is that the wife can find herself homeless in middle age (when the youngest child reaches eighteen or so), with only a share in the proceeds of sale – and a share that may not be enough to buy anywhere else (and a further difficulty may well be that her age and limited earnings prevent her from taking on a mortgage). To try to avoid this problem, some judges prefer to say that the property should be sold only on the wife's death, marriage, or her wishing to move (i.e. no mention of a sale on the children reaching eighteen). Thus the wife has long-term security but at the price of depriving the husband of his share of the capital for what may turn out to be a very long time – and many judges take the view that this is too unfair on the husband.

The problem is, of course, that there is no satisfactory solution – there usually is not enough money available to finance the purchase and maintenance of two homes. Because of these difficulties, sometimes the court will order the husband to buy out the wife and so order a 'clean break' (see page 74). For instance:

The husband moved out after seventeen years' marriage, leaving the wife and the three children in the house (worth £18,500). The trial judge ordered that the property be kept until the youngest child left home and that then it be sold, with the proceeds being divided fifty/fifty. In the meantime, the wife should pay 'rent' to the husband for the use of the house. On appeal, the court decided that this was an impracticable order; the wife would not have the money to pay any rent to the husband. Instead, the husband was ordered to accept the wife's offer to buy out his share in the house for £2,500. This would give him a deposit for a new house, and he would be able to afford mortgage repayments. The wife would be left with the house, which would give her long-term housing security, but no maintenance (she could claim supplementary benefit if necessary). Scipio (1983)

Does it matter whose name the house is in?

It used to matter a lot. Before 1970 the courts adopted a very legalistic approach and were primarily concerned with whose name was on the title deeds. Often a wife was refused a share in the matrimonial home simply because her name was not on the deeds.

After years of agitation by Lord Denning and others, Parliament changed the law. Now the courts are not so concerned with whose name is on the deeds, although it is still a relevant factor.

If the house, or flat, is held in joint names (i.e. both spouses' names appear on the deeds) then it is virtually certain that they own the property jointly. Often the wife will receive half the value of the house plus maintenance, although sometimes the value of the maintenance will be offset against her share and so what she will receive will be nearer one-third than one-half. For instance, the house in one case was in joint names but the wife was deemed to be entitled to only a one-third share. However, if there were no children, and both husband and wife had contributed to the house bills, then both would probably receive half – especially if the wife was working. The wife might get only a small amount of maintenance to get her back on her feet for a short period (e.g. one to two years).

If the house is not in joint names (i.e. it is in the name of only one of the couple) then the position may occasionally be different. The courts will then be more ready to deny the other spouse a one-third share of the home, but this will happen only in exceptional circumstances, such as with a very short marriage, or where the other spouse has behaved very badly or is wealthy and yet did not provide any money for the house.

But in the vast majority of marriages that last more than a few years the wife will be given a half share, whether or not her name is on the deeds. Even though her husband may have put up all the money for the house, it is likely that the court will see her contribution in terms of being a home-maker, cook and mother, and so she will have earned her share in that way. As Lord Denning said in *Wachtel*:

... Parliament recognized that the wife who looks after the home and family contributes as much to the family assets as the wife who goes out to work. The one contributes in kind. The other in money or money's worth. If the court comes to the conclusion that the home has been acquired and maintained by the joint efforts of both, then, when the marriage breaks down, it should be regarded as the joint property of both of them, no matter in whose name it stands.

Although the courts will usually give the wife a half share whether or not her name is on the title deeds, it is preferable for her to insist that the house be in their joint names. But it must be remembered that no two cases are the same; it is impossible to generalize, and there is no rule that says the wife must have a half share. It could be more; it could be less. See the warning on page 100.

The importance of staying at home with the children

The court will nearly always award the house to the spouse who has remained living there with the children. In practice this means that if the wife can remain in the house with the children, and get her husband out, she is almost certain to be awarded the property by the divorce court. As we have seen (above) this is likely to mean either:

• she occupies the house until the children grow up, whereupon it is sold and the proceeds divided between the spouses, *or*

• she becomes sole owner of the house immediately, forfeiting about one-third of her maintenance as payment for her husband's share.

Thus there is every reason for the wife to refuse to move out. Since her husband's legal advisers may well have informed him that if he moves out he is likely to lose the house, there is every likelihood of a domestic confrontation. Quite simply, neither dares move out. When this situation develops the law favours the wife, since she can get an exclusion order ordering the man out of the house if the strain becomes too great, but only if this erupts into actual violence. Otherwise both parties may be advised to sit it out until they reach an agreement or get a court order.

Stopping a sale or remortgage

If the house is not in joint names, but (for instance) in the sole name of the husband, there is an added danger; he may sell the house before the court makes an order and then disappear with the proceeds.

However, this can be prevented. The wife can register her interest in the house and so stop it being sold against her wishes. She can do this at any time – not just when she has fallen out with her husband. Her husband will probably not learn of the registration until he attempts to sell the property or to raise a new mortgage on it.

This system of registration is set out in the Matrimonial Homes Act 1983. It allows the non-owning spouse, whether wife or husband, to register a charge on the property. This gives her (or him) a legal right to occupy the home and so no one would buy the property (or lend money on its security) until she removed her registration. In effect, she can make sure that the property will not be sold behind her back. The only transaction that the registration is ineffective against is if the building society (or other lender) forecloses on the mortgage and repossesses the house because the instalments were not paid. But otherwise it gives her complete protection. Also, if her husband should try to evict her forcibly from the house she can apply to the court for an injunction (see page 106).

This right of occupation can be registered simply, easily and cheaply. It is best done by a solicitor, who should be asked to 'register a charge under the Matrimonial Homes Act'. The solicitor's fee would probably be around £75 (the green-form legal-advice scheme might cover the cost – see page 957).

A non-owning spouse who has any doubts as to the loyalty of the other spouse is always well advised to register a Matrimonial Homes Act charge. If necessary, even after the divorce, if the financial arrangements have not been worked out, this type of charge can be converted to another charge (technically called a 'pending action' charge) to continue the protection of the non-owning spouse's interest until the money disputes are concluded.

Ordering the other spouse out of the home

Once the divorce is heard the court can make whatever order it wishes and it may well order one of the spouses to leave the matrimonial home. Usually, the court will order a spouse out of the home *before* the divorce is granted only if he (or she) has been violent to the other spouse or to the children (see page 106).

Summary

With owner-occupied property, the woman has the following rights even if her name is not on the title deeds:

• she can live in the home until a court order is made evicting her;

• she can ask the divorce court to transfer the home to her sole name;

• in the meantime, she can prevent the home being sold, by registering a charge. She can also obtain an injunction if her husband tries to throw her out of the house.

2. Rented property

The divorce court can order that the tenancy be transferred to one of the spouses.

(a) Privately rented property

The position depends upon the terms of the tenancy, and whether there is any restriction on the tenancy being assigned (i.e. transferred).

If there is no written tenancy agreement. It will be assumed that the tenant can assign the tenancy, even if the landlord does not want this. Thus the court will feel able to transfer the tenancy to the other spouse even if the landlord and the original tenant object.

If there is a written tenancy agreement. The position here is more complicated. There are three possibilities:

• If the agreement does not contain a clause forbidding the assignment of the tenancy, then the tenant is able to assign and so the court will feel able to transfer the tenancy to the other spouse. In other words, the position is identical to that when there is no written tenancy agreement.

• If the agreement contains a clause stating that the tenancy can be assigned only with the consent of the landlord, then the law will imply a qualification to this by saying that the landlord cannot 'unreasonably' withhold his consent. Thus, if the spouse to whom the tenancy would be granted is a 'reasonable' prospect as a tenant, then the landlord cannot object to the transfer of the tenancy. On the other hand, if it would not be 'unreasonable' for the landlord to object (e.g. the spouse cannot supply references, has no money, has previously been a bad tenant) then he cannot be forced to agree to the assignment. If the spouse is a 'reasonable' prospect then the court will feel able to transfer the tenancy, even if both landlord and tenant object. If the spouse is not a reasonable prospect then the court will not agree to the transfer. Usually, of course, there is no suggestion that the spouse (probably the wife) would not make a suitable tenant and so the problem rarely arises.

● If the tenancy agreement contains a clause stating that the tenancy cannot be assigned (and there is no clause saying that the landlord's consent is needed), then the landlord cannot be forced to accept an assignment. Thus, the court will probably feel unable to transfer the tenancy to the other spouse.

(b) Council property

The council will transfer the tenancy from one tenant to another only if a court order has been made. The court can make an order only on divorce or judicial separation. The position will therefore depend upon whether one or both of the spouses are tenants.

● If the council flat or house is in joint names (i.e. both spouses' names are on the rent book) and the court does not order a transfer of the tenancy, then they can both stay there. This is commonly what happens when there are no children; neither spouse has anywhere else to live and so the divorced couple are forced to continue living together. If this happens, the only hope is for one of the spouses to be able to show that her (or his) mental or physical health is suffering as a result of the arrangement. If this can be shown the divorce court may order the other spouse out or the council may agree to rehouse the ill spouse.

● If the council house or flat is in the name of only one of the spouses and the divorce court does not transfer the tenancy to the other spouse, then the other spouse will have to leave if ordered to do so by the spouse who is the tenant, once the divorce has been made absolute. Until that time, he or she has a right to remain in occupation. After the decree absolute, the spouse who is the tenant can apply to the county court for an eviction order (and if necessary an injunction) against the other spouse.

● If the council house or flat is in the name of only one of the spouses and the divorce court transfers the tenancy to the other spouse, then the original tenant will have to leave. Generally, the court will transfer the tenancy to the spouse who has custody of the children and will require the other spouse to leave.

Similar rules apply when renting from a housing association.

Does it matter whose name is on the rent book?

Generally, the answer to this is 'no' for, as explained above, the court can order that the tenancy be transferred from one spouse to another. However, if the rent book or lease is in the names of both spouses, then they can both continue living there unless the court says otherwise. So it is always an advantage for a spouse to have his or her name on the rent book or lease – in the same way that it is always better to have both names on the title deeds if the couple are owner-occupiers.

Sometimes a rented home will be in the name of the husband only and, following a matrimonial dispute, he simply walks out and does not return. When this happens, the wife can continue living in the home and she can insist that the landlord accepts rent from her as though she was the tenant. In effect, she takes over in place of her husband, although she will have to pay off any rent arrears that may have built up. This provision, in the Matrimonial Homes Act 1983, also applies to husbands who are deserted by their wives. However, it does not apply to unmarried couples – the deserted common-law wife cannot insist that she be allowed to remain in her ex-lover's rented house or flat.

Ordering the husband out before there is a divorce.

This is often ordered when the husband has been violent to his wife or the children. The husband can only rarely be ordered out if he has not been guilty of physical violence (see page 106).

SUMMARY: THE FINANCES OF A SPLIT-UP

This chapter has gone through the principles applied by the courts when working out maintenance and the division of the family assets on a matrimonial breakdown. It will be clear that there are numerous factors to be taken into account and accordingly it is impossible to give simplified advice that will apply in every case.

However, several years ago in his book *Divorce and Your Money* (Allen & Unwin, 1979) W.M. Harper attempted an analysis of reported decisions to see whether there are any mathematical constants in the decisions of the judges. Surprisingly, he found that there was an overall consistency in the approach of the judges in typical middle-class cases. His findings are summarized in the chart on page 99, although it should be emphasized that this should not be regarded as an infallible guide to the outcome of any individual case. The chart was prepared for the days before the Child Support Act came into force and so is limited to giving you an idea of the 'old days' type of division. Even so, in particular if the parties are rich or poor, as opposed to being of average income, the chart will not be applicable. Also, the courts have become more flexible in recent years – they are now less likely to adopt rigid ideas of one-third or one-half. They also put greater emphasis on the position of the children and the desirability of the couple becoming financially independent. *So treat this chart with great caution.*

The Finances of the Typical Split-up

Maintenance
– the dependent spouse (usually the wife) receives one-third of joint income, less her own income;
– each child that stays with the wife receives 7½ per cent of the husband's income (less a small reduction if wife has significant income – the reduction could be up to 2 per cent if the wife's income amounts to half of the husband's).

Is the total maintenance figure more than 30 per cent of supporting spouse's (i.e. usually husband's) income?

yes

Final maintenance figure will be average of above figure and 30 per cent of supporting spouse's income (i.e. split the difference).

no

Final maintenance figure will be as calculated with no reduction.

Family assets excluding the home
– major items go to owner, with one-third payable to other spouse;
– minor items are split fifty/fifty.

The home
Are there any children?

no

yes

House goes to spouse with the children.

House goes to the occupier.

Is the spouse awarded the house the dependent spouse (i.e. usually the wife)?

yes

Her final maintenance is likely to be reduced by one-third or more.

no

The dependent spouse is likely to be awarded a lump sum of between one-third and one-fifth of its equity value (i.e. value after deducting mortgages).

Based on a chart in *Divorce and Your Money* (Allen & Unwin, 1979) by W.M. Harper.
Treat this chart with caution! See warning on page 98!

The legal costs of divorce

Going to court for a full-blown battle over money is guaranteed to be very expensive – both emotionally and financially. Many couples have found this out to their cost too late, seeing all the family money swallowed up by lawyers' bills instead of being more fruitfully used for the benefit of the new halves of the family.

Warnings about costs are constantly being made in the courts. One judge, Mrs Justice Booth, issued these guidelines to lawyers in 1990:

- affidavit evidence should be confined to relevant facts;
- professional witnesses should avoid taking a partisan approach;
- extra care should be taken to decide what evidence should be produced – non-material emotive evidence should be avoided;
- avoid duplicating documents;
- both parties' solicitors should agree a chronology of material facts;
- if a case looks to be substantial, have a pre-trial review to see if settlement can be reached.

But what happens if one party wants to be reasonable and settle at a fair figure and the other refuses? The answer: damage limitation! The reasonable spouse can make an offer to the other spouse, called a Calderbank offer. Then, if the other spouse rejects the offer and pushes on to a full court hearing and the court ultimately makes an order of around the figure offered, the rejecting spouse can be penalized by having a costs order made against him or her, thus ending up having to pay most of both lawyers' bills.

Usually costs orders follow the event – so in financial cases in divorce the winner will get an order that the loser should pay his or her legal costs. The amount of the costs ordered to be paid may not meet the full legal bill of the successful spouse, but it will certainly go a long way towards it. By making a Calderbank offer, the other spouse becomes more at risk on costs grounds.

Making a Calderbank offer is a gamble, but an experienced solicitor can help reduce the odds. In some cases the gamble pays off even if the offer is on the low side.

The husband made a Calderbank offer of £400,000, which the wife rejected. After a contested hearing the wife beat the offer and was awarded £435,000. But the judge refused to award the wife her costs because of her refusal to negotiate over the original offer. So she had to pay her own legal bill instead of this being awarded against the husband. S v. S (1990)

Calderbank offers are not just limited to rich families; they can be very useful in any case which involves the dividing up of assets, even just the family home.

An example

The husband earns £150 p.w. gross, and the wife £30 p.w. gross. They have three children. The husband has left the matrimonial home, which is worth £50,000, but subject to a £10,000 mortgage.

Maintenamce. The wife will receive a third of the joint income, less her own: a third of £180 (£60), less £30. Thus, she receives £30 a week. Prior to the Child Support Act coming into force, each child will receive 7½ per cent of her husband's income (i.e. £11.25 each). But there will be a slight discount for the wife's earnings so each is likely to receive £10 a week. For the three this totals £30 per week. Thus the total maintenance is £60. But this is 40 per cent of the husband's income. Final maintenance is likely to be the average of 30 and 40 per cent (i.e. 35 per cent), which is £52.50 a week.

The house. This is likely to go to the wife. But she will then probably lose a third or more of her maintenance. Her final total maintenance is thus likely to be in the region of £30 to £35 a week.

MONEY MATTERS: CONCLUSION AND WARNING

Please remember what has been repeated again and again. In a book of this sort the author can give only general guidance. Please do not think (for instance) that a wife is automatically entitled to one-third income plus half the house. It is not as simple as that. Every case depends on its own circumstances – and the courts will throw away the rule book to do what is best in the particular circumstances.

6 Domestic Violence

The trauma frequently associated with relationship breakdown can occasionally erupt into violence. Domestic violence is no respecter of age or class: it cuts across all strata of society.

There are several remedies available, but before looking at their individual merits, it should be stressed that:

● common-law wives (i.e. a woman living with a man but not married to him) *can* get protection;

● the court procedures in domestic-violence cases are often complicated. It is always advisable to take legal advice and the woman should instruct a solicitor to act for her. Legal aid is available; since the partner's income will be ignored, most battered women will be eligible for free legal advice (see page 969).

HOW THE LAW CAN PROTECT A WOMAN AND CHILDREN

The court can do two things: first, it can order the husband/man to stop assaulting or threatening the woman and/or children. This is called a non-molestation or personal protection order. Secondly, it can order the husband/ man out of the matrimonial home, so leaving the woman and children in peace. This is called an ouster or exclusion order. But the court can make these orders only if the parties have been living together. If they live separately there is a different procedure (see page 104). How effective the court orders will be depends often on how law-abiding the violent partner is (whether or not he will pay attention to a court document) and how determined the woman is to end the cycle of violence once and for all and not accept dishonest promises to change by a habitually violent partner.

Which court to apply to?

There are three different courts that can help in wife-battering cases. The procedure in each court is different, and each has its own particular advantages and disadvantages.

The Family Proceedings Panel of the magistrates' court

The magistrates' court can make a personal protection order and/or exclusion order but only *if the couple are married*. It cannot help if the couple are unmarried and it cannot make an order unless the husband has been violent to the wife or child (or unless he had been violent to someone else and now threatens to use violence on the wife or child). If there is going to be a major dispute over the facts, it is better to go to the county court or divorce court.

The county court

The county court can grant an injunction and/or a non-molestation order *whether the couple are married or unmarried*. Any county court can hear a domestic-violence application, not just divorce county courts or family hearing centres under the new family court structure. The county court can make an order even if there has been no physical violence or threats of violence. For instance, see *Spindlow* (1978), page 104.

The divorce court

The divorce court can make a non-molestation order and/or an ouster order, but only if divorce proceedings have been started. Obviously, this can only apply to *married* couples.

Note: unmarried women can only apply to the county court, not the magistrates' court or the divorce court.

The choice of court will depend upon the circumstances of the individual case. For instance, if the couple are unmarried the woman will have no choice but to apply to the county court. If divorce proceedings have been started, then the application will have to be made to the divorce court (i.e. the High Court in a defended divorce case; the divorce county court in an undefended divorce).

If the couple are married and divorce proceedings have not been started, the wife has a choice. She can apply to either the magistrates' court or the county court. They have broadly similar powers and so it will often be a matter of deciding which is the more convenient. Generally, the county court is preferred.

Procedure in the magistrates' court is very informal and the wife could probably act for herself if she wanted to. However, this would rarely be necessary since she would probably be eligible for legal aid and so could have a solicitor to act for her. A disadvantage of magistrates' courts is that the magistrates are usually part-time amateurs, and there is a lack of consistency in the decisions of magistrates' courts that is not so common in the county court, where cases are decided by experienced professional judges. But the wife may find that the decision is taken out of her hands: the legal aid will probably be for the cheaper court – the magistrates' court.

In addition, the county court can make an order even if violence has not been threatened. In the magistrates' court, an act of violence is usually a precondition of being able to apply for an order.

'Mr and Mrs' Spindlow were unmarried; they lived in a council house with their two children. Mrs Spindlow applied to the county court (under the Domestic Violence and Matrimonial Proceedings Act 1976) for an injunction ordering Mr Spindlow to leave the matrimonial home. There had not been any real physical violence although there was evidence of one incident when Mr Spindlow had pushed Mrs Spindlow on to the settee. But Mrs Spindlow said that unless Mr Spindlow left she would leave with the children and since there was nowhere else for her to go the children would have to go into care. Held: An injunction would be granted. The welfare of the children was the court's main concern, and since Mrs Spindlow was the only person able to look after them, the court would accept the reality of the situation; she would not live with Mr Spindlow and so he would have to go. The 1976 Act allowed the court to order a spouse or cohabitee out of the home even if there had been no violence (cf. the position in the magistrates' court). Spindlow (1978)

One other advantage of the county court is that the magistrates are more likely to want the man to be given advance notice of the application to the court, whereas in serious emergencies a woman can get an *'ex parte'* order from a higher court (the county court or divorce court) without her violent partner being told about the application beforehand (see page 108).

Ex-partners who live separately

The remedies explained above apply only if a husband and wife or a man and woman have been living *as husband and wife* (i.e. living, eating and sleeping together under the same roof). But what happens if an ex-partner starts getting nasty long after the relationship is over or if otherwise the relationship does not fall into these categories (like homosexual relationships or parents of violent children)?

The victim can apply to court only for a *non-molestation injunction* (ouster orders are not available), and the procedure is more complicated. Legal advice must be sought.

Basically, the victim's legal remedy is to make a money claim for compensation for damages caused by the violent partner. As a first step in this claim, the victim asks the court to make a non-molestation injunction. If the injunction is granted, the aggressor has to be served with the injunction in the usual way for it to be effective, but powers of arrest cannot be attached to the injunction, giving this type of injunction fewer legal teeth than the usual domestic-violence type.

The whole process is a bit of a farce as the claim for damages never goes any further than the non-molestation injunction and is usually left inactive on the court files. The process is more expensive than 'normal' domestic-violence cases (although the Legal Aid Board will often be footing the bill). This is an area of law long overdue for reform.

Domestic Violence: Magistrates' Court or County Court?

Giving evidence	The county court is better, since the woman can give written evidence by way of affidavit. In the magistrates' court she must attend in person and give evidence in the witness box. If there is a major dispute over the facts, the case might be transferred up to the county court.
Legal aid	Legal aid is available in both courts. Usually the woman will be eligible for legal aid, since her partner's income and capital will be ignored when considering her finances. In the magistrates' court, financial eligibility will be decided under the green-form rules (see page 957); in the county court it will be under the civil legal-aid rules (see page 964). Because of the difference between the two, the woman should check which is financially more advantageous.
Do-it-yourself	Usually this will not be necessary, because of the availability of legal aid. But if the woman wishes to act for herself, she should choose the magistrates' court, where the procedures are less formal than in the county court.
The court's order	There are two procedural advantages of the county court. First, the county court order may last for three months, whereas the magistrates' court will probably say that the order will last for only a month or so. Secondly, the county court rules on serving the order are better, since they allow the woman's solicitor to serve the order for her. In the magistrates' court the order will be served by the police, and, in practice, they do not regard this as a priority task. Delay often occurs and they may make no great effort to track down the man.
Children	If there are children, the woman should choose the county court. It is generally the better place for making orders affecting children.
If no violence has occurred	Only the county court can make an order if there has not already been violence (see above).
If the parties were not living together	An application will have to be made to the county court (see above).
The court	There are many more magistrates' courts than county courts, so it may be more convenient to choose the magistrates' court.

The county court injunction

If the wife (married or common-law) needs help as a matter of urgency, she should apply to the county court or divorce court for an injunction against the man. An injunction is a court order directing a person not to behave in a particular way; in domestic-violence cases, the injunction tells the husband not to molest the woman and children and/or not to re-enter the matrimonial home.

Orders that could be included in an injunction are:
- not to assault the woman (called a 'non-molestation order');
- not to assault the children;
- to leave the home and not return (called an 'exclusion order' or an 'ouster');
- to allow the woman back into the home;
- to keep away from the home (e.g. not to come within a quarter of a mile of the home).

If the man breaks the injunction (for instance, by hitting the woman or trying to re-enter the home) he can be brought before the court and punished – if necessary, by imprisonment. However, it can take time to summons him before the court, and a more effective way of enforcing the injunction is to allow the police to enforce it. The problem is that the police will not normally intervene in what they call 'domestic disputes', and so they will usually refuse to eject the husband even if he has broken an injunction. The only exception is where the court backed up the injunction by attaching 'a power of arrest' to it. If there is a 'power of arrest' then the police will have no choice but to intervene and enforce the injunction if asked to do so.

Thus it is usual for the wife's lawyer to ask the court to attach a power of arrest to the injunction, so that the husband can be arrested if he breaks it. But, in practice, county courts might refuse to attach a power of arrest, unless the case is particularly serious. Certainly a power of arrest will not be granted unless there is clear evidence that the woman or child has suffered actual bodily harm.

If there is a power of arrest and the man breaks the injunction, the police can keep him in custody for up to twenty-four hours before bringing him before a judge for punishment. If there is no power of arrest, then the police cannot intervene and the woman will have to give the man at least two days' notice if she intends to apply for him to be committed to prison because he has broken the injunction. During that two-day period the woman is often at risk.

Ordering the man out of the home

It is much more difficult to persuade the court to grant an exclusion order, ordering the man out of the home, than it is to obtain a non-molestation or personal protection order, which merely orders him to stop assaulting and threatening the wife and children.

Whether or not an exclusion order will be made will depend on all the circumstances – in particular, how quickly the wife has gone to court, and the extent of the violence. It is important to realize that a domestic-violence injunction is only a temporary remedy; the courts take the view that it is reasonable to evict a man from his home for three months or so but then permanent arrangements must be worked out. For instance:

Ms O'Neill and Mr Williams cohabited in a flat, which they owned in their joint names. In August he assaulted her and so she moved out. She hoped there would be a reconciliation and so it was not until October that she went to see solicitors. They applied for legal aid (to cover the costs of going to court for an exclusion order against Williams) but legal aid was not granted until February. The court then held that it was too late: exclusion orders are designed to give temporary, emergency, relief whilst long-term solutions are sorted out. Now that six months had passed, it would not be right to order Williams to leave the flat in which he had a half-share. So, the injunction was refused and Ms O'Neill would have to apply to the court for an order that the flat be sold and the proceeds split fifty/fifty. O'Neill (1984)*

More recently courts have emphasized that ouster orders will be given only where the situation has reached crisis point and there is no alternative.

An unmarried couple obtained a council tenancy. The woman spent one or two nights there but then returned home to live with her parents. Some time later, a violent dispute broke out and the woman applied for a non-molestation injunction and an ouster order. Orders were made and the man appealed. Held: An ouster order was a draconian order and should be made only after the evidence had been looked at with the greatest possible care and should be made only in extreme circumstances. Tuck v. Nicholls (1989)

Apart from questions of delay or emergency, the court will also look at:

1 Whose name is the property in (whether it be owned or rented)? If the property is in the sole name of the woman she will find it much easier to obtain an order than if it is in the sole name of the husband. This is particularly so if the couple are not married. If the couple are unmarried and the property is in the sole name of the man, the woman may obtain an exclusion order but it will not be permanent. The court will not deprive the man of his property permanently, so the woman can expect only three to six months' protection. The aim of an injunction is to give the woman a chance to find somewhere else to live. This is so whether the house is owned or rented.

2 How large is the property? Could it be divided up so that the couple can lead separate lives?

3 Is there anywhere else for the husband (or boyfriend) to go? Has he friends or relatives he can stay with?

4 What assaults or threats have been made to the woman or children? When was the most recent? Are further attacks likely? If not, there is virtually no chance of the man being ordered out. Has the man since made a sincere

apology and promised to behave himself in the future? If so, what are the chances of his keeping his word?

5 Is it likely to cause mental or physical suffering to the woman and/or the children if the man is allowed to continue living in the same house? In short, is it impossible for her to continue living with him?

Applying 'on notice' or '*ex parte*'

Applications to a court are usually made after notifying the defendant (i.e. the man) of the date of the application and the type of order that the court is being asked to make. Such an application is said to be made 'on notice'.

However, it is not always necessary to warn the defendant beforehand. In emergency cases the application to the court can be made without notice; such an application is said to be made '*ex parte*'.

Usually, of course, the battered woman would prefer that the application be made *ex parte*, so that the man does not know about it until after the injunction or order has been granted. Naturally, she will be worried that he will assault her if he is given notice of the proposed application. However, *ex parte* applications are only for real emergencies – i.e. more-serious-than-average cases where there is real immediate danger of serious injury or irreparable damage. While non-molestation and personal protection orders can be obtained without difficulty *ex parte*, it is much more difficult to obtain an exclusion order *ex parte*. This is because the courts are reluctant to exclude a man from his home without giving him a full chance of explaining himself to the court and of being able to call witnesses to support his version of events. This is particularly so when the home is either rented or owned in the sole name of the man. The woman's solicitor will be able to advise her whether the case is sufficiently grave to justify an *ex parte* application.

Obtaining the injunction

If she wishes, the woman can act for herself and apply to the court without the help of a solicitor. However, in practice it is advisable to use a solicitor since he or she will be more familiar with the procedure and can act more speedily. Legal aid will usually be available (see page 964). Relatively few solicitors specialize in this sort of work so it is advisable to ask at a Citizens' Advice Bureau or Women's Aid Centre for the name of an experienced, competent solicitor. Then:

1 The solicitor will type out an originating application asking the county court to grant an injunction and specifying the type of injunction sought. Two extra copies will be made – one for the court and one for the man.

2 The solicitor will take a detailed statement from the woman, which will then be set out as a formal affidavit to be signed by the woman (see Appendix 2;

note that it does not only deal with the last violent incident but also explains why further violence is likely). Sometimes an affidavit will also be taken from a witness.

3 The solicitor will then take the papers to the court and pay a £15 fee; legal aid may pay the fee. In an exceptional emergency, the application can be made *ex parte*, and the hearing will take place immediately. In less exceptional circumstances the application must be on notice, and the man must be given at least four days' advance warning.

4 The application will be heard before the judge. The hearing will be in chambers, a private room, and not in a public courtroom.

5 If the case is heard on notice, the violent partner may attend and give an undertaking to the court not to attack the victim and/or the children. The drawback of an undertaking is that no power of arrest can be attached to it (see below), so it is usually safer for the victim to try and get a full court order as in 6 below.

6 The judge makes his order. If he grants an injunction (see pages 106, 107), the solicitor will ask him to attach a power of arrest (see page 106). The importance of this is that the police must arrest the man if he breaks the injunction. But courts are reluctant to attach a power of arrest – the Court of Appeal has said it is only for 'exceptional circumstances, where the man or woman persisted in disobeying an injunction'. Even if a power of arrest is granted, it is unlikely to be valid for more than three months.

7 The injunction must be served on the man. Only then does it become effective, unless a power of arrest is attached. The solicitor will usually arrange for service.

8 If the man disobeys the injunction the position depends upon whether the injunction had a power of arrest attached:
   • *if there was a power of arrest* the woman should contact the police, who will already have a copy of the injunction. They should arrest the man (although often they refuse to) and keep him in custody until he appears before the judge, usually within the next twenty-four hours. The woman should attend that hearing, having sworn an affidavit setting out the details of how the injunction was broken.
   • *if there was no power of arrest* the woman will have to go back to the county court. Her solicitor will try to arrange a speedy hearing in front of the judge who granted the injunction. The man must be given at least two days' notice of the hearing and the woman will have to swear an affidavit setting out how the injunction was broken. In practice, there is likely to be a delay of at least a week between the woman contacting her solicitor again and the case being heard by the judge. This is the disadvantage of not having a power of arrest.

Either way, the judge will read the affidavits and listen to what the man has to say. The man may be given another chance or he may be sent to prison for contempt of court. However, if he tells the judge he is sorry and that he will not break the injunction again, he is unlikely to go to prison. Similarly, if he is sent to prison he will probably be released as soon as he apologizes to the court and promises not to break the injunction again.

A set of legal documents from a typical domestic-violence case is shown in Appendix 2.

If the couple are unmarried

If the couple are unmarried, there is a loophole in the legislation that can mean the woman has only a pyrrhic victory. If the furniture in the home belongs to the man the court cannot prevent it being removed on his behalf. So, although the woman will have possession of the house or flat, the court cannot ensure that she also has the use of the furniture. If the woman has limited means – as is often the case – her inability to buy new furniture will make her court order of limited practical value. This is a loophole in the law that should be closed.

If the woman is homeless

The local authority has a duty to house homeless people who have a 'priority need' (see Chapter 62). The government's Code of Guidance says that battered women with children are always a priority need. If there are no children, the woman should be regarded as a priority need if she risks further violence by returning home. Note that the council cannot argue that a battered woman is 'intentionally' homeless in an attempt to avoid their duty to house: the Code of Guidance says 'a battered woman who has fled the marital home should never be regarded as having become homeless intentionally, because it would clearly not be reasonable for her to remain'.

7 Parents and Children

REGISTERING A CHILD'S BIRTH

Within six weeks of a child being born, the birth must be registered with the District Registrar for Births, Marriages and Deaths. Births are usually registered in the district where the child was born. But you can register the birth at a local Register Office.

The registrar will take details of the date and place of birth. The child's sex and names and the mother's details (name, surname and her address) will always be entered. If the parents are married, then the father's details (name, surname and occupation) will also be entered. If the parents are not married, then the father's details will be entered only in the circumstances set out below.

Who can register the birth

If the parents are married, either the mother or father alone can register the birth. If the parents are unmarried, only the mother can register the birth on her own but both parents can register it jointly.

The name of the father of an illegitimate child can be added to a birth certificate only if:
- the father wishes it and the mother consents, *or*
- if the mother asks for his name to be registered and has a statutory declaration sworn by the father in which he declares he is the father, *or*
- on production of a court order showing the man to be the father.

Naming a child

Children ordinarily take and are registered under their father's surname, but this need not be the case. Children can be registered under their mother's surname or a hyphenated version of their parents' surnames joined together. For example, Jane, the newly born daughter of John White and Jessica Black (who kept using her maiden name after her marriage) could be registered as Jane Black-White or Jane White-Black if the parents so choose.

Altering the register

If the child has already been registered but no person has been registered as the father, the register can be altered to show a man to be the father if the mother consents or if a court order is produced proving the man to be the father.

The register can also be changed within twelve months of registration if the parents want to change the name of the child or if there has been an error in the details recorded.

Otherwise, the register cannot be altered unless the child is adopted. A later change of name, even by statutory declaration or deed poll, cannot alter the details on the certificate.

BIRTH CERTIFICATES

There are two types of birth certificate. The short version does not give full details of the parents and thus conceals the fact that a child is born outside marriage. One copy of this is provided free at the time of registration. The long form of birth certificate includes the parents' details. The long and short forms are equally valid.

If a birth certificate is lost, certified copies can be obtained from the register office where the birth was registered or from the Central Register of Births and Marriages at St Catherine's House, Aldwych, London WC2 for a fee (£5.50 for the long form, £3.50 for the short form for applicants in person; a search of the entries will cost £13).

ADOPTED CHILDREN

When a child is adopted, the Registrar General enters the adoption in the Adopted Children's Register, which sets out the date, county, district and sub-district of the birth, the new names of the child, its sex, the name, address and occupation of the adopters, the date when the adoption order was made and the court that made the order. This is the child's new full birth certificate and effectively replaces the original one.

A short form of birth certificate can be obtained which makes no mention of the child's biological parents or of the fact that the child has been adopted.

Adopted people over eighteen can trace the names and particulars of their parents on the original birth register. If the adoption was made before 12 November 1975 this information will be made available only after the young person has seen a counsellor. Counselling services are provided by the Registrar General, local authorities and adoption agencies. Applications can be made to the General Register Office, Titchfield, Fareham, Hampshire.

An Adoption Contact Register has been created by the Children Act 1989, kept by the Registrar General. Both people who have been adopted and their relatives (which includes anyone related by blood or marriage, not only the natural parents) can apply to have their names and addresses put on the

Contact Register. This helps speed up the process for adopted children in tracing their birth family: details of relatives registered will be passed on to adopted children who themselves apply to be registered. But it is not a two-way process: birth parents cannot use the register to contact their adopted child without his/her knowledge and consent.

The information kept on the Contact Register is confidential and will not be disclosed to outsiders. In one rare case, the information was not even disclosed to the adopted person.

A man who had been adopted applied for an original birth certificate. He was being detained in Broadmoor, having been convicted for manslaughter. Held: His application should be refused as there was a real risk that if the information were supplied, the applicant's natural mother would be at risk. R v. Registrar General *ex p.* Smith (1990)

APPLYING FOR A PASSPORT

If the child is entitled to British citizenship, either married parent (or a single mother) can apply for their child to be added to their passport by completing a special form available from post offices and sending it to the Passport Office with the birth certificate and fee (currently £4). Photographs are not required. Only in special circumstances will a separate passport be given to a child under five (say, if she will be travelling separately from her parents). Children over sixteen must have their own passport.

CHILDREN BORN OUTSIDE MARRIAGE

Twenty-nine per cent of children born in the UK are born outside marriage. It seems likely that most of these children were born into stable relationships: seven out of ten were registered by both parents living at the same address.

Since the Family Law Reform Act 1987 came into force on 1 April 1989, much of the legal stigma of illegitimacy has been removed and the law gives marital and non-marital children broadly equal rights – for example, to claim maintenance and inheritance from the father.

But one major difference still remains: if the parents were not married at the time of the birth, then only the mother automatically has the legal rights and duties for the child, which is classed by the law as parental responsibility (see also page 121). If the father wants an equal say in the child's upbringing, then he has to acquire parental responsibility, which he can do either:

- with the mother's agreement, *or*
- by applying to court for a court order (see page 114).

Agreeing to share parental responsibility

If the mother agrees to share parental responsibility, both she and the father must sign a special court form (reproduced on page 13) to make that decision effective in law. She should lodge it (with two copies) at the Principal Register of the Family Division, Somerset House, Strand, London WC2R 1LP. No fee is payable. The mother should think carefully about taking such a step. In so doing she will be giving up her sole right to decide issues about the child and she will not be able to reverse her decision later. The father will have an equal and independent say about the child's upbringing which will last until the child reaches eighteen.

Parental responsibility by court order

If the mother refuses to sign the court form, the father can apply to court for a parental responsibility order. The court will grant this only where it is in the best interests of the child. The father will have to show that his application is not made just on impulse, but that he wants to take and play a useful role in the child's development throughout childhood. Parental responsibility can also be obtained by the father by a successful application for a residence order (see page 148).

Child support for non-marital children

For the mother of a non-marital child to be able to get an order for child support from the father or for the father to apply to court for an order (for parental responsibility, residence or contact, for example), paternity must be proved unless both parents accept that the father is the father. If there is any doubt, this can be resolved by way of a blood test or by the newer and more accurate DNA testing.

Blood tests

By comparing the blood of a man with that of a child it is sometimes possible to show that the man could not be the child's father. But blood tests can never show that the man is the father – their sole use is in showing who could *not* be the father. If the man is not the father, a blood test will have a 93 per cent chance of proving this. But blood tests cannot be proof positive of true paternity.

DNA testing

DNA tests, a comparatively recent scientific development, examine bodily samples (this can be blood, semen or hair) from the parents and child and compare the genetic information. Because each person has a distinctive individual genetic fingerprint, the tests are claimed to be 100 per cent accurate. They are more expensive than blood tests. If the costs of tests are to be met by the Legal Aid Board, it will insist on an undertaking by both parents to abide by the testing authority's findings before authorizing payment of the test.

Taking a test

For blood and DNA tests, samples will be needed from the mother, the father and the child. Consent on the child's behalf will usually be given by a parent or another person with parental responsibility (see page 147). Older children of sufficient maturity and understanding have the right to refuse to submit to testing.

If an application to court is made for a test, the court will usually agree to it. In very rare cases, the court can intervene to stop the blood test if it would be against the child's best interests. Thus if a child is thought to be legitimate and the only effect of the test would be to make him illegitimate, with no father, the court might refuse to allow the test to take place.

Refusing to take a test

The court cannot order a man to undergo a test, but it can draw its own conclusions if he refuses to agree to the test. If he does refuse, the court will usually take this as corroboration of the mother's claim that he is the real father.

Fathers' applications

Under the old law, a man could not apply for a court order declaring him to be the father of an illegitimate child. Since 14 October 1991, when the Children Act came into force, a father can apply to court for a parental responsibility order (see opposite) even in the face of the mother's opposition. A parental responsibility order is not quite the same as declaring him to be the true father, but it does firmly establish his legal connection with the child. He could ask the court to order that a DNA test be carried out so that paternity would not be in doubt.

A father could also apply for a declaration of parentage, which resolves the question of paternity once and for all. In practice very few of these applications are made since they do not give the father any actual rights.

Maintenance for non-marital children.

A father of a child born outside marriage is legally bound to contribute towards his child's maintenance. If he will not agree to pay a reasonable amount of maintenance voluntarily, then under current law either the mother or the DSS can apply to court for an order against him. Once the Child Support Act comes into force (at the time of going to press this is due in 1993), the newly created Child Support Agency will have the power to trace him and collect and enforce maintenance payments, assessed according to a formula (see page 118).

BEFORE THE CHILD SUPPORT ACT 1991 COMES INTO FORCE

Written agreement

Before the Child Support Agency is in force, or if parents otherwise wish to make a voluntary arrangement, the mother should ensure that the father signs a written agreement which can be enforced if the man defaults. Voluntary agreements do not preclude the mother making a later application to court. Agreements will usually be enforced by the courts, though the courts do have the power to alter the arrangement if they think fit – this includes the right to increase the payments.

Generally, the more formal the document, the more likely it is that the court will uphold it. The position is the same with voluntary separation and maintenance agreements between husband and wife. But in any event, there are wide powers of the court available for single parents to apply for financial support for their children.

Unwritten agreements

Where the mother is receiving state benefits there are advantages in the father making voluntary extra payments by purchasing goods or making payments to third parties even if he cannot afford to make regular maintenance payments. The DSS will ignore the value of goods and payments made to third parties for items *not* covered by state benefits (which are supposed to cover payments like mortgage interest payments or rent, clothing and food). So the father could help the mother out by paying for things which are not supposed to be covered by welfare benefits, without the mother suffering a deduction pound for pound of her benefit. For example:

● buying her a washing machine;
● buying her a car;
● paying capital repayments on her mortgage;
● paying school fees.

However, if the father does help the mother in this way, it will still not stop either the mother or the DSS making a claim against him for maintenance through the courts (or, from 1993, through the Child Support Agency).

Applications to court

Until the Family Law Reform Act 1987 came into force, applications for maintenance for non-marital children were called affiliation proceedings. Few mothers actually applied to court, discouraged by the complexity of the law and the restrictions of applying to magistrates' courts (which had only limited powers in comparison to county or High courts), as well as the embarrassment of going to court in the first place.

Affiliation proceedings were replaced in April 1989 and the current law has been much simplified. Mothers can apply for a maintenance order for children born outside marriage in the magistrates' court, county court or High Court. They can also apply for a lump-sum order, secured periodical payments or property transfers (see page 10). Applications for financial relief for non-marital children are made in exactly the same way as applications for children born within marriage, save that paternity will have to be established too if the father denies he is the father.

The test is whether it is probable (not possible) that the man is the father. Corroborative evidence can include:

- an admission by the father of his paternity;
- evidence of sexual intercourse between the parents around the time of conception;
- proof of cohabitation;
- the man's name appearing on the birth certificate.

DNA tests can now conclusively prove whether or not a man is the father. If the father refuses to take a test, his refusal can itself amount to corroboration.

AFTER THE CHILD SUPPORT ACT COMES INTO FORCE

The Child Support Act 1991

The Child Support Act applies to non-marital children as well as to those born within marriage. It was introduced because of the courts' poor record in ensuring that child support was paid – seven in ten lone parents on welfare benefit received no child maintenance from the fathers. If the Act comes into force as scheduled in 1993, it will provide a comparatively simple and even-handed method of calculating and enforcing payment of child maintenance.

All mothers on welfare benefits will have to use the new Child Support Agency. Other mothers will be able to use it if they choose, but may have to pay a fee (likely to be a lot less than solicitors' costs for going to court to get an order for maintenance).

The Agency will provide a form asking the mother for details about the child and the identity of the father. If mothers on welfare benefits refuse to give the name of the father, they will be at risk of having the adult personal allowance of their income support reduced as a penalty (by 20 per cent in the first six months, less thereafter). There are limited exceptions to the penalty – for example, in cases of incest or rape, or if otherwise there is good cause. But mothers can expect to be questioned closely if they are reluctant to tell the Agency about the father.

The Child Support Agency will assess the amount of maintenance the absent parent must pay according to a special, rather complex formula.

Child support formula

The child support formula is complicated to work out. The following just provides a summary, as the Child Support Act was not up and running at the time of going to press. Contact your solicitor or Citizens' Advice Bureau to ascertain whether the Act has been implemented and for further advice.

The formula is based on five different calculations:

1 The maintenance requirement.
2 Exempt income.
3 Assessable income.
4 Deduction rate.
5 Protected income.

1. The maintenance requirement

This represents the day-to-day expenses of raising a child and is based on income support rates. The weekly levels set for the children vary according to the child's age (examples are £13.60 for a child under eleven and £23.90 for a child of sixteen – 1991 figures). Added to the level set for each child is the family premium, £8.70, plus the lone parent premium (where the caring parent is bringing up the child on her own), £4.45, and the adult personal allowance, £39.65 for a woman over twenty-five. The added personal allowance is set at a higher level when the children are young but reduces as they get older. Child benefit is deducted from the maintenance requirement.

2. Exempt income

This applies to both parents' income and represents their own essential living expenses. It covers a personal allowance, for day-to-day living costs, plus the costs of caring for their natural children, plus their actual housing costs.

3. Assessable income

This is the part of a liable parent's income used for calculating the amount of maintenance due. It is the difference between the potential payer's net income (after deduction of tax, national insurance and half of pension contributions) and his exempt income. Assessable income will be divided fifty/fifty between the children and the absent parent up to the amount of the maintenance requirement.

4. Deduction rate

Once the maintenance requirement has been paid, if there is any extra assessable income belonging to the payer, a further sum of maintenance will be payable at a lower rate of deduction – i.e. 25 per cent of the maximum amount of maintenance.

This is an example of the maintainance requirement for two children aged six and four (1991 figures):

child allowances 2 × £13.60	£27.20
family premium	£8.70
lone parent premium	£4.45
adult personal allowance	£39.65
subtotal	£80.00
Less child benefit	– £16.75
total maintenance	£63.25

The actual amount that would be payable by the absent parent depends on his own income and needs, as indicated above.

5. Protected income

This is designed to prevent the payer's income falling to income support levels or below as a result of child maintenance commitments. The payer's income will not be allowed to drop below the protected income level.

There is a ceiling set to the maximum amount of maintenance which the absent parent will pay to the Child Support Agency, calculated by adding an extra amount for each child on to the maintenance bill. If a parent wants to ask for maintenance over and above this formula, then she will have to apply to the courts.

The Child Support Agency

It is the duty of the Child Support Agency to trace the father and collect maintenance payments from him, and enforce arrears if any become due. The Agency is a new and separate body, evolving from the DSS rather than the tax inspectorate (as in other countries where Child Support Agencies have had success in increasing payments made, like Australia). Although it is due to have access to some central records, these may not include tax records, thus limiting the Agency's power to trace fathers who try to slip the net. None the less, it will have much greater powers than individual single parents to ensure prompt payments.

Lone parents on welfare support will have the amount of maintenance deducted pound for pound from income support, although the first £15 of the maintenance will be disregarded (or ignored) when calculating a lone parent's entitlement to family credit, housing benefit and community charge benefit, so here the family will actually be better off.

The Agency will be able to get an order that maintenance collected by the Agency is deducted straight from the father's salary.

The Agency will be useful for cases where fathers are employed (if they are themselves on welfare benefits they will not have to pay). Where they are self-employed and/or work as part of the black economy (cash up front, no questions asked), the Agency is just as likely to experience difficulties as any lone parent trying to extract maintenance on her own.

Voluntary agreements

Once the Child Support Agency is up and running to collect payments, there will be few remaining incentives for lone parents to make voluntary arrangements for maintenance payments with the absent parent. Unless the maintenance payments paid voluntarily are more than the amount which would be fixed by the Agency, there is no advantage to the mother in relying on the father's goodwill in making payments.

ABORTION

A man cannot get a court order preventing his wife or girlfriend from having an abortion. Nor can parents usually obtain an injunction to stop their teenage daughter from having an abortion.

A pregnant sixteen-year-old girl obtained medical approval for an abortion which her parents then tried to prevent. Held: The expectant mother had sufficient intelligence and understanding (both about the abortion and her obligations to her parents) to make up her own mind. Wren (1987)

The 1967 Abortion Act makes it lawful for a doctor to carry out an abortion during the first twenty-eight weeks of pregnancy * *if:*
● the continuance of the pregnancy would involve risk to the mother's life, *or*
● the continuance of the pregnancy would involve risk to the physical or mental health of the mother or her other children [social circumstances can thus be taken into account], *or*
● there is substantial risk that the child would be born with a physical or mental abnormality that would make it seriously handicapped.
The consent of two doctors is necessary. A doctor or nurse can refuse to take part in an abortion on the grounds of conscience. The NHS will not always provide a free abortion and sometimes the mother may have to go to a fee-paying clinic. A mother who is having difficulty arranging an abortion should contact one of the pro-abortion charities, such as the British Pregnancy Advisory Service.

UNPLANNED CHILDREN

On a related topic, what happens if a man or woman has a vasectomy or sterilization operation but then has a child? Some judges have held that it is wrong for the parents then to be able to sue over the child's birth, but latterly the opposing view seems to have gained ground.

---

* A Parliamentary Bill in 1990 to reduce the period for lawful abortions to twenty-four weeks was unsuccessful.

A vasectomy was carried out properly but the doctor forgot to tell the man that it could not be 100 per cent guaranteed that he would not father a child. When a child was born, the man sued for breach of contract. Held: Damages should be awarded. The man and his wife were awarded a total of £8,600 damages (£2,000 for her loss of earnings between the birth and the time the child started school; the rest being the cost of upbringing, based on supplementary benefit [the old equivalent of income support] rates). Thake (1985)

Thus damages can be claimed if a sterilization or vasectomy operation goes wrong.

CHILDREN: WHOSE RESPONSIBILITY?

In the thirty years or so culminating in the Children Act 1989, there has been a dramatic shift in the way the law regulates relationships between parents and children. Children were once viewed as little more than objects over which parents had rights. The law then began to recognize that children had rights too. Thus the right of access to a child for a separated parent was seen as the child's right (not a parent's). Whether access would be awarded by the courts depended on what was in the child's (not the parent's) *best interests*.

Since 14 October 1991, when the Children Act 1989 came into effect, the focus has shifted yet again, with the emphasis now on parents' *responsibilities* towards their children. The Children Act introduced the new concept of parental responsibility – a durable link between parents and children which will not be ended by divorce and which usually lasts until the child is eighteen.

The change in the law is intended to produce a change in the way children and their families are treated by the legal system. So in future the courts will not interfere in the arrangements parents make for their children unless a specific problem arises. On divorce, for example, the courts will not make an order about where the children will live if the parents can agree this between themselves (see page 150).

The new, stronger legal requirement that children's welfare is the court's paramount consideration when considering any question about their upbringing or maintenance aims to put children first. The child's best interests will override the feelings of the parents.

Parental responsibility

Someone has to be legally responsible for a child until it grows up and reaches the age of eighteen. In law, the people responsible are those with parental responsibility.

Having parental responsibility is not the same as being a parent. Not all parents have parental responsibility automatically (see below). Also, people who are not parents can be given parental responsibility.

Parental responsibility is defined as 'all the rights, duties, powers and responsibilities and authority which by law a parent has in relation to the child and his property' (s. 3, Children Act 1989).

121

In practice parental responsibility covers the responsibility and right to, for example:

- maintain and protect the child;
- ensure he or she receives medical treatment;
- appoint a guardian to care for the child after a parent's death;
- make sure the child is educated between five and sixteen years old and choose the child's school;
- name the child and register its birth;
- apply for the child's passport;
- choose the child's religion;
- decide where the child is to live.

Who has parental responsibility?

These people have parental responsibility automatically:

- married parents;
- unmarried mothers.

Married parents both continue to have parental responsibility even if the marriage breaks down. The only ways that they, or unmarried mothers, can lose parental responsibility are if the court makes an order terminating it (this is hardly ever likely to happen) or if the child is adopted.

Note: married parents who divorced before the Children Act came into force on 14 October 1991 will also both have parental responsibility.

Unmarried fathers can obtain parental responsibility by:

- making an agreement with the mother drawn up on a special court form (see page 13), *or*
- successfully applying to court for parental responsibility, *or*
- successfully applying to court for a residence order, *or*
- being appointed a guardian by the mother.

Also, if an unmarried father (i.e. a father who was not married to the mother at the time of the child's birth) had an order predating the Children Act for custody, care and control or parental rights and duties in his favour, then as from 14 October 1991 that order will automatically include parental responsibility.

Stepfathers and stepmothers cannot acquire parental responsibility on its own, but they can apply for a residence order, which then gives them parental responsibility too.

Anyone with a residence order in their favour (this can include a grandparent looking after a child following a family split) will also have parental responsibility. In this case, parental responsibility lasts only as long as the residence order lasts.

If a care order has been made for a child, then the local authority looking after the child in care also has parental responsibility (but the local authority does not get parental responsibility if it is just providing accommodation for a child – the new Children Act term for voluntary care). However, parents do not lose their rights while children are in care; they still continue to have parental responsibility and they and the local authority have to work in partnership (see page 165).

What does having parental responsibility mean in practice?

One of the most important differences about this new concept of parental responsibility is the increased amount of flexibility it gives to anyone who has it. Anyone with parental responsibility can act independently of others with parental responsibility and can make up their own minds about what is best for a child. They do not have a formal legal duty to consult anyone else with parental responsibility before making a decision (e.g. where the child should go to school), although on a practical level good parenting works best if the parents discuss issues about the children and make a joint decision.

It is easy to see how this could work well while the parents are together or, for example, in an emergency. If, say, a mother has to take her child to casualty, she does not have to consult the father and obtain his agreement before giving the medical staff the go-ahead for an operation.

Some parents have expressed concern about how the new concept will work if the parents divorce, especially if the split-up is very bitter. But the important thing to remember is that while, on the one hand, the courts give parents a lot of flexibility to make up their own minds and will not interfere unnecessarily in family life, if disputes do arise which the parents just cannot sort out between themselves, either can apply for a court order. The new court orders that can be applied for are much simpler and the process for applying for them quicker and more streamlined (see page 147)

There are also a few legal restrictions and guidelines about the exercise of parental responsibility:

• The exercise of parental responsibility must not contravene any court order. If, for example, a father has a contact order for weekend access in his favour, the mother cannot disappear with the children at the weekend to frustrate the contact order.

• A person with parental responsibility cannot give it away or transfer it, but they may arrange for some of it to be met by someone else acting on their behalf. Anyone looking after a child may do what is reasonable to safeguard the child.

GUARDIANS

Guardians can be appointed by the parents (under a will or in writing) or by the court to care for the children after the parents die. A guardian will have full parental responsibility just as if he or she were the parent. Not everyone is willing to take on the responsibility of becoming a guardian for children who are not their own, so a potential guardian should be asked in advance whether he or she would be willing to undertake this role. Deeds of appointment or wills can be drawn up by a solicitor, who would probably charge around £50 upwards for preparing it. A blank draft deed is set out opposite.

If the parents were married at the time of the child's birth (even if they have divorced), in most cases the appointment of a guardian does not take effect until after both parents have died. This is to avoid battles between the surviving parent and the newly appointed guardian. But if there was a residence order in favour of the deceased parent, then the appointment of a guardian will take effect straight away. If both parents die and both have appointed different guardians who disagree, an application should be made to court for a section 8 order to decide who should act.

If the parents are not married, then only the mother can appoint a guardian, unless the father has parental responsibility too (see page 122). If he does not have parental responsibility, he will have no rights to look after the children after the mother's death. If the mother wants to appoint him as a guardian she must do so by deed or by will (although she can also appoint anyone else she chooses too). If the father does have parental responsibility, then he will automatically take over legal responsibility for the children after the mother's death as a married father would.

In summary, it is crucial that parents (especially unmarried mothers) do appoint guardians during their lifetime and do not just leave it to fate as to who will care for their offspring in future after their death.

MAINTENANCE

Parents have a legal duty to maintain children (whether or not they were married at the time of the birth). Generally, this duty is enforced by the mother seeking a maintenance order against the father (and after 1993 will most likely be enforced through the Child Support Agency). See page 117. But fathers looking after children alone can also make an application for child support against the mother.

Children over eighteen now also have their own right to ask for a maintenance order against a parent if they are in full-time education or training (whether or not they are earning money too – e.g. by working in a bar) if there was no maintenance order existing before the child was sixteen and the parents have separated or divorced.

So the use that can be made of this legal right is fairly limited. It is really designed to give the child the right to apply for maintenance if he or she has gone on to further education and in the meantime the parents have split up and the father has refused to pay his top-up of the grant.

TREATMENT WHEN ILL

The pre-Children Act test was that the parent must behave as a 'reasonable parent' would. If a reasonable parent would send for a doctor or allow an

Draft Deed of Appointment of Guardian

By this DEED OF APPOINTMENT I............................ (mother's name)
of .... (mother's address) APPOINT .... (guardian's name)
of .... (guardian's address) to be the
GUARDIAN of my (minor/infant) son/daughter .... (child's name)
In pursuance of Section 5 of the Children Act, 1989.

Signed, sealed and delivered by the above named (mother's name) ....
(signature) .... In the presence of .... and ....
....(witnesses' names)

.... (first witness's signature)

....
....

Address of witness

....
....

Occupation of witness

....
....
....

.... (second witness's signature)

Address of witness

....
....

Occupation of witness

....

Dated this .... day of ....19 ....

operation, then so should the child's parent. Now the test is that the child's welfare is the paramount consideration: parents' own views may well have to take second place.

If neither parent will consent to a necessary operation on the child, the hospital may inform the Social Services Department of the local authority. If the local authority has reasonable cause to suspect that the child is suffering, or is likely to suffer, significant harm, then it has a duty to investigate and decide whether it should take action to safeguard or promote the child's welfare. It could apply to the court for a child protection order (like a child assessment order or an emergency protection order). It could also apply for a specific issue order or for the child to be made a ward of court, although the court's permission would first have to be obtained. The court could then consent to the medical treatment on the child's behalf. See also page 165.

SEX AND CONTRACEPTION

Girls over the age of sixteen can consent to sexual intercourse. It is a criminal offence for a man to have sexual intercourse with a girl under sixteen, although the girl herself commits no offence. (There is no specific age limit for boys, although the law does not recognize that a boy is capable of having sexual intercourse until he is fourteen.)

But what if a girl under sixteen intends to have sex and wants contraceptive advice?

Mrs Gillick, the mother of four daughters, wrote to her local Health Authority formally forbidding them from giving any contraceptive or abortion advice to her children whilst under sixteen and asking for their written agreement to her request. Receiving no satisfactory assurance, she commenced proceedings, which were appealed up to the House of Lords. Held: Young people have the right to make decisions about their lives and their bodies if they are old enough to have a mature appreciation of the issues and to make up their own minds. Gillick (1985)

Department of Health guidelines advise doctors that they should normally seek parental consent for contraceptive advice but doctors can give advice and help if the patient 'is capable of understanding what is proposed and of expressing his or her wishes' (Lord Fraser in *Gillick*). The court avoided laying down a specific age limit. Doctors can thus give contraceptives to young people below sixteen but doctors must not in any way encourage a breach of the criminal law. In practice, it will be up to doctors themselves.

SURROGACY

A surrogate mother is a woman who agrees to bear a child for a couple (usually because the woman of the couple is infertile). She agrees to hand over the child after the birth. Surrogate arrangements, although rare, are most often made between family members – say, a sister bearing a child for her sister who cannot carry a child to full term. While the law does not prohibit surrogacy, it prohibits payment to surrogate mothers of anything more than their costs involved in the pregnancy and birth (and for the period caring for the baby, if any). The law also protects the woman, allowing her to revoke her agreement to hand the baby over.

To become recognized as parents by the law, the couple should apply to adopt the child.

ADOPTION

See the chart on page 128 for the procedure on adopting a child. An adoption application can be made by: a married couple (both must be at least twenty-one), parent and step-parent (but often a residence order will be preferred – see page 148), or a single person (must be at least twenty-one and unmarried – or if married, spouse permanently living apart). Unmarried couples cannot jointly adopt a child; however, one of them can apply as a single person to adopt.

In practice, of course, the fundamental problem is finding a child to adopt. Begin by asking the adoption officer in the local Social Services Department to provide a list of adoption agencies.

INJURING THE CHILD

Obviously the parent has a duty to look after the child and to avoid injuring it. Deliberate injury or irresponsible neglect may well give rise to criminal proceedings or the local authority taking action. (Local authorities keep records of non-accidental injuries to children and a child abuse register for children at risk in their area.)

There is also the more general question of the parent's liability should he or she injure the child. The law allows the child to sue the parent for negligent injury. The most common form of this is when the child is a passenger in a car driven by its father and is injured; if the father was driving negligently, then he has broken his duty of care to the child and so he can be sued. In practice, of course, the father will have motor insurance to cover his liability for negligent driving and the child will be able to claim compensation from the insurance company. However, a child cannot sue in its own name (except in certain family proceedings), so the action is brought in the name of an adult who is said to act as the child's 'next friend' for the purposes of the action.

A child cannot sue its parents for injuries caused before its birth. For instance, if a child is born retarded because its mother drank alcohol during pregnancy, the child cannot sue its mother for negligence. But a local authority can take action to protect a child after the birth if the mother endangered its health during the pregnancy.

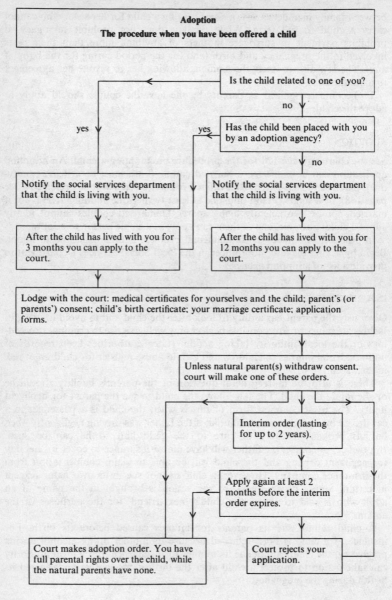

Adoption
The procedure when you have been offered a child

Is the child related to one of you?

no

yes

yes

Has the child been placed with you by an adoption agency?

no

Notify the social services department that the child is living with you.

Notify the social services department that the child is living with you.

After the child has lived with you for 3 months you can apply to the court.

After the child has lived with you for 12 months you can apply to the court.

Lodge with the court: medical certificates for yourselves and the child; parent's (or parents') consent; child's birth certificate; your marriage certificate; application forms.

Unless natural parent(s) withdraw consent, court will make one of these orders.

Interim order (lasting for up to 2 years).

Apply again at least 2 months before the interim order expires.

Court makes adoption order. You have full parental rights over the child, while the natural parents have none.

Court rejects your application.

A mother who was a heroin addict bore a child prematurely: the child was suffering from withdrawal symptoms at birth. The local authority applied for a care order. Held: The child should be taken into care. The court could have regard to events occurring during the pregnancy if they affected a child's health and development after birth. Re D (A Minor) (1986)

CORPORAL PUNISHMENT

Some countries, like Sweden, have introduced special laws to prohibit corporal punishment. Here, the law still allows parents to impose 'reasonable chastisement' on their children. The test is whether a reasonable parent would impose that punishment. So a smack is allowed and will not be an illegal assault on the child. On the other hand, a punch in the face will be unreasonable and will be a criminal offence. In addition, of course, conduct of that sort is likely to lead to the local authority taking action to safeguard the child. Unnatural punishments, such as keeping the child locked up, are illegal.

A mother asked her boyfriend to 'smack' her six-year-old boy for disobedience. The boyfriend hit the boy twice with his belt, bruising him. The social worker saw the bruises and the boy was taken to hospital. The boyfriend was prosecuted for causing actual bodily harm to the boy. Held: He was guilty. Smith (1985)

See page 140 about corporal punishment in schools.

VIOLENT PARENTS

Neighbours and relatives who think that a child is receiving excessive punishment should report their fears to the Social Services Department of the local authority or the National Society for the Prevention of Cruelty to Children. The NSPCC will handle the matter confidentially and cannot be made to disclose a complainant's identity.

The NSPCC received a complaint about the mistreatment of a fourteen-month-old girl. An NSPCC inspector visited the parents and the mother called the family doctor, who examined the child and found it to be unmarked. The mother, who was very upset, sued the NSPCC and demanded to know the name of the informant. The NSPCC refused to disclose the informant's identity. Held: The need for confidentiality overrode other claims and so the NSPCC were not obliged to disclose the identity of the informant. NSPCC (1977)

Since 14 October 1991, NSPCC records can be made available to a *guardian ad litem* in some family proceedings, but this should not affect the confidentiality of an informant's identity.

The NSPCC can itself apply directly to court for a care order for a child (see page 168).

If the father is violent towards the child, the mother can petition for divorce on the fact of her husband's unreasonable behaviour (see page 43). In addition, she will probably be able to obtain an injunction which forbids the father from harming the child and which, in some instances, excludes him from entering the family home (see page 106).

CRUELTY TO CHILDREN

There are numerous criminal charges which can be brought against parents who assault or harm their children. The main offence is the 'cruelty to children' provision in the Children and Young Persons Act 1933, which protects children under sixteen. The accused person must have responsibility for the child (any person who has parental responsibility, or is legally liable to maintain, or otherwise has care of the child) and must have assaulted, ill-treated, neglected, abandoned or exposed the child – which is sufficiently wide to cover general abuse and threats. But, in addition, the prosecution must show that the neglect was 'wilful', in that the act of cruelty was deliberate even though its effect was not anticipated. The offence is triable in the magistrates' court (maximum £2,000 fine and/or six months' prison) or the crown court (up to two years' prison and unlimited fine).

In practice, relatively few prosecutions are brought. The more sensible remedy is to remove the child from the position of danger. This is done either by the local authority taking action to protect the child or by the non-violent parent asking for an injunction stopping the violent parent from hurting the child or excluding them altogether.

THE CHILD'S NATIONALITY

A child takes the nationality (i.e. citizenship) of its father (usually) or the place where it was born. If these are different, the child can choose either, or alternatively sometimes it can have dual nationality by keeping both. This depends on whether both countries allow dual nationality: Britain, for example, allows dual nationality but the US does not; so if a child is entitled to both British and American nationality, eventually it will have to choose one of them only.

If a legitimate child, born abroad, has a mother with British nationality but a foreign father, the parents can apply for the child to be registered as a British citizen. The decision is in the hands of the Secretary of State.

An illegitimate child born in the UK can inherit British citizenship only if the mother is a British citizen or settled in Britain. He or she does not get British citizenship simply by being born in Britain, unless he or she was born before 1 January 1983. An illegitimate child born abroad will be a British citizen if the mother is a British citizen, though this does not necessarily apply if the mother was herself born abroad.

If the child is born on a ship, aircraft or hovercraft which is registered in the UK, that child will be deemed to have been born in the UK. For example, if a child is born in the course of a British Airways flight to Iran, the child will be a UK national. However, if the flight was on an Iranian plane the child would not be of UK nationality unless its father has UK nationality.

GROWING UP

Although the law will rarely allow a contract to be enforced against a child, it does allow children to own money, possessions, and property, but not land (which includes houses). Generally, though, children's possessions are held in trust for them by their parents until the child is old enough to manage its own affairs. If the parent betrays the trust by using the money for his/her own uses, the child can sue the parent for the money lost. The parent is, however, allowed to withdraw money to pay for the child's upkeep, board and education.

Large amounts of money are usually held by independent trustees such as solicitors or bank managers. Generally, they will release money only for the child's maintenance and will not part with other sums unless the permission of the court has been obtained.

Taking a job

For the rules on the employment of children see pages 429–30.

Leaving home

Although the age of majority is eighteen, the courts will intervene only rarely to stop a child in its mid- or late teens from leaving home.

Generally, if the child has reached 'the age of discretion' (approximately sixteen) the court will not intervene. Whilst the parents could apply for a section 8 order (see page 147) or for the child to be made a ward of court (see page 162), the court would be unlikely to intervene unless it could be shown that the child was in danger (e.g. keeping bad company).

Another possibility is for the local authority to take action to safeguard the child (which may involve taking him or her into care) if the child 'is suffering, or is likely to suffer, significant harm' (see page 166).

Generally, the child who has reached the age of discretion, has found a job and is leading a steady life is unlikely to be troubled by the law. The child will not be able to claim income support for himself or herself until aged sixteen, and then only in limited circumstances: where the child is caring for dependent children or is unable to work. Otherwise the child may be able to obtain a discretionary payment of income support to avoid severe hardship (this will depend on whether parents or relatives are willing to support the child).

Growing Up: The Law's Minimum Ages

Age

At birth   A bank or building society account can be opened in the child's name and he or she can own premium bonds.

6 weeks   The child can be handed to prospective adopters.

4½ months   The child can be adopted.

2   The child can join a nursery school.

3   The child must be paid for on public transport.

5   The child must receive full-time education (see page 135) and can drink alcohol in private.

7   The child can draw money from a TSB or PO savings account.

10   The child can be convicted of a crime if it can be shown that he or she knew it was 'wrong' (page 176).

12   The child can buy a pet.

13   The child can open a current bank account, at the discretion of the bank manager.

14   The child:
● can take a part-time job (see pages 429–30);
● can be convicted of a criminal offence as if an adult (although the mode of trial and the sentence will be different); can also be fined up to £400 and (if male) sent to a young offenders' institution;
● can own an airgun;
● can go into a bar with an adult but cannot buy or consume an alcoholic drink.
A boy can be convicted of rape and unlawful intercourse with a girl under sixteen.
The police can take the child's finger and palm prints if they have obtained a magistrates' court order.

15   The child can:
● own a shotgun and ammunition;
● be sent to youth custody;
● be admitted to a film rated 15.

16   The child:
● can marry if there is parental consent (see Chapter 3);
● can buy fireworks;
● can leave school (see page 141) and then work full-time;
● can buy a ticket in a registered public lottery;
● can join a trade union;

- can drink beer, cider, porter or perry in a pub, but only with a meal in a part of the pub that serves meals, not at the bar;
- can drive a moped or tractor;
- can fly solo in a glider;
- can buy cigarettes (he or she can smoke at any age);
- has to pay prescription charges;
- has to pay the full fare on buses, on British rail and on the Underground.

A boy can join the armed forces, with parental consent.

A girl can consent to heterosexual sexual intercourse. (Boys can consent to heterosexual intercourse at any age. There is no law against homosexual intercourse between women.)

17   The child can:

- drive a car or motor cycle;
- go into a betting shop (but not bet);
- have an airgun in a public place;
- fly a plane solo;
- be tried on any charge in an adult court; can also be sent to prison;
- be fined up to £2,000.

A girl can join the armed forces, with parental consent.

18   The child becomes an adult and can:

- vote;
- sue in his/her own name;
- marry without parental consent;
- change his/her name;
- apply for a passport;
- own land (including a house);
- enter into binding contracts;
- obtain credit (including HP) and have a cheque or credit card;
- be eligible for jury service;
- buy drinks in the bar of a pub;
- be tattooed;
- donate blood and organs;
- bet;
- make a will;
- join the armed forces without parental consent;
- be admitted to a film rated 18.

21   The adult can now:

- stand in a general or local election;
- apply for a liquor licence;
- if male, consent to homosexual acts in private;
- drive a lorry or bus.

PARENTS' LIABILITY FOR CHILDREN

Liability for contracts

In legal theory, a parent is liable for his or her children's contracts only if the parent told the child to make the contract or if they allowed the child to appear to be their agent (e.g. if the child orders groceries from the local shop the grocer is entitled to believe that the child is acting on its parents' behalf).

But in practice parents are often made liable for their children's contracts because the parent signs an indemnity or a guarantee agreement. This makes the parent personally liable if the child defaults on payment. Usually, no trader will accept a sizeable order from a child unless the child's parent signs a guarantee or indemnity (in which case the parent is liable).

The child itself is unlikely to be liable to carry out the contract. Only if the contract is for 'necessary' items, or if it is to his/her definite advantage, will it be enforced against him/her. But if a child enters into an unenforceable contract and refuses to pay, the court may order the return of goods. The child can probably enforce the contract against the other, adult, party to the contract, although some lawyers dispute this.

Liability for the child's negligence

Negligence is a failure to take 'reasonable care'. But obviously a different standard of 'reasonableness' has to be applied to a child than to an adult. A child may therefore be able to do an act that injures another person or which damages property and yet not be legally liable, whereas if that same act had been done by an adult, the adult would be legally liable.

So the 'reasonable behaviour' test has to be modified when dealing with children. A seven-year-old boy who injures someone with a catapult will probably not be liable, for the court would be likely to decide that a typical seven-year-old would not appreciate the harm a catapult might do. But if the child was ten, the court might well think that a ten-year-old should have realized the dangers of a catapult and so he would be liable in negligence. The additional problem that arises when suing a child is that the child is unlikely to have any money with which to pay any damages. Usually, the child's parents will not be liable on behalf of their child and so they cannot be made to pay the damages. The practical result of this is that it is only rarely worth suing a negligent child.

But can the parent be sued for the child's negligence? Generally the answer will be 'no'. The parent is not automatically liable for the child's negligence and the parent will be liable only if he or she was negligent. For instance, the court might find that the parent was negligent to give a seven-year-old child a catapult, for if the child is too young to appreciate the dangers of a catapult, perhaps he or she should not be given one. Thus the person injured by the catapult might be able to sue the parent, not for the child's negligence, but for the parent's own negligence in letting the child have the catapult.

The child's education

The Education Act 1944 imposes a duty on parents to ensure that their children are educated and a duty on local education authorities (LEAs) to provide suitable schools. In London, since the Inner London Education Authority (ILEA) was disbanded, its powers have devolved to thirteen London boroughs, which have gained the status of LEAs.

If a child is of compulsory school age (between five and sixteen) he or she must 'receive efficient full-time education suitable to his age, ability, and aptitude'. This duty falls on the person with parental responsibility for the child (usually both parents) and if the local authority thinks that this duty is not being fulfilled, it can give the parent fourteen days to prove that the child is receiving suitable education. If the local authority is not satisfied with the explanation offered, it will apply for an education supervision order on the parents. If this is ignored, the parents will be summonsed to appear in the magistrates' court.

Thus parents cannot refuse their child an education. However, it does not necessarily follow that the child has to go to school; the parents can discharge their duty to provide suitable efficient full-time education by, for example, employing a tutor or teaching the child themselves. The parent who chooses to do this need not notify the local education authority beforehand, but once the local education authority learns that the child is not attending school it will require the parents to prove that the child is being properly educated.

The 1944 Act does not define what is a 'suitable' education, other than to say it must be full-time, and suited to the child's age, ability and aptitude. Much is, therefore, left to the discretion of the LEA, but it cannot insist that the child be taught the same range of subjects as is available at the local school or even that its education be as efficient. There is no need for the parents who are teaching their own children to be qualified teachers, although if they are suitably qualified that will be an important factor in deciding the authority's attitude.

If the parents cannot satisfy the LEA that the child's education meets the statutory standard they may first be given formal warning that the LEA intends to apply for an education supervision order. The parents may be able to delay matters by appealing against the LEA's choice of school, but the end result may well be the service of an education supervision order, to secure that the child is 'properly educated'. This order will usually last for a year, but it can be extended for up to three (see Truancy and School Attendance, page 138). In addition, the LEA could apply for the child to be taken into care if it is not receiving official full-time education.

Types of schools

The Education Acts refer to a confusing variety of schools. Officially, the categories are:

County schools. Entirely financed by LEAs. Most primary and secondary schools come within this category.

Voluntary schools. These get some financial help from the LEA and are of three types:
• *controlled schools:* run by voluntary organizations, but the LEA will nominate two-thirds of the governors and pay all the running costs (and appoint the teachers);
• *aided schools:* receive 85 per cent of their running costs from the Secretary of State or the LEA. Two-thirds of the governors are appointed by the voluntary body (the others by the LEA);
• *special-agreement schools:* these are relatively rare (about 100 or so, mostly Catholic, with some Church of England).

Special schools. For those with a 'learning difficulty' (see opposite).

Direct-grant schools. These receive some grant aid. Most are former grammar schools which opted to go 'independent' rather than be drawn more closely into the county schools system.

There is no duty on LEAs to provide comprehensive education. A 1976 Act did introduce such a duty, but it was repealed in 1979, so now there is just a power for LEAs to impose the comprehensive system.

Choosing the school

The Education Act 1981 gives parents some say in the choice of their children's school. Parents' rights to choose a school for their child are being strengthened but schools still have a discretion about accepting pupils. Many schools operate admissions procedures, with priority being given to children within the locality and whose siblings attend the school, for example. These procedures must be fair. If the parents' chosen school refuses to accept their child, this is taken to be a decision of the local authority and can usually be appealed.

The choice of school is made by the person with parental responsibility for the child, which will usually, of course, be the parents.

Finding out about the local schools. Most parents will find about their local schools through informal contacts – friends, neighbours, etc. But, in addition, the LEA is obliged to provide certain basic information. The Education (School Information) Regulations of 1981 require that the local authority should let inquirers know:
• the number of children that will be admitted to a school in the coming year;
• the admission arrangements for children who do not live in the authority's area;
• transport arrangements (and whether help is given towards travel costs);
• the functions of the authority and the school governors as regards admissions.

The local authority's decision. The education authority need not accept the parent's choice of school. Under section 6 of the Education Act 1981, the authority can use one of three excuses:

1 It would prejudice the provision of efficient education, or the efficient use of resources. This is a very wide let-out clause but it will generally be used when there are no spaces available in the school, or if preference is to be given to children who live more locally to the school.
2 It would be incompatible with the normal admission policy of the school (e.g. a church school that only takes children from a particular parish).
3 The child is refused admission because of 'ability or aptitude' (e.g. if there is an 11-plus exam, which the child has not passed).

Appealing against the authority's decision. The authority should provide details of the appeals procedure, but all appeals must be in writing; a time limit for making the appeal will usually be laid down, but this cannot be less than fourteen days. Usually, a simple letter of appeal will be enough but it is important to give a reason for the appeal. The sort of reasons that are more likely to be taken seriously are that: the child does live in the school's catchment area; brothers and sisters go to the school or to another school in that area; older brothers and sisters had been to the school that was being rejected (i.e. the parents have had one child there and do not want another to go); the child's home is very close to the school; there are genuine medical or social reasons (but try to get a doctor's certificate in support). On the other hand, the sort of reasons that are less likely to make the authority change its mind would include: convenience for mother's shopping or child-minding arrangements; parents wish to have the child educated at a single-sex (or co-ed) school; better sports facilities at a particular school; the child's friends will be going to the school.

In practice, it is difficult to win an appeal for a child who lives outside the school's catchment area. If a written appeal is made, there will eventually be a private hearing at which the parent can argue his/her case. After the appeal, a dissatisfied parent can complain to the Secretary of State for Education that the authority's admission arrangements are 'unreasonable', but in practice such complaints very rarely succeed.

Special schools

The Education Act 1981 saw a change in the way of dealing with children who have 'special educational needs'. The previous policy had been to send them to special schools but the 1981 Act introduced a policy, wherever possible, of keeping such children in ordinary schools (i.e. they are not to be segregated into special schools). In practice, this has been no more than a statement of intent because lack of money has prevented it being implemented.

The LEA can decide that a child has 'special educational needs', in which case the parent must be told, and be consulted. The LEA can then go on to make a formal assessment. The procedures are extremely complex but involve the LEA in preparing a written statement of the child's special needs, which can be appealed by the parent. The parent can also ask for reassessment. Advice on the procedures (and the tactics of appealing) can be obtained from a Citizens' Advice Bureau or from one of the specialist educational advice bodies.

Truancy and school attendance

A parent commits an offence if the child does not regularly attend the school where it is registered, unless, of course, the child is receiving suitable full-time education elsewhere (s.39, 1944 Act).

The offence is committed even if the parents were unaware that the child was not attending school. The only defences to the charge are:

• the child did not attend school because of sickness, *or*

• the child could not attend school because of some unavoidable cause affecting the child (i.e. not affecting the parent), *or*

• the child was absent on days set aside for religious observance (either the parents or the child must follow that religion), *or*

• the school is not within walking distance of the child's home, and the local education authority has not provided transport or arranged for transfer to a nearer school. ('Walking distance' for children under eight is 2 miles, and for those over eight, it is 3 miles; distances are measured by the shortest practicable route, i.e. disregarding heavy traffic – but the child is not expected to use an isolated track.)

In practice, prosecution is a last resort. The first step will be for an education welfare officer to call on the parents to discuss why the child is not attending school. If it is simply because the parents are too poor to pay for a school uniform, the local authority may help with the cost. A prosecution for truancy (i.e. failing to secure regular attendance of a child at school) is a different offence from failing to register a child at school. If the parents do not register the child at school, then they will probably be served with an education supervision order. See page 135.

If it seems to be the *parents* who are at fault, the LEA will usually serve a warning notice on them. If there is no improvement, the parents may be prosecuted (maximum penalty: £400 fine and one month's prison).

If it is the *child* who is at fault, the case will go before the juvenile court. The court will consider reports from the education welfare service and will usually adjourn the case for four weeks to give the child a last chance. Most children heed this warning, but if the child continues to play truant, the next step will probably be a referral to a child guidance clinic. An alternative would be an education supervision order.

School rules

Local education authorities can lay down rules covering such matters as dress, length of hair and discipline, and these rules can apply not just while the child is at the school, but on his or her way to and from the school. If the child breaks these rules (e.g. because they are improperly dressed) then the school can refuse to admit them. The child's parents will then be failing in their duty to ensure that the child is being educated.

The School Regulations of 1959 govern the exclusion of children from school. There are, in fact, three different sanctions available and they have different consequences:

1 Exclusion.
2 Expulsion.
3 Suspension.

Exclusion. A child can be excluded on medical grounds (for instance, if it is infected with vermin, or otherwise medically unfit to be at school). In practice, pregnant girls are often excluded from school on this ground, even though LEAs are under a duty to continue to educate them. Confusingly, some LEAs also use the word exclusion when suspending a child who has not complied with one of the school rules (e.g. as to dress).

Expulsion. This is the ultimate sanction. However, this is reserved for serious breaches of discipline, since if the child is of compulsory school age (see below) he or she must receive schooling from the LEA. This means that if he or she is expelled, the LEA must find another school.

It is not within the power of a head teacher of a school to expel a pupil. The articles of government of the school will lay down who has the authority to expel; it will be either the LEA or the governors, or a combined decision of the LEA with the governors. It will never be the head who expels.

In practice, expulsions are rare and are usually dressed up as suspensions. This avoids the LEA having to provide a place in another school for the child.

Suspension. This is primarily designed for use against children who break school rules (e.g. against the wearing of jewellery). A suspended child remains on the school register and accordingly there is no need for the LEA to find another school place for the child. Accordingly, it is a temptation for LEAs to suspend pupils rather than expel them. However, by suspending a child for an indeterminate length of time, the practical effect is the same as that of expulsion – the child does not attend school.

The procedure for suspending a child will be set out in the school's articles of government. These may differ from one LEA to another but it is likely that they conform to the Model Articles, which state that the head teacher shall 'have the power of suspending pupils from attendance for any cause which s/he considers adequate, but on suspending a pupil s/he shall forthwith report the case to the governors who shall consult the local education authority'. Sometimes the consent of the governors is also needed before a child can be suspended.

A parent has no legal right to see the school's articles of government, although in practice most head teachers will show them to an interested parent.

When a child is suspended, the parent should write to the head teacher asking for details as to why the suspension took place and for how long it is to last. They should also ask whether they have the right of appeal; copies of the letter should be sent to the governors and to the LEA. It is important that the head teacher is asked to specify the length of the suspension; this will help prevent the suspension becoming indeterminate in length.

Corporal punishment

Teachers no longer have a right to inflict corporal punishment on their pupils whose education is paid for from public funds.

Children educated in the state sector or whose education is wholly or partly paid for out of the public purse (e.g. where boarding school fees are paid by the Ministry of Defence or where a local authority pays for a child to board) cannot be physically punished. If their teachers hit them, the teachers can be charged with assault.

Corporal punishment can still be inflicted on pupils whose parents pay all of the school fees. In practice not all private schools do use corporal punishment, but if it is part of the school's practice, parents cannot object if the punishment was 'reasonable'. The general limits were laid down in an 1860 case (R v. Hopley):

If it be administered for the gratification of passion or of rage, or it be immoderate and excessive in its nature or degree, or if it be protracted beyond a child's power of endurance, or with an instrument unfitted for its purpose, or calculated to produce danger to life or limb, in all such cases, the punishment is excessive, the violence is unlawful, and if evil consequences to life and limb ensue, the person inflicting it is answerable to the law.

What is reasonable depends on the circumstances and, often, on the attitudes of individual judges. Boxing the ears has been held to be unreasonable, whereas the inflicting of a blow which broke a boy's jaw in two places was once held to be reasonable – the judge said he had a special duty to protect society from 'an excess of sentimentality or sloppy thinking'.

No girls' schools are known still to use corporal punishment on their pupils.

If parents of fee-paying pupils do not want their children to suffer physical punishment, they should check about the school's policy (usually outlined in the school's rules, or check with the head). If corporal punishment is still used, it is wiser to choose another school. But also relevant is a decision of the European Court of Human Rights in 1982; that case held that corporal punishment must not be used against the wishes of a parent, and also that a child cannot be suspended from school for refusing corporal punishment. That decision is arguably binding in the UK, although no case has tested it.

Starting school

Schooling is compulsory from the beginning of the first term after the child's fifth birthday. In practice, some education authorities are prepared to take children before that age.

Leaving school

The minimum leaving age is sixteen, but a child cannot necessarily leave on his or her sixteenth birthday. By the Education Act 1962:

Date child becomes sixteen	When he or she can leave school
1 September to 31 January	End of spring term
1 February to the end of May	End of May
End of May to 31 August	End of summer term

Sixteen-to-nineteen-year-olds

The duty of the LEA to educate extends to sixteen-, seventeen- and eighteen-year-olds. There is a duty to provide suitable facilities for children of that age group who wish to receive full-time education. As regards those aged nineteen and over, there is a duty to provide further education for those who want it (but since it need not be in the local area, this duty is – in practical terms – meaningless). As for fees, LEAs can charge for non-advanced further education (which means below GCE A-level standard); until recently, few LEAs did charge, but some authorities have now introduced charges.

The National Curriculum

One of the most important changes brought about by the Education Reform Act 1988 (certainly one which has generated much public debate) was the introduction of a National Curriculum. It forms part of an increasing seizure of power by central government of the education sector. The National Curriculum applies only to children between five and sixteen being educated in the state system; the private sector is exempted.

The National Curriculum introduced ten foundation subjects which all children must study at school: English, mathematics, science, technology (and design), history, geography, a modern foreign language, music, art and physical education. From autumn 1989, all schools had to teach pupils aged five to fourteen these foundation subjects. Attainment targets and study programmes for maths, science and English were introduced for five-year-olds and for maths for eleven-year-olds. The Act states that children must be assessed at ages seven, eleven, fourteen and sixteen, partly on the basis of teachers' own assessment and partly on the basis of national tests known as 'standard assessment tests'.

The first national *trial* assessment of seven-year-olds was in summer 1991. Teachers' criticism has led to the likelihood of some of the more time-consuming tasks of assessment being relaxed. The first national assessment of seven-year-olds, where the results will be reported to parents, was due in summer 1992 and by summer 1993 the same should apply to fourteen-year-olds. For further information and publications, contact the Information Section, National Curriculum Council, Albion Wharf, 25 Skeldergate, York YO1 2XL (0904 622533).

The Parents' Charter

Published in September 1991, the Parents' Charter sets out parents' existing rights and responsibilities and talks of a partnership between parents and schools for children to receive the best education. While it proposes changes like regular inspection of schools, written progress reports and annual published tables of performance for all local schools, it does not actually make these changes. Copies of the Charter are available free from Freepost (BS 528/81) Bristol BS3 3YY.

Sex education

Parents cannot insist that their children should not have sex-education lessons. There is no duty on the LEA to provide such lessons, and there is no right for the parent to object to such lessons. In practice, all the parent can do is to attempt to reach an informal agreement with the head that the child be excluded from those classes.

School uniforms

Head teachers can lay down rules that require the wearing of certain items and which forbid the wearing of others (e.g. Doc Marten boots). But the rules must be 'reasonable' and it would not be reasonable for the head to insist that particular types of garment (e.g. a special type of blazer) be worn when cheaper, otherwise similar, items can be bought elsewhere. But schools cannot discriminate on grounds of race, sex, culture or religion. If your religion dictates you must wear an item of clothing, the school cannot forbid it.

An orthodox Sikh boy, suing via his father, applied to court because his school had insisted that he remove his turban and cut his hair. The House of Lords held that this was unlawful discrimination under the Race Relations Act 1976. Mandla (1983)

Similarly a girl refused the right to wear trousers (which boys can wear) would be able to argue that this amounted to unlawful sex discrimination.

With regard to problems of appearance (e.g. long hair, jewellery, make-up), again it is back to reasonableness. In practice, the head teacher is in a powerful position and failure to comply with the school rules as to uniform and appearance may eventually lead to suspension – it being treated as a discipline problem. The concerned parent should begin by discussing the problem with the head. The next step is to ask the LEA for a copy of its *Information for Parents* booklet to see whether the head teacher is complying with it (1981 regulations require that the LEA must publish details of its schools' uniform and dress rules). Otherwise, the only hope is to complain to the LEA.

The child and religion

Parents have no duty to bring children up with religious beliefs. The courts will not interfere unless the child is being exposed to a religious belief that will harm it – but, of course, such cases are few and far between.

Schools are required by law to start the day with collective worship and they must also provide RI classes. Many schools ignore this legal requirement. A parent has a legal right to withdraw the child from the collective worship or from the RI classes. In county schools, the collective worship must be non-denominational.

School records

All schools keep records on pupils, but those records are confidential and need not be shown to either the pupils or the parents, unless the records are filed in a computer, in which case parents do have the right to ask for details.

School charges

State education should be free. In practice, many schools ask parents to contribute towards the cost of books and craft materials, and also to pay for swimming and music lessons. Such charges are probably illegal (certainly, the courts have held that fees for music lessons carried out on school premises are illegal). However, the school can certainly charge for activities and trips which are outside the normal curriculum, and since 1980 schools have been free to charge what they like for school meals (although these must be provided free to children whose parents receive income support). If school milk is provided (fewer and fewer schools do so), it will be charged for. As regards fares for school buses, the LEA cannot charge anything if the child lives further than 'walking distance' (see page 138 for what this means), but otherwise the authority can charge what it wishes.

Size of classes

There is no fixed maximum number of pupils per class; the Schools Regulations 1959 simply state that classes should not be 'overcrowded'.

8 Disputes over Children

A new law, the Children Act 1989, which came into force on 14 October 1991, has made dramatic changes in the law relating to children. Some of the most important changes are the new restrictions which limit when the law can be used to intervene in disputes involving children – both in private law (divorce and separation) and in public law (children in care) – and the greater emphasis on *cooperation*, on parents being encouraged to try and sort problems out themselves without unnecessary court interference.

Many of the aims of the Act will take time to achieve. At the time of going to press, the Children Act has only recently come into effect, so it is difficult to assess how the courts will interpret the new law and in general how far the ideals of the Act will translate into reality. For example, any local authority which takes the Children Act reforms seriously will find its financial resources stretched to their maximum. The courts may find it hard to cope with the extra pressures on their timetables. But the Act has positive underlying messages for consumers (parents and children). Consumer power is considerably strengthened in the legal process: parents now in theory have more legal muscle to demand their

---

Main Aims of the Children Act 1989

- To change the way children are treated by the law, stressing adults' responsibilities towards children.
- To put children first: children's welfare is the court's paramount consideration in resolving disputes about them.
- To speed up the legal process and cut down delays in children cases.
- To reduce unnecessary court interference: courts can make an order only if it is better for the children to do so.
- To simplify the law so children are treated the same in the private (e.g. divorce) and public (e.g. children in care) law.
- To put local authorities under duties to provide services for children and to set local authorities standards that must be achieved.
- To respect family life: local authorities must promote the upbringing of children by their own families.

---

rights and courts have the power to stop endless unnecessary delays in deciding legal cases involving children. (See page 163 for the position on local authorities.)

PART I CHILDREN AND THE PRIVATE LAW: FAMILY BREAKUPS

When parents decide to end their relationship, children can be caught in the middle as mother and father argue over who is to have them.

The law's paramount concern is for the welfare of the children and not the hurt feelings and pride of the parents. Generally the courts take the approach that a child's welfare is best protected by ensuring that he or she retains links with both parents. Studies have shown that children cope much better with the trauma of separation and divorce if they continue to have regular contact with the parent who leaves as well as the parent who looks after them on a day-to-day basis.

The law now gives parents who can cooperate with one another much greater flexibility to make their own arrangements for the children: courts will in future make no court order unless it would be better for the children to do so. On the other hand, if parents (or even interested outsiders, like other family members) disagree over arrangements for the children, then the courts have wider powers to make simple but effective orders to sort out the problems.

The old law

The Children Act abolished the old familiar terms of 'custody', 'care and control' and 'access'. The new legal terms do *not* correspond exactly with the old law. The boxes summarize the old and new concepts.

Old orders for children

Custody

This was the right to take the long-term decisions that affect the child. A parent with custody (properly called *legal custody*) had the ultimate legal responsibility for the child, but it did not necessarily follow that the child lived with that parent, since *legal custody* did not always equal *physical custody* of the child. Usually, the parent with custody also had actual physical custody of the child but not always. The most common order was for one parent to have sole custody, but sometimes a joint-custody order was made (custody to both parents jointly, but with only one of them having care and control).

The sort of decision that the parent with custody could make was choosing the method of education; the choice of religion; administering the child's property; vetoing the issue of a passport to the child; withholding consent to the child's marriage.

Care and control

This covered the day-to-day care of the child, and the responsibility for looking after it. It was called *actual custody* of the child, but did not include the right to make the sort of decisions that went with *legal custody*. Usually, of course, one parent was given both legal and actual custody of the child. But sometimes the court separated the two by making a joint order which gave legal custody to both parents jointly and actual custody to just one of them. By doing this, both parents were able to retain some influence over the child and neither felt totally excluded.

Access

This allowed the parent who did not have care and control to visit the child. The courts would only rarely refuse to allow access for they were always reluctant to sever a child's links with its natural parents. Only if the visits were likely to harm the child would access be refused, for the general rule was that the parent who failed to obtain custody would be granted access.

Usually, the court ordered 'reasonable access' (i.e. no fixed times) and would often allow more access as the child grew older. By the time the child was a teenager, it might be allowed to spend weekends with the parent or go away on holiday with him/her, although this would largely depend on the character and wishes of the child and the parents. These arrangements were usually agreed by parents – not ordered by the court.

The new law

Parental responsibility

Parental responsibility is defined as 'all the rights, duties, powers, responsibilities and authority which by law a parent of a child has in relation to the child and his property' (see page 121–3 for what this means in practice).

Under the new law, all married parents have parental responsibility for their children. This lasts until the child reaches eighteen, whether or not the marriage lasts. (See page 12 for the position of unmarried parents.) The courts cannot take away parental responsibility from married parents unless an adoption order is made. The law thus recognizes the continuing blood tie that exists between children and their parents. The fact that each spouse will always have parental responsibility is intended to encourage absent parents (usually fathers) to take an active interest in their children's welfare. It means that fathers will not lose out on divorce since they keep parental responsibility (unlike under the old law, when they often lost custody).

New orders the courts can make

All of the following orders are under section 8 of the Children Act 1989 and are thus referred to as 'section 8 orders'. They are intended to be much simpler

---

Summary of Old and New Legal Concepts

The old law	*The new law*
Custody	*Parental responsibility (PR)*
'Custody' as interpreted by lawyers meant all the bundle of rights and responsibilities that parents have towards their children. It could be sole (in favour of one parent) or joint (shared between them).	PR means all the rights, duties, powers, responsibilities and authority parents have towards their children.
	PR is not lost on divorce.
Sole custody gave a parent the right to decide issues about the child alone (although he or she should consult with the other parent).	PR can be given to a non-parent.
	A person with PR can act independently of others with PR, but must not break any court order.
Joint custody meant that parents had to discuss and agree issues about the children.	Various 'section 8' orders can be made. The two principal ones are:
Care and control	*1. Residence order*
Care and control meant the day-to-day care of the child. It was sometimes called actual custody. Care and control could not be shared – it was given to one parent alone.	Residence orders state where the child will live and with whom. They can allow shared parenting (where children spend part of their time with Mum and part with Dad).
Access	*2. Contact order*
This allowed the parent who did not have care and control to visit the child and/or have the child to stay.	Contact orders require the person the child is living with to allow the child to visit or stay, or otherwise have contact, with the person named in the order.

than the old court orders and easier to grasp. So instead of the old confusion about, for example, 'custody' – whether this meant legal custody or care and control (actual custody) – there is now a simple order for residence.

Residence order. This spells out where a child is to live. In most cases it will be with one parent (usually the mother). But it can allow for shared parenting, where children divide their time between their parents' homes.

Contact order. This requires the person with whom the child lives to allow contact (thus shifting the burden more to the parent looking after the child). It can be visits or stopovers, or can be by way of telephone calls or letters.

Specific issue order. This gives directions for the purpose of determining a specific question connected with parental responsibility – for example, which school the child should go to.

Prohibited steps order. This has the effect of restraining in some way the actions of a person in relation to the child. No step stated in the order can be taken without the consent of the court.

Both specific issue and prohibited steps orders have their origin in wardship proceedings, which are now thus much less likely to be used.

Although the courts have wide powers to make these section 8 orders, they are supposed *not* to use them without proper consideration. Court orders will in future be made only if it is better for the children to do so. In-built within the new law is a presumption that it will usually be better for the children if their parents can agree between themselves how the children will be looked after. See also page 151.

Pending and old cases

What happens where applications had already been made under the old law and are still continuing or where an order under the old law has already been made?

Pending applications

Applications made before the Children Act came into force (on 14 October 1991) will be dealt with by the old law. So if a divorce or a court application about the children started before 14 October 1991 but has still not yet been resolved, the eventual court order will be for custody, care and control and/or access (see page 146 for an explanation of the old law).

Once a court order is made, for legal purposes it will be treated as having been made the day before the Children Act was implemented – that is, 13 October 1991. If a parent or anyone else later wants to apply to vary (change) the order, the new application will be made under the new law, under the Children Act (say for a residence order or contact order).

Old orders

Where parents were married to each other when a child was born and where there is an existing order (usually an order for custody, care and control or access), then each will have parental responsibility for the child.

Where the parents were not married, the mother will have parental responsibility automatically; the father will have it automatically only if he had obtained an order for parental rights and duties or a custody or care and control order in his favour (but he can now apply for a parental responsibility order or a residence order which would give him parental responsibility.

Again, if a parent or anyone else wants to change the old order, then the new application will be for a new Children Act order.

Who looks after the children on divorce or separation?

On separation

Separating married parents can make their own voluntary agreement as to who will have primary care of the children and how much contact the other parent has. They both continue to have parental responsibility. Sometimes a provision about arrangements for the children is inserted in a *separation agreement* to record formally what the parents agree to do.

Such an agreement is not binding; parents can in any event apply to court for a residence order or contact order to regulate arrangements for the children. They do not have to wait until the divorce has been started to apply. An application can be made to the magistrates' court, a divorce county court designated as a Family Hearing Centre (see below) or the High Court.

The principle that the court will not make an order unless it is better for the children to do so will apply; but if arrangements are disputed, then it is likely that the court will make an order to resolve the problem.

Separating unmarried parents again can make their own agreement. The mother has parental responsibility automatically, so it is up to her usually to decide where the children will live. If the father too has parental responsibility (see page 121), he also has the right and responsibility to make decisions about the children's upbringing, so the parents should try to work out arrangements between themselves. If they cannot, again an application can be made for a residence or contact order.

On divorce

Divorcing parents both continue to have parental responsibility for the children even after the divorce. So they both technically have an equal say in what arrangements should be made for the children – where they will live, who will look after them, how often the other parent will visit and so on. In practice the parent looking after the children on a day-to-day basis has more control over what happens to them.

In theory, this equal say can be exercised independently – that is, both parents can make up their own minds individually. But good parenting necessarily involves co-operation and negotiation, so parents should try to discuss with each other what will be best for the children. If they are still at stalemate, they could consider using their solicitors to try and negotiate for them or try conciliation or mediation (see page 153). If there are still insoluble differences, then either can apply to court for a section 8 order.

No divorce decree can be made absolute without the court considering the arrangements for the children of the family. The court has to look at the arrangements and decide whether it is satisfied that a court order need not be made (see also page 12). In the vast majority of cases the divorce courts will not make court orders about the children but will leave it up to the parents to sort out arrangements between themselves.

'Children of the family' means the couple's own children (including adopted and legitimated children) and any child treated by them as one of the family. So arrangements made for a stepchild will also have to be put before the court.

Normally, only arrangements for children under sixteen have to be put before the court. While parental responsibility lasts during the children's minority (until they are eighteen), court orders (i.e. section 8 orders) will not be made for children under sixteen unless there are exceptional circumstances. But financial applications (e.g. for maintenance) can be made for a dependent child undergoing further education at any age.

When the parents agree about the children

Usually the parents are able to work out some satisfactory arrangement that they can both agree to. For instance, they may agree that the children are to live with the mother, while the father will look after them every other weekend and for a couple of weeks in the summer, alternating Christmas and other special days.

Parents have more flexibility under the Children Act and can tailor-make arrangements to suit their own family. Agreements are encouraged under the new law. If parents agree about where the children will live and who will care for them, they will be given the freedom to do so. The court should not reject arrangements just because they do not conform to traditional family patterns. So if parents want to share care of their children more equally, they can, for example, set up an arrangement so that the children spend term-times with Mum and holidays with Dad. The test is whether the arrangements are in the best interests of the children. If they are, then the court will not interfere. But if the court thinks the proposals will put the children under stress, then it may intervene and will usually ask a court welfare officer to prepare a report to check that the children are coping satisfactorily.

Procedure at court

1 Before starting a divorce, the petitioner prepares a document called a Statement of Arrangements for the children and tries to agree its contents with
  the respondent. This form requires fairly detailed information about proposals for the children's upbringing, including details about:

- the home (the number of living rooms and bedrooms, whether the house is rented or owned, who else lives at the home);
- education (schools attended, any special educational needs, any fees payable);
- childcare details (which parent looks after the children, whether he or she works and, if so, who else looks after the children);
- maintenance (payments made, whether or not under a court order, what agreements have been reached);
- contact (whether the children see the absent parent and how often);
- health, *and*
- any other court proceedings.

Present arrangements and any proposed changes must be set out.

2 If the petitioner and respondent agree the form, they should both sign it. If the respondent does not agree the contents of the form, he or she can file his/her own Statement of Arrangements once the divorce has started.

3 The petitioner starts off the divorce (see page 58), the papers are served by the court on the respondent and the respondent returns the acknowledgement of service.

4 Once the respondent has confirmed his/her consent to the divorce going ahead and the Statement of Arrangements, the District Judge will look at the papers and consider the evidence.

If satisfied that the court does not need to make an order about the children, the District Judge will issue a certificate to this effect and neither husband nor wife has to go to court. No formal court order will be made. It will then be up to the parents to make the arrangements they have proposed work (although they can later apply to court for a court order if there are problems).

If not satisfied that a court order need not be made (i.e. if the arrangements do not look as if they benefit the children or if for some other reason the District Judge has doubts), the District Judge may ask for more information. He or she will either set a date for a court hearing for the petitioner and respondent to attend personally, or ask for other evidence (usually statements) to be sent to court or ask for a welfare report so that a thorough investigation can be made.

5 If a court welfare report is ordered, the court welfare officer (often a trained probation officer) will visit both parents at home and discuss the children and their relationships with them. If the mother or father has acquired a new partner, then the officer may well want to know how he or she feels about looking after the children. The officer will also want to talk to other people who have relevant information, such as a social worker who has been involved with the parents and, sometimes, the child's schoolteacher. The child concerned may also be asked his or her own views, especially if they are old enough to have decided views and be able to express them. The welfare report will then go back to the court. The parents are entitled to copies of the report. If the District Judge is then satisfied, a certificate will be issued.

6 Once a certificate is issued, the final decree of divorce (decree absolute) can be applied for.

For a summary of the steps in a divorce where the parents agree over arrangements for the children, see the chart on page 59.

When parents cannot agree

Conciliation

If parents cannot agree but are reluctant to become embroiled in a full-blown court battle, with its high emotional (and usually financial) costs, voluntary conciliation is an option to consider.

The language used for this alternative means of dispute resolution is unfortunately confusing. There are two problems to bear in mind. First, the term 'conciliation' is different from reconciliation, which means spouses trying to get back together as husband and wife. Secondly, the terms 'conciliation' and 'mediation' are often used interchangeably although the services offered by the National Family Conciliation Council and the Family Mediators' Association (see below) differ.

Conciliation and mediation services are confidential. They involve anything between one and six sessions, depending on need.

Conciliation is a method of resolving disputes involving both parents. With the expert help of a conciliator, who provides a neutral forum for parents to discuss their problems, parents are assisted in working out their own solutions to problems stemming from family breakdown. Conciliation is sometimes offered in-court as a means of establishing whether agreement can be reached in a dispute over children. The in-court version usually offers limited help in comparison to the voluntary out-of-court services. Conciliation is most often sought for problems involving children, but sometimes can touch on problems about the divorce or money matters. Fees vary, often depending on the income of the parents, but tend to be low: some agencies charge around £10 per session, others give free services.

For a list of affiliated conciliation organizations nationally contact:

National Family Conciliation Council (NFCC), Shaftesbury Centre, Percy Street, Swindon, Wilts SN2 2AZ, Tel: 0793 514055

Mediation, as offered by the Family Mediators' Association, is a more sophisticated form of conciliation, pairing specially trained and experienced lawyers and family counsellors to help resolve problems, not only about the children but also about finance and the divorce. Mediators will help the couple put together a full picture of family finances and negotiate a fair division. Mediation is usually more expensive than conciliation but there are schemes for free advice. In any event the fees will be a lot less than the legal costs of a full-blown court case.

For names and addresses of local trained mediators contact:

Family Mediators' Association, (FMA), The Old House, Rectory Gardens, Henbury, Bristol BS10 7AQ, Tel: 0272 500140

Going to court about the children

If the parents cannot reach agreement about arrangements for the children this will *not* make the divorce a 'defended divorce'. But it will mean that the divorce itself will take longer and may well be costlier.

In a disputed case, the petitioner or respondent will make an application for a section 8 order – usually a residence or contact order. The respondent will be able to send to the court his or her own proposals in another Statement of Arrangements. Applications for section 8 orders are best made by a solicitor; legal aid should be available.

Once the court receives an application, it fixes a date for a preliminary hearing. That hearing is usually a conciliation appointment (or 'in-court conciliation'), when a District Judge and/or a court welfare officer will explore whether any agreement between the parents is possible. Other conciliation appointments can be set up if need be. If the dispute is not then resolved, the court will make an order for directions. This will include a timetable for the preparation of evidence and a date when the case will be brought back to court for another hearing. Strict time limits apply. A parent who fails to comply with the time limits runs the risk of being accused of deliberate delay (recognized as being harmful to children by the Children Act) and will be in breach of a rule of court.

Separate representation for children

Children can make their own applications for section 8 orders under the Children Act, either by someone else (known as a 'next friend') or by themselves. The test for the court to hear an application made by a child him- or herself is whether the child has sufficient understanding to make such an application. This depends on the maturity of individual children: adolescents will certainly be covered but an articulate, mature eight-year-old may even be allowed to have a say.

A 'next friend' usually means the child's mother or father, but it could also be the official solicitor, who has power to act in children's cases in the High Court and the county court (but not in the magistrates' court). Legal aid should be available.

Evidence for the court

A welfare report will be prepared (by another welfare officer than the one involved in any in-court conciliation) and copies will be supplied to both parents. The solicitors will draw up formal statements setting out their clients' respective claims to the children and the reasons why the children should go to a particular parent (or whether contact should, or should not, be granted if there is a dispute about access). Sometimes other witnesses may be asked to give evidence – say, a grandparent or schoolteacher.

All evidence will be put before the judge when he or she hears the case, in private, in chambers. The courts try to take a clear, unemotional approach in children cases, even though the subject matter is highly charged for the parties. The judge will want both parents to be present so they can be questioned. The children may also be asked to attend court (usually from about nine years old); the judge may interview them in private but they will not be called in to witness the whole case. Often they will be asked to wait outside the court until the judge is ready to speak to them, so it is a good idea to arrange for an extra pair of hands to help with looking after them at court during the day.

The court's decision

The judge will then usually make an order. He or she will first have to consider whether making an order will be better for the children, but in a disputed case it is unlikely that no order will result unless the parents have reached a proper agreement and are both willing to make the agreement work in practice.

In the great majority of cases, the judge will follow the welfare officer's recommendation. If he or she does not, reasons must be given.

The decision as to who will have primary care for the children will usually be vital in deciding which spouse is to have the matrimonial home (i.e. possible transfer of a tenancy or transfer of an owner-occupied home), since the home will normally go to the spouse who looks after the children.

Which Court?

Divorce
Most divorces are applied for in divorce county courts (or the Principal Divorce Registry at Somerset House in London). Under the Children Act, most divorce county courts have been designated 'Family Hearing Centres' and will be able to deal with contested applications as well as divorces alone. Some, however, will just be administrative centres, dealing with the paperwork for divorces; disputed cases will be transferred to the nearest Family Hearing Centre. Check with the local county court for details.

Children Act applications
Applications under the Children Act can be made in private law in the magistrates' court, Family Hearing Centre or High Court. The High Court is usually reserved for very complex cases or those involving a lot of money. If a divorce has already started, applications should be made in the divorce court. If this is a divorce county court, the court will transfer the case up to the local Family Hearing Centre. Legal aid may be granted only for applications in lower courts (check with your solicitor).

The factors that decide a court case

The overriding principle is 'the child's welfare shall be the court's paramount consideration' (s.1 (1), Children Act 1989). In applying this principle, the court now has a checklist of matters it must look at. In particular:

● the ascertainable wishes and feelings of the child (in the light of the child's age and understanding);

● the child's physical, emotional and educational needs;

● the likely effect on the child of any change in circumstances;

● the child's age, sex and background and any characteristics the court considers relevant;

● any harm the child has suffered or is at risk of suffering;

● how capable each of the child's parents, and any other person in relation to whom the court considers the question to be relevant, is of meeting the child's needs;

● the range of powers available to the court.

The wishes and feelings of the child

The fact that the child's wishes and feelings have been placed at the top of the checklist emphasizes that children should be put first. The judge may ask to see the children in private in chambers without parents or legal advisers present, to talk to them and ask them what they want. More often their wishes and feelings will be explored by the court welfare officer when preparing the report.

The older the child, the more persuasive his or her views. Teenage children in any event 'vote with their feet' (i.e. live at the home of their choice). Little children may be asked to draw their wishes and feelings if they cannot put them into words. Often children will say that they just want their parents to get back together.

If the court suspects that children have been coached by one or other parent, 'their' opinions will carry little weight.

Although children's views will be respected, they should not be forced to choose unwillingly between two people both of whom they love. Ultimately it is up to the adults to make decisions.

The child's needs

The child's physical, emotional and educational needs are second on the list. If the child is very young or sickly or otherwise needs a mother's care, the mother is more likely to get the residence order. A good school near a parent's home where the child would be accepted as a pupil could also strengthen one parent's claim.

Splitting the family is always regarded as undesirable.

When husband and wife separated, one of their two children went to live with the mother, the other with the father. The mother appealed against the court order splitting custody and care and control between the parents. Held: Following divorce, siblings should, wherever possible, be brought up together so that they could give each other emotional support. The mother should have care and control of both children. C v. C (1988)

The effect of change

The courts have long acknowledged that changing the status quo will disrupt the child and thus compound the difficulties of adjusting to the parents' separation. So a parent who is already looking after the children will have a much stronger claim. This, however, does not apply if the children have been snatched from their usual home environment: the courts can act quickly to hand children back if they have been taken away from the parent best able to care for them.

Although the courts will normally want to make an order that will resolve a dispute for the foreseeable future (to ensure that the children are not going to and fro between the parents), in a borderline case the court may be forced to make the best short-term decision.

The wife went to live with another man. The husband stayed behind and looked after the daughter with the help of his mother and a woman friend. The mother applied for custody but failed; the court felt it was wrong to move a child from a home where she was happy to a home where she might or might not be happy. On appeal, held: This was a borderline case, decided on the child's best interests in the short term. The child should stay with the father but either parent could later apply to vary the order. Thompson (1987)

The child's age, sex and background

Generally the courts decide that a child's welfare is best protected by being with the mother rather than the father. This is only a general rule but it applies particularly to young children. It is not, however, unusual for a court order to provide for older boys to live with their fathers. If one parent decides to leave and adopt a different lifestyle from the one the children are familiar with, the courts would take a critical view.

Harm or risk of harm

Alcoholism or violence (whether towards the other parent or the children) will prejudice a parent's case. A parent's homosexuality will be a factor taken into account but not necessarily a decisive one (unless the court thinks the children will be adversely affected).

If there is a risk of sexual abuse by a parent, that parent would definitely not get a residence order. A contact order might be given, but only if it would be in the child's best interests (e.g. if there is a strong bond between parent and child, if the parent is seeking treatment and if the contact is supervised properly).

157

Capability of the parents

This can range from practical factors, like whether either parent works outside the home, to the ability to respond to the child's needs. Overall it is a matter of trying to assess which will be the better parent, and sometimes the claims of both will be equal.

Note: this does not refer to the parents' conduct as individuals and a distinction must be drawn between a person's behaviour as a parent and as a partner.

The husband was a clergyman. His wife had an affair and told her husband she wanted to leave, taking the children with her. The husband applied for custody. Held: Although the husband was of unimpeachable conduct, it was in the best interests of the children that they should be with their mother – despite the fact that she was the 'guilty' party. Re K (1977)

A parent who can offer a stable home life (perhaps particularly if remarrying) will obviously have a stronger claim than a parent who is unreliable. A parent who walks out on the children or puts the interests of a lover above those of the children may well be at a disadvantage when making an application for a residence order.

Where relatives or other people (like nannies or childminders) are involved in looking after the children, their capabilities too will have to be examined.

The courts' powers

The courts' powers under the Children Act are much wider; so they might be expected to come up with more creative solutions than in the past. For example, residence orders can be split between both parents. Thus if both parents are equally capable and the children want to share their time with each parent, the court could make a residence order specifying that the children would spend two weeks with the father and then two with the mother so that the parents have the opportunity of sharing care of the children. But the court would have to be convinced that unusual arrangements are in the children's best interests.

Financial considerations should not weigh too heavily with the courts, as they have powers to make appropriate divisions of capital and maintenance orders so that children are properly provided for where possible.

Appeals

Successful appeals against first-instance decisions are extremely rare. The trial judge has wide discretion and appeals will be allowed only if the first decision can be shown to be 'plainly wrong'. This is so even if the Court of Appeal feels it would have come to another decision itself. But if further important evidence comes to light, then an appeal might work.

Both husband and wife sought custody of the children. The father alleged that the mother had a violent temper and had committed adultery with D. The judge found that the mother was a liar with a bad temper and used bad language, but she would control herself and did not intend a permanent relationship with D. It was best for young children to be with their mother. The husband appealed, showing that D and the mother now lived together and that the mother had been violent. Held: The children should go to live with their father. The fresh evidence undermined the basis of the judge's findings. A v. A (1988)

But usually it will not be worthwhile appealing against an order. A parent unhappy with a court's decision would usually do better to wait for some time to pass (at least a year) and then reconsider whether circumstances have changed so that a fresh application to court might be warranted. For example, a father of a ten-year-old boy, when a residence order was given to his ex-wife, could wait until the boy becomes a teenager and then see if his son wants to come to live with him for longer periods of time.

Stepfamilies

Stepfathers and stepmothers can often occupy a special place, having taken on the burden (and joys!) of an actual parent but without being recognized by the law as such. However, under the new law the greater flexibility of the courts' new powers can be helpful for stepfamilies.

Step-parents do not automatically have parental responsibility during a marriage (or even after divorce) for their stepchildren. Parental responsibility belongs to both the father and the mother (if the parents were married at the time of the birth) or to the mother alone if the parents were unmarried. So step-parents cannot in law make decisions about a stepchild's upbringing themselves, although they will usually be involved in decision-making via the parent (their partner).

To change this and to become recognized by the law as having the role of a parent, a step-parent could apply for a residence order jointly with his or her new partner if the children are living with them. This indirectly gives him or her parental responsibility – residence orders can be made in favour of two people jointly.

The court will have to consider whether making an order is better for the children than making no order at all, but might grant such an application, particularly if the absent parent takes little or no interest in the children and the step-parent is particularly involved. The court would want to be satisfied that the new arrangement is stable.

Another option would be for the step-parent to apply jointly with his new spouse (the parent) for an adoption order. The courts are, however, unlikely to grant this as they are unwilling to terminate the links with natural parents.

On the death of the partner (the parent), the step-parent has no automatic rights *vis-à-vis* the stepchildren. If the parents were married at the time of the birth, then the other parent (not the step-parent) would automatically take over responsibility for looking after the children and the step-parent would be shut out. If the step-parent wanted to continue looking after the children, then again he or she would have to apply for a residence order.

To protect against this, particularly in situations where the absent parent has lost interest in the children, the parent (partner), while living, could make a will or deed appointing the step-parent as a guardian of the child on his or her death. But to make the position watertight, the step-parent and parent should apply jointly to the court for a residence order too, as otherwise the appointment as a guardian will not take effect until the death of the surviving parent (which defeats the object of an appointment).

Applications by grandparents and other relatives

When a marriage ends, sometimes the contact between children and their grandparents ends too, as families place themselves in opposing camps. This is rarely in the children's best interests: often children can be helped to cope with their distress by grandparents (or other mentors) who can offer a sympathetic (and non-partisan) shoulder to cry on.

Grandparents (or for that matter any other interested adult) can apply to the court for a contact order, a residence order or any other section 8 order. They do not have to wait until divorce proceedings have been started (as under the old law). If the parents divorced under the old law, grandparents can now make an application under the new law.

A grandparent (or any other interested adult) has the right to apply automatically to court for a section 8 order if:
- the child has lived with him or her for three years or more;
- they have the consent of the person with a residence order in their favour, *or*
- they have the consent of everyone with parental responsibility.

Otherwise, they have to get the court's permission to apply. The court will take into consideration:
- the nature of the proposed application;
- the applicant's connection with the child;
- the risk of harmful disruption to the child's life.

If grandparents have lost contact with the children over many years or had a bad influence on the children, then it is possible that their application for permission to apply to court will fail. But usually the court will grant permission to apply and leave an investigation of the facts to a full court case.

Applications for contact for grandparents will usually be granted unless there is deep bitterness between the families which would be exacerbated by making a contact order. Contact orders can be in the form of letters, cards and telephone calls, so the court may make an order for contact in stages, building up contact from letters and telephone calls before a face-to-face meeting if there has been no contact for a long time.

Applications for residence orders are unlikely to stand a chance of success unless the natural parents are in support.

Taking a child abroad

The usual rule is that a parent who wants to take a child abroad (this includes going to Scotland) should obtain the other parent's written consent first. This is because it is a criminal offence to remove a child from the country without the written consent of both parents or the consent of the court.

Where a parent simply wants to take the child on holiday, if he or she has a residence order in his or her favour, he or she can take the child abroad for a period of up to a month. If the other parent objects, an application can be made to court for its permission by way of a section 8 order. (See page 163 concerning child abduction.)

If there is no residence order, the civil law says nothing either to permit or to prevent a parent from taking a child abroad. Again, if parents are in dispute, one or other should apply for a section 8 order.

But whether a residence order exists or not, the criminal law still applies.

Emigration

Emigration will of course affect children long-term and different considerations apply.

If a parent looking after the children wishes to emigrate with the children, in the past the court usually allowed him or her to do so, even if this meant that the other parent would have great difficulty in seeing the children in future.

The mother had custody of the two daughters, aged eleven and ten. The father lived locally; he and his parents had regular contact with the children. The mother and stepfather wanted to emigrate to New Zealand and applied to court. Their application was unsuccessful at first; the mother appealed. Held: The mother would be allowed to take the children abroad permanently. In considering the welfare of the children the court had to bear in mind the risk of friction and bitterness resulting from the reasonable proposals of the custodial parent being interfered with. L v. H (1986)

Under the new law, the welfare checklist must be applied. It is arguable that if older children were adamantly opposed to the move and the other parent had sound plans for caring for them, an application to take the children abroad might be refused. But old cases still carry weight with the courts.

Changing the child's name

Under the old law, the position was clear: the child's surname must not be changed unless both parents consented or unless the court gave its permission. This was rarely exercised in practice.

The mother of two children, aged three and four, had remarried. She applied for leave to change their name to that of their new stepfather but the natural father would not agree.

Held: Changing a child's name was a matter of great importance, affecting the best interests and the psychological welfare of the child. The natural father was someone with whom it would be beneficial for the children to maintain a close connection. A marriage could be dissolved but not parenthood. So leave to change the names was refused. L (1978)

Under the Children Act, when a residence order is made parents cannot change the child's surname without consent (of the other parent or the court). But if no order is made, there is no legal requirement specifically preventing a parent with parental responsibility from changing the name. So either parent, so long as they have parental responsibility, can change the child's surname; the other will have to apply to court for a prohibited steps order or a specific issue order to stop the change. As long as this is done quickly, the court will probably agree that the old family name should be kept. But if the child has had a new name for a long time and has adjusted to being known by the new surname, the court would probably take the view that to change the name back again would be confusing and so the new name could be retained.

What if the child itself wants to change its surname? Since the case of *Gillick* was decided, a child of 'sufficient maturity and understanding to appreciate the nature and importance of the proposed change of name' would be allowed to change the surname himself or herself. This would definitely cover teenagers; for younger children it will depend on their own individual maturity and articulateness.

(See page 20 for further details about changing names.)

Emergency disputes

Sometimes the court has to act quickly to protect a child. For example, the parents might break up and one of them might try to snatch the child and perhaps take it abroad. Similarly, the child may need to be prevented from doing something that would be to its own disadvantage – for instance, a sixteen-year-old might be planning to elope with someone wholly unsuitable. Under the old law, the solution was usually to make the child a ward of court, so that the court took over the role of legal parent. Children who were made wards of court were immediately prevented from leaving the country and no significant step could be taken concerning them without the court's permission.

Since the Children Act 1989 came into force, there are other court orders that can be applied for – prohibited steps orders and specific issue orders – that are effective and can be granted in an emergency. It is thus likely that applications for wardship will become less frequent. The new orders can stop children from being taken out of the country but otherwise will not freeze any other action; the remedies are specific, not blanket cover-alls.

The child's welfare will be the court's paramount consideration and the usual governing principles of the Children Act will apply: a court order will be granted only if it is in the child's best interests. Mature children will be given their own say too.

Child abduction

If a parent is suspected of intending to take a child abroad, action must be taken fast. Prevention is far easier than cure. Although there are legal remedies for the return to the UK of abducted children, these are time-consuming at best and useless at worst (if a child is taken to a country outside an international convention where signing countries agree to enforce each other's court orders).

The first step is to get legal advice (legal aid should be available but will be subject to means and merits tests). The solicitor will usually apply for a prohibited steps order, which can be applied for *ex parte* (without telling the other parent in advance) on the same day, even by telephone if necessary. A prohibited steps order can prevent the other parent from abducting the child abroad, but the other parent must be physically served with the document.

If there is a real and imminent danger of the child being abducted (real and imminent means within twenty-four hours) a solicitor (or even a parent) can ask the police to issue a 'port alert'. The police will need personal details of the child and abductor, a description of their appearances and photographs if possible. They will want sight of any court order too. The police can then immediately notify all air and sea ports, whose officials will then be on the lookout for the abductor and child. Their task will be hard if the abductor flees from a busy terminal (and even harder post-1993). If possible try to supply specific details of which flight or boat crossing the abductor plans to take.

PART 2 CHILDREN AND THE PUBLIC LAW: LOCAL AUTHORITIES AND CHILDREN

The burden of the new responsibilities envisaged by the Children Act falls very heavily on local authorities. They have new duties not just towards children in care but towards all children who live in their area, with special extra duties towards 'children in need' (as defined in the Act).

Under the new law, all children have a right to basic standards of care, nurture and upbringing. Where the parents fall short, local authorities are supposed to fill the gap. The services they provide are supposed to meet each child's identified needs and be appropriate in terms of the child's race, culture, religion and linguistic background.

In practice the success of these aims will very likely be much curtailed by local authorities' limited resources. Many social services departments are already stretched to breaking-point, so while the new rights set out here are laid down by law, in reality trying to exercise many of the more idealistic 'rights' will more likely lead to a complaint to the new complaints panels (which the local authorities also have to set up) rather than direct effective action.

163

Local authorities' duties to all children in their area

Local authorities have much greater powers to regulate and control services for all children in their area. Minimum standards of care and safety must be met by childminders and nurseries, all of whom have to register with the local authority. Nurseries and childminders who look after children under eight years old for more than two hours per day for payment must apply for registration with the local authority and be vetted in advance. If they fail to do so the services they offer are illegal and they could face a fine.

Parents can check with the local authority for lists of registered childminders and nurseries (contact the local social services department), which should be provided free. If parents feel that the services fail to meet the standards laid down, they can complain to the local authority, which is under a duty to investigate.

Local authorities' duties to children in need

Children in need are defined by the Children Act thus:
- being unlikely to achieve or maintain or to have the opportunity of achieving or maintaining a reasonable standard of health or development without the provision for the child of services by a local authority;
- if the child's health and development is likely to be significantly impaired or further impaired without the provision for him of such services; *or*
- if the child is disabled.

The local authority is under two special duties towards children in need:
- to safeguard and promote the welfare of children within its area who are in need; *and*
- so far as is consistent with that duty, to promote the upbringing of such children by their families.

Disabled children. Local authorities must maintain a register of disabled children within their area. They must also provide services designed to minimize the effect of their disabilities and to give such children the opportunity to lead lives which are as normal as possible.

Services for children in need

Local authorities must provide three types of services for children in need (these services must be reviewed once every three years):

1 *Services for children in need who live with their families.* Under the umbrella aim of promoting children's upbringing within their own families, the local authority must provide a range of services designed to support the families who look after them. This includes advice and counselling, occupational and

recreational activities, home help (which may include laundry facilities) and assistance enabling the families to have a holiday.

2 *Family centres.* The local authority must provide 'such Family Centres as it considers appropriate' in relation to children in its area. The idea of family centres is to provide within a comparatively informal and homely setting a place where absent parents and children can meet (as an alternative to trailing around the park on a rainy day or McDonald's) and again where services for children can be centred. The law envisages that such services could include activities (occupational, social, cultural and recreational), advice and counselling, and even accommodation.

3 *Day care.* The local authority must provide day care for children in need under five not yet going to school and for those of school age outside school hours and during school holidays.

Local authorities' duties towards children in care

Under the old pre-Children Act law (before 14 October 1991), when a child was taken into care the local authority usually took over parents' rights and responsibilities. This was the case whether the child was in voluntary care or under a proper care order.

Nowadays, parents retain their own rights and responsibilities, which they may share with the local authority. The concept of voluntary care has been abolished, and the right of local authorities to ask for a care order for children has been much restricted. Local authorities must provide accommodation for children who need it (see below under Provision of Accommodation by Local Authorities), but providing accommodation for a child does not give them the right to assume the role of a parent.

Local authorities have to work in partnership with parents. They are under a duty to promote contact between children being looked after by them and their parents. What that means in practice is that they must first exhaust the possibilities of children being looked after by their own families before making other accommodation arrangements for them. Also, if they do make arrangements for children to be accommodated, they must work with the parents rather than making their own independent choices. Parents have to be given opportunities to have regular contact with their children and have a right to be consulted on arrangements made for them.

Provision of accommodation by local authorities. The Children Act stresses the fact that children should be brought up within their own homes and the need for partnership in working with children and their families, and for avoiding court appearances except where necessary to safeguard and promote the welfare of the child.

Local authorities are under a duty to provide accommodation for any child in need (see above for definition) within their area who appears to require accommodation as a result of:

- there being no person who has parental responsibility for him;
- his having been lost or having been abandoned; *or*
- the person who has been caring for him being prevented (whether or not permanently and for whatever reason) from providing him with suitable accommodation or care.

If the local authority provides accommodation for a child in need, both the child's wishes and the parents' role are important. Local authorities must find out what the child wishes to do and properly consider those wishes. The local authority also cannot continue to provide accommodation in the face of an objection from a parent with parental responsibility who is willing and able to provide a home (or arrange for accommodation to be provided).

Even more importantly, any person with parental responsibility for the child can take the child away from local authority accommodation at any time. (Under the old law, twenty-eight days' notice had to be given; now the removal is allowed to take place immediately.) In practice, because local authorities want to have a degree of certainty in making arrangements for the children, they will try to make an agreement with the parent(s) about giving notice to take the child away.

Grounds for taking a child into care

Where local authorities:

1 are informed that a child who lives, or is found, in their area
   - is the subject of an emergency protection order, *or*
   - is in police protection; *or*
2 have reasonable cause to suspect that a child who lives or is found in their area is suffering, or is likely to suffer, significant harm

the authority shall make, or cause to be made, such inquiries as they think necessary to enable them to decide whether they should take any action to safeguard or promote the child's welfare.

Note: the local authority do not have to take action, just investigate.

Before a court will make a care or supervision order, it must be satisfied:

1 that the child has suffered or is likely to suffer significant harm; *and*
2 that the harm or likelihood of harm is attributable to
   - the care given to the child, or likely to be given to him if the order were not made, not being what it would be reasonable to expect a parent to give to him, *or*
   - the child's being beyond parental control.

These grounds have become known as the 'threshold criteria'. They are designed to prevent the knee-jerk response of taking a child into care. So first the local authority must investigate before they can take action. Usually this will involve a full case conference (which the parents would normally be asked to attend). See chart opposite about taking a child into care.

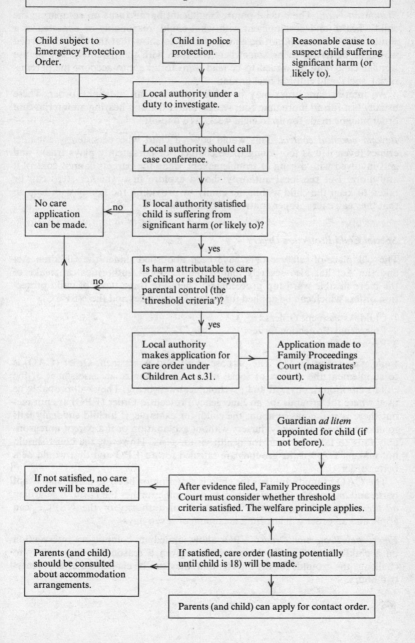

Taking a Child into Care

Child subject to Emergency Protection Order.

Child in police protection.

Reasonable cause to suspect child suffering significant harm (or likely to).

Local authority under a duty to investigate.

Local authority should call case conference.

Is local authority satisfied child is suffering from significant harm (or likely to)?

no → No care application can be made.

yes

Is harm attributable to care of child or is child beyond parental control (the 'threshold criteria')?

no →

yes

Local authority makes application for care order under Children Act s.31.

→ Application made to Family Proceedings Court (magistrates' court).

Guardian *ad litem* appointed for child (if not before).

After evidence filed, Family Proceedings Court must consider whether threshold criteria satisfied. The welfare principle applies.

→ If not satisfied, no care order will be made.

If satisfied, care order (lasting potentially until child is 18) will be made.

→ Parents (and child) should be consulted about accommodation arrangements.

Parents (and child) can apply for contact order.

Significant harm. The crucial phrase 'significant harm' turns on comparing the child's health and development with what could 'reasonably be expected of a similar child'. So it will not be enough simply to show that the child concerned would be better off living somewhere else than with the parent(s). The phrase 'similar child' can be argued to be read so as to take into account the parents' racial, social and cultural background.

An interim care order may be made instead of an indefinite order. These usually last for no more than four weeks, but at the first hearing an interim care order may be made for up to eight weeks as a one-off.

Beyond parental control. This would cover a child who persistently commits crimes (even if it is too young to be charged) or persistently plays truant and gets involved with a gang of troublemakers, when the parents cannot control it any more. But the local authority should explore first whether steps can be taken to keep the child within the family by providing the family with help so that they can exert proper control over the child.

Special Child Protection Orders

The old place-of-safety orders have been abolished under the Children Act and the Act has also severely limited the use local authorities can make of the more flexible wardship proceedings. There are three types of child protection orders which can be applied for by local authorities and the NSPCC:

1 Child Assessment Orders.
2 Emergency Protection Orders.
3 Recovery Orders.

Child Assessment Orders. The purpose of a Child Assessment Order (CAO) is to supplement the powers of social workers to organize an assessment of the child's emotional, physical and psychological well-being. They will probably be used where the grounds for an Emergency Protection Order (EPO) are not met but there is real concern about the child: for example, if a child suddenly fails to attend a local authority nursery without explanation or if a parent unreasonably fails to take the child for health visitor tests. However, the court should not make a CAO if the grounds are satisfied for an EPO and that would be a better order.

The CAO grounds are that the child is suffering or likely to suffer significant harm and an assessment is necessary to determine further the harm. A guardian *ad litem* should be appointed. Only the local authority or the NSPCC can apply and an order will last for a maximum of seven days.

Emergency Protection Orders. EPOs allow immediate compulsory intervention on a child's behalf, while the parents are given a reasonable opportunity to challenge the grounds for the intervention: they can be challenged after seventy-two hours.

They cover two main situations. First (most likely to be used where the child is in hospital and a parent unreasonably threatens to remove the child), if the child is likely to suffer significant harm if he or she does not remain in current accommodation (or if the child is not taken to this accommodation). Secondly, if the local authority's or the NSPCC's inquiries are being frustrated by being denied access to a child. In both cases the significant-harm grounds must also be proved and again a guardian *ad litem* will be appointed. EPOs will last for a maximum of eight days.

Recovery Orders. Recovery orders allow a child to be recovered if someone has snatched the child: they order someone to produce a child who has been wrongly taken away. These are most likely to be used where parents are on the run, trying to avoid the local authority.

Representatives for children

It is not often easy for children to voice their wishes and feelings; even when they do voice them, they can be ignored. To give children a proper say in adult proceedings, the Children Act provides for guardians *ad litem* to be appointed in any proceedings taken by the local authority.

They will act as the children's representatives in court, preparing for going to court by interviewing the parents, the child and anyone else who is concerned. They will have access to files which would otherwise be confidential – the local authorities' and NSPCC files, for example. Unlike in private law proceedings (e.g. divorce or applications for a residence order), there is no test that a child has to satisfy before a representative is appointed for him or her. A guardian *ad litem* will always be appointed to act for the child and the child will also always have his or her solicitor (drawn from a panel of childcare specialists). Legal aid is available without a means test.

Guardians *ad litem* are usually trained family experts drawn from a panel of counsellors. Their role in court proceedings will be powerful and should act as a counterbalance to the adversarial stances often taken by the parents and local authorities respectively.

Where children in care will live

Before the local authority decide where to place a child in care, they have to consult the child itself, the parents, anyone with parental responsibility and even anyone else whose wishes and feelings the authority think to be relevant.

If a child already in a residential home is unhappy with the placement, he or she should complain to his or her social worker. Children can also complain about their treatment while in care: the new complaints procedures are designed to prevent another 'pin-down' occurring.

Contacting a child in care

It is not just the responsibility of parents of children who are in care to have contact with them. Local authorities are under a special duty to promote contact between children in care and their families, unless this is not 'reasonably practicable or consistent with the child's welfare'. If the local authority refuse to allow contact, then parents (including unmarried fathers), anyone who had a residence order made in their favour and even the child itself can apply to court for a contact order automatically (others have to seek the court's permission first). If the application is refused, then the applicant will have to wait for six months before applying again.

When children leave care

Local authorities are under a duty to provide aftercare services between the ages of sixteen and twenty-one to a young person who was in care. They must 'advise, assist and befriend him with a view to promoting his welfare, when he ceases to be looked after by them'. This provision applies to young people who were looked after by a voluntary organization too.

The aim of aftercare is to smooth the transition between institutionalized care (which can often create dependency) and the harsh realities of an independent life in the outside world. The assistance can be in the form of cash. How much will depend very much on the local authorities' resources, and in practice will sadly often be zero.

Contact the local social services department for further details.

9 Children, Safety and the Law

Every day three children die from accidents, 300 are seriously injured and 3,000 are taken to hospital. Levels of injury from accidents have reached what one television presenter (Anneka Rice) described in 1991 as 'epidemic proportions'. Of course, not all accidents can be prevented, but the law does provide some compensation for injuries and does set safety standards in a number of areas.

ACCIDENTS AT SCHOOL

A school is responsible for the safety and well-being of its pupils. If the school or a member of its staff is negligent, then the school will be liable in damages. Similarly, the school will be liable if the premises are unsafe.

Two boys were playing with a swing door. As a result of horseplay, a child put his hand through a glass panel in the door. The glass was an eighth of an inch thick. Held: The school was liable. Whilst the glass was thick enough for normal domestic use, it was not suitable for the rough and tumble of school life. Lyes (1962)

Was it negligent to allow a child – aged seven years and two months to select sharp-pointed scissors for use in an art class? Held: The teacher had been negligent and the education authority was liable for £10,000 damages for the serious eye injury caused. Black (1983)

ACCIDENTS IN PLAYGROUNDS

Parents can reasonably assume that playgrounds are safe. Owners or managers of playgrounds are under a statutory duty to equip and run playgrounds to ensure that children are not exposed to risks to their health and safety. They are liable for any injury which they could reasonably have foreseen; a higher duty of care must be shown towards children (even trespassers) under the Occupiers Liability Act 1984.

If children are hurt because of unsafe equipment or the play area itself (from, say, jagged broken netting surrounding it) or if there was no supervision and there should have been, claims could be made for resulting injuries.

DOGS AND CHILDREN

If a dog physically attacks a child (or adult) it must usually be destroyed: there is no rule that the dog is allowed 'one bite'. But you do not have to wait until a child has actually been hurt before action can be taken against a dog's owner. It is also an offence under the Dangerous Dogs Act 1991 to allow a dog to be dangerously out of control (maximum fine £2,000 or six months' imprisonment). If the dog also causes injury to anyone, this is an aggravated offence with a maximum penalty of two years' imprisonment. So if there are good grounds for suspecting that a dog will injure someone – if the dog's owner refuses to secure the dog and it is trying to attack passers-by, for example – the police can take action. Owners can be ordered to muzzle or leash any breed of dog they consider dangerous (not just the four breeds mentioned below) and owners can be disqualified from having a dog.

Special breeds

Following the vicious attack on six-year-old Rucksana Khan by a pit bull terrier in 1991, the government tightened up laws on some breeds of dog viewed as being dangerous: the pit bull terrier, the Japanese tosa, and the unlikely named dogo argentino and fila braziliero. Owners who wanted to keep their dogs had to obtain a certificate of exemption by 1 March 1992. Strict rules now mean owners of these dog breeds must:
● have third-party insurance to cover against the dog causing injury or damage; *and*
● keep the dog muzzled in public places and keep it on a lead in charge of someone aged at least sixteen.

Breaking any of these rules is a criminal offence and can result in a fine of up to £2,000 and the dog's destruction.

Parents may also have a remedy under the civil law if the dog is bred for fighting (like the American pit bull terrier, the Japanese tosa and 'bandogs'). Under the 1971 Animals Act, the keeper of a dangerous animal (defined as a species or breed not commonly domesticated in the UK and which, when full grown, is likely to cause severe damage unless restrained) is liable in civil law for any injury or damage it may cause.

But what happens if the dog's owner does not have proper insurance cover for the dog? In practice, the first thing to do is see if the dog's owner has a house insurance policy, since this will often cover liability for animals. If the dog owner does not have a policy, it may still be worthwhile making a claim against the owner if the victim has a domestic insurance policy: many of these policies have clauses which will pay damages and costs if the insured obtains a judgement in an action for personal injury and if that judgement remains unsatisfied. It is worthwhile seeking legal advice if a claim is intended to be made.

ALCOHOL AND TOBACCO

There are specific laws which protect young people from the hazards of alcohol and tobacco.

Alcohol

The law allows children to go into pubs only in limited circumstances. It puts much of the responsibility for protecting children from alcohol on publicans (or other licence-holders), who can be fined up to £200 if they break any of the following regulations:

• children under five cannot be given alcohol except on medical grounds;

• children under fourteen must not be allowed in bars (although they can be allowed in a separate room);

• young people over sixteen can go into a bar, but cannot drink alcohol until they are eighteen.

Children can be fined for breaking these regulations too. A young person under eighteen who tries to buy, actually buys or drinks alcohol (thus covering every scenario) in licensed premises is liable to a fine of up to £400.

An older law can be used to punish parents too (although in practice this is hardly ever used). Under the Penalties for Drunkenness Act 1962, a person looking after a child under seven who is found in licensed premises can be liable to a fine of £10 or a prison term of up to a month.

Tobacco

Tobacco cannot be sold to anyone apparently under the age of sixteen, whether or not it is for his or her own use. Shopkeepers can be fined and even owners of cigarette-vending machines face fines if they do not take specific measures to prevent them being used by young people under sixteen.

Park-keepers and police constables have a duty to confiscate smoking materials of anyone apparently under sixteen smoking in a public place.

CAR SAFETY

Some 230 children are killed every year on the roads and 20,000 injured. The laws are being increasingly tightened up in an endeavour to halt the escalating figures.

Driving

Children under sixteen cannot drive a moped and certain tractors. Children under seventeen cannot drive a motorcycle, car or small goods vehicle (age limits for other passenger vehicles or goods vehicles are between eighteen and twenty-one). When learning to drive, the car must be fitted with L plates and the learner-driver must have a learner's certificate issued (available from DVLC, Swansea) and be accompanied by a qualified driver over the age of twenty-one sitting in the front passenger seat.

Seat belts

Legally no person can travel in the front seat (or, since 1 July 1991, in the back seat if seat belts have been fitted) without using a seat belt. There are special extra regulations about children. It is up to the driver of the vehicle (whether or not they are the parents) to make sure that the laws are complied with.

Children in the car cannot be carried on adults' laps but must be restrained in a purpose-built restraint appropriate to the child's weight. An appropriate restraint includes:

• *for children under one year old* a carrycot which is itself restrained by straps or a baby carrier;
• *for children between one and three years* a child seat or safety harness or a booster cushion used with an adult belt;
• *for children over four* an adult belt.

Illustration. *In 1991, a mother was fined £50 because her three-year-old child had undone the safety belt of the child's car seat in the back. A police car waiting next to the mother's car at traffic lights spotted that the child was unrestrained, and the mother was liable even though she had not noticed that the child had got out of her car seat.*

There are some exceptions, so if all the available seat belts are used up (by adults or other children), extra children don't have to wear one. The theory behind adults taking priority in the use of seat belts is that the heaviest unrestrained passengers cause the most injury to others if thrown around in a crash. Children can also be medically exempted from using seat belts (but the child must be disabled and wearing a special belt or must be given a certificate by a doctor). In practice, as with adult seat belt regulations, few such certificates are granted.

CONSUMER SAFETY

It is a criminal offence under the Consumer Protection Act 1987 to supply unsafe consumer goods in the UK, although suppliers can offer as a defence that the product meets safety standards. There are extra regulations for children's goods. Pushchairs must be stable and have adequate brakes, an attachment for a safety harness and two separate locking devices.

Regulations about toys prohibit sharp edges and points, toxic paint and non-securely attached facial features. Plastic bags should also carry warnings about their dangers to young children.

See also Chapter 37.

FIRE

It is an offence for anyone over sixteen, looking after a child under twelve, to leave the child alone in a room with an unprotected heater or open fire if the child is seriously injured or killed.

Children's nightwear (except terry towelling) is protected by special regulations. If a garment is marked 'low flammability to BS 5722', it has passed special safety tests. 'Keep away from fire' shows a less safe garment which has not passed tests.

The Furniture and Furnishing (Fire) (Safety) Regulations 1988 set new standards for furniture with foam filling: tests must prove them not to ignite quickly or emit high rates of toxic fumes.

FIREWORKS

While most restrictions on the sale of fireworks are voluntary controls by the industry, there are a few legal prohibitions. Fireworks must not be sold to any young person apparently under the age of sixteen (leaving the decision up to the shopkeeper) and they must not be discharged in a public place. Fireworks must be packed in approved packaging and only 5 lb of fireworks should be exposed at any one time.

If a big neighbourhood party is planned, there are special rules too. If more than 100 young people under fourteen attend 'an entertainment', the provider of entertainment must ensure there are enough adults in attendance to ensure the children's safety and stop the admission of more children than can be accommodated.

SAFETY AT WORK

Children must be over school-leaving age (i.e. sixteen) before they can:
• work in industry (e.g. mines and manufacturing);
• carry a heavy load, operate a circular saw, handle poisons or use equipment without proper safety regulations.

Department of Health model guidelines (which may be enacted by local authorities as by-laws) propose that children must not work in collecting rubbish, delivering fuels or cleaning windows more than 10 feet from the ground.

10 Children and Crime

If a child is accused of a crime he or she will be treated differently from an adult; the principles and procedures are modified to take into account the age and circumstances of the child.

The laws which deal with children and crime (the Children and Young Persons Act 1969 and the Children Act 1989) are based on the premise that the child who commits an offence probably has social problems. The aim should be to help the child to mend its ways. Prosecution is seen as the last resort. It is used only when the child does not admit guilt or when, having admitted guilt, the 'social-work' approach will not by itself reform him or her. Children should, however, always expect to be prosecuted when they are accused of a *serious* crime.

The Children Act requires every local authority to take all reasonable steps to discourage children from committing offences – for instance, by establishing youth and community services or by supporting parents in their role of encouraging children to steer away from crime. Similarly, local authorities must wherever possible reduce the need to bring criminal proceedings against child offenders. Whether either of these idealistic aims is realized remains in doubt because of local authorities' hard-pressed financial situation.

Children, or 'juveniles' as the law calls them, have different criminal responsibilities depending on their age.

Under ten – children cannot be found guilty of any criminal offence and are immune from prosecution. That does not mean that the child can commit offences with impunity, because the local authority may apply for a child to be taken into care if it repeatedly breaks the law.

Ten and under fourteen – children may be found guilty of a crime but it must be shown that they knew that they were doing wrong. If a child knows that its actions are *seriously* wrong and not just naughty or childish, then it will be assumed to know that they are *legally* wrong.

The courts adopt a common-sense rather than a legalistic approach. The child need not know that it has broken the law. Its actions at the time of the offence (such as planning, concealment or violent behaviour) are often a good indication of its state of mind.

Illustration. *A boy of ten was convicted of murder when the evidence showed that, after killing a five-year-old child, he had concealed the body and told lies about what had happened.*

The closer a child is to the age of fourteen, the more easy it is to show that it knew it was doing something legally wrong, although it is always necessary to look at its mental age. If, for instance, the mental age is under ten, it will be difficult to show that the child has criminal responsibility.

Children of this age cannot be charged with rape, or assault with intent to rape, because the law presumes that they are incapable of committing these crimes. This applies even if the child is physically capable of the acts, although in these instances he could be charged with indecent assault.

Fourteen and under seventeen – adult laws apply. A child is assumed to know the law, and to know what is an offence. It will usually be tried in the juvenile court but, if found guilty, may receive a different sentence from an adult.

Seventeen to twenty-one – the child is an adult in the eyes of the law, but it may receive a different sentence for its offence. It will be tried in an adult court.

POLICE INVESTIGATIONS

Often the first the parent will know of the offence is when the police call at the house. If that happens, the parent should first discuss the case with them, out of earshot of the child. The police may then ask to speak to the child. If they do, then the parent should insist on being present.

It must be established that an offence was committed. For instance, in a shoplifting case, the child may have absent-mindedly left without paying. Here no further steps should be taken because there was no criminal intention. The nature of the offence should be explained to the parents to reduce the possibility of a child wrongly confessing to an offence.

If the offence is serious, it may be best for the child not to answer any questions until a solicitor has been instructed. Free access to a solicitor under the duty solicitor scheme is one of the important rights afforded to any accused person, whether child or adult (see page 132). It is available whether or not the child has been charged.

The police should not interview or arrest suspected juveniles at their schools other than in exceptional circumstances. The consent of the head teacher must be given and the interview or arrest must be in his or her presence.

Detention at the police station

If a juvenile is arrested, his or her parents must be notified as soon as possible, and arrangements made for them to attend the police station. If a person *looks* under seventeen, the police must treat them as a juvenile until they establish otherwise.

During police detention, the child must be kept away from adults charged with an offence, unless child and adult are charged with the very same incidents. This also applies when the child is travelling to court or waiting at court. If the juvenile is a girl, she must be kept in the care of a policewoman at these times.

Suspects are always entitled to read copies of the *Codes of Practice* which spell out their rights. This is especially important as the whole process of police detention and questioning is a frightening enough experience for adults and will be much more so for children. Police stations are a world of their own. Any detained person will in some respects be at the mercy of the police, who are to a great degree in control of what the suspect may or may not do while in the station.

Any juvenile can see the custody record at the end of his or her detention and may also ask to see it for up to one year after the record was made.

Rules for interviewing juveniles

The 'appropriate adult'

The procedures are now laid down by the Police and Criminal Evidence Act 1984 (the PACE Act).

When a child is interviewed or asked to sign a statement, this must be done, if possible, in the presence of an 'appropriate adult'. This applies whether the child is a suspect *or* a witness to a crime. Copies of interview records and statements must be read and signed by the adult. An intimate search can be carried out only in the adult's presence.

The adult's duty is to advise and help the juvenile and to ensure that the interview is fairly conducted. The juvenile can consult privately with the adult at any time.

If the parent or guardian is not available *or suitable*, the 'appropriate adult' could be a social worker or a representative of the local authority. As a last resort the adult may be any independent person over eighteen who is not employed by the police.

A child aged sixteen was interviewed by the police in the presence of his father. They chose not to ask for a solicitor. The father could not read and had a very low IQ. He was probably incapable of understanding the seriousness of his son's position. The High Court decided that he was not an 'appropriate adult' and that the interview was excluded from the evidence. R. v. Morse (1991)

The police may waive the rules if the interview is 'urgent' – if a superintendent or higher-ranking police officer considers that a delay in interviewing the juvenile would involve an immediate risk of harm to people or a serious loss of or damage to property.

'Cautioning'

The police must always 'caution' a suspect before questions are put to him or her. The purpose of cautioning is to make them aware of the importance of what they say. If the police fail to caution, any statements the suspect makes may be rejected by the court. The exact words used for cautioning are: 'You do not have to say anything unless you wish to do so, but what you say may be given in evidence.'

If a juvenile is cautioned without an adult being present, the caution must be repeated in the adult's presence.

The right to legal advice

All suspects must be told of their right of access to a solicitor. A juvenile must be told this in the presence of an 'appropriate adult'. If the adult feels that the child does need legal advice, then it should be provided. The child or the adult should then be allowed to communicate with a solicitor by telephone, letter or in person *at any time* and in private.

There is a duty solicitor scheme for those questioned in police stations. This service is funded by the government and organized by local solicitors, who arrange to be available both day *and* night to attend police interviews at police stations or elsewhere. This service is free to all those detained, regardless of income. The same solicitor who is present at the police station may represent the child in any subsequent hearing – for example, in an application for bail or at the trial. The child may later choose a different solicitor to represent him or her.

If the child admits the offence

If the child admits guilt, the police may simply caution him or her rather than prosecute. This 'caution' is different from the official 'caution', which is explained above. 'Cautioning' in this sense is in effect a 'dressing-down' from a senior police officer. The child is given a severe warning and told that he or she will not be dealt with so leniently next time. The caution does not go down as a criminal record, although reference can be made to it if the child appears before a juvenile or adult court in the future.

If the police are in doubt as to whether to give a caution, they may invite a 'juvenile liaison panel' (consisting of representatives of the probation, social and education services) to review the case. None the less, the police have a complete discretion in deciding whether to prosecute for minor offences. If the juvenile has been arrested and cautioned on several previous occasions (exactly how many varies with the different police forces – three is the usual number) then prosecution will follow. Prosecution *must* follow if the offence is serious (e.g. rape, arson, aggravated burglary etc.).

Sometimes, after cautioning, the child may be referred to agencies which provide guidance, support and involvement in the community. This may be help with accommodation or benefits or work experience.

While cautioning a child as an alternative to prosecuting is clearly sensible, there is one major disadvantage. A caution will be given only to a child who admits guilt and, since many children regard a caution as 'getting off', there is a danger that the innocent child will say they are guilty just to avoid the anxiety and worry of a juvenile court appearance. Thus the caution can sometimes be an inducement to the innocent to admit guilt. But care should be taken as the caution can be used as evidence of previous bad character if the child is prosecuted at a later date.

If the child denies the offence

If the child refuses to admit to the offence, then the police will have to decide whether to prosecute or to drop the matter. The child cannot be given a caution as this would imply that they did commit the offence. In these cases it may be the courts' role to determine guilt or innocence.

Charging detained juveniles

When the police have concluded their investigations the child must be either charged or released. Any action should be taken in the presence of the appropriate adult. Once charged, the juvenile should be free to leave the police station unless the custody officer authorizes further detention on the grounds that:

● the child's address is unknown or uncertain;
● the officer believes that detention is necessary to prevent harm to the officer or others or loss of or damage to property;
● the officer believes the child will fail to attend court or answer to bail; *or*
● detention is necessary to prevent interference with the administration of justice or the investigation of an offence.

A juvenile may also be detained after being charged if the custody officer believes that this would be in the juvenile's *own interest*.

As a general rule, juveniles should not be kept at the police station after being charged. They should be granted bail and released. If the juvenile is remanded in custody (i.e charged with an imprisonable offence), he or she should be sent to local authority accommodation, unless the circumstances justify keeping them at the police station:

A juvenile had been living at a local authority hostel. He had been convicted of a number of offences of theft and burglary, and was under arrest for further serious offences. He was denied bail to prevent him from interfering with witnesses. The local authority wanted him to go back to the hostel but the police custody officer refused. The local authority applied to the High Court to overrule the custody officer's decision. The High Court refused the application and decided that the custody officer had acted properly. R v. Chief Constable of Cambridgeshire *ex p.* Michel (1990)

Juveniles should not be sent to *secure* accommodation (which they are not free to leave) if they are under fifteen. Secure accommodation may be used for juveniles over fifteen but only in respect of those charged with a serious offence or those who have a history of absconding from local authority accommodation. The requirement is usually imposed on a juvenile only when it is necessary to protect the public from serious harm.

When there is not enough evidence to charge the juvenile, the police must release him or her, unless the custody officer believes that detention is necessary to preserve evidence or to carry out further questioning.

GOING TO COURT

If the police decide to prosecute, their next step will be to issue a summons and serve it on the parents. This will tell the parents and the child to attend the juvenile court at the stated date and time. Only in serious cases will the police issue a warrant for the arrest of the child and take him or her to the police station. If this happens, the parents should contact a solicitor at once.

Even if the child is arrested, the police will usually release him or her on bail until the hearing of the case.

If bail is not granted, the child should be kept in the care of the local authority or in a remand centre if he or she is charged with a serious offence.

WHICH COURT?

Most children are tried in a juvenile court and the trial will be by magistrates sitting without a jury – i.e. summarily. The magistrates are drawn from a specially trained panel and have knowledge and experience of children. They must be under fifty (preferably under forty) when appointed and must retire at sixty-five. The bench should consist of two or three magistrates, one of whom at least must be a woman.

In exceptional circumstances a child may be tried in a crown court by a judge and a jury as if he or she were an adult. They may also be tried in a magistrates' court with a normal panel of magistrates (as opposed to a juvenile court).

For instance, a juvenile charged with murder, manslaughter or any offence for which an adult may be punished with a prison sentence of fourteen years or more will usually be committed by the magistrates for trial in a crown court.

Where a child is charged jointly with an adult, he or she may be tried beside the adult co-defendant in a crown court or in a magistrates' court, though he or she may be referred to the juvenile court for sentencing.

Illustration. *A sixteen-year-old (juvenile) and a eighteen-year-old (adult) are accused of stealing a car. The eighteen-year-old can opt for trial in either the magistrates' court or the crown court. If he chooses a magistrates' court trial the sixteen-year-old will be tried with him. But if the sixteen-year-old is found guilty, he will be referred to the juvenile court for sentencing. However, if the magistrates wish to fine him, bind over his parents or give him an absolute or conditional discharge, they can impose that sentence themselves. If the eighteen-year-old elects to go for a crown court trial, the sixteen-year-old will be tried with him. But if he is found guilty, he will almost always be passed back to the juvenile court for sentencing.*

In theory, juveniles should be tried in the crown court only if it is necessary in the interests of justice. In practice, they are nearly always tried in the crown court. This is because the prosecution does not want to risk one offender being acquitted and the other being convicted on the same evidence but in a different court.

Treatment of the sixteen-year-old defendant who turns seventeen

The juvenile court normally hears cases involving children under seventeen. A child who is sixteen (and therefore a juvenile) when charged may have reached seventeen by the time the case is tried. The general rule is that he or she will then be tried as a juvenile even though their age at trial makes them subject to adult procedures. However, the rule is not always followed.

A juvenile was charged with committing an assault ten weeks before his seventeenth birthday. The prosecution papers were ready five weeks later. The Crown Prosecution Service instructed the police to bring him to the magistrates' court (as opposed to a juvenile court) one day after his seventeenth birthday and he was found guilty. The juvenile applied to set aside the decision on the ground that this was an abuse of the court procedures. The Divisional court decided that the Crown Prosecution Service had acted improperly but refused to quash the decision as the juvenile had not been deprived of the protection of the law. R v. Rotherham Magistrates' Court *ex p.* Brough (1991)

PROCEDURE IN THE JUVENILE COURT

The hearing may be either in a court which is used only for juvenile hearings or in a normal magistrates' court. Although the juvenile court will be in the same building as the magistrates' court, it often has a separate entrance. When the juvenile court is in a normal courtroom, no adult criminal proceedings may be held in that room for at least an hour beforehand.

The procedure in the juvenile court is similar to that in the magistrates' court. The magistrates act as both judge and jury (see page 752), and are advised by a legally qualified clerk. Juvenile court cases are tried *summarily* (see above, Which Court?).

The proceedings are less formal than those of the normal magistrates' court. The object is to make the process less intimidating to juveniles. Less legal terminology is used. For instance, juveniles will be asked whether they 'admit' or 'deny' an offence rather than pleading guilty or not guilty. Witnesses will 'promise' to tell the truth as opposed to swearing on oath and juveniles will be referred to by their first name. Juveniles are not 'convicted' or 'sentenced', but are instead euphemistically 'dealt with'.

Hearings in juvenile courts are conducted in private; the general public may not attend. There may still be a surprisingly large number of people in the courtroom: lawyers, legal staff, the accused, his or her parents, the police, a representative of the local education authority and a probation officer. The press are also allowed in court but will rarely attend, as any information which may identify the juvenile (e.g. the name, address or school of the child) cannot be published.

Parents are expected to appear and may even be ordered to do so. If there is a reason why the parents cannot be present (e.g. they are ill), then the magistrates will probably accept another family member, such as an older brother or sister, as a substitute. Should no substitute be available, the case may be adjourned, especially if the child does not have a solicitor representing him or her. In some courts, the child will be referred to the court's duty solicitor, who will then act for them. If the child remains unrepresented and if he or she denies the offence, a parent can help the juvenile with their defence. The helper *and the juvenile* may cross-examine the witnesses for the prosecution on such occasions. The court will generally assist by making sure that the juvenile's case is properly put to the witnesses. In practice it would be unusual for a child to remain unrepresented, as legal aid is generally freely available to juveniles.

Home surroundings reports

If a juvenile is found guilty, the court will (in all but the most trivial cases) consider a report on his or her background and surroundings. If it has not been prepared by the end of the case, the court will adjourn so that social workers can prepare the report. Generally bail will be granted (often with the parents as sureties). The procedure varies according to the age of the child.

Under thirteen – the police must notify the local authority of their intention to start the proceedings. The local authority must investigate the home surroundings, school record, health and character of the child. A report will be sent to the court. The court may ask the local authority to make further investigations. The child's attitude to the offence and any mitigating circumstances will be included in the report, which will in turn be supplemented by other reports produced by the local education authority or other body.

Thirteen and over – prior notice must in this case be given to the probation office, which will then make the necessary inquiries and produce a report.

If the report is available at the hearing, the magistrates will immediately be able to sentence the juvenile. The report need not be read out in court. The parents and the child can even be ordered to stay out of the courtroom while the report is being discussed. The court should, however, tell the parents and the child about any information in the report which will affect the sentence.

Statements by the parents

If the child is found guilty, the parents and child will be given the opportunity to make a statement 'in mitigation' on anything which the report may not have mentioned, to try to persuade the magistrates to deal with the juvenile leniently. This is in addition to submissions made to the court by the child's solicitor. The magistrates will then consider the appropriate treatment for the child.

SENTENCING

A juvenile court can impose some adult sentences. There are also sentences only for juveniles.

Sentences specially for juveniles

Detention in a young offenders' institution

This is available only for youths who have committed an imprisonable offence. It is not available for males under fourteen or females under fifteen. The length of sentence varies according to the age and sex of the offenders. The minimum for males is twenty-one days, but for females it is four months. The maximum can never be more than an adult sentence for the offence, or the maximum sentence the court can impose (i.e six months in a magistrates' court). Depending on the age of the juvenile there are further restrictions on the maximum sentence. For instance, a child under fifteen can receive only four months; between fifteen and seventeen it is twelve months. However, in very serious cases (such as when a child is convicted of an offence carrying an adult penalty of fourteen years' imprisonment) the 'age' limits on the length of sentence can be overridden.

Supervision order (for juveniles of ten to sixteen years)

This is the juvenile court's equivalent to a probation order (see page 770). The aim is to give juveniles long-term help without removing them from their home. The child will be under general supervision. Often conditions will be imposed, such as:

- to live with a certain person for a specified period;
- to have regular appointments with a 'supervisor' (see below);
- to have psychiatric treatment;
- to go to school regularly if of compulsory school age;
- to have a curfew imposed;
- to refrain from participating in certain activities.

These conditions can be imposed only for a period of up to ninety days.

If the child does not comply with the order he or she can be brought back to the juvenile court and a different sentence may be imposed (e.g a fine or an attendance centre order).

A supervision order may last for a maximum of three years. If the offender is under thirteen the 'supervisor' will be the local authority; otherwise the supervisor will be a probation officer.

Supervision order with residence requirement

This is an order requiring the juvenile to live in *local authority accommodation* for a maximum of six months. The residence requirement is intended to help a juvenile whose surroundings are a contributory factor towards his or her behaviour. For example, the residence requirement would help a juvenile who is living rough and stealing to survive, or where there is a lack of parental control.

It can be imposed only on a child who has committed a serious offence (one that would occasion imprisonment for an adult) while under a supervision. The court must be satisfied that the child's home circumstances contributed to a significant extent towards his or her behaviour. A supervision order of this kind may also impose any of the conditions mentioned above – see Supervision Order for (Juveniles of Ten to Sixteen Years, page 184). This sentence can normally be given only to a juvenile who is legally aided.

Detention under the Children and Young Persons Act 1933 (for juveniles of sixteen to eighteen years)

This is the juvenile equivalent of adult imprisonment for children who have committed serious offences (manslaughter and offences which would involve adult prison sentences of fourteen years or more). It will be used when, because of the seriousness of the offence, there is no alternative to prison. The place and conditions of imprisonment are determined by the Secretary of State. It will usually be in a young persons' prison. The term of detention is limited to the maximum for the particular offence.

Detention 'during Her Majesty's pleasure'

This sentence must be imposed on juveniles under eighteen who are convicted of murder in the crown court. The juvenile is held in custody for an indefinite period. The Home Secretary decides when he or she will be released.

Custody for life (for youths of seventeen to twenty-one years)

This is imposed on juveniles and young people between these ages who have committed murder or any other offence which has a mandatory life sentence. It may also be given to those who are convicted of an offence where an adult *could* receive a life sentence (e.g. robbery).

Attendance centre order (for youths of ten to twenty-one years)

This is ordered where the juvenile is guilty of an offence punishable with prison or has broken the terms of a supervision order. A mixture of firm discipline, physical training and the teaching of handicrafts and similar activities is used not only to take away the offenders' leisure time but to try to teach youths less antisocial uses of this time. The usual sentence is for a total of twelve hours, to be served by between one and three hours on alternate Saturday afternoons. It is thus particularly suitable for football hooligans (i.e. when the team is playing at home), but generally it achieves little. An added problem is that few areas have enough attendance centres available (and so some other sentence has to be imposed). This sentence is only available for young offenders who have *not* previously been sentenced to periods of detention. The number of hours normally ranges from twelve to thirty-six in total.

If the child does not attend he or she can be brought back to the juvenile court and a different sentence will be substituted.

'Adult' sentences used to punish juveniles

Community service order (for juveniles of sixteen plus)

This is an order to do unpaid work. The sentence may be used only for offenders who have committed an imprisonable offence and who consent to the order. The offenders will work with volunteers.

The number of hours of community service which may be ordered for an adult is between forty and 240 hours. The maximum for a child under seventeen is 120 hours. Adult rules apply to those over seventeen (see page 780).

Fines

Children may be fined, but in practice their parents will be ordered to pay. The maximum fines are as follows:
- ten to thirteen – £100
- fourteen to sixteen – £400
- seventeen and over – £2,000

Compensation

In addition to (or instead of) fines, the court can order payment of compensation up to £2,000 where injury is caused or property damaged. If an offender cannot pay both, priority will be given to compensation.

Costs

A juvenile may be ordered to pay legal costs. If the juvenile is under seventeen, the amount must not be more than the maximum fine for the offence.

Responsibility of the parent

The parents of a juvenile will be required to pay all fines, compensation and costs imposed on the juvenile unless the parents cannot be found or it would be unreasonable to order them to pay. The parents must be given an opportunity to be heard before a payment order is made.

Discharge

Absolute and conditional discharges (see page 774) are both commonly used in juvenile courts. They follow a finding of guilt. A juvenile granted an absolute discharge leaves the court with no criminal record. If he or she receives a conditional discharge, they will have no criminal record provided that they do not commit another offence within twelve months. Both kinds of discharge amount to a warning to the child while at the same time avoiding the stigma that may be attached to a more serious sentence. Neither form of discharge is equal to an acquittal.

Binding over

The offender gives a written undertaking (or recognizance as it is called) to promise to pay a sum of money (up to £1,000) if he or she reoffends within a given period.

The parents may be bound over to take proper care and control of their child. The parents' consent is not necessary, but if they refuse without good reason to give their consent to its use they are liable to a fine of up to £1,000.

Deferred sentence

This allows the court to put off passing a sentence for up to six months. When the court reconvenes it will be to consider how the child has behaved. If the child has not misbehaved during this time, he or she will usually be given an absolute or conditional discharge, or a fine (see above). In practice the courts seldom use this sentence and will instead give the offender a conditional discharge.

Hospital orders

If during the course of the trial it becomes clear that the juvenile has psychiatric problems he or she may be ordered to be detained in a hospital. If the mental condition is severe, and the court is satisfied that the juvenile committed the offence, the court will make the order without making a finding of guilt.

APPEALS

Appeals against juvenile court decisions are normally made to the crown court. They should be made within twenty-one days and only the juvenile may appeal. If the appeal is against sentence the crown court may decrease or *increase* the sentence. Even if a custodial sentence is given, bail may be granted pending an appeal. In addition, either the juvenile or the prosecution may appeal to the Divisional Court of the High Court on a point of law.

LEGAL AID

Juveniles may apply for legal aid in the juvenile court. The parents may also apply on their behalf. Where the child is under seventeen the court may take into account either the child's *or* the parents' means. In all other respects legal aid is assessed and granted following the same procedures as those used for adults who are charged with a crime (see page 982, Legal Aid). As is the case with adults, a juvenile who is charged with an offence for which he or she may receive a custodial sentence will almost certainly be granted legal aid.

CHANGES IN THE OFFING

The Criminal Justice Act 1991 will make further changes to the legal system.

From 1 October 1992 juvenile courts will be renamed 'youth courts' and the upper age limit of those dealt with by these courts will be raised from sixteen to seventeen.

11 Wills

WHAT IS A WILL?

A will is the legal document by which a person directs what should happen to their property after their death. A person who dies without making a will is said to have died intestate.

A properly made will appoints one or more people to carry out the terms of the will. They are called executors. If there is no will, the rules of intestacy determine who will administer the property of the intestate. They are called the administrators. Both executors and administrators are sometimes called personal representatives.

The property of the deceased is called their estate. Freehold land and leasehold property are described as real estate or realty, and all other property is described as personal estate or personalty. The main duty of the personal representatives is to gather in the assets of the estate, to pay the debts and liabilities and then to distribute what is left to those entitled.

There are various laws which ensure that the personal representatives carry out the duties which have been entrusted to them. These laws often describe the personal representatives as trustees, although the duties of a trustee can continue after the estate has been administered – for instance, when they have to continue looking after property which has been left to a child.

WHAT IS PROBATE?

Probate has two usual meanings. First, it can mean the document which confirms that the will is valid and states who the executors are. It authorizes the executors to gain access to bank accounts, shares, real property and other investments. It is known as 'Probate of the Will' and corresponds to 'Letters of Administration', which are granted to the administrators of the estate when a person dies intestate.

The second meaning of probate is wider and refers to the various laws and courts which deal with wills, intestacy, succession, inheritance, administration and disputes over estates.

While death may be the end of a person's earthly troubles, it can be just the beginning for those left behind. Until 1857 the Ecclesiastical Courts dealt with many probate matters but after that date the civil courts took over. Since that time Parliament has passed numerous laws relating to probate matters.

The probate laws have various objectives:
- to safeguard the dead person's creditors;
- to ensure that the provisions of the will are carried out (if there is a will);
- to ensure that the dead person's estate is shared out according to law (if there is no will);
- to determine what must happen if there is a disputed estate;
- to ensure that inheritance tax is paid (unless the estate is exempt).

The common law laid down its own rules for securing these objectives, but these laws have been replaced by acts of Parliament, mainly of nineteenth-century origin, which lay down rules as to how a valid will is to be made, how personal representatives are appointed, the extent of their powers and duties, and, finally, how the assets are to be distributed and to whom.

WHY MAKE A WILL?

According to a recent Gallup Poll, most of us think we should make a will but only one in three actually does so.

'I haven't decided who to leave it to yet.'

'I'm not going to tempt fate.'

'They can fight it out between themselves when I'm gone.'

'It will all go to the wife anyway.' (Not necessarily!)

Many people who die without making a will have had these phrases on their lips. They can leave a desperate muddle for their families.

If a person dies intestate, the property will pass to his or her relatives in accordance with the rules of intestacy (see page 226). Generally, this means that the surviving husband or wife receives the first £75,000 (or £125,000 if there are no children), plus a life interest in half the balance (or half the balance if no children). Problems, therefore, arise if the deceased does not want his or her spouse to take such a large share (for instance, they might have separated, or the spouse may have a large estate of their own) or wants them to receive a larger amount. Many lawyers these days advise that a surviving spouse should be left all the estate unless it amounts to well over £100,000 or they have significant funds in their own name. This is because inflation can soon reduce the value of that lump sum; even with inflation at only 5 per cent a year, £100,000 today would be worth only £46,500 in fifteen years. So a man worth £100,000 with a wife and child would be well advised to make a will leaving everything to his wife, rather than rely on the intestacy laws (in which case his wife would get only £75,000, plus a life interest in half the balance of £25,000). There are also significant income tax savings to be made by dividing such a sum between husband and wife during their lifetime, so a spouse thinking about making a will should also be thinking about equalization of assets and lifetime gifts. Do not forget the quotation, 'But in this world nothing can be said to be certain except death and taxes.' Think ahead.

So a will is advisable when the intestacy laws will not produce a satisfactory distribution of the estate. Since circumstances can change (for instance, a person might not think his estate is worth more than £75,000 or £125,000, but a few years of inflation can drastically alter the position), it is always sensible to make a will and avoid possible problems in the future. One way of reducing the impact of inflation on a will is to express gifts in terms of fractions or percentages of the estate so that the relative value of each gift is maintained at the same level.

In more complicated situations the advantages of a will are obvious. Apart from ensuring that the estate is given to the right people in the right proportions, a will can avoid family squabbles and jealousies, reduce the amount of inheritance tax payable, and also simplify the task of the personal representatives. An additional benefit is that the person who leaves a will can choose who will be his or her executors; if he or she dies intestate they will be selected by following a statutory set of rules (see page 217).

Making a will is not expensive. Solicitors generally charge from £30 upwards for drawing up a straightforward will, but despite this, many people put off making a will until it is too late: 'I feel better now, doctor' are famous last words. The eventual inheritance tax savings which can be made by having a will professionally prepared can be considerable. A solicitor should also draw attention to other ways in which a person can organize his or her affairs to advantage.

Some people on low incomes or state benefits may be eligible for free or low-cost wills under the Law Society's green-form scheme. Those entitled include single parents, persons over seventy, the blind, the deaf, those with serious illness or disability, people with handicapped children and those on housing benefit and numerous other state benefits.

Do not forget lifetime gifts as an alternative to, or in conjunction with, a will. Annual exemptions are available and great inheritance tax savings can be made by the careful use of gifts. For others there is the simple pleasure of making the gift during their lifetime, when it may be most needed.

MAKING A WILL

The intention

Anybody who is over eighteen and of sound mind can make a will. But not every written document that sets out how one's property is to be disposed of on death is a will, for it must be intended to act as a will and to be its maker's 'last will and testament'.

Unless the document is intended to be a will it will not be enforced by the courts, or, to put this in more legal language, a will is only valid if it is made with the necessary testamentary intention. It must express a person's genuine wishes and they must understand and approve of its contents. Great care must be taken when encouraging an elderly member of a family to make a will to ensure that the will does not set out the wishes of the relative doing the encouraging. Thus, if someone is of unsound mind, or doubtful mental capacity, their will may be invalid. Even a person who is not of sound mind but is a patient under the Court of Protection may have a will made for them under the supervision of the Court of Protection. Because of this, when an aged and perhaps eccentric person makes a will, it is advisable to have a doctor as one of the witnesses, and the doctor should check that the old or infirm person is capable of making a will and that he or she understands what is written in the will. If the doctor makes a record of the examination it may be valuable evidence should the will ever be challenged on the grounds of mental incapacity. If an elderly person wishes to change a well-balanced will in favour of some other person, consideration must be given to ensure that there has been no undue influence.

Foolishness, eccentricity or social pressure is not enough to invalidate a will. However, fear, fraud or coercion is; for instance, a person who signs a will at gun-point is not making a valid will. Thus, if a solicitor or doctor takes advantage of his position of trust so that he benefits under the will, the gift to him will probably not take effect. Similarly, if a person is nagged and pestered by a begging relative or pressurized by someone who is looking after them, that too may amount to undue influence.

The formalities

There are detailed rules on how to sign and witness a will. These are set out in section 9 of the Wills Act 1837. Now, the rules are that:

● the will must be in writing (so a video will would not be valid!); *and*

● it must have been signed by the testator or some other person in their presence and at their direction; *and*

● there must be signatures from at least two witnesses, who both saw the testator sign and who both then signed in his/her presence.

If the will does not comply with these requirements, it will be invalid. Its author will, therefore, die intestate, and his or her personal representatives may be forced by the intestacy rules to distribute the estate in a way that was not intended.

Although the Wills Act requirements seem straightforward, numerous wills have been turned down over the years because of a failure to meet the strict wording of the provisions. Although these rules may seem strict, the rules were even stricter before 1982 and it is likely that in the future many fewer wills will fail than was previously the case. For example, before 1982 testators had to sign at the foot of the will – if they wrote anything after their signature, then that part of the will was ignored. Now, they can sign wherever they like as long as it is clear that they want the whole document to be treated as their will. In practice, of course, the will should still be signed at the end so as to avoid any arguments, but the 1982 changes have meant that if a mistake is made it is now less likely to cause major problems. If the will consists of several pages, it is wise for the testator to sign at the bottom of each page.

Witnesses

As mentioned above, there must be at least two witnesses to the will. Any adult, except someone who is blind, can be a witness, but the witnesses must see the testator sign, and then sign the will themselves. The will is not valid if the witness does not see the testator sign or if the testator signs after the witness.

The witnesses need not see the contents of the will; all they are doing is witnessing the testator's signature, not the contents of the will. They are there as independent witnesses that the person signed the will freely and voluntarily. Because they are independent persons, they cannot benefit from the will, nor can their husband or wife benefit. Any gift to the witnesses (or their spouses) will be invalid and the property that would have gone to them will form part of the residue of the estate. However, if the witness and the beneficiary marry after the will is made this rule will not apply and the beneficiary can take the gift.

It is vital, therefore, that a beneficiary or the spouse of a beneficiary under a will should not witness it. If they do witness it, and so cause the gift to be forfeited, that will not affect the validity of the rest of the will; it will remain valid subject to their (or their spouse's) gift being struck out.

People often ask close relatives to witness their wills. In such a case the witness should check whether they (or their spouse) will benefit from the will; if so, someone else will have to witness the will. This is most important!

Drafting a will

A will that complies with the rules and which was made with testamentary intention will be upheld by the courts as a valid and binding will. Therefore, the personal representatives will have to follow its instructions exactly – even if it is clear that the testator made a mistake when drafting it. This is because the law requires the written directions of the testator to be followed, and if he or she leaves clear and unambiguous instructions they must be obeyed. Only if there is some ambiguity or uncertainty in the will itself can the court consider other evidence, such as letters written by the deceased, or memories of conversations. Thus the language of a will must be clear and unambiguous, and the wording carefully chosen.

If ambiguous words are used, there are two possible consequences. First, the gift might not go to the correct people. For instance, suppose a man leaves his property to 'my children' and at the time of his death he has three children, including one stepchild. In such a case the law will construe 'my children' as meaning 'my own children of the whole blood', and so the stepchild will not receive anything. The property will all go to the other two children. There is a story, perhaps apocryphal, of the original 'lucky bastard'. A man is supposed to have made a will stating, 'I leave everything to my nephew Arthur.' There were in fact two nephews called Arthur, one of whom was illegitimate. On the construction of the will the court decided that the illegitimate nephew was the one intended to benefit under the will.

The second possible consequence of unclear wording is that the gift will fail altogether, because the court cannot decide what the testator meant. For an example of real trouble arising from a real will, look at the home-made will on page 208 and the resulting consequences.

The moral is to avoid difficulties by using clear, unambiguous language when drawing up a will. Sometimes testators fail to see inconsistencies in their wishes. They desire to leave everything to their spouse absolutely but they then contradict that desire by attempting to leave to their children what is left when their spouse eventually dies. They can say what will happen if their spouse dies first but otherwise a trust must be established and the spouse does not get an absolute interest.

Because of pitfalls such as these, words used in a will must be chosen with great care. While the layperson can draft their own will if it is simple (for instance, leaving all their property to one person), it is unwise to draft one's own will if there are several beneficiaries involved, or if the value of the estate is considerable. In these cases it is worth paying a small amount for a solicitor to draft the will. In fact, many solicitors make a loss on will-drafting, but are prepared to do the task cheaply in the hope that they will be asked to take over the rewarding work of administering the estate when the testator dies. There are now firms which offer a will-writing service, but these may not be any cheaper than a solicitor and may not always have the broad view of the law necessary to advise on the best way to arrange one's affairs generally. Bear in mind also that inheritance tax can begin to bite on an estate worth over £150,000. Will-drafting by a solicitor may pay for itself many times over if the solicitor can draw up the will so as to reduce the IHT payable. Generally, therefore, it is wise to use a solicitor for drafting a will; this does not, of course, mean that there will be any obligation to let the solicitor administer the estate when the time comes. A person should think very carefully indeed before allowing their bank to arrange a will to be drawn up. The bank will inevitably put itself forward as executor and this will mean that the estate will have to pay the bank's administration charges, which are usually much higher than those charged by solicitors. A typical bank charge for administering an estate of £200,000, comprising a house worth £150,000 and a building society account of £50,000, could be as much as £6,000.

A person who is not prepared to go to a solicitor and who insists on writing his or her own will should use one of the will forms obtainable from stationers. These forms have the Wills Act requirements incorporated into them and give basic instructions for completion. Despite these precautions, people still make mistakes when using these forms. Also, the forms give little help on how to word the gifts correctly. Before completing one of these forms, however, read the home-made will on page 208, which contains several serious mistakes and ambiguities. Do not take any risks when making your will. Your family may be able to sue your solicitor if he or she is negligent when making your will. They cannot sue you when you are gone.

Do not forget the green-form scheme for those on low incomes or state benefits. See page 957.

Words in wills

Wills drawn up by solicitors sometimes seem verbose and full of antiquated legal jargon. Usually there is a reason for this; the solicitor is carefully using words and phrases that are known to have a well-defined legal meaning, usually as a result of court decisions which have laid down what these phrases mean. Generally, though, most people's wills can be written in modern English, uncluttered by the 'hereinafters', 'abovementioneds', 'hereinbeforementioneds', 'provided howevers' etc., that one frequently associates with legal documents. But whatever words they use – ancient or modern – the person drafting the document will need to choose their vocabulary with care, and also to ensure that the will envisages and deals with all possible eventualities. If you have a will prepared by a solicitor, do not be afraid to ask what a phrase means in ordinary English. It is your will, so you should understand it! If the solicitor can't explain it, do they understand it?

Words that are frequently used

bequeath The word 'bequeath' is used to refer to a gift of anything other than land (i.e. houses, flats, land). If the gift is of land, the word 'devise' is used. For instance, a testator 'bequeaths' a car, or a gift or £x, but he 'devises' his house.

children This includes both legitimate and illegitimate children, whether boys or girls. Adopted children are included if the will was made before or after the date of the formal adoption order, although there can be complications if the will leaves property 'to the children of . . . living at my death'. If the adoption takes place after the death, the child is treated as having been born after the death, even though their actual date of birth was before the death. Step-children do not always come within the definition of 'children' unless all the children are stepchildren and there are no other children alive at the date the will was made, or unless it is clear that the stepchildren were intended to be included.

descendants This means children, grandchildren, great-grandchildren, great-great-grandchildren etc., whether male or female. If property is left to 'all my descendants', each individual descendant will have an equal share of the estate (referred to as '*per capita*'), whereas it may have been the intention of the testator that only their children should have an equal share, so that if a child has died leaving grandchildren, those grandchildren will share their parent's share (referred to as '*per stirpes*').

family This word has been held to have several different meanings. Generally, it means the same as 'children', but the careful will-drafter will avoid using the word 'family' because of the confusion over its meaning. In divorce proceedings, for instance, 'a child of the family' is one treated as one of the family whoever their parents. This can be quite different from 'a child of the marriage', who may be living with another family even though his parents are divorcing.

free of tax Although the law provides for the payment of inheritance tax from the residue of the UK estate, the testator can overrule that provision. If a particular gift is to bear its own proportion of inheritance tax, the will should make that clear.

infant This means the same as 'a minor', i.e. a person under eighteen. People under eighteen cannot own land and they cannot give a valid receipt to the personal representatives for money or chattels. It is, therefore, impossible for a gift to go direct to a minor. In the case of land, it will be held by trustees until the child is eighteen, and with other property the usual device is to word the will so that the gift goes to the parents or other trustees, who are asked to hold it for the child's benefit.

issue This has basically the same meaning as 'descendants', but occasionally it has been held to have a different meaning. Therefore, the word 'issue' is avoided by experienced will-drafters.

legacy This usually means a specific sum left to a beneficiary but it can also be a gift of a specific item.

nephews and nieces The general rule is that this phrase includes only the testator's own nephews and nieces, and not those of his/her spouse. For the avoidance of doubt, it is wise to name the children rather than simply describe them as 'my nephews and nieces'.

next of kin This will be the person who is the closest blood relative of the testator.

residue The residue is what is left after paying the testamentary expenses, the inheritance tax and all the specific legacies and devises (i.e. after all specific gifts have been made).

testamentary expenses These are the expenses of administering the estate: e.g. expenses of the executors, probate fees, lawyers' fees, costs of adverts, tracing beneficiaries, etc.

Making a will: thinking ahead

The person drafting a will has to think ahead and envisage all possible circumstances, such as the death of the main beneficiary, a change in the size of the estate or even a change in the tax laws. These are some of the points that a solicitor would want his or her client to consider:

• Are some people to be allowed to select mementoes or souvenirs from the testator's personal possessions? If so, it is wise to give very clear guidance to the personal representatives to enable them to avoid disputes which might otherwise arise over the identity and value of these items.

● Is there a gift of the *residue*? The residue is the property that is not specifically given away as named items or as money legacies. If there is no gift of the 'remainder of my property', the residue will not pass under the will but be distributed as though the testator had died intestate (see page 226). This is a very common omission in home-made wills, where the testator leaves exactly what they have got when they make the will. Remember that a person may win the pools between making their will and dying.

● Is a gift to bear its own inheritance tax? Under s.211 of the Inheritance Tax Act 1984, all inheritance tax on the UK estate falls on the residue. Would that be fair on the residuary beneficiary? Do not forget that a gift to a spouse is exempt and that there are other exemptions.

● If a house is to be given to a beneficiary, are any mortgages to be paid off? If so, it is the residue that will suffer. Would that be fair? At this point it is worth noting that confusion can arise over the effect of a mortgage protection policy. This is an insurance policy that pays out enough money on death to pay off the mortgage. However, it does not always follow that the insurance money must be used to pay off the mortgage; to avoid doubt it is wise to have a clause in the will which makes it clear that the policy moneys are to be used to pay off the mortgage. In some cases the policy money may not be paid to the estate at all but direct to a spouse or a child, thus avoiding aggregation with the other assets of the estate for inheritance tax.

● Should a particular beneficiary be given a first option to buy a specific item from the estate and, if so, on what terms? This can cause problems if not carefully thought out. It may be better for the testator to make the arrangements direct with the beneficiary before making the will.

● What if a beneficiary should die before the testator? Normally, a dead person cannot inherit under a will. So, if the beneficiary is already dead when the testator dies, then the gift will fail. In this case, the property that should have gone to the dead person will remain in the testator's estate – and go to those people who are entitled to the residue. However, there is one exception. If the gift was to a child (or grandchild) of the testator, then it passes to that child's (or grandchild's) children. But, if the dead child did not have any children, then the gift will fail – it will pass into residue (and not, for instance, go to the dead child's spouse). It is therefore important when making a will to consider making substitutional gifts, to deal with the eventuality of someone dying. Bear in mind that if a specific gift does lapse, it will be added into the residue. Would that be an unfair benefit to the person entitled to the residue?

● What will happen if the person who is to receive the residue should die before the testator? Unless other arrangements are set out in the will the residue would then pass under the intestacy rules (see page 226).

● Are there any adopted, legitimated or illegitimate children? Although such children are assumed to be included in the phrase 'children' (see above), it is best to avoid any doubt by specifically naming them.

- Does the will revoke all previous wills made by the testator?
- Is it possible that the testator will not own the property specifically named when they die? Obviously, if they do not own the property at the time of their death, they will not be able to give it to the beneficiary, and so the testator should consider this possibility by including an alternative gift when drafting the will. Lawyers say that a will 'speaks from death', which means that one must look at the position at the time of death, not at the time the will was written. For example, if a person makes a gift of 'my sports car' but by the time of his death has traded in the sports car for a saloon model, then the proposed beneficiary will take nothing; the correct way to word the will is to give 'my car' or 'my sports car or any other car I may own at the time of my death'. A gift that fails in this way is said to have been 'adeemed'.
- Does the testator have any infant children? If so, should the will appoint guardians in case the other parent also dies and the children are left without parents?
- If the estate is a large one, does it take advantage of the inheritance tax exemptions? In particular, do the respective wills of husband and wife both make gifts to the children in order to make the most of the £150,000 exemption available on each death?
- Is there a gift subject to a condition? Such a clause requires very careful drafting. The solicitor will word it so that the condition is for an event to happen before the gift is made, rather than for the gift to be forfeited on the event happening. Also, the condition should be drafted in such a way that it will be easy for the personal representatives to decide whether or not the condition has been satisfied.
- The will should name the executors. Should substitutes be named in case the named executors have died or are unable to take on the job? Two is generally regarded as the ideal number of executors. Are the executors to be paid for their services? If so, the will must specifically authorize their payment. It is usual to include a 'charging clause' in the will when there are professional executors such as solicitors or accountants. This enables them to make normal charges for their services. Think twice before appointing the bank as executor, as their administration tends to be quite expensive, especially for simple estates. Before naming someone as an executor, the testator should check that the person is willing to be an executor; a person named as an executor can decline to act. It is not essential to name executors: it will still be a valid will even if executors are not named.
- Does the will specifically state that it is 'signed by the testator in our presence and then by us as witnesses in his/her presence'? This confirms that the main requirements of the Wills Act have been observed and is called an 'attestation clause'. Its omission will result in the personal representatives being unable to prove the will until they obtain evidence from the witnesses that the Wills Act rules were observed. Accordingly, an attestation clause will save time, expense and inconvenience after the death.

• Should a trust be set up? It is often done inadvertently in home-made wills by clauses such as, 'I leave my estate to my wife, but if she remarries I leave it to my daughter.' Like it or not, the testator has created a trust which prevents the wife from having access to the capital even if she never remarries. A trust is an arrangement whereby property is given to someone to hold for someone else's use until the occurrence of some event, such as their death. The concept is very simple but, unfortunately, the more one goes into it the more complicated it becomes. Suffice it to say that if I had £100,000 and an ex-wife (I have neither), I might leave the money to a solicitor to hold on trust for my ex-wife until her death. Although the solicitor (the 'trustee') would be the legal owner of the money, it would be my ex-wife (the 'beneficiary') who would receive the benefit of the gift. However, she would not receive the capital sum itself; my solicitor would have to invest the money and my ex-wife would be entitled to receive only the interest or income from it – she could not touch the capital. On my ex-wife's death, the £100,000 would revert back into my estate and be distributed by my personal representatives in accordance with the terms of my will.

A trust is an effective method of giving a person the benefit of property without actually giving them the property itself. The beneficiary of a trust can be anyone – an infant, a Mental Health Act patient, a spouse etc. – but the main use of the trust has been to enable wealthy families to pass their money down through the generations without the risk of it being squandered by one spendthrift member of the family. The trust is also used in schemes to minimize the amount of income tax and IHT paid by members of a family, and was greatly used in estate duty avoidance schemes. If complex trusts are being contemplated, specialist legal advice will be essential. A settlement is a particular type of trust for which there are very complicated rules.

Making a will: a summary of the steps to be taken

1 Draw up a list of the estate. This will be all the assets, such as land, property, business, money, cars, valuables etc., less debts (i.e. mortgage, bank overdraft, bills etc). The net figure is the likely estate.
2 Draw up a list of beneficiaries: the people who are to benefit.
3 Work out who is to receive what. How is inheritance tax to be paid? Check that all eventualities are covered. Is the bulk of the estate to pass under the gift of the residue or is that just a tidying-up clause?
4 Is there any property outside England and Wales (are two wills needed), are there any insurance policies written in trust, is there any jointly owned property (does it pass under the will or to the survivor)? Have any gifts been made in the last seven years which might affect inheritance tax or which might result in one person getting more than their fair share?
5 The will should be set out on a clean sheet of paper. While it can be handwritten, it is advisable to type it and so avoid any problems of illegible handwriting.

6 The first clause of the will should set out the correct and full baptismal names of the testator. If he or she does not always use that name, the words 'sometimes known as . . .' should be stated. To avoid doubt it is best to state specifically that all previous wills are revoked. There is no need to start with the words 'This is the last will and testament of' although many lawyers use these words in order to avoid any doubts if an earlier will remains.

A typical first clause will simply state:

'I . . . (name, address, occupation) revoke all previous wills and testamentary dispositions made by me and declare this to be my last will.'

7 The next clause should appoint the executors. Note that the executor(s) can be beneficiaries under the will (but witnesses cannot, see page 193). In a typical will the testator leaves all their property to their spouse and in such a case it is usual to appoint the spouse as the sole executor or executrix, with a named alternative in case the spouse cannot act for some reason. If a professional executor, such as a solicitor, is to be appointed, then the clause should specifically allow him or her to charge the estate for their work. (If everything is being left to the spouse there is seldom any need to appoint a professional executor.) In such a case, the testator should inquire what the executor's likely fee will be. A person should not be shy to ask what the fees will be if a bank is to be executor. A solicitor's charges will almost certainly be much less.

8 The will should next deal with all the gifts of money and property other than land (which includes houses and flats). These are the legacies – 'chattels' is the word used to describe all such property, except for money. A typical clause will state: 'I give to (*name*) absolutely such of my chattels and effects of personal domestic or household use or ornament as are not hereby otherwise specifically disposed of', and then go on to deal with specific gifts: 'I give the following specific legacies absolutely:

(a) to my daughter (*name*) my gold watch (be very careful to define which watch where the testator may have several gold watches),

(b) to my grandson (*name*) the tools which belonged to my late husband', and finally deal with pecuniary legacies: 'I give the following pecuniary legacies absolutely and free of all taxes:

(a) to (*name*) the sum of £x

(b) to each of my grandchildren living at my death (absolutely and free of all taxes*) the sum of £x.' If the sum is small it may be desirable to allow the parents to receive the legacy on behalf of the infant grandchildren in order to release the executors from long-term trust responsibilities.

9 Next come the devises of real property (i.e. land, houses and flats). Sometimes these devises are held via trusts, in which case complicated provisions may apply. Legal advice is then essential. Often, though, the property (generally the family house) will go to the testator's spouse along with all the other property. Then a typical clause will read: 'I devise and bequeath all my estate both real and personal whatsoever and wheresoever,

* Optional (see page).

subject to the payment of my debts and funeral and testamentary expenses unto my said wife/husband (*name*) but if s/he should fail to survive me the succeeding provisions of this Will shall take effect (*then set out the alternative provisions*) . . .'

10 Who is the residue (i.e. the net estate after making all the other gifts) to go to? Usually it is left to the surviving spouse in which case the above clause can be used. Otherwise, a different clause will be needed, such as: 'I give the residue of my estate to my two sons (*names*) equally, but if either of them dies before me leaving children then those children shall on reaching eighteen take equally the share which their father would otherwise have taken.' If the residue is not left to anybody it will be distributed under the intestacy rules (see page 226). When working out entitlement under the intestacy rules, any benefits received under the will are taken into account. The intestacy rules also take earlier gifts into account even if they were made more than seven years before the death of the testator. For example, if a testator gave his son a business worth £50,000 ten years before his (the testator's) death, that gift will be looked upon as a part payment to that son under the intestacy rules. Or again, if a surviving spouse has already received £20,000 under the will then she will be absolutely entitled only to £55,000 of the residue (£105,000 if there are no children) plus half the residue.

11 What powers are to be given to the executors? There are various acts of Parliament which set down certain powers but these can be quite restricting, so a testator will often want to give his or her executors wider powers, expecially if they have money to invest or a business to wind up.

12 Does a testator have any declaration to make which would influence the executors? Here he or she would indicate, for example, whether they wished to be buried or cremated, and whether they wished to donate their body for medical research.

13 Finally, the testator should sign in the presence of the two witnesses. Remember that neither the witnesses nor their spouses can be beneficiaries. Typical wording is:

In witness whereof I have hereunto set my hand this . . . day of . . . 19—.
Signed by the above-named (*name*) in
our presence and then by us in his/hers: ....
(*signature*)

....
(*signature*)

(*name, address, occupation*)

....
(*signature*)

(*name, address, occupation*)

14 The will should be kept in a safe place; it is advisable to make photocopies. Solicitors and banks will usually hold wills. Alternatively, the will can be lodged for safekeeping with the Principal Registry (at Somerset House) – contact any district probate registry for details of this service (which costs £1). This ensures that the will is available when anyone attempts to become a personal representative and so there can be no risk of the testator dying intestate. The executors and the family should be told where the original will is kept and a note of the place written on a copy of the will kept with the other papers.

15 The really conscientious will-maker will try to make things easy for his/her relatives by making a comprehensive note of all the personal details that might be needed after death – for example, names and addresses of doctor, trade union, bank, accountant, solicitor, landlord, employer, building society, anyone who is a beneficiary or who should be told of the death. Also, where the following documents can be found: birth and marriage certificates, driving licence, insurance policies, title deeds, HP agreements, building-society and bank books, rent book, passport, share certificates, NI card etc.

16 It should be remembered that marriage revokes a will so always make a new will on remarriage (and also on divorce – see below).

REVOKING A WILL

The usual way of cancelling a will is by making a new one and commencing it with the phrase 'I revoke all former wills and codicils made by me.' If the revocation clause was not included, the new will would revoke the earlier will only in so far as it was inconsistent with it.

As might be expected, the deliberate burning, tearing up or destroying of a will is assumed to destroy it. But merely writing 'revoked' across the face of the will may not be enough.

The revocation of a will may not always be effective if it was done on a false assumption. For example, suppose a testator makes a new will and then tears up their old will. If the new will should be held to be invalid for some reason, the testator would seem to be left without a valid will. However, in these circumstances, the court might say that the revocation of the old will was conditional on the new will being valid and, since that is not so, the revocation of the first will would be ineffective and it would still be a valid will. The jargon for this conditional revocation is 'dependent relative revocation' – a phrase that endows a straightforward idea with an unnecessary aura of complexity. For instance:

In August 1966, Mr Carey, a widower, made a will leaving his estate to his sister-in-law. He left the will with his solicitors but in 1972 he reclaimed it saying that he had nothing to leave and so he was going to destroy the will. In 1973 his sister died leaving him £40,000. In 1976 Mr Carey died without leaving a will. The sister-in-law asked the court to enforce the 1966 will on the basis that it had been revoked by Mr Carey in the mistaken belief that he had nothing to leave. *Held: The 1966 will remained valid.* Carey (1977)

Marriage and Divorce

Marriage

Revocation is automatic on the marriage of the testator. The logic behind this rule is that Parliament in 1837 assumed that most testators would want to leave their property to their spouse but a newly married testator might forget to alter their will, which might not mention the spouse as a beneficiary. Thus the Wills Act provides that unless the testator makes a new will after their marriage, they will die intestate and so the spouse will inherit some, if not all, of the estate under the intestacy rules (see page 226). The only exception to this rule is when the gift was clearly made in contemplation of the marriage, for then the testator can be assumed to have had their spouse-to-be in mind when they drafted the will; this applies even if the will leaves nothing to the spouse, for Parliament did not think it proper in 1837 to interfere with the right of a man to dispose of his property as he wished. Now, of course, the family provision legislation allows the courts to award shares of the estate to a spouse and other dependants (see Chapter 13).

If a will is made before a marriage it should always state that 'This will is made in contemplation of my marriage with . . .'. If the marriage does not take place such a will would remain valid, and so it is usual to add 'and is conditional on the marriage taking place within . . . months'. Unless clear wording is used, the courts will not be able to uphold the will as having been made in contemplation of marriage. If a testator asks a solicitor to make a will in circumstances where the testator's cohabitee has taken the same surname, it is important to advise the solicitor, who may otherwise make wrong assumptions about inheritance tax liability and the like. If such a couple subsequently married, the will would become invalid and the intestacy rules would apply – not at all what might have been intended.

Divorce

Divorce does not invalidate a will but may make it largely ineffective. This is because any gift to the former spouse will no longer take effect, and nor will the appointment of the ex-husband/wife as executor. In effect, the ex-spouse is cut out of the will, but the rest of the will takes effect in the usual way. This rule is subject to there being no 'contrary intention' in the will – so if it is made clear that the spouse is to have the gift even if there is a divorce, then the gift will remain valid. Remember, though, that if the divorce is followed by a remarriage then the new marriage will invalidate the will (see above) and so the ex-spouse will get nothing – unless a new will is executed in which a gift is made to them (or unless they can apply to the court under the family provision legislation – see Chapter 13).

If a divorced husband/wife is cut out of the will in this way, then his/her share will go to the person who is entitled to the residue (i.e. all parts of the estate that are not specifically given to other people). Sometimes, of course, this is not what was intended. For instance, suppose a husband makes a will leaving his house to his wife, but if she should die before him, it is to go to the children. The residue is to go to his brother. If they are then divorced and he does not rewrite his will, then on his death the house will not go to the wife. She will have been cut out. However, it will not go to the children – as was probably intended – but will go to the brother (i.e. because he takes the residue). So, if you are getting divorced, your ex-spouse will be cut out of the will – but you should think carefully about what will happen to his/her share. If you do not want it to go to the person who is entitled to the residue, then you should alter your will to deal specifically with the point. If you are paying maintenance under a court order you should seek legal advice on how best to deal with that matter under your will.

Can you agree not to alter your will?

The general rule is that a will is not a contract so disappointed beneficiaries cannot sue for breach of contract if they are not left what they were promised by the testator. This is because a person is free to alter his or her will as he or she pleases. For instance, if a poor relative of a rich person agrees to be housekeeper for that person on the basis that 'you will have the house when I've gone', then the poor relative cannot claim off the estate if, in fact, the house is left to someone else. However, there is one exception to this. If there was a binding contract between the testator and the disappointed beneficiary, then the estate will be bound to honour that contract – and so the beneficiary could sue the estate for the value of the gift that had been promised. For this to happen there must have been a specific contract – and usually this will have to be in the form of a deed (i.e. a professionally prepared document that is formally witnessed etc.). If there was such a document, then the disappointed beneficiary (e.g. the poor relative who had been promised the house) could sue the estate.

But unless there is a formal agreement of this sort, it is generally unwise to rely on a promise of being left something in a will. Ask for a formal deed to be prepared, for otherwise the promise will be worthless.

Alterations

Any alteration to a will should be treated as a new will, with all the Wills Act formalities being observed, even if the alteration or amendment is only minor. An amendment to a will is called a 'codicil'. A codicil is an amending document prepared and signed with all the formalities of a will. Apart from ensuring that the codicil is properly signed and attested, it is wise to state that 'in all other respects I confirm my will' so there can be no suggestion that the codicil was meant to revoke the whole will. However, if the layperson wishes to alter their will, it is better to rewrite the whole will in its amended form than add on codicils.

Three sample wills, one invalid, one defective but valid and one effective and valid, are shown on pages 206–209.

After-death variations

It has always been possible to disclaim a benefit under a will, but the right to vary a will after the death is a comparatively recent development. Under the 1984 Finance Act variations can be made to wills or in the event of intestacy, so that adult beneficiaries can effectively agree who should get what. This redistribution must take place within two years of the death but it does enable the beneficiaries to reorganize the provisions of the will. A variation can be made to an infant's benefit provided the benefit is increased; otherwise the consent of the court will be required. These variations are subject to a number of conditions upon which legal advice should be obtained as soon as possible after the death, but it does mean that a will can be written for the deceased even if he or she never made a will before they died.

Three sample wills

John James wants to leave everything to his cohabitee, and nothing to the wife from whom he is separated

---

An Invalid Will

I John James of 2 Abingdon Cottages, London NE1 make this my Will, as set out in the Schedule hereto.
Signed by me, John James, on the 2nd of November 1991

....

(*signature*)

Witnesses: Mabel Smith
....

              (*signature*)

              Fred Evans
....

              (*signature*)

The Schedule

I give the whole of my estate to my common-law wife Mabel Smith and nothing to my lawful wife Anne James.

Defects in this invalid will

1 The testator, John James, has not signed at the end of the will. It will not be invalid, but the Probate Registry will probably query the signature (causing delay and probably expense).

2 The beneficiary is Mabel Smith, yet she is one of the witnesses. The gift to her would therefore fail and the estate would pass under the laws of intestacy to Anne James, the testator's surviving spouse (and, if the estate was of sufficient size, to children or other relatives; see page 226).

3 Although there are two witnesses, it is not stated that they saw the testator sign and that they then signed in his presence. Whilst such a clause is not essential, the Probate Registry will not grant probate until it has been confirmed that the proper formalities were observed. If the witnesses cannot be traced, this can cause delay and difficulty.

4 The will does not state that it revokes all previous wills. If there is no revocation clause the will only revokes an earlier will in so far as it is inconsistent with it. In this example, it would probably make no difference but it is always wise to avoid doubt by inserting a revocation clause.

5 A properly drafted will would appoint executors.

Summary. The will fails completely. Thus John James will die intestate and all or part of his property will pass to his wife, Anne James, which is precisely what he wanted to avoid. The only hope that Mabel Smith, his common-law wife, will have of inheriting any of the estate is to apply to the court under the family provision legislation (see Chapter 13).

Sydney James wants to make a simple will leaving everything to his wife if she survives him and to his son if she does not

---

A Valid Will

I, Sydney James, of 2 Abingdon Cottages, London NE1, hereby revoke all previous Wills and Testamentary dispositions made by me and declare this to be my last Will.

1 I appoint my wife Emma James of 2 Abingdon Cottages, London NE1 to be the executrix of this my Will but if she should be unwilling or unable to act as my executor I appoint my son, Harry James of 93 Clifton Road, London NE5, to be my executor.

2 I devise and bequeath all my estate both real and personal whatsoever and wheresoever subject to the payment of my debts and funeral and testamentary expenses unto my wife Emma James of 2 Abingdon Cottages, London NE1, but if she should pre-decease me I leave all my said estate to my son Harry James of 93 Clifton Road, London NE5.

In witness whereof I have hereunto set my hand this 2nd day of November 1991

Signed by the above-named
Sydney James in our presence   Sydney James
and then by us in his: ....
                                                          (*signature*)
Fred Evans
(1a Abingdon Cottages, London NE1, postman)

Mavis Evans
(1a Abingdon Cottages, London NE1, housewife)

Note. This will is for illustration purposes only. Do not risk adapting it to other circumstances. Many stationers sell pre-printed wills that can be used to cover most contingencies and one of those forms should be used if a solicitor is not used to draft the will but consider the errors in the defective but valid will will before taking the risk.

Even this will would be an inefficient will in the following circumstances: if the estate of Sydney James was worth £200,000 and if his wife had investments of her own worth £150,000, the death of Sydney before Emma would incur no inheritance tax (all transfers to a spouse are free of tax). However, on Emma's death the combined value of £200,000 and £150,000 would incur inheritance tax of £80,000.

If, on the other hand, Sydney James had left £150,000 to his son and the balance of £50,000 to his wife, there would still be no inheritance tax to pay on his death (£150,000 exemption covers the gift to the son and the balance passing to the wife is also free). On the wife's death she will have a total estate of £200,000 (£150,000 + £50,000), on which the inheritance tax will be £20,000. This represents an overall saving of £60,000! Not all professionally drawn wills can save such a large amount, but a badly drawn home-made will can cost you dear.

A Home-made Will

How *not* to write your own will.

Here is a real example of a home-made will typed on to a will form. Only slight changes have been made for anonymity. The testator was an intelligent man but frugal. In saving the solicitors' fees by making his own will he has dropped several clangers.

This is the last Will and Testament

of me   Edward Johnson

of   Ashfield House, Clodby

in the County of   Nottingham

made this   1st   day of   January

in the year of our Lord one thousand nine hundred and   ninety one

   I HEREBY revoke all Wills made by me at any time heretofore. I appoint
my son Darren Johnson

to be my Executor(s) and direct that all my debts and Funeral Expenses shall be paid as soon as conveniently may be after my

decease.

   I GIVE AND BEQUEATH   unto my son Darren Johnson
all that property known as Ashfield Cottage, comprising house, workshop, buildings and
land on the north side of the communal carriage way with all machinery, tools and all my
money, half of my furniture and domestic goods.
I GIVE AND BEQUEATH unto my daughter Jane Fitzhenry of Ashfield Cottage all that property
known as Ashfield House and paddock all that is at the south side of communal carriage way,
the oak desk and cupboard and half of my furniture and domestic goods.
The communal carriage way is to be included in the property I leave to my son
Darren Johnson.
In the event of my daughter Jane Fitzhenry's death, the property that I leave her shall
not become the property of Silas Fitzhenry, but shall become the property of my grand
daughter Tracey Fitzhenry.
If my wife Winnie survives me she shall have the use of all this property and money during
her life and upon her death this Will shall be executed.

Signed by the said TESTATOR
in the presence of us, present at the same time, who at
his request, in his presence, and in the presence of
each other, have subscibed our names as witnesses.
If necessary to use next page, strike this out

   C. Johnson.

   M. Cantor

   Evelyn Cantor

The real property consisted of several acres of land, comprised in one set of title deeds, on which there were two houses. Ashfield House, occupied by the deceased, was left to his daughter, the other, Ashfield Cottage, was occupied by the daughter and her husband as tenants but was left to the son. The garage for Ashfield House stood at the end (not on the south side and not on the north side) of the communal carriageway. The deceased left money in a building society, but he also left stocks and shares. The value of Ashfield House was approximately equal to the value of Ashfield Cottage plus the money.

The testator has made several serious mistakes:

1 The will gives the daughter an empty house. What if she stays on as a tenant in Ashfield Cottage, left to her brother, and sells the testator's house, Ashfield House? The brother gets a sitting tenant.
2 The testator's garage, which serves Ashfield House, is at the end of the communal drive. It is not to the south or the north of it. Who gets the garage which serves Ashfield House left to the daughter?
3 Inheritance tax was payable. Is it to be paid equally by son and daughter? The daughter had no money so she would have to sell Ashfield House, which she has inherited and hopes to live in, in order to pay the tax. What did the testator intend? Was the son to pay all inheritance tax from his 'money'. If so, the value of his inheritance was much less than the daughter's. The testator appears to have thought that he was sharing his assets out equally and had not thought that tax would be payable.
4 The will leaves the son 'all my money'. In law the meaning of 'money' must be ascertained from the context. What did the testator intend? He makes a mistake common in home-made wills: he tries to dispose of everything he owns at the time of making the will as specific items. He forgets to write in a clause which disposes of the residue of the estate.
5 The testator refers to his daughter's death. Does he mean that the property he leaves to her is to go to his granddaughter if his daughter dies before him or does he mean that his daughter is to get only a life interest in the property he has left to her, in which case she cannot sell Ashfield House? Furthermore, does he mean only the real property or all the property which she receives?
6 The testator's wife, Winnie, died before the testator, but if she had survived him a trust would have arisen which would have left the widow short of money but unable to sell the houses.

When wills like this are written they can cause trouble between families for a generation, and they can and do prove very expensive to adminster, because a dispute of this type would have to go before a Chancery Court at a cost of many thousands of pounds. Do not forget the case of Jarndyce v. Jarndyce in *David Copperfield* (when the costs of the case extinguished the value of the estate before the case was concluded).

The moral of this story is, do not attempt to save the cost of having a will prepared by a solicitor if your estate is likely to incur inheritance tax or if you have any complicated provisions to make. Instead of a will costing, say, £50, the estate had to pay several thousand pounds in additional costs before settling the case. Had it gone to court as a contested case, the costs would have been even greater and would probably have meant the selling of the testator's house left to the daughter. Neither party was happy about the settlement but neither did they want to risk losing any more of the estate in legal costs.

12 When Someone Dies

CHECKLIST OF STEPS TO BE TAKEN ON DEATH

Before personal representatives are appointed (see below) there are several administrative tasks that have to be carried out. Unfortunately, it is not always clear who is responsible for these tasks. Where families are close there should be no difficulty, but in other cases great care should be taken.

When a person dies leaving a will, the executors appointed by the will take on the mantle of authority immediately. If they are not close members of the family they will frequently delegate the funeral arrangements and the like to a member of the family.

When a person dies without making a will there can be difficulties because it may be several weeks or even months before letters of administration are granted, giving legal authority to the personal representatives. During that waiting period the funeral must be arranged. Some equally entitled members of the family may disagree about who should make these arrangements, about the place of burial or even the form of the funeral. More frequently there can be trouble because some members of the family enter the deceased's house and distribute cash and possessions wrongly, believing that they have authority or without understanding the strict rules that apply, perhaps forgetting the rights of the children of a deceased brother. A person intermeddling in this way can be in trouble because others may recollect that grandmother always kept her savings in the blue jug and where has that gone?

1. Immediately on death

If death occurred at home

The informant (usually but not necessarily a relative) should inform:
- the family doctor;
- relatives, and perhaps the priest, vicar etc.;
- the department of anatomy of the local medical school if the deceased had donated his or her body for medical research. If the deceased was an organ-donor the nearest hospital should be informed.
- the police, if the death was violent, accidental or in suspicious circumstances.

If the doctor attended the deceased during their terminal illness, the doctor will give the relatives:

• a free medical certificate, showing the cause of death. This will be in a sealed envelope addressed to the registrar of deaths, *and*

• a formal notice stating that they have signed a medical certificate, and which also explains the procedure for registering the death.

Alternatively, the doctor will report the death to the coroner if:

• the deceased was not seen by a doctor during his last illness, or within fourteen days of death, *or*

• if the cause of death is uncertain, *or*

• if the death was sudden, violent or caused by an accident, *or*

• if the death resulted from an industrial disease.

If death occurred in hospital

The ward sister will inform the nearest relative of the death (the police will do this if the death followed an accident). The relative will have to attend the hospital to collect the deceased's possessions and also identify the body, unless the deceased had been an in-patient.

If the cause of death is clear, the hospital doctor will give the relatives a free medical certificate and a formal notice (as with a death at home, above). In addition, they will usually carry out a post-mortem, if the relatives agree.

Alternatively, they will report the death to the coroner if:

• the cause of death is uncertain, *or*

• the death was sudden, violent or caused by an accident, *or*

• if the death resulted from an industrial disease, *or*

• if the death occurred during the course of an operation or while the deceased was under anaesthetic.

2. If the coroner is notified of the death

Whether the death was in hospital or not, the coroner will usually arrange for a post-mortem to be held; the relatives' consent is not needed, although they can retain a doctor to be present during the post-mortem.

The coroner may also decide to hold an inquest. He or she will generally do so if the cause of death:

• was violent, *or*

• was accidental, *or*

• resulted from an industrial disease, *or*

• remains uncertain.

If an inquest is held, the coroner will normally hold a preliminary hearing within a week or so of death. This hearing will be for purposes of identification only and formal evidence of the identity of the body will have to be given. The coroner will then release the body and so allow the funeral or cremation to take place. The inquest proper will usually take place some weeks later and will be an inquiry into the cause of death. The coroner may decide to sit with a jury. Relatives can attend the inquest and may wish to instruct a solicitor to attend if, for instance, the death was the result of a road accident (no legal aid is available, however).

Before the burial can take place, the coroner must first issue a disposal certificate (either an order for burial or a certificate for cremation). This will normally be provided, free of charge, after the post-mortem or after the preliminary inquest hearing.

In addition, the coroner must also issue a cause of death certificate, so that the death can be registered. There are two possibilities:

● If the post-mortem shows that death was by natural causes, the coroner will normally provide a pink form addressed to the registrar of deaths in a sealed envelope. Sometimes he or she will simply send the form direct to the registrar, in which case the relatives will be notified of its issue.

● If a full inquest was held, the coroner will send a cause of death certificate direct to the registrar of deaths.

3. Registration of the death

Register the death with the local Registrar of Births, Marriages and Deaths (address in the telephone directory).

If the death has been reported to the coroner it cannot be registered until the coroner has provided the necessary pink form or certificate (see above). Thus there is nothing to be done until the coroner notifies the relatives that the pink form or certificate has been issued.

If the death has not been reported to the coroner, it must be registered within five days. Documents needed are:

● evidence of the cause of death (i.e. medical certificate provided by the doctor and/or pink form provided by a coroner);

● the deceased's NHS card, if available;

● the deceased's birth certificate and marriage certificate;

● any war pension order book of the deceased (if applicable and if available).

The registrar will want to know:

● date and place of death;

● deceased's usual address;

● full forenames(s) and surnames of the deceased (and maiden name, if a married woman);

● deceased's occupation (and that of her husband if a married woman or a widow);

● date of birth of deceased's surviving spouse (if applicable);

● whether the deceased was receiving any state benefits.

The registrar will then register the death and provide the applicant with:

● A certificate for disposal, unless the coroner has already issued one. This will have to be produced to the funeral director before the burial or cremation can take place.

• A certificate of registration of death. This is for social-security purposes and upon production at the local DSS office will prove entitlement to widow's benefit. Extra copies can be obtained at this stage for a small fee and may be needed for claims on insurance policies etc. They will cost more once the details have been passed to the Superintendant Registrar.

• Pamphlets on welfare benefits that might be available and form PR 48, which gives guidance on obtaining a Grant of Probate.

4. The funeral arrangements

These cannot be finalized until it is known whether the death will be reported to the coroner, for this will affect the date when the body can be released for burial or cremation.

Check the deceased's will to see if it contains instructions as to whether he or she is to be buried or cremated. Note that there is no legal obligation on the executors or next-of-kin to follow these instructions: it is for them to decide whether to bury or cremate.

It is advisable to use a funeral director who belongs to the National Association of Funeral Directors (NAFD), since they are bound by a code of practice agreed with the Office of Fair Trading. In particular, an NAFD member must provide a full estimate in advance, and this must include the estimate for the cost of a basic, simple, funeral (i.e. exclusive of church fees, flowers, notices in local paper, but inclusive of a coffin, collection or delivery of the body up to 10 miles, care of the deceased, and provision of a hearse and one following car to the nearest local cemetery or crematorium, together with conductors and bearers as necessary).

If the estate has insufficient assets to cover the funeral an application should be made first to the DSS. If a person instructs an undertaker to deal with the funeral, that person is legally responsible for making the payment (although they will be entitled to a refund from the estate if they are the personal representative). Most of the assets will be available only when probate has been obtained, and that will take some time, so discuss the matter with the undertaker first. Most undertakers accept that there will have to be some delay before the bill can be paid. However, some institutions (e.g. building societies, banks) may be prepared to release up to £5,000 worth of assets on production of the death certificate alone (see step 34, pages 225–6).

The funeral cannot take place until a disposal certificate has been handed to the funeral director.

Burial

Check the deceased's personal papers and will to see if he or she has already paid for a plot in a graveyard or churchyard (the documents are called a grave deed or a deed of grant and a faculty, respectively). If not, a plot will have to be bought. The funeral director will provide details.

The burial will take place only when the following documents have been produced:

● either a certificate for burial (the disposal certificate) from the registrar of deaths, *or*, if there has been an inquest, the coroner's order for burial;

● application for burial – addressed to the cemetery and signed by the executor or next-of-kin. The funeral director will provide this form;

● grave deed or faculty, from the cemetery or diocese, which entitles the deceased to be buried in a particular plot.

Remember, some members of the family may have strong views about funerals. Should it be a lavish display or a simple one? Which church? Should it be a cremation? If the deceased was widowed twice, which wife should he join?

In the case of my grandfather, the churchyard was full but after negotiations the vicar agreed to allow him, as the deceased widower and father of eight children, to be squeezed into the only space left, on top of my grandmother, who had died some years before (and was known in the family as 'the hardy annual').

In some cases the relatives expect a good meal after the funeral. 'He was buried with ham' may be heard in Yorkshire after the funeral. This refers to the meal enjoyed by the mourners and not to some strange ritual at the burial.

Remember that a gravestone is not a testamentary expense. The executors must obtain the consent of the beneficiaries before ordering one.

Cremation

A cremation involves more formalities than a burial. It is necessary to have *one* of the following:

● A certificate for cremation (the disposal certificate) from the registrar of deaths, plus two cremation certificates. One is signed by the family doctor and the other by another doctor; both doctors will probably charge a fee.

● If the death was reported to the coroner, then after a post-mortem or inquest he or she will provide a free certificate for cremation.

The following documents are also needed:

● A cremation certificate signed by the medical referee at the crematorium. His/her fee will usually be included in the crematorium's charge.

● Two forms signed by the executor or next-of-kin. One applies for the cremation, while the other confirms the arrangements and gives instructions for disposal of the ashes.

Other steps to be taken

1 Return any pension book or welfare benefit book to the DSS; the book is the property of the DSS.
2 Go through the will to see who has been appointed executor. If no will can be found, make inquiries with likely solicitors and banks used by the deceased to see if they hold a will.

3 Work out who will be the personal representative(s) – see below. If the will appears complicated or if the estate includes a business or farm, you should immediately seek legal advice. If you intend to administer the estate yourself, turn to page 218. If there is no will, you must work out who is to be the administrator and contact them without taking any further steps yourself.

THE PERSONAL REPRESENTATIVE(S)

The personal representatives, whether executors or administrators, are the guardians of the deceased's legal personality. They can sue on his/her behalf (strictly speaking, on behalf of his/her estate) if, for instance, he or she was owed money under a contract and, conversely, they can be sued (i.e. the estate can be sued) by the deceased's creditors.

The personal representatives are not personally liable to pay the deceased's debts, nor can they personally claim any damages recovered; it is the estate that is suing, or being sued, and the personal representatives are the mere nominees through whom the estate acts.

There are two types of personal representatives – those appointed by a will and those not appointed by a will:

• personal representatives appointed by a will are called 'executors' (female singular: executrix (female plural: executrices);

• personal representatives not appointed by a will are called 'administrators' (female singular: administratrix).

Both types (collectively called personal representatives) have similar powers and duties. Only one personal representative is needed to administer an estate, although two will be required if there is an infant beneficiary or if a trust is created by the will or upon the intestacy.

A personal representative's task is similar to that of a trustee. Various statutes lay down detailed rules as to what a trustee or personal representative should, and should not, do. The basic rules are that they should be familiar with the terms of the will and not deviate from them; they must take care to preserve the property and assets as though they were their own; they must keep full accounts and keep the beneficiaries fully informed; they must consult with any other trustees, and not make unilateral decisions, and if in doubt, they should take legal advice. They must not make a profit from their position, unless they are professional trustees and the terms of the will give them the right to charge fees for work done, although they can recover their out-of-pocket expenses; neither must they put themselves in a position where there is a conflict of interest between themselves and the estate – thus a personal representative cannot buy anything from the estate unless all the beneficiaries are adults and they all consent.

If they fail to live up to the high standards required, the beneficiaries can sue them for negligence or fraud. If the claim is upheld they will be personally liable to compensate the estate, unless they can persuade the court that they acted 'honestly and reasonably, and ought fairly to be excused', in which case the court has a discretion to let them off.

Clearly, then, being a personal representative, or the trustee of a trust, is no sinecure. However, the prospective applicant should not be alarmed for, in practice, most estates are straightforward and are simple to administer, involving the personal representative(s) in little or no personal risk. In addition, of course, many personal representatives choose to seek the help of a solicitor and charge up his fees to the estate.

Who will be the personal representative(s)?

Different rules apply depending upon whether there is a will or not.

If there is a will

If the will is valid and appoints you as executor you must decide whether you are going to administer the will yourself without legal assistance. You should not do this if the estate includes a farm or a business or foreign assets. You should think twice before administering any estate on which inheritance tax is payable without at least consulting experts to see how best to mitigate the effects of IHT, perhaps by a post-death variation. However, an executor is not obliged to act and if he or she does not wish to, he or she should make his/her position clear. This is best done by sending a written letter of 'renunciation' to the other people concerned, in case it is suggested that he or she has accepted some of the duties involved and so become obliged to take on all the responsibilities. It is quite common for an elderly widow to renounce probate of her husband's estate in favour of her children if she is bedridden or unable to act for some other reason.

If the will does not name any executors, or if the named executors all renounce the job, someone else will have to apply for the grant. The persons entitled, in order of priority, are:

● the trustees and beneficiaries of any trust set up under the will; in practice, it is rare for there to be such a trust and so those next entitled are:

● the persons entitled under the will to the residue of the estate (see page 196);

● those entitled to inherit the estate under the intestacy rules (see page 226). Whoever takes on the task will be an administrator, not an executor, since he or she was not appointed by will. In such a case an application will be made to the Probate Registry for 'Letters of Administration with the Will Annexed'.

Why appoint an executor? It is sensible to appoint an executor – although it is not compulsory to do so. The best advice is to appoint a capable friend or relative. Alternatively, a bank or solicitor can be appointed. But if a solicitor or bank is appointed then your family will be committed to using that solicitor or bank to administer the estate. In the case of banks, this can be extremely expensive (see below). It might be much better simply to appoint a friend or relative, because at least that person will have the option of administering the estate themselves, rather than incurring professional fees. It is sensible to appoint two executors as there is less chance of both dying before the testator. Very elderly executors should not be appointed, and neither should an executor who lives abroad unless there are strong reasons for doing so. Another disadvantage of naming a particular bank or solicitor is if the person chosen should turn out to be inefficient and slow. If that happens, then there is not much that the beneficiaries (i.e. your family and relatives) can do to hurry matters up. It is very difficult for beneficiaries to bring pressure to bear on a slow solicitor or bank. It would be much better if they themselves were the executors, in which case they could sack the slow bank or solicitor, and transfer the papers to someone who was likely to be more helpful.

If there is no will

If there is no will the estate will be vested in one or more administrators. Parliament has laid down an order of priority between competing applicants based largely on the closeness of the applicant's family links with the deceased. The order of priority is:

- surviving spouse, *next*
- issue (i.e. children, grandchildren etc., whether adopted, illegitimate etc.), *next*
- parents, *next*
- brothers and sisters of the whole blood (or their issue), *next*
- brothers and sisters of the half blood (or their issue), *next*
- grandparents, *next*
- uncles and aunts of the whole blood (or their issue), *next*
- uncles and aunts of the half blood (or their issue).

If there is no person with a beneficial interest in the estate the Treasury Solicitor will apply for the 'Grant of Letters of Administration'. The estate will then pass to the Crown, or the Duchy of Cornwall or the Duchy of Lancaster if the death is in one of those areas.

A creditor of the estate may also apply if those entitled are unwilling to apply.

Between those of equal priority there is no order of priority (e.g. eldest son and youngest daughter have equal priority). Sometimes it may even depend upon who 'gets in first', but it is obviously better if the family can agree as to who will act.

Remember: this is just the order for deciding who is to be the administrator; there is a different order of priority for deciding how the estate is to be divided up (see page 226).

The appointment of the personal representative(s)

Once it has been decided who is entitled to become the personal representative(s), the prospective executor or administrator must apply to the Probate Registry for the court's written confirmation of his appointment. If the prospective administrator (no will) is a child under eighteen, testamentary guardians will have to be appointed to apply for the grant on the child's behalf.

The court's confirmation is in the form of a certificate called a 'grant', and this is the personal representative's formal proof that the deceased's estate is vested in him or her. The grant made to an executor (i.e. if appointed by the will) is called a 'Grant of Probate of the Will', while the grant to an administrator (i.e. when there is an intestacy) is a 'Grant of Letters of Administration'; in addition, there is also a 'Grant of Letters of Administration with the Will Annexed', which covers the hybrid situation of a will but no executors or a will which fails to dispose of the residue of the estate. Although these three grants have different names, their effect is the same – namely, to vest the deceased's assets and liabilities in the personal representative(s) as from the date of death, not just from the date of the grant. Thus there is no period of time when the deceased's legal personality is neither in the deceased nor in the personal representative(s), and so the presumption that death does not destroy the legal personality is preserved. Complications can arise where one person has partly administered the estate, believing that they have a right to do so when in fact they do not. If in doubt, take legal advice.

When there is no need for a grant

It may not be necessary to have a grant, because:
- small sums in National Savings etc. can be paid out without a grant (see page 225). So also can 'nominations' (see page 226);
- cash, jewellery etc. can be divided up between the relatives and beneficiaries (if they all agree) without a grant (see page 225);
- jointly held assets will normally pass automatically to the survivor (e.g. jointly owned house or bank account) and so a grant may not be necessary.

Do-it-yourself probate

Many personal representatives simply instruct a firm of solicitors to supervise the administration of the estate, and the duties of the personal representative are then restricted to signing forms prepared by the solicitors. The solicitor's fees will be paid out of the estate. Alternatively, a bank will usually be prepared to administer the estate, provided all the executors renounce probate and agreement can be reached over payment of the bank's (usually high) fees.

However, the personal representative need not retain a bank or solicitor to help him/her with his duties. He or she can instead do the administering of the estate alone and so save the legal fees that the estate would otherwise have paid. The savings can be considerable (see Legal Fees in Probate Work, below).

In view of the potential liabilities of being a personal representative (above) DIY probate is not something that should be taken on lightly. However, when the estate is small or if there are few beneficiaries, it is usually a straightforward if time-consuming business of writing letters to banks, creditors and insurance companies. On the other hand, there are some more complicated situations when it is inadvisable to do the work oneself, and instead the executor or administrator should instruct a solicitor or a bank to administer the estate. This would generally be so if:

• the estate is worth a large amount (or, conversely, it is not large enough to pay the debts);
• the dead person has set up a trust;
• some of the beneficiaries cannot be traced;
• the dead person did not leave a will and it is known that there are untraced relatives who might have a claim on the estate;
• the testator was under eighteen when he or she made their will;
• the will does not contain an attestation clause (see page 192);
• the will contains unsigned alterations;
• the will shows signs of burning, tearing, erasions or of another document having been attached (e.g. staple holes);
• the will gives a beneficiary a right to reside in a house;
• there is a business;
• inheritance tax may have to be paid;
• the will refers to another document or deals with property outside the UK;
• one of the beneficiaries under the will witnessed the will (or is married to one of the witnesses);
• the will is ambiguous or unclear (see the home-made will on page 208);
• the will does not dispose of the residue of the estate;
• there is a possibility of a relative or dependant making a family provision claim (see pages 230–33).

Legal fees in probate work

The saving of legal fees is likely to be the main reason why a personal representative decides to administer the estate himself.

Solicitors' fees are assessed on the same basis as fees in any other non-contentious (i.e. non-court) legal work, such as conveyancing. The eight factors to be considered when deciding what is a 'fair and reasonable' fee are set out on page 941. But with probate work, the size of the estate is usually taken as the most important single factor. If the solicitor charges on a time basis, the Law Society would generally approve a bill which comprised a charge for the time spent, plus 25–30 per cent typing and services, plus 1 per cent of the value of the gross estate. The total of these figures, in very rough terms, often works out in the region of 2 per cent of the gross estate. Do not expect a City firm (if it even deals with modest administrations) to have similar charges to a small provincial firm. You will be paying for expertise, but you will also be paying for the overheads of the firm acting for you.

If the solicitor is an executor under the will (especially if he or she is a sole executor with added responsibilities) it is usual to increase the 1 per cent charge to 1½ per cent.

Grant only

If the solicitor takes out only the Grant of Probate or Letters of Administration, and takes no part in administering the estate, the 1 per cent is generally reduced to ½ per cent.

As always, to avoid difficulties, it is advisable to obtain a firm estimate from the solicitor before instructing him or her to act. The difficulty for solicitors is to anticipate the complications which might arise and increase the work to be done.

Disputes over fees. Solicitors' fees for probate work come under the general non-contentious costs rules (see page 940). In particular, if the personal representative thinks the solicitor's fee is too high, he or she could ask the solicitor to obtain a remuneration certificate from the Law Society and can ask for the fees to be taxed (see page 943). This is one major advantage of using a solicitor rather than a bank: with banks, there are no controls over the fees charged (and, in any event, they nearly always charge more than solicitors).

Banks

Banks lay down their own scale of fees. Because banks usually charge a lot it is essential to discuss the fee before committing oneself to using the bank. Relatively few people realize just how much banks charge. For instance, in 1991 the National Westminster Bank charged 5 per cent on the first £50,000, 3 per cent on the next £50,000 and 2 per cent on the excess over £100,000. Remember that these fees are calculated on the *gross* estate before inheritance tax is paid. The bank also charges a 3 per cent withdrawal fee when any capital is withdrawn from a trust. There are other discretionary fees. Although the bank may reduce its charges if the estate is *unusually* simple, you should be ready for a very large bill if a bank is the executor. Most other banks have a similar fee structure.

Generally, solicitors' charges are considerably less. As a rough guide, on an estate of £200,000 a solicitor might charge £3,000 (plus VAT) whereas a bank might charge approximately £6,000 (plus VAT). In addition, there would be disbursements (i.e. out-of-pocket expenses) incurred by the solicitor or the bank, the main one being probate fees paid to the court when taking out the grant. These are charged on the size of the *net* estate. The net estate is the amount left for distributing to the beneficiaries after paying funeral, probate and testamentary expenses.

Finally, if the property contains a house or flat, there will be solicitor's conveyancing fees for transferring the property to the beneficiary, or for acting on the sale of the property (see page 276 for conveyancing fees). If the property is sold, the solicitor's conveyancing fee will be calculated on the usual basis. However, if the property is merely transferred to a beneficiary (by what is called an 'assent') the fee will be much less, since little work will be involved.

ADMINISTERING AN ESTATE: A STEP-BY-STEP GUIDE

Obviously, no two estates are the same, but the procedure to be followed will always be similar. This checklist summarizes the main steps to be taken by personal representatives who decides to administer the estate themselves, whether they be an executor (i.e. there is a will) or an administrator (i.e. there is no will). If the estate is complicated or if it includes a business, a farm or a private company, it is essential to obtain professional advice at an early stage. If inheritance tax is payable a post-death variation may be advantageous. Do not be afraid to take professional advice at an early stage. Failure to spot a problem early on can lead to serious consequences for the executor.

Before obtaining the grant

1 Follow Steps to be Taken on Death, page 210.
2 Examine all the deceased's papers and find out where all the property is. A full list of assets and liabilities will eventually have to be prepared. Check that any property is properly insured, remove any valuables to safekeeping, redirect the post and consider whether the water system should be drained if the property is to remain empty.
3. Write to the bank for a statement showing balance, interest and any bank charges. What cheques have not yet been paid in? Ask whether the bank holds any securities for the dead person. Ask a bank to open an executor's account; the account need not be with the deceased's own bank.
4 Find out the details of any life-assurance policies held by the deceased. Write to the company notifying them of the death and enclosing a copy of the death certificate. Ask for details of the amount that will be paid; ask for a claim form. The amount due under the policy will not form part of the estate if either (i) it was taken out by the deceased's spouse, on the deceased's life, or (ii) it was taken out under the Married Woman's Property Act (in which case the policy will be held for the wife and children).
5 Draw up a list of any shares held by the deceased. These will have to be valued as at the date of death; the bank manager will probably be able to find out the valuation. Otherwise, contact the brokers, or look up the shares in the Stock Exchange official list for the date of death.

6 If there is a mortgage, notify the building society and enclose a copy of the death certificate. Ask for details of the amount owed at the date of death. It is wise in all cases to ask at this stage for any forms which may have to be completed before the bank or insurance company will pay out. Otherwise you will be sent the forms after you send the Grant of Probate, thus causing delays and increasing your work.

7 Obtain a probate valuation of any real property, such as a house or flat. The district valuer of the Inland Revenue will agree to fix a valuation after the papers have been lodged with the Probate Registry (see below). Seek expert advice if the deceased owned any property abroad.

8 Contact any pension fund (or employer) enclosing a copy of the death certificate and asking for full details of any sums due on death (e.g. under an occupational pension scheme). Ask whether the sum is to be treated as part of the estate or not, as this can affect the question of tax.

9 If the deceased held any savings certificates, write to the Savings Certificate Office, Durham, enclosing a copy of the death certificate. Ask for a full list of all certificates held, their date of purchase and value at the date of death.

10 If the deceased held any premium bonds, write to the Bond and Stock Office, Lytham St Annes, Lancashire, giving the full name and bond numbers. For the moment the bonds can be left in the draw and only cashed shortly before the estate is distributed to the beneficiaries (bonds can remain in the draw for up to twelve months after death).

11 With savings, as in the National Savings Bank or a building society, send the savings book or deposit book to the institution, enclose a copy of the death certificate and ask for the book to be made up and interest calculated to the date of death. Ask for a withdrawal form.

12 Value all the personal assets of the deceased. A valuer or secondhand-furniture dealer can value the furniture if a personal estimate is felt to be insufficient. Use a garage to value a car, or look up its value in trade publications.

13 Had the deceased made any gifts in the seven years before his or her death? If the deceased left no will, it is essential to know whether he or she made any gifts to any beneficiary during his/her lifetime as that gift will normally be treated as part of the beneficiary's share.

14 Was the deceased entitled to income from any trust or settlement? If so the trust will have certain formalities to complete and the value of the deceased's free estate (the estate he or she can leave as he or she pleases) will be added to the value of the trust assets to determine the total amount of inheritance tax payable.

15 Obtain details of any jointly held property. Does it pass automatically to the other joint holder or does it pass according to the deceased's will? Special rules apply for the valuation of half-shares in real property. Seek specialist advice if you become involved in such a case.

16 Notify the Inland Revenue of the death. Is the deceased entitled to a tax refund or does he owe tax?

17 Draw up a list of people who owed money to the deceased.
18 Draw up a list of people who are owed money.
19 Once all this information has been collected, the personal representative will be in a position to complete the forms needed to apply for probate or for letters of administration.

Applying for probate

20 Find out the location of the nearest local probate registry or probate office from the telephone directory. Write for the necessary forms. There are four forms and a guide (form PA2):
   • form PA1 (white application form);
   • form 44 (blue form for inheritance tax calculations);
   • form 37B (yellow form for listing real property such as houses, flats, land);
   • form 40 (yellow form for listing stocks and shares).

These forms are lengthy but each is straightforward. Do not be frightened by their seeming complexity. Forms PA1 and 44 must always be completed; forms 37B and 40 need be completed only if the estate includes real property and shares. Generally, if the estate, including relevant gifts, is not worth more than £125,000 and the death was after 1 July 1991, it will not be necessary to fill in any inheritance tax forms. (Note: some forms still refer to capital transfer tax, although it has been replaced by inheritance tax.)

21 Send to the Probate Registry (not the probate office):
   • the four forms, duly completed;
   • the death certificate;
   • the will (keep a copy in case the original is lost in the post);
   • a covering letter.

As a personal applicant the personal representative will have to attend an interview, at either the Probate Registry or the probate office. He or she should state which they wish to attend and they should state any dates or times of the day when they cannot attend.

22 The applicant will be given an interview appointment. The object of the interview is to sort out any difficulties or ambiguities and to ensure that the forms have been completed correctly. The applicant will also have to formally swear an Inheritance Tax Account Form, and sign an Inheritance Tax Warrant. The interview will be informal.

23 Some three or four weeks after the interview the applicant will be sent a set of forms. These forms are the application forms for the Grant of Probate. These should be completed and returned. The full list of items to be returned is:
   • the Inheritance Tax Account Form;
   • the forms originally filled in (see 20, above);
   • the Inheritance Tax Warrant, with a copy of the will annexed to it;
   • a cheque for the inheritance tax in favour of the Inland Revenue. The

amount of tax payable is set out on page 12 of the Inheritance Tax Account Form. In fact, few people have to fill in IHT forms – let alone pay any tax. The forms need only be filled in if the estate, including lifetime gifts, is worth more than £125,000, and tax will be payable only if it is worth over £150,000 (1992 figures). However, it is not necessary at this stage to pay tax arising because of land (i.e. house, flat etc.) or certain shares in a private company. The personal representative may have to arrange to borrow money from a bank to pay the tax, for even if the amount in the deceased's own account is enough to meet the bill it cannot be touched until after probate is granted. However, if the account was a joint account the survivor can operate it and may be prepared to advance enough money to pay the tax. There is also a special scheme to allow National Savings and building society accounts to be used to meet the tax bill; for details, contact the tax office.

• a cheque for the probate fee. Make the cheque in favour of the District Probate Registrar;

• a covering letter requesting sufficient office copies of the Grant of Probate to avoid having to wait for the return of the original document every time it is requested by a company, bank or other authority. Each copy costs 25p.

24 Some three weeks later the executor will be sent the Grant of Probate plus the office copies.

Administering the estate

25 Open a bank account in the name of the estate.

26 Collect any debts owed to the deceased, sums payable on insurance policies, sums in banks, building societies, unclaimed pension benefits, premium bonds etc. If you have already obtained the relevant claim forms, you will be expected to send the completed claim form, the office copy Grant of Probate or Letters of Administration, the pass book or insurance policy and, in some cases, an official copy death certificate. Pay the moneys into the estate's bank account, especially if it was overdrawn to pay out the tax and other sums mentioned in 23 above. If the estate is under £5,000, it will not be necessary to produce a Grant of Probate, but the institutions in which the money is held will have their own forms which require completion. Insurance companies will wish to see an official death certificate.

27 Ask the Inland Revenue to pay over any tax refund.

28 Pay the debts owed by the deceased, funeral bills, testamentary expenses and IHT. If there is not sufficient cash available, sell off assets. Unless the will states which assets are to be used, the money should be raised, in order, from:

• property not dealt with under the will (i.e. property in respect of which the testator died intestate), *next*

• the residue, *next*

- property specifically left for the payment of debts (note that this property is *not* the first property used to pay the debts), *next*
- any fund left to pay pecuniary legacies, *next*
- property specifically devised or bequeathed (a proportion of the money from each).

29 Advertise for any creditors. Place adverts in the *London Gazette* and, if the deceased held land, in a local paper in the area. Forms can be obtained from Oyez Publishing Limited; ask for forms Pro. 36A, 36B and 36C. The estate should not be distributed until two months after the placing of the advertisements, for otherwise the executor may be personally liable to the creditor. Once the two months have expired the executor is not personally liable, although the debt remains legally valid and the creditor can sue the estate and, if necessary, recover the money from the beneficiaries. If the advertisements result in claims these must be investigated before the estate is distributed.

30 Consider whether there is any possibility of a family provision claim (see Chapter 13) – that is, are there any children, including illegitimate children, mistresses, ex-wives, or others who might have a claim on the estate? If there is any possibility of there being such a person, do not distribute the estate until six months after obtaining the grant.

31 Sell off assets that are not specifically devised or bequeathed, and which are not wanted by any of the beneficiaries. If they realize more (or less) than their original valuation, additional (or less) IHT may be payable. Apply to the Revenue on form D3.

32 Consider whether a post-death variation could save IHT or achieve a fairer distribution of assets. Remember that all the beneficiaries must agree and be over eighteen, otherwise the consent of the court will be needed (not a simple or cheap exercise).

33 The next step is to distribute the assets. Note:
- the cost of maintaining any property specifically devised or bequeathed (e.g. insurance, packing, repairs) is borne by the beneficiary; similarly, legal fees on conveying land to a beneficiary are borne by the beneficiary;
- if property specifically devised or bequeathed produces income (e.g. dividends on shares), the beneficiary is entitled to all the income since the date of death;
- a pecuniary legacy accrues interest at 6 per cent per annum but generally this arises only from one year after the death.

Small estates – no need for probate

34 Small amounts of money due to the estate from building societies, the National Savings Bank, savings certificates, premium savings bonds, government stocks, banks etc. may be payable without the need to obtain, or produce, a Grant of Probate. If the amount due from each institution is no

more than £5,000, that institution may agree to pay out the money without the need for a Grant of Probate. However, the institution can insist on production of a Grant of Probate if it so wishes. Note that there can be up to £5,000 in each institution, so the total amount coming within this 'small estates' exception can be quite large. Also, any cash and personal effects (e.g. jewellery, furniture) can be dealt with without the need for a grant – provided that all the relatives and beneficiaries can agree on how it is to be split up.

Money 'nominated' before death

35 A person with money in a friendly society, a trade union or an industrial or provident society can instruct the society to pay the money to a nominee when he or she dies. The nominee will be entitled to the money on production of the death certificate; they need not wait until a Grant of Probate or Letters of Administration have been obtained. Thus money 'nominated' in this way can be a useful source of ready cash when someone dies. However, the total amount that can be nominated with each institution is £500. If more than £500 is nominated, probate or administration papers will be required.

A person who wants to nominate money in this way must write to the society or union setting out his/her wishes; some bodies have a special form for this. The nomination can be cancelled at any time by giving written notice to the institution. It will automatically be cancelled if the nominator marries or if the nominee dies first. It is not cancelled by a will which leaves the money to someone else.

When the death occurs, the nominee simply writes to the institution setting out the circumstances and enclosing a death certificate. He or she may be asked to complete a form.

INTESTACY: WHEN THERE IS NO WILL

If there is no will, the personal representatives will distribute the estate in accordance with the intestacy rules laid down in the Administration of Estates Act 1925 and the Intestates' Estates Act 1952. The order of entitlement laid down in these Acts was drawn up after a detailed examination of the way people tended to leave their property in wills, and so these Acts can be said to give effect to the 'presumed intentions' of the deceased – i.e. what he or she would have done had they left a will.

The rules are complicated and are best understood by considering, in turn, the position of the spouse, then the issue, and finally, the other relatives.

The surviving spouse

- *If there are no surviving relatives*, the spouse takes the whole of the estate.
- *If there is issue* (i.e. children or grandchildren), the spouse takes the personal

chattels (which include household goods, car, jewellery, wines, clothes and the like), a fixed sum of £75,000 and a life interest in half the balance. This means that the spouse will receive the interest from half the balance but will not have access to the capital.

● *If there is no issue but other relatives such as parents or brothers and sisters,* the spouse takes the personal chattels, a fixed sum of £125,000 and half the balance.

The issue (i.e. children, grandchildren etc.)

What the issue receive will depend upon whether the deceased parent left a surviving spouse:

● *If there is a surviving spouse,* the issue take one-half of the residue (i.e. the amount left after the spouse has deducted the chattels and £75,000). The other half of the residue will go to the surviving spouse for life and the capital will then pass to the issue on his/her death.

● *If there is no surviving spouse,* the issue inherit the whole estate. The estate is held for them so that they all have equal shares when they reach eighteen or when they marry (if earlier). If any children have already died leaving children, those children will share what their deceased parent would have received. If any of the children are illegitimate there may be difficulties if there is no affiliation order or other acceptable evidence of paternity.

In one recent administration a problem was solved by modern technology. A bachelor died leaving one accepted illegitimate child aged three. The child's mother had obtained an affiliation order against him. Another woman then alleged that her two-year-old child was also a child of the deceased and that she had been about to marry the deceased. Unfortunately she had no affiliation order or other evidence.

Because both children were under eighteen there could be no compromise. The matter was therefore expected to go to court in order for the two-year-old, through his lawyers, to prove to the court's satisfaction that he was the son of the deceased.

The parties then considered genetic fingerprinting. Because the parents of the deceased were still alive, they were able to provide blood samples which, when combined with samples from the two-year-old and his mother, proved he was indeed the child of the deceased.

The matter was therefore solved relatively cheaply, without using up the modest estate in legal fees.

The other relatives (i.e. parents, brothers, sisters or their children)

Entitlement here will depend upon whether there is a surviving spouse and/or any issue (children, grandchildren etc.):

● *If there are any issue,* the other relatives will not receive anything.

• *If there is a surviving spouse but no issue*, the other relatives receive one-half of the residue left after the surviving spouse has deducted the chattels and £125,000. The half will go to the parents of the deceased in equal shares, but if there are no parents living, it will go to the deceased's brothers and sisters in equal shares. If any of those brothers and sisters have already died their share will be divided between their children.

• *If there is no surviving spouse and no issue*, the other relatives inherit all the estate. The order of entitlement is:

• to the parents, *but if none*
• to brothers and sisters, *but if none*
• to half-brothers and half-sisters, *but if none*
• to grandparents, *but if none*
• to uncles and aunts of the whole blood (i.e. brothers and sisters of one of the deceased's parents), *but if none*
• to uncles and aunts of the half-blood (i.e. half-brothers and half-sisters of one of the deceased's parents), *but if none*
• the estate passes to the Crown or, in the appropriate areas, to the Duchy of Cornwall or the Duchy of Lancaster. In practice, the Crown (or the Duchies) will often pay all or part to someone who seems morally entitled to a share.

Note: if, under the intestacy rules, a share passes to a child, brother, sister, uncle or aunt who died before the deceased, then the share passes to that person's descendants (usually their children).

Illustration. *Fred Jones died intestate leaving an estate of £200,000. He was survived by his wife Mabel, but they had no children. Other relatives include two nephews – the sons of Fred's brother Michael – and a niece – the daughter of his brother Frank. The estate will be divided as follows:*

• his wife Mabel *will take the personal chattels plus £125,000, plus one-half of the remaining £75,000 (i.e. £37,500). A total of £162,500 plus chattels.*

• the nephews and the niece *will take the share their parents would have taken. As brothers of Fred, each would have been entitled to an equal share of the £37,500 left after Mabel had taken her share. Thus, the niece inherits £18,750 and the two nephews inherit £9,375 each.*

Mistresses, common-law spouses

The intestacy rules only recognize the claims of relatives. Mistresses, lovers, close friends, and others do not have any claim under the intestacy rules. Contrary to popular belief, the term 'common-law spouse' is not recognized by the intestacy rules. If your partner is not your spouse, you both need wills – badly. They may be able to qualify as 'dependants' and so bring a claim under the family provision legislation for a share of the estate (see below) but there are no certainties and the claim may be expensive to pursue. Spouses of deceased relatives have no claim at all. Consider the following situation. A wealthy widower invites his brother and sister-in-law to come and live with him. They get on well but the brother dies shortly, followed by the widower. The only living relative is another brother, to whom the widower has not spoken for twenty years. Under the intestacy rules the estranged brother gets the whole estate and the sister-in-law gets nothing.

Partial intestacy

If a person dies leaving a will, but the will does not dispose of all his estate, he is said to have died partially intestate. For instance, if the residue is left equally between two people, but one dies before the testator, then his share will pass as on an intestacy, unless the will makes the appropriate provision. Note that if the gift was to the two people jointly, then the survivor would take the whole gift.

The usual rules on intestacy apply to that part of his estate but the spouse and issue must take their benefits under the will into account when working out their shares under the intestacy rules. For instance, a widow who received £10,000 under the will would not take the first £75,000 of the undisposed-of estate, but only the first £65,000.

13 The Family Provision Legislation: Fair Shares for Family and Dependants

Only in 1938 did Parliament decide that a testator's moral duty to provide for his/her family should become a legal obligation.

It had long been a principle of English law that a man could dispose of his property as he wished. Thus a man was free to leave his family and dependants destitute – a principle that was alien to most Continental legal systems and to the laws of Scotland too. The only relaxation of this strict rule was by virtue of several old common-law doctrines (such as dower, escheat and curtesy) that sometimes allowed the spouse and children to claim part of the estate, but these laws were repealed by a series of statutes from 1833 onwards. The law of the nineteenth century was a *laissez-faire* law, in which the right to dispose freely of one's property was inviolable. The family provision legislation of 1938 scotched this notion, and it provides yet another example of the free-enterprise spirit of Victorian law being overturned by a twentieth-century Parliament which is more concerned with social justice than jurisprudential consistencies.

The 1938 Inheritance (Family Provision) Act was replaced in 1975 by the Inheritance (Provision for Family and Dependants) Act. This statute extended the protection to dependants such as mistresses, and did away with some of the more restrictive rules affecting the entitlement to provision and the form the provision was to take.

The 1975 Act (usually called the 'family provision legislation', despite the fact that it includes dependants who are not members of the family) envisages three categories of claimants – the surviving spouse, the children and, finally, other dependants whether members of the family or not. The Act is strengthened by provisions which make it difficult for the testator to concoct schemes that may get around the legislation. Application under the Act is made by way of an originating summons to the High Court, either within the Chancery Division or within the Family Division, unless the net estate does not exceed £30,000, in which case the county court can hear the claim.

The application must be made within six months of the grant being issued by the Probate Registry, although the court does have power to allow late applications in exceptional circumstances (for instance, on the late discovery of a will). This six-month time limit poses a problem to many claimants, such as spouses who have been deserted by the deceased and who may not have heard of his/her death. To prevent the estate being distributed without his/her knowledge, the potential claimant can register a 'caveat' in the Probate Registry, which prevents a grant being made for the following six months without his/her knowledge and approval. An alternative and simpler safeguard is for the potential claimant to make a 'standing search' at the Probate Registry (fee £1) which entitles him/her to a copy of any grant during the next six months, and also to any grant taken out in the last twelve months. The search can, of course, be renewed every six months. If you register a caveat you will be warned if a probate action is commenced. You will then find yourself involved in the action. You would therefore be well advised to seek legal advice before registering a caveat.

Many such actions will be started with the words: 'It's not the money I mind about, it's the principle.' Unfortunately, such principles can be expensive, especially if the case has to be conducted through the Chancery Division of the High Court.

THE SURVIVING SPOUSE

The court will act as though it was considering the financial arrangements to be made on a divorce; thus the factors and principles considered by the divorce court (see Chapter 4) will be applied to the family provision claim. Most important, the issue before the court is not whether the deceased made reasonable provision for the *maintenance* of the spouse, but whether the deceased left his/her spouse (whether by will or under the intestacy rules) a 'fair share of the family assets' – which may, of course, be considerably more than is needed for maintenance alone. This test is more generous than that applied to the children and other dependants, who are only entitled to reasonable provision for their maintenance.

If the surviving spouse was divorced or judicially separated from the deceased, it is probable that there will have been an earlier court hearing when the family assets were divided between them. In such a case, although the surviving spouse can apply under the family provision legislation, the earlier division may well reduce the chances of a successful claim. If the former spouse remarries, he or she automatically loses all rights to maintenance or a share of the assets under the family provision legislation, and any order (e.g. for maintenance) is cancelled.

When deciding the sort of order to be made, the court has similar powers to those of the divorce court in matrimonial cases. For instance, the order can be for periodic payments, a lump sum (or a lump sum payable by instalments), or the transfer and purchase of property. A 'fair share' of the assets is determined on an objective basis, depending on the commitments and wealth of the deceased at the time of his/her death.

THE CHILDREN

The children do not fare as well as the surviving spouse. The test is whether the deceased parent made 'reasonable provision' for their maintenance. This is all they are entitled to – maintenance only, not a share of the family assets. 'Children' in this context includes any child of the family who was maintained by the deceased prior to his/her death; the child's age, marital status or illegitimacy is irrelevant. A child of the deceased who had not been born at the date of the testator's death would be entitled to claim if the will had divided the estate between named children.

OTHER DEPENDANTS

The final category of claimants under the 1975 Act is that of other dependants who were partly or wholly maintained by the deceased at the time of his/her death. This includes common-law wives and mistresses. Many cases of hardship arose from the exclusion of such people from the 1938 Act, for when the deceased died intestate the estate would pass to relatives (e.g. an undivorced, but separated, wife) and not to the common-law spouse. Although the common-law spouse is now included in the legislation, he or she is still discriminated against, for the Act only permits a claim for 'reasonable provision for maintenance', and not for a share of the family assets. In addition, of course, the common-law spouse is wholly excluded from the intestacy rules (above), does not have full protection under the Rent Acts (see page 312), and is not eligible for such DSS benefits as the widow's pension.

FAMILY PROVISION LEGISLATION IN PRACTICE

A woman was brought up by her grandparents having been rejected by her mother. When the mother died her estate was £172,000 but the daughter (then aged fifty-eight) received only a legacy of £200. The woman claimed that her mother had not made a reasonable provision for her. The woman lived on state benefits. The remainder of the estate was left to charities. The court decided that although the mother had no legal obligation to her daughter, there was a moral obligation to fulfil. She was therefore awarded £3,000 in a lump sum and £4,500 per annum maintenance. Re Debenham dec'd (1986)

On the other hand:

A woman left everything to her natural son to the exclusion of her adopted daughter. The adopted daughter was independent and impecunious. She had also been wild, having served a three-month prison sentence. The testator stated in her will why she had left nothing to her adopted daughter. The judge considered the needs and financial resources, the size of the estate, the moral obligations and other matters. The adopted daughter failed to establish a right to be maintained. Williams v. Johns (1988)

A mistress can use the legislation to claim a share of the estate. For instance:

A former mistress claimed from the estate of the deceased. Their five-year relationship had ended two years before his death. She argued that he had promised to provide for her if she would live with him. Her claim failed but the court indicated that she would have succeeded had she been living with the deceased at the date of his death. Layton v. Martin (1986)

Since the cost of taking a disputed case to court can often be a substantial part of the value of the estate, the courts discourage claims over relatively small estates.

PART TWO

HOUSING

14 Home Ownership

This chapter looks at the law for the home-owner. The law on renting a home is dealt with in Chapters 17–19.

The purchase of a house or flat is quite unlike the buying of a car, fridge, caravan or other physical commodity. This is partly because the land on which a house or flat stands is indestructible and will never wear out. In addition, land can be subject to a whole host of rights and liabilities that cannot apply to other things: rights of way, rights of light, restrictive covenants, and so on. Thus the ownership of land (and the houses and flats on the land) can be transferred only by following a set procedure involving inspection and transfer of formal documents of title, a process that usually takes two months or more from start to finish. In comparison, buying, say, a fridge or a car is comparatively straightforward, for then it is largely a question of seeing the item, satisfying oneself that it belongs to the seller, paying the purchase price and then taking possession of the item.

This is why conveyancing has traditionally been such a long-winded and complicated process. But improvements have been introduced in recent years. Indeed, only ten years ago, conveyancing was even more long-winded (and more expensive). A major catalyst for change was the breaking of the solicitor's monopoly, which had effectively meant that only solicitors could act on the buying and selling of properties. Licensed conveyancers were introduced to compete with solicitors. While there are still relatively few licensed conveyancers, the threat of competition was sufficient to make many solicitors look more closely at the conveyancing service they were offering. The result has been a far more competitive price market (with conveyancing fees having gone down in many parts of the country), and attempts by solicitors to speed up the conveyancing process. In addition, the finance houses – the banks and building societies that lend mortgages – have insisted on more streamlined procedures. Perhaps most important of all, the financial institutions (many of which own estate-agency chains) will soon be able to do conveyancing for their customers. This threat of massive competition has forced many solicitors to improve radically the quality of the conveyancing service they offer.

A final impetus for change was the collapse of the property market in 1989–90. Many firms of solicitors were over-dependent on conveyancing work and the property slump meant that many solicitors lost a substantial part of their workload (and income). As a result, many firms have now moved away from a reliance on residential conveyancing, and some have stopped doing it altogether. Those that remain have to compete more fiercely for the work – which means that conveyancing has never been cheaper or more efficient. All of this is good news for the home-buyer and the home-seller.

The fact remains, however, that conveyancing transactions still take at least a month or more. The ultimate goal must surely be for the Land Registry to be accessible by computer link and for the solicitor's profession, the financial institutions and the local authorities to agree on a standard method of electronic communication. Only then will conveyancing become truly speedy.

THE OWNERSHIP OF LAND, HOUSES, AND FLATS

Traditionally, the law has always been concerned with 'land' rather than the houses, flats, garages, and other buildings on the land. Even today, the law technically still looks at the transfer and ownership of the land – not the flat, semi-detached house, or other building on the land. The building is seen as a mere incidental to the purchase of the land. For instance, the standard legal phrase for describing a house is 'all that land situate and known as (*address*) together with the dwelling house situate thereon', as though the land was the important thing to the purchaser, not the house.

So the first step towards understanding conveyancing is to appreciate that when a lawyer talks of 'land', he or she is also referring to the house or flat on the land; 'land' does not just mean allotments, gardens and country estates.

Freehold or leasehold?

Householders can have either a freehold or a leasehold interest.

The freeholder owns the land for ever and has fairly wide powers to do with the land as he or she wishes. The leaseholder owns the land for a fixed period only, and at the end of that period the land will go back to the freeholder (but see the Leasehold Reform Act, page 286). In the meantime the leaseholder will have to pay ground rent to the freeholder and observe the terms of the lease granted by the freeholder.

Clearly, then, a freehold interest is more desirable than a leasehold interest, and it may seem surprising that anyone would accept a leasehold and not insist on having the freehold. The answer lies in the enforcing of obligations and restrictions between neighbouring home-owners. It is very difficult to give one freeholder the power legally to restrict another freeholder's use of his or her land (see Restrictive Covenants, page 363). But with leaseholds the position is different; the leases can be worded to allow one leaseholder to enforce covenants against another leaseholder. This is absolutely essential with flats because, for instance, the owner of a first-floor flat must be able to make the owner of the ground-floor flat maintain that flat so the first-floor flat does not lose its structural support. Conversely, the owner of the ground-floor flat will want to be able to force the owner of the top-floor flat to maintain the roof. Mutual repairing obligations are needed between flat-owners and this is something that the law allows only between leaseholders, not freeholders. Thus, flat-owners nearly always have leases.

Occasionally, however, a house-owner will have a leasehold interest and not a freehold interest. For instance, in a new development of town houses there may be covenants between the home-owners about maintaining a common roof or common forecourt. In such a situation, it may be easier – from a legal point of view – if the home-owners have leases with service charge provisions (see page 351 for the rules on service charges). But it would be possible legally for each home-owner to have a freehold interest and then enter into restrictive covenants with the other home-owners (i.e. binding promises not to do certain things).

In essence, however, the distinction is between leasehold and freehold. In practical terms, leases are for flats; freeholds are for houses. Having said that, however, there is no legal reason why a house cannot be held on a lease; indeed, many are. But it is usually possible for a home-owner to buy the freehold of a house that is held on a long lease (see Chapter 16 Leasehold Reform Act). But a flat-owner cannot normally buy the freehold of an individual flat from the freeholder (although it may soon be possible for several leaseholders to get together and buy a Commonhold interest from their landlord).

The main differences in the positions of freeholders and leaseholders are set out in the table on pages 240–41.

Shared ownership

This is a hybrid form of home ownership – in effect it is a half-way house between owning the house (whether by having a leasehold or freehold) and renting it. It is only available to secure tenants (i.e. council tenants, housing association tenants etc. – but not tenants of private landlords). For instance, a secure tenant may buy a 60 per cent interest in his or her flat from the landlord; under this arrangement, the landlord will retain 40 per cent. When the tenant comes to sell the flat, the landlord will get 40 per cent of the profit.

Shared ownership is relatively uncommon now. It became fashionable in the mid-1980s and was encouraged by the property boom (when tenants were worried about being left out of the home-ownership market). The collapse of the property boom has dissuaded many such people from wanting to own property.

Time-shares

How does a time-sharing agreement fit into these legal structures? The answer is that it doesn't: lawyers have had great difficulty in finding a satisfactory legal framework for time-shares. A time-sharer will have a limited interest in the land (e.g. one week a year for a period of ninety-nine years). Various legal devices have been used but few of them stand up to close examination. In practice, the best schemes will involve the participation of one of the major banks (or some

Freehold and Leasehold: The Main Differences

	Freehold	Leasehold
Mortgage availability	Mortgages on houses should be easy to obtain (subject to satisfactory survey etc.). Mortgages on freehold flats are very difficult to obtain since maintenance and repair of common parts, stairs, structure etc. cannot easily be enforced.	Building societies like there to be at least 30 to 40 years of the lease left *after* the date of paying off the mortgage. They will inspect the maintenance and repair provisions of a flat lease to ensure that they can be properly enforced.
Rent	No rent payable, unless property is subject to a rent charge (unlikely outside Manchester and Bristol).	Annual ground rent payable according to terms of lease; usually increases as the lease expires, generally between £50 and £150 p.a. Will rarely be such that it could be two-thirds of the property's rateable value, since Rent Act protection might then come into effect. In addition, leaseholder may have to pay a maintenance or service charge.
Security	The owner cannot be evicted except by: (i) compulsory purchase (e.g. by the council); (ii) foreclosure by building society if he or she fails to pay the instalments or breaks the terms of the mortgage deed (e.g. by letting the property).	The owner cannot be dispossessed except by: (i) compulsory purchase (e.g. by the council); (ii) foreclosure by building society if he or she fails to pay the instalments or otherwise breaks the terms of the mortgage deed; (iii) eviction by freeholder if he or she fails to observe the terms of the lease (e.g. does not pay the ground rent); (iv) eviction by freeholder when lease expires (unless Leasehold Reform Act 1967 applies; see Chapter 16).
Obligation to repair	None, unless: (i) insisted on by the building society (the mortgage deed will	The lease will probably require the tenant to keep the property in a good state of repair and

	Freehold	Leasehold
	impose repairing and maintenance obligations on the borrower); (ii) if the building is of special architectural or historic note, the local authority can make an order requiring repairs or maintenance to be carried out.	to maintain it properly (e.g. repaint the interior every 3 years). There may also be an obligation to pay a proportionate part of the cost of maintaining/repairing common parts of a block of flats (see page 351. Service charges). In addition: (i) building societies may insist on repairs and maintenance as a condition of their mortgage loan; (ii) if building is of special architectural or historic note, the local authority can make an order requiring repair or maintenance to be carried out.
Alterations, extensions, change of use	Owner can do as he or she wishes, subject to: (i) obtaining any necessary planning permission; (ii) observing any restrictive covenants, rights of light and support etc. that someone else can enforce; (iii) perhaps obtaining the building society's (or mortgage company's) consent, since the mortgage deed may prohibit alterations made without their permission.	Position is similar to that of freeholder, but in addition restrictions will probably be set out in the lease (e.g. that property be used only for residential purposes and that freeholder's consent be obtained for any alterations and extensions).

other reputable institution), which will hold the land and property and then act as trustee; each time-sharer will have a contract with the trustee, and the chances are that there will not be any problems. The difficulties, in practice, arise when the property is held by a management company that is in financial difficulties, or which starts overcharging the time-sharers through excessive service charges. This is especially so with speculative developments abroad. The unfortunate reality is that our old-fashioned system of land law has not been able to adapt sufficiently to meet the new problems of time-share agreements. This is one more reason for being extremely wary of time-sharing!

Commonhold

Many flat-owners would prefer to have a freehold rather than a leasehold. To overcome this problem (and the fact that many leases are now getting unacceptably short for mortgage purposes) the government is planning to introduce a new form of ownership called Commonhold. In effect, Commonhold is designed for a development in which there are two or more units that have a shared management of common parts; typically, of course, this will be a block of flats. Under Commonhold, the owner of each unit (i.e. flat) will own the freehold in that unit plus the legal right to essential services (e.g. gas, water, the right to communal services and, where appropriate, the right to use communal facilities such as parking spaces, common gardens etc.). The main legal title under a Commonhold will be held by a Commonhold Association (similar to a company). Standard Commonhold regulations will be laid down that set out the mutual obligations between all unit holders (e.g. to maintain their individual flats or units; to pay towards the cost of roof repairs and painting the outside etc.).

The plan is that existing flat-owners with leases will be able to get together and buy the freehold from the existing landlord. They will then hold the property under Commonhold. This will therefore mean that flat-owners can buy their freehold (householders with leases have previously been able to do this under the Leasehold Reform Act 1967). But the Commonhold changes are not law yet at the time of going to press.

'Ownership' of land

Beyond distinguishing between freehold and leasehold, it is difficult to define the word 'ownership' when it is applied to land. The non-lawyer may be satisfied with the short dictionary definition of its meaning 'to hold', but the lawyer requires more precision. If a client is spending thousands of pounds on purchasing the 'ownership' of a plot of land, then the lawyer must know exactly what 'ownership' means.

Clearly, there can be no such thing as the *absolute* ownership of land today. The Planning Acts, police rights of entry, public footpaths etc. have all made a nonsense of the claim that 'an Englishman's home is his castle'.

The concept of ownership is also weakened in less obvious ways. For instance, suppose someone buys a flat on a ninety-nine-year lease, with the help of a building society mortgage, and then lets out part of the flat. Who 'owns' that flat? To the non-lawyer the answer is simple enough: the owner is the leaseholder. That is true enough, but consider the position in more detail. The building society has a mortgage deed which entitles it to be repaid in full, and which allows it to enter and sell the property if the instalments are not paid or if any of the other clauses in the mortgage deed are broken. Further, the property is on a lease, so there is a freeholder who may be able to reclaim the flat at the end of the ninety-nine years. In addition, there may be a Rent Act tenant who has possession and who cannot be evicted without a court order. Thus, although we say that the leaseholder 'owns' the flat, the reality is that the building society, the freeholder and the Rent Act tenant all have *rights* over the flat which significantly erode the leaseholder's 'ownership' of it.

Accordingly, to speak in simple terms of 'owning' a home can be misleading. 'Ownership' is a meaningless description until you know what rights other people have over that property. Thus 'ownership' is a relative concept; it can mean one thing to one home-owner and a completely different thing to another home-owner. This is another illustration of the inadequacy of words as a means of accurately describing legal concepts; as Humpty Dumpty said to Alice, 'When *I* use a word it means just what I choose it to mean'.

'Rights' over land

The rights that a freeholder or leaseholder has over his land (to live there, put up new buildings, chop down trees etc.) are limited by:
• the community's rights (e.g. to use the planning laws to control development on the land, to allow the police to enter with a search warrant, to dig trenches for public sewers), *and*
• other people's rights (e.g. the Rent Act or Housing Act tenant who lives there; the next-door neighbour, who can prevent the erection of buildings that obstruct the light to the next-door property; the neighbour who has a right of way to walk across part of the land).

All any home-owner has is a 'bundle of rights' over the land, house or flat. The extent of this bundle of rights will depend on the rights enjoyed over the land by other people and by the community. If 'ownership' can be understood in this way, you can soon appreciate what a conveyancer does when acting for the buyer of a house or flat; the conveyancer looking to see what 'rights' the seller has over the land, how many of those 'rights' will be transferred to the buyer, and what 'rights' other people and the community have over the land which may adversely affect the buyer's use and enjoyment of it. The table on page 244 gives an idea of the sort of 'rights' that can affect land, and how some of these 'rights' are vested in the owner, some in other individuals, and others in the community at large.

The community's rights over private land

Acts of Parliament lay down various rights that apply over all land, such as the law that all houses are subject to planning controls or that aircraft are free to fly over private land and through the airspace that technically belongs to the owner of the land. These rights are of general application, as are the other examples listed in the table, and they are all illustrations of how the traditional sanctity of private property has been eroded.

The Householder Owns a 'Bundle of Rights'

The owner's 'rights'

- to live in the property
- to let the property
- to keep, sell or destroy anything on the property
- to build on the land
- to sell the land to anyone
- to give the land (or part of it) away; to bequeath it by will
- to fish in any river that flows through the land
- to do what he or she likes on the property
- to sue for trespass by other people or their possessions (including tree roots and branches)
- to sue for nuisance, if the 'quiet enjoyment' is disturbed (for example, by noise and vibration) etc.

The 'rights' that other individuals may have over the property

- as tenant under a lease for more than 21 years (the 'rights' will be set out in the lease and in the Leasehold Reform Act 1967)
- as tenant under any other lease (the 'rights' will be set out in the Rent Acts, Housing Acts, and in the lease, if any)
- the building society or mortgage company that lent money on a mortgage (the 'rights' of possession and sale will be set out in the mortgage deed)
- a neighbour's 'right' to prevent the home-owner from reducing the amount of light that enters the neigbour's buildings
- a neighbour's 'right' to prevent the home-owner from removing soil that would affect the support and structure of the next-door property (including, perhaps, any buildings)
- a 'right of way' to pass over the land
- a 'right' of possession gained by 12 years' squatting on the land
- 'rights' under restrictive covenants to control and prevent development on the land or a change in its use
- 'rights' granted by custom, to graze cattle on the land, dig turf for fuel etc.

'Rights' vested in the community

- to enforce standards of hygiene and cleanliness
- to control development, erection of buildings, signs, conversions etc.
- to control a change of use of the property
- to control the quality and nature of building works
- to restrict the type of fuel burnt on the property
- to allow planes to trespass over the land and through its airspace
- to claim gold, silver and oil found on the land
- to claim any treasure trove found on the land, on behalf of the Crown
- to regulate the number of people living there
- to restrict the amount of water that can be taken from any rivers that flow across the land
- to prevent the property being used for certain dangerous purposes (e.g. involving radioactive fuels)
- to sue for nuisance if the landowner disturbs others, or allows dangerous materials to escape from the land
- powers of entry given to police, gas board officials etc.
- the right to compulsory purchase of the land
- the right for certain works to be carried out on the land (e.g. digging of pipes and laying of cables) etc.

Other people's rights over private land

Of more immediate concern to the conveyancer are those rights that other private individuals have over the land. The problem is to find out what rights exist, and whether those rights can be enforced against someone who buys the land. Clearly, not all these rights will survive against a buyer; for example, the seller's building society will have powerful rights of entry and sale under the mortgage deed, but the buyer's solicitor will insist that the mortgage be repaid (and so the building society's rights destroyed) before the purchase is completed. However, some of the other rights might bind the buyer (e.g. a right of way over the land). The list in the table opposite gives some of the more important rights that outsiders may have over private land.

How other people acquire rights over private land

Apart from statute, the main ways in which outsiders can acquire rights over private land are either by deed (as with the building society and its mortgage deed) or by claiming, and using, the right over a period of years.

When the right is created by statute or deed the position is clear enough, since the purchaser simply has to refer to the lease, title document, will, Rent Act or whatever to see the extent of those rights. The problems arise when there is no written statement of the rights, as happens when they are acquired by long usage – by what is called *prescription*.

Prescription assumes that someone has a legal right to do something when they have been doing it continuously over a period of years in such a way as to indicate that they have a legal right to do it. For example, if a person parks his car on his neighbour's plot of land for year after year, he may acquire the legal right to keep on parking his car there and that right may be taken over by whoever owns his house in later years. But if he had first asked for permission to park the car or if he had occasionally bought his neighbour a small gift as a 'thank you', then he would – by implication – have admitted that he did not have the legal right to park there and so he could not acquire the right to park there by prescription. Similarly, if the neighbour had told him not to park there, his claim would be defeated.

The right must be exercised without permission, force or secrecy, before it can become a legal right by way of prescription. In addition, the right must have been exercised fairly continuously over the years; if the householder parks on his neighbour's land only once every few years then he cannot claim the right to do so by prescription.

The real problem is in deciding how long the right has to be exercised before prescription can apply. At common law, the rule was that the right must have existed since 'time immemorial' which – for the sake of convenience – was arbitrarily fixed at the start of Richard I's reign, 1189. This was a hopelessly strict test, and so the courts decided that the right might be assumed to exist if it could be shown to have been in use for as long as could be remembered by those in the area. But these tests were not applied with any uniformity and so Parliament has now passed several statutes laying down specific time periods. Generally, twenty years' regular use will be enough, assuming that it was without permission, force or secrecy in the first place.

The rights that outsiders can acquire

The rights that outsiders can have over other people's land are numerous. Those listed in the table are merely illustrations of the more common rights.

Many of these rights date back to feudal days when, for example, the right to cut turf or to cut wood for making agricultural implements was of some importance. Nowadays, such rights of 'turbary' and 'ploughbote' are few and far between, and the conveyancer will be more concerned with rights of way, rights of light etc. over the land. Even if the right is unlikely to be used by the outsider, the conveyancer will still want to know the full extent of it. The fact that it would be unfair for the outsider to be allowed to exercise his or her right is not relevant, for a court would not consider the merits of the case – only whether the right is valid and enforceable. Thus, for example, it might be unfair for the neighbour of a cricket club to exercise his ancient right of cutting turf for his hearth, but the court would still enforce the right even if it meant destroying the cricket pitch; this can be compared with the French and German legal systems, where rights cannot be exercised if they can have no other purpose than to harm someone else.

See Chapter 21 for when these rights can apply.

TAX RELIEF AND THE OWNER-OCCUPIER

Owner-occupiers receive tax relief on both income tax and capital gains tax liabilities.

Income tax relief

Tax relief is allowed on interest paid to buy or improve the taxpayer's only or main residence. Typically, this will be interest on mortgage repayments.

Detailed points to note include:

• The property must be in the UK or Eire. It need not be a house or a flat but could, for instance, be a houseboat or caravan.

• Only interest on the first £30,000 of the loan is deductible. Married couples are allowed only £30,000 between them, unless they are separated. Unmarried joint purchasers split the £30,000 on the basis of their respective shares in the property.

• The relief does not apply only to loans to buy the property. A loan to improve or develop a property will also be allowed. For instance, installing central heating or double glazing; building a garage, garden shed, extension, swimming pool or patio; converting the house into flats. But the total of all loans on which tax relief can be claimed is £30,000; you cannot claim up to £30,000 per loan!

• The property must be an only or main residence. If you have more than one residence it is a question of fact which is the main residence: you cannot arbitrarily choose for yourself (cf. capital gains tax).

• It does not matter to whom the interest is paid. Typically, it will be a building society or bank, but loans from other sources (e.g. private loans) are also eligible. But tax relief on interest on bank overdrafts and on credit cards is not allowed, so improvements should be financed by a bank loan, not by overdraft or Access/Barclaycard.

• Generally, in order to qualify for relief you have up to twelve months to move into the property after buying it, although the Revenue will often agree a longer period. Generally, up to four years' absence will be allowed if your job requires you to move for a period not exceeding four years, and if you are likely to return to the property at the end of that time. Similarly, if you move into your new home before selling the old home, tax relief will be allowed on both the old and the new loan (usually a bridging loan) for at least twelve months. The old loan will also be ignored for the purpose of the £30,000 limit. The Revenue will usually extend the twelve months' period if there is a genuine difficulty (for instance, if a property slump makes it difficult to sell the old house).

Capital gains tax relief

The general rule is that the profit arising on the sale of any capital item (such as a house) is subject to capital gains tax. However, if the property was the taxpayer's only or main residence during the period of ownership, the whole of the profit will be exempt from tax.

Detailed points to note include:

• If you have more than one residence you can choose which is to qualify for the CGT relief. But you must serve a formal notice on the Revenue within two years of the start of the date when you claim it became your main residence.

• If the property was not the main residence for the whole period of ownership, then tax will have to be paid proportionately on the profit. But temporary periods of absence are ignored. This covers:

– periods (together not exceeding three years) when you were employed outside the UK, *and/or*

– periods (together not exceeding four years) when the you (or spouse) could not live in the property because of the location of your job or because of a condition imposed by your employer, *and*

– the last two years of ownership are always ignored.

If applicable, all of these periods can be added together and claimed cumulatively.

• An apportionment will also be needed if part of the property is used for business purposes (e.g. offices; or let as a flat) since it will not have been used solely as a main residence. Lettings by resident landlords get the benefit of a special relief: the capital gain attributable to the rented property is taxed only if it exceeds £40,000 (1992) or if it exceeds the capital gain attributable to that part of the property used as the main residence (whichever is the lower). Only the excess is taxable.

For instance:

A house was owned for fifteen years; one-third of it was let for ten years. The capital gain on its sale is £180,000; the taxable portion of this is 10/45 of £180,000, that is £40,000. But the first £40,000 is tax-free, and so no tax will have to be paid.

• Land belonging to the residence may not be exempt from tax. Generally, only 1 acre of land can get the benefit of being part of the residence. However, this is not a hard-and-fast rule and professional advice (from a lawyer or accountant) should always be taken. There are also complicated rules to observe when selling off part of a garden for development. In essence, it is important to sell off the garden before selling the house; that way, the part of the garden that is sold will be treated as part of the private residence and so exempt from capital gains tax. On the other hand, if the house is sold first and then the garden shortly afterwards, the Revenue will almost certainly be able to claim that the garden was not part of the home – which means that capital gains tax will have to be paid on the gain relating to the garden. This is a complicated area; professional advice from an accountant or lawyer should always be taken.

• Husband and wife can have only one main residence between them, unless separated. Complications can arise on divorce when the ex-wife is given the right to live in a property partly owned by her ex-husband, with his being entitled to a share in the proceeds when it is eventually sold. Professional advice is needed in such a case.

MORTGAGES

The costs of mortgages vary from time to time, as interest rates and tax rates change. For most young people starting out on the property-buying business, the best advice is to go for the cheapest possible monthly repayment – do not worry about long-term bonus payments etc. A pound or two saved now (when you are hard up!) is probably more valuable than a lump sum in twenty-five years' time. Also, remember that you are not guaranteed to receive an additional lump-sum profit with an endowment policy; in recent years, many people who took out endowment mortgages have woken up to the fact that the original projections for their eventual profit were over-optimistic. Accordingly, the best advice for most home-buyers is to go for the cheapest mortgage you can – which, in practice, is likely to be a straightforward repayment mortgage.

Mortgages: getting into arrears

The property slump of 1989–90 led to many people getting into arrears with their mortgages. Part of the problem was that mortgage companies made mortgages too easily available. It had never been easier to borrow money. The result was that many people took on commitments that they could only just afford. When interest rates went up, people found they could no longer afford to keep up the mortgage payments. To make matters worse, the property slump meant that many homes were worth less than they had been at the time they were bought. Since many people had received mortgages of 90 per cent or 100 per cent of the cost of the home, it followed that these mortgage-borrowers were in a trap: they could not afford to pay off the mortgage interest, but if they sold their home they would still not have enough money to pay off the mortgage company.

The result has been more mortgage repossessions than ever before. Anyone facing problems paying their mortgage should immediately go to the Citizens' Advice Bureau (or a Moneycentre, if there is one nearby). The golden rule of debt-negotiation is to keep the lender (i.e. mortgage company) informed as to what the position is. Do not simply stop paying and then refuse to answer letters.

But, if all else fails, the mortgage company will take the case to court. The usual sequence of events is:

1 Borrower falls into arrears.
2 Lender (i.e. mortgage company) asks that arrears be paid off.
3 Lender threatens legal proceedings.
4 Lender instructs solicitors. They start county court proceedings and a possession summons is served on the borrower. This states the date for the court hearing.
5 At the court hearing the borrower explains his or her problems to the court. It is advisable to make an offer to pay off the arrears, if only by regular instalments. The court is likely to:
   ● dismiss the lender's application if the borrower can immediately pay off the arrears and show he or she is unlikely to fall into arrears again, *or*
   ● grant a suspended possession order if a sensible and realistic offer of instalment payments is made – if the borrower pays the instalments no further action can be taken; if he or she falls into arrears the lender can ask the bailiff to evict without having to reapply to the court, *or*
   ● grant a possession order if there are no prospects of paying off the arrears.
6 The ultimate step is for the bailiff to evict the borrower. The property is then sold, sometimes by auction, which tends to realize a lower price than a private market sale. All the mortgages are then paid off, legal costs are deducted and the balance (if any) is paid to the borrower.

In general terms, the courts do what they can to avoid making repossession orders. But, if there is no likelihood of the mortgage company being repaid, the court will have no choice but to make the repossession order. In practice, however, courts are often persuaded to delay. Anyone facing repossession proceedings might find it useful to go to a few hearings beforehand, and find out the attitude of the judge; in practice, there are some approaches (excuses) that tend to find more favour than others. In particular, the courts are usually ready to accept that there can be delay on the part of the DSS in processing mortgage-interest payments; the courts also get worried if there are serious arguments about the amount of the outstanding instalments, and they will listen sympathetically if it can be shown that a cheque to clear the arrears (or at least part of them) has been sent off in the post. If all else fails, it is possible to appeal against a possession order.

A home-owner facing substantial mortgage arrears may be tempted to do a moonlight flit: in other words, to abandon the property and post the keys back through the mortgage company's letterbox. Unfortunately, this will not wipe out the debt. The legal obligations created by the mortgage deed are not so easily avoided! Having said that, if the arrears are relatively small then a building society might decide that it is simply not worth the expense of pursuing the borrower through the courts. But, that is not something you can rely upon (also, non-building society lenders tend to adopt a much tougher line). The basic point to note, however, is that posting the keys back through the mortgage company's doors does not legally wipe out the mortgage debt.

Finally, it is worth noting that the DSS can make payments to cover interest due on a mortgage. In practical terms, there will normally be a maximum amount that can be paid.

15 Conveyancing

THE CONVEYANCING TRANSACTION

This chapter is not a comprehensive guide to the buying and selling of houses; several excellent books have been written on the subject, and our limited aim here is to reveal some of the mysteries of the conveyancing machinery, which are so often shrouded in obscure legal phraseology. The following description is intended to strike a balance between the detailed knowledge needed by a DIY conveyancer and the over-simplified impression given by the many newspaper articles on the subject, such as the one which started 'a purchaser's solicitor sends a form to the local council and another form to the vendor's solicitor; then he exchanges contracts'. Regrettably, there is more to it than that!

The step-by-step guide illustrates the sequence of events in buying a freehold house. The procedure when buying a leasehold flat (or even a leasehold house) is the same, except that it will be necessary to examine the lease to see how long it has to run, whether there have been breaches of its terms, how much the rent is, how the repairing covenants are to be enforced etc.

But first, there are certain points to be borne in mind:

1 A *conveyance* is simply a written deed. It can also be called a *transfer*.
2 For historical reasons, lawyers sometimes describe the seller as the *vendor*.
3 There are two systems of conveyancing in England and Wales, depending on whether the land (i.e. house, flat etc.) is *registered* or *unregistered*.

Registration of land was first introduced in the 1860s and, in time, all land will eventually be registered; at the moment nearly 90 per cent of homes are registered. It tends to be the rural areas that are still unregistered.

It is easy to find out whether a property is registered or not; telephone the nearest District Land Registry and ask whether the property is in an area of 'compulsory registration', and if so, when it became a registered area. If the property has been sold since then, it will be registered.

If land is registered, the buyer knows that the seller's title has been checked and that it is virtually guaranteed by the government. If the land is not registered, the checking of title is more laborious for it involves inspecting the 'chain of conveyances' to the present seller, although it is necessary to go back only to the first conveyance that is over fifteen years old. For example, if the land was sold as follows:

1950 Henry to Harry
1975 Harry to Freddy
1982 Freddy to Bertie
1985 Bertie to Basil

then a purchaser from Basil would want to see the conveyances of 1985, 1982 and 1975 (since that would be the first conveyance outside the fifteen-year period). Title would be checked by examining these three documents and seeing that the property was properly described in each, that stamp duty was paid on each transaction and so on. This is called 'deducing title' and it obviously involves much more work (and legal knowledge) than the purchase of a registered property. So, the step-by-step guide (below) deals only with registered properties.

The conveyancing transaction is in two halves:

• The first half is the stage between the seller's acceptance of the buyer's offer and the time when they sign binding contracts (called 'exchange of contracts'). During this period the buyer will be arranging a mortgage and perhaps obtaining a surveyor's report, while the buyer's conveyancer will be checking that there are no planning restrictions, road proposals etc. that could affect the property. In short, during this stage, the nature and character of the property are being examined, and either buyer or seller can back out without giving any reason.

• After exchange of contracts, there is the second half of the transaction when the buyer's conveyancer double-checks the seller's right to sell the property (i.e. by looking at the Land Registry certificate or the chain of conveyances) and prepares the transfer (sale) document. Once these inquiries have been completed the transaction can be completed by the buyer paying the balance of the price and the seller signing the transfer deed. During this second stage neither side can back out and they are bound to proceed with the purchase and sale.

The conveyancing Protocol

For many years, solicitors have been criticized for making the conveyancing process unnecessarily long-winded and complicated. In an effort to meet these complaints, the Law Society introduced in 1990 a standardized conveyancing procedure. Apart from a standard form of contract, the Law Society hoped that all conveyancers would use its standardized procedures, set out in a checklist of steps to be taken. This (called the Protocol) is designed to ensure that conveyancing is as quick as it reasonably can be. For instance, under the Protocol, the seller applies to the local council for the local search. The idea is that the seller's conveyancer will send off the search forms as soon as the property goes on the market so the results of the search can be given to the buyer's conveyancer as soon as a buyer is found. Under the old procedure (which, unfortunately, some solicitors still use) the local search forms were sent off by the buyer – which meant that there would usually be a delay before the forms were posted.

Thus the Protocol was a serious attempt by the Law Society to introduce streamlined procedures for conveyancing. But its use is not compulsory. Not surprisingly, therefore, there are still some solicitors and conveyancers who 'think they know best' and therefore refuse to use the Protocol.

The hope must be that as time goes by more and more conveyancers will use the standard procedure set out in the Protocol. In general terms, both buyers and sellers are well advised to tell their solicitors that they must use the Protocol. Solicitors who use the Protocol usually show a TransAction sign (and logo) on the front of their offices; TransAction is the name that the Law Society uses for the Protocol.

In our step-by-step guide to conveyancing, we assume that the Protocol is being used.

BUYING A HOUSE: A STEP-BY-STEP GUIDE TO THE CONVEYANCING PROCESS

The chart on pages 254–5 shows the sequence of events from the buyer's point of view; the seller's steps follow on from what the buyer does. Refer to the chart when reading this step-by-step summary of the conveyancing procedures:

Step-by-step conveyancing: 1
Buyer chooses property, makes offer 'subject to contract', which is accepted by the seller, and pays a small deposit to the estate agent

'Subject to contract'

Any offer to buy or sell a house should specifically state that it is 'subject to contract': this is a golden rule that must be followed. The contract to buy or sell land (including houses, flats, garages etc.) is unlike a contract to buy or sell anything else in that it must be in writing. By s.2 of the Law of Property (Miscellaneous Provisions) Act 1989, a contract to sell or buy land must be in writing; furthermore, it has to set out all the terms (i.e. name of the property and the price) and it must be signed by both sides. What this means is that there must be one written document signed by both buyer and seller (or buyer and seller must each have signed their own identical copy).

The 1989 Act tightened up the rules on making a contract to buy or sell land. Previously, while a contract had to be in writing it did not have to be signed by both sides. Accordingly, a buyer might write to a seller, agreeing to buy the property for a stated price. In that situation, there was always the danger that the seller would then regard that letter as a binding contract – which meant that the buyer could not back out for any reason (for instance, if no mortgage was

The Conveyancing Transaction

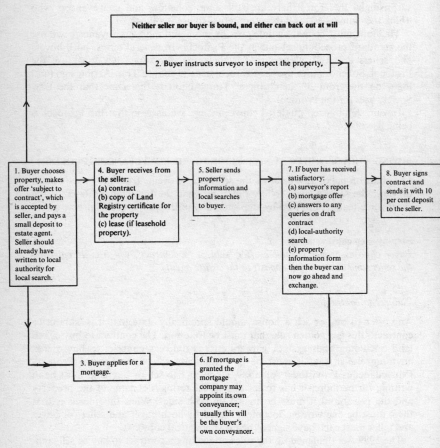

Neither seller nor buyer is bound, and either can back out at will

2. Buyer instructs surveyor to inspect the property.

1. Buyer chooses property, makes offer 'subject to contract', which is accepted by seller, and pays a small deposit to estate agent. Seller should already have written to local authority for local search.

4. **Buyer receives from the seller:**
(a) **contract**
(b) **copy of Land Registry certificate for the property**
(c) **lease (if leasehold property).**

5. Seller sends property information and local searches to buyer.

7. If buyer has received satisfactory:
(a) surveyor's report
(b) mortgage offer
(c) answers to any queries on draft contract
(d) local-authority search
(e) property information form
then the buyer can now go ahead and exchange.

8. Buyer signs contract and sends it with 10 per cent deposit to the seller.

3. Buyer applies for a mortgage.

6. If mortgage is granted the mortgage company may appoint its own conveyancer; usually this will be the buyer's own conveyancer.

Both buyer and seller are bound and neither can back out without the other's consent

9. Buyer's mortgage company insures the property.	

14. Seller sends completion statement to buyer.	

| **10.** Buyer receives signed copy of the contract from the seller. | **11.** Buyer receives permission to inspect the Land Registry certificate for the property. | **12.** Buyer sends queries on title to the seller. | **13.** Buyer prepares draft transfer (i.e. sale deed). | **16.** Completion takes place. | **17.** Buyer can now move in. | **18.** Seller's conveyancer: (a) pays any stamp duty (b) registers buyer as 'registered proprietor' of the land, and the mortgage company as owner of the 'registered charge' (mortgage). |

15. One week or so before completion, buyer writes for certificate to show he is not bankrupt, and inspects the Land Registry certificate by post, to check seller's legal title.

available or if the property failed its survey inspection). Because of these dangers, lawyers and estate agents always advised their clients to write the words 'subject to contract' over any letters or documents concerning land. By adding 'subject to contract', they were ensuring that no contract could be made inadvertently.

However, the 1989 Act now requires that both buyer and seller sign. That being so, it is far more difficult to enter into a contract accidentally or inadvertently. To that extent, there is probably no longer any need to use the words 'subject to contract' when making an offer for a property. But most lawyers and estate agents are cautious – and so they still retain that phrase. However, the general view is that those words are no longer needed.

Only exceptionally will the courts enforce an oral (i.e. spoken) contract for the sale of land, for the general rule is that the contract must be in writing. However, if buyer and seller come to an agreement and one of them unequivocally acts on that agreement (e.g. the buyer pays the purchase price and moves into the property with the seller's consent), the court may uphold the oral contract. But such exceptions are rare.

The important point to remember is that at this subject-to-contract stage of the transaction either buyer or seller can back out. It is only when there is a signed contract that both buyer and seller are bound. Thus if, for example, a buyer finds dry rot in the roof of the house, he or she can refuse to proceed with the transaction.

But once the buyer has exchanged contracts it is too late to back out, and he or she will take the property subject to any dry rot that it contains. Similarly, the seller can change their mind and refuse to sell the property to the buyer until they have signed and handed over a contract; from then on the seller is bound, and cannot back out if, for example, someone else offers a higher price for the house or flat.

The preliminary deposit

The estate agent will probably ask the buyer for a deposit to show the 'seriousness of his intentions'. The payment of a deposit to an estate agent at this stage will not legally commit either the buyer or the seller, and so the paying of such a deposit is no more than an indication of the moral commitment between the parties. Accordingly, there is little reason to pay a deposit at this stage, and if one is required it should be no more than a nominal sum, say £50 or £100. Some agents ask for more (sometimes as much as 5 per cent of the purchase price), but if they do they must give the buyer the interest if it comes to more than £10, and if more than £500 was taken as the deposit (see page 281). Obviously, the buyer should refuse to pay more than a nominal sum and may find it necessary to ask the seller to tell the agents to accept a smaller amount than they want; there is, of course, no loss to the seller in agreeing to this.

If a deposit is paid to an estate agent (or indeed to anyone, including a solicitor) he or she should confirm in writing that they are holding it as 'stakeholder' (i.e. as a neutral agent of the parties), rather than as 'agent for the vendor' (which would be the same as paying it direct to the seller). If the parties should later have a dispute, this makes it less likely that the deposit will be paid to the seller.

If the transaction should fall through before contracts are signed, any preliminary deposit will be returned to the buyer. This is so even if the buyer backs out without any good reason (e.g. simply because of a change of mind).

Step-by-step conveyancing: 2
Buyer instructs surveyor to inspect the property

A buyer takes a house or flat 'as he or she finds it'. The seller gives no guarantee as to the condition of the property unless there are specific claims that turn out to be untrue (e.g. it is said to have cavity-wall insulation, when it does not).

A survey is, therefore, essential; the Royal Institution of Chartered Surveyors and the Society of Valuers and Auctioneers can suggest the names of suitable surveyors. The buyer should not use a surveyor from the firm of estate agents involved in the sale, since that surveyor will not be independent.

Many buyers do not bother to obtain a surveyor's report. This is usually because they begrudge spending money in the expectation of being told that there is nothing wrong with the property. In addition, some people are prepared to rely on the building society's or mortgage company's survey on the basis that 'If the building society are lending their money, it must be all right, mustn't it?' 'Not at all' is the answer, for the building society's survey is a relatively cursory affair that is designed only to check that the building society will recover its money should they ever have to repossess and sell; it will not go into the sort of detail required by most buyers.

As regards 'wasting £150 or more on a report', the buyer should bear in mind that the report may well pay for itself by revealing hidden defects in the property. It may be a remote chance that the house/flat is defective, but property repairs cost so much that few buyers can afford to take the risk. In addition, a well-written survey report can often be used to negotiate a reduction in the price.

However, a survey will rarely be 100 per cent comprehensive, since a complete survey would require removal of ceilings, lifting of floorboards etc., all of which are unlikely to be agreed to by the seller.

Illustration. *Mr and Mrs Gill bought a flat. On the advice of their solicitor they had it surveyed, and the survey report was satisfactory, revealing no major defects. Within a month of buying the flat, the roof of the kitchen extension had fallen in and they were faced with a bill for £600. Their first reaction was to blame the surveyor for not noticing the fault, but closer examination revealed that the fault in the roof-beams could have been discovered only by removing the kitchen ceiling. This was clearly impracticable and so the surveyor had not been at fault.*

With flats, there is the additional problem that a proper survey really requires a full examination of the other flats in the block, since a failure to repair one flat may have disastrous consequences for everyone else in the block. Also, most flat-owners pay a percentage service charge towards the cost of maintaining the whole block of flats, and so they have to pay just as much towards the cost of a structural repair to one part of the building as they do for another part of the building (e.g. the owner of a ground-floor flat usually pays a proportion of the costs of repairing the roof, even though their flat is not directly underneath the roof). So to discover the likely level of the service charge, a surveyor would have to survey the whole block of flats! Usually, it is impracticable to inspect the other flats and so the survey can only be of limited value.

A normal structural survey does not include electrical or gas services, drains or woodworm etc., although these can be inspected at further cost. The buyer should be sure to ask the surveyor exactly what is included in the survey fee.

Most surveyors charge between £125 and £175 for a full written report. However, if the surveyor is also carrying out a survey for a building society or mortgage company, then a lower survey fee will normally to charged to the buyer. If the same surveyor is to be used, it is essential that the building society is informed as soon as the mortgage application is submitted; otherwise the surveyor may have made an inspection for the society without realizing that a private survey report for the purchaser also has to be prepared.

When reading a surveyor's report, the buyer should look for any wording that is open to a double interpretation and try to pin the surveyor down to a definite opinion. If the report finds fault with the property, it is usually advisable to show it to the seller and argue that the price should be reduced. In this way, a survey report can often pay for itself.

The NHBC Buildmark guarantee

The buyer may decide to dispense with a survey because the estate agent tells him that the property has a ten-year National House Building Council (NHBC) Buildmark guarantee. But a buyer should not take such a 'guarantee' as being all-embracing, for it is of limited value except during the two years following its issue, when nearly all defects have to be put right by the builder (but even then not all defects are covered – normal wear and tear, and normal shrinkage, are excluded, as are fences and lifts. Central-heating boilers and any other electrical moving parts are covered only for one year). For the next eight years (i.e. until ten years after construction), the guarantee covers only major structural defects, and not hidden defects such as faulty wiring or poorly connected plumbing. For the guarantee to take effect, the defect must be 'severe' and it must be a structural defect that has caused major damage (e.g. collapse or serious distortion of joists or roof structure; dry rot; failure of a damp-proof course). Subsidence, heave and settlement will be covered only if not covered by the householder's own insurance policy. Minor structural defects, and non-structural problems, are excluded (e.g. leaking gutters, twisted doors, cracked fittings). In short, the NHBC guarantee is not much of a guarantee and, in practice, many people mistakenly think it offers more protection than it actually does. At the end of the ten-year period, the guarantee expires and is of no value at all.

A further weakness is that the maximum cover given by Buildmark is the original price of the house (i.e. the price paid by the first purchaser) up to a maximum price of about £500,000. The cover is index-linked throughout the ten years.

The NHBC Buildmark scheme is therefore of limited value. However, the guarantee does show that a certain level of workmanship was used during the construction of the building and it does provide some protection against major defects. Clearly, though, the mere presence of an NHBC Buildmark guarantee should not necessarily mean that there is no need to have the property surveyed.

Other guarantees

If the property has been treated for woodworm, dry rot or wet rot during, say, the last twenty-one years, there may be a guarantee that goes with the house or flat. The buyer should check the wording of such a guarantee very carefully to see exactly what is promised. The guarantee should specifically state that it benefits future owners of the property and not just the person who originally had the work done. Also the guarantee will usually be worthless without the original survey report and the original estimate, since the guarantee will often state: 'A claim can be entertained only on production of the survey report and estimate.' More often than not, either or both of these documents have been lost. In addition, there is always the risk that the company which issued the guarantee has since gone out of business, in which case the guarantee will be worthless.

Step-by-step conveyancing: 3
Buyer applies for a mortgage

Most people need a mortgage to help finance their purchase of a home. People who have difficulty in obtaining mortgages often use the services of so-called 'mortgage brokers', who advertise that they can 'procure advances'. Unfortunately, many of these firms charge excessive fees (e.g. 1 per cent of the mortgage sum) and should be avoided. Even if no mortgage can be arranged, some of these firms still try to charge for their services, although the Consumer Credit Act does state that if no mortgage is arranged within six months, the customer cannot be liable for a fee of more than £3. Mortgage brokers should not be confused with 'insurance brokers', who receive their fees from insurance companies in the form of commission.

Solicitors and estate agents often have agencies with building societies or mortgage companies, and may be able to help the buyer obtain a mortgage.

The buyer will have to pay a valuation fee to the mortgage company. This covers the fee of a surveyor who will inspect the property for the mortgage company, check its condition and also value it. This fee will have to be paid even if the mortgage company refuses to grant a mortgage and even if the purchase falls through.

The valuation fee will depend upon the price of the property (not the amount of the mortgage). For a property worth £50,000, it would probably be in the region of £75 or so (but the figures do vary from one mortgage company to another). In addition, many mortgage companies will give the buyer the option of having a more detailed survey carried out at the same time – typically, for an extra £75 or so.

Building society (and mortgage company) surveys are relatively cursory. The surveyor is likely to spend considerably less time examining the property than if carrying out a full private survey and the buyer should not rely on the building society's survey as being conclusive proof that the property is in good condition. It is therefore best to arrange a private survey, in addition to the building society survey. However, in practice, only about 10 to 15 per cent of buyers do this.

The building society (or mortgage company) surveyor surveys the property for the building society, not the buyer – although the buyer pays for it. It used to be thought that if the building society (or mortgage company) surveyor carried out the survey negligently, the buyer would not be able to sue the surveyor. But, that all changed in 1981, with this case:

The Halifax was going to lend money so that Mr and Mrs Yianni could buy a house. The Halifax asked a local firm of surveyors to survey the house – for the Halifax, not for the Yiannis. The surveyors were negligent and failed to spot major defects: within nine months there were subsidence cracks, and one wall was eventually rebuilt, and others underpinned. The Yiannis sued the surveyors, who argued that the survey had been for the Halifax, not the Yiannis and, anyway, the Halifax mortgage application form had a printed recommendation that anyone applying for a mortgage should get their own independent survey. Held: The surveyors were liable to the Yiannis. The surveyors knew that their valuation would be passed on to the Yiannis, and that they would rely on it. Yianni (1981)

In response to this decision, most building societies and mortgage companies started printing disclaimers on survey reports. In other words, it was specifically said that the mortgage was being obtained for the mortgage company and therefore the borrower could not rely on that survey. But the courts have since held that such a disclaimer does not stop a surveyor being liable.

A survey was carried out for a mortgage company. The survey had the words 'confidential' and 'solely for the benefit of the mortgage company' written on it. When defects appeared in the building, the buyers sued the surveyors. In response, the surveyors argued that their responsibility was only to the mortgage company – not to the buyers. In any event, they argued that the written disclaimer made it clear that the buyers could not rely upon the mortgage survey report. The House of Lords held that this was wrong. In straightforward house and flat purchases, it is reasonable to assume that the buyer will rely upon the mortgage survey/valuation, and it is not reasonable to exclude the surveyor's liability. Smith (1989)

One point to note is that if a mortgage survey/valuation is negligent, then the buyer sues the surveyor, not the mortgage company (or building society). The only exception to this will be if the surveyor was an in-house surveyor for the mortgage company (or building society).

Step-by-step conveyancing: 4
The buyer's conveyancer receives title documents from the seller's conveyancer

These documents are:
- the draft contract;
- a copy of the Land Registry certificate for the property;
- a copy of the lease (if the property is leasehold).

The draft contract

This is the contract that the seller wants the buyer to sign on exchange of contracts. It sets out the terms of the transaction and what is being sold. Most solicitors use a standard pre-printed contract (called the Standard Conditions, published by the Law Society). The small print of this contract runs to many thousands of words, but in most cases there is no need to refer to that small print. The standard provisions work well enough.

The contract is called a *draft* contract at this stage because the purchaser's solicitor may wish to amend it slightly, although usually there are few changes that need to be made.

A copy of the Land Registry certificate

This is the title deed. See specimen in Appendix 2. The buyer's conveyancer will want to check the plan on the certificate to see that it tallies with what the buyer thinks he or she is buying. In addition, the conveyancer will look for restrictive covenants (see page 363) which might affect the land.

If the property is unregistered, there will be no Land Registry certificate. Instead, the buyer's conveyancer will usually be sent a plan (probably taken from an old conveyance), and a copy of any restrictive covenants mentioned in the deeds.

A copy of the lease

If the property is leasehold, then the buyer's conveyancer will want to see a copy of the lease. This will set out the detailed obligations between the landlord and the tenant (because the buyer will become the tenant).

Leases are long and complex documents. From a landlord's point of view, it is important that the lease contains obligations on the tenant: for instance, to pay the rent; pay the service charge; pay any insurance premium; not make undue noise; only use the flat as a private home; not display placards in the windows; not keep bikes or prams in communal corridors; and so on. From a tenant's point of view, it is important to check that the lease makes it clear who is responsible for maintaining and repairing all parts of the building; who paints the exterior; who maintains the common parts; who insures the building; who administers the service charge fund; and so on.

Step-by-step conveyancing: 5
Buyer's conveyancer receives property information from the seller's conveyancer

The buyer's conveyancer should have already obtained:
- a local search (from the local council);
- a completed Property Information Form from the seller.

The local search

There will be numerous points to be checked with the local authority. For example, is there a possibility of road development? Was planning permission granted when the property was built? Are there compulsory-purchase proposals? Are there any tree-preservation orders? Is the property connected to the mains sewer? Is the road a public highway? Have any public-health orders been made? Is it a slum-clearance area, a development area, a conservation area, a clean-air zone etc.?

Fortunately, all these questions are printed on a standard form that is sent to the local authority. The preferred procedure is for the seller's conveyancer to send the forms off to the local council – before the seller actually finds a buyer. In other words, the seller's conveyancer sends off the forms at an early date, so that any delay in the forms' being processed by the council will not cause undue delay to the conveyancing transaction. Indeed, under the the Protocol (the Law Society's recommended standardized conveyancing procedure) it is always the seller's solicitor who sends off the forms to the local authority. However, it does have to be said that many solicitors have been reluctant to adopt this part of the Protocol. Largely because of the costs involved, they prefer to wait for the buyer's conveyancer to send off the local search forms to a council. But that is often a short-sighted approach since it will generally result in delay.

The cost of the local search will vary from council to council (generally, it is in the range of £35–£75). Also, some councils deal with search forms more speedily than others; generally, a delay of two to three weeks is typical. In the property boom of the late 1980s, search fees were cheaper, but the service from local councils was much worse and there were many instances of local search forms not being returned for six or eight weeks. Now the fees are more but the service is better.

A deposit of 10 per cent is payable when contracts are signed and exchanged

There are 13 Land Registries, each with its own area of the country

Every registered property has its own individual title number

Note the unnecessarily wordy description: the postal address alone would suffice

This means the seller owns the property himself. He or she could be selling as a personal representative or as part-owner, for example

CONTRACT OF SALE
The National Conditions of Sale, Twentieth Edition

Vendor   John David Evans of 200 Morrison Lane, Maida Vale, W.9, in the County of Greater London

Purchaser   Michael Peter Jones and Mary Ann Jones (his wife) both of 12 Springsteen Grove, Lower Norwood, in the County of Greater London

Registered Land		
District Land Registry: Harrow	Purchase price	£ 60,500 —
Title Number: NGL1234567	Deposit	£ 6,050 —
Agreed rate of interest:	Balance payable	£ 66,550 —
	Price fixed for chattels or valuation money (if any)	£ 250 —
	Total	£ 66,800 —

Property and interest therein sold

ALL THAT freehold land situate at and known as No. 96 Clifton Road, Maida Vale, W9, in the County of Greater London as the same is registered at H as Land Registry with Title Absolute.

Vendor sells as   beneficial owner   Completion date: 18th October 1986

AGREED that the Vendor sells and the Purchaser buys as above, subject to the Special Conditions endorsed hereon and to the National Conditions of Sale Twentieth Edition so far as the latter Conditions are not inconsistent with the Special Conditions.

Signed   J. D. Evans

Date   20th September   1986

© 1981
oyez
THE SOLICITORS' LAW STATIONERY SOCIETY, plc
Oyez House, 237 Long Lane, London SE1 4PU
Form Con 14—without special conditions

This form is copyright. It can be purchased only by solicitors

Completion will usually be arranged for 4 weeks after the date of exchanging contracts

This is the rate of interest that the buyer will have to pay to the seller if he or she delays completion (see 274)

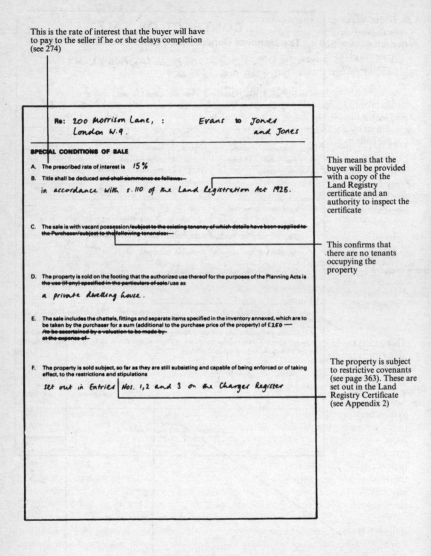

Re: 200 Morrison Lane, :   Evans to Jones
London W.9.   and Jones

SPECIAL CONDITIONS OF SALE

A. The prescribed rate of interest is 15%

B. Title shall be deduced ~~and shall commence as follows:~~

   in accordance with s.110 of the Land Registration Act 1925.

This means that the buyer will be provided with a copy of the Land Registry certificate and an authority to inspect the certificate

C. The sale is with vacant possession ~~/subject to the existing tenancy of which details have been supplied to the Purchaser/subject to the following tenancies:~~

This confirms that there are no tenants occupying the property

D. The property is sold on the footing that the authorized use thereof for the purposes of the Planning Acts is ~~the use (if any) specified in the particulars of sale/~~ use as

   a private dwelling house.

E. The sale includes the chattels, fittings and separate items specified in the inventory annexed, which are to be taken by the purchaser for a sum (additional to the purchase price of the property) of £250 ~~/to be ascertained by a valuation to be made by at the expense of~~

F. The property is sold subject, so far as they are still subsisting and capable of being enforced or of taking effect, to the restrictions and stipulations

   set out in Entries Nos. 1,2 and 3 on the Charges Register

The property is subject to restrictive covenants (see page 363). These are set out in the Land Registry Certificate (see Appendix 2)

If the buyer exchanges contracts (i.e. goes ahead and buys the property), then it is the buyer who will be expected to pay the local search fees. Thus, even if the seller sent off the search forms to the council (which is the recommended procedure), the buyer will normally be expected to reimburse the cost of the search fees when exchanging contracts.

Local search insurance. Generally local searches are reckoned to have a lifespan of three months. But delays in the conveyancing process (e.g. waiting for someone else in the chain to be ready to exchange) can mean that a search is out of date by the time everyone is ready to exchange contracts. When this happens, one solution is to take out insurance to cover the risk of the search now being out of date. The Law Society runs a search validation scheme for solicitors which gives insurance on any loss in value of the property as at the date contracts are exchanged. Thus, if an up-to-date search would now show an entry which would reduce the value of the property, then the insurance will make up that loss. The scheme covers domestic properties (worth up to £500,000), if the search is not more than six months old.

Incidentally, it is worth noting that a cash buyer can avoid any delay in obtaining a search by going in person to the council offices and taking the standard search form from department to department. But a 'personal search' of this sort would not be guaranteed as accurate by the council. Because of this, a personal search will not be acceptable to a building society or mortgage company, which will insist on a formal written search.

Property Information Form

The buyer will want the seller to provide answers to a standard Property Information Questionnaire.

Under the Protocol (i.e. the Law Society's recommended conveyancing procedures) the seller's conveyancer will have sent the seller a standard form. This asks the seller for detailed information about the property. For instance: Who owns the boundaries, and who has accepted responsibility for maintaining them? Have boundaries been altered in the last twenty years? What disputes are there with neighbours? Have any formal notices been received? Are there any guarantees with the property? Are any mains services shared with neighbouring properties? Who else has any claims over the property? Who lives there? Are there any planning problems? Is the seller's sale dependent on a related purchase? This is the sort of detailed information that any buyer (or conveyancer) will want to know.

When the seller's conveyancer receives this completed form back from the seller, it is the job of the conveyancer then to send the Property Information Form to the buyer's conveyancer. This is an important document, because the seller will normally be bound by the replies given in it. Obviously, if the seller (or the seller's conveyancer) is not sure of how to answer a particular question then that will be made clear. Otherwise, however, the buyer can generally rely upon the answers as being accurate.

Fixtures and fittings. Part of the Property Information Questionnaire completed by the seller deals with fixtures, fittings and contents. This part of the form sets out in some detail a list of items about which there might be any dispute when buying or selling a residential property. The idea is that the seller should complete the form and send it to the buyer, so both sides can check that they are in agreement as to what is or is not included in the price.

Usually, it is quite straightforward. However, if no specific arrangements are made then the buyer will be entitled to claim the 'fixtures and fittings' that are permanently attached to the property. This seemingly straightforward test can often be difficult to apply in practice, and the best way to avoid problems is for the parties to make a list of what is included in the price. The value of the curtains, furniture etc. can be taken off when working out the sale price for stamp-duty purposes. (See page 280.)

It will be seen from the table opposite that several items fall into the 'doubtful' category and it is arguable whether or not they are removable. Generally, the answer will depend upon the extent of the damage that would be caused by their removal. For instance, fitted shelves might be held to be removable if the damage caused by taking them was easily made good – for instance, by filling in the holes and repapering – although it would be the responsibility of the seller to do this work.

A person who buys a property and moves in to find that the seller has taken fixtures and fittings should immediately report the matter to his conveyancer. The conveyancer will complain to the seller's conveyancer and demand that the items be replaced, or alternatively that the purchaser be compensated for the loss of value; obviously, this will include the cost of making good any damage caused in removal of the unauthorized items. If the seller refuses to compensate the buyer, then the buyer should consider starting county court proceedings. If the items are within the 'not removable' category, then the purchaser would have excellent prospects of success.

Step-by-step conveyancing: 6
The buyer's mortgage company may appoint its own conveyancer

Usually, the mortgage company or building society will appoint the buyer's conveyancer to look after its interests in the transaction. Sometimes, however, if the buyer's conveyancer is not on its list of approved conveyancers, it will ask another firm of conveyancers to act for it. Also, some of the smaller building societies prefer – as a matter of policy – to appoint independent solicitors, rather than rely on the buyer's own conveyancer.

This is an important point for the buyer, since the mortgage company will expect him or her to pay its legal fees. Thus a buyer who has a mortgage will have to pay his or her own legal fees, plus either:

• an additional fee charged by his conveyancer for acting for the mortgage company, *or*

• a separate fee to another firm of solicitors/conveyancers.

Fixtures and fittings

Removable	Not removable	Doubtful
cooker (unless built-in)	wiring	curtain rails
fridge	plumbing	fitted shelves
washing machine	bathroom suite	greenhouse without
dishwasher	central heating	foundation
hanging light fittings	built-in cupboards	wall lights
(but not the bulb	purpose-built cupboards	fitted decorative wall
holders or sockets)	garden shrubs and plants	mirrors
gas fires (unless built in)	greenhouse on foundations	TV aerial
carpets, lino, curtains	towel rail	
garden furniture	wall-mounted bathroom	
fitted wardrobe designed	heater	
to be removable	coal bunker	
	toilet-roll holder	

If a separate firm is used by the mortgage company, the buyer's own conveyancer will expect his/her client to pay for the extra work arising from the correspondence etc. with the other firm. It is therefore cheaper if a buyer's own conveyancer also acts for the mortgage company or building society.

Step-by-step conveyancing: 7
If the buyer's conveyancer has received satisfactory replies

The buyer will be ready to go ahead once the conveyancer has received satisfactory:
- surveyor's report (see step 2);
- mortgage offer (see step 3);
- answers to any queries on the draft contract (see step 4);
- local-authority search (see step 5);
- replies to property inquiries (see step 5).

Generally, this stage will not have been reached for at least a month after the buyer had his offer for the property accepted. Replies to local authority searches and mortgage applications generally take a month or so to process, and until both have been received the buyer dare not enter into a binding commitment by exchanging contracts.

Step-by-step conveyancing: 8
The buyer signs the contract and sends it with a 10 per cent deposit to the seller's conveyancer

This is the last opportunity for the buyer and seller to back out. Exchange of contracts will take place when the seller has received the buyer's signed contract (plus the deposit cheque), and when the seller's contract has, in turn, been posted to the buyer.

Usually, a 10 per cent deposit is paid (less any preliminary deposit that may have been paid to the estate agents). The buyer will have to raise this money, either from savings or by borrowing it from a bank (a 'bridging loan'). The buyer cannot use any of the mortgage loan since this will not be available until the purchase is finally completed – probably one month later. To avoid the expense and inconvenience of borrowing the full 10 per cent deposit the buyer could try asking whether the seller would accept less (e.g. 5 per cent).

The idea of a deposit is to provide the seller with some security, in case the buyer backs out at the last minute; if that happens, the seller may be able to forfeit the deposit (in practice, this virtually never happens since a buyer will nearly always make some arrangement to avoid losing his/her deposit). In many ways, the idea of paying a deposit is old-fashioned. A much simpler (and cheaper) way of giving the seller some security against the buyer backing out would be to replace deposits with guarantees. Such a guarantee would be provided by the buyer's bank or building society, which would promise to pay up if the buyer defaulted. In fact, Deposit Guarantee Schemes do just this; however, in practice they are used relatively rarely.

One of the changes introduced by the Law Society's Protocol was that a seller would be able to use the buyer's deposit as the deposit on the seller's own purchase. For instance, if a seller is selling for £75,000 and buying for £100,000, then the seller can expect to receive a deposit of £7,500 from the buyer on that sale. On the other hand, on the seller's own purchase, a deposit of £10,000 will be needed. Under the Protocol the seller can use the £7,500 provided by the buyer towards the deposit on that related purchase (i.e. the seller would therefore only have to find an additional £2,500 to make up the full 10 per cent).

Under the Protocol the standard rule is that the seller can use the buyer's deposit on a related purchase. If the seller does not have a related purchase, then there will be no need for the deposit money to be used and accordingly it will be held on to by the seller's conveyancer (or solicitor). Thus the buyer pays the money to the seller's conveyancer, who retains it until the transaction is completed. At that stage the deposit money is paid over – as part of the price – to the seller. Any interest on that deposit money is paid by the seller's conveyancer to the buyer.

In practice, it is often possible to negotiate a deposit of less than 10 per cent. After all, the purpose of the deposit is to provide the seller with security; in most residential transactions a deposit of 5 per cent will be more than sufficient security to cover any losses that the seller might suffer if the buyer was to withdraw and refuse to complete.

The completion date

'Completion' is when the deal is completed – the buyer pays the rest of the money and is then allowed to move in. Normally, this will be four weeks after the day on which the contracts were exchanged. But, this four-week rule is no more than a convenience – if both buyer and seller want it to be more (or less), then that can be agreed. In practical terms, however, a gap of ten days between exchange and completion is likely to be the shortest that can be agreed by the conveyancers, since it usually takes that long to do the searches and to obtain the money from the mortgage company. Also, if there is a chain of transactions, then it is often difficult to get everyone to agree on a specific date, in which case the usual four-week period is adopted. What is important, however, is that everyone should agree on the planned completion date before they exchange contracts.

Moving in before completion

If the house is empty, the buyer might wonder whether it is possible to move in before completion. Generally, the answer will be 'no' – the seller's conveyancer will be worried about the practical difficulties of evicting the buyer should he or she default and refuse to pay up on the completion date! However, the seller may agree to allow the buyer access to measure up, and even have building works done. Normally this can be agreed – but there is no obligation on the seller to agree and it will normally be on the strict understanding that the buyer is not to take advantage of the seller's generosity and move in to the property. It follows that if a buyer wants access to an empty property between exchange and completion, then the buyer's conveyancer should be told before exchange of contracts that this must be a term of the contract.

Step-by-step conveyancing: 9
The buyer's mortgage company insures the property

The buyer has signed a contract to buy the property. From now on he or she is, in theory, the legal owner of the property and the seller holds it for them as a trustee, looking after it until the purchase price is paid. This will usually be some four weeks later, and only then can the buyer move in.

If the property is destroyed or damaged between now and completion it will be the buyer's loss. Accordingly, he or she must insure it straight away, preferably on a 'comprehensive' basis. In fact, this will automatically be done by the building society and so the buyer will not have to do anything about it. But the seller must look after the property until completion takes place. If they do not, they will be liable to the buyer.

Mr Lucie-Smith contracted to buy Mr Gorman's house. Contracts were exchanged with completion to be on 31 January. Gorman moved out on 24 January without notifying Lucie-Smith. Completion was delayed because of a delay on the part of Gorman. Unfortunately the house was flooded early in February when a frozen pipe burst: it turned out that

Gorman had not turned the water off when he had left on 24 January. Lucie-Smith claimed damages for the cost of repairing the damage. Held: Gorman was liable. He should have turned off the water supply. Lucie-Smith (1981)

The seller will probably keep his or her own insurance on during this period rather than risk relying on the buyer's insurance. Generally, the result is that a property will be insured twice: by the seller and by the buyer. While this may seem a waste of money, it is one of those situations in which the risks of failing to insure are so great that both sides' conveyancers will want to ensure that there is no risk of their clients' being uninsured. The Protocol does recommend that the seller remains liable to insure the property until completion, which therefore means that there is no need for the buyer to insure. In practice, buyers' conveyancers are reluctant to rely upon this (and sellers have been reluctant to be legally obliged to insure). The end result, therefore, is that both sides end up with their own insurance!

Step-by-step conveyancing: 10
The buyer's conveyancer receives a signed copy of the contract from the seller's conveyancer

When both the buyer and the seller have signed contracts, their conveyancers can 'exchange contracts'. This means that they swap signed contracts, and both buyer and seller are then fully committed and cannot back out of the transaction.

In the old days, the buyer's conveyancer would go to the offices of the seller's conveyancer and there would be a formal exchange – in person – of the contracts. Nowadays, this rarely happens. Instead, the two conveyancers will speak on the phone and they will exchange contracts on the phone (i.e. they will confirm to each other that they hold contracts signed by their clients; they will then agree to exchange contracts immediately, with both contracts being put in the post, and the seller being sent the buyer's deposit).

If there is a chain of transactions, then the conveyancers throughout the chain will have to speak on the phone so they can synchronize exchange (to ensure that contracts are exchanged in all the transactions – in other words, the related purchases and sales). Often, of course, a deposit on one transaction will be passed up the chain to be used as the deposit on another transaction, and so on through the chain.

The important point to appreciate is that once contracts have been formally exchanged, then both buyer and seller are bound to proceed with the transaction. Both will have a copy of the contract signed by the other.

Step-by-step conveyancing: 11
The buyer's conveyancer receives permission to inspect the Land Registry register

The seller's conveyancer will now give permission for the buyer's conveyancer to contact the Land Registry and check the seller's legal title to the property (i.e. whether the seller is really the owner, and whether any claims have been registered against the title). In fact, the buyer's conveyancer will do more than simply look at the Land Register although simply to look at a Land Register it is not necessary to have the permission of the landowner. Anyone can search the Land Register to find out who owns a particular piece of land. (For the procedure, phone a District Land Registry.)

Apart from looking at the Land Register, the buyer's conveyancer will want to tell the Registry that the buyer will soon be purchasing the property. Obviously, one of the concerns of the buyer will be that no fresh entry (e.g. a mortgage) is registered against the property between the time that his conveyancer looks at the Land Register and the time when the buyer is actually registered as the owner. To overcome this problem, the buyer's conveyancer carries out an Official Search of the Land Registry. Not only does this tell the conveyancer what is registered in respect of that property, but it also gives several weeks in which the buyer can be registered as the owner without being affected by any late entries on the register. So, by carrying out an Official Search, the buyer gets priority over anyone else who has a claim on the property.

Step-by-step conveyancing: 12
The buyer's conveyancer sends queries on title to the seller's conveyancer

The seller is now asked to answer any queries as to the legal title to the property. The buyer's conveyancer will use a pre-printed form that contains most of the usual points arising (e.g. asking when the seller's mortgage will be paid off). These queries are called 'requisitions'. The seller's conveyancer will answer them by filling in the blanks on the form sent by the buyer's conveyancer.

Step-by-step conveyancing: 13
Buyer's conveyancer prepares draft transfer (i.e. the sale deed)

Whereas it was the seller's conveyancer who prepared the draft contract, it is the buyer's conveyancer who prepares the draft transfer (called a 'conveyance' if the land is unregistered). The seller's solicitor may ask for changes to be made, although this rarely happens. There is a specimen form printed in Appendix 2.

Step-by-step conveyancing: 14
The seller's conveyancer sends a completion statement to the buyer's conveyancer

The completion statement sets out how much money has to be paid on completion. Generally, this will be the balance of the purchase moneys (i.e. the purchase price less any deposit already paid) plus a sum to allow for any water rates (and, if leasehold, any service charge, rent or insurance) paid in advance –

or owed – by the seller. These sums will be apportioned so that the seller pays for the period up to completion and the buyer pays for the period from completion.

Water rates are personal debts. This means that they are debts of the individual occupier of a property and do not attach to the property itself. Thus, if the seller fails to pay water rates, the buyer is not liable to the water board for the arrears. The buyer is liable only as from the date of buying the property.

Service charges, rent and insurance on a leasehold property are debts that go with the property. Thus the buyer is liable for any arrears. This means that the buyer will be liable for the seller's unpaid bills – so the buyer's conveyancer will want to check that all bills have been paid up to date. With service charges on flats this can be a problem; often, service charges are invoiced on an annual basis at the end of the year and so neither buyer nor seller will know just how much the eventual bill will be. Either money will have to be kept back (which is highly inconvenient) or buyer and seller will just have to make the best guess that they can.

Step-by-step conveyancing: 15
Buyer's conveyancer checks that the buyer is not bankrupt and that the seller has a proper title

The buyer's conveyancer will need to prove to the mortgage company that the buyer is not bankrupt before they will agree to part with the mortgage money. Thus one week or so before completion the conveyancer obtains a certificate confirming this from the Land Charges Department (Burrington Way, Plymouth), where a register of bankruptcies is kept. The buyer's conveyancer will also check the seller's legal title to the property by posting a search form to the Land Registry. This will show whether there have been any recent changes, or if there are any problems. It will also notify the Land Registry that the buyer is planning to purchase the property (this is an Official Search – see step 11).

Step-by-step conveyancing: 16
Completion takes place

Completion is when the transaction is finalized. In return for the money, the buyer receives the title deeds (and the keys!). Until a few years ago this used to be done by the two sets of solicitors meeting in the office of the seller's solicitor and physically handing over bank drafts, deeds, keys etc. Now, the vast majority of completions take place by post – the buyer's conveyancer simply tells the bank to transfer the money immediately into the bank account of the seller's conveyancer. In return, the seller's conveyancer will phone and promise to put the deeds and other documents in the post. The handing over of the keys will probably be sorted out by the buyer and seller themselves, or by the estate agents. There should be no need for the buyer (or the seller) to have to go to the conveyancer's office since all the signing of paperwork, and paying over of money, should have been sorted out in advance.

Finally, note that completion is usually four weeks from the day when contracts are exchanged. But this four-week period is no more than a traditional convention. Completion must take place on a weekday (i.e. when the parties' conveyancers are open for business) – not on a weekend.

Step-by-step conveyancing: 17
The buyer can now move in

Step-by-step conveyancing: 18
The conveyancers finalize the transaction

To complete the paperwork:
• The seller's mortgage will be paid off. The seller's conveyancer will do this with the money received from the buyer, and afterwards send a formal receipt to the buyer's conveyancer.
• The buyer's solicitor will send the purchase deed to the Inland Revenue, and pay any stamp duty (see page 280).
• Finally, the buyer's conveyancer will send the papers (i.e. the purchase deed, the title certificate, the mortgage deed, the receipt for the seller's paid-off mortgage) to the Land Registry. When the Land Registry fee is paid, the seller will be registered as the owner.

After registration the title deeds are kept by the mortgage company – they do not go to the buyer.

What happens if there is delay in completing?

Sometimes either the buyer or the seller is not ready to complete on the agreed date, which is usually four weeks after the exchange of contracts. For example, the seller may be buying another house and be unable to complete because the seller in that transaction has not yet moved out. When this happens the person causing the delay is liable in damages to all the people affected by his default. For instance:

In a chain of transactions A agreed to sell his house to B, and B agreed to sell his house to C. Contracts were exchanged between A and B, and B and C, with both transactions due to be completed on 12 July. On 11 July, A told B that he would have to delay the completion because A was having difficulty in moving. B immediately told C that they would be unable to complete on the 12th. Unfortunately, C had already sold his house and his furniture was on route in a van to B's house, ready for the expected completion on the 12th. Because completion was cancelled, C was forced to move into temporary accommodation and store his furniture. It was not until 11 August that the two transactions were completed. C then sued B for the extra expense he had incurred; B in turn sued A, arguing that A should indemnify B for the damages due to C. Held: B was liable to C, and A was liable to B. In effect, therefore, A had to pay C's expenses. Raineri (1980)

Thus a person who delays completion may have to compensate other people in the chain as a result of the delay. In practice, it is relatively rare for damages to have to be paid. This is because a compromise deal is usually worked out at the last minute.

If the buyer is delaying completion

If the seller is willing and able to complete, the buyer must pay interest on the money due (i.e. on the purchase price minus the 10 per cent deposit). The rate of interest will be set out in the contract.

Also, the seller can serve a 'notice to complete' on the buyer. This means that unless the buyer completes within (usually) two weeks the seller will be able to forfeit the 10 per cent deposit and sue the buyer for any other losses incurred. The deposit can be forfeited even if the seller resells the property for a profit. A striking illustration of how this can work was provided by a case in which a property company agreed to sell a site for £2,350,000; the buyer paid £235,000 deposit but then refused to complete. The seller then took the deposit and sold the property to another buyer for £2,500,000. Thus, as a result of the original purchaser defaulting, the seller had made an extra £385,000 (the deposit plus the increase in the selling price).

If the seller delays completion

The buyer is in a less strong position since he or she may not be able to demand interest. However, he or she can serve a 'notice to complete' and if the seller does not complete within twenty-eight days the buyer can:

- cancel the contract and have his/her deposit returned, *or*
- sue for breach of contract and obtain damages for any losses, *or*
- go to court for an order that the seller be forced to complete.

However, in practice, the buyer is in a weaker position than the seller, since he or she cannot charge the seller interest if there is delay in completing. While the Law Society (Standard Conditions) contract does envisage that a buyer might be able to claim interest from a seller if completion is delayed, in practice this happens rarely. All too often, the seller's solicitor will have altered the contract – before exchange – to make it clear that the seller cannot be liable for any delay on completion. If this has been done, then the buyer's only remedy is to sue for damages; in practice, this happens only rarely (when the losses involved justify the cost and inconvenience of suing).

Why does conveyancing take so long?

Most conveyancing transactions take about three months from start to finish. Why is this? There are three main reasons:

1 The buyer cannot go ahead without a clear local search. Many authorities, especially the London boroughs, take a month or so to reply.

2 The buyer cannot go ahead without a definite mortgage offer. This will rarely take less than three weeks, will often take four weeks and can exceptionally take longer. During this time the mortgage company (or building society) will check the applicant's income and survey the property.

3 Each transaction will probably be dependent on one or more other transactions. For instance, if A is buying from B, and B is buying from C, and C is buying from D, then A cannot proceed until B, C, and D are all ready to go ahead. They will all want to exchange contracts simultaneously so that no one will be committed to buying without having their sale finalized, and vice versa. So a chain of conveyances can build up, with everyone being held up by one person in the chain.

The only feasible way of reducing the delay would seem to be for local authorities to provide a return-of-post service for local searches (presumably at an increased fee) and for building societies to speed up their process for offering mortgages. This saving of time would then reduce the likelihood of delay in the chain. Conveyancers could also improve the efficiency of the operation by the seller's conveyancer following the Law Society's Protocol and sending off for local searches before a buyer is found. Also the usual twenty-eight-day period between exchange of contracts and completion could be reduced to, say, fourteen days; this can be done now, although generally people do in fact want a month in which to finalize removal arrangements etc. Increased computerization might also help. It goes without saying that the whole process would be quicker and cheaper if all the searches could be done by computer links, and if conveyancers had compatible software systems. These changes are on the way.

The expenses of buying and selling property

As a result of a typical conveyancing transaction, the following bills will have to be paid:

Seller pays

- the conveyancer's fee;
- the estate agent's fee.

Buyer pays

- the conveyancer's fee for acting on the purchase;
- the legal fees for the mortgage work. This will depend upon whether the buyer's conveyancer also acted for the mortgage company. The buyer will pay *either*:
  - the mortgage company conveyancer's fees, plus a small additional fee to his or her own conveyancer for the extra work involved in writing to the building society's conveyancer, *or*
  - his or her own conveyancer's fee for acting for the mortgage company;

- fees for local authority and bankruptcy searches;
- stamp duty;
- Land Registry fee;
- mortgage company's survey;
- perhaps, surveyor's fee.

Conveyancing fees

Until 1973 solicitors' conveyancing fees were on a scale basis: the more the house was worth, the more the solicitor charged. The drawback of this system was its inflexibility and the absurdity of the notion that the complexity of the transaction was related to the value of the property. Its advantage was that everyone knew where they stood; the client knew in advance how much the fees would be and there was little scope for misunderstanding.

In 1973 conveyancing fees were put on the same basis as other non-contentious (i.e. non-court) work done by solicitors. The solicitor should charge what is 'fair and reasonable', having regard to eight factors (such as the complexity of the transaction, its urgency, whether the land is registered etc.). See page 941 for a full list of the eight factors and for how solicitors' fees are worked out.

See page 913 for how to complain about a solicitor's bill. In particular, note that there is a procedure allowing the client to have the bill checked by the Law Society; see Remuneration Certificates, page 942.

Since the scale fees have been abolished, it is not possible to give a detailed guide as to likely solicitor's fees. However, as a general guide one can say that the solicitor's fee for acting on a purchase or sale (exclusive of VAT, stamp duty, building society legal work etc.) is rarely likely to be less than ½ per cent of the price of the property, and it is rarely likely to exceed 1½ per cent of the price. Generally, sales are cheaper than purchases, and usually the fee is likely to be nearer the 1 per cent level until the price rises to over £25,000–£30,000. For instance, a typical price on a £20,000 sale might be £200, and on a £20,000 purchase, £220. For a £40,000 sale the fee might be £300, and for a £40,000 purchase, approximately £350. Some solicitors think in terms of charging ½ a per cent (of the price) plus £50 (for instance, on a £30,000 purchase, this would be £200, plus VAT – plus the fee for acting for the building society). But there is no uniformity in solicitors' charges.

It must be remembered that these are rough guides only. The longer a transaction takes and the more complicated it is, the more the solicitor is likely to charge. Many solicitors' firms keep a time record and charge their clients on the basis of how much time was spent on the transaction. But it does have to be said that many solicitors' firms are now abandoning the practice of charging by the amount of time spent on a transaction. Instead, they are beginning to appreciate that it is possible to give a fixed price at the beginning of the transaction – and then be held to that price.

Accordingly, the best advice one can give to anyone (whether buying or selling) is to ask for a written quote from the solicitor. Indeed, the Law Society always recommends that solicitors should give a written quote so that clients know where they stand. It is important to remember that the written quote may be no more than a best guess as to what the likely fees will be. But the client should be told in advance the basis on which the solicitor will charge. Thus, if the charge is likely to increase (e.g. because the transaction is far more complicated than originally envisaged), then the solicitor should warn the client about this. On the other hand, it may be that the price quoted by the solicitor will be a binding quote – one which binds the solicitor irrespective of the amount of work involved.

The important thing is to get a written quote from a solicitor. Ask the solicitor to set out what the fee is likely to be, and how that fee will be made up (and whether it is a binding, fixed price or not). If a solicitor is not prepared to do this, then he or she is not worth using!

Until relatively recently, conveyancing work used to be a gravy train for solicitors. It was easy work and they charged a lot for it. Furthermore, as house prices went up with inflation, so did the legal fees! As a result, many law firms became over-dependent on residential conveyancing work. Also, of course, there were many vested interests in the legal world that were opposed to any rationalization (i.e. simplification) of the conveyancing process.

Now, however, times have changed. Increasing competition in the legal marketplace means that there is now much more willingness to quote competitive fees. The advent of licensed conveyancers (see below) caused many law firms to modernize their conveyancing departments. Furthermore, the collapse of the property market in 1989–90 meant that many law firms were having to compete with each other for the relatively small amount of conveyancing work that was going on. The third factor has been an increasing public awareness of the need to challenge solicitors over their fees. Ten or twenty years ago, it was extremely rare for a solicitor's client to ask for a written quote and therefore pin down the solicitor as to the likely level of fees. Now, it is the rule rather than the exception in conveyancing.

All of these factors have contributed to ensuring that conveyancing is now no more expensive than it was ten years ago. Indeed, in real terms, conveyancing has never been cheaper.

The moral for anyone buying or selling a property is to shop around, and get firm written quotes.

When getting quotes, remember to compare like with like. One quote may include stamp duty and Land Registry fees, while another quote does not. For instance, a quote on a £40,000 purchase of £700 inclusive of Land Registry fees, stamp duty and mortgage legal fees would be cheaper than a quote of £250 exclusive of them all! In fact, the Law Society has laid down recommended forms for use by solicitors when giving quotes. If those forms are used, then you can be sure that you are comparing like with like.

Do not forget that a solicitor or conveyancer will normally charge for the work done even if the transaction falls through. In practice, most conveyancers will agree to raise only a nominal charge if the purchase or sale does not go ahead. However, this is worth checking out beforehand. It is also worth noting that a few firms do specifically agree that they will waive all their charges (except for money spent on local search fees) if the transaction falls through. It is also possible to take out insurance against wasted legal fees ('abortive conveyancing costs' insurance). Indeed, some building societies have now begun to offer this as part of their mortgage packages.

Licensed conveyancers. Licensed conveyancers are non-solicitors who are licensed to do conveyancing work. Generally, they tend to be former legal executive (see page 922) who have taken extra exams and who specialized in conveyancing. The system of licensed conveyancers was introduced only in 1985. The aim was that competition from non-solicitors would result in a more competitive conveyancing market. That certainly seems to have been the result. In practical terms, the threat of attack by licensed conveyancers persuaded many solicitors that they should market their conveyancing services more aggressively. In fact, the threat from the licensed conveyancers has, by and large, not materialized.

The mortgage company's legal fees

If a purchase is partly financed by a mortgage, the mortgage company (or building society) will instruct a conveyancer to prepare the mortgage deed and generally to protect its interests. They will normally use the buyer's own conveyancer but a different firm might be instructed if, for instance:
• the buyer does not have a conveyancer (e.g. because the buyer is a DIY conveyancer or is using an unlicensed conveyancing firm);
• the buyer's conveyancer is not on the mortgage company's approved list of conveyancers.

The fees will depend upon whether or not the buyer's conveyancer also acts for the mortgage company.

When the purchaser's own conveyancer also does the mortgage company's legal work

Most mortgage companies (and building societies) lay down a scale fee that the buyer's conveyancer can charge the buyer for doing the work on the mortgage. In particular, the Building Societies Association has a scale of fees that the solicitor or conveyancer can charge (when they are also acting for the buyer). Typically the fee for a mortgage of £50,000 would be some £77 (plus VAT). If it is an endowment mortgage, then the solicitor is usually entitled to charge an extra 25 per cent.

When the conveyancer who does the mortgage company's work does not act on the purchase as well

In this case there is no scale fee and the charge must be 'fair and reasonable'. In practice, it is likely to be 50–60 per cent more than the scale fee charged by a conveyancer who also acts on the purchase (e.g. on a £30,000 mortgage the fee is likely to be £115–£120 plus VAT).

When the mortgage company does all the legal work

Recent changes in the law mean that financial institutions (i.e. mortgage companies, building societies etc.) will soon be able to set up their own conveyancing departments. Potentially, this represents an enormous threat to the residential conveyancing workload of many solicitors' firms. However, whether the financial institutions will bother to set up their own conveyancing departments (either in-house or by entering into bulk deals with outside firms of solicitors) remains to be seen.

There is little doubt that, if they choose to do so, the financial institutions could take away most of the conveyancing work done by the typical solicitors' firm. After all, the financial institutions can offer the consumer a far better deal than can a firm of solicitors: in essence, would you rather have your legal costs added to your mortgage and paid off over a period of twenty-five years or pay them straight away to your solicitor? The answer, of course, is that people would normally prefer to have the fees added to their mortgage.

The argument against these changes is that they deprive the buyer (who is also the mortgage-borrower) of independent legal advice. After all, can the buyer really expect to get the same level of service from an in-house lawyer from the mortgage company? Given that the mortgage company has a financial incentive for the purchase to go ahead (i.e. they will make commission from policies sold to the buyer) there is an argument that the quality of legal service received could be diminished. On the other hand, it is probably fair to say that these difficulties are being exaggerated by the solicitors' lobby. What is clear, however, is that there is still an on-going battle between these two different viewpoints.

Commission received by solicitors

Mortgage companies (and their agents) do all they can to persuade buyers to take endowment or life policy mortgages. This is because they can make significant sums from those policies. Normally, the person who arranges the mortgage will receive a commission payment from the mortgage company. This explains why mortgage brokers are always so keen to arrange mortgages (if they are mortgages with policies attached) for buyers.

Solicitors can also arrange these mortgages. However, if a solicitor receives commission, then that commission belongs to the client. It follows from this that a solicitor must always declare any commission to the client. What sometimes happens is that a solicitor will say that the commission will be offset against the legal fees. This is usually a satisfactory arrangement for both the solicitor and the buyer. This assumes, of course, that the mortgage being arranged is the most suitable for the client, and that the solicitor is not trying to foist a policy-backed mortgage on to the client (in fact, solicitors are bound by strong professional rules to give the 'best advice' irrespective of any commission they might receive).

Stamp duty

Stamp duty is paid by the buyer of a property worth more than £30,000. Above that figure, the duty is 1 per cent (e.g. £350 on a £35,000 property, £900 on a £90,000 property etc.). If the property is not worth more than £30,000 then no stamp duty is paid (e.g. on a £29,000 – or even a £30,000 – purchase, no duty is paid). The stamp duty is paid on the whole of the purchase price, not just the excess over £30,000. For instance, the tax on a £30,000 purchase is nil, but on a £40,000 purchase it is £400 (i.e. tax is levied on the whole £40,000, not just the £10,000 over the £30,000).

If the price of the property is at the bottom level of stamp-duty liability (i.e. £30,000), then it might be possible to value the curtains, fittings and furniture separately, and so reduce the price to below the stamp-duty threshold. For instance, on a £30,500 purchase, if £500 can legitimately be apportioned to the furniture, then the price of the property can be stated as £30,000 and no stamp duty will have to be paid (i.e. a saving of £305).

Land Registry fees

These are paid when a buyer of a property is registered as the owner. The fee is on a sliding scale, rising with the value of the house. There are two different scales, depending upon whether or not the property is being registered for the first time (i.e. is it the first purchase since the area became an area of compulsory registration? See page 251). Typical fees would be: £45 on a £20,000 purchase; £90 on a £40,000 purchase; £140 on a £60,000 purchase; £190 on a £80,000 purchase; and £240 on a £100,000 purchase.

Estate agents' fees

Estate agents' fees vary enormously, but are generally very high. Commission is usually 1½, 2 or 2½ per cent of the selling price, although some agents operate a sliding scale (e.g. 2½ per cent on the first £5,000, and 1½ per cent on the rest). In London 2½ per cent is common. Thus, on a £100,000 house, the agent's fee may be £2,500 which, with the addition of VAT, means a bill to the seller of over £2,900! In comparison, the conveyancing fees, Land Registry fees and stamp duty paid by a purchaser can often fade into insignificance!

It is important that sellers agree the agent's rate of commission in advance. They should insist on written confirmation of the rate, and should check that there will be no charge for advertisements etc. placed by the agent. In addition, they should check carefully on the following points.

Sole agency

This means that the estate agent is the only agent for the property. It is advisable to put a time limit on this sole agency.

Sole selling rights

Do not confuse a sole agency with sole selling rights, which means that the agent alone can sell the property. For instance, if the seller sells privately to a friend, the agent can still claim commission. The general rule is never agree to sole selling rights.

Multiple agency

In this case the agent is not the only agent with the property on their books. The disadvantage is that the agent may not try as hard as if they had a sole agency; also, there can be arguments between agents as to which is entitled to the commission if the buyer contacted both of them.

It is also important to agree in advance exactly when the agent should be entitled to commission. Some agents have a standard contract that entitles them to commission on 'introducing a buyer ready, willing and able to buy'. It might be argued that this commits the seller to paying the agent even if the seller changes his/her mind and subsequently withdraws from the transaction or if he or she sells privately to a friend in preference to someone sent from the agents. Such a clause should never be accepted; the seller should insist that the agent is to be paid only if the buyer introduced by him or her actually buys the property.

The Estate Agents Act 1979 makes it compulsory for an estate agent to inform clients of the scale of fees and when they will become payable. This information must be provided before the contract is made with the client; if it is not provided, then the court can declare that the contract is not binding on the client, and so no fee, or only part of the fee, is payable. Estate agents must also:
• pay interest to clients on deposits, but only if the deposit is over £500 and the interest is at least £10;
• declare any personal interest they have in a transaction. For instance, if an estate agent is selling a flat that is owned by an associate (e.g. a nominee company with a different name), then the buyer must be told (although, in practice, this may not be until the buyer is on the verge of signing the purchase contract). The idea of requiring estate agents to disclose their interests is, of course, to make buyers realize that the agent cannot be trusted to be an impartial middleman;
• the agent must keep proper books and accounts and these must be audited every year.

DO-IT-YOURSELF AND CUT-PRICE CONVEYANCING

No one is bound to use a solicitor or a licensed conveyancer when buying or selling a house or a flat; either or both of the parties are free to do their own conveyancing if they so wish.

Before deciding whether to do one's own conveyancing, there are two questions that need to be answered:
1 What is the saving in legal fees?
2 How difficult is conveyancing?

The first question can be answered by looking at the above section, The Expenses of Buying and Selling Property. However, it should be borne in mind that the conveyancer's fee is only one of the expenses arising and that all the other fees (such as the building society's legal charges, stamp duty, the estate agent's fees, Land Registry fees) will still have to be paid by the DIY conveyancer. Thus the saving may not be as great as it seems at first glance.

The feasibility of DIY conveyancing

It is the alleged difficulty of conveyancing that is the real point of contention between those who advocate DIY conveyancing and those who say that it is an unwise and risky venture. The first part of this chapter mentioned some of the complicated adverse rights that can arise in the course of a conveyance, and which go some way towards justifying Dickens's contention that English land law was the son of the devil. Against that, of course, one can argue that most of the legal theory just does not arise in practice when dealing with a typical residential property. For example, a leading textbook devotes 100 pages to a discussion of the complications that can arise with mortgages, yet all buyers of a house need to know is that the seller's mortgage must be paid off by completion and that they should keep up to date on their mortgage repayments! However, conveyancing can be complicated and it should be appreciated that the transaction described above is of the simplest type; frequently, the transaction will raise more difficult problems.

Arguments in favour of DIY conveyancing

• The saving in legal fees can be considerable.
• The vast majority of house conveyances are straightforward and do not raise complicated matters of law.
• There are several good books available on DIY conveyancing, which, if followed carefully, virtually guarantee success.
• Much of the terminology used in conveyancing is less complicated than it seems at first glance (e.g. the words engrossment, abstract of title, peruse, requisitions, all sound more intimidating than they really are).
• Most of the standard forms used by conveyancers can be purchased by members of the public.

The costs of moving: purchasing a house or flat	£	See page
Conveyancer's fee for purchase	...	278
Conveyancer's fee for building-society work	...	278
Local-authority and bankruptcy search fees	...	262, 272
Land Registry fee*	...	280
Stamp duty	...	280
Building society's surveyor's fee	...	257
Surveyor's fee	...	257
Removal firm's charge	...	
Total		

* *Note.* With unregistered property there will be no Land Registry fee (unless the property now has to be registered), but the conveyancer's increased charge for the legal work will offset this saving.

The costs of moving: selling a house or flat	£	See page
Conveyancer's fee on sale	...	278
Estate agent's fee	...	280
Removal firm's charge	...	
Total		

• Many firms use unqualified clerks to do most of their conveyancing, so often the person is not in reality paying for the advice and experience of a qualified solicitor or licensed conveyancer.

• The conveyancing procedure as conducted by conveyancers is not particularly efficient or comprehensive; a person acting for him- or herself can do a more thorough job.

Arguments against DIY conveyancing

• People do not like the responsibility of handling large sums of money.

• The conveyancing transaction takes place over some two or three months and most people would prefer to pay a professional person to take over the responsibility and worry during this time. An analogy can be made with repairs to a car: someone can buy a workshop manual explaining how to repair a car and can then spend many hours working on the car; however, most people prefer to pay a specialist to repair their car for them. So it is with conveyancing; most people who buy and sell property prefer to pay a conveyancer to do the work for them.

• Although most conveyances are straightforward, how does the layperson know that this will not be the exceptional case that does raise difficult legal problems? And will the layperson be able to recognize a defect in the title or a legal problem if one arises?

• The DIY books cannot foresee every problem that might arise. If lawyers' textbooks are several thousand pages long, how can DIY manuals of a few hundred pages cover all eventualities?

• The DIY conveyancer will still have all the other fees to pay (and, in particular, increased mortgage legal fees, see page 278)

• The conveyancer/solicitor does not just provide 'legal' services; in addition he or she will usually advise on insurance, mortgages and surveys, and will be able to arrange a convenient completion date. An experienced conveyancer can do this better than a DIY conveyancer.

A personal opinion

The opinion of this solicitor is:

Buying freehold property (i.e. usually houses). It can be seen from the chart on page 254 that there is much more work to buying than there is to selling. In addition, of course, a mistake will probably have more disastrous consequences for a buyer than for a seller. A distinction should be made between:

• *registered property*. A person of average intelligence can safely do their own purchase, so long as they approach the task with care.

• *unregistered property*. Most people would find the complication of checking a chain of title deeds totally confusing. This work is best left to a qualified lawyer.

Selling freehold property. A person of average intelligence can safety sell a registered freehold property. If the title is unregistered, then there are more complications, but these can be overcome (although, in fact, relatively few people try to do their own unregistered sales). Do not forget that the major expense on a sale is likely to be on estate agent's fees, and these will usually be much more than those of a conveyancer. So anyone trying to save money might be well advised to concentrate their energies on finding a buyer without using an estate agent.

Buying leasehold property (i.e. usually flats). The extra complications with a leasehold property arise from the need to check the clauses of the lease (e.g. have there been breaches of the terms? Are the repairing covenants properly framed and enforceable?). Although these need not be difficult to understand, they usually are – largely because most leases are drawn up in unnecessarily complicated legal jargon. It is probably best to use a solicitor for a leasehold purchase.

Selling leasehold property (i.e. usually flats). The complications of a leasehold title are of more concern to the buyer than the seller. A fair summary of the position might be to say that you can do your own sale of a lease with a registered title, but not of one with an unregistered title.

Buying a new property (whether a house or a flat). This presents extra complications. For instance, the contract may have to be signed before the property is built, and it is then essential to have properly drafted clauses in the contract as to the quality of the building work, specifications, materials to be used, and the date by which it should be finished. In addition, the purchaser will have to sign the NHBC guarantee agreement (see page 258). Because of these complications, it is generally unwise to act for oneself when buying a new property.

In conclusion, there are several points that must be stressed. First, conveyancing can be very time-consuming and it also takes time and patience to familiarize oneself with the terminology used by the legal profession.

Secondly, those who decide to do their own conveyancing should not rely on just one DIY book; there are several guides available and it is best to have as many as possible, together with access to a comprehensive law book for the occasional technical problem.

Thirdly, bear in mind that all the DIY guides assume that there is a solicitor or licensed conveyancer acting for the other party. It is very unwise to risk doing one's own conveyance if the other person is also acting for themselves. If there is a conveyancer on the other side, he or she is likely to stop the DIY conveyancer from completely messing up the conveyance.

Fourthly, if a defect in title is not noticed when the property is bought it can cause considerable delay when the property is sold, for the purchaser will want the defect corrected.

Finally, no DIY conveyancer should be afraid of going to a conveyancer if difficulties arise. The sums of money involved in property transactions make it foolish to risk thousands of pounds for the sake of a relatively small saving on legal fees.

The reality is that much of the impetus for DIY conveyancing has now gone. Ten years ago solicitors' fees for conveyancing were unreasonably high. But increased competition (both from licensed conveyancers and from other solicitors) has meant that the average firm of solicitors is now charging no more than they were a decade ago. All things considered, conveyancing services are now cheap – and represent good value for money.

The bottom line in the DIY conveyancing debate is that conveyancing is no longer as over-priced as it used to be.

16 Leasehold Reform

CONVERTING A LONG LEASE INTO A FREEHOLD

The differences between a freehold and leasehold have already been explained (see page 238). The essential difference is that the leaseholder's interest in the property comes to an end when the lease expires and so the leaseholder may well lose his or her home.

This harshness of the law has been softened to some extent by the provisions of the Leasehold Reform Act 1967. This allows householders who have long leases to buy the freehold to the house or, alternatively, to obtain a fifty-year extension of their leases. The Act is a complicated piece of law; its provisions are technical and no layperson should use them without having taken full legal advice.

The basic requirements of the Act are set out in the chart opposite. There are three basic points:

1 The Act only applies to houses, not flats. As a policy decision flats were excluded, but there is now some pressure for the Act to be amended so as to include them. Not surprisingly, disputes have arisen over what is a 'house', but it seems clear that if a property is divided vertically into separate dwellings, then those dwellings will be 'houses' (as with a terrace). However, if the property is divided horizontally, the dwellings will be flats and so outside the 1967 Act. There are plans to change the law so flat-owners can get together and own the freehold of their leases (see Commonhold, page 242).

2 The lease must be a long lease. It must originally have been for more than twenty-one years, even if it now has only a few years left to run. The annual ground rent paid under the lease must be less than two-thirds of the rateable value as at 1965; if the ground rent is as much as that, then the house will probably be within the Rent Acts and the leaseholder will probably have little need of Leasehold Reform Act protection. As with the Rent Acts, the Leasehold Reform Act does not apply to luxury dwellings (e.g. if the rateable value in 1965 was over £750, or £1,500 in London).

3 The leaseholders themselves, or their family, must have lived in the house for the last three years (or have lived there for a total of three years during the last ten years).

How A Tenant May Be Able to Buy the Freehold to His or Her House

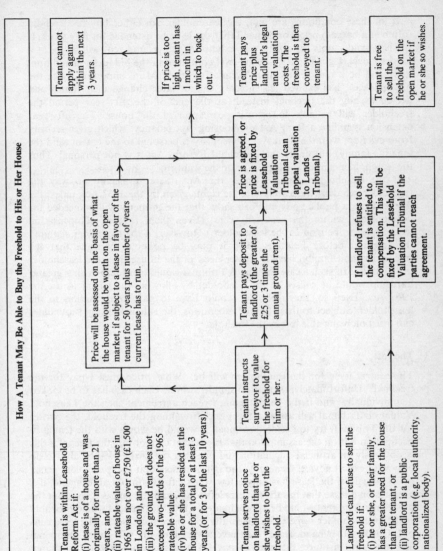

Tenant is within Leasehold Reform Act if:
(i) lease is of a house and was originally for more than 21 years, and
(ii) rateable value of house in 1965 was not over £750 (£1,500 in London), and
(iii) the ground rent does not exceed two-thirds of the 1965 rateable value.
(iv) he or she has resided at the house for a total of at least 3 years (or for 3 of the last 10 years).

Tenant serves notice on landlord that he or she wishes to buy the freehold.

Landlord can refuse to sell the freehold if:
(i) he or she, or their family, has a greater need for the house than the tenant, or
(ii) landlord is a public corporation (e.g. local authority, nationalized body).

Tenant instructs surveyor to value the freehold for him or her.

Price will be assessed on the basis of what the house would be worth on the open market, if subject to a lease in favour of the tenant for 50 years plus number of years current lease has to run.

Tenant pays deposit to landlord (the greater of £25 or 3 times the annual ground rent).

Price is agreed, or price is fixed by Leasehold Valuation Tribunal (can appeal valuation to Lands Tribunal).

If landlord refuses to sell, the tenant is entitled to compensation. This will be fixed by the Leasehold Valuation Tribunal if the parties cannot reach agreement.

If price is too high, tenant has 1 month in which to back out.

Tenant cannot apply again within the next 3 years.

Tenant pays price plus landlord's legal and valuation costs. The freehold is then conveyed to tenant.

Tenant is free to sell the freehold on the open market if he or she so wishes.

If all these conditions are met, the leaseholder can either buy the freehold (often at a bargain price) or demand that the lease be extended for fifty years. If the leaseholder opts for a fifty-year extension, the ground rent will be set at a modern level (e.g. £50 p.a.), not the level contained in the old lease; in addition, there will be a rent review after twenty-five years. More important, once the original lease has expired leaseholders cannot later change their minds and decide to buy the freehold instead; at the end of the fifty-year period the freeholder will be able to recover possession of the house. The fifty-year extension is unlike a Rent Act or Housing Act tenancy, which gives security from eviction; with the Rent Act the security is personal to the tenant (and the tenant's family) but under the Leasehold Reform Act it is not personal. Thus the leaseholder can sell the lease if he or she wants to.

If the leaseholder qualifies under the Act, there is usually no way the freeholder can deny the leaseholder the rights given by the 1967 Act, unless the freeholder is a public body and can show that the property will be needed for development within the next ten years. (Even then, though, compensation would have to be paid to the leaseholder.) However, if the freeholder acquired the freehold before February 1966 it may be possible to argue that the freeholder (and family) have a greater need of the house than the leaseholder (and family). In such a case the Lands Tribunal would consider whether greater hardship would be caused to the freeholder by allowing the tenant to use the 1967 Act. Even so, the freeholder would have to pay compensation to the leaseholder. Subject to these limited exceptions, the rule is that the leaseholder can insist on being able to buy the freehold.

The cost

The central issue for the leaseholder will be: 'What price must I pay for the freehold?' Unfortunately, there is no simple answer. Each case has to be looked at individually, and if the parties cannot reach agreement then the Leasehold Valuation Tribunal will assess a fair price. In valuing the freehold, the parties (or the Tribunal) try to decide how much it would be worth with the tenant in occupation but on the assumption that the tenant cannot buy the freehold; this is obviously an artificial calculation and one that the parties will be able to do only with expert advice. Generally, though, it means that the leaseholder gets a good bargain if the lease has only a few years left to run. As an example, if a house is on a lease that has thirty years left to go, and the rent is £5 p.a. but the modern ground rent would be approximately £100, the freehold would probably cost the leaseholder some £175. Generally, the price increases as the lease runs out. On the other hand, leases that have a very long life will go for a nominal amount – for instance, the price to pay for a lease with 950 years unexpired might be £100 or so. (Note: different valuation rules apply to high-value premises.)

Finally, the leaseholder must pay the 'reasonable' costs and expenses of the freeholder. Thus, the leaseholder must budget for paying the price of the freehold, and also the costs of two sets of solicitors (and probably surveyors as well). It may be because of this that surprisingly few leaseholders have taken advantage of their rights under the Act. In fact, it should not be difficult to borrow money for the purchase, since the lender can always take the newly purchased freehold as security for the loan.

THE ALTERNATIVE: BECOMING A RENT ACT TENANT

The tenant with a long lease may not always be able to take advantage of the Leasehold Reform Act provisions when the lease comes to an end; for instance, if it is a flat rather than a house or if the leaseholder has not lived in the house for three years.

Some long leaseholders can become Rent Act tenants, and so be safe from eviction. Part 1 of the 1954 Landlord and Tenant Act gives this protection to leaseholders whose original lease was for more than twenty-one years, and whose annual rent is less than two-thirds of the March 1965 rateable value of their property. Generally, the Rent Acts and Housing Acts do not apply to such tenants, but an exception is made for long leasehold tenants on the expiry of their leases.

If this provision applies, the leaseholder need not leave on the expiry of the lease. However, on the ending of the lease, the landlord can serve a possession notice on him or her and they will be entitled to evict the leaseholder if one of five situations exists (i.e. 'alternative accommodation', 'breach of tenancy', 'rent arrears', 'nuisance to neighbours', or 'required for the landlord or his family'). Unless one of these grounds exists, the leaseholder can remain in possession.

17 Renting from a Private Landlord

Many rented houses, flats and bedsitting rooms belong to private landlords. Such private landlords include the owner-occupier who has surplus accommodation to let, the owner who is working abroad and letting his or her home while away and the large commercial landlord or company that owns numerous properties for rent. There can be many pitfalls for both landlords and tenants in what has become an extremely complex area of the law.

Here are just a few of the questions that often arise:

1 Can the tenant be evicted when the tenancy ends (or even before it ends)?
2 What is the correct procedure for repossessing tenanted property?
3 What is the position if the landlord attempts to 'harass' the tenant into leaving or tries to evict the tenant without a court order?
4 Can the rent be increased or decreased?

Questions often arise also about repairs and maintenance, but this topic is dealt with in Chapter 19. To answer these questions is not always easy. The law is not contained in any single code or act of Parliament. The law is a combination of old common law (judge-made law), sometimes centuries old, and various acts of Parliament (statutes). However, by answering the above questions *in general terms*, the reader will hopefully gain an introduction as to which sections of this chapter to read. So here we go!

1. Can the tenant be evicted when the tenancy ends (or even before it ends)?

If the tenant will not leave voluntarily the landlord *must* obtain a court order, usually from the local county court. Even if the landlord is entitled to evict the tenant and the case against the tenant is overwhelming, the landlord must still go to court for an eviction order. Without a court order the landlord will be breaking the law and if he or she tries to evict without complying with the legal rules there are several penalties. It is true that there are a few very exceptional cases where the landlord is permitted to 'peaceably re-enter' without obtaining a court order (you will find details on page 322, Excluded Licences and Excluded Tenancies), but even here if the landlord uses any violence he or she is guilty of a criminal offence.

The next question is whether or not the landlord is *entitled* to a court order for possession. In many cases the tenant will be entitled to remain in occupation even if the tenancy expires or is terminated by the landlord giving a notice to quit, and so the landlord will not be entitled to a court order even if he or she applies for one. This right to remain in possession is known as 'security of tenure', but it is not available to all types of tenants. It depends on various factors but, in particular, on *when* the tenancy was granted. If it was granted on or after 15 January 1989 the relevant law in most cases is contained in the Housing Act 1988. Either an 'assured tenancy' or an 'assured shorthold tenancy' can be created under the 1988 Act. These are dealt with in Part 1 of this chapter (page 294). The basic position is that an assured tenancy can be terminated only by the landlord obtaining a court order based on one of sixteen specified grounds for possession. If he or she cannot prove any such ground the tenant is entitled to stay. An assured shorthold tenancy must be for a minimum of six months and when it expires the landlord will need a court order for possession, but he or she will be entitled to this without having to prove a ground. In other words, an assured shorthold tenant has no security of tenure once the court order is made.

If the tenancy was granted *before* 15 January 1989 the position is usually governed by the Rent Act 1977. Such tenancies are usually referred to as 'protected tenancies' or 'statutory tenancies'. Not only can the tenant not be evicted without a court order, but the landlord is entitled to a court order only if he or she can prove one of twenty grounds set out in the 1977 Act. These tenancies are dealt with in Part 2 of this chapter (page 313). Thus in these cases the tenant usually has substantial security of tenure.

But much will depend on the status of the occupier:

● he or she may be an assured or an assured shorthold tenant under the Housing Act 1988;

● he or she may be a protected or statutory tenant under the Rent Act 1977;

● he or she may be a licensee, having no protection under either Act (see page 295).

2. What is the correct procedure for repossessing tenanted property?

In virtually all residential lettings the landlord will need a court order to repossess, but how does the landlord go about obtaining this?

Before starting proceedings, which in most cases must be commenced in the local county court, the landlord will normally have to serve certain notices on the tenant. Failure to give the correct notices may result in the landlord's court action ending in failure and the proceedings being dismissed.

If the tenancy was granted on or after 15 January 1989 and comes within the Housing Act 1988 as an 'assured tenancy', the notice requirements are dealt with on page 305; if it is an 'assured shorthold tenancy', the relevant notice requirements are dealt with on page 308.

If the tenancy was granted before 15 January 1989 and comes within the

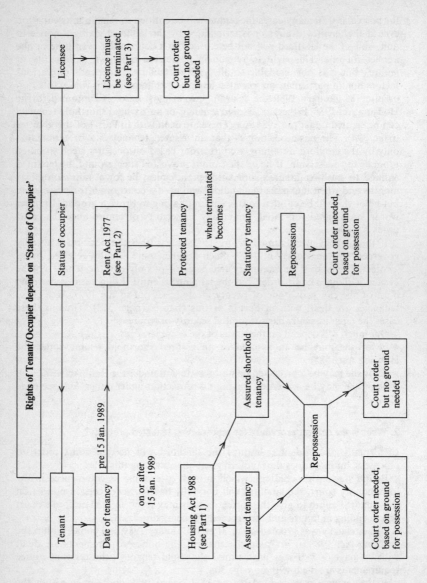

Rights of Tenant/Occupier depend on 'Status of Occupier'

Status of occupier
- Tenant
- Licensee

Licensee → Licence must be terminated (see Part 3) → Court order but no ground needed

Tenant → Date of tenancy

pre 15 Jan. 1989 → Rent Act 1977 (see Part 2) → Protected tenancy → *when terminated becomes* → Statutory tenancy → Repossession → Court order needed, based on ground for possession

on or after 15 Jan. 1989 → Housing Act 1988 (see Part 1) → Assured tenancy / Assured shorthold tenancy → Repossession →
- Court order needed, based on ground for possession
- Court order but no ground needed

Rent Act 1977, the landlord will normally be required to serve a notice to quit, which is dealt with on page 322. However, if the tenancy was for a 'fixed specific period' of time (a fixed-term tenancy) which has already expired before the proceedings were commenced, a notice to quit is not required, but a court order is still needed if the tenant remains in possession.

Exceptionally, certain tenancies do not come under the protection of either the Housing Act 1988 or the Rent Act 1977 (see page 298 for exceptions to the 1988 Act and page 320 for exceptions to the 1977 Act), but even in these cases the landlord will usually have to give some prior notice to the tenant before starting proceedings. The position is covered in more detail in Part 3 of this chapter (page 321).

3. What is the position if the landlord attempts to 'harass' the tenant into leaving or tries to evict the tenant without a court order?

The short answer to this is that all residential occupiers (who are lawfully residing in the premises and who are not squatters) have some very important and valuable rights against a landlord who interferes with the tenant's peace and comfort or who tries to evict without getting a court order and without complying with the strict legal rules. These rights and remedies are dealt with in Part 3 of this chapter. In addition to the possibility of a criminal prosecution, the landlord can be sued for a court injunction to prevent further harassment (or for reinstatement if the tenant has already been evicted). Damages can also be claimed against such a landlord and the amount of these damages can be very large nowadays. (See page 325).

4. Can the rent be increased or decreased?

If the tenancy was granted before 15 January 1989 and is covered by the Rent Act 1977, there is a system known as 'fair rents' so that the landlord cannot always charge what he or she likes. Details of the 'fair rent' system are set out on page 319. Fair rents are registered with the local authority, who keep a register which is open to public inspection.

If a fair rent has been registered, that is the maximum the landlord can charge no matter what the tenancy agreement says. If the tenancy was granted on or after 15 January 1989 and comes within the Housing Act 1988, the landlord is entitled to charge the amount specified in the tenancy agreement (including any increased amount if the agreement provides for rent increases). There is very little the tenant can do to challenge the rent. However, if the tenancy agreement does not provide for increases in rent but the landlord tries to increase the rent later on, the tenant may be able to challenge the amount of the increase. Details are given on page 305.

Further, in the case of an 'assured shorthold tenancy', the tenant may be able to get the initial rent reduced if the landlord is charging *significantly* higher than other comparable rents in the district. Again details are given on page 312.

Rent Act 1977 and Housing Act 1988

It will be seen from the above brief introduction that the main Acts giving protection to tenants are the Rent Act 1977 and the main Housing Act 1988. Most private residential tenancies come under the protection of one or the other, *but not both*. In some cases a tenancy may come under neither Act; here the tenant is not totally unprotected but his or her protection is very basic (i.e. the landlord needs a court order for possession but the court must grant it). It is now necessary to look into it in more detail at:

• when the Housing Act 1988 applies (assured and assured shorthold tenancies – see Part 1 of this chapter);

• when the Rent Act 1977 applies (protected and statutory tenancies – see Part 2 of this chapter);

• the general protection given to tenants, licensees and residential occupiers (whether or not the Rent Act 1977 or the Housing Act 1988 applies against unlawful eviction and harassment – see Part 3 of this chapter).

PART 1: HOUSING ACT 1988

Tenancies granted on or after 15 January 1989 – 'assured tenancies' and 'assured shorthold tenancies'

This Act applies to 'assured tenancies' and 'assured shorthold tenancies'. It is very important to be able to distinguish between the two. *Assured tenants* enjoy substantial security of tenure and cannot be evicted unless the landlord can obtain a court order based on one of sixteen grounds. *Assured shorthold tenants*, on the other hand, have no security when the tenancy comes to an end; the landlord needs a court order but does not need to establish a ground and is therefore entitled to an order for possession as of right.

Meaning of assured tenancy

In order to qualify for an *assured tenancy* the following conditions must be satisfied:

1 There must be a *tenancy* and not a licence (see note 1).
2 The tenancy must be of a *'dwelling-house'* (see note 2).
3 The tenant must be *an individual* (if there is more than one tenant, they must all be individuals) (see note 3).
4 The tenant must *occupy* the property as his or her *only or principal home* (see note 4).
5 The tenancy must *not* be one that is specifically *excluded* from protection under the Act (see note 5).

Note 1: 'a tenancy'

This is a contract under which the landlord gives to the tenant the exclusive use and occupation of the property (or part of the property) either for a fixed specific term – for example, six months or one year (in which case it is referred to as a *'fixed-term tenancy' or a 'lease'*) or on a periodic basis for an indefinite period, for example, from week to week or from month to month (in which case it is referred to as a *'periodic tenancy'*). The contract is normally made in writing but this is not absolutely essential; an oral tenancy is valid if it is a periodic tenancy or is for a fixed term not exceeding three years, provided it was granted at a normal market rent without the landlord charging a premium (i.e. a capital sum over and above rent as a condition of granting the tenancy). Most tenancy agreements will, however, be in writing or will be recorded in a rent book, but the absence of any document does not necessarily mean that the tenant does not have a legal tenancy.

The main requirement of a tenancy is that the tenant does have *exclusive possession* of the property or some specific part of it – for example, a flat or a bedsitter. If the tenant does not enjoy exclusive possession, this may mean that the tenant is merely a licensee. Most licensees do not enjoy protection under the Act. Because licensees are excluded from protection, it is not unusual for some landlords to try to evade the Act by attempting to create a 'licence'. A typical anti-avoidance arrangement is a written agreement described as a 'licence' under which the landlord agrees to give to the occupant a right to 'share' occupation of the premises with other people. The question of whether or not such an arrangement is effective to exclude the Act depends on whether or not there is a genuine arrangement to share with others and what the terms of that 'sharing' agreement are. The fact that a document is called a licence does not necessarily mean that the occupier is without statutory protection. The courts will look to the *'substance and reality'* of the transaction rather than merely the words or form of the agreement that has been signed. An occupier may well in fact have exclusive possession of the property or part of it despite the wording of the agreement. Alternatively, the persons with whom the occupier is required to 'share' may collectively be construed to be the tenants, so that between them they all have a 'joint tenancy' of the property in question. The following examples illustrate the courts' attitude to the question of whether or not an occupier does have a tenancy despite having signed what appears to be a 'licence'.

The case of Street v. Mountford decided by the House of Lords is a clear example of when the courts will hold the occupier to be a tenant, thus having protection, despite having signed a document called a licence. The owner, Mr Street, gave to Mrs Mountford the right to occupy furnished rooms forming part of a house in return for a 'licence fee' of £37 per week subject to termination by fourteen days' written notice and to certain other conditions set out in the agreement. No person other than Mrs Mountford occupied those rooms. The owner provided no services, such as cleaning services etc. in respect of those rooms. The only right which the owner retained in respect of entering the rooms was simply the right to inspect the condition, to read meters etc. and to carry out maintenance work where necessary. The House of Lords decided that Mrs Mountford was in fact the exclusive occupier of the rooms and that the agreement which she had with the owner was in reality a tenancy agreement.

She therefore had legal protection as a tenant. The fact that the tenancy agreement was called a 'licence' could not alter the reality of the transaction. This was despite the fact that the agreement contained the clause saying, 'I understand and accept that a licence in the above form does not and is not intended to give me a tenancy protected under the Rent Acts.' The House of Lords held that (in the absence of exceptional circumstances) if an occupier is given exclusive occupation of a property (or a room) in return for a rent that is a tenancy regardless of what the parties decide to call it.

Although this was a case concerning the Rent Acts the same point applies exactly to the Housing Act 1988 and so, had the agreement been signed on or after 15 January 1989, the result would have been the same. This case, however, concerned only one occupier. What is to be the position if there are two or more occupiers? Much will depend here on whether the occupiers are a married couple (or living together as such) or a family where there is no *real* intention that anyone else will in fact share occupation, or whether the property is to be occupied by several single people or strangers where it is intended that the occupiers should come and go on a regular basis.

In the case of AG Securities v. Vaughan, one large flat consisted of four bedrooms and two living rooms. The owners entered into four separate agreements with four different occupiers. The agreements were called 'licences' in which the owners granted to each occupier the right to 'share' the flat in common with others who might from time to time *be granted similar licences, but without the right to exclusive possession of any part of the flat. The flat was always fully occupied but whenever one occupier left another occupier was brought in to fill the vacancy.* There was a fluctuating body of occupiers. *No single occupier was given exclusive occupation of any part of the flat. It was always a sharing arrangement. The House of Lords held that here the occupiers were only licensees and not tenants and therefore did not have the protection of the Rent Acts.*

Again, had the agreement been signed after January 1989, the Housing Act 1988 would not have applied.

In the case of Antoniades v. Villiers the occupiers, Mr Villiers and Miss Bridger, spent three months looking for a flat where they could live together. In February 1985 they were shown the attic flat in the building owned by Mr Antoniades. This flat lacked a bed but the owner agreed to provide one. Mr Villiers and Miss Bridger (his cohabitee) expressed a preference for a double bed which the owner agreed to provide. The owner entered into two separate licence agreements, one with Mr Villiers and one with Miss Bridger. Both these agreements contained the clause that the 'licensee' did not have exclusive possession of any part of the property and was required to share the accommodation with other licensees introduced by the owner. Both agreements provided that the Rent Acts were not to apply. Furthermore, the flat was declared for use only by single persons 'sharing' and provided that if any occupier married another occupier the agreement was to be terminated! Here the court held that Mr Villiers and Miss Bridger between them had joint exclusive possession of the entire flat; that there was no genuine intention of a third party moving in with them. It was intended for use by a married couple or by persons living together as such. Thus in reality a joint tenancy existed and not a licence. The occupiers, jointly, had the protection of the Rent Acts.

We can see from these three cases that:

1 If there is to be one occupier only of a flat or bedsitting room who has exclusive use of that flat or bedsitter, the fact that the signed document is stated to be a 'licence' will not prevent a tenancy. The same applies to married couples or people living together as such.
2 If a property is to be shared by strangers or a 'fluctuating' group, with no one person having exclusive occupation, the arrangement is likely to be a licence, so that the Rent Act 1977 and the Housing Act 1988 will not apply.

Note 2: 'of a dwelling-house'

The word dwelling-house includes a flat or bedsitting room. However, for the Act to apply it must be let to the tenant 'as a separate dwelling'. The residential unit does not need to be completely self-contained and may involve sharing a kitchen, a lounge, a bathroom or a toilet with tenants or occupiers of other residential units in the same property. However, if there is sharing of a kitchen, lounge, bathroom or toilet, it is important that this is *not* shared with the landlord. If the landlord lives in the same property, at the time when the tenancy is granted, and continues to reside there, he or she will be a 'resident landlord' and the tenancy will not be protected by the Act. If, however, the sharing is not with the landlord but with other occupiers, the tenancy will still be within the Act. The situation regarding resident landlords is dealt with later (see page 299).

Note 3: an 'individual' or 'individuals'

This simply means that *the tenant* must be a human being and not a limited company or a corporation or other corporate association. If the tenancy is in favour of a company, the company has no protection under the Act. It is for this reason that landlords sometimes advertise 'company lets only'. However, company lets must not be used as a disguise to evade protection. Where the tenant is in reality an individual and the company is simply a nominee of the landlord, the court may declare the real tenant to be the individual. For example, if the landlord negotiates a tenancy with an individual who has no connection whatsoever with the limited company named in the tenancy agreement and the limited company belongs to the landlord (i.e. the landlord is the shareholder), the courts will readily regard the arrangement as a 'sham' and will regard the individual as being the real tenant and not the company. On the other hand, if a company takes on a tenancy from a landlord, where the company has no connection with the landlord and the object of the exercise is, for example, to provide accommodation for one of the company's employees as part of his or her employment, then the company is the tenant and the company has no protection under the Act.

Note 4: 'occupy as ... only or principal home'

This requirement is twofold. First, there must be continuity of residence by the tenant throughout the tenancy. Temporary absences such as for holidays, periods in hospital and temporary absences working away will not preclude the tenant from protection. But if the tenant moves out of the property and leaves it totally unoccupied (i.e. by moving out all the furniture) or by sub-letting the entire property, this will take the tenancy outside the protection of the Act. Sub-letting *part* will not take the tenancy outside the Act, but unless the landlord gives his or her consent for such sub-letting this will usually be a breach of the tenancy agreement and may give the landlord a ground for possession.

The second requirement is more difficult: it concerns the tenant who has two homes. In these circumstances it must be established which of the two homes is the tenant's *main* (principal) home. The other house does not itself have to be a tenanted house. The tenant might *own* a house somewhere else or be buying it with a mortgage. It may be that the other house is *in fact* the tenant's main home. For example, the tenant may own or be buying a house out in the country, but may rent a flat or bedsitter in the town where he works during the week. He may have this rented accommodation simply because it is *convenient* for work. His main house may be the one occupied by his wife and children. It is likely that the courts would find that the rented accommodation is merely a second home, not the tenant's 'principal home'. In this situation the tenant would have no protection for the rented accommodation under the 1988 Act. This would be particularly so if the other house was being bought with the aid of a mortgage and the taxpayer was claiming tax relief in respect of the mortgage payments, because here the general rule is that mortgage-interest tax relief can be claimed only in respect of one's only or 'principal' home. A person cannot have *two* main homes, and if the tenant/taxpayer has already elected to treat the mortgaged home as his or her principal home, it may be very difficult to persuade the courts that the rented accommodation is an assured tenancy.

Note 5: 'specifically excluded'

There are certain tenancies which can *never* be *assured tenancies*. The main exclusions are as follows:

● *pre-Act tenancies*. Tenancies granted prior to 15 January 1989. These are usually governed by the Rent Act 1977 (see Part 2 of this chapter).

● *high rateable value*. If the tenancy was granted before 1 April 1990 and the property had a rateable value of £1,500 in Greater London or £750 elsewhere, it cannot be an assured tenancy.

● *high rental tenancies*. If the tenancy was granted on or after 1 April 1990 and the rent is £25,000 or more per annum, it cannot be an assured tenancy.

● *low rental tenancies*. If the tenancy was granted before 1 April 1990 and the rent is less than two-thirds of the rateable value, it is excluded. Similarly, if the tenancy was granted on or after 1 April 1990 but the rent does not exceed

£1,000 per annum in Greater London or £250 per annum elsewhere, it is not an assured tenancy.

● *business tenancies.* If the tenancy includes a shop or an office covered by the same tenancy agreement and occupied by the same tenant (e.g. shop with flat above where a tenant carries on a business downstairs) this is excluded.

● *licensed premises.* If the premises have an on licence this is excluded. Public houses are not protected.

● *farms.* Where the tenancy includes a farm or agricultural land exceeding 2 acres, it cannot be an assured tenancy.

● *certain student lettings.* If a university, college or polytechnic lets accommodation to students, this is exempt. If, however, a *private* landlord lets to students this is not excluded.

● *holiday lettings.*

● *public-sector lettings.* If the landlord is a local authority (or the Crown), the tenancy is not protected under the 1988 Act.

● *resident landlords.* If the landlord lives in the same building and complies with certain conditions, this excludes the Act. These conditions are dealt with in the next paragraph.

Who is a resident landlord?

In order to be a resident landlord (and thus exempt from the definition of an *assured tenancy*) the following conditions must be fulfilled:

1 The property comprised in the tenancy must form a part only of the building. The building must not be a purpose-built block of flats (i.e. must not be a building which was built as a block of flats). A house *converted* to flats is not a purpose-built block of flats, but a building which was designed and built originally as flats is a purpose-built block of flats.

2 The landlord must be an individual (i.e. a person, not a company) who occupies another part of the building.

3 At all times since the tenancy was granted the landlord must have continued to reside in the same building. However, certain periods of absence by the landlord are disregarded in deciding whether or not there has been continuity of residence:

● If the landlord has sold the property to another individual, the new landlord has twenty-eight days from the change of ownership in which to take up and continue residence himself. If the new landlord does not move in within this period of twenty-eight days, the resident landlord exemption will be lost unless within those twenty-eight days the new landlord notifies the tenant in writing of his intention to occupy within six months from the change in ownership and in fact moves in within that period of six months.

● If the original resident landlord dies a successor has two years following the death to move in.

Assured tenancies: what protection is given (security of tenure)?

A tenant under an *assured tenancy* has substantial protection against eviction in that the landlord must normally obtain a court order for possession and this can be granted only if one of sixteen grounds set out in the Act is proved. However, before looking at these grounds in detail, it is necessary to distinguish between those tenancies which were originally granted for a *fixed* term and those which were granted as *periodic* tenancies, such as on a weekly or monthly basis.

Fixed term

If the tenancy was granted for a fixed term (e.g. six months or a year) which has not yet expired, the tenancy can be terminated only in one of the following ways:
• *by surrender.* If the tenant agrees to surrender and give up his or her tenancy to the landlord (with or without payment of money), this will be effective to terminate the tenancy.
• *by court order.* If the tenant will not move out voluntarily, the landlord needs a court order based on grounds 2, 8, 10, 11, 12, 13, 14 or 15 mentioned below (most of these involve some default on the part of the tenant, such as non-payment of rent or breach of obligation). Even if the landlord is able to prove one of these grounds, the court cannot make an order unless the terms of the tenancy agreement actually provide for termination in the event of one of those grounds arising. Further, even if the landlord proves that one of these grounds exists (apart from grounds 2 or 8), he or she must also show that it is reasonable for the court to order the tenant to leave.

What happens if the fixed-term tenancy expires?

If a fixed-term tenancy expires, the tenant does not have to move out. The tenant is allowed to remain in possession at the same rent he or she was paying previously and will become what is known as a 'statutory periodic tenant', which means he or she can continue in occupation unless and until the landlord obtains a court order based on one of the sixteen grounds listed below.

What happens if a tenancy is periodic – for example, weekly or monthly?

Here the landlord *must* obtain a court order based on one or more of the sixteen grounds below if the tenant wishes to remain in residence. If the tenant does not wish to continue in residence he or she can either surrender the tenancy by mutual agreement with the landlord, or alternatively serve on the landlord a notice of his or her intention to quit the premises (see Part 3 of this chapter). It must be emphasized, however, that a landlord in these circumstances cannot give the tenant notice to quit since an assured periodic tenancy cannot be terminated by a landlord's notice to quit. The landlord must obtain a court order on one of the grounds specified below.

The sixteen grounds for possession

The Act lays down sixteen grounds for possession. Grounds 1–8 are mandatory (i.e. the court has no discretion and must order possession if the landlord proves one of them). Grounds 9–16 are discretionary (i.e. the court must also be satisfied that it is reasonable to order possession having regard to all the circumstances).

Ground 1: landlord is owner-occupier or requires property for his/her own occupation

The following conditions must be satisfied:
• *prior notice.* On or before granting the tenancy, the tenant must have been given written notice that possession might be required on this ground. If this notice was not given, the landlord cannot use ground 1, unless the court is of the opinion that it is just and equitable (i.e. fair) to dispense with the notice. For example, if the tenant was told that the property was previously occupied by the landlord, but the landlord failed to give a *written* notice, the court might dispense with the requirements of a written notice.
• *prior residence.* Prior to the tenancy the landlord (or one of them if there is more than one landlord) must have occupied the property as his or her only or principal home. In other words, the landlord must have previously been an owner-occupier. If this is not so, see 'no prior residence'.
• *no prior residence.* If the landlord did not personally occupy the property prior to the tenancy, the landlord must show that he or she now requires possession for him- or herself, or for his or her spouse, as his or her only or principal home. If the landlord already has another house (or the landlord's spouse as the case may be), it may be difficult for the landlord to regain possession on this ground. Furthermore, ground 1 is not available if the landlord bought the property during the currency of the existing tenancy. This is to stop landlords buying up rented property and then seeking to get possession on the basis that they want it for themselves. This is not allowed under the Housing Act 1988.

Ground 2: landlord's mortgage lender requiring possession in order to sell with vacant possession

The following conditions must be satisfied:
• *Existing mortgage.* The house must have been mortgaged to the lender *before* the tenancy was granted. If the mortgage was taken out after the tenancy was granted, ground 2 is not available.
• *Lender selling.* The lender/mortgage company must show that it is entitled to sell the property. This normally means that the landlord/borrower has defaulted in his/her mortgage payments or his/her obligations under the mortgage deed.

● *Vacant possession needed.* The lenders must show they require possession of the house in order to sell it with vacant possession.

● *Prior notice.* On or after the date of the tenancy the tenant must have been given notice under ground 1 or, if no such notice was given in writing, the court must be satisfied that it is just and equitable (i.e. fair) to dispense with that notice. However, this ground cannot be used in the case of a fixed-term tenancy which has not yet expired unless the tenancy agreement contains an appropriate clause allowing the landlord's mortgage lender to repossess before the tenancy ends.

Ground 3: out-of-season holiday accommodation (winter lets)

The following conditions must be satisfied:

● *prior notice.* On or before the date of tenancy the landlord gave a written notice that possession might be recovered on ground 3.

● *fixed term.* The tenancy must be for a fixed term of not more than 8 months. During the twelve months prior to the tenancy, the property must have been occupied for holiday purposes.

Ground 4: out-of-term student accommodation

If the property belongs to a university, polytechnic or college and in the last twelve months the property was occupied by their students, the landlord is entitled to possession if the landlord gave notice that possession might be required on ground 4.

Ground 5: minister of religion's house (vicarages etc.)

If, on or before the date of the tenancy, the landlord gave written notice that possession might be recovered on ground 5 and the court is satisfied that the house is now required for occupation by a minister, the court must make a possession order.

Ground 6: demolition or reconstruction

The following conditions must be satisfied:

● The landlord intends to demolish or reconstruct the entire property or a substantial part of it or to carry out extensive works. If this work needs planning permission, the landlord must normally show that it has been granted.

● The intended work cannot reasonably be carried out while the tenant is still living there or the tenant will not allow the landlord access to carry out the work or is not willing to accept a smaller part of the property not affected by the work.

● The landlord did not *buy* the property subject to the tenancy. In other words, only the original landlord (or someone who inherited on the landlord's death or acquired the property as a gift) can use this ground.

This ground is not available during a fixed-term tenancy that has not yet expired. It can be used only during periodic tenancies or after the fixed term has come to an end. Even if the landlord succeeds on this ground, he or she is required to pay the tenant's removal expenses.

Ground 7: death of a periodic tenant

If the tenancy is periodic (as opposed to a fixed-term lease) and the tenant dies without leaving a resident spouse living in the home, the landlord can seek possession within twelve months of the tenant's death.

This does require some explanation. If a periodic tenant dies leaving a widow or a widower or a person with whom the tenant lived as husband or wife (even if not legally married), the surviving spouse residing in the property will be entitled to take over the tenancy and the landlord cannot prevent this. If, however, the deceased tenant is not survived by a spouse or the spouse does not actually live in the same property (i.e. separated), the tenancy may pass to some other member of the deceased's family. It is only in this case that the landlord can recover possession. The landlord has twelve months to decide whether or not the non-spouse successor who has taken over the tenancy should or should not be allowed to remain. It must be emphasized that ground 7 applies only to periodic tenancies and will not operate where the tenant had a fixed-term tenancy (e.g. six months or a year) which has not yet expired. In the case of an unexpired fixed-term tenancy, the balance of the tenancy will pass to a beneficiary under the tenant's will or intestacy and does not automatically pass to the surviving spouse. The landlord has no grounds for possession in these circumstances.

Ground 8: three months' or thirteen weeks' rent arrears

If the tenant is at least three months or thirteen weeks in arrears with rent when the landlord serves notice that he or she intends to bring proceedings (see page 305) and that amount of arrears still exists at the date of the hearing, the landlord is entitled to possession *as of right*. However, for this purpose the rent must be 'lawfully due'. If the tenant has a valid claim against the landlord for lack of repair (see Chapter 19), this may have the effect of reducing the arrears. It is only if three months'/thirteen weeks' rent is lawfully due at the date of the hearing that the court can grant possession under this ground. A further point which the tenant will need to check is whether or not the landlord has served a notice in writing giving the tenant an address for service on the landlord of documents and proceedings. This is required by s. 48 of the Landlord and Tenant Act 1987.

If no such notice has been served prior to the current proceedings, the rent is not lawfully due unless and until the landlord complies.

Ground 9: suitable alternative accommodation

If the tenant has been offered suitable alternative accommodation but chooses not to accept it the court may order possession against the tenant. The alternative accommodation must be similar in size, quality and proximity to the tenant's place of work and afford to the tenant similar security of tenure. The offer of alternative accommodation may come from the landlord him- or herself, from a local authority or from some other landlord. If the landlord does succeed on this ground, he or she must pay the tenant's reasonable removal expenses.

Ground 10: rent arrears

This applies to any rent lawfully due but unpaid.

Unlike ground 8, where the court has no discretion but to order possession, if the landlord is relying on ground 10 the court does have discretion and it must be satisfied that it is reasonable to order possession in the circumstances. For ground 10 to apply, however, there must again be some rent lawfully due at the time when the landlord served notice of his/her intention to bring proceedings and also on the day when proceedings were begun.

Ground 11: persistent delay in paying rent

Even if there are no rent arrears, the fact that the tenant is persistently late with the rent payments can be a ground for possession.

Ground 12: breach of tenancy obligations

If the tenant has broken the terms of the tenancy agreement (other than failure to pay rent) the court may, if it is reasonable, grant possession on this ground.

Ground 13: deterioration of property through waste or neglect

This ground applies if the condition of the property has deteriorated because of the waste, neglect or default of the tenant or of any person residing with the tenant. It must also be remembered that the landlord will in most cases be liable for major repairs and so he or she cannot rely on this ground to the extent that the condition of the house is due to neglect by him/her of his/her obligation. This is further considered in Chapter 19.

Ground 14: nuisance or annoyance to adjoining occupiers

This applies where the tenant or a person living with him/her has been guilty of nuisance or annoyance to adjoining occupiers or has been convicted of using the property for illegal or immoral purposes.

Ground 15: damage to furniture

This applies where the landlord's furniture has been broken or damaged by ill-treatment by the tenant or a person residing with the tenant.

Ground 16: tenant a former employee of the landlord

This applies where the property was let to the tenant while he or she was an employee of the landlord (or a previous landlord) and the tenant is no longer so employed.

How does the landlord obtain possession?

Assuming the landlord can prove one of these sixteen grounds mentioned above, the landlord cannot evict the tenant without a court order and must, before the proceedings commence, have served a formal notice (under s. 8 of the Act) on the tenant of the landlord's intention to institute proceedings.

The form is as illustrated on pages 306 and 307.

The notice must be served at least two weeks before proceedings are commenced, and in certain cases at least two months before proceedings are commenced. If the landlord commences his/her proceedings without having served this notice, it is unlikely that the court would allow the landlord to proceed until he or she had served a proper notice.

Length of notice

A minimum of two weeks' notice is required if the landlord is relying on grounds 3, 4, 8, 10, 11, 12, 13, 14 or 15 (see page 302). If, however, the landlord is relying on grounds 1, 2, 5, 6, 7, 9 or 16, the notice must be at least two months *and*, if the tenancy is periodic, cannot take effect any earlier than a notice to quit. This means that if, for example, the periodic tenancy is quarterly (i.e. rent payable every three months), the s. 8 notice must be of at least three months' duration to be valid.

Rent increases under assured tenancies

Unlike the Rent Acts, dealt with in Part 2 of this chapter, there is generally no restriction on the amount of rent that the landlord can lawfully charge the tenant. The rent stated in the tenancy agreement is payable. However, this does not mean that the landlord can at any time and under any circumstances unilaterally increase the rent. There is a distinction between fixed-term tenancies – where the fixed term has not expired – and periodic tenancies.

Fixed-term tenancy (or lease). During a fixed-term tenancy the landlord has no right to increase the rent or vary it unless there is a clause in the tenancy agreement or lease allowing the landlord to do this. If there is such a clause

FORM No. 3

Housing Act 1988 section 8

Notice Seeking Possession of a Property
Let on an Assured Tenancy

- Please write clearly in black ink.

- Do not use this form if possession is sought from an assured shorthold tenant under section 21 of the Housing Act 1988 or if the property is occupied under an assured agricultural occupancy.

- **This notice is the first step towards requiring you to give up possession of your home. You should read it very carefully.**

- If you need advice about this notice, and what you should do about it, take it as quickly as possible to any of the following–
  - a Citizens' Advice Bureau,
  - a housing aid centre,
  - a law centre,
  - or a solicitor.

  You may be able to get Legal Aid but this will depend on your personal circumstances.

1. To: _____   *Name(s) of tenant(s)*

2. Your landlord intends to apply to the court for an order requiring you to give up possession of–

Address of premises

- If you have an assured tenancy under the Housing Act 1988, which is not an assured shorthold tenancy, you can only be required to leave your home if your landlord gets an order for possession from the court on one of the grounds which are set out in Schedule 2 to the Act.

- If you are willing to give up possession of your home without a court order, you should tell the person who signed this notice as soon as possible and say when you can leave.

3. The landlord intends to seek possession on ground(s) [   ] in Schedule 2 to the Housing Act 1988, which reads

Give the full text of each ground which is being relied on. (Continue on a separate sheet if necessary.)

- Whichever grounds are set out in paragraph 3 the court may allow any of the other grounds to be added at a later date. If this is done, you will be told about it so you can discuss the additional grounds at the court hearing as well as the grounds set out in paragraph 3.

4. Particulars of each ground are as follows–

Give a full explanation of why each ground is being relied on. (Continue on a separate sheet if necessary.)

- If the court is satisfied that any of grounds 1 to 8 is established it must make an order (but see below in respect of fixed term tenancies).

- Before the court will grant an order on any of grounds 9 to 16, it must be satisfied that it is reasonable to require you to leave. This means that, if one of these grounds is set out in paragraph 3, you will be able to suggest to the court that it is not reasonable that you should have to leave, even if you accept that the ground applies.

- The court will not make an order under grounds 1, 3 to 7, 9 or 16, to take effect during the fixed term of the tenancy; and it will only make an order during the fixed term on grounds 2, 8 or 10 to 15 if the terms of the tenancy make provision for it to be brought to an end on any of these grounds.

To be signed by the landlord or his agent (someone acting for him), or by the tenant or his agent. If there are joint landlords or joint tenants each landlord/tenant or the agent must sign, unless one signs on behalf of the rest with their agreement.

Signed	
Name(s) of land-lord(s)/tenant(s)	
Address of land-lord(s)/tenant(s)	
Tel:	

If signed by agent, name and address of agent

Tel:	Date:
	19

(commonly known as a 'rent review clause'), the landlord can increase the rent only if he or she complies with the terms of that clause. If there is no such rent review clause, then the landlord cannot vary the rent until the tenancy expires. It will then become a periodic tenancy and rent increases will be governed by the restrictions mentioned below.

Periodic tenancies. Some periodic-tenancy (e.g. weekly, monthly) agreements do contain a clause allowing the landlord to increase or vary the rent by giving, say, one month's notice to the tenant. If there is such a clause in the tenancy agreement, then the landlord can increase the rent, provided that he or she strictly complies with the terms of that clause.

If, however, there is no such clause in the tenancy agreement, the landlord cannot increase the rent until at least twelve months have elapsed since the tenancy was created. After twelve months the landlord can serve a notice under s. 13 of the 1988 Act proposing a rent increase. The notice must be in the prescribed form, setting out the tenant's right to challenge the increase.

The notice must be served at least one month before the proposed increase takes effect and, during this time, the tenant can, if he or she objects to the proposed increase, refer the matter to the rent assessment committee. The committee will then determine 'the open market rent' (i.e. what a reasonable landlord would charge a reasonable tenant for this type of property in this locality having regard to the prevailing level of rents). Once the new rent has been determined, it will remain in force unless and until the landlord again serves another notice under s. 13, but this can be done only at twelve-monthly intervals, so the rent will remain constant for at least a year.

Assured shorthold tenancies

An *assured shorthold* of *tenancy* must be for a minimum period of six months. It is an extremely popular way (from a landlord's point of view) of renting property in the private sector. The major distinction between an *assured tenancy* and an *assured shorthold tenancy* is that a tenant under an assured tenancy has substantial protection against eviction in that the landlord must prove one of the sixteen grounds mentioned above, whereas a tenant under an assured shorthold tenancy has no protection once the fixed term has expired. A court order for eviction is needed but the court *must* grant it.

Meaning of an assured shorthold tenancy

There are four requirements:

1 It must be an *assured tenancy* (see note 1).
2 It must be for a *fixed term of not less than six months* (see note 2).
3 It must not allow the *landlord to terminate* during the first six months (see note 3).
4 *Before* the tenancy was granted the landlord served on the tenant the *prescribed shorthold notice* (see note 4).

Note 1: an assured tenancy

This has already been fully dealt with on page 294. In particular, there is a list of tenancies which are excluded (see page 298) and so cannot receive protection. This same list applies also to 'assured shorthold tenancies'. Thus, for example, if the landlord is a 'resident landlord' (see page 299), the tenancy cannot be an 'assured tenancy' and so it cannot be an 'assured shorthold tenancy' either. It is outside the Act completely and the only protection the tenant has is that mentioned in Part 3 of this chapter.

Note 2: minimum fixed term of six months

The tenant must be allowed a full six months from the date when the tenancy was granted. If less than six months has actually been given (even if it was only a day short), this would mean that the tenancy is *not* an assured shorthold tenancy but is an 'ordinary assured tenancy', so that the tenant would have full protection. In other words, the landlord would have to prove one of the sixteen grounds mentioned earlier.

Note 3: no power to terminate

If the tenancy contains what is known as a 'break clause', allowing the landlord to serve notice during the first six months, saying that the tenancy will end before the first six months have expired, this would not be an assured shorthold tenancy. The tenant would have full protection in that the landlord would have to prove one of the sixteen grounds applicable to ordinary assured tenancies mentioned above before obtaining possession. However, it is important to note that many tenancy agreements contain what is termed 'a forfeiture clause'. This provides that if the tenant does not pay his/her rent or breaches his/her obligations under the agreement, the landlord can re-enter. A forfeiture clause allowing the landlord to re-enter for non-payment of rent or breach of obligation during the first six months *is* valid and the tenancy would still be an assured shorthold tenancy.

However, if there are rent arrears or breaches of obligation during the first six months, the landlord would not be automatically entitled to re-enter. He or she would still need to obtain a court order in any event.

Note 4: prescribed shorthold notice

It is absolutely essential that the landlord gave to the tenant, before the tenancy was granted, the prescribed shorthold notice illustrated on pages 310 and 311.

The form of the notice may change from time to time (so do not rely on the notice printed here being up to date!). The purpose of the notice is to warn the tenant of the consequences of having no protection at the end of the fixed term and to tell the tenant of his/her rights to refer excessive rents to the rent assessment committee (see page 312).

What happens when the fixed term of an assured shorthold tenancy expires?

This will depend on whether or not the parties want to renew the tenancy. If both parties want to renew the tenancy and enter into a new agreement, this new agreement does not have to be for a minimum of six months and it does not have to be preceded by a new form of notice. If the parties to the new agreement are the same as under the old agreement, the renewal will be an assured shorthold tenancy despite the fact that it does not comply with the normal initial requirements mentioned above.

If the tenancy is *not* renewed and the tenant does not move out at the end of the fixed term, the tenancy will become 'a statutory periodic tenancy', meaning that the tenant can continue to reside there at the same rent as before. However, the landlord is entitled to repossess the property on giving at least two months' notice requiring possession. Here there is no prescribed form of notice and it could take the form of a letter from the landlord. However, there can be pitfalls concerning this notice requiring possession. It is dealt with by s.21 of the 1988 Act. The Act says it must be a *minimum* of two months. It can therefore be longer. For example, it could have been given during the initial six-month term. It could have been given immediately after the tenancy commenced, stating that at the end of the fixed term the landlord requires possession. Such a

Notice of an Assured Shorthold Tenancy

- Please write clearly in black ink.
- If there is any thing you do not understand you should get advice from a solicitor or a Citizens' Advice Bureau, before you agree to the tenancy.

To:

- The landlord must give this notice to the tenant before an assured shorthold tenancy is granted. It does not commit the tenant to take the tenancy.
- **This document is important, keep it in a safe place.**

Name of proposed tenant.If a joint tenancy is being offered enter the names of the joint tenants.

1. You are proposing to take a tenancy of the dwelling known as:

from [   ] *19* [   ] *to* [/] */19* [   ]   *The tenancy must be for a term certain of at least six months.*

day   month   year   day   month   year

2. This notice is to tell you that your tenancy is to be an assured shorthold tenancy. Provided you keep to the terms of the tenancy, you are entitled to remain in the dwelling for at least the first six months of the fixed period agreed at the start of the tenancy. At the end of this period, depending on the terms of the tenancy, the landlord may have the right to repossession if he wants.

3. The rent for this tenancy is the rent we have agreed. However, you have the right to apply to a rent assessment committee for a determination of the rent which the committee considers might reasonably be obtained under the tenancy. If the committee considers (i) that there is a sufficient number of similar properties in the locality let on assured tenancies and that (ii) the rent we have agreed is significantly higher than the rent which might reasonably be obtained having regard to the level of rents for other assured tenancies in the locality, it will determine a rent for the tenancy. That rent will be the legal maximum you can be required to pay from the date the committee directs.

To be signed by the landlord or his agent (someone acting for him). If there are joint landlords each must sign, unless one signs on behalf of the rest with their agreement.

Signed

Name(s) of landlord(s)

Address of landlord(s)

Tel:

If signed by agent, name and address of agent

Tel: [   ] Date: [   ] 19

Special note for existing tenants

- Generally if you already have a protected or statutory tenancy and you give it up to take a new tenancy in the same or other accommodation owned by the same landlord, that tenancy cannot be an assured tenancy. It can still be a protected tenancy.

- But if you currently occupy a dwelling which was let to you as a protected shorthold tenant, special rules apply.

- If you have an assured tenancy which is not a shorthold under the Housing Act 1988, you cannot be offered an assured shorthold tenancy of the same or other accommodation by the same landlord.

---

letter/notice is valid. Here, if the tenant has not moved out, the landlord can, when the tenancy expires, immediately start proceedings for a court order and the court order must be granted in the landlord's favour. The court has no discretion.

If, however, the landlord does not serve the minimum two months' notice during the fixed term, he or she can give it afterwards, but in this case not only must a minimum two months' notice be given but also the date specified in the notice for requiring possession must be the last day of a period of the tenancy. Thus, if a tenancy began on the 2nd of a month, the last day of a period of that tenancy is the 1st day of a subsequent month and that is the date which would have to be specified in the landlord's notice requiring possession. Some examples may make the point clearer.

Illustration. *An assured shorthold tenancy is granted for a term of six months from and including 2 January 1992. On 3 January 1992 the landlord gives notice to the tenant that he will require possession of the property on 2 July 1992. This notice is valid. If the tenant does not move out on 2 July the landlord can immediately start court proceedings and will obtain an order for possession.*

Illustration. *An assured shorthold tenancy is granted on 2 January 1992 for six months (as in example above). However, the landlord does not serve the two months' notice requiring possession during the first six months. The landlord serves the notice on 3 July 1992. The notice must be for at least two months and must expire on the last day of a period of the tenancy. The last day of a period of this particular tenancy is the 1st of a subsequent month. Therefore the earliest date that can be validly inserted in the notice served on 3 July will be 1 October 1992. A minimum two months' notice expiring on 3 September would not be expiring on the last day of a period of a tenancy and so the earliest such date is 1 October.*

If a defective notice is given, the court *cannot* make an order for possession and the landlord will have to serve a fresh valid notice and start all over again. This will obviously delay the landlord gaining possession, as well as increasing legal costs involved.

Reduction of excessive rent charged under an assured shorthold tenancy

During the initial fixed term of an assured shorthold tenancy (which must be at least six months), the tenant can refer the rent payable to the rent assessment committee if he or she can show that it is 'significantly higher' than other comparable rents payable under assured tenancies in that locality. The rent assessment committee has in its possession information concerning other rents in the locality which can be used to show that the rent being charged is significantly higher than other comparable rents. If the rent assessment committee is satisfied the rent is excessive and reduces the rent, the reduced rent is the maximum that the landlord can charge for the rest of the tenancy. However, once the tenancy expires the landlord will be able to recover possession after having served the usual two months' notice and the landlord cannot be compelled to grant a renewal. Therefore, if the tenant is proposing to refer the rent it is unlikely, of course, that the landlord could be persuaded to renew the tenancy and therefore the tenant will have to leave when the tenancy is terminated.

Death of an assured tenant or an assured shorthold tenant

What happens if a tenant dies? The position depends on two questions:

1 Whether the tenant is a *joint* tenant or a *sole* tenant.
2 Whether the tenancy is a *fixed-term tenancy* or a *periodic tenancy*.

Joint tenancy

If a tenancy is granted to two or more tenants and one of them dies, the surviving tenant or tenants automatically take over the tenancy. The landlord cannot use the death of one as a ground for recovering possession or altering the terms of the tenancy.

Sole tenancy

If the tenancy agreement is in the name of just one tenant alone, the landlord *may* be able to terminate the tenancy but this will depend on whether the tenancy is for a fixed term or is periodic.

Fixed term

If the tenancy is for a fixed term (e.g. twelve months) which has not expired when the tenant dies, the unexpired portion of the term passes to the executors named in the will (or the administrators if he or she dies intestate), who are required to transfer it to the appropriate beneficiary. The landlord cannot prevent this and cannot recover possession simply because the tenant has died.

Periodic tenancies

If the tenancy is from week to week, month to month or on some other periodic basis and the tenant dies, the tenancy will pass automatically to the tenant's spouse (including a common-law spouse) residing with the tenant at the time of the death. The widow/widower thus becomes the tenant. The landlord cannot prevent this and cannot use the tenant's death as ground for possession. When the widow/widower dies, no further passing on of the tenancy is allowed and on that occasion ground 7 (see page 303) can be used to obtain possession. But if the tenant dies without leaving a surviving spouse living with him at death, ground 7 can be used (within twelve months of the date of death) to regain possession (see page 303).

Divorce

The divorce court can order that the tenancy be transferred to the other spouse in certain circumstances. The landlord cannot use this as a ground for possession (see Chapter 4).

PART 2: RENT ACT 1977 – TENANCIES GRANTED BEFORE 15 JANUARY 1989

Protected and statutory tenancies

Tenants get more protection under the Rent Acts than they do under the Housing Acts (which apply to tenancies granted since 14 January 1989).

Most private tenancies granted before 15 January 1989 fall within the protection of the Rent Act 1977. This Act provides wide-ranging security of tenure (i.e. the landlord can obtain possession only by proving certain grounds set out in the Act). In addition, unlike the Housing Act 1988, the Rent Act sets up a system of 'fair rents' so that the landlord cannot charge what he or she likes; if a fair rent is registered for the property, this is the maximum the landlord can charge. Furthermore, when the original tenant dies, the tenancy will pass automatically to the tenant's surviving spouse or, in certain circumstances, to another member of the family. These matters will be considered in turn, but it is first necessary to ascertain which tenancies the Rent Act covers.

Protected tenancies

The Act applies first and foremost to what is known as 'the protected tenancy'. This is 'a tenancy under which a dwelling-house is let as a separate dwelling'. Thus:

1 There must be a *tenancy* and not a licence (this has already been considered; see page 294).
2 The tenancy must be of a *dwelling-house*. This includes houses, flats, and bedsitting-rooms.

3 The dwelling-house must be *let as a separate dwelling*. The property in question does not have to be self-contained. If there is a sharing of accommodation (e.g. a lounge, a kitchen, a bathroom or a toilet) this does not automatically disqualify the tenancy from protection. However, it does depend on whether or not the sharing is with the landlord or with other occupiers. If there is a sharing with the landlord, the tenant will not have full protection but will have some protection (very limited) in the form of a 'restricted contract' (see page 321, Lettings by resident landlords). If there is a sharing with other occupiers, the tenant will have *full* protection.

The protected tenancy is a contract between the landlord and the tenant and the tenancy will continue until the contract is properly terminated in accordance with the law. This will depend on whether the contract of tenancy was granted for a fixed term (e.g. six months, a year or even longer) or whether it was granted on a periodic basis (e.g. week to week, month to month etc.).

If the contract of tenancy was for a fixed term, it will expire automatically at the end of that fixed term. If it was granted on a periodic basis it must be terminated by notice to quit, given usually by the landlord to the tenant. The length of notice to quit will depend on whether it is a weekly, monthly, quarterly or yearly tenancy (see Part 3 of this chapter).

Assuming that the contract of tenancy has either expired or been terminated by notice to quit, the *protected* tenancy comes to an end. However, this does not mean that the tenant has to vacate the property. Once the protected tenancy comes to an end, the tenant is allowed to remain under what is termed a *statutory* tenancy, which gives the tenant the right to continue in residence.

This statutory tenancy can be terminated only by the landlord obtaining a court order on one of the grounds laid down in the Act.

The grounds for possession

These are referred to in the Rent Act as 'cases'; they do not apply to assured (or assured shorthold) tenants under the Housing Act – they have different grounds for possession (see page 301). If the landlord cannot prove one of these 'cases', the only other basis on which he or she can obtain possession is by showing to the court that suitable alternative accommodation is available for the tenant.

Note that cases 1–10 are all *discretionary* grounds. This means that in addition to proving the grounds, the landlord must also satisfy the court that it is reasonable in all the circumtances to order possession against the tenant.

Cases 11–20 are *mandatory* grounds. This means that, provided the landlord proves one of these grounds, the court must order possession against the tenant regardless of whether or not it is reasonable. However, in all these mandatory cases the tenant must have been given notice at or before the beginning of the tenancy that possession might be required on one of these grounds. If no such notice was given by the landlord to the tenant, the landlord cannot rely on these mandatory cases unless, in exceptional circumstances, the court considers that it is reasonable to dispense with the prior notice.

Case 1: rent arrears or other breach of the tenant's obligation

If rent is lawfully due when the proceedings commence or if the tenant is in breach of his/her obligations under the tenancy agreement, this is a *discretionary* ground for possession. This means that the court must be satisfied not only that the rent arrears existed or that the breaches occurred but also that it is *reasonable* in the circumstances to grant possession. In the case of rent arrears, it is normal for the court to make a 'suspended possession order' (i.e. the tenant can remain in possession provided he or she pays off the arrears at a specified rate in addition to current rent).

Case 2: nuisance or annoyance

This is a discretionary ground available where it can be shown that the tenant or a person residing with the tenant has caused nuisance or annoyance to adjoining occupiers or has been convicted for using the house for illegal or immoral purposes.

Case 3: deterioration of the house

If the condition of the property has deteriorated owing to acts of waste, neglect or default of the tenant the court may grant an order for possession. It should be remembered that the landlord is usually liable for most major repairs (see Chapter 19) and so cannot use this ground if the deterioration is due to the landlord's failure to repair.

Case 4: deterioration of furniture

If the landlord's furniture provided under the tenancy has deteriorated because of ill-treatment by the tenant or by a lodger or sub-tenant whom the tenant ought to have removed, this is a discretionary ground for possession.

Case 5: tenant gives his/her notice to quit and landlord sells the house

This is a rare ground for possession. A periodic tenant may terminate the tenancy by giving notice to quit to the landlord. Under the Rent Act, even though the tenant has given his/her own notice to quit, he or she is not obliged to leave if he or she changes his/her mind. However, if the landlord, having received the notice, agrees to sell the house to someone else (believing that vacant possession would be obtained), this is a ground for possession.

Case 6: unlawful assignment or sub-letting

The landlord may claim possession where the tenant has, without the landlord's consent, assigned or sub-let the whole of the property. A sub-letting of part only of the property would not necessarily be a ground for possession, but if the tenancy agreement prohibits any sub-letting (as it probably will), a sub-letting of part would constitute a breach of the tenancy agreement and therefore case 1 would become a ground for possession.

Case 7: this has been repealed

Case 8: job-related tenancy

If the tenancy was granted in consequence of the tenant being an employee of the landlord, but that employment has now been terminated and the landlord reasonably requires possession for another employee, the court may order possession.

Case 9: premises required for landlord or his/her family

The landlord *reasonably* requires possession for occupation as a residence for:
- him-/herself;
- a son or daughter over eighteen;
- his/her father or mother;
- his/her father-in-law or mother-in-law.

If there has been a change of landlord since the tenancy commenced, this ground is not available to the new landlord if he or she purchased the property subject to the tenancy. Furthermore, even if the ground is available, the tenant can object on the ground that he or she would suffer greater hardship than the landlord in having to move out.

Case 10: overcharging sub-tenants

The court may order possession if the tenant has sub-let part of the property and is charging the sub-tenant more than 'the fair rent' which has been registered for the part sub-let.

Case 11: landlord an owner-occupier

The court must be satisfied that:
- prior to the tenancy the landlord resided in the house; *and*
- the house is now required as a residence for the landlord or a member of his/her family who resided with him or her when the landlord last occupied the house.

Case 11 is also available where the original landlord has died and the house is needed by a member of his or her family who resided with the landlord or is required by someone who inherited the house, or is to be sold with vacant possession. It must be noted, however, that if the tenancy was for a fixed term and this has not yet expired, case 11 cannot be used until the tenancy expires.

Case 11 can also be used to gain possession where the landlord had mortgaged the house before the date of the tenancy and the mortgage lender sells the house because the landlord has defaulted on the mortgage repayments. It can also be used where the landlord needs to sell the house because he or she has changed job to another part of the country and needs to sell the house so that he or she can buy another house nearer his/her new place of work.

Case 12: landlord's retirement home

If the landlord acquired the house for retirement and has now retired from regular employment and requires the property as his/her residence, case 12 can be used. It can also be used on the death of the landlord or by his/her mortgage lender in circumstances similar to those mentioned in case 11.

Case 13: winter lets

The house has been let for a fixed term not exceeding eight months and at some time during the previous twelve months the property was occupied for holiday purposes. The object of this ground is to allow owners of holiday accommodation to let it for non-holiday purposes out of season.

Case 14: out-of-term student accommodation

The property belongs to a university, polytechnic, college or other recognized educational institution and has been let for a period not exceeding twelve months and in the previous twelve months was let to students. This is not available to private landlords.

Case 15: minister of religion's house

The house is held for occupation by a minister of religion and the court is satisfied that the house is now required for that purpose. This ground applies where the tenancy is a temporary letting of a vicarage etc. during a vacancy.

Cases 16, 17 and 18: farm houses and agricultural cottages

Basically, if the property is normally used in connection with agricultural work for housing farm-workers or managers and has been let to a non-agricultural worker, the landlord can use one of these grounds if the property is now required for occupation by farm managers or agricultural workers.

Case 19: protected shorthold tenancies

A protected shorthold tenancy is a fixed-term tenancy of between one and five years (granted prior to 15 January 1989). Before the tenancy was granted the tenant must have been given formal notice in writing that the tenancy was to be a protected shorthold tenancy. If a protected shorthold tenancy has been *renewed* since 15 January 1989, it automatically becomes an *assured shorthold tenancy*, governed by the Housing Act 1988 (see page 308). However, if a protected shorthold tenancy has *not been renewed* since that date, the landlord can claim possession under case 19, but to do this the landlord must serve notice requiring possession within the last three months of the fixed term. The landlord must also start proceedings for possession within a further three months from the expiry of that notice. If he or she does so, the landlord is guaranteed possession. If the tenancy has expired but has not been renewed and the necessary notice has not been given within the three months before it expired, the landlord can use case 19 only on a subsequent anniversary of the tenancy and only then if he or she serves the notice requiring possession within the three months prior to such an anniversary and institutes proceedings within three months thereafter. Otherwise, the tenancy will continue from year to year unless and until these rules are complied with. Most protected shorthold tenancies have now been terminated and no new ones can be created. All new shortholds will be *assured shorthold tenancies*, governed by the 1988 Act.

Case 20: landlord a member of the Armed Forces

If the landlord was a member of the Armed Forces when the property was acquired and let, he or she can use case 20 if the landlord now requires it to live in or has died and it is required for a successor or for sale.

Prior notice – an important reminder. With cases 11–20 *above*, the landlord must have given the tenant notice in writing that possession might be needed on one of these grounds. This notice must have been given to the tenants on or before the granting of the tenancy so he or she would know of the risk of possession being required. If such a notice was not given, the court will not grant possession unless it is satisfied that it is just and equitable to dispense with the notice. Furthermore, these grounds cannot be used if the tenancy is for a fixed term that has not yet expired. If the tenancy is periodic, the landlord must give a proper notice to quit in the prescribed form and there must be a minimum of four weeks' notice (see page 321).

Death of a Rent Act tenant

If the original tenant dies leaving a widow or widower (or a person living with the tenant as spouse even if not legally married) residing in the house immediately before the death, the spouse will become a statutory tenant and can remain in occupation. The Rent Acts continue to apply.

If there is no spouse (or the spouse lived elsewhere), another member of the original tenant's family who lived in the house for at least two years before the death is entitled to an *assured* tenancy governed by the Housing Act 1988. When the first successor dies it is possible for a second successor to take over, but only if:

- he or she was a member of the family of both the original tenant and the first successor; *and*
- he or she resided with the first successor for at least two years prior to the first successor's death.

Rent control – the fair rents system

One of the main features of the Rent Act 1977 is rent control. This is known as the system of fair rents. Either the landlord or the tenant can apply to the Rent Officer for a fair rent to be fixed. The amount of the fair rent will be determined by the Rent Officer having regard to the state and condition of the property, its location and the terms of the tenancy. However, a fair rent will normally be less than an open-market rent. An open-market rent takes into account supply and demand of rented property. In other words, if rented accommodation is scarce, this forces the market rent up. The Rent Officer must disregard this scarcity element, with the result, in most cases, that the fair rent will be less than what the landlord would in fact be able to obtain in the open market had there been no system of rent control. This fair rent system applies only to tenancies granted before 15 January 1989 and which come within the Rent Act 1977. It has no reference whatsoever to tenancies granted on or after 15 January 1989, which are governed by the Housing Act 1988 – and which have far less rent protection (see page 312). This is the major difference between protected tenancies and statutory tenancies which are governed by the Rent Act 1977 and assured tenancies and assured shorthold tenancies governed by the Housing Act 1988.

How do I find out if a fair rent has been registered?

Each local authority is required to maintain a register of fair rents which have been registered for properties in its locality. If a fair rent has been registered for a particular property, that is the maximum rent that can be charged for any tenancy granted prior to 15 January 1989. It does not matter who registered the rent or in what circumstances. The registered rent is the maximum which is recoverable in respect of tenancies granted before that date.

What if no fair rent is registered?

Either the landlord or the tenant can apply to the Rent Officer for a fair rent to be registered. If dissatisfied with the Rent Officer's decision, either party can ask for the matter to referred to the Rent Assessment Committee for the area. The Rent Assessment Committee's decision is final. The amount determined either by the Rent Officer or by the Rent Assessment Committee is then registered on the register of rents. If the landlord subsequently charges more than the registered rent, the tenant can recover the excess.

How can the fair rent be increased or decreased?

The registered rent will remain the maximum unless and until there is an application for a different rent to be registered. Normally, such application can be made only after two years from the last registration, although if there is a change of circumstances (e.g. the original tenancy was furnished but the new tenancy is unfurnished or improvements have been made) an application can be made earlier.

Premiums

Under the Rent Act a landlord is forbidden to demand or receive a premium (a lump sum of money over and above rent or service charges – in other words, any capital sum) as a condition of granting a Rent Act tenancy or giving permission for its assignment or transfer. Similarly, a Rent Act tenant cannot take a premium as a condition of transferring the tenancy to another person. This law has now lost most of its importance in view of the fact that no new Rent Act tenancies can be created after 15 January 1989, but the rules are still important for the transfer of old Rent Act tenancies, which continue to be governed by these restrictions. For *new* tenancies granted on or after 15 January 1989, the Housing Act 1988 will apply and, under that Act, there are no restrictions whatsoever on the charging of premiums and lump sums.

Tenancies outside the Rent Act 1977

Some tenancies are outside the Rent Act altogether. Where this is the case, there is no rent control and there is no need for the landlord to establish one of the grounds for possession listed in the Act.

These exceptional cases include the following:
● *Certain properties with a high rateable value.* The rules here are complex but, generally speaking, if the property has a rateable value in excess of £1,500 in Greater London or £750 elsewhere on the appropriate day it cannot be within the Rent Act. The appropriate day varies. It is generally 1 April 1973, or when the property was first rated if later.
● *Low rental tenancies.* The rent is less than two-thirds of the rateable value.
● *Board and attendance.* That is, the rent includes payments for board or substantial payments in respect of attendance. If the landlord provides meals (e.g. bed and breakfast) or personal services, such as daily cleaning of rooms and provision of bed linen, and the cost of these personal services accounts for a substantial part of the rent, the tenancy cannot be within the Rent Act 1977.
● *Student lettings.* Lettings by universities, polytechnics or other approved educational establishments to students. Private landlords who let direct to students do not come within this exception.
● *Holiday lettings.* Where the purpose of the letting was for a holiday.
● *Agricultural holdings.* Farms are excluded.

- *Licensed premises*. Public houses are excluded.
- *Public-sector tenancies* (e.g. councils). See Chapter 18.
- *Lettings by resident landlords*. However, in this case although the tenancy does not have full protection, it does have some limited protection known as 'a restricted contract'. The effect of this is that the tenant has the benefit of the fair rent system and so can refer the rent to a Rent Officer, but the landlord does not need to prove a ground for possession. No new restricted contracts can be created on or after 15 January 1989 and most of the ones prior to that date have now come to an end, so they are virtually obsolete. If the tenancy is granted by a resident landlord on or after 15 January 1989, the tenant has no protection from eviction other than that contained in the Protection from Eviction Act 1977, mentioned in Part 3 of this chapter.

PART 3: PROTECTION FROM UNLAWFUL EVICTION AND HARASSMENT

Regardless of whether or not the tenant has the protection of the Housing Act 1988 or of the Rent Act 1977, *all* residential occupiers have a right not to be unlawfully evicted or subjected to harassment. If the tenancy is protected by the Rent Act 1977 or the Housing Act 1988, then the landlord must obtain a court order before the tenant can be evicted. However, some residential occupiers do not have the protection of the Rent Act or of the Housing Act; they may, nevertheless, have the protection of the Protection from Eviction Act 1977. It applies to all residential occupiers whether they are tenants or merely licensees who lawfully occupy the property.

The need for a court order

Where any premises have been let as a dwelling and the tenancy comes to an end, but the occupier continues to reside in the premises, the owner cannot enforce his/her right to recover possession other than by court proceedings. This prevents the landlord from simply walking back in and repossessing the property. The protection extends not only to tenants but to other residential occupiers – namely a person lawfully residing in the premises when the former tenancy or licence came to an end. It does not, however, extend to squatters or trespassers. Furthermore, there are some specific cases which are excluded. These are referred to as excluded licences or tenancies.

Excluded licences or tenancies

These include:
- where the occupier shares accommodation (e.g. a kitchen, a lounge or a bathroom) with a resident landlord or with a member of the landlord's family and both the landlord and the member of his family also live in the same building;
- holiday lettings;

- where the occupier does not have to pay any rent (i.e. a gratuitous arrangement).

However, even in these excluded cases, although a court order is not required, the landlord cannot use violence to gain re-entry. Using violence to gain re-entry is a criminal offence under the Criminal Law Act 1977. The landlord can be fined or imprisoned if convicted.

Notice to quit – periodic tenancies or licences

If the tenancy or licence is periodic (e.g. weekly or monthly), the landlord must serve a notice to quit before the tenancy or licence can be terminated. This notice must be served before any proceedings are commenced for possession and it must be a *valid* notice to quit. To be valid it must comply with:
- the rules of common law; *and*
- s. 5 of the Protection from Eviction Act 1977.

The common-law rule

At common law, the landlord can terminate a periodic tenancy by giving a notice to quit to the tenant which must be at least equal to the length of a rental period (at least one calendar month in the case of a monthly tenancy) *and* must expire at the end of a rental period. For example, if a tenancy is a monthly tenancy which commenced on 2 January, a notice to quit must be at least one calendar month in length and must take effect on the first or second day of a subsequent month. The tenancy agreement may specify different rules but the tenancy agreement cannot modify the minimum requirements of s.5 of the Protection from Eviction Act 1977.

Section 5 of the Protection from Eviction Act 1977

This provides that no notice by a landlord or a tenant to quit a dwelling is valid unless:
- It is in writing and contains the prescribed information; *and*
- It is given not less than four weeks before the date on which it is to take effect.

The current prescribed information is as follows:

1 If the tenant or licensee does not leave the dwelling, the landlord or licensor must get an order for possession from the court before the tenant or licensee can lawfully be evicted. The landlord or licensor cannot apply for such an order before the notice to quit or notice to determine has run out.
2 A tenant or licensee who does not know if he has any right to remain in possession after a notice to quit or a notice to determine runs out can obtain advice from a solicitor. Help with all or part of the cost of legal advice and assistance may be available under the Legal Aid Scheme. He should also be

[Note: This Form is NOT
appropriate for use in
all cases (e.g. DO NOT
use in connection with
Housing Act 1988 tenancies
as to which see Stat-Plus
Form LTA 202)]

The Notices to Quit Etc.
(Prescribed Information)
Regulations 1988

NOTICE TO QUIT/DETERMINE
BY LANDLORD/LICENSOR OF PREMISES LET OR
OCCUPIED UNDER LICENCE AS A DWELLING

To ....
(name of tenant/licensee)

of ....

....
(address of tenant/licensee)

I/We [as] [on behalf of] [your landlord(s)] [your licensor(s)] ....
(name of landlord/licensor)

....

of ....

....
(address of landlord/licensor)

HEREBY GIVE YOU **NOTICE TO [QUIT] [DETERMINE YOUR LICENCE]** AND
DELIVER UP POSSESSION to [me] [us] [your landlord(s)] [licensor(s)] of the premises

....

....

....
(address of premises)

which you hold as [tenant(s)] [licensee(s)] on the .... day of .... 19....
or at the end of the period of your [tenancy] [licence] which will end next after the expiration of
(*) **four weeks** from the service upon you of this notice.

Dated the.............................day of...............................,19.........

signed..

....
(name of agent)

....

[to be completed by agent if serving notice]   *(address of agent)*

PRESCRIBED INFORMATION FOR TENANT/LICENSEE

1. If the tenant or licensee does not leave the dwelling, the landlord or licensor must get an order
for possession from the court before the tenant or licensee can lawfully be evicted. The landlord or licensor
cannot apply for such an order before the notice to quit or notice to determine has run out.

2. A tenant or licensee who does not know if he has any right to remain in possession after a notice
to quit or notice to determine runs out can obtain advice from a solicitor. Help with all or part of the
cost of legal advice and assistance may be available under the Legal Aid Scheme. He should also be able
to obtain information from a Citizens' Advice Bureau, a Housing Aid Centre or a rent officer.

(*) Note: Save in the case of an excluded tenancy or an excluded licence, at least **four weeks**
notice must be given to quit or to determine a licence of any premises let or occupied under
licence as a dwelling, before it takes effect. *(Protection from Eviction Act 1977, S.5 (1), (1A)
and (1B))*

able to obtain information from a Citizens' Advice Bureau, a Housing Aid Centre or a rent officer.

Failure to provide this information renders the notice invalid.

It is emphasized that four weeks is an *absolute minimum* and that a longer notice may be required in many cases. For example, if the tenancy is a monthly tenancy at least one full calendar month's notice is required at common law and therefore four weeks would be insufficient in most cases.

These rules apply not only to periodic tenancies but also to periodic licences, so that even if the occupier does not have a tenancy in the strict sense, he or she is still entitled to a minimum of four weeks' notice in the prescribed form.

There are, however, some exceptional cases not covered by s.5 of the Protection from Eviction Act 1977. Certain types of tenancies and licences are excluded from these provisions. They are set out on page 322, Excluded Licences and Tenancies.

Even in these excluded cases, though, the landlord must still give a *reasonable* period of notice before seeking possession. What counts as a 'reasonable period' will depend on the circumstances. In some cases one week has been held to be too short for a residential occupier, but each case must be looked at on its own merits.

Assured tenancies under the Housing Act 1988

In the case of an *assured tenancy* under the Housing Act 1988 (see page 294) a landlord's notice to quit is totally ineffective and can be ignored. Instead, the landlord is required to serve a 'notice of intention to commence possession proceedings', which must be done a minimum length of two weeks before the landlord can start court proceedings, and in some cases a minimum length of two months before. The form of the notice and its length are considered in more detail in Part 1 of this chapter (see page 305).

Unlawful eviction

If the landlord evicts the tenant or occupier without a court order (e.g. by turning out the tenant's furniture and/or changing the locks while the tenant is away), this constitutes unlawful eviction. The remedies are dealt with below (page 325).

Harassment

Harassment is any act done with the intention of causing the tenant to give up possession of all or part of the property or to refrain from exercising his or her legal rights. It also includes acts which are *likely* to have this effect even if the landlord did not intend that result to happen.

Harassment can take many forms but here are a few examples:
● locking the tenant out of the building;

- changing the locks;
- assaulting the tenant or his/her family;
- turning off the gas, water or electricity without good cause;
- taking up floorboards every weekend on the pretext of repairing the electric wiring;
- removing slates from the roof;
- deliberately blocking a shared WC;
- leaving a hi-fi on so as to disturb the tenant;
- the landlord kicking the door every time he passes it;
- frequently shouting abuse at the tenant or making threats of eviction;
- interfering with the tenant's hot-water supply;
- removing light bulbs from the hall so that the passage becomes unsafe.

Such acts can amount to the offence of 'harassment' under the Protection from Eviction Act 1977, even if they are not successful and the tenant stays put.

In cases of unlawful eviction and harassment there are several remedies available.

Remedies for unlawful eviction and/or harassment

Court injunction

The tenant/occupier can apply to court for an injunction reinstating the tenant/occupier and/or prohibiting the landlord from continuing his/her unlawful conduct. If an injunction is obtained and the landlord breaches it, he or she is liable to imprisonment. In most cases the county court is the appropriate court.

Criminal prosecution

Criminal prosecutions for unlawful eviction and harassment are normally dealt with by the local authority. Under the Protection from Eviction Act 1977 it is a criminal offence for any person unlawfully to deprive a residential occupier of his/her occupation of premises or any part of it or to attempt to do so. It is also an offence to do acts likely to interfere with the peace or comfort of a residential occupier or members of his/her household or persistently to withdraw or withhold services reasonably required for occupation of the premises if the landlord knows or believes that such conduct is likely to cause the residential occupier to give up occupation of the property or to refrain from exercising any of his/her rights. The offence is punishable by a fine and/or imprisonment for up to six months (and in some cases up to two years). It is a defence if the landlord had reasonable cause to believe that the residential occupier has ceased to reside in the premises. Local authorities are able to bring prosecutions.

Damages

The tenant who suffers loss as a result of being unlawfully evicted or harassed into leaving the premises has always had the right to sue the landlord if the loss actually incurred. However, under the Housing Act 1988, which applies to all residential occupiers and not just to those mentioned in Parts 1 and 2 of this chapter, the measure of damages has been enormously increased. This is intended to deter landlords from unlawful eviction or harassment. For example:

Value of landlord's interest in property with vacant possession (i.e. free of tenancy) £75,000
Value subject to tenancy £44,000
Difference in value £31,000
Thus the unlawfully evicted tenant is entitled to £31,000 damages under the Housing Act 1988. Tagro v. Cafane (1991), Court of Appeal

Some other cases of high damages being awarded under these provisions include £34,000 (Weston v. Maloney, 1991 – Blackpool County Court) and £20,278 (Chappel v. Panchall, 1991 – Preston County Court).

In order to succeed, the tenant/occupier must show that he or she has been unlawfully deprived of possession of the property or has left because the landlord (or someone on his or her behalf) has done acts likely to interfere with the peace and comfort of the occupier or his/her family, or persistently withheld or withdrawn services reasonably required for occupation.

Defences/mitigation of damages under the Housing Act 1988.

● *Belief that residence has ceased.* If the landlord can show that he or she genuinely and reasonably thought the tenant/residential occupier had already moved out before the conduct complained of, this is a defence. It may be difficult for the landlord to prove this.
● *Misconduct by tenant/occupier.* The damages can be reduced if the tenant/occupier or someone living with him or her has been guilty of unreasonable conduct which makes it fair for the damages to be reduced. This must be judged on the facts of each case.
● *Reinstatement.* It is a defence if, before the legal proceedings are disposed of, the tenant/occupier is reinstated or the court, at the tenant's/occupier's request, makes an order reinstating him/her.
● *Offer of reinstatement.* The damages can be reduced if the landlord offers to reinstate the tenant/occupier, who unreasonably rejects that offer. The offer must be made *before* the court proceedings are commenced. If the court takes the view that the tenant/occupier was right to reject the offer (e.g. because he or she feared that the landlord might do the same thing again), there will be no reduction in damages.

Other damages

Apart from being able to claim for the loss of the tenancy, or the right to occupy, the tenant may recover damages for other losses. For example, if the tenant has been assaulted or his/her belongings have been destroyed or damaged as a result of the landlord's actions, additional claims can be made for such items.

18 Council Housing

Whereas the Rent Act 1977 and the Housing Act 1988 – which control relations between landlords and tenants of privately rented properties – are of awesome complexity, the law for council tenants is relatively straightforward. In short, council tenants have considerable protection from eviction, but little or no protection from rent increases.

RENT

A council tenant will have to pay whatever the local authority thinks is 'reasonable'. The tenant must be given four weeks' notice of the proposed rent increase. The increase does not have to be phased, but the notice of increase must be served. Financial assistance with rent is available to council tenants through housing benefit.

EVICTION

A council tenant can be evicted only by a court order. This will be made only in certain well-defined circumstances and if it would be reasonable to evict, or if alternative accommodation is available.

THE PROVISION OF ACCOMMODATION

Local authorities have considerable discretion in deciding to whom they should let council flats or houses. In short the 'general management, regulation and control' of local authority housing is within the hands of the local council, but this is subject to influence and pressure from central government as to the design and layout of the houses.

Sometimes a simple waiting-list is the sole criterion in the selection of tenants, although it is more usual for it to be combined with a *points system* that takes into account such things as:
- room deficiencies, including mixed sleeping;
- whether the family has been broken up as a result of their poor housing conditions;
- the absence of facilities such as a bath, WC, cooker etc.;

- the fact that the accommodation is shared with other people;
- the inadequacy of the facilities provided (e.g. if the cooker is on the landing or the WC is in the back yard);
- personal health, age and disability;
- length of time the family has been living in the borough;
- length of time the family has been on the housing waiting-list.

Different boroughs award different numbers of points for these varying factors, for the government has not laid down any fixed guidelines. Councils must provide written summaries of their selection and priority rules if requested.

Councils are under a statutory duty to give a reasonable preference to persons in insanitary or overcrowded housing, persons with large families, or persons living under other unsatisfactory housing conditions.

When it is decided that an applicant should be offered a house or flat, the usual procedure is for him or her to be visited by a member of the council's housing department. The council official will try to form an impression of the applicant's general desirability as a tenant. Thus tenants are often informally graded, so that a high-quality home will not be given to an unsatisfactory tenant and a tenant with financial problems will probably be offered a cheaper property than would otherwise be the case.

REHOUSING

Generally, therefore, the council has a wide discretion when deciding how to allocate its accommodation. However, there is one restriction on this discretion, for the council must, by law, rehouse any person made homeless by compulsory purchase, redevelopment, demolition etc. on the part of the council; in such a case the council must provide 'suitable alternative accommodation on reasonable terms' if the applicant cannot find such accommodation for him- or herself. Generally, therefore, the council has to rehouse in these cases.

For whether the council has to rehouse in other cases, see Chapter 62.

THE COUNCIL TENANCY: A SECURE TENANCY

In law, a council tenancy is usually called a 'secure tenancy'. The rules on rent and eviction set out in this chapter apply only to secure tenants. This, in practice, includes the vast majority of council tenants.

But the following council tenants are excluded and will not have secure tenancies:

- lettings of non-residential property;
- fixed-term lettings for a period of over twenty years;
- some lettings to students;
- lettings to council employees when 'the house comes with the job'.

In addition, short-term temporary accommodation will not be protected since there will not be a secure tenancy. This covers property let:

● *As short-life lettings pending development of the land.* For instance, many councils allow squatting groups to occupy short-term property that is due for redevelopment or demolition; these squatters would not be secure tenants.

● *To homeless people under the Housing Act 1985.* There is a twelve-month period before they become secure tenants, so during that time the council can evict them more easily. At the end of the twelve-month period (or earlier if notified or rehoused elsewhere by the council) the tenant becomes a secure tenant and so has the benefit of the stricter controls on eviction.

● *To job seekers.* If a person moves into a district or London borough to take up a job, the local authority can give him or her accommodation without their becoming a secure tenant. But he or she must have been given written notice of this before the letting began and, in any event, the restriction lasts only twelve months. At the end of that time, they will become a secure tenant.

● *When the council itself has only a short let.* If the council then lets the property, that tenant will not be a secure tenant.

The terms of the tenancy

When an applicant is offered a council house or flat they will have to accept the terms of the tenancy offered by the council. The terms will vary from council to council since there is no standardized set of terms laid down by central government.

Some councils require the tenants to sign a formal tenancy agreement, while others simply set out the main terms in the rent book. A rent book must be provided if the tenant pays his/her rent on a weekly basis.

The tenant will probably have to pay rent each week on Monday, one week in advance. They will also have to pay the water rates in respect of the property.

Allowing the tenant to make improvements

One of the more absurd clauses that used to be found in council letting agreements was a restriction preventing tenants from carrying out improvements to their homes. The Housing Act 1980 removed this restriction and the Housing Act 1985 now provides that the tenant must ask the council for permission but the council cannot unreasonably withhold its consent.

This applies to any alteration or improvement (e.g. changing bathroom fittings, erecting an exterior TV aerial, painting the outside). But in every case, the council's written permission must be asked for before the work can be done.

The council is not permitted to increase the rent on account of improvements lawfully carried out by the tenant at his/her own expense.

Sub-letting part

A lodger is a person who lives with the family – for instance, someone who shares meals and is taken into the home to live more or less as a member of the family. A council tenant need not obtain the council's prior permission before taking in a lodger. But if part of the property is let off to a sub-tenant, not a lodger, the council's written approval must first be obtained.

So the tenant must ask the council for permission and the council will want to know who is to be the sub-tenant. The council cannot unreasonably withhold its consent, but if there are reasonable grounds for refusing permission (e.g., there would be overcrowding) then the sub-letting will be prohibited. If the council gives a reason that seems unreasonable, the county court will decide the issue, but the burden would be on the council to show that it is not being unreasonable.

If part of the house or flat is sub-let unlawfully (because the council's permission was not obtained or because it was sub-let in defiance of the council's reasonable objections), the sub-tenant will be an 'illegal sub-tenant' (see page 315) and the council will be able to evict him or her. However, the sub-tenant's own landlord (i.e. the council tenant) will not be able to use the illegality of the sub-letting as a ground for evicting the sub-tenant; only the council can do that.

In practice, the sub-tenant will have little security *vis-à-vis* his/her landlord, the council tenant. This is because the landlord will be a resident landlord and so the sub-tenant will have only restricted protection under the Rent Act 1977, or none at all under the Housing Act 1988.

Sub-letting/assigning the whole tenancy

If the tenant parts with possession of the whole of the property, he or she will no longer be a secure tenant, and nor will the person who takes over from them. The council would be able to obtain possession very quickly.

The general rule is that a secure tenancy cannot be given away or sold to someone else, unless, of course, the council will give its consent. But transfer is allowed:
- when one secure tenant exchanges (swaps) with another;
- when the court orders a transfer of the tenancy to the husband or wife in divorce proceedings;
- when the tenant dies and a member of his/her family 'succeeds to the tenancy' (see page 312);
- where the transfer is to a person who would be qualified to 'succeed to the tenancy' if the tenant were dead.

RENT

The tenants of council houses and flats do not have the benefit of rent-control legislation. So the council can increase the rent at any time it chooses and by any amount – subject, of course, to the new rent being 'reasonable'.

EVICTION

The Housing Act 1980 severely restricted the occasions when a council could obtain a court order to evict a council tenant. Before that Act was passed, councils could easily obtain eviction orders and the courts had no choice but to grant the order, even when it was clear that the council was acting unreasonably. The limitations on the council's power to recover possession are set out in the Housing Act 1985.

Evicting the tenant

Like any landlord, the council must obtain a court order before it evicts a tenant. If a tenant is evicted without there being a court order, it will be an illegal eviction and, generally, a criminal offence (see page 325).

The procedure to be followed is in two stages:

1 The council must serve a preliminary notice on the tenant.
2 At least four weeks later, court proceedings can be begun.

The preliminary notice to the tenant

The first requirement is for the council to serve a notice of intention to seek possession on the tenant, stating and giving particulars of the ground on which the council will apply to the court for possession. It is insufficient merely to state the ground. Particulars must be given to indicate to the tenant what, if anything, he or she can do to avoid the commencement of proceedings. It must give at least four weeks' warning of the commencement of proceedings. Exceptionally, the warning period will have to be even longer – for instance, if the tenant pays his or her rent on a quarterly basis, then three months' notice must be given. Proceedings cannot be commenced until the warning period has expired.

The preliminary notice then has a life of twelve months. If proceedings are not commenced within that time, the council will have to serve a fresh notice and wait for the minimum period of four weeks to expire before starting the court proceedings.

The court proceedings

It is for the county court to decide whether a possession (i.e. eviction) order should be made. The general rule is that a well-behaved tenant will not be evicted unless his or her home is needed and even then he or she will have to be rehoused by the council. The detailed grounds for possession are set out on page 333.

Eviction of the tenant's family etc.

What happens if the council tenant dies or leaves the rented property: do the people living with him or her have to leave as well or can they carry on living there?

Members of the tenant's family

When the tenant dies, the secure tenancy can be inherited by members of the tenant's family. Those entitled to inherit are:
● the husband/wife of the dead tenant, provided that it was his/her main home at the time of the death – he or she will always have first claim to the tenancy;
● any other member of the family who lived in the property for twelve months before the death and who regarded it as his/her main home.

'Family' means common-law husband or wife, parents, grandparents, children, grandchildren, brothers, sisters, uncles, aunts, nephews and nieces. If there is a dispute as to which member of the family should succeed to the tenancy, the landlord can select the new tenant.

The tenancy cannot be inherited if the dead tenant:
● had already inherited the tenancy by virtue of the above provisions;
● was a sole tenant who had previously been a joint tenant; *or*
● had the tenancy assigned to him or her, since he or she would then already have been the second tenant to hold that tenancy.

When the tenant deserts his family

The abandoned husband or wife cannot automatically take over the tenancy, but the landlord is obliged to accept rent from him/her and the deserted spouse's occupation is to be treated as occupation by the tenant (Matrimonial Homes Act 1983). Thus the landlord cannot argue that the tenant has left and that accordingly the remaining spouse must also leave.

Although the council must accept rent from the remaining spouse, they may refuse to transfer the tenancy to them unless the court has made an order to that effect. However, the court will make an order only in a divorce or judicial separation proceedings. If there are no divorce or judicial separation proceedings, then the court cannot order a transfer of the tenancy.

Other members of the family have no such right to remain in occupation. For instance, if the tenant is a single woman and she abandons her aged mother, her mother cannot demand to be allowed to stay in the rented property. Since the tenant has ceased to be in occupation, the tenancy has ceased to be secure.

On divorce

The divorce courts can order the secure tenancy to be transferred from one spouse to another, or from joint names into the name of one spouse only. If there are children, the tenancy is likely to be transferred to the spouse who resides with the children. The council is unlikely to transfer the tenancy unless there is a court order.

Common-law husbands/wives

When the tenant dies, the common-law spouse can inherit the tenancy (see the above section).

When the tenant deserts the common-law spouse

The abandoned partner has no legal right to claim the tenancy or to insist that the council accept his/her payments of rent. However, if the unmarried couple originally took out the council tenancy together, then they will almost certainly both have their names on the rent book. Thus the departure of one of them would not affect the other, for he/she would be a joint tenant and would be able to carry on living there.

Notice to quit given by one of two joint tenants

If the tenancy is in joint names and only one moves out, the outgoing tenant can give the council/landlord notice to quit.

This will terminate the tenancy even for the remaining tenant. The remaining tenant should seek a new tenancy agreement in his or her *sole* name.

COUNCIL TENANTS: GROUNDS FOR POSSESSION

Grounds where it must be 'reasonable' to evict

In the following cases the court will make a possession order only if it would be 'reasonable' to do so. For instance, not every act of damage will result in a court making an eviction order; the court will want to be sure that it is reasonable for that damage to lead to the tenant's eviction.

1. Rent arrears

Usually the order will be made only if the tenant has a very bad rent record. If the arrears can be paid off by instalments, the court might make an order but suspend it. The order will then come into effect if the tenant does not pay the instalments. If the arrears are paid off before the court hearing, it is almost certain that no eviction order will be made.

2. Breach of tenancy

The tenant has broken the terms of the tenancy agreement (e.g. sub-letting without consent). However, no order will be made if the breach is only minor and the tenant agrees not to do it again.

3. Nuisance, annoyance, illegality, immorality

The tenant, or anyone living with him or her, has been guilty of such conduct.

4. Damage

The tenant has damaged the property or allowed it to fall into disrepair. If a lodger or sub-tenant was to blame, the tenant must have failed to take steps to evict him or her.

5a. False statement

The tenant made a false statement, knowingly or recklessly, to persuade the council to grant him/her the tenancy.

5b. Selling the tenancy

When the tenant has bought, sold or paid or received money for swapping his/her tenancy.

6. Temporary accommodation

When the tenant has been allowed to live in the property while building works were being carried out to his/her own home, which was itself occupied under a secure tenancy.

Grounds where the council provide alternative accommodation

Here the court will make a possession order only if it is satisfied that the council can offer the tenant suitable alternative accommodation. In short, this means that the tenant must have security of tenure; it will be either another secure tenancy or a private-sector assured tenancy, but not one which the landlord could terminate by invoking a mandatory ground (see page 333), and in addition the property must be suitable for the tenant and his/her family – distance from work, size, terms of the tenancy and any furniture provided will all be relevant.

7. Overcrowding

8. Demolition, reconstruction

The council reasonably needs possession to demolish or reconstruct the premises within a reasonable period.

9. Charitable housing trust

The landlord is not a council but a charitable housing trust and the tenant's occupation conflicts with the charity's objects (e.g. a person in housing for the blind is no longer blind).

Grounds where the council must prove it is reasonable to evict and must also provide suitable alternative accommodation

In these cases, a double test has to be satisfied: reasonableness and provision of suitable alternative accommodation.

10. Disabled accommodation

The property is suitable for disabled persons but the tenant is not a disabled person, and the council requires it for such a person.

11. People difficult to house

If a housing association lets property to people who are difficult to house and the present tenant is either not within such a category or has been offered a secure council tenancy.

12. Special needs

If the property is one of a group let to people with special needs, where special services are provided, but the present tenant does not have special needs, and the council requires it for such a person.

13. Over-housed

The accommodation is bigger than is reasonably needed. But the tenant must have been a 'successor' to the original tenant (see page 312) and the landlord must serve notice of court proceedings between six and twelve months after the death of the original tenant before this ground can apply.

THE REPAIR AND MAINTENANCE OF COUNCIL PROPERTIES

Contrary to popular belief, councils are not exempt from the laws on maintenance and repair of rented property (see Chapter 19).

THE COUNCIL TENANT'S RIGHT TO BUY HIS/HER HOME

The Housing Act 1985 allows council tenants to buy their homes. No such right is given to tenants of private landlords (except where the tenant has a long-term lease).

The tenant (or his/her spouse) must have been in occupation for at least two years. The price to be paid will be the open-market price, less a discount which varies with the length of the tenant's occupation:

● up to two years, 32 per cent discount;

● over two years, 32 per cent discount plus 1 per cent for every year over two years (e.g. ten years equals 40 per cent) subject to a maximum discount of 60 per cent or £35,000, whichever is the lower amount. The discount is greater with respect to council flats, as an encouragement to those tenants to exercise their right to buy (e.g. 44 per cent discount after two years plus 2 per cent for every year over two years subject to a maximum of 70 per cent or £35,000).

The price will initially be fixed by the council but the tenant can appeal this valuation to the District Valuer within three months. The District Valuer's decision is final.

If the tenant resells within three years of his/her purchase he or she must repay all or part of the discount to the council:

Time since purchase.	Percentage of discount to be repaid
under one year	100 per cent
after one year	66.6 per cent
after two years	33.3 per cent
after three years	nil

The tenant can claim a council mortgage to finance his/her purchase. This can be up to 100 per cent of the price, subject to the tenant's income entitling him/her to a loan of that amount. If the tenant cannot afford to buy, he or she can opt for shared ownership instead.

Some housing association tenants also have a right to buy (see page 339).

HOUSING ASSOCIATIONS

Housing associations are now seen as a major provider of state-financed housing. Basically the idea is that a group of people can register themselves as a housing association with a view to constructing new homes or converting existing buildings into modern housing. If the government approves of the scheme, it will finance the building works and capital costs through full grants from the Housing Corporation, and when the work is completed the housing association will rent out the properties.

The concept of housing associations is not new; it dates from the mid-nineteenth century. However, the early housing associations soon found that their economic-cost rents were too expensive for the 'labouring classes', for whom the accommodation was intended. Thus it was left to private foundations such as the Guinness, the Peabody and the Bournville trusts to subsidize various schemes, and it was not until the 1960s that the state began to take an active interest in financing housing associations. Since then, the housing association movement has expanded rapidly.

Since there are many similarities between housing associations and local authority housing programmes, it is not surprising that housing associations are expected to have motives that go beyond the rehousing of the people who formed the association. The government (through the Housing Corporation) will want to be sure that it is lending money to a deserving cause and, in particular, will look for evidence that the association is concerned with improving housing conditions in an area where they are poor. In addition, housing associations are expected to behave like local authorities in allocating housing to those with special needs, such as the infirm and those with social problems that make it difficult for them to find accommodation. However, since the Housing Act 1988, new housing association tenancies are treated as private dwellings.

The position of the tenant in a housing association where tenancy was granted before 15 January 1989

For rent purposes the housing-association tenant receives the protection of a private (Rent Act) tenant, but for eviction purposes he or she is treated in the same way as a public (council) tenant.

Rent

Housing associations charge 'fair rents' as assessed by the Rent Officer (see page 319 for how fair rents are assessed and registered).

Eviction

The tenant of a registered housing association has a 'secure' tenancy and can be evicted only by a court order obtained in certain well-defined circumstances. The position is exactly the same as for council tenants.

Eviction of the tenant's family etc.

What happens if a housing-association tenant dies, leaves the rented property or divorces his/her spouse? Briefly, the position of the spouse and family will be exactly the same as if they were in council housing.

Similarly, the position of a cohabitee is as if the property were rented from the council (see page 333).

The position of the tenant in a housing association where tenancy was granted on or after 15 January 1989

Most new tenancies granted by housing associations on or after 15 January 1989 are governed by the Housing Act 1988 as part of the private sector. These are dealt with in Part 1 of Chapter 17. The new tenancy will be either an *assured tenancy* or an *assured shorthold tenancy*.

Rent

There is no rent control. The tenant is obliged to pay the amount of rent specified in the tenancy agreement. If the housing association wishes to increase the rent, it can do so only if either there is a clause in the tenancy agreement allowing them to do so or the tenancy is a periodic tenancy (weekly, monthly etc.) by serving a notice of proposed increase under the Housing Act.

Eviction

The tenant can be evicted only by court order, but much will depend on whether the tenancy is an *assured tenancy* or an *assured shorthold tenancy*. (See pages 294 and 308).

Transitional cases

If a new housing association tenancy is granted on or after 15 January 1989 it will not be governed by the Housing Act 1988 if:
● it is a renewal of tenancy granted before that date, *or*
● it was entered into pursuant to a contract made before that date. Here, the old rules will continue to apply.

FULLY MUTUAL HOUSING ASSOCIATIONS AND HOUSING ACTION TRUSTS

Tenancies granted by these landlords are exempt from the Housing Act 1988. Thus, if the tenancy was granted on or after 15 January 1989 by such a landlord, the tenant has no statutory protection (other than the protection mentioned in Part 3 of Chapter 17).

REPAIR AND MAINTENANCE OF HOUSING ASSOCIATION PROPERTIES

The normal rules as to the repair and maintenance of the rented property apply to housing associations (see Chapter 19).

THE 'RIGHT TO BUY': HOUSING ASSOCIATION TENANTS

Many housing-association tenants whose tenancies were granted before 15 January 1989 have the right to buy their homes from their landlords – as if they were council tenants. See page 336 for how the discount is calculated, and the rules on resale. But not all housing-association tenants have the right to buy. The rules are complicated and it will usually be necessary to ask the housing association whether it is subject to the right-to-buy provisions. Note that most tenants of charitable or cooperative associations do not have the right to buy their own homes.

19 Rented Property: Repair and Maintenance

The law on repairing rented accommodation is both complicated and difficult to enforce. Ideally, the law should be set out in one easily understood Act. But in practice this is not the case, for the law may be contained in any one of several unrelated statutes or in the terms of a tenancy agreement between the landlord and the tenant. Often a tenant will find that he or she has more than one remedy and that these different remedies originate from different Acts; it will then be necessary to decide which to pursue first.

There are several major repairing remedies that may be available to the tenant; these are set out in the table on page 341. Few of the remedies have any connection with each other; each has its own rules as to when it is available and the tenant has to work his/her way through the list, finding out which remedies are applicable to the particular problem. But to complicate matters further, the different remedies are enforced in different ways, and whereas some remedies are relatively speedy to put into effect, others are not.

So the starting-point is to check which remedies might be applicable to the problem in hand. The next stage is to see which remedy is the most easily enforced in the shortest possible time. (A helpful hint: usually Repairing Remedy No. 1, page 342, will be the most useful starting-point.)

WHAT IF LANDLORD WANTS TO REPAIR BUT TENANT WON'T ALLOW IT?

Most of this chapter deals with the position when a landlord is reluctant to repair and so a tenant has to use a legal remedy to ensure that the necessary repairs are carried out. However, it sometimes happens that the position is reversed, and it is the landlord who wants to carry out building works but the tenant refuses to give his or her consent. What can the landlord do? First, a landlord has the right to enter the property (after giving reasonable notice) and carry out *necessary* repairs if:

● there is a specific clause in a lease or tenancy agreement that gives him that right, *or*

● the repairs are his/her legal responsibility under tenant's Remedy No. 1 or No. 4 (see table, page 341).

Otherwise, the landlord cannot force repairs on the tenant, and if he or she

A Tenant's Possible Repairing Remedies

Remedy	Who enforces it?	Council tenants included?
1 Letting of less than 7 years, so landlord responsible for drains, heating structure, etc.	tenant only	yes
2 Written tenancy agreement with specific clauses on responsibility for repairs.	tenant only	yes
3 No written tenancy agreement, so several implied terms are assumed to apply.	tenant only	yes
4 Lettings at a very low rent, so landlord must keep premises 'fit for human habitation'.	tenant only	yes
5 Breach of the general environmental health laws.	either tenant or local authority	yes
6 Local authority powers for bad housing.	local authority	yes

tries to do so may be liable for harassment (see page 325). Secondly, the landlord might want to *improve, modernize, extend* or *convert* the property, as opposed to merely carrying out repairs. If so, does he or she have the right to enter the property and carry out the work? Generally, the tenant can refuse entry unless there is a specific clause in the lease that allows it. The only exception is when the landlord wishes to install 'standard amenities' (i.e. bath/ shower, washbasin and sink, all with hot and cold water) which are eligible for a local authority grant. If the tenant will not give his or her consent, the landlord can try to obtain an order from the county court. Otherwise, repairs and improvements cannot be forced on a tenant. However, if the tenant has very little security from eviction (e.g. he has a resident landlord), the tenant may have no choice but to agree or be evicted.

REPAIR OR IMPROVEMENT?

Be careful to distinguish between *repair* and *improvement*.
   Repair includes:
● remedying a defective damp-proof course;
● repointing brickwork;
● eliminating dry rot and replacing the affected timbers but not removing the cause (e.g. lack of a damp-proof course);
● renewing crumbling plaster;

- maintaining an existing water heater;
- replacing worn-out fixtures;
- rewiring;
- replumbing.
  Improvement includes:
- putting in a bathroom;
- installing extra electrical sockets when rewiring;
- installing damp-proof course;
- replacing fixtures put in by a tenant.

A TENANT'S REMEDIES WHEN LANDLORD WILL NOT CARRY OUT REPAIRS

There are several major repairing remedies. The tenant must work his or her way through the list and see which remedies apply to the specific case, and then select the remedy that seems to be most effective. In practice, Remedy No. 1 will probably be the most helpful.

Remedies enforceable by the tenant only

Repairing Remedy No. 1

In lettings of less than seven years, the landlord is responsible for maintaining and repairing:
- structure and exterior of the building;
- drains. gutters and exterior pipes;
- water, gas and electricity supplies;
- sanitary installations such as sinks, baths and WCs;
- space-heating (e.g. gas fires) and water-heating appliances.

Most rented accommodation is covered by this, which is based on s. 11–14 of the Landlord and Tenant Act 1985 (repeating similar legislation contained in s. 31–32 of the Housing Act 1961). Note that the obligation on the landlord is only to repair and maintain; he or she need not, for instance, install water heaters or gas fires if they were not there when the tenant first rented the property. Summarized, it makes the landlord liable for the repair and maintenance of the structure of the building (e.g. outside walls, roof, foundations, stairs) and of the electrical, gas and plumbing systems.

The remedy is available only if the original letting was to be for less than seven years (e.g. lease for six years; weekly tenancy), although it still applies if the tenant stays on for more than seven years. It therefore covers all periodic tenancies, and the vast majority of lettings referred to in Chapters 17 and 18. In addition, pre-October 1961 lettings are excluded unless it is a Rent Act tenancy and the Rent Register specifically states that the landlord has agreed to accept the Act's repairing obligations – as it often does.

The landlord cannot evade responsibility by putting a clause in the lease which states that the Act shall not apply.

The tenant's use of the property. However, the landlord will be able to avoid liability if the disrepair arose because the tenant did not behave properly, such as failing to 'behave in a tenant-like manner'.

Thus, if the tenant is going away for the winter, he must turn off the water and empty the boiler. He must clean the chimneys when necessary, and also the windows. He must mend the electric light when it fuses, he must unstop the sink when it is blocked by his waste. In short, he must do the little jobs about the place which a reasonable tenant would do. Lord Denning (1954)

Consequential loss. Even if the landlord is clearly liable to repair the property, there may be a dispute as to the cost of loss and damage caused by the defect. For example, if the roof leaks and rain damage is caused to interior decorations, who pays for the cost of redecorating? Even worse, suppose the roof leaks so badly that a bedroom ceiling falls on the tenant, injuring him. Can he sue the landlord for his personal injury and loss of wages while off work? As regards the cost of repairing the roof and the ceiling, there can be no argument, for the Act clearly makes this the landlord's responsibility. But as regards the consequential loss (i.e. the cost of redecorations, the injury compensation, loss of wages), the landlord will be liable only if he had notice of the defect. Thus, if the tenant had earlier warned the landlord that the ceiling looked unsafe, the landlord would be liable. Or if the landlord's builder had inspected the property and seen the defect (or if he *ought* to have seen it), the landlord would be liable. But not otherwise. For instance:

Mr O'Brien was the tenant of a flat. In 1965 he had complained to his landlord about stamping on the ceiling from the flat above, although he had not suggested that the ceiling was defective in any way. In 1968 the ceiling fell in and Mr O'Brien was injured. He sued the landlord, arguing that there had been a breach of the Act. Held: The landlord was only liable to remedy the defective ceiling when he knew that it was defective; he had not been given notice of any defect and so he was not liable. O'Brien (1973)

So the advice for any tenant is to carry out regular inspections of rented property and give the landlord written notice of any possible defect.

The main drawbacks of this remedy are that:

• it cannot be used to require structural alterations or improvements (and installing a damp-proof course would probably come within this category, although there are cases in which a landlord has had to repair an existing one);

• it cannot be used for consequential loss when the tenant has not given the landlord notice of disrepair;

• it cannot be used to require hot water or space-heating if there was none in the property at the start of the letting;

• generally, it does not apply to communal parts (e.g. shared hallway or a WC on the landing). However, if the tenancy was granted on or after 15 January 1989 the landlord will be liable for communal parts if he or she owns the entire building.

This latter point is very important if the tenancy is of a flat or bedsitter and the landlord owns the whole building. Furthermore, if these repairs cannot be done without gaining access to the flat or flats and such access is refused, the landlord will be able to defend proceedings on the basis that he or she used all reasonable endeavours to obtain access (s.116(2) Housing Act 1988). Moreover, there is no liability unless the disrepair interferes with the enjoyment of the tenant's flat.

Despite these drawbacks, the remedy will often be the main remedy available.

Enforcing the remedy. See page 346.

Repairing Remedy No. 2

When there is a written agreement, there may be a specific clause in the lease or tenancy agreement that states who is responsible for carrying out the repairs.

If a tenant has a lease, it is likely that several clauses will deal with responsibility for repairs – generally imposing many obligations on the tenant but few on the landlord. However, an express clause of this sort cannot override a repairing obligation imposed by an Act of Parliament. For example, Remedy No. 1 (Landlord and Tenant Act 1985, section 11) cannot be evaded by putting in a clause saying the Act shall not apply (see page 343).

Most leases exempt the tenant from responsibility for damage etc. caused through 'fair wear and tear'. This exempts the tenant from liability for repairs that are decorative and for remedying parts that wear and come adrift in the course of reasonable use, but it does not exempt him or her from anything further. If further damage is likely to flow from that wear and tear, he or she must do such repairs as are necessary to stop that further damage. According to Lord Denning: 'If a slate falls off the roof through wear and tear . . . the tenant is not responsible for the slate coming off, but he ought to put on another so as to prevent further damage.' The tenant could, of course, charge the cost of replacing the slate to the landlord.

Implied 'correlative' duty by landlord. If the tenancy agreement makes the tenant responsible for internal repairs and decoration but does not state that the landlord must look after the exterior, the court may imply such an obligation in certain circumstances. The landlord will probably be liable for exterior repairs under Remedy No. 1 but if for any reason Remedy No. 1 is not available, it can be argued that if the internal repairs and decoration would be pointless (because, e.g., penetrating dampness caused from outside means the wallpaper keeps peeling off), it must be an implied term that the landlord must repair the outside in order to enable the tenant properly to perform his or her duties. This 'correlative' implied term has already been successful in at least one case: Barrett v. Lounova 1989.

The tenant's use of the property; consequential loss. The position is the same as under Remedy No. 1 (see page 343).

Enforcing the Remedy. See page 346.

Repairing Remedy No. 3

When there is no written agreement, the law puts several fairly minor repairing obligations on the landlord.

Often there will be no written contract or agreement between the landlord and tenant, and so there is an 'oral' tenancy. In this case, the common law implies several terms into their oral agreement, as being the law's assumption of what they would have agreed had the terms been put in writing.

Furnished lettings. The courts have held that there is an implied covenant that furnished premises are 'fit for human habitation' at the time the letting starts. This should not be confused with the statutory requirement that all dwelling-houses be fit for human habitation (see Local Authority Remedies, page 349). Generally, a lower standard is expected than under the statutory provisions and in practice this remedy is of virtually no use.

Weekly tenancies. There may be an implied term that the landlord will be responsible for the repair and maintenance of the outside structure of the building, if it is a weekly tenancy (i.e. the tenant pays his or her rent week by week, as do most council tenants). However, the law is not clear: one case says there is an implied term making the landlord liable, but another case says he or she is not responsible. Once again, the remedy is of very little practical use. Repairing Remedy No. 1 is much more likely to be of use.

Safety of common parts. The landlord must take reasonable care to keep the common parts (e.g. steps, stairs, passages, roof, shared WC) in a safe condition.

The tenant's use of property; consequential loss. The position is the same as under Remedy No. 1.

Enforcing the remedy. See page 346.

Repairing Remedy No. 4

In lettings at a very low rent there is an implied term that the landlord will keep the premises 'fit for human habitation'.

Remedy No. 4 is based on s.8 of the Landlord and Tenant Act 1985 (but repeating identical legislation in the Housing Act 1957). It applies only if the rent at the start of the tenancy was less than £52 p.a. (£80 p.a. in Greater London), unless the tenancy predates the Act, in which case the rent levels are halved. Thus few tenants come within the scope of this remedy. Even if they do, the standard of repair is not high; all that is required is that the premises should be 'fit for human habitation'. The end result is that this remedy is of little practical use to the tenant.

The tenant's use of the property; consequential loss. The position is the same as under Remedy No. 1.

Enforcing the remedy. See below.

Enforcing Remedies Nos. 1–4

These remedies can be enforced only by tenants themselves. They cannot ask the local authority to enforce the remedies for them. The tenant will probably want to know whether he or she can claim damages and also get the repairs done.

Damages

The landlord is liable in damages as from the date he or she knew of the defect and can be sued, generally in the county court. But the compensation will depend on the circumstances of each case. The tenant may be able to claim general damages for discomfort, ill-health/injury resulting from disrepair, mental distress and disappointment. If the condition is such that he or she has no alternative but to move into temporary accommodation while the repairs are done, he or she can claim the expenses of that temporary move. Any actual expense attributable to the landlord's breach (e.g. cleaning and redecoration) can also be recovered.

Getting the repairs done

This is tenants' main concern. They can either start court proceedings or get the repairs done themselves.

Starting court proceedings. Generally tenants will bring their claim in the county court. They can ask the court for an injunction, which in effect orders the landlord to do the work, as does an 'order of specific performance', which is another type of order that they might ask for. Alternatively, the landlord may agree to give an 'undertaking' to the court to do the repairs, without the need for the case and evidence to be heard. But these three courses of action (the injunction, the order for specific performance and the undertaking) all presuppose that the tenant is able and willing to go to court. Although legal aid (see page 964) may be available, the court case will probably involve expense, inconvenience and – most important – delay. So tenants may do better to get the repairs done themselves.

Doing the repairs yourself. Tenants can get the work done themselves and deduct the cost from future payments of rent. However, the danger of this is that the landlord will say that the tenant has failed to pay the proper rent and serve a notice to quit, with a view to bringing a county court claim for an eviction order. To avoid this danger, the tenant should play safe and give the landlord written notice of his or her intention. The landlord should be given a chance to do the work – say, twenty-eight days, or seven days if it is really urgent. The tenant should obtain more than one estimate for the work and give the landlord a chance to challenge them. Only then should the work be done and deducted from future rent payments. Obviously, the tenant should be sure that the landlord is legally liable to do the work before he or she risks doing the work themselves and deducting the cost from the rent. As a less risky alternative, tenants could still do the work themselves but then sue the landlord in the county court (see Chapter 68 for the procedure) for the cost, rather than deducting the cost from rent payments. That way the tenant cannot be said to have got into rent arrears.

Council tenants have a special 'self-help' scheme for getting repairs done. It applies only to repairs costing between £20 and £200 and details are given in the Secure Tenancies (Right to Repair Scheme) Regulation 1985. Basically, it involves the tenant completing various forms and notices. The council may serve a counter-notice, objecting to the proposed repair or imposing conditions. It is a rather complex procedure, but it is not compulsory for the tenant to use it. It is simply an alternative to the ordinary legal rules. It is probably simpler for the tenant to use the ordinary legal rules and to ignore this scheme.

Remedies enforceable by either the tenant or the local authority

The next two remedies can be enforced by either the tenant or the local authority. They are speedy and effective remedies, and are derived from environmental or public health legislation, which reflects society's concern that everyone should live in hygienic, healthy surroundings. However, in practice, local authorities are reluctant to get involved in anything that might require them to spend money and so often it is only in the worst cases that they are prepared to intervene.

Repairing Remedy No. 5

Has there been a breach of the environmental health laws because the premises are in such a state as to be likely to cause:
- injury, *or*
- a nuisance to the occupiers and neighbours?

The unusual feature of this remedy is that it *requires* the local authority to take action against the landlord if the public health provisions have been broken. The local authority has no discretion.

The remedy applies to two different sets of circumstances: first, when the premises are a legal 'nuisance' (see page 376) and, secondly, when they are 'prejudicial to health'. It is the 'prejudicial to health' claim that is likely to be of most use to the tenant. To the layperson, the idea of a breach of the Environmental Protection Act conjures up images of a house infested with rats and cockroaches, or with foul drains.

Although the Act covers such blatant examples of uncleanliness, it also encompasses much less obvious health hazards that might not, at first sight, seem to be environmental health matters. For example, dampness, defective sanitary fittings, ill-fitting windows or doors, leaking rainwater drains, defective roofs, damp plasterwork etc.

But it must be appreciated that it is not the defect itself that gives rise to an environmental health remedy; it is the *consequence* of the defect that raises a matter of environmental health concern. As an illustration, consider a window that will not open because the wooden frame has rotted. In itself this will not be an environmental health matter, but if that window is the only one in the room, the result will be that there is no ventilation and that could be an environmental health matter (particularly if it is in a bedroom), since it is 'prejudicial to health' to occupy an unventilated room. Similarly, suppose the defect is a holed roof. Of itself, that will not be an environmental health matter, but as soon as it rains and water enters the house, it becomes a public health concern, for the defect has now caused a situation that is 'prejudicial to the health' of the occupants.

But there must be a defect in the property. Otherwise the remedy will be of no use. This can be a particular problem with condensation, as this case illustrates:

Council tenants lived on an estate in which the buildings had gas or electric background-heating systems. These systems were expensive to run and, in practice, none of the tenants used them. The result was that the buildings suffered from condensation. The tenants complained that the buildings were 'injurious to health' because of the extensive condensation. Held: The council was not liable. There was an adequate heating system which was not defective. If the tenants used the heating system provided, then there would be no condensation problem. Even though the court felt that the tenants were not acting unreasonably in not using the expensive heating systems, the fact remained that the council was not liable.
Dover District Council (1982)

Thus a tenant can use the public health remedy only if he or she can tie up the defect to an environmental health aspect. If there is no health hazard resulting from the defect, the remedy cannot be used. An environmental health hazard of this sort is called a 'statutory nuisance' and this is the term that the tenant should use when making a complaint.

Enforcing the remedy: (a) enforcement by the local authority. The local authority must enforce the remedy. If the environmental health officer thinks that the defects amount to a 'statutory nuisance' he or she must serve an 'abatement notice' on the landlord, specifying the defects and fixing a date by when they should be remedied. The landlord has a right of appeal, within twenty-one days, to the magistrates' court if he or she wishes to dispute the notice. If the landlord does not appeal and does not comply with the notice, he or she is guilty of an offence, unless able to show there was a reasonable excuse for non-compliance. It is up to the local authority whether or not to prosecute. Alternatively, or in addition, the local authority can itself do the necessary work and recover the cost from the landlord. But this assumes that the local authority is helpful and prepared to act on the tenant's behalf. If the council fails to serve an abatement notice, the tenant could probably go to the High Court for an order telling the council to carry out its duty. However, this is unnecessarily complicated, for all the tenant has to do is to start proceedings against the landlord.

Enforcing the remedy: (b) enforcement by the tenant. The tenant may find it quicker to take action him- or herself rather than wait for the local authority to do so. The tenant should go to the local magistrates' court and ask them to issue a summons under s. 82 of the Environmental Protection Act 1990. Once the summons has been issued, the court will serve it on the landlord and arrange a date for the hearing of the case. If the magistrates decide there is a statutory nuisance, they must issue an abatement notice. Some magistrates' courts take a fairly robust view of what constitutes a health hazard and is thus a statutory nuisance. However, it must be remembered that several seemingly trivial defects can, when taken together, amount to a statutory nuisance. Although this is undoubtedly the law, some magistrates' courts are reluctant to convict in such cases, and need to be reminded of the law. For instance:

Mr Patel issued a summons against his landlord. At the hearing the evidence was given by a self-employed public health adviser and by the local council's environmental health officer. Both described the property's defects in detail and stated that they were 'prejudicial to health'. Despite this expert evidence, the magistrates did not convict the landlord. They said that it appeared from the unchallenged evidence that the alleged defects to the premises existed and that the standard of those premises was undesirably low. The majority of the defects were trivial and appear to have been contributed to, if not caused by, the neglect of the occupiers (i.e. the Patels). They constituted an inconvenience rather than a health hazard. Mr Patel appealed to the Divisional Court. Held: The magistrates were ordered to convict the landlord. Magistrates should not substitute their own opinion for those of informed expert witnesses. Patel (1980)

From the tenant's point of view, the main problem with this repairing remedy is that it can be very difficult to get the local authority to act (especially if the council is itself the landlord!). The other problem is that legal aid is not available to the tenant who wants to take the case to court him- or herself.

Repairing Remedy No. 6: Bad Housing – Local Authority Action

Local authorities have extensive powers to deal with disrepair and bad housing. The main legislation is now contained in the Housing Act 1985. Getting the local authority to act is not always easy. A local housing advice centre may be able to help in lobbying the Housing Department, the Environmental Health Department, a local councillor or your MP. The tenant could issue a complaint to a magistrate under s.606 of the Act, but do note that legal aid is not available for this.

The various powers that local authorities have are complicated.

Briefly, the main powers are:

● to serve a repair notice;
● to make a closing order;
● to make a demolition order;
● to provide for area clearance.

Many of these powers depend on whether or not the house (or flat) is 'unfit for human habitation'. This is dealt with in s.604 of the Act. A house is deemed to be 'unfit' if, first, *in the opinion of the local authority* it fails to meet one of the requirements listed in s.604 (see below) and, secondly, in consequence, it is not reasonably suitable for occupation.

The list includes:

● structural stability;
● serious disrepair;
● dampness prejudicial to the health of the occupier;
● adequate lighting, heating and ventilation;
● adequate water supply;
● adequate facilities for preparation and cooking of food, including sink and hot and cold water;
● suitably located WC, bath or shower and washbasin;
● adequate drainage.

There are additional requirements in the case of flats in relation to the entire block.

Repair notice

If the local authority decides that the most satisfactory method of tackling the problem is repair, they may serve a 'repair notice' on the person 'having control' of the premises – which means, normally, the landlord or managing agents. The notice must specify what work is needed. The recipient can appeal within twenty-one days to the county court. If the notice is not complied with, the local authority can (if they so choose) carry out the work themselves and recoup the cost from the owner.

The repair notice procedure can also be used in cases where the house is not 'unfit' in the legal sense. Under s.190, it can be used where the property is in such a state of disrepair that although not unfit for human habitation, the condition is such as to interfere materially with the personal comfort of occupying tenants.

Similarly, the procedure can be used where substantial repairs are required to bring the property up to a reasonable standard. Failure to comply with a valid repair notice is a criminal offence and the local authority could prosecute the landlord.

Closing order or demolition order

These measures are worth considering only if the house is unfit for human habitation and the tenant wants to be rehoused. If the local authority resolves to make either of these orders, the result will be that the property will be closed down or demolished (although if the local authority has itself purchased the property, the property can be used for temporary accommodation). There is a right of appeal against a closing/demolition order to the county court if the owner objects. If a tenant is displaced as a result of either type of order, and suitable alternative accommodation is not available, the local authority must provide accommodation, but not necessarily on the same terms as the present accommodation. Compensation may be payable to the tenant.

Area action

If a whole area is affected by bad housing the local authority may resolve to declare the area either a clearance area or a renewal area. A clearance area involves the compulsory purchase and demolition of the houses affected, but if the houses can be renovated and rehabilitated a renewal area can be declared, in which case the local authority can take steps to ensure the properties are modernized. In either case, there will be a process of public consultation beforehand.

Service charges for leases

In the case of flats, the lease or tenancy agreement often contains a clause allowing the landlord to levy a service charge for the maintenance of common parts. This usually includes repairs, electricity, heating costs and painting and redecoration of common parts. There are restrictions on the amount that the landlord can charge for these items and the individual tenants (or a tenants' association if there is one) can challenge excessive amounts. The law is contained in s.18–30 of the Landlord and Tenant Act 1985 as amended by the Landlord and Tenant Act 1987 (Part V). In essence, the landlord can recover service charges if they are reasonable. Further, the landlord has duties to obtain proper estimates and to consult the tenants in certain circumstances.

Reasonableness

The landlord can recover service charges only if the items concerned:
• have been reasonably incurred, *and*

• relate to work done and the work has been done to a reasonable standard and is of a reasonable amount.

The tenant can challenge the service charge in the county court if he or she considers the charges to be unreasonable.

Estimates and consultation

The landlord must obtain estimates and consult the tenants before incurring expenditure over a certain value. The value is £1,000 or £50 per flat in the building, whichever is the greater. This means that if the expenditure does not exceed £1,000 the tenants need not be consulted. But if there are more than twenty flats then the figure is increased (e.g. it would be £2,500 for fifty flats in the block).

For works above that value:

1 The landlord must obtain at least two estimates (one from a person or firm with whom he or she is not connected).
2 Then prepare a notice to the tenants describing the work to be carried out and inviting observations on the work and the estimates. The notice must specify a date (at least one month ahead) as a closing date for observations.
3 Then he or she must send the notice (and copy estimates) to each tenant, or display the notice and estimates in the building in a place where they are likely to come to the notice of all the tenants. In addition, if there is a recognized tenants' association, a copy of the notice and estimates must be given to the association's secretary.
4 The landlord must then wait until the closing date for observations and have due regard to any points raised by the tenants or the association.

If the landlord does not follow this procedure, he or she cannot charge the excess above the £1,000/£50 per flat.

Check the lease/tenancy agreement

Apart from the above restrictions, do bear in mind that the landlord cannot charge *any* service charges unless there is a clause in the lease or tenancy agreement permitting this and the items charged for are included in the wording of the relevant clause. Furthermore, if the lease is for less than seven years, so that Remedy No. 1 (see page 342) applies, the landlord cannot contract out of such obligations and so cannot levy service charges as a condition of doing those repairs.

20 Home Improvements, Modernization and Planning Controls

Householders who wish to modernize, convert or improve their property have three hurdles to overcome before they can put their plans into effect.

First, they must raise the money. A local authority grant (see below) might possibly cover part of the cost, but they will probably need to raise money by loan or mortgage. Once it is clear that finance is available, they must next consider whether planning permission is needed. Finally, they must obtain any other necessary consents: for example, from the building society or from neighbours.

Only then can work start.

RAISING THE MONEY: LOCAL AUTHORITY GRANTS

The grant system was overhauled in 1989. In essence, there are now five types of grants:

1 *Renovation grants.* These are to improve or repair a house or flat (or to help with the cost of converting a house into flats). In practice, a means test is applied depending upon the finances of the applicant (and the criteria used differ for landlords, tenants, and owner-occupiers).
2 *Common Parts grants.* These are to help with the cost of 'common parts' (e.g. stairs, hallways, lobbies) in flats and other buildings containing more than one home.
3 *Disabled Facilities grant.* This is specifically designed to help with the cost of making the property suitable for a disabled person.
4 *Multiple Occupation grant.* These are to improve and repair properties that are in multiple occupation.
5 *Minor grants.* In practice, these cover thermal insulation, and also alterations to enable an elderly person to remain in his or her home.

The days of extensive grants from local authorities for home improvements have gone. The rules have been tightened up, with the result that there is far less money available for local authorities to spend on grants. Also, the criteria for getting grants have been narrowed considerably. In practice, many people who would be theoretically eligible for grants no longer bother to apply.

Special grants for listed buildings

Buildings of 'special architectural or historic interest' may be eligible for special grants. If the building is 'listed' by the Secretary of State, the local authority can give a grant even if the building is not within the council's geographical area. However, if the building is not 'listed', the local authority can only give a grant if it considers it to be of architectural or historic interest, and if it is situated in its area.

In addition, the Historic Buildings Council can award grants for buildings of architectural or historic interest.

RAISING THE MONEY: BORROWING TO FINANCE THE WORK

The first place to try for a loan is the building society that originally gave a mortgage for the house purchase. They may well be sympathetic to a proposal that increases the value of the property. However, building societies lend money only for work on properties that are already mortgaged to them, and it would be most unusual for them to finance repairs and improvements to a house that was mortgaged to another society.

Tax relief can be claimed on interest paid on all forms of home-improvement loan except for a bank overdraft (see page 246).

OBTAINING CONSENT FROM THE LOCAL AUTHORITY

The householder will have to consider whether planning permission is needed.

Planning permission

The wish of the householder to improve, modernize, or convert his or her home must be balanced against the effect the works will have on the local area and its amenities. The control of such development is provided by the planning system introduced in 1948 by the Town and Country Planning Act.

Planning permission is needed for any *development*. However, the word 'development' is given an unusually wide definition by the planning laws. Thus, not only does it cover straightforward building work such as the erection of an extension, but it includes any plan which involves a change of the use to which the building is put. For example, converting a house into two flats, or into an office, will be a change of use and so require planning permission; this is so even if no building work is needed to carry out the change of use.

Thus, when the town-planner talks of 'development' the word is being given a much wider meaning than it has to the layperson. The result of this wide definition is to bring most projects for the improvement, modernization, conversion and repair of homes within the scope of the planning laws. Fortunately, though, the fine detail of the Acts exempts many of the minor household 'developments' from the need to apply for planning permission.

So it is possible for a householder to carry out a 'development' and yet not have to obtain planning permission. The summaries, below, set out the rules that apply to the more usual household developments.

Applying for planning permission

Forms can be obtained from the district council (or London borough council). It is wise to discuss the plans with the council officers before filling in the forms.

Detailed plans will have to be lodged with the application unless outline planning permission only is being sought. For outline permission, the plans need only indicate the size and form of the development. If approved, the outline permission would have to be followed up by a further application to approve all the details; this is called an 'application for approval of reserved matters'. The outline planning permission procedure is not available for a 'change of use' application.

Applications generally take about two months to process. A fee is usually payable. If permission is refused, or is granted subject to conditions, the council must give an explanation to the applicant, who then has six months in which to appeal to the Secretary of State.

Flouting the planning laws

Do not be tempted to ignore the need for planning permission and assume that once the development has been completed the local authority will be unable, or unwilling, to do anything about it. The developer in such a case is likely to be served with an 'enforcement notice' requiring that the property be put back to its original (undeveloped) condition, regardless of the cost and inconvenience of doing so. If the 'enforcement notice' is not obeyed, the local authority may start criminal proceedings against the developer. The local authority can begin by serving a Planning Contravention Notice, which requires that information be given to the council about the use to which the property is being put. If that use is in breach of a condition attached to a previous planning permission, then the council can issue a Breach of Condition Notice, which is a far more straightforward and simple procedure than an enforcement notice.

If the unauthorized development involved *building works*, then an enforcement notice must be served within four years of the works being carried out. Once the four years have expired it is too late for the council to serve an enforcement notice and so the unauthorized development is allowed to stand. However, if the unauthorized development did not involve building works but

Is Planning Permission Necessary?

Advertisements   No.   But separate control-of-advertisements rules might apply (these do not apply to signs for jumble sales etc.).

Aerials   No.

Central-heating tanks   Yes.   Unless all of the following apply:
- the tank must be for domestic heating purposes, and be in the garden;
- it must not exceed 3,500 litres in capacity, or be more than 3 m above ground level;
- it should not project beyond the front line of the house where it faces on to a public road or path, nor be positioned where it might obstruct the view of a road user.

Demolition   No.   Generally permission is not needed unless the building is listed or is in a conservation area.

Detached structures   Yes.   This covers such separate buildings as a shed, greenhouse, aviary kennel, summer-house, swimming pool, sauna cabin etc. However, there will be no need for planning permission if all the following apply:
- the structure is for the use of the residents of the main house, and is connected with the residential use of the home (i.e. it cannot benefit other people or have a business use);
- it does not project beyond the front line of the house, where it faces on to a public road or path;
- the height does not exceed 3 m (or 4 m if it has a ridged roof);
- less than half of the garden is covered by the new structure or other structures built since the erection of the house or since 1948 (whichever is later);
- it does not obstruct the view of road users and is not in a position to cause them danger.

Driveway or path   Yes.   Unless the drive or path gives access to an unclassified road. If the drive or path will cross the footway, pavement, or verge of a road, it will also be necessary to obtain consent from the highway authority.

Extensions   Yes.   But if the extension is for the use of the residents of the house (i.e. it will not be a separate dwelling), there will be no need for planning permission if all the following conditions are met:
- the volume of the house as originally built (or in 1948, if built before then) will not be increased by more than 70 m³, or 15 per cent, up to a maximum of 115 m³, whichever is the greater. Stricter limits apply to terraced houses; then the maximum increases are 50 m³, 10 per cent and 115 m³;
- the extension will not be higher than the original house (but if it will be within 2 m of the perimeter, then it must not exceed 4 m in height);
- it will not project beyond the front line of the house where it fronts on to a public road or path;
- it will not obstruct the view of road users or cause them danger.

Finally, if the extension will go over an existing drain or sewer, special permission will be needed from the district council. (These rules are shown in the diagram on pages 358–9.)

Is Planning Permission Necessary?

Fences and walls	Yes. Unless it is not higher than 1 m if it faces on to a road; otherwise not higher than 2 m. In addition, the fence or wall must not obstruct the view of road users or cause them danger.
Flats	Yes. There is a material change of use. In particular, permission is needed to convert a house into two or more flats. Permission is needed even if no building works are needed for the conversion.
Greenhouse	Yes. See 'Detached Structures'.
Hardstanding for a car	No. Unless a new means of access will be required (see 'Driveway or Path').
Hedges	No. See 'Fences and Walls'.
Improvements	No. Unless the front line of the house is extended in any way. Thus changing flat sash windows into bay windows might require planning permission, whereas a change from sash window to casement window would not. See also 'Internal Alterations' and 'Maintenance'.
Internal alterations	No. Unless there is a change of use (e.g. erecting a new staircase for the purpose of converting a house into a flat and an office) or unless it is a listed building. Otherwise, there is no control over internal alterations. See also 'Extensions', 'Improvements', 'Maintenance'.
Keeping a boat or caravan in the garden	No. Unless the caravan is used as a separate dwelling. However, many local authorities have local by-laws that restrict the keeping of boats and caravans in gardens, so check with the local council.
Loft conversion	No. Unless the volume of the loft will be increased; see 'Extensions'.
Maintenance	No. For example, redecorating the inside and outside, stone-cladding, repointing brickwork, pebble-dashing, sandblasting, fitting shutters to windows, etc. All of these can be done without planning permission, even if the external appearance of the house is altered. Different rules apply in conservation areas.
Office	Yes. Using part, or all, of a house as an office will be a change of use and so will need planning permission. Similarly, a householder who decides to work from home, give lessons at home, or store business goods in a spare room, will technically require planning permission, although councils will often turn a blind eye to minor infringements.
Porch	Yes. Unless all the following conditions are met: • the floor area does not exceed 2 m²; • no part of the porch is more than 3 m above ground level; • no part of the porch is within 2 m of a boundary facing on to a road or footpath.
Shed	Yes. See 'Detached Structures'.
Sun-lounge	Yes. See 'Extensions'.
Tree lopping or felling	No. But check that the council has not made a tree preservation order (see page 386).
Walls	Yes. But see exceptions in 'Fences and Walls'.

Extensions: Is Planning Permission Necessary? (And see page 357)

YES
extension is larger than 15 per cent of the size of
the original house, and is larger than 70 m³

NO
extension is within the 15 per cent (70 m³) size
limit

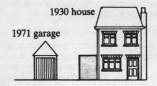

1930 house

1971 garage

YES
extension is within the 15 per cent size limit, but
the limit has already been taken up by the garage

road

YES
extension is above the height of the original house.
Front fence (facing road) can only be up to 1 m
high

road

NO
extension does not exceed height of original house

Extensions: Is Planning Permission Necessary? (And see page 357)

YES
extension is in front of original house, facing a road

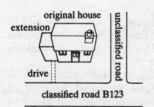

NO
extension does not face a road and is at rear of the original house

YES
extension has a new access on to a classified road

NO
extension has a new access but it is not on to a classified road

Housing: The Householder and the Law

was a *change of use* (e.g. converting an office into a flat) then there is a longer time limit for serving an enforcement notice. An unauthorized change of use can be legal only if the change of use was carried out before 1964.

Unauthorized planning development (i.e. works that were carried out without permission more than four years ago, or a change of use carried out before 1964) can be legitimized by obtaining a certificate of lawful use or development from the council (this used to be called an 'established use certificate').

Is planning permission needed?

The summaries set out the usual position for household developments, *but* bear in mind that:
• they deal with houses (for flats and maisonettes the answers may be different);
• an existing planning permission may cover the property and lay down special conditions that override the normal rules;
• special conditions can apply in conservation areas and to listed buildings; also, the position in London may be different by virtue of the London Building Acts;
• the full details are set out in the Town and Country Planning General Development Orders 1988 (and amendments since then).

Changing the use of a property

Planning permission is needed for 'a material change of use'. Thus it will be needed if, for instance, a shop is to be changed into a residential house or a factory is to be changed into a supermarket. This is so even if no building works are needed to bring about the change.

In particular, the Town and Country Planning Act 1990 states that the conversion of one house into two or more dwellings is a material change of use and so planning permission is needed. All conversions of houses into flats must therefore be approved by the planners.

Not all changes of use are so clearly within the planning laws. The difficulty lies in deciding what is a 'material' change of use. Guidelines were laid down in a ministry circular some thirty years ago:

A proposed change of use constitutes development only if the new use is *substantially* different from the old. A change in *kind* will always be material (e.g. from house to shop, or from shop to factory). A change in the *degree* of an existing use may be 'material' but only if it is very marked. For instance, the fact that lodgers are taken privately in a family dwelling-house would not in the Minister's view constitute a material change of use in itself so long as the use of the house remains substantially that of a private residence. On the other hand, the change from a private residence with lodgers to a declared guest house, boarding house, or private hotel would be 'material'. In the case of a change of use involving only part of a building which would nevertheless continue to

360

be used as a whole ... the question ... should be decided in relation to the whole premises and not merely in relation to the part (i.e. the point at issue is whether the character of the whole existing use will be substantially affected) ... He would not, for instance, regard as constituting a material change of use the use by a professional man – say a doctor or a dentist – of one or two rooms in his private dwelling for the purposes of consultation with his patients so long as this remained ancillary to the main residential use ... The use, however, of a part of a private residence for a shop would clearly be a material change of use since even if the shop were to be confined to part of the building, its establishment would involve a change in the kind of use.

The General Development Order

The basic rule is that any 'development' needs planning permission. But, because the word 'development' is defined so widely, it would cover virtually any works that anyone wanted to do to their property (as well as any change of use). To overcome this, the Town and Country Planning Acts allow certain types of development to be carried out without the need for planning permission. These exceptions – when permission is not needed – are mainly set out in the General Development Order (GDO) 1988.

For instance, the GDO allows certain developments within the grounds of a dwelling house (e.g. enlargement, improvement or other alteration, erection of a porch, enclosure of a swimming pool, within certain limits). Refer to the accompanying diagrams for illustrations of how these rules work.

Similarly, the GDO permits certain minor building operations to be carried out: for instance, the erection of gates and fences, and the construction of roadways to minor roads (subject to height limitations). Once again, the diagrams show how these rules work. Having said that, the rules are extremely complex and one should always double-check with the local planners.

There are also important rules on when one can change the use of premises without the need for planning permission. The basic rule is that any change of use amounts to 'development', and therefore requires planning permission. However, the GDO says that certain types of change of use are exempt from the need to obtain planning permission. The main legal document on changes of use is the Use Classes Order. This categorizes the more common types of usage. For instance, Class A1 cover shops; Class A2 covers financial and professional services; Class A3 covers premises selling food and drink; Class B1 is general business and offices; Class B2 is general industrial. There are many further sub-classes, but these are the main ones encountered.

The rule is that you can change the use of premises within the same use class. For instance, if premises are currently being used as a Class A1 shop, then the use can be changed to any other category A1 shop without the need for permission. On the other hand, it would not be possible to change to a different category (e.g. a shop selling drink or food, which is Class A3) without the need for permission. Similarly, a surveyor's office would be covered by Class B1 (offices), and those premises could be changed to the offices of a market researcher since that would still be an 'office' use, and thus within the same class (B1).

In fact, there are occasions when it is possible to change from one class to another: e.g. it is possible to change from Class A3 (food and drink) to Class A1 (shops); similarly, it is possible to change from Class A2 (financial and professional services) to Class A1 (shops) if the premises have a display window at ground-floor level. It is also possible to change from Class B2 (general industrial use) to Class B1 (business offices).

As can be seen, these are complicated rules. The key point to appreciate is that any development needs planning permission; this includes any change of use of premises. But, the GDO exempts much 'development' from this rule; in particular, changes of use within the Use Classes Order do not need permission.

Because of the complexity of the rules, it is always advisable to check with the local planners before carrying out any 'development' (i.e. building works or change of use).

Finally, it should not be forgotten that any building works carried out should comply with the relevant building standards.

Listed buildings

Listed buildings are subject to special planning controls. There are three grades of listed buildings:
● Grade I: buildings of exceptional interest (only about 2 per cent of listed buildings are in this category);
● Grade II: these are particularly important buildings of more than special interest (some 4 per cent of listed buildings);
● Grade III: these are buildings of special interest which warrant every effort being made to preserve them.

There are over 6,000 Grade I buildings and over 20,000 Grade II buildings.

Conservation areas

A district or county council can designate an area as being of special architectural or historic interest: this is a conservation area. There are about 6,300 conservation areas in England.

If a property is within a conservation area, it follows that the planners will give special attention to the desirability of preserving or enhancing the character of the area whenever they are considering a planning application. The basic rule is to say that the planners start with a presumption in favour of preservation.

The GDO (see above) normally allows certain development works to be carried out without planning permission (e.g. increasing the size of a property by up to 15 per cent). But within a conservation area those exceptions are severely restricted (e.g. the 15 per cent increase limit becomes 10 per cent; stone-cladding is completely prohibited).

In addition, any tree within a conservation area is automatically protected (as though there were a Tree Preservation Order in respect of that tree).

Booklet. Anyone who has a planning-permission query should begin by obtaining a copy of an excellent booklet called *Planning Permission, a Guide for Householders* (free from councils and CABs).

Obtaining other consents

Even if the householder has raised enough money to finance the improvements or modernization, and has obtained any necessary planning permission from the local authority, it still may not be possible to do the work.

There may be other people whose consent has to be obtained before starting work. In particular, it may be necessary to ask permission of someone with the benefit of a restrictive covenant over the land; a ground landlord; the building society that gave the mortgage to buy the property; or a tenant who lives in it. Some, none or all of these consents may have to be obtained.

Restrictive covenants

Restrictive convenants may limit the freedom of the freeholder to do what he or she likes with a property. Frequently, such restrictions are imposed by the developer of a building project when selling off the plots, so as to preserve the character and amenities of the area or of a neighbouring piece of land. In essence, the present owner of land A can stop the present owner of land B from doing what is expressly forbidden by a restrictive covenant in land B's title deeds.

Typical restrictive covenants are shown in the specimen Land Registry certificate in Appendix 2; other restrictive covenants that are frequently met forbid the erection of fences, construction of extensions, use of premises as an office etc.

The law on restrictive covenants is complicated and in some respects out of date. Detailed rules decide when a restrictive covenant is enforceable. The solicitor who acted on the purchase of the property should be able to advise the owner whether the land is subject to any restrictive covenants, and if so, may also be able to say who they benefit.

In practice, many of the restrictive covenants in title deeds are unenforceable because they do not comply with the strict rules as to enforceability; such covenants can be safely ignored by the householder, but obviously this is something that should be done only after taking full legal advice.

If there is a valid restrictive covenant that affects planned building work, then there are four possible lines of action:

1 Approach the holder of the restrictive covenant and negotiate (i.e. buy) permission.

2 Apply to the Lands Tribunal for the restrictive covenant to be cancelled or altered. Basically, the landowner will have to prove that:
 ● there has been a change in the character of the area, *or*
 ● no one would be injured by the cancellation or amendment, *or*
 ● the restrictive covenant impedes the reasonable use of the land.

In practice the landowner has to make out a very good case, and may well have to pay compensation. In any event it will probably cost several hundred pounds to make the Lands Tribunal application and the plans will be held up for months while the case waits to be heard.

3 If the plans involve the conversion of a house into two or more flats or dwellings, the landowner can apply to the county court (and not the Lands Tribunal) for the restrictive covenant to be cancelled or altered. Once again, cost and delay are factors to be borne in mind.

4 The householder can simply insure, so that if the restrictive covenant should be enforced against him or her the insurance company will pay compensation. Obviously, cover is available only when it is most unlikely that the covenant is enforceable. Premiums vary considerably but a typical rate would be £5 per £1,000 covered.

Is a restrictive covenant enforceable? Suppose my land has the benefit of restrictive covenants affecting my neighbour's land. Can I enforce the covenants? Only if:
 ● my neighbour's title deeds make it clear that the restrictive covenant is to benefit my land (unless they were both part of an estate developed and sold off by one person, in which case special rules apply), *and*
 ● the restrictive covenant can be observed without the need for my neighbour to spend money. For example, a clause to 'maintain a fence' cannot be a restrictive covenant since it requires money to be spent, as does a clause 'not to allow a party wall to fall into disrepair'. But compare 'not to use the premises for business purposes' or 'not to build on the garden' – these do not require the spending of money, and so can be valid restrictive covenants.

These are complicated rules, so always take specialist legal advice.

Covenants in a long lease

In the same way that a freeholder's rights may be limited by restrictive covenants, a leaseholder's rights may be limited by clauses in the lease. Moreover, the advantage of a lease is that it allows positive covenants (e.g. to spend money on repairing a fence) to be enforced. This is why most flats are sold on a leasehold, not freehold, basis.

Most long leases (i.e. leases for over twenty-one years) require the leaseholder to obtain the landlord's consent before erecting an extension or carrying out any other building work. Such consent should always be obtained, for otherwise the landlord might be able to terminate the lease for breach of covenant by the tenant; dispense with consent only after taking full legal advice.

As with restrictive covenants, the Lands Tribunal and the county court have powers to cancel and amend such clauses in long leases. The grounds of application are identical to those for restrictive covenants, above.

With most Rent Act and Housing Act tenancies (i.e. lettings for under twenty-one years) the tenant must ask the landlord for permission before carrying out any improvements. However, the landlord cannot unreasonably refuse to give permission for any improvement or alteration.

Mortgage company's consent

Most mortgage deeds require the borrower to obtain the mortgage company's consent before carrying out any alterations or building works. Usually, obtaining consent is no more than a formality since the mortgage company will be only too pleased to approve works that increase the value of the property. However, the consent should always be obtained, for otherwise – in theory, anyway – the mortgage company might be entitled to reclaim its loan.

Party walls

A neighbour may have a 'right of support' from the land or buildings on the householder's land. If so, the householder must not carry out any works that would interfere with that right. In effect, both property owners are prevented from pulling down the party wall.

In London there are special laws that allow a householder to develop a party wall after giving notice to the neighbour. If the neighbour will not consent to the works, permission to carry them out can be obtained from the court, which can also order the neighbour to contribute towards the costs of the works if he or she will benefit from them. Architects and surveyors can advise on how these rules work.

Rights of light

Check that any building works will not interfere with a neighbour's right of light (see page 374).

A tenant's consent

If there is a tenant living in the property, it may well be necessary to obtain their consent before any building work can be carried out. There are strict rules about forcing unwanted repairs and improvements on to tenants (see page 340).

21 Neighbours

Every householder has certain rights, and similarly his or her neighbours will have rights over their property. At times, these rights and interests will clash, and then the law must resolve the ensuing dispute.

But the law is a clumsy instrument for dealing with such a delicate relationship and the aggrieved householder will probably do better to use tact, persuasion and diplomacy, rather than move in with a blunt statement of legal rights. All solicitors know from experience how neighbour disputes can easily erupt into lengthy, expensive and bitter litigation, with the real cause of the argument being lost in a web of hurt feelings and self-justification. Often, too, neither party is satisfied with the outcome.

If the parties cannot reach a satisfactory compromise, what is the legal position? What are the rights and responsibilities of the householder *vis-à-vis* neighbours?

MY RIGHTS – MY NEIGHBOUR'S RIGHTS

We have already seen that there is no such thing as the 'absolute ownership' of land or the complete freedom to do as one wishes in one's house or garden (see page 242). This is because the householder's right to 'use and enjoy' his or her property is subject to the rights enjoyed by the community and by other individuals over that land. A glance back at the table on page 244 will illustrate this; the owner's rights seem at first sight to be all-embracing, but we see that in fact they are subject to:

● rights vested in the community (e.g. to enforce public health standards of hygiene on the property; to control the erection and design of buildings; to allow police and gas board officials to enter the house etc.);

● rights that other individuals have over the property (e.g. a right of way to walk over the land; the power to stop nuisance-making activities etc.). These are the sort of rights that neighbours can have over one's land, and are therefore the concern of this chapter.

Thus my right to use and enjoy my land freely is limited by my neighbour's rights. Conversely, the extent of my rights over my neighbour's land affects the neighbour's ability to use and enjoy that neighbouring property.

The point to be repeated (again and again!) is that the law should be the last

Troublesome Neighbours

Possible legal remedies

Suing for trespass (see below) e.g. to tackle overhanging tree branches; intrusion on to one's land etc.

Suing for legal nuisance (see page 376) e.g. to tackle noise, smells, fumes etc.

Complaining to the Public Health Department (see page 349) e.g. to tackle smells, dirt, dust.

Complaining to the Planning Department (see page 354) e.g. to tackle problems raised by commercial use of a residential house.

Issuing a summons under the Control of Pollution Act (see page 380) e.g. to tackle persistent noise.

---

resort in a neighbour dispute. Conciliation, not confrontation or litigation, is likely to yield the best results.

Trespass

'Keep Out – Private Property' is a concise statement of the law. If someone owns a plot of land, a house, or a garden, it is up to them to decide who can come on to the property. This is, of course, subject to the community's right to send in the police or to allow gas pipes to be laid etc. But as regards other private individuals, such as neighbours, the owner can generally say 'Keep Out – Private Property: You are Trespassing.'

What if the trespasser defies the owner's wishes and comes on to the property; what can be done? First, the landowner can eject the trespasser, after first asking him or her to leave, using no more force than is necessary. But this is unwise, for the trespasser might allege that unnecessary force was used and so prosecute for assault.

Secondly, the landowner could sue the trespasser for damages, to obtain compensation for any loss caused. Unless the intruder had damaged the house, trampled on the garden or broken a fence, it would be unlikely that the landowner would have suffered any loss and so claiming damages would be a pointless exercise. The owner would probably recover only nominal damages of a few pence, and the court might show its disapproval of suing over such a petty matter by not awarding any legal costs.

Does this mean that there is no remedy against the trespasser? Against the casual trespasser – such as the country walker who takes a short cut across a field – the answer is 'yes', for in practice the landowner can do nothing unless real damage is caused. However, the landowner could ask the court for an *injunction* against a persistent trespasser, ordering that person not to trespass in the future; if that order was ignored then the trespasser would be in contempt of court and so be liable to fining or imprisonment. Thus, if a person regularly uses someone else's back garden as a short cut, or if they frequently park their car on someone else's lawn, the law can be used to stop the trespassing.

As for signs that proclaim 'Trespassers Will be Prosecuted', these are pure bluff on the part of the landowner. Trespass is a wrong to the landowner, who can sue in the civil courts for damages and/or an injunction. But the landowner cannot prosecute, since trespass is not, of itself, a criminal offence. Exceptionally, the person who trespasses in a building by squatting may be committing a criminal offence, but the general rule remains that trespass is a civil, not a criminal, wrong.

Squatters' rights

If someone trespasses on land for twelve years they may acquire the legal title or ownership of that land. In fact, there is no need to live there for that twelve-year period, for all that has to be done is to assert one's authority and ownership during that time openly, without acknowledging the owner's right to the land (e.g. by asking permission to stay there or by paying rent). In addition, the owner must not have been in possession or have asserted any rights over the land (e.g. by asking the squatter to leave).

The strict requirements of this *adverse possession* by the squatter mean that it would be most unusual for a squatter in a housing squat to acquire a title in this way, for few householders would completely ignore the possession for twelve years. However, it has been known to happen. In contrast, in agricultural areas it is not uncommon for a farmer to acquire title: for instance, when renewing a fence the farmer may erect the new fence a few yards on the wrong side of a neighbour's boundary, and perhaps acquire the title to the land after grazing animals there for twelve years.

Rights of way

The general rule is that a person who goes on to another's land without permission will be a trespasser. But footpaths and other rights of way allow the use of private land without trespassing.

Private footpaths

A person may have the right to use a footpath across private land. That right can be given by written deed, or it can be acquired by using the footpath for a sufficiently long period.

Some legal rights can be acquired by continued usage over a long period of time – by what the law calls *prescription* (see page 245). So it is with footpaths –

a person who openly crosses another's land for twenty years or more can acquire the right to do so for the years to come. However, for prescription to apply, the person must have acted as though they had the legal right to use the path and the landowner must have impliedly accepted that right (e.g. by not challenging the use or by not doing anything inconsistent with it). So if the trespasser asked for permission or offered payment, or if the owner told him or her to stop using the path, the prescription rule could not apply.

If a person has a right of way across another's land then they will not be a trespasser as long as they keep to the footpath. If they deviate from the path, they will become a trespasser.

Public rights of way

In the same way that an individual can acquire a private footpath right, so the public at large can gain a public right of way. Public rights of way can be created after twenty years' use, but only if the route is used:
• by the public at large (i.e. not just by the landowner's staff), *and*
• as of right (i.e. without permission having been asked for or given), *and*
• over a defined route (cf. general access to a hillside).

After twenty years' use by the public, the law presumes that the landowner has dedicated the land as a public highway (Highways Act 1980). To avoid this happening, a landowner should publicly show that a public right of way is not being created. This can be done by displaying a sign stating that the land is not being dedicated as a public highway, or by depositing a formal notice with the local authority. Alternatively, the landowner can protect his or her position by blocking off the road or path for one day every year (as is done in the Temple area of London), so as to assert ownership and indicate that the use of the path is by courtesy only.

A right of way, whether public or private, can be restricted to a particular type of user. In cases of uncertainty, one should inspect the local authority's definitive map showing all highways in their area. By the National Parks and Access to the Countryside Act 1948 and the Countryside Act 1968 all highways have to be categorized as either:
• *footpaths* – pedestrians only;
• *bridleways* – pedestrians and horses only;
• *by-ways open to all traffic* – i.e. cart-ways open to pedestrians, horses, carts and cars.

The district and county councils keep copies of the definitive map, which shows the location and classification of every public right of way. If a path is marked on a definitive map that will be conclusive evidence that it is open to the public, but just because a path is not on the map it does not follow that it is not open to the public. So public paths can still be created and can therefore exist even when not marked on the definitive map. Obviously, in such a case it is sensible to ask the county council to include the path on the definitive map when it is next revised.

A footpath cannot be lost by disuse; once a footpath exists it remains a footpath, until closed by an order made under a statute. Such an order might be made, for example, to divert a path in order that a building estate can be constructed.

Use of a footpath

A public footpath can be used by anyone, but only for passing along it in the course of a bona fide journey. While the walker can stop for a rest he or she cannot use the footpath for camping on or for some other use unconnected with travelling along the path. If the path is not used for its proper purpose, the walker becomes a trespasser.

A footpath ran beside a field where horses were trained. A journalist walked backwards and forwards over a 15-yard stretch of the path for an hour and a half, making notes on the performance of the various horses. Held: He was a trespasser since he was not just using the path for a bona fide journey. While it would not be unreasonable for a walker to sit down to rest, or even to stop to make a sketch, it was unreasonable to use the footpath as a means of spying on the training of horses. Hickman (1900)

The general rule is that it is a criminal offence to ride a motor bike or drive a car on a footpath or bridleway. Although horse riders are not allowed to use footpaths they do not, in fact, commit any criminal offence in doing so; the only remedies are for the council to put up barriers (but leaving sufficient space for walkers), or for the landowner to sue for trespass. Finally, a walker can take a dog on a footpath, but obviously it must not be allowed to stray on to the neighbouring land.

Maintenance of footpaths and bridleways

The general rule is that it is the duty of the county council, or London borough council, to maintain public footpaths and bridleways in its area; the only exceptions are footpaths created since 1949 which the council has not agreed to maintain. By s.130 of the Highways Act 1980, county councils have a duty 'to assert and protect the rights of the public to the use and enjoyment' of paths in their area and 'to prevent as far as possible the stopping up or obstruction' of paths.

The council's duty is to maintain only the surface of the path. There is no duty to maintain the subsoil on which it rests. For example, if a towpath collapses into a canal the council need not repair the path since it has now disappeared!

A council is not expected to maintain a path in perfect condition. As long as it is safe and fit to carry its usual amount of traffic that will be sufficient. The rambler cannot expect a little-used path to be fully cleared. Ministry guidelines to councils state:

Where paths are used mainly for pleasure by ramblers, it will no doubt generally be sufficient that they should be free from obstructions or impassable water or mud, and that they should be inconspicuously but sufficiently signposted or marked where necessary. The main consideration is clearly that they should serve their purpose, whether business or pleasure, and not that they should conform to some arbitrary standard of construction.

If the county council, as the highway authority, fails to maintain paths to this standard, it can be taken to court by any private individual and ordered to repair the path or bridleway. For instance:

Over the years a public footpath had become increasingly obstructed by fences and buildings put up by adjoining landowners. Since 1969 the parish council, local residents and local organizations had been urging the county council to use its powers and force the landowners to remove the various obstructions. Eventually the parish council sought a court order requiring the county council to take action. Held: Yes. The Highways Act required the county council 'to take proper proceedings' to remove obstructions. It had not done so. The court would order the county council to take action. Surrey County Council (1980)

In addition, if the authority fails to inspect the paths reasonably often and then carry out any necessary works, it may well be liable in damages to anyone injured because of the lack of repair. However, it is rare for such a liability to arise since the courts do not expect councils to carry out frequent inspections of their footpaths.

Mrs Whiting was injured while walking on a footpath. She stepped into undergrowth beside the path to let another walker pass and hurt herself on a concealed tree stump. She sued the council, but the council argued that it had not been negligent. The path had been inspected in July, cleared the following February, and the accident happened a month later. Held: The council had acted reasonably and was not liable. Whiting (1970)

While the duty to maintain the surface of a footpath falls on the council, the duty to maintain stiles and gates rests on the owner of the land. The obligation is to keep stiles and gates 'in safe condition, and to the standard of repair required to prevent unreasonable interference with the rights of persons using the footpath or bridleway' (Countryside Act 1968). The council must contribute at least a quarter of the maintenance costs. If the landowner does not maintain the stiles and fences, the council can give fourteen days' notice and then do the work itself, but at the expense of the landowner and without any contribution from the council. Alternatively, the council or any private individual can apply to the magistrates' court for an order requiring the landowner to do the necessary works.

In theory, county councils are under a duty to put up signposts whenever a public right of way meets a metalled (i.e. tarmac) road. But the Act does not lay down a time period within which this must be done and so, in practical terms, councils cannot legally be forced to put up signposts.

Obstructions on footpaths and bridleways

Anyone who 'wilfully obstructs the free passage along a highway' can be fined up to £400 (s.137 Highways Act 1980). The prosecution need not be brought by the highway authority but can be brought by a private individual or even an amenity group (see page 1005 for how to bring a private prosecution).

It is not necessary that the obstruction should completely block the path; it is sufficient that it blocks part of it or that it makes walking along the path more difficult. For instance, a farmer who dumps refuse on part of the path or who padlocks a gate can be prosecuted. Similarly, if a farmer allows crops to grow on the footpath or bridleway, that too may be an obstruction.

The ploughing up of a path or bridleway is not of itself an obstruction, unless, of course, it makes it impossible to use the route. In theory, ploughing might be a legal nuisance and those affected could start an action in the civil courts for damages and an injunction. In practice, the difficulty and expense of bringing such an action would deter most people from trying to take action against the farmer. Thus there is little that can be done when a footpath is ploughed. If crops have grown where the ploughing was carried out, the walker can walk through the crops provided he or she causes as little damage as possible.

Under the Highways Act 1980 a farmer could plough up a right of way (such as a footpath) provided it was reinstated within a certain period. Because of difficulties in enforcement, the law was changed by the Rights of Way Act 1990. In essence, a farmer can now plough a right of way, provided he does this for the purposes of 'good husbandry' and provided the path is reinstated within fourteen days. If the farmer does not reinstate within fourteen days, then the highway authority can prosecute (but the highway authority can extend the fourteen-day period).

The Rights of Way Act 1990 also makes it an offence for a farmer to allow any crop (except grass) to encroach on a footpath or bridleway so as to make it inconvenient for the public to exercise their right of way. Another offence puts an obligation on the farmer to take necessary steps to ensure that the line of the highway on the ground is indicated. In other words, a farmer cannot simply plant crops and leave it to the public to guess which is the correct line of the footpath. Moreover, the Act lays down minimum widths for footpaths in these circumstances. Note that any individual or organization can prosecute for breach; this is obviously important in terms of pressure groups wishing to preserve rights of access to the countryside.

If a walker or rider comes across an obstruction it can be removed, but only in so far as it is necessary to be able to continue the journey. So if the path is only partly obstructed the walker cannot remove the obstruction if it is possible to continue the walk without removing it. The walker can only do what is essential.

Mr Slama had a café by the seafront in Hastings. Access to the café was by three public footpaths which crossed Mr Seaton's land. Mr Seaton erected a fence which blocked all three paths. Slama took down 180 yards of fence and burnt part of it, claiming that he was exercising his right to remove obstructions from a public footpath. Held: No. The judge said: 'If the gate is locked he may be entitled to break the lock. If there is a fence across the entrance to the way he may be justified in removing a sufficient part of the fence to enable him to have free access to the way.' But he could do no more than that. Seaton (1932)

In addition, this form of self-help is available only to someone who is genuinely using the path for a journey. So a rambler who sets out with the sole object of removing obstructions cannot claim to be acting lawfully; apart from being sued for trespass, the rambler might be prosecuted for criminal damage. In practice, of course, it would be difficult for the landowner to prove that the rambler did not genuinely intend using the path for a journey.

The experienced walker will probably come across two other problems – usually resulting from farmers who resent public use of footpaths. First, there is the 'misleading sign' ploy (e.g. a 'Private' sign). This is illegal if the sign is designed to deter the use of a public right of way marked on the definitive map (see page 369). Report the offence to the county council. The second tactic is the 'bull in the field' ploy. Since 1981 all dairy bulls have been banned from fields that are crossed by public paths, and other types of bull can be permitted only if accompanied by cows or heifers. Prosecution is difficult because no specific criminal offence arises (although the police might decide that the farming business being carried on is endangering the public, and so prosecute under the Health and Safety at Work laws).

Airspace

The rules of trespass are not confined to the land itself. In legal theory, a landowner owns not only the land, but the air above it and the soil beneath it. Thus an unreasonable intrusion into another person's airspace will be a trespass, although whether that person will be awarded any damages will depend upon their being able to show a resulting loss.

Mr Kelsen had a tobacconist's shop in Islington. His landlords allowed a tobacco company to erect a large 'Players Please' sign which projected 8 inches into the airspace above his shop. Mr Kelsen sued for trespass. Held: Yes, it was a trespass and the sign should be removed. Kelsen (1957)

But it is not always necessary to claim damages. Simply getting an injunction may be enough to cause great inconvenience to the trespasser. This has proved to be the case with large cranes. Often, the property developer will install a crane on a plot of land in order to carry out building works. But modern cranes are so large that the booms often overhang neighbouring land. If this happens, there will have been a trespass. It follows from this that anyone who wishes to use a crane must ensure that neighbours give consent before a crane boom passes over their land. If this consent is not given, then an injunction can be obtained against the trespassing crane. In practice, this means that the developer will have to buy permission to use the airspace from the neighbour.

The developers of a major docklands site erected large cranes. But the owner of a neighbouring site objected because the booms of the tower cranes over-sailed his land from time to time. The developer argued that it would be wrong for an injunction to be granted; after all, the crane booms were at such a height that they were in no way interfering with the normal use of the neighbour's land. Held: The crane booms amounted to an invasion of airspace and this was trespass. That being so, an injunction would be granted. Anchor Brewhouse (1987)

When planes first started flying, their pilots faced trespass claims from the owners of the land flown over. To get around this problem, the Civil Aviation Act 1949 exempts over-flying aircraft from trespass claims, for otherwise homeowners near airports would be able to obtain injunctions against the airline operators and so ground all flights. However, the Act does not protect planes that are flying 'unreasonably low' and in that case there may be a trespass; generally, the minimum height for a light aircraft is about 1,000 feet and 2,000 feet for other aircraft except, of course, when landing and taking off.

The protection given by the 1949 Act covers any flight which is at a reasonable height, even when the object of the flight is not just to pass over the land en route to the plane's destination.

Skyviews was a firm that took aerial photographs of people's houses and then offered to sell photographs to the householder. One person whose home was photographed in this way was Lord Bernstein. He took exception to this invasion of his privacy and sued Skyviews for trespass. In their defence, Skyviews relied upon the protection given by the Civil Aviation Act 1949. Held: A landowner has rights only in his airspace to such a height as is necessary for the use and enjoyment of his land. The flight by Skyviews had been at a reasonable height and was thus protected. There had been no trespass. Bernstein (1977)

Light

Although landowners own the airspace above their property, there is no automatic right to have light enter their airspace or land. Thus, if a neighbour wants to build a high boundary wall that will put their house into shade, there may be nothing that can be done about it, beyond opposing the neighbour's application for planning permission to erect the wall (see page 354).

Acquiring a 'right to light'

That would be the landowner's only remedy unless the property had acquired a 'right to light', either by written agreement with the neighbour or by *prescription* (i.e. continuous use) over twenty years or more. So, if the house is over twenty years old, the householder will probably have acquired a right to light and will be able to prevent the erection of any structure that would seriously reduce the amount of light. Similarly, if the house is new but is built on the site of an old property that had previously acquired a right to light, then the new house will normally inherit that right to light, unless it is radically different in size and character from the old house.

This twenty-year rule applies only to rights to light for buildings, and not for gardens and other open spaces, such as allotments; so if the proposed wall would put a rose garden into shadow the landowner could probably never claim a right to light to prevent its erection (but a greenhouse may have a right to light – see below).

The extent of the right

If a right to light exists, it is not a right to prevent any obstruction, but just a right to ensure that a minimum level of light is maintained. If the light is reduced, but the selling and letting values of the house are unchanged and the comfort of its occupants not reduced, then there will not have been any infringement of the right to light. Thus the question is not 'How much light has been taken away?' but 'How much light remains?'

In deciding what is the minimum level required the court will consider such factors as the nature of the locality and the type of room affected: for instance, a bedroom needs less light than a lounge, and this will be so even if, for example, the bedroom is used for an activity that requires good lighting, such as sewing and embroidery.

Conversely, if the normal use of a building requires it to have an unusually high level of light, then the right to light will have been infringed if the level is reduced to a level which is insufficient for its normal use. For instance:

Mr and Mrs Allen had a greenhouse in their back garden. It had been there for over twenty years, so when their neighbours erected a fence beside it, they asked for the fence to be removed on the grounds that it infringed their right to light. In particular, their tomatoes no longer grew properly because the greenhouse was now in shadow. The neighbours refused to move the fence and argued that a right to light only covers a 'normal' amount of light – not the exceptional amount needed by a greenhouse. Held: A right to light extends to the amount of light needed by a building for its normal use. The greenhouse needed a lot of light, and so the right to light had been infringed. The fence had to be taken down. Allen (1979)

(This case also shows that a householder is entitled to sunlight, not just illumination, which could be important if solar heating panels become more widespread.)

If a householder does not have a right to light (e.g. if he or she owns a new house on a new site) there is nothing that can be done to prevent neighbours from blocking off the light, apart, of course, from using this as a ground for opposing the granting of planning permission. If, despite these efforts, planning permission is granted, the householder will just have to accept the resulting inconvenience and reduction in the value of the property.

Finally, a word of warning: it is possible to own a twenty-year-old house and yet not have a right to light. This can happen when the title deeds specifically say that a right to light cannot be acquired. For instance, if a householder sells off half the garden for development, a clause might be inserted preventing a right to light being acquired by the purchaser and his successors; otherwise, if the seller wanted to build on the other half of the garden in over twenty years' time, this might be challenged on the ground that the proposed building would infringe the other property's right to light. By suitably wording the original conveyance a seller can prevent the right to light being acquired. It is not unusual for the conveyance to state that the buyer cannot acquire a right to light over the seller's land, while specifically giving the seller a right to light over the buyer's land.

Mr Howells decided to put up an extension. His neighbours the Pughs objected, pointing out it would interfere with their right to light. Despite clear warnings on this, Mr Howells went ahead. The Pughs then went to court, asking for an order that the extension be removed. Held: The extension did interfere with the light to the Pughs' house. Howells had been given ample warning but decided to go ahead heedless. An order was made that the extension should be knocked down. Pugh (1984)

The other method of stopping a right to light from being acquired is under the Rights to Light Act 1959. This little-used Act allows a landowner to register a notice with the local authority stating that an adjoining building is not acquiring a right to light by the passage of time. The registration lasts only for one year but it would simply need to be renewed every twenty years so as to stop a fresh period of twenty years running.

Protecting a view

English law does not recognize the right to a view from one's house and, unlike a right to light, it is not possible to acquire the right to an uninterrupted view by twenty years' usage.

Thus a householder cannot go to court if a neighbour erects a building or plants a tree that will ruin the view, even if it takes thousands of pounds off the value of the householder's property.

Nuisance

Trespass covers *physical* intrusions by a neighbour but if the interference with a householder's rights is of a less tangible nature, trespass will be of no use; for instance, noise and smells cannot be stopped by bringing an action for trespass since there has been no physical encroachment on to the property. However, for these *intangible* intrusions, the law provides another remedy – bringing an action for 'nuisance'.

When a lawyer talks of a 'nuisance', the word is being used in a well-defined legal sense. Not every antisocial act by my neighbour will be a legal 'nuisance', although I might well regard it as a damned nuisance.

The 'nuisance' claim covers behaviour that causes injury to land or, alternatively, substantially interferes with the enjoyment of land. Vibrations from a nearby factory that cause damage to the foundations of a house; heavy smoke from a coal fire; strong smells from a neighbour's septic tank; noise from machinery in a factory or noise from late-night parties – these are the sort of antisocial acts that can amount to a legal 'nuisance'.

The law expects neighbours to give and take. When people live in close proximity to one another they must be prepared to compromise and to take account of the reasonable wishes of their neighbours. In fact, the word 'reasonable' occurs again and again in the courts' decisions on nuisance cases, for the courts apply an objective test of how the 'reasonable man' (or woman!) would behave and how he (or she) would react to the behaviour in question.

Does a 'nuisance' exist?

The first step is to consider whether the plaintiff (i.e. the complainant) is justified in going to court. Clearly, if he or she or their land has suffered material physical damage, they are entitled to bring a claim (e.g. if crops have died from factory fumes). If the complaint is an interference with the use and enjoyment of land (e.g. unpleasant smells) then the courts will want to be sure that there is a serious or substantial interference, and that the plaintiff is not being over-fussy or fastidious. Thus the extent and duration of the interference becomes relevant (e.g. a party every night is unreasonable, but one a week is probably not). What is the nature and character of the harm? Is the plaintiff's use of the land suitable for the neighbourhood and locality (e.g. he or she may want peace for their animals to graze – in the country this might be reasonable, but in central London it would be unreasonable)? Could he or she have easily avoided the consequences of the neighbour's behaviour or are they just being bloodyminded?

If the plaintiff passes these hurdles on the 'reasonable man' test, the court goes on to consider the behaviour of his troublesome neighbour, the defendant. An important factor will be whether their use of the land is reasonable for the area and locality (e.g. keeping a dozen pigs may be reasonable in the country, but it would be considered unreasonable in central London). Is the defendant's aim innocent or is he or she, in fact, acting with malice by trying to annoy the plaintiff (e.g. is the sole motive for practising drum solos to annoy the neighbour or is the defendant really a music student with nowhere else to practise?)? Has he or she taken all reasonable steps to minimize the effects of their actions (e.g. do they try to muffle the sound of their drums? Do they practise in daylight hours only?)? Once again, a 'reasonable man' test is applied, and if the defendant has not behaved reasonably the court will award damages to the plaintiff and probably grant an injunction ordering the defendant to stop the nuisance-making activities.

Clearly, then, what will be a nuisance in one part of the country may not be a nuisance in another area; what may be a nuisance to one plaintiff will not be a nuisance to another plaintiff. It all depends on the facts of the case and whether our 'reasonable man' (or woman) would tolerate the neighbour's behaviour. But nuisance claims are not confined to such obvious complaints as noise and smells. Anything that substantially interferes with a householder's or landowner's enjoyment of his property can be a nuisance. For instance:

Two prostitutes lived in a house in Mayfair. Their neighbours applied to the court for an injunction ordering the girls not to use their house for prostitution, on the ground that the frequent callers and the general misbehaviour was a legal nuisance. Held: Yes, there was a nuisance, and an injunction was granted. Thompson-Schwab (1956)

A company bought a shop in an area that was residential, but which included restaurants, snack-bars etc. Previously the shop had been a dress shop; the company converted it to a sex shop, with illuminated signs describing its wares. Local residents brought a nuisance claim against the company, claiming damages and an injunction. Held: A sex shop could be a legal 'nuisance'. Anything that was an affront to the reasonable susceptibilities of ordinary people and which interfered with reasonable domestic enjoyment of property could be a nuisance. An interlocutory injunction would be granted. Laws (1981)

A motor company had a lease on premises next to some open land owned by the local council. Gypsies moved on to the land and, despite complaints, the number of gypsies increased over the years. The council got a court order against the gypsies but never evicted them. The garage company sued for damages – complaining that they had suffered a major loss in trade due to the presence of the gypsies. Held: The council were liable in nuisance. They owned the land and should have taken more prompt steps to get rid of the gypsies. Page Motors (1981)

Noise

When considering a nuisance claim for noise, the court will consider all the factors mentioned above. For example, in a 1914 case a hotel was able to stop building operations on an adjacent plot because they prevented the residents from sleeping and after-dinner speakers from making themselves heard. But the court ordered the builders to stop their pile-driving only between 10 p.m. and 6.30 a.m. – so what may be a nuisance at night need not be a nuisance in the daytime.

The nature of the locality will also be important. For instance:

Mr Leeman bought a house in an area that was partly residential and partly rural. His neighbour had an orchard 100 yards away, in which he kept 750 cockerels. The crowing of the cockerels prevented Mr Leeman from sleeping, so he brought a nuisance claim against his neighbour. Held: The cockerels were a nuisance, although they would probably not have been a nuisance in a non-residential area. Leeman (1936)

Why does the plaintiff need peace and quiet? Is a neighbour's noise really a nuisance or is the plaintiff being fussy? For instance, when the vicar of a Brighton church went to court over the hum from nearby electrical machinery, his claim failed because the court did not regard the noise as a sufficiently serious annoyance, since he was still able to preach and conduct services.

Sometimes it is a new neighbour who has just moved into the area who complains about the defendant's noisy behaviour. The defendant might argue, 'I was making the noise before he came; he didn't have to come and live here.' That argument will not succeed, and the defendant will have to stop his antisocial behaviour if it is a nuisance to his new neighbour – as with Mr Leeman's neighbour who kept the cockerels in his orchard (above). The fact that Mr Leeman was new to the area did not prevent him from having an existing nuisance stopped.

Mrs Kennaway owned land beside an artificial lake, which was used by a skiing club. The club had been using the lake since the early 1960s. In 1969 Mrs Kennaway got planning permission to build a house which she started occupying in 1972. From 1969 onwards the motor-boat activities steadily increased and by 1977 the lake was used each weekend for races and practice. In 1977 Mrs Kennaway started court proceedings. She wanted an injunction but the trial judge would only award her damages (£1,000 for past nuisance, and £15,000 for future nuisance). She appealed. Held: An injunction would be granted allowing only limited use of the lake by the club. Damages should only be awarded in place of an injunction in the most exceptional circumstances. Kennaway (1980)

On the other hand, the defendant may be able to use the 'long-usage' defence against a neighbour who has tolerated it for twenty years or more: for example, if Mr Leeman (or the previous owner) had waited twenty years before complaining, he might well have lost his case.

Even noisy children can be a legal nuisance. For instance:

Mr and Mrs Dunton owned a small hotel with a pleasant garden and grazing land beyond it. The council built a housing estate on the grazing land, with a playground next to the hotel garden. The playground was open from dawn to dusk and was used by children of all ages. The noise was so intolerable that Mrs Dunton moved out of the hotel. Mr Dunton brought a nuisance claim against the council. Held: The playground was a nuisance. The council was ordered to limit its use to children under twelve, and to restrict the opening hours to between 10 a.m. and 6.30 p.m. In addition, Mr Dunton was awarded £200 damages. Dunton (1977)

If an injunction is granted, it may be suspended in order to give the defendant time in which to reorganize his or her business:

Mr and Mrs Allison lived in a council house next door to a hospital boiler room. The noise, a continuous low-pitched hum, interfered with Mr Allison's sleep and caused him a significant degree of nervous agitation, as well as bouts of depression. Held: The noise was a nuisance. The hospital would be given twelve months in which to cure the noise, and in the meantime, the Allisons would be paid £850 damages. Allison (1975)

The problem is, of course, that going to court – and asking for an injunction – is usually an expensive process.

Other remedies for noise

Bringing an action for nuisance is only one of the remedies available against noisy neighbours. Because of the cost of bringing such a civil action the householder will probably be reluctant to sue for nuisance and might prefer to try a cheaper remedy. The Control of Pollution Act 1974 contains various provisions that can be used to control excessive noise.

The first step is to complain to the Environmental Health Department of the local authority that the noise is a 'nuisance' under the 1974 Act. Evidence that it interferes with sleep, or causes disturbance, will probably be needed. If the council agrees that the noise is a nuisance, it can serve a noise-abatement notice on the owner or occupier of the building. The notice will forbid the making of the noise, or restrict it to certain noise levels, at certain times of the day. If the noise-abatement notice is not complied with, the council can prosecute in the magistrates' court, and the offender will be convicted unless it can be shown that the 'best practicable means' were used to avoid making the noise (e.g. the latest, quietest machinery was installed with all the usual noise-reduction devices) (maximum penalty £200 fine for first offence, £400 for subsequent offences).

Prosecution under the Control of Pollution Act 1974 is entirely separate from bringing a civil injunction:

Major construction work was being carried out next door to a branch of Lloyds Bank. So much inconvenience was being caused that the bank sought an injunction limiting the hours of building work. The injunction was granted. However, at the same time the local council issued a notice under the Control of Pollution Act 1974 which also limited the hours of work, but which was less strict than the court's injunction. The builders argued that the injunction should now be cancelled. Held: The two legal remedies were entirely distinct and separate. The injunction could remain in force. Lloyds Bank (1987)

If the council refuses to issue a noise-abatement notice, or if it refuses to prosecute for its breach, the householder can complain to the magistrates' court. A summons is issued in the usual way (see how to bring a private prosecution, page 1005) and if the magistrates agree that the noise is a nuisance under the 1974 Act, they will issue a noise-abatement notice. As with a notice issued by the council, the offender can be fined if he or she does not observe the terms of the notice. A householder who applies to the magistrates' court for a noise-abatement order should produce evidence to support the contention that the noise is a nuisance (e.g. statements of other neighbours, a note from a doctor as to the effect the noise is having on the householder and family etc.).

Another way of taking action against noise is to prosecute under local by-laws. Most local authorities have by-laws that can be used to control noise. Usually, a private individual can prosecute for breach of the by-laws, although it is always advisable to try to persuade the council to prosecute. The maximum penalty is usually a £50 fine. The householder should check whether there are relevant by-laws by inquiring in the Environmental Health Department; anti-noise by-laws are usually contained in the 'Good Rule and Government' section of the by-laws. The following are typical anti-noise by-laws:

Radio, stereo etc. Such noise is prohibited if it is so loud and so continuous that it is an annoyance to occupiers of premises in the neighbourhood. Generally, the complainant must first give fourteen days' written notice to the offender that he or she regards the noise as a nuisance, and the notice must also be signed by two other householders within hearing distance. Only if the noise continues beyond the fourteen-day period can the offender be prosecuted in the magistrates' court.

Alarm bells. It is often an offence to leave an alarm bell ringing for so long that it becomes an annoyance to local residents. However, the offender will usually have a defence if he or she can show that the noisy alarm was not his/her fault (e.g. there was an unknown electrical fault).

Noisy animals. It is usually an offence to keep a noisy animal if it causes a serious nuisance to residents in the neighbourhood. As with the radio and stereo by-law, the offender must first be given fourteen days' notice, signed by a total of three householders.

Music near houses. It is usually an offence to play any 'musical or noisy instrument' or sing in a street or public place that is within 100 yards of a house or office. However, the noise must have been sufficient to have interfered with the ordinary activities carried on in the building (e.g. sleeping, if outside a house at night) or to have been otherwise unreasonable.

Two other common sources of noise are also subject to legal restriction.

Car horns. The Road Traffic Act 1974 makes it illegal to sound a horn while the car is stationary or to sound the horn on a moving car in a restricted road (unless there is danger to another moving vehicle) between 11.30 p.m. and 7 a.m. Both offences carry a maximum penalty of a £1,000 fine. Prosecutions are extremely rare.

Chimes and loudspeakers. The Control of Pollution Act 1974 makes it illegal to operate a loudspeaker or chime in a street. The main exception is for food and drink vehicles, which can use loudspeakers and chimes between noon and 7 p.m., but only if the noise does not cause unreasonable annoyance to local residents. Thus short bursts on an ice-cream chime are allowed but long tunes are not. The maximum penalty, on conviction, is a £2,000 fine and £50 for each day the noise continues after conviction.

Noisy vehicles

Maximum noise levels for vehicles are laid down in the Motor Vehicles (Construction and Use) Regulations. The maximum fine for breach is £1,000.

In practice these noise restrictions are of limited value because the police lack the facilities for monitoring noise levels. In addition, it can often be difficult to prove that a particular vehicle was causing excessive noise if it was one of several vehicles on the road at that time.

Complaints about routeing and regulation of traffic should be made to the local traffic authority.

Noise from planes

There is little that can be done about noise from planes. The normal remedies of applying for a noise-abatement order or of bringing a nuisance action do not apply, since various statutes exempt aircraft from these controls.

Complaints about noise from aircraft using an airport should be made to the airport operator. Complaints about military aircraft should be made to the Ministry of Defence or to the station commanding officer.

Grants for insulating against traffic noise

The Noise Insulation Regulations 1975 provide for grants to help insulate homes affected by traffic noise.

The scheme covers only new roads or roads which have an extra carriageway added to them. This is a major flaw, because it means that existing roads which suddenly have more traffic (e.g. because a new motorway exit is opened) are not included.

A complicated noise test is used to determine whether a particular residential building is eligible. When the road (or extra carriageway) is built the local authority must write to the occupiers of all eligible properties offering them the grant. The amount paid will depend upon what would be a 'reasonable cost' for the works.

Local authorities also have a *discretionary* power to make grants to people living near roads that have had their location, width or level altered, and who would otherwise be ineligible for a grant.

For full details see *Insulation against Traffic Noise* (No.5 in the 'Land Compensation – Your Rights Explained' series published by the Department of the Environment).

Smells

What if a neighbour has a compost heap in his garden and, because of the exceptionally dry weather, it smells? Probably there is no nuisance, because it is only a temporary annoyance and it is quite reasonable to have a compost heap in one's garden. However, if the neighbour uses the heap as a general dump for all household refuse, that would probably be unreasonable and so a nuisance.

What is an objectionable smell in one neighbourhood may be perfectly normal elsewhere. A person who lives in a steel town is expected to tolerate smells that would be regarded as a nuisance in other areas; as one Victorian judge said, 'What would be a nuisance in Belgrave Square would not necessarily be so in Bermondsey.' Thus the smell from a fish-and-chip shop was held to be a nuisance, even though it would not have been a nuisance in a less fashionable district one mile away.

As with noise, the householder who suffers from offensive smells in the neighbourhood may have additional remedies apart from an action for nuisance. Complaint should be made to the environmental health officer of the local authority, for there are several statutory provisions that can be used to control the source of the smells.

Building works

The nuisance action can sometimes be of help to the landowner disturbed by nearby building operations. If noise, dust and fumes result, it may be possible to obtain an injunction to stop the work continuing, although the court will probably confine the ban to the night hours and insist that the builders take all reasonable steps to minimize the inconvenience (as in the hotel case on page 378). However, some disruption and inconvenience may have to be accepted by the landowner, for it is not unreasonable to build on one's land (or carry out DIY works) as long as the inconvenience to others is minimized.

Local authorities have special powers to control noise from building sites (under the Control of Pollution Act 1974), so complaint should be made in the first place to the local authority.

Subsidence

But what of the damaging effect that the building works may have on one's own property? If a neighbour digs a hole on their side of a boundary fence, it may well cause subsidence to the soil on the other side. Can the neighbour be ordered to stop digging, in order to prevent the subsidence? The answer is 'yes', for a neighbour cannot excavate land if it will cause another's soil to fall in.

But this *right of support* applies only to earth and soil – it is not assumed to apply to buildings. This may seem ridiculous, but if the excavations cause a neighbour's house to collapse the neighbour may not have any remedy – unless the soil would have fallen in anyway, whether or not there was a building there! In short, the right of support covers only soil and earth, not buildings.

However, it is possible to acquire a right of support for buildings, so that they are protected in the same way as soil and earth. This could be done by a written deed or restrictive covenant (see page 363), but the usual method is to acquire it by twenty years' usage (i.e. *prescription*) in the same way that a right to light is acquired after twenty years (see page 374). If the house has had the benefit of a support for twenty years or more, then the law presumes that it has the right to be supported by next-door's soil. Also, if a house stands on the site of an old house that had itself acquired the right of support, then the new house will probably inherit that right. Once acquired, the right continues for ever. Otherwise there will be no right of support for a house, just for the earth and soil. But there is an exception to this: if subsidence is caused to a house by a neighbour's tree roots, the landowner can sue even if there is no right of support (see below).

Trees

Trees can also amount to a nuisance at law.

Overhanging branches

If the branches of a neighbour's trees interfere with the enjoyment of an adjoining property, it may amount to a legal nuisance.

The usual way of tackling a legal nuisance is to take the matter to court and ask for damages and/or an order that the offending item be removed. This is an unnecessarily complicated and expensive procedure for so small a matter as an overhanging branch. If the neighbour refuses to prune the tree, the landowner is allowed to resort to *self-help* and cut off the branches. However, the branches will still belong to the neighbour (and so will the fruit on them) so the law-abiding landowner should return them to the neighbour.

This is one of the few occasions when the law does not frown upon self-help, for generally the courts do not approve of people taking the law into their own hands. It is, though, important that the landowner be able to show that it was reasonable to chop off the branches; probably the best safeguard is to write a letter to the neighbour setting out the complaint, and stating a date by when the tree should be pruned, failing which the landowner will prune it him- or herself.

If the tree branches do not overhang the landowner's property, but merely block the light, there is probably no remedy for the landowner unless there is a right to light (see page 374).

Tree roots

As with tree branches, so with tree roots; if the roots of a neighbour's tree intrude into another's property, the landowner can either cut off the roots or take the neighbour to court for damages and/or an order that the roots be removed. In view of the cost of digging up tree roots, it is usually advisable for the landowner to obtain a court order beforehand, rather than do the work and then try to recover the cost from the neighbour. Apart from paying for the cost of digging up the roots, the neighbour would also be liable for incidental expenses, such as returfing a lawn.

The tree-owner will also be liable for any damage caused to neighbouring buildings. This does not just apply to trees owned by neighbours; it also applies if the trees are on the council's pavement:

Two old oak trees were growing in the pavement outside a house. They were about 150 years old. The council was told that the trees were causing damage but nothing was done. Held: The council was liable for the damage caused to the foundations. Russell (1984)

But this does not mean that every council is liable for all damage caused by trees on pavements. For example:

Eight metres from a house was a 60-foot-high horse-chestnut tree. In the 1976 drought, the roots dehydrated the soil and caused subsidence. The householder sued for the cost of the £5,000 underpinning. Held: The council was not liable. The risk of this sort of damage arising had been too vague and remote. It would not be right to make the council liable. Solloway (1981)

The moral of this case is to make sure that the council is given good advance notice if there is any possibility that the roots might cause damage.

It is no defence for the tree-owner to argue that the damaged building should have been constructed more soundly.

A block of flats was built near the boundary of a plot of land. On the other side of the boundary were tall trees. Within ten years the foundations of the flats were affected by subsidence, caused by the trees which were reducing the moisture level of the soil. The tree-owner was sued, but he argued that the flats were of faulty construction. Held: The tree-owner was liable. He could not blame the faulty construction of the building; that would be relevant only if the defects had been so overwhelming as to make the effect of the roots insignificant. Moreover, the fact that the trees had been there before the block of flats was no defence in a nuisance claim. The tree-owner was liable for the full cost of repairs. Bunclark (1977)

Nor is it a defence to argue that one's trees were planted naturally (as opposed to having been planted by man). The landowner is responsible for all trees on the land, irrespective of how the trees came to be on the land in the first place.

Falling trees and branches

The owner of any item or piece of property is liable for damage or injury caused if he or she was negligent. So it is with trees, and the householder will be liable for damage caused by a falling tree or branch, if he or she was negligent. So if the accident occurred without warning (e.g. because of an exceptional gale, lightning or other unforeseen weather conditions) there would not have been any negligence. But if the tree fell down because of old age or disease the landowner would probably have been negligent for not inspecting the tree regularly, and so would be liable in damages. The prudent tree-owner would probably be expected to inspect all trees at least once a year and perhaps twice a year.

Tree-preservation orders

A tree-preservation order (TPO) is an order made by the local planning authority which makes it illegal to prune, fell, uproot or lop that particular tree. When a TPO is made the owner is given notice by the local authority, and then has twenty-eight days in which to make representations.

The TPO is binding on all subsequent owners of the land, not just the person who was the owner at the time the order was made. This is so even if the offender does not know of the existence of the TPO:

Mr Mortimer cut down an oak tree that was subject to a tree-preservation order. He was prosecuted but argued that he could not be guilty since he had not known about the TPO. Held: This was not a defence. He was guilty. Maidstone (1980)

The planning department of the local authority can tell you whether a particular tree is covered by a TPO. The maximum penalty for felling a protected tree is a fine of £2,000, or up to twice the timber value of the tree, whichever is the greater. For otherwise damaging a protected tree, the maximum penalty is £1,000 fine.

Even if a tree is not subject to a TPO, the owner may be subject to restrictions on lopping, pruning, felling or uprooting the tree. If it is within a conservation area at least six weeks' notice must be given to the local authority so they can decide whether to make a TPO. Failure to give notice is an offence (same penalties as for breach of a TPO). A person who thinks that a particular tree should be subject to a TPO should apply to the local planning authority for an order to be made. In deciding whether to make a TPO, the authority may refer to a 1966 circular sent out by the ministry. This states:

Local planning authorities can make a tree-preservation order only if they find it expedient in the interests of amenity. The amenity should be one enjoyed by the public at large, and the local planning authority should be able to show that without the order there would be a risk of amenity being spoiled. The degree of risk should be assessed realistically but it is not suggested that orders should be made only when there is an immediate threat of felling. Areas should be chosen with discrimination and not so as to blanket extensive areas with a view to maintaining a general control over a whole district. Orders should not be made for shrubs or bushes but only for trees with real amenity value ... Precautionary orders may be desirable to protect trees of special amenity value, for example in urban areas where trees are few and far between.

Liability for escaping water, oil etc.

If householders choose to store water on their land, will they be liable if it escapes? For example, suppose the householder builds a rock garden with fountains and fish ponds; what happens if the supporting walls give way and the escaping water floods a neighbour's cellar? The courts would say that the householder was liable even if there was no reason to suspect that the walls might give way; thus his having acted 'reasonably', without negligence, would be irrelevant. The court would simply say that if someone chose to store water on their land, they did so in the knowledge that it might cause damage if it escaped. Anyone should appreciate the risks and it would be for the householder to compensate the neighbours if an accident occurred. This strict rule was laid down in a case that is famous among lawyers – Rylands v. Fletcher, 1868.

Mill-owners built a reservoir to hold water for their mill. Unfortunately, the water percolated down disused mine workings and flooded a nearby mine. The mill-owners had not been negligent, but it was held that they must compensate the mine-owner for the damage done. A 'person who for his own purposes, brings on his land and collects and keeps there anything likely to do mischief if it escapes, must keep it at his peril'. Rylands (1868)

Since then, this approach has been extended to cover the storage and escape of other potentially dangerous substances, such as electricity, smuts, gas and even sewage in a septic tank. Similarly, if the householder builds a tank to hold central-heating oil, but the tank fractures and the escaping oil ruins his or her neighbour's garden, then the householder will be liable to the neighbour – whether or not it was the householder's fault.

It is this element of *strict liability* (irrespective of negligence, nuisance, reasonableness and the other usual tests of liability) that makes the rule in Rylands v. Fletcher so unusual. Generally, English law disapproves of strict liability. Normally, negligence by the neighbour must be shown; if it *is* shown then he or she will be liable. For instance:

A basement was used for storing goods. The next-door building was derelict and the basement-owners made lots of complaints about tramps wandering around the next-door building. Eventually, burglars broke through the dividing wall and stole valuable goods. Held: The owners of the derelict building had been negligent in not taking reasonable security precautions. Perl (1983)

Rivers, fishing rights

Although a landowner owns the air above and soil below his or her property, this ownership does not include the water that runs across his or her land in rivers.

Navigation

The public can navigate on a tidal river up to the point where the tide ebbs and flows. Beyond that point the public have a right to navigate only if such a right has been acquired by long usage over the years (in the same way that the public can acquire a right of way over land – see page 369).

Fishing

The public can fish in a tidal river up to the point where the tide ebbs and flows. Beyond that point, fishing rights are vested in the landowner. Even if the public have acquired a right to navigate over this non-tidal part of the river, that navigation right will not include the right to fish.

Abstracting water

A landowner used to be able to take water from rivers and streams that flowed through his or her land. However, the Water Resources Act 1963 now requires the landowner to obtain a licence to abstract from the local water authority, although no licence is needed if no more than 1,000 gallons are abstracted, or if the water is taken for domestic purposes.

Boundary fences and walls

'Good fences make good neighbours,' wrote Robert Frost. But the law does not usually require a landowner to fence property or even to maintain an existing fence or wall.

Despite this, neighbours often have disputes over the responsibility for maintaining their boundary fences. The first point to note is that there is only rarely a legal obligation on a landowner to fence a property. Generally, this will be as a result of a covenant in the title deeds or lease which obliges the landowner to fence. Conversely, the property may be in an open-plan estate, in which case it is likely that the title deeds will contain a covenant prohibiting the erection of a fence.

But in the absence of such a legal obligation, the householder is free to decide whether or not he or she wants to fence a property, and similarly whether to continue maintaining an existing fence or wall.

Fences

If the deeds make no provision, a general guide for deciding the ownership of a fence is to say that it belongs to the land on the side of the vertical support posts.

Boundaries

When it comes to considering the ownership (and even the location) of a disputed boundary, the court will look, first, at the title documents to see if they give any guidance (e.g. 'T' marks). But often the deeds are of little help, being imprecisely worded or incorporating a map of such a small scale as to be useless. However, if there is a hedge and a ditch, the court will assume that the person who dug the ditch did so at the boundary of his or her own land, and then planted the hedge on top of the earth from that ditch; so the boundary is then assumed to run along the edge of the ditch furthest away from the hedge. The rather strained logic behind this rule can be overruled by other evidence;

for example, if the other landowner has traditionally maintained the hedge, it might be held that it – and not the ditch – formed the boundary. Similarly, if the title deeds define the property by reference to Ordnance Survey maps, the hedge-and-ditch rule might not apply, for the OS always draw boundaries along the middle of hedges rather than along the edges of ditches.

RESPONSIBILITY FOR DAMAGE CAUSED BY ANIMALS

What if a pet escapes and causes damage to a neighbour's garden or injures the neighbour; can the neighbour sue? Generally, the answer will depend upon whether the pet's owner was *negligent*, and this will be judged according to the standard set by the mythical 'reasonable man' (or woman).

Thus, if an animal wanders out on to the public highway and causes an accident, the owner will be liable only if their behaviour fell below that expected from the 'reasonable man'. For example, it may be reasonable to leave an untethered dog in an ungated garden if the property is beside a quiet country road; however, if the same behaviour took place in the centre of a town the owner would almost certainly be liable if, for example, the dog ran out into the road and caused a motor-cyclist to swerve and fall off.

Ms Sudron bought a pedigree puppy. To stop it escaping she had repairs done to her fence and gate. One afternoon, when she was out, her boyfriend failed to notice that a visitor had forgotten to close the gate. The puppy darted out and caused a moped-rider to crash. He sued. Held: Ms Sudron was not liable. She had not been negligent since she had taken all the precautions that one could reasonably expect. The injured moped-rider went without compensation. Smith (1982)

Although the animal-owner will normally be liable only if he or she was negligent, there are three exceptions to this rule.

1. Dangerous animals

If a person chooses to keep an animal belonging to a *dangerous species* they do so at their own risk. So they will be liable if the animal escapes and causes damage, even if they were not negligent and could not be blamed for the accident.

Certain animals are obviously dangerous, such as lions, tigers, elephants etc., and so if one of these animals escapes from a zoo, the zoo-keepers would be liable whether or not the accident was their fault. The Animals Act 1971 says that an animal is of a 'dangerous species' if it is not usually domesticated in this country and is, when fully grown, likely to cause severe damage unless restrained.

2. Animals that are normally harmless but for some reason are dangerous

The same rule of strict liability without the need to show negligence will apply to damage caused by animals that are not from a 'dangerous species', yet have unusual characteristics known to the owner. This is because an animal may normally be harmless but, in a particular set of circumstances, can be dangerous. For example, a dog is not normally dangerous, yet if a bitch has a litter of puppies it is quite likely that she will bite an approaching stranger; thus the owner of the bitch should keep her under strict control during this dangerous period. Similarly, a dog with rabies is, in the circumstances, dangerous and so if it bites someone the owner will be liable – assuming, of course, that the owner knew it had rabies.

It is this requirement that the owner should know of the special circumstances that makes the animal dangerous which gives rise to the phrase 'every dog is allowed one bite'. Until that first bite, the owner has no reason to suppose that a seemingly normal dog is unusually aggressive and dangerous; however, after that bite the owner is assumed to know of its dangerous temperament and so should take precautions to ensure that it does not hurt anybody. But there is no need to show that the animal was known to be vicious – merely that it was bad-tempered may be enough.

A groom was injured while leading a horse into a trailer. The horse, which was known to be temperamental and nervous, suddenly became violent and her arm was crushed. Held: The stable-owner was liable. There was no need to show that the horse had a vicious tendency to injure people; it was known to be unpredictable and unreliable, and that made it dangerous. Wallace (1982)

3. Straying livestock

We have seen that an animal-owner is not usually liable if a pet strays, unless there was negligence. However, for *livestock* the position is different, and an owner may be liable even if there was no negligence; this applies when the animals stray on to private property, such as a neighbour's front lawn.

This strict liability rule applies only to livestock, as defined in the Animals Act 1971. The definition includes cattle, horses, asses, mules, sheep, pigs, goats, fowls, turkeys, geese, ducks, pigeons, peacocks and other poultry; it does not include cats and dogs.

Thus, if a householder chooses to keep a goat in the garden, and the goat enters his or her neighbour's garden through a hole in the hedge, the householder will be liable for any damage caused by the goat – even if it was thought that the goat was properly tethered and even if the owner did not know about the hole in the hedge. The only defence would be if it was the neighbour's own fault (e.g. in leaving a gate open), or if the livestock strayed on to the neighbour's land from the public highway (if they were lawfully on it in the first place). Remember that if livestock stray on to the road, then the owner will be liable only if he or she was negligent (page 389).

Guard dogs

The Guard Dog Act 1975 lays down special rules for the use of guard dogs on commercial premises. Unfortunately, the Act does not apply to private houses or to agricultural land.

The main requirement of the Act is that the dog should be under the immediate control of its handler or, alternatively, that it be tethered so it cannot roam freely. In addition, a warning notice must be displayed. Breach of these laws is a criminal offence, triable in the magistrates' court (maximum penalty, a fine up to £2,000). However, breach of the Act does not automatically mean that the dog's owner would be liable in damages if a civil claim was brought (e.g. if someone was mauled by an untethered guard dog). This is because the Act is concerned only with the criminal law, and not with the civil law of damages for injury and loss caused to someone else. Despite this, though, the fact that the dog was allowed to roam freely would probably be regarded as 'unreasonable behaviour' on the part of the owner, if he or she was sued for negligence.

Keeping animals

Most domestic animals need not be licensed. It is a common belief that cats are beyond the law, and that a cat-owner cannot be responsible for the actions of the cat; this is not true, and a negligent cat-owner will be liable in the same way as any other pet-owner, although, in practice, proof of such negligence would probably be extremely difficult.

A local authority licence is needed to keep a dangerous wild animal (e.g. alligator, cobra, cheetah, lion, gibbon, ostrich etc. – a full list is set out in the Dangerous Wild Animals Act 1976). The maximum penalty for not having a licence is a £2,000 fine, plus disqualification from holding a licence.

Any animal imported into the country must go into quarantine for six months. There are no exceptions to this rule: it applies to all live animals (not just dogs and cats), even if they have been inoculated against rabies and other diseases. The importation should be arranged through an authorized 'carrying agent' who will bring the animal in under licence and leave it at approved kennels. The animal-owner is liable for all the costs of importation, kennelling etc.

Most animals from abroad can be imported only under licence (unless the animal comes from Northern Ireland, Eire, the Channel Islands or the Isle of Man, and has been there for the previous six months). Applications for a licence should be made to the Ministry of Agriculture, Fisheries and Food, Government Buildings, Hook Rise, South Tolworth, Surbiton, Surrey. The application should be made at least four (preferably eight) weeks in advance.

It is a criminal offence to evade quarantine (maximum penalty is an unlimited fine or one year's imprisonment).

Dogs and the criminal law

Various statutes contain provisions aimed at controlling dogs, and also at protecting animals from their owners. In practice, prosecutions are rare: apart from the difficulties of identifying the owner of a particular dog, the police tend to refuse to prosecute in all but the most serious cases. The main laws are:

Dogs roaming in the road

Local authorities can designate particular roads as being roads in which any dog must be on a lead. The maximum penalty for breach is a £50 fine.

Dangerous dogs

The Dogs Act 1871 allows the magistrates to take action against dogs that are both dangerous and not under proper control. The mere fact that a dog is dangerous is not sufficient; the magistrates will also want to be sure that it is not under sufficient control. In practice, the easiest way to prove that a dog is dangerous is to show that it has attacked someone; once again, therefore, there is some truth in the adage that 'every dog is allowed one bite'. But it is not essential that injury be caused before a prosecution can be brought.

If the case is proved, the magistrates can order the owner to keep the dog under proper control, or they can order its destruction. Other remedies include ordering that a male dog be neutered, and the magistrates can disqualify the owner from dog-ownership for a period of time. A fine of up to £400 can also be imposed.

The Dangerous Dogs Act 1991 was introduced to deal, primarily, with the threat from particularly vicious dogs – such as pit bull terriers. A registration system has been introduced for such dogs. But a more important change brought about by the 1991 Act was to introduce an offence of having a dog that is dangerously out of control in a public place; this is a more serious charge than anything covered by the Dogs Act 1871. Prosecution can be brought only if the dog was out of control in a 'public place', and if it was also 'dangerously out of control' – a far stricter test than under the 1871 Act. On conviction in the magistrates' court, there is a maximum penalty of £2,000 (or six months' prison); if the dog actually injured someone, then it is possible for the case to be heard in the crown court (which could impose an unlimited fine and imprisonment).

Collarless dogs

Under the Control of Dogs Order 1930 it is compulsory for a dog on a highway or in any 'place of public resort' to wear a collar stating the name and address of the dog's owner. Maximum penalty for breach of the order is a £2,000 fine.

Fouling the footpath

Most local authorities have by-laws which provide that 'no person being in charge of a dog shall allow the dog to foul the footpath ... provided that a person shall not be liable if he satisfies the court that the fouling of the footway was not due to culpable neglect or default on his part'. Maximum penalty is usually a £100 fine. Private prosecutions are permitted.

Noisy dogs

By-laws usually contain provisions that can be used to control noisy dogs.

Worrying livestock or poultry

Under the Dogs (Protection of Livestock) Act 1953 it is an offence for a dog to 'worry' livestock on agricultural land if it could reasonably be expected to cause injury or suffering to the livestock. Maximum penalty is a fine of £200. If the dog actually injures cattle or poultry, or chases sheep, it can be treated as a 'dangerous dog' (see page 392). Private prosecutions are permitted.

The Dogs Act 1926 makes the owner liable if the dog injures poultry, cattle or sheep. The owner can be sued for damages and it is not necessary for the farmer to show that the dog's owner was negligent or that there was reason to think the dog might attack the animals.

A trespassing dog can only be shot if it is worrying or attacking animals or human beings, and if it was reasonable in the circumstances to shoot it.

Cruelty to dogs

Under the Protection of Animals Act 1911, it is an offence to be cruel to any animal, including a dog. The maximum penalty is £50 fine and three months' imprisonment, plus disqualification from keeping a dog for a stated period. Private prosecutions are permitted.

Abandoning a dog

The Abandonment of Animals Act 1960 makes it illegal temporarily or permanently to abandon any animal without reasonable cause, if it is likely to cause unnecessary suffering to the animal. The penalties are the same as for cruelty. Private prosecutions are permitted.

ACCIDENTS AT HOME

What happens if someone is injured because of a defect in the home, such as an uneven path or a falling slate; is the householder liable for the state of the property?

The simple answer is 'yes'. The general rule is that the owner of the premises will be liable if he or she was negligent. This is the rule applied if the person injured is on the road or if he is the next-door neighbour. Thus, if a slate falls off the roof and hits the neighbour's car, the question to be asked is: was the householder negligent? If he or she knew the slate was loose, or had not inspected the roof for a long time, then he or she would be liable. On the other hand, if the falling slate was the result of an unusually fierce storm, he or she might not be liable, since then he or she might not have been negligent.

The same rule applies if a tenant has a flat and is injured by something falling from the landlord's part of the building:

Mrs Cunard was injured when part of the roof and some guttering fell on her. Mr and Mrs Cunard were tenants of part of the building, but the roof and guttering were retained by the landlord. Held: The landlord had been negligent and so he was liable to pay damages to Mrs Cunard. Cunard (1932)

Visitors etc.

Complications arise if the accident involves someone who is visiting the house. While the general rule is that the occupier is liable if he or she was negligent, the rule has to be modified to deal with uninvited guests: burglars, squatters and other trespassers. It would be unfair to make the occupier liable to these trespassers and so the law provides that the occupier is not liable even if there was negligence. For instance, if burglars trip over an uneven step, they cannot sue the householder. But even this rule is subject to exceptions:

1 The occupier cannot take advantage of this freedom from liability deliberately to lay traps that might injure a trespasser. For instance, it is wrong to leave a mantrap to catch a burglar, and the householder who did so would be liable in damages. In short, the householder need not take steps to ensure that trespassers are not injured but must not deliberately take steps that will cause them to be injured.
2 Children cannot be expected to stay off private property. Children are naturally adventurous and curious. The householder must therefore take precautions to prevent children from entering dangerous property – otherwise, if children are injured, it cannot be argued that they were trespassers. The precautions to be taken will largely depend upon the extent of the risk.

But this is not an absolute duty. The occupier (or the owner of the land) just has to take the precautions that a sensible and humane adult would. It is a matter of protecting children from themselves, but there is a limit to the precautions that can reasonably be taken:

Northampton Council owned a rubbish tip. At one end it adjoined houses, but the railings between the two had been broken down. The council knew that children played on the tip, and staff chased them off whenever dumping was being carried out. It would have been prohibitively expensive to fence the whole site. Several children lit a fire on the site and one of them threw an empty aerosol can into it. It exploded, burning one of the children. Held: The council was not liable. The risks did not warrant the expensive precautions required to make the site child-proof. Penny (1974)

So, if a person is injured on someone else's property (or if their property is damaged), they will be able to sue the negligent householder, unless they themselves were trespassers. But, in addition, there may be other people who can also be sued:

The landlord

If the property is rented, the landlord will probably be liable for accidents caused by defects in the property. (See Chapter 19 for when a landlord is obliged to repair a tenant's home.) However, the landlord will only be liable if he or she:

● knew of the defect, *or*
● should have known of the defect (see page 346).

Building contractors

If the householder employs a contractor to carry out work and a visitor is injured through the contractor's negligence, the contractor will be liable.

Building contractors were employed to remove a sloping ramp leading to the front door of a house. They told the householder to use a side route until the work was completed. The side route passed close to a small sunken area. One night a seventy-one-year-old friend of the householder left by the side route and was injured. Held: The negligent contractors were liable to her. Billings (1957)

Professional advisers

They owe a duty to all people who might reasonably be on the property. For instance:

During demolition works, an architect advised that a wall was safe and that it could be left standing. In fact, it was not safe – as any expert should have known. A labourer was hurt when the wall collapsed. Held: He could sue the negligent architect. Clay (1963)

The local authority

The local authority has a duty to take care when it inspects new buildings for Building Regulations approval. If someone is later injured, or suffers loss, the council might be liable if their inspector should have checked the premises more thoroughly.

In 1962 a local authority approved the plans for a block of flats that was built later that year. By 1970 structural cracks had appeared in the walls due to subsidence and it was discovered that the local authority's building inspector had not properly inspected the foundations to see that they had been prepared in accordance with the approved plans. The owners of the flats sued the council for negligence. Held: The council was liable, for it had a duty to the future owners and occupiers of the flats to take care. Anns (1977)

Insurance

Most house-owners have a building policy that provides cover for damage to the home by fire, explosion etc. In addition, this policy is likely to provide cover for liability arising from accidents caused by the defective state of the premises. Thus most house-owners are insured against a claim for damages.

Tenants, however, are often not insured, since they rarely take out a building policy. However, the landlord will be liable if he or she should have known of the defect and if it was his or her responsibility (see above) and it is usual for a landlord to have a building policy. More often than not, therefore, an insurance company will have to pay any damages.

PART THREE

EMPLOYMENT

22 The Worker's Contract of Employment

Despite all the recent legislation, the basis of modern employment law is still the idea that each employee has his or her own contract of employment. The theory is that each employee individually enters into a legally binding contract with his or her employer; the employee provides working skills and, in return, the employer pays wages.

The contract of employment was, and still is, at the heart of the employment relationship or, as it was called until recently, the 'master and servant relationship'.

But the use of the word 'contract' suggests that there was a bargaining session at which employer and employee negotiated the terms of an agreement. This is, of course, not so. The idea of a freely negotiated employment contract is a myth – a legal fiction. Life is not like that. The unemployed worker does not negotiate with the personnel manager to secure the best terms. What is more likely is that he or she will have been sent to the firm by the Job Centre, be told the rate of pay and what the job involves and will then have to take it or leave it. If he or she accepts the job, then the lawyer will say that there is now an employment contract between the employer and the employee, even though there is no written agreement, and even though few of the terms of employment were expressly agreed.

A contract does not have to be in writing to be legally binding, and employment contracts are no different from other contracts in this respect. The law will enforce the terms of the contract, and if the parties did not specifically agree on all the terms, then the law will work out what they intended – the *implied* terms. So terms as to overtime, holiday arrangements, sick pay and discipline can all be implied if no express agreement was reached.

Every employee has a contract of employment with their employer. It is impossible to be an employee without having an employment contract.

Workers who are self-employed are not 'employees'. They do not benefit from all the numerous employment protection rights given to employees. It is not always easy to decide whether a worker is employed or self-employed. See page 411.

THE EMPLOYMENT CONTRACT

The employment contract is important because it is the peg from which all employees' rights hang. It is the starting-point in deciding whether they have been unfairly dismissed or been made redundant. It decides whether they can be forced to do overtime, how much holiday they can take, whether they can demand sick pay, the extent to which they can be disciplined by employers. It is the very basis of the employer/employee relationship, and hardly any employment law dispute can be resolved without considering the terms of the employment contract.

This is, of course, an artificial approach. It virtually ignores the existence of collective bargaining – a grave fault, since a considerable number of British employees still have their conditions of employment determined by reference to collective agreements. All the law can do is to imply some – but not all – of the terms of the collective agreement into the individual's employment contract and so legal theory is half-heartedly reconciled with industrial reality.

Putting the employment contract into writing

It is better for both employer and employee if the contract of employment is set out in writing. Both of them then know where they stand and there is unlikely to be a dispute over the terms and conditions.

Although the law does not insist that the employment contract be in writing, it encourages the employer to set out some of the terms in writing:

1 The employer *must* provide the employee with a written statement of the main terms of the employment contract within thirteen weeks of the employee starting work. This written statement (usually called the 'written particulars') aims to be a true record of the more important terms of the contract, although it is not the contract itself. But often the written statement will be the only written record of what was agreed and so it will, more often than not, be taken as a summary of the employment contract. Since employers have to prepare the written statement they might just as well set out the whole of the contract in writing.
2 Industrial tribunals look with disfavour on employers who do not put the terms of the employment contract into writing. If there should ever be a dispute between employer and employee – such as an unfair-dismissal claim – the industrial tribunal might well give the benefit of any doubt as to the terms to the employee.

Drawing up a written employment contract

Ideally, the written employment contract will set out all the terms and conditions of the employer/employee relationship. It should be as comprehensive as possible. So that nothing is overlooked, it is best to:

1 List all the points that must be included in the written statement, which has to be prepared within thirteen weeks of the job starting. See page 405 for all the matters that must be mentioned in these 'written particulars'. If the written contract covers all these points there will be no need to prepare separate written particulars; the written contract will suffice.
2 Next, consider and deal as appropriate with:
  - the requirements of the job and whom the employee should report to;
  - trade union arrangements;
  - opportunities for promotion and any training necessary to achieve it;
  - social or welfare facilities;
  - fire prevention and health and safety rules;
  - any suggestion schemes.
3 Finally, consider whether there are any other matters that should be included. In practice, employers often forget to ask themselves whether they need specific clauses dealing with:
  - *job mobility*: will employees be expected to move home if their employers want them to work elsewhere?
  - *job flexibility*: will employees be expected to change their duties if asked? If the contract sets out a very narrow job description the employee may be able to refuse to alter his or her duties.
  - *overtime*: will employees be expected to work compulsory overtime when required?
  - *works rules*: works rules and disciplinary codes will probably be *implied* into the contract anyway (see page 405). But to remove any doubt it is best to refer to them specifically in the written contract.
  - *restrictions on future employment*: should there be a clause limiting employees' future choice of jobs (e.g. if they know trade secrets or lists of customers)? See page 453.

When there is no written employment contract: working out the terms

When there is no written contract of employment, the law will look at all the surrounding circumstances and work out what it thinks the parties meant to agree.

These are *implied* terms, and can be derived from:

1 The duties imposed on all employ*ers* by the law.
2 The duties imposed on all employ*ees* by the law.
3 Obvious terms.
4 Custom and practice.
5 The conduct of employer and employee.
6 Collective agreements.
7 Works rules and disciplinary codes.
8 The 'written particulars' supplied to the employee.

1. The duties imposed on all employers

All employers are expected to:
- pay their staff (see page 415 for the law on 'pay');
- provide a safe system of work by taking reasonable care of their staff. This means supplying proper, safe equipment, competent fellow-workers, adequate supervision and proper instruction.

If an employee is injured because the employer failed to provide a safe working environment, the employee can sue the employer for negligence – even if the injury resulted from the negligence of a fellow-employee (e.g. if an employee trips over an uneven floor, is injured by an unfenced machine or knocked over by another employee, then almost certainly the employer – through his insurance company – will have to pay compensation). For examples, see page 443.

Similarly, if an employer breaks the law and the employee is sued as a result, then the employee can demand that the employer pay the damages:

Mr Gregory was injured when a lorry driven by Thomas Hill knocked him off his motor bike. At the time Hill was driving his employer's lorry in the course of his job. Unknown to him, his employers had not insured the lorry. Mr Gregory sued him for damages because of his negligent driving. Could he sue his employers to recompense him for the damages he had to pay Mr Gregory? Held: Yes. It was an implied term of Hill's employment contract that his employer would obey the law and insure the lorry: 'There was an implied term in the contract of service that the employer would comply with [the law] *from which it would follow that the servant would be indemnified . . . for any damage caused by his negligence.'* Gregory (1951)

In addition, employers must obey the law by giving employees the benefit of their rights under the employment-protection laws. Thus eligible staff must be allowed to claim maternity pay and their job back after pregnancy, to be paid a guarantee payment if laid off, or put on short time, to take time off for trade union duties or activities, and so on. But note that there is no general implied obligation on employers to provide their staff with any work (see page 431 or to supply them with references when they leave (see page 452).

2. The duties imposed on all employees

To work. Employees must turn up for work and work to a reasonable standard. But if they are sacked for absenteeism or poor work they may still be able to bring an unfair-dismissal claim (see pages 464–5)

To obey orders. But employees need obey only lawful orders. So if asked to do something dangerous or unlawful – such as operate an unsafe machine or 'cook the books' – they can refuse. Also, the orders must be within the terms of the employment contract: fitters need not obey orders to clean the toilets, because those duties are outside their employment contract.

To take reasonable care. Employees must take reasonable care when carrying out their duties. If they are negligent then they can be sued by their employer for the resulting loss. But they will not be liable if they acted reasonably – the courts 'apply the standards of men, and not those of angels'.

It may seem strange that an employer can sue his negligent employee, but this was laid down in a House of Lords decision of 1957:

Martin Lister and his father both worked for the same Romford firm. While reversing the firm's lorry into a yard, Martin negligently drove into his father. His father then sued the firm, saying it was liable for the negligent acts of its employees. But the company's insurers argued that if they were liable to Martin's father – which they clearly were – then they could recover their losses from Martin himself. Held: Yes. Martin owed his employers a duty to take care. Since he hadn't taken care they could sue him for his negligence. Lister (1957)

Surprisingly, that case remains the law today. This was confirmed in a Court of Appeal decision, when a bank successfully sued a former assistant general manager for £36,000. The employee had been negligent in granting overdrafts and the bank was able to sue him for its losses (*Janata Bank*, 1981). In practice, it is extremely rare for employers to sue their staff in this way; usually the employer will be covered by insurance and insurers do not sue because it is bad for their image! But, legally, the principle remains valid.

Not to betray their employers' trust. Employees must not give away their employers' trade secrets or confidential information. Often there will be an express clause in a written contract of employment restricting employees' future activities (see page 453).

There is *no* general duty on employees to cooperate with their employer. As long as they fulfil the terms of their employment contract that is sufficient. The basic rule is that they cannot be expected to do more than comply with their contractual obligations. However, the court will usually decide that an employee is contractually obliged to do whatever is necessary to keep the employer's business running reasonably smoothly (e.g. as in a 1972 case, railway workers who went on a work-to-rule were held to be in breach of their contracts of employment). In addition, if the employer is under a statutory duty to fence machinery or ensure that safety equipment is worn, then the employee must cooperate to help the employer meet these obligations.

3. Obvious terms

Some terms are so obvious that they 'go without saying'. For instance, if an employer advertises for a lorry driver, it is an assumed part of the employment contract that the employee will be able to drive a lorry. If the employee didn't know how to drive, the employer could dismiss him or her without risk of an unfair-dismissal or redundancy claim.

4. Custom and practice

The custom and practice in an industry as a whole can also be relevant. For instance, if an employer can show that it is normal practice, or customary, for workers of that sort to be 'mobile' then the court will imply such a term into the contract of employment. On this basis a job-mobility clause might well be implied into an actor's employment contract, but not into a solicitor's.

But the courts will only recognize a custom if it is 'reasonable, certain, and notorious'. 'Notorious' means that it must be very well known in the industry.

Traditionally Lancashire weavers had deductions made from their wages for bad workmanship. Nothing was said about this practice in any written employment contract and so one worker took his employer to court arguing that the deductions were unlawful. Held: No. 'A Lancashire weaver knows and has for very many years past known precisely what his position was as regards deductions for bad work in accepting employment in a Lancashire mill.' So it was a valid custom. Sagar (1931)

5. The conduct of employer and employee

The parties' conduct during the employment can be used to work out what they originally agreed. For instance, suppose that an employee is told that he will have to move to a new plant 100 miles away. Whether the employee can refuse to move (and so claim unfair dismissal or redundancy if he is sacked for refusing to move) will depend upon whether his employment contract contains a job-mobility clause. If there is no express clause, then the law looks at, among other things, the past conduct. So, if the employee has previously moved home at the employer's request, that will probably be evidence of an implied job-mobility clause.

6. Collective agreements

Many people still have their terms and conditions of employment set by collective agreements. Do the terms of a collective agreement bind the individual worker?

If the individual's employment contract specifically refers to the 'current collective agreement' then there can be no doubt. He or she is subject to the terms of the agreement even if negotiated without his or her knowledge and against his or her will.

Mr Callison was a first-rate spray painter. He worked for Fords and his employment contract was subject to the terms agreed from time to time between his union and Fords. Fords and the union negotiated a reorganization which made spray painters of his ability unnecessary and so he was regraded as a Class C sprayer. He left, and claimed wrongful dismissal and redundancy. Held: No. The new arrangements had been agreed with the union, and since his employment contract bound him to accept the terms negotiated by the union, the company had not acted wrongly. Callison (1969)

Difficulties arise when the employee's employment contract does not make any mention of a collective agreement. In these circumstances it is more difficult for an employer to argue that the employee is bound by the terms negotiated with the union. But, in practice, employees are usually bound by the terms of collective agreements – especially if they have accepted the terms of the agreements in the past. Often, in the absence of objection (and sometimes in the face of it), the employee will be taken to accept or regarded as bound by the new collective agreement. Generally, this will be so whether or not he or she is a member of the union.

7. Works rules and disciplinary codes

These days, employers are expected to have comprehensive disciplinary codes and disciplinary procedures. To what extent are these, and other works rules, binding on the individual employee?

If the rules are specifically referred to in employees' contracts of employment then there can be no doubt that they are bound by them. So wise employers ensure that their staff have written contracts that state: 'I have read the works rules and regulations contained in the works rules booklet and accept the conditions of employment set out in that booklet.' Also, if employees sign that they accept the job 'on the usual conditions', that will usually be enough to make them bound by the rules.

But not all employers are that legally minded. Sometimes there is no express reference to the works or disciplinary rules. When this happens, the employee will generally be held to be bound by them if they are reasonable and likely to be regarded as binding by the staff. If the rules are on display in the office or factory then they will generally be regarded as binding.

However, this does not mean that the employer can simply alter the terms of the employment contract by pinning up a new set of works or disciplinary rules. If the orders are changed to such an extent that they alter the contract of employment, then the employee can protest.

8. The 'written particulars' supplied to the employee

If there is no comprehensive written employment contract the employer must provide the employee with a written summary of the contract (see below). Often these 'written particulars' are the only written evidence of the contract and so, more often than not, they are accepted as the best evidence of what was agreed between employer and employee unless the employee can convince the industrial tribunal that his or her recollection of what was originally said is correct. For instance:

Mr Rump started work as a heavy-goods-vehicle driver in 1973. The company asked him to sign a contract of employment form which said that he would be liable to work anywhere in the United Kingdom. However, one of the company's managers orally promised him that he would only have to work in the south of England owing to his family circumstances. As a result of this promise, Mr Rump signed the form.

In 1976 Mr Rump signed a copy of his written particulars of employment which stated: 'You may be required to transfer from one workplace to another on the instruction of the employer.'

All went well until February 1978, when Mr Rump was ordered to work outside the south of England. He refused, resigned and then claimed unfair dismissal. Held: It had been an original oral term of his employment that he would not have to work outside the south of England. The 1976 written particulars could not alter the contract of employment. Accordingly, he was justified in resigning once the company insisted that he work outside the south of England. He was entitled to unfair-dismissal compensation. Hawker Siddeley (1979)

If an employee does not agree with the details set out in the written summary, it is important that he or she makes this clear to the employer. If they do nothing they will later find it difficult to argue that the summary is not a true record of what was agreed.

EMPLOYMENT RIGHTS

The longer you have worked for your employer, the more rights you are entitled to.

Period of employment	Rights	See page
1 month	If sacked, you must be given at least 1 week's notice; you are entitled to guarantee payments if laid off, on short time, or if you are suspended on certain medical grounds.	445 420
13 weeks	You should have received written particulars of your contract of employment by now.	407
2 years	You are within the unfair-dismissal legislation.	456
	If sacked, you must be given at least 2 weeks' notice.	445
	You are entitled to demand a written statement of the reason for your sacking.	449
	You are within the redundancy-payments legislation.	498
	You can have reasonable time off to look for a job if you are being made redundant.	511
	You are entitled to maternity pay and also to return to your job after confinement for pregnancy.	435
4–12 years	If sacked, you must be given 1 week's notice for each year of your employment.	445
over 12 years	If sacked, you must be given at least 12 weeks' notice.	445

PROVIDING 'WRITTEN PARTICULARS' OF THE EMPLOYMENT CONTRACT

Employers must provide each member of staff with a written summary of the main terms of their employment contract. This must be provided within thirteen weeks of starting work.

But it is not the actual contract of employment that need be provided. The 'written particulars' are just a summary of the terms of the contract – not the contract itself. However, as already explained, the written particulars will usually be the best record of the terms of the contract and so, for all practical purposes, will be the contract. But in theory they are not.

The written particulars can be handed or posted to the employee within the thirteen-week period. All the particulars need not be contained in one document, so employees can be given a piece of paper that refers them to another document – such as a staff handbook or a pension-scheme booklet. If they are not given a copy of the other document, there must be one available for them to inspect at work and they should be told where it is. So a worker could be referred to 'the terms of the current collective agreement made between the firm and the recognized trade unions, a copy of which is available for inspection in the personnel department offices'.

Obviously, it is better if all employees are given their own individual written particulars with all the information contained in the one document. But, as the law stands, this is not necessary.

Sensible employers will:

1 Prepare the written particulars as soon as the employee is recruited, rather than wait until the end of the thirteen-week period. By serving the written particulars straight away they are reducing the scope for future argument.
2 Include all the other terms in the contract of employment and not confine themselves to those points required by law (see page 410). They will thus end up with a comprehensive, written employment contract.
3 Ask employees to sign that they accept the written particulars as representing the terms of their contract. By doing this employees will almost certainly be committing themselves to accepting the terms set out in the written particulars – even if they are not a true record of what was originally agreed.

If the written particulars are wrong

If employees accept incorrect written particulars they will probably find that they are bound by the error. For instance, suppose that the particulars state that an employee is entitled to sick pay at two-thirds of the normal rate, whereas full sick pay was agreed when he or she was offered the job; if he or she does not query the error he or she will later find it very difficult to prove what was originally agreed. More often than not, silence in not querying the error will be taken as acceptance of the terms.

		Employee's Rights				
	The right	*Written particulars of the employment contract (see page 407)*	*Notice (see page 445)*	*Unfair dismissal (see page 456)*	*Written reasons for dismissal (see page 449)*	*Redundancy payment (see page 498)*
Eligible employees	*(see remedy below)*	1	2	3	4	5
Self-employed; partner; freelance		no	no	no	no	no
Over the normal retirement age for the job, even if under 65		yes	yes	no	yes	yes
Of retirement pension age		yes	yes	no	yes	no
Aged under 18		yes	yes	yes	yes	no
Less than 1 calendar month's continuous employment		no	no	no	no	no
Less than 2 years' continuous employment		yes	yes	no	no	no
Fixed-term contract for over 1 year which specifically excludes these rights		yes	N/A	no	yes†	no

Ineligible employees

In addition various other groups of employees are ineligible: certain Crown servants, the police, public officials, share fishermen and those who work outside Great Britain. So too are 'part-timers', but there is a complicated definition of what is a part-timer (i.e. a person who works fewer than sixteen hours per week, unless employed for five years or more, in which case it is a person employed for fewer than eight hours per week). Also excluded are seasonal workers – that is, employees taken on for a fixed period of twelve weeks or less.

An employee should write to the employer pointing out any errors. If the employer refuses to accept that there is an error, the employee can ask an industrial tribunal to decide who is right.

Mr Churcher was sent written particulars which described him as 'planner and associated duties'. He thought he should be 'senior planning engineer'. The firm did not agree and so he took the matter to an industrial tribunal. Held: His proper job title should be 'planning engineer'. Churcher (1976)

Employee's Rights								
Statutory maternity pay and leave (*see page 435*)	Itemized pay statement (*see page 415*)	Equal pay (*see page 422*)	Guarantee pay on lay-off and short-time (*see page 420*)	Rights on employer's insolvency (*see page 451*)	Trade union activities (*see page 512*)	Time off for union officials (*see page 514*)	Time off for public duties (*see page 430*)	Time off for antenatal care (*see page 433*)
6	7	8	9	10	11	12	13	14
no	no	no	no	no	no	no	no	no
yes	yes	yes	yes	yes	yes	yes	yes	yes
yes	yes	yes	yes	yes	yes	yes	yes	yes
yes	yes	yes	yes	yes	yes	yes	yes	yes
no	yes	yes	no	yes	yes	yes	yes	yes
no*	yes	yes	yes	yes	yes	yes	yes	yes
yes	yes	yes	yes	yes	yes	yes	yes	yes

* Except for SMP at lower rate, where 26 weeks' employment is necessary. † If longer than 2 years.

What sanction can be imposed (usually by industrial tribunal)?

The remedy

1 *Declare what particulars should be*
2 *Sue for wages in county court*
3 *Award reinstatement, re-engagement, or compensation*
4 *Can award up to 2 weeks' pay*
5 *Cash compensation*
6 *Up to 18 weeks' wages – 6 at 90 per cent of net pay and 12 at £46.30*
7 *Award up to 13 weeks' worth of the 'deductions'*
8 *Wage imbalance for up to 2 years*
9 *5 days' pay per quarter*
10 *The Secretary of State can pay the arrears due*
11 *Can award compensation*
12 *Can award compensation*
13 *Can award compensation*
14 *Can award compensation of wages due during time off*

The contents of the 'written particulars'

By section 1 of the 1978 Act, an employee's written particulars must state:

1 The *names* of both employer and employee.
2 The *date* when the employment began. Also whether any previous service will count as continuous employment for working out eligibility for employment law rights.
3 *Pay* – the rate of pay, or the method of calculating it. Also whether he or she is to be paid by the week, month or year.
4 *Job title*. But it need not be a job description. If it is a detailed description of the job, rather than a mere job title, it may well be taken, at a later date, as restricting the employer's ability to ask the employee to do other work. The employee should object if the particulars contain a job description which is very wide since this may restrict his/her right to refuse a 'suitable alternative job' if he or she is made redundant or if she returns to work after pregnancy.
5 *Holiday entitlement*. What are the holidays? Are they paid? When does the firm's holiday year begin?
6 *Pension*. Is there a pension scheme? If so, what are the details? Usually the employee is referred to a separate pensions booklet.
7 *Sickness and injury*. The firm's rules about sickness. Is the employee entitled to sick pay? If so, for how long? Can the employer deduct DSS sickness benefit from the sick pay? What procedure is to be followed for deciding whether an employee is so ill that he or she should be dismissed? What are the rules about production of sick notes? Can the employer insist on a medical examination by the firm's doctor?
8 *Notice*. Both employer and employee must give the other notice if the employment is to be ended by sacking or resignation. The minimum periods of notice must be set out, but they cannot be less than the statutory minimum periods (see page 445).
9 *Hours of work*. What is the length of the normal working week? Employees need not work overtime unless it is a term of their employment contract. So if the employer wants to be able to insist on compulsory overtime, there should be a specific clause saying so.
10 *Discipline at work*. Employers are expected to draw up disciplinary rules and disciplinary procedures. Employees should be told of them. Usually this will be done by referring them to a separate booklet, such as the works rules. They should also be told of the disciplinary appeals procedure.
11 *Complaints*. Employees should be told to whom they can complain if they have a grievance.

If the written particulars are not provided

If the written particulars are not provided, employees can complain to an industrial tribunal. They can complain at any time during their employment, or within three months of leaving the job. The industrial tribunal can then declare what the written particulars should say.

But beyond that, there is no real sanction on the employer who does not supply the written particulars. Employees will probably be reluctant to complain to their employer or to make an issue out of it. Certainly complaining to an industrial tribunal is hardly likely to increase promotion prospects within the firm!

Asking for your 'written particulars'

1 Check that you are entitled to receive written particulars. A few workers (such as part-timers) are excluded: For full details on ineligible employees, see page 408.
2 Check that your employer has not complied with his/her legal obligation by handing you a note which refers you to other document(s); see page 407.
3 Once you have been employed for thirteen weeks you can demand the written particulars. If they have not been supplied check that this is not through an oversight or clerical error.
4 A letter is now needed. Write asking your employer for 'the written particulars of my contract of employment, which you are required to provide to me, in accordance with section 1 of the Employment Protection (Consolidation) Act 1978'. Keep a copy of the letter.
5 If you still do not receive the written particulars you will have to decide how far you are prepared to take the matter. You can complain to an industrial tribunal but you might do best to draw up your own set of written particulars and send them to your employer. You will then have gone on record as setting out what you regard as the main terms of the employment contract. This should safeguard your position for the future. But, whatever you decide to do, it might be sensible to wait until you have been employed for two years. Then you will be eligible for compensation for unfair dismissal and will have some protection if your employer decides you are a trouble-maker and sacks you. Alternatively, you might ask a trade union for help, if it is recognized by your employer.

EMPLOYED OR SELF-EMPLOYED?

Only 'employees' are eligible for the various employment-protection rights (except the discrimination and equal-pay laws), such as unfair dismissal, redundancy, the right to notice, maternity pay and so on.

People who are self-employed cannot claim any of these rights, for they do not have a contract of employment. Instead they are independent contractors, employed on a contract for services.

Usually it is obvious whether a worker is an employee or not. The question can often be answered by simply asking, 'Who pays the national insurance contributions?' and, 'Does he/she pay tax by PAYE?' However, these factors are not conclusive – a worker can have claimed the tax benefits of being self-employed and yet still be held to be an employee:

Mr Davis was a lecturer at the New England College, Arundel. He was taken on as an employee in 1971, but later he asked the college to treat him as self-employed 'for fiscal reasons'. Thereafter the college no longer deducted tax or national insurance contributions from his pay. Later, Mr Davis was sacked and the question that arose was whether he was eligible for unfair dismissal. The college argued that he was self-employed and so not eligible. Held: He was an employee. The relationship between Davis and the college was that of employer and employee, and this had not been altered by the tax and NI arrangements. Davis (1977)

So it is not so much the label that the parties put on their relationship (i.e. employee or self-employed) but the reality of the relationship. For instance:

Under the 'lump' system, building labourers are said to be self-employed, whereas in reality they are treated as employees. The device was widely used as a tax-dodge until the tax laws were tightened up. In one case, a lump worker was injured and sued the contractor for negligence. If the worker was an employee, the contractor would have been liable; if the worker was self-employed, the contractor would probably not have been liable. Held: He was an employee. The mere fact that he was called 'self-employed' could not hide the real nature of the employer/employee relationship. The judge said: 'I regard the lump ... as no more than a device which each side regarded as being capable of being put to his own advantage ... but which in reality did not affect the relationship of the parties ... the reality of the relationship was employer and employee.' Ferguson (1976)

Similarly:

Mr West was a sheet-metal worker. He asked his employers to treat him as self-employed and they did so. He was paid without deductions and he received no holiday or sick-pay entitlement. But otherwise there was no difference between his working conditions and those of his PAYE workmates. The employers told him that they did not need him any more and he claimed unfair dismissal. The employers argued that he was not eligible for unfair-dismissal compensation since he was self-employed, not an employee. Held: West was really an employee – it was impossible to regard him as being in business on his own account – so he was within the unfair-dismissal legislation. Young & Woods (1980)

However, this is probably a more typical case:

An architect worked for a housing association for a period of twenty-one months, averaging twenty-eight hours' work each week. He did not receive sick pay or holiday pay. Was he employed or self-employed? Held: He was self-employed. But this was largely because he did not undertake or promise to turn up at the office at any particular time and nor did he promise to do a particular number of hours each week. Basically, all he had promised was to do architectural work during the hours that he chose to work. WPHT (1981)

Undoubtedly, many people claim to be self-employed and yet they work for only one person, turn up at that person's office, and do the work they are told to do, during the hours laid down for them. Accordingly, it would seem that such people are not genuinely self-employed – and they and their employers

Employed and Self-employed: The Differences

	Employee	*Self-employed*
Tax	PAYE deducted by employer assessed under Schedule E	Pays Schedule D; generally has more deductible expenses and so pays less tax; will usually pay tax in arrears
NI	Paid partly by employer and partly by employee	All paid by the self-employed worker
Occupational pension	Probably entitled to a pension, partly financed by employer	Must pay own pension contributions
Sickness	Entitled to statutory sick pay from employer, or sickness (or supplementary) benefit from DSS	No entitlement to sick pay or statutory sick pay. Can claim sickness (or supplementary) benefit from DSS
Unemployment benefit	Eligible	Ineligible
Unfair dismissal	Eligible	Ineligible
Redundancy payments	Eligible	Ineligible
Holidays	Usually receives paid holiday	Not paid
Notice	Entitled to statutory minimum period of notice (see page 406)	Need not be given any notice, unless contract says otherwise
VAT	Not liable	Must be charged if turnover over £36,000 p.a. (1992)

should beware (because the DSS might claim that the more expensive employee's NI stamps should be paid, and the Inland Revenue might claim that the self-employed person's tax benefits should not apply).

Home workers can be employees; once again, the issue is decided by looking at the totality of the relationship. Most home workers are self-employed but some may be surprised to learn that they are not (or, more likely, their employers would be horrified to learn that the home workers are employees!). For instance:

A clothing factory made men's trousers. Machinists worked in the factory and they were all employees. However, there were also out-workers who worked at home, sewing pockets into the trousers. They were paid on piece-rate and they decided themselves how much work they wanted to do [usually, it was about four to seven hours a day]. There was an argument over holiday pay, and it ended with two of the home workers claiming unfair dismissal. So the question then arose of whether they were employees or self-employed. Held: They were employees. Nethermere (St Neots) (1984)

This decision was greeted with some amazement at the time and so it is probably best seen as an extreme example. The position remains that most home workers are probably self-employed but they may turn out to be employed; a lot will depend upon the extent to which the employer supervises their work and lays down the working hours etc. Similarly, casual workers can also be employees, although they will normally be regarded as self-employed unless they have to work as and when requested by the employer.

Company directors can often be in a difficult position. It is not always easy to decide whether they are employees or self-employed. Usually, the control test (can he or she be told how to do their job?) will decide the issue. If the directors are in reality their own boss, they will not be employees. For instance, a director who owns a majority of the shares in a company will be self-employed.

Full-time directors are more likely to be regarded as employees than part-time directors. But even a full-time director will be self-employed if his or her position is inconsistent with their being an employee.

The three Parsons brothers inherited their father's haulage business and ran it, although most of the shares were owned by their mother. But the brothers argued and Leonard Parsons was voted off the board. He claimed unfair dismissal, but the company argued that he was not an employee and so he was not eligible. Although Leonard did not have a contract with the company he was a director for life. Held: By looking at all the circumstances, it was clear that Leonard was self-employed. His pay was described as director emoluments and he paid tax and NI contributions as a self-employed person; thus he could not claim unfair dismissal. On these facts, the court could not agree that he was an employee. Parsons (1979)

23 At Work

WAGES

Itemized pay statements

Employers must provide their staff with itemized pay statements (s. 8, Employment Protection (Consolidation) Act 1978), specifying:

- the gross pay;
- the net pay;
- any deductions from the gross pay, stating the amounts deducted and why the deductions are made.

Employees should therefore be able to work out how their pay is made up. The itemized pay statement need not repeat the fixed deductions that are made from every pay slip if the employee has been given (within the last year) a 'standing statement of fixed deductions' setting out the amount of the deductions, when they are made and why they are made. So fixed deductions, such as trade union membership fees and staff club contributions, need not be set out separately on every pay slip.

The aim of the legislation is that every employee should be able to work out how his or her net pay is calculated. Unfortunately, the Act does not lay down any standard form of pay slip, and an employer can provide staff with computerized pay statements that comply with the legislation but are nevertheless difficult to understand.

If employees are not given an itemized pay statement, or if they are given an incomplete statement, they can apply to an industrial tribunal (the usual application form, IT1, is used; see page 482). The application can be made at any time during the employment, or within three months of the ending of the employment. The tribunal can decide what the statement should have said. But that by itself is no real sanction. So an additional sanction is provided by allowing the tribunal, in effect, to 'fine' the employer. He or she can be ordered to pay the employee an amount up to the total of all the unnotified deductions made during the thirteen weeks before the application to the tribunal. So the employer can be ordered to pay a sum equal to the employee's tax, NI, pension and other contributions – even though the employer was entitled to deduct them in the first place. For instance:

Mr and Mrs Davies were employed as steward and stewardess at a labour club in Cardiff for three months. They were not given an itemized pay statement despite having asked for one. They complained to an industrial tribunal. Held: The tribunal calculated Mr Davies's unnotified deductions at £181.35 and Mrs Davies's at £62.30. The tribunal awarded Mr Davies £150 and Mrs Davies £50. This was despite the fact that neither Mr nor Mrs Davies had suffered any loss through the club's failure to supply itemized pay statements. Davies (1979)

Ineligible employees. Not all employees can demand an itemized pay statement (e.g. part-timers are not eligible). For a full list, see the chart on pages 408–9.

Deductions from wages

The Wages Act 1986 contains provisions which prevent or limit an employer making deductions from an employee's wages. Shortly put, an employer is not permitted to make any deduction from wages unless:

• this is in accordance with another statute (e.g. an attachment of earnings order), *or*

• there is a term in the contract of employment permitting this (the contractual term must be in writing), *or*

• the employee has consented/agreed in writing to the deduction (including consent to make a payment to a third party where that party tells the employer what amount to deduct).

In addition, the prohibition against deductions does not apply where a deduction is made in order to obtain lawful repayment of any overpayment of wages or expenses, or where the deduction relates to a period when the employee is on strike or taking part in other industrial action.

Even where deductions are allowed, there are provisions in the Act which limit the amount which can be deducted from the wages of employees in retail employment on account of cash shortage or stock deficiency. In such a case, an employer is not allowed to deduct more than one-tenth of the gross amount of wages payable and deductions cannot be made where the shortage or deficiency is more than twelve months old unless it could not reasonably have been discovered in that period. The one-tenth limitation does not, however, apply to a final instalment of wages due to an employee on leaving employment.

Although it may seem simple at first sight, the question of what is a 'deduction' has caused tribunals and the courts a great deal of difficulty in practice. As matters now stand, a refusal/failure to pay wages is a deduction even though, if nothing is paid, the deduction is effectively 100 per cent! 'Wages' include any bonus, commission and holiday pay. However, a failure to pay salary in lieu of notice is not a deduction, since such a payment has not been *earned*. It is in the nature of damages for breaking the contract by not allowing the employee the opportunity to work out the period of notice.

If a deduction has been made from wages which is not permitted by the Act, the employee may make a complaint to an industrial tribunal, but must do so within three months of the payment (or more correctly non-payment) of the wages in question, and the industrial tribunal has the power to order repayment. Where deductions have been made by a series of instalments, provided the last of these is within the three-month time limit, all the previous deductions from earlier instalments can be included in a complaint to the industrial tribunal. There may be some overlap between remedies under the Act and under the Employment Protection (Consolidation) Act 1978 where deductions coincide with a failure to provide an itemized pay statement (see above). Non-payment of salary in lieu of notice is a claim which has to be pursued in the county court. Although it was envisaged at the time of the 1978 Act that industrial tribunals would be given jurisdiction to deal with such claims, as yet regulations for this purpose have not been made.

Special provisions apply when an employer becomes insolvent. His or her staff can claim money due from the Department of Employment (see page 451).

The right to sick pay

Whether or not employees can demand sick pay from their employer will depend upon the terms of their employment contract. If there is a written contract with a clause giving (or denying) them the right to sick pay, then that will be conclusive.

But a number of employees do not have written employment contracts and so the law has to work out what the parties intended the position to be. Usually by far the best evidence of this will be the 'written particulars' of the employment contract, sent to employees within thirteen weeks of their starting work (see page 407). The written particulars should state whether sick pay is payable. In the absence of other clear evidence, the law will accept the position as set out in the written particulars.

If the written particulars do not mention sick pay (or if the employee is not sent any written particulars) the law will look at the custom and practice in the firm or industry, and see what has happened in the past. There is no definite rule that an employee is automatically entitled to sick pay, unless the contract says otherwise. The court will usually be able to come to a decision based on past practice in the firm, what was said when the employee was first offered a job, and so on. But if there is no evidence either way, then the likely outcome is that the employee will be presumed to be entitled to sick pay.

An employee was off sick for seven of his fourteen months' employment, before he resigned. He claimed that he was entitled to sick pay. Held: There was no automatic entitlement to sick pay. One had to look at the details of the case. Since the 'written particulars' did not cover the point, this meant looking at the past history. Since he had not sent in any sick notes, and no one else had been paid whilst off sick, it was decided that there was no implied term that he should be paid whilst off sick. Mears (1982)

Even if there is an implied right to sick pay, it will normally be payable only for a 'reasonable' length of time – not indefinitely. In cases of serious, lengthy sickness the employer may be able to say that the employment has automatically been brought to an end (because the illness has 'frustrated' it). See page 447.

Statutory sick pay

Most employees are entitled to statutory sick pay (SSP). This is a payment made by the employer, for which the employer later claims a refund from the state. It is paid for twenty-eight weeks by the employer, and at the end of that time most employees have to start claiming invalidity benefit.

Since only employees can claim SSP, it follows that self-employed people cannot claim it (instead, they should claim sickness benefit from the DSS). Also a few categories of employees are excluded – see the chart opposite.

SSP is only payable when employees have been ill for four days in a row (note that this includes non-working days, such as Saturdays and Sundays). But they do not actually have to be paid any SSP unless they have been sick for three 'qualifying days' (i.e. days on which they would normally have worked) in any two-week period. Once the employee is eligible it is for the employer to pay the SSP to the employee; this will be at one of two different rates, depending upon the employee's earnings. Considerable discretion is given to employers as to the rules they want to lay down for notification of sickness but the basic requirement is that the employer must be notified no later than one week after the first 'qualifying day' (i.e. within one week of the first work-day being missed). If the illness is for seven days or less, most employers will accept a self-certificate (i.e. a form filled in by the employee stating that he or she was ill); for longer periods, it is usual to ask for a doctor's certificate.

The SSP rules are complicated, but a simple guide to SSP is contained in DSS pamphlet NI244; full details will be found in pamphlet NI270.

Medical suspension pay

Healthy employees might be laid off because of dangerous conditions at work. If so, they can claim full (basic only) pay from their employer for a period of up to twenty-six weeks, unless they have unreasonably refused an offer of suitable alternative work from the employer (s.19, Employment Protection (Consolidation) Act 1978).

This right to medical suspension pay applies only to certain industries such as paint, vitreous enamelling, lead smelting, certain chemicals, india rubber, radioactive substances, asbestos and pottery dust. For instance, an employee working with radioactive substances may be laid off if the radiation levels become too high.

Ineligible employees. Not all employees can demand medical suspension pay (e.g. part-timers). For a full list, see the chart on pages 376–7.

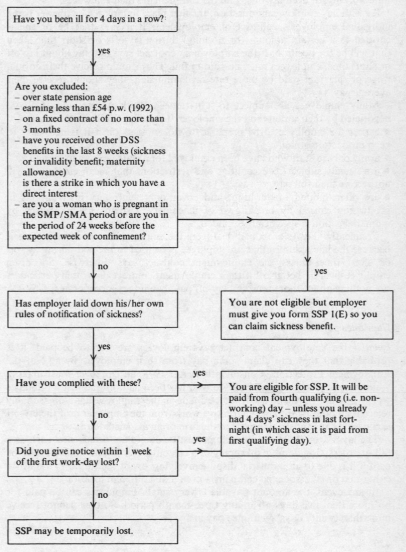

Statutory Sick Pay

Have you been ill for 4 days in a row?

yes

Are you excluded:
– over state pension age
– earning less than £54 p.w. (1992)
– on a fixed contract of no more than 3 months
– have you received other DSS benefits in the last 8 weeks (sickness or invalidity benefit; maternity allowance)
  is there a strike in which you have a direct interest
– are you a woman who is pregnant in the SMP/SMA period or are you in the period of 24 weeks before the expected week of confinement?

no

yes

Has employer laid down his/her own rules of notification of sickness?

You are not eligible but employer must give you form SSP 1(E) so you can claim sickness benefit.

yes

Have you complied with these?

yes

You are eligible for SSP. It will be paid from fourth qualifying (i.e. non-working) day – unless you already had 4 days' sickness in last fortnight (in which case it is paid from first qualifying day).

no

Did you give notice within 1 week of the first work-day lost?

yes

no

SSP may be temporarily lost.

Wages during lay-off or short time

Industrial action, recession, bad weather and breakdown can all lead to short-time working, or even lay-offs. Can the staff demand their full wages?

As with any employment question, the first place to look for an answer is the individual employee's contract of employment. If it says that he or she is entitled to a certain amount (or nothing) during lay-offs or short time, then that will be the position. If the employment contract says nothing about lay-off or short time, employees must be paid in full. They should receive their normal wage or salary; if paid by piece rate or commission, they should receive their average pay.

Many employees are subject to 'Guaranteed Work Agreements' (GWAs) negotiated by their unions and the employer. Typically, GWAs:

● expect the employee to be prepared to do another job if it is necessary to keep production going;

● apply only to staff who have been employed for a stated minimum period;

● are usually subject to exceptions and restrictions that mean employees will not receive their full pay;

● are often limited in duration, and cover only temporary interruptions in production caused by breakdown of machinery. Usually, lay-off caused by industrial action is specifically excluded.

Frequently GWAs are a bad deal from the employee's point of view. This is because the law assumes that an employee is entitled to be paid during lay-off or short time unless the employment contract says otherwise. So, often employees will be better off if their employment contract or written particulars say nothing about short-time and lay-off pay than if they incorporate a GWA.

Guarantee payments

Even if the employment contract says employees are not to be paid, it is probable that they can claim some pay from their employer. By s.12 of the Employment Protection (Consolidation) Act 1978, an employer must make a 'guarantee payment' to an employee who has been laid off and lost a full day's work. But the payment need not be made if the employee has unreasonably rejected an offer of suitable alternative work from the employer or if the lay-off is caused by an industrial dispute in the firm or an associated firm.

The lay-off, or short-time working, must be due to an 'occurrence' such as a fall in orders, fire, flood, bankruptcy of a customer etc. But no money has to be paid if it is due to an industrial dispute involving any of the employer's staff (in either that or an associated company – even if at a different location).

In any event, the amount payable is very small. Employees can be paid for no more than five days off in any three-month period. So they cannot receive more than twenty days' guarantee pay in a year.

More important, the maximum amount that the employer is required by law to pay is £14.10 a day (1992 figures).

Illustration. Frank Jones is a gardener in a private school. He is laid off because a heating breakdown has closed his school. He is paid £2.75 per hour for a basic thirty-seven-hour week. But he usually works an extra four hours each week, at £3 per hour. He can claim a guarantee payment:

$$\frac{\text{pay}}{\text{hours}} = \frac{£2.75 \times 37 \text{ and } £3 \times 4}{41} = \frac{£101.75 + £12}{41} = £2.78 \text{ per hour}$$

The guarantee payment for one day will be 8.2 hours at £2.78 per hour ... £22.80. But the maximum amount payable is £14.10, so that is all he receives.

Guarantee payments need be made only for days when employees' employment contracts require them to work. So if employees *accept* a shorter working week, they cannot then claim a guarantee payment for the days they are laid off:

Mrs Clemens worked a four-day week. But business declined and so she agreed to work a two-day week and this amendment was recorded in her contract of employment. She claimed a guarantee payment for the other two days when she was laid off. Held: No. She was ineligible because she had accepted the shorter working week. Clemens (1977)

If employers do not pay employees their guarantee payment, employees can take their claim to an industrial tribunal, which can order employers to pay them. There is no criminal penalty imposed on the employer.

Ineligible employees. Staff with less than a month's service and part-timers cannot claim guarantee payments. For a full list, see the chart on pages 408–9.

The statutory right to a guarantee payment was a well-intentioned innovation. However, the amounts that are paid are so unrealistically low that the scheme may do more harm than good. This is because some employers are taking the '£14.10 per day and five days per quarter' levels as being the maximum that they should pay staff who are laid off. Some employees seem unaware that they can still claim their full wages from the employer (unless there is a GWA) under the old rule of law that employees are entitled to be paid while laid off unless their employment contract says otherwise. So the danger is that employees will claim only a small proportion of the wages that are actually due to them.

Minimum wages for certain industries

There are some industries in which trade unions are notoriously weak, mainly those employing large numbers of women and part-timers. To protect these workers, Wages Councils were formed to lay down minimum terms and conditions in each industry. However, the relevant legislation was repealed by the Wages Act 1986, leaving in place only Wages Councils in existence at the time and limiting their power to fixing single rates of pay and not other terms and conditions, as previously was the case.

There are some 2½ million workers in the industries that are subject to Wages Councils. There are some twenty-five Wages Councils, and they include most jobs in:

- retail shops (including supermarkets, but excluding chemists and butchers);
- the catering trades (excluding canteens and boarding houses);
- hairdressing;
- clothing trades;
- toy manufacture;
- laundries (excluding dry cleaners and launderettes);
- agricultural jobs (which are largely governed by Agricultural Wages Boards).

The orders made by Wages Councils are enforced by the Wages Inspectorate of the Department of Employment. They can provide a full list of the trades covered by Wages Councils and they can prosecute employers who pay less than the minimum rates. In practice, the inspectors are so few on the ground that they can prosecute only in the worst cases. A much better course of action is likely to be for the employee to sue the employer (in the county court) for the underpaid wages. He (or, more probably, she) can sue for up to six years' underpayments. (See Chapter 68 for how to sue in the county court; legal aid may well be available.)

Equal pay for men and women

The Equal Pay Act 1970 requires equal pay for 'like work' regardless of the employee's sex. That seemingly straightforward aim has, however, been partly frustrated by a series of court decisions that have made the legislation extremely complex and difficult to apply.

The woman can compare herself with a man employed in the same firm, if:

- they do 'like work', *or*
- a job-evaluation scheme has compared their jobs, *or*
- her job is of 'equal value' (i.e. the demands made on her – effort, skill, decision etc. – are of equal value to those made on the man).

There are thus three routes to an equal-pay claim. But the laws are complicated and an employer can often get away with paying the woman less:

1 Regrading of jobs may put women in lower categories, and there are some jobs (e.g. office cleaning) that are rarely done by men. This can make even 'equal value' claims difficult.
2 The Act allows inequality of pay where there is a 'difference of *practical* importance in the work done'. In other words, the employer can then argue that it is not 'like' work. So, if the man is doing a more responsible job, a wage differential is justifiable. If the man can be said to be using different

equipment, to have extra duties or to be working on a different stage of the same work process, there may well be a 'practical difference' justifying the inequality.

3 There may be a 'material difference' between the man's job and the woman's job. A 'material difference' allows a more general, wider, comparison than under the 'practical difference' rules, above. Generally, 'practical difference' relates to the work done, whereas 'material differences' are concerned with who does it. For example, inequality is allowed if:

• the wages include a bonus element, and so the man earns a larger bonus because his output is greater;

• the wages include a 'service' element determined by the length of service with the firm: the man can be paid more if he has worked longer than the woman;

• a new male recruit may be appointed at the same salary as an existing female employee who has better qualifications and more experience, although he cannot be paid more than her.

The employee's remedy

The employee can apply to an industrial tribunal at any time during the employment or within six months of leaving the job. The tribunal can award damages, including pay due to the employee if she is being paid less than a man. No more than two years' arrears can be awarded.

Before going to an industrial tribunal the employee would be well advised to contact the Equal Opportunities Commission (EOC). The EOC can advise as to the prospects of success and, in exceptional cases, will help bring the claim.

Anyone thinking of bringing an equal-pay claim should take specialist advice from a solicitor or trade union representative. The decisions of the courts have made the legislation a minefield for the unwary. Certainly, reading the reported cases one has the impression that the tribunals and the courts have decided to apply a very restrictive interpretation to the Act. Often, 'material differences' and 'practical differences' are found where – to the layperson – they do not exist.

DISCIPLINE

It is an implied term of any contract of employment that employees will obey their employers' reasonable, lawful commands, and will behave themselves at work.

What happens if employees are in breach of this implied duty? If they misbehave or are disobedient, the employer may want to discipline them. But there are legal constraints on the disciplinary action that he or she can take.

1 *Dismissal.* The employer can dismiss the employee, but the employee will probably be able to bring an unfair-dismissal claim. The claim will succeed

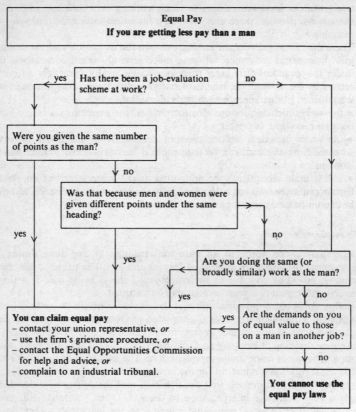

Equal Pay
If you are getting less pay than a man

Has there been a job-evaluation scheme at work? — yes / no

Were you given the same number of points as the man? — no

Was that because men and women were given different points under the same heading? — no

Are you doing the same (or broadly similar) work as the man? — no

Are the demands on you of equal value to those on a man in another job? — yes / no

You can claim equal pay
– contact your union representative, *or*
– use the firm's grievance procedure, *or*
– contact the Equal Opportunities Commission for help and advice, *or*
– complain to an industrial tribunal.

You cannot use the equal pay laws

(Note. This chart can also be used by men who are earning less than women.)

unless the employer can show that the employee's behaviour justified the sacking, and that he or she, the employer, acted reasonably in the way the sacking was carried out. Often, this will mean that the employer has to show that he or she followed the Code of Practice on Disciplinary Rules and Procedures published by the Advisory, Conciliation and Arbitration Service (ACAS) – see page 479.

2 *Suspension on full pay.* Generally, employers are not obliged to supply their staff with work, as long as they pay them their wages (see page 431). So suspension on full pay will be a proper, and legal, disciplinary sanction.

3 *Suspension without pay.* This will usually be unlawful. While employers need not provide their staff with work, they must provide them with their full wages unless their employment contracts say otherwise. So suspension on less than full pay will usually be unlawful – unless specifically allowed by the contract of employment, or unless the employee's behaviour had been so bad that the employer was entitled to dismiss him or her (in which case, of course, the employee might be prepared to accept a day's loss of wages as an alternative to dismissal).

4 *Warnings and reprimands.* Employees cannot object if they are reprimanded and given a warning (written or verbal) by their employer. If they do not think the reprimand or warning is justified, they should say so, preferably in writing. But there is no legal remedy – they cannot, for instance, complain to an industrial tribunal that they have been unfairly told off.

5 *Deductions.* These will be unlawful unless permitted by the employee's contract of employment. A specific clause will be needed and the Wages Act imposes limitations in the case of retail employees where deductions stem from cash or stock losses. See page 416.

6 *Demotion.* This will be a breach of contract on the part of the employer. Employees can thus regard themselves as having been sacked, and so can resign and then claim unfair dismissal.

7 *Transfer to another location.* This also will be a breach of contract, unless a job-mobility clause exists (see page 505).

The importance of disciplinary rules and procedures

ACAS has published a Code of Practice on disciplinary rules and disciplinary procedures. The Code sets out the behaviour required of a reasonable employer.

While it is not illegal to fail to observe the Code, an employer who does so will find it more difficult to defend an unfair-dismissal claim.

Accordingly, the Code is one of the fundamental documents in modern employment law. Both employers and employees should know what it says (see page 426). Anyone involved in a dispute over discipline at work – and in how arguments should be resolved – should always begin by reading through the Code of Practice to see whether the 'other side' have followed it. But the industrial tribunals do not expect 'blind obedience' to the Code – for instance, if the employee has been guilty of a very grave offence, it will probably make little difference if the employer does not follow the procedures recommended by the Code. (For more on this, see page 480.)

The main parts of the Code are set out below, but the most important paragraphs are those on how an employer should deal with a disciplinary matter. The sequence of events is:

1 Tell employees of the complaint being made against them.
2 Give them a chance to explain themselves.
3 Take a decision on what is the appropriate disciplinary action. The disciplinary action will normally be:
  • formal oral warning, *or*
  • formal written warning for 'more serious issues'; the warning should set out the offence and the likely consequences if it is repeated, *or*
  • final written warning, saying that further breaches of discipline will lead to a specified step, such as dismissal or suspension;
  • dismissal (or suspension without pay, if allowed by the employment contract).

The main provisions of the Code of Practice

[Paragraphs 1–5 and part of 6 omitted]

6 When drawing up rules the aim should be to specify clearly and concisely those necessary for the efficient and safe performance of work and for the maintenance of satisfactory relations within the work force and between employees and management. Rules should not be so general as to be meaningless.

7 Rules should be readily available and management should make every effort to ensure that employees know and understand them. This may be best achieved by giving every employee a copy of the rules and by explaining them orally. In the case of new employees this should form part of an induction programme.

8 Employees should be made aware of the likely consequences of breaking rules and in particular they should be given a clear indication of the type of conduct which may warrant summary dismissal.

ESSENTIAL FEATURES OF DISCIPLINARY PROCEDURES

9 Disciplinary procedures should not be viewed primarily as a means of imposing sanctions. They should also be designed to emphasize and encourage improvements in individual conduct.

10 Disciplinary procedures should:
  (a)– Be in writing.
  (b)– Specify to whom they apply.
  (c)– Provide for matters to be dealt with quickly.

(d)– Indicate the disciplinary actions which may be taken.

(e)– Specify the levels of management which have the authority to take the various forms of disciplinary action, ensuring that immediate superiors do not normally have the power to dismiss without reference to senior management.

(f)– Provide for individuals to be informed of the complaints against them and to be given an opportunity to state their case before decisions are reached.

(g)– Give individuals the right to be accompanied by a trade-union representative or by a fellow employee of their choice.

(h)– Ensure that, except for gross misconduct, no employees are dismissed for a first breach of discipline.

(i)– Ensure that disciplinary action is not taken until the case has been carefully investigated.

(j)– Ensure that individuals are given an explanation for any penalty imposed.

(k)– Provide a right of appeal and specify the procedure to be followed.

THE PROCEDURE IN OPERATION

11 When a disciplinary matter arises, the supervisor or manager should first establish the facts promptly before recollections fade, taking into account the statements of any available witnesses. In serious cases consideration should be given to a brief period of suspension while the case is investigated and this suspension should be with pay. Before a decision is made or penalty imposed the individual should be interviewed and given the opportunity to state his or her case and should be advised of any rights under the procedure, including the right to be accompanied.

12 Often supervisors will give informal oral warnings for the purpose of improving conduct when employees commit minor infringements of the established standards of conduct. However, where the facts of a case appear to call for disciplinary action, other than summary dismissal, the following procedure should normally be observed:

(a)– In the case of minor offences the individual should be given a formal oral warning or, if the issue is more serious, there should be a written warning setting out the nature of the offence and the likely consequences of further offences. In either case the individual should be advised that the warning constitutes the first formal stage of the procedure.

(b)– Further misconduct might warrant a final written warning which should contain a statement that any recurrence would lead to suspension or dismissal or some other penalty, as the case may be.

(c)– The final step might be disciplinary transfer, or disciplinary suspension without pay (but only if these are allowed for by an express or implied condition of the contract of employment), or dismissal, according to the nature of the misconduct. Special consideration should be given before imposing disciplinary suspension without pay and it should not normally be for a prolonged period.

13 Except in the event of an oral warning, details of any disciplinary action should be given in writing to the employee and, if desired, to his or her representative. At the same time the employee should be told of any right of appeal, how to make it and to whom.

14 When determining the disciplinary action to be taken the supervisor or manager should bear in mind the need to satisfy the test of reasonableness in all the circumstances. So far as possible, account should be taken of the employee's record and any other relevant factors.

15 Special consideration should be given to the way in which disciplinary procedures are to operate in exceptional cases. For example:

(a)– *Employees to whom the full procedure is not immediately available.* . . .

(b)– *Trade union officials.* . . .

(c)– *Criminal offences outside employment.* These should not be treated as automatic reasons for dismissal regardless of whether the offence has any relevance to the duties of the individual as an employee. The main considerations should be whether the offence is one that makes the individual unsuitable for his or her type of work or unacceptable to other employees. Employees should not be dismissed solely because a charge against them is pending or because they are absent through having been remanded in custody.

For cases of unfair dismissal and disciplinary offences, see pages 465–70.

HOURS

Overtime

Employees must work for the number of hours stated in their contract, but no more. Theoretically, therefore, they can refuse to work overtime unless their employment contract specifically requires them to do so.

The length of the working week, and any overtime requirements, should be included in the written particulars sent to their employees within thirteen weeks of their starting work (see page 410).

But if employees regularly agree to work overtime they might then find that they are unable to refuse overtime in the future. They might be held to have impliedly agreed to change their contract so that overtime is now compulsory:

Mr Tovey was a lorry driver. On 18 November he and other drivers changed to a new wage structure agreed with the company. The new agreement did not deal with the question of overtime payments. Three days later he was asked to do unpaid overtime, but said he would only do overtime if he was paid. He was sacked and then claimed unfair dismissal. Held: Tovey had accepted the new arrangement and there was evidence that other drivers customarily worked short periods of overtime without extra pay. Accordingly, he was now bound to work overtime and his dismissal was not unfair. Tovey (1975)

Senior staff may find it more difficult to refuse to work overtime. The law will often assume that there is an implied term in managers' or senior executives' employment contracts that they will work overtime when required – even if it is unpaid overtime. Whether this will be so will depend on the nature of the job and the practice in the trade or profession.

Employees who need not work overtime but who are dismissed for refusing to do it can claim unfair dismissal. But the tribunal might find their refusal unreasonable and so reduce the amount of compensation they received. This is especially likely to be so if other staff have agreed to work overtime, or if the employer wants to reorganize work arrangements more efficiently. In recent years the tribunals have been more ready to find that employees should cooperate with work-place reorganizations and it is therefore likely that an employee who sticks to the strict wording of his or her employment contract will be treated unsympathetically by the tribunal.

Maximum hours at work

There is at present (EC law may change this) no general restriction on the length of the working week, and previous restrictions relating to hours of work, the maximum length of time that could be worked without a break, overtime and shift work which applied to women and young persons, have been removed. Some vestigial provisions remain. For example, a woman may not be employed within four weeks of giving birth, the employment of women and young persons is prohibited in relation to certain processes connected with lead manufacture, and young persons may not be employed to work at any machine specified by the Health and Safety Executive to be dangerous unless they have been fully instructed as to the dangers and precautions and have received sufficient training in the work or are under supervision. There are also regulations governing the hours of work of those employed in the transport industry.

Children

There are various laws that restrict the employment of children. Unfortunately, the position is complex:
1 Children under thirteen can never be employed unless the local education authority (LEA) has agreed a lower age. This is usually done to allow children to work with their parents in light agricultural and horticultural work.
2 Children between thirteen and school-leaving age generally cannot work:
   • for more than two hours on school days or Sundays;
   • before 7 a.m. or after 7 p.m.;
   • until after school hours on school days, but many LEAs alter this and allow one hour's work before school, thus permitting paper rounds etc.;
   • without obtaining a licence if there is a performance at which a charge is to be made; school performances are exempt, as are performances amounting to fewer than three days in a six-month period.

3 Children between thirteen and sixteen cannot:
  - do any work involving heavy lifting or carrying;
  - work in manufacturing, demolition, building, transport or mining.
4 Children under seventeen cannot take part in street trading (e.g. working at stalls, selling flowers or papers), although children over fourteen can work for their parents.
5 Children under eighteen cannot work in a bar. But a child of thirteen or more can work in licensed premises where drinks are served with meals (e.g. restaurants, canteens).

Taking time off for public duties

An employee can take unpaid time off work to carry out his duties (s.29 Employment Protection (Consolidation) Act 1978) as a:
  - magistrate;
  - local councillor;
  - member of a tribunal;
  - school governor or manager;
  - regional or area health authority worker;
  - National Rivers Authority or river-purification board member

Employees can take only a 'reasonable' amount of time off. Clearly, the size of their firm, position in the firm and the amount of time needed for the duties will all be relevant. Sometimes employees who are members of these various public bodies will also be trade union officials and so allowed to take paid leave for those duties (see page 514). If that is the case, then time already taken off for union duties can be taken into account when deciding what is a reasonable amount of leave for the public duties.

If employees are entitled to time off, employers cannot expect them to work evenings to catch up with work:

A college lecturer asked for time off when he became a local councillor. The employers rearranged his teaching timetable so that he could attend council meetings but he was still required to do the same amount of teaching. As a result he had to work in the evenings and at weekends. He complained to an industrial tribunal that the college had not given him time off work. Held: He was right. The college had not given him time off. All they had done was to swap his hours around. Ratcliffe (1978)

An employee who is refused time off has three months in which to complain to an industrial tribunal (using the usual Form IT1). The tribunal can order the employer to pay cash compensation.

Although there is no Act dealing with the point, employees should always be allowed time off work for jury service (although they need not be paid).

Ineligible employees. Not all employees can claim unpaid leave for public duties. (e.g. part-timers). For a full list, see the chart on pages 408–9.

Time off for other purposes

Officers of recognized trade unions can take paid leave so as to carry out their union duties and to undergo training (see page 514). Members of recognized trade unions can take unpaid time off work to take part in union activities (see page 514). Redundant workers can take unpaid leave to look for a new job or to arrange training (see page 511).

HOLIDAYS

Employees are always entitled to take public holidays as holidays unless their employment contract requires them to work then. (The days covered by this are New Year's Day, Good Friday, Easter Monday, the first and last Mondays in May, the last Monday in August, Christmas Day and Boxing Day.)

Generally, the courts will find that there is an implied right for an employee to take a reasonable amount of paid holiday. So, in practice, unless the employment contract or the written particulars specifically say otherwise, the employee can claim a paid holiday. The amount of holiday will depend on the general practice and custom in the industry; in short, how much holiday do other workers of similar standing and length of employment receive? So, if an employee was sacked for taking a holiday of a reasonable length, he or she would almost certainly win an unfair dismissal claim.

Employees who return to work late after their holidays will obviously be in breach of their contract of employment, but it seems that the tribunals do not regard a twenty-four-hour lateness as justifying dismissal – unless, of course, there are other circumstances, such as a poor attendance record in the past (see Unfair Dismissal, page 467).

GIVING THE EMPLOYEE WORK TO DO

Surprisingly there is no general duty on employers to provide their staff with work. It is sufficient if he or she pays them. Generally, they cannot complain if they are not given enough to do.

This common-law doctrine has come under increasing attack in recent years, but it is still the law, although there would seem to be three exceptions to it:

1 *Actors, writers.* Some people work not just for the money but for the chance and opportunity of becoming better known. Writers, singers, actors, photographers and other artists can thus demand the right to work or compensation for not receiving it.
2 *Skilled workers.* An employee who has a skill can demand work so that he or she will not lose that skill. But the limits of this category are difficult to lay down. It clearly covers such people as airline pilots and surgeons, but it is open to question whether it covers skilled industrial workers. In Langston (1974) a car welder was suspended on full pay for two years. Lord Denning

said he had the right to work because 'in these days an employer, when employing a skilled man, is bound to provide him with work. By which I mean that the man should be given the opportunity of doing his work when it is available and he is ready and willing to do it.' But Lord Denning was in the minority in that case, so his opinion – while of great influence – is not the law.

3 *Piece-rate and bonus workers.* Employees can claim work when their wages are linked to the amount of work they do. But it seems likely that employees could not complain if their employer simply paid them a reasonable sum instead to cover their lost commission. So, to that extent, it may well be that they do not have a right to actual work. The law is unclear.

If employees are entitled to insist on work and are not given it, they can regard themselves as having been dismissed. They can thus leave and then claim unfair dismissal; but even this will not guarantee them the right to work. An employer cannot be forced to reinstate an employee and if he or she defies an industrial tribunal's order to reinstate the worker, the employer can be forced only to pay money compensation.

INVENTIONS AT WORK

The Patents Act 1977 sets out complicated rules as to whether employees can own a patent over something they invented at work. Generally, the answer will be 'no', because the Act says they cannot claim it as their own if:

• they invented it in the course of their normal duties: so if a research chemist creates a new medical compound for his or her pharmaceutical employers, the employer can claim the patent rights, *or*

• they are 'in a position of special responsibility': just what this means is not entirely clear, but it is probably intended to cover senior management staff who instigate research projects.

If the invention belongs to the employer, then the employee can apply for cash compensation if the employer has derived 'outstanding benefit' from the patent, 'having regard among other things to the size and nature of the employer's undertaking'. This is an area for specialist advice, but note that many employees are covered by collective agreements which give more generous terms – so employee inventors should always consider whether they should be in an appropriate union.

A good starting-point for anyone who wants to find out more about patents is to get the free booklet *What is Intellectual Property?* (from the Department of Trade and Industry).

Copyright

Copyright in any work produced by an employee in the course of employment will result in the employer being the first owner of any copyright in the work, unless there is an agreement to the contrary.

24 Maternity

A pregnant employee can have time off work for antenatal care; in addition she can claim maternity pay from her employer and she can also claim her job back after the birth of her child.

Further, she can claim unfair dismissal if she is sacked because she is pregnant (see page 474).

TIME OFF FOR ANTENATAL CARE

The Employment Act 1980 allows all pregnant women to take time off work, with pay, in order to receive antenatal care. However, after the first appointment the employer can demand a medical certificate confirming that the woman is pregnant, together with an appointment card (or other document confirming the appointment for which she wants time off).

If the employer unreasonably refuses paid leave to the woman, she can complain to an industrial tribunal. Note that this right to take time off is not limited to occasions when the woman has complications – it covers any appointment made on the advice of a doctor, midwife or health visitor. Also, this is one of the few rights that is available to virtually all employees – even if they are only part-timers, and even if they have only recently started work with that employer.

The employee was allowed time off to go to antenatal and relaxation classes, but the employers refused to pay her during the time off. She complained to an industrial tribunal. Held: By allowing her to take time off, the employers had conceded that it was reasonable for her to have the time off. Under the Act, she must be paid if it is reasonable for her to have the time off – thus, the employers had to pay her. Gregory (1982)

STATUTORY MATERNITY PAY (SMP)

Most women workers can claim SMP, whether or not they intend to return to work after the birth.

SMP is paid for what is called the 'maternity pay period'. The maximum period is eighteen weeks. The period cannot start earlier than the eleventh week before the expected week of confinement (EWC), but subject to this there is some flexibility as to when precisely the maternity pay period starts. There is a central 'core' period of thirteen weeks, which starts with the sixth week before the EWC. The remaining five weeks can be taken before or after the core period and may be split, with some weeks taken before and some after. There are two rates of SMP. The 'higher' rate is 90 per cent of normal earnings and is payable for six weeks. The lower rate is £46.30 per week (1992 rate), payable for the remaining twelve weeks.

SMP is treated as normal earnings and the employer therefore deducts tax and NI contributions and other sums he or she is entitled to deduct from pay. SMP is paid in the same way and at the same time as wages would have been paid to the employee. Any dispute regarding SMP entitlement will be resolved by reference to the DSS Adjudication Officer or (on appeal) by the Social Security Appeals Tribunal/Social Security Commissioner. If employers cannot pay because they have gone bust, the government will pay the employee (see page 451). For an outline of the way in which the SMP scheme works (with examples), see DSS Booklet NI257, *Employers' Guide to Statutory Maternity Pay* (April 1990).

A woman is not automatically eligible for SMP. She must follow complicated rules:

1 Continue in employment until at least the eleventh week prior to the expected date of birth. If she leaves her job before then she will lose her right to maternity pay. Note that she need not be 'working' at the eleventh week – all that is required is that she should still be employed. So if she is off work sick she will still be employed, and will be eligible even though she is not working. If her employer dismisses her because she is pregnant, and she will thus not be employed on the eleventh week, she should claim unfair dismissal (and also sex discrimination).

She can, of course, work on after the eleventh week if she wishes; her employer cannot force her to leave before she wants to.

2 She must have been employed by her employer for at least twenty-six weeks (or two years to qualify for the higher-rate SMP), continuing into the fifteenth week before the baby is due.

3 *She must tell her employer that she intends to stop work because of her pregnancy.* This must be done at least three weeks before she is due to leave. If she does not give this notice, she will lose her right to maternity pay. In exceptional cases, the three-week period can be waived if she gave notice as soon 'as was reasonably practicable' – for example, if she did not know she was pregnant until a few days before she left. Similarly, the three-week period may be waived if the woman did not know she had to give notice to the employer; however, such claims are treated with great scepticism. The notice to the employer need not be in writing, but it is always advisable to give written notice so that there can be no dispute about whether she did give proper notice. (See draft letter on page 438.) If she does not give written notice, the employer can insist on being given written notice.

4 It is also necessary to provide the employer with a maternity certificate comprising evidence of pregnancy and confirmation of the expected date of confinement, although not earlier than the fourteenth week before the EWC.

Ineligible employees. Not all women can claim maternity pay. In particular, part-timers, and those who have not been employed for 26 weeks or two years (for lower and higher rate SMP respectively) cannot claim. For a full list, see the chart on pages 408–9.

Other maternity money. A pregnant woman who does not qualify for SMP may still be able to claim state maternity allowance from the DSS.

MATERNITY LEAVE: RETURNING TO WORK

An employee who has left to give birth can claim her job back after the birth (s. 45, Employment Protection (Consolidation) Act 1978), but as with the right to maternity pay, there are complicated requirements to be met. She must:

1 Continue in employment until at least the eleventh week before expected date of birth (as with maternity pay).
2 She must then have been employed for at least two years.
3 She must write to her employer that she intends to stop work because of her pregnancy and that she will want to return to work after the birth. As with the maternity pay, this notice must be given at least three weeks before she leaves. The notice must be in writing and it must state the expected date of birth (see draft letter below). If they wish, employers can insist the woman provides a medical certificate stating the expected date of birth.
4 Employers can insist that she confirms her intention of returning to work. The rule is that once seven weeks have elapsed after the expected date of birth the employer can ask her to give written confirmation of her intention to return to work. If she does not give the written confirmation within two weeks of it being requested, she will lose her right to return to work (assuming that the employer warned her that failure to reply within two weeks would result in her losing the right to return). Note that the seven-week period runs from the expected date of birth, as originally notified to the employer, and not the actual date of birth. At this stage she does not have to give a date for her return to work – she simply has to confirm that she still intends to return.
5 She must return to work within twenty-nine weeks of the birth. This twenty-nine-week period is strictly enforced and the woman can extend it only if she can produce a medical certificate confirming that she is not well enough to return to work. But a sick note can only extend the period by four weeks so, whatever happens, the woman will lose the right to return unless she does so within thirty-three weeks of the actual date of birth.

6 She must give her employer at least three weeks' written warning before she does return to work. She must give a specific date – at least twenty-one days in advance. In practice, therefore, the latest deadline for giving this notice is twenty-six weeks after the start of the week in which the child was born.

7 If she works for a small firm, she may not be able to insist on having her job back. If there were fewer than six employees (including her) in the firm at the time when she left, then the employer need not take her back if it is not 'reasonably practicable' to give her the old job (or another 'suitable' job). It will be for the employer to convince the industrial tribunal of this.

When the woman returns to work

On her return, the employee can claim the same rate of pay and the same terms of employment as if she had not stopped work. Thus she will obtain the benefit of any pay increases that have been made since she left. Normally, her contractual pension and seniority rights will carry on as from the date she left (unless her contract says otherwise), so that the period of absence cannot be counted when later calculating length of service for pension entitlement. Redundancy pay and other statutory benefits, however, will continue to accrue during the period of absence.

But only rarely will the woman be able to insist that she returns to the actual job she was doing prior to her leaving. The law says that she must be employed on the same 'terms and conditions' as previously – in other words, her contract of employment must not be changed. But usually the employment contract only defines an employee's job in wide terms. So unless her contract is very specific in defining her job, she will have to accept another similar job, as long as the pay, hours, holidays and other terms are the same. Thus, in practice, the woman will often find that her new job is not the same as her old job.

In addition, the employer can offer the woman an alternative job if it is 'not reasonably practicable' for her to return to her old job. This is intended to cover the situation in which the employer has had to take on permanent staff to cover for the woman while she was off work or where circumstances have made her old job unavailable. However, the employee must be offered a suitable alternative job instead, and if she is not offered a job, or if she is offered an unsuitable job, she can claim unfair dismissal or redundancy. The only exception is in firms employing fewer than six people: in these small firms if it is not reasonably practicable for the woman to return to her old job, and if she cannot be offered a suitable alternative job, then she need not be re-employed and she will not be able to claim unfair dismissal or redundancy. (See 7 above.)

Similarly, if the employer simply refuses to re-employ the woman, the employee can claim unfair dismissal or redundancy.

Ineligible employees. Not all employees can claim maternity leave (e.g. part-timers). See the chart on pages 408–9.

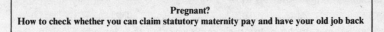

Pregnant?
How to check whether you can claim statutory maternity pay and have your old job back

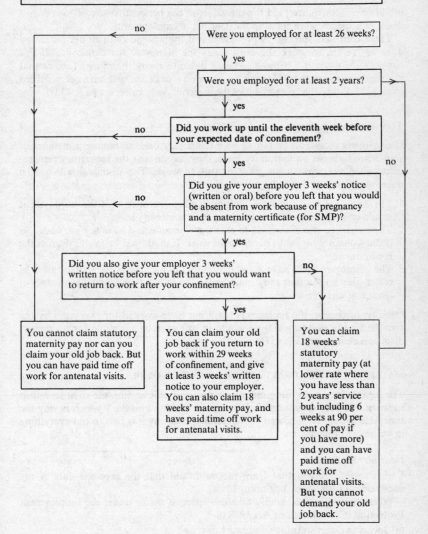

Were you employed for at least 26 weeks? — no

yes

Were you employed for at least 2 years?

yes

Did you work up until the eleventh week before your expected date of confinement? — no

yes — no

Did you give your employer 3 weeks' notice (written or oral) before you left that you would be absent from work because of pregnancy and a maternity certificate (for SMP)? — no

yes

Did you also give your employer 3 weeks' written notice before you left that you would want to return to work after your confinement? — no

yes

You cannot claim statutory maternity pay nor can you claim your old job back. But you can have paid time off work for antenatal visits.

You can claim your old job back if you return to work within 29 weeks of confinement, and give at least 3 weeks' written notice to your employer. You can also claim 18 weeks' maternity pay, and have paid time off work for antenatal visits.

You can claim 18 weeks' statutory maternity pay (at lower rate where you have less than 2 years' service but including 6 weeks at 90 per cent of pay if you have more) and you can have paid time off work for antenatal visits. But you cannot demand your old job back.

If the woman is paid while off work

SMP is paid for eighteen weeks only, but some women (notably in central and local government) who notify their employers that they intend to reclaim their job after childbirth are paid for the whole of the period they are off work, as a result of a specific agreement in the contract of employment.

These contracts sometimes provide that if the woman changes her mind and does not return to work she must repay the money to her employers. If this happens the woman is almost certainly liable to repay the money (except that she need not repay the SMP she has received – since she will have been entitled to be paid during that period under the maternity-pay rules; see page 433).

Temporary replacements

If employers recruit an employee on a temporary basis to replace a member of staff who is absent on maternity leave, they can dismiss the temporary replacement when the woman on leave returns to work. The dismissal will not be unfair dismissal if:

1 The employee was given written notice when recruited that the employment would end when the woman returned from maternity leave.
2 The employee was dismissed so that the woman could have her job back. So if the woman went on to do different work, it might not be fair to dismiss the replacement.
3 The employers must have acted reasonably in dismissing the replacement. In effect, this means that they must have offered him/her a suitable vacancy if there was one available.

Usually, of course, the replacement will not have worked for two years by the time he or she is dismissed, so would in any case be ineligible for an unfair-dismissal claim (see page 457).

MATERNITY RIGHTS: DRAFT LETTER TO AN EMPLOYER

The legal rules on claiming maternity pay, and on claiming the right to return to work, are very complicated. It is easy to make a mistake – which is why the timetable should be followed very carefully, and why it is best to put everything in writing. For instance:

Dear Sir/Madam,

I wish to inform you that I am pregnant, and that the expected date of my confinement is the week beginning (date).

Would you therefore kindly take this letter as notice under the Employment Protection (Consolidation) Act 1978 that:

(a) I wish to claim statutory maternity pay, and

(b) I wish to return to work after the birth of my baby.

In addition, I may need to take paid time off work for antenatal visits. I shall, of course give you notice of the appointments as soon as I am able.

I should be grateful if you would acknowledge receipt of this letter.

Yours . . .

Note 1. This letter must arrive at least three weeks before you plan to leave work.

Note 2. Even if you have previously told your employer that you will not be claiming maternity pay and/or maternity leave, it seems that you can change your mind – assuming, of course, that you comply with the rules and give the employer proper notice. Obviously, it is better to avoid any dispute by not agreeing to forgo any of these rights in the first place.

Note 3. If you notify your employer that you intend to return, but subsequently change your mind, your employer cannot sue you for compensation. It is, therefore, always advisable to state that you intend to return if there is any possibility that you may wish to do so. Remember that there is always the slight possibility of a miscarriage.

25 Accidents at Work

All employers have a duty to take reasonable care for the safety of their staff; if they do not, they can be sued for negligence by an injured employee.

But it is for the employee to show that the employer was negligent, for if negligence cannot be shown the employer will not be liable. In addition, if the court finds that the employee was partly to blame for the accident, it will reduce his or her damages by a corresponding amount. For instance, if an employer was negligent, but the employee was one-third to blame for the accident, the courts would award only two-thirds of the normal damages.

The employers' duty to take reasonable care of their staff has three elements:

- to provide competent work-mates, *and*
- to provide safe equipment and plant, *and*
- to provide a safe system of working.

COMPETENT WORK-MATES

It is the employer's duty to employ safe and responsible staff. If one employee is negligent and so injures another employee, the injured employee can sue his or her employer for the work-mate's negligence. Employers are therefore personally liable for the negligence of their staff, although they may – in theory, if not in practice – be able to sue the negligent employee to recover any damages paid to the injured employee (see page 403). For instance:

Mr Cripps was an electrician. His employers sent him, with an apprentice, to install electric lights in a barn. In the barn were some calves, so Mr Cripps told the apprentice to stand at the foot of the ladder and keep the calves away. A calf bumped into the apprentice, who fell against the ladder, knocking it over. Mr Cripps injured his wrist. He sued his employers. Held: The employers were liable because the apprentice had been negligent. They were responsible for his negligence. Cripps (1974)

If employers know that a member of their staff is a danger to his or her work-mates then they should remove that person from a task where he or she is likely to injure someone, or even, after warnings, dismiss them. For instance, if the employer knows that someone plays practical jokes, the employer will be liable if an accident occurs:

Mr Hudson was injured when a practical joke went wrong. The person who played the joke on him had been employed for some four years, and over that time he had often tripped people up and engaged in horseplay, despite having been told not to by the employer. Mr Hudson sued the employer, arguing that the employer had failed to provide a safe and competent work-mate. Held: The employer was liable. Hudson (1957)

Many claims arise out of motor accidents, when the injured employee is a passenger in a vehicle driven by a work-mate. In such a case the employer is responsible for the negligent driving of employees.

If employers can show that the negligent employee was not acting 'in the course of his employment' at the time of the accident, then they will not be liable. For instance, if the employees without permission leave the work site to drive to the pub and on the way back one of the employees is injured by the other's negligent driving, the employer will not be to blame. Employers are liable for the negligence of their staff only when the staff are acting in the course of their employment. The same applies if it is a non-employee who is injured:

A bus conductor got into a quarrel with a passenger. The bus conductor assaulted the passenger, injuring him. The passenger then sued the bus company, arguing that it was responsible for the acts of its employees. Held: No. The bus conductor had not been acting in the course of his employment by striking the passenger and so the company was not liable. Keppel Bus Co. (1974)

Similarly, if the negligent person is not an employee but an independent contractor, the employer will not be liable. In some cases, the employer will not be liable if the independent contractor is injured, since there will be no employer/employee relationship between them:

Jones was on the lorry on a building site. When a cement mixer broke down, he was told to use another one which was unsafe. Jones was injured. Held: Jones was not an employee and so the normal duty of care did not apply; he could not recover damages. Jones (1973)

See page 411 for how to decide whether or not a person is an employee.

SAFE EQUIPMENT AND PLANT

Employers are liable if an employee is injured because of faulty equipment, plant or premises, if the employers were negligent. For instance, if the floor is slippery or uneven, the employers are liable if they knew of the defect or should have known of it.

Similarly, if employees are injured by defective equipment, they can sue the negligent employer. For instance, if a hammer fractures and a flying piece injures the employee, the employers will be liable if they were negligent; in effect, they will be liable unless they can show that they had inspected the hammer and had no reason to suspect that it was faulty. If the hammer was made in a negligent manner by the manufacturer (e.g. faulty casting, poor-quality metal) then, by the Employer's Liability (Defective Equipment) Act

1969, the employers will be liable to the employee for the negligence of the manufacturer. This allows the employee to sue the employer, rather than the manufacturer, who might since have gone out of business or might be based abroad. The employer may, however, be able to make a claim against the manufacturer.

This common-law duty to provide safe working conditions is often backed up by detailed statutory requirements as to the design, layout and provision of working equipment and facilities. Numerous regulations have been made covering various industries (e.g. under the Offices, Shops and Railway Premises Act 1963; the Mines and Quarries Act 1954; the Agriculture (Poisonous Substances) Act 1952; Mineral Workings (Offshore Installations) Act 1971; Nuclear Installations Acts 1965 and 1969; and so on). Of particular importance is the Factories Act, which covers more than just factories – construction sites, shipyards, docks and warehouses using mechanical power, brickworks, potteries, cement works, paper-making and printing firms, laundries and dry-cleaners, garages, power stations, gasworks, slaughter-houses and railway workshops are all included in the definition of a factory. Among the detailed requirements of the Factories Act are the rules that:

- work places shall be properly ventilated and lit;
- sufficient washing and toilet facilities must be provided;
- moving machinery must be fenced;
- fences must be properly maintained;
- hoists, lifts and ropes must be properly constructed and maintained;
- floors, passages and stairs must be kept unobstructed and free of slippery surfaces. For instance:

Mrs Woodward had a lift to work from a colleague. They parked in the factory car park, close to the footpath leading to the factory entrance. She slipped on ice and injured her back. She claimed damages from her employers, arguing that there was a breach of the Factories Act. Held: Yes, the employers should have gritted the footpath and, since they had not, they were liable to Mrs Woodward. Woodward (1980)

For details of the Factories Act requirements, contact the local health and safety inspector (phone number in the telephone directory). An important point to note about many of the statutory requirements is that employers are liable even if they were not negligent; for instance, if an employee is injured by an unfenced machine, the employers are liable whether or not they were negligent; they would also be liable if, for example, the fencing was wrongly removed by another employee.

A SAFE SYSTEM OF WORKING

It is for employers to supervise how their staff carry out their jobs, and to ensure that they do so in a safe manner. If they negligently fail to ensure that a safe system is in use, then they will be liable in damages to any employee who is injured.

Mr Upson was lifting a metal plate with four work-mates. One of the others let go, and as a result the plate slipped and crushed Mr Upson's fingers. He sued his employers, arguing that the system of work was unsafe. Held: The employers were liable. They should have arranged [through their foreman] for someone to act as a coordinator for the lifting operation. Upson (1975)

Mr Litherland worked for a furniture manufacturer, where he used a glue which was often a cause of dermatitis. The employers did not warn him of this risk, nor did they provide him with gloves or cream to reduce his chances of catching dermatitis. Mr Litherland contracted dermatitis and sued his employers. Held: They had negligently failed to provide a safe system of work and so they were liable. Litherland (1974)

Mr Payne was a labourer in a quarry. One day he was asked to help out by doing the more skilled job of repairing a chain with a steel hammer. He was not supplied with, or told to wear, goggles, nor was he told that if he struck the link-pin, as opposed to the link, it might shatter. Mr Payne hit the link-pin and lost an eye when it shattered. Held: His employers had not provided a safe system of work and so they were liable in damages. A safe system of work requires that untrained workers be told how to look after themselves. Payne (1973)

Mr Charlton was sent by his employers to collect the firm's weekly wages, some £1,500. He was attacked by robbers and injured. He sued his employers, arguing that they had failed to provide a safe system of work. Held: The employers were liable. They should not have sent Mr Charlton alone to collect the wages; they should have made some other arrangement, such as employing a security firm. Charlton (1978)

In many cases the amount of damages the employer has to pay will be reduced because the employee was partly to blame. When this happens, the employee forfeits part of the damages for this 'contributory negligence'.

Mr McGuiness was an eighteen-year-old butcher. He was using a new meat cutter when his hand slipped and he lost the tops of two fingers. He had in the past been told to use a pusher to hold the meat but he had not bothered to do so since the manager never used it. He sued his employers. Held: The employers were liable for not providing a safe system of work. But McGuiness himself had been negligent. He was one-third to blame and so he only recovered two-thirds of the full damages he would otherwise have been awarded. McGuiness (1973)

SUING AN EMPLOYER

Employees who have been injured in an accident at work should always take legal advice as to whether they have the basis of a claim against their employer. It should be borne in mind that the law will often make the employer liable in circumstances in which a layperson might not think that they were to blame. Accordingly, it is important always to take legal advice. Trade union members will usually be able to ask their union to take advice from the union's solicitors, who are likely to have considerable experience of such claims. A non-union member should consult a solicitor privately.

Many employees are very reluctant to sue their employers; they feel that it could cost them their jobs. However, it should be remembered that the employer will be insured against such a claim (the law requires employers to be insured) and so the claim will really be against the insurance company: it will be against the employer in name alone. The employee need not fear that employers will have to pay the damages out of their own pocket.

The injured employee should also claim any welfare benefits that might apply (e.g. injury benefit, disablement benefit).

IF YOU ARE INJURED AT WORK

1 Note down names of all witnesses. Later obtain written statements from each of them. Try to arrange for photographs to be taken of the scene.
2 Report the accident to the employer. Ensure correct details are entered in the firm's accident book.
3 If the accident involved defective equipment (e.g. broken rope) keep it, or make sure it is not thrown away or repaired until your lawyers have agreed. Take photographs of it.
4 Try to find out whether there have been any similar accidents, and whether anyone has ever complained about the hazard that led to your accident. Obtain a written statement from anyone who complained or who had a similar accident.
5 Contact your trade union representative and take legal advice.
6 Claim any welfare benefits for which you are eligible.
7 Keep a note of all your losses and expenses (and those of your family) arising out of the accident. These will form part of your claim.
8 See your doctor if the injury is other than trivial.
9 Do not accept any offer of compensation until you have taken full legal and medical advice.

REPORTING AN ACCIDENT

An employer must notify the local health and safety executive officer if there is:

1 An accident which causes *major injury or death* to anyone (whether an employee or not). A 'major injury' means a fracture of the skull, spine or pelvis; a fracture of any bone (except in wrist, hand, ankle or foot); an injury necessitating the amputation of hand or foot; loss of sight of an eye; or any injury resulting in hospitalization for more than twenty-four hours (unless for observation only). In short, any serious injury must be reported.
2 A *major incident* which endangered anyone working there, even if no one was injured. (This covers serious incidents such as explosions, collapse of cranes and scaffolding etc.)

The notification must be made by the quickest possible means, usually the telephone. It must also be reported in writing within seven days (using form F 2508) and an entry should be made in the firm's accident book.

26 Ending the Employment

Neither the employer nor the employee can end the employment contract unless one gives the other proper notice. In other words, the employer cannot sack the employee and the employee cannot resign unless proper notice is given.

NOTICE BY THE EMPLOYER

An employer who wants to dismiss a member of staff must give proper notice. Unless the employment contract says otherwise, the length of notice will vary with the length of the employee's employment.

Often there is no written contract of employment and there are no written particulars. In this case the statutory minimum will apply, unless the employee can show it was an 'implied' term of the employment contract that he should receive longer notice. Often employees who are paid monthly will be able to argue that they should receive at least a month's notice even if the statutory minimum gives them less than a month. It all depends upon what is regarded as 'reasonable' notice in the trade or profession. Generally, the more highly paid and the more senior the position, then the longer the notice to be given to the employee. For instance, three months has been held to be reasonable for a specialist oil salesman, six months for a photographic journalist and twelve months for a ship's officer.

When employees are given notice they should ask the employer to give written reason for the dismissal (see page 449). The employer's answers may enable the employee to decide whether he or she should bring an unfair-dismissal or redundancy claim.

Statutory minimum length of notice required

Length of employment	Length of notice by employer
Under 1 month	Nil
1 month to 2 years	1 week
2 years to 12 years	1 week for each full year of employment
Over 12 years	12 weeks

(s. 49(1), Employment Protection (Consolidation) Act 1978.)

Ineligible employees. The notice provisions do not apply to all staff (e.g. part-timers). For a full list, see the chart on pages 408–9.

Giving wages in lieu of notice

Normally, employers need not provide their staff with work; they just have to pay them (see page 431). It follows that an employer who wishes to dismiss an employee need not let the employee carry on working during the notice period. The only legal obligation on the employer is to pay the normal wages during that time. This is called 'giving wages in lieu of notice'.

In practice, employees need not work out their notice if they do not want to. They can leave (e.g. to start a new job) and not lose their right to bring an unfair-dismissal claim (although there are special provisions about redundancy). If they do leave, they will of course lose the right to wages in lieu of notice (see page 449).

When the employer need not give any notice

There are two sets of circumstances in which the employer need not give the employee any notice:
● when the employee's 'gross misconduct' justifies 'summary dismissal';
● when the employment cannot continue – for example, if the employee has been sent to prison or is suffering from a major illness.

1. 'Gross misconduct' and 'summary dismissal'

On-the-spot sacking is allowed – without notice – when the employee is guilty of such gross misconduct that it goes 'to the root of the employment contract'. But the employee must have behaved extremely badly for summary dismissal to be justified. Theft at work, assaults on management or gross breaches of discipline might justify summary dismissal.

Generally, the industrial tribunals regard summary dismissal as being only rarely justified. Even if it is justified, the employer should follow the normal disciplinary procedures – such as allowing the employee to give his or her side of the story. (See page 425 for the rules on disciplinary procedures.) On the other hand, if the conduct was very bad and a proper disciplinary inquiry would not have made any difference to the outcome, then the employee would still not win an unfair-dismissal claim (see page 480).

If the summary dismissal is unjustified there are two different claims the employee can bring against the employer:
● a *wrongful-dismissal* claim for wages due to him or her for the period of notice they should have been given (see page 447).
● an *unfair-dismissal* claim for the employer's having sacked him or her unreasonably.

2. When the employment cannot continue

Some outside event might occur which is so serious that it automatically brings the employment to an end. The contract becomes impossible to perform, and so lawyers say it has become 'frustrated'. For instance, an employee may receive a long prison sentence, become incurably ill or lose a particular skill – an opera singer who loses his voice is an example.

But if it is decided that the contract has been 'frustrated' then it will mean that it has simply come to an end – and so the employer cannot be said to have dismissed or sacked the employee. Thus, no unfair-dismissal claim can be brought by the employee. This is why it is serious for employees if it is suggested that the employment contract has become frustrated – they run the risk of not being able to bring an unfair-dismissal claim. Because of the serious effects of holding that employment has been frustrated, the courts have become increasingly reluctant to uphold frustration claims by employers: the courts seem to feel that it is fairer for everyone if the ending of the employment is treated as a dismissal, so employees can at least argue their case before an industrial tribunal.

In practical terms, therefore, frustration claims are rare – and it is even rarer for them to succeed. It is probably in cases of lengthy absence through ill-health that frustration is most often argued. Each case has to be decided on its own facts and the decision reached in one case is not likely to be of much help in another case (e.g. in one case an absence of eighteen months was held not to be frustration; in another case, an absence of four months did amount to frustration!).

Anyone who is unlucky enough to be involved in an argument as to whether an employment contract has been frustrated should seek expert legal advice.

When proper notice is not given

If employers do not give proper notice to employees, they can be sued for breach of contract. They have broken the employment contract and so must pay damages to the employee. The amount of damages will be the employee's losses arising from the breach of contract – the wages they should have been paid for the proper period of notice or for the remainder of their fixed-period contract and the value of any other contractual benefits (e.g. the private use of a company car).

The employee's claim is called a *wrongful-dismissal* claim. It is usually brought in a civil court in the county court. This is the only employment law claim that is not brought in an industrial tribunal. If employees bring a wrongful-dismissal claim, they do not lose their right to bring an unfair-dismissal, or redundancy, claim as well.

The damages claimed by the employee will normally be the wages due for the period of notice. Only exceptionally will they be more. There is one case in the law reports in which the employee in a wrongful-dismissal claim was given additional damages for the 'mental distress' he suffered because of his employer's behaviour:

In July 1963, after seventeen years' service, Mr Cox was promoted and his salary increased by £70 p.a. He was led to believe that he would receive a further substantial increase, and was dismayed when he was awarded only a further £30 p.a. He protested, and the firm retaliated by, in effect, demoting him, although he continued to receive his previous salary. He became depressed and frustrated. In 1975 the firm persuaded him to resign. In effect he had been forced out of his job and so he sued for wrongful dismissal. He was awarded £500 for the depression, frustration and distress caused by the employer's breach of the employment contract. Cox (1976)*

But this case should be treated with caution. Most lawyers feel that it was wrongly decided and, even if it was, it must be borne in mind that the employer's conduct was spread out over a period of ten years. So it is probably of very limited application. However, an employee bringing a wrongful-dismissal claim is probably best advised to claim damages for 'mental distress' in order to inflate the claim, so that he or she can then negotiate a good compromise settlement.

More often than not, the damages in a wrongful-dismissal claim will be less than the wages due to the employee. This is because the damages are supposed to compensate employees only for 'loss'. If they found another job immediately – at a similar or higher salary – they have not suffered any loss, so will not be able to claim any damages.

Usually, the ex-employers will argue that employees could have found another job and that any losses are their own fault. If they can prove this, then the employee's claim will be worthless. Often employees with wrongful-dismissal claims will have to be prepared to compromise their claim, unless they can show that they couldn't be expected to get a job at a similar salary during the period of notice.

Finally, the damages will be reduced by any unemployment benefit received during the notice period, and by the amount of tax and national insurance that would have been deducted from wages. The justification for reducing the damages in this way is that the damages are intended only to compensate for losses; if these items were not deducted the employee might (theoretically) recover more in damages than he or she would have in wages.

Wrongful dismissal and unfair dismissal. The two are distinct claims and must not be confused. Wrongful dismissal is for a specific amount of wages owed, whereas unfair dismissal is a claim for general compensation to cover the dismissal. Other differences are that wrongful-dismissal claims are brought in the civil courts, have a six-year time limit, are within the legal-aid system and normally make the loser liable to pay the winner's legal costs. None of these applies to unfair-dismissal claims.

Giving reasons for a dismissal

Employers must provide written reasons for dismissing an employee (when the employee has worked for them for longer than two years) – but only if the employee asks for them (s53, Employment Protection (Consolidation) Act 1978). The employee's request need not be in writing, although it is advisable for a written request to be made so that there is a record. The employer has fourteen days in which to provide written reasons.

The employer's reply must be in sufficient detail. While the reasons need not be exhaustive, they must be sufficiently comprehensive to be self-explanatory. The Employment Appeal Tribunal has said: 'The document must be of such a kind that the employee, or anyone to whom he may wish to show it, can know from reading the document itself why the employee has been dismissed.' In practice, it is sufficient to refer back to the letter of dismissal if that was sufficiently detailed.

If the employer does not provide the written reasons within fourteen days, the employee can then apply to an industrial tribunal. If the tribunal decides that the employer acted 'unreasonably' in not providing the reasons, it will order him or her to pay the employee two weeks' wages. It may also draw unfavourable conclusions which might damage the employer's credibility if he or she is trying to show that he or she acted fairly.

If the employer does provide the written reasons, but they are inadequate or untrue the employee can complain to the tribunal. The tribunal will decide the issue, and if the complaint is upheld the employee will receive two weeks' wages.

Ineligible employees. Not all employees can insist on being given written reasons for dismissal (e.g. part-timers). For full details, see the chart on pages 408–9.

NOTICE BY THE EMPLOYEE

Employees who want to leave their job must give at least one week's notice if they have been employed for four weeks or more (s. 49(1), Employment Protection (Consolidation) Act 1978). This is unless their employment contract requires them to give longer notice. The *written particulars* of the contract, sent to the employee by the employer (see page 407). should state how much notice they must be given, and often this will be more than the statutory minimum.

If there is no written provision as to notice, the law may decide that senior members of staff should give more than one week's notice during their first two years with a firm.

If the employee resigns without giving proper notice

If employees do not give notice of their resignation, then they are in breach of contract and can be sued by the employer. The position is similar to a wrongful-dismissal claim brought by an employee who has been sacked without proper notice (see page 447).

Employers can sue employees for damages. But their provable 'losses' are unlikely to be large. Employees will usually be able to show that employers could have cut their losses by recruiting a replacement. Even if employers can show a direct loss (e.g. no replacement was available; a major order was lost; they incurred advertising and job agency costs), they are unlikely to sue. First, suing the ex-employee might worsen labour relations in the firm. Secondly, the courts tend to be unsympathetic to such claims and usually find a way of ensuring that the employee is not penalized for resigning their job.

In practice, all the employer can easily do is to refuse to provide the employee with a reference. Although in at least one case the employer refused to accept the employee's resignation and obtained an injunction from the court preventing the employee joining a rival business for the duration of the notice period. However, such cases will in practice be rare. Prior to the Wages Act the employer might have withheld accrued wages and holiday pay. However, absent a term in the contract permitting deductions, the employee can claim reimbursement of accured monies deducted by the employer by means of an application to an industrial tribunal, and in such circumstances the employer may not subsequently bring proceedings to recover, as losses caused by the employee, any amount which an industrial tribunal has held to be an unlawful deduction.

ENDING A FIXED-TERM CONTRACT

A fixed-term contract is for a definite duration. There is no need for either employer or employee to give notice when the fixed term expires since they both know when it is due to end. The only way the contract can be ended before the due date is if the employee is guilty of gross misbehaviour or if 'frustration' – such as serious illness – occurs, although some fixed-term contracts have notice periods which can operate *during* the fixed term – if no notice is given the contract will simply expire (see page 447).

Note that employees with fixed-term contracts may be able to claim unfair dismissal if their contract is not renewed when it runs out (see page 464).

DEATH OF THE EMPLOYER OR EMPLOYEE

If either employer or employee dies, the employment contract automatically comes to an end. Note that if an employee is employed by a company, the fact that his or her own boss dies will not mean that the employer has died. The company is separate from its directors and managers, and cannot die other than by going into liquidation.

If the employer dies

The employees can make redundancy claims against the employer's estate, unless they decide to carry on working for the business if the estate carries on running it. Employees can carry on with an unfair-dismissal claim made before the employer died, or if they had been given notice of dismissal before the employer's death.

All debts due from the employer (such as wage arrears) can be claimed from the employer's estate.

If the employee dies

The employee's personal representative can carry on with any unfair-dismissal or redundancy claim which the employee had made or could have made.

THE INSOLVENT EMPLOYER

If an employer goes bust, generally speaking the contracts of employment of the staff automatically come to an end. But special protection is given to employees to ensure that money owed to them by the employer, and any redundancy pay they could claim, is paid. This is done by:
- allowing most claims to be paid by the Department of Employment;
- making some of the claims priority debts.

These various rights benefit only an employee whose employer becomes insolvent. They do not protect the employee whose employer simply disappears (as sometimes happens in the building trade), unless someone is prepared to start bankruptcy proceedings against the absent employer.

1. Claiming from the Department of Employment

The employee can claim (under s.122, Employment Protection (Consolidation) Act 1978):

1 Wage arrears for up to eight weeks, at a maximum rate of £205 per week (1992). This includes wages owed in respect of medical suspension payments, guarantee payments for lay-off, pay due for time off to union officials and to redundant staff looking for new jobs.
2 Notice: wages due for the period of notice which the employee should have been given, up to £205 per week (1992). But the employee can only claim in respect of the statutory period of notice, not for any longer period allowed under his or her employment contract.
3 Holiday pay for up to six weeks, up to £205 per week (1992).
4 Unfair dismissal (basic award only) and redundancy payment.

The employee should first ask the liquidator or receiver for the amount due.

The liquidator or receiver will calculate the amount due, and if the employee agrees the figures, the Secretary of State sends the money direct to the employee. If the employer does not have a receiver or liquidator, the employee should apply direct to the Secretary of State, via their local Department of Employment office. If payment is still refused, complain to an industrial tribunal.

Ineligible employees. See the chart on pages 408–9.

2. Claiming priority debts from the employer's receiver or liquidator

When a company goes bust, there is an order of priority among the various creditors. Only when the *preferential* creditors have been paid in full can the other creditors claim a share of the remaining assets. Certain debts to employees are preferential debts, but the maximum amount that can be treated as a priority debt is £800. These debts include:

- wage arrears for up to four months;
- holiday pay;
- pension contributions for up to four months.

Any excess will be an ordinary debt.

Claiming from a liquidator or receiver can take a long time. Also there may be other preferential debts (such as tax owed to the Inland Revenue and claims by other members of staff) so that there may not be sufficient assets to pay all the preferred creditors. When this happens, they all get a percentage of the amount due to them.

REFERENCES AND TESTIMONIALS

There is no legal obligation on employers to provide their staff with references or testimonials when they leave.

This can cause hardship. In one case, a man had worked for ten years as a security guard. His immediate superior was replaced by a different person with whom he had a row. So the employee fixed up another job and left. Unfortunately the new job fell through and so he had to look for employment with other security firms. But all the firms he approached contacted his previous employers for a reference, and the supervisor with whom he had argued would reply: 'Mr X worked with us for ten years and left of his own accord.' While this was true, it was a damning reference; by making no mention of his honesty, reliability and integrity, it by implication cast doubts on his suitability. As a result, he was unable to obtain a job as a security guard despite his excellent record. He was, in effect, unemployable as a security guard because he could not insist on a proper testimonial, and yet he had no legal redress.

If employers do provide a reference they should tell the truth. But honest, discreet employers need have no fears as to their legal liability for giving a reference. In theory, employees could sue them for defamation if the references contained an unprovable allegation. However, references are covered by 'qualified privilege', which means employers would be liable only if they acted 'maliciously' (i.e. without believing that what they were saying was true). Employees' difficulty in proving 'malice' and the absence of legal aid for defamation cases make the chances of their suing an employer very remote. As a result, a case in 1992 saw the ex-employee sue the former employer for negligence (where 'malice' is not required to succeed in a claim) in preparing his reference; he won. A practical way for employers to limit this risk is to give the reference verbally on the phone, for employees will then find it extremely difficult to prove what was said about them.

Employers might also have a legal liability to the person to whom they give the reference. If they tell the new employer that an employee was 'trustworthy and honest' when in fact he was sacked for stealing at work, they may be liable in negligence. Although in legal theory they would be liable, it seems unlikely that the courts would hold them responsible. Certainly, there is no record of a case in the law reports in which the ex-employer was held liable to the new employer. The ex-employer may be able to limit any liability by writing 'without responsibility' across the top of the reference or some other disclaimer. This will make it clear that new employers rely on the reference at their own risk.

If employers deliberately provide false testimonials they can be prosecuted in the magistrates' court under the Servants' Character Act 1792. So also can an employee who forges or alters an employer's reference (maximum penalty for both offences is £50 fine).

RESTRICTING THE EMPLOYEE'S FUTURE WORK

Sometimes employers will try to restrict the type of work that their staff can do when they leave. They might insert a clause into the contract of employment that ex-employees are not to work within a stated distance of their employer's office, that they won't set up their own competing business within a stated period, and that they won't approach their ex-employer's customers for business once they have left the firm. Restrictions of this sort are called 'covenants in restraint of trade'.

The courts frown on any action that has the effect of limiting someone's freedom of work – to do the work they want to do, for whomsoever they choose. This was the principle behind the decision in the Kerry Packer 'cricket circus' case:

Kerry Packer recruited top star cricketers to play for his commercial cricket teams. The Test and County Cricket Board retaliated by altering its rules so that any cricketer who played for Packer would no longer be able to play first-class cricket in the UK. Packer, and several of his recruits, challenged the validity of the action. Held: The bans were in restraint of trade. They prevented the cricketers from seeking employment elsewhere and they were not in the interests of the cricketers or the public. Thus the clauses were invalid and could not be enforced. Greig (1977)

If employers insert a restraint-of-trade clause in employees' contract of employment, the courts will examine it critically. Only if employers can show that it is reasonable and necessary for the protection of their trade interests will it be upheld – but only if it is not against the public interest. The courts' dislike of these clauses was forcibly expressed by Lord Denning in a 1956 case:

During the last forty years the courts have shown a reluctance to enforce covenants of this sort . . . if these covenants were given full force they would tend to reduce the employee's freedom to seek better conditions, even by asking for a rise in wages; because if he is not allowed to get work elsewhere, he is very much at the mercy of his employer.

The more widely drafted the restriction, the more likely it is that the courts will decide that it is unenforceable. In short, the less ambitious the covenant, the more likely it is to succeed. Most clauses fail because:
- they are not *solely* designed to protect trade secrets or trade connections;
- they last for an unreasonably long time;
- they cover an unreasonably wide geographical area.

The seniority of the employee will often be an important factor in assessing the reasonableness of the clause:

Mr Greer had worked for a dry-cleaning business for some twenty years. In 1974 he was offered the chance of becoming a director, which he accepted. His contract of employment as a director contained the following clause: 'In view of the access to trade secrets and secret processes which the employee may have during the course of his employment . . . he shall not within a period of twelve months from the termination thereof either directly or indirectly, neither alone nor in association with any other person, firm or company engage in any part of the United Kingdom in any business which is similar to any business involving such trade secrets and/or secret processes carried on by the company.' Shortly afterwards, Mr Greer left and joined another dry-cleaning firm. Was the clause valid? Held: No, the clause was too wide. Greer (1979)

In this case the main defect was the clause saying that it applied 'in any part of the United Kingdom'. The company could, however, have protected its position by restricting the clause to the local area in which Mr Greer had worked. They had not done so, and so the clause was not binding on him.

By way of contrast is the following case, in which the restriction clause was upheld by the court:

Mr Harris was in charge of preparing Littlewoods' mail-order catalogue. It was a senior post, giving him a directorship. He was approached by Littlewoods' big mail-order rivals, who offered him more money and a company car. He accepted. Littlewoods then sought an injunction to stop him working for the competitors, on the basis that he had signed a restraint-of-trade clause which prevented him joining any rival firm for twelve months. Held: The twelve months' restriction was reasonable for a man of his seniority. The covenant was valid and so he could not join the rival firm. Littlewoods (1977)

Estate agents often seem to have arguments about these restrictions:

Mr Luck was employed by Mr Davenport-Smith in his estate agent's business. Mr Luck left the firm and set up in competition. Mr Davenport-Smith claimed damages on the grounds that Mr Luck was in breach of a covenant that he would not work as an estate agent for three years within one mile of each of Davenport-Smith's offices in Saltdean, Peacehaven and Patcham. Held: The three-year restriction was unreasonable and so the clause was void. Luck (1977)

A less ambitious clause would have worked. For instance:

An ex-employee of a firm of estate agents set up in business 150 yards away. He had signed an agreement not to set up in competition within a one-mile radius. His former employers applied for an injunction against him. Held: An injunction would be granted. The one-mile radius was reasonable. Anscombe & Ringland (1984)

However, even limited geographical areas are not always the solution.

The branch manager and a consultant employed by an employment company in London had a restraint clause in their contracts which was to operate within a 1,000 metre radius of the branch where they worked. Held: Invalid – the branch where they worked was in the City of London and a 1,000 metre radius therefore covered most of the City and was accordingly too wide. Office Angels (1991)

The net effect is that many restraint-of-trade clauses are unenforceable. Even clauses drafted by skilled lawyers are often held to be invalid. In practice, these clauses are used more to discourage the employees than to restrain them legally.

27 Unfair Dismissal

The first unfair-dismissal legislation was introduced in 1971. Until then, employers had been free to dismiss staff subject only to their being given notice and any redundancy payment that might be due to them. But that was the full extent of the employers' obligations. The fact that they were behaving unreasonably or immorally was irrelevant in the eyes of the law. The Industrial Relations Act 1971 altered this position. The present law on unfair dismissal is contained in the Employment Protection (Consolidation) Act 1978, although that Act has since been progressively changed. But the basic principles of unfair-dismissal compensation remain as they were in 1971.

The employer must be able to justify the dismissal to a public body, the industrial tribunal. If the tribunal finds that the dismissal was unfair, the employer can be ordered to pay cash compensation to the employee, or even to re-employ him or her. The unfair-dismissal legislation has thus transformed the law on dismissals. In the early 1970s, the industrial tribunals acquired a reputation of being pro-employee and anti-employer. Since then there has been a subtle but marked change in the attitude of the tribunals, and many would now argue that the tribunals have reversed this trend. Be that as it may, there can be little doubt that it is now significantly more difficult to win an unfair-dismissal claim than it was in the 1970s and early 1980s, almost certainly because many employers have learned the value of applying fair disciplinary procedures, the absence of which caused them to lose more cases in the early years.

Summary: The basic principles of the unfair-dismissal rules are straightforward. An employee who is sacked after *two years' service* has three months in which to complain to an industrial tribunal. If he or she can show the tribunal that he or she has been '*dismissed*', the employer will then have to justify the dismissal. To do this, the employer must show that he or she had a 'fair' reason for sacking the employee (e.g. because the employee was incompetent or dishonest). Then the tribunal will consider whether the employer acted reasonably in deciding to sack the employee; generally, this means checking that a fair procedure was followed. If the tribunal decides that the dismissal was unfair, then it can order the employer to give the employee his/her job back or to give him/her another job. Usually, though, the employee receives cash compensation. The amount paid will reflect the fact that he or she has now lost his/her job and will also compensate him or her for their losses, although the compensation will often be reduced if the employee's own conduct contributed to the dismissal.

THE REQUIREMENTS OF A SUCCESSFUL UNFAIR-DISMISSAL CLAIM

There are four hurdles to be overcome by an employee who brings an unfair-dismissal claim:

1 Is he or she within the unfair-dismissal legislation? (See below.)
2 Has he or she been 'dismissed' by the employer? (See page 459)
3 Was there a 'fair' reason for the dismissal (i.e. misconduct, disobeying orders, non-cooperation, poor timekeeping, drunkenness, violence, swearing, dishonesty, incapability, incompetence, lack of qualifications, ill-health, industrial action or some other substantial reason)? (See page 464)
4 Did the employer behave 'reasonably'? (See page 479)

Hurdle No. 1. Is the employee within the unfair-dismissal legislation?

Not all employees can claim for unfair dismissal.

The main requirement is that employees must have been employed for at least two years, otherwise they cannot claim unfair dismissal, however unreasonably their employer behaved. Because of this two-year qualifying period many employers review the position of new staff shortly before the two-year period expires.

In deciding whether the employee has worked for two years, the tribunal will add the period of his/her statutory notice on to the time when he or she was dismissed. So, if he or she is dismissed without notice after 103 weeks, then the one week's notice to which he or she is entitled by statute (see page 445) will be added to his/her 103 weeks' service, and he or she will be held to have been employed for two years.

Part-time workers

Part-timers are defined as those employees who do not work more than sixteen hours a week. If an employee works sixteen hours or more then he or she is a full-timer and thus able to claim unfair dismissal. If he or she works between eight and sixteen hours a week (on average) then he (or more probably, she) can claim unfair dismissal – but only if he or she has worked for the employer for at least five years. So, in such cases, the normal two-year qualification period is extended to five years. If the part-timer works fewer than eight hours a week then he or she cannot claim unfair dismissal – however long he or she has worked for the employer.

Retirement age

If an employee is sacked after he or she has reached the 'normal retirement age' for that category of employee, then he or she is not eligible to claim unfair dismissal. The retiring age must be the same whether the employee is a man or a woman. The (rather harsh) rule is that it is the retirement age for similar employees that matters – not the retirement age for that particular employee.

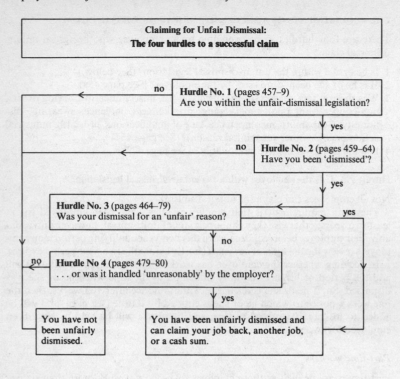

So in one case a woman aged sixty-one could not claim unfair dismissal even though her employment contract envisaged her working until age sixty-five, because the 'normal' retirement age was stated to be sixty. If there is no normal retiring age, then sixty-five applies as a barrier to claims.

When there is no qualifying period

If the employee claims he or she has been sacked because of his/her trade-union activities, or because of race, sex or marriage discrimination, then there is no qualifying period (i.e. there is no need to have worked for two years).

Illegal contracts

If the contract of employment is illegal then no claim for unfair dismissal can be made. This is primarily aimed at tax fiddlers. For instance:

An employee brought an unfair-dismissal claim. At the industrial tribunal hearing the employers showed that the employee, as well as being paid her normal wage, had received an extra £5 cash per week gross. No tax or NI deductions were made from that extra £5. Held: There was an agreement to defraud the Inland Revenue and thus, as a matter of public policy, the whole contract of employment was illegal. No unfair-dismissal claim could be brought. Corby (1980)

Ineligible employees Not all employees can claim for unfair dismissal. Apart from those who have not worked for long enough, part-timers are the main group that cannot claim. See page 408–9 for a full list.

Hurdle No. 2. Has the employee been 'dismissed' by the employer?

Usually it is obvious whether or not an employee has been dismissed. Normally he or she is sacked, given proper notice and handed his/her P45 tax form.

It is not always so straightforward. If the employer did not specifically tell the employee that he or she was sacked, the tribunal will have to decide whether or not the employer did mean to sack him/her. For instance, if the employer tells the employee to 'get out of my factory' it will probably be a dismissal. On the other hand, if the employee is told to 'join a f– union and get some overalls on' the position will be less clear-cut; it will depend on the surrounding circumstances (e.g. if the words were said to a manager it would probably be taken as a dismissal, but not if said to a labourer on a building site where such words might be taken as part of everyday vocabulary). So it is not the words alone that matter – you must also look at the surrounding circumstances.

Mrs Simpson had been unwell and she was recovering from a major illness. She overheard an argument between an employee and her son, so she rushed into the room and shouted at the employee, 'Go! Get out! Get out!' He left, and claimed unfair dismissal. Held: He had not been dismissed. Mrs Simpson's words had to be looked at in the overall context – she was unwell and they were spoken in the heat of the moment. J. and J. Stern (1983)

Mr Martin had a heated row with a director of the company; it ended with the director sacking him. Five minutes later – when he had calmed down – the director realized he had not acted properly and so he saw Martin and told him he was suspended for two days, but not sacked. Martin would not accept this, and claimed unfair dismissal. Held: There had not been a dismissal. The surrounding circumstances showed that it would be wrong to treat this as a dismissal – words spoken in the heat of the moment can be withdrawn if a mistake has been made (provided this is done quickly). Martin (1983)

'Dismissal' is not confined to the cases in which the employer sacks the employee. An employee can still regard him or herself as having been dismissed (and so be eligible for unfair dismissal) if:
• he or she is entitled to resign because the employer has broken the contract of employment; this is called constructive dismissal, *or*

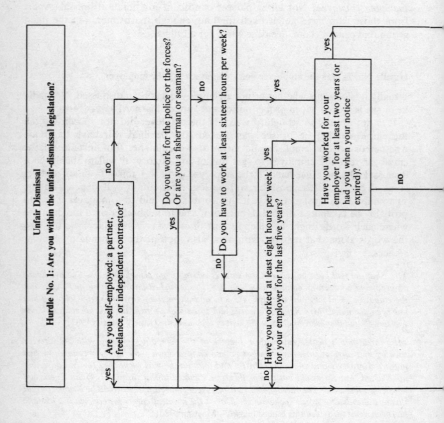

Unfair Dismissal

Hurdle No. 1: Are you within the unfair-dismissal legislation?

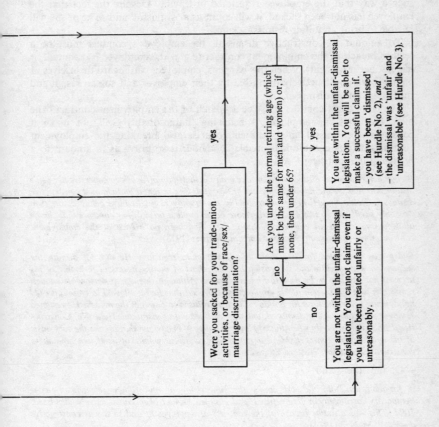

Were you sacked for your trade-union activities, or because of race/sex/ marriage discrimination?

yes →

no →

yes →

Are you under the normal retiring age (which must be the same for men and women) or, if none, then under 65?

no →

yes →

You are within the unfair-dismissal legislation. You will be able to make a successful claim if,
– you have been 'dismissed' (see Hurdle No. 2), *and*
– the dismissal was 'unfair' and 'unreasonable' (see Hurdle No. 3).

You are not within the unfair-dismissal legislation. You cannot claim even if you have been treated unfairly or unreasonably.

● the employer fails to renew the employee's fixed-term contract when it expires (but see page 464).

Justified resignation – constructive dismissal

Sometimes the employer does not sack the employee but, instead, behaves in such a way that the employee is justified in leaving. Despite the fact that the employee has not been sacked, it will count as a 'dismissal' and so he or she will be able to bring an unfair-dismissal claim.

To amount to constructive dismissal, the employer's conduct must be a serious breach of the employment contract (e.g. if the employee is demoted, or has his/her wages cut). When this happens, employees can regard themselves as having been constructively dismissed by their employer and so can resign and then claim unfair dismissal.

The employer's conduct must be a breach of the employment contract. The mere fact that the employer is behaving 'unreasonably' will not make it constructive dismissal unless the employer is also breaking the employment contract, or unless the unreasonable behaviour is so grave as to amount to a breach of the contract.

A shop assistant was refused leave to take a day or half-day off work to supervise her son's insulin injection on the day he came out of hospital. She resigned and claimed constructive dismissal. Held: No. However unreasonably the employers might have behaved, the firm was only small and so it could not therefore be an implied term of her contract that she be allowed time off in an emergency. Since there had been no breach of the employment contract, there was no constructive dismissal. Warner (1978)

Sharp was suspended for five days as a disciplinary measure. He did not dispute the suspension, but because the suspension left him short of money he asked for some of his accrued holiday pay to be paid to him in advance. Although this was a reasonable enough request, it was not a term of his employment contract that he be allowed to claim accrued holiday pay before he took his holiday. The firm refused to pay him the money. He resigned saying it was constructive dismissal, and then claimed unfair dismissal. Held: No. Constructive dismissal arises only when the employer is guilty of behaviour that breaks the very basis of the employment contract. Mere unreasonable behaviour would, of itself, not amount to constructive dismissal. Western Excavating (1978)

On the other hand:

A foreman was told to work under the supervision of an ordinary electrician, as a 'temporary' arrangement. He refused, and claimed he had been constructively dismissed. Held: This was a major breach of the contract of employment and so it was constructive dismissal. McNeil (1984)

Mr Jones was a fleet sales director, but he was subjected to gradual demotion, being moved to more cramped offices with fewer and fewer facilities. In the end he was unable to do his job properly and so he resigned. Held: This was constructive dismissal (and so he could claim unfair dismissal). Wadham Stringer (1983)

In legal theory, it is not the unreasonableness of the employer's behaviour

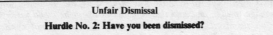

Unfair Dismissal
Hurdle No. 2: Have you been dismissed?

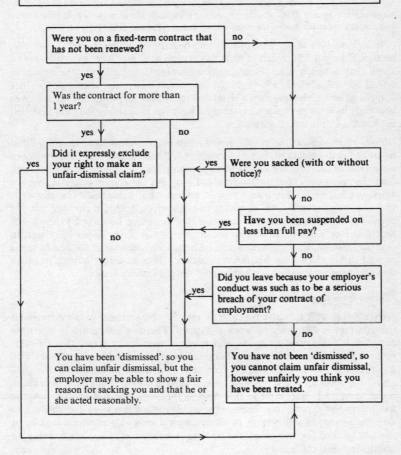

that decides whether or not the employee is justified in leaving. The law requires that there must have been a major breach of the contract of employment – but, in practice, an implied term in the contract (e.g. trust and confidence) will probably be found by the industrial tribunal to cover a situation where the employer has behaved badly, so that the employee can claim unfair dismissal on the basis it has been broken.

Cedron was a night-club worker. He was insulted by the manager, who used foul and abusive language to him, and said that if he didn't like it he could leave. Cedron left, and claimed unfair dismissal. The employers argued that it was not constructive dismissal because even if the manager had behaved unreasonably, he had not broken the terms of the employment contract. Held: It was constructive dismissal. The manager's behaviour was so bad that it went to the root of the employment contract. Palmanor (1978)

If an employee is thinking of resigning because of his employer's behaviour, he should keep a full record of what has occurred, as it will be up to him/her to show that it was a case of constructive dismissal. Accordingly, the employee would be well advised to write to the firm before resigning, setting out his/her complaint and giving the firm a chance to reconsider its position. The employee will then have some written evidence to back up allegations that the firm had broken the employment contract.

'Resign or be sacked.' An employer will often make it clear to an employee that he or she is to be sacked, but the employer will then suggest that the employee resigns so as to avoid the embarrassment and stigma of having been dismissed. Can the employee claim unfair dismissal – or can the employer argue that the employee left of his/her own free will, and was not dismissed? The answer is that the tribunal will look at all the circumstances, and if it decides that the employee was pressurized into resigning (i.e. 'resign or be sacked') then it will be treated as a dismissal, and so the employee can claim unfair dismissal. In practice, though, the employee would be better advised to wait until he or she is sacked rather than offer his/her resignation – thus avoiding having to prove that he or she was, in fact, sacked and did not voluntarily resign.

When a fixed-term contract ends

An employee with a fixed-term contract may be able to claim unfair dismissal if the contract is not renewed when it expires. The only exception is when the contract is for a year or more, and when it specifically states that its non-renewal will not give rise to an unfair-dismissal claim. In effect, employees with a contract for more than one year can sign away their unfair-dismissal rights, and if the contract is not renewed when it expires they will not be able to claim unfair dismissal. But, even in this case, if the employee is sacked before the fixed term has expired (e.g. because the employer has less work for him/her to do), the employee will be able to claim unfair dismissal – provided that he or she has worked for two years (the minimum period for being able to bring an unfair-dismissal claim).

If the fixed-term contract is for less than a year then the employee cannot sign away his/her rights – and so will be able to claim unfair dismissal if the contract is ended early or if it is not renewed when it runs out.

Hurdle No. 3. Was there a 'fair' reason for the employee's dismissal?

Once the employee has surmounted Hurdle No. 1 (is he or she within the unfair-dismissal legislation?) and Hurdle No. 2 (has he or she been 'dismissed' by the employer?), it is for the employer to show that there was a fair reason for the dismissal: This is Hurdle No. 3.

So, once Hurdle No. 2 has been passed, the burden of proof passes on to the employer. It is up to him or her to show a 'fair' reason for the dismissal.

The usual 'fair' reasons for a dismissal are:
- misconduct by the employee
  - disobeying orders (see below)
  - non-cooperation (see page 466)
  - poor timekeeping (see page 467)
  - drunkenness (see page 468)
  - violence and swearing (see page 468)
  - dishonesty (see page 468);
- the employee is incapable or incompetent, or lacks qualifications (see page 470);
- other 'capability' problems, such as ill-health (see page 472);
- industrial action, such as striking (see page 476);
- it would be illegal for the employee to continue working (see page 477);
- there is 'some other substantial reason' justifying dismissal (see page 477).

Misconduct by the employee: disobeying the employer's orders

It is an implied term of every employee's contract of employment that he or she will obey the employer's orders – assuming that the orders are both lawful and reasonable (see page 402). In addition, though, the order must be one that is authorized by the contract of employment. For instance, if a man's employment contract states that his job is to operate a lathe, it will not be an authorized order if he is told to clean the lavatories instead. If the employer insists that the employee obey this unauthorized order, the employee can resign. He can then regard himself as having been constructively dismissed (see page 462) and can claim unfair dismissal.

If the employment contract (and in practice that usually means the 'written particulars' sent to the employee) does not define the job, then the employee may well be obliged to obey the employer's instructions. If he or she refuses to do so, the employer will then have a 'fair' reason for dismissing him. So it can be very important from the employee's point of view that his/her job be fully described in the written particulars (see page 407).

Similarly, if the employee breaks the rules of conduct or disciplinary rules laid down by the employer, his/her dismissal may not be unfair. Obviously, each case must be decided on its own facts and the tribunal will consider the 'reasonableness' of the decision to sack. For instance:

Ladbroke's disciplinary rules forbade the staff from placing their own bets. In the course of an abortive investigation into allegations of fraud it was learned that several employees had placed bets in breach of the disciplinary rules. They were dismissed, that being the penalty laid down in the disciplinary rules. They claimed unfair dismissal. Held: Their dismissal was unfair. It was not sufficient that the disciplinary rules authorized dismissal for the dismissal to be fair. Ladbroke Racing (1979)

If an employer is complaining about a particular matter of conduct, it must be related to the employee's job. For instance, in one case a petrol-pump attendant was learning to drive and she drove off from work in the family car – but collided with the petrol pumps, causing damage worth £6,000. It was held that her dismissal was unfair – her bad driving was not relevant to her job.

Misconduct by the employee: non-cooperation

Non-cooperation can take various forms. The mere fact that an employee does not work cheerfully or with good grace does not amount to non-cooperation; employees are legally obliged to do their work, but not to do it with a smile on their face.

Whether an employee is not cooperating will depend upon the terms of his/her employment contract. For instance, if one refuses to cooperate and do occasional overtime, the position will depend upon whether their contract obliges them to do overtime when required. If overtime is voluntary, then this non-cooperation will not make a dismissal 'fair'.

Mr Martin's written terms of employment stated that 'you will be expected to work such overtime as is necessary to ensure continuity of service'. Throughout his employment with the firm, Mr Martin was reluctant to work overtime, but did so on some occasions after persuasion. He was eventually sacked after refusing to work on one Friday or Saturday evening. He claimed unfair dismissal. Held: The dismissal was fair because Martin had not complied with what was a term of his employment contract. This was so even though the firm had not sought to force him to work overtime before and had in fact condoned previous refusals. No warning was necessary. Solus (1979)

The tribunal will have little sympathy with employees who rigidly stand on their contractual rights when it is clear that they are acting unreasonably by not cooperating in a change of contractual arrangements. For instance:

The RAC emergency service was inundated with work. The RAC decided to reorganize the service and reached an agreement with the staff association which was acceptable to the majority of staff. However, it involved staff in working extra hours; three employees refused to agree to the changes, because their thirty-one-and-a-half-hour week was increased to a forty-two-hour week. After being sacked, the three men claimed unfair dismissal. The Employment Appeals Tribunal ruled that it did not necessarily follow that they were entitled to win their claims because their contracts of employment had been altered. As long as the RAC demonstrated to the employees with patience and understanding that the reorganization was sensible and in the interest of employees generally, and had listened to and weighed up their views, then the dismissal would be fair. Martin (1979)

Most cases of non-cooperation take the form of niggling, petty incidents – in short, bloody-mindedness. Only if the conduct continues over a long period of time will it be regarded as a 'fair' reason for dismissal. Even then the tribunal will look closely at the reasonableness of the employer's conduct (Hurdle No. 4, page 479). They will ask why the employee has been behaving in that way. Has the employer been authoritarian, inconsiderate or rude? Has the employer tried to discuss the problem with the employee? Have the employees been given a chance to explain why they are discontented? Most important of all, have they been given a clear 'this can't go on' warning? In short, what would the reasonable employer have done?

Misconduct by the employee: poor timekeeping

As with bloody-mindedness, poor timekeeping will not be a serious disciplinary matter unless it continues for a long time. Dismissal for lateness will almost certainly be unfair if employees were not given an express warning and told that they would be dismissed unless their timekeeping improved. Also, the tribunal will want to know why the employee has been arriving late – for instance, is it a temporary problem caused by domestic upheavals?

The nature of the employee's job will also be relevant. It will be a more serious matter if he or she is a senior employee or in a position of responsibility. An extreme example:

Two maintenance fitters were both long-serving employees with excellent records. But one afternoon they both went absent for two and a half hours without permission and were summarily dismissed. They claimed unfair dismissal. Held: No. They held important positions of responsibility, and as such, were paid to be on call at any time. An absence of two and a half hours could not be excused – especially since there were clearly displayed notices warning staff that they would be instantly dismissed if they went absent without permission. Morrison (1973)

If the tribunal decides that the lateness or absenteeism did not justify dismissal, then the employee will win the unfair-dismissal claim. However, if the employee was persistently late, the tribunal might well find that his/her own conduct contributed to the dismissal and so reduce the compensation paid (see page 492). As always, the tribunal will consider the case by reference to what the 'reasonable' employer would have done. (See Hurdle No. 4, page 479.)

Clocking-in offences are regarded in a different light; they are always serious offences and often justify summary dismissal (because of the 'dishonesty' involved). For instance:

Mr Stewart was a bus driver. Although his shift was due to end at 9.45 p.m. an inspector could not find him at 7 p.m. On the following night he was watched by two inspectors, who saw him hand in his cash and time cards much earlier than he should have done. The same thing happened a few days later. He was reported to the district traffic superintendent and, following a meeting, he was sacked. He claimed unfair dismissal. Held: It was not unfair dismissal. False clocking in and false claims about hours worked are always serious offences of dishonesty, which can often justify instant dismissal. This was so, even though the company had not followed its own disciplinary procedure – in that it should normally have challenged Mr Stewart and asked him for an explanation after he was first seen by the two inspectors. Stewart (1978)

In practice nowadays compliance with procedure is important and can render a dismissal unfair even where the underlying facts clearly merit dismissal of the employee. This can always be reflected in the amount of compensation the industrial tribunal decides to award.

Misconduct by the employee: drunkenness

Drunkenness does not normally, of itself, justify dismissal. But persistent drunkenness will. A lot will depend upon the nature of the employee's job; an airline pilot who is found drunk would be liable to summary dismissal, whereas a packer in a factory should probably only be given a reprimand for a first offence.

The tribunal will want to know whether it was a one-off offence. Has the employee been given a warning in the past and specifically been told that further drunkenness would lead to dismissal? Has the management turned a blind eye to drinking in the past? Did the employer give the employee a chance to sober up and give an explanation before sacking him her (perhaps drugs prescribed by a doctor caused 'drunken' behaviour, for example)?

Misconduct by the employee: violence and swearing

These are similar to drunkenness. How serious was the offence? Certainly, bad language of itself must be particularly serious to justify dismissal. Who was the person attacked or insulted? The more senior his/her status, the more seriously should the offence be regarded. Has such conduct been condoned in the past? Has the employee been given a chance to explain his/her conduct and to apologize? Was he or she given a formal warning that repetition would lead to dismissal?

This is the sort of question that the tribunal will want to have answered. The members of the tribunal will be realistic and be aware that some swearing (and even horse-play) is accepted in industry. They will want to be sure that the alleged bad language is not being used as a mere excuse for getting rid of the employee.

Serious fighting at work might be sufficiently grave to justify dismissal for a first offence, although the tribunal might want to check that the employee realized fighting would lead to dismissal. Mere arguing will rarely justify dismissal:

Two employees started arguing. A heated row developed but there was no violence. Both were dismissed. Was it unfair dismissal? Held: Yes. The misconduct was not sufficiently grave to make the dismissal fair. The chairman of the tribunal said: 'Here we have found that there was not a fight, merely a tussle.' Till and Walters (1978)

Misconduct by the employee: dishonesty and other offences

Theft is always a serious matter. Usually a theft at work will justify summary dismissal, but the employer must still act 'reasonably' and handle the incident in the proper way (see Hurdle No. 4, page 479). The amount involved is usually not the important point: it is the principle of dishonesty that matters. Thus, in one case, a dismissal for a fiddled travel-expenses claim of £1.48 was held to be fair.

If employers suspect an employee of theft, they should not act as an instant prosecutor, judge and jury. The employee should be given full details of the allegations, all witnesses should be interviewed and the employee should be given a chance to explain his/her conduct. If employers do not follow the proper procedures, they may well lose the unfair-dismissal claim, although it is likely that the tribunal will reduce the employee's compensation because his/her own conduct contributed to the dismissal (see page 492).

A supermarket cashier failed to ring up eighteen items on a customer's bill. The area controller asked her to explain herself and she said she had been unwell. The police were called and later that day she was sacked. But the police eventually decided not to prosecute. Was it unfair dismissal? Held: Yes. She should have been given a proper chance to explain, since she had 'not been herself' when interviewed by the area controller. The firm should have waited a few days before asking her to explain. Since the proper disciplinary procedures had not been followed, the dismissal was unfair. Obviously, if she had been caught red-handed the position would have been different and she could have been dismissed without an investigation and without being given a chance to explain herself. Tesco (1977)

Employers do not have to wait for an employee to be found guilty in a criminal court before they dismiss the employee. It will be 'fair' for employers to dismiss the employee if they have 'reasonable grounds' for believing the employee is guilty. They need not have evidence that would convince a jury; all that is needed is to have 'reasonable grounds' for believing that the employee is guilty. As Lord Denning has put it, 'If a man is dismissed for stealing, as long as the employer honestly believes it on reasonable grounds, that is enough to justify dismissal. It is not necessary for the employer to prove that he was in fact stealing.'

The rules on how to deal with suspected dishonesty by an employee were laid down in a 1980 case called Burchell v. BHS. The dismissal will not be unfair if, first, the the employer reasonably believed that the employee was guilty and, secondly, he or she carried out 'as much investigation as was reasonable in the circumstances'. So the important point is not whether the employee was actually guilty or not; it is whether the employer was reasonably entitled to think that he or she was guilty.

Even if the employee is subsequently acquitted by a court, the dismissal will be 'fair' if the employer can show that he or she had reasonable grounds, at the time of the dismissal, for thinking the employee was guilty. The Employment Appeals Tribunal has justified this seemingly harsh line:

At first sight those not familiar with the problem say that it is wrong to dismiss the employee until the guilt has been established. Further experience shows that this is impracticable. In the first place, quite apart from guilt, involvement in the alleged criminal offence often involves a serious breach of duty or discipline. The cashier charged with a till offence, guilty or not, is often undoubtedly in breach of company rules in the way in which the till is being operated. The employee who removes goods from the premises, guilty or not, is often in breach of the company rules in taking his employer's goods from the premises without express permission; and it is irrelevant to the matter that a jury may be in doubt whether he intended to steal the stock.

The same criteria apply to employees who are suspected of vandalism:

An employee was suspected of committing acts of vandalism at his work place. He was sacked. Subsequently he was acquitted of the criminal charge brought against him. He claimed unfair dismissal. Held: No. The employer was not required to prove that the employee was the vandal – all that the employer had to do was show that he had reasonable grounds for believing the employee to be guilty. Ferodo (1976)

Normally, employers should investigate the alleged offence. They are expected to investigate the most obvious and likely explanations of what happened and should do so with an open mind. They should not set out to prove that the employee was guilty, but simply try to gather evidence from the more obvious sources. At the end of the day the industrial tribunal will ask, 'Was there anything more a reasonable employer would have done?' A mere suspicion of dishonesty will not justify a sacking. For instance:

An anonymous tip-off led to a spot check being carried out on a till-girl who had worked for the firm for many years. There was a £22 shortfall and the girl offered no explanation. So she was sacked. Held: It was unfair dismissal. There were no reasonable grounds for suspecting her of dishonesty in view of her previous good work-record, and, most important, there had not been a proper investigation. Peebles (1984)

Criminal convictions for offences outside the employment can sometimes justify dismissal. But the tribunal will want to be sure that the conviction is relevant to the employment. For instance, does it affect the employer's reputation? (As in the case of a shopfitter who was convicted of stealing from one of his employer's customers: it was held that the dismissal was fair.) If the employee is in a position of trust or responsibility then his/her dismissal is more likely to be fair, but if the offence does not affect the employer's trust in him/her, it will probably be unfair to dismiss him/her.

Sexual offences are regarded in a particularly serious light:

A bus conductor was sacked following his conviction for gross indecency in an out-of-work incident. His dismissal was held to be fair. The chairman of the tribunal said that the conductor 'came into close contact with the public and there would be occasions when the bus would be at lonely spots, and it would be understandable if members of the public should be apprehensive of entering buses where he was a bus conductor'. Potts (1978)

The employee is incapable, incompetent, or unqualified

Even if an employee is clearly incompetent, it is important that the employer acts reasonably (see Hurdle No. 4, page 479).

The most difficult cases are those involving employees who are doing their 'incompetent best'. If employees are not up to the job, then much will depend upon the wording of their employment contract. If they are employed, for instance, to operate a particular machine and are incapable of doing so, then their dismissal is likely to be 'fair'. On the other hand, if their duties are described in a vague, general way, the employer will probably be unable to dismiss them for not being able to operate one type of machine when they can operate other machines that come within the job description.

The employer will generally be expected to do all he or she can to help employees. They should be given a chance to improve their performance, and receive encouragement and training from management. They should also be sent a clear warning letter, making it clear that they will be dismissed if their performance does not improve.

But how long a period should incompetent employees be given in which to 'pull up their socks'? There is no hard-and-fast rule; much will depend upon the seniority of the job, how long the employee has been doing it, and the other surrounding circumstances. In one case, a three-month period was held to be appropriate for a sales director who had been employed for two years; in another case, six months was appropriate for a works director employed for six years. Conversely, in another case involving a works director of six years' standing, a five-week period between warning and dismissal was not enough and so he won his unfair-dismissal claim.

In fact, there is a further problem for employees in this position. If they are not given enough warning (i.e. sufficient time in which to improve performance), then they may well win an unfair-dismissal claim. But, if the tribunal decides that a longer period of warning would have made no difference – because the employee wouldn't have improved his/her performance sufficiently – then only limited compensation will be awarded. See page 492 for how compensation is assessed (e.g. if someone should have received six months' warning but was given only two months', then the compensatory part of the award will be only four months).

If employees are promoted, they should be given a fair chance to adjust to their new responsibilities. If they cannot cope then they should be offered their old job back, if at all possible. But if all else fails, the employer will be entitled to dismiss them and the dismissal will be fair. It should be emphasized that this is despite the employee not having done anything 'wrong' or otherwise being at fault; that is not how the unfair-dismissal laws work. For instance:

Mr Cook was manager of a non-food depot. After eight years he was promoted to be manager of a food depot despite his having no experience of managing food depots. He could not cope with the new job and so the firm offered him another job as a non-food depot manager, but at the higher food-depot manager rate of pay. He refused on the grounds that

it would involve him in inconvenient travel. He claimed unfair dismissal. Held: No. The
employers had acted reasonably. Cook (1977)

What mattered in this case was that the employer had lost confidence in the employee. The Employment Appeals Tribunal commented: 'It is important that the operation of the unfair-dismissal legislation should not impede employers unreasonably in the efficient management of their business.'

If employees are dismissed for lack of qualifications, the tribunal will want to know when it was decided that they must have the qualifications. If it was decided after they started the job, then the dismissal is likely to be unfair. On the other hand, if they were told before they started work that they would have to obtain certain qualifications, it will probably be fair to dismiss them if they fail to qualify. But, as always, the employer must act 'reasonably' (see Hurdle No. 4, page 479). In short, what would the reasonable employer have done in these circumstances?

Other capability problems, including temperament and ill-health

Employees can be efficient and hard-working, and yet have the wrong personality for the job. If so, it may be 'fair' for the employer to dismiss them.

Industrial tribunals approach such cases with great reserve. The tribunal will want to be sure that it is not the employer who is being unreasonable or 'difficult'. Has the employee been asked to mend his/her ways? Has the problem been explained to him/her? Is it possible to transfer him/her to another job? Has he or she received a formal, written warning? How long has his/her personality been tolerated without complaint?

But there comes a time when the employer can say 'enough is enough'. Often the dismissal can be justified on the basis of 'some other substantial reason' (see page 477).

Ill-health is another area of difficulty. Employers are expected to provide reasonable job security for sick members of staff. Before sacking a sick employee the employer should:

1 Fully investigate the nature of the sickness and how long it is likely to last. The employee should be consulted and given a chance to give his/her views as to the prospects for recovery.

An employee started work as a cold-metal handler in October 1974. In January 1975 he
slipped a disc and went off sick. In March 1976 he told his employer that he was expecting
to be operated on soon, and that he would then be able to return to light work. On 28 June
1976 he was given his notice, expiring on 11 July 1976. He claimed unfair dismissal. Held:
Yes. There was no reason why the firm should not have consulted with him before deciding
to sack him. They had not done so, and so it was unfair dismissal. Williamson (1977)

Only when consultation would be completely pointless – such as when the employee is seriously ill – can the employer dispense with it. For instance:

Mr McInally was a barman at a camp for North Sea oil workers in Shetland. During the six months prior to his dismissal, he suffered from asthenia, which, in the opinion of both the company doctor and his own doctor, made him unfit to carry out his job. Subsequently, he was dismissed without any further consultation by his employers. He claimed unfair dismissal. Held: Further consultation was unnecessary. Since it had been overwhelmingly established that Mr McInally was medically unsuited to the job, consultation was not needed. The purpose of consultation is to establish the facts of the case, and 'if it is clear that the purpose cannot be achieved, the need for a consultation diminishes or disappears'. Taylor-plan Catering (1980)

2 Give the employee written notice that the illness, or repeated absence from work, may lead to his/her dismissal. But, once again, this might not be necessary if the illness is particularly serious.
3 Obtain full information, usually from proper medical reports.
4 Every effort should be made to find alternative work for the sick employee. For instance, if an employee is no longer able to do heavy work the employer should try to find light work for him, if such work is available. But the employer cannot be expected to create a new job for the employee.

An electricity board inspector had worked for the board for thirty-eight years when he was dismissed. He had been absent for all but two weeks during the last year of employment, because of a heart condition. He claimed unfair dismissal, arguing that his employers should have found him suitable alternative work, especially in view of his long service. The judge who heard the appeal said 'no'. 'It cannot be right that . . . an employer can be called upon by the law to create a special job for an employee, however long serving he may have been. On the other hand, each case must depend on its own facts. The circumstances may well be such that the employer may have available light work of the kind which is within the capacity of the employee to do, and the circumstances may make it fair to at least encourage him or to at least offer him the chance of doing that work.' However, on the facts of this case, the employee was not unfairly dismissed. Merseyside and N. Wales E.B. (1975)

5 It is not so important to follow these procedures if the employee is often absent owing to unconnected minor ailments rather than one major illness. This is so even if the unconnected absences are all covered by medical certificates. In such a case, there comes a time when the employer is entitled to say 'enough is enough' and, assuming warnings have been given, he or she can fairly dismiss the employee.

Mrs Thompson was absent from work for about 25 per cent of her working time. Throughout this period she had numerous minor illnesses. She was given a number of warnings about her attendance record; eventually she was sacked for failing to improve her attendance. She had been given a final warning. She claimed unfair dismissal. Held: No, it was not an unfair dismissal. In cases of this sort, with intermittent illnesses: 'Firstly, there should be a fair review by the employers of the attendance record and the reasons for it, and, secondly, appropriate warnings, after the employee has been given an opportunity to make representations. If there is no adequate improvement in the attendance record, it is likely that in most cases the employer will be justified in treating the persistent absences as a sufficient reason for dismissing the employee.' Int. Sports Co. (1980)

The net effect of these rules is that if employers follow the proper procedure they can fairly dismiss a sick employee unless there is alternative work that could have been offered to the employee. So sick employees have relatively little job security. To protect themselves as much as they can, sick employees should ensure that they keep their employers fully informed of the medical position. They should send in sick notes regularly. They should make it clear that they intend to return to work, and that they do not regard the employment as coming to an end. They should also keep in touch with their work-mates so that they can find out if there is any suitable alternative work available in the firm that they could do.

For rules as to sick pay, see page 417; for SSP, see page 418.

Pregnancy

Normally it will not be fair to dismiss a woman because she is pregnant. So the sacked employee will win her unfair-dismissal claim (provided she has worked for two years). However, the dismissal of a woman for reason of her pregnancy may also amount to sex discrimination, entitling her to bring a claim under the Sex Discrimination Act 1975 (SDA), where the qualifying period of two years' employment is not a requirement. This is a complex and developing area of law where European law also plays a part, with two European cases, Dekker and Hertz (both 1991), confirming the possibility of a claim under the SDA or the Equal Treatment Directive on which the SDA is based.

In fact, relatively few employees are dismissed solely because they are pregnant. It is usually a consequence of the pregnancy that causes the employer to sack the woman. For instance, the pregnancy may affect the woman's concentration, it may increase her absenteeism or it may make it difficult for her to work without frequent rests. Usually, however, the sacked woman can successfully claim unfair dismissal:

An employee who was pregnant was absent from work for a month, because of hypertension brought on by the pregnancy. Held: She had been dismissed for a reason connected with her pregnancy and so the dismissal was unfair. Elegbede (1977)

And this will be so even if the pregnancy is the 'last straw' for the employer:

An employee had a bad absenteeism record. She had been given a verbal warning and also a final written warning that any further absences would lead to her dismissal. She then became pregnant and went into hospital as a result of a miscarriage. Because of this absence from work, she was dismissed. She claimed unfair dismissal. Held: Yes. She had been sacked as a result of the miscarriage, which was a reason connected with her pregnancy. Accordingly, it was unfair. George (1977)

Compare:

An employee was frequently absent owing to ill-health and this caused substantial disruption at her workplace. She received several warnings from the employer. In April 1979 she was off sick again, and produced a medical certificate in support. On 10 April her supervisor recommended that she be dismissed. On 11 April she phoned to say she was pregnant. On 17 April she was sacked. She claimed unfair dismissal on the basis that the principal reason for

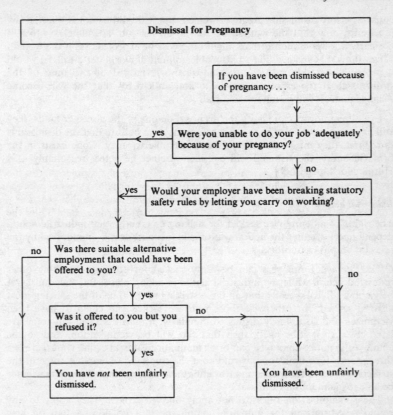

Dismissal for Pregnancy

If you have been dismissed because of pregnancy ...

Were you unable to do your job 'adequately' because of your pregnancy? — yes

Would your employer have been breaking statutory safety rules by letting you carry on working? — yes / no

Was there suitable alternative employment that could have been offered to you? — no

Was it offered to you but you refused it? — yes / no

You have *not* been unfairly dismissed.

You have been unfairly dismissed.

her dismissal was her pregnancy. Held: No. The employers learned of her pregnancy only after it had been decided to sack her. Her pregnancy was not the principal reason for her dismissal. Del Monte Foods (1980)

So, generally, a dismissal for a reason connected with a pregnancy will be unfair. However, there are two exceptions to this, when it will be fair for the employer to dismiss the pregnant woman. But even in these cases, the employer must offer the woman another suitable job, if there is one available:

1 If the woman cannot carry on doing her job without breaking the law, it will not be unfair to dismiss her. For instance, if her job involves working with radiation levels that could be dangerous to the unborn child.
2 If the woman is incapable of doing her job, or of doing it adequately, the dismissal will not be unfair. In practice, this is the provision that employers

use to justify dismissing pregnant women. But it should be noted that the law requires only that the woman be able to do her job 'adequately', which is clearly a lower standard than might otherwise be expected. So, if the woman can show that she is doing a reasonable amount of work, her dismissal would probably be unfair. Also, the 'adequacy' is judged at the time of the dismissal. If the employer rushes in and anticipates that she will become inadequate, it will be unfair dismissal.

Even if employers can justify the dismissal on one of the above grounds, they still have two more hurdles to cross before they can be sure that the dismissal is fair. First, they must offer the woman a suitable vacancy if one exists in the firm. Secondly, the tribunal will consider whether he acted 'reasonably' (i.e. Hurdle No. 4, page 479).

Industrial action

The rights of an employee sacked for striking or taking other industrial action depend upon whether the action was official (i.e. authorized or endorsed by the relevant union) or unofficial.

Official action. Employees can be fairly sacked for striking or taking other industrial action while the industrial action is taking place. But they must not be victimized. This means that *all* those striking at the time of the sacking must also be sacked, for otherwise those who are sacked can claim to have been victimized and so unfairly dismissed. Similarly, if all are sacked but some are later given their jobs back, then that too will be victimization, and so the employee(s) not re-employed can bring an unfair dismissal claim. (But there is a three-month time limit for this rule, so if the employer re-employs some of the strikers, but more than three months after their sacking, then the others will not be able to claim unfair dismissal.)

These victimization rules do not apply only to strikes. They apply to any employees dismissed for industrial action, be it a go-slow, a ban on new machinery or whatever. Unless all the staff involved in the industrial action are dismissed, dismissals may be unfair.

Different rules apply to dismissals that take place after the dispute has been resolved. If an employer sacks a striker after his or her return to work, then the dismissal will have to be justified as being fair. But it may be fair to make former strikers redundant before making 'loyal' employees redundant.

Unofficial action. Where the strike or industrial action is unofficial, the employee has no right to complain of unfair dismissal if, at the time of dismissal, he or she was taking part in unofficial industrial action. It does not matter that the individual concerned was selected because he or she was a ring-leader or an activist.

Sometimes an employer will argue that striking employees have dismissed themselves by going on strike, since the strike is in breach of their contract of employment. This argument is totally false – striking employees are not assumed to have dismissed themselves.

Finally, it should be noted that these victimization rules all deal with dismissal (i.e. sacking); they do not cover less drastic sanctions imposed by an employer. So, docking a day's pay may, for instance, be allowable, since it will not legally count as victimization. In practical terms, therefore, the safeguards that are designed to stop the victimization of those involved in industrial action are of limited effect.

It would be illegal for employees to do their job

The obvious example of this is the lorry driver who is disqualified from driving. He is thus unable to do his job without breaking the law. His dismissal will therefore probably be fair.

Even so, the tribunal will want to be sure that the decision to sack was a reasonable one (i.e. Hurdle No. 4, page 479). How long would the ban last? Could a temporary replacement be employed? Is there another job that could be given to the employee?

The Hearing Aid Council Act 1968 forbids hearing-aid dispensers from employing unqualified dispensers. An employee who had been a trainee dispenser was sacked after he failed to qualify. He claimed unfair dismissal but the employers argued that the dismissal was fair because it would have been illegal for them to employ him as a dispenser. Held: The employers had not acted reasonably. They could have applied for the employee's training period to be extended and, besides, it was unlikely that they would have been prosecuted. So it was unfair dismissal. Sutcliffe (1977)

There is 'some other substantial reason' justifying the dismissal

This is a catch-all provision. It allows an employer to dismiss employees when the complaint against them does not fit into any of the normal 'fair' reasons justifying a dismissal.

The courts have not defined what 'some other substantial reason' means. It has deliberately been left vague so that it can continue to be used as a long stop for the unusual cases. It can sometimes be used to justify seemingly hard decisions – as in the case of the fireman who was sacked for refusing to agree to work longer hours under a collective agreement negotiated between his union and his employers. It was held that this was 'some other substantial reason' justifying the dismissal, even though it was accepted that the union could not negotiate as his agent and so bind him to accept the change in his employment contract.

'Some other substantial reason' is often used to justify dismissal when there is an incompatibility between staff. So in one case it made the dismissal of a female employee 'fair' when she had upset her male colleagues by frequently boasting of her sexual exploits with a younger man. In another case it was used to justify the dismissal of an employee in an old people's home whose behaviour upset the aged residents. Another example:

Mr Saunders was a handyman at a children's camp. He was sacked when it was discovered he was a practising homosexual. Mr Saunders argued that he was not interested in young people and was able to keep his private life separate from his work. He claimed unfair dismissal. Held: The dismissal was fair. The tribunal was entitled to find that many employers would feel that the employment of homosexuals should be restricted, especially when they had to work closely with children. Saunders (1981)

In reaching that decision, the Employment Appeals Tribunal made it clear that, in borderline cases, if employers approach the matter fairly and properly they cannot be faulted for doing what they consider to be just and proper. Potentially, 'some other substantial reason' can be used to justify a wide range of dismissals. For instance, in one case an employee had been given a wage rise above government guidelines and the firm was being threatened with withdrawal of government subsidies. The firm therefore reduced his wages and he resigned. It was held that it was not unfair dismissal.

Occasionally, the tribunals have allowed 'economic necessity' of a firm faced with a crisis to be treated as 'some other substantial reason' justifying dismissal. Staff who have refused to vary their employment contracts to allow more efficient work practices to be introduced have been held to have been fairly dismissed. For instance, see the case of Mr Martin on page 466. Similarly, dismissal may be justified where employers need to reorganize their businesses and an employee refuses to cooperate:

Mr Hollister was a local secretary of the farmers' union in Cornwall. His main source of income was commissions from an insurance company. Other local secretaries in Cornwall complained that local secretaries in other parts of the country were able to earn more because they had different insurance commission arrangements. Accordingly, the Cornwall branch agreed to alter the secretaries' contracts of employment so that a new commission scheme could be introduced. Hollister refused to accept the change and was sacked. He claimed unfair dismissal. Held: The dismissal was fair. The reorganization of the business justified the decision to sack him. Hollister (1979)

This was an important decision by the Court of Appeal. The dismissal was held to be fair despite the fact that Mr Hollister was having the terms of his contract of employment changed against his will, and despite the fact that the employers did not carry out the full consultation envisaged by the Code of Practice then in force. The tribunals have made it clear that employers who have to reorganize business have little to fear from the unfair-dismissal laws. Thus in one case an employee was sacked for refusing to do voluntary (i.e. not compulsory) overtime and it was held that this was not an unfair dismissal – the needs of the business required that the overtime be worked. Similarly, if employers come under pressure from their main customer, then the dismissal will probably be fair – however unfair it may be on the employee. So, in one case a firm of North Sea oil contractors sacked a worker because BP (their main client) wanted the man to be sacked; this was held not to be an unfair dismissal since it had been a 'fair' decision for the employer to make in the light of his business requirements (i.e. the mere fact that it was unfair on the employee did not make it an unfair dismissal).

Hurdle No. 4. Did the employer behave 'reasonably'?

The last hurdle in an unfair-dismissal claim is the 'reasonableness' of the employer's behaviour. Even if employers have surmounted Hurdle No. 3, and shown that they had a 'fair' reason for the dismissal, they cannot be sure that the dismissal was fair. The industrial tribunal will ask itself whether they acted 'reasonably'.

Of course, if the employers failed to surmount Hurdle No. 3 and were unable to show a 'fair' reason they will have lost the case, so there will then be no need to go on and consider whether they acted 'reasonably'.

General guidelines on what is the 'reasonable' behaviour expected of an employer are set out in the various codes of practice published by ACAS. The most important of these codes is the one dealing with disciplinary rules and disciplinary procedures; extracts from it are set out on page 426.

It is important to remember that:

1 The decision whether the employer acted reasonably is taken from the employer's point of view. The test is, 'What would a reasonable employer have done in these circumstances?' The decision to sack does not have to be fair from the employee's point of view.

2 The 'reasonableness' of the decision to sack will occasionally involve a consideration of whether sacking was too severe a penalty. But usually the tribunal will be more concerned to see that the proper procedures are followed.

3 The employee must be warned about his/her conduct in all but the most exceptional cases (e.g. guilty of gross misconduct) or where a warning would have been irrelevant because of the employee's 'irredeemable incapacity'.

4 In other cases, consultation may be necessary: for instance, with an employee suffering from long-term sickness. This is also the case when the employer wants to reorganize the business and requires the staff to change the terms of their employment contracts. But in the final analysis, tribunals will not allow the unfair-dismissal legislation to prevent the proper and reasonable reorganization of a business (for instance, see the case of Mr Hollister, page 478).

5 Generally, employees must be given a chance to put their side of the story before any decision is made to sack them. But even this may not be necessary if it is obvious that the decision to sack them would have been the same even if they had been allowed to argue their case.

When a proper inquiry would not have made any difference

The Code of Practice sets out the standard of practice and 'reasonableness' expected of employers. When it was first introduced, the Code was regarded as the standard expected of all employers, regardless of their circumstances. However, the tribunals have, since then, at times adopted a less rigorous standard. For instance, it has not been unusual for a dismissal to be held fair, despite the fact that the proper procedures (e.g. consultation, investigation) were not followed, where the tribunal has been satisfied that following the procedures would have made no difference to the eventual decision to sack. In short, where the tribunal felt that dismissal would have resulted even if the employer had followed a proper disciplinary procedure, then the procedural irregularity has on occasion been ignored. If the procedural shortcomings would have made no difference, then they would probably not make a 'fair' dismissal into an unfair dismissal.

However, tribunals are expressly required to take into account the size and resources of the employing firm when deciding whether a dismissal was 'reasonable'. One result is that less emphasis is placed on procedures in such cases.

28 Industrial Tribunals: Bringing an Unfair-Dismissal Claim

Industrial tribunals hear virtually all employment law disputes. Most of their work consists of hearing unfair-dismissal and redundancy-payment claims.

The tribunals are designed to be relatively informal and to hear employer/ employee disputes with the minimum of cost, delay and legal formality. To achieve these aims, the tribunals have several important rules:

1 Non-lawyers can represent the parties. So employers or employees who do not want to act for themselves need not instruct a solicitor. Instead they can ask a trade union official, friend or other person to act as their advocate.
2 Everybody pays their own legal costs. In other courts, the winner of a case usually has his or her costs and expenses paid by the loser. But industrial tribunals award costs only in exceptional circumstances. The idea of the no-costs rule is to discourage the use of professional lawyers. In practice, though, employers usually do instruct lawyers, whilst employees more often go unrepresented, unless their union provides representation.
3 An unfair-dismissal claim must be made within three months and a redundancy claim must be made within six months.
4 Once the employee has shown that he or she was 'dismissed' by the employer, it is in effect for the employer to show that the employee is not entitled to an unfair-dismissal or redundancy award. In other words, the burden of proof is, in practice if not in theory, on the employer.
5 The hearing of cases is relatively informal when compared to the procedure in a normal court. While the hearing is not a round-the-table discussion, it will avoid the formalities of a court. In particular, the rules of evidence are less strict and so hearsay and written evidence will usually be allowed.
6 Legal aid is not available. So however poor the employee may be, he or she cannot get legal aid to finance the claim. However, advice and assistance in filling in the forms and in preparing the case might be available under the green-form scheme.

APPLYING TO AN INDUSTRIAL TRIBUNAL

To claim unfair dismissal, employees must make their claim within three months of dismissal. The claim is made by sending in an application form to an industrial tribunal – not to the employer.

The three-month period for claims

The application form must arrive within three months of the dismissal. The tribunal can extend the three-month period, but only when it was 'not reasonably practicable' for the employee to apply in time. The tribunals apply the rules strictly and allow late claims only in exceptional circumstances. The sort of excuse that is likely to be accepted is if the employee has had a serious illness, or if the employer told him/her to delay starting the industrial-tribunal proceedings because 'we might be able to work something out'. On the other hand, the mere fact that negotiations were taking place, or the fact that the employee had thought he or she would easily find another job, will not be a reason for extending the time limit – and nor will the employee's ignorance of there being a time limit.

Sometimes employees do not apply in time because they took advice and were not told that there was a time limit. When this happens, the tribunal will consider the status and qualifications of the person who gave the advice. If it was a 'skilled' adviser (such as a lawyer, trade union official or Citizens' Advice Bureau worker) then the late claim may be turned down. The employee will not be able to claim unfair dismissal but will probably be able to sue the skilled adviser for negligence in giving bad advice. If the advice came from an 'unskilled' source (such as a work colleague) then a late claim may be allowed.

Before making the claim

To win their claim, employees will have to show that they were employed for at least two years and also that they were dismissed. It is therefore advisable for them to:

1 Collect together the relevant papers. These will usually include the letter of appointment, the written particulars of their employment contract, copies of the firm's disciplinary rules and procedures, staff handbook works rules and pension booklet; their last wages slip, their P45 form and any letter of dismissal that was sent. If necessary they should ask the employer for copies.
2 Ask the employer to provide written reasons for dismissal. The employer must provide this information (see page 449). The answers will let the employee know how the employer intends to defend the claim. The answers should be checked with any letter of dismissal to see if there is any inconsistency.

Filling in the application form

The application form is called an IT 1. Its full title is 'Originating Application to an Industrial Tribunal'. Copies can be obtained, free, from any Job Centre, employment office or unemployment office.

The IT 1 form is largely self-explanatory. There are only two questions that are worthy of mention:

IT 1 question No. 1: 'Say what type of complaint(s) you want the tribunal to decide.'

Usually the answer will simply be 'unfair dismissal' or 'redundancy payment'.

IT 1 question No. 10: 'Give full details of your complaint.'

The employee should set out a brief summary of the case. There is no need to reveal all the details of the case, but it should provide the employer with enough information to enable him or her to defend the claim properly.

The employee should remember that the tribunal will look at the IT 1 when it hears the case. They will be looking to see whether the employee has been consistent in the grounds for his/her claim, and has not changed the story since filling in the form.

The application form should be sent to the Secretary to the Tribunals, Central Office of the Industrial Tribunals (England and Wales), Southgate Street, Bury St Edmunds, Suffolk IP33 2AQ. For Scotland the address is St Andrew House, 141 West Nile Street, Glasgow G1 2RU. The application will be registered and sent to the employee's local tribunal, which will acknowledge receipt of the IT 1. It is vital that the form arrives within the three-month period.

The employer's response

A copy of the IT 1 is sent to the employer. He or she then has fourteen days in which to reply to the claim. Usually, this is done by filling in form IT 3 (sent to the employer with the IT 1).

Employers must first decide whether they intend to argue that there was no dismissal – perhaps because the employee resigned. But often the employer will admit that there was a dismissal, going on to argue that it was a 'fair' dismissal.

The employer will need to take great care in stating the reason for the dismissal. The reason given on the IT 3 should be the same as the reason originally given to the worker when he or she was dismissed or when supplied with written reasons for the dismissal. For instance, suppose the original reason was bad timekeeping, but the employer now gives the reason as insubordination. If this happens the tribunal will be suspicious of the employer's consistency and, in addition, it may well decide that the employer never gave the employee a chance to answer the insubordination charge. If that were so, the employer would not have acted 'reasonably' and so the dismissal would be unfair.

Employers should also check whether they gave the employee a reference. If

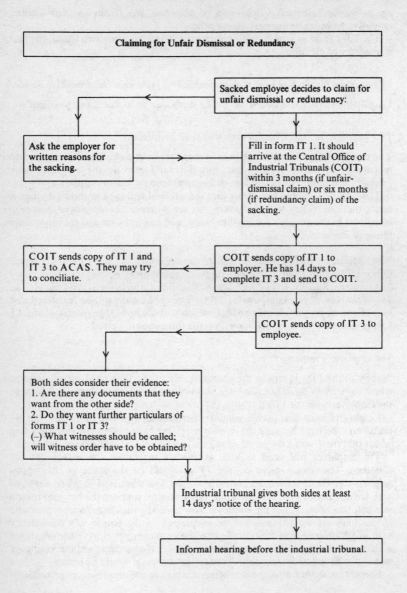

Claiming for Unfair Dismissal or Redundancy

Sacked employee decides to claim for unfair dismissal or redundancy:

Ask the employer for written reasons for the sacking.

Fill in form IT 1. It should arrive at the Central Office of Industrial Tribunals (COIT) within 3 months (if unfair-dismissal claim) or six months (if redundancy claim) of the sacking.

COIT sends copy of IT 1 and IT 3 to ACAS. They may try to conciliate.

COIT sends copy of IT 1 to employer. He has 14 days to complete IT 3 and send to COIT.

COIT sends copy of IT 3 to employee.

Both sides consider their evidence:
1. Are there any documents that they want from the other side?
2. Do they want further particulars of forms IT 1 or IT 3?
(–) What witnesses should be called; will witness order have to be obtained?

Industrial tribunal gives both sides at least 14 days' notice of the hearing.

Informal hearing before the industrial tribunal.

so, they should make sure that the reference is not inconsistent with what is said to be the reason for the dismissal. For instance, if the reference describes the employee as 'reliable and hard-working' the employer can hardly give 'incompetence' as the reason for his dismissal.

Conciliation

A copy of the IT 1 is also sent to a conciliation officer of ACAS, who will try to negotiate a settlement if asked to by either employer or employee, or if he or she 'considers that he [or she] could act with a reasonable prospect of success'. The officer will ask both employer and employee whether he or she can help by conciliating. There is no obligation on either to discuss the case with the conciliation officer or to cooperate with him/her in any way. The tribunal will not be told of a refusal to cooperate. Any information given to the conciliation officer is confidential, so there is no danger of its being revealed to the tribunal.

Generally, it is sensible to use the conciliation officer's service. He or she can provide objective advice (but will not say if an offer is high enough!) and can have a calming influence on injured feelings.

Settling out of court

Many claims are settled without the case being heard by a tribunal. However, a settlement will not be binding on the employee unless it is approved beforehand by a conciliation officer. This is so even if the employee signs a receipt that he or she accepts the offer 'in full and final settlement' of the claim.

The practice which grew up during the 1980s of getting a conciliation officer to 'rubber stamp' a settlement already concluded between the parties (albeit that with the involvement of ACAS the settlement terms were invariably fair) has ended, and unless there is a real dispute between the parties (with or without an IT 1 having been submitted to the industrial tribunal) and the settlement is genuinely referred to the conciliation officer for settlement, ACAS will not bless any settlement concluded between the parties.

Preparing for the hearing

Both employer and employee should prepare their cases well in advance. To do this they will want to find out as much as they can about each other's evidence and arguments.

Obtaining all the relevant documents

Either employer or employee can ask for copies of the other's relevant documents. This is called 'discovery of documents'.

For instance, employees could ask for their personnel file, copies of internal memos, time and motion studies, time sheets, disciplinary records, disciplinary letters sent to them, and the employer's note of what happened at any disciplinary meeting or appeal. They could also ask for a copy of the written particulars of their employment contract (or the employment contract itself, if it was in writing) should they have mislaid their own copy.

An employer might ask to be given copies of sick notes, medical reports and details of the employee's efforts to find a new job.

In short, any document that is relevant can be asked for. To obtain discovery of documents the employer or employee should first write to the other, setting out the documents required. If the letter is ignored or the request is refused, the next step is to write to the secretary to the tribunal, enclosing a copy of the previous letter and asking that an order be made. Normally, the order will be made without the need for a hearing.

Obtaining further particulars

Either employer or employee can ask for more detail of the other's case. This is done by asking for 'further and better particulars' of the answers given on forms IT 1 and IT 3.

For instance, suppose an employer's IT 3 states that the employee was unable to cope satisfactorily with her duties and that her attitude to the job was wrong. In such a case, the employee can ask for more information – 'In what way is it alleged that I could not cope with my duties'? and 'In what way is it alleged that my attitude to the job was wrong'? The employer will then have to reply with specific instances.

It is often advisable for an employee to ask for further and better particulars to show whether employers followed the proper disciplinary procedures. If they did not, they may not have acted 'reasonably' and so may lose the case.

It will therefore often be useful for an employee to ask: 'State the date and nature of any warnings that were given to me, by whom they were made, and in whose presence. State when the decision to dismiss me was taken and by whom. State when I was advised that I could appeal against the decision, and by whom.' Questions of this sort can tie employers down and cause them considerable difficulties.

Applying for 'further and better particulars' is done in the same way as applying for discovery of documents.

Witnesses

It is helpful to go through witnesses' evidence with them before the hearing. But witnesses cannot be made to cooperate. Although they can be forced to attend the tribunal hearing, they are under no obligation to speak to either employer or employee before the hearing.

The witnesses should be asked to attend voluntarily, without a *witness order* being made. But sometimes it will help witnesses if they are ordered to attend.

For instance, a shop steward will be reluctant to attend to give evidence for the employer since it may put him in an embarrassing position with his members. By obtaining a witness order, the employer allows the shop steward to say that he had no choice but to attend.

To obtain a witness order the employer or employee should write to the industrial tribunal stating that witnesses are unwilling to attend without an order, and also explaining why their evidence is required. The tribunal will normally make the witness order and it will then be for the employer or employee to serve it on the witnesses. If there is any doubt about a witness being willing to attend, the order should be handed to him or her in person (not posted).

Working out how much the case is worth

Both sides should decide how much the claim is worth. Many claims are settled at the last minute, often a few minutes before the hearing is due to start. So both employer and employee should know the figure (if any) at which they would be prepared to settle.

In many claims the real issues in dispute will be
- did the employees contribute to his or her own dismissal?
- has the employee done all he or she can to reduce his or her losses?

Employees should therefore go prepared to fight both these suggestions. In particular, they should have written evidence of their efforts to find a new job and the number of interviews they have attended, as well as receipts for all their expenses.

The pre-hearing assessment

Sometimes there will be a preliminary hearing before the case is properly heard. This is an informal hearing designed to weed out the hopeless cases.

A preliminary hearing is not held in every case. It can be held either at the request of one of the parties (usually the employer) or if the tribunal thinks such a hearing would be useful. No evidence is heard and the tribunal members consider the merits of the case on the basis of the originating application (IT 1) and notice of appearance (IT 3). They cannot prevent the applicant from continuing with a claim, nor can they give judgement. However, they can advise either party as to the weakness of a case and remind them that costs can be awarded at the tribunal hearing if the claim (or defence) is 'without merit'.

Indirectly, therefore, hopeless claims are warned off.

The hearing of the claim

Both employer and employee will be given at least fourteen days' notice of the hearing. Both should ensure that their witnesses can attend on that date. If they can't, then the hearing should be postponed.

Who speaks first?

The hearing usually begins with the tribunal chair making a short introductory speech and then asking both sides to make an 'opening statement'. The idea is that the tribunal, and the other side, should have an idea of what each party will say and the evidence that will be produced. The case then begins in earnest.

Who speaks first will depend upon whether 'dismissal' is at issue. If the employer denies that the employee was 'dismissed' (e.g. it could be argued that he or she resigned), then the employee presents his/her case first and calls witnesses. But if the employer admits that the employee was 'dismissed', then the issue to be decided is whether the dismissal was 'unfair'. So, in that case, the employer presents his/her case first and calls his/her witnesses.

When a witness has given his/her evidence he/she can be cross-examined by the other side, as in any court case. But the normal rules of evidence are relaxed in tribunal hearings. Thus *hearsay* evidence is allowed (e.g. 'John told me he had seen Brian hit the foreman' will be allowed, although it would still be better to call John to describe what he saw).

Written evidence is also acceptable. But the tribunal will prefer the evidence of a witness in person to that of a written statement, since there can be no cross-examination of what is said in a written document.

The employee should be sure to take all relevant documents to the hearing, such as:

- contract of employment;
- pay details (e.g. wage slips, P 60);
- details of fringe benefits (e.g. luncheon vouchers, use of car, travelling expenses);
- pension and superannuation documents;
- details of income tax refunds received;
- particulars of unemployment benefit received;
- receipts and documents connected with expenses in looking for a new job (e.g. travel expenses, household removal expenses).

The decision

When both sides have presented their evidence they will be allowed to make concluding statements. Then the members of the tribunal will retire and probably announce their decision a few minutes later. In complicated cases the tribunal may *reserve* its decision, which means that the parties will be sent a written decision at a later date.

Costs

Each party will normally have to pay their own legal costs (if any) whether they win or lose. Only when a party has acted *frivolously*, *vexatiously* or *unreasonably* will costs be awarded against them. For instance, an employee who presses on with a claim despite being warned at a pre-hearing assessment that the case is hopeless might well have to pay some of the employer's legal costs.

In addition, costs and expenses can be awarded when a postponement was asked for without good reason. For instance, if the employer turns up at the hearing and then decides that he or she wants to be legally represented, the tribunal might agree to a postponement but order him/her to pay the employee's wasted costs. But even these orders are rare.

Limited expenses, however, are often ordered for the parties and their witnesses. The expenses of representatives are only allowed if the representative was not a lawyer or a full-time trade union or employers' association official.

Anyone thinking of bringing an unfair-dismissal claim should read *Industrial Tribunals Procedure* (free from the Department of Employment or COIT).

29 Winning An Unfair-Dismissal Claim

If employees win their unfair-dismissal claim, the industrial tribunal can make one of three orders:

1 That they be re-employed by the employer and given their *old job* back (reinstatement).
2 That they be re-employed by the employer, but given a *different job* (re-engagement).
3 That they be paid a *cash sum*.

The decision on which order to make will depend on the wishes of employees and the circumstances of the case. The tribunal will explain the differences between the three remedies and ask employees which one they would prefer.

1. REINSTATEMENT

If employees ask for their old job back, the tribunal will consider whether it would be practicable and also whether the justice of the situation would make it fair on the employer. For instance, if the employee's own behaviour contributed to his/her dismissal, the tribunal might well decide it would be unfair on the employer to insist on reinstatement.

The 'practicability' of reinstatement can include such matters as harmony in the workplace and the feelings of the other staff. The fact that the employer has taken on a replacement for the dismissed employee can also be relevant, but usually employers will have to show that they did not realize the employee would ask for the job back. This is why it is advisable for employees to ask for reinstatement when they fill in the unfair-dismissal application form.

However, in practice, reinstatement is virtually never ordered.

2. RE-ENGAGEMENT

This can be ordered by the tribunal at the request of the employee, but only if the job is suitable and the terms and conditions are comparable to those of the employee's old job.

Similar considerations arise as with an order for reinstatement. In practice, it is virtually never ordered.

3. CASH COMPENSATION

A cash award is made in over 99 per cent of successful claims.

The total cash sum will be made up of two separate amounts:
- the *basic* award (up to £6,150) (1992);
- the *compensatory* award (up to £10,000) (1992);

In practice, few awards reach these maximum figures; £1,000 or so is a typical award. The award will be tax-free.

Calculating the basic award

The basic award gives employees the amount of redundancy payment they would have received if they had been made redundant instead. The size of the redundancy payment (and thus the basic award) will depend upon the age of the employee, the length of service and the amount of the weekly net wage. He or she will receive a certain number of weeks' wages depending on age and length of service. The table on page 493 sets out how the award is calculated.

The maximum award is thirty weeks' wages. However, an additional restriction is imposed because the maximum net wage allowed is £205 p.w. (1992).

Illustration. *Mr Jones earns £65 p.w. net. He is aged twenty-four and has worked with the firm for two years. His basic award is thus two weeks' wages (see table): i.e. 2 × 65 = £130.*

Illustration. *Mr Smith earns £225 p.w. net. He is now aged fifty-five and has been with his employers for seventeen years. His basic award is thus twenty-four weeks' wages (see table), but up to a maximum of £205 p.w.: i.e. 24 × 205 = £4,920.*

However, the tribunal can reduce the basic award if it is felt that the employee's own conduct contributed to his/her dismissal. For instance, if the employer had a fair reason for dismissal but failed to follow the proper procedures, the employee might win the case but forfeit some (or all) of the compensation because of his/her behaviour. Similarly, the award can be reduced if the employee unreasonably refuses an offer of his/her job back. See When the Employee's Behaviour Reduces the Compensation, page 492.

Employees near retirement age

An employee who is within one year of his/her sixty-fifth birthday will lose one twelfth of his/her compensation for each whole month after his/her birthday.

The basic award will also be reduced by any amount that the employee has received as a redundancy payment. So an employee who is unfairly selected for redundancy would normally receive no basic award.

Calculating the compensatory award

This is intended to cover the employee's losses resulting from dismissal. The maximum award is £10,000.

The compensatory award will usually be made up of:

• *Lost earnings to the date of the hearing.* This is the net wage loss. It is the amount that employees would have received had they carried on working, after allowing for tax, national insurance, other deductions, and also any earnings from their new job (if any). If employees were not paid during the period of notice (see page 445), then they should receive full compensation for those lost wages – even if they found another job and so did not suffer any actual loss during the notice period. But once the notice period ends, other earnings are taken into account. For example: an employee should have been given four weeks' notice, but is sacked on the spot. His wages were £100 p.w. but he gets another job paying £70 p.w. for a period of seven weeks, after which he gets another job paying £100 p.w. His lost earnings will be £490 (i.e. 4 × £100, plus 3 × £30).

• *Future loss of earnings.* If employees are still out of work, or if they have taken on a new job at a lower wage, they will have a continuing wage loss. Tribunals are generally reluctant to apply strict mathematical calculations when working out the loss, and will only rarely allow more than five years' loss. In practice, tribunals tend to round down rather than round up, and so employees receive less compensation than a strictly mathematical calculation would entitle them to.

If the tribunal feels that employees have not done all they could to 'mitigate their loss' (i.e. keep losses to a minimum) it will usually reduce the award. Thus a tribunal will often decide that employees should have made greater efforts to find another job or that they should have accepted a lower rate of pay (as in a wrongful-dismissal claim, see page 447).

• *Loss of employment protection rights.* Employees will have lost the right to notice built up by the length of their service. They will also have lost the other employment protection rights which are given only to staff who have worked for qualifying periods (see the table on pages 408–9). For instance, employees will have no entitlement to redundancy payments in their new job until they have worked there for two years. A fairly notional figure in respect of the value of these rights is applied in practice: about £100.

• *Expenses in looking for work.* Looking for a new job can be expensive. Travel, phone calls, advertisements and subscriptions to trade journals can all be expenses arising from the dismissal. Sometimes the cost of moving home to take up a new job will be recoverable in part.

When the employee's behaviour reduces the compensation

The industrial tribunal can reduce the basic award and the compensation if it is felt that the employee's behaviour contributed to the dismissal. The courts have

Compensation for unfair dismissal: how many weeks' wages?

Age (*years*)	*Service (years)* 2	3	4	5	6	7	8	9	10	11	12	13	14	15	16	17	18	19	20
20	1	1	1	1															
21	1	1½	1½	1½	1½														
22	1	1½	2	2	2	2													
23	1½	2	2½	3	3	3	3												
24	2	2½	3	3½	4	4	4	4											
25	2	3	3½	4	4½	5	5	5	5										
26	2	3	4	4½	5	5½	6	6	6	6									
27	2	3	4	5	5½	6	6½	7	7	7	7								
28	2	3	4	5	6	6½	7	7½	8	8	8	8							
29	2	3	4	5	6	7	7½	8	8½	9	9	9	9						
30	2	3	4	5	6	7	8	8½	9	9½	10	10	10	10					
31	2	3	4	5	6	7	8	9	9½	10	10½	11	11	11	11				
32	2	3	4	5	6	7	8	9	10	10½	11	11½	12	12	12	12			
33	2	3	4	5	6	7	8	9	10	11	11½	12	12½	13	13	13	13		
34	2	3	4	5	6	7	8	9	10	11	12	12½	13	13½	14	14	14	14	
35	2	3	4	5	6	7	8	9	10	11	12	13	13½	14	14½	15	15	15	15
36	2	3	4	5	6	7	8	9	10	11	12	13	14	14½	15	15½	16	16	16
37	2	3	4	5	6	7	8	9	10	11	12	13	14	15	15½	16	16½	17	17
38	2	3	4	5	6	7	8	9	10	11	12	13	14	15	16	16½	17	17½	18
39	2	3	4	5	6	7	8	9	10	11	12	13	14	15	16	17	17½	18	18½
40	2	3	4	5	6	7	8	9	10	11	12	13	14	15	16	17	18	18½	19
41	2	3	4	5	6	7	8	9	10	11	12	13	14	15	16	17	18	19	19½
42	2½	3½	4½	5½	6½	7½	8½	9½	10½	11½	12½	13½	14½	15½	16½	17½	18½	19½	20½
43	3	4	5	6	7	8	9	10	11	12	13	14	15	16	17	18	19	20	21
44	3	4½	5½	6½	7½	8½	9½	10½	11½	12½	13½	14½	15½	16½	17½	18½	19½	20½	21½
45	3	4½	6	7	8	9	10	11	12	13	14	15	16	17	18	19	20	21	22
46	3	4½	6	7½	8½	9½	10½	11½	12½	13½	14½	15½	16½	17½	18½	19½	20½	21½	22½
47	3	4½	6	7½	9	10	11	12	13	14	15	16	17	18	19	20	21	22	23
48	3	4½	6	7½	9	10½	11½	12½	13½	14½	15½	16½	17½	18½	19½	20½	21½	22½	23½
49	3	4½	6	7½	9	10½	12	13	14	15	16	17	18	19	20	21	22	23	24
50	3	4½	6	7½	9	10½	12	13½	14½	15½	16½	17½	18½	19½	20½	21½	22½	23½	24½
51	3	4½	6	7½	9	10½	12	13½	15	16	17	18	19	20	21	22	23	24	25
52	3	4½	6	7½	9	10½	12	13½	15	16½	17½	18½	19½	20½	21½	22½	23½	24½	25½
53	3	4½	6	7½	9	10½	12	13½	15	16½	18	19	20	21	22	23	24	25	26
54	3	4½	6	7½	9	10½	12	13½	15	16½	18	19½	20½	21½	22½	23½	24½	25½	26½
55	3	4½	6	7½	9	10½	12	13½	15	16½	18	19½	21	22	23	24	25	26	27
56	3	4½	6	7½	9	10½	12	13½	15	16½	18	19½	21	22½	23½	24½	25½	26½	27½
57	3	4½	6	7½	9	10½	12	13½	15	16½	18	19½	21	22½	24	25	26	27	28
58	3	4½	6	7½	9	10½	12	13½	15	16½	18	19½	21	22½	24	25½	26½	27½	28½
59	3	4½	6	7½	9	10½	12	13½	15	16½	18	19½	21	22½	24	25½	27	28	29
60	3	4½	6	7½	9	10½	12	13½	15	16½	18	19½	21	22½	24	25½	27	28½	29½
61	3	4½	6	7½	9	10½	12	13½	15	16½	18	19½	21	22½	24	25½	27	28½	30
62	3	4½	6	7½	9	10½	12	13½	15	16½	18	19½	21	22½	24	25½	27	28½	30
63	3	4½	6	7½	9	10½	12	13½	15	16½	18	19½	21	22½	24	25½	27	28½	30
64	3	4½	6	7½	9	10½	12	13½	15	16½	18	19½	21	22½	24	25½	27	28½	30

not laid down any guidelines as to what is conduct justifying a reduction in the amount of the award. In practice, the tribunal has a considerable discretion and the 'contributory fault' rule will often be used to reduce an employee's compensation to what the tribunal members regard as being reasonable. This is all part of the rough-and-ready approach that tribunals take when calculating compensation.

The contributory fault need not amount to a deliberate act by the employee, although he or she must have been blameworthy or culpable. But employees can be found to have contributed to their dismissal even when they did not mean to exacerbate the situation.

An employee won his unfair-dismissal claim but had his compensation reduced by 40 per cent because his character and personality had contributed to his dismissal. He appealed, saying that his character and personality were beyond his control and so shouldn't be taken into account. Held: The tribunal acted correctly in reducing the award by 40 per cent. Moncur (1978)

Only exceptionally will contributory fault exceed 80 per cent. But it can be as much as 100 per cent.

The employee was dismissed unfairly. Shortly after his dismissal the employers discovered that he had been taking secret commissions from the customers. He won his unfair-dismissal claim but he received nothing because the contributory fault was assessed at 100 per cent. W. Devis & Sons (1977)

Similarly, if the employer offers to give the employee his/her job back but the employee unreasonably refuses to accept, the compensation can be reduced by whatever percentage the tribunal thinks fair. But in this instance, it is only the basic award that can be reduced; the compensatory award cannot be reduced.

Because of the contributory-fault rule, employees bringing an unfair-dismissal claim should be ready to rebut all allegations that their employers may make against them. The problem is that if employers make enough allegations against them, the tribunal may eventually believe some of them, and so reduce the award.

Extra cash in exceptional cases

Occasionally, the employer will have to make an additional cash payment to the employee. This happens when a tribunal has ordered the employer to re-engage or reinstate the employee, but the employer has not done so. The employer can be ordered to pay extra compensation of between thirteen and twenty-six weeks' wages. If the refusal to re-employ is because of sexual or racial discrimination, the extra compensation is between twenty-six and fifty-two weeks' wages. (As usual, there is a maximum rate of £205 (1992) p.w.) Exceptionally, the employee may be entitled to even more compensation – if it is a trade union-related case (i.e. because he or she was – or was not – a member of a union; or, because of union activities). Special rules apply but the minimum award is £2,700 plus compensation of up to £10,000 and where the employee applies for re-engagement or reinstatement (it is not necessary that this should be ordered) if the tribunal does not order it, a 'special award' of 104 weeks' pay or £13,400 (1992), whichever is the greater, but subject to a maximum of £26,800 will be made. If ordered, and the employer fails to comply, an award of 156 weeks' pay or £20,100 (1992), whichever is the greater, will be made.

Enforcing the cash award

Both employer and employee have six weeks in which to appeal against the tribunal's decision. Once that period has expired, and if no appeal has been made, the employee can sue the employer for the cash owed. If the employer does not pay up, the employee should sue in the civil courts in the usual way for any debt. The claim will be brought in the county court.

Criticisms of the unfair-dismissal legislation

The major weakness of the legislation is its technicality, which makes it difficult for both employer and employee to know just what the law is. As the president of the Employment Appeals Tribunal has said: 'Unfair dismissal is in no sense a commonsense expression capable of being understood by the man in the street ... In fact, it is narrowly, and to some extent, arbitrarily, defined.' But it is difficult to see how this complexity can be avoided. The alternative is to scrap the detailed rules and give the tribunals a greater discretion, but at the price of even greater uncertainty as to the law.

Many people argue that the cash awards made by tribunals are too low. Although in theory the awards can run into thousands of pounds, typical awards are around £1,700. Certainly there are arguments for increasing the amount of the basic award.

Some of the rules as to who is excluded from the legislation are rather arbitrary (see pages 408–9). The exclusion of part-time workers effectively ensures that many women workers have no unfair-dismissal rights. The exclusion of those past retirement age, while perfectly logical, often causes a sense of grievance.

Is it fair that employees should have to be employed for two years before they come within the legislation? Why have any qualifying period? The present two-year rule encourages employers to sack staff before they have been employed for 104 weeks and replace them with other temporary staff. This is especially true in the hotel and catering trades.

Even if employees are within the legislation, will they bother to use it to enforce their rights? There are two disincentives:

1 There is no legal aid for industrial tribunal cases. If employees do not have a trade union that will act for them, they will have to act for themselves or pay a solicitor to represent them. Many employees are reluctant to act for themselves, and since the sacked employee may well have financial problems, and be living on state benefits, he or she will be in no position to instruct a solicitor, so incurring legal costs.
2 If employees are legally represented, and win the case, they will not have their legal costs paid by their employer. They will have to come out of the compensation.

Employers also have their criticisms of the legislation. Many argue that it is too easy for an employee to bring an unfair-dismissal claim. They suggest there should be a small registration fee to deter the cranks and those with hopeless cases. Some would like to see the losing employee paying part of the employer's legal costs.

The cost to an employer of defending a claim can be considerable. Apart from the expense of legal fees, the employer may have senior staff and personnel wasting time at the hearing of the case as they wait to give evidence.

Sometimes an employer will decide it is cheaper to 'buy off' the claim rather than go to the expense and inconvenience of defending it. In short, they argue that they are being blackmailed into settling hopeless cases for their 'nuisance value'. Against this it can fairly be said that many employers incur lawyers' fees unnecessarily, when they could easily defend the case themselves or through a member of staff.

30 Redundancy Payments

The redundancy-payments scheme was introduced in 1965 to compensate redundant workers for the loss of their jobs. This simple aim was initially frustrated by a series of court decisions that applied a narrow, restrictive interpretation to the key sections of the legislation. However, in recent years, most of these difficulties have been overcome, although the redundancy-payments scheme remains a highly technical and complex form of compensation. The modern law is set out in the Employment Protection (Consolidation) Act 1978.

Apart from giving employees some 'property' rights in their job, the redundancy-payments scheme was also designed to increase job mobility by cushioning the financial effects of redundancy. However, it seems unlikely that the scheme has encouraged mobility of labour, because the mere fact that employers might have to make a redundancy payment is likely to encourage them to retain staff rather than make them redundant.

WHAT IS NEEDED FOR A SUCCESSFUL CLAIM?

There are three hurdles that need to be met by employees who want to claim redundancy payments:

1 Are they within the redundancy-payments legislation or are they ineligible?
2 Have they been 'dismissed' by their employer?
3 Were they dismissed because they were 'redundant'?

Once the employee has cleared the first two hurdles, it is for the employer to show that the employee was *not* dismissed because of redundancy. The burden of proof is on employers; if they cannot show that it was not a redundancy situation, then they will lose the claim.

If the employee's claim is successful, he or she is entitled to a cash sum, the amount of which varies with their age and the length of service with the employer. It is irrelevant that he or she may have obtained another job, even if it is better paid. He or she is being compensated for the loss of job – not for a period of unemployment.

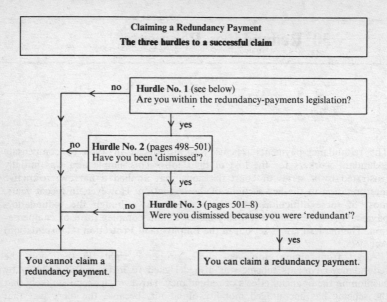

| **Claiming a Redundancy Payment** |
| **The three hurdles to a successful claim** |

Hurdle No. 1: Are employees within the redundancy-payments legislation?

Not all employees are eligible. Part-timers and those beyond retirement age are among those specifically excluded. For full details of ineligible employees see the table on pages 408–9 and the chart on page 499.

In practice, the most important restraint on eligibility is the two-year qualifying period. Employees can claim a payment only if they have been continuously employed, by the employer, for at least two years.

The qualification period is therefore the same as with an unfair-dismissal claim – two years.

Hurdle No. 2: Have the employees been 'dismissed' by their employer?

A redundancy payment can be claimed only if the employees have been 'dismissed'. In law, 'dismissal' is not restricted to sackings but also covers the situation where employees have been forced to resign because of the conduct of their employer ('constructive dismissal', see page 462). Generally, for the legal meaning of 'dismissal', see Unfair Dismissal (page 456), where similar principles apply. Do not forget that people with fixed-term contracts will count as having been 'dismissed' if they are not offered a new contract:

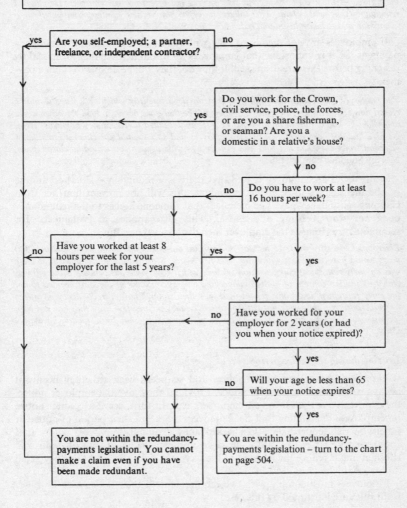

Are You within the Redundancy-payments Legislation?

yes ← Are you self-employed; a partner, freelance, or independent contractor? → no

Do you work for the Crown, civil service, police, the forces, or are you a share fisherman, or seaman? Are you a domestic in a relative's house? ← yes

no ↓

Do you have to work at least 16 hours per week? ← no

Have you worked at least 8 hours per week for your employer for the last 5 years? → yes

no ←

↓ yes

Have you worked for your employer for 2 years (or had you when your notice expired)? ← no

↓ yes

Will your age be less than 65 when your notice expires? ← no

↓ yes

You are not within the redundancy-payments legislation. You cannot make a claim even if you have been made redundant.

You are within the redundancy-payments legislation – turn to the chart on page 504.

Mr Lee was taken on as a temporary lecturer in a teacher-training college for one year. At the end of that year he was offered another one year's employment, although he realized that the declining number of students would mean that his services would not be needed in the future. At the end of the second year he was not offered a new contract. He claimed redundancy payment. Held: The failure to offer him a new contract amounted to a 'dismissal' and so he could claim a redundancy payment. Notts CC (1980)

If employees are not dismissed they will not be able to claim a redundancy payment. So it is important that employees do not anticipate their dismissal by resigning before they are dismissed. If they do, they will be unable to claim a payment:

The employee was told by his employers that the department in which he worked would be closed down some time in the future. The employee therefore began to look for other work, and when he had arranged another job he left, and claimed a redundancy payment. Held: No. He had not been dismissed by his employers and so he could not claim a redundancy payment, since they had not told him exactly when his department would be closed down. Morton Sundour Fabrics (1967)

However, if an employee is told that there is a redundancy situation and he or she then agrees to be made redundant, this will not prevent him/her from claiming redundancy pay. The mere fact that someone agrees to the redundancy does not stop it being a dismissal. This also applies to 'volunteers' for redundancy, as long as the employer then dismisses them. But:

Liverpool University wrote to its staff saying that cut-backs had to be made and that 300 posts would have to be lost within the next few years. Staff were also reminded that there was an early-retirement compensation scheme, which gave generous benefits if the job was ended by mutual consent of both employer and employee. Some of the staff decided to opt for early retirement under this scheme and they then claimed normal redundancy payments as well. Held: No, they were not entitled to redundancy payments – since they had not been 'dismissed'. The jobs had been ended by mutual agreement, not by dismissal. Liverpool Univ. (1984)

Leaving during the notice period

If employees have been given notice, and so been dismissed, they need not always work out the period of notice. Provided they give the employer notice, they can leave early. However, employers can, in turn, serve a counter-notice on employees demanding that the employees work out their period of notice or otherwise risk jeopardizing their redundancy claim. If employees ignore that counter-notice, they can still claim a redundancy payment, but an industrial tribunal might reduce the amount of the payment if it is decided that they acted 'unreasonably'.

Employees must comply with two requirements if their notice is to be valid. Both rules are illustrated by this case:

An employee was given four and a half weeks' notice, although under the statutory rules as to notice (see page 445) he was only entitled to two weeks. The employee found another job and gave his employers oral notice a week after they had given him notice of his dismissal. Held: He was ineligible for redundancy because:

● *the notice to his employers should have been in writing, not oral*; and
● *the notice to his employers had to be served during the statutory period of notice (i.e. the last two weeks). He had served the notice before the statutory period had started and so the notice was invalid.* Lobb (1966)

Clearly these rules as to the employee's notice are unnecessarily complicated and are a pitfall for the unwary. Full details are in s.85 of the 1978 Act.

The effect of misconduct and industrial action

Employees may jeopardize their redundancy rights if they are in breach of their employment contract by misbehaving at work or by taking part in industrial action.

The effect of their breach of contract will depend upon whether it takes place before they are dismissed:
● *misconduct and/or strikes before the redundancy is announced* will cause employees to forfeit their right to a redundancy payment;
● *misconduct and/or strikes after the redundancy is announced* will not necessarily cause employees to forfeit their redundancy payment. However, an industrial tribunal will award them only what it regards as a 'just and equitable' amount, so the gravity of their breach of contract – and the circumstances in which it occurred – will determine the amount received.

The rules on striking against redundancy are complicated and they are a pitfall for the unwary. Workers should take expert advice – but bear in mind that dismissal of all the strikers where industrial action is official or selected participants during industrial action where it is unofficial will not be unfair dismissal (see page 476), so they clearly run the risk of forfeiting both redundancy and unfair-dismissal entitlements.

Hurdle No. 3. Were the employees dismissed because they were redundant?

In a redundancy claim, an industrial tribunal will assume that the employee was 'redundant' unless the employer can show otherwise.

Usually it is easy to decide whether employees have been made redundant. The simple test that will normally answer the question is to ask, 'Has the dismissed employee been replaced by another employee?' If they have, it will not be redundancy. If they have not, then it will probably be redundancy.

But this test will not cover every situation. It is possible for an employee not to be replaced and yet not be redundant:

Mr Hindle was a craftsman with a lifetime's experience of boat building. But his employers decided that he was 'too good and too slow' for their requirements. So he was dismissed. No replacement was taken on, but the remaining employees worked overtime to make up for the loss of his services. Held: This was not redundancy. The employer had shown that redundancy was not the reason for the dismissal and that was sufficient to defeat Mr Hindle's claim. The Court of Appeal said: 'All an employer must do is to prove that redundancy was not the main cause and he does this by proving that the requirements of the business for workers of the relevant kind had not diminished. It is not the policy of this Act to reward long service and good conduct, as such, but only to compensate an employee who is dismissed for redundancy.' Hindle (1969)

Note that this decision was reached in 1969, some two years before the unfair-dismissal legislation was introduced. There can be little doubt that if Mr Hindle was dismissed in the same way today, he would be able to claim unfair dismissal and so recover compensation from his employers. This is a point that should always be borne in mind; if employees are not 'redundant' they may be able to claim unfair dismissal. They will be better off for doing so since unfair-dismissal compensation usually exceeds redundancy compensation.

Unfair dismissal and redundancy

It will be remembered that to defend an unfair-dismissal claim, employers must show that:
- they had a fair reason for dismissing the employee, *and*
- they behaved reasonably.
- 'Redundancy' is a 'fair' reason for dismissing employees. So usually redundant employees cannot claim unfair dismissal. However, they will be able to do so if the employer did not behave 'reasonably' (if, e.g., the employee was unfairly selected for redundancy). In such a case employees can claim a redundancy payment and also unfair dismissal, although the amount of their unfair-dismissal compensation will be reduced by the amount of their redundancy payment (see page 491).

So while most redundant employees cannot claim unfair dismissal, in the exceptional case the employee who has not been treated 'reasonably' can claim both redundancy and unfair dismissal.

Selection criteria

If the employee is unfairly selected for redundancy then an unfair-dismissal claim may be brought. This will involve looking at the reasonableness of the criteria used by the employer for deciding who should be selected. 'Last in, first out' used to be the usual criterion and tribunals will normally accept this as a fair method of selection. Recently, more discretionary criteria have become widespread (e.g. 'capability, qualification and performance' of relevant staff), in which case there is much more scope for the employee to argue that the criteria are unfair. For instance, an employee who is generally uncooperative and unhelpful could not be properly selected on the basis of 'performance' since those personal characteristics will not normally be relevant to how he or she performs the job.

As a generalization, the tribunals will expect an employer to follow these five principles of good industrial-relations practice:

1 Give as much warning as possible of the possibility of redundancies.
2 Consult with the union as to what should be the selection criteria.

3 Use objective criteria for selection (e.g. attendance record, length of service), not personal opinions.
4 Follow these criteria closely when deciding who is to be made redundant.
5 Check that there are no other alternative jobs available.

One point to note is that a 'part-timers first' rule will almost certainly run into difficulties – not from the redundancy-payments laws, but from the sex-discrimination laws. Nationally, over 80 per cent of part-timers are women, and a 1982 case held that it would therefore be 'grossly discriminatory' to have a 'part-timers first' rule when deciding which staff were to be made redundant.

When does 'redundancy' exist?

'Redundancy' is defined in s.81 of the Employment Protection (Consolidation) Act 1978. The effect of the section is that redundancy exists when:
- the firm closes;
- in certain circumstances where the business is taken over;
- the firm moves;
- the employee's work is reduced;
- the employee is laid off or put on short time.

The firm closes

There is usually no problem in recognizing a redundancy when the firm closes down. However, complications arise if the firm is taken over.

The business is taken over

This is one of the areas of employment law where European legislation is having an influence. If a business is transferred as a going concern, the Transfer of Undertakings (Protection of Employment) Regulations 1981 (based on an EC directive) transfers the contracts of employment of those working in the business to the new owner and there is no 'dismissal' as a result of the transfer. This is not the case where what is sold is merely assets (i.e. the business does not transfer as a going concern) and in such a case the workforce will usually be redundant and able to claim redundancy payment.

Where the business is being sold as a going concern (i.e. with the benefit of stock, goodwill, existing contracts and customer contacts), if during the course of the transfer of the business either the old or the new owner dismisses employees as redundant, they will be entitled to a redundancy payment, except where the new owner offers continued employment before the notice given to employees expires. In fact, however, the 1981 Regulations provide that a dismissal in such circumstances is automatically unfair except where it is for an 'economic, technical or organizational reason entailing changes in the workforce' (which would cover a genuine redundancy situation). The 1981 Regulations are

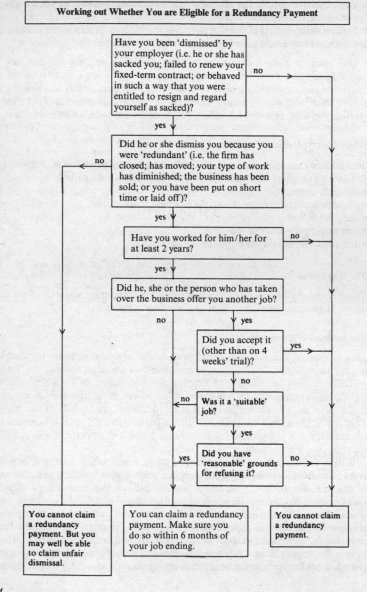

Working out Whether You are Eligible for a Redundancy Payment

Have you been 'dismissed' by your employer (i.e. he or she has sacked you; failed to renew your fixed-term contract; or behaved in such a way that you were entitled to resign and regard yourself as sacked)? — no →

yes ↓

Did he or she dismiss you because you were 'redundant' (i.e. the firm has closed; has moved; your type of work has diminished; the business has been sold; or you have been put on short time or laid off)? ← no

yes ↓

Have you worked for him/her for at least 2 years? — no →

yes ↓

Did he, she or the person who has taken over the business offer you another job?

no ↓   yes ↓

Did you accept it (other than on 4 weeks' trial)? — yes →

no ↓

Was it a 'suitable' job? ← no

yes ↓

Did you have 'reasonable' grounds for refusing it? — no →
yes ←

You cannot claim a redundancy payment. But you may well be able to claim unfair dismissal.

You can claim a redundancy payment. Make sure you do so within 6 months of your job ending.

You cannot claim a redundancy payment.

complex in their operation and also lay down requirements for information to be provided to and consultation to take place with any recognized trade union before any transfer takes place. Such is the complexity of this area that specialist advice is always needed. So seek expert help in a situation such as this.

The firm moves

A firm may transfer its operations to a different plant in another place. Can the employees refuse to move and declare themselves to be redundant?

The answer will depend upon the terms of the employees' contract of employment. If it contains a job-mobility clause, requiring them to move when requested, then they will be in breach of contract if they refuse to move. So they will be unable to claim redundancy. On the other hand, if it does not contain a job-mobility clause, then their employers cannot insist that they move, and they can claim redundancy, unless the move is so trivial as to make it unreasonable to refuse (e.g. a move to the next street). Relatively few employment contracts have specific job-mobility clauses. Generally, an employer will try to *imply* a job-mobility clause into the contract, but a lot will depend on what is the practice in the particular industry.

Two employees worked in a firm's north-western area office, which covered an area from mid-Wales to Cumberland. The office was in Liverpool, and their work allowed them to return home every day. However, work in the Liverpool area declined and so the employers decided to move the office to Barrow-in-Furness, 120 miles away. The two employees claimed a redundancy payment. The employers argued that it was an implied term of the employment contracts that the men would be prepared to work well away from home. Held: No. The only clause that could be implied was that the men would work within daily travelling distance of their homes. So while the employers could move the office from Liverpool, they could not move it so far away. So the redundancy claims succeeded. O'Brien (1968)

When there is a job-mobility clause, then the employee who refuses to move will have no right to a redundancy payment. So an engineer moved from RAF Marham to RAF Kinloss and an atomic-energy worker transferred from Orfordness to Aldermaston were both unable to claim redundancy.

The employee's work is reduced

Reorganizations, productivity agreements and new working methods can all lead to a reduction in the number of staff needed, or to a reduction in the need for the particular kind of work done by an employee.

When this happens there will almost certainly be redundancy. But a mere reorganization will not be redundancy unless the amount of work to be done is reduced. Altering the hours of work cannot of itself be redundancy – although if the imposition of a new working schedule is not authorized by the employment contract, the employee may be able to claim unfair dismissal.

An employee worked a five-day week from 9.30 a.m. to 5.30 p.m. Her employers changed her to a six-day week, from 8 a.m. to 3 p.m. and noon to 8 p.m. alternate weeks. She refused to accept the change and was dismissed. She claimed she had been made redundant. Held: No. The employers needed just as many employees as previously, it was just that they were needed at different hours. So this was not redundancy. Johnson (1974)

Even if the reorganization leads to a shorter working week, it will not be redundancy unless the length of the week is reduced below that promised by the employment contract.

The makers of Matchbox Toys reorganized their production system because of a decline in sales. The effect of the changes was to alter the hours of work and, more important, to reduce the overtime that the men worked. Six men refused to accept the changes and claimed redundancy, saying that the decline in overtime resulted from the fall in sales. Held: This was not redundancy because the employers were under no obligation to provide overtime work. Lesney Products (1977)

Difficulties can arise when the employer still needs employees to do a particular type of work, but decides that the employee is no longer suitable for that type of work. An example is Mr Hindle, who was 'too good and too slow' and yet his dismissal was not due to redundancy (see page 501). Other examples include:

A barmaid was sacked after eighteen years' service. The management wanted to change the image of the pub and so decided 'young blondes and bunny girls' should serve behind the bar. The sacked barmaid claimed redundancy. Held: No. The employers still needed barmaids so it could not be a case of redundancy. Vaux Breweries (1968)

The workshop manager of a garage was dismissed when new owners took over the garage business, despite his having worked there for thirty years. He was unable to do crash-repair estimates, which his previous boss had done, and so his new employers found him to be unsuitable. He claimed redundancy. Held: No. The work of the repair shop had not diminished and so it could not be a redundancy situation. North Riding Garages (1967)

Note that some of these cases were heard before the unfair-dismissal laws were introduced. So today those employees would be able to claim unfair dismissal as an alternative to claiming redundancy. Often such a claim will succeed, on the basis that it was unfair to reorganize the working arrangements. But not always: if the bulk of the rest of the staff accept the changes then the tribunal will probably decide that it is not unfair dismissal. For instance, in a 1984 case, a shift supervisor refused to change from night shifts to day shifts because of her family commitments. It was held that this was not redundancy but nor was it unfair dismissal (since the reorganization had been agreed with the unions and supported by 80 per cent of the staff in a ballot).

Generally, if the dismissed employee is replaced by another employee, then that will be clear evidence that the amount of work has not diminished, and so it cannot be a case of redundancy. However, this applies only if the dismissed employee is replaced by another *employee* – not if he or she is replaced by a self-employed contractor, or lump labour (i.e. self-employed contractors).

Two painters and decorators were sacked by their employer. He replaced them with lump labour, and argued that it could not be redundancy since there had been no decline in the amount of work – as was evidenced by his having replaced the two men. Held: This was redundancy. The two men had not been replaced by employees, so there was a decline in the amount of work available for employees. Bromby (1971)

The employee is laid off or put on short time

Occasionally employees who have been laid off or put on short-time working can claim redundancy payment. This is so even if their employment contract allows their employer to lay them off or put them on short time (see page 420). The law is set out in s.88 of the 1978 Act. The section is complicated and an employee who is thinking of making a redundancy claim under it should take advice from a solicitor or trade union official.

Basically, s.88 allows employees to declare themselves redundant if they have been laid off (i.e. received no pay) or put on short-time working (i.e. received half a week's pay or less) for:

● four consecutive weeks, *or*
● six of the last thirteen weeks.

Employees have four weeks in which to serve a notice on their employer. The notice must be in writing and state that they intend to claim a redundancy payment; in addition they must give in their notice of resignation. The employer then has seven days in which to serve a written counter-notice saying that he or she will dispute the claim and that, within the next four weeks, full-time working will resume and will continue for at least thirteen weeks without lay-off or short time.

If the employer does not serve a counter-notice, then employees are entitled to their redundancy payment. However, if a counter-notice is served the industrial tribunal will consider the matter and the employees may well lose their payment if work was in fact available as promised by the employer.

The offer of another job

Employees may lose their redundancy payment if they turn down the offer of another job from their employer.

If the new job is *identical* to their old job and they refuse it, they will definitely forfeit redundancy payment.

If the new job is in any way *different* from their old job, then they can try it out for a 'trial period' of up to four weeks. If they decide to reject the job, they will lose their redundancy payment if the job was 'suitable' for them and if they acted 'unreasonably' in refusing it.

The offer must be made by the employer or by the person taking over the firm. The employer cannot try to evade his/her liability to pay redundancy money by finding a job for the employee with a different firm.

In addition, it will be a valid offer only if:

- it is made before (and not after) the old job ends;
- the new job will start no later than four weeks after the end of the old job;
- the offer describes the new job in sufficient detail. It must be more than a vague offer of employment.

If the employer does not fulfil these conditions, then the 'alternative job' rules will not apply. So even if the employer is certain that the employee will reject the new job, he or she must go through the formalities of offering it to the employee.

Refusing the offer

If the new job is identical to the old job, employees will lose their redundancy payment if they refuse to take the new job.

The complications arise when the new job differs from the old job. Then employees can try it out for up to four weeks. If at the end of that four weeks they decide to reject the new job, they can apply for their redundancy payment. They are not obliged to try out the new job on a trial period – they can simply refuse it as soon as it is offered to them. However, if they do this, it is more likely that the tribunal will decide that they acted 'unreasonably' in rejecting the job.

If employees reject the new job, they will forfeit their redundancy payment only if:
- the new job was '*suitable*', and
- they were '*unreasonable*' in refusing it.

Whether a job is 'suitable' will depend upon its terms and conditions; such matters as pay, fringe benefits, the job description and the place of work will all be relevant. The question of whether it was 'reasonable' for the employee to reject the job will depend more on the employee's personal circumstances; the travel involved in the new job, its effect on his/her home life and any loss of status will all be relevant.

In practice, industrial tribunals treat 'suitability' and 'reasonableness' in similar ways. Rather than consider them as two separate criteria they tend to be amalgamated into a general test of whether the employee should have accepted the new job.

Claiming a redundancy payment

Employees must claim their redundancy payment within six months of the end of their old job. If they do not, they may well forfeit their right to a payment.

The claim can be made either to the employer or to an industrial tribunal. Either way the claim should be in writing and should be made within the six-month period. If the claim is made to the employer and the employer does not make the payment, the employee can then apply to an industrial tribunal even if the six-month period has expired by then.

The time for claiming

The general rule is that redundancy claims must be made within six months of dismissal (unlike unfair-dismissal claims, in which there is only a three-month time period). This six-month period can be extended, but the sensible advice is to avoid any difficulties by making a claim to the industrial tribunal within the six-month period.

The amount of the redundancy payment

The amount of the payment is worked out by allowing employees a fixed number of weeks' wages for the number of years they have worked for the employer:
- each year worked between the ages of eighteen and twenty-one gives the employee half a week's pay;
- each year worked between the ages of twenty-two and forty gives the employee one week's pay;
- each year worked between the ages of forty-one and sixty-five gives the employee one and a half weeks' pay.

Service below the age of eighteen does not count, and the maximum number of years of service that can be taken into account is twenty. The table on page 493 sets out how these rules work. When assessing the amount of the payment, any weekly wage in excess of £205 (1992) is ignored.

Illustration. An employee joined a firm at the age of fifteen. At the age of thirty-five he is made redundant. At the time of his dismissal he earns £210 p.w. He has twenty years' service but service under the age of eighteen is ignored, so he only has seventeen years' allowable service. Referring to the table, it will be seen that an employee of thirty-five with seventeen years' service is entitled to a payment of fifteen weeks' wages. However, the maximum weekly wage allowed is £205, so his redundancy payment will be 15 × 205 = £3,075.

The redundancy payment will usually be tax-free.

Employees Near Retirement Age

Employees who are near retirement age will lose part of their redundancy payment. A woman or a man aged sixty-four will lose one-twelfth of the payment for every additional month of their age. Thus an employee aged sixty-four years and nine months will lose three-quarters of his or her redundancy payment.

If the employer is insolvent, employees can still claim their redundancy payment. If necessary, the Department of Employment will make the payment to the employee and then try to recover the money from the employer.

REDUNDANCY: THE EMPLOYER'S DUTY TO CONSULT

Every employer who is planning to introduce redundancies has a general duty to 'give as much warning as possible to the employees concerned'. This was recommended by the old industrial relations code of practice and if employers ignore the principle they may be found to have behaved 'unreasonably' and so lose an unfair-dismissal claim (see page 502).

In addition, there is a more specific duty to consult with the trade unions, but only if the unions are recognized by the employers. If the employers have recognized union(s) then if they are planning:

● to make 100 or more employees redundant within a period of ninety days,
or

● to make ten or more employees redundant within a period of thirty days, they must notify the union(s) (and the Department of Employment) at least ninety days and thirty days (respectively) beforehand.

S. 99 of the 1978 Act requires the employer to provide the union with details of:

● the reasons for the redundancies;
● the number of employees to be made redundant and the type of work they do;
● the total number of staff doing that type of work;
● how it is proposed to decide who should be selected for redundancy (e.g. 'last in, first out');
● how the dismissals are to be carried out and over how long a period.

Sanctions

If employers do not comply with these consultation provisions, the union (but not the individual employees) can complain to an industrial tribunal. Employers will lose the case unless they can show that there were 'special circumstances' why they couldn't comply with s. 99 (perhaps because of a sudden bankruptcy) and that they took all 'reasonably practicable' steps.

In addition, the tribunal can order employers to pay compensation to the individual employees. This is called a *protective award* and can be the employees' wages for the length of notice that should have been given (i.e. up to ninety days' pay if ninety days' notice is appropriate; up to thirty days' pay for thirty days' notice; up to twenty-eight days' pay in any other case).

In practice the consultation provisions are largely ignored and most employers simply close down without notice, but pay their staff the compensation which would be required if a protective award were made. Thus the consultation rules are generally a financial rather than a procedural obstacle to declaring redundancies.

GOLDEN HANDSHAKES

Redundancy payments are always tax-free. In addition, employees may receive termination payments from their employers when made redundant or sacked;

generally, this is called a 'golden handshake'. Often the employee will pay little or no tax on this sum because the first £30,000 (inclusive of a redundancy payment) (1992) received is tax-free.

Note that money in lieu of wages will generally be regarded as a golden handshake and not normal taxable earnings, even though strictly speaking it is taxable. Accrued holiday pay will be taxed.

TIME OFF TO LOOK FOR A JOB

If employees with two years' service have been given notice of redundancy, they are entitled to take paid time off work to look for a new job.

The employer must allow time off for the employee to:
• look for new employment, *or*
• make arrangements for job training (note: they are allowed time off only to *arrange* the training – they cannot demand time off for actual training).

The employer must pay the employee during the time off.

The difficulty arises in deciding what is a 'reasonable' amount of time for the employee to be allowed off. While this will depend on the facts of the individual case, it seems that a total of two days will often be the maximum.

If the employer refuses to allow the employee to take time off, the employee has three months in which to complain to an industrial tribunal. The tribunal will penalize the employers only if it was 'unreasonable' of them to refuse the time off, so if there was a staff shortage or other crisis they might be able to refuse time off.

If employers are found to have been 'unreasonable' they can be 'fined' by being ordered to pay the employee up to two days' wages. Because this is the maximum penalty, the clear implication is that more than two days' leave will be an unreasonable amount of time off.

31 Trade Unionism and the Law

THE RIGHT TO BE A TRADE UNIONIST

Every employee has a legal right to join an independent trade union. An employer who interferes with this right can be ordered to pay compensation to the employee (s.23, Employment Protection (Consolidation) Act 1978).

It is not only straightforward sacking for trade union activities that is prohibited. Less draconian measures which amount to victimization of the unionist, such as unfair disciplinary measures, excessive zeal by a supervisor and unjustified refusal of promotion, are also unlawful.

But the law protects the employee only if the trade union activities are taking place outside working hours or, if in working hours, the employer had previously given his/her consent to such activities taking place. So normally the trade union member who carries out union activities during working hours will not be protected.

A new employee in a bus firm joined the TGWU and actively tried to recruit new members amongst his work-mates. The firm did not recognize the union and to thwart the employee's efforts he was transferred to another job which isolated him from the other staff. He claimed that the firm had victimized him because of his trade union activities. Held: Yes. He had been victimized, but he could not receive any redress from the law. His union activities had taken place during working hours and accordingly it was not unlawful for the employers to victimize him. Robb (1978)

Occasionally tribunals have held that management have implicitly given their consent to union activities during working hours, but such cases are rare and the activist would be unwise to rely on such an implied permission.

'Working hours' is confined to the hours when employees work; it does not include their meal, rest and tea breaks. So they can complain if they are dismissed or victimized for trade union activities carried out during off-work periods, even if these activities took place on the employer's premises (e.g. meeting in the canteen during the dinner break).

Unfortunately the Employment Protection (Consolidation) Act does not define what 'trade union activities' are permitted. It would seem that the usual union organizational work of collecting subscriptions and distributing union literature is protected. But beyond that, the law is unclear; the test laid down in some cases has been that permitted union activities must not cause 'substantial inconvenience' to the firm – hardly a clear guideline to those involved. In practice, the tribunals tend to apply a narrow and restrictive meaning to the phrase so that unofficial action over a pay claim would probably not be a permitted activity.

However, concern over health and safety matters will probably count as trade union activities.

Mr Drew was a parks gardener. During his three months' employment he frequently made complaints over health and safety matters. He was eventually sacked when he refused to clear snow during an official go-slow. He claimed unfair dismissal, arguing that he had really been sacked because of his health and safety complaints, and that these were trade union activities. Held: It was not unfair dismissal. While health and safety matters were 'trade union activities', only trade union officials and safety representatives could bring them forward. Individual union members, such as Mr Drew, could pursue such matters only outside working hours. The 1978 Act protected unionists only if their trade union activities took place either:

● *outside working hours, or*
● *within working hours with the employer's consent.* Drew (1980)

If Mr Drew had been acting in an official trade union capacity he would, of course, have been protected.

The right to take part in union activities applies only to members of *independent* unions. These are unions that have been certified by the government's certification officer as being independent of employers and employers' organizations. The union need not be recognized for its members to be protected. However, if the union is recognized then additional rights accrue; members can take part in certain activities during working hours and officials can take paid leave to deal with their union duties (see page 517).

When activists are dismissed or victimized they should complain to an industrial tribunal within three months.

If they have been *dismissed* there is a special procedure available which is designed to reinstate them in their job until the proper, lengthy hearing of their claim. This is called an application for 'interim relief' and it must be made within seven days of the dismissal. At the full hearing of the unfair-dismissal claim it is for the employee to show that the employer dismissed him or her for trade union reasons (i.e. union membership or activities). In practice it can be extremely difficult to do this and few employees succeed in doing so. It is usually fairly easy for the employer to argue that there was some other reason for the dismissal, such as misconduct or poor time-keeping.

Do not forget that if the activist is on strike, or taking part in industrial action, it will not be unfair dismissal (where the action is official) if *all* those still out on strike are sacked. Mass dismissals are permitted; victimization is not (see page 476). (However, if the action is unofficial the position is different (see also page 476.

If the employee has not been dismissed but has been *victimized*, he or she has three months in which to apply to the industrial tribunal. It will be for the employer to prove to the tribunal that the action taken against the employee was not motivated by anti-union intentions. If the employer cannot do so, the employee will win the case (cf. dismissal, above, where it is employees who must prove their case). But the tribunal will want to be sure that the employers *intended* to victimize the employee; so even though the effect of their actions was to victimize unionists, they will not be liable if they can show that this was not the intention. If the employee's complaint is upheld, the employers can be ordered to pay compensation (there is no maximum limit).

Ineligible employees. Not all employees are protected against victimization and dismissal for union activities. In particular, part-timers are excluded. For full details see the table on pages 408-9. The protection is also not available to prospective employees.

A well-known trade union activist used a false name when applying for a job. He did this because he knew that he would not get the job if the employers knew his true identity. But soon the employers found out who he was and told him he could not have the job. He claimed he had been dismissed for his trade-union activities. Held: No. The law protected staff only from dismissal and victimization *resulting from trade union activities, not against* being refused employment *on those grounds.* City of Birmingham (1977)

Time off work for union duties and activities

If employers recognize a trade union, they must be prepared to allow members and officials of the union to take time off work for their duties and activities.

Union officials

Union officials, as opposed to mere members, can take 'a reasonable' amount of *paid* time off work for:
● industrial relations duties between employer and employees (e.g. collective bargaining, talking to members about negotiations, appearing before tribunals, lecturing new employees), *and*
● industrial relations training on a course approved by their union or the TUC.

The description 'union official' is not restricted to paid officials of the union. It covers any lay union official who has been constitutionally appointed or elected. So it includes shop stewards and staff representatives but probably not branch secretaries.

ACAS have published a Code of Practice which gives guidance on how the rules are to be applied. However, the code does not define what is a 'reasonable' amount of time – that will depend on such factors as the size of the firm, the employee's position, the pressure on the firm etc.

Union members

Union members can take a 'reasonable' amount of *unpaid* time off work to carry out their trade union activities. The ACAS Code of Practice does not define 'union activities' but the term usually covers attendance at policy-making meetings of the union, representing the union on committees, voting in union elections and sometimes attendance at union meetings. (For further information, see the ACAS Code of Practice, obtainable from HMSO.) If employees are not allowed to take time off they can complain to an industrial tribunal within three months. The tribunal can order the employer to award cash compensation.

Ineligible employees. These time-off provisions apply only if the employer has recognized the union. In addition, certain employees (such as part-timers) are excluded. See the table on pages 408–9.

The closed shop

1988 saw the removal of the last vestiges of the legislation legitimizing the closed shop, so long a part of the industrial relations scene. Total priority is now given to individual freedom in that the employee's right not to join a union means that it is unfair to dismiss an employee for refusing to join a trade union and unlawful for an employer to take action short of dismissal to compel an employee to join a union. Similarly, there is the right not to be unfairly dismissed or victimized for refusing to make a payment in the event of failure to become or ceasing to remain a member of a trade union. In addition, where a non-unionist wants to become a member of a union in order to obtain or retain employment, he or she has a statutory right not to be excluded from the union in question. Aside from this, the Independent Review Committee of the TUC will hear complaints, if the applicant has exhausted the union's complaints procedure. The Committee can recommend that the individual be admitted to the union, but the recommendation is not legally binding. However, the TUC say that there is a 'clear responsibility' on unions to accept the Committee's recommendations.

Against this background, while there is no reason why a closed shop should not be created (it is not unlawful), there is in practice no way of keeping it in place, save by the will and the consent of all those involved.

LEGAL PROTECTION FOR UNIONS AND STRIKERS

During the nineteenth century it was virtually impossible for trade unions to take effective industrial action and yet be acting within the law. As soon as they found a means of bringing pressure to bear on employers, the judges would decide that this new activity infringed an old common-law rule. Accordingly, the police could bring prosecutions and the employers could sue the unions and their members, and also obtain injunctions preventing the action from taking place. Such obscure civil laws as conspiracy, procuring breach of contract, intimidation and unlawful interference with trade were all used to make trade union activities unlawful.

In the end Parliament had to step in to protect the unions from these common-law offences – and indeed from the ingenuity of the judiciary, who kept finding ways of curbing union activities. The first major piece of legislation to protect the unions was the Trade Union Act 1871, which led to the Trades Disputes Act 1906, and the protection given by that Act has survived as the basis of the modern law on trade union immunity, until rewritten by the 1982 Employment Act (itself amended further still in 1988 and 1990).

The 1982 Act gives trade unions immunity from being sued for nearly all the old common-law offences, but only if they are pursuing legitimate trade union objectives. In the words of the Act, they must be acting 'in contemplation or furtherance of a trade dispute'.

Over the years there have been numerous decisions as to what is, or is not, a 'trade dispute'. Obviously, a trade dispute exists when there is an argument as to the terms of work, allocation of work, sackings, discipline at work or the provision of union facilities. The 1982 Employment Act gave the phrase 'trade dispute' a narrower meaning than had previously been the case. So an inter-union dispute (i.e. one not involving an employer) is not a trade dispute, and nor is a dispute involving an employer who does not have any staff involved in the dispute (e.g. if he or she is a supplier of another employer whose staff are on strike). Similarly, if the motives behind the union's actions are political or personal, then it will not be a trade dispute.

The union representing BBC engineers intended to ask its members not to transmit the Cup Final unless the BBC agreed that the programme should not be relayed to South Africa. The BBC sought an injunction preventing the ban. The union argued that there was a trade dispute and so the court could not grant the injunction. Held: There was no trade dispute. The action was due to political motivations and an injunction would be granted. BBC (1977)

Similarly, a one-day protest strike against the Industrial Relations Act was held not to be a trade dispute. In another case, a union strike pressurized an employer into sacking an employee but this was held not to be a trade dispute because the union's action was motivated by the individual officer's personal grudge against the employee concerned.

The important point to grasp is that if it is a 'trade dispute' then the union will be protected from some of the old common-law claims for damages that could otherwise be brought against it – provided there was a strike ballot beforehand (see page 518). But, even then, if it acts unlawfully (e.g. by taking secondary action – such as blacking a firm that supplies the firm whose employees are on strike), then it can be liable in damages. If the union fails to repudiate such unlawful action then it can be sued. Obviously arguments can then arise over whether the union did approve of the unlawful action, but the Employment Act 1982 tackles this by making it liable where the Act has been authorized or endorsed by any person empowered by the union's rules to do so, the principal Executive Committee, the President or General Secretary of the union, any other committee of the union or any official (whether employed by the union or not), and has not been repudiated by the union without delay and in the manner provided for in the EA 1982.

To summarize, one can say that unions now have only limited protection from being sued. If they ballot and they are involved in a genuine trade dispute (i.e. action taken for industrial reasons by staff against their employer) then the union will be exempt from being sued (e.g. for any lost profits caused to the company by the strike). But if the action becomes unlawful, then the union can be sued – for instance, for those lost profits. And even then, the union might be liable if it did not hold a secret ballot before the industrial action took place (see page 518).

One thing that will be obvious to any reader is that the whole area of trade unions and the law has become absurdly complicated – largely because successive governments have altered the law to favour their own views. Specialist advice is needed to anyone who is thinking of entering this legal minefield.

Union recognition

It is to a union's advantage to be recognized by an employer. It then has certain rights that are denied to a union that is not recognized:

1 It can demand to have certain bargaining information disclosed to it.
2 It must be consulted over proposed redundancies (see page 509–10).
3 It must be informed and consulted when all or part of the employer's business is to be transferred.
4 Its members and officials can take time off work to carry out their union duties and activities (see page 514).
5 It must be consulted over the provision of occupational pension schemes.
6 The employer must, on request, allow his/her premises to be used for secret ballots held by the union (if in connection with strikes, industrial action, union and staff representative elections, or the rules of the union).
7 It has the right to information and to be consulted under the health and safety legislation.

But employers cannot be made to recognize a union, even if the majority of their employees are union members. Recognition of a union can be only a voluntary act by the employer.

The legal effects of going on strike

Suing

Employees who go on strike, or take other industrial action, are likely to be in breach of their contract of employment. Theoretically then, their employer could bring a civil action against them and sue for breach of contract. However, if they were sued, the damages payable would be the cost to the employer of hiring substitute labour, but the court might well express its disapproval of the employer's claim by refusing to award costs.

Apart from the breach-of-contract claim, strikers (and their supporters) could be sued for various torts – such as inducing breach of contract, interference with trade and conspiracy. Many of these torts were 'invented' by the judges in the nineteenth century when trying to extend the liability of strikers and unions. However, the Trade Disputes Act 1906 gave a defence to such tort claims if the defendant was acting 'in contemplation or furtherance of a trade dispute'. As we have seen above, the definition of what is a 'trade dispute' has been narrowed in recent years and so too has the extent to which unions (and their officials) are protected from being sued (e.g. by an employer who has lost sales because of a strike). A union will be safe from being sued only if:

- there is a genuine trade dispute, *and*
- a secret ballot was held no more than four weeks beforehand.

The need for a strike ballot. The Trade Union Act 1984 requires there to be a ballot before any strike or industrial action (i.e. anything that breaks the contract of employment) takes place if the union is to avoid being sued. The ballot must be secret; it must be no more than four weeks before the action is taken; only those likely to take part in the action can vote; postal votes must be accepted. In short, there are detailed rules as to how the ballots are to be held and if these rules are not followed then the union will lose its immunity from being sued (e.g. by an employer who has lost profits because of a strike). So whereas prior to 1984 a union was immune from being sued if the strike was a genuine 'trade dispute', now there is a second hurdle to be overcome – was there a secret ballot?

If there isn't a genuine trade dispute, or if there was not a secret ballot, then the union can be sued for damages.

Secondary action. The press often talk about 'secondary action'. This is when union action is taken against an employer who is not a direct party to the dispute (i.e. someone who does not employ the striking staff but might, for instance, supply their employer with materials). Since 1990 secondary action has been unlawful except where it occurs in the course of lawful picketing. As a consequence, the union can be sued for it. (See page 517.)

Wages

Strikers lose the right to be paid while they are on strike. Whether or not they will be able to demand strike pay from their union will depend upon whether the union has made the strike 'official' and, if so, whether the union has exercised its discretion to award strike pay.

Dismissal

Employers can dismiss a striker, and if they do so while the employee is still on strike, the dismissal cannot be held unfair, unless the employer did not dismiss *all* the striking employees (i.e. everyone who is still out on strike) in circumstances where the industrial action is official. An employer can selectively dismiss trade union officials or activists while engaging in industrial action where this is unofficial.

Social-security benefits

Unemployment benefit

People laid off because of a strike cannot claim unemployment benefit if they are either participating in the strike (e.g. on strike, refusing to cross a picket line), or if they are directly interested in the outcome (e.g. if they will receive higher wages themselves through a knock-on effect).

Statutory sick pay

A person receiving SSP when the strike starts will continue to be entitled to it. But strikers who fall ill after the strike has begun cannot then claim SSP unless they can show that they are neither participating in the strike nor directly interested in it (see above). They will still not be eligible for SSP when the strike ends – instead they will be entitled to sickness benefit from the DSS.

Family credit

A striker receiving FC when the strike begins continues to be entitled to it until it next has to be renewed (it normally runs in a twenty-six-week period of entitlement). No new FC claim can be made by a person on strike, but the partner or spouse may be able to claim it.

Education and health benefits

Entitlement to help with fares, free school meals, prescriptions etc. is unaffected by a strike – and indeed many strikers will immediately become eligible for these benefits.

Housing benefit

Entitlement should not be affected by there being a strike (except that housing-benefit supplement may be lost). Many strikers will find it advisable to claim housing benefit.

Tax rebates

PAYE refunds are no longer made at the start of a strike.

Income support

There are severe restrictions on the claiming of IS by strikers and their families. The basic rule is that there is no entitlement to benefit if there is a trade dispute – assuming that the person is participating in the dispute, or is directly involved in it (i.e. as with unemployment benefit – above). As far as single strikers are concerned (i.e. no family), there will be no entitlement to benefit except that in a few urgent cases payments may be available (although housing benefit should be paid in full). For strikers with families, there are complicated rules but the basic effect is that IS is available for the family but not for the striker. Normally, the family will get IS, but without the amount that would usually be included for the striker (generally, of course, the man) and in addition there will be a further deduction of £22.50 (1992), which is supposed to represent the amount of strike pay the union is assumed to be paying.

Payments from the Social Fund

Budgeting loans, crisis loans and community care grants are generally speaking not payable to claimants or their partners who are involved in or affected by a strike or industrial action, although funeral and cold weather payments remain payable.

Working out entitlement to social-security benefits is always extremely difficult, because the system is so complicated. When strikers are involved the position is even worse and it therefore follows that strikers and their families should always seek expert help on their benefit entitlements (rather than rely on what the DSS says). Unions, CABs, law centres and the Child Poverty Action Group are obvious starting-points when looking for this specialist help.

ON THE PICKET LINE

It is on the picket line that trade unionists are most likely to fall foul of the law.

Picketing, of course, can mean different things to different people. The word originates from a military term used to describe guards who man an outpost so as to give advance warning of an attack. Today, simple picketing involves a few strikers standing at the work gates to remind their fellow workers that there is a strike in progress and perhaps to persuade them to support the pickets by not working. 'Mass picketing' is simple picketing but with numerous pickets taking part and so physically blocking the work entrance. In addition, there are 'flying pickets' and 'ghost pickets', each of which has different characteristics.

There are two ways in which pickets can become involved with the law:

• if the picketing is unlawful, the employer can use the *civil law* to obtain an injunction ordering the picketing to stop;
• if the pickets break the *criminal law*, the pickets can be prosecuted.

Picketing and the civil law

The basic rule is that there is no legal right to picket. Thus the civil courts will grant an injunction ordering the pickets to stop. The only exception is when the picketing comes within s.15 of the Trade Union and Labour Relations Act 1974, which makes it lawful for 'a person in contemplation or furtherance of a trade dispute' to attend at or near his or her own workplace 'for the purpose only of peacefully obtaining or communicating information or peacefully persuading any person to work or abstain from working'.

In short, workers can picket their own workplace, but not someone else's. Secondary picketing (i.e. when employees of A picket workplace B) is therefore illegal and the employer can obtain an injunction to stop the picketing.

For the picketing to comply with s.15, it must come within each of the three following categories. If it does not, an injunction can be obtained:

1 *The only people who can picket are*:
   • employees;
   • full-time union officers and national officers of the union, who can join their members on the picket line;
   • ex-employees sacked during the dispute (unless they have since found other jobs).
2 *The only places that can be picketed are*:
   • the workplace – that is, the entrances to the premises but not inside the premises, since that would be trespass;
   • if there is more than one place of work (e.g. if the pickets are van drivers, building workers) or if it is impractical to picket the workplace (e.g. if the pickets are miners or seamen) then they can picket other premises. The Code of Practice suggests they picket 'those premises of their employer from which ... their work is administered. In the case of lorry drivers, for example, this will usually mean in practice the premises from which their vehicles operate'.
3 *The only picketing that is lawful is*:
   • for the purpose *only* of peacefully obtaining or communicating information or peacefully persuading any person to work or abstain from working. For instance, if the picket goes beyond peaceful persuasion it will be unlawful. In this respect, the recommendations of the code are of great importance. Violence and disorder on the picket line is more likely to occur if there are excessive numbers of pickets. Wherever large numbers of people with strong feelings are involved there is a danger that the situation will get out of control .. particularly so wherever people seek by sheer weight of numbers to stop others going into work or delivering or collecting goods. .... Accordingly pickets and their organizers should ensure that in general the number of

pickets does not exceed six at any entrance to, or exit from, a workplace; frequently a smaller number will be appropriate.' Whilst the code is not legally binding, a court will give great weight to it when deciding whether to grant an injunction to stop the picketing.
• if it is 'in contemplation or furtherance of a trade dispute' (see page 516). Thus political and consumer pickets are unlawful and can be stopped by an injunction.

Section 15 of the 1974 Act does not allow pickets to stop vehicles so that they can then communicate with, or persuade, the drivers of the vehicles not to enter the employer's premises. In theory this seriously limits the protection given by s.15 since the stopping of supplies in lorries is usually a main objective of a picket line. In practice, however, the police use their discretion to allow the stopping of vehicles as long as it is done in an orderly manner.

Broome was picketing a building site. He tried to persuade a lorry driver not to enter but the driver refused. Broome then stood in front of the lorry, still arguing with the driver. He was arrested and charged with obstructing the highway. He was found guilty, for although he was trying to 'peacefully persuade' the lorry driver not to cross the picket line, he was also trying to stop the driver and detain him against his will. It was said that the section 'does not confer any right on any picket to stop anyone or to stop any vehicle in order to try to persuade persons not to work'. Hunt (1974)

Picketing and the criminal law

Completely separate from the civil law (above) is the criminal law. If pickets commit a criminal offence the police can prosecute them irrespective of whether they are protected by s.15 of the 1974 Act from civil action. Thus a picket can be protected by s.15 and yet act illegally. As the Code of Practice says: 'If a picket commits a criminal offence he is just as liable to prosecution as any other member of the public who breaks the law. The immunity provided by the civil law does not protect him in any way.'

In practice, it is the risk of prosecution for obstruction of the highway and/or breach of the peace that is the real threat to industrial picketing. Generally, the right to picket depends upon the discretion and tolerance of the police present. The crucial element is the decision of the police on whether or not to allow the pickets to remain, or to prosecute, although usually the police are prepared to turn a blind eye to what are technical infringements of the law. However, pickets cannot be sure that their picketing will not lead to a criminal charge, however peacefully they may carry out their picketing. The two criminal charges that are most likely to be brought against a picket are obstruction of the highway and/or breach of the peace.

Obstructing the highway

It is an offence wilfully to obstruct the highway (s.137 of the Highways Act 1980 – maximum penalty £400 fine, see page 372). The offence does not apply to *every* obstruction of the highway but only to an *unreasonable* obstruction of the highway. Lord Parker has said: 'It depends on the circumstances, including the length of time the obstruction continues, the place where it occurs, the purpose for which it is done and, of course, whether it does in fact cause an actual, as opposed to a potential, obstruction.' So it is a question of fact.

But the courts are usually willing to accept the evidence of the police as to whether there was an obstruction of the highway.

Some forty pickets were circling the outside of a factory. A police officer considered that they were obstructing the highway and asked them to stop, saying he would only allow two or three people to picket. The leader of the pickets, Mr Tynan, refused to obey this instruction and was arrested for obstructing the highway. He was found guilty. It was held that section 15 did not protect Tynan because the pickets were there not merely for the purposes allowed by the section, but also in order to block off part of the highway. Tynan (1967)

In that case the pickets were moving; they were circling the factory. They did this because they thought it would reduce their chances of being accused of obstructing the highway. They argued that since they were on the move they were using the highway for a legitimate purpose and so could not be guilty of obstruction. The decision in the case shows that their supposition was wrong.

Mass pickets are usually unlawful because the numbers involved are an indication that there is an intention to block the highway. In practice, though, mass pickets, while often illegal, are usually effective, because mass arrests are rarely carried out for fear of inflaming the situation. However, if picketing takes place on private land (e.g. on a private entranceway to factory gates) then there can be no obstruction charge (since it is not the public highway that is being obstructed).

Conduct likely to cause a breach of the peace

It is the duty of the police to prevent a breach of the peace. 'Breach of the peace' is a very wide term and it allows police to order someone to stop doing something that is itself perfectly legal, if they think that it is likely to lead to a breach of the peace (i.e. it is likely to lead to the commission of any offence) (see page 831). So if an offence is likely to result, pickets can be told to stop. If they refuse they may be charged with conduct likely to lead to a breach of the peace or with obstructing a police officer in the execution of their duty.

The organizers of a picket had agreed with the police that the number of pickets should be limited to two at each of the two entrances to the factory. Bates wanted to join the two pickets at one of the entrances and refused to accept the limitation on numbers imposed by the police. He was not obstructing the highway, nor was he acting violently or threatening violence. He was arrested for obstructing a police officer in the execution of his duty. Held: He was guilty. It was sufficient that the constable could reasonably anticipate a real possibility of a breach of the peace. Piddington (1961)

Even if pickets are able to avoid falling foul of the two offences detailed above, there are other charges that can be used against them – for instance, if there is any violence a charge of unlawful assembly can be brought; if abusive language is used it can be threatening behaviour (see page (833). Similarly intimidation, possession of an offensive weapon (e.g. banner), criminal damage and obstructing the police can often be brought into play.

Extracts from the Code of Practice on Picketing

B. Picketing and the civil law

9 The law sets out the basic rules which must be observed if picketing is to be carried out, or organized, lawfully. To keep to these rules, attendance for the purpose of picketing may only:
  (i) be undertaken in contemplation or furtherance of a trade dispute;
  (ii) be carried out by a person attending at or near his own place of work; a trade union official, in addition to attending at or near his own place of work, may also attend at or near the place of work of a member of his trade union whom he is accompanying on the picket line and whom he represents.

Furthermore, the only purpose involved must be peacefully to obtain or communicate information, or peacefully to persuade a person to work or not to work.

10 Picketing commonly involves persuading workers to break, or interfere with the performance of, their contracts of employment by not going into work. Picketing can also disrupt the business of the employer who is being picketed by interfering with the performance of a commercial contract which the employer has with a customer or supplier. If pickets follow the rules outlined in paragraph 9, however, they may have the protection against civil proceedings afforded by the 'statutory immunities'. These rules, and immunities, are explained more fully in paragraphs 11 to 30 below.

11 Picketing is lawful only if it is carried out in contemplation or furtherance of a 'trade dispute'. A 'trade dispute' is defined in law so as to cover the matters which normally occasion disputes between employers and workers – such as terms and conditions of employment, the allocation of work, matters of discipline, trade union recognition.

12 The 'statutory immunities' do not apply to protect a threat of, or a call for or other inducement of 'secondary' industrial action. The law defines 'secondary' action – which is sometimes referred to as 'sympathy' or 'solidarity' action – as that by workers whose employer is not a party to the trade dispute to which the action relates.

13 However, a worker employed by a party to a trade dispute, picketing at his own place of work may try to persuade another worker, not employed by that employer, to break, or interfere with the performance of, the second worker's contract of employment, and/or to interfere with the performance of a commercial contract. This could happen, for example, if a picket persuaded a lorry driver employed by another employer not to cross the picket line and deliver goods to be supplied, under a commercial contract, to the employer in dispute. Such an act by a picket would be an unlawful inducement to take secondary action unless provision was made to the contrary.

14 Accordingly, the law contains provisions which make it lawful for a peaceful picket, at the picket's own place of work, to seek to persuade workers other than those employed by the picket's own employer not to work, or not to work normally. To have such protection, the peaceful picketing must be done:

a. by a worker employed by the employer who is party to the dispute; or

b. by a trade union official whose attendance is lawful.

15 Where an entrance or exit is used jointly by the workers of more than one employer, the workers who are not involved in the dispute to which a picket relates should not be interfered with by picketing activities. Particular care should be taken to ensure that picketing does not involve calls for a breach, or interference with the performance, of contracts by employees of the other employer(s) who are not involved in the dispute. Observing this principle will help avoid consequences which might otherwise be damaging and disruptive to good industrial relations.

16 It is lawful for a person to induce breach, or interference with the performance, of a contract in the course of attendance for the purpose of picketing only if he pickets at or near his own place of work.

17 The expression 'at or near his own place of work' is not further defined in statute law. The provisions mean that ... lawful picketing must be limited to attendance at, or near, an entrance to or exit from the factory, site or office at which the picket works. Picketing should be confined to a location, or locations, as near as practicable to the place of work.

18 The law does not enable a picket to attend lawfully at an entrance to, or exit from, *any* place of work other than his own. This applies even, for example, if those working at the other place of work are employed by the same employer, or are covered by the same collective bargaining arrangements as the picket.

Lawful purposes of picketing

24 In no circumstances does a picket have power, under the law, to require other people to stop, or to compel them to listen or to do what he asks them to do. A person who decides to cross a picket line *must* be allowed to do so. In addition, the law provides a remedy for any union member who is disciplined by his union because he has crossed a picket line.

25 The *only* purposes of picketing declared lawful in statute are:

• peacefully obtaining and communicating information: and

• peacefully persuading a person to work or not to work.

26 The law allows pickets to seek to explain their case to those entering or leaving the picketed premises, and/or to ask them not to enter or leave the premises where the dispute is taking place. This may be done by speaking to people, or it may involve the distribution of leaflets or the carrying of banners or placards putting the pickets' case. **In all cases, however, any such activity must be carried out *peacefully*.**

C. Picketing and the criminal law

41 If a picket commits a criminal offence he is just as liable to be prosecuted as any other member of the public who breaks the law. The immunity provided under the civil law does not protect him in any way.

42 The criminal law protects the right of every person to go about his lawful daily business free from interference by others. No one is under any obligation to stop when a picket asks him to do so or, if he does stop, to comply with the picket's

request, for example, not to go into work. Everyone has the right, if he wishes to do so, to cross a picket line in order to go into his place of work or to deliver or collect goods. A picket may exercise peaceful persuasion, but if he goes beyond that and tries by means other than peaceful persuasion to deter another person from exercising those rights he may commit a criminal offence ...

44 A picket has no right under the law to require a vehicle to stop or to be stopped. The law allows him only to ask a driver to stop by words or signals. A picket may not physically obstruct a vehicle if the driver decides to drive on or, indeed, in any other circumstances. A driver must – as on all other occasions – exercise due care and attention when approaching or driving past a picket line, and may not drive in such a manner as to give rise to a reasonably foreseeable risk of injury.

D. Role of the police

45 It is not the function of the police to take a view of the merits of a particular trade dispute. They have a general duty to uphold the law and keep the peace, whether on the picket line or elsewhere. The law gives the police discretion to take whatever measures may reasonably be considered necessary to ensure that picketing remains peaceful and and orderly.

46 The police have *no* responsibility for enforcing the *civil* law. An employer cannot require the police to help in identifying the pickets against whom he wishes to seek an order from the civil court. Nor is it the job of the police to enforce the terms of an order. Enforcement of an order on the application of a plaintiff is a matter for the court and its officers. The police may, however, decide to assist the officers of the court if they think there may be a breach of the peace.

47 As regards the *criminal law* the police have considerable discretionary powers to limit the number of pickets at any one place where they have reasonable cause to fear disorder. The law does not impose a specific limit on the number of people who may picket at any one place; nor does this Code affect in any way the discretion of the police to limit the number of people on a particular picket line. It is for the police to decide, taking into account all the circumstances, whether the number of pickets at any particular place is likely to lead to a breach of the peace. If a picket does not leave the picket line when asked to do so by the police, he is liable to be arrested for obstruction either of the highway or of a police officer in the execution of his duty if the obstruction is such as to cause, or be likely to cause, a breach of the peace.

E. Limiting numbers of pickets

51 Large numbers on a picket line are also likely to give rise to fear and resentment amongst those seeking to cross that picket line even where no criminal offence is committed. They exacerbate disputes and sour relations not only between management and employees but between the pickets and their fellow employees. Accordingly pickets and their organizers should ensure that in general the number of pickets does not exceed six at any entrance to a work-place; frequently a smaller number will be appropriate.

F. Organization of picketing

Functions of the picket organizer

54 Wherever picketing is 'official' (i.e. organized by a trade union) an experienced

person, preferably a trade union official who represents those picketing, should always be in charge of the picket line. He should have a letter of authority from his union which he can show to police officers or to people who want to cross the picket line. Even when he is not on the picket line himself he should be available to give the pickets advice if a problem arises.

56 Whether a picket is 'official' or 'unofficial' an organizer of pickets should maintain close contact with the police. Advance consultation with the police is always in the best interests of all concerned. In particular the organizer and the pickets should seek directions from the police on the number of people who should be present on the picket line at any one time and on where they should stand in order to avoid obstructing the highway.

57 The other main functions of the picket organizer should include ensuring that:

● the pickets understand the law and the provisions of this code and that the picketing is conducted peacefully and lawfully;

● badges or armbands, which authorized pickets should wear so that they are clearly identified, are distributed to such pickets and worn while they are picketing;

● employees from other places of work do not join the picket line and that any offers of support on the picket line from outsiders are refused;

● the number of pickets at any entrance to, or exit from, a place of work is not so great as to give rise to fear and resentment amongst those seeking to cross that picket line;

● close contact with his own union office (if any), and with the offices of other unions if they are involved in the picketing is established and maintained;

● such special arrangements as may be necessary for essential supplies, services or operations are understood and observed by the pickets . . .

Non-industrial pickets

If the picket is not connected with a 'trade dispute' then the civil immunities conferred by the 1974 Act do not apply. This means that, in addition to the criminal liabilities set out above, the pickets can have civil proceedings taken against them (i.e. they can be sued for damages and an injunction can be obtained ordering them to stop picketing). This also applies to industrial pickets who take action that is not in contemplation or furtherance of a trade dispute.

So political pickets (e.g. a picket outside an embassy) or a consumer picket (e.g. a picket outside a shop that charges excessive prices or discriminates against non-whites) are usually unlawful. The leading case involved an Islington firm of estate agents:

Pickets were outside the office of a firm of estate agents which was alleged to be associated with property speculators who winkled out tenants (i.e. bought them out for cash inducements). The picket was peaceful and orderly. The police did not intervene so the firm started civil proceedings. They claimed that the picketing was a 'legal nuisance' (see page 376) and asked for an injunction ordering the picketing to stop. The Court of Appeal granted the injunction, partly because the pickets would not have had sufficient money to pay any damages awarded to the estate agents. Hubbard (1975)

Sit-ins and occupations

Until 1977 it was not a criminal offence for a worker (or student) to stage a sit-in or occupation – assuming, of course, that there was no violence and that the premises were not broken into. The only sanction that could be used against them was a civil one; the owners could seek an injunction (and damages) ordering the occupiers to leave or use reasonable force to eject them as trespassers.

The Criminal Law Act 1977 introduced criminal sanctions for sit-ins and occupations in certain circumstances. Section 6 of the Act creates the offence of 'using or threatening violence to secure an entry' (maximum penalty six months' prison and a fine of £2,000). The section has been criticized because it covers the mere threatening of violence when there is someone on the premises – even if the people staging the occupation do not know anyone is there. For instance, suppose a security guard sees a group of people approaching the premises equipped with what could be taken as offensive weapons, such as spanners; in this case, the offence has been committed. Mere weight of numbers could also be taken as a threat of violence. So people entering premises should make it obvious that they are not threatening any violence. They should not carry anything that could be mistaken for an offensive weapon and they should enter in small groups.

If, however, workers refuse to leave a factory at the end of their shift they cannot be prosecuted under the 1977 Act, since their entry was not unlawful.

THE TRADE UNIONIST AND HIS/HER UNION

Disciplinary proceedings against members

When people join a trade union they agree to be bound by its rules, as set out in the rule book. The rule book forms a contract between the member and the union. The rules will usually allow the union to discipline the member for misconduct, failure to pay subscriptions, or 'conduct detrimental to the union'. The ultimate disciplinary sanction is expulsion from the union.

The courts have been very critical of trade union disciplinary procedures and have always insisted that the strict wording of the rule book be followed. In addition, the courts have repeatedly stated that the rules must comply with the requirements of 'natural justice' – basically that accused members be given a fair hearing and an opportunity to answer the charges against them.

Thus, in one case, expulsions were set aside because the members had not received advance notification of the charges and because there was no proper hearing. In another case the expulsion was overruled because the general secretary acted as both prosecutor and judge, by presenting the case against the member and then sitting as chair of the meeting. Another expulsion was invalid because the member had not had a proper opportunity of refuting the allegations. In short, the courts will bend over backwards to ensure that the member is treated fairly by the union. The judicial justification for this was summed up by Lord Denning in a 1952 case: 'A man's right to work is just as important to him as, if not more important than, his rights of property. These courts intervene every day to protect rights of property. They must also intervene to protect the right to work.'

However, some commentators have suggested that the courts have shown themselves to be over-zealous when protecting individual union members by applying the rules of natural justice. They note that the courts seem less concerned in applying the rules of natural justice in other cases, for instance, to immigrants refused entry and to students facing expulsion from college.

In addition, the Employment Act 1988 has introduced for trade union members the right not to be 'unjustifiably disciplined' by the union for certain specified actions. Examples are failing to support or take part in a strike, or alleging that a union official has broken the union's rules or acted unlawfully. Disciplinary action may take the form of expulsion from the union, imposition of a fine etc. A claim may be made by the union member who is disciplined to an industrial tribunal (it must normally be presented within three months of the infringement of the right), and if it is upheld a declaration is made and compensation may be claimed within six months of the declaration. The amount which can be awarded will be the sum considered to be just and equitable in the circumstances, but it is subject to a maximum of £16,150 (1992), and where the union has not reversed its action as a consequence of the declaration that the disciplining was unjustified, a minimum award of £2,700.

The 'political fund' – 'contracting out'

The Trade Union Act 1913 allows unions to set up separate political funds if a majority of their members approve of such a step. However, not every union member may want part of his/her subscription to be allocated towards a political party that they oppose. Accordingly, any member can demand to be allowed to contract out of the political fund and cannot be victimized, punished or expelled for doing so.

The Trade Union Act 1984 has made it mandatory for unions to hold regular ballots on whether the political levy should continue. There must be a ballot at least every ten years; the first ballot must have been held by 31 March 1986 (unless a ballot was held in the ten years prior to that date).

Trade union elections

The 1984 Trade Union Act introduced rules requiring that certain trade union elections be by secret ballot. Note that the rules apply only to the election of voting members of the union's 'principal executive committee' (i.e. usually the NEC) and they must have been elected by secret ballot within the last five years. Similarly, office holders on the committee (typically a president or general secretary) must have been elected by secret ballot to that office within the last five years.

PART FOUR

THE CONSUMER

32 The Consumer and the Law

As the law goes, consumer law is quite a recent addition to English law. Some of the statutes date from the late 1960s, such as the Misrepresentation Act 1967 and the Trade Descriptions Act 1968; many important ones from the 1970s, such as the Unfair Contract Terms Act 1977, the Fair Trading Act 1973, the Consumer Credit Act 1974 and the all-important Sale of Goods Act 1979. The 1980s brought the Supply of Goods and Services Act 1982 and the far-reaching Consumer Protection Act 1987, while the 1990s started well with the Food Safety Act 1990.

The names of several of these acts of Parliament have been around for some time with a different date at the end. From the Sale of Goods Act 1893 (now 1979), for example, it can be seen that the essence of the relationship between buyer and seller is still based on the same express and implied terms as it was 100 years ago.

Some new acts, such as the Consumer Credit Act 1974, sweep up an existing ragbag of previous legislation, sort it out, shake it up and bring in new concepts, all in one fell swoop. That is a slight exaggeration: although the act has been around for nearly two decades now, it came into force bit by bit, some parts of it only as recently as 1985. This act, as others relevant to consumers, allows for new statutory regulations and orders to be made under its provisions. So there is a constant, if irregular, growth of consumer legislation, including some that arises from EC directives.

Other comparatively recent developments are the codes of practice which trade associations have introduced, some of which are drawn up in conjunction with, or are monitored by, the Office of Fair Trading. Most of the codes of practice are voluntary. If traders contravene one, they are not breaking the law; but their professional or trade association may impose sanctions – from a gentle tut-tut, to a fine or even expulsion from the association.

The law is compartmentalized; real life is not. There is statute law, derived from acts of Parliament and statutory instruments, and the common law and case law, based on precedents (cases that have been decided one way or the other). Then there is the civil law, which confers rights and duties on individual people, and the criminal law, which is concerned with behaviour that is harmful to the community as a whole and is punished by the state. There is the (civil) law of contract (which underlies the Sale of Goods Act) and there is tort, a civil wrong which deals with the situation when someone injures another person physically or economically. In the consumer context, it is the tort of negligence that we are most concerned with. And in the consumer context, a situation may well arise which involves all the above aspects of the law at the same time.

One fundamental difference between civil and criminal law is that in a civil action it is up to consumers themselves to take the trader to court; nobody else will or can do so for them. With criminal cases, it is generally the trading standards department or the police who take action and prosecute.

CONSUMER PROTECTION

Because consumer law has developed piecemeal over the years, the different forms of consumer protection are largely unrelated and often overlap.

Under the law of contract, the shopkeeper who sells defective or unsuitable goods or the trader who supplies unsatisfactory services is in breach of contract and must compensate the customer (see page 553).

Under the law of negligence, the seller and the manufacturer of goods are liable for defects that ought to have been avoided: someone injured by a negligently made product can sue either or both (see page 550).

The criminal law deals with aspects of consumer protection in the widest sense: health, food, hygiene. It lays down the standards of safety and quality for many products, and prohibits false descriptions or misleading indications of price (see page 570).

Credit control laws impose strict rules regarding hire purchase or credit agreements (see page 576).

33 The Contract between the Customer and the Trader

Any purchase or sale involves making a contract. Contracts do not have to be complicated documents drawn up by solicitors, and they generally need not be in writing. Only contracts for the sale of land, hire purchase agreements and some insurance agreements need to be in writing.

So shoppers who buy potatoes from the grocer, sweets from a confectioner, papers from the newsagent, a train ticket at the station etc. are making a contract. Similarly if they buy cigarettes from a machine, they are making a contract with the machine-owner, and if they buy goods through the post they are making a contract with the mail-order firm. In each contract they are contracting to pay the purchase price, while the retailer, or whoever is the other party, is contracting to supply the goods. Retailers and consumers are all the time entering into contracts with each other, and if either side breaks the contract, the other can sue for breach of contract.

WHEN IS THE CONTRACT MADE?

A typical consumer contract will be made informally.

Customer: 'A pound of apples, please.'
Shopkeeper: 'That will be 55p, please.'

The customer hands over 55p and the shopkeeper hands over the apples; in the eyes of the law, the customer and shopkeeper have made a contract. The customer offered to buy the apples; the shopkeeper accepted the offer; the apples were then exchanged for money. The requirements of a binding contract were present: an offer and an acceptance, together with value given and received.

Suppose that a shop has a washing machine marked at £350. If a customer goes into the shop and tells the shop assistant that she will buy the machine, that constitutes her offer, the first stage in the making of a contract. But there is no contract until that offer has been accepted, so the customer has until then to change her mind and back out of the deal. When the shop assistant accepts the order, there has been an acceptance of the offer, and so the contract is made. The customer cannot now change her mind and demand her money back (unless, of course, when she takes the machine home, she finds it is defective – see page 540). Similarly, the shopkeeper cannot now back out of the contract. If the machine should have been priced at £450 and the £350 was an error, he cannot demand an extra £100 from the customer. It is too late: a binding contract has been made.

Can customers change their mind?

Customers cannot call off the deal once their offer has been accepted by the shopkeeper. Only if they tell the shopkeeper that they have changed their mind before the shopkeeper has accepted the offer are they free to back out, without cost or obligation.

In practice, therefore, it is important to know when the offer is accepted. Usually this is obvious: it will be when the shopkeeper accepts the money from the customer. In a self-service shop or a supermarket, consumers who have taken goods from the shelves can change their mind and put the goods back. But once they have brought them to the check-out desk and an assistant has taken their money, there is a contract and customers cannot change their mind. In buying from an automatic vending machine, the contract is concluded when buyers put their money in the slot.

If goods are ordered through the post by mail order, the contract is made (i.e. the consumer's offer to buy is accepted by the firm) when the firm posts to the customer an acceptance letter, confirmation, receipt (or the goods themselves), not when the firm's letter is received by the customer. Even if the firm's letter of acceptance is lost in the post, there is still a contract. Goods ordered by post can be cancelled without obligation if the customer notifies the suppliers (by phone or letter) before they post the goods or a letter of acceptance. However, under the Mail Order Traders Association's code of practice, goods which have been ordered from a mail-order catalogue should be sent 'on approval' and the buyer given the right of cancellation within a specified time (at least two weeks after receipt of the goods). If a buyer does cancel, the purchase price or deposit paid should then be refunded promptly. A code of practice is not legally binding (see page 563).

At an auction, the customer's bid is the offer for the goods. This bid is accepted when the auctioneer knocks down the goods to the bidder, usually by tapping a hammer on the auction desk. So a bid can be withdrawn any time before the hammer comes down.

A customer who backs out of a contract after it has been made will be liable to pay compensation, in the form of damages, to the shopkeeper. The amount of the damages will depend on the amount of the seller's loss.

Special rules apply to goods bought on credit at home (i.e. not in a shop or other trade premises). Although the contract is made when the seller agrees to sell the goods, customers usually have five days in which they can change their mind and cancel the contract (see page 580).

Similarly, under a piece of legislation with the pithy title Consumer Pr (Cancellation of Contracts Concluded away from Business Premises) Regulations 1987, the consumer has the right to cancel after an unsolicited visit by a trader (such as a high-pressure doorstep salesman or 'cold callers') to the consumer's home or place of work, or when a contract is signed during an excursion organized by traders away from their own business premises. The consumer has seven days following the making of a contract for over £35 in which to cancel (as against five days and over £50 in a credit transaction). This has to be done in writing, and a notice of cancellation takes effect at the time of posting, irrespective of when it reaches the trader.

Can shopkeepers change their mind?

Shopkeepers, too, are bound by the rules. Once they accept the customer's offer, they cannot change their mind. If they do try to back out of the contract, they will be liable in damages.

Although shopkeepers have to go ahead and sell the product once they have accepted the buyer's offer, they do not have to accept the offer in the first place if they do not want to. The practical importance of this is that shopkeepers are not obliged to sell items just because they have them on display. Thus, in the example of the washing machine earlier, if the shopkeeper had realized that he had made a mistake and that the price was incorrectly marked before he accepted the customer's offer, he could have refused to sell it for £350. The mere fact that he has 'For Sale £350' on a sign, or attached to the machine, does not make him legally liable to sell it at that price. His 'For Sale' sign is no more than an 'invitation to treat': an invitation to the customer to make him an offer. In effect, the shopkeeper is saying, 'If you make me an offer of £350, I may well accept it, but I need not do so.'

Although traders do not have to sell you their goods, if they deliberately display a lower price than the price they actually charge for something, as a come-on to entice customers into the shop, they commit an offence under Part III of the Consumer Protection Act 1987 (see page 570). It is illegal to mislead customers as to the price they can be expected to pay; displaying false price labels is a criminal offence.

Shopkeepers would be in trouble for not selling goods, at the marked or whatever price, if their refusal to accept the offer was because of the customer's race or sex (see page 805).

THE TERMS OF A CONTRACT: EXPRESS AND IMPLIED

When the consumer bought the washing machine, she did not discuss the terms of the contract with the shop assistant. It was left unsaid that the machine should wash clothes properly and that it should be safe to use. But although these terms were not specifically agreed upon, the law implied them into the contract. These implied contractual terms form the basis of the consumer's protection against faulty goods (see Chapter 34).

As long as there is sufficient certainty as to the basics of the transaction, the law will imply the other terms. But if there is not sufficient certainty, there will not be a contract. For instance, suppose a customer goes into a shop and asks how much kitchen units are and then asks whether the shopkeeper could supply them if necessary. In such a case there is insufficient certainty: they have not agreed which kitchen units, how many, or at what price. However, if it was only the price that had not been agreed, there might be sufficient certainty for a contract; the law would simply make it an implied term that the customer would pay a 'reasonable' price, bearing in mind what other shops charge for those units. So the price need not necessarily be agreed in advance. For example, when a cottager orders a load of firewood, he may not know exactly what the bill will come to until the wood is delivered. Or if you take a bicycle to be repaired and do not get an estimate, you will not know the cost until after the work is done. Where the price is not agreed in advance, there is an implied term that a fair price, 'the going rate', will be payable. But if consumers agree a price at the time the contract was made, they cannot later claim a reduction or try to cancel the contract, even if they realize that the price was unreasonable and elsewhere they would have got the article for less or would have had to pay less for the work. It is what was agreed that counts.

Sometimes the terms of the contract will be expressly agreed between retailers and their customers. For instance, a hire shop is likely to have a standard order form setting out its conditions of hire. Or a bus company may have a notice on its tickets reading 'For conditions see over' and then on the reverse side travellers are told that they travel 'in accordance with the current conditions of business laid down by the company, a copy of which can be inspected at the company's offices'.

There are clear advantages in having express terms in a consumer contract. It avoids doubt as to what has been agreed and it reduces the scope for misunderstandings. In large or unusual transactions, it is sensible to have comprehensive express terms, rather than have to rely on implied terms. For instance, when arranging for building work to be carried out, it is advisable to set out the terms in writing before any work is done. But for express conditions to be binding on consumers, the conditions must have been brought to their attention *before* the contract was made.

If the customer learns of the conditions only after the contract has been made, then obviously they cannot form part of the contract. For instance, if a hotel has a notice stating that 'All valuables are left in rooms at owner's risk', then that sign should be displayed at the reception desk, or wherever the guest books in, not the bedrooms, for the contract has been made by the time customers enter their room. Similarly if a dry-cleaner's has a sign limiting its responsibility for damage to clothes, that message should not be on the back of the entrance door, for then customers would see it only when they had left the shop after making the contract.

No unfair conditions, please

The conditions must be fair. They must not take away the customer's statutory rights – for example, that goods will be of proper quality or that work done will be to a proper standard. A clause that attempts to do this will be ineffective, and in addition the shopkeeper will be committing a criminal offence. Moreover, any condition which limits retailers' liability to their customers is put to a 'fair and reasonable' test; if it is unfair then it is ineffective (see page 548).

Until not all that long ago, shopkeepers could avoid being liable for the quality and fitness of the goods they were selling. Traditionally, the law said that the seller sold the goods, and the buyer bought them, on the terms agreed in their contract. And, although the courts might imply a term that the goods were of proper quality or fit for use, it was possible for these implied terms to be specifically excluded from the contract. So it became common – especially, but not only, in the motor trade – for receipts and order forms to contain *exemption clauses* which specifically said that there were to be no implied terms as to the quality of the goods. Usually the exemption clause would be in small print and worded in legal jargon that made its effect incomprehensible to the consumer.

Customers often did not realize that an exemption clause was taking away their legal rights, but even if they did, there was little they could do about it; most retailers sold goods subject to exemption clauses and so the consumer had no choice but to accept the position.

The law allowed this unfair system on the basis that the customer and the shopkeeper had freely bargained and entered into a contract with one another, and should be bound by the terms of that contract. Today we recognize that freedom of contract exists only when there is equality of bargaining power; it is nonsense to suggest that the individual consumer can freely bargain and negotiate with large retail concerns.

In the 1970s new laws stepped in to help safeguard the consumer. The consumer is no longer bound by clauses that exempt the shopkeeper from liability for faulty and defective goods. Signs and notices (of which there are now fewer, but they still happen) saying, for instance, 'All conditions and warranties are hereby excluded', or 'We will not in any case be liable to pay compensation for any loss or damage whatsoever sustained by the purchaser', or 'No money can be refunded', are ineffective: the retailer remains liable for breach of contract if the goods are faulty.

Moreover, the shopkeeper who displays such a notice may be committing a criminal offence. By the Consumer Transactions (Restriction on Statements) Orders 1976 and 1978, it is illegal for a supplier of goods to try to take away a customer's rights under the Sale of Goods Act (see page 542) or to apply terms which are void by virtue of s.6 of the Unfair Contract Terms Act 1977 (see page 548).

The 1976 Order covers any notice that misleads customers as to their Sale of

Goods Act rights. So, 'No refunds', 'No complaints considered once you have left the shop', 'Any complaint must be made within seven days of purchase', are all illegal. For example, in 1978, Abbey Fashions in Leeds had a sign reading, 'We willingly exchange goods but regret that money cannot be refunded.' The proprietor was fined £5 and ordered to pay £15 costs since the sign implied that purchasers of defective goods could not claim their money back, which of course they can. Similarly, a Shrewsbury umbrella-maker was found guilty after displaying a sign which read, 'All umbrellas must be checked before leaving till. No returns can be accepted after use.'

These regulations do not apply to trade purchases – in other words, when the goods are bought in the course of business and not as a consumer purchase. With a business purchase a trader can insert an exclusion clause, although even then the clause will be subject to a 'fairness and reasonableness' test and if it is unfair on the buyer, it will be ineffective (see page 548).

WHEN A CONTRACT IS BROKEN

If either customer or retailer breaks the contract, the other can sue for breach of contract. For instance, if the washing machine is faulty, the customer can sue the shopkeeper. If the customer's cheque bounces, the shopkeeper can sue the customer. Moreover, under the Theft Act 1968 it is a criminal offence to issue a cheque knowing that there are not sufficient funds in the bank to honour it or intending to 'stop' the cheque. When consumers stop their cheques they will have broken their contract by not complying with their side of the bargain.

Only the parties to the contract can sue for breach of contract. For instance, if the washing machine had faulty wiring and the customer was injured, she could sue the shopkeeper for breach of contract – namely, for breach of the implied terms that the machine was reasonably fit for the purpose intended and also that it was of merchantable quality (see page 545). Even if the wiring defect was the fault of the manufacturer, the shopkeeper would be liable. He could not tell the customer to sue the manufacturer. Instead, the customer can sue the shopkeeper and the shopkeeper can then in turn sue the manufacturer.

But suppose the machine was bought by a husband and it was his wife who was injured when using it. The wife would not have been a party to the contract made with the shopkeeper and so she could not sue him for breach of contract. Her remedy would be either to sue the manufacturer (and perhaps the shopkeeper) for negligence in marketing an unsafe machine or to invoke the Consumer Protection Act 1987, under which the need to prove negligence has disappeared (see page 550 and page 566).

34 Buying Goods

In many respects the legal position of the consumer is the same when paying for services or repairs as when buying goods. It is a question of contract and depends on what the parties agreed. The contract may be classified as a contract for work, or work and materials, rather than for the sale of goods. When a hairdresser cuts a woman's hair and gives her a shampoo and blow-dry, it is for the hairdresser's skill that she pays rather than the negligible cost of the shampoo. When an artist is painting a portrait, he is supplying his skill with the brush and the sitter pays for that service rather than the oil paint and canvas. (On the other hand, if a client comes to the artist's studio or a gallery, selects one of the finished pictures there and pays for it, that is a sale of goods.)

Sometimes it is quite difficult to decide whether one is paying for goods or for services. If a car is damaged and the motorist takes it to a garage for repair, the garage will provide the necessary new parts (goods) and fit them in position and perhaps respray (service and repair). The payment is for the skill and labour in repairing the car and for the cost of the parts.

The legal rules for the work half of the contract and the goods half are different. For the provision of work, there is an implied term that the supplier will carry out the service with reasonable care and skill (under s.13 of the Supply of Goods and Services Act). For the second half, the provision of materials, s.4 of that Act stipulates that the goods in question must be of merchantable quality and fit for the purpose – a phrase that also lies at the heart of the Sale of Goods Act 1979.

THE SALE OF GOODS ACT

The Latin phrase *caveat emptor* (let the buyer beware) has always been good consumer advice, and particularly so before the first Sale of Goods Act, the 1893 one, came into force. Although that act was more concerned with regulating commercial transactions between traders than with the unequal bargaining status of consumers, it gave protection to the buyer by implying a number of terms into all contracts for the sale of goods. The implied terms include that the goods are reasonably fit for the purpose for which they were bought and that the goods are free from any defects rendering them unmerchantable. However, the parties could exclude the implied terms from their transaction if they wished, and it was the traders who often so wished, leaving the buyer at a considerable disadvantage. Most retailers sold goods subject to exemption clauses and the consumer had no choice but to accept the position. It was not until the 1970s that Parliament stepped in. Now the Unfair Contract Terms Act 1977 prevents the retailer inserting exemption clauses into a contract which purports to exclude or limit the customer's Sale of Goods rights (see page 548). And a new Sale of Goods Act came into force on 1 January 1980 (as it was passed the previous year, it is called the Sale of Goods Act 1979). The Act implies the following terms in a contract of sale:

• that the seller has the right to sell the goods (s.12 and s.21 (1));
• that the goods will correspond with the description (s.13);
• that the bulk of the goods will correspond with the sample (s.15);
• that the goods are of merchantable quality (s.14 (2)) and fit for the purpose (s.14 (3) and (6)).

The last point is the most important.

Seller must have the right to sell

Another Latin maxim used by lawyers is *nemo dat quod non habet* (nobody can give what he does not possess). It is a basic rule of law that a person can sell only what belongs to him or her. If the goods do not belong to the seller, the buyer does not acquire 'good title' – that is, ownership of them – however innocently he or she may have acted. For instance, if my watch is stolen and then sold to various innocent purchasers, the watch will still belong to me. If I find out where the watch is, I can claim it back. The person who had innocently bought the watch would have to go back to the person who sold it to him and claim damages (his money back). The seller would have no defence to the claim, for the Sale of Goods Act 1979 makes it an implied term on the part of sellers that they have a right to sell the goods. The seller could, in turn, claim from the person who sold him the watch, and so on, down the line of innocent buyers and sellers.

So in theory, and in law, consumers who have bought goods may find themselves faced with a claim to ownership by someone who has a better right to possession than the seller from whom they got the goods. In practice, it is likely to involve a lot of trouble and expense to trace sellers along the line and enforce the right.

There are several exceptions to the *nemo dat* rule. The most obvious one is selling with the true owner's consent. This is written into s.21(1) of the Sale of Goods Act: '... where the goods are sold by a person who is not their owner and who does not sell them under the authority or with the consent of the owner ...'

Another exception is contained in s.22(1) of the Sale of Goods Act: '... where goods are sold in market overt, according to the usage of the market, the buyer acquires a good title to the goods provided he buys them in good faith

. . .' This market overt exception is a leftover from long-ago law and custom in England (it does not apply in Wales) and is full of anomalies and technicalities that reflect its sixteenth-century origins rather than the realities of today. For example, the 'overt' part of the phrase means 'open' – a public market or fair legally established by charter or custom – but includes the shops in the City of London. 'By charter or custom' is also not without its problems. In the 1990 case of Long v. Jones a sale from a private stall adjoining a market was held not to be market overt and therefore the buyer who bought there did not get good title.

The sale must take place between sunrise and sunset. This ancient pre-electric light rule was applied in the case of Reid v. Metropolitan Police Commissioner (1973):

A pair of elegant glass candelabra was stolen. A couple of months later, they were sold at the New Caledonian Market in south London, a legally constituted market which is open on Fridays from 7 a.m. onwards. Dealers tend to go early, to get the best bargains. On the day in question, which happened to be Friday, 13 of February, sunrise was at 8.19 a.m. Some time later, when the earlybird dealer who had acquired the candelabra was about to resell them, the original owner appeared and claimed that they were his. The police took them away and the court had to decide the case between the original owner and the dealer who had bought the candelabra at the New Caledonian Market. It held that the market sale having taken place before sunrise, the dealer who bought them was not protected by the 'market overt' rule and the candlesticks still belonged to the original owner.

Incidentally, people who buy stolen goods are not committing an offence unless they know or believe them to be stolen. If they bought them very cheaply from someone who assured them they'd legitimately fallen off a lorry, they would probably be taken to have believed them to be stolen if brought before the court on a handling charge.

The market overt rule applies equally to a private buyer or a trader. In another of the exceptions to the *nemo dat* rule, there is a difference depending on whether the next purchaser is a private individual or a trade purchaser. It applies only to motor vehicles bought on hire purchase (which is an area where a consumer can most easily be conned by buying a vehicle that turns out to have been stolen).

When an item is on HP or a conditional sale agreement, it belongs to the finance company, not the buyer. Only when all the instalments have been paid off will it become the buyer's property (see page 576). If the item is sold before the HP is paid off, the new buyer will not acquire ownership. But exception is made for cars, motor-bikes and other motor vehicles (by Part III of the Hire Purchase Act 1964 as amended by the Consumer Credit Act 1974). A private purchaser who buys a car from a hire-purchaser (i.e. *not* from a crook) without knowing of the HP agreement (or that it has not been paid off) acquires ownership of the car, and so it cannot be repossessed by the finance company. If the car is bought by a trade purchaser, however, the trade purchaser will not be protected; but if that trade purchaser then sells it on to an innocent private purchaser, the private purchaser will acquire ownership.

There is a way of avoiding the risk of buying a motor vehicle that is on HP rather than relying on redress via the Hire Purchase Act 1964, Part III. A company called HPI (Hire Purchase Information), set up by and for finance companies, has a register of subsisting hire purchase agreements and can pass on the information to its motor-dealer member. A dealer who is considering buying a car can contact HPI and check if on the register there is an HP agreement related to that car. This information is not available to the public, but Citizens' Advice Bureaux and the motoring organizations can phone HPI on behalf of their clients and members, so someone contemplating buying a secondhand car can ask for a check to be made.

Goods must correspond with the description

The goods which the consumer buys must be as the seller has described them. If shoes made of man-made materials are described as leather, that is a breach of s.13 of the Sale of Goods Act, and so would a 1985 model of car being advertised as a 1989 one. A coat described as 'waterproof' must not let in the rain. The description may be by word of mouth, perhaps the shop assistant's, or in writing or print, as in a display advertisement or on the label, the box or other packaging. Where buyers take items from a supermarket shelf, it is considered a sale by description even though the buyers have themselves decided which articles to select.

It may still count as a sale by description if the buyers carefully examined the goods, as long as there was some reliance on the description. This is particularly relevant when buying a secondhand car. The implied term that goods must correspond with the description is not limited to a transaction between trader and consumer but also applies to purely private sales. The description with which the goods must comply need not necessarily be inclusive of everything that can be said about a particular article but the essential characteristics – quantity, composition, origin ('Scotch' salmon, say) – must correspond with the description.

There is some overlap between misdescription under the Sale of Goods Act, the Misrepresentation Act 1967 (see page 547) and the Trade Descriptions Act 1968 (see page 567).

The bulk must correspond with the sample

Simply showing a sample in the course of negotiations will not make the transaction a sale by sample unless the parties agree this and, where there is a written contract, include this in the writing. But where there is a contract for sale by sample, s.15 of the Sale of Goods Act provides that there is an implied term that the bulk of the goods will correspond with the sample in quality and that the buyer will have a reasonable opportunity of comparing the bulk with the sample. The goods must be free of defects rendering them unmerchantable which would not be apparent on reasonable examination of the sample.

If any defects which the buyer could reasonably have discovered on an examination of the sample are such as to make the goods unmerchantable, this would activate s.14 (2), the one concerned with merchantable quality.

Merchantable quality and fitness for the purpose

S.14 is the supreme section of the Sale of Goods Act as far as two important implied terms are concerned: that the goods supplied shall be of merchantable quality and fit for the purpose. The two concepts go together and overlap. What they amount to is that the goods will work properly and will be free of major unexpected defects. Defects which are specifically drawn to buyers' attention before they actually buy are excepted, and so are defects which they ought to have discovered if they had examined the goods before buying. (They do not *have* to examine them but, if they do, any defect that the actual inspection ought to have revealed is excluded.) The moral of this is: customers should either not examine goods at all or, if they do examine them, do so properly. If they only examine them half-heartedly, they cannot complain about defects that would have been revealed in a more thorough examination.

Wrong or misleading instructions supplied with the goods can make them unfit for their purpose. But the customer's case would fail if there are clear warnings or 'Do not use after . . .' instructions (as in the case of Wormell v. RHM Agriculture, 1987, where a farmer's herbicide failed to kill the wild oats because it was used too late in the season).

Special purpose, multi-purpose

Where the buyer does not rely on the seller's skill and judgement and firmly says, 'I want this or that' (rather than, 'I want something that'll remove the oil stains from my jacket'), the seller is exonerated from any responsibility that the product is fit for the purpose.

Where goods are being bought for some unusual purpose and the consumer expressly informs the shopkeeper what that purpose is, then the goods must be fit for that particular purpose.

Goods that can be used for a number of different purposes should be reasonably fit for their various purposes but will be unmerchantable only if they are unfit for *all* their normal purposes. This was decided in the 1987 case of M/S Aswan Engineering Establishment v. Lupdine Ltd, where goods sold to A were packed in plastic pails which collapsed when stored at very high temperatures in Kuwait (A's place of business). If the plastic pails had needed to be fit for *all* common purposes to which such pails could be put, they would have had to be fit for export to the heat of Kuwait as well as to cooler places. The Court of Appeal, however, held that it is sufficient if goods are fit for *any* of their common purposes.

(We have not heard the last of this. The Law Commission is considering whether the somewhat outmoded concept of 'merchantable quality' in the context of consumer sales should not be replaced by 'acceptable quality'. In their proposal, quality would include fitness for *all* the purposes for which goods of the kind are commonly supplied.)

If the paintwork of a new car is scratched, that scratch will not affect the car's performance and it is therefore fit for the purpose. But obviously a new car should not be scratched, so is it of merchantable quality? However, an item can be fit for its purposes and yet not of merchantable quality. If a new car will not start or the gears jam, it is not fit for its purpose, nor is it of merchantable quality. Consumers have become accustomed to accept 'the usual teething troubles' of cars, but being of merchantable quality should mean more than that goods can be repairable in order to become so.

Some recent cases have shown that the courts will pay attention to what might be considered cosmetic defects and aesthetic considerations. In Rogers v. Parish (Scarborough) Ltd (1987), the appeal judge said:

One would include in respect of any passenger vehicle not merely the buyer's purpose of driving the car from one place to another, but of doing so with the appropriate degree of comfort, ease of handling and reliability and, one might add, of pride in the vehicle's outward and interior appearance. What is the appropriate degree and what relative weight is to be attached to one characteristic of the car rather than another will depend on the market at which the car is aimed . . . Deficiencies which might be acceptable in a secondhand vehicle were not to be expected in one purchased as new.

Private sales, secondhand goods

Generally, the implied terms of the Sale of Goods Act cover secondhand goods bought from a trader, but a lower standard is applied, depending on the price and description of the goods.

S. 14 of the Sale of Goods Act (the section with the implied terms of fitness for purpose and merchantable quality) protects the consumer if the seller sells in the course of a business. If not and it is a private sale, *caveat emptor*!

When buying from a private individual rather than from a trader, terms regarding fitness for purpose and merchantable quality are not implied by law into the contract. This led to some trade sellers (of, e.g., secondhand motor vehicles, furniture, electrical appliances) masquerading as private sellers (using small ads and giving only their private addresses), so that they could get away with selling something of a lower standard, or even defective goods. Such a practice is now a criminal offence under the Business Advertisement (Disclosure) Order 1977 and advertisements must make it clear when goods are being sold in the course of a business.

MISREPRESENTATION

False sales talk has been around since the serpent and Eve. The law accepts that salespeople often use exaggerated language and meaningless hyperbole –

that is all part of the language of the marketplace. The customer is expected to take phrases like 'She's a beauty', 'The best around', 'Fantastic value', 'One of our most popular models', and so on, with a pinch of salt. The law will dismiss that sort of sales talk as mere 'puff', and the customer cannot return the goods just because they are not 'the best around'.

In practice, the difficulty about bringing consumer claims based on misleading sales talk is that you have to prove that the salespeople said what they did. This is why it is useful for customers to have someone with them when making a major purchase, particularly of secondhand goods, so that there is a witness to what was said and promised.

But the law will intervene if salespeople make false statements of fact which induce customers to buy goods. So if a salesman says, 'You will get thirty-eight miles to the gallon from this model' or, 'The element needs to be replaced only once a year', then the customer can complain if these statements turn out to be untrue. The law calls them 'misrepresentations', and if they induced customers to buy the goods, then shopkeepers are liable even if they (or their staff) did honestly believe that the car would do thirty-eight miles to the gallon or that the heating elements would last at least a year. Even if sellers are acting innocently, and to the best of their knowledge, they are responsible if their representation is untrue (Misrepresentation Act 1967).

Misrepresentions can be made fraudulently, negligently or innocently. The differences are relevant mainly in relation to what the consumer can claim as a result: rescission (that is setting aside) of the contract and rejecting the goods, plus damages as well, or damages instead of rescission.

An American businessman (as reported in *The Times* in November 1991) successfully sued a firm of specialist dealers in London for fraudulent misrepresentation. He discovered that the vintage car, sold to him for £51,000 in 1983 as a 1913 model Rolls-Royce Silver Ghost was a fake; it was a 1922 model, worth half what he had paid for it. The judge said (among other things), 'I am sure beyond reasonable doubt that the false representations were made knowingly', and awarded the buyer the difference between the current value of the fake (£75,000) and what a genuine 1913 model would be worth (£135,000).

EXCLUSION CLAUSES

A large number of contracts are brought about by means of preprinted forms containing standard conditions. Details of the variables, such as price, delivery date, description of goods, are filled in at the front of the order form or other document. At the back is the list of conditions, exclusions and exemptions which only the most ardent consumers would read – and then not necessarily understand the implications. Such standard forms of contract are used not only in a buyer/seller situation but for house purchase, building contracts, insurance, furniture removal and hire purchase. The trader or company can cut down on administrative costs by not having to negotiate each contract individually.

Often a ticket or a receipt would have conditions and exclusions printed on the back, but these are effective only if they are brought to the consumer's attention before the contract is agreed; afterwards it is too late.

Exemption clauses were open to abuse because consumers would unwittingly sign away their rights and before 1978 the courts leaned over backward to lessen the harsh effect of such clauses on consumers. On 1 February 1978 the Unfair Contract Terms Act 1977 came into force and with it the need for the courts to control exemption clauses became much less important.

The name of the Act is slightly misleading: it deals with negligence as well as contract, but not with *all* unfair terms. It covers only exemption clauses and notices; for all practical purposes it does not apply to contracts of insurance and dealings in land (which, in legalspeak, includes houses).

The restraining effect of the Unfair Contract Terms Act is that the consumer's 'inalienable rights' under s.12–15 of the Sale of Goods Act (the right to sell, true description, correspondence to sample, quality and fitness) cannot be excluded in any circumstances.

Customers have more legal protection if they buy an item 'as a consumer' than when they buy as a trader or for a business, because for non-consumers the seller can insert quite significant exclusion clauses. Dealing as a consumer is defined in s. 12 of the Unfair Contract Terms Act as someone who is acquiring the kind of goods that are ordinarily bought for private use or consumption, and where the seller is in business but the buyer is not, nor pretends to be. For example, Basil decides to improve the insulation of his house. If he buys the double-glazing sheets and drill, hammer and other tools from a DIY shop or discount store, it will be a consumer purchase. But if the store has a trade counter and Basil uses it (to get a trade discount, perhaps), he will not be dealing as a consumer. If he buys the tools from his friend, a retired sea-captain, it will not be a 'consumer purchase' since the friend is not in the handyman-tools business. It is up to the seller who claims that the other party does not deal as a consumer to show that the customer is not a 'consumer'.

Is it fair and reasonable?

Where the buyer does not deal as a consumer, any exemption clause or condition which excludes or restricts the Sale of Goods Act's implied terms as to description, quality and fitness will have to satisfy 'the requirements of reasonableness'. The Act itself offers guidelines for the reasonableness test, including the relative strengths of the bargaining positions of the parties and whether the customer's requirements could have been met elsewhere; whether the customer knew or should have known the existence of the exclusion clause and realized what it meant, perhaps through some custom of the trade or previous dealings with the seller.

It is for sellers to show that their exclusion clause is reasonable, not for customers to show that it is not.

An exclusion clause limiting liability to 'the cost of', with nothing for disappointment or distress, would not pass the reasonableness test. For example, in the case of Woodman v. Photo Trade Processing (1981), Mr W took photos of his friend's wedding, intending to give the photos to the friend as a wedding present. The film was taken to a chemist's shop, which acted as collecting agent for a national firm of film processors. On the side of the envelope into which the film was put there was an exclusion clause stating that the company was liable only for the value of the film. When the films were returned it was obvious that many of the photos had been lost. Mr W sued, but the company merely offered him the value of the ruined film. The court held that the exemption clause was 'unreasonable' and therefore it was invalid. Mr W was awarded £75 damages for the distress and loss of enjoyment arising from the loss of the wedding photos.

A recent case (Smith v. Bush, 1990) which was mainly about something else – namely whether a building society surveyor who makes a valuation for purposes of a mortgage owes a duty of care to the house-buyer as well as the building society – also dealt with reasonableness: can the surveyors prove that their exemption clause satisfied the reasonableness test? The answer was no, because, among other things, the two parties did not have equal bargaining power because the intending house-buyer had no effective power to object.

The one kind of liability which cannot be excluded or limited or contracted out of is liability for death or personal injury resulting from negligence. Any other loss or damage which a person may suffer as a result of another's negligence can be restricted or excluded only in so far as that would satisfy the test of reasonableness. That 'other' can be a trader, a retailer, a manufacturer, a builder, a garage, a bus company, a holiday tour operator – anyone in business. Business is defined in the Act as including a profession and the activities of any government department or local or public authority.

British Rail does not fit into this list and BR's 'Conditions of Carriage' have some wide-ranging exclusions, such as no responsibility for trains being cancelled without notice, or for trains not arriving or starting at the time specified in the timetable. A ticket does not entitle the passenger to a seat, but passengers who travel without a ticket commit an offence if they do not intend to pay the fare.

These austere conditions do not mean that in practice BR may not compensate a passenger with a genuine grievance. And the Passenger's Charter, introduced in March 1992, makes provisions for passengers to receive compensation for 'poor performance' (mainly in the form of travel vouchers and season ticket extensions). The Passenger's Charter is a first step in fulfilling the requirements of the government's Citizen's Charter, and BR's Conditions of Carriage and complaints procedure are likely to be revised in the light of the Charter.

NEGLIGENCE

In the Unfair Contract Terms Act, negligence is defined as the breach of any contractual obligation or common-law duty to take reasonable care or exercise reasonable skill. The concept of duty of care is at the heart of liability in negligence generally.

It is a part of the law of contract that only the parties to the contract have any rights and duties against each other – for example, the buyer and seller, but not the buyer's wife or the seller's supplier, or any other third parties. Both the buyer and third parties can, however, seek redress under the law of negligence. The case of the snail in the ginger beer bottle (Donoghue v. Stevenson, 1932) decided that the manufacturer of a product owed a duty of care to the ultimate consumer.

'You must take reasonable care to avoid acts or omissions which you can reasonably foresee would be likely to injure your neighbour,' said Lord Atkins, who, in the same judgement, also laid down the 'who is my neighbour?' test to be applied. 'The answer seems to be,' continued the law lord, 'persons who are so closely and directly affected by my act that I ought reasonably to have them in contemplation.'

In practice, it is very difficult for a plaintiff to prove that the manufacturers were negligent in the legal sense. This is because victims have to show not only that there was a duty of care owed to them but also that this duty had been breached by the manufacturer and that this breach had in fact caused their injury or loss. No liability arises under the law of negligence without proof of fault.

Take, for example, the thalidomide claims; the deformed children would have been able to win their claims in court if they could have shown that Distillers had been negligent. Because of their inability to prove negligence, the claims dragged on for years as the children's lawyers tried to negotiate a compromise settlement. (However, if the mothers who purchased the drug had been injured by it and they – rather than their children – had been suing, it might have been a different matter. The mothers, as customers, might have been able to sue the chemists who supplied the drugs for breach of contract in selling goods that were not of merchantable quality; there would then have been no need to prove negligence.) Things are different now.

It had long been obvious that the fault system of compensation for victims of defective products was unsatisfactory. What was needed was a system of strict liability – that is, manufacturers having to pay compensation without there being need to prove negligence against them.

Product liability

The breakthrough came mainly via Brussels, the EC's Directive on Liability for Defective Products, implemented in the UK by the Consumer Protection Act of 1987, Part I. It states that where any damage is caused wholly or partly by a defect in a product, the producer will be liable for the damage and so will anyone who has held him- or herself out to be the producer by putting their name on the product or its packaging, or using a mark (such as an own-brand label) in relation to it.

Damage means death, personal injury or any loss of or damage to any private property caused by defective goods. Defective does not mean unfit or unmerchantable in the Sale of Goods Act sense, but unsafe or dangerous. An article may be unsafe if it is supplied without proper instructions or warnings, and vice versa. If a warning about how to deal with a potentially dangerous product is clearly provided, it ceases to be unsafe.

As befits a piece of legislation that arose out of an EC directive, liability for an unsafe product remains with anyone who imports it from outside the EC into one of the member states in the course of business. What is more, if consumers are not sure who imported the defective product (which may in fact have been re-exported), they have the right to ask the supplier to identify that party.

Time for claiming

The injured party must bring a claim within three years of the date when the cause of the action occurred. Generally that is not from when consumers bought the product, but from when they discovered the relevant facts, or could have done so. There is also a long-stop relevant time limit of ten years from the time when the product was brought into circulation by the manufacturer or own-brander or importer.

It is, of course, possible that the defect did not yet exist at the relevant time, or that at that time the state of scientific and technical knowledge was not advanced enough for anyone to know of the hazards of the product or some of its component parts. Technically this is known as the 'state of the art defence', and it bristles with problems.

The Act can be invoked only where the cash amount that would be awarded as damages is more than £275. This is a practical point, aimed at discouraging small claims.

Where the Consumer Protection Act does not apply (under £275 damages or out of time), the consumer would probably be back to invoking the laws of negligence and contract to try and get redress.

REDRESS FOR FAULTY GOODS

The first thing to be done is to complain. Many shopkeepers will not argue if a reasoned complaint is made to them, but it is important that the complaint be made without delay. Once the customer has accepted the goods, it is too late to reject them. Acceptance need not be in words; it may be inferred by the buyer's action – for example, when, as s. 35(1) of the Sale of Goods Act puts it, the buyer 'does any act in relation to them which is inconsistent with the ownership of the seller', such as using the goods in a way that makes it impossible to take them back and ask for a refund. Thus, if a dressmaker buys a length of material and starts cutting it up in order to make a skirt and jacket from it, she could then not reject the cloth if she discovers that it is wool and nylon rather than pure wool (i.e. it does not comply with the description).

S. 35(1) of the Sale of Goods Act goes on further to define deemed acceptance: '. . . or when, after the lapse of a reasonable time, he retains the goods without intimating to the seller that he has rejected them'. That seems fine on the face of it, but when does the 'reasonable time' start to run? At the moment of buying? Or when the defect comes to light, which may be many weeks or even months later? If, within the year of purchase, an electric motor fails, or a chair collapses, or holes appear in its upholstery, such faults show that the goods were probably not merchantable at the time of buying them. But as the law stands, it is then too late for consumers to reject the goods and get their money back. This is particularly irksome where the retailer tries – and fails – to put right fault after fault till it is too late.

The court may decide (as it did in Bernstein v. Parsons Motors Ltd, 1987) that three weeks is a reasonable time for trying out a new car.

Mr B's car was delivered on 7 December. He could not use it over Christmas because he was ill. On 3 January, after 140 miles of use, the car broke down because of a major mechanical failure (a seized camshaft). Mr B tried to reject it as not being merchantable. The motor traders, P Ltd, said it was too late for rejection and that Mr B had 'accepted' it. The court agreed with P Ltd, but agreed with Mr B that the car was unmerchantable. P Ltd repaired it under the manufacturers' warranty and Mr B was paid damages to compensate him for his extra expenses arising from not having the car when needed and also something for the vexation he suffered.

The consumer's long-term right to reject goods with a latent defect was not established by the Bernstein case. However, a recent Law Commission report, while not dealing with the question of time for rejection, includes the proposal that 'an attempt by or under an arrangement with the seller to cure the defect should not destroy the right to reject'. In the meantime, consumers who agree to allow repairs to be carried out on their brand-new goods, perhaps under a guarantee, would be wise to make it a condition that the repairs will not rob them of their right to reject the car, washing machine or whatever it is, if the repairs do not put it totally right.

On the question of guarantees, a manufacturer's guarantee is always an extra and cannot take away or restrict any Sale of Goods Act rights. Sellers remain responsible for the goods under their contract with the buyer.

Under a guarantee

By signing a guarantee, customers do not forfeit any of their other legal rights. In fact, it is a criminal offence for the guarantee to suggest that it takes away any of the consumer's legal rights – which is why some guarantees have a phrase stating, 'This guarantee is in addition to your statutory rights.'

Sometimes a guarantee will go further than the statutory rights. For instance, suppose a watch breaks down after two years. It might be that, under the implied term that goods are of proper quality, two years is a reasonable time for such a watch to last. But if the manufacturer has given a three-year guarantee, there will be no need to argue with the shopkeeper about whether the goods are of proper quality; the customer can simply send the watch back to the manufacturer.

If the watch that went wrong was bought as a gift for someone else, there is no contract between the seller and the recipient of the gift. So the recipient does not have the right to take it back to the shop, even if the watch does not work properly right from the start. But he or she can invoke the guarantee.

Damages

Damages for breach of contract and cancelling the contract are consumers' only two remedies recognized by the law. It follows that customers are not obliged to accept a replacement item from the shopkeeper. In law, they are entitled to either damages or money back; they need not accept an exchange. The same applies if the shopkeeper offers to repair the defect.

If customers have not accepted the goods, they can demand their money back. If they have accepted them, they can insist on damages. The damages will usually be the cost of repair, plus any incidental expenses. They need not have the repair carried out by the shopkeeper but can, if they wish, have the repair done elsewhere and make the shopkeeper pay the bill. If they do this, they must, of course, ensure that the repair work is done at a reasonable price, so they should obtain estimates from several sources.

Credit notes

Since a credit note is not one of the two remedies recognized by the law, it will be either less or more than the customer is entitled to. If customers have not accepted the goods, they can demand all their money back, in cash. So they need not accept a credit note if they would rather have cash. However, if customers have 'accepted' the goods, then they will be entitled only to damages.

Once customers have agreed to take a credit note they cannot demand that it be exchanged for cash. They have said they would accept goods to the value of the credit note and cannot later change their mind.

How much damages?

If goods are faulty and it is too late to cancel the purchase, customers can claim damages for all losses naturally and directly flowing, in the ordinary course of events, from the breach. The object of damages is, by paying compensation, to put them into the position they would have been in if the contract had not been broken.

For example, Mrs Jones buys a washing machine. Three months later it overheats, ruining the clothes inside it. Clearly the shop is liable since the machine is not of merchantable quality. It is too late for her to get her money back, but she can claim the cost of the engineer's visits in inspecting the machine and repairing it; the value of the clothes that have been ruined; the additional cost of taking her clothes to a launderette while her machine is out of order; the postage and phone bills involved; her lost wages while off work (e.g. to let the engineer in). If she did not lose time off work she could claim a nominal sum for the inconvenience involved – say, £10 per half-day. All of these would be losses naturally flowing from the shop's breach of contract. Mrs Jones would, of course, be under a duty to keep her losses to a minimum (e.g. postpone doing her washing for a day rather than incur extra launderette bills).

Mrs Jones in the example claims not only for financial costs, the amounts of which are easily identified, but also for inconvenience, which is less easy to calculate in monetary terms. Damages for breach of contract can also include compensation for disappointment, inconvenience, distress (including mental distress) and discomfort and loss of enjoyment. An example of this would be a claim where the ecstatic text of a holiday brochure was in no way matched by the reality of the resort.

35 Paying for Services

In a contract for services, or for work and materials, the consumer's rights and supplier's duties are governed by the Supply of Goods and Services Act 1982. It too (like the Sale of Goods Act) has several implied terms which protect the consumer. S. 13 reads: 'In a contract for the supply of a service where the supplier is acting in the course of a business there is an implied term that the supplier will carry out the service with reasonable care and skill.'

REASONABLE CARE AND SKILL

A person who follows a trade or profession must exercise the ordinary skill of a reasonably competent member of that trade or profession. But whereas there is an implied term as to 'reasonable care and skill', there is no implied term that the professional person will achieve the desired result.

Although the customer can expect a reasonable standard of workmanship, this is a notoriously difficult test to apply. It is so vague that it allows for considerable dispute as to what is 'reasonable' and what is not.

Where a repairer fails to solve a problem and, for all his skill and efforts, cannot trace – let alone cure – an elusive fault, the customer cannot refuse payment for the work and time spent. He must pay a reasonable amount, unless the problem was not solved due to the incompetence of the repairer.

If customers do not think that the work done is of the proper quality, and the firm will not accept their complaint, they should obtain evidence to show that the work was not of a reasonable standard. This is best done by asking another firm, in the same line of business, to inspect the work and say what, in their opinion, is wrong. If they also give a quote for remedying the faults, that will be a good starting-point for deciding how much damages are due.

The Supply of Goods and Services Act applies not only to 'pure' services, such as dry-cleaners, laundry, cobbler or electrician, but also to those which include the provision and use of at least some materials and goods. The goods and materials of such a contract must meet the quality, fitness and description criteria of the Sale of Goods Act. These are a strict liability – not in the sense of being onerous but of being strictly binding on retailers even if they have taken all reasonable care and the fault lies with, say, the manufacturer.

The idea of 'reasonable skill and care' extends to taking care of the articles entrusted to a trader for servicing or repairing. If they are lost, destroyed or stolen while there, traders would have to prove that they (or their staff) had not been negligent (in the technical sense of negligence – see page 550). If they cannot, they would have to pay compensation to the customer.

Some repairers, contractors and servicers use exclusion clauses in their order forms in an attempt to exclude their liability for lost or damaged goods (e.g. 'Customers' goods and valuables are left at their own risk'). Under the Unfair Contract Terms Act these exemption clauses must pass the 'reasonableness' test; if the clause is unreasonable it will be struck out and so be totally ineffective.

A QUESTION OF TIME

In s. 14 of the Supply of Goods and Services Act there is an implied term that the supplier will carry out the service within a reasonable time; the contract itself can, however, stipulate the time. So if a motorist wants her car serviced by the Friday evening when she is due to go away on holiday, she should make this clear to the garage. If the car is then not ready in time, she would be entitled to deduct damages (e.g. the cost of hiring a substitute car) from the bill.

Stipulating a time by which a service must be carried out, repairs completed or goods delivered is called 'making time of the essence'. It is best to do so in writing (so as to have written proof) but word of mouth is sufficient. Then if you are let down, you can cancel the contract, get back any money paid and claim compensation for any loss suffered or extra expenses incurred.

ESTIMATES, QUOTES, PRICE TO BE PAID

When major work is to be carried out, or if the work is of a technical nature, it is usual for customers to obtain an estimate or quote from contractors. They are not the same thing, although it is not uncommon to find quotes and estimates regarded as being mere guides as to the eventual price.

A quote is binding on the parties, even if the job should turn out to involve considerably more, or less, work than was originally envisaged. A quote is a fixed price, unless it specifically says that the quotation 'is not a fixed price', or that the quote can be 'increased to reflect increased cost of materials'.

With estimates, the position is less clear-cut. In legal theory, an estimate is similar to a quote in that it is a pre-arranged, fixed price. However, in practice, an estimate is regarded as no more than a 'statement of intent' as to what the price will be, and it seems unlikely that customers could treat an estimate in the same way as a quote. If the eventual bill is higher than the original estimate, customers will have to pay the increased amount – assuming, of course, that it is a 'reasonable' price for the work done. If the price greatly exceeds the estimate, the consumer should ask the contractor to justify the increase.

When customers agree an estimate, it is advisable for them to stipulate, where appropriate, that 'Extra work shall be carried out only on my written instructions.' This will reduce the scope for arguments if the contractor should later charge for work that was not asked for.

A customer, for example, may have asked only for a coat to be dry-cleaned and yet be requested to pay extra because it has been retextured as well. When this happens, the customer is not responsible for the extra work and need not pay for it. However, this assumes that he can prove what was said when the original order was made. In practice, it may be difficult for the customer to show that he did not ask for the coat to be retextured, unless there was a witness who heard him ask for it to be dry-cleaned only.

Similar rules apply when a garage carries out expensive work to a car without prior authorization. If the customer takes a car into the garage for them to investigate a particular noise, the garage cannot go ahead and remedy the defect without the owner's authority: he has asked only that the noise be investigated, not that the work be done. Likewise, if the customer asks the garage to contact him if the cost is likely to exceed a specified sum, the garage must do so. Often there is no pre-arranged agreement about the price to be paid for the work done. Either the price is not mentioned or the contractor says it is impossible to give a price until work has been started and it becomes clear what is involved in the job. The problems arise when the customer thinks the bill is too high.

A reasonable price

In the absence of a specific agreement as to the price, the customer must pay a 'reasonable amount' – in other words, the amount that a similar firm would charge for the work done. The law says that when a price is not agreed in advance, then 'there is an implied term that the (customer) will pay a reasonable charge' (s. 15, Supply of Goods and Services Act 1982). So if customers think the bill is too high, they should ask other local traders what they would have charged, and then offer the contractor what seems to be the average price.

Obviously, it is important to compare like with like. For instance, a person who employs a twenty-four-hour plumbing service to repair a leaking pipe must expect to pay more than if he had employed a local, day-time plumber. What is a reasonable price for the work done will depend on all the circumstances of the case.

If the parties agreed beforehand on a specific price, the 'reasonable amount' rule does not apply. Both sides are bound by the agreed price. If the price is excessive for the work done, then the customer has no legal redress (assuming, of course, that the work is to a standard that one would expect for that price); conversely, if the agreed price is very cheap for the work done, the customer cannot be made to pay more.

557

Deposits and the unpaid seller

Paying a deposit is more than a formality or a sign of good intentions; it is usually part of a binding contract.

Customers may want to put down a deposit to reserve an article in a shop for which they do not have enough money till next payday. Shopkeepers can say 'no' to this proposal, but if they say 'yes', neither side can back out. Or customers want something not actually available in the shop and the retailer orders it or gets it made specially for them on condition that a deposit is paid. If those customers then change their mind, they will forfeit their deposit to the retailer, who can offset it against his loss (the full price of the goods if he cannot sell them to another customer).

Builders or decorators may ask for an advance payment before they even put brush to paintpot (the cash advance may indeed be necessary before they can buy the necessary brush and paint). If you then decide not to go ahead with the work, the builders can sue you for their losses, which would be compensation for loss of profit and the cost of extra materials bought that they could not use on another contract.

Under s. 49 of the Sale of Goods Act, where goods have been ordered and the consumer wrongfully refuses to accept them (i.e. without valid reason for rejection) and refuses to pay, the retailer can sue for the price of the goods. Moreover, under s. 50 of the Act, the seller can claim damages for the estimated loss resulting from the buyer's breach of contract.

Sellers are 'unpaid' within the meaning of the Sale of Goods Act (s. 38) when the whole of the price has not been paid or tendered, or when the cheque for it has bounced. They then acquire a lien on the goods (a right to keep them). This in itself does not rescind the contract, but where unpaid sellers give notice that they intend to resell the goods to someone else, that second buyer acquires good title to them as against the original buyer. So if the original buyer were to say, 'These goods really belong to me', he or she would not be right.

Waiting for delivery

Sometimes customers order an item and are then told it is out of stock and cannot be supplied for some time. Can they back out of the transaction and take their custom to another shop that can offer immediate delivery? Generally the answer will be no, for there is already a binding contract with the shopkeeper and the customer cannot back out – unless, of course, it was specifically agreed that the goods should be ready by a particular date, or the customer has made time 'of the essence' (see page 556).

Once a contract has been made and a price agreed, the traders cannot ask you to pay more than the price you saw when you placed your order. They would have had to make it clear when you placed the order that you are expected to meet any price rises which occur before the goods are delivered. (A change in VAT can, however, be passed on.)

But when ordering from a catalogue or brochure which says something open-ended like 'subject to price fluctuations' or 'prices correct at the time of going to print', the customer may have to pay the new current price in order to receive the goods.

Sometimes you are asked to sign for goods when they are delivered. There is no reason to refuse, as long as the signature is no more than proof of delivery. Not so if it is a satisfaction note stating that the goods are satisfactory or in good order. Unless there is a chance to look at them properly first, it is better to write 'goods not examined', in case they turn out faulty and you want to take action.

BUYING BY POST

The first thing to remember is that the consumer's Sale of Goods Act rights are the same when buying from home by mail order as when buying in a shop. This is particularly relevant for the implied terms that the goods are not faulty and are as described. Wrong descriptions should be reported to the local authority's trading standards department (see page 573). When ordering goods by post, it is advisable to keep the catalogue or advertisement that describes the goods and to make a note of what you ordered, when, and how you paid for it.

The name and address of the business must be given where an advertisement, circular or catalogue invites orders for goods for which payment is to be made before they are dispatched. That seems to be all the law has to say specifically about mail order; the rest lies in various codes of practice. A consumer buying from a catalogue published by one of the mail-order companies which belong to the Mail Order Traders' Association is protected by the MOTA code of practice (see page 563 for codes of practice generally). Under that code, the goods should be sent 'on approval', allowing the customer to return them within a specified time (fourteen days plus). Refunds for unwanted or faulty goods should be made promptly, goods damaged in transit replaced at no extra cost. The delivery dates quoted in the catalogue should be met and if there is likely to be any undue delay, the customer should be told.

The Association of Mail Order Publishers represents many firms that sell books, periodicals, records (including videos and cassettes) by post. Before joining such a so-called 'club', read the terms and conditions carefully: they form the basis of your contract, which generally you may terminate only after one year or after you have bought the agreed number of books (or other items).

There may be a condition that club members will accept – and pay for – the 'choice of the month' book or cassette, which will be sent automatically unless they say 'no' within a set time. (This is a different thing from what is generally known as 'unsolicited goods' – see page 561.)

The majority of book clubs are registered with the Publishers Association and have to follow certain regulations of conduct: the minimum period of club membership must not be less than six months (but can be, and generally is, longer) and members must buy not less than three book club choices within the first year of membership.

The Association of Mail Order Publishers' code of practice covers the way goods are advertised and dispatched and the publisher-members' debt-collecting methods, to ensure that customers are not being bothered without good reason.

Mail Order Protection Scheme (MOPS)

When paying in advance for goods offered in a newspaper or magazine advert, customers risk losing their money if the advertiser has stopped trading. There are, however, various mail-order protection schemes run by some publishers of newspapers and magazines. The aim is to protect readers who have no chance of receiving either the goods ordered or their money back because the trader has gone into liquidation or become bankrupt. This applies only to adverts in the newspapers or magazines which belong to one of the participating trade associations, and not if the advertisement appeared as a small-ad in a classified column or is for perishable foods or medical products. There is a time limit for claiming; the publications which participate in the 'protection scheme' carry details about how to claim.

If the complaint is a more general one about the wording of the advertisement, it should be directed to the Advertising Standards Association, which enforces the British Code of Advertising Practice. That code is intended to ensure that adverts are 'legal, decent, honest and truthful'. The advertising practice code requires mail-order traders to deliver goods (except plants and made-to-measure items) within twenty-eight days, or to tell the customer if they cannot do so.

DOORSTEP SELLING

Of course, not all doorstep selling is roguery. But, 'Good evening, I'm doing some research', or 'Good evening, I have come from the council to advise on security', may well be ways for rogues to insinuate themselves into the home of an unsuspecting consumer. The Direct Selling Association's code of conduct requires sales representatives to carry an identification card, and common sense requires the householder to examine it carefully, preferably before the caller's foot is through the door.

Goods sold by any trader must be of merchantable quality, fit for their purpose and 'as described'. Services ('I see your roof needs retiling') must be carried out with 'reasonable care and skill'. But these legal rights are not much use if the doorstep seller has moved on or disappeared. So ask callers for their full name and find out whom they represent, and keep a note of the firm's address. If there is a lot of pressure or the whole thing seems fishy, do not buy, and report the incident to the local trading standards department.

Do not sign anything without first reading it carefully, and if you do not understand it fully, do not sign at all. Following an unsolicited doorstep sale of over £35, and also where a trader calls after making a telephone appointment based on something like, 'Good evening, you have won a prize . . .', the buyer has the right to cancel. This cooling-off period is seven days when payment was in cash or by cheque. For HP or other credit agreements signed at the buyer's home, not in a shop or other trade premises, there are five days in which to cancel. Where the purchase was made at an organized selling-party in somebody's private home, ask if the business that sells the goods is a member of the Direct Selling Association, as many such businesses are. There should then be a fourteen-day cooling-off period with offer of full refund.

UNSOLICITED GOODS

Goods arriving on the doorstep or through the letter box that had not been ordered need not be paid for. The Unsolicited Goods and Services Act 1971 says that the recipient can use them, deal with them or dispose of them as if they were unconditional gifts. However, unlike a true unconditional gift, which can be thrown in the wastebin or destroyed the minute it arrives, unordered goods have to be retained for six months and kept safe so that the sender can come and collect them back at any time during that period. Alternatively, the recipient can write to the sender of the goods, stating that the goods were unsolicited, giving the address from which the sender should collect them. If this does not happen within thirty days, the goods really become the recipient's – to use, sell, give away or throw on the bonfire.

Moreover, the Unsolicited Goods and Services Act has a criminal sanction: a trader commits an offence if he or she demands payment for goods knowing them to be unsolicited, or makes any threats about non-payment. A consumer should take any bill or demand for payment for unsolicited goods to the local trading standards office (see page 573).

36 Complaining

Being cross or upset without doing something about it is unlikely to get you any compensation. If you think you have a reasonable complaint, take it up with the shopkeeper or other seller, or, in the case of a service, with the contractor or other provider of the service. Even if you do not know exactly which bit of the law is at issue – breach of contract, negligence, non-compliance with section X or Y of this or that statute – if something is faulty you are not asking a favour when trying to have it put right; you are simply claiming your rights.

These may be: money back (which also means returning the goods) and/or damages to recompense you for any extra expenses (e.g. hiring a car) and/or for actual financial loss (e.g. pay deducted for a day off work waiting for a service engineer who does not turn up) and recompense for distress or disappointment. This is more difficult to quantify and more difficult to enforce and may need threatened – or actual – court action (see Chapter 68 for a guide on taking a case to court, with or without a solicitor).

For a claim that involves only a small amount (at present £1,000 or less) the county court – where most consumers' civil actions are heard – offers an arbitration procedure. This is less formal than a full-blown court action and has the advantage that no 'costs' will be awarded. So, win or lose, neither side can be ordered to pay the other's legal costs. For a case where the amount claimed by the consumer is more than £1,000, the trader would have to give his or her agreement that the case be dealt with by 'small claim' arbitration.

ARBITRATION

Going to court should be a last resort, and is generally the exception. There are less drastic routes for settling disputes.

Some public utilities (even some of the now-privatized ones), such as gas, electricity, telephones, the post office, the railway, have a consumer or consultative council (or it may be a users' committee) to help sort out problems. The local contact point and brief instructions are usually on the back of the current bill.

Many trade associations have set up their own schemes for resolving disputes between traders and consumers. Such a scheme may be conciliation under a code of practice (see below for codes of practice). If that fails, the next step may be arbitration. Such 'code of practice' arbitration is something quite different from what takes place in the county court. An independent arbitrator decides the rights and wrongs of the case, and the level of damages, on the basis of documentary evidence submitted by the trader and the consumer.

The arbitrator is not a member of the particular trade association but an independent professional arbitrator appointed by the Institute of Arbitrators. Usually a smallish fee is payable, but it may be returned to the consumer if his or her complaint is eventually upheld by the arbitrator.

Arbitration is on the terms of the contract that was concluded between trader and consumer. That means that, for example, the validity of any exclusion clauses or limitation clauses cannot be challenged, as would be possible at a court hearing.

Arbitration can take place only if both parties agree. Under the Consumer Arbitration Agreements Act 1988 any term in a trader's standard contract that future differences (between trader and consumer) are to be referred to arbitration cannot be enforced, and if consumers do not want to go to arbitration, they cannot be compelled to. (Such a compulsory arbitration term used to be common in, e.g. furniture-removers' contracts.)

CODES OF PRACTICE

Trade associations and professional bodies exist largely for the benefit of their members. Many have a voluntary code of practice – rules which their members should follow and which should provide a better deal and improved standards of service for customers. The codes are entirely voluntary and have no legal standing but are of great practical importance, not least because they can include provisions not covered by law (such as how to deal with complaints promptly and politely, or to have spare parts available for the servicing of new models of cars).

Many of the codes have arisen via a statutory requirement in the Fair Trading Act 1973 for the Director of Fair Trading to encourage trade associations to prepare 'codes of practice for guidance in safeguarding and promoting the interest of consumers'. The public relations value to the particular trade of a good code of practice is an essential by-product.

Nearly thirty voluntary codes of practice have been negotiated with the Office of Fair Trading and are sponsored by trade associations concerned with cars, caravans and motor cycles, direct marketing, mail-order and direct selling, dry-cleaning and laundering, electrical goods, double-glazing, funerals, furniture, photography (seven different codes), shoes and – much needed – travel.

The travel trade's code

The ABTA (Association of British Travel Agents) code for tour operators requires that brochures should be clear, comprehensive and accurate, with the prices quoted to include airport taxes; and that holidays should not be cancelled except in very rare (*force majeure*) circumstances after the balance of the price becomes due (generally one and a half to two months before departure), unless the tour operator pays compensation to the holidaymaker. (*Force majeure* includes war, civil strife and terrorist activity, industrial dispute, natural or nuclear disaster, fire and adverse weather conditions.)

Similarly, where there are material changes to the confirmed arrangements about travel and accommodation, they should be notified to the traveller not later than a fortnight before the beginning of the holiday (except for *force majeure*).

If such changes are made at any time before the balance of payment is due, the client shall be given the option of cancelling the tour, or travel arrangements, and getting back all the money so far paid. Where the reason for the proposed change is other than *force majeure*, or it happens later than by the allowed date, the code asks the tour operator to offer 'reasonable compensation' on a rising scale – the nearer to departure date, the higher the amount of compensation.

The ABTA code requires the tour operator to settle disputes amicably and as quickly as possible; there are even time limits for the to-and-fro of complaints correspondence. One clause of the code exhorts not only that 'all members shall ensure that the public receive the best possible service' but also that they 'shall take no action that might adversely affect the reputation, standing and good name of the Association and its members'.

Under the ABTA code, the association offers a free conciliation service where there is serious disagreement and previous negotiations have failed. ABTA cannot, however, compel members to offer customers compensation, but would point them to the documents-only arbitration scheme. Using the conciliation service does not take away the right to take legal action. The ABTA arbitration scheme, on the other hand, is an alternative to going to court; once you have opted for arbitration you cannot sue. A case for arbitration has to be submitted within nine months of returning from the holiday. The conciliation and arbitration procedures apply to tour operators and to travel agents (the two lots of holiday and travel providers have two different codes).

And what are the sanctions if the code is breached? In ascending order, the penalties are: investigation by the ABTA secretariat, reprimand, fixed-fee penalty (£300 at present), suspension or even termination of membership. So, look out for the ABTA symbol and the firm's ABTA number when you make a booking. If there is none, beware; the travel agent or tour operator is either defrocked or never was a member of the trade association.

The motor trades code

The code of practice for the motor industry deals with all the potential bugbears: new car sales, used car sales, repairs and servicing, replacement parts and accessories and a complaints procedure complete with conciliation scheme and independent arbitration. The Office of Fair Trading gives this practical advice to consumers:

● Give the garage a clear description of the problem or the work you want done. It's best to do it in writing.

● Make sure you know beforehand what the service includes. Tell the garage if you want the manufacturer's recommended servicing schedule to be carried out – and agree items (if any) that can be left out.

● Get a quotation (a fixed price) or estimate (a good guess), in writing if it's a big job. Check that labour, parts and VAT are included.

● Find out how long the job will take or agree on a set time for collection.

● Leave a phone number. Tell the garage to ask for your permission before carrying on with the work if the cost is likely to exceed the estimate.

● Get a detailed invoice, listing all work carried out, showing parts and labour costs.

CODES OF PRACTICE: ADVANTAGES AND DISADVANTAGES

Although not a law, a code of practice can have a very useful role in trades where there is an effective control method, such as with ABTA. It is almost impossible for travel agents or tour operators to run a business in this country unless they belong to ABTA; if they do not, they will not get the necessary air travel licences needed to book charters. In other areas, such as the motor trade, codes work less well, mainly because garages do not have to belong to a trade association in order to be in business at all.

Codes of practice are not carved in stone; they can be, and have been, renegotiated and adjusted as needs arise, and as circumstances change, within and outside the particular trade or industry. And while the law is not carved in stone either, to change it tends to take time. The consumer can invoke the law in any confrontation with suppliers and traders, but cannot invoke the code of practice of the trader's association against him or her.

The main disadvantage is that the codes are voluntary and do not have the force of legislation. Not all members of an association always honour their code, nor do the associations themselves check whether this is done. The most serious disadvantage is that not everyone who carries out a particular trade is a member, and it may well be the rogues in the trade who are not.

Apart from the voluntary codes of practice of trade associations, there are statutory codes (see page 571 for an example).

37 Crimes: Safety, Description, Price

The criminal law discourages behaviour which is likely to be harmful to everyone by punishing those who commit an offence. An offence is a breach of the rules of the criminal law. While the criminal law does not give consumers any individual rights, it does protect them as members of the community.

There are many criminal statutes which apply to the manufacture, description and distribution of consumer goods, and also to their weights and measures, pricing, labelling, advertising and safety. The responsibility for enforcing these laws and their various rules and regulations rests largely, but not exclusively, with the local authorities (see page 573).

PRODUCT SAFETY

Various pieces of legislation, from the early 1960s onward, have brought some statutory control over unsafe products supplied to consumers, mainly by making it possible for regulations to be made setting out this or that safety standard on an ad hoc basis. These include safety regulations (made under two Consumer Protection Acts, 1961 and 1971, and the Consumer Safety Act 1978) for carry-cot stands, nightdresses, oil heaters, babies' dummies, fireguards, electric blankets, pushchairs, aerosol dispensers, upholstered furniture, motor tyres and fireworks.

Part II of the Consumer Protection Act 1987 has kept alive – with improvements – many regulations of previous legislation, consolidated it and brought in new provisions. The main innovation is the formalizing of a 'general safety requirement': 'A person shall be guilty of an offence if he supplies any consumer goods which fail to comply with the general safety requirement.'

Supplying goods includes offering to supply them, or simply having them there for the customers to see. 'Safe' is defined as no risk, or risk 'reduced to a minimum' of the goods or the way they are used causing death or personal injury to anyone.

Secondhand goods are excluded from the general safety requirement, but the government can make specific safety regulations for secondhand goods – and any other goods. Regulations can be made about composition or contents, design, construction, finish of goods and even their packing, and can require that a mark, warning or instruction, or other relevant information, be put on or accompany the goods (and that inappropriate information is not given in relation to goods by misleading marks or in any other way).

Action points

The Secretary of State can issue a *prohibition notice* (preventing the supply of unsafe goods) or a *notice to warn* (that the goods are considered unsafe). The trading standards officers (see page 573), who are the enforcing authority for this piece of legislation, may serve a *suspension notice*, specifying that the goods in question may not be supplied for six months. If all else fails, the enforcing authority can apply to the magistrates' court to issue an *order for forfeiture* so that the goods will be suspended from supply or, more likely, destroyed.

Because unsafe goods may be imported into the UK, customs officers may seize imported goods that they suspect to be unsafe, and hold them for two working days. This might then be followed by a six-month suspension notice.

TRADE DESCRIPTIONS

Whenever goods are for sale, anything relevant that is said about them is a trade description. Trade descriptions, in whatever way they are made, must not be false. They may be by word of mouth (sales talk) or in writing/printing, such as a brochure, label, display card, instruction leaflet, poster, circular, catalogue, price list or other advertisement, including TV advert. Even a picture can amount to a trade description. In Queensway Discount Warehouse v. Burke (1986) a newspaper advert showed the finished product of DIY assembly furniture, which is delivered to customers packed flat. The court held that this amounted to a breach of the 'composition' requirement in s. 2 of the Trade Description Act 1968.

The Act specifies in great detail what is included in the concept of a trade description, including:

• *quantity or size* – that is, not only number but also length, width, height, area, volume, capacity and weight (and there is some overlap with the Weights and Measures Act 1985, a criminal statute under which it is an offence to sell short weight or inadequate quantity when goods are sold by weight, number or other measurement). Certain foods (such as salt, sugar, milk) when sold prepacked must be in prescribed quantities and all prepacked foodstuffs (in pack, bottle, tin) must be marked with their weight or quantity;

• *fitness for purpose* – strength, performance, accuracy; any indication of how effective the goods will be – 'waterproof', 'non-stick', 'shrink-resistant', 'stainless' – must be true;

• *date and place* of manufacture, production, processing or reconditioning: that would apply to a secondhand car and to the age of a priceless antique; and so would

• *other history* – including previous ownership or use ('one lady owner' or 'army surplus');

- *composition* – which generally refers to what materials the goods are made of ('leather uppers', 'man-made soles', 'four star petrol').

A claim that an article has been tested or approved by anyone must also be true. And it is an offence to give a false 'by royal appointment' indication.

On the whole, s. 2 of the Act lists attributes of which the truth or falsity can be established as a matter of fact. Less clear-cut matters of opinion (such as 'extra value' on the wrapper of a chocolate bar) may not be caught by the definition of a (false) trade description. A trade description can be false within the meaning of the Act if it is actually false 'to a material degree' or merely likely to be misleading to a material degree.

Falsely described motor vehicles and motor accessories are the largest category of convictions under the Trade Descriptions Act.

S. 2 of the Trade Descriptions Act contains clear echoes of the Misrepresentation Act 1967 and s. 14 of the Sale of Goods Act 1979, and a situation that amounts to a criminal offence under the Trade Descriptions Act may at the same time give rise to a civil action between consumer and trader. The Misrepresentation Act gives consumers rights which enable them to cancel the contract and/or claim damages (see page 553). Similarly, they may have the right of action under the Sale of Goods Act. However, prosecution under the Trade Descriptions Act would not directly help the consumer (but see page 574 for the criminal courts' power to award compensation). A contract for the sale of goods is not invalidated, nor does it become unenforceable, just because there is a contravention of the Trade Descriptions Act.

The Trade Descriptions legislation relates to any person in the course of trade or business – that is, business suppliers only, not a private seller. The offence of applying a false trade description can be bipartite. In the first place, manufacturers who put the labels on their product, or prepare the promotion literature, can be prosecuted if they contain false information. And so can the retailer who then sells these same goods. Moreover, shopkeepers become responsible if they simply offer for sale or display in their shops goods carrying a false trade description, even if nobody has come forward to buy these goods. Where the description is oral, perhaps by zealous shop assistants, and it can be shown to be false, they commit an offence.

It is, however, a defence if traders can prove that they took all reasonable precautions and exercised all due diligence to avoid the commission of such an offence by themselves or any person under their control, and that the offence was due to a mistake or reliance on someone else's information (who might then have to carry the can), or due to an accident or 'some other cause beyond his control', or if they can prove that they did not know and could not with reasonable diligence have known that the goods did not in fact conform to the description given of them.

Descriptions of services, just like descriptions of goods, must be accurate. If a sign in a photo-shop promises 'one-hour developing', or that a shoemaker will repair your boots 'while you wait', the jobs must not take longer to complete.

Travel agents' brochures, too, have to comply with the requirement of no false statements. S. 14 of the Trade Descriptions Act makes it an offence for any person in the course of any trade or business to make any statement which he knows to be false, or recklessly to make a statement which is false as to the nature or provision of any services, accommodation or facilities (and their location or amenities) provided in the course of any trade or business.

This part of the Act relating to false statements about services is more lenient than that relating to the strict offence of applying false descriptions to goods. The false statement about services has to be made knowingly or recklessly. A reckless statement does not necessarily involve dishonesty. It is one made regardless of whether it is true or false, or whether or not the person making it had reasons for believing that it might be false.

Estate agents are different

The Trade Descriptions Act does not deal with land or buildings and so it does not cover estate agents' descriptions of houses for sale. In view of the imaginative prose of estate agents' literature and the persuasive oral statements of some, this was for a long time a bone of consumer contention and a cause for consumer lobbying. Then 1991 saw the passing of the Property Misdescription Act (to take effect in the summer of 1992). The Act makes property-sellers legally responsible for the accuracy of their descriptions (like sellers of goods and services being responsible under the Trade Descriptions Act) and covers estate agents, builders, property developers and also solicitors when selling property.

The three estate agents' professional bodies have all drawn up quite stiff codes of conduct for their members.

Estate agents are not obliged to belong to these associations, but the majority of them do, and all estate agents are bound by the Estate Agents Act 1979. Under that Act, estate agents must disclose any interest they (or any of their employees, or any relative) have in the property they are trying to sell.

Estate agents' ombudsman

One of the new ombudsman schemes is the Ombudsman for Corporate Estate Agents. Corporate, in this context, means being part of another corporate body such as bank or building society, or large enough to be quoted on the stock exchange. So far, twenty-seven estate agency chains belong, with about 4,300 shops between them.

It was introduced in September 1990 'to provide an independent service for dealing with disputes between member agencies and buyers or sellers of residential property in the UK'. Complaints can be considered where clients think that the agency has infringed their legal rights, treated them unfairly, was inefficient or caused undue delay.

It does not cover complaints where the dispute is about a survey, or claims above £100,000. The top limit of compensation, if awarded by the Ombudsman, is £100,000. The estate agent would be bound to pay. Clients can reject the Ombudsman's decision and take legal action against the estate agent if they prefer.

Anyone can set up as an estate agent, but under the Estate Agents Act the Director General of Fair Trading is empowered to prohibit unfit persons from doing estate agency work.

THE OFT AND THE FAIR TRADING ACT

The post of Director General of Fair Trading was created by the Fair Trading Act 1973. The Act is more concerned with trader-to-trader aspects than with the trader-to-consumer angle. But the Director must keep on the lookout for trade practices which may be detrimental to the economic and other interests of consumers. He can, and does, arrange for the Office of Fair Trading to publish information and advice for consumers. Many such OFT publications are available free from libraries and Citizens' Advice Bureaux.

Where a trader's conduct is persistently unfair to consumers, the Director can demand an assurance (in writing) from the offender that he or she will cease the conduct in question. If traders refuse to give their assurance, or fail to honour it, the Director may bring proceedings against them.

While the OFT does not deal with individual consumer complaints, a record is kept of such complaints, and they may lead to an investigation into rogue trading activities.

For the Director General's role in connection with consumer credit see pages 577, 582.

PRICES

The Trade Descriptions Act 1968 had an important section (s.11) dealing in some detail with false or misleading indications as to the price of goods. The offences were over-charging, false comparisons with a recommended price (e.g. the 'list price' for white goods or electrical appliances) or with the trader's own previous price (e.g. 'sales' goods which were not really reduced in price but specially bought in). The provisions were cumbersome and a wily trader could wriggle out with impunity. They were supplemented with a clumsy piece of subsidiary legislation, the Price Marking (Bargain Offers) Order 1979. Eventually this Order and s.11 of the Trade Descriptions Act were repealed by Part III of the Consumer Protection Act 1987, which is wider in scope and simpler in approach.

There is still the basic offence (s.20 of the Act) of giving, by any means whatever, to any consumer an indication which is misleading as to the price at which any goods, services, accommodation or facilities are available. S.22 of the Act gives details of what is meant by misleading in various circumstances and s.25 approves the issuing of a code of practice for the purpose of giving practical guidance with respect to any of the requirements of s.20.

This is a statutory code, unlike the trade associations' codes of practice discussed on page 563, which are voluntary.

The prices code

The way a statutory code works is that there is a general legal provision – in this case, the law says that shops must not use misleading price indications – and the code then takes over and lays down, in a relaxed way with lots of examples, all the things that the trader should and should not do. For example, 'Do not make statements like "sale price £5" or "reduced to £39" without quoting the higher price to which they refer . . . crossed-out higher prices should be used only if they refer to your own previous price.'

For any comparison with the trader's own previous price the code says: 'The product should have been available to consumers at that price for at least twenty-eight consecutive days in the previous six months . . .' (the twenty-eight days may include bank holidays and days of religious observance when the shop was closed).

The code asks traders not to 'call a promotion an introductory offer unless they intend to continue to offer the product for sale after the offer period is over and to do so at a higher price . . .' It deals with prices for special groups of people; with sales – 'do not use general notices saying "up to 50 per cent off" unless the maximum reduction quoted applies to at least 10 per cent of the range of products on offer'; and with free offers – 'make clear to consumers, at the time of the offer for sale, exactly what they will have to buy to get the "free offer" and if there are any conditions attached to it'.

The code commands, 'Do not compare your price with an amount described only as "worth" or "value"', and, 'Do not use a recommended retail price in a comparison unless it has been recommended to you by the manufacturer or supplier as a price at which the product might be sold to consumers.' It warns against incomplete information and non-optional extras, such as a service charge in a hotel or restaurant: '. . . Incorporate the charge within fully inclusive prices wherever practicable.' And where this is not practicable, the charge should be shown as prominently as other prices on any list or menu.

For holiday and travel prices, if the tour operator or travel agent wants 'to reserve the right to increase prices after consumers have made their booking, state this clearly and include prominently in your brochure full information on the circumstances in which a surcharge is payable.'

The code says that all price indications given to private consumers, by whatever means, should include VAT. If a trader's price indications become misleading because of a change in the general rate of VAT or other taxes paid at point of sale, the correct price indication should be made clear to any consumers before they are committed to buying the product.

Effect of the prices code

There is a presumption that traders who can show that they comply with the code are not giving a misleading price indication (and therefore not guilty of an offence under the Consumer Protection Act) and, conversely, those who are in breach of the code are *prima facie* – but not necessarily – guilty of the offence.

The code seems to work in practice rather better than the previous, much discredited, detailed regulations governing bargain offers and similar matters.

Other rules about price marking

Misleading price indications are also held in check by statutory instruments such as the Price Marking Order 1991 (made under the Prices Act 1974) which implements EC directives requiring the selling price, and in some cases the unit price, of goods offered for sale to consumers to be indicated in writing. For goods displayed for sale, if the selling price is not shown on the goods themselves, or on a ticket on them, it should be on a list nearby, clearly legible to a prospective buyer. Also goods not on display, which are brought to the counter at the request of the customer, must either have the price on them or it must be shown to the customer in a catalogue, price list or visual display.

The Order applies to virtually all goods offered for retail sale. Antiques and works of art are excepted and there are special provisions for articles of jewellery and precious metals: if displayed in a shop window, the price need not be shown if it is more than £2,500 (but must be made available to prospective buyers by, e.g., showing them a price list).

The Order requires retailers to display the unit price of goods sold from bulk or prepacked in variable quantities. Fruits and vegetables (excluding mushrooms and herbs), meat, fish and cheeses all have to be unit-priced by reference to the kilo or the pound. Where the unit price of food is expressed in metric units, there must also be a unit price in imperial units. (This dual marking may be phased out in due course under the EC Units of Measurement Directives.)

FOOD

Some of the requirements of the Food Safety Act 1990 (which deals with more than food and more than safety, and which has retained many of the diverse regulations made under the earlier Food Act 1984) show an overlap with other legislation. For example, it is an offence to have a false or misleading description of the nature, quality or substance of food, and an offence if the nature, quality or substance of the food is not of the standard demanded.

It is an offence to supply food which is:
• unfit for human consumption;
• injurious to health;

- contaminated to the extent that it cannot reasonably be used for human consumption.

This 'general food safety requirement' echoes the 'general safety requirement' concept brought in by Part II of the Consumer Protection Act 1987 (see page 566).

In addition to any criminal sanctions, if customers buy food that is bad, the shop should refund their money. Buying food that is has gone off is just the same as buying any faulty goods, and the customer has the same legal redress against the shopkeeper (see page 553) under civil law; the environmental health officer will be enforcing the criminal law.

The environmental health departments of local authorities also enforce certain laws that cover public health matters, such as inspecting places where food is stored, prepared and sold, and also cleanliness in other establishments used by consumers, such as hairdressing and beauty salons. In the London boroughs, the division of work between environmental health departments and trading standard departments varies.

TRADING STANDARD OFFICERS

All local authorities have a trading standards department, generally with a fair trading, a product safety and a metrology division, and sometimes a consumer protection officer. Metrology is the new name for weights and measures. Official controls over traders' weighing and measuring equipment have been around for hundreds of years and the origin of the modern trading standards service goes back to this root. Inspectors have to check the accuracy of every petrol pump, pub measure, shop scale, packing machine and yardstick before it is allowed to be used, and make subsequent spot checks.

The trading standards officers make test purchases in shops and investigate complaints relating to the laws they enforce regarding false descriptions, prices, short weights and measures, quantity frauds, some aspects of the safety of consumer products, and some food matters such as composition and labelling. Usually one officer specializes in consumer credit (see page 576) and the TSO's areas of responsibility may include accuracy testing of weighing and measuring equipment used for trade purposes, disguised trade sales, unroadworthy car sales, cigarette sales to children, mock auctions, unsolicited goods and cowboy tradesmen.

Here are a few examples of matters investigated in one year (1990) by the fair trading division of a north London borough.

1 Unfair trading practices:
  - companies that disappeared with customers' deposits;
  - salesmen who would not leave the home;
  - mail order which never arrived;
  - car dealers who masqueraded as private sellers;

- cowboy builders who claimed to be on an 'approved' list.
2 false descriptions:
  - diver's watch that was not even splash-resistant;
  - imported products labelled 'made in Britain';
  - supermarket prices that were higher at the checkout;
  - a 93,000-mile car that was clocked to show 25,000;
  - fake 'branded' products complete with counterfeit labels and trademarks.
3 Consumer credit (see page 576):
  - credit adverts that misled and confused;
  - debtors harassed by bogus 'official documents';
  - pensioners with crippling repayment problems.

Trading standards departments keep a record of complaints and this information may then become relevant to the Director of Fair Trading. Although trading standards departments are not funded to deal with civil complaints, the officers may be able to advise on the validity of consumers' complaints against a shop and may even take some steps on their behalf if the other party is a known 'problem' trader or there is a criminal element in the complaint, such as a misdescription. The intervention of the TSO may help consumers to get their money back.

Where there is an offence, it is the trading standards officer who prosecutes, if necessary. The main aim is to put things right, so in some cases there may not be a prosecution but a warning. TSOs give advice to local traders, particularly regarding new legislation (to pre-empt the new law being broken – or, if broken, there would then be no excuse).

A complaint to a trading standards office can be made on the telephone, in person, by letter or even by fax. If, later, the citizen's complaint should lead to a prosecution, he or she will be asked for a witness statement, but it is uncommon to have to go to the magistrates' or Crown Court as a witness. And if, later still, the prosecution leads to a conviction, the court may make a compensation order to the consumer.

Compensation orders

The basis of early English criminal law is thought to have been the payment of compensation by the offender to the victim. As there was no central authority to set the appropriate punishment to fit the crime, pecuniary compensation ruled. Amounts depended on the seriousness of the injury and the social standing of the parties involved. When the criminal law evolved to concentrate on offenders and their offence (their injury against society rather than an individual), the victim was left to seek redress through the civil courts, where possible.

The Criminal Justice Act 1972 introduced the compensation order, whereby the court can order the offender to pay compensation to the victim. As the law now stands (s. 35 of the Powers of Criminal Court Act 1973), the court can make such an order instead of or in addition to any penalty imposed, up to £2,000 in the magistrates' court, and an unlimited amount in the higher courts.

There is no laid-down procedure for applying for a compensation order. All that the consumer needs to do is to indicate to the magistrates' clerk (or the prosecutor) that he wishes for a compensation order. The court may even make such an order where it has not received a specific application for one. Conversely, the magistrates are not compelled to make such an order and can use their discretion to say 'no'. The victims of the crime are then left to pursue their own remedy through the civil courts – in other words, the consumer can sue, helped by the knowledge that the trader's conviction of whatever the criminal offence was may be used as evidence in the civil proceedings.

38 Consumer Credit and HP

Buy now, pay later has been a commercial reality since money was invented, and straight borrowing is probably even older. All aspects of buying on the never-never, and buying on tick, now come under the heading of consumer credit. Credit is simply another name for debt, and never-never is misleading: at some point the debt will have to be repaid, with interest, plus probably some other charges.

DIFFERENT FORMS OF CREDIT

Hire purchase agreement

The customers technically hire the goods while they pay for them by instalments and own them only when they exercise their option to purchase and the last instalment has been paid. Interest is normally at a fixed rate throughout the agreement (see later regarding APR) and is part of the regular repayments. Buyers cannot end an HP agreement unless they are up to date with payments and have paid at least half the total amount owed. When one-third or more of the total amount payable has been paid, if the buyer then defaults, the finance company cannot reclaim the goods without a court order. It is usually a finance company, because when the consumer buys on HP, the retailer sells the goods to the finance company, who then lets the consumer have them on whatever HP terms are agreed. But in some cases retailers finance the HP agreement themselves.

Conditional sale agreement

For practical purposes this is the same as HP, but without the notional hiring. The purchase price for goods (or land) is payable by instalments and the goods (or land) will belong to the buyer when the conditions of payment etc. are fulfilled.

Credit sale agreement

Again, this is similar to HP but the crucial difference is that the goods belong to the buyer straightaway, as soon as the agreement is concluded, usually when the deposit is paid.

Since customers acquire immediate ownership of the goods, they can sell them before they have paid off all the loan – unlike with goods bought on HP – although they will of course remain liable to pay off the outstanding instalments. However, it will probably be a term of the credit-sale agreement that they pay off in one go all the remaining instalments as soon as they sell the goods.

The Consumer Credit Act 1974, which had an exceedingly slow parturition, being implemented bit by bit over more than ten years, is now the one statute dealing with virtually all aspects of credit, with the help of numerous orders, regulations and a licensing system. It brings under one umbrella practically all the various consumer credit agreements, up to a credit ceiling of £15,000: HP, conditional sale, credit sale, credit cards and credit tokens, bank overdraft, charge cards, store cards, loans from bank, building society, finance or insurance company, and even pawnbrokers. The Act controls ordinary hire agreements (although, unlike HP, hirers do not in the end buy the goods they have on hire) where the hire agreement is capable of lasting for more than three months. Hiring of goods is also taken care of by other legislation, such as s.9 of the Supply of Goods and Services Act 1982.

Licensing of lenders

The Consumer Credit Act 1974 has introduced an extensive system of licences for all people and firms who provide credit, hireage services, credit brokerage, debt-counselling and debt-collecting services. In effect *anyone* who provides credit, or lends money (e.g. under an HP agreement), must have a licence from the Office of Fair Trading. If there is no licence, then any credit agreement will be *unenforceable*, and so the customer can simply refuse to pay the instalments due. Then the lender can enforce an agreement only if the Director General of Fair Trading says so. In addition, the lender commits a criminal offence.

While all the reputable credit firms do have licences, some of the 'fringe operators' have not obtained licences, either because they do not realize that they need them or because their unsatisfactory credentials would bar them from obtaining a licence. A customer who is in dispute with such a firm might find it worthwhile checking whether they do have a consumer credit licence.

Certain agreements are valid even if there is no licence. For instance, building societies do not need a licence. Nor is a licence needed if the rate of interest was relatively low. In addition, the Consumer Credit Act applies only when credit of up to £15,000 is involved. So if more than £15,000 is lent (e.g. on a second mortgage) no licence is needed.

HOW MUCH DOES CREDIT COST?

There are strict rules about how the cost of borrowing is brought to the consumer's attention. The total charge for credit includes the interest that has to be paid, plus any charges for setting up the credit agreement, any cost of

577

security for the loan, compulsory insurance premiums, a credit broker's fee. The annual percentage rate (APR) is calculated from the total charge for credit via a complicated formula laid down by regulations which also take into account the fact that each repayment reduces the amount of debt, while the instalments remain the same throughout the loan. In practice, the APR works out at very approximately 1.8 times (i.e. nearly twice) the rate of interest.

To enable the consumer to compare like with like, the APR has to be stated prominently in advertisements, in quotations and the agreement itself. Where the APR is not fixed for the duration of a credit agreement, there must be a clear statement that it is variable.

Expressions such as 'interest free' must be used only where the total amount a credit customer will be liable to pay is not more than the cash price, and there are no hidden charges, such as a lower part-exchange allowance, that would not apply to a cash buyer.

Too much?

There are no rules about the interest rate charged. For example, in difficult circumstances a short-term loan might work out at an APR of 48 per cent (which the old Moneylenders Acts would have considered 'harsh and unconscionable'). That is as nothing to the APR of 1,407 per cent reported in a *Which?* article in August 1988 or an APR of 4,822 per cent uncovered by a trading standards officer in the Midlands. What is more, that particular lender was not a loan shark but a firm trading with an OFT credit licence. For a loan of more than £30, a trader must have a credit licence and it is illegal to split up a larger loan into several smaller ones in order to qualify for the less-than-£30 exemption.

The Consumer Credit Act provides for 'extortionate credit bargains' to be reopened and for the county court to alter the terms of the credit agreement – for example, by reducing the rate of interest.

The onus of proof is not on the debtor that a credit bargain is extortionate, but on the creditor that it is not. The Act itself does not clearly define what is extortionate, but uses the phrases 'grossly exorbitant' and 'grossly contravenes ordinary principles of fair dealings' and gives guidelines for the court to take into account the relative bargaining powers of debtor and creditor, and factors such as:
* the interest rates prevailing at the time the agreement was made;
* the debtor's age and health, experience and business capacity and the nature and extent of financial pressure on him or her when the agreement was made;
* the degree of risk accepted by the creditor.

Credit brokers and mortgage brokers

Anyone who finds credit facilities for someone else is a 'credit broker'. For instance, a mortgage broker who arranges mortgages and an electrical dealer who arranges HP finance for his customers are credit brokers.

The Consumer Credit Act imposes restrictions on the charges that can be made by credit brokers. But these restrictions apply only if the credit involved does not exceed £15,000. If it does, then there are no restrictions on fees. However, a major exception to this is for mortgages; mortgage brokers' fees are controlled whatever the size of the mortgage.

If credit brokers fail within six months to obtain credit for the customer, their fee cannot exceed £3. The same applies if the broker raises credit for the customer, but the customer then decides not to enter into the agreement. For instance, if a mortgage broker finds a mortgage for a client, but the client then decides not to take up the mortgage, the most the broker can charge is £3. However, if the credit broker finds credit for the customer, and the customer takes it up within six months, the credit broker can charge a fee, and then there is no restriction on the fee that can be charged – however high it may be.

Cancellable agreements

The agreement which the prospective debtor or hirer has to sign must contain all the terms of the agreement and relevant information: description of goods, deposit, total charge and APR, the period of the loan, amount and frequency of payments, and a warning in the signature box.

This is a Credit Sale Agreement regulated by the Consumer Credit Act 1947. Sign it only if you want to be legally bound by its terms.

Signature of buyer   Date of signature

This is a Hire Purchase Agreement regulated by the Consumer Credit Act 1947. Sign it only if you want to be legally bound by its terms.

Signature of debtor

Date of signature

The goods will not become your property until you have made   payments. You must not sell them before then.

If the agreeement is a cancellable one, there must be another 'box' near the signature with the message:

YOUR RIGHT TO CANCEL

Once you have signed this agreement you will have, for a short time, a right to cancel it. Exact details of how and when you can do this will be sent to you by post by the creditor.

The Consumer

The buyers or hirers can cancel their agreement when it was made after 'oral representations' (i.e. any kind of face-to-face talk, but not by phone) between the prospective customer and the dealer or creditor, and the customer signed the agreement away from the dealer's or finance company's premises. But it does not apply where the agreement was entirely negotiated by post, as in a mail-order transaction. The cancellation provisions are mainly aimed at doorstep sellers but would apply if, for example, the consumer is in a shop, listens to what the sales person has to say, takes away the agreement and then signs it at home.

If the agreement was signed off trade premises, a copy of it must be left with the customer straight away, and another copy of the signed agreement, or a statutory notice of cancellation rights, must be posted to him or her within seven days. There is then a five-day 'cooling-off' period, during which the debtor can inform the would-be creditors, or their agent, of his or her intention to cancel. There is no laid-down form for giving notice of cancellation, but it would be common sense to send it by recorded delivery or to obtain a certificate of posting from the post office (as proof of the date of posting within the allowed time limit).

If a credit agreement is signed on – rather than off – trade premises, the customer cannot cancel. So the consumer who has been persuaded by a doorstep sales person should be careful of an invitation to 'come down to the shop to sign the agreement'.

Withdrawing at an earlier stage

Until there is a formal contract, with offer (by consumer) and acceptance (by finance company), either party can simply withdraw. Unlike the contract made when buying a pound of apples from the greengrocer, where offer and acceptance follow each other within seconds, with consumers who ask for credit there may be a few days' delay while the finance company checks their creditworthiness and processes their application for credit. During that time they can revoke the offer, and if they have put down a pre-contract deposit, get it back in full.

After cancellation

The general effect of the agreement being cancelled (or withdrawn from) is that no further sums are payable and the money the consumer has paid must be returned. Linked transactions (such as a maintenance contract) are cancelled along with the agreement. Until that has happened, consumers can hold on to the goods they have on HP. They must take reasonable care of the goods for twenty-one days from the date of cancellation and do not have to do the sending back, but must allow the owner access to collect them.

If the credit purchase involved a trader in part-exchange, those goods must be returned to the customer. If they are not returned within ten days in the same condition, the customer can claim the agreed cash trade-in value from the dealer.

No credit?

Before selling goods on credit, many firms and finance companies check the customer's creditworthiness by getting information from one of the credit reference agencies. This may be done on a system of 'credit-scoring' – so-many points for different items of information on the application form, and the customer is turned down if the score is not high enough.

Credit reference agencies do not give an opinion on whether or not a person should have credit; they have no blacklist and there is information about good payers as well as bad. It is the shopkeeper or finance company who decides on the person's creditworthiness.

The large agencies keep computer information about almost every address in the UK; often there is nothing recorded on a person's file (but it may be important for a lender simply to have confirmation that a would-be borrower really lives at the address given on the credit application form). Details of previous credit accounts can show how well or badly a customer has paid in the past. Records are kept of county court judgements and bankruptcies. When someone has been taken to court for not paying debts, the agency may keep the judgement on its files for years after the debt has been paid off.

Nobody has an automatic right to credit, and lenders do not have to say why they have turned someone down. But a would-be debtor has the right to know the name and address of the credit reference agency that was approached for details.

Credit reference agencies: action plan

● Within 28 days of the last time you contacted them about the credit deal, write to the shop or finance company and ask for the name and address of any credit reference agency that has given information about you;

● within seven working days they must tell you that name and address;

● at any time (also if you have not been refused credit) you can write to the agency, sending £1 (non-returnable). It helps to trace your file if you give not only your full name and address, with postcode, but also any previous addresses within the past six years;

● within seven working days from when it receives your letter, the agency must send you your file (in plain English – not, e.g. in code or on a computer tape) or tell you that it has no information about you;

● if the facts on your file are incorrect, you can write to the agency asking them to remove or change any entry which you think is wrong, and that you are likely to suffer as a result of the entry (if relevant and possible, enclose proof of payment);

- within twenty-eight days the agency should reply that it will remove or change the entry;
- if there is no reply within those next twenty-eight days, or if the agency says it will not remove or change the file entry, send a 'notice of correction' to be added to the file. It is a statement of up to 200 words: your side of the story. The agency can reject it if it seems incorrect, frivolous or defamatory. If the agency does not want to add the notice of correction to your file, it must get the permission of the Director General of Fair Trading;
- if the agency amends your file or adds the notice of correction, it must use the new details in future and must, within ten working days, send the details to anybody who has made an inquiry about you in the previous six months;
- if the agency does not reply within twenty-eight days to the letter with the notice of correction, you can ask the Director General of Fair Trading to intervene. There is no fee. Say that you are writing under s.159(5) of the Consumer Credit Act 1974 and give full details of what is incorrect on your file and why it should be changed (copies of correspondence will help speed things up).

Faulty goods and credit

Buying on credit does not take away from the buyer's rights against the seller regarding any misrepresentation and that the goods shall be as described, of merchantable quality, fit for the purpose. Where goods are bought on HP, the finance company providing the credit is in law the seller (unless the shop itself finances the credit, so that supplier and seller are one and the same person). So the shopkeeper and the finance company have equal liability and the consumer can take action against either. This is particularly useful if the shopkeeper has become bankrupt, gone into liquidation or just refuses to cooperate when there is a complaint.

This joint liability for breach of contract or misrepresentation, or breach of duty of care, is not restricted to goods bought on HP. It applies to all credit purchases where the cash price is over £100, including goods or services bought with a credit card and even goods bought with the help of a bank loan earmarked for that particular purchase. It does not apply to goods bought on an ordinary bank overdraft where the cash was not specifically provided to finance that particular purchase.

Wanting to end it all

At any time the customer can ask for an up-to-date statement to find out:
- how much he or she has paid so far, *and*
- the amount he or she should have paid so far, *and*
- when unpaid instalments become due, *and*
- the total amount that would need to be paid to discharge the indebtedness under the agreement, *and*

• details of any rebate he or she is entitled to for early settlement of the HP or credit sale debt.

Customers can pay off the amount owed at any time. All they have to do is give written notice of their intended early settlement.

Apart from this right to early settlement (i.e. paying up in full and becoming the owner of the goods on HP), with a hire purchase agreement or a conditional sale agreement there is the right to terminate the agreement at any time before the final payment falls due. The Consumer Credit Act allows this on condition that:

• all amounts that were due up to that moment have been paid;

• at least half the total price has already been paid or, if not, the necessary additional sum will now be paid to bring the total payment to one-half of the total price or to the amount of the creditor's loss of profit on the transaction if that is less than 50 per cent of the total price;

• damages are paid for the decreased value of the goods if the debtor has not taken reasonable care of them. The goods are not the customer's property until all the instalments are paid off, so if the agreement is terminated before then, they have to be returned so that they can be resold to someone else.

Falling into arrears with payments

If the customer gets into arrears, the legal position will depend upon whether the agreement is for credit sale or HP.

Under a *credit-sale agreement*, the goods already belong to the customer and so the finance company cannot reclaim them or sue for their return. All the company can do is to start court proceedings for the amount still due.

With a *hire-purchase agreement*, the position is different. The goods will not be the customer's property until all the instalments have been paid. Accordingly, the goods still belong to the finance company and they can be repossessed, or reclaimed, if the customer falls into arrears.

However, to protect the customer, when goods are on HP:

• if an instalment is overdue, the finance company must give the customer seven days' notice before it takes any steps against him or her;

• if the customer has paid one-third (or more) of the credit price, the finance company must obtain a court order before it repossesses the goods. If less than one-third has been paid, the company need not apply for a court order, although its representatives are not allowed to enter the customer's home (or other premises) to seize the goods, unless the customer agrees.

If the finance company applies to the county court for a repossession order, the judge will not necessarily make the order. He or she will listen to the customer's explanation and, if there is any reasonable prospect of the money being paid off, will probably make a 'time order'. This is an order for the debt to be paid in instalments.

If the case does go to court, the customer will probably have to pay the company's legal costs. However, if customers previously make a written offer of smaller instalments over a longer period, and that offer is similar to the order eventually made by the judge, it is unlikely that they will be ordered to pay the legal costs. It is, of course, illegal for a finance company to harass a customer who is in arrears.

Standing surety for someone else's credit agreement

Often a finance company will provide credit only if customers can persuade a friend or relative to be a 'surety' for them. This is usually done by the surety being a 'guarantor' – he or she agrees to pay if the customer defaults on the credit agreement (e.g. is in arrears with the instalments). Alternatively, the surety may be asked to give an 'indemnity', in which case he or she agrees that the finance company can approach him or her direct for payment, without involving the customer. Another possibility is that he or she is asked to deposit money to cover the customer's possible default.

People who act as a surety must be given a copy of the customer's credit agreement, which is the source of their own liability. In addition, the finance company must provide them with two copies of the surety agreement, one signed by the company and the other by themselves. If these copy documents are not provided, the surety cannot be sued for the customer's debts.

The surety (or guarantor) is liable for the customer's default, and to this extent he or she stands in the shoes of the customer. They cannot be made to pay more than the customer would have had to pay. For instance, if the customer legally cancels the agreement because it was signed 'off trade premises' (see page 580) then the surety cannot be sued to meet the company's loan. The surety is no more liable than the customer.

However, being a surety can often be very risky. It is unwise to stand surety unless one is sure that the customer – even if he or she is a friend – can, and will, pay the instalments. If not, and the surety has to cover the finance company's losses, the surety can sue the customer for the amount paid out. Often, of course, this right to sue is valueless since it is usually the customer's lack of money that led to the default in the first place.

Finance companies do not hesitate to enforce agreements against sureties. Once the sureties have agreed to stand surety, they cannot later change their mind and demand to be released from their obligation.

CREDIT CARDS

There are various types of cards. Some fall outside the purview of the Consumer Credit Act. The true credit cards (such as Access, Barclaycard, American Express gold) are caught – and the consumer is protected – by the Act.

The plastic outsiders are:
- debit cards (such as Switch, Connect, Delta) – the amount of any payment

made with such a card is immediately debited to (bankspeak for taken out of) the customer's current account, as with a cheque but quicker, so that the bank does not provide any credit;
• cheque cards – here, too, the bank does not provide any credit, but merely guarantees to honour cheques up to a stated amount;
• cash cards – for getting money from a hole-in-the-wall cash dispenser (official name: automatic teller machine). The money comes straight out of the customer's own account, no credit is involved. And with cash dispenser cards, if the card or PIN (personal identification number) is lost or stolen, the customer will not be reimbursed for any sums taken (fraudulently) before the bank or building society has been informed of the loss or theft. After notification customers will not be liable, but only if they have not written down their PIN number. Since the new banking code of practice came into effect in March 1992, a £50 limit for loss through unauthorized use applies to all cards.

Under the Consumer Credit (Exempt Agreements) Order 1989, other exempt agreements include cards such as:
• Diners Club or American Express green card – where repayment has to be made in a single payment of the whole amount of the month's accrued credit;
• some shopper's charge cards – where the customer has to settle the monthly account in full with a single payment.

Getting a credit card

It is an offence to send promotional literature or other documents to minors (anyone under eighteen years of age) inviting them to borrow money or get goods or services on credit, or even encouraging them to ask for information or advice on how to obtain credit.

The card companies spare no efforts to persuade people (over eighteen) into having and using their cards. They are not allowed, however, to send an unsolicited card (as against promotional literature about it) to anyone who has not asked for one, in writing. Filling in an application form counts as writing, but after that another signature will be necessary when the card arrives. Until they sign the card, card-holders are not responsible for it. So if it is lost before they sign it and an unauthorized person uses it to buy goods, card-holders are not liable, and the loss falls on the credit-card company. Thus the instructions to a new card-holder always say, 'Sign the card immediately.'

In practice, a card is usually valid for two years and a new one is then sent – to be validated by the customer's signature. The credit card company or bank reserves the right to vary the agreement at any time as long as the client is notified of the changes either in writing or by whatever other means are appropriate (such as newspaper advertisements). Clients can terminate the agreement whenever they wish, by giving notice in writing and paying off the outstanding debt. The card will have to be cut in two and the pieces sent back.

What does it cost?

There is now a fee for most – but not all – credit card accounts. The amount is added as a debit when the account is opened and annually thereafter. A monthly statement of how much has been charged up to the card is sent to the customer, with a 'pay by' date (usually within approximately twenty-five days), but only a small percentage needs to be paid. If the whole outstanding balance is repaid by close of business on the specified date, there is no interest payable. But even one day late will attract interest at a stated rate which seems low but, if translated into APR, may work out at around 26 per cent or higher.

What is more, with some cards the interest is now calculated on a daily basis, not from the date of the monthly statement, but from the date on which the transaction was charged to the credit card account. This makes the credit more expensive than that of a card which may have the same APR but which charges interest only from the date of statement.

Using the card

Not all shops or other outlets accept credit cards. Those that do have to pay a service charge or commission to the card company. They are now allowed to offer a lower price for cash, or an increase for credit card payment. Where a retailer or a restaurant has introduced such differential pricing (or dual pricing, as it is also called), a clear notice with full details must be displayed.

On the whole, garages and petrol stations rather than shops and stores tend to take advantage of this provision; they have to abide by the statutory requirements about price indication for motor fuel. If a cash price is marked at the pump of, say, 50p per litre and a credit card price of 52p is charged, a clear and legible notice must be displayed at the point of payment stating either that the credit card price is 52p a litre, or that the credit card price is 2p more (or that it is 4 per cent more) than the cash price.

The rules about filling in a credit card sales voucher and signing it are commercial rather than legal. Some theatres and travel agents allow the card to be used over the phone in order to offer the customer an instant confirmed booking. There is a risk of abuse in over-the-phone credit transactions, and consumers should never give their credit card number and details over the phone without knowing exactly to whom and for what.

Similarly, when signing the credit card voucher, make sure that the 'amount' has not been left blank and that the total is correct. Many shops give a separate receipt with a credit card voucher, but they do not have to. There is no legal obligation on the part of retailers to give any receipt (cash or credit purchase), nor for the customer to produce one as proof of purchase.

Misusing the card

The Consumer Credit Act (s. 84) and the card companies' conditions of use ('the credit agreement') jointly offer reasonable protection if a credit card is misused by someone who has found or stolen it. The credit agreement must contain details of how, where and to whom a lost or stolen card should be notified. If this is done by phone, it should be confirmed in writing within seven days. Until such notice is received at the card company's end, the card-holder is liable. But the liability is limited to £50.

Where the card is misused by someone who had it with the card-holder's knowledge or consent, the card-holder will be liable for the full amount of debts run up.

Special advantages of paying by card

The joint liability of seller and finance company for defects in goods, under s. 75 of the Consumer Credit Act (see page 582) extends to credit card transactions. Where the purchase price is over £100, the card company or bank is responsible for the trader's misrepresentation or breach of contract (which includes breach of the implied terms of proper quality and fitness for purpose). So, if the goods bought are defective or cause damage, the buyer can claim against the credit card company or bank as well as, or instead of, suing the shop or other supplier. This is particularly important where the supplier has gone into liquidation or ceased trading by the time the claim arises. So, holidaymakers whose tour operator goes bust will get their money back if they paid by credit card, while their neighbour who paid in cash may be left high and dry.

Does s. 75 apply where the defective goods were bought from a trader outside the UK? There is no authority on the matter, but the answer seems to be no. The Banking Ombudsman, who had some cases where the purchase was made overseas, has said: 'I am satisfied that it was not intended by Parliament that section 75 should apply to claims involving a foreign element.'

OMBUDSMEN

The Banking Ombudsman scheme

The main object of the Office of the Banking Ombudsman is to receive unresolved complaints about the provision of banking services and 'to facilitate the satisfaction, settlement or withdrawal of such complaints'. Excluded from his brief are complaints about a bank's interest rates, or commercial judgement about lending, or security (e.g. for a bank loan).

A complaint has to be made within six months of deadlock having been reached between bank and customer, and within six years of the customer first making a complaint to the bank about what it had done or failed to do. There must be a specific complaint that something has gone wrong, causing injustice to the person who is complaining.

The Ombudsman's decision is binding on the bank but consumers can reject it. By taking their complaint to the Ombudsman, they do not lose their right to take legal action.

The banking services include credit card services and the Ombudsman has been known to offer recommendations to banks and to clients.

The Banking Ombudsman gives the following common-sense advice to cash cardholders:

- destroy the PIN (personal identification number) notification;
- do not write the PIN anywhere; if you cannot remember it without a written record, keep that record hidden and entirely separate from the card and not, for example, in your handbag or wallet. If a handbag with card in it is stolen, the thief can usually use the card successfully within minutes afterwards if the handbag also contains an address book in which the card-holder has entered his/her personal identification number. A PIN masquerading as a telephone number, for example, is a disguise which a thief is likely to decipher without difficulty;
- never disclose the PIN to anyone, not even a bank employee, relative or spouse, and never lend the card to anyone else;
- check the withdrawal shown on the bank statement as soon as you receive it;
- notify the bank immediately of any discrepancy in the statement, loss of the card or compromise of the PIN.

If a card has been stolen, card-holders may be tempted to notify the police before notifying their bank. By the time they notify the bank, the fraudster may have successfully withdrawn £200, perhaps at the very time when the card-holder was conscientiously giving a statement to the police.

A general guide to the Banking Ombudsman scheme can be obtained from the Office of the Banking Ombudsman, Citadel House, 5/11 Fetter Lane, London EC4A 1BR (071 583 1395).

Building Societies' Ombudsman scheme

Unlike some other ombudsman schemes, this one is statutory under the Building Societies Act 1986, and all building societies are members of the scheme.

Consumers can contact the office of the Building Societies' Ombudsmen (there are two) if they believe that a building society has infringed their legal rights, treated them unfairly, or has been guilty of maladministration, including inefficiency or undue delay, that resulted in inconvenience, expense or financial loss. It does not deal with questions of general creditworthiness.

Automatic teller machines (cash dispensers) feature prominently in the list of complaints dealt with by the Ombudsmen. Up to 1991 the ATMs were the heading of most frequent complaints – frauds, phantom withdrawals or the machine having produced the correct print-out slip but no money.

Information and a complaint form can be obtained from the Office of the Building Societies' Ombudsman, 35–37 Grosvenor Gardens, London SW1X 7AW (071 931 0044).

Insurance Ombudsman Bureau

A consumer who has a dispute with an insurance company, or about a policy underwritten by Lloyd's, may be able to refer it to the Insurance Ombudsman if all else fails. This has generally to be done within six months of the complaint having been left unresolved in negotiation between the insurers and the consumer.

Most but not all insurers are members of the Insurance Ombudsman Bureau. Not all matters can be dealt with, but unfair treatment by the company, or maladministration, is on the list, and so is poor service; commercial decisions and actions by some insurance intermediaries are not.

The Ombudsman will investigate the papers and the other details set before him by both sides, and then adjudicate on the case. He can make binding awards up to £100,000, or £10,000 a year in permanent health insurance (a euphemism for long-term disability insurance) cases. His decision is binding on the insurer but not on the consumer, who can still go ahead and take the case to court.

The address of the Insurance Ombudsman Bureau is 135 Park Street, London SE1 9EA (071 928 7600 and 071 928 4488).

Another organization that may be able to help resolve a consumer's insurance dispute is the Personal Insurance Arbitration Service, if the insurance company is a member of the service (about thirty-five are). The insurer would have to agree to arbitration, unlike referring a dispute to the Ombudsman, where the insurer has to go along willy-nilly.

The address is PIAS, 24 Angel Gate, City Road, London EC1V 2RS (071 837 4483).

39 Insurance

For all the mystique surrounding it, insurance is a contract. Consumers pay a set sum to the insurers, who undertake to indemnify them or to pay out an agreed amount if a particular circumstance happens. The terms of the contract are set out in the insurance policy. When consumers agree to pay the premium, they accept the terms of the policy (whether they have read them or not) and the insurers undertake to cover the risk.

Contracts of insurance are 'contracts of utmost good faith' (*uberrimae fides* is the Latin phrase used for this). It means that every relevant fact which could influence the insurers in setting the premium, or in deciding whether or not to accept the risk, has to be disclosed. Risk can mean the property to be insured, the likelihood of the occurrence of the specified hazard and its likely effects (e.g. fire in a thatched cottage), and the the person insured (some occupations, such as actors, are considered a bad risk).

Disclosure

Even facts not actually asked for on the proposal form have to be disclosed if they could materially affect the risk, so consumers have to be mindreaders about what else they are supposed to disclose.

The renewal of a policy reaffirms by implication that all the details remain correct. At each renewal, the policyholder has to disclose any new relevant facts; ditto if anything significant happens during the validity of the policy (significant to the possible risk, such as someone with a household contents policy deciding to take in a student lodger).

When a policy is for one year, as most motor insurances and householder's are, the contract comes to an end and a new one starts when the next annual premium is paid. The insurance company can unilaterally vary the terms by an endorsement to the policy, or increase the premium, or refuse to renew. Consumers can vote with their feet and take their insurance business elsewhere, or simply decide not to take out any insurance. In law, only motor insurance is compulsory. And housebuyers must insure the building as part of their mortgage contract. Most building societies charge a sum of around £25–£35 (the 'freedom of agency charge') if consumers want to insure their mortgaged home otherwise than under the building society's block policy.

Claiming

Taking out insurance cannot stop any disasters from happening; it can only give you the money towards making good the damage.

Indemnifying means that the insurers pay an amount, up to the sum insured by the premium, that should put you financially into the position you were in before the event, neither better nor worse off. So, making a claim is asking the insurers to reimburse you for your loss.

Many policies have a time limit for making a claim, or at least stipulate that notice of a claim must be given as soon as possible. Usually you have to give a lot of details and state the amount of the loss on the claim form. Insurers are good at spotting frauds. Over-valuation does not necessarily constitute fraud, but the insurers will thoroughly investigate any claim that seems exaggerated.

It is at claim-time that insurance companies seem often to discover reasons for not paying, or paying a reduced amount, such as:

* exclusion clauses hidden in a policy;
* deemed failure to disclose 'relevant' facts;
* insufficiently high premium;
* lack of proof of the loss;
* non-compliance with the terms of the policy.

Problems of construction and interpretation often arise under motor policies. For instance, what is 'social and domestic use' of the car?

Mr Binions was a carpet layer. One day he was working on a job with an employee of his, and Mr Binions's father had also called in to help out. The employee had a bad toothache so it was agreed that Mr Binions senior would drive the employee home in his son's car. On the way to lunch, the car crashed. Mr Binions senior's policy covered only 'social and domestic use'. Held: His policy did not cover him, since he was using the car for two purposes. First, the social use of going to lunch and, secondly, the non-social use of taking the employee home. The material character of the journey was to take the employee home and so his insurance did not cover the accident. Seddon (1977)

Another case illustrated how the wording of a policy can be of crucial importance. The owner of a Rolls-Royce was tricked into parting with it by a con-man, in return for a forged bank draft. He then claimed on his insurance policy with the Commercial Union, only to be told that the policy covered 'theft', but his car had not been stolen – it had been obtained by fraud, and, in addition, he had parted with it voluntarily.

Sometimes the insurance company can declare the policy void on the grounds of 'public policy' – i.e. that it would be wrong for the customer to be allowed to claim.

Mr Geismar took out insurance for some valuable items. When they were stolen, he claimed on the policy. The insurance company discovered that he had imported them into the UK without having paid customs duty on them. So they refused to pay up, arguing that it would be wrong to compensate him for the loss of 'illegal' items. Held: They need not pay him. Geismar (1977)

What is more, since the Geismar case, insurers have often refused to meet claims for lost or stolen property if the items in question were bought overseas, even if no import duty was payable on them.

Some insurance words explained

---

all-risks. Insurance that covers loss or damage by any accident or misfortune not specifically excluded by the policy.

averaging. The amount paid in settlement of a claim being reduced by the proportion of any under-insurance (e.g. a piece of property worth £10,000 is insured for £5,000, and £5,000-worth is stolen; under the average clause, payment will be only £2,500).

betterment. The amount by which an insured person would be better off after a claim; it has to be repaid, or will be deducted from settlement (e.g. old car in accident, after repair paid for by insurance, car has new wing instead of the rusty old one, so consumer has to pay appropriate proportion of cost).

excess. A specified amount of a claim – say, £25 for storm damage – which the insured person will bear him- or herself; if the whole claim comes to less than that amount, nothing will be paid by insurer.

ex gratia. Payment made as a gesture of goodwill when the insurer does not have to do so on a strict interpretation of the terms of the policy.

index linking. The sum insured goes up automatically in line with increased prices or building costs.

knock-for-knock. In motor insurance where two cars are involved, an agreement that the two insurers will each pay their client's claim, irrespective of which one was to blame for the happening.

ombudsman. See pages 587–9.

uninsured loss. In motor insurance, amounts not met by the policy (e.g. hire of substitute car while damage done is being repaired).

PART FIVE

BANKRUPTCY

40 Bankruptcy

In 1986 the laws on bankruptcy and insolvency were updated. There is a basic distinction between the position of individuals and companies:
- individuals – a person who is insolvent can be made bankrupt;
- companies – a company that is insolvent can be put into administration or into liquidation.

HOW THE BANKRUPTCY LAWS WORK

If an individual person is insolvent (i.e. cannot pay off debts), then someone who is owed money (a creditor) can start the legal process of petitioning the court for the person who owes money (the debtor) to be made bankrupt. This is called a Creditor's Petition, because the petition is presented to the court by a creditor who is owed money.

Alternatively, the individual who is in financial difficulties may decide that bankruptcy is the only realistic outcome. In this case, it is possible for the person who owes the money (the debtor) to apply to the court to be made bankrupt. Since this step is taken by the debtor, it is known as a Debtor's Petition.

Accordingly, either the creditor (the person owed money) or the debtor (the person who owes the money) can start the bankruptcy process.

Making someone bankrupt

A creditor who is owed money can start the legal process that will end in bankruptcy. But, before the creditor can petition the court, it must be shown that there is a valid debt that has not been paid. This can, of course, be proved by having got a court judgement against the debtor; if the money ordered to be paid by the court has not been paid to the creditor, then the creditor can use that 'judgement debt' as sufficient justification for bringing a Creditor's Petition for bankruptcy.

But it can be a time-consuming and long-winded process to sue over a debt and get judgement from a court. Accordingly, there is an alternative approach, which will often be much more attractive to the creditor. Instead of having formally to sue (and win in court), the creditor for £750 or more can simply serve a formal demand for payment on the debtor. This is called a Statutory Demand.

The statutory demand

A Statutory Demand is a formal written demand for the money owed. The Insolvency Act lays down rules about the wording and style of the Statutory Demand. In essence, the creditor fills in the blanks on a pre-printed form bought from a law stationer. That form is then served on the debtor (this is best done in person). The debtor then has twenty-one days in which to pay the money that is owed, failing which the creditor can present a Creditor's Petition and start the bankruptcy process.

Needless to say, it is far easier to fill in a form and serve it on a creditor than it is to go to court and get a formal court judgement. In practice, it is also much speedier as well! There is another major advantage in that, in practice, debtors take the threat of being made bankrupt far more seriously than a threat of court proceedings. Because of this, someone who is owed money may be far better advised to serve a Statutory Demand on a debtor than start court proceedings.

A Statutory Demand can also be served on a company that owes money (although it is a different pre-printed form that is used). If the company then does not pay the debt within twenty-one days, application can be made for the company to be wound up.

One point that should be made clear is that a Statutory Demand can be served only if there is no real argument that the money is owed (e.g. a loan has not been repaid in time, goods have been supplied but not been paid for etc.). But if there is an argument over the amount of money owed, then it is not possible to use the Statutory Demand procedure (e.g. if the debtor can show that the money is not yet due or that the goods supplied were defective). So, in cases of dispute the creditor will simply have to take the case to court and get a court judgement for the debt before being able to start the bankruptcy procedure. The other problem is that a Statutory Demand can be used only if the debt is at least £750. If less than £750 is owed, then the case will have to go to court, and the bankruptcy procedure cannot be started until there is an unpaid court judgement.

The table on page 597 sets out the steps in making someone bankrupt under a Creditor's Petition.

Making yourself bankrupt

Many people think that bankruptcy can be brought only by someone who is owed money (a creditor). In fact, the bankruptcy proceedings can be brought by the person who owes the money (the debtor). So, someone can petition for their own bankruptcy – a Debtor's Petition.

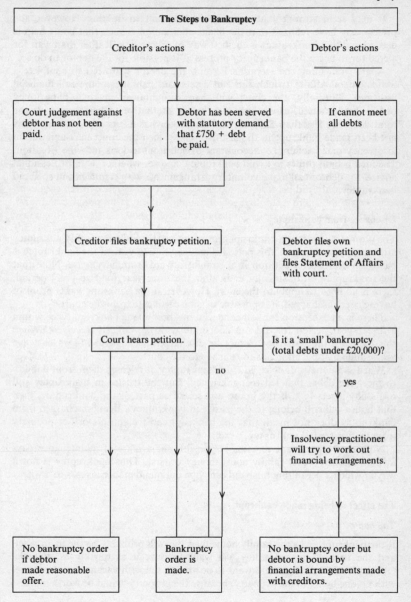

The Steps to Bankruptcy

Creditor's actions

Debtor's actions

Court judgement against debtor has not been paid.

Debtor has been served with statutory demand that £750 + debt be paid.

If cannot meet all debts

Creditor files bankruptcy petition.

Debtor files own bankruptcy petition and files Statement of Affairs with court.

Court hears petition.

Is it a 'small' bankruptcy (total debts under £20,000)?

no

yes

Insolvency practitioner will try to work out financial arrangements.

No bankruptcy order if debtor made reasonable offer.

Bankruptcy order is made.

No bankruptcy order but debtor is bound by financial arrangements made with creditors.

It may seem strange that someone would want to do this. However, the person may have realized that the financial situation is such that court help is needed and that bankruptcy is the best way of proceeding. Rather than wait for a creditor to begin the bankruptcy process, it is possible for the debtor to do so.

Apart from filing the Debtor's Petition the debtor will need to complete a Statement of Affairs (which sets out assets and liabilities – the full financial position). Normally, the court will then straightaway make a bankruptcy order. But in 'small' cases there may be an alternative to bankruptcy. If the total debts are less than £20,000, and the debtor has assets of £2,000 (and has not been made bankrupt in the last five years), then the court may appoint an insolvency practitioner (i.e. accountant or solicitor) to look into the situation. The idea behind this is to avoid bankruptcy, and see whether, with professional advice, the debtor can make voluntary arrangements with creditors and so avoid bankruptcy.

Discharge from bankruptcy

The normal rule is that a bankrupt gets an automatic discharge from bankruptcy after three years. In fact, this period is reduced to two years if the bankruptcy is based on a Debtor's Petition in a straightforward (summary) case. Note that the bankruptcy automatically ends after the three-year (or two-year) period; there is no need to apply to the court. However, if the bankrupt wants proof of having been discharged, it is possible to get a certificate from the court.

There is an exception for someone who has been made bankrupt twice within a fifteen-year period (or did not cooperate with the Official Receiver). When this happens, the bankrupt cannot be discharged for a period of at least five years, and an application has to be made to the court.

When someone is discharged from bankruptcy, it releases them from liability to meet the debts that led to bankruptcy. But the trustee in bankruptcy still owns any assets (e.g. if the house was seized as part of the bankruptcy, then that house will still belong to the trustee in bankruptcy). Being discharged from bankruptcy does not mean that the bankrupt can reclaim his or her property from the trustee in bankruptcy.

Note that a bankrupt remains responsible for arrears of maintenance payments (and any other family court money orders). Thus bankruptcy is not a way in which a defaulting husband can wipe out maintenance arrears to a wife.

The effect of being made bankrupt

The home

If the bankrupt owns the family home then this will probably be the main asset, and the trustee in bankruptcy will want to seize it as quickly as possible. Obviously, the trustee would want to be able to sell with vacant possession (i.e. with no one living in the property) because the property would be worth more.

If there is a spouse (usually a wife), an ex-spouse or a child (under eighteen) living in the home, then the trustee in bankruptcy cannot get possession for at least twelve months after the bankruptcy. Thus in most family cases there can be no eviction for at least one year. But if there is no spouse (or ex-spouse or child), then the trustee in bankruptcy can apply for possession of the home without delay. In practice, therefore, if the bankrupt lives alone, or lives with a co-habitee or adult children, then there is no twelve-month gap before possession can be sought.

If there is a spouse (usually a wife), then that spouse may be able to claim a share of the property. Certainly, if the property is in joint names, then it will be generally accepted that the spouse does have an interest in it. If it is not in joint names, then it is more difficult to prove that the spouse has a share (but not impossible). Either way, the court will take into account all the circumstances before deciding whether or not to evict and give possession to the trustee in bankruptcy. The court has a discretion, but it is clear that possession will be refused only in 'exceptional circumstances'. The mere fact that the wife and children would have to be evicted and that they have nowhere else to go would not make the circumstances 'exceptional'.

If the wife does own a share in the home, then one possibility might be for the wife to try and buy her husband's share from the trustee in bankruptcy (perhaps with a loan from parents or friends). While this is often not a realistic possibility, it should not be forgotten that it is one option that might be available.

The furniture

The trustee in bankruptcy can seize items such as cars, boats and caravans. But the Insolvency Act allows the bankrupt to retain basics such as clothing, bedding, furniture and household equipment. So the bankrupt can retain all such 'basic' items. Just what the word 'basic' means in this context is open to argument. In practice, secondhand furniture realizes very little and it is often not worth the trustee's while to incur the costs of removing furniture and selling it. But this exception for basics cannot be used to justify the bankrupt keeping antiques. For instance, if the bankrupt has an antique dining table the trustee can purchase a basic replacement (perhaps from a discount warehouse) and then seize the valuable antique.

Bear in mind that it is only the bankrupt's assets and possessions that can be seized. Thus, if furniture or other items belong to, say, a husband or wife, then they cannot be seized. Accordingly, it is important for the bankrupt's spouse to make clear what items are not owned by the bankrupt.

Earnings

The trustee in bankruptcy can intercept some of the bankrupt's earnings by asking the court to make an Income Payments Order. This is, in effect, an Attachment of Earnings Order, requiring the employer to pay some of the wages direct to the trustee in bankruptcy. Obviously, the court would take into account the personal circumstances of the bankrupt (including family obligations) for making an order and in deciding how much should be paid.

Divorce

It is common to find that a marital breakdown follows hard on the heels of a financial breakdown. Indeed, as soon as a husband gets into financial difficulties there may be a temptation to transfer assets – in particular, the home – to the wife, and then divorce. What should be remembered, however, is that the court can set aside property transactions, and this is likely to be done if property was transferred at an undervalue. Accordingly, someone who is in financial difficulties should not think that they can simply give away all their assets to relatives and so avoid those assets being seized by the trustee in bankruptcy at a later date.

The main penalty of being a bankrupt is, of course, that all assets have to be handed over to the trustee in bankruptcy (apart from a few 'basics'; see above). Another problem is that it becomes difficult to get credit. In particular, the fact of bankruptcy must be disclosed when trying to get credit of £250 or more; for practical purposes, disclosing this information means that the bankrupt will not be given HP or credit sale. It can also cause problems for bankrupts who are still trying to run a business, since 'credit' includes being paid in advance for services. For instance, if the bankrupt is still carrying on in business as a self-employed plumber, it would be wrong to ask a customer for £250 in advance to cover the cost of plumbing work.

In practice it is extremely difficult for a bankrupt to carry on in business. First, any existing business will have become the property of the trustee in bankruptcy. Secondly, a bankrupt can run a business only by using his or her full name; using a business or trading name could be regarded as an offence (since the idea behind the bankruptcy laws is that a bankrupt has to disclose his or her full name so customers can check on the credit worthiness). An undischarged bankrupt cannot act as a company director, which therefore means that it is virtually impossible for a bankrupt to run a business through a company.

If the bankrupt is able to carry on in some form of business (typically, as a self-employed skilled tradesperson), then he or she can keep tools, books, vehicles and other equipment that are necessary for that business. Obviously, the trustee will look closely to see what items are being kept back, and the trustee can insist that the bankrupt gets cheaper replacements.

As a final point, a bankrupt cannot be an MP, local councillor or GP.

Company insolvency

An individual person who is insolvent can be made bankrupt. For a company, there are two alternatives: liquidation or administration.

A winding-up is a formal closing down of the company with the assets being sold off. Typically, a compulsory winding-up will be brought by a creditor. However, it is possible for the shareholders in the company to agree a voluntary winding-up.

Administration is a way of trying to salvage near-dead businesses. If an Administration Order is made, then a temporary freeze is made on all debts owed by the company. In effect, there is moratorium while the administrator looks at the state the business is in. The aim is to see whether proposals can be drawn up that will enable the company to continue trading. The overall aim is to avoid winding up. In some cases, it may allow a more orderly running-down of the business, and mean that assets can be sold for more than would be the case if it was a liquidation sale.

PART SIX

BUSINESS

41 Starting up a Business

The number of self-employed rose dramatically in the 1980s from around 1.9 million in 1980 to around 3.1 million in 1989, since when it has fallen back (as many self-employed were forced into bankruptcy by high interest rates and the recession in the 1990s). But even in times of a recession, new businesses which are carefully prepared for have a better chance of success than those started off without much planning.

Many people want to put their redundancy money to good use by setting up their own business or are anxious to leave the shackles of employment for the relative freedom of being self-employed. If the new business is intended to be in competition with that of a former employer, the first hurdle to cross is checking whether the former employer can do anything to prevent the business venture from getting off the ground.

GOING INTO COMPETITION WITH A FORMER EMPLOYER

Employers usually try to guard against an ex-employee starting up a business in direct competition with them and it is not hard to see why. An employee can, through being employed, gain skills and experience and build up contacts with the employer's customers. If the employee leaves and offers a similar or better deal to those customers, then it will not just be a once-valued employee that the employer will be losing.

Practically, the employer can be stung into taking direct action against the employee by trying to squeeze him or her out of the market in a cost war. The ex-employee can do nothing legally to prevent this.

Legally, however, there are two ways in which an ex-employer can potentially stop an ex-employee from competing:

1 *If the ex-employee had a contract with the ex-employer which restrained future competition.*
2 *If the ex-employee uses confidential information learned during the employment.*

Employment contracts which stop competition

Many employment contracts have a special clause which limits future competition if the employee leaves employment: these are called covenants in restraint of trade. But the law does not allow blanket restraints of trade; it allows only those that are reasonable in terms of distance and length of time. What is 'reasonable' is not strictly defined, but depends on the circumstances. So it would not be reasonable to stop an ex-employee who was employed in Glasgow setting up a competing business in Sheffield, but it would be reasonable to stop them from setting up a business within a 1-mile radius of their ex-employer. Also a time limit of four years would not be reasonable but a time limit of one year probably would be.

Using confidential information

If there was no special restrictive covenant, the employer can sometimes argue that the ex-employee owes special duties of good faith and trust towards the ex-employer. But without a contract the ex-employer faces an uphill task in stopping competition from an ex-employee, who will usually be able to get away with it. For example:

A sales manager had built up a van sales operation supplying fresh chickens. He and his ex-employer parted company bitterly. The sales manager set up in competition with the ex-employer, employing former colleagues, using knowledge of the company's customers and prices and selling along identical delivery routes. The employer had had no restrictive covenant in the contract with the employee, so the company tried claiming damages for breach of contract for misuse of information and for conspiracy to injure goodwill by abuse of confidential information. The employer lost. Faccenda Chicken Ltd *v.* Fowler (1985)

This particular area of law is also shaped by public policy. Generally the law tends to the view that competition in the market is a good thing, thus overall leaning in favour of an ex-employee. But ex-employees should get legal advice to check on their vulnerability as against a former employer.

CHOOSING A BUSINESS STRUCTURE

Anyone who sets up in business will want to know whether it will be best to form a company or stay as a sole trader (or a partner if the business is shared with someone else). The answer will depend largely upon such factors as the size of the business, the risks of the business and tax advantages.

The main differences between companies and sole traders or partnerships

Who is in control and who owns what?

A sole trader is in sole command of the business and solely owns it too. He or she can decide exactly how it will operate.

When a sole trader enters into a partnership, then each of the partners is treated automatically as an equal. That means not only becoming an equal owner and being entitled to an equal share of the profits but also being equally liable for all the business debts and obligations (even if incurred by other partners). If partners wish to own the business and/or divide the profits in unequal shares, then they will have to make a partnership agreement. Making a partnership agreement is also very important to exclude the automatic tax treatment of the partnership coming to an end if the partnership changes – say, if a partner leaves or a new partner joins (see Tax and VAT, page 645).

Partnerships are usually managed by all the partners in partners' meetings. The larger the partnership, the more problematic the principle of equality between partners, especially if all the partners want a say in every decision. Larger partnerships can be more unmanageable, whereas the structure imposed by a company can help to divide responsibilities clearly and make the business easier to run.

A company is a separate legal body which exists independently of its owners (the shareholders) and its managers (the directors). The management of a company is carried out by its director or board of directors. Usually the board will appoint different people to be responsible for different aspects of running the business, but that will not absolve any one director of responsibility for other areas, particularly finance. Sleeping partners and directors have equal responsibilities with their colleagues.

The risk of bankruptcy

The sole trader, or partner, risks bankruptcy if the business fails, and the effects of bankruptcy will not be confined to the loss of personal money and property. It will have other disadvantages, such as making the trader or partner ineligible to be a company director and unable to obtain credit of more than £50 without disclosing the bankruptcy. A person made bankrupt will find it difficult to borrow money in the future – for a house mortgage, for example.

The equivalent of bankruptcy for a company is insolvency. Generally, the director or shareholder of an insolvent company will not face any personal stigma as long as the director has taken every step to minimize creditors' losses (see Extra Duties of Directors, page 615). This is because in a limited company the shareholders' and directors' personal liability is strictly speaking limited to their shares. In practice, however, if the company has borrowed money, then the bank will almost always insist on personal guarantees being given by the directors, secured on their own homes. So if the company becomes insolvent, then the directors will have to pay the debts. If they cannot do so they will be declared bankrupt and so they will be no better off than if a company had not been formed.

But a company does give some extra financial protection to directors against claims by outsiders. If the company is sued (e.g. for damages caused by goods it sold), the directors will not usually be personally liable for the claim, but see below (Extra Duties of Directors).

A company effectively acts as a shield for the directors. Shareholders can find themselves liable to pay up for a claim, but only to the extent of their unpaid shareholding and only if the company cannot pay the claim itself. So a shareholder who owns £1,000 worth of shares but has paid only one quarter of the amount due (£250) would be liable to pay up an extra £750 to cover an outsider's claim that could not be met by the company.

A sole trader or partner, on the other hand, is fully liable on a claim up to the whole extent of his or her assets. So for ventures which potentially involve consumer claims, the company format is usually preferable.

The size of the business

There is no restriction on the size of any firm in the number of employees, value of assets held etc. There used to be a limit on the number of partners in a business (the old maximum being twenty). Now there is no limit. The maximum number of people who can be directors in a private company is limited to twenty for a private company and fifty for a public company. In practice these restrictions are not decisive. Most businesses have less than twenty shareholders or partners and the choice as to what business structure is preferable will depend on other factors.

Raising money

Because the sole trader or partner is personally liable for the business debts, one would have thought that he or she would find it easier to borrow money than would a company. Surprisingly this is not so. This is because of a device known as a *floating charge* which provides an effective security for a loan but which can be created only by a company. A floating charge gives the lender a continuing security against all the assets of the company, including, for example, stock in trade. The company can deal with its assets in the usual way by buying and selling its assets as it chooses, even though there is a floating charge on them. This would not be possible with a normal mortgage or charge of the property as the lender's consent would be needed for the sale of each item – something that would be clearly impracticable with the changing stock in trade of any business.

A floating charge is therefore a very effective but flexible form of security. It allows the company to trade in the normal way without having to obtain consent from the lender, and conversely it provides the lender with a security tied to all the assets of the firm.

In legal theory both sole traders and partnerships could create floating charges, but detailed provisions in the law make it uncertain whether the lender would have a complete safeguard for their security. The practical effect of this is that floating charges are not available to sole traders or partners and are confined to companies.

Remember that if a small company borrows money, the directors will probably be asked to provide personal guarantees and thus their personal fortunes will be at risk if the company fails.

The expenses of formation

It is easy for a sole trader to start up a business and the same applies to a partnership. The position is much more complicated for a company: there are sizeable fees to be paid, documents to be drawn up and procedures to be followed.

There is no doubt that it is more expensive and difficult to form a company (see below). But the extra formalities of running a business under a company structure do not stop at formation. A company must keep its statutory books up to date (this is basically a register of directors and secretaries, shareholders and their shareholdings and certain debts of the company). There is also the necessity of having the accounts audited every year (which will cost at least £1,500 in the South-East, perhaps less elsewhere). Every year audited accounts and the annual return have to be filed with the Registrar of Companies (annual fee currently £32), with hefty penalties for late filing or failure to file accounts (see below). There are also requirements on companies about informing the Registrar of Companies about certain actions or changes in the company – for example, changes of directors or secretaries or an increase in share capital must be notified.

Publicity of accounts

All limited (and some unlimited) companies must file audited accounts with Companies House each year whether they are trading or not, unless they fall into the strict classification of dormant companies (see page 617). (All unlimited companies are required to prepare acounts but only those which are connected to a limited company have to file accounts at Companies House.) Once filed at Companies House, these accounts are open to public inspection.

In the old days this added requirement for companies was not taken particularly seriously; most accounts at Companies House were at least a year out of date. But late-filing penalties have now been introduced by the Companies Acts of 1985 and 1989, so that companies who fail to file their accounts on time can face fines up to £1,000 for private companies; fines against public companies are up to five times higher (see box page 610).

Fines payable for late filing or failure to file company accounts

---

The fines are fixed according to a sliding scale based on the delay between the due date for filing the accounts and the date the accounts are actually filed at Companies House.

	Private	*Public*
Up to 3 months late	£100	£500
Up to 6 months late	£250	£1,000
Up to 12 months late	£500	£2,000
More than 12 months late	£1,000	£5,000

Even if a company is only a few days overdue, the fines are likely to be applied. Late-filing fines are payable by the company, but if the directors fail even to submit accounts, they themselves are personally liable to extra penalties fixed by the court of up to £2,000 per offence. They can also be disqualified from managing a limited company for a period of between two and fifteen years (the average period is five). The penalties are all part of the more efficient – and tougher – regime operated by Companies House.

Conversely sole traders or partners can keep their accounts confidential and theoretically need not disclose them to anyone. In practice, sole traders and partners are likely to find that accounts have to be disclosed to various people. Lenders are probably the main category of people likely to want to refer to a company's accounts. If a sole trader or partner wants to sell the business or bring in a new partner, the potential buyer or partner will want to look in detail at up-to-date accounts. In addition, the activities of credit-rating agencies are such that it is usually possible to find out the credit rating or standing of a sole trader or partnership. In some ways it could be argued that it is better to have accounts on public view and so reduce the risk of unjustified assumptions being made on the basis of gossip or rumour.

Using the firm's money

A sole trader can draw money and capital out of the business as and when he or she chooses; so too can a partner as long as the other partners do not object. The director or shareholder of a company is in a less flexible position. There are rules in the Companies Acts which forbid loans to directors and a reduction in the share capital of the company. If shares are sold to raise money, there might be a liability to capital gains tax and corporation tax.

Taxing the profits of the business

The sole trader or partner pays tax on all profits even if the profits are not taken out of the business. The rate of tax will depend on the earnings and will be taxed at 20 per cent on the first £2,000 of taxable income, 25 per cent on taxable income up to £23,700 and 40 per cent on taxable income above that (1992/3 figures).

In a company the directors pay tax on their earnings in the same way as any other employee but the excess profits can be kept in the company, where they will be subject to corporation tax (currently 25 per cent, unless the annual profits exceed £250,000 – 1992/3 figures).

The net effect of these tax rules is that if the firm's profits are such that the sole trader or partners are in the higher tax bands, they would be well advised to convert the business into a company.

Conversely, there are several tax advantages that the sole trader or partner has over a company:

• the sole trader or partner will pay less in national insurance contributions as a self-employed person than the combined contributions of the company and him- or herself if he or she were a director employed by the company;

• the sole trader, or partner, pays tax on a preceding-year basis, which means paying last year's tax this year (if incomes are going up this gives a useful cash-flow advantage); the employee of a company (which includes a director) pays tax on his or her salary as it is earned under the PAYE system;

• it is easier for the sole trader or partner to claim that a spouse works in the business and pay him or her an income equal to the personal allowance (£3,445 – 1992/3 figures);

• a sole trader or partner can offset losses in one business against profits in another, which cannot be done with a company;

• the sole trader or partner can generally claim more expenses and fringe benefits than can a company director.

Pensions

Pensions provide one area where a company has a tax advantage over a partnership or a sole trader if major contributions are wanted to be paid. The amount of contributions a company can make to a pension scheme is limitless and can all be set off against tax as an allowable expense. Added to the contributions made by the company, a company director can invest up to 15 per cent of salary and get full tax relief at the highest income-tax band. This contrasts with the position of a sole trader or partner, whose tax relief is limited to between $17\frac{1}{2}$ per cent and 40 per cent of own income.

Death and retirement

Because a company is a legal entity in its own right, as such it can never die; it can come to an end only when it is wound up. The company is therefore technically unaffected by the death or retirement of directors or shareholders; the company continues if necessary with new directors and new shareholders (although if a former director used the company as his or her vehicle and was particularly strong and influential, then practically his or her loss will of course have an effect on the future prospects of the company).

If a sole trader or partner dies, the firm will also die. The remaining partners will have to reconstitute the partnership and there may be difficulties in the valuation and transfer of assets, such as buildings plant and machinery and bank accounts.

Value Added Tax

Any business which has a turnover of £36,600 (1992 figures) or more is liable to pay VAT and must charge VAT on its services or sales. This is so whether the business is run by a sole trader, partnership or company. However, when a person operates several different businesses, although each business may have a turnover below the VAT limit their combined turnover is over the VAT limit. It may therefore be advantageous for him or her to separate the different businesses so that they are not treated as one single business. This can be done most easily if there are different companies set up for each different business as then there can be no argument that each is trading on its own. But the separation can also be done by a sole trader or partnership as long as the different businesses are truly run distinctly.

Having to register for VAT is not always a disadvantage, especially if the business is supplying other businesses which are also registered for VAT rather than the general public (few of whom are VAT-registered). Having to charge VAT means that the business can also offset the VAT it has to pay on items like telephones, computer software and stationery. Even if these were paid for up to nine months before the business was registered for VAT, they can be used to reduce the first VAT payment due to customs and excise.

Illustration. *Andrea Black plans to set up her own business as a graphic designer on 1 October. For six months beforehand, she still works for her old employer during the day but works on her own business at evenings and weekends. Between 1 April and 1 June she pays £1,250 plus VAT (£218.75) for a computer and £750 plus VAT (£131.25) for desktop publishing software. She also spends £100 plus VAT (£17.50) on an answerphone and her phone bill is going through the roof. She works out her first outside printing costs for her own stationery will be £950 plus VAT (£166.50). She works very hard on the business and by the end of August she can tell that by her planned start-up date she will have already earned £4,000 and she has future contracts and reliable promises of work of £26,000 all for large companies. Even though she has not yet reached the threshold level, she would probably do well to register for VAT: she can claim back the £533.75 that she has already paid out and will be able to reduce future amounts by the VAT element of her later telephone bills and all other VATable items.*

Registrations for VAT can be made in advance of a start-up date and can be made voluntarily even if the turnover or expected turnover does not exceed the threshold level. VAT returns must usually be completed every three months; the necessary forms are sent out in advance by the VAT office. Although registration for VAT certainly involves greater paperwork (an undeniable 'con') and a skill in numeracy, there are balancing 'pros'. The discipline involved in preparing VAT accounts every three months can encourage businesspeople otherwise prone to procrastination to keep up to date with their accounts and to ensure that their book-keeping remains in a reasonable state. There is also extra cashflow generated by adding VAT, some of which may not need to be paid for up to four months. (See also page 659)

Employed or self-employed?

A sole trader or a partner will be self-employed; a company director will normally be employed. See the table on page 413 for the main differences between the two. Note in particular:

• the combined national insurance contributions of an employer and an employee are more than those of a self-employed person;

• a self-employed person is not eligible for as many welfare benefits as an employed person – in particular unemployment benefit and sickness benefit are denied to the self-employed;

• a director, as an employee, can receive a golden handshake of up to £30,000 tax-free on being made redundant (although if the sum is paid on retirement it may be taxable); there is no such golden-handshake provision for the sole trader or partner, who would have to pay income tax on the amount received.

Bringing a husband or wife into the business

Some married men have wives who are not earning because they are largely involved in bringing up the children but may also be involved to a greater or lesser extent in running the business. Less frequent, but growing in number, are role swaps, where married men stay at home to care for the children while their wives are out there running their own businesses; these husbands too may be involved in helping out with the business side of things.

If the working husband or wife is self-employed, he or she can pay a spouse a salary for all the work carried out as a self-employed assistant. This could be just enough to use up the single person's tax-free allowance (£3,445 – 1992/3 figures). This is especially tax efficient where the 'non-working' spouse has no income of his or her own. Generally the Inland Revenue accept this as a legitimate ploy, although obviously some work must be carried out for the business.

A company director as an employed person cannot do this unless the company employs his or her spouse. Then there will usually be an immediate liability for national insurance too.

If a spouse puts a considerable amount of time into the business, the best arrangement would be for him or her to be in partnership, especially if the self-employed spouse would otherwise be in higher-rate tax bracket. Half the profits can then be paid to the spouse, thus reducing the overall tax bill (see also page 64).

Setting up as a sole trader: checklist

This is easy and straightforward. Sole traders should:
• tell their local tax inspectors when they are becoming self-employed (address in the telephone directory under Inland Revenue). Ask for form 41G;
• inform the local DSS office (listed in the telephone directory under Social Security, Department of). Self-employed people who earn more than £3,030 annually (1992/3 figures) must sign a form in favour of the DSS for them to pay national insurance contributions. This used to be by way of getting a book stamped every week. The term 'paying a stamp' still lingers, though most self-employed national insurance contributions are collected through direct debits from bank accounts. The amount thus paid – £5.35 per week – covers the amount of national insurance contributions due if the sole trader earns less than £6,120. The full amount of national insurance will be calculated once the sole trader files accounts. If the amount is over and above the minimum, a further amount of national insurance will be due assessed at 6.3 per cent of profits between £6,120 and £21,060 (1992/3 figures).
• check with the planning officer that the place of work is suitable (see chapter 20);
• consider whether or not to register for VAT.

Setting up as a partnership: checklist

Setting up as a partnership involves very similar steps to setting up as a sole trader, so refer above. In addition, future partners should agree the terms of a partnership agreement to ensure that their responsibilities and rights are clearly set out. A solicitor should be instructed (who will probably charge around £250 upwards). The agreement should cover:
• the names of the partners, the name of the business and its activity;
• the date the partnership starts and how long it will last (e.g. if there is an agreement that the partners will retire at sixty);
• the capital put into the business and whether the partners will be entitled to any interest on it;
• the profits' split;
• the management and control of the business;
• holidays;
• pension rights and any other benefits;
• what happens when a partner retires, dies or wants to leave.

Usually the partners should agree to sign a 'continuation election' to make sure that the partnership is not treated by the Inland Revenue as coming to an end (see page 653).

Setting up as a company: checklist

Again the businessperson should:
• tell the local tax inspector;

- check with the local planning officer that the place of work is suitable;
- consider whether to register for VAT (see above under sole trader).

To tailormake your own company, a 'starter pack' is available from Companies House, Crown Way, Cardiff CF4 37A. Most companies are *private limited companies*. *Public limited companies* must have an authorized share capital of at least £50,000 and a quarter must be paid up for each share (i.e. £12,500 is the minimum investment for a plc).

To start up a company you will need two people. Although a director can also act as a secretary, a sole director cannot act as a secretary too.

To register the company from scratch, the following have to be sent to the Registrar of Companies:

- *Memorandum of Association.* This states the name of the company, the registered office, the objects, the fact that the company has limited liability, the share capital and details of the first issued shares.
- *Articles of Association.* These contain the detailed rules about internal management of the company. If no special articles are drawn up, the standard format set out in the Companies Acts will apply.
- *Form 10.* This gives details of the first directors and secretary (including their names, addresses and occupations, dates of birth, nationality and details of other directorships held within the last five years) and the registered office.
- *Form 12.* This confirms compliance with all requirements.
- *Registration fee.* This procedure is likely to take several weeks (although Companies House do offer a same-day service at a considerable extra cost).

As an alternative, most new businesses buy a ready-made company 'off the shelf' from a company agent. Here the basic company has already been formed and all that needs to be done is change the name of the company (the fee for which is £50), register the new shareholders and appoint the new directors and secretary. This is a quicker process, although it will take around two weeks for the Registrar of Companies to change to the new company name.

To make the changes, you will need to call an annual general meeting or an extraordinary general meeting and pass a special resolution. Within fifteen days, a signed copy of the resolution should be sent to the Registrar of Companies, together with completed forms showing the appointments of the directors and secretaries (Form 288) and any allotment of shares (Form 88(2)).

Extra duties of directors

There have been a number of changes in recent years in how directors are regulated by law. In practice a director's general obligations are not much worse than they are for a sole trader or partner, and indeed they can be better because their assets are separated from the business assets (see page 606). But directors' own assets are safe only if they behave in a way which could be summed up by the term responsible business behaviour.

In summary, extra duties for directors are:

● *To act in the interests of the company.* This means putting the company first if there is a conflict between what would be best for the company and what would be best for the director personally. For example, if a director is offered a contract to do work personally for a customer instead of the company (which already has the promise of a contract), then the director should refuse.

● *Not to deceive shareholders or others.* Company directors should report to the shareholders every year at the AGM. The report should be honest and should not attempt to disguise any business difficulties or even additional profits.

If a company director is deceitful to an outsider, he or she can face claims personally. For example:

A firm of architects, Thomas Saunders Partnership, engaged Mr Harvey's company to install a cavity floor for the owners of new office premises. Mr Harvey falsely confirmed that the flooring met with certain specifications. The architects succeeded in their claim that Mr Harvey should be personally liable to indemnify them for the damages which they had to pay to the building owners even though Mr Harvey argued that his representation had been made on behalf of the company. Thomas Harvey Partnership v. Saunders (1989)

● *To have regard for the interests of company employees.*

● *To comply with the requirements of the Companies Acts.* Thus ensuring proper accounting records are set up, that companies' accounts are filed and that the necessary paperwork is sent to Companies House.

● *Not to carry on company business intending to defraud creditors or for any other fraudulent purpose.*

● *Not knowingly to allow the company to trade while insolvent ('wrongful trading').* Directors who do so may have to pay for the debts incurred by the company while insolvent. There is a more serious version of this called fraudulent trading but this is rarely used against directors as it has to be proved that the directors knew subjectively that the company was going bust. 'Wrongful trading' covers the more general situation where the company directors have been financially unrealistic.

The directors of a company Produce Marketing Consortium Limited continued to trade even though the accounts showed the company to be insolvent. The company's auditor had warned about the possibility of personal liability for the directors seven months before the company stopped trading. The judge found the directors had been overly optimistic and made them pay £108,000, which were the losses incurred after the directors should have been aware of the situation. Produce Marketing Consortium Limited (1990)

Directors have also found themselves personally liable for cheques they signed personally but which did not properly set out the full details of the company.

In settlement of a claim against a company, the company agreed to give five post-dated cheques to a creditor: all were temporary cheques containing the company's numbered account but not its name. A director signed all five cheques: two were met but three bounced before the company went bust. The creditor successfully sued the director who had signed the cheques. Rafsanjan v. Reiss (1990)

The moral to this is always ensure that any cheque (and any other document promising payment) contains the company's full and correct name; watch out especially for temporary chequebooks.

Dormant companies

Occasionally a sole trader or partner may want to buy a company, intending to use it as a vehicle for the business later. The main benefit in buying a company now rather than later is to buy a particular company name to protect against someone else using that name. So, for example, a partnership trading as Red and Amber could find out when they did a company search that the company name Red and Amber Ltd was currently not being used. They could thus buy a company, register its name as Red and Amber Ltd and keep their options to trade under the name of that company open for the future. But in the meantime, what do they have to do with the company?

They will still have to meet Companies Acts requirements, but there are less rigorous standards to comply with for dormant companies (i.e. companies which have no income and no expenditure). The directors can pass a special resolution exempting the company from filing audited accounts and from holding annual general meetings and send this to the Registrar of Companies within fifteen days. Then the only forms which will need sending to the Registrar of Companies are a balance sheet signed by a director confirming that the company was dormant throughout the financial year plus the annual return (Form 363a).

A free booklet, *Dormant Company Accounts*, from Companies House is useful.

Forming a co-op

A co-operative is a kind of enterprise which is controlled by all its members. They tend to be set up where all the members have idealistic aims; their essential features are democratic equality and mutual self-help. Co-ops are primarily of two kinds. First, workers' co-ops, in which all the staff own a share in the business: these have sometimes been used when the staff buy out a business which is about to close. Secondly, consumer co-ops, such as housing co-ops, in which the members jointly purchase, develop and manage a pool of properties.

A legal structure is usually necessary and there are two main alternatives:

1 Registration as a Friendly Society (under the Industrial and Provident Societies Acts). Most co-ops which adopt this form of structure will use

model rules prepared by the Industrial Common Ownership Movement (ICOM) or by the Co-operative Development Agency (CDA).

2 Registration as a company limited by guarantee. This is the same as an ordinary company except that no shares are issued. All the members guarantee a nominal sum (usually £1) towards the company's debts and that is the extent of their personal liability.

Both these legal structures ensure that there is a written legal framework for running the co-op and both offer the advantages of limited liability towards the participants. In practical terms there is virtually nothing to choose between the two methods. It is cheaper to form a company limited by guarantee and that method is more popular (£150 would probably cover the formation costs). Registering as a company means that the co-op will be under a duty to submit annual returns and audited accounts to Companies House, but it may be easier to borrow money as this particular structure is better understood by banks (who will, as ever, usually require some security).

FINDING OUT ABOUT A BUSINESS

It is not always easy to find out who owns a business, even though this may be vital information for a supplier or customer. In most cases it is possible to check the position simply by looking at the firm's notepaper. If the name ends in 'Ltd' or 'plc', then it should be a company (although this is not a foolproof check since some businesses wrongly claim to be companies when they are not). The next step is to check with the records at Companies House. Postal and telephone searches are no longer possible directly, so if checking in person it will be necessary to go along to the Registry (in London or Cardiff; or to check whether the local main library has an index of all registered companies. As an alternative, there are a number of company agents who can carry out an up-to-date search on your behalf; this will cost around £20 for an ordinary company search.

Companies in theory should provide quite a lot of information about themselves at their place of business and on their notepaper and invoices (see page 633), and there are also rules for partnerships and sole traders. Not all do comply and there is in any event no need usually for directors' names to be shown. Thus it is not always easy to find out who owns a business.

Disreputable businesses (which are more likely to be sued or have complaints made against them) are just the sort of firms who will not bother to display the true owner's name and address. In such cases it can be extremely difficult to find out exactly who runs a business, even though the trader is probably committing a criminal offence by failing to provide his or her name. Although it is theoretically possible to bring a private prosecution against such a wrongdoer, it is more effective to complain to the trading standards officer and hope he or she prosecutes.

42 Franchises

The idea behind franchising is simple, and when it works it works like this. The franchisor has developed a tried and trusted formula for operating in a particular type of business and has developed a good reputation for a particular business name. The franchisee buys the right to use the well-known business name and also the right to use the franchisor's experience and know-how to create a successful business run by the franchisee him- or herself.

The main benefits are that the franchisor can expand the network of businesses trading under its name; whilst the franchisee does not have to start a new business from scratch but can utilize a platform already built by the franchisor. The chief disadvantage for the franchisee is the cost: franchisors will be looking for a considerable upfront payment plus a creaming-off of the franchisee's profits in several ways (see below, Franchisee's Costs). The risk for the franchisor is that a new business might not meet the standards attained by all the others and thus might ruin the overall established reputation. Both the franchisee and the franchisor are united in their desire to see the new business succeed; if the franchisor is skilled in providing training and on-going support and supervision, this can give the new business the boost it needs.

Overall, franchised operations have statistically been shown to have a greater chance of success than the average new business (the UK Franchise Directory states that while the average failure rate for new businesses is 25 per cent, that for franchises is 10 per cent).

But buying a franchise gives no immunity from a harsh business climate and a potential franchisee will need to calculate carefully whether the high costs of a franchise can be realistically borne by the new business.

THE CONTRACT

Many of the bigger franchisors produce standard franchise agreements which they say they will refuse to change. Because franchising is a fairly specialized area of law, it is worthwhile going to a solicitor to check through the terms and conditions of a proposed agreement. The solicitor can also test how adamant the franchisor and their advisers are about amendments. Checking through the small print is highly important particularly to work out how much extra the franchisee will be paying to the franchisor over the period of the agreement.

Accurate projected costing will help work out whether the business has good prospects for making a profit.

The contract should cover:

- the type of business, its name and how it can be used;
- the territory where the franchisee will operate;
- the time limit of the franchise agreement;
- what the franchisee has to pay;
- what the franchisee agrees to do;
- what the franchisor agrees to do;
- what happens if the franchisee wants to sell;
- how the contract can otherwise be ended.

The business

This section of the contract describes what is basically for sale as a franchise, indicating whether the franchisor has registered a trademark or patent. The franchisee usually has to agree not to sell any products belonging to a competitor. The very fact that the franchisee will have no alternative but to use the franchisor's products means that the franchisee cannot benefit from shopping around to buy cheaper products from a competitor.

The franchisee's territory

The contract will usually specify that the franchisee will have sole and exclusive rights to operate the franchised business in a particular area and will be prevented from operating elsewhere (where perhaps other franchisees have their businesses). It is obviously in the franchisee's best interests to negotiate for as wide an area as possible, while the franchisor will be keen on limiting the territory so that they can sell other franchises nearby.

It is not just the franchisee that the franchisor is up against over granting exclusive territorial rights; both the Government and the EC are aiming to limit exclusive territorial rights. Franchisors have to register agreements under the Restrictive Trade Practices Act if exclusive rights are being granted, and the EC is also planning to restrict what exclusivity can be granted. The problem remains that unless the franchisee has some territorial safeguards then the business becomes more risky as the franchisee is more vulnerable to competition.

Time limits of the agreement

Franchise agreements typically run for a period of five years and can usually be renewed after that subject to the franchisee having performed satisfactorily and being willing to carry on. An option to renew should be insisted on, as should clarity about what standards of satisfactory performance the franchisee will be expected to meet. Unless the franchisee has some security, like a longer lease, without an option to renew it will be hard to sell the business as a going concern because the franchisee will no longer have any rights to use the name or the business format.

Sometimes the contract will specify that other sums must be spent on the premises or for refurbishing the premises. Again, these need to be clarified in advance.

Franchisee's costs

In addition to the initial upfront costs paid by the franchisee, the franchisor will usually charge a service fee (also called a continuing fee or royalties) over the period of the agreement. The franchisee may also have to meet advertising levies, product mark-ups and other hidden costs. The overall costs of a franchise in the package to the franchisee can often prove a deterrent. But less is not necessarily more. Successful franchisors have invested heavily in training and on-going support for their franchisees, and have to pass these costs on to the franchisees themselves. Cheaper franchises may be little more than a demand for payment of goodwill, leaving the franchisees having to fend for themselves.

Upfront costs

The upfront costs of franchises vary enormously, from a few thousand for lesser-known products to several hundred thousand for a fast-food beefburger franchise. More respectable franchisors take around 10 per cent of this capital payment as profits, investing the rest in the cost of training and supervision, for example. Added to this premium, franchisees will have to pay the costs of fitting out the premises and equipment, initial stock and legal fees.

Service fees

Again the parameters are fairly wide, but a franchisee could expect to pay around 10 per cent of *sales* (not profits). Sales figures are easier to check than profits from a franchisor's standpoint, but this can result in penalizing payments for the franchisee if business expenses exceed estimates. If, for example, business expenses (like salaries, heat and light, stationery etc.) represent 60 per cent of sales, then 10 per cent of sales means in practice a quarter of the profits.

Some agreements with an option to renew specify that for the renewal period the sales percentage payable as service fees will increase. This should be resisted where possible.

Advertising levies

It is said that only about half of all sums spent on advertising is productive. The problem is that no one knows which half is profitable and which half is basically thrown away, so large sums continue to be spent on advertising budgets.

The promotion of a brand name is part and parcel of a successful franchise operation. Most franchisors organize this either by advertising on a regular basis or advertising as and when necessary (if the latter, check carefully what the trigger points are for an advertising campaign to begin).

Franchisors may undertake to spend a certain share of the service charge each year on advertising, but many franchise packages also charge a separate advertising levy, again calculated as a percentage of profits. It is worthwhile exploring whether the levy is actually spent for the purpose it was designed for. This can be done by asking to see the franchisor's audited accounts and looking for a separate item for advertising and public relations costs on the profit and loss account.

Product Mark-ups

Buying in bulk by the franchisor gives the opportunity for bulk-buy discounts and cheaper supplies, which could be passed on to the franchisees. Alternatively franchisors may add on a mark-up which means they, not the franchisees, get the financial benefits. Check by getting quotes for alternative supplies.

Hidden costs

Some franchisors have set up arrangements with banks or finance companies to offer financial deals to incoming franchisees. These often involve the franchisor receiving a commission which might be paid for by the franchisee from more expensive interest or arrangement fees charged by the lender. In practice it is not always possible to find alternative sources of funding, but finding out on what terms other banks or lenders would lend can help widen the franchisee's options.

What the franchisee and franchisor agree to do

The agreement should state clearly what both the franchisor and franchisee agree to do to meet their own sides of the bargain: breaching any of these terms will be grounds for getting out of the contract (often with certain financial penalties).

Most franchisors have prepared operations manuals, which set out guidelines for how the business will be run. These are really summaries of the essential principles to operate the franchise, distilling the experience and know-how of the franchisor on such areas as the business itself (e.g. how to cook a hamburger), accounting systems, recruitment and customer service. The contract will usually contain a commitment by the franchisee to adhere to the manual. As a rough rule of thumb, the more regularly the operations manual is updated, the more interested and committed the franchisor.

Franchisees will usually have to attend periods of training, weighted towards the time of the business start-up, but this may be ongoing too. Franchisors should have set up a back-up and support service (e.g. for advice, troubleshooting, and research and development) which franchisees can use without any extra costs.

If the franchisee wants to sell

Most franchise agreements include a clause allowing the franchisee to sell before the agreement has gone its full term. Many will insist on a first option being given to the franchisor. It is not in the franchisor's interests to handcuff a franchisee to a business he or she is unwilling to continue running, but equally the franchisor will want to have certain safeguards about the skills of an incoming buyer. The buyer will usually have to undergo some similar training and sign a similar agreement, but in practice a new buyer is unlikely to have to meet exactly the same rigorous standards that the original franchisee did. Watch out for a clause permitting the franchisor to charge hefty transfer fees on sale. In reality, this will block a sale to anyone else except the franchisor, usually at well below the market value.

Ending the contract

This should cover what would happen if the franchisee were to die or become incapable of running the business and may also allow other get-outs. The first draft of the agreement is likely to be unfavourable to the franchisee, who should try and ensure that the final agreement is as fair as possible. The contract will also lay down the conditions for the franchisor being able to end the contract: if the franchisee fails to meet minimum performance targets, for example. The franchisee should try to insist that he or she is given the opportunity to rectify any problems before the contract is finally terminated.

PREMISES

Different franchisors have different practices when it comes to business premises. Some prefer the franchisees to own the leasehold or freehold; others prefer to keep control of the premises themselves, which they then lease to the franchisees. The more respectable franchisors usually have strict standards about what sort of area the premises should be based in and will carry out their own searches to find suitable outlets.

If the franchisor owns the freehold or a long leasehold of the premises, then when the time comes for renewal the premises can be used for another business. Basically, the franchisee's options are much wider. On the other hand, when the franchisor owns the premises, if the agreement is ended then the franchisor keeps the benefit of a valuable site.

RAISING FINANCE

All the clearing banks have specialist franchise units (often based separately from individual branches) and can usually offer a reasonable degree of experience when advising. Applications for finance to start off a reputable franchise operation are often dealt with slightly more sympathetically than applications for one-off business start-ups because of the proven record of certain franchises. Lenders will still apply stringent tests to would-be applicants (see Chapter 43).

WOULD-BE FRANCHISORS

The British Franchise Association, Thames View, Newtown Road, Henley-on-Thames, Oxon RG9 1HG (0491 578050) sells a franchisor's manual costing £22 (including p + p).

43 Raising Finance

The process of raising money for a business venture may well be one of the most time-consuming tasks of starting a business, but the least part of this should be the time involved in sitting in front of a bank manager. If sufficient time has been invested in the preparation of a sound financial and business plan with budget forecasts, then potential problems will have been thought through and the meeting with the bank should be a comparatively painless experience.

The money required will need to cover not only the expensive one-off costs of starting up, like the costs of equipment, premises and furniture, legal and professional costs and initial marketing expenditure, but also working capital to meet the day-to-day running costs of the business until it is generating healthy profits.

PREPARING A FINANCIAL PLAN

Financial plans are based on both known facts and also intelligent guesses (which will be tested by the bank manager's questioning and by the market if the plan overcomes that hurdle). It should begin with a budget statement setting out sales forecasts, proposed prices, trade credit periods, stock-holding and replacement costs, drawings, salaries, interest payments and other expenses (monthly, quarterly and yearly), tax liabilities and capital expenditure requirements. This will then show what investment needs to be made in the business:

- *short term* – to provide working capital for day-to-day running;
- *medium term* – to buy equipment and machinery and possibly for improvements to the premises;
- *long term* – to buy an established business or the freehold or long leasehold of new premises.

There is a plethora of books on the market offering advice to business start-ups. Useful ones are *The Lloyds Bank Small Business Guide*, by Sara Williams (Penguin) and *The Guide to Running Your Small Business*, by David Porter (Holyoake).

Bank Presentation: Checklist

---

1 Summary of plan, highlighting the most important attractions of the business.
2 Personal details:
   ● age, education, business experience (highlighting successes to date and showing how previous problems, if any, have been overcome), specialist skills, health record;
   ● assets and liabilities;
   ● personal investment in proposed business.
3 Details of the planned business:
   ● the type of business;
   ● reasons why the business will be sound and viable;
   ● management ability;
   ● relevant experience.
4 Details of others involved in the venture:
   ● their personal details;
   ● the nature of their interest.
   If no others, the plan should state who will cover in the event of sickness or other absence.
5 Business plan:
   ● budget and cashflow forecast broken down on a monthly basis to show expected income and expenditure;
   ● profit projections;
6 Marketing:
   ● whether any trademark or patent will be sought;
   ● potential demand, backed up by market research if obtained;
   ● details of competition;
   ● what competitive advantages the new business has over the competition (including any identified gaps in the market).
7 Anticipated problems:
   ● identify if possible and explain contingency plans.
8 Business premises:
   ● location;
   ● whether freehold or leasehold;
   ● planning (and licensing) position.
9 Amount of loan:
   ● how much needed;
   ● when it will be needed (over what period of time);
   ● for what purpose.
10 Repayment:
   ● back-up ability to repay principal within loan period;
   ● back-up ability to repay interest (even if interest rates go up) and any bank charges.
11 Security:
   ● what you are willing to offer (e.g. insurances, shares etc.), with independent valuations if need be;
12 Proposals to insure:
   ● business premises and assets and those involved in or employed by the business.

Note: sketches and photographs may be required in support.

GETTING THE MONEY

New business start-ups have traditionally got their long-term capital from two sources:

- savings that they themselves have made or from relatives or friends, *and/or*
- a secured bank loan.

Working capital, on the other hand, is more frequently funded by a combination of bank overdraft and trade credit (the time gap between receiving the goods and paying for them).

Savings

Unless a potential business-owner is willing to invest personally in the business, then a bank is highly unlikely to do so either. Personal investment in practice is often made up not only of the assets of the businessperson him- or herself but also of those most likely to trust in that person's judgement – close family and friends. While those closest may be the easiest to convince, they can also be the cause of greatest domestic upset if plans go wrong. Agreements should be clearly made about whether the investment is a gift or a loan and, if the latter, how much interest will be paid and whether any security will be offered. The terms also need to cover what should happen if the business fails.

As a rough rule of thumb, the absolute most a new business could expect to raise will be five times the amount of the personal investment. In practice banks are often reluctant to see the ratio exceed twice that of the personal funds, even if there is sufficient security.

Secured loans

If at the outset it is unlikely that a loan can be repaid in the short term but, longer term, the profits generated will be able to meet capital and interest repayments, then a longer-term loan would be more suitable. Loans can be for any term between two and thirty years, but the lender (usually a bank) will insist on some form of security which cannot 'walk': land, for example, cannot disappear but vehicles can (and, in the lenders' experience, often do just before a business fails).

Lenders will want more security; borrowers should try to get away with offering less. Avoid where possible the loan being secured on the house, and offer shares and/or insurance policies as an alternative. If the loan is secured on the home, then the home will have to be sold if the repayments are not paid up to date and the lender calls in the loan.

The repayment of the loan and the interest payments will be arranged at the start, either at a fixed rate or at a certain percentage point above the bank's base rate. Sometimes there are financial penalties for redeeming (paying off) the loan before its term ends. It is occasionally possible to have a capital 'holiday', where the capital repayments do not have to be made for an initial cushioning period of, say, a year. But of course the interest will still have to be paid and there will be extra interest over the whole period because of the delay in starting to pay off the capital. Always check the small print carefully.

Overdrafts

Overdrafts tend to be quicker to arrange and used to be fairly cheap, but many small businesses have more recently found that they have been charged penal rates of interest by their banks. The major drawback of an overdraft is that it is repayable on demand and will usually need regular renegotiation (at least annually). Most banks will insist on some form of security and will usually ask for personal guarantees from company directors (sole traders and partners will be personally liable anyway). Banks are often wary of taking shares as security and will want more substantial security like debtors or property (see above).

Agreeing an overdraft constitutes a contract between the business-owner and the bank manager. There will be an upper limit which should not be exceeded without the prior permission of the bank manager. If it is exceeded, the banks will at best charge a fee for advising the customer that the account is over the limit and add extra monthly charges, and at worst can call in the overdraft. The terms and rates of interest are up to negotiation so it could be worthwhile getting quotes from different banks to arm you for negotiating with a chosen bank.

Business Expansion Schemes

Individuals who wish to invest in or lend money to small businesses have been offered generous tax incentives by the Government to do so. Investors can get full income-tax relief on investments of up to £40,000 per year in newly issued ordinary shares of new or small unquoted companies at up to the investor's highest rate of tax (currently 40 per cent – 1992/3 figures). The investment must be kept in the business for a minimum period of five years. After that, assuming the shares increase in value, the investor will not have to pay capital gains when the shares are sold. The tax incentives are available only to outsiders and not to paid directors or employees of the company. The BES scheme is, however, only available up to 1 April 1994.

There are limitations on the types of businesses that can qualify. The scheme is limited to companies alone and they must carry on business mainly in the UK. The companies must not operate in certain fields – for example, certain types of financial investment, insurance, leasing or hiring. The disadvantages from the viewpoint of the business-owner is that an investor will almost always want to liquidate the assets after the five-year period and will usually want some control of the business (often via a directorship) as well. Most schemes are arranged through specially set-up BES funds, which pool individual investors who would not otherwise have the contacts with businesses wanting to use the BES scheme. The BES funds frequently prove an expensive way of raising money, as the managers of the fund usually want some shares in the company (e.g. an option on an extra 2 per cent of the shares) plus expensive arrangement and non-executive director's fees.

Venture capital

About half of all venture capital is raised through the Business Expansion Scheme as above. The remainder is provided by money put up from pension funds, banks and other major investors. In both cases the investors will usually be looking for established companies that want to expand rather than new business start-ups. The criteria they look for are companies with very good management with a proven track record operating in a market which is either very large or fast-growing (i.e. companies which could reach profits of £300,000 upwards in three to four years).

Venture capitalists will normally require ordinary shares plus preference shares, plus an appointment of a non-executive director to the board (annual fees will be around £7,500, which the company will have to bear) plus payment of their own costs of investigating the company and their legal and professional fees. Added to that the fact that most will want their money back comparatively quickly too, venture capital funding becomes of interest to only a small minority of companies.

Other sources of financial help

Nationally

Towards the end of the 1980s and early 1990s, governmental moves were made away from nationally orchestrated financial help for businesses towards a patchwork of different locally organized schemes (see below), with the overall aims of concentrating help where it was most needed and designing local schemes to fit different communities' requirements. The main remaining national scheme organized by the Government is the Loan Guarantee Scheme, which is administered by the banks. Not all businesses will qualify.

A loan under this scheme can be for up to £100,000 and lasts for between two and seven years. There can be a capital 'holiday' of up to two years before the capital is repaid, so only interest is payable during that time. The Department of Employment guarantees 70 per cent of the outstanding amount due to the lender (85 per cent in some inner-city areas), which will be paid if the business fails. The drawback is the extra cost: the interest rate set by the bank must be paid plus the guarantee premium required by the government (currently 2.5 per cent on the guaranteed part of the loan or 2 per cent if the loan is in one of the qualifying inner city areas).

Locally

Free advice is available from the local Enterprise Agency, while applications for money should be directed to the local Training and Enterprise Council (TEC).

One of the most useful forms of regular financial help for a new business start-up used to be called the Enterprise Allowance Scheme (EAS). This has now been scrapped, since the TECs have been set up in different parts of the country; there are eighty-two in all. All TECs are private-sector led and are supposedly geared to each different community's needs. So each TEC has its own individual rules about providing financial help for business start-ups, but as many of them are offering a variation on the old Enterprise Allowance Scheme, it may be useful to explain this.

To qualify under the old EAS, the potential businessperson should have been unemployed for at least eight weeks (and have signed on during that time at the employment agency) and must have a minimum of £1,000 to invest in the business (this could be raised by borrowing from the bank). The business must have been brand new, not one which was taken over. If those conditions were met, then the successful claimant received a taxable sum of £40 per week for one year and access to free business counselling.

Many of the TECs call their own versions of the old EAS scheme NBOs, or new business opportunities. Some of them now last for six months, whereas some still last for a year. Some have increased the weekly payments; others have kept the same amount. Ask at the local Enterprise Agency or TEC for further information.

Some areas have also been designated Enterprise Zones. Once designated, the zones last for ten years from the date they were started (most were set up in the early to mid 1980s). If a business sets up in one of these zones, it will receive considerable benefits, like no business rates to pay, capital allowances of up to 100 per cent claimable in the first year and easier planning applications. The original areas included London Docklands, Rotherham, North West Kent, Sunderland, Telford, Milford Haven Waterway and Workington. Other initiatives exist to encourage the growth of new businesses and jobs in particular locations, like regional enterprise grants (available for firms employing less than twenty-five people) which can finance investments, give guidance to new businesses, and help with rents and reductions in the business rate.

In addition to the above there may well be other sources of help for your particular business. The Prince's Youth Business Trust, for example, offers help to young businesspeople and there are competitions run by banks, accountants and the media offering financial help. The Enterprise Agencies should be able to give further details.

44 Business Image

CHOICE OF NAME

The way a business presents itself to the outside world shapes public perceptions of the business and its products or services. Owners can choose whether to use their own names for the business name or to pick another name which better promotes the image they want to achieve.

The choice of business name has more to do with marketing than the law, which places few restrictions on business-owners. There is no longer any legal necessity to register business names with anybody. The requirements of the old Business Names Act 1916 were ended back in 1982. While this gives greater freedom in the choice of a business name, there are drawbacks in not being able to check quickly in advance whether another business already exists in the same field with the same chosen name unless the business is a company. New businesses cannot register a company name identical to that of an existing company. This can be checked by looking at the index in the public search rooms of Companies House at Cardiff or London.

Limitations on choice of name

Business names cannot lay claim to connections which they do not have. So any business name which gives the (untrue) impression that it is nationwide (like English or National), an institution (like University) or connected with royalty (like Royal or Windsor) will be out unless the business can substantiate those claims. Business names which could be considered offensive or illegal will also be out.

In practice one of the more important limitations on a choice of name is given by the law of *passing off*. A business cannot pretend to be an existing established business in the same field. The law is not so straightforward when it comes to setting up a business in another field, so it is arguable (if potentially dangerous) that a new business could use an established business name if it operates in an entirely different part of the country selling entirely separate products.

So a new business cannot set up as 'Marks and Spencer' and sell clothing and food, nor can it copy existing Marks and Spencer-type packaging or copy a trademark (see also page 666) to sell a different and cheaper brand of products.

There are five requirements for a successful passing-off action. There must have been 1. a misrepresentation, 2. made in the course of trade, 3. to prospective customers, 4. calculated to injure the business or goodwill of another trader and 5. which causes actual damage to the business or goodwill of that trader. The underlying question is whether the buying public have been fooled into thinking the new business or its products are the same as the old, established, successful one. In practice passing-off actions are rarely successful, but the following example is one case where it was:

The defendants made drawings of humanoid turtles similar in appearance to Teenage Mutant Ninja Turtles (whose copyright belonged to the plaintiffs) and licensed these similar drawings for designs on clothes. The plaintiffs asked for an injunction stopping the defendants from carrying on these activities as they were passing off their drawings as the original ones and for breach of copyright. The court decided to grant the injunction because it found that the public mistakenly believed that the goods were genuine as a result of the defendants' misrepresentations. Mirage Studios *v.* Counter-Feat Clothing Company Limited (1991)

There are also some added requirements on owners in disclosing the ownership of the business (see diagram opposite, which summarizes the disclosure requirements).

Sole Traders

These requirements do not apply to a sole trader operating the business under his or her surname alone. So, for example, if David Black trades as 'Black', 'D. Black' or 'David Black', he is not affected. But if he calls his business 'D. Black Painters and Decorators', then he will have to give his own name and a business or other address. A married woman who is normally known by her married name but carries on business under her maiden name also should give her married name if she normally uses it.

Partnerships

As with sole traders, if a partnership operates the business solely under the surnames of the partners (with or without forenames and initials), then they need not separately disclose their names and addresses. But if they do anything else, then they will have to.

Companies

If a company operates under its own name, then again it is not affected, but a company which trades under another name will have to disclose the name of the company too. Companies must in any case disclose their registered office, registered company number and state that the company is registered in England and Wales. Directors names do not need to be disclosed unless they are foreign (when they must be shown), but if any of the company directors' names are shown, then all the others must be included too.

Examples of Business Letterheads, Disclosing Required Details

---

1 Business owned by a sole trader

D. BLACK BAKERY
(Prop. D. Black)
21 High Street
Barchester
Barset BA1 2AB

---

2 Business owned by a partnership

BLACK AND WHITE PAINTERS AND DECORATORS
Partners: D. Black and S. White
43 Castle Street
Barchester
Barset BA2 3CD

---

3 Business owned by a company

BLACK AND WHITE STORAGE
Unit 4, Castle Industrial Estate
Barchester
Barset BA3 4EF

(At the bottom of the letterheaded page, details to be disclosed as required by the Business Names Act 1985 and the Companies Act 1985)

Black and White Storage (Barchester) Limited
Registered in England and Wales
Registration number: 7654321
Registered Office: 65 Regent Street,
Barchester, Barset BA4 5GH

LOGOS

Logos are symbols for a business. It may be nothing more than a word, the name of the company or product, always shown in the same colour or typeface or within a distinctive shape. The idea is to create a memorable symbol that will be quickly recognized and will eventually be associated with a quality product or service. Again, the only restriction placed by the law is that the logo should not *pass off* or pretend that the product or service is someone else's (see above).

Obviously, you will require other details like telephone and fax numbers and maybe a business logo, but the above examples just set out what must be included so that letterheads comply with all the necessary requirements.

This information should be stated not only on letterheads but also on invoices and demands for payment, written orders for the supply of goods or services and also at the premises where the business is carried on.

The Companies House booklet *Business Names and Business Ownership*, available free from Companies House, is useful.

45 Business Premises

WORKING FROM HOME

Many small businesses start off from a back room at home, the main advantages being cost and convenience. But what was at one time convenient may turn out to be wildly inconvenient later on as the space and time demands of work compete with those of home.

Aside from personal requirements, the major potential legal obstacle to using the home for a business base involves planning. Planning laws limit the use of different properties, one of the main functions of the planning laws being to keep residential and work areas distinct. If operating the business from home involves a major change of use – say, if you were to take over the whole premises to run a factory from them – then the local authority could serve an enforcement notice, requiring you to turn the premises back to a residential property. But the planning laws do not stop you, for example, from working as a graphic designer, a carpenter or knitwear producer in the back room at home. As long as you keep a low profile and your business is not very noisy, does not annoy your neighbours or involve a lot of people coming to visit you, planning permission for a change of use is probably not necessary.

Other possible hurdles which may need checking are:
- whether there is a restrictive covenant on the property which prohibits your intended use – check with the title deeds or with the solicitor who bought the property for you;
- whether the mortgage stops you from working at home – check with the bank or building society;
- whether your insurance policies have any particular restrictions – you can always change the policy;
- whether you may be liable for capital gains tax on the part of the house used for the business when you sell your home (see page 651).

FINDING BUSINESS PREMISES

The search for premises which are vacant and meet your own specific needs can involve a lot of work, but there are an increasing number of organizations which can assist. In addition to combing through local newspapers, estate agents' particulars and looking at post office windows, some local authorities keep lists of local vacant commercial premises, and local Enterprise Agencies should also be able to help. Especially in areas of high unemployment, there are a number of national and local agencies who can help with the provision of premises.

Very often, though, once you have targeted a particular area that you want to move your business to, the most effective method for finding your own premises is to go round the area by car, bike or foot.

Requirements for Business Premises: Checklist

---

1 Space and cost:
 • number of square feet required (allow approximately 100 sq. ft. per employee for an office);
 • maximum price prepared to pay per sq. ft. (add on running costs: service charges, heat and light and maintenance etc.);
 • maximum price prepared to pay as premium (add on costs of refurbishment, legal costs of purchase) – check how long the lease is for and when the next rent review is due.
2 Ease of access:
 • check on ease of access for pedestrians (and disabled access if necessary), proximity to motorways, rail (underground) and bus links, parking and delivery facilities.
3 Environment:
 • check on image (appearance), light, noise, cleanliness (especially of common parts if sharing a building with others), fire hazards and neighbours. If you are planning to start a particular type of business – say, an art gallery – it can often be a good (not bad) sign that there are other similar businesses nearby. That way the area acquires a reputation for art galleries and the number of visiting customers increases.
4 Facilities and services:
 • Fittings/partitions (if wanted, already installed), central heating, telephone, electrical points, cooking facilities (and perhaps a shower), air-conditioning, burglar alarms.

Renting Business Premises

Very few business start-ups can afford the high cost of purchasing their own premises. For the vast majority, the only option is to lease or rent. But a tenant can still get some security of tenure to give stability when establishing the business.

The Rent Acts apply only to residential lettings. The law on business letting is set up in the Landlord and Tenant Act 1954. This Act applies to all commercial letting, whether the premises be an office, factory, studio, shop, warehouse or whatever. If the premises are used partly for residential purposes and partly for business purposes, then the tenant will not be able to claim Rent Act protection (see page 297). However, the tenant will usually be able to claim business-tenancy protection unless he or she falls foul of one of the following:

• if the lease specifically prohibits the premises being used for business purposes, so the tenant is using the premises in contravention of the terms of the lease;
• if the landlord and tenant together agree to opt out of the provisions of the Landlord and Tenant Act 1954 and a court order is obtained to this effect;
• if the tenancy is a licence only or a tenancy at will (see below).

If the tenant is occupying the premises in one of these three ways, then the tenant will have no protection under the Landlord and Tenant Act (or even under the Rent Acts) and so he or she will have to leave when the lease or licence expires or when the periodic tenancy (e.g. weekly, monthly etc.) is brought to an end by a notice to quit.

When deciding how long a period to take on a lease for, the tenant of a new lease should be aware that he or she will be liable for all the responsibilities (covenants) under the lease for the whole of the lease term. This applies even if the business fails or if the original tenant assigns the interest in the lease to a buyer. Often where a new business is concerned, it may be better to settle for a shorter period rather than risk taking on very long-term (and thus onerous) obligations (see Assigning a Lease, page 640).

Anyone taking on a business lease should get legal advice from a solicitor; business tenancies are complicated and many landlords try to impose extremely harsh terms on their tenants. In practice most business tenants are fully liable to maintain and repair their premises as though they owned them and it is usual to have a rent review after, say, three to five years. The solicitor will be able to advise as to whether the repairing obligations, the rent review provisions and the other terms of the lease (e.g. any restrictions as to the type of business that can be carried on) are acceptable. If the landlord is trying to get round the business-tenancy protection by offering a licence instead of a lease, the solicitor will also be able to advise whether the form of the licence really does exclude the protection of the Landlord and Tenant Act or whether the courts might construe it as a lease anyway.

WHEN THE LANDLORD AND TENANT ACT APPLIES

The 1954 Act applies to all business lettings with only limited exceptions:
• if the tenant is given a fixed-term tenancy of up to six months, the Act will not apply. Thus the tenant will have no security of tenure and is reliant on the landlord's discretion about renewing the lease. The landlord can use this way of evading the Act only twice: once the tenant has been in occupation for more than twelve months the tenant acquires full rights under the Act.
• if the tenant is given a fixed-term tenancy and the court has agreed that the 1954 Act should not apply. Both the landlord and the tenant must together apply to the court before the tenancy begins for formal confirmation that the tenant will not have any rights to stay on at the end of the lease. In practice the courts usually rubber-stamp these agreements and the whole procedure need only take a month or so. But note that this procedure applies only to a

fixed-term letting (e.g. a lease for a year); it cannot be used for a periodic letting (e.g. a weekly or quarterly letting that could be ended on a week's or quarter's notice).

• if the tenant occupies under a licence or a tenancy at will. Sometimes the landlord will allow the tenant to occupy premises before an agreement has finally been reached for a formal tenancy or sometimes the landlord is prepared to offer only a licence instead of a proper tenancy. The courts are very reluctant to let landlords off the hook of the protection of the Landlord and Tenant Act and thus will scrutinize any agreement expressed to be a licence or a tenancy at will very carefully. If there is non-exclusive occupation (i.e. the 'landlord' keeps the right to come in to the premises at any time and does not give the 'tenant' any rights to stay more than temporarily in the property), then the courts may agree that the business tenancy protection does not apply. But if there is any doubt, the courts usually come down on the side of the tenant and would usually imply that there is a periodic tenancy.

How the 1954 Act works

One of a business tenant's main concerns is not to be evicted at the end of the lease or by service of a notice to quit. The tenant is likely to have built up a clientele and goodwill at the premises and therefore will usually want to stay in occupation. The 1954 Act gives the tenant this security except in certain very limited cases (see 4 below).

If the tenant has a fixed-term tenancy it will carry on when the term expires. The landlord can only end an expired fixed-term tenancy or a periodic tenancy by serving a special notice on the tenant and then applying to the court.

The procedure is:

1 The landlord must serve a statutory notice to quit (in a prescribed style and format available from law stationers or solicitors) on the tenant. This must state a date when the tenancy is to end, and this must be between six and twelve months ahead. The notice must also state whether the landlord would oppose an application by the tenant to court for a new tenancy and, if so, on what grounds.

2 Within two months of receiving the notice, the tenant must give a written counter-notice stating whether or not he or she will give up possession. Note that all these time limits are applied very strictly. For example if the tenant does not serve the notice in time, then the right to claim a new tenancy will be lost (it is a mistake often made, but it can none the less be disastrous).

3 Unless the tenant comes to a satisfactory agreement with the landlord the tenant must within two to four months of receiving the notice also start county court proceedings for a new tenancy. Once again, the tenant must make sure that the time limits are not missed. If they are, the tenant loses the right to demand a new lease.

4 The court will grant the tenant a new tenancy unless the landlord can show that one of the following grounds for possession exists:
- failure to repair and maintain as required;
- persistent delay in paying rent;
- other substantial breaches of the terms of the tenancy;
- suitable alternative premises can be provided;
- the tenant is a sub-tenant of part only of the premises and the landlord needs possession so that the landlord can sell the whole premises;*
- the landlord wants to demolish or reconstruct the premises and needs access to do so;†
- the landlord wants the premises for his or her own business or residential use (unless this landlord purchased the interest in the lease from the previous landlord within the last five years).‡

5 If the court grants a new tenancy, it will fix the terms of the tenancy. These need not necessarily be the same as those of the old tenancy, although the court will 'have regard' to them as well as 'all the relevant circumstances'. The new tenancy will start three months after the court hearing, and in the meantime the old tenancy will continue (except that the court can order a new rent to apply in the interim). The new rent will be an open market rent (i.e. what the premises will be let for, disregarding the fact that the tenant has been in occupation and that he or she has built up goodwill; improvements carried out by the tenant are also ignored).

If the court refuses to grant a new tenancy, the tenant will have up to twenty weeks in which to leave. If the tenant does not leave by then, the landlord can apply to have the tenant evicted.

It cannot be stressed too much that all the above time limits are applied very strictly. For instance, a tenant who does not apply to the court within two to four months of receiving the landlord's notice will forfeit the right to apply to the court for a new tenancy. Even if the landlord and tenant agree between themselves to waive the time limits of the Landlord and Tenant Act, their agreement will not be upheld by the courts.

If the tenant's original tenancy was for a fixed term of over one year, or if he or she has continued from year to year, the tenant can him- or herself initiate the procedure under the 1954 Act; the tenant need not wait for the landlord to serve a notice (i.e. 1 above). Instead the tenant can serve a notice on the

---

* In these cases the landlord must compensate the tenant for evicting him or her. The compensation will depend on how long the tenant has been in business at the premises and when the tenancy was granted.

† If the tenancy was granted after 1 April 1990, the compensation will be: for *less than fourteen years*, the amount of the Uniform Business Rate multiplied by the number of years occupying the premises; for *fourteen years or more*, double the UBR multiplied by the number of years occupying the premises.

‡ However, if the tenancy was granted before 1 April 1990, then the tenant can opt for compensation assessed under the old rules: that is, for *less than fourteen years*, the amount of the old rateable value multiplied by eight, multiplied by the years of the tenancy; for *more than fourteen years*, the amount of the old rateable value multiplied by sixteen, multiplied by the years of the tenancy

landlord (the notice must again be in a special prescribed form) asking for a new tenancy. The landlord then has two months in which to serve a counter-notice stating whether such an application will be opposed and, if so, why. The procedure then continues in the usual way (i.e. 3, 4 and 5 then follow).

If, for some reason, the tenant does not want the tenancy to continue, then the tenant should give the landlord at least three months' notice before the date it is due to expire. But if the tenant waits until after that time, the three-months' notice must still be given to expire on a quarterday (25 March, 24 June, 29 September, 25 December). Even if the tenant leaves before the end of the expiry period, the tenant will be liable for rent until the tenancy properly expires.

The above is just a summary of the provisions of the 1954 Act. It is a complex piece of legislation; there are time periods to be observed and special forms to be used. Accordingly, it is important to obtain legal advice when dealing with any business-tenancy matter.

ASSIGNING A LEASE

If a tenant wants to sell off the business, the usual intention is to sell the remaining term of the tenancy with the business as a package. But an original tenant of a lease must beware: original tenants remain liable under all the covenants in the lease (including the payment of rent and responsibilities to repair), at least until the original lease period has expired but if the period has been extended under the Landlord and Tenant Act 1954, possibly until even the end of the renewed tenancy.

An original tenant will also be bound by any increases of rent fixed following the rent review clause in the lease. This means that if the original tenant assigns his or her interest in the lease and then the new tenant (or even a later assignee) goes bust, the landlord will have the right to ask the original tenant for any arrears of rent and to pay for any necessary repairs, even if the original tenant is no longer in business and has no desire whatsoever to occupy the premises again.

If a tenant has taken out a long lease and does want to assign, the tenant's solicitors will try to protect the tenant's position as best they can by requiring an indemnity from the incoming tenant. This means that if the landlord tries to recover money from the original tenant under the lease, the original tenant will have the right to counter-claim against the assignee tenant. This can be a useful device, especially where there is a chain of assignments and the tenant finally in occupation of the premises goes bust. But the original tenant will still be protected only to the extent that his or her assignee is financially sound.

This very harsh rule has received a lot of criticism but as yet there are no definite plans to change it. If the original tenant wants to leave the premises before the end of the lease, he or she should try asking the landlord whether they would be willing to accept a surrender of the lease so that the original tenant's covenants come to an end. However, this is often not possible, as landlords would usually prefer the premises to be occupied and thus the rent to be paid; there are few incentives for landlords to accept a surrender.

If a tenant does want to assign the lease, the tenant will first have to obtain the landlord's consent to the assignment. The standard arrangement is that the landlord will not be able to 'unreasonably withhold' consent. The assignee (the purchaser) will usually have to provide the landlord with three or four business references to prove the assignee's suitability as a tenant. The landlord will then sign a formal licence which authorizes the assignment: the fees of the landlord's solicitors will usually have to be met by the existing tenant. Only once the licence is formally given can the existing tenant sign a deed assigning the tenancy to the buyer. If the assigning tenant is a company and one of the directors has given a personal guarantee to pay the rent etc. to the landlord, the individual(s) should ask the landlord for a termination of the guarantee(s) in writing, otherwise they will continue to be liable too.

The seller and buyer will have to bear their own legal fees unless there is an agreement in writing to the contrary (Costs of Leases Act 1958). It is not uncommon for the seller to insist that the buyer pays the seller's and the landlord's legal fees. When this happens, the buyer should insist that a maximum figure is agreed in advance; otherwise the buyer risks being overcharged by the solicitors. If the buyer is overcharged, he or she would not have the usual remedies against the seller's and the landlord's solicitors that they would have had against their own solicitor (see Chapter 66).

LEGAL FEES

Generally a solicitor will work out the fees in a similar way as for the purchase of a residential property (see page 276 for how the fees are calculated).

If the business premises are being bought under a lease, fees have traditionally been worked out according to a fairly complex calculation often resulting in expensive bills for the client. For example, the charges were likely to be on the basis of the time spent, plus 25–35 per cent for checking the lease and carrying out all the other necessary work, plus $\frac{1}{2}$ per cent of the purchase price, plus 1 per cent of the annual rent multiplied by the length of the lease up to a maximum of twenty years. For instance, on the purchase of a shop lease for twenty-one years for £25,000, with the rent at £7,500 p.a., the work involved being nine hours at an hourly charge of £60, the fee might be:

9 × 60	£540.00
plus 25 per cent	£135.00
plus $\frac{1}{2}$ per cent of £25,000	£125.00
plus 1 per cent of £7,500 × 20 years	£1500.00
Total (excl. VAT and disbursements)	£2300.00

More recently, with increasing competition among solicitors' firms, the bills are likely to be calculated just according to the time spent, sometimes with a mark-up of between 25 and 50 per cent. However, the hourly charges of the solicitors who specialize in this type of work have gone up quite considerably. Hourly charges of £175 upwards are not unusual in some City of London firms, but they should be less elsewhere. Using just a time basis, the bill would be worked out, using the same example as above, like this:

9 × £100	£900.00
plus 30 per cent mark-up	£270.00
Total (excl. VAT and disbursements)	£1170.00

It is well worth while asking for quotes from several firms about how much they would charge. By shopping around it should be possible to get a cheaper price (probably more like £750 plus VAT and disbursements). As always, get a firm estimate from the solicitor before formally instructing him or her to go ahead.

If the client thinks the fee is too high, the solicitor can be asked to obtain a remuneration certificate from the Law Society (see page 942). It can sometimes be productive trying to negotiate the amount of the fee with the solicitor first.

RUNNING THE BUSINESS

Once the business is up and running, there are a number of regulations and laws that have to be complied with. This section gives an idea of some of the more important ones, as well as some pointers about insurances, but checks should be made about whether there are others that apply in a particular line of business. (See also Part Four).

The work environment

The Health and Safety at Work etc. Act 1974 defined and extended employers' duties towards their employees at work. The Offices, Shops and Railway Premises Act 1963 also applies to offices and shops where people are employed. Where the business involves using machinery, the Health and Safety at Work etc. Act lays down requirements about fencing and guarding the equipment.

As there are various duties and regulations, guidance should be sought from the local authority's environmental health department.

Essentially, employees should work in reasonable safety and comfort: premises should not be too hot, cold, damp or noisy. Welfare and catering arrangements and toilet facilities should be reasonably clean and safe. All employees should know where there is a first aid kit and employers employing more than 5 staff should set up a Health and Safety Policy, which not merely delegates responsibility for safety matters but also sets out the employer's aims and objectives.

Food Hygiene Regulations

Food Hygiene Regulations affect anyone running, managing or carrying on a food business (i.e. where food is sold for human consumption). The Regulations are available from HMSO.

Insurance

Certain types of insurance are compulsory.

Employers' liability

If staff are employed, the employer must have insurance to pay out for legal liabilities if one of the employees is injured or made ill as a result of work. The amount of cover is generally unlimited but must be at least £2 million.

Motor insurance

Liability to others (i.e. third-party) occurring because of a car crash or other vehicle accident is compulsory. This includes death or injury to anybody and damage to others' property (including other vehicles). Failure to tell the insurance company what the vehicles are actually used for can mean that it will be able to escape having to pay out on a claim.

Although not insisted on by the law, topping third-party insurance up to cover fire and theft or even comprehensive insurance (the latter covers all accidental damage regardless of who is to blame) is worth considering.

Insurance needed by contracts

Some contracts will insist on insurance being taken out. Others are well worth considering (what follows is not an exhaustive list).

Public liability and Product liability. Public liability provides cover for civil liability claims (e.g. injury to a member of the public while on the premises). Product liability provides cover against damage caused by a product to a member of the public (recent cases in this country have awarded damages of up to £1 million; elsewhere, for instance in the United States, awards are astronomical).

Engineering equipment. By law certain engineering equipment, like lifting-tackle and pressure vessels, has to be inspected and passed as safe at regular intervals. Although not strictly necessary, the maintenance can be combined with an insurance policy to cover against the risk of explosion, accidental damage and breakdown.

Fire and theft. This would cover destruction or damage by fire (other risks, like storms etc., can also be covered) and burglary – although the premiums can be very high for the latter in high-risk areas.

You could also consider taking out insurance for other potential losses arising, like legal expenses, computers and computer records, directors' liability, goods lost in transit, fidelity claims etc. etc.

46 Tax and VAT

PAYING TAX ON SPARE-TIME EARNINGS

If tax-free income is earned from working in your spare time, your tax inspector must be told how much was earned within twelve months of the end of the tax year (tax years run from 6 April to 5 April) in which the income was received. So if extra income was earned over a summer holiday in 1992 (even if this was received in cash) and no tax was deducted by an employer, the recipient must inform the tax inspector of the amount of those earnings by 5 April 1994. The burden is on the earner of income to declare the income; the fact that no tax return has been received is unfortunately no excuse. The stick for not telling the tax inspector in time and of your own free will is that a financial penalty may be charged on top of any income tax due (and tax inspectors have the right to go back at least six years against unpaid tax bills; longer if there has been some fraud involved). But you will be charged tax only if the amount of your income exceeds the exemptions you can set off against tax (see page 648).

Your tax inspector is either the tax inspector for your employer (if you are already employed – the name and address can be obtained from the accounts office or personnel) or, usually, your nearest tax inspector, whose address can be found in the telephone directory under Inland Revenue.

If you are planning to test the waters for a new business venture – for example, if you are already employed and want to increase your earnings or if you are looking after children at home but want to start a business part-time – from a tax viewpoint it is better to try and persuade the tax inspector that you are working on a properly self-employed basis. Describing your work as a business or profession, getting headed notepaper for correspondence, carefully keeping book-keeping records and showing the tax inspector that your sales will repeat and grow can help to influence him or her.

The advantages of the tax inspector treating your income on a self-employed basis is that you will be taxed on a preceding-year basis (see Tax and the Sole Trader, page 646). You will be able to set off a number of expenses against profits to reduce the amount of tax to be paid, and any losses made can be set off against your overall income tax payments. If your profits rise over time, then the preceding-year basis has considerable cashflow advantages as you will have to pay tax only on the lower profits earned earlier, while you are generating increasing profits.

If, on the other hand, the tax inspector does not accept that your additional income is from self-employment, the extra income will be treated as occasional or irregular and you will be taxed on a current-year basis (under Schedule D case IV). Although you will be able to set off expenses necessarily incurred in getting the income, losses can be set off only against profits from the same source of income.

For example, if you are making and selling knitwear from home in addition to working in employment, if you make a loss on the sales of knitwear and the tax inspector is treating your income as occasional, then you would be able to offset that loss only against past or future profits from knitwear sales, not against your tax bill as an employee. If the tax inspector were to treat you as being self-employed, on the other hand, you would be entitled to claim a tax refund from your PAYE tax already paid.

TAX AND THE SOLE TRADER

Income tax

Sole traders (and partners) do not pay tax on their drawings (or payments to themselves) from the business accounts but on the actual profits of the business. Even if the profits are not taken out of the business, the sole trader (or partner) will be liable to pay tax on all the profits.

Ideally the amount that sole traders draw out of the business should be an amount that the profits of the business can support, leaving in the business sufficient to cover bills, tax and other expenses. Sole traders are able to make loans for their own benefit from the business; if partners want to make a loan, they will have to agree the terms of it with the other partners. But as sole traders (and partners) are liable for all the business debts, personally as well as on a business footing, they cannot argue to the Inland Revenue that the business should be treated differently from themselves.

Sole traders and partners are actually treated more leniently by the tax system than companies as they usually pay income tax on a preceding-year basis (i.e. there is a delay between the time when the profits are earned and the time when the tax is actually payable, thereby producing cashflow advantages). The preceding-year basis can be lawfully manipulated by fixing the business's accounting year to result in the longest possible delay between earning profits and paying tax on them. The greatest gap is usually if the year end is just after 5 April. However there are several factors to bear in mind.

1 Sole traders usually pay tax on profits earned during tax years, not during the accounting year of the business. Tax years run from 6 April to the following 5 April. If the chosen accounting year is different from the tax year, then the Inland Revenue will sometimes apportion percentages of income earned in the accounting years that straddle the tax year.

2 Confusingly, the preceding-year basis does not start to work until the business has been up and running for at least a couple of years. The rules that the tax inspector uses are:

● for the first tax year (6 April to 5 April), you will pay tax on the profits made during the first tax year;

● for the second tax year (6 April to 5 April), you have a choice whether to pay tax either on the profits made during the second tax year (option 1) or the profits made during the first twelve months of business (option 2);

● for the third tax year (6 April to 5 April): if you chose option 1, then you will be taxed on actual profits made in the third year too; if you chose option 2, then you will be taxed on the profits made in your accounting year which ended in the last tax year. If the first accounting year has not yet finished, you will usually be taxed on the profits made in the first twelve months of trading.

3 The preceding-year basis works well if profits are increasing, because, while the income is going up, the tax bills are relatively low. But if the profits drop, then you can face hefty demands for tax which will have to be paid out of reducing income. Also when you cease trading, either if you sell or retire (or if a partner leaves), then the tax bills will catch up with you and you may have to pay several years' worth of tax in one big lump.

4 Sole traders normally pay income tax bills in two chunks, on 1 January and 1 July. This can be quite an adjustment to make for an ex-employee used to having tax deducted by PAYE. Any initial cashflow advantages of later payment of tax will soon vanish if you do not plan ahead for the tax which will be due and simply spend the income as it comes in. It is useful to contact your tax inspector in advance (the nearest one will be listed in the telephone directory under Inland Revenue) rather than wait for the tax inspector to start chasing you. If you submit no accounts or are late in filing accounts or tax returns, the tax inspector is typically likely to sting you into action by sending you a high tax assessment, which must be paid or appealed against within thirty days. Interest is charged on late payments at 9.25 per cent per annum.

Illustration. *Frederica Bloggs opens her new business on 1 November 1992 and looks at three different options for the end of her accountancy year:* (a) 31 October; (b) 31 December; (c) 30 April.

After the first few years of trading, this is when tax would be due on her profits:

(a) If she chooses 31 October as her year end, for the income she earns in the year to 31 October 1993 she would pay 50 per cent of the tax on 1 January 1995 (fourteen months after she gained the profits) and the remaining 50 per cent on 1 July 1995 (a gap of twenty months).

(b) If she chooses 31 December as her year end, for income earned in the year up to 31 December 1993 she would pay 50 per cent of the tax on 1 January 1995 (twelve months after the profits were earned) and the remaining 50 per cent on 1 July 1995 (a gap of eighteen months).

(c) If she chooses 30 April as her year end, for income earned in the year up to 30 April 1994 she would pay 50 per cent of the tax on 1 January 1996 (twenty months after the profits were earned) and the remaining 50 per cent on 1 January 1996 (a gap of twenty-six months).

Obviously the year-end date of 30 April looks the most attractive, but she will want to be reasonably confident that her profits will increase rather than go down before deciding to go for 30 April as her accounting year end.

The above is only a limited example and does not look at, for instance, what reliefs can be available for trading losses nor apportioning the tax over tax years. Tax is a complex area and you should obtain specialist advice from an accountant, who will also be able to advise on the overall tax position, like what capital allowances you can claim, keeping accounting records and how to deal with tax losses.

CLAIMING BUSINESS EXPENSES

Anything that is paid out 'wholly and exclusively' for the business can be claimed as a business expense, although there are a number of exceptions (see chart opposite). When in doubt, try and claim it; you do not get anything unless you ask for it.

CAPITAL ALLOWANCES

The full cost of buying capital equipment cannot be set off against tax as a business expense, but a percentage of the initial purchase price can be used to cut the tax bill: this is called a capital allowance. Capital equipment really means any substantial asset that will be around for some time, like office furniture: desks and filing cabinets, plant and machinery, cars etc.

If you have started a business and plan to use any equipment for the business which you owned privately before, you should assess a market value of the item for the date when the business is started; a capital allowance can then be claimed on that figure. Market values do not have to be too scientific; it is just the price someone else would pay for the item. So if you have a car which you will use for the business, you can estimate the market value by looking at car prices in newspapers or a major car-price guide like *Glass's*.

To qualify for a full capital allowance, the equipment must be used 'wholly and exclusively' for the business. But if there is an item which you will be using partly for the business and partly for your own personal use, then you should assess a division of the different uses and claim the proportion for business use. So if you use a car 60 per cent for work and 40 per cent for home, you can claim 60 per cent of the full capital allowance for a car.

The amount of capital allowances varies depending on what is being claimed for, but most principal capital allowances (like for cars up to £8,000, plant and machinery) are set at 25 per cent (1992 figures). This percentage is

What Can be Claimed as a Business Expense	What Cannot be Claimed as a Business Expense
All staff costs: e.g. wages, bonuses, gifts, redundancy payments, pensions, national insurance contributions (NIC) except as opposite, entertainment and contributions for staff.	Drawings for self and half own NIC (if a sole trader or partner). Taxes, fines and penalties. Own living costs.
Business postage, stationery, graphic design and printing costs.	Business entertainment.
Cost of computer software if bought separately from the hardware.	Computer hardware (and software bought with hardware), word-processors etc. and all capital equipment (but you can get capital allowances). Depreciation on capital equipment.
Professional fees (e.g. legal and accountancy fees) except as opposite. Premium for grant of lease.	Legal costs on forming a company, drawing up a partnership agreement or acquiring assets like a long leasehold. Accountancy costs for tax investigation by HMIT involving reopening previous years.
Relevant books, magazines, periodicals, subscriptions to professional organizations.	
Work travel costs except as opposite. Running costs of car apportioned for business use.	Travel expenses between home and work or to lunches. Holiday travel costs. Running costs of car apportioned for domestic use.
Bank charges on business accounts, interest on loans and overdrafts for the business and cost of arranging them except as opposite.	Interest paid to a partner for capital put into the business or interest on overdue tax. Interest and bank charges etc. paid on own account.
Business insurance except as opposite.	Insurance on own life or for accident or sickness insurance.
Bad debts claimed specifically.	General reserve for bad debts.

If you work from home

Proportion of home expenses, like telephone/fax, light, heat. But note potential CGT problems (page 651).	Personal community charge or personal council tax.

If you work from an office or factory

Heat, light, cleaning, rent, business rate, telephone/fax, normal repairs and maintenance.	Personal community charge or personal council tax.

VAT

If you are not registered for VAT, include the cost of VAT in what you claim as it is a business expense which you cannot recover from the VAT system. But if you are registered for VAT, do not include the VAT element of your expenses (e.g. on items like stationery, telephone bills etc.) and claim back only the cost of the item less VAT.

deducted, in the first year, from the full purchase price or market value of the equipment. In later years, the percentage is deducted from the net value (i.e. less the percentage already deducted).

WORKING OUT THE AMOUNT OF INCOME TAX

Income tax is payable on the gross turnover of the business, less allowable business expenses and capital allowances and half of national insurance contributions paid for your own benefit.

You will need to include as profits any bank interest paid without deduction of tax at source (e.g. from a foreign account). Some grants (like the old Enterprise Allowance and New Business Opportunities – see page 630) are taxable but should not be included in the business accounts. They (and any other personal, non-business income, like interest on savings) should instead be included in the special spaces provided on your tax return.

What happens if you make a loss?

When starting a new business

The costs you can claim as business expenses are not just the costs that you incur once the business is up and running. You can also claim pre-trading expenditure incurred up to five years before the business was started, as long as it was started after 1 April 1989.

If you make a loss in the first four tax years of a new business, you can get a tax refund from income tax paid (e.g. as an employee) for up to three years before the business began.

Claims for refunds must be made within two years after the year when the loss arose and you should set the loss off against the earliest year first (leaving your options open for later years).

When the business is established

If the business has already been going for a number of years, you can either set the loss off against other income or carry the loss forward and set it off against future trading profits from the business. If you have a choice, it is usually preferable financially to set off the loss against other income as otherwise it may be some years before you see an actual cash benefit.

NATIONAL INSURANCE CONTRIBUTIONS

Unless your yearly earnings are below a certain threshold (£3,030 in 1992/3), self-employed people have to pay regular Class 2 national insurance contributions (NIC). This can be done the traditional way by buying a stamp each week from the post office or by paying by direct debit. The important thing to remember is that the Department of Social Security will not contact you and ask you to pay contributions; you have to apply to your local DSS office for a form and tell them when you will be starting work on a self-employed basis.

If your earnings are then between a higher level (£6,120 in 1992/3) and an upper limit (£21,060 in 1992/3), you have to pay an additional percentage of your profits as Class 4 contributions (set as 6.3 per cent in 1992/3). Above the higher level, no further NIC is payable. The extra NIC will be collected by the tax inspector in the same way that you pay tax.

Half the cost of your own NIC can be used to reduce your income tax bill. Paying NIC entitles the self-employed to basic sickness and invalidity benefits and basic maternity allowances and retirement pensions. Broadly the self-employed cannot claim unemployment benefit (but see leaflet FB30, *Self employed*?, available from DSS offices).

CAPITAL GAINS TAX

If you work from home

Individuals are not usually charged capital gains tax on the gain they make when they sell their own home, because of an exemption called the principal private residence exemption. But if you use part of your home *exclusively* for business purposes, then you may be liable for capital gains tax for the gain on the business proportion of the house.

As a rough example, if you have a house with six main rooms and you use the basement, comprising two rooms plus a lavatory, exclusively as offices, then you may be liable to pay capital gains tax on two-sixths of the gain you make when you sell your house. You will, however, be able to use any other exemptions you have, like the annual exemption (£5,800 in 1992/3) plus a previous year's annual exemption (if unused) to reduce the tax bill.

You can avoid paying capital gains tax if you are able to prove that where you worked was an integral part of the home (i.e you did not use it only for the business). If you follow this route, you will usually be prevented from claiming as capital allowances any costs you incur in substantially renovating the business area (like building new walls) but you will be able to claim the costs of decorating and refurbishing. You can claim the running costs of the business as a proportion of the running costs of the home (see above) without the risk of being liable for CGT.

In times of recession, occasionally the need to avoid the payment of capital gains tax may be far less important than trying to get tax relief on an actual loss made. So if you, for example, bought a property which you used partly for your home and partly for your business and then sold the property at a price less than you paid for it, you may be able to offset the CGT losses on the part of the loss attributable to the part of the house used for the business against other tax payable. Seek legal or accounting advice if you are in any doubt about whether or not CGT may be payable (or may be used as a loss against other tax).

If you work from an office or factory

If you sell or otherwise dispose of (this covers exchanging, giving away or even losing) land, plant and machinery or goodwill, you may be liable for CGT for any 'gain' you make. Gain here includes a deemed gain, so you could be liable for CGT even if you never see a penny. For example, even if you give the asset away, the tax inspector treats the gift as a disposal and thus a deemed gain, and will want to know what the market value of the asset was when it was disposed of so that the deemed gain can be calculated.

There are some reliefs available. So if you sell in order to buy another business property, then you can usually 'roll over' the tax to the new asset and thus delay having to pay it. Other reliefs are available on retirement. If you have owned the business (or were a full-time working director in a company in which you owned shares) for at least a year and are over fifty-five or are retiring on grounds of ill-health, then the amount of CGT will be reduced, and will be payable only on gains over £150,000 (1991/2 figures). The older you are and the longer you have worked in the business, the greater the CGT relief. This area is fairly complex, so seek advice from your accountant.

TAX AND THE PARTNERSHIP

The tax treatment of partners is very similar to that of sole traders, so refer to the previous section for most information. However, there are added considerations for partners to bear in mind:
- who is responsible for paying tax?
- what happens if the partnership changes?
- what happens if the partnership makes a loss?

Who is responsible for paying tax?

Every partner is jointly and severally liable for all the debts of the partnership; this includes the partnership tax bill. So if one partner does not pay his or her share of the partnership tax bill, then the tax inspector is perfectly within his or her rights to recover the unpaid amount from the other partner(s). However, this strict rule applies only to the profits of the partnership; it does not apply to the personal tax bills of the partners for income earned outside the partnership, or for capital gains tax bills or tax bills for other non-trading income (like investment income) for individual partners. Here the Inland Revenue has rights to claim only against the individuals, not the partnership.

Most partners will usually agree how to split the tax bill. But if there is no agreement about who is responsible for how much tax, then the tax inspector will look at what percentages of profits the partners share in the current tax year (if there is no specific agreement it will be assumed that the profits are divided equally). This can cause problems as the tax bill is actually calculated on a preceding-year basis. So if the division of profits has recently changed, then one partner could find him- or herself strictly due to pay more than his or her fair share of the tax. This is why it is important to make an agreement where possible.

Illustration. *Shirley and Lucy are partners in a design consultancy. Up to 1991, they split profits in a ratio of 75:25 because Shirley worked longer hours in the business than Lucy. But from April 1991 onwards, as Lucy is working similar hours to Shirley, they decide to split the profits equally. Both have other incomes but do not come within the higher tax bracket. For the 1990/91 tax year, their profits were £8,000, which they divide up so that Shirley receives £6,000 while Lucy receives £2,000. But when the tax inspector assesses their tax bills, he will be charging them equal amounts of £1,000 (£8,000 divided by 2 ... £4,000 x 25 per cent) because he is looking at the division of profits for the 1991/92 tax year, which is 50:50. But Shirley and Lucy can of course decide to share out the tax bills to reflect the old unequal profit share for the previous tax year, so that Shirley pays £1,500 (£6,000 x 25 per cent) and Lucy pays £500 (£2,000 x 25 per cent).*

What happens if the partnership changes?

If a partner dies or leaves or if a new partner joins the business, then from a tax viewpoint the 'old' partnership is treated as if it had automatically come to an end. This means that all the tax due up to the date of the change will have to be paid immediately – which can have particularly adverse tax consequences for partnerships taxed on a preceding-year basis, who will probably have at least two years' tax bills to pay. However, the partners can elect to be treated by the Inland Revenue as if the partnership is carrying on if they fulfil two conditions:

• at least one of the old partners is continuing with the new business, *and*
• all the partners before and after the change agree that it should continue and sign a continuation election.

A continuation election needs to be made in writing to the tax inspector within two years of the change. The partners should agree who will pay the tax due up to the date of the change even if the tax bills are not going to be sent until later. Either the old partners can indemnify the new partners for their share of the tax due before the change or the new partners can agree to take this on as part and parcel of the business.

What happens if the partnership makes a loss?

Partnership losses are dealt with by the Inland Revenue in the same way as losses for sole traders (see page 650). Partners share the losses in the same proportions as they have agreed to share the profits in the year in which the losses arise. Losses cannot be carried back against previous years' profits if the partnership continues.

Individual partners can choose how they wish to have the losses treated: whether to set them off against other income or carry them forward against future partnership profits.

TAX AND THE COMPANY

The tax that companies have to pay is called corporation tax. It has to be paid both on the income or profits of the company and on its capital gains. So corporation tax is like a combination of income tax and capital gains tax. Corporation tax is usually paid earlier than the tax paid by established partnerships and sole traders because the tax is charged on a current-year basis, and there are also different rules relating to the way salaries are paid out to directors, who cannot operate in the flexible way that sole traders and partners can. But apart from these differences, the way in which the amount of income and gains is worked out is similar to that used with sole traders and partnerships, as is the treatment of capital allowances.

Paying a director

As a director of a company you will not be able to draw money out of the business as and when you want to. Directors are treated as employees of the company and thus have to be paid a salary. However, they also have the option of drawing extra money out as dividends on their shares and can pay themselves indirectly by way of fringe benefits. There are financial incentives in keeping some profits within the business, as even the maximum rate of corporation tax of 35 per cent (payable by companies with profits of over £1,250,000 (1992/3 figures) is less than the maximum rate of tax payable by individuals (40 per cent in 1992/3). The small companies' rate (25 per cent in 1992/3) for companies with profits up to £250,000 (1992/3 figures) gives an even greater differential and can thus reduce the overall tax bill considerably. (The tax rate for corporation tax increases on a sliding scale between £250,000 and £1,250,000 of profits.)

Salary

As a director, you receive a salary which has to be paid on a PAYE basis and is usually paid monthly. Company directors cannot provide services on a self-employed basis to the company. If a member of their family enters into a contract with the company, the director must declare an interest in the contract at a board meeting of the company. The company is free to pay whatever salary it wants to directors but the amount paid should be justified by the profits and the amount of work done by the director. Occasionally the Inland Revenue may refuse to accept an excessively high director's salary as an allowable expense against corporation tax.

The most tax-effective salary to pay (although this may either be too much for directors of newly started companies or too little for directors of more successful businesses) is an amount which is below the level at which the higher rate of personal income tax (40 per cent in 1992/3) bites (£23,700 in 1992/3). Given that an individual would have personal allowances to set off against tax, like the personal allowance (and possibly the married couple's allowance), plus

allowances for pensions etc., the actual most tax-effective top-level salary paid
will exceed that.

A spouse who works in the business can also be paid a salary, which again
must be paid by way of PAYE. However, if the spouse is paid less than the
personal allowance (£3,445 1992/3) then no income tax will be payable and the
spouse can claim back any income tax deducted at the end of the tax year.

Fringe benefits

Fringe benefits to directors can be tax-effective, particularly if they involve
pension contributions. There is no limit to the amount that a company can pay
into a company pension scheme for its employees (who include directors) and
the payments can be fully offset against tax. Life insurance payments paid on
behalf of directors are also fully tax-deductible.

Directors (or other employees) earning less than £8,500 p.a. will not be taxed
on fringe benefits. If they earn more than £8,500 p.a. then broadly the individuals will have to pay tax on the cost to the company of providing the benefit less
anything paid as an employee towards the cost. Cars are, however, treated
differently, depending on their age and power. A notional extra amount is
added to the higher-paid director or employee (see below).

What if a company director who earns more than £8,500 p.a. and his wife,
who is also a director (earning less than £8,500 p.a.), agree that they should have a
car as a fringe benefit? She will not pay any extra tax for the car, but her
husband might have to. Unless he is able to slip through under a tax concession
which gives relief if there is a policy decision throughout the company to give

Car and Fuel Scale Benefits for Directors and Employees Earning £8,500 p.a. plus

Car benefits *†	1992/3	
Age of car on 5 April	Under 4 years £	4 years or more £
Up to 1400cc	2,140	1,460
1401–2000cc	2,770	1,880
Over 2000cc	4,440	2,980
Original market value		
£19,251–£29,000	5,750	3,870
Over £29,000	9,300	6,170
Fuel benefit †	Petrol	Diesel
Up to 1400cc	500	460
1401–2000cc	630	460
Over 2000cc	940	590

* 1.5 × scale if business use 2,500 miles or less and for second car
† 0.5 × scale if business use 18,000 miles or more

the same fringe benefits for all similarly employed staff, then the husband-director will have to pay tax at a penal second car rate on 150 per cent of the value of the car.

Dividends

From a company's viewpoint, dividends are less tax-effective than paying salaries or fringe benefits as they can be paid only out of the profits of the company. They are not an allowable expense, so they do not reduce the company's tax bill. The company has to pay advance corporation tax (ACT) on any dividends paid out. The recipient of the dividends will be given a tax credit for the ACT paid, which can be used to reduce his or her income tax bill.

There are some advantages to individuals in receiving extra cash by way of a dividend rather than a salary bonus or otherwise (see example below). The first is that any extra tax payable on the dividends (this arises only if the recipient pays tax at a higher rate; otherwise the individual has to pay no extra tax at all as he or she has an ACT tax credit) will not have to be paid until the end of the tax year when the dividends are declared to the Inland Revenue on the tax return. Secondly, and more importantly, national insurance contributions do not have to be paid by the director on dividends, whereas they do on salaries. Remember that dividends do not count as pensionable income and so for an individual director, say in his late forties or fifties, the payment of dividends will reduce the final salary for determining retirement benefits under an occupational scheme. Also a long period of time without payment of NICs may affect an individual's entitlement under the state-related pensions scheme and other benefits, such as unemployment benefit.

Taking extra profits out of the company

If the company has some extra profits that the director wants to take out, there are three different options of paying out the extra cash: either by way of a bonus, as dividends or as a loan. At first glance, it might seem best to pay the extra cash by way of a loan, thus avoiding payment of tax (either income tax or advance corporation tax) and national insurance contributions. But in practice, if the company is a close company (i.e. there are five or less people controlling it, either as directors or as shareholders), this is not so, as a basic-rate tax deposit has to be paid to the Inland Revenue at the time the loan is made, calculated on the amount of the loan. Take this example:

Say there are additional profits of £50,000 in a close company which it is agreed that a director will take out. Using 1991/92 tax figures:
- if she takes it as a salary bonus, then income tax at 40 per cent plus national insurance contributions would have to be deducted – this would leave her a net sum of £27,162;
- if she takes it out as dividends, then advance corporation tax at 25 per cent

plus the balance of the director's higher-rate tax liability (40 per cent − 25 per cent = 15 per cent) would have to be paid, leaving her a net sum of £30,000;
• if she takes it out as a loan, the company would have to pay advance corporation tax (at 25 per cent), plus a deposit of income tax for the balance (again at 25 per cent), which would give her a net figure of £28,125. In addition, because the director is receiving a benefit in kind, she would also have to pay £1,238 as well. So her net benefit reduces to £26,887, being the least tax-efficient method of payment.

There are other financial restrictions on close companies. If one of the people deemed to be controlling the company gets extra fringe benefits (like the right to occupy a flat owned by the company), then the Inland Revenue can treat the benefit as a distribution of the company and make the beneficiary pay tax on it as if it was a dividend.

The rules and regulations about payments to directors (and members of their families) are very complex. If you want to look at more creative ways of payment (i.e. reducing the overall tax bill as much as possible), you should seek specialist tax advice from an accountant.

How corporation tax is worked out

Corporation tax is payable on the actual profits of an accounting period, which is usually twelve months. Companies can choose which accounting period they will have, but if they fail to exercise their option to choose the Registrar of Companies assumes that the accounting period runs up to 31 March. Unlike with individual sole traders or partners, the rules for the payment of tax are much stricter and there is less room to manoeuvre in delaying payment of tax. Tax is payable, on a current-year basis, nine months after the end of the accounting year or thirty days from a notice of assessment (unless appealed against). If tax is overdue, interest is charged at 9.25 per cent.

Corporation tax is chargeable on the taxable profits of the company, which means:
• the trading income, *and*
• capital gains (called chargeable gains), *and*
• some investment income, like rents from lettings and interest from deposit accounts.

When calculating the trading income, deduct all allowable business expenses (see list on page 649) and capital allowances and any loss reliefs (see below).

Capital gains are worked out in much the same way as an individual's capital gains. If assets were disposed of during the accounting period, then corporation tax will potentially be charged on the gain in value of the asset since 1 April 1982 (gains made before then are ignored). Although companies, unlike individuals, do not have annual exemptions from tax on capital gains, they can reduce the corporation tax payable by deducting from the gain an amount allowable for inflation (called indexation relief).

Company accounts are complex and proper accounting advice should be sought. Each company has to file annually audited accounts with the Registrar of Companies and pay an auditor to prepare these accounts. The extra cost of auditing (over and above any book-keeping costs) will be at least £1,500 in London and the South-East, but should be less elsewhere.

What happens if the company makes a loss?

Trading losses are worked out in the same way as trading profits, but the company itself has more options about how the losses will be dealt with than sole traders or partners. The company can:
● set off the loss against current profits (e.g. from other income or chargeable gains).

If there is still a loss left over, the company can:
● carry back the loss against previous profits, usually only against the last accounting period.

If the company wants to exercise either of these choices it must do so within two years. As another option the company can carry forward the loss against future profits; it has six years within which to decide to do this.

Because of the time periods allowed, it may be worthwhile continuing trading and then working out what the different tax bills would be using the different options. An accountant's advice should be sought.

Remember too that a company cannot continue trading if it is insolvent and the directors can be personally liable if they are involved in wrongful or unlawful trading (see page 615).

If the company closes, losses from the last twelve months' trading can be carried back against profits from the preceding three years if none of the above options can be exercised. Losses from a company cannot be used to reduce individuals' (like directors') own income tax bills.

VAT

VAT as a tax does not generate much public enthusiasm among the business community. It is time-consuming to administer and makes goods more costly to the consumer. It is, however, here to stay as all the European countries within the EC operate a similar system. The EC is aiming to standardize VAT rates across the community, which may even result in a percentage increase of the tax as the UK's standard VAT rate (17.5 per cent in 1992) is lower than many other countries' and the UK also exempts certain goods from VAT which are VATable elsewhere across the Channel.

In essence the VAT system is operated by businesses acting as tax collectors for the government. It is an indirect tax charged on sales of goods or services. From a purchaser's viewpoint, the VAT paid on purchases cannot be claimed back unless the purchaser lives abroad or is registered for VAT (very few members of the public are). But as a businessperson registered for VAT, VAT paid on supplies for the business can be deducted from the amount of VAT charged to your customers. The amount of VAT charged and received can help with cashflow in the early months for new businesses because VAT is usually payable every quarter, one month in arrears. That early cashflow assistance is soon caught up with for established businesses, who typically dread the coming around of the next date for paying VAT.

In 1992 there were two rates of tax: the standard rate of 17.5 per cent and the zero rate (applicable for only a few types of supplies and goods).

Who must register for VAT

Although there are some goods and supplies which are exempt from VAT (see table below), the vast majority of businesses supply goods or services on which VAT is potentially chargeable. But a business has to charge VAT (and thus register for VAT) only if the amount of sales or invoices goes above a certain limit.

The thresholds for registering in 1992 were:
• if the value of the business's taxable supplies in the last twelve months exceeded £36,600, or
• if there are reasonable grounds for believing that the value of taxable supplies in the next thirty days will exceed £36,600.

If the business fails to register there are financial penalties payable to Customs and Excise on top of the VAT which will also have to be paid. Taxable turnover should preferably be reviewed monthly if the business turnover is creeping towards the VAT threshold. But while business start-ups do not have to register for VAT until their sales cross the financial barriers, there can be advantages in registering for VAT in advance, either voluntarily even if the business is not expected to meet the threshold sales figures or if the projected turnover is fairly high.

Examples of Zero-rated Supplies

• most 'essential' food and drink – this excludes chocolate, crisps and hot take-away food;
• books and newspapers;
• children's clothes and footwear;
• transport (except taxis and hire cars);
• construction and sale of new residential homes;
• heat and light (except when supplied to businesses);
• prescriptions;
• mobile homes and houseboats;
• exports.

Deciding to register for VAT voluntarily

The extra administrative burdens involved in keeping VAT records and making VAT returns, combined with the bogymen reputation of Customs and Excise officers, warn off many potential voluntary registrations. But there are advantages in choosing to register for VAT even if you are not obliged to do so. The principal one is the right to claim back VAT paid on your own purchases.

The costs of setting up a business can be very high; many of the start-up costs include goods or services for which you will be charged VAT. For example, the bills for investing in a computer and software, printing (and possibly graphic design) costs, installing a telephone, your solicitor and accountant will all have VAT added. Registering for VAT means that you will probably be able to claim a VAT refund in the first few months before your own sales start to gather momentum. As long as what you paid exceeds what you earned, you will be able to get a VAT refund. Even if your sales in the early months are welcomingly high, you will be able to reduce the VAT you owe by the amount of VAT you have paid out.

If you are in the minority of businesses which involve the sale of VAT-exempt (i.e. zero-rated) goods or services, registering for VAT is again worthwhile as the customer will not be charged any extra but you will again have the right to apply for VAT refunds for supplies on which you paid VAT. If your only or major customers are VAT-registered, as most large businesses are, then charging VAT again should not mean that you lose business. It is only if you supply the general public that you either have to swallow the amount of VAT in your sales figures or increase prices, thus making your goods less competitive.

It is also arguable that registering for VAT creates a more favourable impression in the outside business world. Some larger organizations will not take a new potential supplier who is not registered for VAT seriously. VAT registration implies that the business is sound and has a reasonable turnover. The actual income can be kept a secret for the Inland Revenue Customs and Excise and the like.

Paying VAT

Any VAT due is payable to Customs and Excise usually within one month of the end of the quarterly period. Most payments are made by cheque, but Customs and Excise have introduced a system which allows payment to be made by bank credit up to a week later as long as the VAT return is submitted on time.

Consistently late payments eventually result in painful financial penalties. Warnings are given after two late returns in any one year; the next late payment attracts a surcharge of 5 per cent, with increasing surcharges if there are further delays.

VAT concessions for small businesses

Small businesses (classified in 1992 for VAT purposes as those with a turnover of less than £250,000 p.a.) can be treated more favourably by Customs and Excise. The first and most important concession is that they can pay VAT on a *cash-accounting basis*. This means that VAT needs to be paid only on monies actually received during the period, instead of on invoices. In practice this is particularly useful if payments for your goods or supplies are not made immediately on delivery – for example, if you work in the service industries where payments for invoices can, and frequently are, made late. VAT also does not have to be paid on bad debts.

Customs and Excise have to approve an application for cash accounting in advance and the system cannot be operated until approval has been given. For business start-ups, approval can be applied for before the business actually gets going. Existing businesses who want to apply will have to show that their VAT returns and payments are up to date.

Small businesses can also elect to pay VAT once a year instead of quarterly. This can help considerably with cashflow, as long as savings are made during the year to meet the annual amount due. Other more specific schemes operate for different types of businesses, like retail. Application forms and further information are available from Customs and Excise offices.

WHAT RECORDS MUST BE KEPT

The main additional records required for VAT (and copies of these should be kept for six years) are:

- tax invoices for sales or supplies;
- a VAT account for each tax period;
- the VAT returns to be sent to Customs and Excise showing the amounts payable or refunded.

Tax invoices

If goods or services are supplied directly to the public, no formal tax invoice has to be provided unless it is asked for, and nor do detailed invoices have to be kept for sales of less than £50. Otherwise, VAT invoices should show the supplier's and the customer's names and addresses, the invoice number, the VAT number, what is supplied (showing any discount), the amount payable, the rate of VAT and the amount of VAT charged. The invoice should also show the 'tax point', which is usually the date on which you supply the goods or bill the client, unless you are operating the cash-accounting system, when this will be the date you actually get paid.

Copies of invoices must be kept by the supplier.

VAT accounts

VAT accounts need to show the totals of input tax and output tax (how much you have paid and how much you have charged). You do not have to include everything in your VAT accounts – for example, bank charges and bank interest do not count when it comes to declaring your inputs. But most businesses usually find it is easier to operate just one umbrella book-keeping system rather than separate systems for VAT and for everything else.

Most expenses incurred necessarily for the business as inputs can be used to reduce the VAT due. But there are some expenses on which VAT cannot be claimed back, like VAT on the purchase of a car (and petrol costs unless an extra payment is made to Customs and Excise) and on business entertainment expenses. Payments made up to nine months before the business began can be included as claimable inputs on the first VAT return, so the VAT on payments made for printing stationery or buying a word processor, for example, can reduce the VAT bill or can be used to make a VAT refund claim. A list should also be kept of all the assets of the business as at the date of the start-up: for example, any car, word processor, telephone or fax machine etc.

VAT returns

Blank VAT returns are sent out by Customs and Excise well in time for completion for each particular VAT period (usually three months). They are one-page forms showing spaces for the totals of input tax and output tax and the sales and payments made during the period.

Customs and Excise officers are likely to arrange visits to ensure all the books are kept in order and the accuracy of the figures supplied to them. The first visit is usually within the first six months of registration, and thereafter every few years, unless they become suspicious, in which case more frequent checks can be expected. When an inspection is carried out, the inspector will want a competent person around to be able to answer any queries. This could either be the businessperson him- or herself or a book-keeper if he or she has prepared the books.

47 Credit Control and Collecting Debts

If your business operates on anything other than a straightforward cash on delivery basis (like a shop), then you will have to create an effective system for credit control. Proper credit control (i.e, ensuring that you do not have to wait too long for your debts to be paid) is one of the keys to business success. Without it, cashflow problems have forced many businesses to go under, even when they were doing well in terms of sales. In times of recession it is often particularly important to keep tight reins on credit control wherever possible, as many customers will try to get away with late payment to help their own cashflow problems.

INVOICES

Invoices should set out clearly the specific terms of payment (i.e. when payment should be made by, with possibly an interest clause if payment is delayed). The terms can include the right to keep ownership of the goods until full payment is made. To be able to sue on the invoice including any extra terms, you will have to show that the terms were clear, specific and understood by the customer. Ideally you should show the terms at the place of sale as well as on the invoice and should go through the terms with the customer when the goods or services are supplied.

Some firms have found that printing their initial invoices in red helped improve the speed of payment.

KEEPING YOUR OWN CHECKS ON CREDIT CONTROL

Both top and bottom limits should be put on credit. Trying to recover small amounts through the courts if all else fails is often not worth the expense of time and money, and allowing customers to build up very high amounts of credit can sink your own business. Insist on the production of a banker's card whenever cheques are issued: the card number should be written on the back by the payee (not the customer). Banker's cards guarantee payment only up to the face value of the card (usually still £50) and the cheque should be linked to only one invoice up to the stated limit. If a series of cheques are issued for the same single item (even if a series of invoices are issued too), the bank can repudiate liability altogether. Checks should also be made that the signatures on the cheque and on the card are the same, because the bank can again avoid responsibility if the signatures clearly differ.

An upper limit should be put on running credit accounts beyond which the account will not be extended unless payment is made. Credit reference checks should also be made on customers for whom credit is given (see page 581). Cut-off points should also be instituted for taking legal action if necessary. Regular reminders of outstanding amounts and telephone calls to debtors can help bring payments in, but it is an offence unlawfully to harass debtors (i.e. threatening them with criminal proceedings or upsetting them or their families by the frequency or methods of demand). But actually taking civil legal action to recover debts is, of course, not unlawful harassment.

What happens if the debtor offers a cheque for a lower amount?

Sometimes a debtor offers a cheque for a lower amount than the full amount: for example, he or she may offer a cheque for £750 in 'full and final settlement' of an invoice for £1,000. Obviously it is tempting to accept the cheque, as an up-front cash payment could be worth more in real terms than dragging a claim through the courts. But can the creditor accept the cheque and then sue the debtor for the remainder?

Surprisingly there is no legal case which decides this point conclusively. But the answer is probably that the creditor will be barred from claiming the further sum due (in the above example, £250) if the cheque proffered is simply banked. But if the creditor complains (preferably in writing) before processing the cheque then he or she should be entitled to persist with the claim for the balance. This will work only if the debtor has not been devious by offering the lower cheque conditionally, on the grounds that if the cheque is banked then it must be accepted as full and final settlement of the claim, with the creditor abandoning any further claims. If such conditions are attached, the creditor has a choice of either accepting the lower amount and forgetting about the balance, or rejecting the cheque and suing for the whole sum due.

Alternative Action

As an alternative or a complement to your own internal procedures, you could consider *factoring* or *invoice discounting* your debts. Clearing banks and other factoring companies offer this service.

The aim is to provide an immediate increase of your cashflow. Both factoring and invoice discounting involve the bank (or other factorer) giving the business an immediate lump sum representing a percentage of the overall debts of the business. If the debts are factored, then the business legally assigns the debts over to the bank (or factorer), which is then responsible for recovering the debts; if the debts are invoice discounted, then the business usually keeps responsibility for the debts and for their collection. The bank or factorer will usually also require some extra security for the debts, like a floating charge on a company's assets.

Although the terms of factoring or invoice-discounting arrangements vary according to what is negotiated, usually the factorer will pay up front between 70 per cent and 85 per cent of the overall debts. It will then charge interest to the business on the outstanding amount of the debts until they are paid off and will also charge a commission of between 1 per cent and 4 per cent of the overall debts as an extra fee. The services are usually available only where the debts are comparatively high – say, at least £100,000 – and the factorer may want to make investigations about how likely the debtors will be to pay. These services, then, may be available only for a limited number of businesses, but they can sometimes be useful.

Legal Action

For the harder-core debts where chasing and reminding has not worked, legal action is the next stage. The recovery rate through the courts, taking into account court fees and time, is likely to be considerably less than the full amount of the debts, but some large organizations take and threaten legal action for even comparatively small amounts on the basis that a 50 per cent rate is justified if there are efficient procedures (the legal costs can be fairly minimal if DIY action is taken). Gaining a reputation for effective and tough debt-chasing can also reduce the number of times that customers try to take advantage of you.

Starting proceedings in the courts need not be the first step. Sometimes a letter written by a solicitor can be sufficient to make the debtor come up with payment. Solicitors will usually charge around £35 upwards (plus VAT) for sending a letter.

Before starting proceedings, if you choose not to instruct a solicitor, you should yourself send a final letter to the debtor, asking for payment and stating that unless payment is made within seven days, then action will be brought against him or her in the court. This is the debtor's final opportunity to pay and until that happens nothing further should be supplied – not even for cash.

The procedure for debt-collection in the courts is straightforward: county courts should be used for debts of up to £50,000 and the High Court for higher amounts. See Chapter 68 for an explanation of the procedure for taking a case in the courts.

48 Patents and Trademarks

Where a supplier is involved in the design and manufacture of new goods, there are steps which can be taken to ensure that others do not steal the ideas and capitalize on them. But the protection of intellectual property (as it is known in legal jargon) cannot apply to ideas themselves, only to ideas or new products which have in some way taken on a material or artistic form.

PATENTS

Patents temporarily protect a technological invention which is capable of industrial application. The invention must be in some way superior to previous products or manufactured by a superior process. Novelty decides whether you can get the patent and how wide a monopoly against other competitors it will give. The longer the period a patent is granted for, the greater protection afforded to the inventor. Rivals will not, however, be prevented from researching and designing to produce their own products rather than copy the patented article. Patents must be registered before they become effective. The process of registration is time-consuming and can be fairly costly.

COPYRIGHT

Copyright protection is given automatically to a literary, dramatic, musical or artistic work (a concept wide enough to include industrial designs in the form of plans and drawings). To obtain protection a work must be recorded in writing or otherwise (copyright includes protection for computer programmes although there is considerable debate still going on about how far it should be extended in this field). Subject to some exceptions, the author is the first copyright owner. Copyright, broadly, makes restriction on copying the work (apart from 'fair dealing', which allows some limited copying for the purposes of private study and research and education), issuing copies to the public, performing, broadcasting or adapting the work. There is no need for registration.

TRADEMARKS

Trademark protection is given for a word or other symbol which identifies the goods as being marketed by a particular company or other business. The mark must be distinctive of the goods, not merely descriptive, its purpose being to show the origin of the goods and to act as a guarantee of quality. Trademarks need registration to provide protection.

PASSING-OFF ACTIONS

If someone else uses a similar name or description in such a way as to cause confusion to the public, a passing-off action can be brought against the 'pretender' to stop them from using that name. If the name is particularly well known, the action may be successful even where there is no common field of activity, but, broadly, passing-off actions are usually successfully brought only against a competitor in the same field. No registration is necessary (see also page 631).

NEW PROTECTION FOR 'MORAL RIGHTS'

The Copyright, Designs and Patents Act 1988 gave additional protection to creative people by protecting their reputations by what are called 'moral rights'. There are essentially four categories of 'moral rights':
• paternity right, which gives the right of an author of a literary, dramatic, musical or artistic work or a director of a film to be identified as such whenever the work is exploited;
• integrity right, which gives authors the right not to have their works added to, deleted, altered or adapted in a way which is prejudicial to the honour or reputation of the author;
• false attribution – this covers false statements being made about the true authorship or directorship of works;
• right to privacy – this very limited right applies when someone has commissioned photographs or a film to be made of themselves; they can control the number of copies being made available to the public

In practice these new moral rights do not give much extra protection. Journalists, for example, are excluded from protection by paternity or integrity rights; they cannot insist on being given a byline nor prevent their copy from being changed by editors. The right of privacy (unlike more extensive rights in many other countries) is particularly restricted. It would give no protection, for example, to a famous female TV presenter from having her naked spare tyre photographed. But the Act was used to stop a megamix of different sections of his records by George Michael in 1991.

The area of intellectual property is very complex and highly specialized. Booklets which contain summaries of current law are available from The Patent Office, 25 Southampton Buildings, London WC2 1AY.

Further advice, if necessary, should be obtained from a specialist patent agent or solicitor.

PART SEVEN

MOTORING

49 Putting the Car on the Road

ESSENTIAL DOCUMENTS

The driving licence

Anyone over the age of seventeen can apply for a driving licence unless suffering from epilepsy, severe mental handicap, disabling giddiness or fainting or bad eyesight (i.e. unable to read a number plate at 20.5 metres in daylight while wearing glasses).

A learner driver receives only a provisional licence (valid until age seventy), but is required to display L-plates and be accompanied by a driver in possession of a full licence who is twenty-one or over and has held a full licence for three years. (To charge for instruction a person must be registered with the Department of Transport if he or she is a professional driving instructor.) On passing the driving test, motorists are entitled to a full driving licence, and this will not be renewed until they reach their seventieth birthday. After seventy, it can be renewed every three years, but applicants must disclose any disabilities and may be required to submit to a medical examination and agree to their doctor's medical records being examined.

A licence must be signed as soon as it is received by the licence-holder. If the licence-holder changes his or her address (or name), he or she must return the licence and supply the new particulars. The penalties for driving-licence offences are set out in the penalty chart (page 708 below; in particular, see page 709).

Producing a driving licence

The police can demand to see a motorist's driving licence if the motorist has been driving on the road (or supervising a learner who was driving), or the police reasonably believe that:

● either the motorist was the driver of a motor vehicle when an accident occurred because of its presence on the road;

● or the motorist had committed a motoring offence.

The main point to note is that anyone driving a car can be asked to produce their licence. However unreasonably the police may be acting, motorists should comply. When asked to produce their licence motorists can either produce it there and then or select a police station where they will take it within the next seven days. However, they cannot send the licence to that police station; they must take it in person.

Road fund licence

Road tax, properly called a vehicle excise duty, must be paid for any vehicle kept, parked or used on the road. This includes an 'old banger' that needs mechanical attention before it will go. The only occasions when a licence is not needed are when the motorist is driving to and from a prearranged MOT test, or when the car is being used during the fourteen days' grace allowed after expiry of the last licence. Note that the period of grace applies only if a new licence was applied for before the old one expired, not if the application is made in the fourteen days following expiry of the licence. During the fourteen-day period the old licence should be displayed on the windscreen; it is not enough to display a 'licence applied for' sign.

Application for a new licence can be made by post or in person at local vehicle licensing offices (in the telephone directory under 'Transport, Department of') and at some post offices. Documents required are the vehicle registration document, insurance certificate, MOT certificate (if applicable), the completed form and requisite fee, and the old licence (if applying at a post office). Failure to tax a car, and failure to display the tax disc, are separate offences (see the penalty chart on page 709). If a tax disc is lost, a replacement can be obtained by completing form V20. If a licence is surrendered before its expiry date, a refund can be obtained for complete calendar months by completing form V14.

Displaying a tax disc on a vehicle which is taken from a separate vehicle is a serious offence, even in circumstances where the latter has been scrapped with an unexpired period on the tax disc. The proper course is to claim a refund and obtain a licence for the second vehicle rather than use self-help methods.

MOT certificate

A current MOT certificate is needed for any vehicle that has been registered for three or more years. The requirement arises at the vehicle's third anniversary; it is not sufficient to wait until the next vehicle excise licence application after that date. Similarly, cars imported from abroad need an MOT certificate as soon as they are three years old; the three years does not run from the date of importation.

The test covers steering, brakes, tyres, lights, seat belts and anchorage points, exhaust, flashers, washers, wipers, warning lights, horn, body and suspension. It is not a certificate of roadworthiness, and the possession of a current MOT certificate will not be a defence in a prosecution for a vehicle defect even if the defect in question was the subject of a recent test.

The police can ask motorists to produce the MOT certificate on the same occasions they can ask to see their driving licence (see page 671). Penalties for MOT offences are set out in the penalty chart on page 709.

Registration document

Some people still use the term 'log book', although the registration document is no longer a book. It shows who is the registered keeper of the vehicle but it does not show who is the owner. Although a registration document should always be handed over when a car is sold, it is not proof that the seller owns the car. When a car is sold the DVLA must be told immediately, by both the seller (who fills in the tear-off part of the registration document) and the buyer. Buyers cannot simply wait until they next need to tax the car.

Great care should be taken by both seller and buyer to make sure that the DVLA are notified. It is unsafe to rely upon assurances that the other party will see to the notification, even if the other party is a car retailer. Every week hundreds of former owners are issued with fixed-penalty tickets that should belong to someone else, because the DVLA records are used by all police forces to trace owners and, like all computers, the DVLA computer will continue to give false information until it is given the new data.

The number of former owners of a vehicle is noted on the registration document, but their names and addresses are not stated (except for the last owner). The registered keeper can obtain these details, free of charge, by writing to the DVLA. Lost registration documents can be replaced by applying on form V62. Penalties for registration document offences are set out in the penalty chart on pages 709.

INSURANCE

The law tries to ensure that anyone who suffers injury through a motorist's negligent driving should recover damages for any serious personal injury that is caused. Parliament has insisted that all motorists insure against that possible liability; this is known as third-party liability. It is all that the law requires – simply insurance against injury to other people (including passengers). The motorist need not be insured for damage to other people's property and possessions, although in practice most policies do cover damage to property and possessions.

Using a vehicle without insurance

While this offence clearly covers the person who drives a car without insurance, it goes further and includes a person who has a car on the road which is capable of being used.

A car was left jacked up on the road, without it being covered by a valid certificate of insurance. The defendant argued that he could not be guilty of 'using' the car since it could not be driven. Held: He was guilty. The car could be moved and so insurance was needed and he was guilty of 'using' it without insurance. Elliott (1959)

On the other hand, if a car is completely irreparable, and cannot be moved, then the owner cannot be said to be using it. The test seems to be, was the vehicle available for use in the sense that it could have been made to move under its own power with a reasonable amount of repair?

The compulsory insurance laws are applied strictly. Even if motorists believe they are insured but in fact are uninsured, they will still be committing an offence regardless of making an honest and genuine mistake. For instance, if Smith borrows a car from Jones after being told by Jones that the insurance covers Smith, then both will be guilty of breaking the compulsory insurance laws. However, it may be that Smith, but not Jones, can avoid endorsement and penalty points if he was misled. Anyone who is misled rather than mistaken over the existence of insurance should seek legal advice.

Failure to have insurance is a serious offence and will lead to the endorsement of penalty points (between 6 and 8), and sometimes disqualification (see the penalty chart on page 709). However, there is a special defence for employees who innocently drive their employer's vehicles without insurance. For this defence to succeed, employees must satisfy the court that it was more likely than not that:
- the vehicle did not belong to them, and they had not hired or borrowed it, *and*
- they were using the vehicle in the course of their employment, *and*
- they did not know, and had no reason to believe, that they were not insured.

Causing or permitting a vehicle to be used without insurance

This offence is aimed at the person who lends out his or her car without checking that the driver is insured. If owners tell drivers that they cannot use the car until they obtain insurance, then the owners will not be liable. But this would need to be clearly and expressly stated; casual comments and assumption will not excuse an owner.

What happens if a car is loaned to a person for a third party to use?

Fisher loaned his car to another on the understanding that the other person would provide a driver with proper documentation. An uninsured driver used the vehicle and, when prosecuted, Fisher claimed he had made a proper arrangement with the person to whom he loaned the car. Held. This did not help Fisher. He had permitted his car to be used without any direct contact with driver so he could not have satisfied himself about the insurance. Fisher (1991)

The obligation to insure (and indeed to have a driving licence and MOT certificate) applies only to a vehicle that is on a road, as opposed to private land. In 1968 a classic border-line case arose when a lorry was half on private land and half on a road at the time of an accident. It was held that the lorry was on a road and so insurance, tax and MOT certificate were all needed. A 'road' may also be a car park or some other place to which vehicles have access which is not clearly kept as private.

How the motorist's insurance can be invalid

The law on motor insurance is no different to that on other types of insurance. Chapter 39 sets out the position. The basic rule is that the insured person must act in the utmost good faith and so tell the insurers of anything that could be relevant to their insuring him or her. Thus they must tell the insurers of all accidents and convictions, even if they are not asked about them, and the information they give to the insurers (e.g. as to where the car is to be garaged or whether the car was used for business) must be 100 per cent correct. Otherwise the insurance will be invalid. Thus the insurance company may not have to pay out if sued, or if they do pay out then the unfortunate motorist may have to reimburse the insurers. However, if the insurance policy is invalidated in this way it is most unlikely that motorists will face a criminal prosecution for not being insured. The police will take the view that they were insured until the time when the insurance company repudiated liability or cancelled the policy. Therefore, while the insurance policy may be invalid as regards a civil claim for damages, it will be valid against a criminal prosecution for being uninsured.

The law reports contain many cases of motorists who thought they were insured but whose insurers were entitled to repudiate liability. Generally this was because they had fallen foul of one of the following rules:

1 The duty to disclose every relevant detail (even ones you are not asked about). For instance:

● *the motorist failed to disclose that a previous proposal for a different type of policy had been turned down.* Locker (1936)
● *the insured did not mention that her husband would be driving the car and that he had a bad accident record.* Dunn (1933)
● *a bookmaker described himself as a dealer, since he knew that the company would not insure him as a bookmaker.* Holmes (1949)

2 False statements (even when you don't know they are false). For instance:

● *the insured completed the proposal form and in reply to, 'Has anyone who to your knowledge will drive the car been convicted of driving offences?', he put 'No.' However, unknown to him, his son, who would drive the car, did have several motoring convictions. Held: The answer was wrong and so the insurers could cancel the policy and repudiate liability.* M & M Insurers (1941)

A motorist who knowingly makes a false statement to obtain insurance commits an offence.

3 Breach of the conditions of the policy. Motor policies always contain small print imposing various conditions on the motorist. The motorist will often be unaware of these conditions and so may not realize that he or she is invalidating his/her insurance. For instance:

● the use to which the vehicle is put. If the policy is limited to 'social, domestic and pleasure' purposes, it will not cover a business trip.

Mrs Levinger's motor policy was limited to use on 'the business of the insured'. Mrs Levinger then turned her business into a company, so legally it was no longer her business. Held: The insurers could repudiate liability since the car was no longer being used on the business of the insured. Levinger (1936)

● that the vehicle be kept in roadworthy condition. Many policies require that the car be kept 'in a proper state of repair', and that it is not used 'in an unsafe condition'.

A car was carrying several extra passengers so that it was overloaded and this affected the steering. It was involved in an accident. The insurers then claimed that the insured had been in breach of the roadworthiness condition of his policy. Held: Yes. He was uninsured. Clarke (1964)

In one case, the front brakes of a coach became worn because the owners failed to carry out normal maintenance. The insurers were able to avoid liability when the defective brakes caused an accident. Even worse, it seems that the insurers can escape liability even if the defect was not the owner's fault because no amount of maintenance would have prevented the defect (e.g. if lights fail). This is, of course, a ridiculous situation. Also, the defect need not even cause the accident or be responsible for the claim being made. For instance, if a car with faulty lights is stolen, the insurers can repudiate liability, even though the failure to maintain was unconnected with the theft! The law is unfairly biased in favour of the insurance companies.

The companies argue that they rarely enforce their policies in such a strict way. Their code of practice says that in the absence of fraud, deception or negligence they will not unreasonably repudiate liability to indemnify a policy-holder where the circumstances of the loss are unconnected with the breach. But why should motorists have to rely on the good practice of insurers? Why not alter the law and remove the privileged legal position of insurers?

4 Most policies require the insured to notify the company of an accident or claim within seven or fourteen days. This provision can be applied strictly:

● *Mr Brooke went to see the branch manager of his insurers to make a claim. He told the manager about the claim and the manager gave him a claim form to complete. He went away, filled in the form and returned it, but by then the time limit had expired. Held: The insurers could repudiate liability.* Brooke (1946)

The duty to report any accident to the insurance company applies even when motorists do not want to claim under the policy. For instance, if they have a comprehensive policy but decide to claim from the other motorist involved, or when they decide to pay the other motorist's damage themselves rather than lose their no-claims bonus. In such a case motorists might write to their insurers: 'I am reporting this accident to you as required by the terms of my policy. However, please note that I am not making a claim under the policy and I should therefore be grateful for your confirmation that my no-claims bonus will not be affected by my reporting this accident to you.'

For how to make a claim after an accident, and the apportionment of blame for accidents, see Chapter 51, page 716.

The effect of motor insurance being invalidated

If a motorist's insurance policy is invalid for some reason, then he or she will be committing a criminal offence if they use the car after the insurance company has cancelled the policy or repudiated liability. But until that time they will not be criminally liable. But what about the injury or damage they cause – can the insurance company avoid paying compensation to the innocent parties? The answer is partly yes and partly no.

As regards claims for personal injury, the insurance company must pay any damages awarded against the uninsured motorist. So the innocent person who is injured can be sure that they will receive compensation from the insurance company. However, the insurance company can, in turn, sue the uninsured motorist in an attempt to get him/her to reimburse them (in practice, of course, he or she probably won't have enough money to make it worth suing).

If the claim is not for personal injury but is for damage to property or possessions, the insurance company need not pay any damages awarded against the motorist. The innocent person will therefore receive compensation only if the motorist has sufficient assets to pay the damages.

Illustration. *Mr Brown had his car insured for 'social, domestic and pleasure use'. One day he delivered a package for his employer in the car and had an accident on the way. The accident was his fault. His insurers repudiated liability because the car was not being used for social, domestic or pleasure purposes. In the accident Mr Brown drove into a car driven by Mr Smith, who claimed damages for:*
- *pain and suffering caused by a broken leg;*
- *lost wages for the time he was off work;*
- *the cost of a suit ruined in the accident;*
- *the value of his written-off car.*

The first and second items will have to be paid by the insurance company, although they can claim reimbursement from Mr Brown. The third and fourth will have to be paid by Mr Brown. If Mr Brown does not have sufficient money to pay, Mr Smith will go uncompensated unless he himself has a comprehensive insurance policy that he can claim on. This would, of course, probably involve him in paying an excess (see below) and also in the loss of his no-claims bonus.

Uninsured motorists

If Mr Brown had never taken out the insurance policy, then Mr Smith would obviously have been unable to claim any of his damages from the insurance company. However, he would not have gone uncompensated. He could claim from the Motor Insurers Bureau (MIB), which exists to compensate the victims of uninsured and untraced motorists. The MIB would meet Mr Smith's claim for damages under the first two items, although it would of course be able to claim reimbursement from Mr Brown, assuming he had sufficient assets.

No-claims and 'excesses'

Most motor policies offer a no-claims discount, whereby the premium is reduced according to the number of preceding years in which no claim was made. Typical reductions are:

1 year – 30 per cent reduction
2 years – 40 per cent reduction
3 years – 50 per cent reduction
4 years – 60 per cent reduction

The important point to note is that the no-claims bonus, or a proportion of it, is lost as soon as the claim is made. It is wrong to suppose that the bonus is lost only if the accident was not the insured's fault; it is a no-claims bonus, not a no-fault bonus. However, many insurance policies now provide that only a part of the no-claims bonus is lost in the event of a claim. A further deterrent to small claims is the 'excess', where a company requires the policy-holder to pay the first £50 of any claim.

A complication can arise, however, because of 'knock for knock' agreements. These are agreements between insurance companies, whereby they consent to meet claims made by their own insured even when, legally speaking, the accident was the fault of a motorist insured by another insurance company. In effect, each company pays out on its own claims and so all the companies avoid the expense and inconvenience of claiming from one another. So motorists may have their claims paid by their own insurers even though it is the other negligent motorist's insurers who should really be paying. They will, of course, lose their no-claims bonus and their excess, since a claim has been made on their policy. In theory, if they can convince their insurers that they were in no way to blame for the accident, the insurers will agree to reinstate the no-claims bonus, but in practice they can do this only by recovering their own excess from the other motorist (or the insurers). Thus innocent motorists may have to sue for the few pounds of their excess if they are to preserve their no-claims bonus.

Car-sharing

It used to be unlawful for motorists to share the cost of travel with their passengers. Since 1978, non-profit car-sharing has been allowed if no more than eight people travel in the vehicle and charges are agreed before the journey starts. There must be no profit, but drivers can charge for more than just the petrol. For instance, they can recover a contribution towards servicing, insurance and road tax proportional to the use of the car. But the owners must incur the expenses; they cannot charge their passengers for costs that they do not incur (e.g. if their employers provide them with free petrol), since they would then be making a profit.

The driver's insurance will not be invalidated by car-sharing if it meets the above requirements. Advertising for car-sharers is allowed, provided the advertisements do not amount to plying for hire, like a taxi.

VEHICLE MAINTENANCE

The duty to have a safe and roadworthy vehicle is not limited to the time of the annual MOT test. The Road Vehicle (Construction and Use) Regulations set out – in some 109 provisions and fourteen schedules – the legal standards required at all times from any car on the road. Many of these detailed regulations will be met by the vehicle manufacturer and are unlikely to concern the motorist (e.g. the dimensions and turning circles of vehicles). However, the regulations insist that these requirements are met at all times and both the owner and the driver of the vehicle can be prosecuted for any breach.

The Construction and Use Regulations cover virtually all aspects of vehicle design, safety and maintenance; the provisions on horns, brakes, overloading, steering, tyres, mirrors and noise are of particular importance. A similarly detailed set of regulations deal with lighting requirements. Most of the offences do not carry penalty points (or endorsement), although the rules on dangerous loads, brakes, steering and tyres are exceptions to this. For penalties see page 708.

Motorists can be convicted of using a vehicle in breach of the Construction and Use Regulations even when they did not know of the vehicle's fault. This is because they are absolute offences: either the offence was committed or it was not – there can be no half-way house. The charge is one of 'being in breach of the Regulations', not 'knowingly being in breach of the Regulations'. For instance, headlights must be in perfect working order during the day, and not just at night; motorists driving in the daytime may not know if their headlight bulb has broken since they last used the lights, but they will still be guilty of an offence. However, in such a case, the court will usually find the motorist guilty but give an absolute discharge, recognizing technical guilt but not imposing punishment.

If the charge is one of 'causing or permitting' the vehicle to be used by someone else in breach of the regulations, then the defendant must be shown to have 'known' of the fault. Whereas 'using' the vehicle is an absolute offence, 'causing or permitting' its use is not.

Spot checks

Breaches of the Construction and Use Regulations usually come to light when the police inspect a vehicle after an accident or during a spot check. A uniformed police officer can, at any time, stop a vehicle and ask to check its brakes, steering, silencer, tyres, exhaust, lights and reflectors. However, the driver can say that it would be inconvenient to have an immediate inspection and can insist that it be arranged at any convenient time in the next thirty days, unless the police officer feels that the vehicle should be checked immediately either because it has been in an accident or because it seems to have a serious defect. If so, the inspection cannot be postponed. If serious defects are found, the police may order that the vehicle not be driven any further.

Brakes

The handbrake and the brakes on the four wheels must be effective and capable of stopping the car in a reasonable distance. As a guide, the Highway Code gives the shortest stopping distance of a typical car with good brakes, including thinking time, as 75 feet at 30 m.p.h., 175 feet at 50 m.p.h., 315 feet at 70 m.p.h. Precise requirements will depend upon the type and age of the vehicle. In general, the more modern the vehicle the more stringent the requirement.

Horn

All private motor vehicles must have a horn capable of giving proper warning of the vehicle's position. Bells, two-tone horns and sirens are not allowed. There are restrictions on sounding horns at night and sounding them unnecessarily. Anti-theft alarms must have cut-off devices to limit the time for which they sound to five minutes.

Lights

Both lights and reflectors must be kept clean and in full working order, even in daytime. It is illegal to have a red light at the front of the car or a white light at the rear (except when reversing). It is also illegal to have rear fog lights that are wired to the brake lights. Lighting-up time is the period between sunset and sunrise. Dipped or full headlights are compulsory at night outside built-up areas (i.e. where the street lights are more than 200 yards apart), and in all areas if there is poor visibility, such as fog or heavy rain.

When parked at night, a car must have sidelights on unless it is on a road with a 30 m.p.h. speed limit, in the light of a street lamp and not on a main bus route. It must also be parked at least 10 metres from any junction and be facing the correct direction.

Mirrors

All vehicles must have a rear-view mirror; modern vehicles and all goods vehicles and large passenger vehicles need wing mirrors in addition. Modern vehicles require an off-side wing mirror and either an internal mirror or a near-side mirror. The internal mirror must be of safety glass and all mirrors must be adjustable.

Number plates

These must have the vehicle's number in regulation-approved size and style of lettering. An offence is committed if the vehicle is driven with number plates that are so dirty as to be unreadable. Clearly using number plates from another vehicle is a serious offence.

Silencer

An effective silencer is compulsory. The precise performance required of a silencer will depend upon the vehicle's age. Clearly standards have risen sharply in recent years to match environmental concerns.

Speedometer

A speedometer must be fitted to nearly all post-1937 vehicles and vehicles first used after 1 April 1984 have been required to show speed in kilometres per hour as well as in miles per hour.

Windscreen wipers

Wipers are compulsory unless the driver can see clearly over or through the windscreen without them. Windscreen washers are also compulsory. The test is whether the two devices used together can effectively clear the windscreen, so therefore blades must be adequate in the wiper and the washer tank has to contain water.

Seat belts

The fitting of seat belts in new cars has been compulsory for many years (generally since 1964). But it is only since 1983 that the wearing of seat belts in the front of a car has been compulsory. There are only a few exceptions: when reversing; for delivery roundsmen, taxi drivers, police and other emergency services; and if a medical-exemption certificate can be produced. In practice few people are entitled to medical certificates, since most GPs apply the rules strictly. Since 1991 the wearing of seat belts in the rear is also compulsory for adults where a belt is fitted. If a person does have a certificate of exemption, then it must be shown to the police on request (or produced at a police station within seven days).

Persons engaged in local rounds of deliveries need not wear seat belts.

'W' was a newsagent; he collected bundles of newspapers and was returning to his premises when stopped by the police for not wearing a seat belt. Held. Rounds meant a series of visits or calls and 'W's' trip did not qualify whatever use the vehicle might be put to at other times. Webb (1988)

Children under twelve months are not allowed to travel in a front seat (even if securely held by an adult). Children aged between one and thirteen inclusive are allowed in front seats, but must be strapped in (as, of course, must any adult). If a child is not strapped in, then the driver can be prosecuted. All rear-seated children must be belted if belts are fitted.

Except where the passenger is a child the driver is not criminally liable where a passenger fails to use a seat belt provided. The normal rules of 'aiding and abetting' are disapplied to this law. However, the driver would be in serious difficulty regarding his or her civil liability if no attempt to encourage the use of a belt had been made. Failure to wear a belt seriously weakens a person's position in any legal action as it will be regarded as contributory negligence.

THE MOTORIST AS A CONSUMER

A car is a consumer item and thus its purchase and sale are subject to the consumer laws set out in Chapter 34. One point to watch particularly carefully is that many secondhand cars are bought and sold from private individuals, not from motor traders. That being so, the purchaser will not have the benefit of the Sale of Goods Act protection which would apply to a purchase from a trader.

If repair work is carried out by a member of the Motor Agents' Association (MAA) or of the Society of Motor Manufacturers and Traders (SMMT), there may be an additional remedy. These bodies have produced a code of practice which, among other provisions, sets out minimum standards expected of their members. If customers feel that a member has broken the code they can apply for arbitration. Even if the garage is not a member of one of these organizations, the code can be relevant because it shows the standards expected of a 'reasonable' garage and this can be extremely useful to the consumer who is suing in the county court.

Major recommendations in the code

The words in square brackets are not part of the code.

Repairs and servicing (excluding work carried out under a manufacturer's warrant)

Dealers must bear in mind that when supplying parts or accessories in connection with repairs or servicing work for consumers, they have a similar responsibility to that which exists under a contract for the sale of goods to ensure that the goods are of merchantable quality and fit for the purpose for which they are required and that work is performed in a proper and workmanlike manner.

Manufacturers accept a responsibility for ensuring the reasonable availability of spare parts to the distribution chain.

Dealers will provide at least an estimate of the cost of labour and materials for all major repairs and manufacturers' recommended servicing. A firm quotation should be offered wherever possible. It must be made clear to the customer whether an estimate or quotation is being made and whether it is inclusive of VAT and where applicable the rate at which this is chargeable. Quotations should always be in writing, identifying the dealer. If requested, estimates will be in writing. It should be remembered that an estimate is a considered approximation of the likely cost involved, whereas a quotation constitutes a firm price for which the work will be done. If a charge is to be made for the estimate or quotation this must be made known to the customer before his instructions are accepted. Any dismantling costs which are necessary to arrive at such estimates or quotations should be notified to the customer in advance on the clear understanding whether or not dismantling costs are to be charged on an estimate or quotation which is refused. If, during the progress of any work, it appears that the estimate will be exceeded by a significant amount, then the customer should be notified and asked for permission to continue with the work. [Of course, there is scope for different views about what is a significant amount and the customer should set a figure over which he or she should be contacted.]

Parts replaced during service or repair will be made available for return to the customer until the customer has taken delivery of the car unless a warranty claim is involved or unless the parts have to be submitted to the supplier because replacement parts are being supplied on an exchange basis. Dealers should notify customers in advance of work being done what their arrangements are in regard to retention and disposal of parts replaced.

Invoices should be clearly written or typed and give full details of the work carried out and materials used. The amount and rate of VAT should be clearly indicated. Dates and recorded mileages should always be noted where applicable.

Dealers should exercise adequate care in protecting customers' property while it is in their custody, and must not seek by disclaimers to avoid their legal liability for damage or loss. Dealers should carry adequate insurance to cover their legal liability and should strongly advise customers to remove any items of value not related to the car.

Repairs must be guaranteed against failure due to workmanship for a specific mileage or time period, which should be stated on the invoice. Dealers are advised to ensure that they are adequately insured against consequential loss claims arising from any such failure.

A dealer's rules as to the method of payment he will require on completion of the work should always be notified to the customer before the work is accepted.

When it is necessary to sub-contract work, the dealer will agree to be responsible for the quality of the sub-contractors' work. Any estimate given to the customer must include sub-contracted work and in the event of any increase in charge for the work, the principles [of reporting to the customer] must apply.

Handling complaints

Manufacturers and dealers must ensure as appropriate that effective and immediate action is taken with a view to achieving a just settlement of a complaint. To this end there will be, from the point of view of the customer, an easily identifiable and accessible arrangement for the reception and handling of complaints. In addition, manufacturers must give every assistance to their dealers in handling complaints under warranty, or those in which the manufacturer is otherwise involved.

When complaints are raised through a third party (e.g. the Automobile Association, the Royal Automobile Club, a trading standards officer or a Citizens' Advice Bureau), willing guidance must be given to that body and every attempt should be made to re-establish direct communication with the complaining customer and to reach a satisfactory settlement with him.

In the event that a complaint is not resolved manufacturers and dealers must make it clear to a customer that he has a right to refer the complaint to the appropriate trade as-sociation.

Where conciliation has failed to resolve a dispute the SMMT, the MAA and the SMTA have agreed to cooperate in the operation of low-cost arbitration arrangements which will be organized by the Chartered Institute of Arbitrators.

Customers must always be advised that they have the option of taking a claim to the courts.

The award of the arbitrator is enforceable in law on all parties.

Arbitration

1 A customer who has a complaint about the quality of the goods or service to his motor car should in the first place and at the earliest opportunity refer it to the dealer concerned.
2 The complaint, preferably in writing, should be addressed to a senior executive, a director, a partner or the proprietor. Some dealers will have an executive specially appointed to deal with complaints.
3 If the complaint relates to warranty on a new car and the dealer is unable to resolve the matter, the customer should take his complaint direct to the manufacturer concerned.
4 If attempts to reach a satisfactory solution fail, the customer has a right to refer his complaint to one of the trade associations which subscribe to the code of practice for the motor industry, if the dealer concerned is a member of that association. Any such complaint must be in writing.

5 All complaints referred to the appropriate trade association (SMMT, MAA or SMTA) within a reasonable time of the cause for complaint arising will be considered.
6 If the trade association fails to resolve the complaint, its members will agree to go to arbitration except in those cases where the trade association is of the opinion that it would be unreasonable for the member to be required to do so.
7 The award of the arbitrator is enforceable in the courts by any party.

50 Prosecution for Motoring Offences

In the eyes of the law, motoring offences are no different from other offences. If the defendant is guilty, then he or she has committed a crime. Society, of course, generally takes a more lenient view and regards motoring offences as being different from other criminal offences, presumably on the basis of 'There but for the grace of God go I.' This ambivalent attitude to motoring offences is reflected in the fact that Parliament has had to create a special offence of 'causing death by reckless driving' because of the refusal of juries to convict motorists of manslaughter, even when there is clear evidence of gross negligence.

However, there is one legal difference between many motoring offences and most other offences, in that motoring offences are generally not concerned with the intention or knowledge of the accused. Whereas most crimes involve, first, an illegal act and, secondly, an intention to commit the illegal act, most motoring offences need only the illegal act and not the intention to commit it. For instance, motorists who drive at 40 m.p.h. in a 30 m.p.h. zone cannot expect to be acquitted because they did not know there was a 30 m.p.h. limit, or because their speedometer was working incorrectly (in itself an offence under the Construction and Use Regulations). The court would be concerned to know only: was there a 30 m.p.h. limit in force and was the accused exceeding 30 m.p.h. If so, then a conviction must result, although obviously the circumstances of the offence would be relevant when deciding on a suitable penalty.

Similarly, take the example of the motorist who does not know that her insurers have gone 'bust', and that she is therefore driving without insurance. She may be morally blameless but in the law's eyes will be guilty of driving without insurance and a conviction must result. Her excuses will be relevant only after conviction, when the court is considering what penalty to impose.

However, this is not a universal rule, for there are a few motoring offences that require a guilty knowledge or intent on the part of the accused before they can be convicted. But such offences (e.g. reckless driving, 'causing or permitting' charges) are the exception rather than the rule, whereas in non-motoring offences the reverse applies.

While in legal theory all motoring convictions are criminal convictions, a distinction is in fact made between the various categories of motoring offences, and this distinction is reflected in the way in which they are recorded.

1 Convictions usually regarded as 'criminal', mostly those for which imprisonment could be ordered, are recorded at Scotland Yard and at the regional police headquarters around the country. Thus offences such as causing death by reckless driving and taking a vehicle without consent would be recorded in the national criminal records.

2 Convictions resulting in an endorsement or in disqualification are recorded on the DVLA computer at Swansea. Every driver has a driver number, and the police or courts can apply for a computer print-out of his or her driving record. Some offences are recorded both in criminal records and at the DVLA.

3 Minor offences are not recorded in a central register.

Convictions do not remain on a driving licence (or in the DVLA computer) for ever. Most offences are removed when a licence is exchanged four or more years after a conviction. The main exceptions are drink-driving offences, which remain on a licence for eleven years.

WHEN PROCEEDINGS ARE BEGUN

Because motoring offences are, in the eyes of the law, similar to other criminal offences, proceedings are begun in the same way (see page 751 for ways in which criminal proceedings can be commenced). However, since most motoring offences carry relatively small penalties, they are usually begun by way of a summons.

Only in the more serious cases (such as reckless driving or breathalyser offences) is the motorist likely to be arrested and taken to the police station. If motorists are arrested they are likely to be bailed to court and, apart from the question of warning, the points made below apply to the charge sheet they will receive instead of the summons. For motorists who are detained legal advice may be available at the police station from a duty solicitor.

When served with a summons there are two preliminary points that the motorist should consider before deciding whether to plead guilty or not guilty.

1. What exactly are the charges against them?

The charge will often be set out in legalistic language, so motorists should read it carefully and, if necessary, seek legal advice. Often it will be important to check whether they are being prosecuted for 'using' the car, 'driving' the car, 'being in charge' of the car (e.g. when it is parked) or 'permitting' its use (e.g. when they allow someone such as an employee to use it). It is worth checking that the correct wording is used for the facts of the particular case.

2. Should the police have notified them of likely prosecution?

With certain offences, motorists must be warned that they might be prosecuted so that they can take steps to contact witnesses and collect evidence before too much time elapses. The warning can either be a verbal warning from the police at the time of the offence (typically; 'The facts will be reported with a view to consideration of the question of proceedings being taken against you') or a written notice of intended prosecution (or even a summons), served within fourteen days of the offence. The notice is usually sent by recorded-delivery post and will simply state that the police intend to prosecute. But just because a notice of intended prosecution is served, it does not necessarily mean that the police will prosecute, for the service of the notice simply allows the police to keep their options open while they decide whether or not to prosecute.

A warning of possible prosecution is needed only for the following offences:
- reckless, careless or inconsiderate driving (or cycling);
- failure to comply with a traffic sign;
- failure to comply with the directions of a police officer regulating traffic;
- leaving vehicle in a dangerous position;
- speeding offences.

However, no notice is needed if an accident occurred at the time of the offence. So if, for instance, motorists are involved in a collision, however slight, they need not be warned that they might be prosecuted for careless driving. However, if they had not hit the other vehicle and there had been no accident, then they would have to be warned.

In practice it is difficult for motorists to have a summons dismissed because no notice of intended prosecution was given. It is for them to show that the notice was not given, and if the police can show that the notice was sent by recorded delivery to their address, the court may find that it was served properly even if it was in fact returned by the post office.

Should the motorist defend the charge?

Once motorists have checked these technicalities, they will have to decide whether to defend the charge and whether to instruct a solicitor. In all but the most obvious cases it is advisable to take legal advice, either from a solicitor, a Citizens' Advice Bureau, or from the AA or RAC (if they are members). If the prosecution follows a serious accident, the motorist's insurance company may be prepared to instruct a solicitor to represent them since their liability to pay damages could be affected by the outcome of the criminal prosecution.

Points to be borne in mind at this stage:

1 Is it worth paying legal fees to defend the charge? In a magistrates' court prosecution motorists should recover all their legal costs if they are acquitted. Legal aid will be available only for the more serious motoring offences.
2 What is the maximum possible penalty, and also what is the likely penalty? Refer to the penalty chart on page 708.
3 Do they have any previous motoring convictions that will affect the penalty? In particular, do they have any penalty points that could lead to disqualification under the 'totting up' rules (see page 694)?

4 If the offence is very trivial, is it worth incurring the inconvenience of defending it? For instance, with a parking summons it might be cheaper and more convenient to plead guilty rather than go to the inconvenience of attending court to defend the charge. (However, a court should not accept a plea of guilty based upon convenience even for a trivial offence. If a motorist says, 'I plead guilty but . . .' and then goes on to give a defence, he or she will be asked to attend court to contest the case.)

5 Do they have a defence to the charge? There is no point in pleading not guilty when there is no hope of acquittal. Indeed, such a course of action usually rebounds; the court may feel its time has been wasted and so impose a stiffer penalty, as well as ordering the defendant to pay the costs of the prosecution (which would probably have been lower had he or she pleaded guilty). This is especially true of breathalyser prosecutions, where many defendants plead not guilty when they clearly are guilty. An early guilty plea, if appropriate, will be seen by a court as straightforwardness and a sign of regret; it should obtain the most lenient penalty.

6 If motorists are going to plead guilty, can they do so by post? It is possible to plead guilty by post to most motoring offences where the prosecutor allows this option, but it is important that defendants write to the court in good time and enclose their driving licence. Remember, it is not possible to plead 'not guilty' by post. A 'not guilty' plea means attendance at court by the defendant.

PENALTIES

The penalty chart on page 708 sets out typical penalties for first-time offenders. But it does not set out the possible maximum penalties, which may well be much greater. This is because the vast majority of motorists are not fined the maximum amount (e.g. some obstruction charges can carry a maximum penalty of up to £2,000 but in practice typical penalties are in the £20–£30 bracket). So maximum penalties are usually misleading.

Bear in mind that the typical penalties set out in the penalty chart are no more than very rough guidelines. Different courts take different attitudes to the same case. It is not uncommon for a solicitor to have two clients with seemingly identical cases and find that one client, in one court, gets a sentence considered 'worth' twice that of the other client, who had the good fortune to appear in a different court. In any event, the penalty imposed will depend on the facts of the incident, the court's impression of the accused, any previous convictions and also that particular court's view of the seriousness of the offence in question. It is, therefore, impossible to set out a list of normal penalties, but the penalty chart does set out 'typical penalties' as a rough and ready guide, although the limitations of these figures should always be borne in mind.

If the offence is one for which a fixed penalty could have been imposed, the court will often wish to impose a penalty significantly above the fixed-penalty levels, which are currently £20 for a non-endorsable offence and £40 for endorsable offences. If a fixed penalty was not offered because, for example, the officer did not have a pad of tickets, this needs to be pointed out to the court; if it is, the court may limit its penalty to the fixed-penalty level.

Apart from fine or imprisonment, endorsement and disqualification are usually the major penalties that can be imposed on motoring offenders.

Endorsement

An endorsement can be imposed for most motoring offences, the major exceptions being for parking, obstruction, no road-fund licence, no MOT certificate, no lights and most construction and use offences.

For relevant offences an endorsement will be ordered unless the court decides that there are special reasons (see page 693) for not endorsing. The endorsement is entered on the motorist's driving licence and also on DVLA records, although the motorist can apply for it to be removed from the licence after four years (eleven years if endorsement was for a drink-driving offence).

What is an endorsement?

An endorsement means that the conviction is 'endorsed' (i.e. written) on the motorist's driving licence. As such, an endorsement is not by itself much of a penalty, except for the fact that each endorsement has a number of penalty points that accompany it. Motorists will want to do all they can to avoid getting an endorsement as the penalty points can accumulate to the point where disqualification is normally ordered.

How can an endorsement be avoided?

The court has very little discretion to refuse to endorse if the law states that the offence carries endorsement. In the penalty chart on pages 708–10 there is a column headed 'Endorse?' and this shows the offences for which the court has to endorse. However, even in those cases, the court can refuse to endorse if it is convinced that there are 'special reasons' surrounding the way in which the offence was committed. So, if motorists can convince the court that there were special reasons, then the court will not endorse their licence, and – probably more important – the court cannot then impose any penalty points. In practice, very few motorists are able legitimately to argue that there were special reasons (see below, page 693, for the rules on special reasons).

One other, very narrow, escape route from endorsement applies to offences of defective steering, brakes and tyres under the Construction and Use Regulations. In such a case if motorists can prove that they did not know of the defect and had no cause to suspect it, they may avoid endorsement. However, the court will expect good vehicle maintenance to be established and the plea is effectively limited to sudden mechanical failure.

PENALTY POINTS

Before 1982 the rule used to be that motorists would lose their licence if they had three endorsements in three years. Now it is if they have 12 penalty points in three years.

The more serious offences carry more points. To see whether a particular offence carries points, refer to the penalty chart on pages 708–10. If the offence is listed as having an endorsement, then points will normally have to be imposed.

Most offences carry a fixed number of penalty points (e.g. defective brakes carries 3 points). But a few offences carry a range of penalty points and the court has a discretion as to the number of points to impose within that range. The offences are:

careless driving	3–9 points
failing to stop after an accident	8–10 points
failing to report an accident	8–10 points
driving while uninsured	6–8 points

In these cases, the court has a discretion. It will obviously take into account the circumstances of the case, the seriousness of any damage caused, and, in some courts, the previous driving record of the motorist. So if motorists are being prosecuted for one of these offences they would be unwise to plead guilty by post, in case the court imposes maximum penalty points. They should appear in court to explain the mitigating circumstances and why a lower number of points should be imposed. To take the example of careless driving, the outcome for the motorist could be 3 points or 9 points or anything in between; 3 points is one-quarter of the way towards a totting-up disqualification, 9 points is three-quarters of the way towards a ban – a difference worth an appearance at court (see table on page 692).

Convictions for more than one offence

Often motorists will face more than one charge as a result of one incident. The question then arises of how many points should be imposed. The answer is that they will get the points only for the most serious offence; they will not also get points for other offences committed on the same occasion.

The penalty points system was introduced in 1982 and since that time the points value that the law has fixed for offences has changed from time to time.

Illustration. *A motorist is stopped on the motorway for speeding. When the police examine his car they discover that his brakes are not working. He is subsequently convicted of speeding (which carries 3 points) and for a breach of the Construction and Use Regulations (which also carries 3 points). In fact, he will receive only 3 points (i.e. not 6 points).*

Illustration. *A motorist is involved in a serious accident and subsequently prosecuted for reckless driving (which carries 10 points) and for speeding (3 points). She will receive 10 points (i.e. not 13 points).*

Motoring

	Penalty Points for Common Offences
4	Any offence involving automatic disqualification (see page 695)
10	Reckless driving
3–9	Careless or inconsiderate driving
10	Being in charge when unfit through drink
10	Being in charge with alcohol above prescribed limit
4	Failure to supply specimen for breath test
10	Failure to supply specimen for analysis
1	Illegally carrying passenger on motor-cycle
3	Failure to comply with traffic directions
3	Leaving vehicle in dangerous position
8–10	Failure to stop after an accident
8–10	Failure to give particulars or report accident
3	Contravention of Construction and Use Regulations
2	Driving without a licence
2	Failure to comply with conditions of licence
2	Driving with uncorrected defective eyesight
2	Refusal to submit to eyesight test
2	Driving when disqualified as under-age
6	Driving when disqualified by court order
6–8	Using/causing/permitting use of uninsured motor vehicle
3	Contravention of motorway traffic regulations
3	Contravention of pedestrian-crossing regulations
3	Failure to obey school-crossing patrol sign
2	Contravention of street playground order
3	Exceeding the speed limit
8	Taking a conveyance without consent
8	Going equipped for stealing with reference to theft or taking of motor vehicle
8	Stealing or attempting to steal motor vehicle

This rule apples only if the offences are 'committed on the same occasion'. For instance, suppose a motorist drives from Bristol to London, and is seen driving carelessly in Bath and speeding near Heathrow. The offences were not committed on the same occasion and so he or she will incur points (between 3 and 9) for the careless driving and 3 points for the speeding. On the other hand, if the two offences had happened at more or less the same time, then it would count as only one conviction for the purpose of points. The difficulty, of course, lies in deciding when offences are 'committed on the same occasion' and when they are different occasions. When there is a dispute on this point, the court has to decide the issue.

Can points be avoided?

If the offence carries penalty points then the court must normally impose those points; it cannot decide that the offence was not serious enough to merit points. Refer to the penalty chart on pages 708–10 to see which offences carry penalty points. But points can be imposed only if the motorist's licence is also endorsed. So if motorists can persuade the court not to endorse their licence (see page 690), then they will also avoid incurring points. However, an endorsement can be avoided only if motorists can persuade the court that there were 'special reasons' in their particular case. This is not as easy as it may seem because it is not the hardship to the individual motorist that matters (e.g. it may threaten his or her job) but the circumstances of the offence.

Special reasons

The fundamental rule on special reasons is that the circumstances must be connected with the offence and not with the offender. The reason must be special to the offence and not the offender. Thus the mere fact that the offender will lose her job if her licence is endorsed cannot be a special reason, as it is a circumstance that relates to the offender not the offence. On the other hand, the fact that the offence was committed after the motorist had drunk laced drinks could be a special reason, since it relates to the circumstances of the offence and not the offender's own personal circumstances.

Many motorists convince themselves that there are special reasons why they should not have an endorsement, but only occasionally will they be correct. The best way to illustrate how strictly the rules on special reasons are applied is to consider these examples of what have been held not to be special reasons:

- the motorist has been driving for many years without complaint or accident;
- he is a professional driver and will otherwise lose his job;
- he is disabled and relies on his car for transport, or he is disabled and only drove the car at the time of the offence because there was no public transport available;
- he will suffer financial hardship, or serious hardship will be caused to the defendant's family;
- he is a doctor and endorsement resulting in disqualification would cause medical services in his area to deteriorate;
- he is a soldier serving in Northern Ireland and must be able to drive on duty;
- domestic circumstances (such as a babysitter waiting at home) forced him to drive the car at the time of the offence;
- endorsement would result in disqualification and that would be too severe a penalty;
- the accident that occurred was not his fault;
- he was the person who actually summoned the police;
- the offence occurred late at night when there were few people about.

Special reasons are not just important when an endorsement is being considered. In the more serious motoring offences for which disqualification is mandatory (e.g. drunken driving, see page 703) motorists can argue that there are special reasons why they should not be disqualified. Once again, the principle to be applied is that the special reason must be relevant to the offence, not to the offender. See page 705 for more examples of special reasons.

12 POINTS EQUALS DISQUALIFICATION

The basic rule is that motorists who acquire 12 penalty points in a three-year period will lose their licence for at least six months. This is what is sometimes called 'totting up'. In fact, it is an oversimplification to say that 12 points in three years equals six months' disqualification. In many cases it will, but often the rules are complicated to apply.

The three-year period

In most cases, it is simply a matter of seeing whether the motorist has had points within the last three years. But special provisions have had to be built into the rules so as to prevent cunning lawyers from trying to get an advantage by postponing their clients' court appearances (and so moving to a different three-year period). However, the basic rule is that offences committed within three years of the date of the latest offence – not the date when it comes to court – are taken into account. (In fact, the rules can be difficult to apply, so anyone with a borderline case should take legal advice.) Nevertheless, if the motorist has already been disqualified in the last three years, then that disqualification wipes the slate clean as regards points incurred before disqualification. So if a motorist had 10 points one year ago, but was disqualified nine months ago, then only points imposed in the last nine months – since his or her disqualification – will be counted.

The length of disqualification

The normal rule is that 12 points in three years leads to a minimum of six months' disqualification. Note that this is the minimum period, although in practice it is usually six months (not longer) that is imposed. But if the motorist has been disqualified before, within the last three years, then the minimum period is longer. The basic rule is:

> no disqualification in last three years – six months minimum
> one disqualification in last three years – one year minimum
> more than one disqualification in last three years – two years minimum.

A disqualification has two consequences. First, it wipes the slate clean so that past penalty points no longer count. Secondly, it means that if there is another disqualification in the three-year period, then the court must impose a longer disqualification next time.

The minimum periods of disqualification apply in the vast majority of totting-up cases. But the court does have a discretion, and it is allowed to impose a shorter period, or not to disqualify at all, if it can be persuaded that there are mitigating circumstances. This allows the court to take into account the personal circumstances of the motorist. But it must be emphasized that the court will look for serious and exceptional hardship if that is to be sufficient reason for not disqualifying. It will not be impressed by vague talk of hardship and inconvenience; it will want clear evidence of exceptional hardship.

'Mitigating circumstances' for not disqualifying under the totting-up rules should not be confused with 'special reasons' for not endorsing a licence (see above). The important restriction on 'special reasons' is that they must be special to the circumstances of how the offence was committed (e.g. laced drinks) and not to the offender himself (e.g. he is a commercial traveller). With 'mitigating circumstances' for not disqualifying, it is different: the personal circumstances of the motorist are relevant and not the facts of the offence. Thus nearly every example on page 693 of what was not a 'special reason' could be a valid example of a 'mitigating circumstance' for not disqualifying.

Anyone who is facing disqualification under the totting-up rules should consider instructing a solicitor to argue their case, if they think they might be able to raise mitigating circumstance as to why they should not be disqualified.

SUMMARY: ENDORSEMENTS, POINTS AND TOTTING UP

The sequence of events is:

1 The motorist is convicted of an endorsable offence (see the penalty chart on pages 708–10 to check whether an offence is endorsable or not).
2 The magistrates will then endorse his or her licence, unless he or she can show there are special reasons for not doing so (see page 693 for what counts as a special reason).
3 If the licence is endorsed, the magistrates will then impose the penalty points shown on the penalty chart. But if no endorsement was ordered, then no points can be imposed.
4 If points are imposed, the magistrates will then go on to see whether the motorist should also be disqualified under the totting-up rules (i.e. 12 points in three years). If so, he or she will normally be disqualified for at least six months, unless they can show that mitigating circumstances apply (see above for what this means).

AUTOMATIC DISQUALIFICATION FOR SERIOUS OFFENCES

There are three ways in which motorists can be disqualified from driving. First, they can be disqualified under the totting-up rules (i.e. because they have received 12 penalty points in the last three years, (see above). Secondly, they may be disqualified for a single offence, if the court believes it serious enough. Thirdly, the law requires that for some offences the court must disqualify a motorist.

The second type of situation, where the court feels an offence so serious that it should impose a discretionary disqualification, is difficult to generalize about as different courts may see offences differently. While any offence that is endorsable may be the subject of a discretionary disqualification, very few motorists need worry about this as a realistic outcome; disqualification cannot be imposed in a motorist's absence without specific warning, so a motorist will have an opportunity to seek advice should such a disqualification be indicated. Probably the most common example of this type of disqualification is extremely high speed: motorists driving at more than 30 m.p.h. over a speed limit may well find that they are required to attend court to say why they should keep their licence.

A glance at the penalty chart (pages 708–10) will show that the court, surprisingly often, has the power to disqualify, if it wants to. In practice, of course, the court will only occasionally disqualify for these offences and much will depend upon the circumstances of the particular case. But there is a growing school of thought that a short period of disqualification can be a far more effective penalty than a fine, and so it is becoming more frequent for courts to impose short disqualifications. The sort of offences that come within this category are: failing to stop after an accident; driving while disqualified; crossing double white lines; reckless driving; deliberate no-insurance; speeding if more than 30 m.p.h over the limit; traffic-light offences; and taking a vehicle without consent. It may be reassuring to note that only about 1 per cent of speeding offenders are disqualified; about 1 per cent of those convicted of careless driving; and about 8 per cent of no-insurance offenders.

The third situation deals with offences that are so serious that Parliament has said that they should normally result in automatic disqualification. Drunk-driving is the best-known example. That offence and certain others (e.g. death by reckless driving and failing to provide a police station breath specimen) carry an automatic twelve months' (minimum) ban. However, even with these serious offences the court can decide not to ban if there are 'special reasons' relating to the offence (e.g. laced drinks). Refer to page 693 for examples of what can be (and more important, what cannot be) special reasons. There are more examples of special reasons in the section on drunk-driving, page 705.

The effect of disqualification

If a court disqualifies, then the ban comes into effect immediately. Motorists cannot even drive from the court house to garage their car! If they defy the ban, and are caught, there is a fair chance of their going to prison (about a 10 per cent chance, if they are tried in the magistrates' court). Even when the period of disqualification ends, they cannot simply get in their car and start driving again. A disqualification revokes a motorist's driving licence and he or she will have to get a new licence from the DVLA at Swansea. They may even have to take a driving test (if that was ordered by the court) or a medical (if the DVLA believe the motorist has a 'high risk' of alcohol abuse).

Removing the disqualification

Motorists who have been disqualified can apply to the court for the ban to be lifted early. The application is made to the court that imposed the ban and it will be for offenders to convince the court that their character and recent conduct justify the return of their licence. The seriousness of the original offence and any pressing reason why they need their licence back will also be taken into account. The application cannot be made until at least two years have expired. The minimum periods to be served are:

disqualified for under 4 years – can apply after 2 years
disqualified for 4 to 10 years – can apply when half the period has expired
disqualified for over 10 years – can apply after 5 years

When the court hears the application, the procedure is that the Crown Prosecutor in court will outline the circumstances of the original offence (including any mitigating or aggravating circumstances). They will also say whether the applicant has been in trouble since his or her disqualification. Next, the applicant will be asked to state the grounds of their application and why they need to be able to drive. Usually, this will be because it will increase their chances of getting a job, in which case it is advisable to have strong supporting evidence from a prospective employer. Instead of removing the disqualification the magistrates may decide simply to reduce its length. Alternatively, of course, they may refuse to change the length of the ban (if so, the applicant cannot appeal, but can apply again in three months' time).

Legal aid is not available for an application to remove a disqualification, although a motorist can choose to pay for a solicitor to attend.

THE PRINCIPAL MOTORING OFFENCES

Reckless driving

S.1 of the Road Traffic Act 1988 creates the offence of causing death by reckless driving, and s.2 covers reckless driving when death does not result.

For a motorist to be guilty of reckless driving, it must be shown that more than mere carelessness or bad driving was involved. The driving must have involved the motorist taking an obvious and serious risk of injuring someone or doing serious damage to property. One judge has defined it as deliberately doing something knowing that there was a risk of losing control of the vehicle. In effect, the driving must have created an obvious risk, which the motorist did not give any thought to (or if he or she did realize the risks, then simply carried on regardless). For instance:

A motor-cyclist sped through Lowestoft at about 75 m.p.h. He was in a 30 m.p.h. speed limit. He hit and killed a pedestrian. Held: This was reckless driving. It was such an excessive speed as to amount to a serious and obvious risk. Lawrence (1981)

The sort of situations that lead to a reckless-driving charge (as opposed to the less serious charge of careless driving) are: a major accident caused by going through red lights, overtaking on a bend, going the wrong way on a dual carriageway, and so on. Often the charge is brought with a charge of the lesser offence of 'careless driving' and it is then left to the court to decide whether the driving was so bad as to be reckless.

Reckless driving is an offence that can be tried in either the Crown Court or the magistrates' court. The charge of causing death by reckless driving can be heard only in the Crown Court. The attitude of courts (and the public) to offences involving death or serious injury has hardened significantly in recent years. Imprisonment is a strong probability where death occurs and a distinct possibility, alongside community penalties such as community service, in a case of simple reckless driving. Disqualification will always be considered and often the court will disqualify and order the offender to retake the driving test. If the motorist is not disqualified then 10 points will normally be imposed. Refer also to the penalty table (page 708).

Careless driving

This offence derives from s.3 of the Road Traffic Act 1988, where it is described as driving 'without due care and attention, or without reasonable consideration for other persons using the road'.

This is a charge that is frequently brought after a minor accident. The test to be applied is, did the motorist exercise the care and attention that a prudent driver would have done? If the answer is 'no', they are guilty. Thus bad driving can lead to a conviction even if there was no accident. Basically, even the most minor error of judgement will be careless driving and although not every breach of the Highway Code will be sufficient for a conviction, the offence is one that is easy to commit, for the 'prudent motorist' is assumed to observe the Highway Code. Many motorists commit the offence every day of the week. It is all a matter of degree. For instance, in the case of the motor cyclist driving through Lowestoft at 75 m.p.h. referred to above, that was reckless driving; if he had been doing 40 m.p.h. then that would have been careless driving. Similarly running into the back of the car in front is careless driving; but driving into the back of it at a high speed, after a dangerous overtaking manoeuvre, would be reckless driving.

Learner drivers doing their incompetent best are subject to the same standards as other drivers (see page 715). So too are the drivers of emergency vehicles. Police, fire-brigade and ambulance drivers cannot, for instance, jump red lights; they are subject to the same standard of driving care as other road users.

A policeman answered an emergency call on a motorway. He drove along the hard shoulder and collided with a stationary lorry. The policeman was prosecuted for careless driving but argued that he was on an emergency call and so had a defence to the charge. Held: No. The policeman's standard of driving must be the same as that of other road users. There are no special standards for policemen. [Note that with speeding there is an exception, for emergency vehicles can exceed the speed limit if their use would otherwise be 'hindered'.] The policeman was guilty. However, the fact that he was on an emergency would be very relevant in determining what was the proper sentence. Wood (1977)

In practice, careless driving is a difficult charge to defend. Endorsement will be ordered unless there are special reasons. A fine of between £100 and £120 (plus 3–9 points) will usually be imposed (see the penalty chart, page 709).

The allied offence of inconsiderate driving covers drivers who, for example, do not bother to dip their headlights at night or do not slow down to avoid splashing pedestrians.

Speeding

The opinion of two people (whether police officers or not) is enough to secure a conviction. However, more usually the evidence will be that of one police officer who followed the accused for three-tenths of a mile and was watching the police vehicle's speedometer, or who noted the speed on radar equipment.

Chief constables have produced guidelines on the action to be taken against speeding motorists: when to use a caution, when to use a fixed penalty and when to send a case to court. The individual officer still has discretion in individual cases but the general scheme is as follows:
- up to 10 m.p.h. over the limit – the motorist will receive a warning or caution, which may be a signal from an officer operating a radar gun, or a firm ticking-off from a traffic officer on the motorway or a written warning;
- over 10 but less than 25 m.p.h. over the limit – the motorist will be offered a fixed penalty (see 707);
- over 25 m.p.h. over the limit – prosecution will normally follow.

Since speeding is an absolute offence, it is no defence to argue that the speeding did not cause danger to anyone. If the speeding was dangerous, then the more serious charge of careless or reckless driving may also be brought.

In built-up areas, if the street lights are less than 200 yards apart one can be fairly sure that there is a 30 m.p.h. speed limit unless there is a sign to the contrary. If the lights are over 200 yards apart then it will usually be a de-restricted zone, or, to use the language of the Highway Code, the national speed limit will apply.

It is notoriously difficult to defend a speeding charge successfully. Police officers have little difficulty in finding motorists who are speeding and so it is difficult to persuade a court that the police are committing perjury and that the offence was not committed. Usually, it is alleged that the motorist was breaking the limit by at least 10 m.p.h. and so it is difficult to argue that there was a mistake, or that the police officer's speedometer was inaccurate. It is particularly difficult to defend the charge if the motorist was caught in a radar trap. Then the only hope is for the motorist to suggest that the police pulled in the wrong car, but few magistrates are impressed by such an argument.

A conviction will result in endorsement, and 3 penalty points, unless special reasons apply (see the penalty chart, page 709).

Taking a motor vehicle without consent

The Theft Act 1968 created a special offence of taking a vehicle without consent. This is because the normal charge of theft can apply only when the offender intended to 'permanently deprive' owners of their vehicles. Obviously, the joyrider has no intention to permanently deprive, and so cannot be guilty of theft. It is also an offence, and one generally considered as serious as taking a vehicle, for a person to allow themselves to be carried in a vehicle knowing it to have been taken without consent.

Defendants will have a defence if they can show that they believed they had the owner's permission to take the vehicle, or that the owner would have consented had they known the circumstances. The defendant has to prove only one of these points on a 'balance of probabilities' to be acquitted.

If the owner's consent is obtained by trickery, offenders cannot be prosecuted for taking the vehicle, although they can be prosecuted for deception.

Disqualification is common, although the youth of many offenders leads many courts to avoid disqualification so as not to damage employment (and thus rehabilitation) prospects. Since joyriders often damage the cars they borrow, it is worth remembering that the court can order the offender to pay compensation to the victim. Where damage or injury occurs after a vehicle is taken the more serious offence of aggravated vehicle taking is committed. For the penalties, see the chart on page 710.

Parking

The offence generally called 'illegal parking' encompasses many different offences. Road-side parking has different rules to off-street parking, local by-laws play a large part and London has a separate scheme from the rest of the country. A few basic generalizations are possible.

The mere absence of a 'no parking' sign does not mean parking is always permitted. Local by-laws will often lay down the details of parking zones and ignorance of these is no defence. Similarly, the rules as to parking meters vary from place to place, but generally motorists cannot feed the meter (i.e. add money for a second time) or move their car directly into a bay in the same group of meters (a different group will be marked by two white lines).

If the parked car causes an obstruction, motorists can be prosecuted for the offence of obstructing the highway. In practice, though, they are more likely to be charged with a similar offence contrary to the Road Vehicles (Construction and Use) Regulations 1986. This covers 'causing unnecessary obstruction of a road'. It is for the magistrates to decide whether the car did cause an 'unnecessary obstruction', but the law can be applied strictly. For instance, in one case a taxi driver was found guilty when he had waited in the road to turn right, so holding up heavy traffic. In another case, a doctor answering an emergency call parked his car so as to cause an obstruction and was found guilty. Likewise a motorist who boxed in another car by bad parking was convicted of causing an obstruction and fined. The fact that ten other cars were doing the same thing, or that others parked after you and created the problem will not alter the basic situation.

Often the offence commonly called parking is the breach of a local 'no waiting' order. However, these orders almost always have an exception to allow for the loading and unloading of vehicles. Not within the exception is the purchase of items, use of a bank or a bank machine or indeed anything other than loading and unloading.

When a ticket is written out, motorists can opt to pay the fixed penalty (usually £20) within twenty-one days. If they do so, there will be no offence and no conviction. However, if they do not pay the fixed penalty and are subsequently fined in the magistrates' court, this will count as a criminal conviction and, theoretically, will need to be reported to their insurers before their policy is renewed.

The offence is not endorsable and the typical fine is about £30. If the obstruction involved a complete disregard for other people (e.g. blocking a fire station access) a heavy fine would be imposed. A heavy fine is also likely where the road involved is a London priority route – the so-called 'red routes'. Parking within a pedestrian crossing or where a double-white-line system is used is endorsable and a typical fine will be £50.

Failing to stop and give particulars after an accident

Motorists whose vehicle is involved in an accident must stop for long enough to allow the other people concerned to ascertain their name and address. Not only must they stop, but they must exchange particulars with anyone reasonably requesting them. In addition, even if the motorists do stop, they may be obliged to report the accident to the police. If they fail to do so, this would be another charge that could be brought against them (see below).

The sensible motorist will, of course, stop after any accident, however small, and exchange particulars with anyone else involved. Legally, though, the obligation to stop and to provide particulars exists only if the accident caused:
• injury to anybody or to an animal (which is restricted to horse, cattle, ass, mule, sheep, pig, goat or dog but not a cat), *or*

• damage to any vehicle (except the motorist's own car) or to other property which is attached to the road or adjoining land (e.g. if a wall, fence, tree, building or street furniture is damaged).

So to take an extreme example, a motorist who runs over a cat, and then collides with a piece of furniture left on the pavement, damaging both it and his own car, need not stop to provide particulars; nor indeed, need he report the accident to the police.

If motorists are obliged to stop, they must give their name and address and that of the owner of the vehicle, plus the vehicle number to anyone who reasonably requires it – in practice, other motorists and those who have suffered injury or damage. Motorists should remain at the scene for a reasonable time to allow time for persons to approach them. They are not required to give particulars of their insurance or to produce their driving licence to the other motorist.

In practice, of course, sensible motorists will do so, if only because by producing their insurance certificate they will usually remove the need to report the accident to the police (see below).

What is the position if the driver believes he has been recognized?

Scarll was involved in an accident which required that he stop and exchange particulars. Believing that the other driver knew him and would be able to contact him should he wish to do so, Scarll did not stop as required. Held. The driver was obliged to comply with the section even if he genuinely believed that he was known to a relevant party. Scarll (1989)

Both failure to stop and failure to provide particulars are endorsable offences, and an endorsement (plus 8–10 points) will be imposed unless there are special reasons (see page 693). If motorists can satisfy the court that they did not realize there had been an accident, they must be acquitted, but in practice that is a difficult defence to prove. See the penalty chart on page 708.

Failing to report an accident

A accident must be reported to the police if:
• someone was injured and at the time of the accident the motorists did not produce their insurance certificate to a police officers or someone reasonably entitled to ask for it (e.g. a traffic warden, someone injured), *or*
• they did not give their name and address at the time of the accident to someone reasonably entitled to ask for it.

So, if full particulars were exchanged at the time of the accident (including insurance details if someone was injured), motorists need not report the accident to the police. If there was no one present at the scene of the accident, and so there was nobody to ask for the particulars, motorists must report it to the police.

If the accident has to be reported, motorists should do so as soon as possible, and in no circumstances can they wait more than twenty-four hours. The accident must be reported in person; it is not good enough to phone the police station. If motorists are found guilty of failing to report the accident, their licence will be endorsed (and they will receive 8–10 points) unless they can show special reasons for not endorsing.

Note: for what to do when there is an accident, see page 712.

Drunk-driving

All solicitors have a steady flow of clients who come into their office with a drunk-driving summons, expecting that some sort of defence can be put up to the charge. For the vast majority of these people, the best advice that can be given is to plead guilty and not waste money on legal fees. It may be a difficult fact for the disgruntled motorist to accept, but in the overwhelming majority of drunk-driving cases there is no defence to the charge and they would be well advised to start the inevitable period of disqualification as early as possible.

In practical terms, once the police can show that the motorist was 'over the limit', then the chances of acquittal are virtually nil. The only possible defences are based on legal and scientific technicalities, but these apply only in the most exceptional cases.

There are five basic offences:

1 Driving or attempting to drive with excess alcohol,
2 Being in charge of a vehicle with excess alcohol,
3 Driving or attempting to drive while unfit through drink or drugs,
4 Being in charge of a vehicle while unfit through drink or drugs,
5 Failing to give a specimen (of breath, blood or urine) at a police station (there is a less serious offence of failing to give a roadside specimen).

The 'being in charge' offence covers motorists who are not driving – perhaps because they are so drunk that they are slumped across the steering wheel.

All of the first four offences must have been committed in a public place. So if the motorist was on private property all the time, no charge could be brought. In practice, of course, this is highly unlikely. Note that whether a place counts as 'private' or 'public' does not depend upon whether it is privately owned. If the public have access then it is likely to be a 'public' place (e.g. a pub car park is likely to be a public place during opening hours). Many offences may be committed in a 'public place' as well as a road.

'B' was seen driving in a multi-storey car park operated by a private company at 12.45 a.m. when only two other cars were parked in the car park. The prosecution produced evidence of use of the car park by the public and the absence of a barrier. Held. The car park was a public place. Bowman (1991)

In theory, the police cannot carry out random breath tests. In practice, however, they need have very little justification to carry out a test. All the police need to show is that they had suspicions that the driver had consumed alcohol. Note: they need not have suspected that the driver was over the limit; it is enough that they suspect the driver has had some alcohol, and so merely leaving a pub car park may be sufficient grounds for suspicion.

Alternatively, they can always carry out a test if there has been an accident or if the motorist has committed a moving traffic offence (e.g. one wheel crossing over a white line or a flickering rear light). It can be seen that these powers are extensive, and while the police cannot simply set up random breath tests as and where they wish, they do in practical terms have more than sufficient powers to stop drunk drivers. The net effect is that it is almost impossible for motorists to raise a defence based on the argument that the breath test was not legally justified, unless they can show that the police acted in bad faith.

Under the old breathalyser laws there were various technical defences that were successfully put up to breathalyser charges; despite the fact that the law was changed in 1983, there is still a popular belief that there are loopholes which any lawyer can exploit. In fact, the drunk driver will almost certainly be convicted. For instance, there used to be a dodge known as the 'hip flask defence', under which the motorist would have a quick drink after being stopped by the police and before having a breath test. Under the present law, the chances of that defence working have been drastically reduced since motorists must now prove that they would otherwise have been under the limit – and in practical terms that is often very difficult to prove. Similarly, under the old law there were complicated procedural steps that the police had to take, and the smallest breach of those rules would make the breath test invalid; under the new rules, minor procedural mistakes are ignored.

The level of alcohol

There are various ways of measuring the alcohol level, but they are all equivalent. Motorists will be guilty if they have more than 80 milligrams of alcohol in 100 millilitres of blood; 107 milligrams of alcohol in 100 millilitres of urine; or 35 micrograms of alcohol in 100 millilitres of breath. In practice, it is the last of these three levels that is applied, usually via use of the Intoximeter machine. To avoid the risk of mistakes, the police do not prosecute if the breath reading is less than 40 micrograms (even though the legal requirement is only 35 micrograms). In practice, therefore, there is little chance of a motorist being wrongly convicted.

Where a breath specimen provided at the police station shows a reading of less than 50 micrograms of alcohol in 100 millilitres of breath, the motorist will be offered an opportunity to provide an alternative specimen. The police will choose between a blood or urine specimen if the motorist takes this option. If it is offered the option should be taken, as alcohol is absorbed in the body over time, the new specimen should show a lower reading. While this new reading will rarely be below the limit, it is the alternative specimen's measurement which will be given to the court and the penalty will be related to it.

The penalty

Motorists convicted of driving with excess alcohol, driving whilst unfit or failing to give a police station specimen face a maximum penalty of up to six months in prison, a fine of £2,000 and disqualification for at least one year. The penalties for being in charge of a vehicle (i.e. not driving) are less. Note that the motorist who refuses to provide a breath specimen still faces automatic disqualification. In practice, these maximum penalties are rarely imposed. But disqualification is nearly always ordered – and it will be for at least twelve months (three years if the second disqualification in a ten-year period). Refer to the penalty chart on pages 708–10 for typical sentences for first-time offenders.

The crucial question for motorists is not likely to be, 'Will I be found guilty?' (because in practice, they will almost certainly be found guilty), but, 'Will I be disqualified?' Once again, the answer is that it is extremely likely that they will be disqualified. However, there are occasions when the court can find that there were special reasons surrounding the commission of the offence and that this justifies avoiding disqualification.

But the special reasons argument can be raised only in a few cases. This is because the 'special reasons' must apply to the way in which the offence was committed, and not to the effect that disqualification will have on the motorist. (Refer back to page 693, where there is a section on what can be a special reason for not having an endorsement, since identical principles apply when arguing that there are special reasons for not disqualifying drunk-driving. The essential point to grasp is that the special reasons must, in some way, explain how the offence was committed; they are not to be confused with the special circumstances of individual motorists that would make disqualification particularly inconvenient for them.

In practice, few motorists are able to argue 'special reasons'. For instance, these are all examples of cases in which motorists were not able to show special reasons (and so they lost their licences):

• the defendant is a careful person who would not have driven had he realized that he had drunk too much;

• he is a diabetic;

• although he failed the breathalyser tests, his driving ability was unimpaired;

• the excess alcohol level in the defendant's blood or urine was very small;

• drinking on an empty stomach caused the drinks to have an unusually powerful effect.

However, a sudden emergency can amount to a special reason. But it is for the defendant to prove that they would not otherwise have driven, and that they were forced to do so by a sudden medical emergency. A mere errand of mercy, or other non-medical emergency, will not be enough. For instance:

A motorist had been drinking. He heard that his business partner was stranded with his aged and ailing mother in a remote part of the country, having run out of petrol. He went to fetch them but was breathalysed en route. Held: This was not an emergency, since a garage, the A A, the R A C or the police could have assisted. Bains (1970)

The court considers the acuteness of the emergency, whether there was an alternative means of transport or help, and the standard of the defendant's driving.

Laced drinks can also be a special reason. But it is for defendants to prove that their excess alcohol level is due to alcohol that was put into their glass unknown to them. So in one case when a defendant thought he was drinking lager and lime, whereas in fact the drink contained vodka, he was able to claim a special reason and persuade the court not to disqualify him. It needs to be remembered that a person who laces another's drinks when they know that they are driving can themselves be prosecuted.

The following was a borderline case:

Mr Krebs was given a Harp lager by a friend. His glass was refilled four times and Mr Krebs thought the refills were also Harp. In fact they were Lowenbrau, a stronger lager. When breathalysed his reading was 92. Expert evidence was given that if the drinks had been Harp as Krebs believed, the reading would have been only 20. Held: Mr Krebs had shown a 'special reason' and so he was not disqualified. Krebs (1977)

Since drunk-driving is an absolute offence, it makes no difference whether the prescribed limit is exceeded by a large or a small amount. In either case the accused is guilty and the court will consider the amount of the excess only when deciding on the length of disqualification and the punishment. Similarly, it is irrelevant that the drink consumed did not affect the driving of the accused. Disqualification is automatic on conviction (see penalty chart on pages 708) for at least twelve months, unless the conviction is the motorist's second drunk-driving conviction in the last ten years, in which case the disqualification will be for at least three years.

Prison for drunk-drivers

In most parts of the country repeat offenders and those with very high alcohol readings will be sentenced to more than just a fine and disqualification. A second offence within a few years or a reading of twice the limit places motorists in difficulty and they cannot safely assume they will receive a fine. Even though they have no defence to the case, a solicitor may be necessary to seek to avoid prison. Aside from prison, the more constructive outcomes of community service and alcohol education programmes as a requirement of a probation order are now widely used.

CYCLISTS

Cyclists are subject to the same laws as other road users and, although they cannot be imprisoned or disqualified, they can be fined. For instance, a cyclist who disobeys a police officer's signal is subject to the same maximum fine, £400, as a car driver. There are, of course, various provisions that apply only to cyclists.

Dismounted cyclists who are pushing their bikes are legally 'riders', not 'pedestrians'. Thus they commit an offence if they wheel their bike past red traffic lights. However, there is an exception for cyclists who wheel their bikes over pedestrian crossings; for those purposes they are not cycling.

Cycles are subject to special parking controls. It is illegal to leave a bike in a dangerous position, on a footpath or on a traffic clearway. But cyclists need not obey painted yellow lines. Thus cyclists can leave their bike on the kerb beside a double yellow line unless it is a dangerous position or a clearway.

A cyclist can be convicted of being drunk in charge of a bike. But the normal breathalyser laws do not apply and of course there can be no disqualification (merely a fine of up to £400).

FIXED PENALTIES

Fixed penalties can be given for a great many road traffic offences. Since 1982 endorsable offences including speeding are among the offences which can be dealt with in this way. There will be even more 'tickets' issued in the future. Plans are well advanced to detect offences of speeding and crossing red traffic lights by means of cameras and computers which will process 'offenders' like sausage machines. What if a motorist is offered a fixed penalty?

To accept a fixed penalty is to accept guilt for the offence in question. The considerations discussed on page 688 apply but with the difference that the motorist knows in advance the penalty. If the fixed penalty is being offered for an endorsable offence, the effect of the penalty points will make these considerations all the more important. For most motorists who have offended, a fixed penalty represents a bargain offer and should be snapped up. It avoids costs and a fine which would almost certainly be more than the fixed penalty.

A mistake made by many motorists is ignoring a fixed penalty. If a motorist is wrongly 'ticketed' it is up to the motorist to take action (indicated on the ticket) to seek a court hearing. If no action is taken proceedings will automatically go through to the point where bailiffs or police officers call for the penalty, which at that point will have been increased by at least 50 per cent and will be treated as a fine.

PENALTIES FOR MOTORING OFFENCES

How to use the penalty chart

The penalty chart on the next few pages sets out the main motoring offences and gives rough guidelines for sentences for first offenders. It cannot be emphasized too strongly that these are no more than very approximate guidelines, and under no circumstances should they be seen as definite recommendations. The aim of the penalty chart is simply to give an approximate indication of the author's guess of 'going rates' in 1992. In the near future a 'unit fine' system will apply nationwide which will relate fines directly to offence facts and the defendant's income.

Offence	Endorse? (points)	Disqualify?	Maximum penalty	Likely penalty
ACCIDENTS				
Fail to stop	Must (8–10)	May	£2,000	£150
Fail to report to police	Must (8–10)	May	£2,000	£150
ALCOHOL				
Driving while unfit	Must (4 if no disq.)	Must 12 months	£2,000 6 months prison	£250 prison and longer disq. possible
Driving while over limit	Must (4 if no disq.)	Must 12 months	£2,000 6 months prison	£250, + prison + longer disq. for high levels
Failing to give specimen at roadside	Must (4)	May	£500	£100
Failing to give specimen at police station	Must (4 if no disq.)	Must 12 months	£2,000 6 months prison	£250, + prison + longer disq. for high levels
In charge while unfit	Must (10)	May	£2,000 3 months prison	£200
In charge while over limit	Must (10)	May	£2,000 3 months prison	£200
DEFECTIVE PARTS				
Defective brakes (private vehicle)	Must (3)	May	£1,000	£60
Defective steering (private vehicle)	Must (3)	May	£1,000	£60
Defective tyres (private vehicle)	Must (3)	May	£1,000	£60
Defective brakes (goods vehicle)	Must (3)	May	£2,000	£150
Defective steering (goods vehicle)	Must (3)	May	£2,000	£150
Defective tyres (goods vehicle)	Must (3)	May	£2,000	£150
Defective (or no) lights	No	No	£2,000	£50
Other parts offences	No	No	£1,000	£30

Offence	Endorse? (points)	Disqualify?	Maximum penalty	Likely penalty
DISQUALIFIED DRIVER				
Driving while disqualified	Must (6)	May	£2,000 6 months' prison	£300 + options including prison
DOCUMENTS				
Failing to produce licence or insurance or test certificate	No	No	£500	£25 each
No insurance	Must (6–8)	May	£1,000	£200
No driving licence (no entitlement)	Must	May	£500	£80
No excise licence ('road tax')	No	No	£500 or 5 × duty lost	relates to duty lost
No test certificate	No	No	£500	£40
Failing to notify ownership change	No	No	£500	£60
DOUBLE WHITE LINES				
Failing to comply	Must (3)	May	£500	£60
DRIVING				
Reckless driving	Must (10)	May*	£2,000 6 months' prison	£400 + options including prison
Careless or inconsiderate driving	Must (3–9)	May	£1,000	£120
PARKING				
Parking in dangerous position	Must (3)	May	£500	£60
Parking within pedestrian crossing	Must (3)	May	£500	£60
Obstruction	No	No	£500	£50
SAFETY EQUIPMENT				
No safety helmet	No	No	£200	£30
No seat belt	No	No	£200	£30
SPEEDING				
Excess speed	Must (3)	May	£500	£3 for each m.p.h. over limit, disq. for high speeds

Offence	Endorse? (points)	Disqualify?	Maximum penalty	Likely penalty
TRAFFIC SIGNS				
Failing to obey traffic lights	Must (3)	May	£500	£60
Other traffic signs	*	*	£500	£50
MOTORWAYS				
Driving in reverse	Must (3)	May	£1,000	£200
Driving in wrong direction	Must (3)	May	£1,000	£300 disq. likely
Driving off carriageway	Must (3)	May	£1,000	£100
Driving on sliproad in prohibited direction	Must (3)	May	£1,000	£100
'U' turn on motorway	Must (3)	May	£1,000	£200
Stopping on hard shoulder	No	No	£1,000	£60
Unlawful use of third lane	Must (3)	May	£1,000	£150
Walking on motorway	No	No	£1,000	£50
DISHONESTY				
Taking vehicle without consent	No	May	£2,000	*
Aggravated vehicle taking	No	May	£2,000	*

* Powers depend upon exact circumstances of offence or record of offender.

51 Road Accidents

Most drivers like to think that accidents happen to other people and not to them, but the statistics tell a different story. Even the most careful motorist is likely to be involved in an accident at some time and it is only sensible to know what to do when an accident occurs.

See page 712 for what to do and what not to do when an accident happens.

The lawyer's basic advice is, 'Say nothing – write down everything.' Remember that responsibility for the accident (and for the resulting losses, expenses and injuries) will depend upon who was to blame. What motorists say in the heat of the moment can be distorted and used against them in a court months or even years later. For instance, most people's natural inclination when speaking to a person injured by a collision with their car is to say, 'I'm sorry', but this can easily be misconstrued as meaning, 'I am sorry I caused the accident', rather than, 'I am sorry you have been injured.'

The motorist should take a note of the names and addresses of the other parties. Vehicle registration numbers and insurance details should also be recorded, if possible. The names and addresses of witnesses should also be obtained or, failing that, a note should be made of their car numbers so they can be traced through the Vehicle Records Office (see page 693). All the details of the accident should be recorded. There should be a sketch plan showing the positions of all vehicles, road signs, road widths, obstructions to vision, position of witnesses, the location of any wreckage or debris, and so on. It is also useful to make a note of the road and weather conditions, the damage to other vehicles and the apparent extent of anybody's injuries.

Vehicles should not be moved until their positions have been recorded on a plan or marked on the road surface; evidence as to the point of impact is often crucial in working out how an accident occurred and whose fault it was.

Unless the accident is trivial, it is advisable to call the police, even though they are not obliged to attend and may refuse to do so if there are no injuries and if the damage is small. If the police do attend, it is advisable to make a note of the officers' numbers. The police will probably ask those involved to make short statements, but motorists should remember that what they say will be written down and a copy will eventually be supplied to the other motorist's insurers and lawyers. That being so, it is best to say nothing at this stage, beyond politely explaining to the police officer that you would rather not make a statement for the moment. However, the police can demand to be told the motorist's name and address (and that of the owner, if different), plus the vehicle, insurance and MOT particulars. This information should obviously be provided if requested.

IF YOU ARE INVOLVED IN A ROAD ACCIDENT

Don't:

1 Assault or abuse the other driver.
2 Apologize, offer excuses or say anything that could later be used to suggest that you admitted responsibility for causing the accident – unless, of course, you clearly were to blame.
3 Move the vehicles until their positions have been recorded.
4 Make a statement to the police at this stage. Wait until you have calmed down. However, you are obliged to give your name, address and vehicle registration number, and to produce your driving licence, MOT certificate and (if anyone has been injured) your insurance certificate.

Do:

1 Stop and remain at the scene for enough time to allow anyone else involved to speak to you.
2 Call the police and note number of police officer attending.
3 Note names and addresses of everyone involved. The other drivers must give you their names, addresses and vehicle registration numbers, and (if anyone has been injured) provide insurance details; similarly, you must provide them with this information on request.
4 Ask witnesses for their names and addresses. If these are not available, note their vehicle registration numbers if they are in cars, so that they can be traced at a later date.
5 Write down any comments or explanations made by any party to the accident or by a witness.
6 Note the apparent damage to any vehicles and the apparent extent of injuries suffered.

Afterwards

1 While the facts are still fresh in your mind, make a full description of exactly what happened. Note time, road conditions, road layout, signposts, damage to vehicles, any vision obstructions, other traffic, road markings, point of impact etc. If you have a camera, take photos.
2 Report the accident to your insurance company.
3 Write to the motorist who is to blame, claiming damages for any loss, expenses and injury suffered.
4 If you have any injury see a doctor. The examination may provide vital evidence to be used at a later stage.

Reporting the accident

To whom should the accident be reported? If the police attend there will be no need to notify them, but if they did not attend and particulars were not given to the other people involved, then the accident will have to be reported as soon as possible. See page 701 for the duty to stop after an accident to provide particulars to other people, and to report the accident to the police.

It will also be necessary for motorists to report the accident to their insurers. Most policies require that the accident be reported within seven days or else the insurance will not cover that accident or future accidents. Further, if the policy is renewed with no mention of the accident having been made to the insurers, then the motorist will not have acted in 'perfectly good faith' and so the insurers will be able to declare that the policy is invalid (see page 675). 'Reporting' an accident to insurers is, of course, different from 'claiming' under the policy and will not, itself, affect the motorist's no-claims bonus. For a specimen letter to the insurance company see page 677.

When filling in the insurer's accident report form, motorists should be perfectly honest and provide all the information that supports their version of how the accident happened. If the accident was not their fault, then they should say so clearly and unambiguously. The accident report form will contain questions similar to those asked when the proposal form was completed on the insurance being taken out. The insurers may well compare the two sets of answers to check that the motorist has not been in breach of the policy in any way (e.g. by using the car for unauthorized business travel) and that full and truthful answers were given when the insurance was first taken out. Any discrepencies may allow the insurers to 'repudiate liability' under the policy and so refuse to meet any claims.

APPORTIONING BLAME

Motorists who have been involved in a road accident will recover compensation for their injuries, losses and other damage only if they have a comprehensive policy or can show that someone else was to blame for the accident.

If they have a comprehensive policy and a motorist claims on that policy, they will generally lose part of their no-claims bonus and will have to pay the excess – the first few pounds of the claim. If motorists have a third-party policy, it will indemnify them only for damages due to another person as a result of their own negligent driving; it will not compensate them for their own losses, however caused.

If they can show that someone else was to blame for the accident, they will be able to claim from that person's insurers.

So unless motorists have a comprehensive policy they will have no automatic right to compensation. Generally, therefore, the right to compensation will be dependent upon showing that someone else was to blame for the accident. If that can be proved, then that person (and their insurers) will have to pay compensation.

Before dealing with the mechanics of making a claim against another motorist, one must first understand how the law apportions and fixes 'blame' for motoring accidents.

Negligence

The law says that all motorists have a duty to take reasonable care to avoid injury, loss and damage to other road users. If they do not, they must compensate those other road users for the injury, loss and damage incurred. In short, they must pay them damages for their negligence.

The problems arise when one tries to apply that seemingly simple idea to practical events, for it is always a question of deciding whether or not the duty to take care has been broken. Clearly, if the 'reasonable' man or woman would not have acted as the motorist did, then there will have been a breach of the duty of care, and thus negligence, but the concept of this 'reasonable' individual is not as simple as it sounds. As a starting-point ask yourself, 'Who was to blame, bearing in mind that the "reasonable" motorist never disobeys the Highway Code and is always alert to the possibility of other motorists being less careful that they should be?' Usually, common sense will supply the answer. Frequently, an accident will not be due to the 'negligence' of just one motorist; the other motorist(s) may have contributed to the accident by being less careful than they should have been, and so they are to a degree to blame themselves. In such cases, the law apportions the blame between the motorists and each will lose a corresponding proportion of their damages for the 'contributory negligence'.

Illustration. A Ford pulls up and a Vauxhall runs into the the back of it. Every motorist has a 'duty of care' to drive in such a way that he or she can pull up in an emergency without hitting the car in front. The Vauxhall's driver is in breach of this duty and thus negligent, and so liable to pay damages to the Ford's owner.

But suppose the accident occurred on the motorway and that the Ford stopped in the carriageway without giving any signal. Then the Ford's driver would have been in breach of his duty – first, not to stop on the motorway and, secondly, to signal his intentions, while the Vauxhall would have been in breach of her duty to keep a lookout for obstructions on the road and to take avoiding action. Thus a court might find both sides equally to blame and give them both only 50 per cent of their full damages.

However, suppose that the Ford had pulled up at a pedestrian crossing, and that the Vauxhall's driver had seen this and tried to brake but hit the Ford because of a brake failure. If the Vauxhall owner had no way of knowing that the brakes were faulty, and had the car serviced regularly, she could not be said to be to blame. She had taken 'reasonable care to avoid injury, loss and damage to other road users' and this accident arose through an entirely unforeseeable failure of her brakes. Thus the Vauxhall would not be negligent and the Ford could not recover damages from her. The only way the Ford would be able to recover any compensation is if he could:

● claim under his own comprehensive policy (but this would cost him his excess and no-claims bonus), *or*

● show that someone else, other than the Vauxhall, was negligent and that this negligence caused what was a reasonably foreseeable accident.

For example, if the Vauxhall was new then the Ford might have a claim against the Vauxhall manufacturers because they were in breach of their duty to the general public to fit sound brakes to new cars. Alternatively, if the Vauxhall was not new, a garage that had recently serviced its brakes might owe a duty to the Ford's driver (as a road user) to ensure that the Vauxhall brakes were working correctly.

All road users, whether motorists or pedestrians, have a duty to take care. For instance, if a careless pedestrian is injured by a careless driver, then the pedestrian will forfeit some, if not all, his or her damages.

Mrs Clifford stepped on to a pedestrian crossing when Mr Drymond's car was some 25–30 yards away and travelling at 26–30 m.p.h. She was hit by the car when she was on the crossing. Held: Mr Drymond was negligent because the reasonable motorist keeps a proper lookout for pedestrians when approaching a pedestrian crossing. But Mrs Clifford was also negligent because the reasonable pedestrian does not step on to a crossing without first checking that the oncoming cars can stop in time. Liability was apportioned with Mr Drymond being 80 per cent to blame and Mrs Clifford 20 per cent to blame. So Mrs Clifford recovered only 80 per cent of the normal damages. Clifford (1976)

What about learners?

The duty of care owed by a learner driver is the same as that owed by any other 'reasonable motorist'. Learners cannot escape liability by arguing that they were doing their incompetent best.

Mr Nettleship agreed to give Miss Weston driving lessons. She was a careful learner but on the third lesson she failed to straighten out after turning left; the car hit a lamp standard and Mr Nettleship's kneecap was broken. He sued Miss Weston for damages but she argued that she was not in breach of her duty to take care – she had taken all the care that she, as a learner, could take. Held: No. She was liable. As a motorist, she was required to drive to the standard of the 'reasonable' motorist not the 'reasonable learner motorist'. Nettleship (1971)

Breaking the Highway Code

Generally, the fact that a motorist did not obey the Highway Code will be a good starting-point for fixing blame. But it does not always follow that the 'reasonable road user' would have observed the Highway Code and so negligence may not attach. For instance:

Motoring

Miss Powell was struck by a car while walking along the left-hand side of the road at night. She had not been walking on the pavement because it was covered by snow, and she was not wearing light-coloured clothes. The car had been travelling quickly and without proper lights. The motorist argued that she was 25 per cent to blame for not observing the Highway Code. Held: No. Whilst she was in breach of the Highway Code she had not been negligent, and so she recovered 100 per cent damages from the negligent motorist. Powell (1972)

Mechanical defects

The essence of attaching blame is that the defendant failed to take proper care. Generally, therefore, if an accident happens because of a latent mechanical defect that he or she could not have known of, they cannot be liable in negligence. However, it will be for the defendant to show that they took all necessary steps to stop the danger arising, for otherwise they will be liable. For example:

A five-year-old lorry suffered a brake failure and killed George Henderson. His widow sued the owners of the lorry for negligence. They argued that they were not to blame since the accident had been caused by a latent defect in the brakes. They had visually inspected the brakes every week, but the failure occurred in a hidden pipe that could not be seen. Held: They were liable, since they had not conclusively shown that they had taken all steps to avoid the risk of brake failure. Henderson (1969)

On the other hand:

Mr Saville bought a seven-year-old car (which had done about 75,000 miles) for £650. It went well enough. There were no odd noises, and it had eight months' MOT left. Three weeks later he lost control of the steering and crashed into a parked car. Examination showed that the steering arm had collapsed. Was he liable (in practice, of course, was his insurance company liable) in damages to the owner of the parked car? Held: No. In the circumstances, he had acted reasonably since he had no reason to think there was any problem with the car. It was unreasonable to expect anyone who bought a car with a recent MOT to have it examined by an expert engineer. So, he was not to blame – and the innocent motorist went uncompensated. Rees (1983)

When both motorists could have been to blame

Often there is no clear proof of who was to blame – perhaps because there were no witnesses and the drivers cannot clearly recall what happened. When this happens, liability is often divided fifty/fifty between them and they both recover half their normal damages from each other. This is often applied when two vehicles meet head-on in a narrow country road or collide at crossroads of equal status.

Two cars collided head-on at night. There were no witnesses; one driver was killed and the other was so seriously injured that he had no recollection of what happened. There was no evidence of what happened apart from marks on one side of the road. Held: It was no more probable that the accident had occurred on one side of the road than in the middle of the road, and accordingly both drivers were equally to blame. Both insurance companies had to pay 50 per cent damages. Howard (1973)

Flashing headlights

It is common for motorists to flash their headlights as a 'come on' sign. What happens if a driver obeys the signal only to find that it is not safe to do so and collides with another motorist? The answer is that the mere flashing of lights does not absolve motorists from their normal duty of care to other road users. In fact the motorist who is hit by the car will usually be able to sue the motorist who acted on the flashing lights, and occasionally even the motorist who negligently flashed their lights when it was not safe. However, this presupposes (as always) that they were negligent, and exceptionally this will not be so.

A car was in a side street waiting to cross a congested main road. A bus driver in the main road stopped and flashed his headlights at the car to indicate that he would let him cross. The car pulled out very slowly but collided with a motorcyclist that was overtaking the stationary bus. Could the motorcyclist sue the car driver and/or the bus driver? Held: No. On the particular facts of the case neither driver had been negligent. The car driver had come out with very great care and so did nothing wrong. The bus driver was also not negligent because the court held that the flashing of lights did not mean, 'It is safe for you to cross', but merely, 'Come on as far as I am concerned.' The motorcyclist did not receive any compensation. Clarke (1969)

Not wearing seat belts

While all road users have a duty to take care not to harm other people, they also have a duty to look after themselves. An obvious way of reducing the severity of injuries received in a car accident is to wear a seat belt; people who do not do so will probably be held not to have taken sufficient care to look after themselves. Thus they too will have been negligent and so any damages they receive will be reduced proportionately to allow for their own negligence.

This assumes, of course, that there were seat belts fitted to the car, and also that wearing the seat belt would have minimized the injuries. If it can be shown that the seat belt would not have prevented injury, then the negligence in not wearing it will be ignored as being irrelevant. But such cases are rare and the general rule is that failure to wear a seat belt will result in a 25 per cent reduction in damages.

Mr Froom was injured in a car crash but he was not wearing the seat belt fitted to his car. He suffered head and chest injuries and also a broken finger. The medical evidence was that, apart from the broken finger, the injuries would probably have been prevented if he had been wearing the seat belt. In reply Mr Froom argued that he did not like wearing a belt for fear of being trapped in the vehicle after a crash and besides, he did not drive at more than normal speed. Held: The reasonable motorist guards against the possibility of negligence by other road users by wearing a seat belt, since statistics show that the chance of injury increases fourfold when a seat belt is not worn. Where injuries would have been totally prevented by wearing a seat belt the damages should be reduced by 25 per cent. When the injuries would have been 'a good deal less severe', the damages should be reduced by 15 per cent. In Mr Froom's case a reduction of 20 per cent should be made. Froom (1975)

For the criminal penalties on not wearing a seat belt see page 681.

When the negligent motorist cannot be traced

The victims of hit and run accidents may have no one to sue, since the negligent motorists will have disappeared. Similarly, if the motorists stopped but gave false particulars, the victim will be unable to sue them.

When this happens the Motor Insurers' Bureau (MIB) will compensate the victims. The MIB is funded by the insurance industry and it will nominate an insurance company to deal with the claim as though the untraced motorist was insured with them. However, as with claims against uninsured motorists, the claim must be restricted to compensation for personal injury and damage to property exceeding £175.

The 'negligence' basis of compensation

Under our legal system victims of a road accident have no automatic right to compensation. Unless they can show that someone else was to blame for the accident, their only source of financial help is likely to be DSS benefits such as sickness benefit, and perhaps some compensation from their insurance company if they were motorists with a comprehensive insurance policy. If no one else can be blamed for the accident, then the law will not entitle them to receive compensation.

A five-year-old boy ran out into the road from behind a parked car; he was running to an ice-cream van on the other side of the road. He was seriously injured by a passing car, even though the car was travelling only at 15 m.p.h. He sued (through his parents), arguing that the motorist had been negligent. Held: The motorist had not been negligent and so the little boy was not entitled to any compensation. The only way the motorist could have avoided hitting the boy would have been if he had been driving at 5 m.p.h. It was not reasonable to expect that, and so he was not liable. The five-year-old went without compensation. Kite (1983)

Even if the injured person can show that someone else was to blame, they may be held to have been negligent themselves and so forfeit some of their damages. For instance, motorists who do not wear their seat belts are likely to lose between 15 and 25 per cent of their damages (see page 717).

The present system of compensation is based on blame, and negligence denies compensation to thousands of people every year. There are some 400,000 road accident injuries every year, including 7,600 fatal accidents. Of these, only about one-quarter of the victims obtain compensation. The others either are unable to show that anyone else was negligent or do not bother to sue – presumably because of the costs and delay involved.

CLAIMING COMPENSATION

If you intend to make a claim against another road user, then:

1 Drive or tow the car home or to a garage and keep any receipt.
2 Report the accident to your own insurers. If you have a comprehensive policy, notify them that no claim is being made against them (see letter on page 677).
3 If the claim is substantial or involves anything other than very minor personal injury, consult a solicitor. If the claim is successful, and it is for more than £1,000, the other side will have to pay most of your legal costs.
4 Ask the garage for a written estimate of the cost of repairs. If the vehicle is a write-off, ask for their written confirmation that it is 'beyond economical repair' and their estimate of its pre-accident value.
5 Write to the other motorist, claiming damages. A typical letter might read:
I refer to the accident on – – – – – at – – – – – involving motor car no. – – – – – . This accident was caused by your negligent driving of a motor vehicle and accordingly damages are claimed for the personal injury, losses, expenses and inconvenience arising therefrom.
The wreckage is at present with Messrs – – – – – at – – – – – and can be inspected by you or your insurers on an appointment being made with Mr – – – – – . Please ensure that an inspection is made within the next fourteen days, failing which the necessary repairs will be put in hand (or the wreckage will be disposed of).
6 Keep a full note of all losses and expenses arising out of the accident.
7 Do not have the repairs carried out until you are fairly sure that the insurers will meet the cost or that your claim will be successful, for the garage bill will be your responsibility.
The insurers will be evasive and slow correspondents, but do not let them slow down the handling of the claim. If necessary, you should pester them with letters. If the repairs will involve replacing worn parts with new parts, the insurers will expect you to pay 'betterment' (i.e. a contribution to the cost) since the car will now be in a better condition than it was before the accident. They are entitled to insist on such a contribution, but always check that they are not charging too much.
8 Alternatively, if the vehicle is a write-off, try to agree a figure for its pre-accident value. Use local newspaper advertisements and garage estimates to support your valuation. Also check your insurance proposal form to see what valuation you placed on the car then. Do not be unrealistic about the valuation; insurance engineers can accurately assess the pre-accident condition of a vehicle from the wreckage and will detect untrue statements about

the car's recorded mileage, interior condition etc. Once the insurers agree that the vehicle is 'beyond economical repair', then take steps to dispose of the wreckage, as the insurers will not be liable for storage charges from that date.

It may be that you cannot afford to buy a replacement vehicle until the insurance moneys are received. But you probably cannot recover extra compensation for the increased period of inconvenience when you are without a car, nor for the cost of interest on money borrowed to buy the replacement car. As far as the law is concerned, your financial status (or lack of it) is irrelevant and the defendant should not have to pay higher damages just because you are hard up.

9 If the car has been repaired, you will generally be expected to pay the garage and to recover the amount afterwards from the insurers. Losses and expenses incurred in collecting the car will form part of the claim.

10 Formulate the amount of the claim. Include all losses and expenses reasonably incurred as a result of the accident, unless they are too unlikely. Items that can be legitimately claimed include the cost of travel home after the accident, travel to pick up the car, wages lost, stamps, telephone calls, private medical fees, prescriptions, new clothing to replace clothing damaged in the accident (but allow something for the fact that the damaged clothing was not new), cost of hiring a replacement vehicle (it must be of a suitable type; i.e. a Mini owner shouldn't hire a Rover), and also losses and expenses incurred by members of your family, although strictly speaking they should be separate claims. If a vehicle isn't hired while the damaged car is being repaired, then claim the cost of bus, rail and taxi fares incurred, plus a small amount for inconvenience. However, allowance must be made for the money saved on not having to buy petrol, oil etc. A figure of £20 per week for inconvenience and compensation for loss of use of the car is generally acceptable.

If possible, all these items of expense should be proved by receipts. Wage losses can be proved by a letter from the employer setting out the net (i.e. after tax) loss. If any DSS benefits were received (such as sickness benefit, invalidity benefit) as a result of the accident, then one-half of their total should be deducted from the wage loss; unemployment and supplementary benefits are deducted in full when working out the wage loss.

Set out all these financial losses (called 'special damage' by lawyers) in list form and send them to the insurers. If there was any injury sustained in the accident, try to negotiate a suitable figure for that as well, but it is important to remember that all but the most trivial personal injury claims should be handled by a solicitor. As a layperson you may, unwittingly, settle your case for less than it is worth or you may not appreciate that what seems to be a trivial injury could have serious long-term consequences.

11 The insurers will probably handle the claim very slowly. If you have a claim that is sound on liability (i.e. the other motorist was definitely to blame) you

may well find it best to commence county court proceedings against the other motorist. This will almost certainly cause the insurance company to deal with the claim without any further delay. The steps to be taken to sue in the county court are set out in Chapter 68. The specimen pleadings in Appendix 2 are from a claim arising out of a minor road accident.

Insurance brokers

Sometimes a motorist's insurance broker will offer to negotiate the claim with the insurance company for him or her. The motorist should check in advance what the broker's fee will be.

These brokers do not have to belong to a professional body and accordingly motorists should try to ensure that their broker is competent and honest, for otherwise they may find that their claim has been under-settled. If the accident involved any personal injury, it is advisable to use a solicitor rather than a broker.

If the broker cannot negotiate a proper settlement and the next step is to start court proceedings, he or she will no longer be able to act. Only a solicitor can sue on behalf of someone else. There is thus a temptation for brokers to under-settle claims and so recover commission, when a solicitor might have commenced proceedings and ended up with a larger amount of compensation for the client.

On-the-spot settlements

When an accident happens negligent motorists may offer innocent motorists an immediate cash settlement on a 'let's not bother with the police' basis. If motorists are offered such a settlement, they should reject it. First, it may be an offence not to report the accident to the police (see page 701) and, secondly, the claim may be worth much more than they are being offered. Only when a mechanic has inspected the car and a doctor checked any injuries should such a settlement be contemplated. Whether or not the offer is accepted, the accident will still need to be reported to the motorist's own insurers (see page 713).

Negligent motorists who offer on-the-spot settlements may do so because they want to retain their no-claims bonus. If so, they should settle the claim by writing to the other motorist as follows:

I refer to the motor accident at ----- on -----. As agreed, although I am not admitting any liability, I am prepared to pay you £----- in full and final settlement of all your claims arising from that accident, and accordingly I enclose a cheque for that amount. Please acknowledge safe receipt by signing the attached copy of this letter and returning it to me.

This ensures that the other motorist cannot come back and claim more money at a future date.

PART EIGHT

CIVIL LIBERTIES

52 Police Powers and Individual Liberty

HELPING THE POLICE

The general rule is that no one is obliged to help the police with their inquiries. It may be one's social or even moral duty to do so, but there is no law which says that one must. All the law requires is that one should not give false information to the police or waste police time (anyone who does is liable to a fine of up to level 4 – see page 772 – and up to six months' imprisonment).

But of course most people do help the police. If everyone stood on their constitutional rights and refused to cooperate, the task of the police would become impossible.

When the police stop someone in the street and ask them to 'Come down to the station and help us with our inquiries', that request can be refused. The only way the police can make someone accompany them to the police station is to *arrest* them, and that can be done only in certain circumstances.

The Police and Criminal Evidence Act 1984 changed the rules on the treatment of people who are 'helping the police with their inquiries'. But it still preserves the right of the suspect to refuse to help the police with their inquiries, and to leave the police station. The Home Office Code of Practice (issued under the Act) says:

Any person attending a police station voluntarily for the purpose of assisting with an investigation may leave at will unless placed under arrest. If it is decided that he should not be allowed to do so then he must be informed at once that he is under arrest ... If he is not placed under arrest but is cautioned ... the officer who gives the caution must at the same time inform him that he is not under arrest and that he is not obliged to remain at the police station but that if he remains at the police station he may obtain legal advice if he wishes.

So the basic rule is that the police can keep someone in the police station only if arrested or if they voluntarily agree to being held by them. (But see Searching Someone, page 735).

The police have considerably more powers in dealing with suspects accused of terrorist offences (see below).

A SUSPECT'S RIGHTS – ARREST

The police cannot arrest anyone unless they have lawful authority to do so, for otherwise they run the risk of being sued for damages for false imprisonment and/or assault. With the more serious offences (generally those for which the maximum sentence could be five years or more in prison), a police officer automatically has power to arrest a suspect (see the list below). The police can also obtain an arrest warrant from a magistrate, although the powers of the police to arrest are now so wide that it is rarely necessary for them to do so. A warrant is obtained by 'laying an information': the police will hand in a written statement to the court and give evidence on oath. If the magistrate decides that there is a prima facie case against the accused, the warrant will be issued. The police can then serve the warrant on the accused and arrest the suspect.

Arrest without a Warrant

The police can arrest someone without the need for a warrant if:

1 The person has committed, is in the act of committing, or is reasonably suspected to be committing, any 'arrestable' offence. An arrestable offence is an offence that could lead to five years', or more, imprisonment. Also included are: armed assault, arson, actual bodily harm; burglary; death by reckless driving; demanding money with menaces; dishonest handling; drug offences; grievous bodily harm; living off immoral earnings; manslaughter; murder; some firearm offences; rape; indecent assault, and other serious sex offences; taking a motor vehicle without authority; theft (including shoplifting); and wounding. (Note: this is not a complete list of all arrestable offences.)
2 The person is guilty or is reasonably suspected of being guilty of an arrestable offence which has already taken place.
3 The person is reasonably suspected of being guilty of an arrestable offence which the police officer reasonably suspects has occurred.
4 The person is or is reasonably suspected of being about to commit an arrestable offence.
5 The person is seen breaching the peace or is acting so that a breach of the peace is likely to occur. A breach of the peace occurs 'whenever harm is actually done or is likely to be done to a person or in his presence to his property or a person is in fear of being so harmed through an assault, an affray, a riot or an unlawful assembly or other disturbance'.
6 The person: is drunk and incapable of caring for him- or herself; refused to take (or fails to take) a breath test; is soliciting; or refused to give his or her name and address when legally obliged to (e.g. a motorist involved in an accident).
7 The person is suspected of driving while disqualified or under the influence of drink or drugs.

8 The person is suspected of committing: an offence relating to the control of alcohol at sporting events, an affray, disorderly behaviour or conduct or failing to comply with lawful directions given by the police in respect to marches and demonstrations.

A variety of other obscure powers also give police officers and others powers of arrest.

A private individual can arrest someone without the need for a warrant (a 'citizen's arrest') if the offence comes within paragraph 1, 2 or 5 above.

In addition a police officer can arrest a person for any offence if the police officer has reasonable doubts either about a suspect's name or address or about whether the summons procedure can be used at the address given. A person can also be arrested by a police officer if there are reasonable grounds for believing that it will prevent: the person injuring him- or herself or others, suffering any other injury, harm to any vulnerable person, loss or damage to property, an offence against public decency or the obstruction of the highway.

A person who is arrested must be informed of this fact and of the grounds for the arrest either at the time or as soon as practicable.

Rights on detention

As soon as a suspect is detained, he or she must be told why, and also that the following rights now apply:
● the right to see a solicitor (see page 732);
● the right to have someone told of the detention (see page 737);
● the right to look at the codes of practice that the police should follow (in particular, to read the detailed detention code – see above).

In addition, the custody officer (i.e. the police officer responsible for all detained suspects – a different police officer from the one dealing with the suspect's case; usually a sergeant) must give the suspect a written note of these three legal rights. That written note will also include the usual caution (i.e. 'You do not have to say anything unless you wish to do so, but what you say may be given in evidence').

Police questioning

A suspect cannot be made to help the police. If he or she simply refuses to answer the police questions then there is nothing (in theory, anyway) that the police can do about it. First, there is a fundamental legal principle which says that a suspect's silence is not to be held against him or her. In other words, the mere fact that he or she did not answer questions is not to be used as an argument that he or she must have something to hide! Secondly, the police should not use force or pressure to get answers to their questions. For instance, the code says: 'No police officer may try to obtain answers to questions . . . by the use of oppression, or shall indicate, except in answer to a direct question, what action will be taken if . . . the person makes a statement or refuses . . .'

If a person agrees to help the police (or if they are arrested), there are rules of conduct governing the manner in which they are to be questioned. The Police and Criminal Evidence Act 1984 sets out basic guidelines that have to be followed, and these are backed up by a detailed code of practice on the detention, treatment and questioning of detainees (generally called the detention code). The code sets out the rules that the police should follow, but these rules are not totally binding on the police. (But see Remedies: Police Complaints, page 731.) So if a police officer conducts an interview that does not follow the rules, it does not necessarily follow that the evidence obtained will be inadmissible – that is for the trial judge to decide. The judge will probably rule it out only if the interview was oppressive or where it would be unfair to include it.

There are other rules that the police have to observe, many of which are aimed at ensuring that unfair pressure is not put on suspects. For instance, cells must be clean. There should be two light meals and one main meal each day. The suspect must be allowed at least eight hours' rest each day; interview rooms must be properly heated; suspects are not to be made to stand; there must be a break from interviewing at normal meal times and – as a general rule – there should be short refreshment breaks every two hours. The code sets out extremely detailed guidelines that should be followed. Another safeguard for the accused is that police must give a verbal 'caution'. The caution reminds the suspect of the fundamental legal right not to answer questions – 'You do not have to say anything unless you wish to do so, but what you say may be given in evidence.' If the suspect has not been arrested but is merely 'helping the police with their inquiries' (i.e. voluntarily agreeing to be questioned – see above), then the caution must state the fundamental legal right: the right to leave the police station (and also to take legal advice).

To summarize, the caution always tells the suspect that he or she does not have to answer questions. But if the suspect has not been arrested, then he or she must also be told that they are free to leave. The caution has to be repeated at various stages of the police investigation. In particular, it has to be given (and repeated):

● when a suspect is arrested;

● when a suspect is about to be interviewed;

● if there is a short break in the interview then he or she must usually be reminded he or she is still under caution when the interview restarts.

The police often ignore these rules. If the police should conduct their questioning in an improper manner, it is difficult for the suspect to prove afterwards that the rules were broken. And, of course, even if he or she can prove that the rules were not followed, the judge who hears the case may still allow the evidence to be heard.

STATEMENTS AND ANSWERING QUESTIONS

A suspect need not give a statement to the police or answer any questions and, unless there is a straightforward explanation, he or she is usually best advised to 'say nothing'. There are several reasons for this:

• He or she will probably be upset and shaken by having been held in a police station and questioned. It would be unwise to make a statement in this disturbed condition – much better to wait until he or she has received legal advice and had a day or two in which to recover his or her composure.

• The statement will probably reveal how he or she intends to defend him- or herself should the case go to court. Since the whole procedure at a criminal trial is based on the adversarial principle of 'your side' against 'their side', it is obviously bad tactics to reveal one's case this early in the proceedings.

• If the suspect does make a statement or answer questions he or she should check that the record is accurate before signing it, or write it out him- or herself (and so avoid arguments about its accuracy).

Obviously, the police will urge the suspect to answer their questions but he or she should not be afraid to insist on his or her legal right to remain silent – even if it means that he or she remains in custody for a longer period. For instance, the police may refuse to grant 'police bail', which may mean a stay in custody overnight. Refusing bail for this reason would be unlawful but the police sometimes suggest that the more cooperative and person is the quicker they will be released.

In virtually all cases the interview will take the form of a question and answer session which will be tape-recorded. The questions are likely to start with the details of the suspect's name and address and lead on to more important questions. It is not advisable to answer some questions and refuse to answer others. Apart from being difficult to do, if some questions are answered but not others this may have a very prejudicial effect at the trial. It is also difficult to remain completely silent in the face of questioning. Many lawyers advise their clients to answer 'no comment' to every question and many suspects find this more acceptable.

Finally, suspects should not be tempted to 'make a deal' with the police whereby they make a statement admitting guilt in return for the police not bringing a more serious charge, unless legal advice has been taken. In any case it is important to consult a solicitor before answering any questions or making a statement).

Verbals

Following on from the problem of statements to the police is the vexed question of *verbals*. This is the word used to describe admissions, or incriminating statements, that the police falsely allege to have been made by the accused.

When the police question, arrest or charge a person, they keep a written record of the events and conversations. For example, the notebook might read, 'When charged, the accused said, "Fair enough, I did it,"' but the accused may later deny ever having said those words. Either he or she is lying or has been verballed by the police.

The end result has been that many criminal trials have revolved around whether the accused did make an admission or was 'verballed' by the police. In effect, there are mini-trials within the main trials, with police officers being accused of giving false evidence. Although tape-recording has cut down on the numbers of challenged 'verbals', there are an increasing number of cases in which a statement was allegedly made by the suspect at the time of arrest, on the way to the police station or in the police cell. For obvious reasons it is very important to say nothing at these times or at the very least to think carefully before doing so. The police should show the notes that they have made to the suspect and ask the suspect to sign them. It is obviously important to sign them only if they are correct and to think very carefully before doing so. In many cases it will be better to speak to a lawyer before signing anything.

BEING HELD BY THE POLICE BEFORE CHARGE

We have already seen that there are three fundamental rights given to all suspects:

1 You cannot be detained and held by the police unless you have been arrested (unless, of course, you are prepared to help voluntarily by answering questions).
2 You need not answer any police questions.
3 You can be detained only if there is not sufficient evidence to charge you and the police have reasonable grounds for believing that they need to detain you to obtain or preserve evidence or to obtain evidence by questioning you.

In fact there is another basic right given to people held in detention against their will (i.e. arrested). This is the right not to be held for an unreasonably long time before being charged in writing for a specific offence. In general, a suspect cannot be held for more than twenty-four hours between being taken to the police station after arrest and being charged with a specific offence. At the end of that twenty-four-hour period the police should either charge or release the suspect – unless they are being held for a 'serious' offence (see below), in which case the police may be able to hold the suspect for longer. In these 'serious' cases, a senior police officer can authorize detention for up to thirty-six (not twenty-four) hours, and at the end of that time the police can ask a magistrates' court to agree to further detention without charging (up to thirty-six hours per application) up to a maximum of ninety-six hours (i.e. four days of detention and questioning without being charged). This court hearing is in private (i.e. relatives and friends cannot attend) but the suspect's lawyer can appear and argue why the detention should not be extended any further.

During detention the police must conduct regular reviews of the detention. These reviews are carried out by an inspector who is not involved in the case. The reviews are intended to consider whether the detention should continue and are held after the first six hours and then every nine hours thereafter. The suspect and his or her lawyer are entitled to make representations to the review officer. Unfortunately such reviews seldom lead to release and are often irrelevant. Nevertheless, the suspect should use them to put pressure on the police to release them.

With the exception of terrorist suspects, very few suspects are held for longer than twenty-four hours. If someone is held for longer than is allowed under the legislation, then an application to the High Court for Habeas Corpus or Judicial Review should be made. Unfortunately, the practical difficulties of getting to court and obtaining an order mean that these protections are virtually worthless in practice.

Remedies

1. Suing for wrongful arrest (assault and/or false imprisonment)

If a person is wrongly arrested and detained by the police, then he or she may be able to sue for damages. However, this is possible only if the police acted unlawfully – in other words, if they did not have reasonable grounds for the arrest or to continue the detention. Just because a person is detained, and subsequently released, it does not follow that he or she is entitled to compensation from the police.

The number of successful cases against the police has dramatically increased over the last few years. Anyone who has been arrested and detained, particularly anyone who has been assaulted by the police, should consult a solicitor. In many cases legal aid will be available.

Damages awarded in such cases can sometimes be very high and between £350 and £1,000 per hour be ordered by the court for unlawful detentions by the police.

It is also possible to sue the police for 'malicious prosecution' if they charge and prosecute without reasonable and probable cause. That is, the police must have prosecuted for an improper or dishonest motive.

2. Police complaints

If someone is treated badly by the police that person can make an official complaint about that officer's conduct. Complaints can be made for: unjustified assault, verbal abuse, racism, lying, releasing confidential information, corruption, oppressive behaviour, drunkenness and criminal conduct. Breaching the codes of practice is also a disciplinary offence. The procedure is to put the complaint in writing and send it to the chief constable. Serious cases will be supervised by the Police Complaints Authority but in all cases the investigation will be carried out by other police officers. The complainant will be interviewed by the police and a statement will be taken. If the complaint is upheld the officer will be disciplined. Police officers can also be prosecuted if the investigation reveals that criminal offences have occurred.

Legal advice should be sought before proceeding with a complaint, particularly if other court or criminal proceedings are going on at the same time. It is important to note that a malicious complaint could lead to action for libel (see Chapter 61, page 835).

Suspect's rights

Apart from the right to refuse to answer questions (see above), all detainees are entitled to:

- see a solicitor;
- have someone told about the arrest;
- be released if not charged within twenty-four hours (see above).

'Serious' offences: when the suspect has fewer rights

For serious offences, these rights are not taken away – but they are reduced, largely because the police can postpone them. For instance, the police can delay the suspect's rights to see a solicitor, or have someone told of the detention. But this happens only if he or she is suspected of 'serious arrestable offence'. Unfortunately, the law does not set out a neat, clear-cut definition of what is a 'serious' offence (i.e. 'a serious arrestable offence'). Obviously, some particularly grave crimes are specifically mentioned (e.g. murder, rape, incest, death by dangerous driving); other crimes have to be looked at on their own merits to see whether they are 'serious'. The Police and Criminal Evidence Act 1984 gives only vague guidance – for instance, has the offence caused serious harm or financial loss to anyone? If so, then it will be a 'serious' offence, and so the police will be able to postpone some of the detainee's legal rights. However, pause for a moment and consider what amounts to a serious financial loss: to a millionaire the loss of £50 is not serious, but to someone who is not working, it might be a disaster!

The right to see a solicitor

The detention code (made under the 1984 Act – see Chapter 53) is quite clear about the right to see a solicitor: 'Any person may at any time consult and communicate privately, whether in person, writing or on the telephone, with a solicitor.' In fact, when the suspect arrives at the police station, the custody officer must give him or her a written notice setting out their legal rights, including the right to see a solicitor (see page 727). The suspect must be asked whether he or she wants to see a solicitor; if they say no, then they should sign so there is a written record of this. If they refuse to sign, then the police should assume that they do want to see a solicitor and they must make the necessary arrangements. In short, the general rule is that the suspect must specifically sign away the right to see a solicitor.

Unfortunately, research findings have shown that police officers often have a tendency to discourage suspects from seeking legal advice. This is a breach of the code of practice and suspects should insist on their right to see a solicitor.

However, as is usually the case, there is an exception to this basic rule. If it is a 'serious' offence then a superintendent can give authority for the suspect to be denied access to a solicitor (see above for what is a 'serious' offence). The officer can do this if he or she thinks that allowing access to a solicitor would:

• interfere with the evidence, *or*
• alert other (unarrested) suspects, *or*
• hinder the recovery of stolen property.

Although it was once frequently used by the police as a device to prevent suspects obtaining legal advice, a decision at the Court of Appeal has considerably reduced the police's ability to delay access to a solicitor.

Research suggests that it is used in less than 1 per cent of cases and in order to justify its use the police would need to show that allowing a particular solicitor to have access would lead to any of the above consequences.

Perhaps more important, in any case (i.e. whether or not it is 'serious') a senior officer can decide that the interviewing of the suspect can go ahead, even though the solicitor has not yet arrived, if he or she thinks 'there is a considerable risk of harm to persons or serious loss of damage to property', or that 'awaiting the arrival of a solicitor would cause unreasonable delay to the processes of investigation'. If the police try to take advantange of this provision, the suspect should not answer any questions or make a statement until he or she has seen a solicitor. Faced with someone who will not speak until they have seen a solicitor, the police will usually wait for the solicitor.

If suspects want to see a solicitor then they can choose any solicitor they like. If they do not know the name or telephone number of a solicitor, or their chosen solicitor cannot be contacted or cannot attend, there is a duty solicitor on call twenty-four hours a day. The duty solicitor will be someone who specializes in criminal law and is in private practice in a local firm which takes part in a rota scheme to provide the service. Where there is to be an interview or some kind of identification procedure, or there is some suggestion of maltreatment by the police, the duty solicitor is obliged to come to the police station. Whether or not the suspect uses his or her own solicitor or the duty solicitor, the service can be provided free under the legal-aid scheme.

Obviously the competence of solicitors varies and in some cases the solicitor will send someone to the police to advise the suspect who is not a qualified solicitor. Some such clerks can provide a very expert service (even better than many solicitors), but many do not. Nevertheless, it is very important to obtain the legal advice because decisions made at this stage can have a fundamental influence on the outcome of the case.

The right to have someone told of the detention

The code explains that the suspect has 'the right not to be held incommunicado'. It goes on to say, 'A detained person may on request have one person known to him or who is likely to take an interest in his welfare informed at public expense as soon as practicable of his whereabouts. If that person cannot be contacted the detained person may choose up to two alternatives.' But, as expected, there is an important exception. If it is a 'serious' offence that is being investigated (see above for what this means), then a senior police officer can decide that the right is not to apply; on the same basis that he or she can deny access to a solicitor (i.e. in order not to interefere with evidence; alert suspects; hinder recovery of property – see above). However, the senior officer cannot do this simply because they think it would cause 'unreasonable delay', although they can use this ground to deny access to a solicitor (see above).

The code also says that the suspect should be given writing materials to write letters or messages, if he or she asks for them; those letters are then to be sent (at the suspect's expense) as soon as is practicable, although the police can read them. Likewise, the code says that a suspect can speak on the phone to one person, although the police can listen in to the conversation. Once again, if it is a 'serious' offence, a senior officer can take away these rights (i.e. on the grounds given above). Similar rules apply when relatives or friends of a detainee inquire of the police if they are holding him or her; the basic rule is that they must be told (assuming the detainee agrees), but this need not happen if it is a 'serious' offence.

Bail

For the rules on granting bail, see page 747.

Taking fingerprints, photographs and samples

The law now gives a wide right to take fingerprints. A senior police officer can authorize the taking of a suspect's fingerprints if he or she thinks the person has been involved in an offence, provided the taking of the fingerprints may tend to prove (or disprove) that guilt. Once a suspect has been charged, in writing, with a specific offence, the police have even greater powers. If the offence is of the sort that is recorded in police records (most non-trivial offences), then they can take fingerprints.

If the suspect is subsequently acquitted of the charge against him or her, then the fingerprints must be destroyed. The suspect can insist on witnessing the destruction.

Roughly similar rules apply to the taking of photos. If it is a recordable offence that he or she has been charged with, then the police can take photos. Once again, the photos must be destroyed if he or she is subsequently acquitted of the charge. Although the police can use force to take a suspect's fingerprints there is no legal right for them to use force to take a photograph. So, if suspects refuse to cooperate (e.g. putting their hands in front of their face), then in theory there is nothing the police can do, and if they use force the suspect would be able to sue for damages for assault.

An intimate sample (blood, semen, urine, pubic hair) may be taken only by a doctor if the superintendent authorizes it *and* the suspect consents. The authorization may be given only if the officer has reasonable grounds for believing the sample will confirm or disprove involvement in a serious arrestable offence.

If the suspect refuses to consent the court or jury may 'draw such inferences from the refusal as appear proper'. That is, the court is allowed to conclude that a refusal to give a sample is evidence of guilt.

Non-intimate samples (hair other than pubic hair, sample from a nail or under a nail or a swab taken from part of a person's body other than an orifice) can be taken *without consent*. It can be authorized by a superintendent if the officer has reasonable grounds for believing the sample will confirm or disprove involvement in a serious arrestable offence.

Searching someone

The police do not have a general power to search members of the public. However, the Police and Criminal Evidence Act 1984 does give them fairly extensive powers to stop and search suspected individuals. Detailed guidelines are set out in a code on stop and search, but the basic effect is that a police officer can search someone if the police officer has reasonable grounds for thinking the person is carrying certain ('prohibited' is the word the Act uses) items. This covers offensive weapons (e.g. knife, razor, sharpened comb etc.) or any item that could be used to commit an offence involving dishonesty, such as theft, stealing a car, burglary etc. It follows that this could cover a screwdriver (it could be used to force a window), or a bundle of car keys. In practice, it is a vague criterion and gives the police a wide discretion in deciding whether to search.

The code says that the citizen must be told why he or she is being searched and why the constable is entitled to carry out the search; the constable must also identify him- or herself. The search can extend to the suspect's car. In public the search is limited to removal of outer coat, jacket and gloves, but a more detailed search – as far as a complete strip search – can be carried out, in which case it must be by a police officer of the same sex and out of public view (e.g. in a police van or at the police station).

The code lays down detailed guidelines for the police to follow (but remember that the courts can still allow evidence to be given even though it was obtained by breaking one of the codes). It says:

It is important that powers of stop and search are used responsibly. An officer should bear in mind that he may be required to justify the use of the powers to a senior officer and in court, and also that abuse of the powers is likely to be harmful to the police effort in the long term. This can lead to mistrust of the police by the community. It is also particularly important to ensure that any person searched is treated courteously and considerately.

These words are obviously aimed at the over-use of police powers against young blacks. In this connection it is necessary to remember that the police can stop and search only if they have 'reasonable grounds for suspicion'. If they do not have those grounds, then the search will be unlawful. What the code says is that:

Reasonable suspicion can never be supported on the basis of personal factors alone. For example, a person's colour, age, hairstyle or manner of dress, or the fact that he is known to have a previous conviction for possession of an unlawful article, cannot be used alone or in combination with each other as the sole basis on which to search that person. Nor may it be founded on the basis of stereotyped images of certain persons or groups as more likely to be committing offences.

The vital point is in deciding what are 'reasonable grounds' for suspicion, for the mere fact that the police officer does not find what he or she is looking for will not, of itself, mean that he or she did not have reasonable grounds for carrying out the search. But how is the citizen to know whether the police officer has 'reasonable grounds'? For example, the police may have just received a report that someone looking like the citizen recently committed a theft in the vicinity. In those circumstances they might well be acting reasonably in searching him or her, but it puts the individual citizen in an impossible position.

Apart from this general power of stopping and searching, the police have additional powers that come into effect as soon as someone is arrested. A constable may search an arrested person on reasonable grounds that the person presents a danger to him- or herself or others or that the person may have concealed anything on him or her which might be used to escape or which might be evidence of an offence. Once at the police station, the police have further rights to search.

Reasonable force can be used to search a person who has been arrested and is in the police station. It has to be by a person of the same sex and reasons must be given for the search. A strip search may occur only if the police consider that it is necessary. An intimate body search (of the anus, vagina, mouth, ear or nose) can occur only if authorized by a superintendent who has reasonable grounds that the suspect has concealed something which could cause injury or has concealed class A drugs (e.g. heroin or cocaine). Intimate searches must usually be carried out by a doctor or nurse.

ENTERING AND SEARCHING PROPERTY

The same basic rule applies as with the searching of a person, namely that the police have no general right of search. If they carry out an unauthorized search they will be trespassers, and so can be physically ejected and sued for damages (see page 367).

But, as always, there are exceptions. The best-known exception is when the police obtain a search warrant. For a search warrant to be granted the police will have to show that the search is likely to uncover evidence which will be of substantial value in the investigation. The police will also have to explain why a warrant is necessary (e.g. the owner of the house cannot be contacted; the owner should not be given any advance warning etc.). Unless the police can satisfy the court on all these points, then no search warrant should be granted. One point to note is that there must have been a 'serious' offence; the police cannot get a search warrant for a trivial offence.

Unfortunately, the police can now in many instances carry out a search without applying for a search warrant first. For instance, to catch an escaped prisoner, to save life or prevent injury, to prevent serious property damage, to arrest a trespasser who has an offensive weapon, to prevent a breach of the peace (see page 831 for what this means).

Finally, the police also have a right to search the home (or other premises) of anyone who has committed an arrestable offence, to look for evidence. The police can also search the premises where the person was arrested or where the person was immediately before he or she was arrested, provided they have reasonable grounds for believing that they will find evidence relating to the offence. The search should not take place without written authorization from a police inspector, although there are exceptions to this rule.

Whenever the police carry out a search they should comply with the code of practice. For instance, this says:

Premises may be searched only to the extent necessary to achieve the object of the search . . . searches must be conducted with due consideration for the property and privacy of the occupier . . . and with no more disturbance than necessary . . . if the occupier wishes to ask a friend, neighbour or other person to witness the search then he must be allowed to do so, unless the officer in charge has reasonable grounds for believing that this would seriously hinder the investigation. A search need not be unreasonably delayed for this purpose.

Bear in mind, however, that this code (as with all codes) is not totally binding on the police. If they break it they cannot necessarily be sued, and – more important – the chances are that any evidence improperly obtained will still be usable against the suspect.

Some evidence is subject to special safeguards and an order to search will be required from a crown court judge. This will include material subject to legal privilege – that is generally communications between lawyers and their clients, personal and confidential records held by third parties and confidential material held by journalists.

The police can use reasonable force to effect a lawful search. That means that if they are not invited in they can break in. Compensation will be available if the search was unlawful. The police must also, before leaving, be satisfied that the premises are secure either by arranging for the occupier to be present or by repairing any damage.

A record must be made at the search and must include the statutory authority for the search, the names of the officers, a list of articles seized, whether force was used and a list of any damage caused.

The Serious Fraud Office also has very wide powers to force individuals to provide information and documents for its investigations.

Police seizure of property

Generally, if the police carry out a lawful search (i.e. a search authorized by search warrant, written authority etc.), then they can take anything they find which is material evidence or the fruit of a crime. This can be evidence of *any* crime, not just the crime for which the person has been arrested, or for which a search warrant was granted. The property can be kept for as long as is necessary for the police to complete their investigations. In practice, it seems that the police sometimes seize goods when they have no clear authority for doing so. When this happens the owner of the property can apply to the magistrates' court for an order to force the police to return the property. However, it is often better to take proceedings in the High Court or county court. Legal aid may be available for proceedings in the High Court or county court but not for such applications in the magistrates' court.

Special powers under the Prevention of Terrorism Act

This Act covers the whole of the UK and it gives the police greater powers in terrorist cases. A police officer can arrest a person on suspicion that he or she is involved in the 'commission, preparation or instigation of acts of terrorism' connected with Northern Ireland or any foreign country.

Once arrested the suspect can be detained for up to forty-eight hours and then for up to a further five days with the consent of the Home Secretary. The police can take any 'reasonably necessary' steps to identify the suspect (photography, fingerprints and measurements). There is no absolute right to legal advice until after forty-eight hours and the right to have someone informed of your arrest can be delayed even beyond this period.

It is a criminal offence not to give the police specific information about people or events concerned with acts of political violence, although this does not apply if the information would incriminate the suspect personally. This offence applies only to terrorism connected with Northern Ireland.

Examination and detention at ports and airports

Under the PTA a person can be stopped, questioned and detained by examining officers (police, immigration or Army) to find out whether they have any connection with, or information about, the use of violence in relation to Irish or international affairs.

The examining officer can require the person to give their name, address, occupation, name of employer, purpose of their trip; search baggage and ask any reasonable questions. The officer can detain a person for up to twelve hours in the absence of any suspicion. As with PTA arrests elsewhere reasonable suspicion allows detention for up to forty-eight hours and up to seven days with the authority of the Home Secretary.

The Act also allows the Home Secretary to use an exclusion order to expel a person from either Great Britain or Northern Ireland or from the whole of the UK.

IDENTIFICATION EVIDENCE

A suspect cannot be made to take part in an identification parade. However, if he or she refuses the police may well arrange for him or her to be seen among a group of other people by the witness, in which case the witness may well make an identification. So it is generally advisable for a suspect to agree to an ID parade rather than allow an informal identification to take place. It is essential to take legal advice before agreeing to take part in an ID parade.

A suspect can insist upon there being an ID parade in any case, unless it would be 'impracticable'. This means that if identification may be an issue at the trial, the defendant can insist on an ID parade.

A code of practice sets out the detailed rules on how an ID parade should be conducted. Perhaps its most important statement is that a 'suspect must be given a reasonable opportunity to have a solicitor or friends present'. The fundamental piece of advice for anyone asked to take part in an ID parade is to consult a solicitor as to whether they should agree, and also to arrange for the solicitor to be present.

The code also says that:
• the suspect should be given a leaflet setting out the suspect's rights;
• the witness should not be allowed a chance of seeing the suspect before the parade takes place;
• 'the parade shall consist of at least eight persons (in addition to the suspect) who so far as possible resemble the suspect in age, height, general appearance and position in life';
• one suspect only should be included in a parade unless there are two suspects of roughly similar appearance, in which case they may be treated together with at least twelve other persons;
• 'the suspect may select his or her own position in the line';
• the line should be visited by only one witness at a time;
• the witness should be told that the suspect may, or may not, be in the line;
• if the witness asks to see members of the line moving, or to hear them talking,

he or she should first be asked whether he or she can identify the suspect by appearance only; the witness should then be told that the members of the line were selected for their physical appearance only – not their similar voices;

• once the witness has left, the suspect should be told that he or she can change position in the line before the next witness inspects the line;

• at the end of the ID parade, the suspect can have his or her comments on the parade noted by the officer in charge.

If the guidelines are not followed, the trial judge may decide that the identification evidence obtained should be ignored. In effect, therefore, the position is the same as with a breach of any other code of practice.

In practice, it can often be difficult for a suspect to refuse to take part in an ID parade. The police will say that if he or she refuses, then they will confront the witness with him or her and ask the witness whether this is the correct person – which can be extremely risky from the suspect's point of view! Another practical problem can arise when, say, a young black is held as a suspect, because the police might have great trouble in finding enough black youngsters to make up an ID parade. When this happens the suspect is often offered a 'group identification', as an alternative to an ID parade. For instance, the witness will wait beside the ticket barrier in a train station and the suspect will walk out of the station, mingling with other passengers. The code of practice sets out guidelines on how such group identifications are to be conducted, and any suspect who is offered one should seek the help of a solicitor, who can give practical help and ensure the procedures are followed correctly.

The code also lays down guidelines for when a witness is shown a selection of photographs:

• photo-identification should not be allowed if an ID parade can be arranged;

• the witness should be shown not less than twelve photos at a time; the photographs used should 'as far as possible all be a similar type' – for instance, a snapshot should not be included in a bundle of 'mug-style' criminal photographs;

• the witness should be told that the suspect's photo may or may not be included in the bundle;

• once a witness makes a firm identification by photo, he or she should then be asked to attend an ID parade and once one witness has made an identification, other witnesses should not be shown photographs but should take part in an identity parade instead.

Identification evidence in criminal trials

Identification evidence is notoriously unreliable. It has been shown on many occasions that people who positively identify a suspect are wrong because the suspect could not have been present at the time of the original sighting.

There are therefore the following safeguards. First, if identification is an issue in the case, the accused can insist on a full old-style committal before the magistrate commits the defendant for trial in the Crown Court. A simplified committal must not be used (see page 758). Secondly, 'dock identifications' can occur only in very rare cases and should always be resisted (except in 'old style' committals – see page 760 for what this means). This means that the witness cannot be asked if he or she sees in court the person he or she saw, unless they have previously picked out the suspect in an ID parade. Thirdly, judges must remind jurors of the weaknesses and dangers of identification evidence. The judge should go through the identification evidence during the summing up, reminding the jury of any weaknesses in it.

53 The Criminal Law

Everyone knows what a 'crime' is. In the words of the *Oxford English Dictionary*, it is an 'act punishable by the law'. But people usually associate the word 'crime' with the more sensational or serious offences, such as murder, manslaughter and arson, and forget that such petty offences as careless driving, parking violations and leaving litter are also crimes. The only difference is in the severity of the punishment meted out to the offender.

The same principles of criminal justice apply to murderers as to shoplifters and others accused of comparatively trivial crimes. In the eyes of the law, a crime is a crime, however grave or trivial the offence may be.

PRINCIPLES OF CRIMINAL PROCEDURES

- the accused is presumed innocent until proved guilty;
- to prove guilt, the prosecution must show beyond reasonable doubt that he or she committed the offence. This means that if there is a reasonable doubt as to guilt, then there must be an acquittal (cf. the lighter burden of proof in civil cases, page 888);
- no one is under a duty to help the police with their inquiries, or to make a statement to them; further, this lack of cooperation cannot be held against them at the trial;
- a suspect can remain silent and it cannot be held against them;
- a defendant is tried on the facts of the case, not on the evidence of previous convictions; the court will not be told of any 'record', since that might create prejudice. Only if found guilty will 'form' be relevant, when it may influence the court sentences; but the accused will forfeit the benefit of this rule if he or she falsely tells the court they are of good character, or if they attack the character of the prosecution witnesses;
- the trial is based on the oral evidence of witnesses; generally, written evidence is not allowed since there is no opportunity for its maker to be cross-examined. It is allowed, however, when the contents of the written statement are not in dispute; also, the evidence of a witness must be of what he or she saw or heard and not hearsay (i.e. secondhand evidence). For instance, B cannot give evidence to say that A saw the defendant commit the crime. A has to come to court to give his or her own evidence;

- the accused is protected from trial by newspaper; the contempt of court rules prevent the papers from reporting anything other than the evidence given in the case; speculation by the press is prohibited.
- there are various protections that regulate the manner in which the police can detain and question a suspect (see Chapter 52).

These safeguards are given to all people, whether they are murderers or litter-bugs. The underlying principle is that it is better for some guilty people to go free than to take the risk of one innocent person being wrongly convicted. The principles are also designed to try to offset the inevitable imbalance of power between a prosecution taken by the state and the individual.

Criminal proceedings

There are two ways of bringing the suspect before the court: either by a summons or, alternatively, by arrest and charge (see the chart on page 744).

Issuing a summons

Firstly, there is the *summons* to appear in court at a certain date and time. To obtain a summons, the police go before a magistrate and state where and when the accused committed the offence. This is called laying an information, and ordinarily must be done within six months of the offence. If the magistrate thinks there is a prima facie case (which is very likely because the suspect will never be present to contradict anything that the police might say), the summons will be issued commanding the accused to appear in court, usually at least one week after. The police then serve the summons on the accused, usually by post.

Obviously, this procedure is used only in the less serious cases where there is no risk of the offender absconding. The accused person must attend the court on the dates given in the summons; if he or she does not, an arrest warrant can be issued. The only exception to the rule is when the summons states that the defendant can plead guilty by post, in which case there is no need to attend court in person (see page 756).

Arresting and charging

The second way of starting criminal proceedings is to arrest and charge the suspect. This is normally done in more serious cases, when a summons would be inappropriate. However, there are some occasions when an offence is not serious, but when a summons would not be suitable (e.g. the suspect's name and address may be false – in which case the police will want to be able to hold him or her while they check the details). Unfortunately the police will arrest and detain a person rather than using the summons procedure even though there is no real justification for this. However, the general rule remains that a

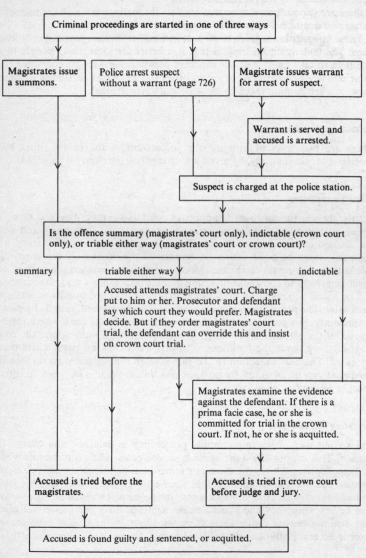

How Criminals are Taken to Court

Criminal proceedings are started in one of three ways

Magistrates issue a summons.

Police arrest suspect without a warrant (page 726)

Magistrate issues warrant for arrest of suspect.

Warrant is served and accused is arrested.

Suspect is charged at the police station.

Is the offence summary (magistrates' court only), indictable (crown court only), or triable either way (magistrates' court or crown court)?

summary

triable either way

indictable

Accused attends magistrates' court. Charge put to him or her. Prosecutor and defendant say which court they would prefer. Magistrates decide. But if they order magistrates' court trial, the defendant can override this and insist on crown court trial.

Magistrates examine the evidence against the defendant. If there is a prima facie case, he or she is committed for trial in the crown court. If not, he or she is acquitted.

Accused is tried before the magistrates.

Accused is tried in crown court before judge and jury.

Accused is found guilty and sentenced, or acquitted.

summons is used for the less serious cases, whereas arrest and charging is used for the more serious cases. Arresting and charging are two different steps in the prosecution process. The suspect is arrested when the police take him or her into custody – in other words, by making it clear that the suspect has to go to the police station. The charging occurs in the police station: the custody officer reads out the formal description of the offence and hands the suspect a copy of the charge. It is thus a two-stage process – arresting, followed by charging at the police station (see page 726 for more on arrest powers).

TIME LIMITS ON CRIMINAL PROSECUTION

There are different rules for magistrates' court cases and for other cases.

Offences that must be tried in the magistrates' court

These must generally be prosecuted within six months of the offence being committed. This means that the prosecutor must lay information before the magistrates and ask that a summons be issued within six months of the offence. However, there is no need for the summons to be served on the accused within the six-month period, or to be tried within that period. But, if the information is not laid within six months, the offender cannot be prosecuted for the offence.

However, with certain motoring offences the prosecution must be careful to give the accused notice of intended prosecution. This must be in the form of an oral warning at the time of the offence or a written warning (or summons) served within fourteen days of the offence being committed (see page 687).

The six-month rule in the magistrates' court is subject to a few minor exceptions, when statutes lay down longer or shorter periods.

Offences that need not be tried in the magistrates' court

These are not, generally, subject to any time limit. Thus a person can be charged with a serious offence that was committed many years ago, although often prosecutions will not be started if the time-lag is substantial. However, there are a few offences that are subject to time periods.

Undue Delay

In any case, if the delay before prosecution is considerable or caused by the prosecution, the case can be stopped by the court on the basis that it is an 'abuse of process'. It will usually be necessary to show that the defendant has been prejudiced by the delay (i.e. the memory of witnesses has failed or an important witness has died).

Bringing a private prosecution

The vast majority of criminal prosecutions are brought by the Crown Prosecution Service (CPS) – in fact, about 99 per cent of the total. But the law allows private individuals to prosecute for most offences, for it has long been a principle of our laws that all citizens should have access to the criminal courts.

Most private prosecutions are started by the issuing of a summons in the magistrates' court. (See page 752 for the procedure to be followed.) Once a summons has been issued, the case will proceed in the normal manner for any magistrates' court case. The only difference would be that the private individual is prosecuting instead.

Mischievous private prosecutions can be stopped in an indirect way. The Director of Public Prosecutions has the power to take over the conduct of any criminal prosecution if he or she so chooses. Thus, if a private prosecution was thought to be against the public interest, the DPP might take over the case but then not present any prosecution evidence when it came to trial. The accused person, would, of course, have to be acquitted.

No one should embark on a private prosecution lightly. It is always preferable to get the Crown Prosecution Service to prosecute. The private prosecutor should bear in mind that:

● if the case is lost he or she may have to pay the accused's legal costs;

● the prosecutor may be sued for damages if it can be shown that he or she acted 'maliciously' in bringing the prosecution. In addition, if a citizen's arrest was made, a damages claim for false imprisonment could follow;

● even if the prosecutor wins, he or she is unlikely to recover all of the legal costs and expenses;

● often the accused will make counter-allegations against the prosecutor (e.g. in the typical dispute between two neighbours who are both making accusations against each other). When this happens, the magistrates frequently find it impossible to sort out who is in the right and who is in the wrong and it is common for the magistrates to bind over (see page 775) both the prosecutor and the accused;

● if the accused is able to opt for a crown court trial (see page 758) and does so, the private prosecutor will have to instruct a solicitor and barrister to act in the crown court. This could be very expensive.

Shoplifting

Shoplifting charges used to be brought by the individual shop-owners (i.e. as private prosecutions) rather than by the authorities. However, these days most prosecutions are brought by the Crown Prosecution Service. If, however, the shop-owner is prosecuting, then the normal rules about private prosecutions will generally apply. That is, in the event of an unsuccessful prosecution, the shop could well face a damages claim for malicious prosecution and false imprisonment.

Bail

Once the accused has been arrested and charged, the question arises of whether he or she is to be released or held in custody. In legal terminology: *remanded on bail* or *remanded in custody*. If the prosecution was started by summons, the problem will not arise for the accused will not have been taken into custody; instead, they will simply have been told when they are to appear in court.

If the arrest was by warrant, the magistrate who issued it may have written on the back that the accused should have bail; if the warrant is 'backed for bail' in this way, the police have no choice but to release the accused after charge. If it is not backed for bail, then the police cannot release the accused on bail.

If the arrest was not by warrant it is for the police to take the initial decision whether to keep the person in custody until the next hearing of the court. Bail is granted entirely at their discretion and it is then called *police bail*. But if police bail is refused, the prisoner must be brought before a magistrate within twenty-four hours (forty-eight hours at weekends and public holidays) and given a chance of asking the magistrate for bail. So when an accused person is arrested and charged, the power to hold them in custody is initially with the police.

Special rules apply to children and young people:
* children under fourteen must be granted police bail unless charged with murder or manslaughter;
* a young person between fourteen and seventeen must be granted police bail unless a senior police officer believes that:
   (i) the young person should be detained in his or her own interest, *or*
   (ii) the young person would not turn up in court if released, *or*
   (iii) it would defeat the ends of justice to grant bail, *or*
   (iv) the young person has committed murder, manslaughter or some other 'serious offence'.

Being detained in custody before charge

There are detailed rules on how long a suspect can be held in custody (see page 730.)

Asking the magistrate for bail

Bail is very important. Keeping a person in custody before he or she has been convicted is a very serious step. It may result in the suspect losing his or her job and will have an inevitable effect on the accused's reputation.

Accordingly, the basic principle is that no one should be refused bail unnecessarily. Apart from the libertarian reasons for this, there are also practical (and financial) reasons for not putting remand prisoners into the already overcrowded prisons. The aim is that 'the number of persons remanded in custody should be kept to the minimum compatible with the interests of justice'. The Bail Act 1976 sets out the rules.

When deciding whether to grant bail, the magistrate will first look at the offence with which the accused is charged:

1 If the offence does not carry a possible prison sentence, bail should be refused only if the accused has previously been given bail and failed to turn up in court when required *and* the court now believes that it will happen again.

2 If the offence could carry a prison sentence, the magistrate need not grant bail if:

- there are *substantial grounds* (i.e. more than mere suspicion) for believing he or she would abscond, commit an offence or obstruct the course of justice (e.g. 'get at' witnesses), *or*
- there has been insufficient time since charging for the police to have collected information about his or her suitability for bail, *or*
- he or she has previously jumped bail, *or*
- if the case has been adjourned for a report to be prepared (such as a social-welfare, medical or probation report), then bail can be refused if it would be impracticable to make the inquiries or the report without the accused being kept in custody, *or*
- he or she should be kept in custody for his/her own protection.

In all other cases, the accused must be granted bail.

If bail is refused

The court must give its reasons for refusing bail, and a written note of these must be given to the defendant. The defendant will then go to prison but as a remand prisoner and will have special privileges not enjoyed by convicted prisoners (see Chapter 54). The time spent as a remand prisoner will count as time served if he or she is subsequently convicted and sent to prison for the offence.

The remand in custody is normally for eight days at a time, and the prisoner will then come back before the magistrate. He or she will normally be remanded for a further eight days, and so on, until the case is ready for trial. However, the accused can opt to avoid these eight-day remands by agreeing to the remand being for a longer time: this will save the inconvenience of trips from prison to the court, and should not delay the trial in any way. The court can now also order remands every twenty-eight days, provided the defendant is legally represented and at court when remanded for the longer period.

The court must consider the matter of bail on each occasion on which the defendant is remanded. However, a prisoner may only make two applications as of right. The first of those must be made on the defendant's first appearance at court. The second can be at any subsequent remand at which the defendant is present. Any further one must result from a change of circumstances.

A prisoner cannot make repeated applications for bail, unless there are new grounds. If there is a change of circumstances (e.g. someone who will stand surety; the defendant has fixed up a job) then a fresh application for bail can be made, but not otherwise. In practice, therefore, most prisoners see little point in insisting that they be re-remanded every eight days, and so they will often agree to being remanded for a longer time.

Appealing. If the magistrates refuse bail, then their decisions can be appealed to the crown court. Legal aid will normally cover the legal costs.

A prisoner's friends and relatives will often urge the solicitor to appeal straight away, but this is not always wise. If the crown court judge upholds the magistrate's decision, it is unlikely that the magistrates will be persuaded to change their minds at a later date. So it might be much better to collect evidence that answers the magistrates' reasons for refusing bail and present this at the next hearing, rather than rush off and appeal to the crown court. It is also possible to appeal to a High Court judge but legal aid is very rarely available.

If bail is granted

The defendant will be given a written note of the court's decision and told when he or she should next appear in court. If the defendant does not turn up on that day but absconds, he or she will be guilty of an offence (maximum penalty three months' prison and/or £5,000 fine in a magistrates' court, twelve months' prison and an unlimited fine in a crown court). In addition, bail is unlikely to be granted again.

Often the bail will be granted subject to conditions. For instance, the defendant may have to surrender his or her passport, report to the police station once a day, agree to live in a certain place, agree not to go near a particular place, or deposit cash or valuables as security. The Bail Act states that 'no condition should be imposed unless it is necessary', but it seems clear that many magistrates impose conditions when they are not strictly necessary. When this happens, the accused should suggest to the magistrate that the conditions are unnecessary. The defendant can refuse to accept the conditions and, if remanded in custody, can apply to the crown court judge for bail to be granted free of conditions. Not surprisingly, few defendants are prepared to do this, and most simply accept the magistrate's conditions, however unreasonable they may be.

Often bail will be granted only if the defendant can find one or more sureties. A surety is a person who agrees to forfeit a fixed sum should the accused not turn up to court. The surety does not have to deposit any money with the police while the accused is on bail, for it is only if the accused fails to answer bail and the magistrates decide to enforce the surety's bond that he or she will have to produce the money. The amount at risk is called the 'recognizance'.

The surety will have to go either to the court or to the police station as the police will want to check that he or she is suitable. The Bail Act says that a surety's suitability will be based primarily on:

- financial resources (does he or she have the money to pay the recognizance if it should be enforced?);
- character and any criminal record;
- proximity (whether in terms of kinship, place of residence, or otherwise) to the person for whom he or she is to be surety.

The correct procedure is for the court to decide on the amount of recognizance required, bearing in mind the nature of the offence, the defendant's record and so on. The court should then consider the suitability of the sureties. The court should not decide that a large recognizance is needed simply because a particular surety is well off.

If the accused absconds and does not answer to bail, the surety may forfeit the sum due; this is called having the 'recognizance estreated'. The surety will have to appear before the magistrates and argue why the recognizance should not be forfeited. Forfeiture is not automatic, for the court will want to know the extent to which the surety was to blame for allowing the defendant to abscond.

Mrs Green stood surety for her husband, who was accused of importing cannabis. She told the court that her share of the family home was worth £3,000 and so she was accepted as surety for a recognizance of £3,000. Her husband later absconded. The magistrates ordered Mrs Green to forfeit the full £3,000, and she appealed against that decision. Held: The magistrates' decision would be overturned. They should have considered the extent to which Mrs Green was to blame for her husband defaulting. Moreover, magistrates should not accept a wife as a surety on the basis of matrimonial property. Since Mrs Green had done all she could to secure her husband's attendance, Lord Denning ordered that the recognizance should not be estreated. Green (1975)

However, that decision was very much a borderline case and subsequent decisions have made it clear that the 'blameworthiness' of the surety is not the only factor to be considered. Strictly speaking, if the surety has any doubts as to whether the accused will answer bail, he or she should take the accused to the police station and ask to be released from the surety. The police will then, of course, take the accused into custody until a suitable replacement surety can be found. In practice, magistrates are reluctant to allow sureties to be let off if the defendant absconds. Clearly, therefore, no one should stand surety unless they are sure that the accused will not abscond.

If the magistrates do insist that bail will be granted only subject to a surety, the defendant must be told why this is so, and then be given a written note of the reasons.

Legal aid

The vast majority of people who are prosecuted for the more serious criminal offences get legal aid. See page 982 for the procedure. But legal aid is not available for all criminal charges. Many magistrates take a fairly tough line and refuse to grant legal aid unless the charge is serious. Anyone who is tried in the crown court can expect to receive legal aid (assuming they pass the means test), and can also expect to receive legal aid if up on a serious charge in the magistrates' court. If there is an element of dishonesty involved in the offence (e.g. theft, fraud, taking a car etc.), then legal aid will probably be granted. But someone charged with, say, drunk-driving would not normally get legal aid. If legal aid is refused and the offence is one that could be tried in the crown court (see below), the refusal can be appealed to the area committee of the Legal Aid Board. For cases that can be heard only in the magistrates' court, there is no appeal, although a detailed letter from a solicitor about the case will sometimes result in legal aid being granted.

THE TRIAL OF THE CASE

Where will the case be tried?

What happens next will depend upon the type of offence, for this will determine whether the case is tried before the magistrates in a magistrates' court or before a judge and jury in the crown court. Magistrates hear the less serious cases – some 96 per cent of all criminal cases.

The offence will be:

- triable in the magistrates' court only (*a summary* offence), *or*
- triable in the crown court only (*an indictable* offence), *or*
- triable in the crown court or the magistrates' court (an offence *triable either way*).

All criminal cases start in the magistrates' court. If the offence is *summary*, then the trial will also take place in the magistrates' court. If it is *indictable*, the trial will take place in the crown court, but only after the magistrates have confirmed that there is the basis of a case against the accused and committed them for trial in the crown court.

With offences *triable either way*, the position is more complicated. First, the charge is put to the accused in the magistrates' court. Second, both the accused and the prosecutor can say which court they think should hear the case. Third, the magistrates then say where they think the case should be tried. If that is in the magistrates' court, the fourth step is for the accused to be given the chance of overriding the magistrates' decision and insisting on the right to a jury trial in the crown court. With juveniles (i.e. under seventeen) different problems arise: see Chapter 10 for juvenile-court cases.

Opting for magistrates' court or crown court trial

If the defence is *triable either way* the defendant has to weigh up the pros and cons of trial in the magistrates' court and in the crown court.

Advantages of trial in the magistrates' court

Speed. If the plea is guilty; if the plea is not guilty, it can take just as long (or even longer) to get the case heard by magistrates as in the crown court.

Cost. It is cheaper to run a case in the magistrates' court. Many defendants obtain legal aid and therefore cost is not a major factor, although if found guilty they are likely to pay a significantly larger contribution towards legal aid costs in the crown court than in the magistrates' court.

Penalty. Generally, lighter penalties are imposed in the magistrates' court. But sometimes the magistrates commit the defendant to the crown court for sentencing, in which case that advantage is lost.

Advantages of trial in the crown court

Acquittal. The chances of being found not guilty are considerably higher in the crown court. Thus if the defendant has a lot to lose if convicted, he or she should always opt for crown court trial if it is available.

Evidence. If evidence is to be challenged (i.e. the defendant challenges a confession alleged to have been made to the police), this can be dealt with properly only in the crown court. This is because the judge can decide on whether the jury should hear the evidence at all. In the magistrates' court, although it is possible to ask the magistrates to exclude evidence, they will have to hear it first before they do so and thus are very likely to be influenced even if they decide to exclude it.

Also in a crown court case the defence will be given all of the prosecution statements, not just a summary of the case, which may be all that is given if the case is tried in the magistrates' court.

Legal aid. There is much more chance of getting legal aid if the case is to be tried in the crown court.

Trial in the magistrates' court

Whether the accused is being prosecuted by way of summons or by arrest and charge, the day will come when the case is listed for hearing in the court's daily case list – the list of cases to be tried on that day.

Generally, the defendant must attend court on the date fixed for trial. The only exceptions are where he or she intends to plead *guilty* and:
● has been offered the choice to plead guilty by post and has done so (see page 756), *or*
● sends a solicitor or barrister to represent him or her in court and is going to plead guilty.

Otherwise the court will usually issue an arrest warrant should the defendant not appear. Sometimes the case will simply be heard in the defendant's absence and he or she will be found guilty. However, this will normally be done only for a petty offence and when it is clear that the summons was properly served.

It may be that either the prosecution or the defence is not ready to proceed with the trial, perhaps because witnesses are not available or because the lawyers have not had sufficient time in which to investigate the case. If so, they may be able to persuade the magistrates to grant an adjournment and fix a new date for the trial.

The prosecution case will always be presented by a solicitor or barrister from the Crown Prosecution Service.

The police officer in charge of the case will have obtained full statements from all witnesses and will also have prepared a brief summary of the facts, setting out the main circumstances of the crime. This will have been served on the accused, usually with the summons. The CPS may not have given the defendant a copy of all the witness statements. Thus he or she may not know all the evidence against them until it is revealed in the course of the trial as the prosecution witnesses give their evidence. This makes it extremely difficult for the defence to prepare its case in advance (cf. the position in the crown court, where the defence always receives the prosecution statements before the trial begins). However, defendants facing *either way* offences are now given copies of the statements.

If the offence is at all serious, the accused will probably have taken legal advice, although he or she does not need to be represented by a lawyer and can act for themselves if they so wish.

The defendant may be tempted to plead 'guilty' just to 'get it all over and done with', but should avoid this temptation unless he or she really is guilty. Conversely, the case may be hopeless and the defendant may decide to plead 'not guilty' on the basis that he or she has nothing to lose. This is wrong, for there is something to lose. On conviction, the magistrates are unlikely to be sympathetic to a defendant who has wasted their time and that of the police and witnesses. In addition, the defendant may well be ordered to contribute to prosecution and witness costs – something that would probably have been avoided if he or she had pleaded guilty.

The procedure in the magistrates' court is fairly informal. In fact, the dictionary definition of 'summary' is a fair description of magistrates' court summary trials – 'brief, dispensing with needless details and formalities: done with dispatch'. Lawyers have long argued about the quality of trials in magistrates' courts, with many practitioners arguing that the magistrates are willing to accept police evidence, and that they are too overworked to be able to give each case the care and attention it deserves.

The case begins with the prosecution giving a brief explanation of the case to the magistrates. Prosecution witnesses are then called to give evidence, with the defence being able to cross-examine each of them. After all the prosecution witnesses have given their evidence, the defence can call its witnesses. They in turn can be cross-examined by the prosecution. At the completion of their evidence, the prosecution and the defence both make short speeches summarizing the reasons why the magistrates should return a verdict of guilty or not guilty.

The defendant does not have to call any witnesses and does not have to give evidence him or herself. It is up to the prosecution to prove the case and

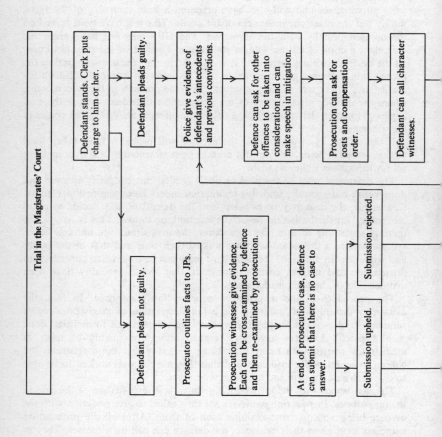

Trial in the Magistrates' Court

Defendant stands. Clerk puts charge to him or her.

Defendant pleads guilty.

Police give evidence of defendant's antecedents and previous convictions.

Defence can ask for other offences to be taken into consideration and can make speech in mitigation.

Prosecution can ask for costs and compensation order.

Defendant can call character witnesses.

Defendant pleads not guilty.

Prosecutor outlines facts to JPs.

Prosecution witnesses give evidence. Each can be cross-examined by defence and then re-examined by prosecution.

At end of prosecution case, defence can submit that there is no case to answer.

Submission rejected.

Submission upheld.

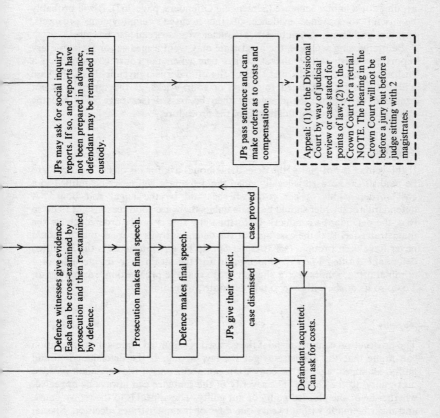

JPs may ask for social inquiry reports. If so, and reports have not been prepared in advance, defendant may be remanded in custody.

JPs pass sentence and can make orders as to costs and compensation.

Appeal: (1) to the Divisional Court by way of judicial review or case stated for points of law; (2) to the Crown Court for a retrial. NOTE. The hearing in the Crown Court will not be before a jury but before a judge sitting with 2 magistrates.

Defence witnesses give evidence. Each can be cross-examined by prosecution and then re-examined by defence.

Prosecution makes final speech.

Defence makes final speech.

JPs give their verdict.

case proved

case dismissed

Defendant acquitted. Can ask for costs.

therefore the defendant can sit back and let them try to do so. Obviously, in many cases it is important for the defendant to give evidence and to call witnesses who support his or her side of the case.

The magistrates then give their verdict. If they find the accused guilty, the Crown Prosecution Service will read out any previous convictions recorded against the defendant. The defence can then make a speech in mitigation, arguing for a lighter sentence (Sentencing Offenders, page 767). It will probably be useful to produce evidence of the accused's employment prospects, earnings and family commitments; character witnesses can also be called.

Before passing sentence, the magistrate may want a medical or social inquiry report prepared; this is almost always true when the court is considering a custodial sentence for the first time or the offender is a juvenile. If so, the case will have to be adjourned for three or four weeks, if the report was not prepared in advance. Sentence will then be passed (see page 767). See the chart on pages 754–5 for full details of the procedure.

Acquittal

If the verdict is not guilty, the defendant should ask for his or her legal costs to be paid. If the accused is legally aided the defendant will never be entitled to a costs order as his or her costs will be paid by the Legal Aid Board. A defendant's cost order should be made unless there are good reasons not to do so (e.g. the defendant's conduct). Unfortunately, this is rarely ordered unless the magistrates feel that the case against the defendant was so weak that it should never have been brought (see Chapter 66). In no circumstances is the acquitted defendant entitled to any compensation for the strain of being accused of a criminal offence unless he or she can prove that the prosecution was malicious. To do so he or she will have to take separate proceedings.

Appeals

The prosecution cannot appeal if the accused is acquitted, unless the prosecution can argue that the magistrates got the law wrong. If the defendant is found guilty, an appeal against the conviction can occur only if the defendant pleaded 'not guilty' to the charge. The severity of the sentence can always be appealed, whether he or she pleaded guilty or not guilty. The appeal is to the crown court, and must be made within twenty-one days of the magistrates' decision. Special points of law may be appealed direct to the Divisional Court of the High Court (Queen's Bench Division) by either the prosecutor or the defendant.

Pleading guilty by post

The defendant may be given the opportunity to plead guilty by post if the charge against him or her is a summary offence that does not carry a maximum penalty of more than three months' imprisonment. Generally, the option of pleading guilty by post is offered only in the less serious motoring offences (e.g. careless driving). It is never possible to plead *not guilty* by post: to plead not guilty, you should appear in court in person. Also, it is not every defendant who can opt to plead guilty by post; it is for the prosecutor to decide whether to allow the defendant the choice to plead guilty by post. If this happens the sequence of events is:

1 The prosecutor serves on the accused:
    • a statement of facts, being a short summary of the facts of the case. This will form the basis of the evidence against the accused should he or she agree to plead guilty by post, *and*
    • a notice explaining that accused can plead guilty by post if he or she wants to but is not obliged to do so.
2 The defendant then decides whether he or she wishes to plead guilty by post. A letter must be sent to the court with the form attached to the notice of prosecution. In motoring cases, the driving licence will usually have to be sent. It is advisable for the defendant to reply well before the date fixed for the hearing, for otherwise he or she may have to pay the costs and expenses of witnesses who attend court unnecessarily. The defendant can withdraw the postal plea at any time before the trial of the case

    The defendant need not agree to plead guilty by post but instead can attend in person to plead either guilty or not guilty. It is not possible to plead not guilty by post.
3 If a postal plea is received, the court notifies the prosecutor.
4 When the case is tried, the clerk of the court will read to the magistrates the statement of facts and the defendant's plea in mitigation and details of his/her financial circumstances.
5 The magistrates then find the defendant guilty and consider the appropriate sentence. Usually the magistrates will pass sentence straight away, but sometimes they will adjourn the hearing so that the defendant can be present when sentenced. This will often be done if the magistrates feel they need more information, but it must be done if a severe sentence is to be imposed. The accused must be present in court if he or she is to be sentenced to:
    • prison, detention centre or a suspended prison sentence, *or*
    • disqualification. This is usually a disqualification from driving, but it also includes disqualification from owning an animal.

For instance, if the defendant pleads guilty by post to a charge of speeding, but already has 10 penalty points, the magistrates would then adjourn the hearing for up to four weeks so that a new date could be fixed when the defendant could attend court and argue why he or she should not lose their licence. If the accused does not appear at the new hearing date, a warrant may be issued.

Trial in the crown court

Nearly every case that is tried in the crown court must first pass through the magistrates' court. (From October 1992 cases involving violent or sexual offences against children will be dealt with slightly differently and the test of the sufficiency of evidence will be heard in the crown court at a pre-trial hearing.) The magistrates will check that there is sufficient evidence against the accused to justify his or her being tried for the offence, if there is, they will commit him or her for trial in a crown court, but if there is not the case will be ended and the defendant discharged.

The committal proceedings

The committal proceedings are not a trial of the case by the magistrates. The magistrates' function is to see whether there is a prima facie case against the accused – in other words, to weed out the prosecutions that have no real chance of success. Thus the purpose of the committal is to test the strength of the prosecution evidence and so, indirectly, to give the defendant a warning of the evidence that the prosecution will bring against him or her in the crown court trial. The defendant is thus given a preliminary view of the prosecution evidence and an opportunity to prepare their defence. This, of course, cannot be done in a magistrates' court trial since the accused may have been given only a summary of the evidence.

In the old days, committals were always lengthy and time-consuming. The prosecution had to call its witnesses to give oral evidence to the magistrates and the evidence would be written down. This was so even when the defence agreed that there was a case to answer and had no objection to the case being committed to the crown court. To remedy this situation, the Criminal Justice Act of 1967 introduced an alternative procedure. The position now largely depends upon whether the defendant agrees that there is a prima facie case justifying committal. In many cases there will be sufficient evidence and the defendant will agree to the committal.

When the defence agrees to the committal

The 1967 Act introduced a short form of committal for such cases. This allows the magistrates to commit the accused without having to consider the strength of the evidence. Thus the defendant voluntarily forgoes the examination of the evidence by the magistrates, but the court will let him or her do this only if all the defendants are legally represented at the committal hearing.

For the short form of committal to be available the prosecution must have previously served the defence with copies of all the statements made by relevant prosecution witnesses. The defence can then consider the strength of the prosecution evidence beforehand and so be able to decide whether there is the

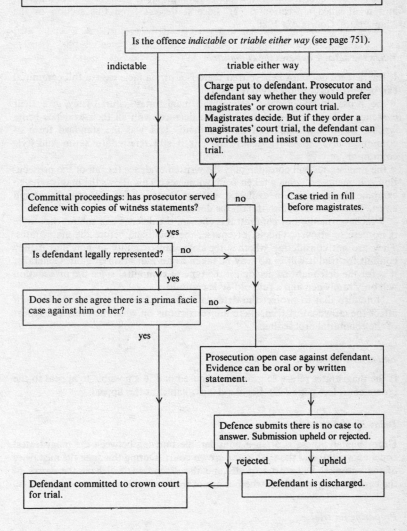

Committal Proceedings

Is the offence *indictable* or *triable either way* (see page 751).

indictable

triable either way

Charge put to defendant. Prosecutor and defendant say whether they would prefer magistrates' or crown court trial. Magistrates decide. But if they order a magistrates' court trial, the defendant can override this and insist on crown court trial.

Committal proceedings: has prosecutor served defence with copies of witness statements?

no

Case tried in full before magistrates.

yes

Is defendant legally represented?

no

yes

Does he or she agree there is a prima facie case against him or her?

no

yes

Prosecution open case against defendant. Evidence can be oral or by written statement.

Defence submits there is no case to answer. Submission upheld or rejected.

rejected

upheld

Defendant committed to crown court for trial.

Defendant is discharged.

basis of a case against the accused. If there is, then they will almost certainly agree to a short-form committal. These days this is the usual form of committal, and it is called a 'section 6 (2)' since it derives from this section of the Magistrates' Courts Act 1980.

When the defence opposes the committal

If the defence does not believe that there is a prima facie case, a full committal can be held. This can take two forms:

● the prosecution witnesses attend the magistrates' court. They give their evidence and are cross-examined by the defence, with all their evidence being written down and then read over to them. This was the standard form of committal prior to 1967. Accordingly, it is still referred to as an 'old-style committal', *or*

● the magistrates will consider only the written evidence (i.e. all of the prosecution statements previously taken from witnesses). This allows the magistrates to examine the prosecution evidence without the need for witnesses to attend court. This is called 'committal on the documents'.

Whichever method of committal is chosen, the defence can submit that there is no case to answer. This is, of course, the sole issue before the magistrates. They are not considering whether the defendant is guilty or not, and if they commit for trial it will in no way be taken as an indication of guilt. Generally, it is for the defendant to decide on the type of committal since the prosecution will only rarely demand a full, old-style committal.

Note also that to protect the defendant from adverse publicity which might affect the crown court trial, there are restrictions on what the press can report of the committal proceedings.

Bail after committal

If the magistrates refuse to grant the accused bail it is possible to appeal to the crown court (see page 749). Legal aid is available for this appeal.

Delay in coming to trial

Unfortunately, there is often a considerable time-lag between the magistrates' court committal and the trial in the crown court. During this time the memories of the witnesses will start to fade, and the defendants will have the worry of the case hanging over them whether or not they are held in custody.

Preparing for trial

After the committal from the magistrates' court the accused will probably be granted legal aid (virtually no applications are turned down), which will cover the greater part – if not all – of the legal costs (see Legal Aid, page 700). The solicitor will go through the prosecution statements and prepare the defence accordingly.

Note that the defence does not have to disclose any of its evidence to the prosecution unless there is an alibi defence or expert evidence is to be given. In the former case the prosecution must be given advance warning. This is supposedly to stop the defendant concocting a false alibi and then springing it on the prosecution during the crown court trial, when it would be too late for the police to obtain evidence to refute it. Accordingly, if the defendant intends to rely on an alibi he or she must give details of it to the prosecution within seven days of their committal by the magistrates (although this period can often be extended).

Where the defence wishes to use expert evidence at the trial, the expert's report must be served in advance at the trial.

The accused's solicitor will instruct counsel (i.e. a barrister) to appear at the crown court hearing since at present only barristers are allowed to do the court work. If the case raises any difficult points the solicitor may well have a conference (i.e. a meeting) with counsel, probably with the accused also present.

There will normally be little warning before the case comes up for hearing; cases come on in turn and not by pre-arranged appointments. Thus the defendant and his or her lawyers may be told of the trial only a few days before it is due to start, and so have to arrange for all their witnesses to come to court at short notice. Frequently, the barrister instructed by the solicitor will be engaged in another case and so be unable to represent the accused at the trial: if so, the brief (i.e the barrister's bundle of papers) will have to be passed on to another barrister, who will have no knowledge of the case and have only a short time in which to familiarize him- or herself with it.

Fraud cases

Serious fraud cases are now dealt with slightly differently. The Criminal Justice Act of 1987 set up a Serious Fraud Office (SFO) to investigate offences. The SFO has considerable investigatory powers, including a requirement to force any person to attend and answer questions. The Fraud Investigation Group, part of the Crown Prosecution Service, has a similar function and powers.

Where a fraud case is particularly serious or complex the case will be transferred by the SFO from the magistrates' court to the crown court without the need for committal proceedings. The defendant will be served with the prosecution evidence in the normal way and can apply to the crown court to dismiss the case on the basis of insufficiency of evidence. If the defendant wishes to call oral evidence as a part of such an application, the consent of the judge will be necessary. These transfer proceedings, however, can be set aside if the defendant feels he or she has been treated unfairly.

THE TRIAL

To start the trial

When the day of the trial arrives the accused will be brought before the judge and the charge will be read out in the form of an indictment. It is possible that this will contain additional charges that have been added since committal, but the indictment should have been sent to the defence before the trial. Should the defendant be charged with any offences triable only in the magistrates' court but arising out of the same incident, they also may be included in the indictment so all the charges can be dealt with together.

The accused then pleads to the charge – either guilty or not guilty. If the plea is not guilty a jury will be sworn comprising twelve members. It is no longer possible to challenge the jury except where the defendant believes a particular juror is unlikely to try the case justly (e.g. because he or she is a friend of the victim).

Prosecution case

Next, the prosecution barrister opens the case by outlining the facts to the jury. Once he or she has done this, he or she then calls the prosecution witnesses. Each witness gives his or her evidence in the form of answers to questions put to them by the barrister. Once they have given their evidence they will usually be cross-examined by the defence. During examination, any evidence which is in dispute must be put to the witness so that they can give their own version of the facts and accept or refute any statements put to them. These days nearly all interviews with suspects take the form of tape-recorded interviews. Rather than play tapes of the interviews in court, it is often quicker to read through a transcript. The prosecuting barrister plays the part of the defendant and the interviewing police officer plays himself. Any points of law concerning the admissibility of evidence are usually dealt with as they arise and always in the absence of the jury. Once the jury has left the court, both barristers argue for/ against the inclusion of the particular piece of evidence. The judge then rules on that point. Such a hearing is known as a 'voir dire' 'trial within a trial'. It is always preferable to avoid these when possible and instead the barristers can reach agreement between themselves before the trial starts.

Once the prosecution has concluded its evidence, the defence may wish to make a submission of 'no case to answer' on the basis that, after hearing all the prosecution evidence, no reasonable jury could go on to convict the defendant. The purpose of this is to prevent the jury from coming to a perverse decision at the end of the case and to save court time (currently valued at £2,600 per day). If the submission is successful, a formal verdict of not guilty is returned without the defence calling any evidence.

Defence case

If the 'no case' submission is unsuccessful or one is not made, then the defence will present its case. The defendant is under no obligation to give evidence but should he or she choose to do so, then they will be called first and any other witnesses follow the procedure of examination, cross-examination and re-examination – the same as for the prosecution witnesses.

It is worth mentioning that, as a general rule, the defence does not need to prove all parts of the alleged defence 'beyond reasonable doubt'. Should the prosecution manage to do this, it would be very unwise for the defence not to call any evidence to refute the prosecution case. Any evidence the defence does call, however, needs only to create a reasonable doubt in the minds of the jurors. The defence does not have to prove anything beyond that. This principle should be explained to the jury several times during the course of the trial.

Speeches and the summing-up

Once all the evidence has been heard the barristers then go to make their closing speeches. The defence always goes on to make its speech after the prosecution. However, in very short trials, the prosecution makes no speech at all.

The judge then sums up the case to the jury. First, he or she will summarize the evidence – any comments he or she may make at this stage are merely there to help and guide the jury, and can be adopted or dismissed as the jury wishes. The second part of the summing-up concerns the law and on this the jury must take the judge at his or her word. As far as they are concerned, he or she is the final arbiter on all legal matters.

The jury's verdict

After the judge has finished his or her summing-up, the jury retires to consider its verdict, preferably a unanimous one. If they have not all agreed on a verdict within two hours, the judge may – if he or she wishes – call them into court and tell them that he will accept a majority decision of ten of the jury. The jury then retire again to see if they can now reach a verdict. But if they still cannot reach a verdict, they will have to sit on until the judge agrees that no decision can be reached. When that happens the hung jury is discharged and a new trial is ordered.

The verdict

If the defendant is acquitted, he or she will be freed and that will be the end of the case. The prosecution cannot appeal. Surprisingly though, the accused will not receive any compensation for the worry, strain, inconvenience and loss suffered, even if he or she has been kept in prison for several months. Only if it can be shown that the police acted 'maliciously' in prosecuting could the defendant sue them for damages – and usually the chances of proving 'malice' are difficult. However, the defendant will probably be awarded costs (i.e. legal expenses; see page 953).

If the defendant is convicted (i.e. found guilty), the judge will ask the police what is known about the prisoner. This is a request for details of the prisoner's criminal record. The prisoner's barrister will then make a speech in mitigation, asking for a lenient sentence. At this stage, the judge may well adjourn the case so that a medical or social inquiry report can be prepared on the prisoner. Often this will have been prepared in advance, but if not, the hearing will be adjourned, probably for two weeks or so. The defendant may be released on bail during this time but it is more usual to be remanded in custody since it will be 'administratively' more convenient to prepare the report if in prison.

The report will be of vital importance. The judge will pay great attention to it when deciding on sentence. It is therefore surprising that a copy of the report is usually not given to the defence before the trial, even when it is known that the accused intends to plead guilty. Moreover, it is usually the case that the social worker who wrote the report is not in court to be cross-examined on the conclusions, prior to sentencing.

Appealing

The defendant can appeal to the Court of Appeal, Criminal Division, against the severity of the sentence, the decision of the jury or on a point of law. The prosecution can appeal to the Court of Appeal if they believe that the sentence was 'unduly lenient'. The prosecution can also apply to the Court of Appeal to clarify a point of law that has arisen in the case, but this will not affect the acquittal of the defendant.

JURIES

Eligibility to serve

Anyone between the ages of eighteen and seventy and who is on the electoral register is liable to jury service. In addition, the person must have lived in the UK for a continuous period of five years since the age of thirteen; this condition is aimed at weeding out those people who do not have a proper understanding of the English language.

But certain groups of people may be excused from serving, or may be unable to serve.

Ineligible people

Judges, JPs, solicitors, barristers, police officers, the clergy, legal executives, prison officers, prison governors, probation officers and members of boards of prison visitors are among those whose jobs make them ineligible for jury service. The person remains ineligible for ten years after leaving the job, except for ex-judges and JPs, who remain ineligible for life.

Disqualified people

Anyone who has been sentenced to prison (or detention centre, youth custody, community service or a suspended sentence) within the last ten years is disqualified from jury service. So too is anyone put on probation within the last five years. Also, a person sentenced to more than five years in prison is disqualified for life.

Excused people

Peers, MPs, members of the forces, doctors, dentists, nurses, midwives, chemists and vets can apply to be excused from jury service if they wish. So also can a person who has sat on a jury (excluding a coroner's jury) within the last two years.

Being called for service

Usually about six weeks' notice is given. A person who is ineligible or disqualified should notify the court office. He or she must do this, for if they sit on the jury they will be committing a criminal offence. The summoning officer can excuse a person from jury service if there is 'good reason' for doing so. However, mere inconvenience will not be sufficient and the officer will want to be satisfied that severe inconvenience or great hardship would be caused. Good reasons would generally include holiday arrangements, exams, an illness in the family, pregnancy or a business that would otherwise have to close down. If the officer refuses to excuse the juror, application can be made to the High Court for the jury summons to be set aside. If the juror is excused service, it is likely to be only a temporary reprieve.

A person who fails to comply with a jury summons can be fined. The mere fact that an employer will not release a juror from work is not a defence; however, the employer might well be punished for contempt of court.

On the date stated in the jury summons, the juror should attend court. He or she will form part of the jury panel – namely, all the prospective jurors. The jury for a case is selected by ballot, and once the twelve jurors needed for a jury have been selected, they take the juror's oath, in turn. Once the oath has been taken the juror cannot be challenged, but at any time before then either the defence or the prosecution can challenge the juror. Any challenges must be justified to the judge. The prosecution can also challenge jurors by asking them to 'stand by for the Crown', which means that the juror goes back to the jury panel and will have to serve only if there are insufficient people in the panel to make up a jury. Like the defence, the prosecution is also able to challenge 'for cause'.

Although a jury is normally composed of twelve jurors, it can be made up of fewer. At the start of the case there must be twelve jurors, but the trial can continue as long as there are nine jurors. So up to three jurors can fall ill or be released.

The judge has power to release a juror during the course of the trial if it would not interfere with the administration of justice to do so. This favour is only exercised occasionally; for instance, if a juror faces a domestic crisis or falls ill. However, it can also be exercised to allow a juror to go on holiday:

A juror was called for jury service on 16 July and was told that she would probably not be needed after 30 July. Her first case, on 16 July, was a theft offence, and the trial was expected to last only three or four days. But it had still not finished on 30 July. The juror told the judge that she had arranged to go on a camping holiday in Somerset with her family on the next day. She asked to be discharged and the judge agreed. The trial continued with eleven jurors. The defendant was convicted and appealed to the Court of Appeal, arguing that there had been an irregularity in the trial, namely the releasing of the juror. Held: No. 'Those summonsed to serve as jurors are entitled to such consideration as it is within the power of the courts to give them. If the administration of justice can be carried on without inconveniencing jurors unduly it should be. Discharging a juror whose holiday arrangements would be interfered with by having to stay on the jury after being sworn no longer hinders the administration of justice: trials can go on as long as there are nine jurors. Anyway an aggrieved and inconvenienced juror is not likely to be a good one.' Hambery (1977)

The finances of jury service

Compensation is fairly limited. It is made up of three different elements:
- *daily travelling allowance*: second-class bus fare or, for car users, a specified rate per mile (but parking fees may not be recoverable); *plus*
- *subsistence allowance*

If absent from home:
for up to 5 hours – £1.80
5–10 hours – £3.90
over 10 hours – £8.60
overnight (Inner London) – £68.50
overnight (elsewhere) – £63.15

- *Financial Loss Allowance*: the actual net loss (i.e. after tax etc.) up to a maximum of £38.50 per day (or £19.25 if absent four hours or less). After ten days, up to £77.00 can be paid (1991 figures).

The importance of jury service

As Lord Devlin said:

Each jury is a little Parliament. The jury sense is the parliamentary sense. I cannot see one dying and the other surviving. The first object of any tyrant in Whitehall would be to make Parliament utterly subservient to his will; and the next to overthrow or diminish trial by jury, for no tyrant could afford to leave a subject's freedom in the hands of his countrymen. So that trial by jury is more than one wheel of the constitution; it is the lamp that shows that freedom lives.

SENTENCING OFFENDERS

The punishment of offenders has four main aims:

1 To deter the offender and others from committing crimes.
2 To prevent further crimes (e.g. by taking away a person's driving licence).
3 To exact retribution for society.
4 To reform the offender via rehabilitation and training.

Making a speech in mitigation

Before a convicted person is sentenced he or she (or their lawyer) can make a speech in mitigation to the court. The purpose of mitigation is to persuade the court to impose a lighter sentence than it might otherwise have done. It is not an occasion for the defendant to repeat 'I didn't do it'; it is too late to argue about guilt, for the only matter to be decided is the sentence.

There are two elementary rules of mitigation:

1 Do not say too much.
2 Do not call too many character witnesses. Usually one will suffice. But make sure that the character witness is unrelated; for instance, the mother of the accused is hardly likely to be viewed by the court as an impartial observer.

Prison

Most offences have a fixed maximum prison sentence, but usually the offender will receive less than the maximum period.

Generally, a magistrates' court cannot impose a sentence of more than six months per offence, although the magistrates can sometimes get around this by committing the prisoner to the crown court for sentence in the hope that the judge will pass a longer sentence. If the accused is being sentenced for several offences, the maximum magistrates' court prison term is a total of twelve months.

If a prisoner is sentenced to prison for several offences at the same trial, the judge will say whether the sentences are to run *concurrently* or *consecutively*. This is best explained by an example: if a prisoner receives two sentences of one year each, he or she will serve only one year if the sentences run concurrently, but will serve two years if the sentences are to be consecutive. Most prison sentences are concurrent.

Prison should be seen as the last resort when sentencing an offender, partly because prison is not generally regarded as a reforming influence and also, of course, the cost of keeping someone in our crowded prisons is very high. Accordingly, there are many rules that limit the powers of the courts to send offenders to prison. Nevertheless, our prison population remains very high and our prisons are overcrowded.

First-time imprisonment

This cannot be imposed unless the accused is legally represented (unless he or she did not bother to apply for legal aid or was rejected on financial grounds) and, in addition, the court feels that no other sentence would be appropriate. If the court feels that only prison would be appropriate, it must say why. Usually it will be because of the gravity of the offence or because of the defendant's previous record. Normally, first-time prison cannot be imposed.

An alternative to sending someone to prison is for the magistrates to have him or her held in the police cells (i.e. not in prison) for up to four days. It amounts to a short sharp shock, and some magistrates have started to use this tactic as a weapon against drunk-drivers, who, apart from losing their licences, are given four days in the police cells.

Suspended sentence

Rather than send the offender to prison, the judge may sentence him or her to prison but say that the sentence will not come into effect if he or she behaves themselves for a fixed period of between one and two years. This option of suspending the prison sentence is only available if the sentence is for no more than two years. In order that the offender does not seem to go unpunished, a suspended sentence should usually go hand in hand with an order for compensation or a fine. If the offender commits another imprisonable offence during the fixed period, the court may bring the suspended sentence into effect and send him or her to prison.

If the prison sentence is for six months or less (as any magistrates' court prison sentence must be), the judge may suspend the sentence unless one of several exceptions applies. The most important exceptions cover crimes of violence and criminals who have previously received prison or borstal sentences; the net effect is that most first-time offenders in the magistrates' court do not go to prison. After October 1992, the partly suspended sentence ceases to exist.

Strangely, those under twenty-one cannot receive a suspended sentence. This becomes more anomalous after October 1992, when the guidelines for determining whether a young offender should go to prison become the same as those for an adult.

The basic rule with any suspended sentence is that if the offender commits another imprisonable offence within the one-to-two-year period, he or she will go to prison for the original offence. However, this will not always be so, for the court:

• *cannot* activate the suspended sentence if he or she receives an absolute discharge, conditional discharge or probation for the subsequent offence;

• *need not* activate the suspended sentence if it would be 'unjust' to do so. Thus the court has a wide discretion, and often this will be exercised in the offender's favour if the subsequent offence is of a different type and nature from the first offence, or if the court does not feel that the subsequent offence by itself justifies a term in prison.

Early release

From October 1992 parole and remission will be abolished but prisoners will continue to be entitled to early release. The new rules provide for a higher proportion of prisoners to be supervised on release and the rules attempt to restore meaning to the sentence imposed by the court. All offenders are now at risk of being recalled right up to the end of the sentence should they commit a further imprisonable offence. Rules vary according to the length of sentence and are as follows:

• under twelve months – automatic unconditional release. Generally, any time spent 'on remand' will still count in full towards a prisoner's early release date. The system is the same for young offenders, except that if they are under twenty-two at the time of release they must be supervised for at least three months by the probation services. Prisoners are automatically released after serving half their sentence. They are not released on licence and do not need to be supervised, but they are liable to have the remaining part of their sentence reactivated if they reoffend before it expires (in addition to the sentence for the new offence).

• more than twelve months and under four years – automatic conditional release. These prisoners are released automatically on licence at the half-way point of their sentence. The release date can be delayed only by 'additional days' being imposed for breaches of prison discipline. The release is subject to licence conditions and will be supervised by the Probation Service up to the three-quarters point. The prisoner is liable to recall or fine if the conditions are breached. Any such breaches will be dealt with in the magistrates' court.

• four years or more – discretionary conditional release. Prisoners will become eligible for parole between the half-way and two-thirds points of the sentence. Should the prisoner be refused parole, he or she will be automatically released on licence at the two-thirds point of the sentence. They will be subject to licence conditions and supervised up to the three-quarters point, and liable to recall if the licence conditions are breached. The unexpired portion of the sentence can be reactivated if they reoffend between the three-quarters and full-term points.

There are separate rules which can apply to people convicted of sexual offences which can result in their having to serve the whole of their sentence if parole is not granted.

Generally, any time spent 'on remand' will still count in full towards a prisoner's parole eligibility date. The system is the same for young offenders, except that if they are under twenty-two at the time of release they must be supervised for at least three months by the probation services.

These rules apply only to prisoners sentenced after October 1992.

Life sentences

Different rules apply to prisoners who receive life sentences. Although life sentences are mandatory for murder, they can be given by a judge in other cases (e.g. rape, buggery, arson, attempted murder and manslaughter). A mandatory life-sentence prisoner – that is, one given a life sentence after a conviction for murder – has less clearly defined rights than a discretionary life-sentence prisoner. For both kinds of life sentence the judge will indicate the tariff – that is, the minimum number of years that the person should serve for the purposes of punishment. After that period has ended the person should be kept in custody only if they remain a danger to the public. In mandatory cases the decision to release them will be made by the Home Secretary following a recommendation by the Parole Board. The decision will be made in secret. However, in discretionary cases from October 1992 the review will be carried out by a tribunal of the Parole Board, and the prisoner will be entitled to see the reports written about him or her, attend the tribunal and be represented by lawyers with legal aid if necessary.

Non-custodial sentences

From October 1992 the law will change in relation to non-custodial sentences (to become known as community sentences). Such a sentence will comprise one or more community orders, which are:

1 Probation Order.
2 Community Service Order.
3 Combination Order.
4 Curfew Order.
5 Supervision Order.
6 Attendance Centre Order.

These sentences are no longer treated as alternatives to custodial sentences but fall somewhere between custodial sentences and financial penalties. They form part of a structure of available sentences, so that each order or a combination of different ones can be used to make the punishment more appropriate to the offence and offender. Pre-sentence reports prepared by the probation services will usually be required before these sentences can be imposed and are sometimes mandatory.

1. Probation Order

Probation can be for up to three years. But if the offender is over sixteen years old, he or she cannot be put on probation unless he or she agrees. Sometimes conditions are imposed, such as residence in an approved hostel, or that the offender will keep in touch with the probation officer as required by the officer, or attend a probation centre, or undergo treatment for medical conditions, drug or alcohol dependency.

If the offender commits further offences while on probation, the court can impose a fresh punishment for the original offence. Similarly, if the offender does not comply with the terms of the probation order (e.g. does not attend appointments with the probation officer) he or she can be resentenced for the offence. Alternatively, the court might leave the probation order in force and impose a fine (up to £400).

From October 1992 probation becomes a sentence in its own right. The qualifying age becomes sixteen rather than seventeen.

2. Community Service Order (unpaid work to benefit the community)

This is no longer instead of prison, but should be used in circumstances where restriction on a person's liberty is appropriate. The court will impose a sentence of between forty and 240 hours, to be served within twelve months. The offender cannot insist on being able to do community service. It is available only when offered by the court, and after a presentence report has recommended him/her for it. It is available only to offenders aged sixteen and over.

If the offender does not carry out the terms of the Community Service Order, the court can impose a fresh sentence for the offence, including a fine or custody. Alternatively they can order him/her to persevere with the order.

3. Combination Order

This is a new sentence available to the court and is essentially a mix of probation and community service. The purpose is both to punish the offender and to provide help and guidance to lessen the likelihood of reoffending. The probation part of the sentence must be for not less than twelve months, and not more than three years; and the community service part not less than forty hours and not more than 100. This order can also be combined with other community orders or with financial penalties.

4. Curfew Order

Another new sentence available to the court is the power to impose a curfew on offenders of sixteen years or over. A pre-sentence report must be obtained and considered before such a sentence is passed. The maximum duration of an order is six months and the period of curfew is between two and twelve hours. These orders can be used in consultation with Community Orders and financial penalties. It is intended that these orders may, when necessary, incorporate the use of electronic monitoring (at the time of writing, proposals for tagging have been shelved).

5. Supervision Order

The order places a child under the supervision of a probation officer or social worker to advise, befriend and assess the child for an initial period of one year (which may be extended to three if appropriate). It can be imposed on those of seventeen years and younger. Various requirements can be inserted into the order (e.g. residence, residential courses or merely to attend school regularly).

6. Attendance Centre Orders

Their purpose is to impose a loss of leisure time on young offenders and juveniles by ordering that they attend a centre for two or three hours alternate Saturdays and in that time to teach them the constructive use of leisure. Such an order can be imposed on anyone between ten and twenty-one years with a maximum of twenty-one hours for anyone up to the age of fifteen and thirty-six hours for those between sixteen and twenty-one.

Breach of Community Order may result in:
● £1,000 fine;
● sixty hours (provided total does not exceed 240 hours);
● court may revoke order and deal with him/her for original offence;
● if offender is under twenty-one the court may impose an attendance centre order.

Financial penalties

In practice this is by far the most important form of sentence, since 80 per cent of magistrates' court sentences are fines. The means of an offender will affect the amount of a fine but it should not influence the decision of whether or not to fine him/her.

Unit fine system

The power of the magistrates' court to impose fines is controlled by statute. Therefore, each offence punishable by the magistrates has a statutory maximum fine. From October 1992 the overall maximum is to be increased from £2,000 to £5,000 and a new system of determining the level at which the fine will be set is to be introduced. The system allows the offender's means to determine the ultimate amount of the fine, the idea being that the poor are not then seen to be treated unduly harshly and the rich unduly leniently.

The system marks the gravity of the offence by fining the defendant in terms of units rather than a specific amount. Each unit represents the defendant's disposable income and each offence is punishable with a maximum number of units. For instance, two offenders who commit the same offence of theft (maximum 50 units) are both fined 20 units. The first offender is unemployed with a weekly disposable income of £5; the second is a shop manager with a weekly disposable income of £20. The first will be fined a total of £100 (£5 x 20) and the second a total of £400 (£20 x 20). The advantage of this system is that when the court passes sentence offenders are seen to be given similar punishments for similar crimes – for example, 20 units. However, even though the resulting fines may differ considerably in value, they should be equally financially burdensome to those who commit the same or similar crimes.

Maximum penalties

Rather than each offence having a statutory maximum fine, they now have a statutory maximum number of units in accordance with the following scale.

> Level 1 – 2 units   (max. £200)
> Level 2 – 5 units   (max. £500)
> Level 3 – 10 units   (max. £1,000)
> Level 4 – 25 units   (max. £2,500)
> Level 5 – 50 units   (max. £5,000)

Offences triable either way (triable in both the magistrates' and crown court) are the more serious classes of offence and so are almost always Level 5, whereas less serious offences, such as street trading without a certificate, are Level 1.

The calculation of the offender's disposable income will be in accordance with rules made by the Lord Chancellor. But in any event the minimum value of a unit is £4 and the maximum £100. Reduced amounts are to be fixed in relation to juvenile offenders.

Enforcement

Usually if offenders are in a position of financial hardship, they will be given time to pay, generally in instalments. If the instalments are not kept up, the court is likely, on application, to allow further time in which to pay. Another alternative is to place offenders under the care of a probation officer who can encourage them to sort out their financial affairs.

A further alternative is an attachment of earnings order which can be made when the defaulter has steady long-term employment. Payments are deducted straight from the defaulter's income by the employer. The amount is set by the court. The court will also set a 'protected earnings rate' which ensures the defaulter's take-home pay never falls below a certain amount as a result of the fine (e.g. no payment towards the fine will be made if the person is sick and does not collect a full week's wages).

If all else fails, however, the defaulter who does not pay his or her fine can be, and often is, sent to prison. The sentence maxima are as follows.

Not more than 2 units – 7 days
More than 2 but not more than 5 units – 14 days
More than 5 but not more than 10 units – 28 days
More than 10 but not more than 25 units – 45 days
More than 25 but not more than 50 units – 3 months

Committal to custody for non-payment of fines will be imposed only when the court finds that there has been a wilful refusal to pay or culpable neglect.

The court can also impose a committal for a set number of days, and then suspend it on certain terms (e.g. on the payment of regular instalments). If the fine defaulter does not make regular payments, then he or she can be arrested and imprisoned without further notice. However, the defaulter is often brought back before the court to say why they should not be imprisoned. If the defaulter is having difficulty making payments, it is therefore very important that he or she apply to the court to vary the terms (e.g. the amount or frequency of payments) of the suspended committal.

For unpaid fixed-penalty fines (e.g. speeding, parking offences) and other small fines, the court may issue a distress warrant. This means that bailiffs will be sent to collect the money. This automatically increases the amount payable as the defaulter must pay both the fine and the bailiffs' costs.

Conditional discharge

If probation would be inappropriate, the offender may receive a conditional discharge instead. The conviction will stand but he or she will be released without punishment for a period of up to three years. If, during that time, he or she commits any other offences then they may be brought back and given a sentence for the original offence. This may or may not be prison.

Absolute discharge

Although the offender has been convicted of the crime, the court may feel that it would be wrong to punish him or her. If so, they may receive an absolute discharge.

For example, the driver of a fire engine might pass through red lights on the way to an emergency call. Technically, he is guilty of an offence, for the law does not allow drivers of emergency vehicles to drive with any less care than ordinary road users (see page 714). But the court may feel that the police should have turned a 'blind eye' to the offence, or perhaps merely cautioned the driver, rather than prosecuted him. If so, the court might give the driver an absolute discharge.

Deferred sentence

The court may decide to postpone sentencing for up to six months. But this can be done only so that the court can take into account:
• conduct after conviction (e.g. making reparation for the offence), *or*

• any change in circumstances (e.g. more settled home life or a new job).

A sentence can be deferred only once and it cannot be deferred for successive periods of up to six months.

Binding over

Strictly speaking, an order that a person can be 'bound over to keep the peace' is not really a sentence at all. It is more in the way of preventive justice, for it allows the magistrates to warn citizens as to their future good conduct. If the person fails to keep the peace or to be of good behaviour during a stated period (up to twelve months) he or she may forfeit a sum of money. This sum is called a recognizance. Thus a typical order would be to be 'bound over for nine months in the sum of £50'.

Before the binding-over order is made, the court must allow the person a chance of arguing against it. If the person does not agree to being bound over, he or she can be sent to prison for up to six months.

The important point to note is that one does not have to commit a criminal offence to be eligible for binding over. The court has wide powers to bind over, given by two different Acts:

• the Justices of the Peace Act 1361 allows an order to be made whenever the magistrates think there is likely to be a further breach of the peace;

• the Magistrates' Courts Act of 1980 allows an order to be made if the magistrates hear evidence that satisfies them that the original complaint against the person was justified.

These are, then, extensive powers. They are often used in inter-neighbour disputes. The typical course of events is that Mr A issues a summons for assault against Mr B; but Mr B then replies with a summons for assault against Mr A. Both cases are heard together and the magistrate is faced with two families arguing out their private feud in the courtroom. Finding it impossible to decide who is in the wrong, the magistrate orders both Mr A and Mr B to be bound over. Naturally, both Mr A and Mr B are furious with the outcome, since they interpret the binding-over order as a finding of guilt.

In addition, binding-over orders are often used against peeping Toms, poison-pen writers and rejected suitors who will not take 'no' for answer. About 8,000 orders a year are made under the 1361 Act.

Clearly, there is a danger that magistrates might misuse their wide powers. Demonstrators and protestors have been bound over for no good reason and, in effect, powers have been used to take away the right of free speech and protest (e.g. it was frequently used against Greenham Common women during the peace demonstrations in 1984).

Young offenders

There are various rules about the sentences that can be imposed on people aged under twenty-one (see Chapter 10).

CRIMINAL PENALTIES
Maximum penalties for criminal offences tried in the magistrates' courts:

Absconding: £5,000 and 3 months
Abusive words or behaviour: £5,000 and 6 months
Actual bodily harm: £5,000 and 6 months
Affray: £5,000 and 6 months
Air guns: £1,000, forfeiture
Airport security (breaches of): £5,000
Ammunition: £5,000 and 6 months, forfeiture
Animals (cruelty to): £5,000 and 6 months
Animals straying on highway: £1,000
Article with blade in public place: £1,000
Assault on police constable or person assisting police constable:
      £5,000 and 6 months

Bankrupt (undischarged obtaining credit): £5,000 or 6 months
Begging: £1 or 14 days before one magistrate; £1,000 or 1 month if
      before two or more magistrates
Brothel: £1,000 and 3 months; £2,500 and 6 months (previous conviction)
Builder's skip
   depositing on highway: £1,000
   not complying with a condition: £1,000
   unlit on highway: £1,000
Burglary: £5,000 and 6 months

Children (cruelty to): £5,000 and 6 months
Common assault: £5,000 or 6 months
   Indictable common assault: £5,000 and 6 months
Computer misuse unauthorized access: £5,000 and 6 months
   with intent to commit further offences: £5,000 and 6 months
   unauthorized modification: £5,000 and 6 months
Crossbow (buying, hiring or possession by person under 17): £1,000, forfeiture
Criminal damage
   value of property under £2,000: £2,500 and 3 months
   value of property over £2,000: £5,000 and 6 months
Cruelty to animals: *see* Animals
Customs duty (avoiding): three times value of goods or £5,000 and 6 months

Dangerous machinery: £5,000
Deception (obtaining by): £5,000 and 6 months
Dishonestly handling: £5,000 and 6 months
Disorderly conduct: £1,000
Dogs
   breeding or parting with fighting dogs: £5,000 and 6 months
   dog licence: £200
   dog worrying livestock: £1,000
   out of control in public place: £5,000 and 6 months
Drugs
   Class A: £5,000 and 6 months
   Class B: £2,500 and 3 months

Drunk: £200
　At football match: £500
Drunk and disorderly: £1,000

Earnings of prostitution (living on): £5,000 and 6 months
Enclosed premises (found on): £1,000 or 3 months
Evasion of liability, obtaining by deception: £5,000 and 6 months
Excessive noise (nuisance order): £5,000
Exposure (indecent): £1,000 or 3 months

False alarm of fire: £2,500 and 3 months
False statement to obtain social security: £5,000 and 3 months
False weighing or measuring equipment: £5,000 (and 6 months if deliberate fraud)
Firearms (forfeiture for each of the following)
　in public place: £5,000 and 6 months
　purchasing, possessing etc. without certificate: £5,000 and 6 months
　trespassing in a building: £5,000 and 6 months
　trespassing on land: £2,500 and 3 months
Food (selling food not of quality demanded): £5,000
Football spectators
　indecent or racialist chanting: £1,000
　throwing missiles: £1,000
Forgery: £5,000 and 6 months
Found on enclosed premises: £1,000 or 3 months

Game (trespassing on land in daytime in search of game): £200;
　£1,000 if five or more trespassers
Glue (offering to supply to person under 18 for purpose of inhalation): £5,000 and 6
　months
Going equipped to steal: £5,000 and 6 months
Grievous bodily harm: £5,000 and 6 months

Handling stolen goods £5,000 and 6 months
Harassing residential occupier: £5,000 and 6 months
Highway
　builder's skip (depositing or leaving unlit): £1,000
　straying animals on: £1,000
　wilful obstruction: £1,000

Indecency (gross between males): £5,000 and 6 months
Indecency with child: £5,000 and 6 months
Indecent assault: £5,000 and 6 months
Indecent exposure: £1,000 or 6 months
Insulting words or behaviour: £5,000 and 6 months
Interference with vehicle: £2,500 and 3 months
Intoxicating liquor
　possessing at or on way to a designated sporting event: £1,000 and three months
　selling outside permitted hours: £1,000
　selling to person under 18: £1,000 (and forfeiture of licence on second conviction)
　selling without a licence: £2,500 and 6 months (and forfeiture of liquor and containers)

Kerb crawling: £1,000

Landlord and tenant
 unlawful eviction or harassment: £5,000 and 6 months
Liability, obtaining evasion of by deception: £5,000 and 6 months
Litter (including car dumping)
● Environmental Protection Act 1990: £2,500
● Refuse Disposal (Amenity) Act 1978: £2,500 and 3 months
Living on earnings of prostitution: £5,000 and 6 months

Making off without payment: £5,000 and 6 months
Malicious communications: £2,500
Measuring equipment (false or unjust): £5,000 plus 6 months if fraud (and forfeiture)

National Insurance
● failing to pay contributions: £1,000 plus two years' arrears
● failing to return card: £1,000
Noise: £5,000

Obscenity – exposing person: £1,000 or 3 months
Obstructing a constable (or a person assisting a constable): £1,000 and 1 month
Obstructing highway: £1,000
Obtaining evasion of liability by deception: £5,000 and 6 months
Obtaining pecuniary advantage: £5,000 and 6 months
Obtaining property by deception: £5,000 and 6 months
Obtaining services by deception: £5,000 and 6 months
Offensive weapon: £5,000 and 6 months' forfeiture

Payment, making off without: £5,000 and 6 months
Pecuniary advantage (obtaining by): £5,000 and 6 months
Pedlar: £1,000 or 1 month before two or more magistrates
Poaching: £200, £1,000 if five or more trespassers (if violence used £2,500 and 6 months)
Point, article with, in public place: £1,000
Possessing anything to damage or destroy property: £5,000 and 6 months
Prostitutes
 living on earnings of: £5,000 and 6 months
 soliciting by prostitutes: £500/£1,000
Public telephone (fraudulent use of): £5,000 and 6 months
 indecent or false telephone calls: £1,000

Railway offences
 avoiding fare: £1,000 or 3 months
 giving false name or address: £1,000 or 3 months
Resisting a constable or a person assisting a constable: £1,000 and 1 month

School attendance (parent not ensuring): £1,000
Shotgun
 loaded shotgun in a public place: £5,000 and 6 months, forfeiture
 purchasing or possessing without licence: £5,000 and 6 months, forfeiture
Skip
 depositing on highway: £1,000
 not complying with a condition: £1,000
 unlit on highway: £1,000

Smuggling: three times value of goods or £5,000 and 6 months
Social Security
  false statement to obtain: £5,000 and 3 months
  persistently refusing or neglecting to maintain oneself or a dependent: £2,500 and 3 months
Soliciting by prostitutes: £500/£1,000
Statutory nuisance (noise): £5,000
Stealing: £5,000 and 6 months
Straying animals on highway: £1,000

Taking motor vehicle or conveyance: £5,000 and 6 months plus endorsement and 8 penalty points
Tattooing a minor: £1,000
Telephone
  fraudulent use of public telephone: £5,000 and 6 months
  indecent or false calls: £1,000
Television licence: £1,000
Theft: £5,000 and 6 months
Threatening to damage or destroy property: £5,000 and 6 months
Threatening words or behaviour: £5,000 and 6 months
Trade description
  applying false trade description: £5,000
  supplying goods with false description: £5,000
Trespassing with a firearm
  in a building: £5,000 and 6 months
  on land: £2,500 and 3 months
Trespassing on land during daytime in search of game etc. £200;
  £1,000 if five or more trespassers

Undischarged bankrupt obtaining credit: £5,000 and 6 months

Vehicle interference: £500 and 3 months
Violent disorder: £5,000 and 6 months

Wilful obstruction of highway: £1,000
Wilful obstruction of police constable (or person assisting police constable): £1,000 and 1 month
Wounding: £5,000 and 6 months

Sentencing Offenders: The Sentences That Can Be Imposed

	Age of the offender						
	under 10	10–13	14	15	16	17–21	over 21
Absolute discharge (no punishment imposed)		●	●	●	●	●	●
Attendance centre order (attendance for several hours per week in leisure time)		●	●	●	●	●	
Binding over (offender or sureties forfeit money if he or she misbehaves)		●	●	●	●	●	●
Care order (child goes into care of local authority)	●	●	●	●	●		
Community service order (unpaid community work)					●	●	●
Compensation order (compensation to the victim)	●	●	●	●	●	●	●
Conditional discharge (no punishment if offender behaves him- or herself)		●	●	●	●	●	●
Criminal bankruptcy (denying the offender the proceeds of his or her life of crime)						●	●
Deprivation of property (offender loses property used when committing the crime)		●	●	●	●	●	●
Fine (financial penalty)		●	●	●	●	●	●
Guardianship order (commits the accused as a mental patient)					●	●	●
Prison (full-time detention)							●
Probation (supervision by a social worker)						●	●
Restitution order (restores stolen property to its owner)	●	●	●	●	●	●	●
Supervision order (a junior form of probation)		●	●	●	●		
Suspended prison sentence (threat of prison if offender commits further offence)							●
Young offender institution			●*	●	●	●	

* From October 1992 must be 15.

54 Prisoners' Rights

Prisoners retain fundamental legal rights as citizens despite their imprisonment, apart from those taken away by a specific law or a necessary implication of the law.

The Prison Act (1952) and Prison Rules (1964) both limit and confer rights. For instance, the Prison Rules give rights to food, clothing, exercise, a specified minimum number of visits and letters, and a fair hearing in disciplinary procedures.

Serious breaches of the above rights may be taken before the courts for judicial review. The courts will review decisions by the prison authorities which are unfair or legally wrong. Topics which have been taken to court include disciplinary adjudications, transfer, censorship and the separation of a woman from her baby. Unless there are exceptional circumstances applications for judicial review should be lodged within three months of the date of the decision in question.

COMPLAINTS

Requests/Complaints Procedure

The prison authorities advise that requests or complaints should be dealt with by speaking to prison staff (i.e. your wing, landing or personal officer and then a governor grade) in the first instance. If this does not resolve matters then a written request/complaint should be made on the forms available. Requests/complaints dealt with inside the prison should be answered within seven days. If the response is unsatisfactory then the next stage is to appeal to the area manager on a request/complaints appeal form. Request/complaints forms can be sent direct to the area manager if they are about 'reserved subjects' which cannot be dealt with inside the prison (i.e. parole), or under 'confidential access' (if you do not want to disclose the request/complaint to staff on your wing or landing). However, it should be noted that an area manager may disclose the contents to the prison if he or she feels it is appropriate.

Outside Agencies

MPs in your home constituency or in the constituency where the prison is situated may take up a serious complaint with the Minister concerned. MPs can also ask the Parliamentary Commissioner for Administration (Ombudsman) to investigate complaints of maladministration including breaches of the Prison Rules.

Solicitors may be consulted for advice and representation.

The Commission for Racial Equality may be consulted where there are allegations of racial harassment or discrimination.

The Queen or Parliament may be petitioned. Prison staff should have copies of the procedures involved.

MEPs may be petitioned.

The European Convention on Human Rights guarantees certain fundamental rights, some of which are relevant to prisoners. In order to make an application all domestic remedies must have been exhausted. Applications to the Commission (the first stage in the procedure of getting a case heard in the European Court of Human Rights) should be made within six months of the alleged breach.

ACCESS TO LAWYERS

You have a right of access to a lawyer in criminal and civil proceedings. There is no need to air complaints internally before consulting with a solicitor/legal adviser. Prisoners who are party to legal proceedings will not have correspondence with their legal advisers read or stopped unless there is reason to suppose that the correspondence does not relate to the proceedings.

DISCIPLINE

The list of offences against prison discipline, including the new offence of mutiny, is set out in Rule 47 of the Prison Rules (Rule 50 of the Young Offender Institution Rules). Prison governors deal with the less serious charges; more serious matters are referred to the police and Crown Prosecution Service for prosecution in the outside criminal courts. Boards of Visitors no longer have any part in the prison disciplinary process, nor in applications for restoration of lost remission.

Prisoners must be charged with any offence as soon as possible and within forty-eight hours of the alleged offence being discovered (except in exceptional circumstances). You should be segregated only pending adjudication if it is justifiable under Rule 43, for the purpose of 'good order and discipline', and the reasons for your segregation should be clearly recorded. Segregation for more than three days must be authorized by a member of the Board of Visitors or the Secretary of State.

You should be allowed to see statements or written material which will be used in evidence against you (except where the author of a medical report considers it should not be disclosed). You should be given sufficient time to prepare for the hearing, if necessary by asking for an adjournment. You may also apply for legal representation, or the assistance of a friend or adviser (a 'McKenzie Friend'), but this is not available as of right. If granted, a solicitor may be able to advise you under the green-form scheme.

If the matter is referred to the police/CPS and a decision is made not to prosecute because the evidence is unsatisfactory, then you should not face a prison disciplinary charge. However, if criminal charges are dropped for other reasons, it will still be open to the Governor to proceed with a disciplinary charge. But once evidence has been presented in court by the CPS, the prisoner will not be at risk of it being pursued against him as a disciplinary offence.

If found guilty of a disciplinary offence you may be punished by: caution; loss of privileges for a maximum of twenty-eight days (fourteen days in YOI); stoppage of earnings for maximum of twenty-eight days (fourteen days in YOI); cellular confinement for a maximum of three days; loss of remission for maximum of twenty-eight days; exclusion from associated work for a maximum of fourteen days. In addition, those in a YOI may be removed from activities for a maximum of fourteen days; be given up to two extra hours work a day for up to fourteen days, or removed from their wing or unit for up to fourteen days.

A prisoner may appeal to the area manager against a finding of guilt on the basis that the procedure was unfair or contained an error, and/or appeal against the punishment imposed. Where the adjudication has been conducted unfairly or illegally, it may be possible to go to the High Court to review the decision.

Correspondence

All correspondence sent to or from prisoners in the dispersal system, Category A prisoners, prisoners in units housing Category A prisoners, and prisoners on the Escape List will normally be read (except where it is legally privileged). There is no routine reading of mail at Category B (non-dispersal) prisons, Category C prisons, open prisons and designated women's prisons and YOIs, and only a very small proportion of letters will be read in those establishments. In certain circumstances letters may be stopped (see Standing Order 5), and if this happens you will be told and may be allowed to rewrite the letter in question.

Categorization

On reception to prison you will be given a security categorization ranging from A (the highest) to D (the lowest). Category A prisoners have extra security restrictions, including the vetting and approval of their visitors by the police. Categorization is reviewed from time to time and you can be moved to a higher or a lower security categorization.

Allocation

Prisoners have no right to choose the prison or the location in which they will be held. However, if your allocation causes particularly severe problems (i.e. to your family because of their age, illness or pregnancy) you can ask for a transfer. It is helpful if you provide the relevant material to support your case (i.e. medical evidence) in such circumstances. If you are unsuccessful you may wish to ask a solicitor, legal adviser, MP etc. to intervene.

Transfers

Transfers may not be used as a form of punishment, but prisoners may be transferred in the interest of 'good order and discipline' under CI 37/90. In extreme cases allocation or transfer may be reviewed by the courts.

Segregation

Rule 43 of the Prison Rules (1964) (Rule 46 of the YOI Rules, 1988) provides for the segregation of prisoners either 'in the interests of good order and discipline' or at their request for their 'own protection'. Segregation under this Rule should not be for more than three days without the authority of a member of the Board of Visitors or the Secretary of State.

Women prisoners

Women prisoners may be allowed to keep their babies with them until the age of nine months or eighteen months, depending upon the prison where they are held. Women and girls do not wear prison uniform but the prison will provide clothing if your own clothes are unsuitable or if you do not have enough clothes of your own. Women cannot be forced to have their hair cut unless the medical officer makes an order to that effect and certain toiletries and sanitary protection will be provided by the prison.

Young Offenders' Institutes

YOIs are governed by a separate set of rules (YOI Rules 1988) which are very similar to the Prison Rules. If you are under seventeen years of age arrangements will be made for participation in education or training for at least fifteen hours within the normal working week.

Race relations

The Prison Service has a public policy statement about race relations which should be displayed in every prison. This states that the Prison Service is committed to a policy of racial equality, and that all prisoners should be treated with humanity, respect and without discrimination. All prisoners have a right to practise their faith and should have equal access to facilities. It is a disciplinary offence for prison staff to use racially abusive language or conduct. All prisons have a race relations liaison officer and a race relations management team, who should meet regularly to check that the policy is being implemented.

Remand prisoners

Remand prisoners are those who are unconvicted, those awaiting extradition, deportation or removal from the UK as illegal entrants, and civil prisoners (i.e. in prison for not paying community charge, tax or maintenance). Those who are convicted but unsentenced are treated as convicted prisoners.

Although unconvicted, remand prisoners may still be disciplined under the procedure outlined above.

Clothes

Remand prisoners are allowed to wear their own clothes if they are suitable, clean and tidy. Clothes may be sent in from the outside or brought in by visitors and exchanged for ones which need washing. Male prisoners on remand may be issued with a prison uniform if they wish.

Visits

Remand prisoners are allowed visits totalling one and a half hours per week and no visiting orders are needed. These must be on at least three days each week and include the opportunity of a weekend visit at least once a fortnight. Visitors do not need a visiting order and up to three adults and the prisoner's children will be allowed at any one time.

Some prisons will allow visitors to hand in cigarettes, tobacco and toiletries, whereas in others they should be sent in by post. Money can also be sent into the prison and can be spent in the prison canteen.

Letters

Remand prisoners may send and receive as many letters as they like. Two second-class letters per week will be provided at public expense and any more will be paid for from prison earnings or private cash. Letters to legal advisers normally have to be paid for, but if a prisoner has no private cash the governor may allow letters essential to the defence to be sent at public expense. Letters are not usually read unless the prisoner is treated as a category A or is on the escape list.

Work

Remand prisoners do not have to work unless they wish to do so. If they do work they will be paid a small amount of money, but in practice there is very little work available. If no work is available, remand prisoners will be paid a very small sum to cover basics. If they refuse to work when offered, this money will be stopped and the prison is not obliged to offer any further work.

Medical treatment

Remand prisoners can apply to be treated by the doctor or dentist of their choice at their own expense although they can use the Prison Medical Service.

Convicted prisoners

Visits

Standing Order 5 (which should be in the Prison Library) sets out the minimum number of visits (and letters) allowed – one thirty-minute visit every twenty-eight days (every fourteen days for young offenders). A visiting order must be sent out to your visitors and they should bring this with them when they visit. Special visits may be allowed in the following circumstances: where there are personal or business difficulties which need to be sorted out after conviction, if they are necessary to the conduct of legal proceedings or the welfare of you and your family, or on the advice of a medical officer where a prisoner is seriously ill.

If the prison where you are held is a long way from your friends and family, you may save up your visits and apply for a temporary transfer to a local prison in order that visits can take place there. Category A prisoners are subject to special procedures. Visits may not be stopped as part of a punishment, but may be deferred if the punishment includes a period of cellular confinement.

Letters

You may send one second-class letter per week at public expense and at least one extra letter paid for out of prison earnings or private cash. The total number of letters allowed will vary from prison to prison and 'special letters' (i.e. extra letters at public expense) may be available in certain circumstances.

Work

Convicted prisoners are required to work unless a medical officer excuses them. It is a disciplinary offence for a prisoner to fail to work properly on purpose or to refuse to work. However, the prison is under no obligation to provide you with work.

Medical treatment

The Prison Medical Service is not part of the NHS, although prison doctors and medical officers can refer prisoners to NHS hospitals or ask specialists to see you if they feel that a second opinion is appropriate or are unable to deal with your medical problems. Treatment by opticians and dentists is also available. All treatment in prisons must be with your consent.

55 Criminal Records

DISCLOSURE AND USE OF PAST CONVICTIONS

The Rehabilitation of Offenders Act 1974 was an attempt to counter, at least in part, the prejudice that 'a leopard never changes its spots'. It was considered unfair that people who at some time in the past had acquired a conviction should have to carry it 'around their necks' for the rest of their lives. However, while the 1974 Act provides an opportunity for offenders to wipe the slate clean for certain purposes, it is very detailed and contains numerous exceptions to this basic principle.

How a sentence becomes 'spent'

The Act applies to all types of sentences, whether custodial, a fine, probation, absolute or conditional discharges, findings in a juvenile court that an offence has been committed, and convictions for certain offences relating to the Armed Services. (Separate rules apply to findings in care proceedings.)

The rehabilitation period depends on the sentence and runs from the date of conviction. When the period has expired, the sentence becomes 'spent' and need not be revealed in the future – for example, when applying for most jobs, completing an insurance proposal form, applying for credit facilities or for the tenancy of a property. However, there are *many* exceptions to this rule. For example, where a person applies for a job which involves substantial access to children or applies to become a member of certain professions.

The table on page 788 details the rehabilitation periods which are set according to the sentence imposed. Certain periods are reduced by half where the offender was a juvenile (i.e. under the age of eighteen at the date of the conviction). The Act applies not only to convictions in this country, but also to convictions before courts outside the UK. The foreign sentence is treated as equivalent to the sentence which most nearly corresponds with it under UK law. However, the Act does not apply outside the UK: for example, to an application for a job or a visa in a foreign country.

The rehabilitation period applicable

Certain sentences can *never* become spent. They are as follows:

Examples of Sentences and the Rehabilitation Periods Applicable	
Sentence	*Rehabilitation period*
A sentence of imprisonment for more than 30 months	Never
A sentence of imprisonment or youth custody of more than 6 months but not more than 30 months	10 years for an adult, 5 for a juvenile (i.e. under 18)
A sentence of imprisonment or youth custody of 6 months or less	7 years for an adult, 5 for a juvenile
An order of detention in a detention centre	3 years
A fine	5 years for an adult, 2½ for a juvenile
A community service order	5 years for an adult
Probation, bind-over to keep the peace or to be of good behaviour, and conditional discharge	The date the order or bind-over ceases or 1 year, whichever is the longer
Hospital orders under the Mental Health Act 1983	5 years from the date of conviction to 2 years after the order expires, whichever is the longer
Absolute discharge	6 months
Disqualifications and other orders imposing disability prohibition or other penalty	The date the order ceases to have effect
For the Armed Services	
A sentence of imprisonment in the Armed Services	Same period as for other prison sentences (see above)
A sentence of detention arising from disciplinary proceedings	5 years for an adult, 2½ for a juvenile
A sentence of discharge with ignominy or dismissal with disgrace	10 years for an adult, 5 years for a juvenile
A sentence of dismissal from the service	7 years for an adult, 3½ years for a juvenile

• a sentence of life imprisonment;
• a sentence of imprisonment, youth custody (or the former sentence of corrective training) for a term of more than thirty months;
• the former sentence of preventive detention;
• a sentence of detention during Her Majesty's Pleasure for life;

- a sentence of custody for life.

It should be noted that it is the *length of the sentence imposed by the court* that is relevant and not, for example, the length of imprisonment actually served.

If a person is given a sentence which can never become 'spent', this also prevents any earlier unspent conviction from becoming spent.

Under the law a sentence counts in the same way irrespective of whether you are sent to prison or the sentence is 'suspended'. The periods of rehabilitation for either are therefore the same as shown in the table.

Where a person receives two or more prison sentences in the course of the same court case, the rehabilitation period depends on whether the sentences are ordered to take effect 'concurrently' (i.e. at the same time) or 'consecutively' (i.e. one after another). For example, if two six-month prison sentences are ordered to take effect concurrently, the sentences are treated separately, giving each conviction a rehabilitation period of seven years. However, if the two sentences are ordered to take effect consecutively, the sentences are treated as a single term of twelve months, with a rehabilitation period of ten years.

Committing further offences

The essence of rehabilitation is that the person who has been convicted does not offend again. Therefore any subsequent conviction *during the rehabilitation period* of a previous conviction *may* extend the rehabilitation period of the first conviction. Whether it does depends, for example, on the seriousness of the subsequent conviction and the sentence imposed.

The effect of rehabilitation

The general principle under the Act is that a person who has become rehabilitated (i.e. their conviction has become spent) shall be treated as a person who has not committed, or been charged with, prosecuted for, convicted of or sentenced for, the offence concerned. Again, there are many exceptions to this general rule, with spent convictions being treated in different ways in different circumstances.

Evidence in legal proceedings

In proceedings before the civil courts or before a tribunal, arbitration, voluntary association, disciplinary or similar hearing you cannot be asked questions concerning any spent conviction and you can refuse to answer such questions – unless the court, tribunal or hearing is satisfied that justice cannot be done except by hearing the evidence involving the spent conviction.

This general rule does not apply in:
- criminal proceedings (but the Lord Chief Justice has ruled that no one should

refer in open court to a spent conviction without the authorization of the judge, which authority should not be given unless the interests of justice so require);
• proceedings relating to adoption, the marriage of any minor, exercise of the High Court's discretion with respect to minors or the provision by any person of accommodation care or schooling for children;
• Armed Services' disciplinary proceedings.

Employment

Questions are often asked by potential employers with respect to a person's previous convictions. The general rule under the Act is that you can treat such questions as *not* relating to spent convictions. Therefore, if you decide not to disclose a spent conviction, you cannot be denied employment or subsequently dismissed on the grounds that you failed to disclose it. (Although in exceptional circumstances, you may be prosecuted for the criminal offence of 'obtaining a pecuniary advantage by deception'.) Likewise, failing to disclose a spent conviction will not be proper grounds for excluding you from any office or profession. Nor can a spent conviction be grounds for prejudicing you in the way you are treated in any occupation or employment.

If, therefore, you are excluded or dismissed from employment on the grounds of a spent conviction, you may be able to take the matter to court for compensation or to an industrial tribunal as wrongful dismissal. If you wish to pursue such action, you should first seek the assistance of a solicitor.

However, many occupations and offices are specifically excluded from this general rule and these are dealt with below. You should read these carefully.

Some employers are adopting the practice of asking prospective or existing employees to obtain a copy of their criminal record under the provisions of the Data Protection Act 1984, which allows people the right to see their own computerized files. This record will list all your convictions, including those that are spent. Although this practice is not unlawful, it is a misuse of the data protection laws and could be highly prejudicial to yourself. If you are concerned about agreeing to such a request, you should seek assistance from a union official or the Data Protection Registrar's Office at Springfield House, Water Lane, Wilmslow, Cheshire SK9 5AX.

Services

Some contracts, such as proposals for insurance, are governed by the legal principle that all relevant information will be disclosed by the person seeking insurance whether it is asked for or not; otherwise the contract could be treated as invalid. Clearly the existence of a driving offence or an offence for dishonesty may well be relevant to an insurance company. However, the Act specifically states that although the existing law requires that you disclose all relevant information in this situation, this does *not* extend to disclosing spent convictions.

Going abroad

It is important to remember that the Act applies only to the UK and has no effect so far as the laws of other countries are concerned. This means, for example, that applicants for immigration, work permits and travel visas to the USA are still obliged to make full disclosure of their criminal record, including spent convictions. Some foreign countries have legislation similar to the Rehabilitation of Offenders Act, but to discover what safeguards apply it is necessary to consult the laws of the country concerned – for example, by asking their embassy in this country.

Defamation proceedings

A reference to a spent conviction in a newspaper article, for example, can give rise to a claim for damages for defamation. However, in order to protect free speech, the Act states that a person who is sued in defamation proceedings for disclosing a spent conviction may rely on the defences of 'justification' (i.e. the statement is true) and/or 'fair comment' (i.e. the statement was a fair comment on a matter of public interest). In order to succeed when such a defence is raised, you would have to prove that the statement was published with *malice* – that is, it was published with some irrelevant, spiteful or improper motive.

In addition, the reporting of certain events and the making of statements in certain circumstances can give rise to the defence of 'absolute' or 'qualified privilege'. For example, fair and accurate newspaper reports of judicial proceedings are absolutely 'privileged' (i.e. protected) against a defamation action.

As the law relating to defamation is complex, you should seek specialist legal advice. Legal aid is not available for defamation actions.

EXCEPTIONS TO THE ACT

The Act is frequently criticized for the many and wide exceptions made to the general principle that a person can become rehabilitated. If you fall within any of the exceptions, you will be treated as if the Act had never been passed and you are not entitled to rehabilitation for the spent conviction. These exceptions are listed in the Orders made by a relevant Government minister and largely relate to matters of national security, the care of those who are considered to be vulnerable and the administration of justice.

Excepted professions, occupations and offices

A number of professions, occupations and offices have been excepted from the general rule that a person does not have to disclose a spent conviction – see

Excepted professions, occupations and offices	
Medical practitioners	Veterinary surgeons
Lawyers	Opticians
Accountants	Nurses and midwives
Dentists	Pharmaceutical chemists
Judicial appointments	Traffic wardens
Police constables	Teachers
Prison Board of Visitors	Probation officers
Prison officers	Firearms dealers
Dealer in securities	Director, controller etc. of insurance
Manager or trustee of unit trust	company or building society

above. The table above lists the professions, occupations and offices which are excepted.

If you apply, therefore, to join one of the professions, occupations or offices listed you will normally be asked (and must be told why) to disclose all previous convictions, including spent convictions, in order that your suitability for the position may be assessed. Furthermore, a spent conviction may be considered grounds for excluding or dismissing you from any profession, occupation or office listed.

Other excepted occupations include:

• Any office or employment where the question is asked for the purpose of safeguarding *national security* – for example, a person employed by the UK Atomic Energy Authority, the civil Aviation Authority or an officer of the Crown;

• certain types of work in *health and social services* where the work involves access to people over sixty-five, to people suffering from serious illness or mental disorder, alcoholics or drug addicts, to the blind, deaf and dumb, or is concerned with the provision to persons under eighteen of care, leisure or recreational facilities (see below for further details);

• applications for certain certificates and licences (for example, concerning firearms, explosives and gaming), require that spent convictions be disclosed and can be taken into account by the licensing authority. Failure to disclose a spent conviction in these circumstances could result in the refusal or loss of the licence, certificate etc. or even in prosecution for non-disclosure.

Disclosure of criminal background of those with access to children

Since 1986 procedures have been adopted to check any possible criminal background with local police forces of those applying for work (including volunteers) with substantial access to children in the statutory sector (i.e. local authorities or health authorities) – for example, staff of day nurseries, playgroups, children's homes and social workers, school teachers, community and youth workers. Since 1989 this has been extended to similar work with voluntary organizations. The check also applies to prospective foster parents, adoptive parents and childminders, including other adults in their households.

Where a police check is required in relation to such a job with a local authority or health authority, you will be requested to list any convictions (including those that are spent), bind-over orders or cautions and be asked to give your consent in writing for a police check to be carried out. It should also be drawn to your attention that by virtue of an exception to the Rehabilitation of Offenders Act, spent convictions will be disclosed by the police and be taken into account in deciding whether to employ you.

Where the information provided by the police differs from that provided by yourself, this must be discussed with you before a decision is taken to employ you. If you consider that the police information is incorrect, you are entitled to make representations to the police through a nominated person. The police may also disclose *'other relevant information'* concerning you. This must be restricted to *factual information* which the police would be prepared to present as evidence in court, or details of acquittals or decisions not to prosecute where the *circumstances* of the case would give cause for concern.

It is for the prospective employers to decide your suitability, taking into account only those offences which may be relevant to the particular job in question — for example, they will consider the nature of the offence, when it occurred and the frequency of offences. The fact that you have a criminal record does not automatically render you unsuitable for work with children. On the other hand, it is not only sexual offences which may render a person unsuitable.

If you are concerned that a prospective employer may take into account a conviction that you consider to be irrelevant to the job applied for, you should attach a note to your original disclosure form which explains the circumstances of the offence and why you consider it to be irrelevant. If you are denied employment on the basis of a conviction which you consider to be irrelevant, you should seek legal advice as, in limited circumstances, it may be possible to challenge the decision.

Prospective employers may also use the Department of Health's Consultancy Service and the Department of Education's *List 99* as a further check on a person's suitability. These hold lists of people who, because of a previous conviction or incident, are considered unfit to work with children and young people. You should have been informed at the time by the department concerned that your name had come to their attention and why. You should also have been given the opportunity to make representations about the incident which they wish to record.

For further information, see Home Office Circular No. 102/88, *Protection of Children: Disclosure of Criminal Background of those with Access to Children* (in the statutory sector), and Home Office Circular No. 58/1989 (in the voluntary sector). Copies of these circulars are obtainable free from F2 Division, the Home Office, Queen Anne's Gate, London SW1H 9AT.

Police reporting of convictions

The general rule is that police information (including information on convictions) should not be disclosed unless there are important considerations of *public interest* to justify departure from the general rule of confidentiality. Exceptions to this rule are made where there is a need:

- to protect vulnerable members of society;
- to ensure good and honest administration of law;
- to protect national security.

The effect of this means that under Home Office Circular No. 45/1986, *Police Reports of Convictions and Related Information*, the police may disclose, when it is requested, information on a person's past convictions, cases pending and other such background information as would be admissible in court in the circumstances listed in the table below.

Under the same circular, the police are asked to report convictions as they occur to the professional bodies of those groups listed in the table below, particularly where the offences involve violence, dishonesty, drink or drugs, as they may reflect on a person's suitability to continue in a profession or office.

Police Disclosure of Convictions is Proper in Respect of:

- Those to be appointed to positions with substantial access to children (see above).
- Persons involved in the case of (or member of the same household as) a child subject to a case conference on non-accidental injury to children.
- Parents (and their co-habitees) to whom a local authority proposes to return a child in care.
- Applicants for compensation for criminal injury.
- Applicants to join the police.
- Applicants for certain licences: for example, gaming, lottery, sex establishments and entertainment licences.
- Applicants for, and holders of, licences as Heavy Good Vehicles and Passenger Service Vehicle Operators.
- Applicants for licences as dealers in securities.
- Applicants for consumer credit licences.
- Applicants for casual post office work.
- Potential jurors in cases including national security and terrorism.
- Social inquiry reports and other reports by probation officers.
- Welfare reports for courts determining care and custody of children.
- Those subject to national security vetting.

Reporting Convictions of Those in Certain Professions and Occupations	
Teachers (including student teachers) and ancillary staff	Midwives and nurses
Youth workers	Dentists
Social workers	Lawyers
Probation officers	Magistrates
Medical practitioners	Civil servants
Staff of the UK Atomic Energy Authority and British Nuclear Fuels Limited	Staff of the Civil Aviation Authority
Pharmaceutical chemists	British Telecom staff
Post Office staff	

Unauthorized disclosure of convictions

The Act makes it an offence if:
• an official in the course of their official duties unlawfully discloses someone else's spent conviction – the penalty is a maximum fine of £2,500 (as from October 1992);
• any person obtains details of spent convictions from any official record by means of fraud, dishonesty or a bribe – the penalty is up to six months' imprisonment and/or a maximum fine of £5,000 (as from October 1992).

If someone wrongfully reveals that you have a past conviction, you can:
• report the matter to the police and ask that the incident be investigated with a view to the person being prosecuted;
• sue the person concerned for *defamation* (see above);
• make a formal police complaint.

If, for example, the police reveal a conviction to an employer who is not within the categories set out in the table, you may be able to bring a claim for damages. Although this has yet to be tested in the courts, you should consult a solicitor to see if it is possible in your circumstances.

56 Victims of Crime

COMPENSATING THE CRIMINAL'S VICTIM

The criminal law is concerned with bringing offenders to justice and ensuring that they do not go unpunished. The criminal law is therefore dealing with the offender rather than with the victim.

But what of the victims? They will want compensation if they have been injured or if their property has been stolen or damaged. There are three ways in which they can go about obtaining compensation:

1 They can ask the criminal court to order the criminal to pay compensation: a criminal compensation order.
2 They can sue the criminal for damages in the civil courts. Exceptionally, they might even be able to sue the police for not taking steps to prevent the offence.
3 They can claim from the state-financed Criminal Injuries Compensation Board (CICB) if they suffered personal injury.

1. Obtaining a criminal compensation order

The criminal court that convicts the offender can order him or her to pay compensation of up to £5,000 (this limit is set in effect by paragraph 40 of the Magistrates' Court Act 1980 as amended by the Criminal Justice Act 1991 s.17 (3) (2)) to the victim (Powers of the Criminal Courts Act 1973, s.35). In principle, this sounds an excellent scheme, and indeed Lord Scarman has described s.35 as 'a convenient and rapid means of avoiding the expense of resorting to civil litigation when the criminal has the means which enable the compensation to be paid'. Actually, the section is not as useful as it would appear, partly because few offenders have 'the means which enable the compensation to be paid', and partly because the criminal courts have been reluctant to use their powers to the full.

In practice, orders are made mainly in cases of criminal damage, fraud, burglary, theft and robbery. In fact, about 70 per cent of magistrates' courts convictions for criminal damage lead to compensation orders being made, although the vast majority are for less than £50.

The power to order compensation is surprisingly wide, and does not cover only damage to property and personal injury. For instance, a terrified (but uninjured) householder was awarded £25 for the terror he suffered when a man had entered his garden and thrown a stone through his window. However, the court must have evidence of the victim's distress. In a 1990 case a compensation order in favour of two people who witnessed a serious act of public disorder was quashed, on the basis that the court was not entitled to speculate about their terror or distress without hearing specific evidence of it.

The court is under a duty to consider the issue of compensation in most cases, and to state its reasons when a compensation order is not made. But the court still has a complete discretion whether or not to order any compensation. A court can give compensation after a road accident only in very limited circumstances, and it will not order compensation if:

• there is some doubt as to the defendant's responsibility for the damage or loss (e.g, if they deny that they stole some of the items, or insist that some of them have been recovered), *or*

• it is unlikely that the defendant will be able to pay the compensation. An order will not be made if it would have to be paid by instalments over a long period of time (say, more than two to three years), or if its effect on the accused would be so serious that it might encourage him or her to commit further crime to pay off the compensation order. In practice, in 1991 it was unusual for an unemployed defendant to be ordered to pay compensation at a rate of more than £5 per week, which clearly limits the scope of the amount which can be awarded; *or*

• if the defendant receives a prison sentence and does not have sufficient assets to pay compensation at the beginning of that sentence. Before making a compensation order in these circumstances, the court must have evidence that such assets exist (assets such as the offender's matrimonial home will not be taken into account). There have been cases where evidence as to offenders' expensive lifestyles before their apprehension have been enough to satisfy the court that they must have enough to pay the victim some compensation.

With regard to compensation for loss to property, the main points to note were expressed in a 1981 case: compensation orders are 'designed for the simple straightfoward case where the amount of compensation can be readily and easily ascertained'. Plucking a figure out of the air will not do. In one case the owner of a car valued it at £3,000, but the defendant had sold it, in bits, for £600. The magistrate decided it was worth £1,000 without having heard any further evidence. The Court of Appeal overturned that compensation order since an order should have been made only if the value was clear. If property is recovered undamaged, there will be no compensation, even if the victim of the theft was distressed by its temporary loss.

Compensation orders for personal injuries are very low, and invariably represent only a fraction of what a civil court would award if the offender was sued. However, the courts are encouraged to use the CICB guidelines, if a compensation order is appropriate (see page 798).

Compensation in the Magistrates' Court: Guidelines Suggested by the CICB (1990)	
Type of injury	*Amount*
Graze	up to £50
Bruise	up to £75
Black eye	£100
Cut, depending on whether scarring or stitches	£75–500
Sprain, depending on loss of mobility	£100–750
Loss of non-front tooth, depending on cosmetic effect on victim	£250–500
Other minor injury, causing 2–3 weeks off work	£550
Loss of front tooth	£1,000
Facial scar (however small)	£550 +
Nasal fracture, displacing septum	£1,500
Wrist, simple fracture	£1,750–2,500
Little finger, simple fracture	£750

Often the court will have to choose between imposing a fine and making a compensation order, since it will feel that the defendant is too poor to be able to afford both. When this happens the court should opt for the compensation order, although it is fair to say that in practice there is often reluctance to award compensation. Where both a fine and compensation are ordered, the money paid off by the offender will go to the victim first.

Restitution orders

A restitution order is an order that stolen property be restored to its owner. As with compensation orders, so criminal courts seem very reluctant to use these powers and the result is that a restitution order will be made only in the plainest of cases, when there can be absolutely no doubt as to where the property is and to whom it belongs.

A restitution order can also be made when the property has come into the hands of the police (Police Property Act 1897). In this case there is no need for the property to have been stolen; it might, for example, be an item that was taken by the police to use as evidence. So the order can be made in favour of the accused, as well as the victim or witness.

2. Suing for damages

A crime of violence will give the victim a civil claim for assault, and a crime involving theft of property or damage to property will usually give the victim a civil claim for wrongful interference with goods (trespass or conversion). Victims of crime will thus always have a civil remedy which they can pursue in the civil courts, where they will, of course, ask for damages against the offender.

In practice, civil claims by victims are rare, presumably because few victims realize they can sue the offender and also because few offenders are worth suing. There is little point in suing an offender who does not have the resources to pay the damages (and any legal costs incurred).

If offenders are insured then it would, of course, be a different matter, for their insurers will usually have to meet any judgment obtained against them. The usual instance of this is in motoring cases: the offender will have committed a criminal offence by reckless driving and the victim can bring a claim for negligence. The damages will probably be paid by the offender's insurers, or the Motor Insurers' Bureau. In some cases household insurance will provide cover; this is worth checking.

Suing the police

If you are a victim of some form of police brutality, a claim will lie for damages for unlawful acts committed by officers in that police force. Space does not permit consideration of this topic in any length, but the usual types of claim are for assault, false imprisonment and malicious prosecution. Although difficult to sustain, these claims, if successful, can attract large awards of damages, which are assessed by a jury. In such cases the victim may be entitled to exemplary damages (which are intended to punish the wrongdoer, rather than just compensate the victim). Where the victim is on a low income, legal aid will be available for such a claim.

Another civil remedy that may be open to the victim is to sue the police. An obscure piece of nineteenth-century law, the Riot (Damages) Act 1886, allows the owner of property damaged in a riot to obtain compensation from the police (in effect, from the local community-charge payers). But, for the claim to succeed, it must be shown that:

1 There was a 'riot' – in other words, there were at least twelve people using or threatening unlawful violence for a common purpose, which would cause a person of reasonable firmness to fear for his or her personal safety. Football hooligans or violent demonstrators could come within this category.
2 The rioters behaved 'tumultuously'. This means that the number of people, or the way in which they were behaving, should have put the police on their guard and so they should have taken steps to stop the damage occurring.

There is no need for the rioters to have been prosecuted for riot. For instance, if a gang of hooligans is prosecuted only for criminal damage, or even if the gang escapes detection, the police can still be liable if there was legally a 'riot' and it was 'tumultuous'.

3. Applying to the Criminal Injuries Compensation Board

The CICB is a state-run body that pays compensation to people injured as a result of a crime of violence, or the apprehension of an offender or suspected offender, or an offence of trespass on a railway.

The CICB performs a vital role in providing compensation where the wrongdoer is either absent, insolvent or uninsured. In the year from March 1989 to March 1990, some 53,655 claims were received by the CICB.

Generally speaking, the crime causing the injury must be a 'crime of violence', but the courts have interpreted this phrase widely, so that a non-violent crime which leads to injury can come within the scheme. The courts are very reluctant to interfere with any decision of the CICB as to what constitutes a crime of violence. It will be a matter of fact in each case.

The fact that no one was prosecuted or convicted for the offence does not affect the CICB's obligation to compensate the victim. The fact that assailants are not themselves held responsible for the crime under the criminal law is irrelevant for the purposes of compensation. Thus the violent activities of a child under ten years old (who will not be prosecuted) or a person adjudged to be insane are covered by the scheme.

The CICB is obliged to pay out even when the injury arose out of a 'suspected crime'. So compensation can be paid even when it turns out that no crime was actually committed:

PC Ince was driving a Panda car in central London when he received a call that people were breaking into a Territorial Army depot. PC Ince rushed towards the scene, but was killed in a collision when he jumped a red traffic light. In fact, the alarm call was a false one – there was no break-in. His widow claimed compensation from the CICB, but the CICB argued that the death did not result from an offence or an attempted offence. Mrs Ince appealed. Held: The CICB should compensate her. It was sufficient that PC Ince had honestly believed that an offence was taking place and had taken action to prevent it. Although his negligent driving had been the direct cause of his death, the suspected break-in had been an indirect cause and so his death was within the CICB scheme. Ince (1973)

It should also be remembered that many trivial actions are in fact crimes and so give rise to a CICB claim. For instance:

Tony Killingbach was playing soccer for his office team. During the game, which was a hard one, Killingbach was deliberately kicked in the course of a high tackle when he was off the ball. Killingbach fell and broke his arm. After the game, Killingbach's team mates reported the incident to the police but he decided not to press charges. Subsequently, he claimed from the CICB. Held: He had been injured as a result of a crime of violence (the tackle being an assault) and so he was entitled to compensation from the CICB. Killingbach (1978)

One claimant was awarded over £7,000 compensation after having had a lump of mud thrown at his back by a workmate (because, of course, that amounted to an assault – a crime of violence!). However, the scope of crimes of violence is not infinite. For example, failure to keep a dog under control or a dog joining in a fight will not be a crime of violence. To qualify, the dog-owner must set the dog upon the victim as if using a weapon.

The provision that the CICB must pay out for injuries attributable to the apprehension of an offender widens the scope further:

Ms Schofield was shopping in a department store when she was knocked down as a store detective chased a suspected shoplifter through the shop. It was unclear who knocked her down. Held: The CICB should compensate. There is no requirement that the suspected criminal should cause the injury. Schofield (1971)

The scheme was revised in 1990, and the scope of the CICB extended to cover 'an offence of trespass on the railway'. This resolves the unfortunate problem in existence until that date which provided no compensation for train drivers who suffered psychological distress as a result of suicides or accidents occurring to people trespassing on the railway.

Cases which are excluded from the CICB scheme

Cases worth less than £1,000. In order to cut down administrative work and expense, these small-value claims are excluded. For instance, an undisplaced nasal fracture with no resultant financial loss may fail to attract the necessary damages of £1,000 limit unless there was also a substantial wage loss involved.

Claims for damages to and loss of property. The CICB scheme is primarily designed to compensate for bodily injury and losses resulting from those injuries (e.g. loss of earnings while off work). It does not cover loss or damage to valuables. So if someone is mugged, they cannot claim compensation for their lost wallet and money, but they can claim compensation for any injury suffered.

Offences not reported to the police. The CICB will not pay compensation unless the crime was reported to the police 'without delay'. Any delay in reporting the offence can result in failure or reduction of the CICB claim. This rule is applied very strictly and the offence must be reported, even when the victim knows that the police will not be able to help – for instance, if the attacker was not seen by the victim and has since disappeared. In practice, it is vitally important that the victim reports the incident without delay.

Claims not made within three years. A claim must be made to the CICB within three years. This rule is similar to the three-year limitation period that applies to the bringing of court proceedings in injury cases. There are exceptional circumstances where the limit can be waived (e.g. cases of sexual abuse in the family, although it must have occurred after 1979), but there is no appeal if the Board refuses to do this.

Traffic offences. Generally, traffic offences are excluded because the victim will usually be able to claim from the offender's insurance company or, if they are uninsured, from the Motor Insurers' Bureau.

Provocation or misconduct by the victim. If the victim provoked the violent crime, he or she cannot expect CICB compensation. Similarly, if they were misbehaving, they will not come within the scheme – for instance, a participant in a gang fight cannot expect compensation if he is injured in the course of the fight. However, it is not clear to what extent 'contributory negligence' by the victim will apply. It might be thought that victims would lose some of their compensation if they themselves were negligent, as, for instance, in the case of PC Ince, who was killed as a result of his negligent driving when rushing to the scene of a crime (see above). But this is not so. In Ince's case, Lord Denning specifically said that the CICB should not be influenced by concepts of contributory negligence unless the conduct of the applicant involves something 'reprehensible or provocative'. So it seems that only 'reprehensible' negligence should be taken into account. In practice, one feels that the CICB does take into account contributory negligence, even when it is not 'reprehensible', and award lower sums to such applicants.

Dubious characters. Finally, the CICB has a wide discretion to refuse compensation (or to reduce the amount awarded) because of the 'conduct of the applicant before, during or after the events giving rise to the claim, or to his character and way of life'. What this means is that the CICB may penalize claims by 'doubtful characters' – generally, people with criminal records, those who associate with criminals or lead a debauched life. For instance, one man was refused compensation for a broken leg caused through an assault by his drinking companion; he had convictions for dishonesty both before and after the incident, and even though those convictions were irrelevant to his claim, he was refused compensation. Not surprisingly, many commentators feel that this is too wide a discretion and that it is open to abuse.

Violence in the family

Until 1979 the victim could not make a CICB claim if he or she was living with the assailant as part of the same family. Battered wives and children were thus excluded. This was obviously unfair and the position now is that a victim can make a claim even if living with the offender as 'members of the same family'. But to guard against fraud the CICB will pay out only if:
● the offender was prosecuted (but they need not have been convicted), *and*
● if the victim is an adult, the victim and the person responsible stopped living together before the application, and appear unlikely to live together again, *and*
● the Board is satisfied that the offender will not benefit from the award, *and*
● when the victim is a child, the CICB will want to be sure that it is in the child's best interest that an award is made.

How much compensation?

In theory, the CICB aims to pay victims a sum roughly equal to the damages which they would be awarded if they sued the offender in the civil courts. In practice, the CICB is much less generous than the courts. The CICB award will cover:
● compensation for the pain and suffering caused by the injury, *plus*
● lost earnings resulting from the injury (net wage loss, minus all social security and NI benefits received by the victim), *plus*

Type of injury	Example award
Undisplaced nasal fracture	£650
Displaced nasal fracture	£1,000
Loss of two front upper teeth (plate or bridge)	£1,750
Elevated zygoma (following injury to cheekbone)	£1,750
Fractured jaw (wired)	£2,500
Simple fracture of the tibia, fibula, ulna or radius with complete recovery	£2,500
Laparotomy (exploratory stomach operation and scar)	£3,000
Scar, young man, ear to mouth	£6,000
Scar, young woman, ear to mouth	£9,000
Total loss of hearing in one ear	£11,500
Total loss of taste and smell (skull fracture)	£12,000
Total loss of vision in one eye	£15,000

• a sum to cover loss of earnings in the future, and/or an additional sum to reflect the difficulty they will have in obtaining a job in the future.

If the claimant is the widow or dependant of a person killed as a result of a crime, the CICB award will comprise:

• for the benefit of the victim's estate, funeral expenses;

• the value of the claimant's dependency on the victim (e.g. the proportion of the victim's salary spent on his wife and children).

It will not include damages for bereavement.

Compensation for pain and suffering will include damages for any (diagnosed) psychological trauma resulting from the crime. Awards for psychological trauma are most often made in cases of rape or sexual abuse. A rape victim who conceives and keeps a child will not receive money to maintain that child, although she will receive the sum of £5,000 for each child. She will also be compensated for any psychological consequences of the attack itself.

When assessing damages, each case has to be judged on its merits and the CICB try to ensure that their awards reflect the amounts being awarded by the courts in civil claims. Some guidance was given by the CICB in 1990 as to the amounts paid out.

But these figures are only a guide, and are minimum figures. A particularly nasty attack on a pensioner in her home is likely to be far more serious than an assault during a football match, even if the physical consequences are the same. Each injury has to be assessed individually. Also, awards increase with inflation each year.

Making the claim

An application form should be obtained from the CICB at Whittington House, 19 Alfred Place, London WC1E 7LG (071 636 2812). This should be completed and returned as soon as possible; there is no fee. The board staff are helpful and will deal with any questions.

A member of the board's staff will investigate the application and collect together all the relevant papers (e.g. proof of loss of earnings from employers, record of the offence being reported to the police, medical reports). In serious cases it is often worth the applicant obtaining his or her own medical report from a consultant to ensure that the medical evidence before the Board is complete.

The papers then go before a member of the CICB who makes an award, generally without having seen the applicant. The applicant is then told how much he or she is being offered. If they are dissatisfied with the amount, they can ask a three-member hearing of the Board to review the award. This is, in effect, an appeal and both the Board and the applicant can supply further information (such as additional medical reports) for the hearing. The applicant can attend the hearing and can bring a lawyer or friend if he or she wishes. The decision of the Board is final and cannot be appealed to the courts unless there is a dispute over the application of the scheme, not just the amount awarded.

In most serious cases, it is advisable to have the help of a solicitor. He or she has experience in presenting claims and collecting evidence, and their knowledge of levels of damage may well be invaluable.

Unfortunately, legal aid is not available for CICB claims. However, the green-form scheme, which generally allows up to two hours of legal advice, can be used. In practice, the solicitor may well be able to have the two hours extended, but if the compensation is awarded the money will have to be used to repay the cost of the free legal advice to the Law Society (see page 975). Other possible sources of advice are victim support schemes (for details of local schemes, ask the police, or contact the national office, Victim Support, Cranmer House, 39 Brixton Road, London SW9 6DZ), Citizens' Advice Bureaux and law centres.

Overall, the CICB scheme is a good starting-point for compensating victims of crime. However, it should be considerably improved, and it could be made the basis of a more generalized compensation scheme. For instance, why not allow legal aid to be granted for CICB applications? Why not allow CICB cover to extend to all claims in which insurance does not apply (e.g. if employers do not insure against accident claims by their staff)? Why not allow the compensation to be paid in instalments rather than simply in a lump sum? Why not allow the damages to be awarded on exactly the same basis as a court would (e.g. allow compensation for bereavement on death; no upper maximum on loss-of-earnings figures)? Many of these may seem small points, but in practice they do seriously limit the effectiveness of the CICB scheme. Many commentators feel that if these changes could be introduced, we would have the basis of a system that could replace the present antiquated procedures for suing for personal injury in ordinary accident claims.

57 Discrimination and the Law

The law is prepared to intervene to remedy three types of discrimination: namely, discrimination based on a person's race, sex or marital status. But the law never makes it a criminal offence to discriminate. If the discrimination is unlawful, the person discriminated against may be able to bring a civil claim for damages but no criminal prosecution can be brought (although, exceptionally, there might be a prosecution for inciting racial hatred).

The anti-discrimination laws are set out in the Race Relations Act 1976 and the Sex Discrimination Act 1975 (as subsequently amended by the Sex Discrimination Act 1986 and the Employment Act 1989). Both Acts adopt a similar approach, and so the same basic principles apply in all discrimination cases. The Acts tackle discrimination at two levels. First, they allow an individual to take legal action against someone who has discriminated against him/her, and, secondly, each creates an overall watch-dog body to monitor and advise on the general problems of discrimination. For racial discrimination, the national body is the Commission for Racial Equality, while its equivalent for sex and marital discrimination is the Equal Opportunities Commission.

But the primary responsibility for enforcing the legislation rests with the individual, and this is probably the major weakness of the laws, for many people will simply not bother to take action against a discriminator. To win the case, complainants must show not only that they have been discriminated against but that the act of discrimination was unlawful and not exempted from either of the two Acts. However, these statutory exemptions for discriminatory behaviour have been virtually eliminated by subsequent amendments.

WHAT IS 'DISCRIMINATION'?

Unlawful discrimination occurs when people are treated less favourably than they would otherwise be, simply because of their:
• race (i.e. because of colour, race, nationality or citizenship, or ethnic or national origin);
• sex (i.e. for being a man or a woman);
• married status (i.e. for being married and not single).

Discrimination can be direct or indirect; discrimination may be unintentional. Direct discrimination is straightforward discrimination (e.g. advertising a flat with a 'no blacks need apply' sign). Sexual harassment is direct discrimination. Discrimination against a woman because of pregnancy or maternity is direct discrimination. Indirect discrimination is more subtle: a person may appear to treat people equally but, in fact, be indirectly discriminating because they impose an unjustifiable condition that effectively limits the opportunities of a particular sex or racial group, or of married people. For instance, if eligibility for membership of a club is dependent upon a certain number of years' residence in the UK, that condition may well be indirect racial discrimination. Likewise, it would be indirect sex discrimination if an employer treated part-time workers less favourably than full-time workers and a higher proportion of part-time workers were women. Indirect discrimination is lawful if it can be justified by proving that it is necessary to achieve a significant business objective which cannot be achieved by non-discriminatory methods.

The headmaster of a private school would not allow a Sikh boy to attend unless he removed his turban and cut his hair, since turbans and long hair were against the school's rules. Held: These rules amounted to indirect discrimination against Sikhs. In addition, the House of Lords held that Sikhs did make up an 'ethnic' group – the Act did not just protect those of a particular race, but extended to groups with a definite cultural tradition, such as Sikhs. Thus the school rules had to be changed. Mandla (1983)

When deciding whether there is indirect discrimination the complainant will have to prove that 'in practice' it is harder for the discriminated-against group to comply with the conditions than other people. For instance:

The Civil Service laid down an upper age limit of twenty-eight for entry into the service as an executive officer. Ms Price was thirty-five and she complained that this was indirect sex discrimination since many women gave up work to look after their children during their twenties. Held: It was clear that 'in practice' it was harder for women to comply with the age limitation than it was for men. Thus it was indirect sex discrimination and the Civil Service was asked to review its policy on age restrictions. Price (1977)

When it is not unlawful to discriminate

The Race Relations Act and the Sex Discrimination Act do not ban all racial, sex and marital discrimination. There are exceptions when discrimination is allowed.

Sport

Sporting teams can be selected on the basis of nationality, birthplace and residence, but not colour. Competitive events can be limited to one sex if physical stamina or physique is important (so single-sex tennis is allowed, but single-sex snooker is not).

Insurance

Sex and marital discrimination is allowed if justifiable on statistical grounds (e.g. women live longer than men, so they can be charged less for life insurance).

When required by an act of Parliament

Discrimination is not unlawful if it is authorized by a statute.

Marital discrimination

The laws on marital discrimination apply only in the employment field. So discrimination on marital grounds in non-employment matters is allowed when racial and sex discrimination would be unlawful.

Communal accommodation

Residential accommodation is exempted from the sex and marital discrimination laws if it is communal and if, for reasons of privacy and decency, it should be used by one sex only. But racial discrimination on this ground is not allowed.

Positive discrimination

Training boards, employers and trade unions can take limited action to encourage the training of groups that have been under-represented in certain fields. But this provision is of limited effect and does not permit reverse discrimination (e.g. employer recruiting staff so as to achieve a balance between the sexes).

Charitable bequests and foundations

Generally charities can discriminate in handing out benefits, unless they impose a colour bar.

Employment

Additional exceptions apply in the employment field (see below).

European Community law

Equal pay and sex discrimination law is strengthened by the law of the EC. Article 119 of the Rome Treaty requires that there is equal pay for the same work on work of equal value and that there is no discrimination direct or indirect in matters of pay. The Equal Treatment Directive prohibits discrimination in non-pay areas on grounds of sex. Claims may be brought directly under Article 119 in industrial tribunals. This has been particularly useful when the discrimination relates to retirement provisions or pensions which are excluded from the Equal Pay Act.

Discrimination in the employment field

The racial/sex/marital discrimination laws apply throughout the employment field. They cover all steps from the recruitment of staff (e.g. notifying only boys' schools of vacancies might be discrimination against girls), the advertising of vacancies (e.g. wording of the advertisement; instructions to an employment agency), the selection of applicants for interviews and the actual hiring to treatment of employed workers, including selection for training, transfers and promotion, as well as selection for layoff, redundancy, short-time working, death or retirement benefits (e.g. age of retirement), severance pay etc. For instance:

Workers had to be laid off. Instead of a 'first in, last out' rule, the firm decided to make part-timers redundant before full-time staff. Held: This was sex discrimination. In practice, it is women who are part-timers (nationally, 80 per cent are female) and so this was indirect discrimination against the women members of staff. Clarke (1983)

Following theft by a black employee, British Leyland planned to increase security by requiring all its black workers to be searched on leaving work. Held: This would be racial discrimination, since white workers were not being treated in the same way. BL Cars (1983)

A new head was to be appointed to a school. Four men and one woman were interviewed; the woman was asked about her relationship with her husband, whether she was Miss or Mrs, was she legally separated from her husband, and did she intend to have a family in the future. The men were not asked questions of this sort. Held: The questions were discriminatory and should not have been asked. Gates (1983)

But there are exceptions when the discrimination will not be unlawful. These are in addition to the general exceptions listed above.

Certain jobs

Some jobs are partially excluded from the sex and marital discrimination laws, but not from the racial laws. For instance, the police force and prison service can lay down height requirements; while both men and women can be midwives, sex and marital discrimination is permitted when recruiting staff. The employer must prove that these requirements are justifiable in relation to the job. Employees of religious bodies are outside the sex discrimination laws if their employment would conflict with their religious doctrine or offend a significant number of the religion's followers. In addition, the forces are excluded from the sex and marital discrimination laws.

Pregnancy, childbirth

Employers can give special treatment to women in connection with pregnancy and childbirth.

Genuine occupational qualifications

It may be that being of a particular racial group or sex is a necessary qualification for the job – but marital status can never be a genuine qualification (e.g. 'single men only' is unlawful) unless it is a married couple that is to be employed (e.g. 'married couple required' is lawful).

Racial group

This can be a qualification when selecting actors for a play or choosing a model, when authenticity requires someone from that racial group. Similarly, bars and restaurants can select a person from a particular racial group (e.g. a Chinese waiter in a Chinese restaurant).

Sex

Sex can be a genuine occupational qualification when selecting actors and models. Also, if a job involves physical contact with the opposite sex (e.g. frisking staff for security checks) or if the work is such that members of the opposite sex might object to a person of that sex (e.g. woman attendant in a male lavatory), then the discrimination will not be unlawful. In addition, there are detailed exceptions for single-sex establishments, such as hospitals.

These anti-discrimination laws do not apply to employees only; they also cover the self-employed, including contract workers and partners. Trade unions, employers' organizations and professional bodies are also forbidden to discriminate in, for example, the terms of membership, benefits for members, expulsion and so on. One point to note is that physical strength and stamina can never be a 'genuine occupational qualification' – so a woman cannot be turned down for a labourer's job merely because she is a woman (but she can be turned down if she isn't strong enough).

Pay

Sex discrimination in the employment field is also governed by the Equal Pay Act 1970. This was passed before the Sex Discrimination Act and it bans sexual discrimination in respect of pay rates and other terms of a contract of employment (see page 422). The term 'pay' has been broadly construed by the courts to include any compensation received directly or indirectly in relation to employment (e.g. pensions, redundancy payments). If the jobs are similar, or of equal value, then a man and woman of similar status (e.g. qualifications, length of service) must work on equal terms unless there is a 'material difference' in what they do. The Sex Discrimination Act did not repeal the Equal Pay Act, and so both Acts work side by side. However, it would have been much simpler if Parliament had tidied up the legislation so that there was only the one Act covering sex discrimination in employment. Under the present law, if the discrimination arises before a job is given (e.g. a woman is refused an interview) that is under the Sex Discrimination Act; but if it arises during the employment (e.g. a woman not given a pay rise) then it comes within the Equal Pay Act!

Discrimination in providing goods, facilities, services and premises

The sex and race discrimination laws – but not the marital discrimination laws – apply in all these fields, subject to the general exceptions listed above.

Goods, facilities and services

This covers an enormously wide field, such as access to and use of hotels, restaurants, boarding houses, shops, public buildings, schools, night classes, cinemas, pubs, theatres and banking services, as well as credit, finance, grants, mortgages and insurance.

El Vino's wine bar refused to serve women at the bar; they had to sit down at tables. Held: This was less favourable treatment of women, and so it was sex discrimination. Gill (1983)

Mrs Quinn bought a suite of furniture in a department store. She asked to pay by HP. The store agreed – provided her husband would guarantee the loan, even though Mrs Quinn had a steady job. The store admitted it would not have asked for a woman to guarantee a husband's HP agreement. Held: This was sex discrimination. Quinn (1981).

Clubs

If a club is genuinely private, and not public, it is not unlawful to discriminate on the grounds of sex in the selection of members and the provision of facilities, including drinks. So a men's bar will probably be legal in a private golf club, but unlawful in a pub.

Special rules apply to racial discrimination in clubs. The basic rule is that racial discrimination laws apply unless all the following are met:

● the club is not an organization of workers, employers or a trade body, *and*

● it is not open to the public or a section of the public, because it has a constitution limiting admission to members, and 'membership' is defined so that 'members' do not constitute a section of the public, *and*

● it has fewer than twenty-five members.

Otherwise, racial discrimination in a club is unlawful. It is worth noting that the Race Relations Act contains detailed provisions to ensure that membership rules cannot be abused so as to avoid the legislation. However, special rules

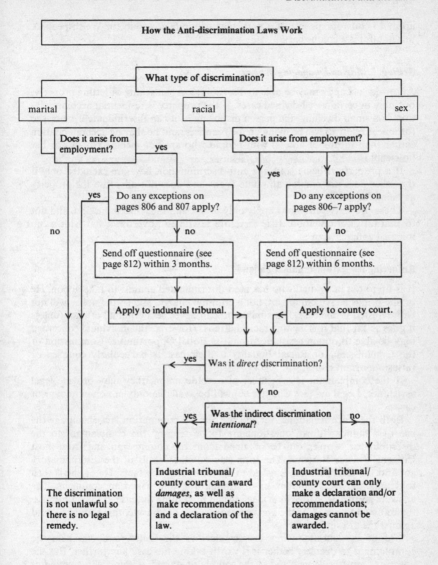

How the Anti-discrimination Laws Work

What type of discrimination?

marital · racial · sex

Does it arise from employment?

Does it arise from employment?

yes

yes · no

Do any exceptions on pages 806 and 807 apply?

Do any exceptions on pages 806–7 apply?

yes

no · no

Send off questionnaire (see page 812) within 3 months.

Send off questionnaire (see page 812) within 6 months.

Apply to industrial tribunal.

Apply to county court.

yes · Was it *direct* discrimination?

no

yes · Was the indirect discrimination *intentional*?

no

The discrimination is not unlawful so there is no legal remedy.

Industrial tribunal/county court can award *damages*, as well as make recommendations and a declaration of the law.

Industrial tribunal/county court can only make a declaration and/or recommendations; damages cannot be awarded.

no

apply to clubs for people of a particular group (e.g. a club for Welsh people), but not if it is a colour bar.

Selling, letting and managing property

An owner-occupier may be able to discriminate when selling or letting property, but only in certain well-defined cases. If the property is residential accommodation in a small dwelling, the person disposing of it can discriminate if he or she (or a near relative) will be living on the premises, and be sharing accommodation (other than means of access) with people who are not members of his or her household.

If a property is being sold, the anti-discrimination laws are excluded only if the seller does not employ an estate agent and does not advertise the property as being for sale.

These property provisions apply only to sex and race discrimination, and not to marital discrimination. It is therefore lawful to advertise a flat with a 'no married couples' sign.

Enforcing the anti-discrimination laws

It is up to the individual who has been discriminated against to take action. He or she brings a civil complaint, not a criminal charge, and so the police will not be interested in the case. Discrimination can never be a criminal offence (unless it goes so far that it is inciting racial hatred). However, the individual concerned may be able to obtain assistance from the Equal Opportunities Commission or the Commission for Racial Equality if their case is particularly complex or raises important issues.

If the complainant is a member of a trade union, they may provide legal assistance. Legal aid (see Chapter 66) will be available only in non-employment cases.

Both the Race Relations Act and the Sex Discrimination Act encourage the use of a standard-form questionnaire to be sent by the complainant to the discriminator. Copies can be obtained from the commission and from most Citizens' Advice Bureaux. The form sets out the details of the discriminatory act and the discriminator is asked to agree or deny the facts. He or she is then told why the facts amount to discrimination, and asked to comment. The answers given can be used as evidence when presenting the case. If the discriminator refuses to answer or the answers are evasive or abusive, this should be held against the discriminator.

Use of the questionnaires usually clarifies the issues, and can help the complainant to decide whether it is worth taking the case any further. But the questions must be served, and so the complaint started, within a short period of the act of discrimination. In an employment case there is a three-month time limit for claims under the Sex Discrimination Act and Race Relations Act.

Claims under the Equal Pay Act have to be brought within six months of the termination of employment. In non-employment cases the period is six months.

All employment cases (e.g. equal pay, race or sex discrimination) are heard before industrial tribunals (see page 481). Non-employment cases are heard in the county court.

The hearing

Whether the case is heard in an industrial tribunal or a county court, the complainant will have to prove his/her case 'on a balance of probabilities' (see page 888). The complainant at all times bears the burden of proof, but tribunals are encouraged to draw legal inferences from the facts as direct evidence of discrimination is rare.

If the tribunal or court decides that there has been discrimination, it will usually award compensation. It may also make a declaration setting out the rights of the parties. It may recommend that the discriminator takes certain action (e.g. that the discriminating employer recruits the complainant by a certain date), but rarely does so.

In cases of direct discrimination damages can always be awarded, but in cases of indirect discrimination damages can be awarded only if the discriminator acted 'intentionally' (i.e. knew they were discriminating; see page 805 for the distinction between direct and indirect discrimination). The damages can cover loss of earnings, expenses incurred etc. and also a sum for injured feelings. The amount awarded for injured feelings may be several thousand pounds.

Bringing a discrimination claim – a word of warning

In the past it had been notoriously difficult to win a discrimination case as English judges were initially inclined to give narrow, restrictive interpretations to both the Race Relations Act and the Sex Discrimination Act. Recently, however, the influence of the European Court of Justice has led to a gradual improvement in domestic courts' receptivity towards cases of discrimination. Generally, race discrimination cases are harder to win than sex discrimination cases.

58 Mental Health and the Law

The law on mental health is set out in the Mental Health Act 1983. This continued the reforms that had been made by the Mental Health Act 1959, which had been a pioneering Act, for it attempted to shift the care of the mentally ill out of special institutions and into the community. Also, as much treatment as possible was to be on a voluntary basis, with compulsory detention being used only when essential. In the words of the 1957 Percy Report, which led to the 1959 Act, 'Compulsory powers should be used in future only when they are positively necessary to override the patient's own welfare or for the protection of others.'

The 1983 Act deals with mental disorder. In fact, the Act defines four different sub-categories of mental disorder, but the important point to remember is that people can be detained against their will only if they appear to be suffering from a disorder so severe that it warrants assessment or treatment, and it would be in the interests of their health or safety or for the protection of others, that they should be detained. People are not to be treated as having a mental disorder merely because of their sexual behaviour, or because of a dependancy on alcohol or drugs.

ADMISSION TO HOSPITAL

Admission can be voluntary (informal) or compulsory (formal). About 90 per cent of admissions are voluntary and, in these cases, the patients are free to discharge themselves at any time – even against medical advice.

There are several ways in which compulsory admission can be authorized: each method is derived from a particular section of the 1983 Act. The question of which section was used to authorize the admission becomes important when considering whether the decision to detain the patient can be reviewed and how he or she may be discharged.

The types of compulsory admission

Admission for assessment (s.2)

Application is made by the nearest relative or an approved social worker, supported by the recommendations of two doctors, one of whom must be approved by the local authority as having experience in dealing with mental disorder. Patients admitted for assessment cannot be held for more than twenty-eight days without their case being reviewed. This is the most frequently used ground for compulsory admission. The patient's nearest relative will be, in this order, the spouse, child, parent, brother or sister, grandparent, grandchild, uncle or aunt, nephew or niece. A person who has been living with the patient for six months as a spouse will be regarded as such if the real spouse is permanently living apart. The criteria for admission are that the patient has a mental disorder which justifies detention to enable the doctor to decide what treatment is needed, if any, and that detention is in the interests of the patient's health or safety or for the protection of others. The patient can challenge the detention by applying to a Mental Health Review Tribunal within the first fourteen days.

Admission for treatment (s.3)

Application is made by the nearest relative or an approved social worker, plus the recommendations of two doctors. The section is used for the more serious cases of mental disorder – about 3 per cent of all compulsory admissions. The criteria for admission are that the patient is suffering from a mental disorder so severe that it warrants treatment in hospital and treatment is necessary in the interests of his or her own health or safety, or for the protection of other people. Thus the doctors' certificates must specifically state why treatment in hospital is necessary and why no other action will suffice. The initial admission can be for up to six months, and this can be renewed for a further six months, and then extended for a year at a time. Patients can apply for their detention to be reviewed once during each of these periods.

Emergency admission (s.4)

Application is made by the nearest relative or an approved social worker, and one doctor (who must have seen the patient within the last twenty-four hours). A patient admitted in an emergency can be detained for seventy-two hours only, unless a second doctor gives his or her recommendation; if they do, then the patient can be held for up to twenty-eight days (i.e. under s.2 admission for assessment, see above). The procedure is designed to deal with emergency cases in which the normal procedures for admission for assessment would involve undue delay.

Compulsory detention of voluntary patients (s.5)

Patients who were voluntarily admitted can usually discharge themselves at any time. However, if the doctor in charge thinks they should be compulsorily detained, he or she can detain them for up to three days. If there would be delay in fetching a doctor, a senior nurse is authorized to detain the patient for up to six hours.

People who are thinking of going voluntarily into a hospital should bear in mind that they may not be free to leave as and when they wish. Often patients who intend to leave will be told that unless they agree to remain in the hospital as a voluntary patient, they will be 'sectioned' (i.e. a compulsory order will be made), and the threat of this will induce many people to agree to stay in. Obviously, if patients feel that there are no medical reasons justifying a formal (compulsory) admission under s.2 or 3, they should apply to the Mental Health Review Tribunal.

Detention by police or social worker

An approved social worker can apply to a JP for the police to be allowed to enter premises and take someone to a 'place of safety' (i.e. hospital, police station, residential home). This is done when the patient has been ill-treated, neglected or is living alone and unable to care for him- or herself (s.135). But, more important, the police can detain any person found in a public place whom they reasonably believe to be mentally disordered, and put them in a 'place of safety' for up to seventy-two hours (s.136). This is potentially a very wide power, for it allows the police to remove and detain someone who has not committed an offence. It is entirely a lay decision by the police: no medical evidence is needed to justify any action.

Criminal court admissions

Any criminal court can make a hospital order, which is a compulsory admission order, on a defendant. In addition, a crown court can add restrictions if it considers it necessary to do so in order to protect the public from serious harm. There are also provisions allowing unconvicted defendants to be remanded in hospital, and for existing prisoners to be transferred to hospitals.

Detention in the hospital

The compulsorily admitted patient cannot choose which hospital to go to. Once in the hospital, the patient must be told – as soon as is practicable – which section of the 1983 Act is being used to justify the detention. Written information must also be given about discharge, appeals, treatment and other rights in hospital.

As will be seen from the summaries above, there are different periods for the detention of different categories of patients (e.g. seventy-two hours for emergencies; twenty-eight days for assessment; six months for treatment); but once the patient is in hospital, the hospital can extend the period of detention. If patients wrongly absent themselves, they can be brought back by the police, an approved social worker or a member of the hospital staff. However, there is a twenty-eight-day time-limit for doing this; after that time, a fresh compulsory-detention order has to be made.

The patient's nearest relative (see page 815 for who this is) can sometimes discharge the patient. This applies to patients who are detained for assessment or treatment, but it does not apply to emergency admissions. The nearest relative has to give at least seventy-two hours' advance notice of the intention to discharge the patient, so that the doctor can have sufficient time to decide whether to block the discharge (by issuing a 'barring certificate'). This prevents the relative discharging the patient, and all the relative can do is appeal to the Mental Health Review Tribunal (unless the patient is detained for assessment, in which case the relative cannot appeal).

Treatment in hospital

A physically ill patient can refuse treatment. If the staff ignore his or her wishes and carry out the treatment, they can be sued for assault if it can be shown that the staff 'touched' the patient without his or her informed consent. If the patient is unable to give consent – for instance, they are unconscious – the doctor can proceed without consent if treatment is urgently necessary. But it will then be for the doctor to defend his or her actions; they will have to show that the urgency of the need for treatment and the impracticability of obtaining consent left no choice but to carry out the treatment. This is usually best done by showing that if the doctor had not carried out the treatment he or she would have been guilty of professional misconduct.

Usually, of course, consent will be given by the patient. But such consent must be real: the doctor must explain, in broad terms, what he or she intends to do, and what the implications are of those actions – in effect, the patient must be told of the risks involved. If the patient is not given this information, then he or she cannot be said to have consented to the operation and so an action for damages might be possible. Thus a proforma signed by the patient consenting to the operation, 'the effect and nature of which has been explained to me', will not deprive the patient of the right to sue if, in fact, no explanation was given.

In a psychiatric hospital the position is different. Patients with mental disorders can be treated against their will for those disorders, but they cannot normally be treated for unrelated complaints. For instance, if a mental patient needs a leg operation the hospital cannot force the operation on him, unless the patient is not competent to make a decision and, in addition, the illness threatens his life.

Voluntary patients cannot be given treatment without their consent (which should be obtained once the patient understands the nature, purpose and probable effects of the proposed treatment). In cases of necessity (e.g. in order to save life) treatment can be given without the patient's consent.

The rules for all mental patients are as follows:-

• psychosurgery and the implantation of hormones to reduce male sexual drive may be given only with the consent of the patient *and* a second opinion from a doctor;

• the administration of medicine for three months or longer and electro-convulsive therapy may be given only with the consent of the patient *or* a second opinion.

Any other treatment can be given if the doctor thinks fit.

These provisions do not apply to patients detained under the short-term powers in the Mental Health Act; and the first rule (relating to treatment which requires consent and a second opinion) does not apply to voluntary patients.

THE PATIENT'S CIVIL RIGHTS

There are various restrictions on the civil liberties of in-patients in mental hospitals.

The right to visits

Patients have no legal right to visits, except to give them assistance where the decision to discharge is involved, or when they make a complaint.

Letters

A postal packet sent *by* a detained patient may be withheld if a request to do so has been made by the person to whom it is addressed. If the patient is detained in a special hospital (Broadmoor, Rampton or Ashworth), it may also be withheld if it is likely to cause distress or danger to anyone.

Post sent *to* a patient in a special hospital may be withheld if it is necessary for the patient's safety or the protection of others.

No letters to or from the following people can be withheld under any circumstances: an MP, an officer of the Court of Protection, the various ombudsmen, a Mental Health Review Tribunal, the managers of the hospital, a lawyer instructed by the patient, the European Commission of Human Rights or the European Court of Human Rights.

Voting

Detained patients cannot have their names on the electoral roll and so cannot vote. Voluntary patients can register on the electoral roll at their former address and can go to the polling station or vote by post.

Jury service

Mentally disordered people who are resident in a psychiatric hospital, or who regularly receive treatment from their GPs, cannot serve on a jury.

Driving licences

An applicant for a driving licence (or a person applying to renew a licence) must declare whether he/or she is receiving in-patient treatment for a mental disorder, or is suffering from a mental disorder that could lead to their being detained. In such a case the Secretary of State for the Environment will usually refuse to grant a licence.

Clothes

Both detained and voluntary patients have the right to wear their own clothes and cannot be forced to wear bedclothes (or hospital-provided clothes) all the time.

Property

Patients' property cannot be interfered with unless they consent or someone is authorized to do so by the Court of Protection (a specialized branch of the High Court which deals with the administration of the property of people who are unable to manage their own affairs).

Access to the courts

Patients may feel they have been dealt with so badly in some way that they want to take the hospital to court. Permission is needed from the High Court for a civil case, or from the Director of Public Prosecutions for a criminal prosecution. In order to win a case, the doctor or nurse must be shown to have acted in bad faith or without reasonable care. The advice of a suitably experienced solicitor is essential. For more information, contact MIND (071 637 0741) or a Citizens' Advice Bureau.

Access to medical papers

Except for a limited number of cases, patients are entitled to see any of their medical notes made after the end of October 1991. They are also entitled to see their section papers.

Type of case	Who can apply to MHRT?
Assessment (s.2)	Patient can apply in first 14 days. Nearest relative cannot apply.
Treatment (s.3)	Patient can apply once in first 6 months, once in next 6 months, and once a year thereafter. Nearest relative cannot apply.
Emergency (s.4)	Patient cannot apply. Nearest relative cannot apply.
Barring of relative's discharge	Patient cannot apply (except in first 14 days of assessment). Nearest relative can apply within 28 days (unless patient is being assessed).
Reclassification of type of mental disorder	Patient can apply within 28 days. Nearest relative can apply within 28 days.

THE MENTAL HEALTH REVIEW TRIBUNAL

Mental Health Review Tribunals (MHRTs) are independent bodies. Each MHRT has a legal member, a medical member and a lay member and will review decisions on detaining patients. The 1983 Act sets out the occasions when the patient or the patient's nearest relative can apply to the MHRT. The main occasions are outlined in the above table.

The hearing

The tribunal must discharge a patient detained for assessment (see above) if it is satisfied that he/or she is not suffering from mental disorder severe enough to justify detention for assessment, or that detention is not necessary for the patient's health or safety or for the protection of others.

In all other cases (except restricted patients, see above) the tribunal must discharge a patient if it is satisfied that he/or she is not suffering from mental disorder severe enough to justify detention for treatment, or that it is not necessary for the health or safety of the patient or for the protection of others that such treatment should be given.

A tribunal must order that a restricted patient be given either an absolute or a conditional discharge if the statutory criteria are fulfilled. In the latter case the tribunal can defer the direction for conditional discharge until the necessary arrangements have been made (s.73).

The only appeal against a decision of a tribunal is on a point of law.

The hearings are normally held in private at the patient's hospital. The applicant may ask for a public hearing, but this may be refused by the tribunal if it considers that it would be contrary to the patient's interests. The tribunal conducts the proceedings as it thinks best, but the patient and the hospital doctor are entitled to hear each other's evidence, to question each other and to call witnesses.

A solicitor can arrange an independent psychiatric and/or social work report if necessary (legal aid will generally cover at least one).

The tribunal has power to take evidence on oath, to order witnesses to appear and to produce any documents. The medical member examines the patient before the hearing date and inquires into all relevant aspects of his or her health and treatment.

Advice and representation

It is most important that a patient should receive advice and representation when appealing to a tribunal. This can be given by a solicitor under the Legal Aid Act by using the scheme known as Advice by Way of Representation. There is a panel of solicitors approved by the Law Society as having experience of representing patients at tribunals. Details can be obtained from the Law Society or MIND.

Expenses may be paid to the nearest relative, representatives of the patient or their nearest relative (unless they are lawyers) and any witnesses whose evidence the tribunal feels has been helpful. Expenses consist of rail fares, subsistence and any loss of earnings agreed by the tribunal.

59 Immigration

Under the Immigration Act 1971 the Home Office has very broad powers to decide who can enter and who can stay in the United Kingdom. People subject to immigration control must get 'leave' or permission to enter the UK at their port or airport of arrival. They can be detained while immigration officers consider their positions and can be swiftly removed if permission is refused. Those who enter without leave or who obtain it illegally can also be removed as 'illegal entrants'. When leave is given, it is often limited to a specified period or is subject to other conditions (such as a prohibition on taking employment). Applications to extend time or vary the other conditions are considered by Home Office civil servants at Lunar House in Croydon. Immigration control is backed up by the power to deport. People who overstay their permitted time can be deported. There are also powers to deport non-British citizens who are convicted of imprisonable offences by a court which recommends their deportation. Deportation is not confined to these categories. There is an ill-defined power to deport any non-British citizen whose presence in the UK the Home Secretary considers 'not to be conducive to the public good'.

BRITISH CITIZENS AND OTHER TYPES OF BRITISH NATIONAL

This battery of awesome powers can (in general) be used only against non-British citizens. Consequently, it is always important to check whether a person is or is not a British citizen. This is often very difficult and needs specialist advice. What follows is only a very basic and incomplete guide.

A person will be a British citizen if:
• before 1983 they were a citizen of the UK and Colonies with the right of abode in the UK (see below);
• after 1983 they were born in the UK *and* one or other parent was settled in the UK;
• after 1983 they were born outside the UK and either mother or father was connected with the UK (i.e. born, naturalized or registered as a citizen here) at the time of their birth.

If none of these apply, a person may still be a British citizen by one of a number of other routes which space does not permit us to describe here.

The terminology of nationality legislation is very confusing. Currently there are five categories which include the word 'British' but which are *not* the same as British citizen:

● *British Dependent Territories Citizens* are people connected with one of Britain's remaining colonies;

● *British Nationals (overseas)* are certain people connected with Hong Kong;

● *British Overseas Citizens* are people who were citizens of the UK and Colonies under earlier legislation but do not have sufficiently close links with the UK or an existing colony to be one of the other categories of British now;

● *British subjects* is *now* a small category of people mainly from Ireland. The term used to be, but is not now, synonymous with 'Commonwealth citizen' (see below);

● *British Protected Persons* are people who used to be connected with a British protectorate.

Being 'British' in any of these senses is not sufficient to be exempt from immigration control. This is confusing, particularly as these people may carry a 'British' passport. If a person has been recognized as a British citizen, this should be stamped inside the passport.

PATRIALITY

Passports issued before 1983 had a different set of terms. People born in or otherwise connected with either Britain or its colonies had a common citizenship: 'Citizenship of the UK and Colonies'. 'Patriality' or 'the right of abode' was the key term which identified the sub-category who were free of British immigration controls. In very broad terms, citizens of the UK and Colonies were patrial if they were or one of their parents was born, naturalized or registered in the UK or if they had lived in the UK without immigration restrictions for five years. Citizens of other Commonwealth countries could also be patrial. In their case they had to show a parental connection with the UK or (if a woman) marriage to a patrial. A Commonwealth citizen or a citizen of the UK and Colonies who was a patrial in any of these senses before 1983 will still be free of immigration controls, but the category is now closed and no one since then has been able to become a patrial.

A passport is important evidence of nationality and an immigration officer can demand production of a passport or a certificate of patriality or entitlement before accepting that a person is free of immigration control. However, people are not British because they have a British passport but because they satisfy the criteria described above or in some other way come within the statutory definition. This means that many people are British (even British citizens) without having a British passport or (in some cases) without knowing that they are British. Britain, unlike certain other countries, allows someone to have more than one nationality, so that people's perceptions of themselves as, say, Bangladeshi or Irish do not exclude the possibility that they are also British. Whenever someone has immigration difficulties, it is always worth checking their nationality status, especially if they, or one or other of their parents or grandparents, were born in the UK.

While only British citizens are free of immigration control, three other groups have preferential status.

EC nationals

Nationals of other member states of the European Community have the right to come to the UK for employment or self-employment to provide or to receive services. From July 1992 these rights are considerably expanded to cover students, retired people and indeed almost any other EC national who has sufficient means of support. These free-movement rights include the right to be accompanied by family members (whatever their nationality). There are circumstances in which people exercising these rights can be deported, but the criteria are much narrower and the procedural requirements much more stringent than would otherwise be the case. EC rights are extremely valuable and for anyone with a family connection with another EC country or its territories, it is worth checking whether they have the status of EC national.

Irish

Since Ireland is a member of the EC its nationals have free movement rights in the UK. There is, in any case, a common travel area between the UK and the Republic, so that (generally speaking) the Irish do not require leave to enter. However, unless they are also British citizens they can still be deported. More importantly, they can be banned from entering the UK or Britain under the special powers in the Prevention of Terrorism legislation.

Commonwealth citizens

Commonwealth citizens are subject to immigration control unless they are patrial (see above). However, those who have a grandparent born in or otherwise connected with the UK will have a right under the Immigration Rules to work here.

IMMIGRATION RULES

The Immigration Rules rather than the Immigration Act are what set out the categories of people who may be given leave to enter the UK and the conditions which apply to each category. The Rules are usually published as a House of Commons paper and are distributed through HMSO. There are provisions for visitors and students, for family members, for refugees, for workers, businesspeople and returning residents, as well as a number of other groups. It is important to remember that the Home Office has a general discretion to admit a person or to allow them to stay in the UK even if they satisfy none of the rules.

Visas and entry clearance

There is no general requirement for a visa or other advance approval before arrival in the UK, but the nationals of an increasing number of countries (both foreign and Commonwealth) are required to have a visa from a British embassy or consulate before they come. A list of these countries is set out at the back of the Immigration Rules. These nationals must have a visa whatever the purpose of their visit. Those who come (from whatever country) for settlement in the UK must similarly receive prior clearance from a British diplomat. People coming to work have to obtain a work permit through a scheme organized by the Department of Employment. Permits are allocated sparingly.

Most importantly, children and spouses of people settled in the UK (including British citizens) need entry clearance before arriving in the UK. DNA testing has largely removed the controversy which often arose over the claims of children, but the Immigration Rules for spouses still generate a great deal of misery. Applicants must show not only that their marriage is genuine but also that the primary purpose of the marriage was not to secure entry of the immigrant spouse to the UK. In most cases it will also be necessary to show that the spouse and/or children can be supported in the UK without recourse to public funds. It is no secret that the real reason for placing such a high burden on applicants is to minimize the number of black, Asian and other minority immigrants. In any other circumstances the heartache caused by years of family division would be considered intolerable.

Carriers who bring to the UK a person who does not have a valid passport or a necessary visa can be made to return the person at their own cost and can also be made to a pay a penalty of £2,000.

Refugees

Refugees do not need advance clearance. By signing a UN treaty Britain has undertaken not to return refugees to countries where they fear persecution. To qualify as a refugee a person must have a well-founded fear of persecution on grounds of race, religion, nationality, political opinion or membership of a particular social group. These claims are considered by the Home Office, rather than immigration officers. The Home Office has taken an increasingly abrasive attitude as the number of claimants has increased. For instance, since 1990 it has been extremely unwilling to consider applications except from those who have arrived directly from a country where they fear persecution. Others who have merely passed through or spent a few hours in some safe third country have not had their claims considered at all. A convention signed in Dublin in 1990 has formalized this approach among the EC member states.

Appeals

Many but by no means all of the Home Office's decisions in immigration matters can be appealed to an Immigration Adjudicator. In some cases there is a right of appeal, but only after the person concerned has left the UK. The main cases in summary are:

• no appeal right – refusal of naturalization; refusal to allow a person to enter or stay outside the immigration rules; deportation on national security grounds; refusal of work permit.

• appeal right only after departure from the UK – illegal entrants; refusal of leave to enter (unless entry clearance or visa held):

• appeal right within the UK – refusal of leave to enter where entry clearance or visa is held; refusal to vary leave to enter *if application to vary was made before the leave expired*; against the destination specified in a decision to deport.

A refusal to grant entry clearance or a visa can also be appealed although in the great majority of cases the appellant will not be able to attend the appeal, which will be held in the UK.

Deportation cases are more complex. A person who has been in the UK for less than seven years at the time of the decision to deport can argue that there is no power in law to deport him or her. A refugee claimant can seek review of the refusal of asylum (see below). A person who has been in the UK for more than seven years can ask for a review of the whole decision, including the balance between the need to enforce immigration control and the compassionate circumstances of the individual case.

It is likely that a new Asylum Bill will became law in 1993. This is expected to give an opportunity to appeal to those who are refused asylum or entry to the UK. However, it is also likely to make all asylum appeals (port refusals, variation of leave, deportation) subject to a filter process. Leave to appeal will probably have to be obtained and the process for doing so confined to a very tight timetable.

It is a galling fact of life for those who deal with immigration matters that while the Home Office can be extremely slow in processing applications, applicants face severe consequences if they do not comply with time-limits. In particular it is important to remember:

• applications for variation of leave to enter or remain should be made *before the current leave expires*; Later applications can be made, but a refusal will not be appealable;

• a right of appeal should be exercised within the time specified in the decision; appeal rights are likely to be lost if the notice of appeal *does not reach the Home Office* in this period.

Judicial review

Judicial review by the courts is an alternative where other remedies are non-existent or insufficient. However, judicial review cannot directly consider whether the decision was right or wrong, but only whether the correct procedure was followed and was lawful in all other respects. Even this limited review is not given to refusals on entry. The courts will not short-circuit the rule that appeals can be brought only after departure from the UK. This attitude is not invariable and will not, for instance, prevent asylum-seekers from arguing on judicial review that their removal is unlawful. A more far-reaching review is conducted of decisions to remove illegal entrants. A person who has what appears to be a perfectly valid leave to enter is entitled to insist that the Home Office prove to the court's satisfaction that his or her entry really was obtained illegally. Here the court must decide whether the Home Office was right.

FURTHER HELP

Immigration and nationality are complex matters. The details of the law (which have been here omitted or glossed over) can be all-important. Help can be obtained from solicitors specializing in immigration (consult the Law Society, 071 242 1222, or Immigration Law Practitioners Association, 071 250 1671); Citizens' Advice Bureaux or law centres (if they have an immigration specialist); Joint Council for the Welfare of Immigrants (071 251 8706); United Kingdom Immigration Advisory Service (071 357 6917).

60 Political Demonstration and Protest

Although there is no statutory or specific common-law right to demonstrate, judges have referred to the existence of fundamental rights in general and to the rights of peaceful assembly and public protest in particular. Article 11 of the European Convention on Human Rights states that everyone has the right to freedom of peaceful assembly. Demonstrations are legal only if they do not involve a breach of the law, however trivial that breach may be – for instance, obstructing the highway.

The Public Order Act 1986 creates a set of rules which must be followed before a public procession can take place and offences which are committed if those rules are not adhered to. In s.13 of that Act, the police have the power to ban processions if the chief officer of police reasonably believes that any conditions he or she might impose are insufficient to prevent serious public disorder. Any decision by the police to ban a demonstration may be challenged by way of judicial review in the High Court.

This chapter is concerned with the offences that demonstrators might commit. The hope is that awareness of the possible charges will enable demonstrators to minimize their chances of acting illegally. The main offences are:

- committing a breach of the peace;
- obstructing the highway;
- obstructing/assaulting the police;
- insulting words and/or behaviour;
- affray;
- riot;
- violent disorder;
- picketing offences (see page 524).

Meetings and processions

If the meeting is to be on private property, the permission of the owner of the land must be obtained first, for otherwise the people at the meeting will be trespassers (see page 367); they can be thrown off the land and sued in the civil courts for any loss occurring.

The Public Order Act 1986 s.39 makes it an offence in certain circumstances to enter land as a trespasser and to fail to leave it after a request by the occupier and a directive by the police to do so. The maximum penalty is three months' imprisonment.

If the meeting is to be on public land there may be a local by-law or a local Act that requires the organizers to give the local authority and the police thirty-six hours' notice. Failure to do so will be a criminal offence (usual maximum penalty £50 fine).

So far as processions and marches are concerned, the Public Order Act 1986 provides that organizers must give advance notice to the police. Conditions such as rerouting can be imposed if the police reasonably believe there will be serious public disorder, or serious damage to property, or serious disruption to the life of the community, or if the purpose of the organizers is the intimidation of others. The police can ban a proposed procession if the chief officer reasonably believes there will be serious public disorder and that conditions will not prevent it.

The 1986 Public Order Act creates new controls over public assemblies and gives police the right to impose conditions on those organizing or taking part in an assembly. A public assembly is a meeting of more than 20 persons in a public place wholly or partly open to the air.

In London further restrictions apply, mainly derived from nineteenth-century Acts:

● when Parliament is sitting, no open-air meeting of a 'political nature' with more than fifty participants can be held north of the Thames within 1 mile of the Houses of Parliament;

● any open-air meeting or procession that obstructs the free passage of MPs to the House, or which causes disorder or annoyance in the neighbourhood, is illegal;

● special Department of the Environment permits are required for meetings etc. in Hyde Park and Trafalgar Square.

Cooperating with the police

In the face of these extensive police powers, it is clearly wise for organizers to cooperate with the police and do more than merely notify them of the intention to hold a public meeting or procession. For, however well-intentioned the organizers may be, they cannot foresee how their supporters (and, indeed, their opponents) will behave. So it is only common sense to liaise with the police before the event.

Private Meetings

If the meeting is on private premises, anyone present can be told to leave; if they refuse, the organizers can eject them as trespassers. If they have paid to enter the meeting then they might have a contractual right to stay; to avoid this, the organizers would be well advised to display a notice at the entrance reserving their right to refund money and to ask people to leave.

Police do not have the right to enter private property without a warrant unless it is necessary to do so *inter alia* for the purpose of saving life or to prevent serious damage to property. There are other powers of entry – for example, to recapture a person unlawfully at large or to arrest for an arrestable offence – but these are not relevant to meetings. Police may also enter premises to deal with or prevent a breach of the peace. A Home Office circular in 1909 expressed what is still the police point of view; namely, a 'preference for the policy of non-interference in ordinary political meetings, although on exceptional occasions it may become necessary to station police inside a meeting for the purpose of maintaining order'.

Organizations

Stewards

Stewards can be appointed at both public and private meetings. In practice, stewards are a very important means of controlling a crowd. The organizers should liaise with the police as to the number and organization of the stewards. Obviously, the stewards have the same status as other private individuals and are not accorded any special legal powers. Thus they cannot use force to ensure compliance with their wishes.

Fly-posting

Sticking posters in public places is illegal under the Town and Country Planning Acts (i.e. because they are treated as adverts – and planning permission is needed for any advertising hoarding), and often under local by-laws as well. The placing of posters and stickers is potentially criminal damage. Exceptions are advertisements for non-commercial events, including political, educational, social and religious meetings, if the prior consent of the owner of the hoarding, window etc. is obtained. There are usually other detailed requirements, the most important of which is that the poster should be no more than six square feet in size. The local authority will provide further details. Posting an advertisement on someone else's property (e.g. window, lamp post) without permission is punishable – under the planning permission laws – by a fine of up to £1,000 in the magistrates' court.

Spray-painting

Painting slogans is likely to be illegal under local by-laws. In addition, it is likely to be criminal damage. The cost of repairing the damage can be high; water-based paint soaks into brickwork.

Collecting signatures

A person organizing a petition should take care not to obstruct the highway (see below).

Selling pamphlets etc.

This does not require a street-trading licence, but there is always the risk of obstructing the highway. In the Metropolitan Police area, a licence is needed for charitable (or other benevolent) collections, but not for selling political papers etc.

Picketing

There is a right to picket, but the right to picket is restricted to industrial disputes involving those doing the picketing, and in particular does not cover non-industrial pickets (e.g. consumer picket, political picket). See s.14 of the Public Orders Act 1986 with regard to the effect on pickets.

Offences arising from meetings, demonstrations etc.

Committing a breach of the peace

There is a breach of the peace whenever harm is actually done or is likely to be done to a person or in their presence to their property, or a person is in fear of being so harmed through an assault, an affray, a riot or other disturbance.

Generally, though, there must have been some physical force used or at least some behaviour that would lead one to expect a disturbance involving force – but even with that qualification it is still a widely drawn offence. The offence ranges from minor assaults, threats or obstructions through to more serious offences such as riot and affray. In practice, of course, a person committing a more serious offence would be prosecuted for that offence rather than face the more minor charge of breaking the peace.

A person who is guilty of a breach of the peace will be bound over to keep the peace or to be of good behaviour. If they refuse to be bound over they can be sent to prison.

Obstructing the highway

In the eyes of the law, the highway (including the pavement) is to be used for 'passing and re-passing' – a quaint phrase which means that it is to be used only for travelling from one place to another. Thus it is not to be used for parking one's car, holding a meeting, talking to a neighbour or selling newspapers from a stand, since all of these activities do not involve the use of the highway for 'passing and re-passing'. All are thus obstructions of the highway.

To make the offence even wider, the courts have held that it is not even necessary for anyone to have actually been obstructed by the unauthorized act.

It is thus an offence that is easily committed. In practice, though, the court will consider whether the defendant was using the highway 'reasonably' and this will mean taking into account the amount of traffic present, the time of day and the size of the road. Thus a person washing a car in a suburban road on a Sunday morning may be technically obstructing the highway, but will generally be held to have been using the highway 'reasonably', and so would not be prosecuted by the police. But for demonstrators who may be peacefully taking part in a demonstration or lobby, the law is usually less understanding. The very vagueness of the charge makes it difficult to defend, and if a police officer tells the court that he or she thought the demonstrator was causing an obstruction, it will be extremely difficult for the demonstrator to avoid conviction. For this reason, an 'obstruction of the highway' charge is probably the most frequently used charge against demonstrators. Also, it has the added advantage from the police point of view that the offender can be arrested on the spot, without the need for a warrant.

A procession which keeps moving is less likely to be an obstruction of the highway, for the participants can then argue that they were indeed using the highway for 'passing and re-passing'. For this reason, a procession or march is usually a legally safer form of protest than a rally or a lobby. The maximum penalty for obstructing the highway is a fine of £1,000.

Obstructing/assaulting a police officer in the execution of his or her duty

The important words here are 'in the execution of his or her duty'. If the police officer was not acting in accordance with his or her legal powers and duties, then the charge must fail. For example, the person who refuses to allow a PC to search their bags will not be obstructing the police officer in the execution of his or her duty, unless the PC has legal authority to search the bags.

Policemen saw two teenagers going from house to house, so one of the policemen challenged the boys and asked them what they were doing. The boys ran off, thinking that the policemen were thugs. The policemen gave chase and caught the boys, who then hit them. When prosecuted for assaulting an officer in the course of his duty, the boys argued that the policemen were not acting in the course of their duty, since the police can use force only to arrest someone, not to detain them for questioning. Held: This was correct and the boys were acquitted. Kenlin (1967).

A youngster was shouting and swearing on a bus. A plain-clothes policeman told him to get off. He began to do so but then the policeman tried to detain him; the youth hit the policeman. Was he guilty of assaulting a policeman in the execution of his duty. Held: No. The policeman had not arrested the youth and had no legal right to detain him. The policeman was therefore acting illegally in trying to detain the youth – and so was not 'acting in the execution of his duty'. Ludlow (1983)

Note that the accused need not know that the PC was, in fact, a police officer for an offence to be committed. So if I hit someone who turns out to be a plain-clothes police officer on duty, I can be prosecuted for the offence; but if he or she is not on duty, I will only face prosecution for simple assault. Both offences can be tried only in the magistrates' court. It has often been suggested that the offences should be triable in the crown court, before a jury, since they are both of a serious nature. The maximum penalty for assaulting a police officer is six months' prison and £5,000 fine; the maximum for obstructing a police officer is one month's prison and £1,000 fine.

Insulting words and/or behaviour

S.4 of the Public Order Act 1986 creates an offence of threatening behaviour. A person is guilty if they use towards another threatening, abusive or insulting words or behaviour or distribute or display to another person any writing, sign or other visible representation which is threatening, abusive or insulting and:
• they intend that person to believe that immediate unlawful violence will be used against him or her, *or*
• they intend to provoke the immediate use of unlawful violence by that person or anyone else, *or*
• whereby that person is likely to believe that such violence will be used, *or*
• whereby it is likely that such violence will be provoked.
This offence can be committed in private as well as in public places, but not in a dwelling house, unless the words or behaviour are directed outside (e.g. abuse from window). The maximum penalty for a s.4 offence is six months' imprisonment and/or a fine of £5,000.

S.5 of the Public Order Act 1986 creates an offence of disorderly conduct. It penalizes threatening, abusive or insulting words or behaviour or disorderly behaviour within the hearing or sight of a person likely to be caused harassment, alarm or distress. The maximum sentence on conviction is a fine of £1,000. Conduct which is disorderly is not criminal within this section unless it tends to annoy or insult such persons as are faced with it sufficiently deeply or seriously to warrant the interference of the criminal law. A person is guilty of s.5 only if he or she intends their words or behaviour to be threatening, abusive or insulting or is aware that it may be threatening, abusive or insulting. The offence is not arrestable unless the person ignores a warning. It is a defence for the defendant to prove that their conduct was reasonable.

Affray

S.3 of the Public Order Act 1986 creates an offence of affray. A person is guilty of affray who uses or threatens violence towards another so as to cause a person of reasonable firmness to fear for their personal safety. The offence is triable in either the magistrates' or the crown court and the maximum sentence which can be imposed in the latter is three years' imprisonment and in the former six months. There is no requirement of numbers, as with riot or violent disorder.

Violent disorder

The Public Order Act 1986 s.2 creates an offence of violent disorder. This is intended to deal with serious outbreaks of public disorder. A person is guilty who uses or threatens violence where three or more persons present together use or threaten violence so as to cause a person of reasonable firmness to fear for their personal safety. The offence is triable in either the magistrates' or the crown court, and the maximum sentence is five years. This offence was introduced to deal with group violence.

Riot

The Public Order Act 1986 s.1 creates an offence of riot. A person is guilty of riot when he or she uses violence where twelve or more persons present together use or threaten violence for a common purpose so as to cause a person of reasonable firmness to fear for their personal safety. The offence is triable only in the crown court and the maximum penalty is ten years' imprisonment. A person is guilty of riot only if he or she intends to use violence or is aware that their conduct may be violent.

61 Freedom of Expression

There is no right to freedom of speech in Britain. The nearest equivalent is the right to free speech guaranteed by Article 10 of the European Convention on Human Rights. Even there, the right is subject to a number of exceptions.

DEFAMATION

Defamation is the collective word for libel and slander. It is the medium through which the defamation is made that determines whether it is libel or slander.

Traditionally, the law distinguished between the spoken word (slander) and the written word (libel), with libel being regarded as the more serious because of the permanence of the written word, as opposed to the transience of the spoken word. However, that classification broke down with the introduction of new forms of communication in the twentieth century. As for films, it was decided in a 1934 case that defamation in a film was libel, even though it was based on the spoken word. Similarly, it has been decided (this time by Act) that defamation on the TV is libel, and not slander. Defamation in cable, video and satellite transmissions is best seen as being libel, not slander. Despite these complications, the basic distinction remains between spoken and written defamation (including TV, films, etc.); spoken is slander, written is libel.

With libel, the plaintiff (i.e. the person suing) need not show that the defamation caused loss or damage; it is enough to show that the words were defamatory. But with slander the position is different; the plaintiff can sue only if the spoken defamation caused loss or damage (e.g. it led to the loss of a contract). Mere injured feelings, embarrassment or hurt pride are not sufficient to justify a slander action. Slander, by its nature, is spoken and thus is only temporary, and so the plaintiff is encouraged to forget the incident rather than litigate.

However, if loss or damage can be shown, an action is possible. In addition, certain types of slander are assumed to cause damage and so legal action can be taken even though loss or damage cannot be proved. For instance:

- an allegation that the plaintiff has committed an imprisonable offence (e.g. 'You are a thief');
- an allegation that the plaintiff has VD;

- disparaging comments about the plaintiff's office, profession, trade or business;
- an allegation that an unmarried woman is not a virgin or that a married woman has committed adultery.

Otherwise, the same laws apply to slander as to libel. In practice, though, libel is the more important of the two; few people litigate over verbal insults and so slander actions are rare.

Suing for defamation

Defamation cases are relatively few. There are two reasons for this:

1 Legal aid is not available for defamation actions. However bad the libel or the slander, the plaintiff cannot get legal aid. Thus the case will usually have to be privately financed. This effectively dissuades most private people (apart from the rich or those with wealthy bankers) from suing for defamation.
2 A defamation action is a civil case (see Chapter 64). But it can be brought only in the more senior (and more expensive) of the civil courts – namely, the High Court. The plaintiff cannot sue in the cheaper county court, however small the claim for damages.

Anyone who thinks they have been defamed should bear these two points in mind. This is why many allegations of defamation do not get past the stage of the solicitor's letter.

What is a defamatory statement?

There is no simple test for deciding whether words (whether written or spoken) are defamatory, but a good general rule is to ask: 'Is it a false statement that discredits the plaintiff?' Falsity by itself is not enough; the words must tend to lower the plaintiff's reputation

When a defamation case is tried, either side has the right to ask for a judge to sit with a jury – one of the rare occasions when a civil case has a jury. The judge decides whether the statement is capable of being defamatory, but it is the jury that then decides whether it was actually defamatory – and if so, how much damages the plaintiff should receive.

Bringing a defamation action

Plaintiffs have to prove three things: first, that the statement had a defamatory meaning; secondly, that it referred to them; and thirdly, that the defendant was responsible for 'publishing' the words (publication in this context means saying or showing them to at least one person who is not the plaintiff). The first two parts of a defamation action that need to be proved are dealt with below. Proof of publication is a question of fact and evidence.

The statement is defamatory

The law will assume (until the defendant proves the contrary) that the words are false, but it will be for the plaintiff to show that they are defamatory.

Usually, showing that the statement had a defamatory meaning is not sufficient. The defendant may agree that the words might be defamatory but argue that he or she has a defence to the action, such as that the statement was justified (e.g. the plaintiff is a drunkard). See below for defences.

Sometimes the meaning is less clear-cut, and the plaintiff argues that by implication the words are defamatory. In effect, it is the innuendo that causes the defamation.

In the 1920s Tolley was a famous amateur golfer. Fry's the chocolate-makers produced an advertisement which showed Tolley playing golf, with a bar of Fry's chocolate sticking out of his pocket. A limerick on the advertisement suggested that the chocolate was as good as Tolley's drive. Tolley sued for defamation because the advertisement had been prepared without his knowledge or consent. Fry's argued that the advertisement was not defamatory. Held: The advert was defamatory. The implication behind the advert was that Tolley had been paid to consent to its publication, and so he had prostituted his reputation as an amateur golfer. Tolley (1931)

A racetrack photographer took a photo of a couple. The man said his name was Corrigan and that he was engaged to the lady. Subsequently, the photo appeared in the Daily Mirror *under the caption 'Mr Corrigan and Miss X, whose engagement has been announced'. In fact, Corrigan's real name was Cassidy and he was separated from his wife. Mrs Cassidy sued the* Daily Mirror *for libel, arguing that the implication behind the photograph was that she was not married to her husband, but was merely his mistress. Held: The photograph and caption were defamatory. Mrs Cassidy was awarded £500 damages.* Cassidy (1929)

The Daily Mail *published an article in which it was alleged that Michael Foot, MP, had received private treatment in an NHS hospital. Held: This was defamatory. The implication was that Mr Foot was hypocritical and insincere in his advocacy of equality.* Foot (1978)

The plaintiff is the subject of the statement

Apart from showing that the statement is defamatory, the plaintiff must also show that he or she was identified as the subject of it. Often this will be obvious, as when the plaintiff is referred to by name. But if his or her identity is ascertainable, then that will be sufficient. This is so even if the defamation was unintentional. For instance:

The Sunday Chronicle *published an account of a Dieppe motor-racing event. In describing the crowd, the correspondent wrote, 'There is Artemus Jones with a woman who is not his wife . . . Who would believe, by his goings-on, that he was a churchwarden at Peckham? . . . Here, in the atmosphere of Dieppe, he is the life and soul of a gay little band that haunts the casino and turns night into day, besides betraying a most unholy delight in the society of female butterflies.' In fact, the correspondent made all this up; it was a figment of his imagination. But there was in North Wales a barrister called Artemus Jones who used to write for the* Sunday Chronicle. *He sued for libel, saying that although he was not a churchwarden and not resident in Peckham, people would take the article as referring to him. Held: It was defamatory. He was awarded £1,750 damages. (Note: today the paper could have avoided paying damages by printing an apology; see below.)* Jones (1909)

The Observer *had an article with the headline 'Corruption: three M Ps escape prosecution – exclusive', and in the article was a large photograph of Reginald Maudling, M P. Although the article made it clear that he was not one of the M Ps referred to, Maudling sued for libel. Held: The* Observer *was liable. The position of the photo was such that readers could have inferred that Mr Maudling was one of the corrupt politicians.* Maudling (1978)

Defences to a defamation action

Anyone who is threatened with proceedings for defamation or libel should take legal advice. If the complaint is justified and the statement was defamatory, the best course of action is to write a letter of apology immediately.

If the action is to be defended, there are five main defences that can be raised: justification, fair comment, absolute privilege, qualified privilege and, finally, that the defamation was unintentional.

Justification

This means that the statements are true. For instance:

A newspaper article stated that Mr Loughans, who had a criminal record, had committed a murder. Loughans had been acquitted on that murder charge in 1944. He sued for libel. The paper pleaded justification as a defence. It was pointed out that in a criminal case (which the murder trial had been) a very high standard of proof was needed to secure a conviction – the jury had to be convinced 'beyond reasonable doubt' that he was guilty. But in a civil case (such as the defamation trial) a lower standard applies; the jury simply had to be satisfied on a 'balance of probabilities' that Loughans had committed the murder. This the jury did by upholding the plea of justification and so defeating the claim for defamation. Loughans (1963)

The Rehabilitation of Offenders Act 1974 has complicated the defence of justification. The Act provides that a criminal can sue for defamation if a 'spent' conviction is revealed. However, the plaintiff can win the defamation case only if it can be shown that the defendant acted maliciously, and so it is very difficult for the ex-offender to obtain an injunction to stop a paper publishing details of any previous convictions – especially when there is some 'public interest' justification.

Fair comment

It is a complete defence to a defamation claim if the words were written or spoken on a matter of public interest, in good faith and without malice. The logic behind this defence is that a person is entitled to opinions and free to tell people of them if, but only if, they are on a matter of public concern. For instance:

A newspaper wrote, 'Sugar for Silkin. From these humble Tories I turn to a lordly socialist. Forward the first Baron Silkin. Observe the return to Britain of the Heinkels. Not in the skies but on the rolling roads. These economical little runabouts are selling briskly in the petrol famine. They are seen everywhere – even in New Palace Yard, Westminster, where MPs park their cars. What has this to do with Lord Silkin? Why, he is Chairman of Noble Motors, who market the Heinkels in Britain. And his son, former socialist candidate Mr John Silkin, is a director. Oh, the eloquence that solemn, portly Lord Silkin has churned out in the House of Lords against arming the Germans. He has said that part of his case is "emotional". "I feel that it is wrong that so soon after the events of the war, we should join hands with them today for the purposes of combining our forces." Of course, when Lord Silkin joins hands with the Germans now, he represses his emotion. It is just good solid business. From which, no doubt, he makes a fine profit.' Lord Silkin sued. Held: The defence of fair comment applied. What mattered was not whether the jury agreed with the opinion expressed, but whether the writer had honestly held that opinion. The claim failed. Silkin (1958)

To succeed with a defence of fair comment the words complained of must be an expression of opinion and not an assertion of fact. In many cases this will be difficult to ascertain. The comment must be based on and in the context of other *facts* contained in the publication. The comment must be one that, on the basis of those facts, could be held by a reasonable person. Finally, the defence can be defeated if it can be shown that the comment was made maliciously.

Absolute privilege

A defamation claim cannot be brought against statements made:
● in the House of Commons or the House of Lords;
● in connection with judicial proceedings (e.g. by a witness in a court case);
● in newpaper, radio and TV fair, accurate and contemporaneous reports of judicial proceedings;
   All such statements and reports have absolute privilege. Their originators cannot be sued, even if the statements are totally untrue and are said out of spite or malice.

Qualified privilege

This protects statements made in circumstances that demand they be privileged. For instance, reports of parliamentary proceedings, reports of meetings of public concern (e.g. a TUC conference), non-contemporaneous court reports or reports of official bodies; also the reference given by an ex-employer to another employer. Similarly, statements genuinely made on matters of public concern can be privileged: for example, a complaint made about a police officer using the official complaints procedure or reporting on allegations of a criminal offence made to the police. However:

Nigel Flood complained about the behaviour of WPC Robson: 'She was rude and abusive and the title pig really sums her up. She has no place in the force and would be better on a butcher's hook. Her attitude is what makes decent citizens turn against the police.' WPC Robson won £500 damages, £4,000 costs and a full apology. The complaint was protected by qualified privilege. The police officer's case was based on her allegation that the complaint was motivated by malice.

The general principle is that society recognizes that there must be occasions when the public interest demands that honest beliefs (even if mistaken) should be reported. Only when the plaintiff can show that the defendant acted out of malice can he or she succeed in a defamation claim if qualified privilege exists. For instance, if your employer wrongly described you as a 'bad timekeeper' in a reference, you could not sue for defamation unless you could prove that it was said maliciously (i.e. in order deliberately to hurt you) rather than through an innocent mistake.

Unintentional defamation

The fact that the defamation was not intentional is no defence to a defamation claim. For instances of this, see Cassidy and Jones cases above. But since the Defamation Act 1952, the defendant has been able to make amends and so avoid having to pay heavy damages to the plaintiff.

If the defamation arose innocently, the publisher of a libel can immediately make a suitable 'offer of amends', such as an offer to publish a suitable correction and apology. If this is done, the plaintiff will not be entitled to damages.

This defence will be available only if the person publishing the words did not know that they would be taken to refer to the plaintiff or of the special facts that made the words defamatory. The publisher has also to demonstrate that they exercised all reasonable care to avoid the defamation.

OBSCENITY AND INDECENCY

Commercial dealing in obscene items, or possession of them for these purposes, is an offence. With or without a prosecution, the items can be seized under a magistrate's warrant and, after a hearing to determine whether they contravene the statute, can be forfeited. The statute is the Obscene Publications Act 1959 (amended in 1964).

The test of obscenity – 'deprave or corrupt'

Does the article have a tendency to deprave or corrupt the persons who are likely to read, see or hear it? There must be more than an immoral suggestion or persuasion or depiction: it must constitute a serious menace. It is difficult to predict in advance whether juries or magistrates will be persuaded that this has been satisfied, which in turn can lead to incompatible decisions in different parts of the country.

The statute requires courts to have regard to the effect of the item taken as a whole (where the article – for instance, a magazine – consists of two or more distinct items, they can be viewed separately). Again, what matters is the likely reader or audience, and a publisher is entitled to rely on circumstances of distribution which will restrict those into whose hands the article might fall. The prosecution's case is not made out by showing that the odd stray copy might be read by a more impressionable person; it is necessary to show that it would have the tendency to deprave or corrupt a *significant proportion* of the likely audience.

Defence of merit

The most important change introduced by the 1959 Act was a new defence that publication (in the case of magazines and books) is in the interests of science, literature, art or learning or of other objects of general concern. A similar but rather narrower defence (interests of drama, opera, ballet or any other art, or of literature or learning) applies to plays and films. The use of this defence was demonstrated in the first major case under the 1959 Act, when the publishers of D. H. Lawrence's *Lady Chatterley's Lover* were acquitted at the Old Bailey.

Obscenity – drugs and violence

Obscenity cases do not necessarily involve sex. There have been occasional prosecutions and forfeitures of books which advocated the taking of prohibited drugs. In 1968, while allowing the appeal of the publishers of *Last Exit to Brooklyn*, the Court of Appeal said that the encouragement of brutal violence could come within the test of obscenity, and in recent years video 'nasties' have been dealt with under the Act.

Children

There are special and much more rigorous offences to try and stop the taking or distributing of indecent photographs of children.

Indecency offences

Obscenity is concerned with the harmful effect of the article on its reader or audience; another group of offences regulates *indecency*, where the complaint is more that the material is offensive to public susceptibilities – a nuisance rather than a danger. No easy definition of indecency exists. The courts have said that it is something that 'offends against the modesty of the average man ... offending against recognized standards of propriety at the lower end of the scale'. It depends on the circumstances and current (and in some cases, local) standards. This vagueness is dangerous. Posters for causes such as animal rights which are deliberately intended to shock their audience have sometimes had to contend with indecency prosecutions.

There is no general crime of trading in indecent articles (as there is with obscene ones), but a number of specific offences incorporate the indecency test. Thus it is a crime to send indecent matter through the post, or to put it on public display unless entry is restricted to persons over eighteen and payment is required, or the display is in a special part of a shop with an appropriate warning notice. The indecency offences do *not* apply to television broadcasts (although both the BBC and private TV companies operate under internal prohibitions on indecent matters), to exhibitions inside art galleries or museums, exhibitions arranged by or in premises occupied by the Crown or local authorities, performances of a play or films in licensed cinemas.

In addition to these offences, local councils can adopt powers to regulate sex shops and sex cinemas in their areas. Council licences always prohibit the public display of indecent material and licences can be revoked for breaches of these conditions. Similarly, the music and entertainment licences granted by local authorities will often be conditional on the licensee ensuring that no indecent display takes place. Breach of this condition is both an offence and a ground for withdrawing the licence.

There are also offences of acting to corrupt public morals and outraging public decency. It is a criminal offence to act in such a way as to openly outrage public decency or injure public morals. The offence must be committed in public. It is also against the law to conspire with others to commit such acts. It is very unclear what is covered by these ancient provisions.

Illustration. *In 1990 a sculptor had designed a human head and to each ear he had attached an earring made from a freeze-dried human foetus of three to four months' gestation. The sculpture was displayed in an art gallery. Both the sculptor and owner of the gallery were convicted of outraging public decency.*

Customs regulations also prohibit the importation of indecent articles. However, these restrictions have been somewhat undermined by the EEC provisions on free trade. A cardinal principle of the EEC is that one member state should not set up trade barriers to goods from another member state if there is a legitimate internal market in the same goods. In the case of the UK there is a legitimate market in indecent (but not obscene) articles as long as the traders observe the restrictions noted above. Consequently, Britain cannot discriminate against the importation of the same, indecent, goods from other EEC countries; European law prevails over the British customs regulations.

Blasphemy

Blasphemy is another anachronistic relic of the common law of libel. It applies to outrageous comment or immoderate or offensive treatment of the Christian faith. More particularly, it protects only the sensibilities of the followers of the Christian religion and, possibly, only the Church of England. The intentions of the publisher are irrelevant. Moderate or reasoned criticism of Anglican doctrine is not a crime and the court must consider the likely audience in order to decide whether the publication would produce the necessary outrage.

For newspapers and periodicals there are the same procedural protections as with criminal libel. Consequently, the prosecutor must first get permission to bring the case from a High Court judge, who must be persuaded that the evidence is clear 'beyond argument', that the offence is a serious one and that the public interest would justify a prosecution.

Racial hatred

The offences of inciting or stirring up racial hatred prohibit the use of threatening, abusive or insulting words, behaviour or displays with the intention of stirring up racial hatred or where racial hatred is likely to be stirred up.

The acts do not have to be done in public, but they are not crimes if done in a private dwelling and cannot be seen or heard from the outside. In addition, it is an offence to possess racially inflammatory material unless ignorant of its contents. The police can obtain a search warrant for such material and magistrates can order its forfeiture.

Contempt of court

Contempt of court covers a multitude of sins, but all of them share the common feature that they are regarded by the courts as a threat to the administration of justice. Publication of a secret document in defiance of an injunction prohibiting its disclosure would thus be punishable as contempt.

JUDGE-MADE LAW

Using this branch of contempt, the courts have invented offences of disclosing the identity of blackmail victims who had remained anonymous in court, day-by-day re-enactments on television of court hearings and (in certain circumstances) of disclosing details of a jury's deliberations.

Obviously *deliberate interference with current legal proceedings* constitutes contempt.

The manifestation of contempt which most frequently restricts what the papers can say is that known as 'strict liability contempt'. For specified periods before and during the time that a case is going through the courts, the media are liable if they publish anything which would cause a substantial risk of serious prejudice to the proceedings, irrespective of the intention or even (in most cases) the degree of care which they exercised. During these periods the case is 'active', although the older phrase *sub judice* is still used.

Criminal proceedings are active from the time an arrest takes place, or a warrant or summons is issued. Civil proceedings do not become active until a date is fixed for the hearing. The degree of restriction that this imposes depends on the court or tribunal which will hear the case. If it will be tried by a jury, nothing should be written or broadcast which might prejudice the jury against the defendant; in particular, no past misdeeds should be referred to, and care should be taken that reports do not assume the defendant's guilt. At the other end of the spectrum are cases on appeal. These will be heard by professional judges, who are trained to exclude extraneous considerations such as press reports.

Defences to a strict liability contempt

There are two important special defences to charges of strict liability contempt. The first is that a *discussion in good faith of public affairs* or other matters of general public importance will not be contempt if the risk of prejudice is merely incidental to the discussion.

A second, important defence is that it is not generally contempt to publish a *fair, accurate, good faith and contemporaneous report of legal proceedings held in public*. This is important because things are sometimes said in trials which might reflect adversely on either participant in those proceedings or in other active cases. However, the media's freedom to report is subject to the power of the court to make a postponement order. These can delay full reporting until the end of either the proceedings in question or the others which are at risk of prejudice.

Special cases

In rape cases the victim must remain anonymous unless the court orders otherwise. Until 1988 the defendant was given the same protection (unless convicted). The press (unlike the rest of the public) have a right to attend youth court hearings, but are prohibited from identifying defendants or witnesses, or from publishing their photographs. Young people do not have automatic anonymity in other courts, but the courts can make orders in specific cases.

SECRETS AND CONFIDENTIALITY

Secrecy, it is sometimes said, is the British disease. The scope of the law for preventing and punishing the disclosure of private and governmental confidences represents one of the most important restrictions on free speech. We will look at the criminal and civil dimensions in turn.

The Official Secrets Act

The Official Secrets Act of 1911 slipped on to the statute book in a single day, borne along on a wave of anti-German spy fever (although its gestation had been much longer). This Act is now restricted mainly to espionage cases. A new Act passed in 1989 now protects only the following classes of information:

- security and intelligence;
- defence;
- international relations and criminal investigations.

Members and former members of the security and intelligence servces are guilty of offences if they disclose any information whatsoever – they have a lifelong duty of confidentiality. Others – that is people who have obtained information in other ways (journalists, friends etc.) – are guilty only if the disclosure is damaging or if disclosure of that kind of information would be damaging to the operation of the services (although the Act is complicated and there are exceptions to this).

In the case of information relating to defence, international relations and information about criminal investigations, a person will be guilty of an offence only if the disclosure is a damaging one – that is, a disclosure which is likely to prejudice the capabilities of the Armed Forces or the interests of the United Kingdom abroad, or to result in the commission of an offence or to impede the prevention or detection of offences or offenders.

Other secrecy offences

Apart from the Official Secrets Acts, there are dozens of specific statutory offences of disclosing information in the hands of the Government. Frequently, they are imposed where a Government department has powers to acquire information under compulsion.

THE CIVIL LAW OF CONFIDENCE

Unlike the criminal law, the civil law of confidence will generally protect only material which is still confidential. It was the widespread publication of *Spycatcher* which powerfully influenced the House of Lords to refuse a final injunction to the government.

Pre-trial injunctions

If the plaintiff can find out in advance that publication of a leak or other alleged breach of confidence is planned, and is willing to go to court, then the inevitable first step will be an application for an injunction to stop publication until trial. The test which the courts apply in deciding whether to grant such injunctions is extremely favourable to plaintiffs. Usually the judges will grant an injunction unless there is clear evidence of public interest, and in the case of the *Spycatcher* pre-trial injunction even that was not sufficient. The argument for this 'balance of convenience test' is that at the pre-trial stage the evidence is incomplete and the court is often required to make a hasty decision because publication is imminent. The objection is that the time between injunction and trial is usually so great that the story will have gone cold by the time that full argument on the merits is heard. This in turn means that the defence is not pursued and there never is a full hearing of the case.

Copyright

Copyright, in brief, gives the owner of the work the right to stop others reproducing it without his or her consent.

Copyright does not exist in ideas as such, although the law of confidence has recently been developed to protect those who provide well-worked-out and practicable suggestions for others to develop and exploit. The law of copyright does not operate until the ideas have been reduced to some material form, and then it is generally the reproduction of that form which is restricted. This means, for instance, that newspapers do not have a monopoly even in their 'exclusive' news stories. They can stop others using their photographs, their text (or a substantial part of it) or a colourable imitation of their work, but the information conveyed is not theirs to control.

Copyright is not infringed if the owner *consents* to the copying. This sounds simple, but it can be a complicated business finding out who the owner is. In some works (e.g. a television play) it is possible for different people to own the copyright in the script, the photographs, the sound-track, the dramatic screenplay, the film recording the play and the broadcast. Even if the owners can be identified, there is generally no obligation on them to sell reproduction rights.

Copyright is also not infringed by the use of reasonable extracts for research or private study, criticism, review or the reporting of current events.

It is also a defence to a charge of copyright to show that it is in the 'public interest'. One example of this would be to expose injustice. Documents supplied by 'moles' will generally be subject to copyright, but newspapers publishing extracts might be able to defend a claim by arguing that the publication of the document was in the public interest.

In addition to copyright protection, the law will prevent one trader passing off its goods as those of another. These commercial disputes often have little to do with free speech, but their over-zealous application (or the minimal investigation of a plaintiff's claim on an application for an interlocutory injunction) can lead to the suppression of parody, spoof and satire.

Controls on broadcasting, films, videos and cable

The Independent Television Commission (ITC) by statute and the British Broadcasting Corporation (BBC) by its charter are intended and expected to 'censor' programmes. Unlicensed broadcasters are prohibited. A radio transmitter is still one of the cheapest ways to reach a large audience, but the radio pirates have to keep one step ahead of the Department of Trade inspectors, who can confiscate equipment as well as prosecute for infringements. The Government has a residual power to direct that certain matters should not be broadcast. It used this power in 1988 to ban spoken comment by or in support of Sinn Fein, the UDA or any of the organizations proscribed under the anti-terrorism laws.

The ITC will replace the old Independent Broadcasting Authority at the end of 1992. The ITC is a licensing body and not a publisher. It is not required to exercise pre-judgement over programmes. The ITC will regulate not merely in the interests of high-quality and diverse television but in order to ensure fair and effective competition in the industry.

The ITC is under a duty to see as far as possible that nothing is included in its programmes which offends against good taste or decency or is likely to encourage, or incite to, crime or lead to disorder or be offensive to public feeling. Its news programmes must be presented with due accuracy and impartiality. Due impartiality must be preserved on the part of persons providing programmes on matters of political or industrial controversy or relating to current public policy. Unlike newspapers, which can openly propagate their own views, neither the TV companies nor the IBA editorialize on matters (other than broadcasting) which are of political or industrial controversy or relate to current public policy. Subliminal messages are prohibited and religious broadcasting is specifically controlled.

The Broadcasting Complaints Commission

Radio or television programmes put out by the ITC or the BBC can be reviewed by the Broadcasting Complaints Commission. This was created by Parliament in 1981 to consider complaints of unjust or unfair treatment or unwarranted infringements of privacy in, or in connection with, the obtaining of material included in sound or television broadcasts. Any complaint must be made by a person affected.

The Commission cannot order the payment of any money to the complainant, but they can insist on the responsible body publishing the Commission's findings and, more significantly, can insist on an approved summary being broadcast at a stipulated time.

The British Board of Film Classification

The British Board of Film Classification (BBFC) is a hybrid system. There is no general requirement that a *film* must have a BBFC certificate before being shown, but this position is achieved indirectly by the power of local councils to license cinemas. Most licences have a condition attached that only films with a BBFC certificate will be shown.

The BBFC has been given an enlarged role in relation to video cassettes.

Here, it is a censor in law as well as in practice and it is an offence to supply an unclassified video or to breach any restrictions which have been imposed by the BBFC (as to minimum age, type of supplier etc.). Videos concerned with sport, religion, music and education are exempt, but not if they show or are designed to encourage human sexual activity (or force or restraint associated with it), or mutilation, torture or other gross acts of violence towards humans or animals. Videos are not exempt either if they show human genitalia or human urinary or excretory functions. The BBFC has to consider whether videos are suitable for viewing in the home. There is an appeal structure for those who submit videos to the BBFC but the sizeable fees charged by the Board and the delays that the process necessarily entails can cause grave difficulties for producers.

The regulatory framework for cable has been established on a similar model to that for broadcasting. Thus the Cable Authority has the power to license operators. It must do all that it can to see that its licensees do not include in their programmes material which offends against good taste or decency or is likely to encourage, or incite to, crime or lead to public disorder or to be offensive to public feeling. Subliminal images are, again, banned. News must be presented with due accuracy and impartiality, but only if it originates in the UK. Non-news programmes are considerably less inhibited than broadcasts: instead of a requirement of 'balance' there is only the duty to see that undue prominence is not given to the views and opinions of particular persons or bodies on religious matters or matters of public controversy or relating to current public policy. Editorializing on religious, political, industrial controversy or current public policy is, as with broadcasting, prohibited.

The Cable Authority has the ultimate sanction of withdrawing an operator's licence if these or the other conditions are broken.

62 Homelessness

Since 1977 local authorities have been obliged to provide permanent accommodation for some categories of homeless people. These duties are currently contained in Part III of the Housing Act 1985. A code of guidance issued by the Department of the Environment (latest edition issued in August 1991) sets out the way these provisions should be applied in practice.

QUALIFYING FOR HOUSING

Councils must provide housing for those who are:
- homeless, and
- in priority need, and
- are not homeless intentionally.

When a local authority receives an application for housing it is bound to investigate and decide whether these three key requirements are satisfied (they are explained below). If the three requirements are not all satisfied, there is no obligation to provide permanent accommodation. If homelessness is established, the authority will be under limited duties to provide the applicant with assistance in finding accommodation and/or with temporary rehousing (normally for no more than a matter of weeks). The duties that apply in each of the situations that can arise are set out on the chart on Pages 850–51.

Applying for housing

The application should be made to the housing department of the local authority. It does not have to be in any particular form and need not be in writing, although this may be advisable for clarity.

The meaning of 'homeless'

A person is homeless if he or she has no accommodation in England, Wales or Scotland.

People may be treated as having no such accommodation, and therefore homeless, even if they have somewhere to live in the following situations:
- when those who either live with them or could reasonably be expected to live

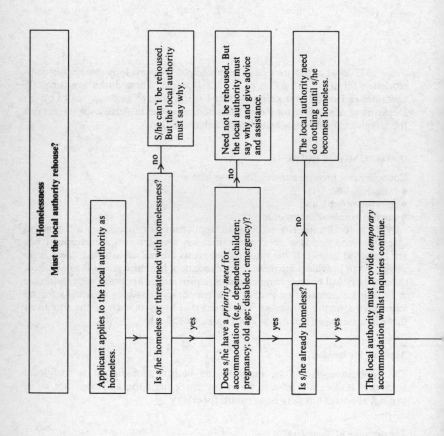

Homelessness

Must the local authority rehouse?

Applicant applies to the local authority as homeless.

Is s/he homeless or threatened with homelessness? — no → S/he can't be rehoused. But the local authority must say why.

yes ↓

Does s/he have a *priority need* for accommodation (e.g. dependent children; pregnancy; old age; disabled; emergency)? — no → Need not be rehoused. But the local authority must say why and give advice and assistance.

yes ↓

Is s/he already homeless? — no → The local authority need do nothing until s/he becomes homeless.

yes ↓

The local authority must provide *temporary* accommodation whilst inquiries continue.

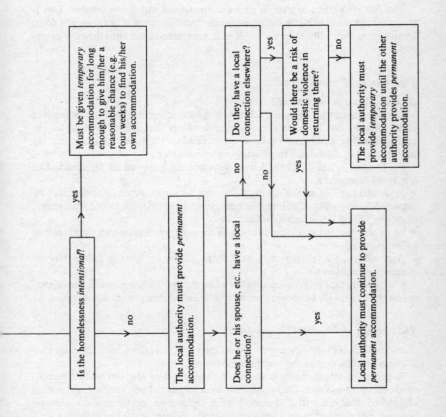

The flow chart contains the following boxes and decisions:

Is the homelessness *intentional*?

- yes → Must be given *temporary* accommodation for long enough to give him/her a reasonable chance (e.g. four weeks) to find his/her own accommodation.

- no → The local authority must provide *permanent* accommodation.

Does he or his spouse, etc., have a local connection?

- no → **Do they have a local connection elsewhere?**
  - no → Local authority must continue to provide *permanent* accommodation.
  - yes → **Would there be a risk of domestic violence in returning there?**
    - yes → (back to) Local authority must continue to provide *permanent* accommodation.
    - no → The local authority must provide *temporary* accommodation until the other authority provides *permanent* accommodation.

- yes → Local authority must continue to provide *permanent* accommodation.

with them as members of their family cannot occupy the accommodation as well; membership of the same family may arise not only through blood or marriage ties but also, for example, through cohabitation or fostering arrangements, *or*
• when it is not reasonable for them to continue to occupy the accommodation – for instance, because of bad disrepair or overcrowding or threat of violence.

The Act also refers to people who are threatened with homelessness. This is the case if they are likely to become homeless within the next twenty-eight days. In any event they will not be provided with accommodation until they are homeless.

The meaning of 'priority need'

A person has a priority need if:
• he or she lives with or could reasonably be expected to live with a dependent child; this covers, for example, younger brothers and sisters, as well as the applicant's own children – children are dependent until the age of sixteen (or nineteen if they attend full-time school or training), *or*
• she (or one of the family she lives with or could reasonably be expected to live with) is pregnant, *or*
• he or she (or one of the family he or she lives with or could reasonably be expected to live with) is vulnerable because of a reason such as old age, youth, disability, illness or domestic violence, *or*
• he or she became homeless because of an emergency such as a flood, fire or other disaster.

Accordingly, a single person is unlikely to qualify for housing unless they are pregnant or vulnerable.

If it appears that priority-need exists when the application is made, the council is obliged to provide temporary accommodation while it arrives at a decision.

The meaning of 'intentional homelessness'

If an applicant is intentionally homeless they will be entitled only to temporary accommodation even if they are in priority need.

A person is intentionally homeless if they left their last established accommodation through their deliberate actions or neglect. Their conduct will not be classed as deliberate if it stemmed from unforeseen problems or a genuine ignorance of relevant facts. Common examples of intentional homelessness are:
• eviction because of a wilful or persistent refusal to pay rent or mortgage repayments;
• leaving accommodation that it was reasonable to occupy in this country or abroad without making adequate alternative arrangements;
• eviction because of anti-social behaviour (such as unacceptable levels of noise, harassment, damage to the premises).

On the other hand, homelessness would not be intentional where:
- arrears problems arose through unforeseen difficulties such as job loss, illness or family breakdown;
- property was vacated in the genuine belief that there was other accommodation available.

Occupiers should be careful not to give up accommodation too readily. Councils generally apply this provision very strictly in order to avoid full housing obligations arising. For example, many local authorities require occupiers facing court possession proceedings to contest the claim fully. A failure to do so is treated as deliberate neglect and therefore intentional homelessness.

The duty to house

If an applicant establishes that he or she is homeless, in priority need and not homeless intentionally, the local authority must secure accommodation for him or her and those members of the family who are referred to under the above section on the meaning of homelessness.

This does not necessarily mean that the local authority will provide its own accommodation. It may arrange for others, such as a housing association, to let their accommodation.

If the applicant has a local connection with another local authority and not the one that he or she has applied to, that other authority will be responsible for providing the accommodation. The only exception is in cases where there is a risk of domestic violence in the other area.

A local connection exists with another area if a person:
- was normally resident there in the past, *or*
- has a job there, *or*
- has family associations or other special connections with the area.

The accommodation that is provided must be suitable. Accommodation could be unsuitable if it is in bad disrepair, overcrowded or poses a health risk. However, applicants should be very careful about rejecting accommodation that they are offered. If they reject accommodation that is in fact suitable, the local authority will not be obliged to make them any further offers. Councils are entitled to house people initially in bed-and-breakfast or other temporary accommodation until permanent accommodation becomes available.

When housing is refused

If a local authority decides that it does not owe a duty to provide an applicant with permanent housing, he or she should consider the following options:

1 Challenging the decision. Many local authorities have internal appeal procedures. It may be possible to have the decision quashed by the High Court. If the latter course is contemplated, specialist legal advice should be

sought promptly. As a general rule the Court requires that proceedings are started within three months of the original decision.
2 Making an application to a different local authority. The decision of the first authority does not bind the second authority (they are obliged only to take note of it).
3 Where the refusal is on the ground of intentional homelessness, bringing a fresh application for housing in the name of another member of the proposed household. If that person did not play a part in the deliberate act or neglect, a full duty to house may arise.

PART NINE

THE ENGLISH LEGAL SYSTEM

63 Introduction to the English Legal System

So far this book has dealt with the law and the rights and obligations it gives and imposes. This section covers the system of justice: the background to the law, the increasing role of Europe, how cases are decided, and the procedures and principles.

This country, unlike America and some European countries, has no written constitution; there is no single document setting out what a citizen's rights are. Our system of justice is like a huge, simmering stock-pot. It is on the boil the whole time and new ingredients are being constantly added. Gradually its taste – its nature – is changing, but this is a slow process.

The English legal system has its roots in antiquity. Magna Carta (1215) is still referred to in text books. There are Acts of Parliament in force which are several hundred years old. The legal system has elements of Roman, French and Danish law in it. Over the centuries it has evolved into what it is today. In recent years European law has begun to make its mark. The European Convention on Human Rights imposes a form of constitution on the English legal system (at least so far as human rights are concerned). This is considered later in the chapter (see page 869).

English law is a mixture, but nevertheless it has a cohesive structure of interlocking rights and duties. Although there is no written constitution, there is an unwritten constitutional system which works as follows.

The monarch

Technically and notionally, the head of state is the Queen – the monarch. Although the monarch does not play much direct part in the legal constitution now, the institution of the monarchy is still a valuable check on Parliament and the Government. The Queen is privy to much Government business, and can offer her opinions to the prime minister of the day. Technically the Queen has power to dissolve Parliament and to appoint a prime minister.

Her functions are largely ceremonial, but if there were a serious constitutional crisis, it is feasible that ceremony could give place to real intervention.

The Queen's speech

At the beginning of each new session of Parliament the Queen's speech outlines the laws which the Government proposes to introduce in the coming session. This speech, while delivered by the Queen, is no longer written by her. It is a statement of the policies and proposals of the Government in power. Parliament is not limited or restricted by the contents of the Queen's speech. This right to choose is symbolically preserved by the reading of a 'Bill for the Suppression of Clandestine Outlawries' *before* the reading of the Queen's speech to the House of Commons.

The executive and the Government

In practice the country is run by the Government – the executive. The Government is *not* Parliament. It is the combined activities of the various Government departments (both central – e.g. the Department of Social Security – and local – e.g. the activities of a district or parish council) and the Cabinet.

The Government is not all-powerful. It must rule in accordance with the laws in force at the time. If it exceeds its powers or breaks the law, it is just as much subject to the law as any private individual.

Furthermore, members of the Government can be called to account by Parliament.

Parliament

Parliament is made up of two tiers, consisting of the lower house, the House of Commons (with elected representatives), and the upper house, the House of Lords (with non-elected members). The duties of Parliament are to keep the Government in check and to pass new laws (called legislation). There is an interrelation between the House of Commons and the House of Lords. Most new laws start in the House of Commons in the form of Bills.

Bills are proposed Acts of Parliament. The Bills must be 'read three times' in both Houses of Parliament and become law only when they receive the Royal Assent (the Queen's formal approval).

The progress of Bills

Bills all have to go through a series of prescribed steps in their journey through both Houses of Parliament. The main steps are as follows.

First reading. Normally the Bill is presented in 'dummy' – that is, a sheet of paper with the name of the MP and the title of the Bill (unless it is a private member's Bill, in which case it will have been printed in full).

Second reading. The Bill is not actually read but its principles are discussed. If no one objects, it can be 'read' a second time when unopposed business is taken. Otherwise it can be considered only on one of the days fixed for taking opposed Bills.

The committee stage. Generally once a Bill has passed its second reading (which it will do virtually automatically if it is a Government Bill) it goes to one of the standing committees of the House of Commons. The committee stage is the time for discussing details and proposing amendments.

Report stage. The Bill is then 'reported' to the House of Commons.

Third reading. After the Bill has been amended and has been considered on report, it is put down for a third reading. A motion is put, 'that the Bill be read a third time'. If it is carried, the Bill is deemed to have passed the House of Commons.

Procedures in the House of Lords. The procedure is similar. If the Bill remains unopposed, it goes for the Royal Assent and then becomes law. Note, however, that some Acts of Parliament are not brought into effect for a considerable length of time. It was well over ten years before the Consumer Credit Act 1974 was fully brought into effect.

The House of Lords used to have the power to veto the bills it received from the House of Commons. It now has only a power of delay, but discussions in the House of Lords are none the less valuable. It is not so entrenched by party politics, and thus can be more impartial. It can allow too for more reflective and informed debate.

The role of Europe

Parliament is no longer the supreme law-maker. Since the United Kingdom became a full member of the European Community, it has been subject to EC law. If there is a clash between national law (the law passed by Parliament) and Community law, the Community law takes priority. Community law gives rights to individuals to which member states must give effect. EC law will become increasingly important in the lives of the citizens of the UK.

EC law has its origins in the Treaty of Rome of 1957. It aims to establish throughout the member states the freedom of movement of people, goods, services and capital (such as savings). Its provisions were largely incorporated into English law in 1972 by the passage of the European Communities Act.

The idea of a united Europe is not new. It can be traced back to the Middle Ages. The real impetus came after the Second World War. What started simply as an economic union now embraces many aspects of domestic and commercial law.

The European Community is administered as follows.

The Council of Ministers

It is the main decision- and law-making body of the EC. It generally meets in

Brussels and is made up of Government ministers from the member states. It can make laws and decisions which are binding not only on member states but also on individuals and organizations in the member states.

The European Commission

This is the civil service of the EC and is based in Brussels. It must act independently of any individual member state. Its functions are:

- carrying out measures passed by the Council of Ministers;
- putting into effect the provisions of the Treaty of Rome;
- enforcing the rules which outlaw unfair trade practices.

The European Parliament

European Members of Parliament (MEPs) are directly elected by voters in each country. There are eighty-one MEPs from the UK. The European Parliament has no powers to make laws. It can consider laws prepared by the European Commission and the Council of Ministers. It can question the European Commission, which is obliged to answer. It can also, by a two-thirds majority, dismiss the whole group of European Commissioners. It can also reject the Community's budget.

It is considered in some quarters that the powers of the European Parliament should be strengthened, so as to make it a legislative body in the same way as any other Parliament, and thus turn the EC into a true democracy.

Judges

Judges are an important part of the constitution. They are independent of Government. Strictly speaking the role of judges is to interpret the law laid down by Parliament and established legal principles, and make their decisions accordingly.

Yet within the legal system judges have power to make decisions against the Government. Ministers of state can be ordered to attend in courts. Injunctions (court orders commanding or forbidding certain actions) can be made against individual ministers or Government departments. In November 1991 the Home Secretary was held by the Court of Appeal to be personally in contempt of court after the Home Office had broken an undertaking not to deport a man who was seeking political asylum. The Home Secretary was ordered personally to pay the costs. The Master of the Rolls Lord Donaldson said: 'Ministers and civil servants are accountable to the law and to the courts for their personal actions.'

The separation of powers: the executive, the judges and Parliament

There is a child's game which involves assuming at random the function of stone, paper or scissors. No one function is paramount. Stone blunts scissors, but can be wrapped by paper; scissors cut paper. The principle of the separation of powers is similar. Judges can overrule the executive, but Parliament can change the law and effectively disarm the judges. The executive appoints judges. Judges are not permitted to sit in the House of Commons.

The theory of this separation of powers is that no single element of power is supreme. Each is subject to control by the others.

RULES OF NATURAL JUSTICE

Any person or body which is charged with the duty of deciding on disputes between, or the rights of, others must act fairly and in accordance with the rules of natural justice. These rules apply to all courts and tribunals. They also apply to other situations where disputes are resolved, such as internal disciplinary procedures, the conduct of clubs and societies and trade union affairs. The rules involve particular consideration of the following:

- *A party must have reasonable notice of the case against him or her.* They must also be given the opportunity of stating their own case. It does not necessarily mean that a person is entitled to be heard orally. The courts have decided that in many instances the rules are satisfied if written representations are made. In criminal cases this principle is expressed by stating, 'No one ought to be condemned unheard.'
- *No man or woman shall be a judge in their own cause.* A judge must always declare any interest in the subject matter of the dispute before them. In Dimes v. Grand Junction Canal (1852) a decree by the Lord Chancellor confirming ownership of a company was set aside by the House of Lords on the ground that he owned shares in the company, even though there was no suggestion that he was influenced in any way by the fact that he was a shareholder.
- *Open justice.* It is a fundamental principle that justice should not only be done but also be seen to be done. It is one of the chief safeguards of the impartial administration of justice for the public and the press to be allowed to attend a court hearing and to be able to publish accurate reports of and fair comment on court proceedings. The courts do have a discretion to hear proceedings in camera (i.e. with press and public absent) but this must be exercised carefully (e.g. where secret information might endanger the state). Decisions to exclude the press and public are open to challenge in higher courts.

Over the years it has become necessary to restrict the open court policy to protect individuals from unfair publicity. The public are generally excluded from juvenile cases (but the press are entitled to report them so long as the juvenile is not identified; see page 183). Most domestic cases in the county court

and magistrates' courts are held in private, though the press may publish limited information about the cases. Special rules apply to specific cases:
● committal proceedings (see page 758) – the public is allowed to attend, but the press may publish only limited information, such as: names of the parties, their lawyers, whether bail was granted and the charges against the accused if he or she is committed for trial. The accused may request reporting restrictions to be lifted. If the magistrates agree, then a full report of the proceedings may be published;
● rape cases – until a verdict is given neither the accused nor the victim may be identified without the court's consent. If the accused is found guilty he or she will be named, but the victim will remain anonymous whatever the verdict;
● indecency – the press are prohibited from publishing indecent matter (including medical evidence) if publication would be 'calculated to injure public morals';
● sub judice – the laws of contempt of court restrict what a newspaper may publish. If, for instance, a paper were to publish details of an accused man's previous convictions for dishonesty during a fraud trial, it would clearly be in contempt of court. The laws of contempt were tightened by the Contempt of Court Act 1981, which gave the court powers to order the press not to publish certain parts of the evidence or the names of witnesses. This provision has been severely criticized as being too far-reaching. It is felt that it allows the courts to gag the press when there is no real justification for doing so.

SOURCES OF THE LAW

There are four sources of law in this country: common law, statute law, equity and European law.

Common law ('judge-made' law)

> We ourselves of the present age chose our common law, and consented to the most ancient Acts of Parliament, for we lived in our ancestors 1,000 years ago, and those ancestors are still living with us.
> Sir Robert Atkyns, English jurist (1686)

Early developments

The origins of our common law can be traced back to the Norman era. Prior to the arrival of the Normans, there was little contact between the various villages and towns scattered throughout the country; each shire and each hundred had its own local court, dispensing its own justice in accordance with local custom and the wishes of the local barons.

It was the Normans who set about imposing a national system of law. By the Assize of Clarendon (1166) and the Assize of Northampton (1176) the basis was laid of a system whereby judges of the realm went on regular journeys through the country to bring the king's justice to every citizen. The aim was that there should be a common system of law throughout the land: common law. These developments took place at a time when there were few forms of written law. A body of principles and maxims (clichés, some would say) evolved which provided an answer to most legal problems. In time, the decisions of the judges came to be written down and their decisions would subsequently be used by other judges as evidence of the law. The decisions of one generation of judges would be adhered to by later generations.

The law could not remain static; there had to be some flexibility to meet the needs of changing times. Accordingly, the judges would still follow earlier decisions but they would distil general principles from the decisions which would then be adapted to meet the new circumstances. The process continues to this day; the common law is continuously developing in the courts.

Growth of the system of precedent

As a hierarchy of courts developed it was natural that the decisions of the senior courts should be regarded as binding on the junior courts. Thus the *doctrine of precedent* was created: the decisions of the House of Lords are binding on all the other courts trying similar cases; if no relevant House of Lords decisions are on record, then the appropriate decision of the Court of Appeal would be binding, and so on, down through the hierarchy of courts.

The advantage of the system of precedent is that there is a consistency in the way the courts apply the law. The disadvantage is that it can lead to inflexibility, if a junior court is bound by an old House of Lords decision that has not been reviewed for a long time. Unfortunately, this has tended to happen. To make matters worse, the House of Lords and the Court of Appeal considered themselves bound by their own previous decisions. Thus change became impossible and judges had to resort to finding semantic devices or artificial differences in cases to justify not following an old decision. It was not until 1966 that the House of Lords finally decided that it was not bound by its old decisions and that it could reinterpret the law if it wished.

Can the Court of Appeal overrule its previous decisions? As long ago as 1944 the Court of Appeal decided that it is bound by its previous decisions except in three instances. Namely:

1 If decisions of its own conflict with one another, it can choose between them.
2 It should not follow its own previous decisions if they conflict with decisions of the House of Lords, even if the Lords have not expressly overruled the Court of Appeal decision.
3 If it made a mistaken decision it is not bound by it.

Young v. Bristol Aeroplane Company, 1944

These principles, reached in the case, are still observed by the Court of Appeal.

Development of the common law

The classic illustration of how the judges have made law is the history of the 'negligence' claim. Basically the law of negligence allows a victim to sue someone who has taken less care than he or she should have done (see page 714). But this is a relatively recent concept. Until the nineteenth century there was no such action; there was merely a variety of situations in which negligence might give rise to liability. But the nineteenth century saw a drawing together of these actions under the overall category of the negligence claim. Slowly standardized tests for determining liability were worked out.

It was not until 1932 that the House of Lords laid down a system of principles for the negligence claim that was the real starting-point of the law of negligence as we know it today. The House of Lords decision in Donoghue v. Stevenson (1932) created the modern law of negligence.

To lawyers Donoghue v. Stevenson is one of the best-known cases. It involved a young lady who became ill when she discovered a snail in the bottom of a bottle of ginger beer which she was drinking. She sued the manufacturer for damages. The case went all the way to the House of Lords, where it was decided that her claim should succeed.

As the years have gone by the principles in Donoghue v. Stevenson have been extended. For instance, in 1932 the negligence action did not apply to negligent statements as opposed to negligent acts, but in 1964 the judges of the House of Lords held that it did cover negligent statements (Hedley Byrne v. Heller).

A solicitor was asked by a garage to give a reference for a client of his who was involved in buying an expensive car. The solicitor knew his client was on a fraud charge but as he did not believe it would affect his performance of the proposed contract, he did not mention it in the reference. The client defaulted and the solicitor had to pay £13,000 damages for giving an unreliable reference. Edwards and others *v.* Lee (1991)

As the law develops, so the scope of claims for negligence can be expanded:

A householder was burning off paint with a blowlamp. By mistake he set fire to his house. A fireman was injured in the efforts to put out the blaze. The fireman sued the householder for damages and the House of Lords decided that his claim should succeed. He was awarded £12,900. Ogwo *v.* Taylor (1987)

Common law decisions are not confined to the decisions of English courts. Decisions of other 'common-law' countries (notably Australia, New Zealand, Canada and Hong Kong) are often considered by English courts.

Common law is not paramount. Its principles can be cancelled, changed or extended by statute law. Nevertheless, it allows considerable opportunity for judges to alter and to make law.

Statute law (Acts of Parliament)

Statute law overrides the common law; if the common law says one thing and an Act says something else, the judges must follow the Act.

Who is to decide what these Acts of Parliament *mean*? The answer is that the judges decide. Judges can therefore create law by the way they interpret statutes. For instance:

● the judges consistently refused to apply the Sex Discrimination Act as it was intended by Parliament; Lord Denning (the former Master of the Rolls), in particular, consistently defied the clear wording of that Act;

● the history of legal protection for trade unions is one of constant conflict between the unions and the judges. When Parliament passed laws to protect the unions, the judges often interpreted the Acts so as to minimize (if not emasculate) the intention of Parliament.

Words are necessarily an imperfect vehicle for setting out the law. It is a difficult task for the drafters of a statute to prepare an Act that covers all possible circumstances. Inevitably there will be ambiguities and unforeseen situations. An arbitrator – the judge – then has to decide what the law should be.

Nevertheless, rules have been developed about how judges should set about the interpretation of Acts of Parliament when the meaning is not clear. Parliament has itself laid down certain guidelines. The Interpretation Act 1978 spells out fundamental rules – for instance, that male equals female and singular equals plural (and vice versa) in all Acts. It also contains a glossary of words which are given official meanings. For instance:

month means calendar month

writing includes typing, printing, lithography, photography and other modes of representing or reproducing words in visible form, and expressions referring to writing are construed accordingly.

No comment is offered as to whether this second definition makes matters clear! The judges too have formulated rules. These are known by different names:

● *The context rule.* A statute cannot be asked to explain itself in the same way that a person can be asked what they mean. It is therefore necessary to look at a word or phrase in its setting. As Henry Fielding said: 'A word may be known by the company it keeps.'

● *Fringe meaning.* If a judge has difficulty in finding the meaning of a statute he or she may try to divine what Parliament intended when the Act was passed. An example of the sort of problem which gives rise to this difficulty is in the definition of a word like 'building'. Normally, that would present no problem if the structure were a bungalow or a school. But what about a shed, or a caravan with its wheels removed, or a converted railway carriage? In such circumstances it may be necessary to look further to try to find what was intended.

Not all judges agree that this is a correct approach. According to Lord Simon in Farrell v. Alexander (1977): 'The court is concerned to ascertain ... not what [Parliament] meant to say, but the meaning of what they have said.'

• *The mischief rule.* This rule was first developed in 1584 and is known as the 'Rule in Heydon's case'. What the judges have to do is see what the law was before the Act was passed and ascertain the 'mischief' which resulted in the change in the law. They cannot of course trawl through the history of the passage of an Act through Parliament. They can, however, look at Royal Commissions and departmental reports for details of the mischief at which the new law is aimed.

• *The literal rule.* This is an unpopular method of interpreting the law. It is the 'nothing added, nothing taken away' approach; stick to the law, however absurd the result may be. According to Glanville Williams in *Learning the Law*. 'The literal rule is a rule against using intelligence in understanding language. Anyone who in ordinary life interpreted words literally, being indifferent to what the speaker or writer meant, would be regarded as a pedant, a mischief maker or an idiot.'

• *The golden rule.* If on the face of it the words of an Act produce an absurd meaning, the courts are allowed to use an interpretation which avoids the absurdity. The sensible meaning has to be linguistically possible; the court cannot completely rewrite the Act so as to make it make sense. Lord Denning put it this way in *'The Changing Law'*: 'The judges are too often inclined to fold their hands and blame the legislature, when really they ought to set to work and give the words a reasonable meaning, even if this does involve a departure from the letter of them. By doing so they are more likely to find the truth.'

The skill and foresight of the parliamentary draftsmen is of considerable importance. Standards vary. Sometimes the wording is appalling:

The following provisions of this Act shall extend only to shops that is to say those provisions of section 6 and section 8 which relate to the approval by occupiers of shops or orders made under these sections the provisions of paragraph (c) of subsection 1 of section 7 and the provisions of paragraph (a) of section 12.

Small wonder that with passages like that to interpret the judges are left by Parliament to make the law. As Lord Justice Mackinnon said of another Act, the Trade Marks Act 1938:

In the course of three days' hearing of the case, I have, I suppose, heard section 4 read, or have read it myself, dozens if not hundreds of times. Despite this iteration, I must confess that, reading it through once again, I have very little notion of what the section is intended to convey and particularly the sentence of 253 words, as I make them, which constitute subsection 1.

Fortunately some of our present parliamentary draftsmen are trying to improve the standard of legislative drafting. Mr Francis Bennion, in particular, has produced the Consumer Credit Act 1974, which is little short of a masterpiece; despite having to deal with topics of great complexity, he has produced an Act which is clear, logical and seemingly free of ambiguities.

Every year up to eighty new Acts of Parliament are passed. Many of these are tortuously worded and a nightmare for lawyers, let alone the layperson. It is not surprising that so much court time is spent in establishing what an Act is trying to say. None the less, however well drafted the Act may be, the judges can interpret it as they will and Parliament may have to pass another Act to close the loophole opened by the judges.

Statutory instruments

These are regulations made by the Government under powers conferred by Acts of Parliament. They carry the force of law, and usually deal in detail – for instance, in the construction of vehicles or hygiene provisions for the sale of food. They far outnumber Acts of Parliament and are often even more difficult to understand than the Acts themselves.

Statutory instruments are seldom considered in detail by Parliament, though MPs do have the power to check them before they are brought into force.

Equity

Equity is a 'gloss' on the common law. Primarily it is a system of fairness which steps in to supplement the common-law rules where common law fails to provide an effective solution. Equity used to be administered by the Chancery court. Since 1873 equity and common law have both been administered together by a single civil-courts system. None the less equity is still relevant today, because its rules can prevail over common law where there is a conflict between the rules of equity and the common-law rules. Equity acts according to a number of principles, which are expressed as 'maxims'. Most equitable remedies are discretionary (as opposed to being 'as of right'). Included are: injunctions (orders to do or refrain from a particular activity), rectification (putting right mistakes in legal documents) or rescission (cancellation of contracts).

Equitable maxims

Equity will not suffer a wrong to be without a remedy.
He who comes to Equity must come with clean hands.
Equity, like nature, does nothing in vain.
Equity regards the balance of convenience.
Equity looks to the intent rather than the form.

European law

> The Treaty of Rome is like an incoming tide. It flows into the
> estuaries and up the rivers. It cannot be held back. Parliament has
> decreed that the Treaty is henceforward to be part of our law. It is
> equal in force to any statute.
>
> Lord Denning in Bulmer v. Bollinger (1974)

The principles of European law are laid down by the Treaty of Rome, which
gave the governing bodies the legal power to make laws on areas of economic
importance. These laws override national laws where there is a conflict between
them. Regulations passed by the Council of Ministers (see above) do not have
to be confirmed by individual countries. The British Government can refuse to
put a Community regulation into effect only if it can show that the regulation is
contrary to community law.

The Single Market

The Single European Act, which came into force in 1987, aims to achieve the following:
- the elimination of frontier controls;
- the mutual recognition of professional qualifications;
- the harmonization of product specifications, largely by the mutual recognition
of national standards;
- free movement of capital;
- harmonization of VAT.

The Single European Act also extends the powers of the EC into fields of
technology, the environment and regional policy.

Although the EC was originally economic in its aims the laws have considerable effect on private individuals, and their effect on citizens of this country is
set to increase.

Examples of European law already in existence

Travel. All EC citizens are entitled to travel freely among member countries.

Work. A UK citizen may live and work in any other part of the European
Community without a work permit, and be accompanied by his/her spouse and
children.

Tax. British citizens who pay tax in another EC country may escape tax in
the UK even if they send some of their income back to this country;

Professionals. Under the Treaty of Rome all EC citizens have the right to set
up a business anywhere in the Community. That rule is not yet fully in force
(1992) because member states have yet to reach agreement on professional
qualifications. Already barristers and solicitors may appear in court professionally in any Community country.

Workers' rights. The Treaty of Rome requires member states to ensure equal pay for men and women doing similar work. A directive of the European Commission requires that companies making more than ten workers redundant must give at least thirty days' notice to the workers and the Department of Employment; another directive (80/987/EEC) sets minimum levels of protection in the event of an employer's insolvency.

The Italian government had failed to implement directive 89/987. In November 1991 the European Court of Justice decided that although private individuals could not rely on that provision in their own courts [because the law had not been brought into effect in Italy], the member state was none the less required to make good damage to individuals caused by its failure to bring the law into effect. Francovich v. Italian Republic (1991)

Health and social security. Social security contributions made in one member country count in all others. Thus an Englishman who pays contributions in France for four years and then returns to England is entitled to the same benefits as if he were in this country the whole time.

Mr Newton, a UK national, suffered complete tetraplegia following a road accident in France. He applied in the UK for mobility allowance. The allowance was granted. Later he moved to France permanently. The Department of Social Security cancelled his mobility allowance. One of the grounds was that he no longer met the residence conditions for the benefit. The matter was referred to the European Court of Justice. Held: The UK authorities were precluded from withdrawing benefit on the ground that Mr Newton was resident in a member state other than the UK. Newton v. Chief Adjudication Officer (1991)

HUMAN RIGHTS

In 1948 the United Nations proclaimed the Declaration of Human Rights. In 1950 the Council of Europe signed the European Convention on Human Rights and Fundamental Freedoms. Since then further rights have been added by eight *protocols* to the convention. Citizens and residents of signatory countries (which include the UK) now have the following rights:

● *Life.* No one shall be deprived of their life intentionally except in the execution of a sentence following conviction of a crime. Even this exception has been curtailed by Protocol No. 6, which declares that the death penalty has been abolished. The death penalty may be used only in time of war.

● *Liberty.* Article 5 states that no one may be deprived of their liberty except under due process of the law. Those arrested shall be informed promptly (and in a language they understand) of the reasons for their arrest. Anyone detained is entitled to trial within a reasonable time, or to be released pending trial. Any person who is arrested or detained in breach of Article 5 shall have an enforceable right to compensation. Under Protocol No. 4 no one shall be deprived of their liberty on the ground of inability to fulfil a contractual obligation. Imprisonment for debt has been abolished in the UK for a number of years but civil courts do have power of committal for breach of orders. It therefore follows that there should be no imprisonment if the breach stems from a contractual obligation.

● *Fair administration of justice*. Article 6 guarantees a fair and public hearing of both civil and criminal cases. Judgement must be pronounced publicly. Those who cannot understand English are entitled to the free use of an interpreter. Legal aid is also guaranteed in criminal cases for those of insufficient means and when the interests of justice require.

Mr Granger appeared as a prosecution witness in a trial relating to murder, arson and other offences. In the witness box he denied all knowledge of the crimes. Later he was convicted of perjury in relation to his evidence at the trial and was sent to prison. He appealed against conviction but was refused legal aid on the ground that he had insufficient grounds for appeal. He therefore conducted his appeal himself. During the course of the appeal it became clear that there were complex matters to be decided. Yet he continued to be denied legal aid. Held: The European Court of Human Rights concluded that there had been a violation of Article 6: legal aid should have been granted. Granger v. United Kingdom (1991)

● *Respect for private and family life*. Under Article 8 no public authority may interfere with this right (which includes the right of privacy of correspondence) unless it is done in accordance with the law *and* is necessary (e.g. for national security, for public safety or the economic well-being of the country).

Mr McCallum was serving a six-year sentence for assault and robbery. During his sentence he spent two periods in solitary confinement, during which the prison authorities stopped five letters written by him, delayed two others and withheld from him two letters written on his behalf. He complained to the European Court of Human Rights. Held: This amounted to a violation of Article 8. McCallum v. United Kingdom (1991)

● *Marriage and founding a family*. Men and women of marriageable age are granted the right to marry according to national laws.

● *Education*. No one shall be deprived of the right to education. Authorities are required to respect the right of parents to ensure that teaching is in conformity with their own philosophical and religious convictions.

● *Enjoyment of possessions*. Under Article 1 of Protocol No. 1 no one may be deprived of their possessions except in accordance with the law and in the public interest. The state is permitted, nevertheless, to enforce such laws as it deems necessary to control the use of property in accordance with the general interest or to secure the payment of taxes or 'other contributions or penalties'. It is not made clear whether this prohibits a bailiff from taking possessions to enforce a civil debt!

● *Free elections at reasonable intervals*. This right was added by Article 3 of the first Protocol.

The convention also generally guarantees freedom of:

● thought, conscience and religion;
● expression and opinion;
● assembly and association with all others.

It gives freedom from:

● torture, inhuman and degrading treatment and punishment;

- slavery, servitude and forced labour;
- retrospective criminal legislation.

Under the Convention, anyone whose rights are violated shall have an effective remedy before a national authority. Britain is a signatory to the Convention. Even though Parliament has never enacted the convention into English law, it is binding on Britain.

How to complain about violation of human rights

Complaints are administered by the European Commission on Human Rights. This is under the general control of the Committee of Ministers (the decision-making body of the Council of Europe; the Committee consists of the Foreign Ministers of the member states of the Council).

The Commission can deal only with complaints relating to the rights listed in the Convention and Protocols. It is not a court of appeal from national courts and cannot overrule or modify their decisions. It cannot intervene directly with the authority or body complained about.

The Commission considers complaints only about matters which are the responsibility of a public authority (administration, legislature, courts of law etc.). It cannot deal with complaints against private individuals or organizations. On the other hand, it can deal with a complaint by someone who is not a national of the country in which the violation occurs.

All national remedies must have been tried before a complaint can be brought. This includes taking the complaint to the highest court which can deal with it. There is no need to try to reopen a case involving conviction or sentence if all the normal appeal procedures of the courts have been followed. Nor is it necessary to use other avenues of redress, such as a complaint to an MP or referral to an ombudsman. None the less, a complainant must make correct use of the available remedies; time limits and procedural rules must be complied with.

Complaints must be made *within six months* of the final decision. This time runs from the final court decision in the ordinary appeal process and not from the date of any later refusal to reopen the case. This time-limit is strict: the Commission has no power to extend the time-limit.

Making the complaint

The procedure is free: no fees are charged. All that is needed initially is a letter addressed to: The Secretary, European Commission of Human Rights, Council of Europe, BP 431 R6, F-67006 Strasbourg Cedex, France.

The letter should:

1 Give a *brief summary* of the complaints.
2 Indicate which of the Convention rights have been violated.

3 State what remedies have been used.
4 List the official decisions in the case, giving the date of each decision, the court or authority which took it and brief details of the decision itself. Attach a copy of these decisions to the letter.

The Secretary to the Commission will acknowledge the letter and may ask for more information. He or she may also explain how the Convention has previously been interpreted in similar cases, and may advise if there is an obvious obstacle to the *admissibility* of the complaint.

If it seems that the complaint could be registered as an application, a formal application form will have to be completed. This requires fuller details of the case, the name of legal representatives, a statement of the object of the application (e.g. compensation for wrongful detention) and an indication of preferred language (the Commission has two official languages – English and French – but the Secretariat conducts correspondence in a number of languages).

Before a decision is taken on whether or not to admit the complaint the Commission will often ask the parties for information or observations.

Once an application is declared admissible, the Commission's next task is to establish the facts. Parties may be invited to send in further evidence. Hearings may be held or on-the-spot investigations mounted (including the examination of witnesses or experts).

One of the roles of the Commission is to conciliate and to attempt to secure a friendly settlement on the basis of respect for the rights guaranteed by the Convention. If there is no settlement the Commission prepares a detailed report, including a presentation of the facts underlying the dispute, and a legal opinion on whether there has been a violation of the Convention. The report is sent to the Committee of Ministers and to the state or states involved. At this stage it remains confidential and is not sent to the applicant or his/her lawyers. The case may then within three months be referred to the European Court of Human Rights. Only the Commission itself or one of the states concerned may refer it to the court. Private individuals do not at present (1992) have the power to refer cases direct to the court. However, that will change when the ninth protocol to the Convention is ratified; individuals will then be able to refer cases to the court, but only if their complaints have been declared admissible.

The European Court of Human Rights

This is also based in Strasbourg. It consists of one judge from each member state of the Council of Europe. Usually seven judges hear a case.

Normally the parties or their lawyers will be permitted to present written and oral argument. The complainant may be required to attend as a witness.

The Commission's function in the court is as advocate-general. It does not act as a party to the case, but presents its impartial opinion (which could well be that there has been no breach of the Convention). Once a case has been referred to the court, the Commission's report to the Committee of Ministers is usually made public.

872

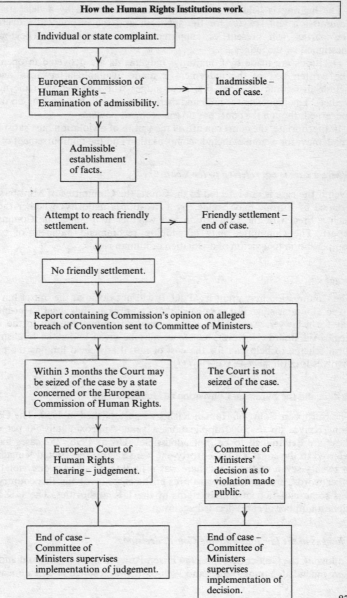

How the Human Rights Institutions work

Individual or state complaint.

European Commission of Human Rights – Examination of admissibility.

Inadmissible – end of case.

Admissible establishment of facts.

Attempt to reach friendly settlement.

Friendly settlement – end of case.

No friendly settlement.

Report containing Commission's opinion on alleged breach of Convention sent to Committee of Ministers.

Within 3 months the Court may be seized of the case by a state concerned or the European Commission of Human Rights.

The Court is not seized of the case.

European Court of Human Rights hearing – judgement.

Committee of Ministers' decision as to violation made public.

End of case – Committee of Ministers supervises implementation of judgement.

End of case – Committee of Ministers supervises implementation of decision.

The hearing is held in public. This will be attended by a delegate of the Commission and lawyers for the applicant and the respondent Government. The parties will present or supplement their submissions. They may be questioned by the judges.

Decisions are made by a majority. Judgements are delivered in open court. The written text of the judgement is made available afterwards, and may include dissenting opinions (i.e. from judges who disagree with the majority verdict). The judgement is final and there is no appeal. It is binding on the state concerned, though the court has no enforcement powers.

If appropriate, the court can afford the victim of a violation 'just satisfaction', which may, for example, include compensation and the reimbursement of costs.

Where a case is not referred to the Court

Even if the case is not referred to the Court, the Committee of Ministers of the Council of Europe may decide (by a two-thirds majority) whether there has been a breach of the Convention and whether to publish the Commission's report. The Committee may in addition recommend payment of costs or compensation to a victim of a violation of human rights.

Legal aid

The Commission may grant legal aid. It will not do so at the outset but it may do so at a later stage if it is satisfied that an applicant has insufficient means to pay for a lawyer. Application is made to the Commission, *not* to the English Legal Aid Board. However, assistance may be given under the English green-form scheme to help pay for the cost of initial advice so long as the problem involves English law (see page 957).

Britain and the European Convention on Human Rights

The European Court of Human Rights was established in 1959. The Commission receives up to 5,000 applications a year. Approximately 90 per cent of these are determined to be 'not admissible'. Up to 1990, 252 cases had been referred to the court. Of these, forty-one were against the United Kingdom and in twenty-seven of the cases there was a finding of at least one violation. In other words, in more than two-thirds of the cases involving this country, there was some violation of human rights by the UK authorities. The UK has the highest number of cases decided against it.

Changes in the law following the Court's decisions

Following the Golder case the 1964 Prison Rules in force in England and Wales were amended. Young, James and Webster (1981) resulted in amendment of the employment legislation in the Employment Act 1982. After X v. the United Kingdom (1981) the Mental Health laws were changed. The Prison Department announced in 1984, following the cases of Campbell and Fell (1984), that legal aid would be available before Prison Boards of Visitors and that their findings would be published.

Relationship to the UK law

Several European countries have enshrined the European Convention on Human Rights and Fundamental Freedoms into their own legislation, so that citizens may have access to it directly through their own courts. Many of the principles in the Convention are contained in various UK Acts of Parliament, but the rights are not generally incorporated into the English legal system. In view of the United Kingdom's unimpressive record on human rights has the time now come for this step to be taken?

THE COURTS

If conflicts cannot be resolved in civil matters or if offences are tried in criminal cases, decisions have to be made by the courts. There are many different types of court. There are also other bodies for deciding disputes which are not courts, but at which legal principles are still applied. These are all described in more detail in the Courts Guide later in this chapter.

How courts decide

Unlike some European legal systems, the courts in this country (with some exceptions) make decisions on an *adversarial basis*. Quite literally this means that there is a contest between the opposing parties (prosecutor/accused and plaintiff/defendant). The court acts as umpire, and success or failure depends on the strength of the case and the way it is presented.

It is not for nothing that lawyers refer to contested cases as 'fights'. The lawyer on each side presents his or her client's case and aims to demolish the opponent's case. There are strict rules to ensure fair play.

In a typical criminal case the prosecution lawyer will give an opening speech describing the offence and giving an account of how he or she will prove the accused's guilt, and will then call his/her witnesses to give evidence. All may be cross-examined by the defence lawyer. When the prosecution case is closed, the defence lawyer calls his/her witnesses (who are also subject to cross-examination). At the end of the evidence the defence lawyer makes his/her closing speech (and the prosecution has a right of reply if points of law are argued).

On the Continent the alternative *inquisitorial system* is used. Here the judge will play a much more active role in the proceedings, which will take the form of an inquiry into the circumstances. A coroner's inquest on the cause of death takes the form of an inquisitorial hearing (see page 883), as do some public inquiries, especially those looking into such matters as the cause of a disastrous fire or plane crash.

Both systems have their advantages and disadvantages. For the adversarial system it is said that a case is properly tested according to set rules, and therefore justice is likely to be achieved. The critics of the system will point to the many miscarriages of justice which the system produces and will argue that a party should not win or lose simply because of the qualities of the lawyers on the case.

Those supporting the inquisitorial system will say that it is fairer, and does away with much unnecessary posturing by the parties. Its critics will say that too much depends on the judge who decides the case, and that there is a real risk that issues will not be thoroughly investigated.

There are many proposals for reform of our legal system, but at the moment none suggests a change in the basis of deciding cases. The adversarial system remains.

Whether the court is civil or criminal the rules are largely the same. All cases must be 'proved' on the evidence. The 'burden of proof' is normally on the person bringing the case: the prosecution in a criminal case, the plaintiff in a civil case. In criminal cases the level or standard of proof is much greater. Guilt must be proved 'beyond reasonable doubt' (the court must be 'sure'). In civil cases the standard is the 'balance of probabilities' (the court must find that it is more likely than not that the plaintiff is right).

COURTS GUIDE

Besides distinguishing between civil and criminal courts, there are various ways of categorizing English courts. There are *inferior* courts and *superior* courts. An inferior court is any court which is not the High Court (and, of course, the appeal courts), the Central Criminal Court or a crown court. Other lesser-known courts are superior courts, such as the Chancery Courts of Lancaster and Durham. Inferior courts are subject to the supervisory jurisdiction of the Divisional Court (see below).

There are also *courts of record*. These can be either superior or inferior courts. The High Court is a superior court of record. The Liverpool Court of Passage and the Salford Hundred court are examples of inferior courts of record. A court of record keeps a permanent record of its proceedings.

Criminal courts

Magistrates' courts

There are more than 650 magistrates' courts in the country. The number is declining because it is administratively more convenient to concentrate the courts in central areas. In country districts this means that those involved in magistrates' court hearings will have to travel further for their hearings. There will be less of the element of 'local justice' which has characterized magistrates' courts.

Magistrates' courts are the most junior in the hierarchy of courts, and yet they are very important. They deal with most criminal cases. Magistrates have power to fine up to £2,000 and to sentence to imprisonment for up to six months. Sitting as a juvenile court (to be renamed *Youth courts*), the magistrates can impose special orders in relation to young offenders (see Chapter 10).

There are two types of magistrate: lay magistrates and stipendiary magistrates. Lay magistrates are not legally qualified (although they receive some training) and are paid only their travelling expenses and a subsistence allowance. Stipendiary magistrates are legally qualified, are usually solicitors and tend to be appointed to sit in the large, urban magistrates' courts. They have a reputation for being tougher and faster than lay magistrates.

About 98 per cent of all criminal cases are heard in the magistrates' court, and every criminal case must start there, even if the case is eventually tried in the crown court. See Chapter 53 for how criminal proceedings are begun and how committal proceedings take place.

Although there are now training courses and instruction books for magistrates, most justices of the peace have little knowledge of the law, other than what they have picked up over the years as they hear cases. For legal advice they rely on the clerk who sits in every magistrates' court and is there to assist and advise the magistrates. Generally the clerk will be a solicitor or barrister with at least five years' experience.

The justices' clerk is in a position of some power, for he or she may easily influence the magistrates in their decision, although, of course, he or she should not do so.

Crown courts

Crown courts are superior courts of record. The crown court system replaced Courts of Assize and Quarter Sessions. Crown courts deal in the main with criminal cases, though appeals from some civil decisions of the magistrates' courts (e.g. matters such as affiliation and licensing) lie to the crown courts. All indictable offences are tried by the crown court. It also hears criminal appeals from the magistrates' and juvenile courts.

Crown Courts deal with four classes of case. The type of case determines the court in which it is tried and the level of judge to hear it:

• Class 1 – examples: murder, treason. These cases are the most serious and are always tried by a High Court judge.

• Class 2 – examples: incitement to mutiny, piracy, manslaughter. These cases are tried by a High Court judge unless a particular case is released by the presiding judge for trial by a circuit judge.

• Class 3 – examples: criminal damage with intention to endanger life, indecent exposure, kidnapping. A case in this category may be tried by a High Court judge but the presiding judge may give general directions permitting cases to be tried by a circuit judge or a recorder.

● Class 4 – examples: obtaining property by deception, destroying or damaging property, abstracting electricity. These are the least serious cases and are not tried by a High Court judge unless the consent of the judge or the presiding judge is given. These cases are normally heard by a circuit judge or a recorder.

For the hierarchy of judges see page 933. Crown courts always sit with a jury when trying criminal cases.

Civil courts

Magistrates' courts

For the constitution of magistrates' courts, see under Criminal Courts above. On the civil side, magistrates' courts have an extensive matrimonial and family jurisdiction. They can make maintenance and affiliation orders and adoption orders, and can also make orders restricting a violent husband's access. In addition they have jurisdiction to hear other miscellaneous matters, such as community charge claims and recovery of unpaid income tax and national insurance contributions.

When dealing with civil matters relating to children and families the magistrates will sit as a *Family Proceedings Court*. Magistrates sitting in these courts are drawn from a specially trained Family Panel.

Committees of local magistrates also deal with such matters as liquor and betting-licence applications.

County courts

County courts were established in 1846 to handle the smaller-value civil claims. Their jurisdiction used to be limited both geographically and financially. Under the Courts and Legal Services Act 1990, proceedings can be issued in any county court in the country, regardless of where the subject matter of the dispute is or where the other party lives (but a defendant may then apply for the case to be transferred to his or her home county court).

Under the same Act the county courts now have power to hear most cases without financial limit. These courts are presided over by a circuit judge who tries the larger value cases (now generally over £5,000). Much of the routine work and all the lower-value cases are tried by the district judge (the former title of this office was 'district registrar'). County courts hear most types of cases, from divorce to debts, from bankruptcy to boundary disputes. Not all county courts have the same status: some are restricted in the level of cases they may try.

The patents county court. New procedures have been introduced to enable patents disputes to be considered in the county court, instead of the High

Court. The only county court which has been appointed as a patents county court is the Edmonton county court, London N22.

The High Court

The High Court hears the more important civil cases, and it also has a small jurisdiction to hear criminal appeals. Its work is split between its three divisions: Queen's Bench, Chancery and Family.

Queen's Bench Division. This division (known as the QBD) is the busiest. It hears all contract cases, tort claims (such as claims for negligence or nuisance) and claims for the recovery of land (such as the eviction of squatters). However, it hears only claims which are above the county court jurisdiction, or which are considered suitable for High Court trial. In 1991 Judge Kennedy ordered that all claimants in the tranquillizer (Benzodiazepene) cases should start their proceedings in the High Court even though many would be likely to attract damages only at the county court level.

Although some lower-value cases (cases worth less than £5,000 and *not* involving personal injury) may be brought in the High Court, they are discouraged and litigants are likely to forfeit some or all of their costs.

There are specialist courts within the Queen's Bench Division:

● *The Commercial Court* hears major commercial disputes, such as insurance claims. Its judges are drawn from those who are experienced in the commercial field. The court may take hearings in private if the circumstances require it (e.g. if the case involves trade secrets). The judge may also sit as an arbitrator if the parties wish it. This makes the proceedings more informal, and the normal rules of evidence are relaxed.

● *The Admiralty Court* hears maritime disputes.

● *The Official Referee* handles cases which require the detailed examination of documents (such as lengthy building disputes).

Chancery Division. This developed from the former Chancery Court, which administered the system of equity (see page 867). It still specializes in 'equity' matters, such as:

● contracts for buying and selling land;
● disputes over wills and the administration of estates;
● trust fund disputes;
● bankruptcy and winding up of companies;
● Inland Revenue disputes.

The Chancery Division also has a number of specialist courts:

● *The Court of Protection* protects and administers the affairs and property of the mentally disordered (known in this context as 'patients'). It is normal to appoint a 'receiver' (usually a relative) to look after the patient's affairs.

● *The Bankruptcy Court* hears cases involving insolvency in the London district. Cases outside London are heard by county courts with bankruptcy jurisdiction.

• *Companies Court*, where cases are tried by a single judge with special knowledge of company law. The court's work is divided into company liquidation proceedings and other company matters.

Restrictive Practices Court

This is a superior court of record (consisting of judges and lay members) set up by the Restrictive Trade Practices Act 1956. The law aims to prevent manufacturers entering into agreements which restrict free competition and tend to fix prices for goods. The court has power to enforce its rulings by injunction.

Since 1973 it has had the additional function of considering the EC competition rules under the Treaty of Rome.

Appeal Courts

Employment Appeal Tribunal

This is a superior court of record. It hears appeals from any decision of an industrial tribunal. It decides on questions of law only. It consists of a legally qualified chair and two lay members, one from each side of industry.

Divisional court

Each of the three divisions of the High Court has 'divisional courts', which consist of two or more judges.

Divisional Court of the Queen's Bench Division. This hears appeals on points of law on cases stated by magistrates' courts and the Crown Court (i.e. statements of the relevant facts for the opinion of the higher court). It also has a supervisory role over inferior courts, and other bodies. It can put right their mistakes or failings by what are known as the prerogative orders. It can, for instance, quash a decision or order a retrial.

Divisional Court of the Chancery Division. The court hears bankruptcy appeals from county courts (except in London). The bankruptcy court of the Chancery Division hears appeals from London.

Divisional Court of the Family Division. This court hears appeals from the Family Proceedings Courts.

Court of Appeal

The civil appeals court is known simply as the Court of Appeal. It can hear appeals from county court decisions and civil decisions of the High Court. The appeal is technically a 'rehearing' of the case, but this is a misnomer, for the court does not hear the evidence of the witnesses again. The court normally listens to legal argument from barristers and any dispute as to the evidence is decided by reference to the notes or transcript taken at the original trial. Most appeals relate to points of law, but some are based on the argument that the judge him- or herself drew the wrong inference from the facts or that the 'learned judge misdirected himself'.

The Court of Appeal has jurisdiction to hear appeals from:
- the county court on all matters except bankruptcy;
- the High Court on all civil matters;
- various tribunals (see below), in particular the Employment Appeals Tribunal, the Lands Tribunal and the Restrictive Practices Court.

Most appeals are heard by three judges, though some (e.g. appeals from county court decisions) can be heard by only two judges. Decisions need not be unanimous. The head of the court is the Master of the Rolls – arguably the most influential appointment in the legal system.

Court of Appeal (criminal division)

The court hears appeals from the Crown Court against conviction and sentence. The Attorney-General may also refer a case to this division for an opinion on a point of law where the case ended in an acquittal. The Court of Appeal may now increase a sentence either when hearing an appeal by the accused or on an application from the Attorney-General where it appears that the Crown Court has been too lenient.

House of Lords

This is the ultimate appeal court from all courts in Great Britain and Northern Ireland (except criminal courts in Scotland). It consists of the Lord Chancellor and all the Lords of Appeal in ordinary (the Law Lords). In 1991 there were nine Law Lords, who were paid £97,000 each per annum.

Civil cases. The House of Lords hears appeals from the Court of Appeal, the Court of Session in Scotland and the Supreme Court of Northern Ireland. Before the House of Lords will hear a case, the lower court must certify that a point of law of public importance is involved, and either the lower court or the Appeal Committee of the House of Lords must give leave. In addition, where all parties and all courts consent, there is a direct appeal from the High Court to the House of Lords under what is known as the leapfrogging procedure.

Criminal cases. The House of Lords hears appeals from the Court of Appeal (criminal division) and the Divisional Court of the Queen's Bench Division.

The Judicial Committee of the Privy Council

This is the court of final appeal from courts of the United Kingdom dependencies, courts of independent Commonwealth countries which have retained the right of appeal, courts of the Channel Islands and the Isle of Man, some professional and disciplinary committees and church sources.

Its judges include all the judges of the House of Lords, certain other Commonwealth judges and other UK senior judges (though in practice it is the House of Lords judges who make the decisions).

Decisions of the Judicial Committee are accorded great respect by all countries whose legal systems are based on our own, even though they are not bound by its decisions.

There have been various proposals to merge its functions with the House of Lords, or to turn it into a peripatetic Commonwealth court, but none has so far been implemented.

European Courts

The European Court of Justice

This court is based in Luxembourg. It deals only with Community law and does not concern itself with the laws of individual states. There are twelve judges, who are drawn from each of the member states. Its main roles are as follows:

1 Interpreting Community law if a national court cannot decide on its meaning. Its decisions are binding on all member states.
2 To make sure that the institutions of the EC act lawfully. Community laws themselves may be challenged before the court, on the ground of conflict with the Treaty of Rome. Challenges can be made by member states, the Council of Ministers or the European Commission. Individuals and companies can challenge the laws only if they are of 'direct and individual concern' to them.
3 To ensure that member states enforce the Community law. If a country fails to uphold the Community law, another member state or the European Commission may refer the matter to the court.

There is more emphasis on written submissions than there is in the English courts and the proceedings are more *inquisitorial* (see page 875) than they are here.

The Court of First Instance

Also based in Luxembourg, this was set up in 1988. It is attached to the European Court of Justice and has jurisdiction to hear and determine certain categories of case brought by natural or legal persons (e.g. companies), as opposed to cases brought by member states. It may deal with cases brought by European Community officials, damages claims against a Community institution, or cases on competition law. Its decisions are subject to appeal (on a point of law only) to the European Court of Justice.

The European Court of Human Rights

This is based in Strasbourg. It was established by the Convention for the Protection of Human Rights and Fundamental Freedoms in 1959. It has no connection with the European Community or the other European courts. See page 885 for further details.

International Court

The International Court of Justice

This is often confused with European courts. Based in the Hague, it is the principal judicial organ of the United Nations and was set up under the United Nations Charter. Its judges are appointed by the General Assembly and the Security Council.

Other Courts (and means of resolving disputes)

Coroners' courts

Coroners' courts date back to 1194. Their chief function is to inquire into cases of violent, unnatural or suspicious death, or death without apparent cause. Coroners must be informed of these, and also deaths:

- where the deceased had not been seen by a doctor in the two weeks before his or her death;
- occurring during a surgical operation;
- caused by industrial poisoning.

A coroner can be a lawyer or doctor. He or she is appointed by the local authority. A coroner's hearing is called an inquest. It is not a trial and takes the form of an inquiry. A coroner may take evidence from witnesses. He or she takes a much more active part in the proceedings than a judge of an English court. It is the coroner who decides when to hold the inquest and what evidence to call.

Not every sudden death results in an inquest being held. If, after ordering a post-mortem (autopsy), the coroner is satisfied about the cause of death, he or she may issue a certificate to permit burial and conclude matters.

If buried treasure is found, it is the coroner who holds a *treasure trove* inquest. If the inquest finds that the treasure was accidentally lost, it is deemed to belong to the owner of the land. If, on the other hand, it is found to have been buried deliberately, the inquest will return a 'treasure trove' verdict and the treasure passes to the Crown (though compensation is usually paid to the finder).

Tribunals

Tribunals are not courts, but they function in a similar way. Most are specialist bodies for deciding disputes in a particular area of the law. For instance, industrial tribunals settle employment disputes; social security tribunals decide on cases of refusal to pay benefits.

Although there were some tribunals in the nineteenth century, they are largely a twentieth-century phenomenon. The post-war period has seen a substantial increase in the number of tribunals and in the type of work they do. The expense, inaccessibility and formality of the conventional courts have led to the introduction of more and more tribunals, aimed at providing a cheap and informal means of resolving disputes. That is the justification for not allowing legal aid for tribunal cases: the argument is that an extension of legal aid would result in the tribunals becoming over-lawyered, and that in time the tribunals would acquire the less desirable features of ordinary courts. The counter-argument is, of course, that it is absurd to allow legal aid for a trivial magistrates' or county court case, and yet deny it for a tribunal case which might be of great significance (e.g. industrial tribunals can award thousands of pounds of compensation – much more than the £1,000 limit in the county court, which is normally regarded as the threshold at which legal aid will be granted).

Although tribunals are outside the conventional courts system, they are subject to control by the courts. Some tribunal decisions can be appealed direct to the courts, but usually a question of law (not fact) must be involved.

In addition the Divisional Court of the Queen's Bench Division exercises a general supervisory role over all tribunals and will quash the decision of a tribunal that exceeds its powers, acts improperly or refuses to hear a claim.

While legal aid is not generally available for tribunal cases, there are some exceptions. Hearings before the lands tribunal and the employment appeal tribunal are covered by legal aid.

Criminal Injuries Compensation Board

The Criminal Injuries Compensation Board exists to compensate victims of violent crime. It is funded by the government. In theory, though not always in practice, it awards compensation to victims at the same level as if they were awarded compensation by the courts. It makes nearly 40,000 awards a year. In the year 1990/91 it paid out £109 million in compensation.

It is criticized as being very slow. It has a chronic backlog. At the end of March 1991 there were 81,828 cases awaiting action. No costs are payable to applicants (though legal aid green-form advice may be available to those of limited means to help with the completion of the necessary forms). The minimum compensation is £1,000. It does not, therefore, deal with minor injuries. Applicants who are not satisfied with awards may use the Board's appeals procedure and have a full hearing.

The Motor Insurers' Bureau

This is financed by the insurance industry and provides for victims of uninsured and untraced drivers. It pays compensation for injuries. It also pays the cost of property damage (e.g. repair to a car), but not the first £185 and not at all if victims had their own insurance.

Arbitration

This way of resolving disputes is used mainly in commercial situations, such as building disputes. Instead of a judge, an arbitrator decides the issues between the parties. He or she need not be a lawyer, and often is not. In a building case the arbitrator might be a surveyor with knowledge of the subject matter of the dispute. The advantages of arbitration are that proceedings are always private, and that the arbitrator will have much more specialist knowledge than a judge.

A dispute can be resolved by arbitration only if the parties agree (either as a term of the original contract or at a later stage). It is not likely to be cheaper than taking a case through the courts. Lawyers will still be employed and in addition the arbitrator will have to be paid – probably several hundred pounds a day.

The award of an arbitrator can be enforced through the courts. Arbitration proceedings are governed by the law (the Arbitration Acts 1950 and 1979).

Arbitrations can take place within the court system. There is provision for arbitration in the commercial court (see page 879) and in the county court under the small claims procedure.

Alternative Dispute Resolution (ADR)

Going to court is both expensive and an ordeal for many. Court procedures are often a crude way of deciding on disputes, leaving the parties impoverished and frustrated. There is no satisfactory alternative for major cases, but in other situations what is needed is for an impartial umpire to take stock of the problem and point the parties in the right direction. In a dispute between neighbours, for instance, a full court hearing is likely to poison relationships permanently; but intervention by a conciliator might defuse the problems.

ADR schemes are not new. For instance, the Advisory, Conciliation and Arbitration Service (ACAS) has for years intervened in employment disputes. However, unless proper funding for such schemes can be found, ADR is unlikely to become a widespread alternative to court disputes. There must also be proper monitoring and training for those involved in mediation.

The Law Society has drawn up plans to encourage the spread of ADR, such as, for instance, to introduce court-annexed mediation and extend legal aid to cover its cost.

See Appendix 1.

Ombudsmen

The first ombudsman was appointed in 1967 to check on abuses of power by government departments (the Parliamentary Commissioner). The original concept comes from Sweden, where the first ombudsman was appointed in 1809. Ombudsmen have been appointed to intervene in a number of areas of official and commercial activity. Currently there are ombudsmen who cover:

- Government departments;
- local authorities;
- legal services (barristers and solicitors);
- the health service;
- the stock exchange;
- insurance companies;
- building societies;
- banks;
- estate agents;
- pensions.

See Appendix 1 for addresses.

It costs nothing to complain to the ombudsman. However, the system is often criticized for being too restrictive: complaints are often outside the scope of the terms of reference of the particular ombudsman.

64 Civil Law and Procedure

Even as there are laws of poetry, so there is poetry in the law
Joseph L Baron

The law of this country is divided into two separate types: civil and criminal. Of the two, criminal law has the more exciting image (perhaps because it is associated with popular police television programmes and crime novels). Yet to those who become involved in civil disputes the law is just as important in their lives.

The two branches of the law have their own separate terminologies. You are *prosecuted* if you are considered to have *committed an offence*. If you are *guilty* you will be *punished* and *sentenced*, probably to pay a *fine* or serve a term of *imprisonment*.

On the other hand, if you have committed a civil wrong you will be *sued* by a *plaintiff* in *High Court* or *county court* proceedings, where you will be named as a *defendant*.

There are many misunderstandings about the differences between civil and criminal law. Take the sign which hangs on the gates of many farms: TRESPASS-ERS WILL BE PROSECUTED. There is no crime of trespassing in a farmer's field, so long as no damage is done. Yet the warning on the gate is written in the language of criminal prosecutions.

The same action can be both a criminal offence and a civil wrong, and its consequences will decide which way the case is seen in eyes of the law. A careless driver who injures a pedestrian may be guilty of the *offence* of driving without due care and attention, but he or she will be found guilty only if a successful prosecution is brought against him/her.

The same driver may also have committed the *civil wrong* (or tort) of negligence and the pedestrian may sue for damages. However, if the police decide not to prosecute the driver, or if the pedestrian does not make a claim, he or she may not be subjected to any legal process.

IS IT NECESSARY TO GO TO LAW?

'I will take it to the highest court in the land.' This is the vow of many who find themselves embroiled in a dispute which is getting out of hand. In reality most problems are solved without going anywhere near a court. The very existence of a network of courts in this country is enough to encourage many to come to a settlement without a court trial.

Nevertheless, thousands of cases are tried every year, and in many more court proceedings are started but the case is settled 'out of court'. Sometimes this is literally at the court's door.

Some cases have to involve court procedures: it is impossible to deal with divorce and most family disputes without a court order. For others, there may be different ways to resolve the problem – and save the trauma and expense of going to law (see Alternative Dispute Resolution and Ombudsmen, pages 885–6).

This chapter describes the procedures and mechanics of civil claims in the High Court and county court; how private individuals can have access to the system of civil justice, and how it works. For practical guidance on how to bring a civil claim, see Chapter 68.

Evidence

All courts must reach their decisions on the basis of evidence presented to them in the correct way. Courts assume very little knowledge of their own. All material facts have to be presented as evidence. The weight given to the evidence depends on its type and quality.

Most disputed evidence is given directly to the court by the witnesses, who are closely questioned (cross-examined). Evidence can also be given by written statements or by sworn statements (known as affidavits). These are often used in the less controversial parts of cases, where both sides agree.

Rules of evidence used to be very restrictive and hidebound, making it difficult to get to the truth of the matter. The rules are now being relaxed, so as to permit, for instance, children to give evidence by a television link instead of attending court. Video recordings are now often played in court. This would have been unthinkable even fifteen years ago.

Hearsay evidence (written or oral statements of witnesses not called to give evidence) used to be absolutely forbidden. Since the passing of the Civil Evidence Act 1968, hearsay evidence may be given of:

- statements made outside the court;
- a witness's previous statement;
- statements contained in records;
- statements produced by computers.

Either party may object to this type of evidence being used; the court will then decide whether it can be called.

Standard and burden of proof

There is a fundamental difference between criminal and civil cases in the level of the evidence which has to be presented to the court. In criminal cases it has to be proved 'beyond reasonable doubt' that the accused is guilty of the crime as charged. In other words, the court has to be *sure* that the case is proved. In civil cases the standard of proof is the balance of probabilities. Here the test is that it must be more likely than not that a particular thing has happened. Another way of putting it is that the chances must be better than 50 per cent. If they are 49 per cent, then the party making the claim will lose.

That may not be easy. The person suing (the plaintiff) must prove the case. He or she therefore has to satisfy the court that the propositions and evidence being put forward are true. It is not enough to show that they are possible, or even likely. They have to be 'more likely than not'.

Illustration. *Mary's car collides with Susan's. Mary was drunk at the time. Susan is badly hurt. She was knocked unconscious and could not remember anything about the accident. Both cars ended up in the middle of the road and there was no evidence as to where the cars were immediately before the accident. Susan's claim failed because she could not satisfy the court that 'it was more likely than not' that Mary's bad driving caused the accident.*

The way the court tilts the balance depends on who carries the burden of proof. Normally the person who makes the claim must prove it, but there are circumstances where the burden of proof shifts. An example is contributory negligence.

Illustration. *Denise is injured at work when she slips on some fat which has been left on the floor. She has to prove that her employers were at fault in not ensuring that her working conditions were safe. But her employers claimed that she was guilty of 'contributory negligence' because she was running at the time she fell. Here the burden of proof shifts, and the employers have to prove that she contributed to her injury.*

Witnesses

Witnesses are required to be sworn before they give evidence. If they object to taking the oath, they may *affirm* instead. Young children may give unsworn evidence if the court is satisfied that they do not understand the nature of the oath. There is no age limit to be a witness. The test is whether the witness has sufficient mental understanding.

A witness is not normally allowed to listen to court proceedings until after he or she has given evidence.

If a witness is reluctant to attend court he or she may be ordered by a *subpoena* (in the High Court) or a *witness summons* (in other courts) to give evidence. If they fail then to attend they are liable to imprisonment for contempt.

Witnesses normally give evidence as to the facts which they have observed. *Expert witnesses* are called to interpret the facts. There is no limit to the type of expert. In addition to medical experts, engineers, accountants, architects, actuaries and even lawyers can be called as experts. Experts usually attend throughout a case; it is often important that they hear the evidence which is given.

A *hostile witness* is a witness 'whose mind discloses a bias towards the party examining him'. Normally one is not entitled to cross-examine one's own witness, but if a witness becomes hostile, he or she may be cross-examined provided the court agrees.

The examination of witnesses

There are three stages of giving evidence:

1 *Examination in chief.* The witness is first questioned by the lawyer representing the party on whose behalf he or she is being called. At this stage the witness is telling the story: recounting the facts and events. The lawyer is not allowed to ask leading questions. If the lawyer wants the witness to describe an accident, he or she cannot ask the witness: 'Was Mr White on the wrong side of the road at the time?' Instead they have to prompt the witness by questions like: 'What happened next?' It can sometimes be a very frustrating process if the witness suffers a mental block at the wrong moment! It is not permitted to cross-examine one's own witness, however uncooperative he or she is, unless leave is given to treat him/her as hostile.
2 *Cross-examination.* The lawyer for the opposing party may then challenge what the witness has said. He or she must put to the witness all the facts which his/her client will be raising in evidence. If the lawyer does not, it may be necessary to recall the witness at a later stage, or his/her client may be barred from giving some of their evidence.
3 *Re-examination.* This is a chance for the first lawyer to clear up any points which may have been raised in cross-examination. It is not a second bite at the cherry. He or she cannot use it as an opportunity to raise matters which were overlooked in his/her examination in chief.

In addition the judge may ask questions at any time. If he or she does so at the end of a witness's evidence, both lawyers should be given an opportunity to ask additional questions on the matters raised by the court.

Juries in civil cases

Until 1854 all civil cases were tried by jury. Since then the use of juries has declined. By 1965 only 2 per cent of cases were tried by jury. Now the use of juries has all but been abandoned in civil cases. The notable exception is in defamation (libel and slander) cases. Juries in libel cases regularly award hundreds of thousands of pounds in compensation for what are often no more than injured feelings. In order to receive compensation of that level in an accident case a person would have to suffer horrific injuries, such as the amputation of two limbs or complete loss of sight. This difference between jury awards for defamation and judge's awards for injury cases has caused much ill-feeling and some lawyers have suggested that jury trials should be used in injury cases. It seems that the courts have set themselves firmly against extending the use of jury trials:

H suffered a serious injury to his sexual organs as a result of negligent medical treatment by his employers, the Ministry of Defence. He applied to have his case heard by a jury. But the Court of Appeal, noting that no personal injury case had been tried by jury for twenty-five years, refused to order a jury trial. But it did leave the door open a crack: 'If, for example, personal injuries resulted from conduct on the part of those who were deliberately abusing their authority, there might well be a claim for exemplary damages and this could place the case in an exceptional category . . .' Lord Donaldson, Master of the Rolls, in H v. Ministry of Defence (1991)

Thus it is still possible to contemplate a case where jury trial might be appropriate in a civil case, but almost all will be tried by a judge alone.

Parties to actions

The person bringing a claim is usually called the plaintiff, and the opponent is called the defendant, but there are exceptions. In divorces, they are the petitioner and respondent.

Different types of organization can be parties to court proceedings, and individuals can be sued in different capacities, as follows.

The Crown

The Crown (i.e. the Government) may sue and (with few exceptions) be sued in the same way as any private organization or individual.

Companies

Companies are regarded as separate legal entities and can sue and be sued independently of their shareholders or directors. In claims involving breaches of the Companies Acts directors and shareholders may be sued personally. If a company is involved in a High Court case, it *must* be represented by a solicitor (and a barrister where appropriate).

Trustees

Trustees may sue and be sued, but their liability is generally limited to the assets of the trust which they are administering, unless they are guilty of improper behaviour, such as fraud.

Partnerships and businesses

Partnerships may sue or be sued in the business name or as individuals (e.g. A. White and B. Black trading as Black White & Co.). A single partner may be sued on their own, but they might be entitled to a contribution from their fellow partners.

Clubs and societies

The legal position depends on whether the club is a proprietor's club (i.e. the club is owned by a single individual or a company) or a members' club. With a proprietor's club, proceedings are brought by or against the owner in the usual way. With members' clubs the position is more complicated. The club itself has no separate legal status. If a club is sued it would be necessary to apply to the court to bring a 'representative action', naming individual members of the club (e.g. the committee), who are taken to represent the body of the club. It is very difficult for one club member to bring an action against the club – for, say, an injury at the club premises. Usually the committee owes no duty of care to individual members.

Trade unions

It has long been established that trade unions have a legal entity which enables them to be sued in the courts for the wrongful acts or omissions of their officials.

Children

Children under eighteen can sue and be sued, but they must do so in the name of an adult. A child sues by his or her *next friend* and if the child is sued, the court appoints a *guardian ad litem*.

Mental patients

The rules relating to mental patients are similar to those covering children.

Vexatious litigants

If the court is satisfied that a person has persistently instituted vexatious legal proceedings or made vexatious applications in a court case, they can order that he or she take no steps to issue or continue with legal proceedings without the permission of a judge. There are many cases where individuals have become involved in dozens of court cases. The application to impose this procedure has to be made by the Attorney-General.

Limitation – time-limits

There has to be an end to litigation. The threat of claims should not hang over a wrongdoer indefinitely. As time goes by, memories fade; witnesses die;

documents are lost. The law therefore lays down time-limits within which to bring proceedings, and to conclude them once they are started.

The time-limits for bringing proceedings are called limitation periods. They can be very short – only three months in an unfair dismissal case – or very long – twelve years for a claim for possession of land. Some common limitation periods are as follows:

> Claims in transport cases (e.g. carriage by sea or air) 2 years
> Claims for personal injury 3 years
> Claims in contract or tort 6 years
> Claims against trustees for breach of trust 12 years

There are three points to note:

1 In injury cases the time does not start to run until the victim has acquired the necessary knowledge – of the nature of the wrong, the significance of the injury and the identity of the person who caused it.

Mrs Stephen received treatment at hospital which involved a mammography in March 1977. She had some knowledge of radiography. She believed she had been injured by the mammography, but she was repeatedly assured that it was not the cause of her symptoms. It was not until 20 February 1985 that an expert supported her. Her writ was issued on 15 February 1988. The hospital applied to strike out the proceedings. Held: Her belief was not enough to fix her with knowledge. She did not have the necessary knowledge until February 1988. Her case was therefore not time-barred even though proceedings were not issued until nearly eleven years after the treatment which caused the injury. Stephen v. Riverside Health Authority (1989)

None the less a victim should never delay. He or she may be found to have 'constructive knowledge'.
2 If an accident victim is under eighteen at the time of the injury, the three-year period does not begin to run till he or she reaches their eighteenth birthday.
3 The only way of stopping time running is to issue proceedings. Nothing else preserves rights under these rules.

Which court?

Until 1991 the small cases were dealt with in the county courts and the large or complex cases were heard in the High Court. The county courts were restricted to dealing with disputes where the property or value was £5,000 or less. From 1991 onwards it is likely that county courts will decide on most disputes; they have been given power to deal with cases involving unlimited value – even millions of pounds. As a further encouragement to use the county courts, no cases may be begun in the High Court where the value of the claim is less than £50,000.

There are still some cases which *must* be dealt with in the High Court. These include libel and slander, cases relating to 'tolls, markets and franchises', and cases involving complex procedures, such as Anton Piller orders (see page 899).

There has always been a feeling among lawyers and clients that the quality of justice in the High Court is better than that in the county court. Certainly the requirements to become a High Court judge are more stringent. Many also feel that the High Court is speedier and more effective than the county court. There is something more dramatic about serving a High Court writ than issuing a county court summons. High Court sheriffs are considered more able to persuade recalcitrant debtors to pay up than county court bailiffs.

In cases where the High Court is available, it is likely that solicitors and their clients will still opt to use it. Even if it is not possible to conduct the cases in the High Court, it may still be possible to use High Court remedies to enforce judgements or orders.

Running a case

Before the trial of a case, a number of preliminary stages have to be gone through. The object is to make each side define their case as clearly as possible, so that both sides can know exactly what is at issue. As Lord Donaldson, Master of the Rolls, said in Davies v. Eli Lilly & Co. L., 1987:

In plain language, litigation in this country is conducted 'cards face up on the table'. Some people from other lands regard this as incomprehensible. 'Why,' they ask, 'should I be expected to provide my opponent with the means of defeating me?' The answer, of course, is that litigation is not a war or even a game. It is designed to do real justice between opposing parties and, if the court does not have *all* the relevant information, it cannot achieve this object.

There is often little to be gained by keeping part of a case secret from the other side. The rules discourage the springing of last minute surprises; indeed to do such things now might well put one's own case in jeopardy.

How a case is started

It is technically possible to get court proceedings under way within hours of seeing a solicitor. In emergencies this often happens. For instance, in cases involving domestic violence or kidnapping of a child by one of the parents, every minute can count.

In other cases it is sensible to prepare the ground first. New court rules also demand preparatory work. In all injury cases it is a requirement that medical reports and statements of expenses and losses (special damages) are filed at the same time as the proceedings. In many other cases it will be necessary to obtain the report of an expert before it is possible to define exactly where the claim lies.

During the preparatory stages, exchanges of correspondence take place between the solicitors, and sometimes a dispute can be resolved then.

If the preliminary work is completed and the opposing party remains unyielding or uncooperative, then the only effective sanction is to issue proceedings.

In the High Court, proceedings are usually started by issuing a writ, though for some more specialized cases (such as infant settlements, applications under the Companies Act and mental health applications) an originating summons is issued instead.

In the county court proceedings are started by filing a request form and Particulars of Claim (there are also the equivalent of originating summonses, called originating applications). Divorces are started by *filing a petition*.

The consequences are as follows:

● Time stops running for the purposes of the time-limits laid down by the Limitation Act.
● Default procedures come into operation. If the opponent ignores the proceedings or the time limits laid down (see below), judgement in default may be entered or an application can be made to strike out a case.
● Costs: see Chapter 66. The fundamental rule is that 'costs follow the event', or the loser pays the winner. This would apply too if someone starts proceedings and then loses heart and does not see them through. They would risk having to pay their opponent's legal costs as well as their own.

Service of proceedings

No steps may be taken (except in some emergency situations) in a case until the proceedings are 'served' on the opposing party. In both the High Court and the county court the requirements are similar, except that the county courts will undertake service of proceedings (unless the plaintiff's solicitor elects to arrange for the proceedings to be served). A copy of the proceedings sealed by the court must be given to the defendant, along with accompanying forms explaining what steps must be taken if the defendant wishes to defend.

Proceedings may be served in different ways. If the rules are not followed, an application can be made by the defendant to set aside any judgement obtained in default. Service must generally be at the defendant's address, but with companies it must be at the registered office, and with other businesses it is the principal place of business.

Service may be carried out as follows:
● *Personal service.* The proceedings are handed to the defendant personally. This is clearly the most effective way of serving proceedings because there can then be no possible doubt that he or she has received them. However, it is expensive and time consuming.
● *By post.* This is the most usual method. Service may be made by first or second-class mail; and the law presumes that first-class mail will be delivered two working days after posting, and that second-class mail will arrive four days

after posting. It has been remarked that this is a modern example of a legal fiction!

• *By delivering to the address of the defendant.* It is sufficient if the documents are put through the letter box, but it must be a letter box (and not the cat flap or an open window). The proceedings must be in an envelope addressed to the defendant personally.

• *By sending to a solicitor.* If a defendant's solicitor agrees to accept service, the proceedings may be sent to the solicitor direct. As between solicitors service may take place by document exchange (an alternative to the postal system widely used by solicitors) and by fax.

• *Substituted service.* If the address of the defendant is not known the court may make an order for 'substituted service'. It may, for instance, order that an advertisement be placed in a newspaper circulating in an area where the defendant is known to be living; or it may order documents to be served on the defendant's solicitor, even if he or she has not agreed to accept service.

• *Service outside England and Wales.* It used to be freely permissible to arrange for proceedings to be served on defendants abroad. The Civil Jurisdiction and Judgements Act 1991 ratifies an international treaty (the Lugano Convention) and provides that for most EC countries a defendant must be sued in the country in which he or she is domiciled (i.e. the proceedings must be brought in that country).

Acknowledging the proceedings

A defendant who wishes to contest all or part of the proceedings must within fourteen days of service send back to the court the form, duly completed, saying that he or she wishes to defend. If they do not, the plaintiff may ask the court to enter judgement. Even if defendants admit the claim they may none the less ask for time to pay or a stay of execution. Different procedures apply in the High Court and the county court.

Default procedures

If a defendant fails to acknowledge the proceedings within fourteen days of service (in High Court cases) *or* to put in a defence after a further fourteen days (High Court), *or* to put in a defence fourteen days *from service* (county court), the plaintiff may enter 'judgement in default'. The effect of a judgement in default is that the court does not need to decide on liability: a plaintiff can proceed immediately to enforce a judgement for a fixed sum (such as a debt) or to apply to have damages assessed by the court where compensation is being claimed (such as in accident cases).

Although application can be made to set aside a judgement, it is never wise to let time run out: a court may impose conditions, such as requiring the amount claimed to be paid into court to await the outcome of the case.

Pleadings

These are the core of the case. They spell out the issues, and consist sometimes of several documents which together build up and define what the dispute is about.

Statement of Claim (High Court); Particulars of Claim (county court). This document is prepared by or for the plaintiffs. It defines what they are claiming, the grounds for the claim and the statement of the amount (if known; otherwise they can claim simply 'damages'). It can also include claims other than money (e.g. for a possession order). It must show a viable legal and enforceable claim against the defendant. Like all pleadings, it must be carefully prepared; it is always embarrassing to change a case once it has been started because the pleadings did not accurately reflect a party's contentions.

In a divorce, the equivalent document is a *petition*.

Defence. This is the defendant's answer to the claim, and can consist of a complete denial, or a full or partial admission. The primary object of the defence is to tell the plaintiff how much of the claim is admitted and how much is disputed, and to state the grounds and facts on which the defendant relies to defeat the claim of the plaintiff. Sometimes there is such a big discrepancy between the statement of claim and the defence that it is tempting to think that the argument is over two completely unconnected cases!

Few divorces are contested; if they are, the respondent will file an *answer*.

Reply to defence. The plaintiff may serve a reply in answer to the defence. This does not simply reinforce the original claim, and is only necessary if the defendant has raised new matters in the defence which need specifically to be dealt with.

Counterclaims and third-party notices. Many disputes involve a complex interplay of problems. The defendant may have a claim against the plaintiff. Rather than issuing a separate set of proceedings, he or she can tack a counterclaim on to their defence. That in turn will give the plaintiff the right to deliver a defence to the counterclaim.

On the other hand, the defendant may argue that he or she is not liable to the plaintiff, but that the real responsibility for the claim rests with someone else. By issuing a third-party notice they can join that someone else in the court proceedings. This can lead to third-party pleadings (similar to those considered here) being created.

Further and better particulars. If opponents are not satisfied with the information in the initial pleading, they can serve a 'request for further and better particulars'. This process can sometimes be prolonged, with additional information being repeatedly requested. It is not unknown for pleadings to include a document with the following unwieldy name: *request for further and better particulars of further and better particulars of particulars of claim.*

These requests cannot be used as fishing expeditions: requests have to be limited to matters raised in the first place, and it is not permitted to ask for particulars of a blunt denial.

If one party is not satisfied with the answers given, they can apply to the court for an order. It will then be for the court to decide what (if any) further information must be given.

Close of pleadings

The court rules ensure that pleadings do not run on indefinitely. At a certain point the pleadings are 'closed', so that the action can move on to the next step. This normally takes place fourteen days after the service of the defence or reply.

Documents

Each party must let the other have details of the documents they hold which are relevant to the case. This is known as 'discovery of documents'.

Not all documents have to be shown. Documents which are not relevant and those which are privileged need not be produced. Privileged documents include correspondence between solicitors and clients, and barristers' opinions. There are inevitably grey areas, and sometimes arguments in court as to what documents should be revealed.

The plaintiff's solicitors by mistake supplied original documents to the defendant's solicitors. These documents came into the 'privileged' category. The defendant's solicitors made copies and refused to hand back the originals. The plaintiff applied to the court for an order preventing the defendant using the documents at the trial. Held. The court ordered the return of the documents and prohibited their use. The defendant's solicitors were not entitled to take advantage of an obvious mistake. Derby v. Weldon (1990)

Discovery normally takes place fourteen days after close of pleadings (see above), but it is possible to apply to the court for an order for discovery of documents before proceedings are even started. This is appropriate in cases such as medical negligence actions, where plaintiffs may not be able to formulate a claim until they have seen the hospital records.

Inspection of documents. After each side has revealed what documents they possess, their opponent has a right to see the originals. Normally photocopies are supplied, but it is sometimes worthwhile to see the originals. For instance, an entry in an accident book may be surrounded by details of many similar accidents – an indication of lack of safety-consciousness by an employer.

Interrogatories

In addition to discovery of documents, the parties may require discovery of *facts*. In appropriate cases one party may be required to answer a series of written questions about the case. There are two main objectives: to obtain admissions to facilitate the proof of a case, and to ascertain as far as possible what the opponent's case is. Interrogatories must be relevant to the questions in dispute. They must not be used to try to create a case which did not exist before. Interrogatories are fairly rare.

Interlocutory applications

During the course of any court case one or other party may make applications to the court. These may be preliminary points, or they may ensure that the case is brought to a swift conclusion.

Interim payments. In any type of case a plaintiff may make an application for interim damages (i.e. a payment on account of the eventual damages). Before the court will order this, it has to be satisfied that the plaintiff will win at the eventual trial. It is common in injury cases for these applications to be made, but the court must be satisfied that the defendant is:

* insured, *or*
* a public authority, *or*
* is wealthy enough to pay interim damages.

Preservation of property. There is a risk in a contested case that an opposing party will remove the subject matter of the dispute beyond the jurisdiction of the courts. The High Court has power to order a defendant not to remove assets or otherwise dispose of them before the case is heard. These orders are known to lawyers as *Mareva injunctions*.

If there is a threat that vital documents or materials will be destroyed the High Court may also make an order allowing a plaintiff forcibly to enter a defendant's property to inspect, copy or even seize documents. This is known as an *Anton Piller order*. It is made only in extreme circumstances. Undertakings have to be given to ensure that the defendant is protected in the event of damage or wrongful removal of documents.

Subpoenas. If witnesses are reluctant to attend court to give evidence, an order may be made against them to attend court. They must be given their expenses. If they fail to attend, they may be arrested. This order is called a subpoena in the High Court and a witness summons in the county court. The order may include a direction to bring documents to the court.

Security for costs. There are limited powers for the court to order a party to give security for the costs of the proceedings.

Summary judgement. If the plaintiff considers that there is no defence to the claim (even though a defence may have been served) he or she may ask the court to enter judgement. This procedure is useful if the defence is simply a straight denial without details, or if it is clear that the defendant is playing for time. Even if the court does not enter judgement, it may impose conditions on the defendant before he or she is allowed to continue with their case (such as requiring them to pay money into court).

Striking out. The courts have a general power to strike out all or part of a case for a number of reasons:
● there is no reasonable cause of action or defence;
● it is frivolous, scandalous, vexatious or an abuse of the court procedures;
● a party has been guilty of delay in proceeding with the claim.

In a complex building dispute the plaintiffs claimed that they had suffered damage caused by the defendants' delay. The plaintiffs had difficulty in isolating the periods of delay and were unable to provide more than outline information. The defendants asked the court to strike out the claim. Held: The claim was struck out. The fact that information was difficult to ascertain was no excuse. Wharf Properties *v.* Cumine Associates (1990)

Directions. In some High Court and county court cases the court will take stock of the case and make orders as to future conduct. In the High Court this is called a directions hearing, and in the county court it is known as a pre-trial review. The functions are similar: the court will give directions over such matters as the number of experts to be called, the exchange of witness statements, the type and estimated length of the trial.

In injury cases the directions are 'automatic': the rules set down a timetable and procedures which must be followed by both sides. If there are unusual aspects to a case, then even in automatic cases, the court can be asked to make an order or give directions.

Trial process

Many cases are settled out of court; others stubbornly rumble on and the only way to finalize them is to obtain a verdict from the court. No trial can take place until pleadings are closed (see above). In civil cases, the hearing does not happen automatically; it has to be requested. There is often a delay of many months between setting down for trial and the hearing date.

In the county courts, cases are heard at the court in which the proceedings have been issued (unless they are transferred to another court). In the High Court, hearings are in London, or in one of twenty-four trial centres throughout the country.

High court cases are listed according to their seriousness:
● Listing Category A – case of great substance or great difficulty or of public importance;
● Listing Category B – case of substance or difficulty;
● Listing Category C – other cases.

The majority of cases are tried before a judge alone in open court. Parties are represented by a barrister in the High Court and by a barrister or solicitor in the county court. The procedure is similar in both levels of court. The judge is robed. The lawyers wear gowns (and wigs if they are barristers) and there is considerable formality. It is only when a small claim is heard by arbitration that the formality is relaxed.

The party presenting the case (usually the plaintiff) opens the case and calls evidence. The defendant then replies with their evidence and both sides address the court at the conclusion of the evidence. The judge will either give his or her judgement immediately or 'reserve judgement' (which means that the judge needs time to consider).

Remedies/orders

A court can make a wide range of orders and judgements at the conclusion of a case.

Damages

This is the most common element of any claim. The objective of damages is to put claimants in the same position as they would have been if the wrong or breach had not been committed. Where the claim is for a specific sum of money that presents no difficulty, but in injury cases the exercise is necessarily artificial. Damages divide into two types.

General damages. This is the 'compensation' element. In injury cases it embraces things like pain and suffering, loss of amenity, loss of future earnings, distress and loss of opportunity on the job market.

Special damages. These are the sums which can be calculated, such as expenses and actual loss of wages.

The distinction between the two types of damages is important because wholly different methods are used to assess them, and payment of interest on them is treated differently.

W fell 12 feet through a defective floor and suffered a burst fracture of one of her vertebrae. She spent three months in hospital, almost completely immobile. Long-term effects included weakness in her left arm and fingers, and an ache at the site of the injury. It was likely that she would suffer degenerative changes by the time she was sixty (she was thirty-six at the time of the accident). She had had to put off getting married and her chances of having children were slim. She received general damages of £20,000 and special damages (medical expenses, loss of wages etc.) of £10,978. Wolf v. Anafield Builders (1989)

Injunctions

Orders 'to do or refrain from doing' certain acts can be made during or at the end of proceedings. The general rule is that injunctions will not be made where monetary compensation will be a sufficient alternative. But in some cases, such as encroachment on land or domestic violence, injunctions are the only possibility.

Eviction

If a tenant is behind with the rent, or a borrower has not kept up the mortgage payments, the landlord or the lender can apply to the court for a possession order. There are safeguards: no one may be evicted without a court order, and the courts generally have a discretion to give time to solve financial problems. Anyone faced with a summons for possession should take immediate legal advice. Do nothing and the inevitable will happen, but those who act positively stand a much better chance of keeping their property.

Forfeiture

This is similar to eviction, and applies mainly to commercial leases. If a tenant breaks the terms of the lease (e.g. by using the premises for a prohibited purpose), the landlord may apply to forfeit the lease. A tenant can ask the court to 'grant relief from forfeiture'.

Bankruptcy/winding up/receivership

Under the insolvency laws and the Companies Acts, the courts may order individuals to become bankrupt, or companies to go into liquidation.

Sequestration

Seizing assets and money. This is a temporary remedy, used to enforce compliance with a court order. It has often been used against trade unions who have defied orders in industrial disputes.

Rectification/rescission

Mistakes do happen. Occasionally lawyers prepare documents which do not reflect what was agreed. There is an equitable jurisdiction with the courts to order that mistakes be put right, or that obligations wrongly entered into be cancelled.

Divorce/nullity/custody etc.

In family cases there are a range of orders which can be made relating to the children and financial resources of the parties to the marriage. See Chapter 4.

Enforcement

The courts do not automatically enforce the orders they make. The winning party has to initiate the procedures. If one fails, another can be tried, though it is always sensible to keep in mind the costs. Every step in a case costs money in terms of court and legal fees.

Most of the ways of enforcing judgements are described in detail in Chapter 68. In summary they are:

- bailiff/sheriff – seizing the debtor's goods;
- garnishee orders – diverting money held by the debtor;
- attachment of earnings – the court equivalent of pay-as-you-earn;
- charging orders – securing the debt against the debtor's home.

65 The Lawyers

Lawyer: one skilled in the circumvention of the law
Ambrose Bierce, *The Devil's Dictionary*

The word 'lawyer' is the general expression which describes anyone who is versed in the law. The main kinds of lawyers practising in this country are solicitors and barristers. Judges are also lawyers.

SOLICITORS

One of the main objects of the Society is to ensure that the profession is manned by persons of integrity and a high sense of responsibility, free so far as possible from the temptations that arise through anxiety over financial problems. The maintenance of proper standards of remuneration on the one hand and of proper standards of conduct on the other, therefore, are complementary and must be two of the main functions of the Law Society and the absence of either of them would profoundly affect the public standing of the profession.
from *Guide to the Professional Conduct of Solicitors,*
Law Society, 1974 (omitted from later guides)

The expression 'solicitor' first came into being towards the end of the sixteenth century. There were two types of lawyers practising in the High Courts: attorneys and barristers. In the eighteenth century attorneys were prevented from joining the Inns of Court (see Barristers, page 925). The attorneys in retaliation formed the Society of Gentlemen Practisers in the Courts of Law and Equity. Included in the membership of the Society was a growing group of lawyers called solicitors. Solicitors were employed to solicit favourable decisions on behalf of litigants bogged down in the court process. The name 'attorney' had acquired unpleasant connotations and went out of usage in England, in favour of the 'gentler' term solicitor. The only relic of these former days is the Attorney-General, the Government's chief law officer.

In England and Wales (Scotland has a different system) there are some 48,000 solicitors practising in about 11,000 different firms. There are a further 9,000 solicitors who are not practising but employed (e.g. in government departments or industry). Almost 50 per cent of all new solicitors are women. Solicitors are controlled by law (the Solicitors Act 1974) and governed by the Law

Society, which decides on standards of conduct. The Law Society issues rules covering the keeping of accounts, publicity, insurance, disciplinary procedures etc.

All practising solicitors must have a valid practising certificate. Before this is issued the Law Society requires an accountant's certificate (to confirm that client's money is being properly handled) and proof that the solicitor is insured. The Law Society may impose restrictions in a practising certificate.

Solicitors, unlike barristers (see page 925), practise in partnerships. This means that solicitors are personally liable to their clients if they are negligent. The next few years may, however, see solicitors practising through corporate bodies (such as limited companies). In November 1991 regulations were passed enabling the Lord Chancellor to bring in procedures to permit this development. All solicitors are insured, but if their insurance cover is insufficient, they must at present personally make up the shortfall.

A popular definition of the distinction between solicitors and barristers is that barristers do the court work and solicitors do the office work. In practice, the major volume of court work is done by solicitors and barristers do much 'office' work. At present no solicitor, however experienced, may represent a client at a full hearing in any of the higher courts. On the other hand, a barrister, however inexperienced, may represent clients in the House of Lords. Under the Courts and Legal Services Act 1990 provision is made to enable solicitors (and others) to represent clients in all the higher courts. These proposals have not yet been brought into force.

Another way of putting the distinction between the two branches of the profession is to describe solicitors as the general practitioners of the legal profession – though even this will not remain true for long. More and more solicitors are becoming specialists. It is the solicitors who have the first and direct contact with their clients. Barristers are brought in as and when they are needed – by solicitors.

It is not always popular to talk of the distinction between professional and commercial occupations. It smacks of snobbery (on the part of the 'professionals'). None the less, being a solicitor does not simply involve acquiring a knowledge of the theory and practice of the law. It also requires high standards of conduct and an onerous obligation to the courts. The full title of a solicitor is 'Solicitor of the Supreme Court'. All solicitors are automatically officers of the court. They have duties to the court which sometimes override the duties to their clients. For instance, solicitors must not knowingly allow their client to tell lies in the witness box. If a client confesses their guilt to a solicitor, the solicitor would be committing an offence if he or she then called the client to give evidence that they were innocent.

Solicitors' monopolies

Solicitors have had the exclusive right to carry out certain types of work for clients. If anyone else attempted it then they ran the risk of prosecution, however competently they may have done it. The monopolies were in conveyancing, probate work and representing clients in court (and preparing court documents). There has been considerable public concern over these monopolies. Solicitors would say that they are there to protect the public; critics would say that they simply protect solicitors!

Few people criticize the monopoly on court work. It is generally accepted that it is desirable to have professionals conducting court cases: they weed out the hopeless cases and ensure that cases are conducted efficiently and fairly. The counter argument is that many court cases (especially in the magistrates' court) do not require specialist advocates and that lay advisers, trade union representatives and social workers would be capable of making speeches in mitigation and of defending in the more straightforward cases. They might also encourage the demystification of the legal process and reduce the amount of legalese used in the courts. In industrial tribunals (which deal with unfair dismissal cases) non-solicitors can represent clients – though statistically the chances of winning are considerably improved with representation by a lawyer.

The critics are succeeding. The monopoly on conveyancing has already gone and there are powers under the Courts and Legal Services Act 1990 to permit non-solicitors to handle court appearances and to apply for probate. In truth the public does have to be protected – and not just from lawyers. If these changes are introduced, there will undoubtedly be safeguards which may well result in much of the work still being handled by solicitors.

The work that solicitors do

Solicitors' work falls into two broad types:

1 *Court work*. At the moment (1992) solicitors can appear as advocates (i.e. present the case in court themselves) only in the magistrates' courts and county courts – and to a limited extent in the crown courts. Only barristers may represent clients in the higher courts. The Courts and Legal Services Act 1990 will enable solicitors (and others) to appear for clients in every court.
2 *Non-court work*. This is also called 'non-contentious work'. The difference between the two categories is important, especially when it comes to considering legal costs. Non-contentious work is all the other legal work, such as conveyancing (property transactions), probate and wills, business and financial advice and also *preparing for* court cases.

Solicitors' practices

It is not easy to say what is a typical firm of solicitors. Politicians love to refer to solicitors as being stuck in the quill-pen era. In many firms the reality is quite different. Solicitors' practices have gone through a slow revolution. Many factors have contributed to this.

The end of the conveyancing monopoly

For about 100 years solicitors had a monopoly on the right to transfer the ownership of land and houses for clients. Until the early 1970s the fees for carrying out this work were fixed and solicitors could be disciplined if they departed from the scale of charges (even if they charged less). This situation was seen by the public and consumer pressure groups as unhealthy. These restrictive practices were eroded away, first by the abolition of fixed scales of charges, and then by the abolition of the monopoly itself.

In 1985 the law changed to allow *licensed conveyancers* to carry out the legal work on property transactions. The Courts and Legal Services Act 1990 contains provisions to enable a much wider range of individuals and organizations to perform this service for the public. It is envisaged that bodies such as building societies, banks and estate agents might all eventually be doing this work.

Whether that is in the interests of the public remains to be seen. Huge sums of money can be made in commissions on loans and life insurance. Those in favour of opening up the system would argue that sharing or crediting the commissions might be a means of reducing costs to the home buyer. None the less, there is great scope for the unscrupulous to put undue pressure on house-buyers to undertake commitments which are inappropriate to their needs or resources. Solicitors are required to give impartial advice to their clients. They are not allowed to permit conflicts of interest to arise (between themselves and clients, or between different clients) and they have to account to their clients for the commissions that they receive. Solicitors may not reward anyone who gives them business, by payment of a commission. Besides, nothing is ever free: if commissions are paid, the cost has to be covered, either in reduced benefits under the policy or in increased premiums.

The economic climate

In the 1960s and 1970s solicitors were guaranteed a comfortable living for not too much effort. It probably is not unfair to say that at the time most of the work in solicitors' offices was done by clerks, while the partners attended in a leisurely way between about 10 a.m. and 4 p.m. That has all changed. In real terms most solicitors now earn less than they did then but work much longer hours. There is now strong competition for the easy work, and prices have been forced down.

The complexities of the law

The law has become more complicated. It is no longer practical for one solicitor to attempt to handle all his or her clients' problems. Solicitors within firms are increasingly allocating types of work among themselves and so developing an expertise in a limited area of the law.

Pressure and initiative from the Law Society

The Law Society is the governing body of solicitors. It has had its critics (and still does), but it has undertaken to improve standards in the service provided by solicitors and to penalize solicitors who fall short of those standards.

Solicitors in the 1990s

Use of technology

Solicitors deal in words. Word processors are a vital weapon in the armoury of a solicitors' office. Almost every firm in the country now uses fax machines to transfer copies of documents by telephone. Indeed, many years after the commercial introduction of fax machines, the court rules have caught up and acknowledged that this is a legitimate way of serving legal documents on an opponent. Some solicitors subscribe to computer databases which can sometimes save days of research. All solicitors have to comply with strict requirements when keeping accounts. Most now use specially designed accounts packages on their computers.

Types of firm

Apart from the traditional high street offices, there are now:

Large city firms. There are twenty or thirty firms of solicitors each with more than 100 partners and a staff of up to 1,000 people. These firms deal mainly in very important commercial matters. They have governments, the clearing banks and the largest industrial corporations as their clients. They are as remote from the average firm of solicitors as a department store is from a village shop. They represent the big business of the law.

Niche firms. This expression describes the firms which specialize in a small area of the law. Unlike the traditional firms, niche firms will deal with a chosen area of activity and nothing else. They might be experts in a patent law, or international oil futures litigation (there is one firm which specializes in just that), or they might act in so-called disaster cases (a drug which has produced unexpected side effects or a transport accident with many casualties).

Consortia. Many solicitors' firms are combining with others to share their skills and knowledge. Some become partners of a large organization. Others simply group together in a loose federation to share what they can without threatening their independence.

Sole practitioners. One-man-band solicitors' offices exist in many places. Claims on the Solicitors' Compensation Fund (see below) and on indemnity insurance are disproportionately high in respect of the activities of sole practitioners. There may be many reasons for this.

Some solicitors set up on their own because they are expelled from their previous partnership for incompetence or other problems. Others may simply buckle under the pressure of work. It is difficult for a sole practitioner to take holidays. He or she has no partners to turn to if they encounter problems. Financial pressures are probably greater for a sole practitioner than for several solicitors in a partnership.

Most sole practitioners are extremely efficient and competent and do their work just as well as solicitors in larger firms. Yet if a solicitor has recently set up on his or her own and has no track record, you may well be advised to be a little cautious in dealings with them.

Most people will deal with the ordinary high street solicitor whose main areas of activity might include the following:

Conveyancing. The legal side of home-buying and selling is still mainly handled by solicitors. This used to provide more than 50 per cent of an average firm's income. The proportion is now diminishing as solicitors expand into other activities. If a client is *buying* a house, the solicitor's job will be to make sure that the ownership is transferred without any hidden snags – planned motorways going through the front room or undischarged mortgages owed by the previous owner. He or she will carry out numerous checks and inquiries, and take charge of the day-to-day handling of the transaction as it progresses. In the *sale* of a house the procedures will be reversed, with the solicitor dealing with the inquiries raised by the other side.

Probate and wills. There is no legal requirement for a will to be prepared by a solicitor. Some banks have a will-drawing service.

Nevertheless, it is sensible to ensure that the work is done properly. Solicitors claim that they make more money out of sorting out the problems caused by home-made wills than they ever do from preparing the wills.

Probate work involves distributing and managing the assets of someone who is dead. Apart from applying for probate (i.e. obtaining the official court approval to collect together and dispose of the assets of the estate) a solicitor will deal with matters of inheritance tax, transfers of property (shares, the family home and so on) and cashing in and closing accounts. Sometimes it is necessary to consider adjusting the terms of the will if the family wish it. There are circumstances where a deed of family arrangement can save a lot of inheritance tax.

Solicitors as executors. Many people appoint their solicitor to be their executor. A solicitor is one of several possibilities. Most banks will act as executors, as will accountants. Before making a decision, consider what you want, and find out how much it will cost. Banks generally are much the most expensive, but a solicitor may agree to charge little extra for acting as executor if he or she is instructed to deal in the estate.

Family and divorce. About 200,000 people start divorce proceedings every year. Changes in the law over the past twenty years have made the process of divorce much easier, but the problems of deciding on the future of the children and resolving who gets what of the family assets are invariably complex.

Criminal cases. It might be a parking fine or a murder. Any case which involves the possibility of a punishment is classed as criminal. Most criminal cases are dealt with by magistrates' courts, where clients are usually represented by solicitors. More serious cases are dealt with by the crown court, where a solicitor is likely to instruct a barrister to represent his or her client.

Civil disputes. These include employment problems, quarrels between neighbours, accidents and disagreements between landlords and tenants. It is not usually economical to use a solicitor in a dispute where the value of the claim is under £1,000 as clients will have to pay costs even if they win the case. Some solicitors will throw a little muscle into sorting out small problems for their existing clients without charging, but that cannot be guaranteed (see Chapter 68).

Restrictive practices by solicitors

The Law Society has been criticized in the past for laying down rules which restrict free competition between solicitors. These criticisms focused on the following areas.

Advertising

Solicitors were not allowed to advertise at all until 1985. If they did, they would be liable to disciplinary proceedings and risked being struck off. Under considerable opposition – from solicitors – the right to advertise was granted. Initially it was very restricted – mainly to 'tombstone' advertisements (the kind that simply give the name, address and telephone number of the solicitor).

Advertising is governed by the 1990 Solicitors' Publicity Code. Solicitors may use any medium they wish (including television). Some solicitors now advertise on the sides of buses or have leaflets delivered with free newspapers. Solicitors may claim that they specialize in a particular area of the law so long as the claim can be justified. They may also quote their fees publicly, and accept payment by credit card.

There are still some restrictions:
- they may not refer to their success rate;
- they may not make comparisons with or criticisms of another solicitor (but there seems to be nothing to stop a solicitor using the technique employed by manufacturers of washing powder, and making comparisons with 'Brand X'!)
- no mention may be made that any member of a firm has a judicial appointment;

- they may not name clients unless the clients give their consent and there would be no risk of prejudice to the clients;
- they may not publicize their practice by unsolicited visits or telephone calls.

Price-cutting

Solicitors are free to compete with each other on price – and they do. Remember that if a solicitor's fee is considerably less than that of his or her competitors, they may have to reduce the level of service to cover the cost. On the other hand, the most expensive solicitor is not necessarily the best.

Sharing office services

Solicitors may share office services, even with non-solicitors, but they have an overriding duty to keep their clients' affairs confidential. Solicitors are still not permitted to go into partnership with people who are not solicitors. Nevertheless, these *multi-disciplinary partnerships* are envisaged by the Law Society in its strategy document 'Succeeding in the 90s'. It is likely that from 1993 onwards foreign lawyers will be able to go into partnership with English solicitors.

Solicitors' fees

For details of how solicitors' fees are calculated and how to challenge a bill, see Chapter 66.

Client care

A new rule (Rule 15) of the Solicitors' Practice Rules introduced in 1991 requires solicitors to

1 Operate a complaints handling procedure and ensure that clients are told whom to contact if they have a problem with the service provided.
2 Ensure that clients:
  (a) know the name and status (i.e. solicitor, partner, legal executive etc.) of the person responsible for the day-to-day handling of the case and who is in overall charge;
  (b) are kept informed of the progress and problems of a case.

These rules include a package of client-care procedures designed to ensure that some of the most frequent criticisms of solicitors – failure to keep in touch and failure to provide proper information on fees – are laid to rest, or at least reduced.

The Law Society recommends that information about all these matters is given in writing, so that clients have the fullest and clearest possible information (see specimen letter on page 912).

A client care letter

Carrot, Turnip and Swede, Solicitors

Dear Mr Pritchard

Thank you for instructing this firm to act for you in connection with your accident claim. I and everyone else here at Carrot, Turnip and Swede will do our best to see that everything proceeds as smoothly as possible.

Responsibility for the work

I shall carry out most of the work in this matter personally, but you can also contact my secretary, Carol, who will be familiar with the file. If she is unable to help you herself, she will be pleased to take a message for you.

The partner of this firm with ultimate responsibility for this matter is Mr Rufus Carrot. We aim to offer all of our clients an efficient and effective service and I am confident that we will do so in this case. However, should there be any aspect of our service with which you are unhappy, and which we cannot resolve between ourselves, you may raise the matter with Ms Tina Turnip.

Fees

Our charges will be calculated mainly by reference to the time spent by me and by other solicitors and executive staff dealing with this matter. This includes advising, attending on you and others, dealing with papers, correspondence, telephone calls, travelling and waiting time. I attach a list of this firm's staff and their charge rates and the rates for routine letters and telephone calls. These rates do not include VAT, which will be added to the bill.

As I have said, I shall carry out most of the work in this matter personally and, as a partner, my charge rate is £75 per hour. The charge rates that I have quoted are reviewed annually and therefore if this matter has not been concluded before April, when the next review will take place, they will rise. I shall let you know the new rates which will apply to work done from then as soon as they have been set.

In matters such as this it is difficult to estimate how many hours of work will be necessary to complete the matter. At the present time I estimate that in the region of 10 hours' work will be required. However, this estimate may change as the matter proceeds and it becomes clearer how much time is likely to be needed. I will let you know if it becomes apparent that we will have to spend substantially more time on this matter than I have currently estimated.

Terms of business

It is normal practice to ask clients to make payments on account of anticipated costs and disbursements. It is helpful if you can meet requests promptly but if there is any difficulty please let me know as soon as possible. At this stage please could you let me have £100 on account.

We shall deliver bills to you at regular intervals for the work carried out during the conduct of the case. This assists our cash flow and enables you to budget for costs. I am sure you will understand that in the event of a payment not being made we must reserve the right to decline to act any further and that the full amount of the work done up to that date will be charged to you. Accounts should be settled within 14 days. Interest will be charged on bills that are not paid within that time at 15 per cent.

Orders for costs

I should also explain that at the conclusion of this matter, and in the event that you are successful, it may be that you will be entitled to the payment of your costs by some other party. However, it is rare for the system of 'taxation' of costs, as it is known, to result in the other party having to pay anything like the full amount of your costs. This is a complex subject which I shall be happy to explain further if you wish.

In the event that you are successful and the costs of the matter fall to be paid by the other party, we will be able to claim interest on those costs to be paid as from the date on which the order for costs was made. To the extent that any of our charges have not been asked for and paid on account we will retain this interest.

Agreement

The charges set out above are an estimate based on the information that I have at present and I will inform you in writing if any difficulties arise or if anything occurs which makes it necessary to revise this estimate. They do not constitute a contentious business agreement – which could have the effect of restricting your rights to challenge them – and if you are not satisfied at the conclusion of the matter you may seek to challenge them by way of taxation.

As confirmation that you would like us to proceed on this basis, I should be grateful if you would sign the extra copy of this letter enclosed and return it to me. At the same time please forward your cheque payable to this firm as requested.

Yours sincerely

[Based on a specimen letter recommended by the Law Society]

Complaints against solicitors

In 1990 there were 13,852 complaints from the public about solicitors. The chief areas of complaint concerned delay, poor communications and negligent or inadequate services.

Complaints against solicitors used to be handled by the Law Society, which also represents the interests of solicitors. In the public mind these two roles undoubtedly conflicted, and the person making the complaint felt that the Law Society was protecting the solicitor.

These conflicts have to a large extent been resolved by the creation in 1986 of the Solicitors' Complaints Bureau. It is funded by the Law Society but acts independently in handling complaints against solicitors.

Since 1991 the case work and appeals handled by the Bureau have been supervised by its Adjudication and Appeals Committee. It works through sub-committees. One sub-committee, the Policy Advisory Committee, has a majority of lay members and gives advice on policy.

The roles of the Solicitors' Complaints Bureau

Conciliation

This is now the preferred route for dealing with complaints. If a problem seems open to discussion, the Solicitors' Complaints Bureau will refer it to a conciliation officer (usually a solicitor) who will try to help the client and solicitor reach an amicable solution to the problem. This is entirely voluntary, and either client or solicitor may discontinue it at any time. If the complaint cannot be resolved in this way or if more serious matters come to light, the conciliation officer will refer back to the Solicitors' Complaints Bureau for further action.

Investigation

If conciliation is not available, the complaint will be investigated more formally by staff at the Solicitors' Complaints Bureau.

Adjudication

Among its powers the Solicitors' Complaints Bureau can:
● order the inspection of a solicitor's accounts;
● in cases of delay, send in an agent, at the expense of the solicitor, to recover money and papers for the client;
● require the solicitor to cooperate in the investigation of a complaint or face disciplinary proceedings;
● if a solicitor has given inadequate professional services, order him or her to reduce or refund fees, or require a solicitor to put right a mistake at his/her own expense, and/or award compensation of up to £1,000;
● rebuke a solicitor for bad conduct;
● set conditions on his/her practising certificate (e.g. that they act only as an employee, not as a partner);
● require a solicitor to pay interest to his/her client;
● refer serious cases to the Solicitors' Disciplinary Tribunal.

Solicitors' Disciplinary Tribunal

A solicitor used clients' money for his own purposes, and for the purposes of other clients. He had sworn an affidavit which contained misleading statements, and had made misleading statements in correspondence to clients. He had been guilty of unreasonable delay in dealing with clients' affairs, and he had failed to deliver accountants' reports to the Law Society on time. He was ordered to be struck off the roll of solicitors and to pay costs.

Solicitors' Disciplinary Tribunal decision 4936/91

This is typical of the cases which are regularly reported in legal magazines. In 1990 the Solicitors' Complaints Bureau instituted 161 sets of proceedings in the Solicitors' Disciplinary Tribunal. In the same year forty-three solicitors were struck off the roll (the most serious penalty available to the Tribunal).

The Tribunal is also independent of the Law Society. Cases are heard by two solicitors and one lay member. Hearings are usually in private.

The tribunal can:
- reprimand a solicitor;
- fine him/her up to £5,000 on each 'offence';
- suspend him/her from practice (usually for between six months and 5 years);
- strike him/her off the roll of solicitors.

The solicitor can appeal against the decision of the Solicitors' Disciplinary Tribunal to the Divisional Court of the Queen's Bench Division (see page 880).

Unlike the decisions of the Solicitors' Complaints Bureau, the findings of the Solicitors' Disciplinary Tribunal are made public, and are frequently given wide publicity.

Suing a solicitor

A continuing cause of dissatisfaction is that complaints procedures do not cover negligence (where a client loses money or incurs expense because of errors by a solicitor).

All solicitors are insured against negligence, but clients who have been the victims of negligence still have to pursue their claim in the same way as an accident victim or a claimant in a medical negligence case. Not everything which goes wrong will amount to negligence by a solicitor. He or she must be shown to have fallen below the standard of competence and expertise demanded of a typical solicitor. Clients also have to show that their loss was *caused* by the negligence. None the less, where a client is unable to obtain damages because a solicitor failed to issue proceedings within the limitation period, or where a business has to move because a solicitor fails to give the necessary notice under the Landlord and Tenant legislation, a client should have little difficulty in obtaining redress.

The courts accept that the negligence of a solicitor can cause the client considerable upset and mental distress:

Miss H was being pestered by a former boyfriend. She went to local solicitors and asked them how the boyfriend could be prevented from pestering her. She was seen by an unqualified clerk who handled the case badly; he spent eleven months trying to obtain a court order against the boyfriend in the High Court. An efficient solicitor would have been able to obtain an injunction in the county court within two or three weeks. She sued the solicitors for professional negligence. Held: The solicitors were liable. She was awarded £125 damages (1992 value: £433) for the distress and upset caused to her. Heywood (1976)

Mr and Mrs Buckley were selling their house and buying another. They told their solicitor not to exchange contracts for one without simultaneously exchanging contracts on the other. Negligently the solicitor exchanged on the sale but not on the purchase, which subsequently fell through. The Buckleys were eventually forced to buy a completely unsuitable property because nothing else was available. They sued the solicitor for negligence. Held: The solicitor was liable. The judge awarded them £355 for out of pocket expenses, such as removal fees, petrol and telephone calls and £1,000 for the loss of money on their new house. In addition he awarded them £750 (1992 value: £2,235) each for the distress, anguish and inconvenience: they had had to live in an unsuitable house for two years. Mrs Buckley had suffered from anxiety; Mr Buckley had been forced to store his business tools (he worked at home) 50 yards away. Buckley (1977)

It is always wise to use a solicitor to make a claim against another solicitor. That solicitor will be represented by the firm acting for the insurers. A client making a claim will therefore be fighting *two* firms of solicitors.

The public view is that solicitors will not sue other solicitors. This may have some truth in a small community where local solicitors are well known to one another, but a client ought never to have difficulty in finding a solicitor to investigate and take on a claim for negligence.

The Negligence Panel

The Solicitors' Complaints Bureau has set up a panel of solicitors who are prepared to sue other solicitors and who will make an initial investigation of a claim. The first interview (up to an hour) is free of charge. After that interview, normal payment is required but legal aid may be available (see Chapter 67). The Solicitors' Complaints Bureau makes referrals where clients are seeking help.

This scheme is not available to limited companies or businesses.

The Compensation Fund

This is funded by the solicitors' profession. The basic object of the fund is to replace clients' money misappropriated by solicitors or one of their employees. The scheme is run by the Law Society, which has a complete discretion whether to make payments out of the fund. It is a 'fund of last resort'. No payment will be made where the loss is an insured risk, or where recompense can be obtained from someone else (such as the partner of a dishonest solicitor).

The requirements are:
* the loss must be caused by the dishonesty of a solicitor (or one of his/her staff);
* there must be an actual loss in money (or equivalent);

- the dishonesty must be substantiated (e.g. by a conviction of the solicitor or some other evidence);
- the loss is not recoverable from any other source.

To apply, notice must be sent to the Law Society as soon as possible after the loss is discovered. Even if the exact amount of the loss is not known, the giving of notice should not be delayed. Besides setting out the full circumstances, the notice should name the offending solicitor and give the full names and address of the client who has suffered loss. It should state the belief that the loss has been caused by dishonesty and confirm that the client has suffered hardship as a result. The notice should include a formal request for payment out of the compensation fund. It must be signed by the client or his/her new solicitor.

Legal Services Ombudsman

Complainants who are not happy with the way the Solicitors' Complaints Bureau (or the Professional Conduct Committee of the Bar Council; see page 929) has handled their complaint may now refer the matter to the Legal Services Ombudsman, who is neither a solicitor nor a barrister.

He can be asked to examine the Solicitors' Complaints Bureau's treatment of the complaint and decide whether it was investigated fully and fairly. He can recommend further action if he thinks the matter has not been dealt with properly.

A complaint to the Legal Services Ombudsman must be made within three months of receipt of the decision of the Solicitors' Complaints Bureau. The Ombudsman then sends out a form, which must be completed and returned to him. The address is The Legal Services Ombudsman, 22 Oxford Court, Oxford Street, Manchester M2 3WQ.

Changing solicitors

If clients are dissatisfied with the service or advice they obtain from solicitors they should think about changing solicitors. Before taking this step, they should try to resolve the problem with their solicitor. A common criticism of solicitors is that they have failed to keep a client informed of what is happening. The solicitor may nevertheless be working competently.

Do not change solicitors simply because you do not like the advice you have been given. The solicitor may be right. If you are concerned, try asking for a second opinion – from a barrister, for instance. Remember that it can be expensive to change solicitors; a new solicitor will have to read him or herself into a case and the outgoing solicitor may exercise a lien on the papers (see below). In a successful court case it is unlikely that a court will order the unsuccessful opponent to pay the costs of changing solicitors in addition to the normal costs.

If you have a complaint against a solicitor do not just turn up at the office and demand to see him or her. Solicitors are busy and often have many appointments during a day. Write a letter itemizing your grievances, and follow it with an appointment if you do not get a satisfactory reply. If that does not work, then consider changing to another solicitor. If the case is complex, a solicitor experienced in that sort of work should be used. Some solicitors do not like to turn work away, and consequently become bogged down in unfamiliar cases. Consult the local Citizens' Advice Bureau. It has experience of the specialists in the locality. The Citizens' Advice Bureau can give an idea of the standards and time-scale which might be normal for a particular type of case.

Procedures for changing solicitors

No formal procedure is required. A letter addressed to the solicitor requesting him or her to hand over the papers to the new solicitor is sufficient. Alternatively, papers may be collected personally. If there are court proceedings, the court and the other parties have to be given formal notification of the change. If the former solicitor had obtained a legal aid certificate for his/her client, an amendment to the certificate is required showing the new solicitor to be nominated as acting.

Papers to be handed over

The Law Society gives guidelines to solicitors as to what should be handed over. This includes all papers and possessions belonging to a client. The solicitor should also account for all money held by him/her.

In addition solicitors should pass to their clients all correspondence (except correspondence between the solicitor and the client), briefs and instructions to barrister (and the barrister's advices and opinions).

Title deeds and other securities should be handed over, but a solicitor may not be able to do so if there is a third-party claim on them – for instance, if the deeds are mortgaged to a building society. Similarly if a solicitor has given an undertaking in respect of property or money, he or she will need to have this released first.

Solicitors are not normally required to give their clients the originals or copies of internal office documents, such as diary notes, attendance notes and office memoranda.

The solicitor's lien

If solicitors are owed fees they are entitled to keep the documents and papers until they have been paid. The solicitor may not sell or destroy the papers; his/her only right is to hold them. Furthermore, the courts have power to order the solicitor to hand over papers, securities or money even if the bill has not been paid. This might be appropriate if the solicitor has been negligent and is not entitled to be paid for the work that has been done.

If clients cannot pay their former solicitor immediately, the solicitor may be prepared to accept an undertaking from the new solicitor to 'preserve the lien'. This means that the new solicitor must keep the papers and not part with them without the previous solicitor's permission.

Where a client has legal aid, a solicitor is entitled to claim payment when he or she stops acting. The Law Society therefore advise that no undertaking about costs is appropriate on a change of solicitor.

A solicitor is not entitled to charge for removing files from storage for collection by a former client, but a reasonable charge may be made for the cost of sending the papers to the client or other solicitor. A solicitor may also charge for retrieving documents from the client's file at the request of the client.

Sworn documents etc.

Certain formal documents, such as affidavits (sworn statements) and statutory declarations, have to be witnessed by a Commissioner for Oaths. Formerly, only solicitors and notaries public were able to undertake this work. Under the Courts and Legal Services Act 1990 the following have the right to use the title 'Commissioner for Oaths':
- solicitors with practising certificates;
- notaries public;
- authorized advocates and authorized litigators (e.g. barristers and others authorized by the Lord Chancellor to conduct court proceedings).

A Commissioner for Oaths is not permitted to witness documents prepared by his/her own firm. Clients must therefore go to another firm to have their documents sworn. The fee (1992) is £3.50 plus £1 for every document attached to the affidavit.

The procedure is arguably a safeguard against fraud, but in other jurisdictions, notably the United States, there is no restriction on documents being sworn by another lawyer in the same firm as the one in which the document was prepared. It is questionable whether it is really necessary for documents to be sworn in the office of another firm. The important thing is for clients to realize the nature and significance of the document they are signing, and the consequences of making a false statement. Their own solicitor could spell these out perfectly adequately.

A notary public is a lawyer who witnesses deeds and other documents for use abroad; the fees are greater. Most notaries are solicitors, but there are few of them. In a medium-sized town there is likely to be only one notary.

Becoming a solicitor

There are three ways to become a solicitor (see chart opposite).

The law-degree route

About 75 per cent of solicitors qualify in this way. Law graduates will have to take a one-year full-time Law Society Finals Course. They must then sit the Law Society Finals Examination (due to be abolished after September 1992). After that date they will have to enrol on a Legal Practice Course. This will be based more on practical procedures than at present and will last for an academic year. Before or after taking this course trainee solicitors will have to spend a two-year period training as an 'articled clerk'. After that they will be qualified solicitors.

The non-law-degree route

This process takes one year longer. About 15 per cent of solicitors qualify in this way. The process here is the same as above except after obtaining their degree graduates will additionally have to take a one-year course leading to the Common Professional Examination, covering six 'core' subjects of the law.

The non-graduate-route

Someone who has four GCSEs (not required of those over twenty-five) can become a student member of the Institute of Legal Executives and train to be a Legal Executive (see below). Once qualified as a Legal Executive they may then either attend the Law Society's Finals Course (or Legal Practice Course; see above) or serve two years' articles and prepare for the Finals Examination as an external candidate. This method provides a route of entry into the profession for school-leavers, non-graduates and even graduates who do not want to take the Common Professional Course, or law graduates who are unable to study for the Finals Course. This route usually takes at least two years longer than either of the other routes.

The 'articles' stage is the period of training in a solicitor's office. Ideally, the academic emphasis of the degree course and the practical emphasis of the Law Society Finals Course or Legal Practice Course will be supplemented by the real-life experience of working in a solicitor's office. Trainee solicitors will sit in with their employer, see how the office is run and gradually build up expertise and a clientele of their own. Unfortunately, it is rarely like that. The quality of the articled clerk's training varies enormously, and it is often a matter of luck, depending on the particular solicitor to whom the trainee is articled. Often the articled clerk is given the menial tasks that none of the qualified solicitors want

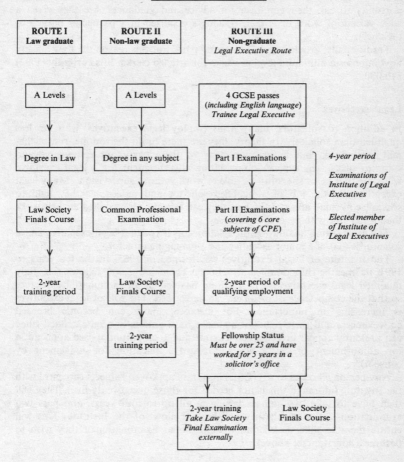

BECOMING A SOLICITOR

| ROUTE I
Law graduate | ROUTE II
Non-law graduate | ROUTE III
Non-graduate
Legal Executive Route |

| A Levels | A Levels | 4 GCSE passes
(including English language)
Trainee Legal Executive |

| Degree in Law | Degree in any subject | Part I Examinations |

4-year period

Examinations of Institute of Legal Executives

| Law Society
Finals Course | Common Professional
Examination | Part II Examinations
(covering 6 core subjects of CPE) |

Elected member of Institute of Legal Executives

| 2-year
training period | Law Society
Finals Course | 2-year period of
qualifying employment |

| | 2-year
training period | Fellowship Status
Must be over 25 and have worked for 5 years in a solicitor's office |

| 2-year training
Take Law Society Final Examination externally | Law Society
Finals Course |

For information about a career as a Legal Executive, you should contact: The Institute of Legal Executives, Kempston Manor, Kempston, Bedford MK42 7AB to do, and there is little Law Society supervision of the quality of the training given – e.g. are clerks given their own cases? Are they allowed the opportunity to ask their employer for advice and guidance? Are they given a wide variety of work or is their training specialized in a particular branch of the law?).

Traditionally, articled clerks are poorly paid. For this reason the Law Society now imposes a minimum level of wages for articled clerks. It is currently (1992) £10,000.

Legal executives

In addition to solicitors, many firms employ legal executives, who are less qualified than solicitors. In theory, they are there to do the routine, run-of-the-mill legal work, but in practice many of them carry out responsible and complex tasks. The typical job-recruiting advertisement for a legal executive will state that he or she 'must be able to work without supervision'. Many legal executives do the job of a qualified solicitor and indeed, as they tend to specialize in small areas of the law, they can become more skilled at their work than a solicitor with general experience.

The most fitting analogy of the relationship between a legal executive and a solicitor is that of a junior executive and a managing director.

The Institute of Legal Executives was formed in 1963. In the ten years to 1991 its membership doubled to 21,000. There are 5,000 fellows (i.e. fully qualified legal executives). The Institute has set up an examination structure so that the competence of members can be verified. The role of legal executives is increasing in importance. For instance, many can become licensed conveyancers and their rights of audience have gradually been extended (they can presently appear before a county court judge on an unopposed application for adjournment or on a straightforward application for judgement by consent).

Any person who has four GCSEs in certain approved subjects can enrol with the Institute (although this is not needed for those over twenty-five). They will then have to take two courses lasting in all up to four years, and pass two examinations, after which they will be a 'Fellow' of the Institute. This will entitle them to take the Common Professional Examination if they wish to become a solicitor (see above).

Licensed conveyancers

Licensed conveyancers are authorized to carry out property transactions on behalf of their clients, in exactly the same way as are solicitors. They are licensed by the Council of Licensed Conveyancers (Golden Cross House, Duncannon Street, London WC2N 4JP), which regulates their conduct and has disciplinary machinery to deal with complaints.

Finding a solicitor

A good solicitor can make a real difference to the way a matter is handled, whether it is a house purchase or a criminal charge. Complex cases involve much prolonged contact between solicitor and client. If it is clear from the outset that there is going to be a clash of personality, or that the solicitor is not going to inspire confidence, it may be better to stop at that stage, before things have a chance to go wrong.

Personal recommendation is often a reliable indicator, but make sure that the solicitor is good at the problems which need to be solved. However warmly he or she is recommended, the solicitor who expertly handled a house transaction is unlikely to be equally skilled at medical negligence cases.

Some types of work are covered by solicitors on specialist panels set up by the Law Society. Already there is a child-care panel, and a panel of insolvency practitioners. In order to be on the panel, solicitors have to satisfy the Law Society that they have special skills in the areas covered. There are proposals for personal injury and medical negligence panels.

The Law Society always sets up a hot-line whenever there is a national emergency which involves legal claims. Claimants are helped to find solicitors to take on their cases. The Law Society also coordinates other types of case, such as those involving individuals who have suffered side effects from a drug or have a rare industrial injury.

There are also organizations which exist to help people with particular problems. The following may be able to provide assistance in finding the right specialist solicitor:

Action for Victims of Medical Accidents
Age Concern
The Childrens' Legal Centre
MIND
National Head Injuries Association (HEADWAY)
(For the addresses see Appendix 1: Doctors, Miscellaneous.)

Citizens' Advice Bureaux generally have experience of local solicitors, and can either make a specific recommendation or provide a list of solicitors who specialize.

Before making an appointment with a solicitor check that the firm or solicitor handles the particular work and what the charges are likely to be. Many solicitors make no charge for a first interview. Under the client-care rules, solicitors are obliged to provide information about how they charge.

There is sometimes reluctance on the part of clients to ask whether the solicitor does a particular type of work, or to tell the solicitor's receptionist what the problems are. This can result in time being wasted; solicitors are now often specialized and they may not take on work which is outside their sphere of activity.

OTHER SOURCES OF LEGAL ADVICE

Solicitors are not the only people who provide advice, and there are also schemes for obtaining advice from a solicitor free or at a reduced fee (see generally Chapter 67). The following are other agencies which might provide help.

Citizens' Advice Bureaux

Many Citizens' Advice Bureaux have professional staff who can provide a skilled, free service. Local solicitors often attend 'surgeries' and give free preliminary advice on problems.

Law centres

These are usually in inner-city areas. They tend to specialize in the type of work which is not adequately serviced by solicitors (e.g. tenants' cases, welfare benefit claims, consumer complaints). They are staffed by qualified lawyers. If they take on a case, they will provide a service similar to that of a private solicitor, except that it may be free! They also operate under the legal-aid schemes.

Advice centres

These are usually open part-time – in the evenings, for instance. Typically, local solicitors will provide free legal advice, but the solicitors cannot become involved in direct action (such as issuing proceedings). If those steps are needed, the client will have to see the solicitor in his/her office and either pay privately or obtain legal aid.

Trade unions

Many trade unions provide legal advice and help on employment-related matters (e.g. accidents at work, unfair dismissal claims). The advice is usually free to union members. Some unions also underwrite legal fees if the involvement of a solicitor becomes necessary. Be sure to study the application form provided by the union. You may find that your choice of solicitor is restricted by the union, and that if you change solicitors you will have to pay off the union's solicitor.

Specialist advice centres

There are numerous advice centres giving specialist advice in particular areas of the law, especially in the housing and consumer fields.

BARRISTERS

> If you ask two barristers for advice you will get two or three opinions.
>
> Anonymous barrister

Barristers are the smaller branch of the legal profession. There are currently about 7,000 practising barristers. Barristers are termed *counsel* when appearing in court or advising clients. They practise from *chambers* not offices. When they are admitted they are *called to the bar*. Their governing body is the General Council of the Bar (known as the Bar Council). Every practising barrister must pay a subscription to the Bar Council and be a member of one of the four Inns of Court: Lincoln's Inn, Inner Temple, Middle Temple and Gray's Inn. The Inns of Court are voluntary unincorporated societies, with the exclusive right to call to the bar (i.e. to appoint barristers).

Many barristers regard themselves as belonging to the senior branch of the legal profession (a view not shared by all solicitors!). Traditionally, it is said that barristers were drawn from the upper classes in society and solicitors came from the middle classes. It takes less time to qualify as a barrister than to become a solicitor, but it takes much longer to start to earn a living wage. Barristers are not allowed to practise in partnerships. They all operate independently; barristers from the same set of chambers can appear on opposite sides in a case.

Barristers are *tenants* of their chambers. Between them they employ clerical staff and a clerk. The clerk is the barrister's managing agent, and is traditionally always called by his first name. He deals directly with solicitors and negotiates on fees, taking a commission (usually about 10 per cent) from the fee. It used not to be considered etiquette even for a solicitor to discuss fees with a barrister. This kind of restriction is at last disappearing.

Barristers used to be allowed to accept work only through solicitors. Now they may also deal direct with members of a number of professions approved by the Bar Council (e.g. chartered accountants, members of the Institute of Taxation, architects, engineers and actuaries). This is known as 'direct professional access'. Many ombudsmen may also instruct barristers direct. Barristers are still not allowed to accept instructions from members of the general public.

Barristers' work falls into two categories:

1 *Court work*. Barristers can appear as advocates in any court. They presently have a monopoly over appearing in the higher courts.
2 *Non-court work*. Not all barristers spend their working day in court. Barristers are asked to advise on difficult points of law or on how a particular case should be conducted. In addition barristers prepare formal pleadings – the documents which make up a court case.

Conduct of work

> A barrister must at all times promote and protect fearlessly and by
> all proper and lawful means his lay client's best interests.
>   from 'The Barristers' Code of Conduct'

Barristers must not take on work which they are not competent to handle, do not have time to perform or cannot deal with because of pressure of other work.

They must promptly read all briefs and instructions, and tell their instructing solicitors immediately if they will not be able to do the work (many solicitors would say that this rule is honoured more in the breach than in the observance!).

Unlike solicitors, they may not make any comment to the media on any current matter in which they are involved (though barristers are now permitted to advertise their services freely and with very little restriction).

In preparing court documents barristers are forbidden to 'devise facts' to assist a client's case. In particular they may not include:

● statements not supported by the client or his/her solicitor;
● contentions which they do not consider properly arguable;
● accusations of fraud against another party unless they are clearly asked to do so and have credible material which establishes fraud on the face of it.

How to instruct a barrister

Even if someone knows a barrister and wants to use him or her on a case, the instructions still have to go through a solicitor (unless they use the direct professional access route; see above).

The 'cab rank' rule

The rule compares barristers to taxis in a rank: they must take the next passengers, whoever they are. Thus all practising barristers must (irrespective of whether the client is privately paying or legally aided):

● accept any brief to appear before a court in which they profess to practise;
● accept any instructions;
● act for any person on whose behalf they are briefed.

They must do so regardless of their own beliefs, the nature of the case or character of the person on whose behalf they are instructed.

There are so many exceptions to this rule that it is generally always possible for barristers legitimately to turn down cases. The rules forbid them to take on a case if in doing so they would be 'professionally embarrassed'.

Professional embarrassment includes a lack of sufficient experience, inadequate time or opportunity to prepare the case, a risk of breach of confidences entrusted by another client and conflicts of interest. Barristers may also decline to accept a case if the fee offered is not a proper one to reflect the complexity of the case or the seniority of the barrister. In legally aided cases, the fee paid is automatically considered to be a proper fee.

Dealings with a barrister

Technically all communications with barristers must be through solicitors. If a meeting is held with a barrister (called a *conference*), a representative of the solicitor has to be present. If a barrister has a query on a case he or she must not telephone a client direct but must ask the solicitor to find the answer. This can often duplicate work quite unnecessarily.

Barristers should not discuss cases with any witnesses (except their client or expert or character witnesses). In a *civil* case only, if barristers consider it in their client's interest, they may discuss a case with a witness, so long as they have been provided first with a full statement from the witness. None the less, they must not put witnesses under any pressure or coach them in any way.

The barrister in court

The normal rule is that a barrister may appear in court only when attended by a solicitor (or other professional client; see page 925). Barristers may now agree to appear alone in the magistrates' court or the county court (and in any other court if they have been provided with all necessary witness statements).

When conducting a case, barristers
• are personally responsible for the conduct of their case;
• must not express their personal opinion unless asked by the court to do so;
• must ensure that the court is told of all relevant law (statutes and cases) of which they arc aware, even if these are against the client's interests. They should also bring any procedural irregularity to the attention of the court, and not wait to appeal it later;
• must not ask scandalous questions or questions intended to 'vilify, insult or annoy' a witness;
• must where possible avoid naming people not involved in the proceedings whose character might be called into question. They should not attack the character of a witness unless the witness has been given the opportunity to reply in cross-examination.

Queen's Counsel

About 10 per cent of barristers are Queen's Counsel (QCs). Queen's Counsel appear in court wearing silk gowns. Junior barristers wear gowns made of cotton. When a barrister becomes a QC he or she is said to be 'taking silk'. QCs are known as *leaders* because until 1977 a QC could appear in court only if a junior barrister (i.e. a barrister who is not a QC) also appeared with them.

Nowadays a QC can appear without a junior, but it is not encouraged. In any event, the QCs can refuse to appear by themselves if they would be otherwise unable to:

- conduct the case, or other cases, *or*
- fulfil their professional or other commitments.

In short, QCs must insist that they have a junior if they are already overworked! In practice it is rare for a QC to appear in court without a junior.

Becoming a QC usually results in an increase in barristers' income, because they can charge higher fees and, by delegating to a junior, can spend less time on research and preparation. However, there is a risk that their clients will go elsewhere rather than pay the increased fees (plus those of a junior). QCs can find that they have priced themselves out of the market.

The earnings of barristers vary enormously; it is a profession of extremes. Top QCs can earn well over £250,000. Some junior barristers in their first few years may well qualify for family benefit!

Barristers' monopolies and restrictive practices

The main monopoly enjoyed by barristers is over rights of audience in the higher courts. Barristers can appear in all the courts, but solicitors can appear only in the magistrates' courts, county courts and, exceptionally, the crown courts (if the hearing involves an appeal or committal for sentence from a magistrates' court case and the solicitor appeared as an advocate).

The arguments in favour of this monopoly are that:
- it is in the public interest that the more important cases should be handled by independent experts, as it ensures a more efficient hearing of the case and a weeding out of hopeless cases;
- it is in clients' interests that their case should be handled by a barrister; apart from being a specialist in advocacy, the barrister can look at the case objectively and give sensible advice; solicitors cannot do this because they have handled the case from the beginning and are often emotionally involved in it.

The arguments against the monopoly are more convincing:
- many solicitors are as competent at appearing in court as are most barristers;
- many clients would prefer to be represented by the solicitor they know, rather than a barrister they do not know;
- it is wasteful for two lawyers to be retained to do the work that one barrister could do. Since over 40 per cent of barristers' fees come from legal-aid work, financed by the state, this represents a substantial waste of public money.
- most solicitors are experienced enough to know when a case is so difficult that a specialist advocate is needed; they could then advise clients that a barrister should be instructed.

The law has also changed (the Courts and Legal Services Act 1990) to provide for ending the monopoly, but it has not yet been brought into force.

Complaints against barristers

These are heard by the Professional Conduct Committee of the Bar Council (the PCC). It consists of members of the Bar Council and Lay Representatives, drawn from a panel appointed by the Lord Chancellor.

A complaint should be made in writing and should:

● identify the barrister;

● set out in detail the nature of the complaint;

● give details of any witnesses who can support the complaint;

● be accompanied by any relevant documents or letters (send copies not originals).

It costs nothing to make a complaint (even if it is not upheld). There is a form to use when making a complaint, but this is for convenience and is not compulsory. The complaint should be sent to The General Council of the Bar, 3 Bedford Row, London WC1R 4DB (071 242 0082).

When complaints are made, barristers are notified of them and asked for their comments in writing. Barristers are required by their code of conduct to respond promptly to complaints. Further information may be obtained from the person making the complaint or witnesses.

When all necessary information is gathered, the PCC investigates the complaint to decide first of all whether there has been professional misconduct. If it decides that there has, it will, depending on the seriousness of the case:

● direct the barrister to attend on the chairman of the PCC 'for advice or admonishment' (the least serious cases), *or*

● refer the matter to a summary tribunal (where the charges are not likely to result in suspension or disbarment), *or*

● refer the matter to a disciplinary tribunal (in the most serious cases, or where there is a serious dispute over the facts).

The disciplinary tribunal

This has five members, including in each case: a judge, a lay representative and three barristers. The proceedings are normally held in private.

Sentence. If a charge of professional misconduct is proved against a barrister, he or she may be:

● disbarred (i.e. struck off);

● suspended;

● fined up to £5,000;

● ordered to repay or forgo fees;

● reprimanded, admonished or advised as to his/her future conduct;

● excluded from carrying out legal-aid work.

Sentences of suspension and disbarment are published in the press; other sentences are not published unless recommended by the tribunal or requested by the barrister.

Financial compensation. There is no provision in the disciplinary procedures for financial compensation to be paid to clients (see Suing a Barrister below).

There are usually about 300 complaints against barristers each year. About two-thirds of these relate to the quality of work done (e.g. bad advice, acting against instructions, lack of courtesy, delay). A sixth relate to professional etiquette (e.g. touting, abuse of qualifications, refusing to act); only 1 per cent relate to fees. The figure is rising.

The Legal Services Ombudsman

The Ombudsman oversees complaints against barristers as well as solicitors. Similar requirements apply as for solicitors, and there is the same three-month time limit (see page 917).

Suing a negligent barrister

Barristers are not technically able to sue for their fees, which have long been considered to be in the nature of an honorarium. From that notion arose the idea that barristers could not be sued for negligent work. The House of Lords, in Rondel v. Worsley, decided in 1967 that a barrister could not be sued for incompetence in court. The House of Lords did subsequently decide in the case of Saif Ali v. Sydney Mitchell & Co., 1978, that a barrister could be sued for giving bad advice:

Saif Ali was injured in a car accident. He instructed solicitors to represent him and they in turn asked a barrister to advise. The barrister failed to advise that the driver of the car, as well as the owner, should be sued and as a result Saif Ali found that it was too late to claim damages. He sued his solicitors, who joined the barrister into the proceedings. The barrister applied to strike out the claim on the ground that the law gave him immunity from being sued. The House of Lords decided that the barrister had no immunity where the claim arose not from conduct in court but from pre-trial advice.

Solicitors are much more likely than barristers to be in the firing-line of claims by dissatisfied clients. It remains difficult to obtain redress against barristers. A more recent case illustrates this point:

A barrister and a solicitor both gave advice to a client on whether he should plead guilty to a charge. The Court of Appeal indicated that the barrister's advice was immune from liability; but that the solicitor's advice was not! Somasundaram v. M. Julius Melchior & Co. (1988)

The moral is clearly sue your solicitor first!

Becoming a barrister

As with the solicitor's branch of the legal profession, most intending barristers

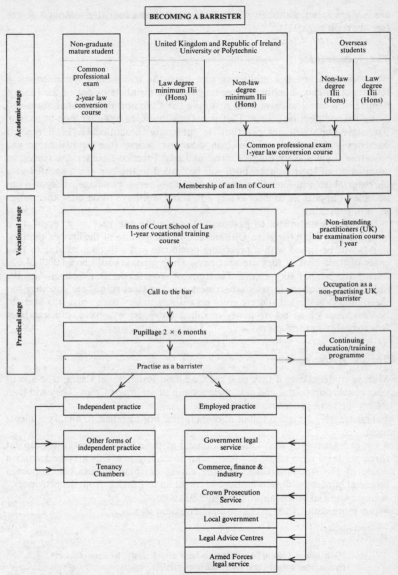

BECOMING A BARRISTER

'A barrister in independent practice must make his practice in England and Wales or in the Courts of the European Community his primary occupation and must hold himself out as being and must be willing at all times in return for the payment of fees to render legal services to the public generally in England and Wales' (Code of Conduct of the Bar, paragraph 208)

are law graduates, although it is possible to become a barrister without a degree (see chart on page 931).

The graduate route

Both law and non-law graduates who have the minimum requirement of a lower-second-class honours degree may become members of one of the Inns of Court. Non-law graduates must first take the Common Professional exam and a one-year conversion course. They may then choose to be either 'non-intending' barristers (who will not practise) or 'intending' practitioners. Each type of barrister will take his or her own one-year course (the equivalent to the solicitors' Law Society Finals Course or Legal Practice Course). On successful completion of their courses, both will be 'called to the bar' (i.e. admitted as a barrister), but 'non-intending' barristers will not serve 'pupillage'. They will not be able to appear as counsel in any court and will have to describe themselves as 'non-practising'.

Barristers who intend to practise will serve for one year as a 'pupil' to a qualified practising barrister. On satisfactory completion of the first six months, pupils will be issued with a practising certificate and will then be able to take cases of their own (if they are sent any). Their income could be £3,000–£4,000 during the second six months. The Inns of Courts, the Bar Council and the individual chambers in which barristers work all provide some funding, but these funds are limited and are given on a discretionary basis only. It is likely to be two years or so before newly qualified barristers will have sufficient brief fees to maintain themselves.

The non-graduate route

Mature students can, if they pass the Common Professional Exam, take a two-year conversion course and gain membership of an Inn of Court. They will then follow the same procedure as a graduate.

This training system is full of idiosyncrasies. For instance, to qualify students must:
- eat at least twenty-four 'dinners' (a meal at their Inn of Court); they can eat three per legal term (there are four terms in each year). This may be seen as a waste of the student's time, and the eating of these dinners can impose a financial burden on those who have to travel up to London from the provinces;
- buy a wig and gown (approximately £800 if new);
- pay more than £3,500 in course and admission fees.

JUDGES

> Four things belong to a judge: to hear courteously, to answer wisely,
> to consider soberly and to decide impartially.
>
> Socrates

The hierarchy of judges

House of Lords

There are (1991) nine Law Lords, headed by the Lord Chancellor. They are the most senior judges in the country.

Appeal Court judges

There are twenty-seven Lord Justices of Appeal. The head of the Court of Appeal is the Master of the Rolls.

High Court judges

The senior judge of the High Court is the Lord Chief Justice. A single judge will try civil cases which are heard in the High Court. High Court judges (or red judges) also try the serious (Class 1) criminal offences in the crown courts. For instance, they try murder and treason cases.

Circuit judges

They are appointed by the Queen on the advice of the Lord Chancellor from barristers of at least ten years' standing, or from Recorders who have held their post for at least three years. Circuit judges try county court cases and the less serious crown court cases.

Recorders

They are part-time appointments from barristers or solicitors of at least ten years' standing. They have the same jurisdiction as circuit judges but in the crown court they will hear the less serious offences.

District judges

They are usually solicitors. They deal only with county court cases. They handle procedural matters and the smaller cases. Under the Children Act 1989 most disputes arising out of domestic and divorce cases are now handled by a district judge.

All professional judges were, until the passing of the Courts and Legal Services Act 1990, recruited from the legal profession, mainly from barristers. That Act will enable anyone with sufficient advocacy experience (i.e. experience in exercising rights of audience in representing a party in court proceedings) to be appointed a judge. In practice it is likely that judges will be recruited from the legal profession for the foreseeable future. Although the Act currently contemplates advocates being drawn from solicitors and barristers, there are provisions in the Act to extend to other professions.

Appointment

The present rule is that judges are appointed from barristers of at least ten years' standing. However, either a solicitor or a barrister can be appointed a recorder and, after five years as a recorder, he or she can be promoted to circuit judge. Solicitors may therefore become judges, but only at the most junior level. In reality, most judges have been practising barristers for more than twenty years before they are appointed.

The appointment of senior judges is made by the Government (i.e. the politicians). Appointment to the Court of Appeal, to the House of Lords, or as Lord Chief Justice or President of the Family Division of the High Court, is made by the Prime Minister after consultation with the Lord Chancellor, who alone is responsible for all other judicial appointments. The Lord Chancellor is a political appointee, with a seat in the Cabinet, who will previously have been in practice as a barrister.

In practice the Lord Chancellor has only a limited number of names to choose from when selecting a High Court judge. He will be looking for an able barrister (almost certainly a QC), aged at least forty-five, who is prepared to take on the job. A High Court judge earns £84,250, which is considerably less than the earnings of a top QC. However, the attraction of a knighthood for senior judges and a state pension is usually sufficient to ensure that few QCs turn down a judicial appointment. None the less, the Lord Chancellor may have fewer than a dozen suitable contenders to choose from.

Social background

Many commentators have pointed out that judges tend to come from the upper echelons of society. There can be little argument about this. In 1969 Henry Cecil carried out a random survey of thirty-six judges in the High Court and Court of Appeal: 86 per cent had been to public school, and 92 per cent were Oxbridge graduates. In a random survey of county court judges, the figures were 75 per cent from public school and 81 per cent from Oxbridge.

In practice, only barristers can at present become senior judges, and it will be some considerable time before the reforms introduced by the Courts and Legal Services Act 1990 will bring about any change. The expense of becoming a barrister and low initial income will ensure that the bar remains, over all, an aristocratic or upper-middle-class profession, whereas solicitors tend to be middle class. Only recently have the extension of higher education, the introduction of more scholarships for young barristers and the growth of legal aid to provide income for the junior bar meant that those without private incomes have been able to contemplate becoming barristers. Until those barristers become middle-aged, the social composition of the judiciary cannot change. Besides, twenty or so years at the bar might have made those barristers upper middle class by then.

Until the beginning of the 1980s barristers, like solicitors, were mainly men, but that situation is changing. Now approximately 25 per cent of all barristers are women. Yet it will take a considerable time for changes to be made in the ratio of men to women holding judicial office. In 1991 there were only three female High Court judges. Of the spring 1992 crop of appointments of new QCs (the senior barristers from whom judges are selected) there were only seven women out of a total of more than seventy. With all the most senior judicial positions held by men, the stranglehold of the male sex on the English legal system is likely to continue far into the future.

The changes introduced by the Courts and Legal Services Act 1990 are unlikely to affect substantially the constitution of the courts. Although judges will be drawn from 'advocates' (instead of just barristers), there will still be a court basis of their experience. In other words, it is most unlikely that academics or others in public life will become judges under the present laws – unless they spend many years practising in court.

More radically, consideration could be given to appointing laypeople as judges, or even to holding elections for judicial office – as happens in the United States. Consideration might also be given to recruiting younger people as judges. At the moment, the average age on appointment is fifty-three. Not surprisingly the judges at the top of the judicial hierarchy are the oldest: the average age of the Court of Appeal judges is sixty-five and that of the Law Lords is sixty-eight.

Retirement of judges

Magistrates must retire at seventy; circuit judges at seventy-two (exceptionally this may be extended to seventy-five); and the senior judges must retire at seventy-five.

It is difficult to sack a judge once he or she has been appointed. Circuit judges and recorders can be removed by the Lord Chancellor for incapacity or misbehaviour, but other senior judges hold office 'during good behaviour' and can be removed only by the sovereign following a vote by both Houses of Parliament – something that has not happened in modern times.

Suing a judge

In private life judges have no different status from anyone else. If they negligently run over a pedestrian, they may be sued. If they drive while over the limit, they will be prosecuted. But in court the position is different: a judge cannot be sued for bad decisions or the mistakes he or she makes in court. This has long been a principle of our law:

William Penn, the Quaker leader, was on trial. The judge ordered the jury to find Penn guilty, but they refused and acquitted him. The judge showed his displeasure by fining and imprisoning the jurors. One of the jurors sued the judge for false imprisonment. Held: His claim failed since judges of the senior courts could not be sued for acts done while acting judicially. Bushell (1670)

Since then the principle has been refined, but the basic rule remains; judges have immunity from liability if the acts complained of were done by them in their capacity as a judge, in good faith, albeit mistakenly.

A judge was hearing an appeal against deportation. The appellant was on bail but the judge ordered him to be kept in custody although he had no power to do so. The judge was sued for false imprisonment. Held: Although the judge had clearly acted wrongly, he could not be sued because he had been acting in a judicial capacity. Lord Denning said: 'Every judge of the courts of the land – from the highest to the lowest – should be protected to the same degree. If the reason underlying this immunity is to ensure "that they may be free in thought and independent in judgement", it applies to every judge, whatever his rank. Each should be protected from damages when he is acting judicially ... So long as he does his work in the honest belief that it is within his jurisdiction, then he is not liable to an action. He may be mistaken in fact. He may be ignorant in law. What he does may be outside his jurisdiction – in fact or in law – but so long as he honestly believes it to be within his jurisdiction, he should not be liable.' Sirros (1974)

A confluence of lawyers

The day has arrived. Two weeks ago a bundle wrapped in traditional legal pink ribbon arrived at the chambers of Ivan Lettuce, barrister at law, in the Middle Temple in London. It was marked 'brief to counsel'. Mr Lettuce's clerk noted with satisfaction the fee endorsed on the brief.

At 9.45 a.m. Mr Lettuce walks the short distance from the Temple to the Strand. He strides through the entrance to the Law Courts, pausing momentarily to remove his keys from his pocket after they have set off a security alarm. He disappears into the robing room and emerges a few minutes later wearing his wig and gown. He glides confidently upstairs towards one of the courtrooms.

Earlier in the day Mr Rufus Carrot, solicitor, had struggled on to the milk train, trailing behind him his client Mr Pritchard. The client was nervous. Mr Carrot was nervous too but tried to appear reassuring. The effort made him go slightly pink. The train arrived late. The taxi became stuck in heavy traffic.

At 9.50 they are disgorged outside the Law Courts. Mr Pritchard's penknife and Mr Carrot's mobile telephone both set off the security alarm. Perspiring and out of breath they rush upstairs to the court and into the cool presence of Mr Lettuce.

In carefully modulated aristocratic tones he outlines his final strategy to Mr Carrot and Mr Pritchard: 'Of course, with old Jaundice we have to be very careful to spell out exactly what the issues are. He's a little deaf.'

At 10.10 Sir Jeremy Jaundice, Judge of the Queen's Bench Division, arrives at the judge's entrance to the Law Courts. Down the judge's corridor he exchanges not entirely judicial pleasantries with other judges before his clerk helps him on with his wig and his robes.

The clock moves round to 10.30. Last minute efforts at compromise in the gloomy corridor come to nothing. The parties assemble in the court. On the front bench are the barristers. Behind sit the solicitors, and behind them the parties to the action are gently smouldering. At 10.32 the judge's clerk nods to the court Associate.

'Silence!' shouts the Associate to the hushed assembly. On cue, the barristers, the solicitors, the protagonists and the few members of the public in the back row all stand up. Slowly, and looking faintly like Father Christmas in his red and white robe, Mr Justice Jaundice walks into the courtroom, bows and sits down.

'Pritchard versus Pilchard,' announces the Associate.

'Yes, Mr Lettuce,' says the judge.

'My Lord, I appear for the plaintiff Mr Pritchard. My learned friend Mr Spinach appears for the defendant Mr Pilchard. This case involves a dispute which first started in 1987 . . .'

And so begins another High Court trial, bringing together the forensic efforts of barristers, solicitors and a judge. To outsiders it can represent either a dignified display or a curious charade.

That is the system in the early 1990s. Will it be different in the next millennium?

Probably not!

66 Legal Costs

Agree, for the law is costly

Thomas Fuller; *Gnomoglia*, 1732

This chapter deals mainly with the costs of civil proceedings, for it is here that most issues on costs arise. Some aspects of criminal cases are considered at the end of the chapter.

WHAT ARE 'COSTS'?

When a client receives a bill from a solicitor, that bill, or the statement accompanying it, will list not just the fee charged by the solicitor but also 'disbursements' and possibly other costs (such as estate agents' fees) which have been paid by the solicitor in the course of the transaction or case. The fee charged by the solicitor will be shown on a VAT invoice and it may form a relatively small part of the total bill. The total will include the following:

• *Disbursements*. These are the solicitor's out-of-pocket expenses – sums spent by the solicitor on the client's behalf. For instance, in a house purchase the solicitor might pay search fees to the local authority, the Land Charges Registry and the Land Registry; he or she might also pay stamp duty and a Land Registry fee for registering the ownership of the property. In addition there may be miscellaneous expenses, such as travel costs, telephone calls and postage. Not all solicitors will charge for miscellaneous items, as they will absorb them in the general fee. In a High Court case the disbursements might include court fees, barrister's fees, expert witnesses' fees, expenses incurred by other witnesses and so on.

• *Profit costs*. This is the solicitor's professional charge for doing the work. It is his/her fee and is separate from disbursements. The phrase 'profit costs' is used in all the regulations which deal with solicitors' costs, but it is misleading. It is not 'costs', as the solicitor has not been charged anything; and it is not profit, since a fairly small proportion of a solicitor's fee is profit (usually it is between a third and a fifth of the sum that is charged). Before solicitors see a penny in profit, they have to pay their wages, insurance, rent, stationery costs, postage and telephone charges, and many other overheads.

● *VAT*. Finally the client will have to pay VAT on the whole of the solicitor's profit costs, and on those of the disbursements which are subject to payment of VAT (e.g. a barrister's fee).

Argument over the bill

Any argument will usually be over the solicitor's profit cost figure, since the disbursements and VAT are generally not disputed. Machinery exists to control the amount of the profit costs. There are three different ways of controlling the fees. The type of case dictates which is the appropriate method:
● *Fixed fees*. For some legal work (in particular, undefended divorces and debt collection) there are fixed fees setting out the amount a solicitor may charge. Generally these fixed fees apply only when the costs are paid by someone other than the solicitor's own client (e.g. when the loser of a case is told to pay the winner's legal costs). If the solicitors' costs are more than the fixed fee, they can usually charge the excess to their client.
● *Scale fees*. For some legal work there are scale fees, under which the fee increases with the value of the item involved. For instance, there is an unofficial scale governing solicitors' costs in work done for a client's building society when a property is being bought (see page 278).
● *Control by the Law Society and the courts*. In court cases (which are called 'contentious cases') the court can check a solicitor's bill. When a court does this it is said to 'tax' the costs. This has nothing to do with the Inland Revenue; it simply means that the court checks and assesses the costs. In non-court cases the bill can be referred to the Law Society, who will decide whether it is fair and reasonable. The society will issue a remuneration certificate setting out what it regards as the proper fee. If either side is still dissatisfied the fees may be reviewed by the courts, which will tax the costs.

Contentious and non-contentious costs

All civil work done by a solicitor can be described as either 'contentious' or 'non-contentious'. Contentious means that court proceedings have actually begun (and it makes no difference whether the client is suing or defending). 'Non-contentious' indicates that court proceedings have not been involved. The distinction in reality is between court and non-court work, though in all the regulations it is always described as 'contentious' or 'non-contentious' work. Examples of the different categories of legal work appear on page 940.

The importance of the contentious/non-contentious distinction is that it involves different methods of assessing and reviewing legal costs. A solicitor's bill in a contentious case will be totally different from the bill in a non-contentious case, and so also will be the way in which the client can complain about it.

Contentious	Non-contentious
Defended divorce	Conveyancing
Undefended divorce	Preparing a will
Applying for maintenance	Probate and winding up an estate
Suing for a debt	Advice on letting a house
Suing for breach of contract	Legal *advice* on anything (even if it
Suing a doctor for negligence	might have led to court proceedings
Suing for accident compensation	Compulsory purchase
Libel and slander	Tax advice
Any other court case	Taking a case to a tribunal (e.g. an
An arbitration hearing	unfair dismissal or redundancy claim)

Solicitors' costs: how much?

It is impossible to give guidance as to the likely charge for different types of work. Most solicitors charge largely on the basis of the time spent on that particular task, and hourly rates vary between £50 and £250 in most firms (the latter being the level of fees charged by big City firms).

LEGAL COSTS: (1) NON-CONTENTIOUS (NON-COURT) WORK

The solicitor's bill

The first stage is for solicitors to send a bill to their client. Solicitors must send a written bill, and they are also required to comply with the VAT regulations. The bill (or statement which accompanies it) should show all disbursements. It must be detailed, but it need not itemize everything. In a 1955 case Lord Denning said a non-contentious bill:

must contain a summarized statement of the work done, sufficient to tell the client what it is for which he is being asked to pay. A bare account 'for professional services' between certain dates, or for 'work done in connection with your matrimonial affairs' would not do. The nature of the work must be stated, such as, advising on such a matter, instructing counsel to do so and so, drafting such and such a document, and so forth.

Clients who are unhappy about their bill should first check the bill itself. Does it set out what the solicitors did for their money? If not, the solicitors should be asked for more detail. Under the client-care principles laid down by the Law Society, a client should be told at the outset either what the fees will be or the basis to be used for charging (e.g. the hourly charging rate). If the bill does not match up with that information, the solicitors should be asked for an explanation.

What is a fair and reasonable fee?

Solicitors should charge their clients only a 'fair and reasonable' fee, taking into account all the circumstances. Non-contentious fees are covered by the Solicitors' Remuneration Order 1972. This provides that in assessing what is 'fair and reasonable' the following should be taken into account:

   (i) the complexity of the matter or the difficulty or novelty of the questions raised;
  (ii) the skill, labour, specialized knowledge and responsibility involved;
 (iii) the time spent on the business;
 (iv) the number and importance of the documents prepared or perused without regard to length;
  (v) the place where and the circumstances in which the business or any part thereof is transacted;
 (vi) the amount or value of any money or property involved;
(vii) whether any land involved is registered land within the meaning of the Land Registration Act 1925; and
(viii) the importance of the matter to the client.

In practice, of course, this is a hopelessly vague test and of little help to clients who think they have been overcharged. They should have been given guidance at the outset if the case was started after July 1991. If the case started earlier than this, no obligation is imposed on the solicitors to give information about charges. In those cases all clients can do is try to find out what the going rate is for that kind of work. If other solicitors would charge less, then they might conclude that the charge is not fair and reasonable.

The mark-up

One of the mysteries of solicitors' charges is that they charge an hourly rate and then add a 'mark-up' of a percentage of the total bill. It smacks of thinking of a number and doubling it.

The rationale is that the hourly rate is the base cost. The mark-up is the add-on element to reflect the special features of the case. Take an extreme example:

Illustration. A solicitor (whose hourly rate is £50) spends an hour sorting out a consumer dispute over a washing machine worth £250. He will almost certainly limit his fee to £50. On the other hand, if he gives financial advice for an hour, as a result of which the client saves £100,000 in tax, the solicitor would undoubtedly charge much more.

The mark-up can be challenged in the same way as the rest of the fee.

Time-costing

Many solicitors now keep time records of how long they spend on each individual case. If records have been kept, solicitors can use this hourly rate as the basis for their charge. There are different systems and different applications.

Some solicitors simply use time-recording to monitor their work; others use it as a guide for charging; and some base all their charges on time records. In practice it is very difficult for solicitors to keep a record on their time sheet of every telephone call and every step in an action.

Well-organized solicitors will ensure that their files tell the whole story, and that there are proper time and attendance notes to show what has been done.

Querying the solicitor's bill

Clients who think their bill is too much should first take up the matter with their solicitor. Once a full explanation is given, the bill may be accepted. Alternatively, the solicitor (who is after all in business to provide a service and keep his/her goodwill) may be prepared to reduce the charge.

If the solicitor is not prepared to make any reduction, then the client can:
● accept defeat and pay the full bill *or*
● not pay, and ask the solicitor to submit the bill to the Law Society for them to say what is a fair and reasonable charge; this process is called 'obtaining a remuneration certificate'. There is a time-limit, so clients must make sure they comply with it (see below), *or*
● do nothing and not pay the bill. The solicitor cannot sue for the money owed without giving the client formal notice of his/her right to apply for a remuneration certificate from the Law Society and to have the bill taxed by the court. The recommended wording of this notice is follows:

This constitutes notice of your right under paragraph (1) of Article 3 of the Solicitors' Remuneration Order 1972 to require me within one month of the receipt hereof to obtain a certificate from the Law Society stating that in their opinion the costs charged are fair and reasonable or, as the case may be, what lesser sum would be fair and reasonable. Also there are provisions in Sections 70, 71 and 72 of the Solicitors Act 1974 relating to taxation of costs which give you the right to have the bill checked by an officer of the High Court.

That notification must score nought out of ten for clarity and ease of comprehension. If it was designed to be off-putting to a client it could not have been better worded! If clients receive a notice in that form they must act quickly (see below).

Remuneration certificates

This is a certificate stating whether in the view of the Law Society the amount charged is fair and reasonable for the work done. This is an excellent remedy from the client's point of view because:
● the Law Society cannot increase the bill but can only confirm or reduce it;
● there is no fee payable and the solicitor cannot charge for the extra cost and inconvenience of obtaining a remuneration certificate, even if the Law Society confirms that the fee is correct.

It is most important to make the request promptly – within twenty-eight days of receiving the notification set out above. Write to the solicitors, telling them you are dissatisfied with the bill and requesting them to obtain a remuneration certificate. As this is an important letter, send it recorded delivery or deliver it personally. Taking this step does not prevent negotiations over the bill, but do not pay it, even 'under protest'. Once the bill is paid, the right to a remuneration certificate is lost – except where payment is made to the solicitor involuntarily: where, for instance, a solicitor takes his/her fee without prior authority from the proceeds of sale of a house before accounting to a client for the balance. That does not count as 'payment', but the twenty-eight-day time-limit still applies. Ask immediately for a remuneration certificate.

It is for the solicitors to make the application. They fill in the requisite form and send it to the Law Society, which in turn sends a copy to the client and invites their comments. The client's comments are then passed to the solicitor, who has a right of reply. A special committee of the Law Society (consisting of practising solicitors) examines the solicitor's file and then issues the remuneration certificate. As there is always a backlog, there is often a delay of several months. The solicitor may take no steps to claim payment from the client until the certificate is received. However, provided that the solicitor has given the requisite notice (see above) interest is payable twenty-eight days after the bill is delivered on the amount of the bill or the reduced sum in the remuneration certificate.

The remuneration certificate does not deal with:
- VAT charged;
- disbursements;
- whether the solicitor has carried out his/her instructions;
- who is liable for the payment of the bill.

Generally, both solicitor and client will regard the remuneration certificate as final. However, either can take the matter further by asking the court to 'tax the costs'.

Taxation: asking the court to assess the costs

It is necessary to start court proceedings to tax the costs. A client should start the proceedings:
- before judgement is obtained by the solicitor for the costs, *or*
- before payment of the bill, *or*
- within twelve months of the bill being delivered, whichever is earlier

If these time-limits are not followed the court may not review the bill except in special circumstances (e.g. gross blunders in the bill). Whatever the circumstances, the bill may not be taxed if more than a year has passed since payment.

There are court fees to be paid on a taxation. Generally the client must pay. However, if the solicitor's total bill is reduced by a fifth or more, the solicitor pays. The 'costs' include the court's taxing fee, which can be large: 5 per cent of the bill. This also has to be paid by the losing party. In practice few clients or solicitors resort to this means of deciding on the bill. There are usually only about 150 applications of this kind each year. See page 949, How the Court Vets Legal Costs, for more information on how a taxation works.

No statistics are available, but relatively few clients are thought to use remuneration certificates as a means of checking their bills. Perhaps they are left in ignorance, after reading the formal notification which the Law Society recommends solicitors to use. It is understandable if solicitors are not keen to publicize this right for their clients; if every client with a non-contentious case exercised the right to obtain a remuneration certificate, the delays in payment could cause solicitors to go bankrupt.

The procedure is weighted against solicitors. Imagine the chaos to commercial life if every customer were given the right to challenge the cost of all goods and services bought!

A client can demand a remuneration certificate on entirely capricious grounds. The solicitor then has to go to the time and expense of making the application, checking and sending the file to the Law Society, dealing with the comments made by the client, only to be told several months later that the bill is correct!

A fairer procedure for both sides might involve:

● *For the client.* Much clearer information about this right, such as a simple notice:

If you do not accept the amount of this bill, you are entitled as of right to ask your solicitor to obtain from the Law Society a certificate stating what is the fair and reasonable sum you should pay. This will cost you nothing, and the bill may not be increased. If you want this certificate, you must within twenty-eight days ask your solicitor (in writing) to obtain it.

● *For the solicitor.* The right as a precondition of obtaining a remuneration certificate to payment of a proportion of the bill – say, two-thirds. The procedure would have to contain protection for the client in the form of a refund with interest if the bill is reduced by more than a third.

Paying someone else's costs

A client may have to pay the fees of the client of another solicitor. This happens with business tenancies (the tenant has to pay the landlord's costs of preparing a lease) or in mortgages where the lender is represented by a separate solicitor (the borrower has to pay the lender's legal fees). Here the remuneration certificate procedure does not apply. The only way of assessing the bill is through taxation in the courts (see above). If clients are faced with that situation they should:

● agree the fee in advance, so that they know exactly what their commitment will be;

● not agree to pay the fee until they know they are going ahead with the transaction. Most third party's solicitors will ask for a guarantee that their fees will be paid in any event. It is therefore important to make sure that money will not simply be thrown away!

LEGAL COSTS: 2. CONTENTIOUS (COURT) LEGAL WORK

As a general rule in court cases (where proceedings have actually started) the loser pays the winner's legal costs. This is known as the 'costs rule'. Losers therefore end up paying two sets of legal costs: those of their own lawyers and those of the winner's lawyers.

This rule is complicated by the fact that there are different ways of assessing the legal costs. The amount to be paid will depend on the basis used. If any party is legally aided, other rules and considerations apply.

The ways of assessing costs

One of the complicating factors about costs is that if the loser is ordered to pay the winner's costs it is most unlikely that he or she will have to pay all of them. There is invariably a shortfall between the amount a court will award on a taxation (see above) and the amount a solicitor is entitled to charge his/her own client. This can be illustrated by an example:

Illustration. *Caroline is badly injured in a car accident, caused entirely by the bad driving of John. In spite of the fact that he has no real defence to the claim, John, through his insurers, makes Caroline take the case all the way to a court hearing. As expected, Caroline wins and is awarded £10,000 damages, and her costs. These are awarded on the standard basis (see below) and the court fixes these at £3,510. Caroline's solicitor is, however, entitled to costs on an indemnity basis and his costs (also approved by the court as being fair and reasonable) come to £4,590. Who pays the shortfall? Not John, because the court has assessed his liability at £3,510. It is Caroline who has to make up the difference (by losing more than £1,000 of her damages, even though she has not wasted time or been guilty of any misconduct in her case.)*

Caroline's case illustrates the difference between the two bases of assessing costs, and the unfairness of the system of costs. The difference between the two methods of fixing the costs is subtle, but highly significant. The bases are as follows:

- *Standard basis*. Here the court will allow a reasonable amount of all the costs reasonably incurred. If there are any doubts as to what is 'reasonable' the paying party (i.e. the loser) shall have the benefit of those doubts.
- *Indemnity basis*. Under this basis the court will allow all costs 'except in so far as they are of an unreasonable amount or have been unreasonably incurred'. This time the receiving party (i.e. the winner) is entitled to the benefit of any doubt as to whether the costs or expenditure is reasonable.

Whichever way the costs are fixed, they must be 'reasonable', but the shift in the balance of doubt factor gives scope for a large variation in the amount of the costs. This, as has been seen, can work unfairly for the winning party.

The answer to the problem would seem to be simple: order all costs to be paid on an indemnity basis. Unfortunately, the court rules do not permit this. The default situation (i.e. if the basis is not spelled out) is that costs are paid on a standard basis only. Thus, if the court simply orders the loser to pay costs, it will not be on an indemnity basis.

The indemnity basis is used sparingly and is generally limited to the following cases:
- the fees payable by a client to his/her solicitor;
- the costs of an executor or trustee;
- the costs of a solicitor acting for a minor under eighteen or someone incapacitated under the Mental Health Act;
- costs incurred where the paying party is in contempt of court;
- cost incurred where the conduct of the paying party has been 'oppressive or unmeritorious' (here the conduct has to be very bad indeed: the normal uncooperativeness of an insurance company when dealing with a claim is not sufficient!).

Contentious costs in practice

Whenever there is a celebrated court case the media invariably estimate the legal costs to be some astronomical figure. Understandably there are many worries about costs for people embarking on litigation. Under the client-care procedures, solicitors are now required to give very full information at the outset to clients, so that they can as far as possible make informed decisions. The illustration given above shows how the system can work unfairly when the loser has to pay on a standard basis only. Below are further instances where the costs rules are not straightforward and are sometimes unfair.

If the loser is not ordered to pay the winner's costs

Usually 'costs follow the event' – in other words, the loser pays – but that is not automatic. Costs are always in the discretion of the judge who hears the case. If he or she feels that the winner was technically right, but had an unmeritorious claim, he or she can make no order for costs. Then each side will have to bear their own costs. Similarly, if the amount of compensation is so low that it is below the costs threshold (£1,000), the court is again unlikely to award costs. If the case was started in the High Court, when the amount at stake should have put it in the county court, the court will again impose penalties as to costs.

If the loser does not pay the costs

If the loser refuses to pay, the same means of enforcement are available as for any civil claim (see page 999); but if he or she has no money, goes bankrupt or simply disappears, it may be impossible to enforce an order for costs against him/her. The winner will then be left with a worthless judgement and liability to pay his/her own solicitor, barristers, experts and court fees out of his/her own pocket. Unfortunately, the rules do not prevent a party with no money contesting a case. The court can order a plaintiff only (not a defendant) to give security for costs in only the following circumstances:

● it is a limited company;

● he or she is resident outside England and Wales or has given an incorrect address with a view to evading the consequences of any liability for costs.

Where the loser has made a payment into court

The loser will not have to pay the winner's costs if he or she previously paid into court the same amount or a larger sum than the winner received in damages.

Illustration. *Peter was injured in a car accident and he sued the negligent driver. Peter's solicitor valued the claim at about £5,000 but the driver's solicitor thought he would receive only £4,000 in damages. They paid £4,000 into court. Peter then had a choice. He could accept the £4,000, and the driver would have to pay all Peter's legal costs to date. Alternatively, if he rejected the £4,000, the case would have to go to trial but the judge would not be told how much had been paid into court. If he awarded Peter £4,000 or less, then Peter would receive that lesser figure and would also have to pay all the legal costs (both his own and the driver's) as from the day the money was paid into court. Peter decided to reject the payment. At the trial the judge awarded him £3,900. Consequently Peter had his costs paid by the driver only up to the date of the payment into court. But he had to pay his own and the driver's costs from the date of payment in. These included the substantial costs of the trial. Consequently, by failing to accept the payment in, Peter had little to keep from his damages.*

By making a payment in at an early stage of the case a defendant can put the plaintiff in considerable difficulty. If the amount paid into court is slightly less than the claim is worth, the plaintiff might well accept it; he or she dare not risk taking the case to court and winning no more than was paid in.

No solicitor will guarantee that a case is watertight. All they do is give their best estimate of what they think will be the outcome. But strange things can happen at a trial. Witnesses can change their stories; experts can backtrack; judges can be sympathetic or hostile; and of course the client may or may not make a good impression to the court. If the battle is over whether the defendant is liable, as well as over the amount of damages, a plaintiff takes an additional risk in not accepting a payment into court.

To accept or not? The final decision has to be the client's. It is inevitably a gamble and the stakes can be high.

Where the loser has offered a fair settlement

Not all cases can be resolved by a payment. If two neighbours have a dispute over where the boundary fence should lie, they will be asking the court to determine the question. In those cases one party may want to protect themselves on costs by offering a sensible solution to the problem. They can do this without jeopardizing their position by making an offer 'without prejudice save as to costs'. The letter containing this offer is often referred to by lawyers as a *Calderbank letter* (after the name of the case which set the precedent). The existence of this offer, like a payment into court, may not be communicated to the judge until the case reaches the stage where costs are to be decided. If the offer is in line with the final court decision, the party which made the offer will be in a strong position to argue that their costs should be met from the date the offer was made. Again, the opposing party has to decide whether to accept the offer or to press on with the case.

Where there is more than one defendant

In some cases there might be a number of people to blame, as can be seen from this example:

Illustration. *Richard has an extension built on to his house. The work is carried out by Ken the builder, supervised by Archie the architect and approved by the building control department of the local authority. Within six months large cracks start to appear in the walls and the roof begins to sag. Clearly something has gone wrong, but who is liable? Richard contacts all three possible parties, and each blames the other two. There is no clear evidence as to who is responsible and eventually he issues proceedings against Ken, Archie and the local authority. After a long trial the judge finds that the sole fault lies with Ken and orders him to pay compensation. As Richard has not succeeded against Archie and the local authority, the judge orders Richard to pay their costs. The end result is that Richard will be substantially out of pocket.*

In a case like Richard's a judge might order the builder to indemnify him against the costs of the other parties; but if the builder becomes insolvent in the meantime, that order will be of no use to Richard. He will still have the primary responsibility for the costs.

Where the loser is on legal aid

The legal-aid regulations restrict the orders for costs which may be made against a party who has a legal-aid certificate. The position is that a legally aided party shall not be ordered to pay more than a court considers it reasonable for them to have to pay, having regard to their finances (and the finances of the other parties to the proceedings), and to the conduct of all parties. In practice few orders are made against legally aided parties; even then a court may order that costs shall not be enforced without leave. A non-legally aided client with a legally aided opponent is really on a hiding to nothing so far as costs are concerned.

But note that where non-legally aided clients will suffer 'severe financial hardship' if their costs are not paid, the court may in exceptional circumstances order the Legal Aid Board to pay the costs. The court exercises this power sparingly and there are many preconditions to payment:

• if the loser had not been on legal aid, there would have none the less been an order for costs against him/her;

• the proceedings must have been started by the party in receipt of legal aid (unless the costs related to an appeal);

• the court must be satisfied that it is 'just and equitable' that costs should be paid out of public money.

How the court vets legal costs

Taxation of costs is the legal term for describing the checking and assessing of costs by the court. The winner's solicitor will prepare a detailed bill setting up how his/her costs are made up. The bill will be divided into sections covering the fees for preparing paperwork and documents, attending on the client, attending the barrister's chambers and court; preparing for trial; attending on the trial itself; and a sum covering general care and attention. The bill is lodged with the court and will be vetted by a court official (a taxing officer or the district judge), who can disallow part of the bill – for instance, if the work was not necessary. The court will never *increase* the bill.

If either party disagrees with the court's assessment, a hearing will take place so that representations may be made. The level of costs is ultimately in the hands of the court, though it has to follow guidelines set down in the rules. There are also scales and limits for certain types of work.

In assessing contentious costs the courts consider similar factors to those in non-contentious costs:

(a) the complexity of the item or of the cause or matter in which it arises and the difficulty or novelty of the questions involved;

(b) the skill, labour, specialized knowledge and responsibility required of, and the time and labour expended by, the solicitor or counsel;

(c) the number and importance of the documents (however brief) prepared or perused;

(d) the place and the circumstances in which the business involved is transacted;

(e) the importance of the cause or matter to the client;

(f) where money or property is involved, its amount or value;

(g) any other fees and allowances payable to the solicitor or counsel in respect of other items in the same cause or matter, but only where work done in relation to those items has reduced the work which would otherwise have been necessary in relation to the item in question.

In some types of case, such as matrimonial, the rules lay down what fees may be allowed. For instance, the standard fee for a junior barrister to attend on an uncontested injunction is £84.50. The standard fee for a full day's hearing in court is £352.50. However, there is nothing to prevent a barrister or solicitor agreeing a higher figure.

If clients have legal aid, their solicitor is not allowed to charge them over and above the fee payable by the Legal Aid Board. Legal-aid costs are taxed in the same way as other costs, though the legal-aid office may assess costs where the total is less than £1,000. If the costs payable by the loser are less than the amount allowed to the legally aided client, the shortfall may have to come out of the compensation (see Chapter 67).

Because of the large amount of paperwork involved, and because of the taxing fees (5 per cent of the amount of the costs claimed), solicitors will often try to agree costs to avoid taxation. In non-contentious matters clients should always start by obtaining a remuneration certificate if they are unhappy with their solicitor's bill.

Being sued for an unpaid bill

Non-contentious matters

If clients fail to pay their bill, their solicitor may sue them for payment. Before they do so, solicitors must comply with the following requirements:
• they must send the bill to the client at their home, business or last known address;
• the bill must be signed, or must be sent with an accompanying and signed letter which refers specifically to the bill;
• they must give the client the notice under the Solicitors' Remuneration Order 1972 (see page 942) and then wait twenty-eight days. If the notice is not given correctly, the court will refuse to order the client to pay the costs and the solicitor will have to start all over again. The notice does not have to state that the solicitor intends to sue. Indeed, the notice is now often given on the original bill itself – which entitles the solicitor to sue twenty-eight days after sending in their bill.

Exceptions to the rule requiring solicitors to give notice are where they have reasonable grounds for believing:
• that clients are about to leave England and Wales, become bankrupt or to compound with their creditors;
• that clients are about to do any act which would tend to prevent or delay the solicitor in obtaining payment.

Contentious matters

The same considerations as for non-contentious matters apply except that clients are not entitled to a remuneration certificate. Their only sanction is to ask the court to tax the bill. However, clients are entitled to require solicitors to deliver an itemized and detailed bill. This request must be made within three months of the bill being delivered and before any proceedings claiming payment are served on the client.

Agreeing a fee

Solicitors may agree with their clients a fee for the services they provide. It must be in writing and signed by both solicitor and client. This will then be binding on both sides and cannot be challenged (e.g. by a remuneration certificate) unless the court decides that the solicitor obtained the agreement unfairly or that the terms are not reasonable. Solicitors may not increase their fee, even if they have to do the work at a loss.

Few solicitors will agree to do work for a fixed fee except in very straightforward and predictable matters (such as making a will), because they have no way of knowing in advance how much time and effort will be involved.

Estimates

Estimates are not binding on solicitors. They should confirm an oral estimate in writing. The Law Society has stated that the final amount of the bill should not vary substantially from the estimate unless the client has been informed of the changed circumstances in writing.

Putting a limit on the costs

The Law Society recommends that clients should be told that they have a right to put a limit on the costs which may be incurred without further reference to them. If a limit is imposed, solicitors should not exceed it, and should also tell the client if the limit is insufficient to cover the work to be done. A decision can then be made whether to continue with the matter.

Interest on unpaid costs

In a non-contentious matter solicitors may charge interest on outstanding accounts (both on the fees and on the disbursements), provided that:
- they have given the required notice to clients (see page 942) of their right to obtain a remuneration certificate, *and*
- a month has passed since the bill was delivered.

Interest is payable at the same rate as interest on judgement debts (15 per cent in 1992).

In contentious matters solicitors may not charge interest unless:
- they have expressly reserved the right when obtaining original instructions, *or*
- the client has later agreed, for a contractual consideration, to pay interest, *or*
- the solicitors have sued for costs and have been awarded interest by the court.

When should a solicitor pay interest to a client?

If a solicitor holds money belonging to a client for longer than the periods set out below:

Number of weeks	Minimum balance
8	£500
4	£1,000
2	£5,000
1	£10,000

he or she must either:
- deposit the money in a separate deposit account and pay the interest to their client, *or*
- pay interest to their client at the rate publicly offered by the solicitor's bank or building society for a small deposit which is held in an account subject to the minimum notice for withdrawals.

Certificates of interest

Any client is entitled to apply to the Solicitors' Complaints Bureau for a certificate stating whether interest ought to have been paid to him/her, and if so how much.

The solicitor receives commission payments: who benefits?

A solicitor is required to account to his/her client for any commission received over £10 unless, after the solicitor has told the client the details of the commission, the client agrees that the solicitor may retain it.

In practice, commissions are something of a windfall and solicitors will often reach agreement with their clients to share it.

HOW TO KEEP COSTS DOWN

- Don't use solicitors as slaves. Every telephone call made to the solicitor adds to the bill. If there is work which can be done by the client (e.g. sorting through documents, taking photographs etc.) a client should consider offering to do it.
- Be sure to deal promptly with queries from solicitors. If they have to write reminders, it simply increases the bill unnecessarily.
- Remember that time is money. If a client takes an hour going over and over the same points with a solicitor, when the job could be done in half an hour, there will be wasted costs. Solicitors aim to strike a balance between giving all the help and support that is needed and not wasting time.
- Be flexible. In many cases, a little give-and-take and common sense solve the most difficult problems. The only people who really benefit from contests over matters of principle are the lawyers.

• Keep legal aid in mind. If you come within the financial limits a solicitor can apply for legal aid at any time. It is not backdated, but can be a great help in future expenses.

Costs in criminal cases

In civil cases the general rule is that the loser pays the winner's costs. In criminal cases this rule cannot be applied rigidly. Often the convicted defendant will not be able to pay because he or she has no money or is going to prison.

The costs of the acquitted defendant

If the accused is acquitted the court can:
• award him/her no costs, so they have to pay their own costs (unless they are legally aided);
• order the prosecutor to pay their costs. If the prosecution is brought by the Crown Prosecution Service, they will have to pay the costs; otherwise the body prosecuting (such as the Department of Social Security, the local authority, Customs and Excise etc.) will have to pay;
• order that costs be paid from central funds (i.e. by the Government).

The court has a considerable discretion in deciding which order to make. Magistrates' courts have tended to be reluctant to make costs orders. However, with legal aid becoming more difficult to obtain, there has been a shift of emphasis in favour of paying costs to an acquitted defendant. Crown courts have always been more willing to award costs.

Whenever there has been an acquittal, the defendant should automatically ask his/her solicitor to apply for costs; the court will never award them unless asked to do so!

If a court orders a prosecutor to pay costs, it is sometimes taken as a sign of disapproval of the conduct of the prosecution. In the crown court the basic rule is that an acquitted defendant should receive his/her costs, from central funds. The court might make a different order if:
• the prosecution acted spitefully or brought the prosecution without reasonable cause. Then the costs would almost certainly be paid by the prosecutor and not out of central funds;
• the defendant brought suspicion on him- or herself by their own conduct, misleading the prosecution into thinking it had a stronger case against him/her than it really did. Here it would be normal for a defendant to pay his/her own costs;
• the defendant was acquitted on a technicality, even though there was ample evidence to convict him/her. Again, the defendant would normally have to pay his/her own costs.

If defendants have legal aid, they can still have their costs paid by the prosecution or out of central funds, but the amount of costs will be no more than could be obtained from legal aid. The amount of the costs recoverable can also include work done from the time of arrest, witness expenses and the accused's own expense, but loss of wages cannot be claimed.

The costs of the successful prosecutor

If the defendant is convicted then the court can order, in respect of the prosecution's costs:

- that no order is made – the prosecution bears its own cost, *or*
- that the costs are paid by the defendant: except in substantial trials (with rich defendants!) this will generally mean the defendant paying a fixed contribution towards the prosecution costs, *or*
- that costs be paid out of central funds.

67 Legal Aid and Help with Legal Costs

> If a solicitor had himself for a client he would not be able to afford his own fees.
>
> Tony Holland, *former president of the Law Society*

Legal fees are costly. Many people are deterred from going to law by fear of what they might have to pay. This chapter covers mainly legal aid, but there are other ways that people may reduce their legal costs. They may join the relevant trade union, the AA, the RAC or any other similar organization which pays legal fees. They may also take out a legal expenses insurance policy.

There are voluntary and charitable organizations which offer free legal advice. Local law centres, run by lawyers, are one example, but these are mainly confined to poor areas in large cities. Then there are Citizens' Advice Bureaux in most towns. The staff are not lawyers but have had some training. They deal with problems of all kinds, a third of which are legal.

There are also two schemes run by solicitors:

● *Accident Legal Advice Service* (ALAS). This is a voluntary scheme run by solicitors to give accident victims a chance to have their cases assessed before they decide to take them further. Solicitors who participate will offer a free first interview. If clients decide to continue, then later work will be charged for in the usual way. This service is available to everyone, regardless of their finances. If legal aid is available, the solicitor will be able to advise on it at the first discussion.

● *£5 fixed fee interview.* A client is given up to half an hour of advice for a fixed fee of £5 including VAT. As it may cost more than £5 to make the necessary book entries, most solicitors have now abandoned the scheme, or simply give the first interview free.

LEGAL AID

The most far-reaching form of help is provided by legal aid itself. It enables the poorest (and most vulnerable) sections of society to be in the same position as a private client. Legal aid currently costs more than £1,000 million a year and the figure is rising.

The legal-aid scheme was introduced shortly after the Second World War. It is a system of Government funding for those who cannot afford to pay for legal advice or representation.

Civil legal aid (including the green-form scheme) is administered by the Legal Aid Board, which has its headquarters in London and area offices around the country. The area offices handle the day-to-day administration of legal-aid applications. They are headed by an area director. There are also area commit- tees (consisting mainly of practising lawyers) which deal with appeals against the refusal to grant legal aid, or appeals against the discharge of legal-aid certificates.

Criminal legal aid is the responsibility of the Lord Chancellor and is generally administered by the criminal courts, which decide whether to grant criminal legal aid.

There are four kinds of legal aid:

1 *The green-form scheme.* This might be considered as 'legal first-aid'. When a client consults a solicitor, this is the first thing which should be considered. If the solicitor does not mention it, the client should raise the matter. A solicitor might not offer legal aid if clients have a prosperous look about them!

If the problem comes within the scope of the scheme (see page 960), the solicitor will carry out a simple means test and cover can be given instantly to those who are eligible, but with a contribution payable by those over the 'free' limit. This varies according to the applicant's income.

The green-form scheme does not allow the solicitor to take any steps in court proceedings. For this, full legal aid or ABWOR (see below) is needed. It does, however, cover preliminary advice, writing letters and help in applying for legal aid for court proceedings.

ABWOR – Assistance by Way of Representation – is a hybrid of the green- form scheme. This pays for a solicitor to prepare a case *and* represent a client in most non-criminal cases in magistrates' courts (such as claims for maintenance and paternity suits) and for some cases in county courts where the court has given authority. It also covers Mental Health Tribunals and prisoners who are facing disciplinary charges. Although ABWOR may be used for proceedings under the Children Act 1989, civil legal aid is more likely to be used. ABWOR may also be used for certain criminal matters. A solicitor will advise on when it is appropriate.

2 *Civil legal aid.* This is generally called 'legal aid' and is available for those involved in civil (i.e. non-criminal) court cases. Civil legal aid usually covers High Court and county court cases, but it can also cover some specialized courts, such as the lands Tribunal, the Commons Commissioners and the Employment Appeal Tribunal. It does not cover ordinary tribunal hearings (such as the industrial tribunals or the social security appeal tribunals). Certain types of cases are also excluded from the legal aid scheme: defamation

(libel and slander), inquests before a coroner and arbitration proceedings. Certain procedural steps are also excluded: county court judgement summonses and other county court proceedings where only the time and method of payment are in dispute.

Applicants can apply for legal aid whether they are suing or being sued. Eligibility will depend upon the merits of the case and a means test. The application is generally prepared by the solicitor. It is sent to one of the area offices of the Legal Aid Board.

3 *Criminal legal aid.* This is for criminal proceedings. Only a defendant can apply, so legal aid cannot cover the costs of bringing a private prosecution. Eligibility will depend upon the requirements of 'justice' and a means test. In practice, it is virtually always granted for crown court cases; it is less likely to be granted in magistrates' courts in cases where liberty and livelihood are not at stake (see page 982).

4 *The duty solicitor scheme.* Duty solicitors are available to attend at police stations and most magistrates' courts to give free legal advice.

Legal advice and assistance (The green-form scheme)

This scheme, which is named after the colour of the application form (first introduced by the Legal Advice and Assistance Act 1972, but now incorporated in the Legal Aid Act 1988), enables people of small or moderate means to obtain help from a solicitor free or at a reduced rate. It normally gives cover for a total of two hours' worth of work (three hours in undefended divorce proceedings). A person who passes a means test will be entitled to advice or assistance from a solicitor in both civil and criminal matters.

Solicitors may refuse to give legal advice and assistance under the scheme, and need not give reasons. The legal-aid office may check that the refusal is justified.

If solicitors agree to give legal advice and assistance, it is they who then decide on the work to be done. For instance, they may:

● give general advice and apply for legal aid;
● write letters;
● negotiate;
● vet or draft a document;
● get a barrister's opinion;
● prepare a written case for a client to present in a court or tribunal (but not themselves take any steps in the proceedings);
● help a DIY litigant (see page 986) who wants advice on how to fill in court forms and how to present a case;
● go to a police station to advise a client who is being questioned by the police (this is more likely to be covered by the duty solicitor scheme).

The scheme covers most English legal problems, such as divorce or maintenance and, in certain circumstances, making a will (see page 960).

How the green-form scheme works

Anyone who wants legal advice can go to a solicitor's office and ask for advice under the scheme (look for the legal-aid logo).

The interview with the solicitor. The solicitor will complete the form before starting to give advice. The form requires the client's name and address, details of finances and answers to a few questions. The solicitor will check that the problem is covered by the scheme (see below).

How the finances are assessed. Eligibility will be determined on the basis of the applicant's 'disposable capital' and *weekly* 'disposable income'.

Disposable capital

All savings (e.g. cash, investments, money in a bank or the National Savings Bank etc.) and anything of substantial value (such as furs and jewellery) come into this category. The following are not included:
● the house the client lives in;
● all household furniture and effects, clothing and any tools used for work;
● the object on which advice is being sought. For instance, if the client is in dispute about who owns an antique table, the value of the table is not included.

Allowances for partner, dependent children and other relatives. The following amounts may be deducted from the total of the savings:

1 dependant	£335
2 dependants	£535
3 dependants	£635
for each extra dependant	£100

'Dependants' are a spouse (or partner) and dependent children.

'Disposable capital' is the amount of savings left after making these deductions. If it is more than £1,000, the client will be above the limit and not eligible for legal advice and assistance under the scheme, however small his or her income.

Assuming the disposable capital is *under* £1,000, the client's 'disposable income' next has to be assessed.

Disposable income

If applicants are on income support or family benefit, they will be automatically eligible for free advice, so long as the disposable capital is less than £935.

Disposable income is the client's weekly income from all sources and their spouse's or partner's income. 'Partners' are a man and a woman living together in the same household as husband and wife. The income of the spouse or partner is not counted if there is a 'conflict of interest' (e.g. he wants a divorce from her). The following are deducted:

• income tax and national insurance contributions (these are usually taken from the last pay slip);

• £40.69 for the client's partner, whether or not there is a conflict of interest, but if the client is separated or divorced and paying maintenance, the weekly maintenance paid should instead be deducted;

• allowances for dependent children:

under 11	£18.19
between 11 and 15	£26.75
between 16 and 17	£31.94
18 and over	£42.00

The disposable income is what is left after making these deductions.

Disposable income		Contribution
over	*but not more than*	
£75	£80	£5
£80	£86	£12
£86	£92	£19
£92	£98	£25
£98	£104	£32
£104	£110	£38
£110	£116	£45
£116	£122	£51
£122	£128	£58
£128	£134	£64
£134	£140	£70
£140	£145	£75

Note: if disposable income is more than £145, legal advice will not be available under the scheme.

Contributions (*1992 figures*)

If the disposable income is £75 or less, then help under the green-form scheme will be free. Otherwise a contribution will be needed as above.

Solicitors will expect to be paid the contribution at once, but if this is not possible then they have a discretion to accept payment later by instalments. Once the formalities are dealt with, solicitors can immediately start work. If at the end of the case the contribution is more than the solicitor's bill, he or she will return the balance to the client. While the green form is in force solicitors are not allowed to charge clients separately for work done on the case. They must also charge at legal-aid rates of pay.

Children

Children may also apply. In most cases children under sixteen need their parent or guardian to apply on their behalf. If children are over sixteen they will be treated as adults and may sign their own application. If solicitors are asked by children under sixteen to advise them under the green-form scheme they must first obtain permission from the legal-aid authority, unless the children are being held at a police station.

Is the problem covered by the green-form scheme?

Legal advice and assistance is available in England and Wales and applies only to questions of English law (though it will cover help in applying for legal aid in some European countries; see page 985). It does not cover the law of Scotland, nor that of any other country. The scheme does not permit a solicitor to start court proceedings (subject to certain exceptions; see below). However, the scheme does cover advice on how to start and run a court case. Special rules apply to certain types of work:

Conveyancing. This is excluded from the scheme except where the work relates to a rental purchase agreement or conditional sale agreement for the sale of land *and* conveyancing services are necessary (because of the agreement or a court order).

Wills. These are excluded apart from the following cases:
● the applicant is over seventy;
● the applicant (or the applicant's children) is blind, deaf or dumb or suffers from a serious physical or mental handicap;
● the applicant and his/her wife are separated and he or she wants to appoint someone other than their spouse to be guardians of the children.

Probates and estates. Advice and assistance are permissible to enable a client to make a personal application, but the client is responsible for paying the probate fees.

Undefended divorce and matrimonial cases. Solicitors who do legally aided work on straightforward, undefended divorce cases will do so under the cover of the green-form scheme. This is because civil legal aid is not available for undefended divorces (see page 53). To compensate for this, green-form cover in such cases is initially for three hours' worth of work instead of the usual two hours.

As the green-form scheme does not allow solicitors to start divorce proceedings, they cannot use the scheme to cover their fees in handling the divorce for their client. All they can do is to tell the client how to do his or her own divorce. The solicitor will fill in the forms, but the client will sign them. The solicitor will advise the client as to the steps which need to be taken, but throughout the proceedings the client is technically handling the case him- or herself.

Advice and assistance in court. Normally the scheme does not cover the solicitor in court. Following the case McKenzie v. McKenzie (1970) (see page 990), the green form can usually be extended to cover a solicitor informally advising a client in court without actually representing him/her. The Legal Aid Board is unlikely to allow this if the client would be better served by a full legal-aid certificate or if the case is not complicated enough for the client to need legal help of this kind.

Increasing the number of hours of cover

As soon as solicitors realize that the work will exceed the initial limit, they may contact the legal-aid area office to request an increased maximum amount which they will need to charge. The extension will be granted if the area office agrees that it is reasonable for the advice and assistance to be given *and* that the estimated costs to be incurred in giving them are reasonable.

Illustration. *Tom and Geraldine have had a turbulent marriage. Geraldine consults a solicitor under the green-form scheme. It takes Geraldine nearly two hours to tell the story of the marriage, and it will take the solicitor much longer to help finalize the forms. It is obvious that the solicitor will be undertaking much more than three hours of work for Geraldine. The solicitor applies to the legal-aid area office for an 'extension to the equivalent of five hours' worth of cover'. This extension is granted. His fee will be paid by the office and the client will have to pay no more than the original contribution.*

When the case is over: the total cost of advice

When a case is over and solicitors have finished their work, they will calculate their fees. If the fee is less than the amount of the contribution paid by the client, the solicitor will refund the balance to the client. Accordingly, the client will have paid the full cost of the legal advice him- or herself. For instance, if the contribution paid is £45 and the solicitor's fee is £30, the solicitor will refund £15.

It is more usual that the contribution is less than the solicitor's bill. Here the solicitor must take the shortfall from any money or property which he or she has recovered or successfully defended for his/her client. The solicitor is said to exercise a *statutory charge* over the money or property, in the same way that the Legal Aid Fund has a statutory charge over any money or property recovered in a civil legal-aid case (see page 975).

Illustration. *Mrs Smith consulted a solicitor over the cost of the repairs to a coat which was damaged by dry-cleaners. Her contribution under the green-form scheme was nil as she was on income support. The solicitor wrote to the dry-cleaners and persuaded them to settle Mrs Smith's claim for £22. The solicitor's fee is £15. He must deduct the £15 from the £22 and so Mrs Smith receives only £7.*

The effect of the statutory charge is that it is rarely worth using the green-form scheme for claims of small value. If such a claim is successful, the legal fees are likely to take away from the client most, if not all, of the money recovered. It is thus of great importance that the client is aware of the implications of the statutory charge before he or she considers pursuing a claim.

Illustration. *Mrs Poole was owed £25 by Burt for a sofa which he had agreed to buy. He refused to pay for it. She saw a solicitor under the green-form scheme and paid a contribution of £5. The solicitor managed to persuade Burt to pay, but only after lengthy correspondence. The solicitor's fee was £35. His fee was paid, first with the £5 contribution, secondly with the £25 reclaimed and thirdly with the balance of £10 from the Legal Aid Fund. Mrs Poole was left with nothing.*

If no money or property is recovered, then there can be no statutory charge. The solicitor will be paid the shortfall by the legal-aid area office. In these cases the client will in total pay no more than the amount of his/her original contribution.

Items which are exempt from the statutory charge

The duty a solicitor has to claim his/her costs from the client's settlement money can cause the client great ill-feeling towards the legal system. To ease the hardship which can be caused, some things are exempt from the statutory charge. For example, solicitors cannot take their fee from the following:
● maintenance payments;
● any property which is the client's main or only home, or any household furniture or tools of the trade;
● the first £2,500 in any family proceedings (e.g. if a husband agrees to give a lump sum to his wife to cover her share of the family home);
● most welfare benefits;
● one-half of any redundancy payment made.

Illustration. *A wife and her two children have been abandoned by her husband. Her solicitor advises her under the green-form scheme and as a result she successfully claims income support and obtains a maintenance order against her husband from the magistrates' court. Her total income as a result is £65 per week. The solicitor's fee is £50. The fee will not come out of her income support or her maintenance as both are exempt from the statutory charge. The solicitor's fee is paid in full by the legal-aid area office.*

Waiving the statutory charge

In some circumstances the legal-aid area office also has the power to authorize a solicitor not to enforce the statutory charge. The power will be exercised in any case in which it 'would cause grave hardship or distress to the client to enforce it' or in cases where there 'would be unreasonable difficulty in enforcement because of the nature of the property' (e.g. in the case of a valuable pet dog that was recovered for the client, it was agreed that it would be unreasonable to expect the dog to be sold to pay for the legal costs!). On the whole, luxury items are unlikely to be exempt from the charge. A person who receives advice under the green-form scheme and who thinks that they come within these exceptions should ask the solicitor not to apply the statutory charge. The solicitor will then apply to the legal-aid area office for permission to waive the statutory charge.

Assistance by way of representation (ABWOR)

The 1979 Legal Aid Act increased the scope of the green-form scheme to cover *representation* in court. This development of the green-form scheme became known as 'assistance by way of representation' or ABWOR. Originally the representation applied only to domestic proceedings in magistrates' courts, but in 1982 the scheme's cover was extended to include preparing a client's case and representing a client in most civil cases in magistrates' courts. These cases include separation, maintenance and defended adoption proceedings. Some criminal proceedings are also covered by ABWOR, as are some county court proceedings. It is also available to those who appear before mental health tribunals and to prisoners facing disciplinary charges in front of 'boards of visitors' (see Chapter 54). Proceedings under the Children Act 1989 may be covered by ABWOR but as civil legal aid (see below) is also available, this is more likely to be used.

How to apply for ABWOR

Solicitors operating the green-form scheme will also deal with ABWOR. The financial limits are the same as for the green-form scheme, except that the disposable capital limit is £3,000 (not £1,000). The statutory charge will also apply in the same way as it does under the green-form scheme.

When applying for ABWOR, the solicitor will fill in the green form, and also the form ABWOR 1, which will be sent to the legal-aid area office. The area office has a discretion as to whether to grant ABWOR, but if an application is refused, the applicant can appeal to the area committee.

The courts themselves can grant ABWOR in cases of urgency in the magistrates' and county courts. The right to ABWOR is automatic in the case of duty-solicitor representation and where the police are applying for extended detention in custody.

A person who is granted ABWOR subject to contributions, and who already has or is at the same time applying for legal advice and assistance under the green-form scheme, needs to pay only one contribution for both schemes.

Illustration. Hilda wants to separate from her husband. She goes to a solicitor, who finds from her disposable income and capital that Hilda is eligible for advice under the green-form scheme, although she has to pay a £12 contribution. As Hilda feels she will need to be represented in court she also applies for ABWOR. The solicitor works out that she is entitled to ABWOR but also subject to a £12 contribution. However, as Hilda is already paying towards the green-form scheme, she does not have to give a further sum towards ABWOR. The £12 she pays will cover both schemes.

Merits test

ABWOR will be refused if applicants cannot establish that they have reasonable grounds for taking, defending or being a party to court proceedings.

Withdrawal of ABWOR

Unlike green-form cover, ABWOR may be withdrawn. For instance, this will happen if the client:

- no longer has reasonable grounds for taking, defending or being a party to court proceedings;
- has had a reconciliation with his/her opponent (in domestic proceedings);
- refuses to accept advice not to proceed.

Legal Aid in Civil Cases

If a client is likely to be involved in civil court proceedings and ABWOR is not appropriate, then civil legal aid will be applied for.

The overall purpose of the civil legal-aid scheme (called simply legal aid) is to enable people to sue in courts, and to defend claims made against them, when they could not otherwise afford to do so. The aim is that the person on legal aid should be in the same position as the person of 'adequate means' (but see page 966). This scheme is separate from the green-form scheme and ABWOR. A person who has cover under either the green-form scheme or ABWOR, or both, may also be eligible for legal aid.

Even if legal aid is available, applicants may have to pay a contribution towards their costs. Often this contribution is so substantial that it deters people from taking up their offers of legal aid.

The roots of the present legal-aid system are buried in the inter-war period. At that time there were only two sources of legal assistance in civil cases. First, there were the 'poor man's lawyer' advice centres, where solicitors would voluntarily dispense free advice at evening meetings. Secondly, there was the 'poor person's procedure', which was a primitive form of legal aid, subject to a stringent means test. More important, it was only available for High Court actions, and therefore excluded the vast majority of civil claims, which were (and still are) heard in the magistrates' courts and county courts.

The reform of the system was brought about by the Second World War. During the war, the three Armed Services set up legal-aid schemes for their officers and men. Most of the cases involved divorce, and to ease the burden the Law Society set up a Services Divorce Department, which took over this work. Soon a Civil Section was established at the Law Society to handle cases for people who were not in the services and, by the end of the war, the Law Society found itself with a substantial legal practice. It had changed from being the solicitors' professional body into a state-financed body of practising solicitors.

Clearly, changes were needed, and the Rushcliffe Committee was appointed to review the position. It was reported in 1945, and set out the recommendations which became the basis of the Legal Aid and Advice Act 1949. Rushcliffe proposed that:
● legal aid should be available in all courts and in such a manner as will enable persons in need to have access to the professional help they require;
● this provision should not be limited to those who are normally classed as poor, but should include a wider income group;
● those who cannot afford to pay anything for legal aid should receive this free of cost;
● there should be a scale of contributions for those who can pay something towards costs;
● the cost of the scheme should be borne by the state, but the scheme should not be administered either as a department of state or by local authorities.

These are the fundamental principles of the present-day legal aid scheme.

Applying for legal aid

Anyone who wants to apply for legal aid should fill in the relevant forms. There are different application forms for different types of cases. Although it is possible to apply for legal aid without consulting a solicitor, it is not generally feasible to do so as it is a requirement that a solicitor has to sign all applications, and supply information about the case to the Legal Aid Board (e.g. an assessment of the chances of success and an estimate of what the costs will be). For how to find a solicitor see page 923.

Solicitors will provide the forms and give help in completing them. They will know best how the questions should be answered, and the sort of information that should be attached in support of the application. Unless all the relevant facts are marshalled in support, the application might be rejected because the case looks weaker than it is. For instance, in an accident case the applicant may not have obtained a statement from the witness who can confirm the identity of the person at fault.

In addition to the application, a form giving financial details will have to be filled in, along with confirmation of wages from employers.

The cost of employing a solicitor to help complete the form will not be covered by legal aid because a certificate does not cover work done before it was issued. Clients will have to:

• pay the solicitor themselves, at the normal rate charged by a solicitor; however they may be able to find a solicitor who operates the '£5 for half an hour' scheme (see page 955), *or*

• obtain legal advice and assistance under the green-form scheme. This will cover some, if not all, of the solicitor's fee, but only if the applicant comes within the strict financial limits of the scheme (see page 958).

Often solicitors will not charge for helping to complete a legal-aid application. They know that if legal aid is granted they will act for the client and perhaps earn other fees, which will be paid.

The completed application forms are sent to the nearest area office of the Legal Aid Board. Apart from any solicitors' fees, it costs nothing to apply for legal aid.

There are two stages to the decision on whether to grant legal aid:

• *Merits assessment.* The application is considered by officers at the Legal Aid Board.

• *Financial assessment.* This is carried out by the Department of Social Security, who may write direct to the client if they need further information.

There are, therefore, two hurdles to surmount before legal aid can be granted. However, there are some cases involving children where there is no merits test and others where there is no means test (see page 969).

Hurdle No. 1: the merits of the case

In deciding on the merits of a case the Legal Aid Board applies two tests. If either fails, legal aid will not be granted.

1 *Does the client have reasonable grounds?* The area office must be satisfied that there is a case which should be put before a court for a decision. The office has to assume that the facts are as stated by the applicant; it is in no position to be a judge. It has to be shown that there are reasonable prospects of success, assuming the facts are proved.

The area office also tries to decide what a private, non-legal-aided client would be advised to do, by asking the question: 'What advice would I give to the applicant if he or she were a private client possessed of sufficient means to pay their costs?' If a private client would be advised to press on with the claim, then legal aid should be granted. If he or she would be advised to take no further steps, then legal aid should be refused.

2 *In the circumstances is it reasonable to grant legal aid?* Legal aid is likely to be refused if:

• the applicant has an illegal motive for applying;

- the proceedings are not likely to be cost-effective;
- the only matter at stake is loss of stature, dignity or reputation;
- the applicant can get legal help elsewhere (e.g. from a trade union);
- a solicitor should not be employed in the case (e.g. where the case simply involves mathematical calculations, such as mortgage arrears);
- the proceedings should be taken in some other court where the costs are lower;
- the applicant is a defendant, and has no means to satisfy a judgement made against him/her;
- the applicant would get no personal benefit from the outcome of the proceedings.

In some cases where ABWOR is available, the applicant will be directed to apply for it instead.

Limited certificates. If the area office of the Legal Aid Board has doubts as to the merits of a case, it may grant a 'Limited certificate', which allows certain steps to be taken. No further work can be carried out until the area office has authorized it. This gives the area office the chance of reviewing the case at a later date when more evidence has been collected. For instance, if a case does not look very strong, a certificate may be issued limited 'to investigating the case and obtaining counsel's opinion'. This would allow the solicitor to investigate the evidence and interview witnesses. The papers would then go to a barrister, who would give a written opinion on the prospects of success. Once that was done, the papers would go back to the area office and it would decide – largely on the basis of the barrister's opinion – whether the legal-aid certificate should be extended to cover court proceedings.

Hurdle No. 2: financial eligibility

Applicants will also have to show that they come within the current means-test limits.

As with the green-form scheme, financial eligibility will be worked out from the applicant's disposable income and disposable capital, but the limits are more generous to applicants.

Disposable income. If applicants are receiving income support they will automatically be financially eligible.

Unlike the green-form and ABWOR schemes, disposable income for legal aid is calculated on the basis of the applicant's likely income during the next twelve months and not from his/her weekly earnings. The finances of both husband and wife (or partners) are added together (see below). Income includes maintenance payments received and most welfare benefits. The following will be deducted from the gross income:

- income tax;
- national insurance contributions;
- work expenses (usually fares);

- housing costs, including
  - rent or mortgage payments,
  - water rates,
  - an allowance of £4.52 weekly for repairs to house,
  - service charges and ground rent where appropriate;
- community charge;
- trade union membership and pension contributions;
- maintenance payments;
- child care expenses incurred because of work;
- allowances for dependants
  - £40.69 for a partner,
  - £18.19 for each child under 11,
  - £26.25 for each child aged 11–15,
  - £31.94 for each child aged 16–17,
  - £42.00 for each child or dependant aged 18 or over.

The final, net figure is called the 'disposable income' (see page 973 for a specimen calculation showing how these rules work). If the disposable income is (1992 figures) more than £6,800 (or £7,500 where the application is for a case involving a claim for personal injury), then the applicant is not eligible for legal aid. If it is £3,060 or less, the applicant is not required to make a contribution out of income. Between the two limits, the applicant will be offered legal aid but will be expected to pay a contribution from income of one-quarter of the difference between the top figure (either £7,500 or £6,800) and £3,060.

Disposable capital. This is the value of all the applicant's and his/her partner's possessions (e.g. cash, bank accounts, National Savings, shares, antiques and jewellery – but not wedding or engagement rings – boats, caravan etc. – but not usually the car – the sum that can be borrowed on security of an existing life policy).

The following are ignored: the house, household furniture, personal clothes, tools used for work.

The net figure is called the 'disposable capital'.

If the disposable capital is (1991 figures) over £6,750 (£8,560 in personal injury cases), the applicant is unlikely to be eligible for legal aid, although there is a discretion. If it is £3,000 or less then he or she will not be required to make a payment from capital. If the disposable capital is between those two figures, then he or she will be offered legal aid but will be expected to make a contribution towards costs (this will be the excess over £3,000).

Retired people. Special provisions apply to men over sixty-five and women over sixty if their disposable income is less than £3,060 (excluding income earned from capital). For them certain savings are disregarded, even though the total may be over the normal capital limit. The amounts disregarded are as follows:

Thus, if a man aged sixty-six has a disposable annual income of £1,100 (apart

Annual disposable income (excluding net income from capital)	Amount of capital disregarded
Up to £350	£35,000
£351–£800	£30,000
£801–£1,200	£25,000
£1,201–£1,600	£20,000
£1,601–£2,050	£15,000
£2,051–£2,450	£10,000
£2,451 + *above*	£5,000

from income from savings), he may have disposable capital of up to £28,000 (i.e. £25,000 + £3,000) and still have free legal aid.

Note that regulations forbid the disposal of resources with the intention of becoming eligible for legal aid.

The husband's, wife's or co-habitee's income and capital. If the applicant is married, or living in the same household with a partner and as man and wife, then the capital and income of the applicant's partner will be taken into account. Thus a housewife who does not work will have her financial eligibility assessed on the basis of her husband's income and their joint capital. This is not the case if the couple have separated and are living apart, or if the applicant's partner has a contrary interest in the dispute for which the application for legal aid is being made. So if a wife wants legal aid to divorce her husband, her financial eligibility will be based solely on her own income and capital. Her husband's finances will be ignored, since the couple are in dispute. Likewise, if a woman who has lived with a man decides to leave him, and wants legal aid to start custody proceedings over their child, only her own income and capital will be considered for her application. The effect of this is that most women involved in family disputes get free legal aid without having to pay any contribution.

Children. If legal aid is required for a child, only the child's finances are considered, not the parents' (as used to be the case). Most children are now financially eligible for legal aid, irrespective of their parents' means.

Children Act cases. Legal aid is available for all proceedings under the Children Act 1989. It is available without a means test or a merits test (i.e it is completely free, and does not depend on the strength of the case) to parents, children and others with parental responsibility in the following applications:

- care and supervision orders;
- child assessment orders;
- emergency protection orders;
- duration and discharge of emergency protection orders.

There are also other circumstances where a means test only is applied, or where legal aid is available to a child only on a non-means test and non-merits test basis.

Examples of Gross Weekly Incomes which Qualify for Civil Legal Aid

Rented home	for free civil legal aid	for civil legal aid with a contribution
Single person	£110.46	£219.42
Lone parent with two children aged 4 and 12	£154.67	£263.17
Couple	£168.00	£276.96
Couple with two children aged 4 and 12	£227.25	£336.23
Owner-occupied home		
Single person	£202.71	£311.69
Lone parent with two children 4 and 12	£246.46	£355.42
Couple	£260.23	£369.19
Couple with two children aged 4 and 12	£319.52	£427.77

When the case involves property or money. When calculating the disposable income and disposable capital, the DSS disregard the value of anything that is 'the subject-matter of the proceedings'. For instance, if the applicant wants legal aid to sue a marina over a defective boat which he bought from them, then the value of the boat will not be taken into account when working out his disposable capital.

It is not always easy to decide whether something is the subject matter of the proceedings. The test for deciding is to ask the question: 'Is it in jeopardy as a result of the case?' If it is, then it should be ignored when assessing financial eligibility. Maintenance paid to a spouse under a court order is, however, taken into account, even when the legal-aid application relates to fresh maintenance proceedings.

Illustration. *Mrs Jenkins receives £60 per week maintenance from her ex-husband. However, Mr Jenkins is not as well off as he was so he applies for the maintenance order to be varied (i.e. he wants the weekly payment to be reduced). Mrs Jenkins applies for legal aid to defend the case. When working out her disposable income, the £60 per week maintenance will be taken into account, even though the maintenance payment is put in jeopardy by the court proceedings.*

Illustration. *A husband and wife agree to divorce. Since it is an undefended divorce, only advice and assistance under the green-form scheme is available and not legal aid (see page 957). However, they cannot agree on how to divide up the family property, including the properties they own, their savings in the building society and cash in the bank. Accordingly,*

the wife applies for legal aid so that she can ask the court to make a property order dividing the family assets between the two of them. When working out the wife's financial eligibility, the DSS assessment officer will:
* *ignore the husband's income, since 'they have a contrary interest', and*
* *ignore the value of all the family property (e.g. houses, savings, cash, furniture) which is 'the subject matter of the dispute.'*

Unless the wife has income or capital of her own, she will almost certainly be eligible for free legal aid. But she may in the end have to pay towards her legal costs if the statutory charge applies (see below).

Contributions. If applicants are financially eligible, they will pay a 'contribution' if their disposable income exceeds £3,060 and/or if their capital exceeds £3,000 (1992 figures).

The size of the contribution will depend upon the amount by which these figures are exceeded. Usually the contribution is:
* disposable income – a quarter of the excess over £3,060,
* disposable capital – all the excess over £3,000 (it is likely to be less only if the applicant's solicitor can certify that the costs will in no circumstances exceed a certain figure – something the solicitor is unlikely to be able to do).

The illustration on page 973 shows how the contribution is worked out in a typical case.

If legal aid is approved, the applicant will be sent an offer of legal aid, setting out the amount of his/her contribution. It will also state how the contribution is to be paid. Generally, contributions based on disposable capital must be paid in a lump sum straight away, but contributions based on income are normally paid in twelve monthly instalments.

There is no right of appeal against the amount of contributions, but the area office will usually check the figures if asked.

The amount of contribution will not necessarily be the maximum amount that applicants will have to pay in legal costs, although often it will be. If they lose the case they may have to pay something towards the winner's legal costs. The maximum they could be ordered to pay will be the same as the maximum amount payable towards their own costs.

If they win they will usually receive back their contribution, unless the loser does not pay all the legal costs. For instance, suppose the contribution is £50 and the costs £100, but the loser pays only £75 towards the costs: the applicant will have £25 returned. If the loser paid nothing towards the costs, the applicant will lose the £50 contribution and also £50 of the damages.

Sometimes the contribution will exceed the estimated costs of the case. For instance, the contribution may be £1,000, and yet the area office estimates that the legal costs will not be more than £750. At first glance, there might seem no point in accepting the offer of legal aid, but there are still advantages in obtaining it:

● If the case is appealed to the higher courts, and even to the House of Lords, the maximum contribution will still be only £1,000. By accepting legal aid – even with a large contribution – the applicant has some safeguard against escalating legal costs.

● By being on legal aid the applicant's risk of liability to pay his/her opponent's costs if he or she loses is, in practice, drastically reduced.

● The existence of a legal-aid certificate shows the other side that the applicant has the resources to take the case to court if necessary, and that he or she will not have to give up because he or she is financially exhausted.

Emergency legal aid

Normally, it takes two months or more for a legal-aid application to be processed. But not all legal claims can wait that long. For instance, if a tenant is illegally evicted by his landlord he needs an injunction immediately, to order the landlord to allow him back into his home. For cases of this sort, legal aid can be granted without delay, even over the telephone.

When there is an emergency, the applicant should first find a solicitor who is prepared to act for him/her and to apply for an injunction as soon as legal aid is granted. After the solicitor has taken note of the facts of the case, and checked the client's financial eligibility, he or she will telephone the Legal Aid Board and ask for legal aid. If legal aid is granted in this way, a written application will still have to be sent to the appropriate area office. Once an emergency certificate is granted, the solicitor can begin to act for the client and take the steps necessary to obtain an injunction immediately.

This emergency procedure is mainly used on behalf of illegally evicted tenants and women who have been beaten up by their husbands or lovers.

The emergency certificate is no substitute for legal aid and it will normally cover only taking the limited steps necessary to deal with the emergency. If further action is needed, a normal legal-aid certificate must be obtained.

The rules for financial eligibility are the same as for a civil legal aid certificate. If it is later discovered that applicants were not eligible for legal aid, they may have to pay the legal costs themselves.

Illustration. *Kevin is married, with a boy of eleven and a girl of eight. He also supports his mother-in-law. His gross salary is £18,000. His payments towards his mortgage, community charge, national insurance and tax add up to £10,544. He has work expenses of £10 per week. He has £2,300 in a building society and his wife has shares worth £2,800. After deducting the £10,544, a £6,214 allowance for his dependants (£1,287 for the eleven-year-old, £870 for the eight-year-old, £2,030 for his mother-in-law and £2,037 for his wife) and the £520 work expenses, he is left with a disposable income of £722. As this is under £2,860, he will not have to make a contribution from his income. As his disposable capital (which includes his wife's savings) is £5,100, he will be liable to pay up to all of the amount by which this figure exceeds £3,000 – that is, up to £2,100.*

Example	
Married man with 2 children aged 11 and 8	

Income	
Earnings	£18,000
Child benefit	£907.40
	£18,907.40
Wife	£2,122
Child aged 11	£1,395
Child aged 8	£948
Allowances for mortgage, community charge, national insurance contributions and tax say	£10,103.94
	£14,568.94
Disposable income	£4,338.46
Less	£3,060
	£1,278 ÷ 4
Contribution	= £319.50

Note: this example also applies to cohabitees.

When legal aid is granted

All legal-aid certificates have a reference number unique to the case. For example 11 01 92 12345 E. The reference has a number of parts to it:

11   the number of the legal-aid office (Cambridge, in this example).
01   the type of certificate (a full certificate).
92   the year of issue.
12345 E   the number of the case; if a client has more than one legal-aid certificate, they will all carry different numbers, though the area office will cross-reference them.

The certificate reference should be quoted in all correspondence with the legal-aid office.

If contributions are to be paid, clients will have the option to accept or decline the offer of legal aid. If they turn it down, legal aid will be cancelled. If they accept, they must pay the first instalment to the legal-aid accounts office in London (not to their solicitor). That will trigger the issuing of the legal-aid certificate to the applicant and their solicitor. While a legal-aid certificate is in force solicitors are not permitted to ask their clients for any payment for work done on the case (though they may do so if they are doing something else for the client, such as making a will).

If no contribution is required, the legal-aid certificate will be sent to the client and solicitor as soon as approval is given.

Legally aided clients can expect much the same service from the solicitor as if they were private clients, paying for themselves. The drawback is that as solicitors' rates of pay for doing legally aided work are lower than for private work, not many solicitors do legal-aid work. There is also a complication: apart from having a duty to help their clients, solicitors will also have a duty to avoid wasting the public money in the Legal Aid Fund. Occasionally, the solicitor's two duties clash and he or she will then have to put their duty to the Legal Aid Fund above their duty to the client.

Illustration. A client is suing his employer over an accident at work. Legal aid is granted, but the solicitor then interviews the witnesses and discovers that the employer was not at fault as the accident was the client's own fault; the case is hopeless. He must then tell the legal-aid area office what the witnesses say, even though the probable result will be that his client's legal-aid certificate will be withdrawn, to avoid wasting any more money on the case.

The same applies if the client refuses to accept a reasonable offer in settlement. The extra cost of taking the case to trial might not justify refusing the offer and the solicitor must put his/her duty to the Legal Aid Fund above that to the client.

Nevertheless, in some ways legally aided clients are in a better position than privately paying ones, since the latter have to pay their way (both legal fees and disbursements, such as experts' fees) as the case progresses while the former do not. Private clients risk having to pay their own costs and their opponent's costs if they lose. A legal-aid client has considerable protection on costs.

The duties of a client who has a legal-aid certificate

Legal aid is not an unrestricted licence to run up legal fees. The grant and acceptance of legal aid carries responsibilities on the part of the client:
• all contributions must be paid, even if clients decide to abandon the case after a few months – this includes any increased contributions if clients' finances change during the currency of the certificate;
• the legal-aid area office must be notified immediately of any change in financial or personal circumstances (e.g. if a client is no longer liable to support his children, he may have a bigger contribution to pay towards the cost of legal aid);
• changes of address should be notified to the area office and to the solicitor;
• legal aid may be withdrawn if clients do not cooperate with the area office or their solicitor.

When the case is over: the total cost of being on legal aid

Not until the end of the case do legally aided clients know exactly how much they will have to pay. They will probably have already paid a 'contribution', but whether they have to pay any more will depend upon whether they win or lose the case and on the amount of costs paid by their opponent.

Winning a case on legal aid

The general rule is that the winner's legal costs are paid by the loser. If the legally aided client wins his/her case he or she will probably find that the judge orders the other party (the loser) to pay all their costs.

Any damages awarded will be paid to the solicitor and not to the client. The solicitor will then pass the money on to the Legal Aid Board and it will not be paid out to the client until all the legal fees have been paid. But if the solicitors will limit their costs to a maximum figure, the Legal Aid Board may allow part of the damages to be released to the client.

The solicitor will work out the costs. Assuming these costs are approved either by the Legal Aid Board or by the court, this is the amount he or she will receive from the Legal Aid Board for acting for the client. The loser will have to pay the solicitor's costs, but there is bound to be a gap between what the court decides the loser should pay and the amount allowed to the winner's solicitor. The loser will pay the costs to the solicitor, who will then pass them on to the Legal Aid Board. The winner's solicitor will be paid in full, but if there is a shortfall it will come from:

1 *The client's contribution.* If the contribution was £100 and the shortfall £30, the client would receive a refund of £70. If the client paid no contribution, or the contribution is insufficient to pay the shortfall, the balance will be taken from:
2 *The damages.* The damages and other proceeds of the case will have been paid by the solicitor to the legal-aid office. It will take any shortfall on costs from this money. The office is said to have a *statutory charge* over the proceeds and it can use this statutory charge to claim a share of the proceeds to pay any unpaid costs.

Illustration. *Suppose the shortfall between the costs due to the solicitor and the costs paid by the loser is £50. The client has paid a £30 contribution, and won £1,000 damages. The shortfall of £50 is met, first, by using the £30 contribution and, secondly, by using the damages. The client thus loses his contribution and receives only £980 damages.*

But note that where clients have a 'financial interest' in their solicitor's fees (e.g. because they will lose out financially if there is a shortfall and the statutory charge is exercised), the solicitor *must* before applying to the Legal Aid Board or the court for approval of his/her fees:
● supply a copy of the bill to the client, *and*
● inform the client of the extent of his/her financial interest and of his/her right to make his/her views known on the bill.

If the loser does not pay. This can be because he or she:
● is ordered to pay the costs but doesn't (e.g. has not got the money to do so, goes bankrupt or disappears), *or*
● is not ordered to pay costs. Although the loser is usually ordered to pay the costs, there are some exceptions (e.g. in matrimonial cases).

When this happens, the shortfall between what the Legal Aid Board receives and the amount they pay the solicitor for his/her costs can be considerable. As always, the shortfall will be met, first, from the client's contribution and, secondly, from the damages and proceeds of the case. The end result can even be that the winner loses all the damages.

Illustration. *Mr Green was granted legal aid to sue Shady Carsales over a defective car which he bought from them. His contribution was £75. Mr Green wins the case, is awarded £600 damages and Shady Carsales are ordered to pay £350 of the damages but then go bankrupt. The Legal Aid Board will pay the solicitors their £400, and recover that money from the contribution (£75) and the damages (£350). Mr Green is then left with £25 (i.e. £50 less than if he hadn't bothered).*

It is because the damages might have to go towards the legal costs that they are paid by the solicitor to the Legal Aid Board. The Legal Aid Board will release the money to the client only when it is clear that there will not be a shortfall. This will usually be some time after the hearing. Clients may well feel aggrieved that, having won their case, they have to wait several months before damages are paid to them.

The statutory charge – the right to take the legal costs out of the damages – can cause great hardship, as well as great bitterness. To a limited extent the hardship is mitigated since some damages and awards (such as maintenance payments) are exempt (see below). However, the Legal Aid Board has no power to waive the statutory charge, however much hardship it causes. All it can do is to agree to postpone the statutory charge.

Illustration. *Mr and Mrs Brown have divorced. The court has ordered that the family house should be sold so that Mrs Brown can use her share of the proceeds to buy a flat in which to live with the children. No order for costs was made, so the proceeds of sale are liable to be used to pay Mr Brown's solicitor's costs, although the first £2,500 of the marital settlement is exempt (see below). However, to do this would defeat the purpose of the court order. The Legal Aid Board agrees that Mrs Brown can buy the flat, and the Legal Aid Board will then have a charge on the flat. If the flat is sold, the debt must be paid off with interest. In effect, Mrs Brown is able to postpone paying the legal costs.*

The statutory charge in matrimonial cases

It is in matrimonial cases (i.e. when husband and wife go to court to sort out disputes over children and property) that the statutory charge causes the greatest problems. The first difficulty is that the wife will normally have been granted free legal aid (i.e. legal aid without having to make any contribution towards the costs). This is because the husband's income is ignored, and because the value of the family assets is also ignored (see page 968). The wife may therefore be misled into thinking that she will never have to pay anything towards the legal costs (after all, she has free legal aid!). Solicitors are now under an obligation to advise on the statutory charge.

In matrimonial cases the court often decides that each side (i.e. husband and wife) should pay their own legal costs. If a wife (or husband) is legally aided, then the 'property preserved or recovered' (i.e. the share in the family home, any lump sum settlement etc.) will be subject to the statutory charge – and be liable to be used towards paying the legal-aid costs. Thus the legal aid will not be free; it might have been free initially, but the wife (or husband) will have to pay for that legal aid if she (or he) receives any of the family assets as a result of the court case. For instance:

In 1972 Mrs Hanlon started divorce proceedings. The case was not finished until 1977, by which time it had been to the Court of Appeal. Mrs Hanlon was on legal aid but so was her husband and thus he was not ordered to pay her costs – amounting to some £8,000. In the course of the divorce hearing, the court had ordered that the matrimonial home (worth some £10,000) be transferred to Mrs Hanlon. The Legal Aid Board claimed that the £8,000 should be paid by Mrs Hanlon from the proceeds of the litigation. Accordingly, a charge was registered against the house. Mrs Hanlon contested the Legal Aid Board's right to do this. Held: The statutory charge applied. Only the first £2,500 was exempt (see below) and the balance could be used to meet the legal fees. Thus, after five years' litigation, Mrs Hanlon had virtually nothing to show for it. Hanlon v. Hanlon *(1980)*

If the house is to be sold straightaway, then the Legal Aid Board will demand immediate repayment of the legal costs. But if the house is not to be sold (usually because it is to be transferred into the sole name of the wife), then the Legal Aid Board will not insist that the house is sold. Instead, it will register a mortgage against the house and wait until it is eventually sold, but simple interest will be charged on the amount outstanding at a rate of 12 per cent per annum (reduced to 10.5 per cent for interest accruing after January 1992).

The Legal Aid Board may agree to wait an even longer time and allow its mortgage to be put on the replacement home instead. Again interest will be charged at the same rate. But it will agree to this only if:

• the new home will have sufficient equity (i.e. value after repaying the mortgages) to cover the amount of the statutory charge, *and*

• the new home is to be occupied as the sole residence of the applicant, together with at least one unmarried child who is under eighteen (or in full-time education if over eighteen), or if it is necessary for the applicants or their dependants to move for reasons of health, disability or employment, *and*

• it will be just and reasonable to agree to postponing the charge again and it would cause 'hardship' to the applicant if that were not done.

Only in the most exceptional circumstances will further postponements be granted (i.e. on a sale of the substituted property).

A wife (or husband) will be much better off if she (or he) receives the house in the matrimonial proceedings rather than a mere share in the house. For instance, if she has the whole house put into her name, then the Legal Aid Board will normally agree to postpone the repayment of the legal-aid costs until it is sold (or even later; see above). On the other hand, if the outcome is that she has a percentage of the value of the house and it is to be sold and the proceeds split, then the Legal Aid Board will demand immediate repayment of the legal-aid costs; it will not accept a mortgage on her own house (i.e. bought with the proceeds of the old house) instead. The moral is that it will often be better for the wife to take the whole of the house (and so avoid it being sold) and 'buy out' her husband's share by agreeing to go without maintenance.

The fundamental point is that legal aid is not necessarily free: the proceeds of the case will be subject to the statutory charge, and so be used to pay the legal costs. The answer is to keep the legal costs to the minimum. It is crazy for husbands and wives to litigate over the family assets, since they are merely increasing the legal costs and reducing the amount that will be left to be divided between themselves.

Exemptions from the statutory charge

The proceeds of the case are exempt from being used to pay the legal costs in a few instances. The main exemptions are:
- maintenance payments to a wife or child;
- the first £2,500 of a matrimonial settlement (i.e. when the family property is divided up and some of it is transferred to the wife – or husband; only the excess over the £2,500 will be used to pay outstanding legal costs;
- various social-security benefits (e.g. disablement benefit, income support);
- interim payments: if the court orders a 'payment on account' of compensation, this will be paid direct to the client even if he or she is on legal aid.

Illustration. *Mr and Mrs Jones both agree to a divorce based on two years' separation. However, they cannot agree over the family property and Mrs Jones is granted legal aid to cover the costs of applying to the court for a property order. The judge awards her maintenance of £1,000 per annum plus £5,000 cash, but does not make any order as to costs. Her solicitor's costs are £500. The Legal Aid Board can apply the statutory charge but the maintenance is exempt and so is the first £2,500 of her cash. However, the balance of the cash is sufficient to pay the first £500, and so she receives only £4,500 cash. If the judge had ordered that she receive £2,500 per annum maintenance she would not have to pay anything towards the costs since all the maintenance would be exempt.*

Losing a case on legal aid

Normally, the loser of a case is ordered to pay the winner's costs, but when the loser is on legal aid the rules are different. The judge will order the legally aided loser to pay only 'a reasonable amount' towards the winner's costs. In deciding what is a reasonable amount, the judge will consider the financial resources of the winner and the loser, and also their conduct in the case. In considering resources the court will ignore the value of the assisted person's dwelling house, clothes, household furniture and the tools and implements of his/her work. More often than not, the judge will decide that a reasonable amount for the loser to pay would be an amount equal to the contribution he or she made when granted legal aid. The loser's total expenditure on the legal costs will then be twice his/her contribution (i.e. the original contribution to the Legal Aid Fund towards his/her own costs and the contribution ordered by the court

Legal-aid costs: A summary

Winner	Loser	By whom winner's costs paid
Assisted	Assisted	By the loser, to the limit of his or her means. The balance is found by the winner out of his contribution and the statutory charge.
Assisted	Unassisted	By the loser, to the limit of his or her means. The balance is paid by the winner out of his or her contribution and the statutory charge.
Unassisted plaintiff	Assisted defendant	By the loser, up to an amount considered reasonable by the court given his or her means. The balance of the costs incurred are paid by the winner out of his or her own resources or damages recovered.
Unassisted defendant	Assisted plaintiff	By the loser, up to an amount considered reasonable by the court given his or her means. The balance of the costs incurred are paid by the winner out of his or her own resources unless the court makes an order against the Legal Aid Fund on the ground of hardship.

towards his/her opponent's costs). That will be the limit of the legally aided loser's liability. His/her own solicitor's costs will be paid by the Legal Aid Fund and he or she will not have to make another contribution to cover those costs.

Note that costs are always in the courts' discretion. A judge can always decide not to make an order for costs.

Settling the case

Many cases are settled without a court hearing or an order for costs. In those cases it is often part of the settlement terms that the winner's costs are paid by the loser. If costs are paid in full, the procedures may be shortened, because the area office can agree to matters being dealt with by means of a 'book entry'; in other words, the damages will go to the client directly, because there will be no claim for costs out of the Legal Aid Fund. Any contribution will then be returned to the client.

Discharge of the legal-aid certificate

A legal aid certificate will of course be cancelled once the case is ended, but the certificate may also be discharged for other reasons. The area office may discharge the certificate where the client:
• is over the financial limit;
• no longer has reasonable grounds for proceeding;
• is demanding that the case be conducted unreasonably;
• has obtained legal aid on the basis of false statements;

- has died;
- is behind with contribution payments.

In some circumstances the area office may *revoke* a certificate (where, e.g., there has been a false statement). The effect of this is that the client will have to refund to the Legal Aid Board all costs which have been incurred.

In most cases the area office will send a letter to the client giving him/her an opportunity to 'show cause' (i.e. to ask for the certificate to remain in force).

There may also be an appeal to the legal-aid area committee against a discharge of the certificate.

Civil legal aid: what needs to be done

The legal-aid system seems to be permanently in crisis. Lawyers complain that it is under-funded and that the rates of pay are too low. The Government complains that it costs too much. Clients complain that it is too restrictive: it is not available for many important types of cases, such as libel or for industrial tribunals and social security tribunals. The statutory charge frequently removes much of the benefit of legal aid.

An effective system of justice requires that those who use it have access to proper legal representation. It is a myth that justice will consistently be done fairly where one party is represented and the other is not. The problem is that legal aid is a demand-led service. It must be granted to all who are eligible. If, because of publicity, a greater percentage of the population decides to exercise its right to claim compensation for accidents (less than half do at present), the cost of legal aid would inevitably rise. The Government can control costs only by restricting eligibility or the types of case covered by the scheme.

The cost of legal aid must be seen in context. At around £1,000 million a year it seems a huge expense. Yet compared to the cost of the National Health Service (£20,000 million a year and rising) it is not large. It is also important to place the cost of legal aid into the overall social setting. Take accidents. Around 30 million days' work are lost through accidents each year. On top of that the social cost of serious injuries and fatal accidents runs to thousands of millions of pounds. Much of this is borne by the Government (i.e. the taxpayer). Those who make successful claims for compensation will often be freed from dependence on state benefits. This is especially so since the Compensation Recovery Unit was created. It is now a requirement that most social security and other benefits paid as a result of accidents are repaid to the Government out of the compensation. If claims for compensation are not brought, there will be no repayments.

Where legal aid is granted for accident cases, less than 30 per cent of the costs are ultimately borne by the Legal Aid Board; most accident claims are successful.

It is also said that clients receiving legal aid are in a privileged position. However, it has been estimated that the value of tax relief to businesses which use legal services is just as great as the total cost of legal aid. If a businessman consults a solicitor he can obtain tax relief on the bill (a saving to him of up to 40 per cent of the bill) and he can also reclaim the VAT (a further saving of $17\frac{1}{2}$ per cent).

Legal aid is expensive, but its real cost to the country is much less than at first appears. Nevertheless, there is still a large percentage of the population denied legal aid and yet too poor to afford to take a case to court. For such people there are various possibilities.

Contingent fees

This is the system operated in the USA whereby the lawyer is paid a percentage of the winnings, but nothing if the case is lost. Provision for introducing this method of charging is included in the Courts and Legal Services Act 1990. Most lawyers do not believe it would work under the English legal system. The damages awarded in English courts are much lower than in the USA. If lawyers took a percentage as part of their fee, they would either be paid very little or clients would have their compensation drastically reduced. Besides, it would mean that lawyers would take on only those cases where there was a good chance of success. Borderline or difficult cases would never see the light of day.

Contingency legal aid

A proportion of the successful winnings would be ploughed back to the Legal Aid Fund to finance the legal-aid scheme. This idea has its appeal, but why should winners (who have not been at fault in any way) have to pay the costs of others? – especially when in some types of case the Legal Aid Fund almost always has to pay out (e.g. children's cases).

The safety-net scheme

Here those who are above the legal-aid limit would be required to spend their capital down to a certain figure; then they would apply for legal aid. This system would seem to be fraught with difficulty. What if legal aid is not granted? What if clients lose their nerve and give up before their disposable capital is low enough? There really seems to be no advantage to a person who has a modest amount of capital.

There are no easy answers, but many problems could be solved with more flexibility. There should be a sliding scale of eligibility depending on the nature of the case. Currently most people earning more than £20,000 a year are denied legal aid. A major injury case could cost thousands in legal fees. Therefore the financial limit should be lifted to enable clients with a relatively large income and/or savings to benefit. It is right that clients should make some contribution. It is not right that they should be denied legal aid. On the other hand, the same clients should not receive legal aid to argue with a neighbour about some overgrown conifers on their boundary.

Legal aid in criminal cases

Legal aid has been available in criminal cases since 1903, when the Poor Prisoners Defence Act provided a limited legal-aid scheme for those accused of serious crimes. Prior to that date, the only form of criminal legal aid was the *dock brief*. In 1930 criminal legal aid was extended to the magistrates' courts for the less serious crimes. The test for eligibility was whether it was 'desirable in the interests of justice'. This remains the overall test under the present legal aid provisions, which are set out in Part V of the Legal Aid Act 1988.

In addition to full criminal legal aid (see below) a client may receive advice from a solicitor under the green-form and the duty solicitor schemes.

Full criminal legal aid

An accused person can apply for full legal aid to pay his/her legal costs. The decision whether to grant legal aid is taken by the courts themselves (i.e. the magistrates' or the crown court).

Legal-aid forms are available from the court (most solicitors who practise in the magistrates' courts have a supply of them). A client must give information to satisfy the merits test and the financial requirements. It costs nothing to apply for legal aid. If the application is turned down on the first occasion, further applications can be made right up until the trial. In serious cases (i.e. those which can be tried by the crown court) there is an appeal against refusal to the area committee of the Legal Aid Board.

Clients can select their own solicitor, or the court will appoint a solicitor for them. If they are charged jointly with others, and there is no clash of interest, the court may require one solicitor only to represent all defendants. It may, however, allow defendants to have different barristers in the crown court (even if the barristers are all instructed by the same firm of solicitors).

The merits test in criminal legal aid

Before the 1988 Act, the courts followed the principles laid down in 1966 by the Widgery Committee, which carried out a review of the criminal legal-aid system. These principles are embodied in s. 22 of the Legal Aid Act 1988, which sets out the factors which should be considered in deciding whether it is 'in the interests of justice' to grant legal aid:

(a) if the defendant is convicted he is likely to go to prison or lose his livelihood; *or*

(b) where the case involves complex legal issues; *or*

(c) where the accused is unable to understand the proceedings and state his own case because of his inadequate knowledge of English, or he is suffering from mental illness, or other mental or physical disability; *or*

(d) where the nature of the defence involves tracing and interviewing witnesses or expert cross-examination of a witness for the prosecution; *or*

(e) where legal representation of the accused is desirable in the interests of someone other than the accused as, for example, in the case of sexual offences against young children, where it is undesirable that the accused should cross-examine the witness in person.

This means in practice that legal aid is granted by magistrates for the more serious cases – or to someone who faces a serious penalty if convicted (i.e. because of previous convictions). But those charged with relatively minor offences will not get legal aid. This is especially true with motoring prosecutions; very few accused motorists can get legal aid (even if they qualify financially).

A further complication is that different courts take different attitudes to the granting of legal aid. Some are generous, others less so. A local solicitor should be able to advise on the prospects of getting legal aid for a particular offence. Virtually any case that goes to the crown court is likely to be serious, and have serious results for the defendant. Legal aid is nearly always granted (over 97 per cent of crown court defendants receive legal aid).

Legal aid in magistrates' court cases can be granted either by the magistrates or by their clerk. Only the magistrates, not their clerk, can refuse legal aid.

Legal aid in crown court cases can be granted either by the magistrates, when they commit the defendant for trial to the crown court, or by the crown court.

The means test in criminal legal aid

Criminal legal aid is granted only to defendants who meet the means test. The rules on financial eligibility are similar to those for civil legal aid (see page 967). Both income and savings are taken into account. Changes in financial circumstances while the certificate is in force have to be notified to the court.

Anyone on income support or family credit will automatically be financially eligible to receive free legal aid. Otherwise, a means test will be applied.

Children and criminal legal aid

If children of sixteen or under need criminal legal aid, their parents or guardians will have to make the application for them. Their finances will be taken into account. They may also have to pay any contribution which is due.

Contributions

Defendants can be ordered to make a contribution towards their legal aid costs, either when they are granted legal aid or when the case has finished – even if they are acquitted. If a contribution is required when legal aid is granted, the defendant will normally pay it in instalments over twenty-six weeks. The contribution is:

● all the client's disposable capital over £3,000 (e.g. if it is £5,000, the client will have to pay £2,000), *and*

● one-quarter of the client's disposable weekly income over £65. If his/her disposable income is £105 per week, he or she will have to pay £10 per week for twenty-six weeks.

Any contribution made under the green-form scheme will count towards these contributions.

After the case has been heard, a defendant may be ordered to pay additional costs. The sentence imposed on him/her will have to be taken into account when deciding whether an order for a contribution should be made. Clearly, if someone is sent to prison and has no savings, there will be little point in ordering them to make a contribution.

There is no appeal against a contribution order. This can cause hardship and it seems an unfair rule. For instance, a defendant might be prosecuted and because of the nature of the case, the trial could take several weeks. He or she may be found guilty and given a relatively minor punishment (such as a fine or a conditional discharge). Nevertheless, the judge can punish him/her indirectly by imposing a high costs contribution. The defendant cannot appeal against that contribution order, even though it may amount to a much more serious penalty than the sentence imposed by the court – against which, of course, it is possible to appeal.

Illustration. *Mr King is arrested on a serious charge of fraud (which can be tried only in the crown court). He is taken to a police station. Mr King requests a solicitor to visit the police station to advise him while he is being questioned. The solicitor's fee is paid under the duty solicitor scheme. It will cost Mr King nothing even if he is very rich. Eventually, he is charged and the next day he appears before the magistrates. They refuse to give him bail and order that he be kept in custody. The duty solicitor scheme covers the first court appearance. The solicitor then applies to the magistrates (or their clerk) for criminal legal aid. This is granted in principle and the magistrates order him to make a contribution. If he had been on income support he would not have to pay a contribution; however, in Mr King's case, he is employed and is expected to pay a contribution. This is paid in instalments over the next twenty-six weeks.*

Mr King can use the duty solicitor for subsequent court hearings or he may choose his own solicitor.

His solicitor decides to appeal against the refusal of bail. The appeal is to a judge in the crown court. The costs of this are covered by the legal aid granted by the magistrates.

Eventually the date for the committal hearing is arranged. At this hearing the magistrates will decide whether Mr King should be committed to the crown court. His solicitor represents him, his fees being paid by the legal-aid order. When the magistrates commit Mr King, his legal aid is extended to cover the costs of the crown court case.

If Mr King is acquitted at the crown court hearing he may still have to make a contribution to the costs of his defence. However, if the court feels that the defence's costs should be paid from central funds, he will not be ordered to make a contribution and any money he has paid will be returned to him.

If Mr King is convicted *he will probably have to make a contribution to his legal costs, unless he is sent to prison. Should Mr King decide to appeal to the Court of Appeal, his existing legal aid will cover advice from his lawyers as to the prospects of his appeal. But it will not cover the costs of the appeal. He would have to make a separate application.*

Duty solicitor scheme

A person who is questioned by the police about an offence at a police station or anywhere else – whether or not they have been arrested – has a right to free legal advice. There is no means test. The person questioned may ask for a solicitor they know, the twenty-four-hour duty solicitor or may choose a solicitor from a list kept by the police. Under the codes of practice laid down by the Police and Criminal Evidence Act 1984, the police are required to notify all suspects of these rights.

If a person has to go to the magistrates' court on a criminal case there will often be a duty solicitor available, either at the court or on call, to give free legal advice and representation on the first appearance. Again, there is no means test and no contribution will be payable under the scheme.

Legal aid abroad

If legal aid is required to bring proceedings in a European country, the application should be made to the English Legal Aid Board. Under the European Agreement on Transmission of Applications for Legal Aid, countries which participate will cooperate in handling legal-aid applications for people who live in other countries.

The countries which have ratified the agreement are Austria, Belgium, Denmark, Eire, France, Greece, Italy, Luxembourg, Norway, Portugal, Spain, Sweden and Turkey.

If a client has a dispute in France, for instance, and wants to apply for French legal aid, they should send their application to the Legal Aid Board at the London office (29/37 Red Lion Street, London WC1R 4PP). It will then transmit the application to the French legal-aid office. Applications are prepared in the same way and using the same forms as for an English application. Most countries will accept applications in English, though France requires statements etc. to be accompanied by French translations.

The green-form scheme may be used for help in completing the applications.

68 DIY: Legal Action without a Lawyer

> 'Settling disputes by agreement between the parties is almost always
> in the interests of *all* parties'
> Lord Donaldson, Master of the Rolls, in Davies v. Eli Lilly & Co. (1987)

It is always possible to go to law without a lawyer. The single exception to this is that companies must be represented by solicitor and barrister in the High Court. It is not even necessary to have a lawyer to take a case to the House of Lords (though this chapter does not tell you how to do it!). Like any skilled activity, there is much more to it than meets the eye. Law is not just a set of procedures; it is almost a culture – a system that has taken hundreds of years to develop. After the five or six years it takes to qualify, solicitors are still only at the beginning of their knowledge of the law. It takes many more years to become proficient at it. Do not expect to match the skills of a solicitor after a few hours of background reading and research.

Even with a small claim, there can be unexpected complexities and it is wise to fill in a little background before taking on a case by yourself. Give yourself a flavour of what is involved first by reading this chapter, and also Chapters 63 and 64. Read up too the parts of the book which cover your problem – consumer, road accidents or whatever. Try to get in your mind the framework of the system.

This chapter mainly covers bringing a claim in the county court from the point of view of the claimant – 'the plaintiff'. It also covers, to a lesser extent, some other procedures in the magistrates' court – again from the claimant's point of view. If you are defending a claim you will also gain assistance from the chapter, because the procedures are the same whether a case is being brought or defended.

When not to act for yourself

Some cases should be handled only by lawyers unless there is absolutely no alternative. It is not advisable to act for yourself when there are important matters at stake or when the case involves complicated legal issues. On this basis D I Y litigation is not for:
• *Defended divorces.* These are heard in the High Court. The procedure is more complicated than in the county court.

• *Children and property disputes.* Even in undefended divorces there can be disputes over custody of the children and division of the family assets. These are important and often emotional matters, best left to a professional lawyer. Legal aid may be available.

• *Injunctions.* Injunctions are for emergencies only, such as to stop an illegal eviction or to prevent further wife-battering. The procedure to be followed is complex, even in the county court, so it is advisable to retain a lawyer.

• *Housing tenancy cases.* The law of landlord and tenant is notoriously complicated. While it is possible for landlords to act for themselves in possession proceedings if the tenant is not disputing the claim, they would be best advised to retain a solicitor if the tenant does defend the case. Tenants should always take legal advice if possession proceedings are begun; they may well have a legal defence to the claim which they do not know of.

Finally it is pointless to act for yourself if free legal aid is available. Check whether you are eligible for legal aid (see Chapter 67).

When to act for yourself

In the following cases litigants are encouraged to act for themselves

• *Industrial tribunals.* These hear, among other things, cases alleging unfair dismissal, redundancy and sex discrimination in employment. Legal aid is not available (although it may be possible to get an extension under the green-form scheme; see page 957). Alternatively, trade unions may help members. If they win the claim, claimants will have to pay their own legal costs; the normal rule that the 'loser pays the winner's costs' does not apply in the industrial tribunals. By this means the use of lawyers is discouraged.

• *Undefended divorce.* These cases are heard in the county court. Only green-form legal advice is available to help with the legal costs, but this does not allow solicitors to take steps. The court procedures have been simplified so as to encourage people to do their own divorces. However, if children are involved or if large sums of money are in dispute, legal advice should always be obtained. If there is an argument over the children or money, legal aid will usually be available.

• *Claims for £1,000 or less.* These claims are also heard in the county court, by an arbitrator. Whenever the amount claimed is no more than £1,000, each side will have to pay their own legal costs, so the normal rule that the 'loser pays the winner's costs' will not apply. This is called the small-claims rule. It is designed to discourage the use of lawyers in claims which involve relatively small sums, when the legal costs could exceed the amount in dispute. The small-claims rule applies to all actions in which the plaintiff (the person suing) claims damages only, whether the damages are for breach of contract, negligence, trespass or whatever. However, the rule does not apply to:

– *complex cases*: in difficult and unusual cases either party can ask the court to order that legal costs be awarded, even if no more than £1,000 is involved;

- *claims for an order other than damages*: the small-claims rule is restricted to damages-only claims. For example, it would not apply to cases in which a battered wife obtained an injunction against her husband or a landlord obtained a possession order against his tenant.

The advantages of DIY litigation

The main reason for acting for yourself is to save money. Most solicitors charge between £50 and £90 per hour. In addition, much of the work involved in preparing a case for trial is routine – writing to witnesses, preparing copies of relevant papers etc. – and can be done as well by a layperson as by a lawyer. Solicitors are likely to charge £250–£450 for handling an undefended divorce and a similar amount for a consumer claim worth several hundred pounds. Their fees for a morning in the magistrates' court might well be £100. So the savings that can be made are significant.

Many people have little choice but to act for themselves. If they cannot obtain legal aid or legal assistance from a trade union, they have no real choice. No one should be frightened of acting for themselves; any reasonably intelligent person can present a case in a satisfactory way. The main points to stress are: know your limitations and prepare the case properly; try to discuss it with a lawyer; be prepared to put in a lot of work; do not try to be Rumpole in the court room; present the case in a logical and coherent way; and ask the judge if in any doubt what to do next.

The disadvantages of DIY litigation

Competence

You cannot be expected to know the law and the court procedure as well as a lawyer. However much you read law books and rehearse the presentation of the case, you can never be sure that you have not, through ignorance, overlooked a basic flaw in the case. Similarly, when you get to court, you are bound to be nervous and apprehensive. You are unlikely to be able to present the case and your evidence to the judge expertly. You will not know how to cross-examine witnesses, how to address the judge or how best to present your case. The danger is that you will lose the case when a lawyer might have won it.

Against this, though, it must be said that it is easy to exaggerate the difficulties facing the DIY litigant. These days judges are sympathetic to laypeople who handle their own cases and will often go out of their way to help DIY litigants. Also, you will have one advantage over a lawyer: you will know the facts of the case intimately, while the lawyer is likely to have only a cursory knowledge of them.

Detachment

One of the reasons for employing a solicitor is to be given objective advice: a detached, realistic opinion of the prospects of success. You will be very closely involved in your case and will find it difficult to look at the claim in an objective way, but it is only by doing so that the weaknesses of a claim can be seen.

One way to overcome this problem is to discuss the case with a lawyer. Rather than asking the lawyer to handle the claim, you simply ask him/her to advise on the weaknesses of the claim, how those weaknesses can be strengthened (e.g. what new evidence should you try to obtain?) and the tactics you should adopt (e.g. should you be prepared to negotiate or should you put on a show of strength by pressing on with the proceedings?). By taking legal advice like this you can go some way to overcoming the disadvantages that you face.

Time

You will take considerably more time to prepare your case than a lawyer would. You will have to start from the beginning: first, finding out the law; secondly, applying it to the case; and thirdly, collecting the relevant evidence. Lawyers will be able to undertake the first and second steps in a very short time; they are likely to have the general legal knowledge and experience to enable them to assess the prospects of success in a few minutes. You will not have this advantage.

Before you start

Consider whether there will be anything to be gained. If the person you are claiming against has no job, no money and does not own their house, you will simply be wasting money and time by starting court proceedings.

Will you really benefit by doing it yourself? You must be prepared to spend time researching the law, finding out about court procedure and, probably, rehearsing the presentation of your case. It will take you much longer than a lawyer to do the work. You may have to take time off from your job (and lose pay). If you put a value on your leisure time, consider whether you will be making a real saving by doing it yourself.

Organizing for the case

Keep a file, arranging it so that you know where everything is: court documents, original invoices etc. Correspondence should be kept separate. If possible have everything typed. If your papers are well presented, it will be easier for the court to follow what the issues are.

Keep notes of the time you spend; you may be able to claim something for your time. Make sure you know how long it has taken you to prepare the case, interview witnesses etc.

Make copies. It is vital to have your own copy of all letters and documentation. When preparing for a hearing you will need additional sets of papers.

Keep diary notes. If you have a key conversation with your opponent, make a note of what was said as soon as possible afterwards. This will be a help to you if there is a conflict over the evidence.

Assemble your information. This chapter tells you of the forms you will need, all of which are obtainable from the county court. Pay an early visit to the court to obtain them. Ask if they have any other material to assist people acting without a solicitor. Some courts have their own specimen documentation. There are a number of leaflets obtainable free from the county court:

- *What is a small claim?*
- *How do I make a small claim in the county court?*
- *No reply to my summons. What should I do?*
- *The defendant admits my claim. What must I do?*

There are also booklets entitled *Small Claims in the County Court* (fairly out of date) and *Enforcing Money Judgements in the County Court*. A charge is now to be made for these booklets. The 'Bible' for county court proceedings is *County Court Practice*. This is produced every year and costs more than £150. It contains all the rules and procedures and is written for lawyers. It is prohibitively expensive for a DIY claimant, but a copy may be available in the local reference library for those who want to look up particular points.

You might find it useful to sit in on another county court trial to see how the case is presented and how the court procedure works.

How a friend can assist in court

Most DIY litigants are nervous when they first go into the court room. It is difficult to take a note of what the witnesses say, to decide what questions to ask in cross-examination, and to follow the arguments of the other side. Yet all of these things have to be done.

Consider taking a friend or helper into court. Because few people do it, some courts might challenge your right to have a helper. It is true that a court has a discretion to regulate its affairs, but it must act 'reasonably'. If the court seems reluctant, ask why it would be unreasonable to have a friend in court and refer to the case of McKenzie (1970). This was a Court of Appeal decision which confirmed the right of a layperson to have a helper in court. However, the friend cannot address the court or examine the witnesses.

Mr McKenzie was petitioning for divorce, but he was not on legal aid. The facts were complicated and his wife defended the divorce proceedings. Mr McKenzie decided to act for himself despite the fact that the case would be complicated; in fact it lasted ten days. At the start of the case Mr McKenzie went into court with a clerk who worked for Mr McKenzie's ex-solicitors. The clerk came as a friend – the solicitors were not acting for Mr McKenzie – and he intended to advise Mr McKenzie on how to present the case. The trial judge ordered the clerk to leave, saying that Mr McKenzie must either act for himself or use a lawyer; he could not have help from another layperson. Mr McKenzie lost the case and appealed, saying that he should have been allowed the assistance of the clerk. Held: Yes. Every litigant can have a friend beside them. This case was corrected: 'Any person, whether he be a professional man or not, may attend as a friend of either party, may take notes, may quietly make suggestions, and give advice; but no one can demand to take part in the proceedings as an advocate.' McKenzie (1970)

Since this case, such lay advisers are generally called 'McKenzie men'. The right to have a friend in court was reaffirmed by the Court of Appeal in 1991, when it quashed a decision by magistrates after they had refused to allow a helper in court (R. v. Leicester City Justice, ex parte Barrow and another).

Being paid for the work involved

The usual rule in civil cases is that the 'loser pays the winner's costs' (see page 946). But what happens if the winner has no legal costs because he or she acted for themselves? Until 1975 the answer was that the loser did not have to pay any costs to the winner, even if the winner had devoted hours of their spare time to preparing the case. Partially to remedy this unfair situation, the Litigants in Person (Costs and Expenses) Act 1975 was passed to allow DIY litigants to claim reasonable compensation for the work put into the case.

To ensure that the loser is no worse off paying costs to a DIY litigant than he or she would have been to a legally represented opponent, the Act restricts the costs that are payable. First, the DIY litigant will be paid costs only if they could have claimed costs if legally represented; in particular, the small-claims rule applies and no costs can be recovered in claims of £1,000 or less (see page 998). Secondly, the DIY litigant's costs cannot exceed those of a solicitor; the loser is not to be made to pay extra because a disproportionately high number of hours' work was put into the case. Also, while they can claim up to £8 per hour for the time reasonably spent on the case, DIY litigants cannot claim more than two-thirds of the amount a solicitor could charge for handling the case.

In short, therefore, the litigant's bill can be cut down if he or she is claiming for too many hours' work, and/or their hourly wage loss exceeds two-thirds of the amount a solicitor would have charged. His/her disbursements (see page 938) will normally be allowed in full if they would have been reasonably incurred by a lawyer. However, if he or she spends money unnecessarily (e.g on expert's reports), the expense will not be allowed. Nor will he or she be able to recover the cost of law books bought for the case.

The DIY litigant's costs may be assessed by the judge at the end of the case, so he or she should have a log of the time spent working on the claim. The alternative is to have them taxed (see page 943). Generally, assessed costs are lower than taxed costs, but it is time-consuming and expensive to have costs taxed.

DIY IN THE COUNTY COURT

The county court now has unlimited jurisdiction to hear most cases, regardless of the amount of money at stake. Cases where the amount involved is £25,000 or less will always be tried in the county court unless they are of special importance or complexity. Accordingly, this is the court that the DIY litigant with a civil claim is likely to sue in. In addition, county courts hear undefended divorce petitions for the steps to be taken in an undefended divorce).

You will usually want to sue for *damages* (i.e. money compensation). Typical DIY claims are for:
- non-payment of a debt (e.g. for money lent and not repaid; for payment of a bill delivered for work done or for goods supplied);
- faulty goods (e.g. defective electrical items or poor-quality consumer goods);
- poor service (e.g. failure to repair a car or radio properly; failure to do the job to a proper standard);
- negligence (e.g. a motorist's car is damaged by the negligent driving of another motorist; while they may be insured, they might decide to sue the negligent motorist and so avoid claiming on their policy, which might lose them their no-claims bonus);
- breach of contract (e.g. a ruined holiday where the accommodation and facilities fall far short of the brochure description);
- wages owed (e.g. an employee may be sacked without proper notice, in which case he or she can claim the wages due; this is a 'wrongful dismissal' claim, not to be confused with an 'unfair dismissal' claim, which is brought in an industrial tribunal).

Whom to sue

The person sued is called the defendant. It is important that he or she is named properly in the court papers and that the address is correct. A private individual's name and address can often be checked from the telephone directory or the electoral register, kept at the town hall.

Businesses

With businesses it is important to sue the correct person(s) or firm.

Partnerships

All the partners in a firm are responsible for each other's business debts and liabilities incurred on the firm's behalf. However, the claim must be against the firm name or against all the named partners; otherwise the other partners will not be liable. For instance, if Brown, Smith and Jones carry on business as 'BSJ Builders', the action should be against 'BSJ Builders' (a firm) or against 'Brown, Smith and Jones'. If it was against Brown and Smith, Jones would not be liable.

Companies

When starting proceedings you have to give the court the registered office of a company. This will appear on the company's letter heading or it can be found out by writing to the Registrar of Companies (see Appendix 1). A company can usually be identified by the fact that it has 'plc', 'Ltd' or 'Limited' in its name. Many firms use 'and Co,' after their names, but this does not necessarily mean that they are companies (see Chapter 44).

Firms

If a business is not a company it will be a one-man business, a partnership or a firm owned by a company. If the name of the firm does not consist of the full names of all of the partners, or of the sole trader, the firm should be sued in its business name. See page 618 for the problems that can arise when trying to trace the owner of a business.

Which court to sue in?

Since July 1991 proceedings may be started in any county court in the country, regardless of where the defendant lives or where the dispute arose. However, if the amount claimed is 'liquidated' (i.e. a fixed amount – like a debt), the case will automatically be transferred to the county court for the area where the defendant lives if he or she puts in a defence to the claim. If the amount claimed is unliquidated (such as a claim for compensation for a spoilt holiday), the automatic transfer provisions do not apply (but if judgement is obtained in default – see below – the case is transferred to the defendant's home court if he or she applies to set the judgement aside).

If you anticipate that the case will be contested, consider starting the proceedings in the defendant's home court.

Dealings with the county court

Once your proceedings are started your case will be given a case number. This should always be quoted to the court in any inquiry about your case.

When making applications through the post, be sure to send a stamped addressed envelope (of sufficient size) for the reply.

The court staff will assist with procedures, but they will never advise on the law. You have to satisfy yourself on that before starting proceedings. Consult a lawyer or Citizens' Advice Bureau.

Most decisions will be made by district judges. They hear the smaller cases (those below £5,000, though they now have power to assess damages without limit) and handle most procedural matters before the trial proper. A circuit judge handles the larger value and more complex cases (see Judges, page 933).

Remember that the county court takes no step of its own to progress the case or enforce its judgements. The initiative must come from the plaintiff. But if there is a delay in setting the case down for trial, the court may strike it out (see page 997).

Bringing a default action in the county court

1 Write to the defendant, setting out details of the claim and giving him/her a time-limit to admit liability or to pay up. Seven to fourteen days is enough. Do this even if the defendant has already verbally denied liability. It will assist on the question of costs, because it will put on record that a formal warning was given before proceedings were issued.

2 If the defendant does not pay, you will then have to issue a 'default summons'. This must be accompanied by written details of your claim. This document is called a 'Particulars of Claim'. It should set out neatly and concisely the basis of the claim. It should state what is claimed and why the defendant is liable, but it need not give the evidence in support of your claim (see Appendix 2 for a specimen).

Prepare the Particulars of Claim in numbered paragraphs. This is how lawyers do it, and it has the advantage of making the document easier to understand. In addition, lawyers usually express the claim in the third person (e.g. 'on 3 May 1992 the plaintiff purchased . . .'). However, this is no more than a legal convention. If you prefer, you can set it out in the first person (e.g. 'on 3 May 1992 I purchased . . .'). Look at the specimen Particulars of Claim in Appendix 2 to see how the document should be set out. You will also find a selection of useful precedent Particulars of Claim in the booklet *Small Claims in the County Court* (available from your local county court).

Ensure that it is neatly typed. Put the name of the court in the top left-hand corner and then put the names of the parties in the centre – as in the specimen. Write 'Case No. . . .' in the top right-hand corner; the court will insert the reference number of the case. You will need at least three copies: one for you, one for the defendant (or each of them if you are suing more than one person) and one for the court.

If the claim is very simple (e.g. for money owed for goods sold and delivered), you may be able to incorporate the Particulars of Claim in the box provided in the Request Form for Issue of Default Summons (see below).

You may claim interest up to the date of judgement at the rate allowed by the county court rules (15 per cent in 1991), but you have to say so specifically.

Add to your Particulars of Claim: 'the plaintiff claims interest pursuant to Section 69 of the County Courts Act 1984'. If you can calculate it, so much the better (e.g. 'interest to date on £746 at 15 per cent for 128 days, £39.24, and continuing at the rate of 30.65 pence per day'). Interest can be ordered on sums unpaid after judgement, but only if it is for £5,000 or more.

Consider whether you should abandon any part of the claim which exceeds £1,000. This would keep the claim within the scope of the small-claims procedure, and minimize the risk of a costs order against you if you lose. On the other hand, you would not be able to claim your costs if you won.

To help D I Y litigants, many county courts have standard Particulars of Claim forms which cover the usual D I Y claims. Ask for copies of these standard forms and, if they are suitable, use them.

3 You can now start the court proceedings. Decide which court you are going to sue in (see page 993). The address of the court will be in the telephone directory under 'courts'. Take or send to the court:

● *Request Form for Issue of Default Summons* (obtainable from the court). This is your request that proceedings be commenced. The court will supply the correct form.

● Three copies of the *Particulars of Claim* (unless you incorporate them into the request form; see above).

● Court fee, paid in cash or postal order. Cheques are not acceptable, unless they are from a firm of solicitors. The fees are (1991):

10 pence for every £1 claimed (minimum fee £7.00)

Exceeding £300 but not exceeding £500 – £37

Exceeding £500 (or unlimited) – £43

4 The court officials will then prepare a Notice of Issue of Default Summons (formerly known as a Plaint Note). There are two versions of this form, depending on whether you are claiming a fixed amount (such as a debt) or for damages generally (such as for a spoilt holiday). The appropriate notice will be sent to you, to confirm that proceedings have been begun and that the summons has been sent to the defendant. It will have been sent with a copy of the Particulars of Claim.

5 What happens next depends on what the defendant decides to do.

● *If the defendant does nothing.* If the defendant does not answer the claim within fourteen days of receiving the summons, you can enter judgement in default. How you apply depends on whether you are claiming a fixed amount or just damages. If you are claiming a fixed amount the Notice of Issue will itself contain the request to enter judgement (on the reverse of the form). Follow the instructions on the form, complete the boxes and return it to the court.

No fee has to be paid to enter judgement. You can ask that the defendant pay the amount owed immediately, or instalments at a frequency you suggest. The court will make this order and tell the defendant. It is not necessarily wise to ask for the whole sum to be paid immediately; if you have doubts as to the defendant's ability to pay, it is better to accept realistic instalments.

If you have claimed damages, complete form N234 (obtainable free from the court). This asks the court to enter judgement on liability and to fix a date for the assessment of damages.

● *If the defendant admits the claim in full.* One of the forms sent to the defendant is an Admission Form. He or she sets out their income and financial liabilities on the form, and can make an offer in payment (e.g. £5 per month). The defendant sends the form direct to the plaintiff. If the offer is acceptable, ask the court to enter judgement. The form will require you to certify that the information is correct (e.g. that the amount is still owing).

If you decide not to accept the defendant's offer, you must give the reasons for your rejection on form N205A (combined notice of issue/request to enter judgement), which must be completed and sent to the court, along with a copy of the admission form (N9A) sent to you. The court staff will then fix the rate of payment by applying standard guidelines to the statement of finances supplied by the defendant. If either party objects, they must notify the court within two weeks and the court will then fix a disposal date. This is the date for an informal hearing when the district judge can decide how the defendant should pay the debt. You can question the defendant as to his/her finances, but in general it is better to accept the offer of realistic instalments rather than obtain an order for instalments that the defendant cannot meet. You need not attend the 'disposal', but it is essential that you write to the court asking that the district judge deal with the case in your absence. The order made is then binding on the parties.

● *If the defendant denies all or part of the claim.* The defendant may deny liability. Often he or she will simply fill in the form that was sent to him/her by the court. On the other hand, he or she might instruct solicitors – in which case, they will probably prepare a formal typewritten defence (a specimen is shown in Appendix 2). If he or she does put in a defence, then the court will fix a date for a preliminary hearing – a pre-arbitration review if the amount claimed is £1,000 or less and the case will automatically be referred for arbitration after further directions have been given at this short appointment. Either plaintiff or defendant can object and ask for it to be tried by the court in the usual way. It will be for him/her to show that the case is not suitable for hearing by an arbitrator (e.g. because it is particularly complicated or involves difficult questions of law). If the claim is for more than £1,000, then arbitration will not be ordered unless either plaintiff or defendant makes an application to the court asking for arbitration.

Note: if the defendant has put in a totally spurious defence, it is possible to apply to the court to enter judgement without the need for a trial. Application is made to the court to enter 'summary judgement'. The plaintiff has to file an affidavit in support of his/her application. The defendant may resist the application. The court will give judgement only in clear-cut cases where there is likely to be no real dispute on the facts. The specimen affidavit in Appendix 2 is in support of such an application.

Automatic Directions Timetable

Period of time from close of pleadings	Act to be done
28 days	Make and serve list of documents on other parties.
35 days	Inspection of documents.
70 days	Disclose experts' reports.
6 months	Request hearing date giving estimated length of hearing and number of witnesses. (This time can be extended by agreement between the parties.)
15 months	*Action automatically struck out* if no request made for hearing date. (This happens even if the parties have agreed to allow further time.) Therefore if more time is needed it is *vital* that before the deadline an application for further time is made to the court.

Period of time before hearing	Act to be done
14 days	Defendant to inform plaintiff of documents to be included in bundle for the court.
7 days	Plaintiff to file paginated (i.e. with numbered pages) and indexed bundle of relevant documents together with two copies of Particulars of Claim, defence (and requests for additional information), interrogatories, witness statemens, experts' reports and legal-aid certificate.

6 If the claim is for over £1,000 *automatic directions* apply. The county court rules set down a timetable of steps which must be taken in the action. These take effect when 'pleadings are closed' (i.e. normally fourteen days after the delivery of the defence. The directions are as follows:

Notes: *Discovery of documents* consists of preparing lists of the relevant and disclosable documents and sending them to the other side. You do not have to disclose documents which are 'privileged'. Privileged documents include correspondence with experts and your own solicitor. If in doubt, take legal advice on what should be disclosed.

The list of documents is county court form N265. It is in three parts:

Schedule 1 [Part I] This is the list of documents which must be disclosed.

Schedule 1 [Part II] This lists the documents which you object to producing. It must state the ground for objecting (e.g. that they are by their very nature privileged).

Schedule 2 This lists the documents which you have had in your possession but no longer have. Commonly this would be the originals of letters sent to others. You are required to state what has happened to each document and when it was last in your possession. A specimen list of documents is given in Appendix 2.

Note: *inspection of documents*. Each party must allow the other access to see his/her documents. In practice this is often handled by sending each other photocopies of documents. However, it is sometimes useful to see the originals, especially if there is any doubt about their completeness or authenticity.

7 If the value of the claim is less than £1,000, the case will be heard by arbitration. Before the main hearing the court is likely to fix a 'pre-arbitration review', at which the district judge will take stock of the case and give directions as to how it is to be conducted. Many of the formal procedures outlined above (such as discovery of documents) are unlikely to be ordered. However, it is still necessary to have all the relevant information and the court might well make orders about the type of evidence to be called.

The arbitration hearing. Arbitration is a much more informal hearing than the normal trial of a case. Rather than being a formal trial with all the rules of evidence (e.g. no hearsay evidence), arbitration is more relaxed and less legalistic. If there is a choice, it is normally advisable to have the case heard by arbitration rather than by trial. The case will be heard by the same person (the district judge) but the procedure will be much less intimidating. The two important points about arbitration are:

• only rarely can the arbitrator's decision be appealed;
• solicitor's costs will not normally be allowed if the claim is for not more than £1,000.

8 You must prepare thoroughly for the trial (or the arbitration hearing). All evidence should be collected together in readiness. Witnesses should be warned of the date of the hearing; the parties will be notified of the date by the court.

9 *How to present a case to the court*. You can take a friend along to advise and assist (see page 990). Start by telling the judge very briefly who you are and what the case is about. If he or she is a district judge, you should call them 'Sir' or 'Madam'. Circuit judges are addressed as 'Your Honour'. The judge may have read the papers before the case starts. If not, offer to read them out. There is no need to make a long speech, but it is sometimes helpful to tell the court how you propose to prove the case, and what evidence you will be bringing.

Move straight on to your evidence. This will normally start with you in the witness box. You may not be allowed to read out your statement: most evidence is given without reference to notes, unless they were prepared at the same time as the event happened. Be sure to remember to bring out all the issues.

Witnesses. See page 890 for the sequence of examination of witnesses. In many civil cases a witness may be allowed to sit in court while waiting to be called, but check with the judge that no objection will be taken to this. The defendant can cross-examine the witnesses.

Then the defendant and his/her witnesses give evidence and they can be cross-examined by you. At the end of the evidence, both you and the defendant may make a closing speech. The district judge will probably deliver his/her judgement immediately. The winner should ask for his/her costs to be paid by the loser. However, if the claim is for no more than £1,000 no costs will be awarded.

Enforcing a money judgement

Obtaining judgement does not necessarily mean that the plaintiff will recover the damages or the debt owed. If the defendant does not pay, the plaintiff will have to ask the court to enforce the judgement. There are various ways of enforcing a judgement but they are all useless if the debtor does not have any money or assets. If the debtor is penniless there is no point in suing him/her, let alone in trying to to enforce a judgement against them: the money spent on court fees (and any lawyer's charges) will be wasted.

If the amount of the judgement is £5,000 or more, interest can be claimed on amounts overdue and unpaid. This should be claimed when using one of the methods of enforcement below. The cost of enforcement, and the fees paid to issue the proceedings, can be claimed as part of the judgement.

Judgement should be enforced only by legal means. Threats of violence can lead to prosecution for threatening behaviour, extortion or even blackmail. There is a criminal offence of 'harassing a debtor'. By s. 40 of the Administration of Justice Act 1970, it is an offence to try to coerce a debtor into paying up by:

• making demands which 'are calculated to subject him, or members of his household to alarm, distress, or humiliation'. The frequency of the demands and the way they are made will be crucial. For instance, it would be harassment to call late at night with rough-looking men; it might be harassment to park a van marked 'debt collector' outside the debtor's house or to keep phoning up throughout the day.

• falsely suggesting that the debtor could be prosecuted for not paying. It is not a criminal offence to owe money, even if a court has entered judgement.

• falsely pretending to be acting in an official capacity or to have an official document in order to enforce payment. For instance, it would be harassment for the creditor to call at the debtor's home, claiming to be a court bailiff and producing what looked like a court order allowing them to seize the debtor's possessions.

Harassment prosecutions are brought in the magistrates' court. The maximum penalty is a £2,000 fine.

Methods of enforcing a county court judgement

There are seven principal methods of enforcing a county court judgement. Remember that the prerequisite is to obtain a judgement (see the procedural steps above). Legal aid may be available to pay a solicitor to enforce the judgement.

The oral examination: finding out the debtor's means

Once judgement has been entered, the creditor (i.e. plaintiff) may ask the court to hold an inquiry into the debtor's means. The debtor can be ordered to produce his/her books and papers. He or she can be asked relevant questions if 'fairly pertinent and properly asked'. The hearing is intended to be a searching cross-examination as to the debtor's property and means. In an extreme case, refusal to answer a proper question could result in the debtor being sent to prison for contempt by a judge.

The hearing is in private before a court officer. The debtor's answers are written down and then read over to him/her. They will be asked to sign the transcript.

Application is made to the county court covering the area where the debtor lives. The application is made on form N316 (obtainable from the court). A fee of £12 is payable. Formerly the debtor had to be paid 'conduct money' (i.e. travel expenses to the court). Under rules introduced in 1991, this is no longer necessary unless the debtor specifically requests it. The amount of any conduct money is added to the judgement debt. A request for an oral examination can be made personally by attending at the court or by applying through the post. The court normally sends the attendance order (and the conduct money if any) to the debtor. At the examination the creditor should ask for an order that the debtor pay his/her legal costs.

Often the debtor will fail to attend the examination. When this happens, the court will adjourn to a new date and give notice to the debtor that he or she may be committed to prison if they do not attend. The maximum sentence is two years. This court notice must be served personally on the debtor, at least five days before the new hearing date. In practice the warning is usually enough to persuade the debtor to attend the new hearing. The debtor is then taken before the judge, suitably admonished and immediately ordered to attend before the district judge or court executive officer, so that the oral examination can take place without delay.

Putting a charge on the debtor's home (a charging order)

If the debtor owns a house or flat, the creditor may apply to the court for an order charging (i.e. mortgaging) the property with the judgement debt. The procedure is complex and is not recommended for the inexperienced. The following is an outline only.

If the judgement debt remains unpaid, the creditor may apply to the court for the creditor's property to be sold to pay the debt. This is so even if the debtor owns the property with someone else (e.g. jointly with his/her spouse or partner).

If the debtor does own property, this can be an effective sanction; the possibility that he or she might lose their home will often ensure that the debtor does all he or she can to pay off the debt. However, in practice the court will very rarely order the property to be sold.

Before applying for a charging order it is wise to carry out an index map search to find out if the ownership of the land is registered and, if so, to obtain copies of the ownership details. This will assist in providing accurate information in the affidavit and the subsequent registration of the charging order (see below). If the ownership is not registered, there is no satisfactory way of establishing the ownership of the land. Sometimes a Land Charges search will show up other debts owed by the debtor, and give clues as to the names of owners and details of the property.

To apply for a charging order, the creditor must swear an affidavit (for a specimen of an affidavit see Appendix 2). The county court staff may advise on the correct wording but the following must be put in the affidavit:

• the name and address of the debtor and, if known, of every creditor of his/ hers whom the applicant can identify, along with details of anyone else with an interest in the property (e.g a building society or the debtor's spouse);

• confirmation of the amount due under the judgement and the amount still outstanding;

• details of the property which will be subject to the charging order;

• confirmation that the debtor does own the property or a share in it.

The affidavit (and two copies plus an extra copy for anyone else who must receive notification of the application; see below) must be sent to the court with the fee (£12 in 1992) and the Notice of Issue of summons and judgement.

If the papers are in order, the district judge will make a 'charging order nisi', and fix a date for consideration of the matter (and to allow the debtor to make his/her own representations). This must be served on the debtor personally at least seven days before the hearing date. Copies must also be served on anyone else who has an interest in the property (for e.g the debtor's spouse, the building society and any finance company or individual who has a charge on the property). The court does not arrange service and it will be necessary to arrange for personal service – usually by an inquiry agent. An affidavit of service will be required.

At the hearing the district judge considers the debtor's position and that of other creditors. If appropriate he or she will make a 'charging order absolute'. If the creditor then wants the property to be sold, he or she must make a separate application to the court.

Note: it is most important to ensure that the application and subsequent orders are protected by registration at the Land Charges registry (if the land is not registered) or the Land Registry (if the land is registered). If they are not registered, the debtor (or another creditor) may be able to sell the land and the charging order will become ineffective.

Issuing a warrant of execution: sending in the bailiff

The creditor can ask the court to send the bailiff in, to seize the debtor's goods, and then auction them off to meet the judgement. This is called *levying execution* or, if the judgement is for arrears of rent, *distress against goods*. The creditor fills in form N323 (available from the court), sends the court the Notice of Issue of Default Summons and Judgement and the required fee (15 per cent of the debt with a minimum of £5 and a maximum of £38). There is no court hearing. The court will then 'issue execution', which authorizes the bailiff to enter the debtor's premises. There is sometimes a considerable delay – up to two months – before the bailiff takes action.

Bailiffs can enter the premises either by day or by night, but not on a Sunday. They cannot break into the premises, although they can climb through an unlocked window. Once inside they can break down internal doors, if necessary.

They can seize any goods or possessions belonging to the debtor (including money, bank notes, bonds, securities etc.) except:

● items *necessary* for use personally by him/her in their job (e.g. tools, books, vehicles and other items of equipment which are necessary for use in their job);

● items *necessary* for satisfying the basic domestic needs of the debtor and his/ her family (e.g. clothing, bedding, furniture, household equipment and provisions).

Items such as stereo equipment, televisions, video recorders or microwave ovens (where there is also a conventional cooker) are not usually considered to be *necessaries*. It is for the debtor to satisfy the bailiff that these items are actually necessary (as opposed to being merely desirable or helpful). This applies particularly to vehicles: the bailiff must be satisfied that no real alternative is available.

Bailiffs cannot seize goods belonging to someone else, so if the debtor's wife says they belong to her, the bailiff will probably not risk taking them. Similarly, hire purchase items (which legally belong to a finance company; see page 576) cannot be seized.

It is usually advisable to have an oral examination of the debtor before sending in the bailiffs (see above). Then if, for instance, the debtor claims *his* car is on hire purchase, the creditor can demand to see the agreement. Note that hire purchase is not the same as credit sale (see Chapter 38) and goods being bought on credit can be seized. In recent years hire purchase has declined in popularity (although many people who buy goods by instalments mistakenly think they are on hire purchase, even though they are being bought on credit sale).

When sending in bailiffs, give them as much information as possible (e.g. colour, make, registration number of the debtor's car).

Bailiffs impound the goods and, if the debt is not paid off within five days, they can be sold by auction. In practice, the goods are usually left on the debtor's premises rather than being carried away. This is known as 'taking walking possession'.

Note: if the amount of the judgement is for £5,000 or more, the execution must be carried out by a sheriff of the High Court. You probably will need to instruct a solicitor to help you with the transfer and procedures.

Attachment of earnings

The court may make an order that regular deductions be made from the debtor's pay packet by his/her employer, and that the debt be paid off in this way. In effect it is 'pay as you earn' via the courts. The amount of the judgement debt must be £50 or more.

An attachment of earnings order is only of use if the debtor has a steady job. If he or she is out of work, or changes jobs frequently, an order will be of no use.

The creditor applies for an order by sending two copies of form N337 (obtainable from the county court) to the county court where the debtor lives. If it is a different court from that where the proceedings were issued, ask for a transfer. In addition the Notice of Issue of Default Summons and Judgement must be produced to the court. The fee is 10 per cent of the debt (minimum fee £5, maximum £40). The creditor must also swear an affidavit confirming the amount owing (form N321, also available from the court). A copy of the application is sent to the debtor, together with a reply form. This requires the debtor within eight days to set out details of his/her employment, income and financial commitments. The debtor is also asked how much he or she would be prepared to have deducted from their wages on a regular basis.

If the court feels that more information is needed, it can ask the debtor, his/her employer and other people to provide information.

Where the court has sufficient information a provisional order is made, and this becomes operative, if no objection is received, within ten days. Otherwise a hearing date is fixed, when the district judge will decide how much the debtor can afford to pay. This will be done by, first, calculating the 'protected earnings' figure – the amount below which the debtor's income should not fall. Often this will be equal to the income support rates for the debtor and his/her family. Then the district judge will fix the 'normal deduction rate', which will be the amount usually deducted from the debtor's wages.

The debtor can never be left with less than his/her protected earnings figure. For instance, suppose the debtor earns £60 per week on average and the district judge fixes a protected earnings figure of £50 per week and a normal deduction rate of £10. If in a particular week the debtor earns only £55, the deduction will be £5. If next week he earns £65, the deduction will still be £10 not £15.

Once the court makes an order, a copy is sent to the debtor's employer. The employer then has seven days in which to start making deductions. The money is sent direct to the court, which then forwards it to the creditor. The employer must tell the debtor of all deductions, and he or she can charge the debtor 50 pence for the administrative work of each deduction.

If the debtor leaves his/her job, the employer has ten days in which to notify the court; failure to do so is an offence carrying a fine of up to £100. The debtor can also be fined up to the same amount (and even be sent to prison) if he or she does not tell the court when he or she finishes or changes jobs.

In practice, attachment of earnings orders are usually of limited value. The sort of people who tend to get into debt rarely have steady jobs. Those who do, often change jobs and disappear.

Attachment of earnings orders can also be made for maintenance orders.

Garnishee orders – intercepting money owed to the debtor

A creditor can apply to the court for an order that debts (exceeding £25) owed to the debtor be paid direct to the creditor, and that money in a bank account be paid out to him/her. This is called a garnishee order.

Generally garnishee orders are little used. In fact, they can be very useful against a debtor who has the money or who is so hopelessly in debt that he or she does not bother to collect the few debts that are owed to them. Garnishee orders are usually used against firms and companies.

In practice the difficulty for the creditor is to find out who does owe money to the debtor or whether he or she has a bank account which is in credit.

The creditor applies for a garnishee order by swearing an affidavit (form N349, available from the county court), and delivering this to the court with the judgement and Notice of Issue of Default Summons. The fee is £12. If the proceedings are in a different court, the creditor should ask the original court for a certificate of judgement and produce it when applying for the garnishee order. This is then served on the person who owes the debtor the money or the bank holding his/her money. If this person – called the garnishee – does not pay up, the case proceeds to a full trial, when the judge decides whether the garnishee should pay the money to the creditor.

If the money is held by a bank or similar institution, it may deduct £30 for its administrative charge in complying with the order. If it holds no funds, it may give notice of no money held – which will effectively put an end to the application.

Bankruptcy

This is a drastic step and it will rarely be worth making the debtor bankrupt unless the sums involved are large. A bankruptcy petition is best handled by a solicitor. Note that creditors can petition for bankruptcy only if they are owed £750 or more, unless they are petitioning with other creditors who between them are owed £750 or more. A creditor who brings bankruptcy proceedings is not in a stronger position than any others who are owed money by the same debtor; furthermore, the preferential creditors (Inland Revenue, employees of the debtor etc.) may take all he or she has.

The court fees are substantial compared with other means of enforcing a judgement (a fee of £45 *plus* a deposit of £270 to the official receiver). However, merely taking the first step (i.e. serving a statutory demand on the debtor; see page 596) can sometimes bring a result, assuming, of course, that the debtor has the money. This first stage costs little and may be a worthwhile ploy, but it is usually not worth going further and actually commencing bankruptcy proceedings. Generally, see Chapter 40.

Making an administration order

Debtors can ask the court to help them organize their liabilities. They tell the court of all their liabilities and the court then stays all other proceedings against them. Arrangements are then made for the debtors to pay off their debts in instalments, often by an attachment of earnings order. The result is that debtors get creditors 'off their back' by telling the court of their financial problems, and the court will then fix a realistic timetable for repayment of the debts by instalments.

The application for an administration order can be made only by the debtors themselves. However, it might be worth a creditor suggesting to the debtor that an administration order would give him/her breathing space and a chance to put his/her affairs in order – which would be of benefit to both debtor and creditor.

STARTING PROCEEDINGS IN THE MAGISTRATES' COURT

The DIY litigant will find that the procedure for starting proceedings in the magistrates' court is straightforward. Typical DIY cases include:
- wife's application for maintenance;
- affiliation application by mother of illegitimate child;
- private prosecutions;
- complaints about noise or other types of pollution;
- footpath and highway obstructions.
  The procedure in all cases is basically the same.

1 Telephone the local magistrates' court and ask about the local procedure for issuing summonses. Sometimes it is necessary to attend before a magistrate; other times courts will arrange for the magistrate to issue the forms without a personal attendance. If a personal attendance is necessary, ask what time of day the court hears applications for summonses. This varies from court to court, but usually it is either 10 or 10.30 a.m., although some courts hear them at 2 p.m., the start of the afternoon session.
2 At the court, ask for the warrant officer's office. Tell him/her you want a summons issued and ask which court to go to.

3 Go to that court. There will probably be a court usher at the door of the court. Tell him/her you want to issue a summons. He or she may want to know your name, address and the nature of your application. It is helpful if you can give the statutory authority for your application, but this is not essential (e.g. if you were a tenant applying for a statutory nuisance order against your landlord, you would say you wanted to issue a summons under s.99, Public Health Act 1936).

4 Wait inside the court. Eventually your turn will come and your name will be called out by the usher. You should then go to the front of the court and explain to the magistrate (or their clerk, if the magistrate is not sitting) why you want a summons issued. By telling the magistrate about the case you are said to be 'laying an information' in a criminal case (i.e. a private prosecution), or 'making a complaint' in any other case. The magistrate will want to be sure that you have the basis of a case, although he or she will not expect you to prove your case at this stage. It might be useful to show them any documentary evidence in support of your application, and offer to call witnesses to support you.

The magistrate should be referred to as 'Your Worship', unless he or she is a stipendiary (professional magistrate), in which case use 'Sir' or 'Madam'.

If the magistrate decides that you have an arguable case, he or she will agree that a summons should be issued. If he or she turns down your application, you will have to obtain more detailed and convincing evidence and then apply again.

5 The police officer in the court will have written down details of the magistrate's order. He or she will give you his/her note. Take it to the general office of the court and tell the clerk that you have been granted a summons. Discuss the wording of the summons with the clerk and ask him/her to issue the summons against the defendant.

6 The clerk (or sometimes the warrant officer) will fix a date for the hearing of the case. He or she will then issue the summons and serve it on the defendant for you.

7 Attend court on the date of the hearing with your witnesses. Don't forget that you can take a friend or helper into court with you (see page 990). The trial will be as in a criminal prosecution.

MORE SERIOUS CRIMES

Private prosecutions can also be brought for cases that are tried in the crown court, but once the magistrates have committed the case to the crown court for trial (see page 758) the Crown will take over the prosecution and the private prosecutor will play no further part, unless, of course, he or she is called as a witness by the prosecution. If the Crown does not approve of the prosecution, it can simply offer no evidence when the case becomes before the judge; the prosecution will then be dismissed.

APPENDICES

APPENDIX 26

1 Useful Sources of Information

There are numerous records and registers that are open to public inspection. What follows is an A–Z summary of the more useful of these sources of information.

Unless otherwise stated, a fee is usually payable but details of fees and charges are not given here because they change so frequently. It is advisable to phone before making a search, to ascertain the amount of the fee.

Highly recommended is the *Directory of Registers and Records*, by Trevor Aldridge (Oyez Longman), which contains full details of virtually all the numerous types of records that can be made available.

Addresses

The DSS has an address for nearly every person over the age of fifteen. However, this address will normally be revealed only if it is needed for court proceedings (such as maintenance, affiliation, divorce cases).

The DSS will sometimes forward letters to the recorded address if a sufficiently good reason is provided. The letter to be forwarded should be in a sealed envelope, and it should be sent with a covering letter to the DSS, Special Section A, Records Branch, Newcastle-upon-Tyne. There is no fee.

Other possible sources of a person's address are the NHS records and the military sources. However, an address will normally only be revealed for the purpose of court proceedings.

See also 'Electoral Register'.

Adoption

There are two registers. The Registrar-General has kept the Adopted Children Register since January 1927 and a copy certificate (showing date and court of adoption, child's adopted name, names and addresses of adopting parents) can be supplied to any applicant. The second register cross-references the entry in the Adopted Children Register to the Births Register and enables the child's parent(s) to be identified. The cross-reference register is not open to the public although the adopted person may be able to make a search in it.

Certificates from the Adopted Children Register can be obtained either in person (from the Registrar-General's office – see address in 'Births, Marriages and Deaths') or by post from the General Register Office, Registration Division, Titchfield, Fareham, Hants.

Alternative Dispute Resolution (ADR)

Mediation UK is a network of projects, organizations and individuals interested in mediation and other forms of conflict resolution. They can be contacted at 82A Gloucester Road, Bishopston, Bristol BS7 8BN (0272 241234).

Then there is ACAS, the Advisory, Conciliation and Arbitration Service, at Clifton House, 83 Euston Road, London NW1 (071 388 5100).

See also page 885.

Bankruptcy

The presentation of bankruptcy petitions and the making of receiving orders are recorded in a central registry. Anyone can make a postal search of the alphabetical index by writing to the Superintendent, Land Charges Dept, Burrington Way, Plymouth.

Receiving orders are recorded in a register at Thomas Moore Building, Law Courts, Strand, London WC2, which is open to personal inspection by anyone.

Barristers

Complaints against barristers should be addressed to the General Council of the Bar, 3 Bedford Row, London WC1R 4DB (071 242 0082).

Births, marriages, deaths

Copy certificates are available from the Registrar-General, General Register Office, St Catherine's House, 10 Kingsway, London WC2 (071 242 0262). Personal searches can be made on weekdays between 8.30 a.m. and 4.30 p.m. Search can also be made by post, either using the free application form or by sending a letter stating (at least) the date and place of the event and the full names.

Generally, the registers date back only to 1 July 1837; where the event occurred abroad, registers were only kept from July 1849. A separate register of still-births was started on 1 July 1927, but this register is not open to inspection unless the Registrar-General's permission is obtained.

See also Adoption; Divorce; Inquests and Post-Mortems; Parish Records; Probate and Letters of Administration; Wills.

Cars

The name and address of the registered owner of a car can be obtained from the Drivers and Vehicle Licensing Centre, Swansea (0792 782523). The names and addresses of previous owners can also be supplied. Application can be made only by someone with reasonable cause for needing the information.

See also Hire Purchase.

Change of name

There is no comprehensive register of changes of name. If the change of name was by deed poll it may have been enrolled with the Supreme Court, but this is not compulsory. Personal search can be made at Room 81, Royal Courts of Justice, Strand, London WC2 or, if the deed poll was enrolled more than three years ago, at the Public Record Office, Chancery Lane, London WC2.

Other sources of information are:
● *An Index to Change of Name 1760–1901* (W. P. W. Phillimore and E. A. Fry, 1905) lists changes recorded in private acts of Parliament, publications etc., but is not completely comprehensive;
● private acts of Parliament;
● Register of Change of Name by Royal Licence kept by the College of Arms, Queen Victoria Street, London EC4.

Charities

Many charities are registered with the Charity Commissioners. Anyone can apply for the name of the charity, its constitution, objects, approximate annual income and the name and address of the person to whom any correspondence should be addressed.

A personal search should be made at the Charity Commission (Registration Division), St Alban's House, 57–60 Haymarket, London SW1 (071 210 3000).

Common land

County councils keep records of all common land and village greens, showing the land affected and the rights claimed, and giving details of anyone claiming to be the owner of the land.

Anyone can search in the register. Apply by post on form CR1 to the county council (they will supply the form).

Companies

Every company has a file with the Registrar of Companies. This gives detailed information as to its constitution, capital structure, shareholders, directors, secretary, registered office, accounts, auditor's reports, director's reports, mortgages and debentures, and associated companies.

A personal or postal search can be made with the Companies Registration Office, Cardiff (0222 380801). Copies of some of the documents on file are also available for inspection in Companies House, 55–71 City Road, London EC1Y 1BB (071 253 9393).

In addition, every company has to keep a register of charges, register of members, register of directors and secretaries. These registers can be inspected by anyone, even if not a shareholder. Often these records are more up to date than those on the files of the Registrar of Companies.

Conveyancers

See Chapter 15.

Also contact the Council of Licensed Conveyancers, Golden Cross House, Duncannon Street, London WC2N 4JP.

Divorce

Anyone can apply for a copy of a decree nisi or decree absolute. The decree will show the name of the parties to whom the decree was granted, the grounds, and the date.

Personal application is made to the Principal Registry, Family Division, Room A44,

Somerset House, Strand, London WC2 (071 936 6000). Once the applicant has found the entry in the index he can ask for a copy.

Doctors

The General Medical Council keeps a register of all medical practitioners, showing their names, address, qualifications, and date of first registration. Apply to General Medical Council, 44 Hallam Street, London W1N 6AE (071 580 7642).

Action for Victims of Medical Accidents gives assistance in medical negligence claims to both victims and their solicitors. They can be contacted at Bank Chambers, 1 London Road, Forest Hill, London SE23 3TP (081 291 2793).

Electoral Register

Anyone can inspect the Electoral Register, compiled by the appropriate local authorities. Copies are usually available for inspection in main post offices, public libraries, and the town hall. The register shows the names of every person living at a particular address who is eligible to vote.

Finance and stock brokers

The organizations which regulate those involved in financial matters are as follows:

Stock brokers

Complaints against stock brokers should be addressed to The Complaints Bureau, The Securities and Futures Authority, The Stock Exchange, Old Broad Street, London EC2N 1EQ (071 256 9000).

Life Assurance and Unit Trust Regulatory Association (Lautro), Centre Point, New Oxford Street, London WC1A 1DD (071 379 0444/Complaints Department: 081 686 9309).

Financial Intermediaries, Managers and Brokers, Regulatory Association (Fimbra), Hertsmere House, Hertsmere Road, London E14 4AB (071 538 8860).

Highways and rights of way

Every district council and London borough council keeps a list of the highways in that area that are maintainable at public expense. Inquiry can be by post or in person; there is no fee. Rights of way are shown on the 1:50,000 Ordnance Survey maps, and on the statutory maps kept by the local authority under the National Parks and Access to the Countryside Act 1949 (see page 369).

Hire purchase

There is no general index of items that are currently on HP. However, there is a register of cars that are on HP (see page 544).

HP information on cars may be obtained from Hire Purchase Information plc, but this can be done only through a Citizens' Advice Bureau.

Housing associations

Housing associations are required to register with the Housing Corporation. This register can be inspected by anyone. It shows the association's registered office, its address for correspondence, the type of dwellings provided, its constitution and accounts for the last three years.

Application is made to the Housing Corporation, Registration and Supervision Division, 149 Tottenham Court Road, London W1 (071 387 9466). More limited information is available from the regional offices of the Housing Corporation.

Human rights

See page 869.

For more information contact The Secretary, European Commission of Human Rights, Council of Europe, BP 431 R6, F-67006 Strasbourg Cedex, France.

Inquests and post-mortems

A coroner is obliged to keep all documents concerning an inquest, including any post-mortem report. These will include the coroner's own notes of the evidence given by witnesses at the inquest.

The documents can be inspected free of charge by a person with a legitimate interest, but not by any person who is merely curious. Copies can usually be supplied on payment of a fee. The documents are kept for fifteen years and then may be destroyed.

Legal aid

See Chapter 67.

The London area office/headquarters are at 29/37 Red Lion Street, London WC1R 4PP (071 405 6991).

Legal stationery

Legal forms and books on law can be obtained from any Oyez shop (head office: Oyez House, 49 Bedford Row, London WC1 (071 242 7132).

Naturalization

When a person is naturalized, details of his or her full name, address, country of origin and date of naturalization are published.

Prior to 1961 annual lists were published by HMSO, but since then monthly lists have been published in the *London Gazette*. Inquiries to Home Office, Lunar House, Wellesley Road, Croydon (081 681 3421).

Ombudsmen

See page 886.

The Banking Ombudsman

Citadel House
5/11 Fetter Lane
London EC4 A 1BR
(071 583 1395)

The Building Societies' Ombudsman

35/37 Grosvenor Gardens
London SW1X 7AW
(071 931 0044)

The Estate Agents' Ombudsman

PO Box 1114
Salisbury
Wiltshire SP1 1YQ
(0722 333306)
He handles complaints against corporate estate agents – such as banks and building societies, and members of the estate agents' organizations. Membership is voluntary, so he does not have power to intervene against *all* estate agents.

The Health Service Ombudsman

Church House
Great Smith Street
London SW1P 3BW
(071 276 3000)
He handles complaints against the health service. Complaints may be made direct but should be in writing. A leaflet is available.

The Insurance Ombudsman Bureau

City Gate One
135 Park Street
London SE1 9EA
(071 928 4488)

The Legal Services Ombudsman

22 Oxford Court
Oxford Street
Manchester M2 3WQ
(061 236 9532)
He reviews the handling of complaints against solicitors and barristers. Complaints should first be addressed to the Solicitors' Complaints Bureau or the General Council of the Bar (see page 917).

The Local Government Ombudsman (The Commission for Local Administration in England)

The Local Government Ombudsman investigates complaints from members of the public about injustice caused by maladministration of local authorities. A free booklet describing how to make a complaint is available from Citizens' Advice Bureaux or from the following addresses:

For Greater London, Kent, Surrey, East and West Sussex
Dr D.C.M. Yardley
Local Government Ombudsman
21 Queen Anne's Gate
London SW1H 9BU
(071 222 5622)

For the South-West, the West, the South and most of central England
Mr F.G. Laws
Local Government Ombudsman
The Oaks
Westwood Way
Westwood Business Park
Coventry CV4 8JB
(0203 695999)

For the East Midlands and the North of England
Mrs P.A. Thomas
Local Government Ombudsman
Beverley House
17 Shipton Road
York Y03 6FZ
0904 630151

For Wales
Mr E.R. Mosely
The Commission for Local Administration in Wales
Derwen House
Court Road
Bridgend
Mid Glamorgan CS31 1BN
(0656 661325)

The Parliamentary Commissioner

Church House
Great Smith Street
London SW1P 3BW
(071 276 3000)
He handles complaints against central government departments. Complaints must be in writing and must be referred via a Member of Parliament. A leaflet is available on application.

The Pensions Ombudsman

11 Belgrave Road
London SW1V 1RB
(071 834 9144)
He deals only with occupational and personal pensions.

Parish records

Records of burials, marriages, and baptisms are kept in many parish churches, but the extent and completeness of the records varies considerably.

Anyone can apply to inspect the records. Application is made to the incumbent, but if he does not have the records, or does not know where they are, application is made to the Diocesan Record Office or the County Record Office.

Many nonconformist registers are now in the Public Record Office.

Planning applications

Local planning authorities keep registers of all applications for planning permission, and records of whether they were granted. Anyone can inspect the register and obtain copies for a fee.

Police

Complaints against the police are handled by the Police Complaints Authority, 10 Great George Street, London SW7P 3AE (071 273 6450).

Probate and letters of administration

Records are kept of every grant, including the name and address of the deceased and the personal representatives, and the value of the estate. Postal or personal application should be made to the Principal Registry, Family Division, Somerset House, Strand, London WC2 (071 936 6000).

Registered land

Anyone can inquire whether a particular piece of land has a registered title. Apply in writing to the appropriate Land Registry (see page 251). The register itself, showing who is the owner of the land and any mortgages or charges affecting it, is not open to public inspection. Only the proprietor (i.e. the owner), or someone applying with his/her written consent, can obtain a copy.

Registered rents

The rent tribunal fixes rents for tenants with resident landlords; the rent officer fixes rents for other tenants. (See Chapter 17.) The rent officer keeps records of all rents he or she has fixed, including a brief description of the premises, the rent payable, any part of the rent which is for services provided by the landlord, the names and addresses of the tenant and the landlord, and particulars of any furniture and services provided by the landlord.

In the same way, the rent tribunal keeps a register of the rents they have fixed. The rent tribunal's register will also specify which parts of the property are occupied by the tenant alone and which parts are occupied jointly with the landlord.

The registers can be searched by anyone on personal application.

Road accidents

If the police took details of an accident a copy of their notes and any witness statements can be obtained. The notes will usually show the names and addresses of those involved and any witnesses, the time, place and date of the accident, any injury or damage caused, and the insurance particulars of the driver. The report will generally not be provided until any criminal prosecution arising from the accident has been completed.

Apply by letter to the chief constable of the district, specifying the date, time and location. The cost of a full police report (1992) is £41.

Service records

Army

Full service records on non-officers who were discharged before 1900 are kept in the Public Record Office, Chancery Lane, London WC2 (071–405 0741). Thesee records are open to anyone.

Post-1990 records and the records of officers are only available to the soldier, someone applying with their consent or to their next-of-kin. The inquiry should be addressed to the record office of the regiment or corps concerned unless it relates to an officer, in which case application is made to the Army Records Centre, Hayes, Middlesex.

Navy

Similar restrictions apply as with the Army, above.

Air force

Records can be inspected only by the service personnel or someone applying with their written consent. For officers, application is made to PM(AR)1b(RAF), RAF Barnwood. Eastern Avenue, Gloucester. For airmen, apply to P(Man)3e(2)a, RAF Personnel Management Centre, RAF Innsworth, Glos.

Sewers and pipelines

Local authorities keep maps showing the routes of sewers and pipelines. Anyone can inspect these maps free of charge.

Solicitors

The Law Society keeps a computerized roll of the names of all solicitors. Anyone can search the roll, free of charge, at the Law Society, 113 Chancery Lane, London WC2 (071–242 1222).

Complaints are handled by The Solicitors' Complaints Bureau, Portland House, Stag Place, London SW1 (071 834 2288).

Tree-preservation orders

If a local authority has made a tree-preservation order, anyone can inspect the order at the council's office and pay for a copy. The order will identify the tree concerned.

Appendices: 1

Victims of crimes

Two organizations provide compensation for victims of crimes (see Chapter 56). They are the Criminal Injuries Compensation Board, 19 Alfred Place, London WC1E 7EA (071 636 9501) and the Motor Insurers' Bureau, 152 Silbury Boulevard, Central Milton Keynes MK9 1NB (0908 240000).

Wards of court

A Ward Book is kept of all infants who have been made wards of court. Application for information can only be made by a person with a legitimate interest.

Apply in person to Room 169, Royal Courts of Justice, Strand, London WC2. There is no fee.

Wills

Copies of wills lodged when probate or letters of administration were taken out can be obtained by any applicant.

A personal search is first made at the Principal Family Registry, Family Division, Strand, London WC2 (071 936 6000) for the reference number of the will. A copy can then be inspected. Application can also be made by post.

Wills and Their Whereabouts, by B.G. Bourne, revised by Anthony J. Camp (3rd edn, Phillimore, 1965), has details of the location of wills of people who died before 1858.

The Principal Probate Registry operates a scheme that allows people to deposit their will with the registry so that there is no danger of its being lost on their death (see page 202). The index of people who have deposited a will is open to inspection by anyone (apply in person to Room 28 Somerset House, or by post to the Record Keeper, the Principal Probate Registry) but the will cannot be inspected.

Miscellaneous advice organizations

Age Concern
Astral House, 1268 London Road,
Norbury,
London SW16 4ER
Telephone: 081 679 8000

Child Poverty Action Group
1–5 Bath Street,
London EC1V 9PY
Telephone: 071 253 3406

The Childrens' Legal Centre
20 Compton Terrace,
London N1 2UN
Telephone (advice service): 071 359 6251

MIND (National Association for Mental Health)
22 Harley Street,
London W1
Telephone: 071 637 0741

National Head Injuries Associatiion (HEADWAY)
200 Mansfield Road,
Nottingham NG1 3HX
Telephone 0602 240800

2 Specimen Legal Forms

Acknowledgements

The form on pp. 1022–3 is reproduced by permission of the Solicitors' Law Stationery Society Ltd. The form on p. 1025 is Crown copyright and reproduced with the permission of the Controller of Her Majesty's Stationery Office. The form on pp. 1026–7 is reproduced by permission of Shaw & Sons Ltd. The certificate on pp. 1028–9 is reproduced by permission of Her Majesty's Land Registry.

Divorce petition

Before completing, this form, read carefully the enclosed NOTES FOR GUIDANCE

In the   KING'S LYNN   ~~County Court~~   *Delete as appropriate

~~In the Principal Registry~~   No.

(1) On the   10th   day of   February   19 90   the petitioner
Elizabeth constantine Dereham   was lawfully married to
Eustace Rose Charles Dereham   (hereinafter called "the
respondent") at The Register Office in the District of Gazymede in the County of
Rutland.

(2) The petitioner and respondent last lived together as husband and wife at "The Haven", 34
Manea Road, Gazymede, Rutland.

(3) The petitioner is domiciled in England and Wales, and is by occupation a
Fashion Designer   and resides at "The Haven", 34 Manea Road, Gazymede,
Rutland   and the respondent
is by occupation a   Financial Consultant
and resides at "The Haven", 34 Manea Road, Gazymede,
Rutland.

(4) There are no children of the family now living ~~except~~

Lucinda Rian Dereham (D.O.B. 17/06/90)

(5) No other child, now living, has been born to the petitioner/respondent during the marriage
so far as is known to the petitioner ~~except~~

SPECIMEN

Divorce petition (continued)

(6) There are or have been no other proceedings in any court in England and Wales or elsewhere with
reference to the marriage (or to any child of the family) or between the petitioner and respondent with
reference to any property of either or both of them ~~except~~

(7) There are no proceedings continuing in any country outside England or Wales which are in respect of
the marriage or are capable of affecting its validity or subsistence ~~except~~

(8) (This paragraph should be completed only if the petition is based on five years' separation.) No
agreement or arrangement has been made or is proposed to be made between the parties for the support
of the petitioner/respondent (and any child of the family) ~~except~~

(9) The said marriage has broken down irretrievably.

(10) The Respondent has behaved in such a way that the Petitioner cannot reasonably
be expected to live with the Respondent.

SPECIMEN

Divorce petition

(11) Particulars

1 From the commencement of the marriage the Respondent has failed to accept the responsibilities of married life and has continued to enjoy the existence of a bachelor leaving the Petitioner to care for their young child and to run the home.

2 The Respondent goes out every evening and weekend, and frequently stays away from the former matrimonial home over night, without advising the Petitioner of his intentions. The Petitioner remains at home worried as to the Respondent's whereabouts and not knowing whether or not he is to return.

3 The Respondent has just completed a 2 week holiday from work, in which time he spent no time whatsoever at the matrimonial home nor with the Petitioner and the child.

4 The Respondent leaves the running of the home entirely up to the Petitioner including the payment of all bills and offers the Petitioner no moral support whatsoever. There is a total lack of communication between the Petitioner and the Respondent, and the Respondent shows the Petitioner no love nor affection.

5 The Respondent is constantly criticising the Petitioner causing the Petitioner to feel "useless" depressed and lonely.

6 The Petitioner has attempted on numerous occasions to talk to the Respondent about her feelings of loneliness and rejection and to persuade the Respondent to change his ways, but the Respondent has refused to take note and considers that he is behaving within the marriage reasonable and properly. Following the Respondent's absence from the matrimonial home during his 2 week holiday the Petitioner has finally concluded that the marriage has irretrievable broken down.

SPECIMEN

Divorce petition (continued)

Prayer

The petitioner therefore prays

(1) **The suit**

That the said marriage be dissolved

(2) **Costs**

That the .... may be ordered to pay costs of this suit

(3) **Ancillary relief**

That the petitioner may be granted the following ancillary relief:

(a) an order for maintenance pending suit

a periodical payments order

a secured provision order

a property adjustment order

a lump sum order

(b) For the children

a periodical payments order

a secured provision order

a lump sum order

(4) **Children**

Signed ....

The names and addresses of the persons to be served with this petition are:-

Respondent:— c/o Fipps, Chism & Keshupp, 40 Market Square, Ganymede, Rutland

Co-Respondent (adultery case only):—

The Petitioner's address for service is:— c/o Peek & Neate, 29 Market Square, Ganymede, Rutland

Dated this .... day of .... 19......

Address all communications for the court to: The Chief Clerk, County Court.

The Court office at ....

is open from 10 a.m. to 4 p.m. (4.30 p.m. at the Principal Registry) on Mondays to Fridays only.

SPECIMEN

Affidavit

In the matter of the Domestic Violence and Matrimonial Proceedings Act 1976

B E T W E E N :

PETRA MORRIS	Applicant
- and -	
MICHAEL MORRIS	Respondent

A F F I D A V I T

I, PETRA MORRIS unemployed of 4 Abingdon Cottages, London NE1 the above-named Applicant, herein MAKE OATH and SAY as follows:

1. On the 16th March, 1968 I married Michael Morris, the above-named Respondent. There is one child of the marriage, Michael Joseph Morris born on the 12th February, 1969.

2. For a very long period of time I have been subjected to violent assaults and abuse by the Respondent. On the 19th December, 1977 I petitioned in the Willesden County Court for divorce on the grounds that my marriage had irretrievably broken down by virtue of the Respondent's behaviour towards me. A copy of that Petition is now produced and shown to me marked 'PM1' the contents of which are true and to which I crave leave to refer...

4. In the course of the divorce proceedings before the Willesden County Court I agreed to attempt a reconciliation with the Respondent and the said Petition was dismissed by consent before the Learned Registrar on the 5th September, 1978.

5. The reconciliation never really worked and the Respondent continued his drunken violent behaviour towards me. The Respondent has received I estimate between £17,000 to £18,000 at the end of 1977 for agreed damages for injuries sustained in an accident and he is in the process of drinking his way through that money. I estimate he has about £4,000 remaining. He has continued to get drunk almost every day and every night and the beatings have hardly stopped...

11. I have myself been drinking heavily recently because I am so shattered by the Respondent's behaviour. My General Practitioner has now prescribed tablets to prevent me drinking so heavily which have been successful. I remain terrified of the Respondent and dread him coming home...

13. The Respondent is not working at all. He is just drunk the whole time and frequently collapses unconscious in the matrimonial home, defecating and vomiting over his clothes and the furniture. I understand that the Respondent draws Supplementary Benefit in respect of me and the child.

14. I have attempted on several occasions now to reconcile with the Respondent. I now believe that my marriage to him is completely at an end and I shall instruct my Solicitor shortly to prepare a Petition for divorce. I also believe that unless restrained by order of this Honourable Court the Respondent will continue to assault and injure on every occasion that the opportunity to do so arises. I accordingly pray for an order in the terms of my application.

SWORN at *100 Hill Street, London NE1*
this *23rd* day of *October* 1980   } *Petra Morris*

Before me J Jones, SOLICITOR

Injunction

BEFORE <u>HIS HONOUR JUDGE TAYLOR</u> SITTING IN CHAMBERS

County Court

No. of Matter: 89356247

Power of arrest attached to injunction under Section 2 of
Domestic Violence and Matrimonial Proceedings Act 1976.

Applicant: PETRA MORRIS

Respondent: MICHAEL MORRIS

(SEAL.)

[here set out the injunction]

UPON HEARING Counsel for the Applicant and the Respondent in person and on the
Respondent undertaking for a period of six months from today.

1)   Not to assault or molest the Applicant PETRA MORRIS.

2)   To vacate the premises situate at 4 ABINGDON COTTAGES, LONDON NE1 by not
     later than 2.00 p.m. on the 14th September 1980.

3)   Not to enter or attempt to enter the said premises after he has vacated
     them as aforesaid except for the purpose of access to <u>MICHAEL JOSEPH MORRIS</u>
     in accordance with arrangements agreed to in writing by the Applicant and/or
     her Solicitors or a Court Order.

AND IT IS FURTHER ORDERED

     that there be no order as to costs (save that the costs of the Applicant be
     taxed on a Common Fund Basis in accordance with the provisions of the 2nd
     Schedule to the Legal Aid Act 1974)

AND LET THE RESPONDENT <u>MICHAEL MORRIS</u> TAKE NOTICE THAT UNLESS HE OBEYS THE
DIRECTIONS CONTAINED IN THIS ORDER HE WILL BE GUILTY OF CONTEMPT OF COURT AND
WILL BE LIABLE TO BE COMMITTED TO PRISON.

DATED THIS 12th DAY OF SEPTEMBER 1980

~~POWER OF ARREST~~

~~AND the Judge being satisfied that the Respondent has caused actual bodily harm to the Applicant (or the child concerned)
and being of opinion that he is likely to do so again, a power of arrest is attached to this injunction whereby any constable
may arrest without warrant a person whom he has reasonable cause for suspecting of being in breach of the injunction as
mentioned in Section 2(3) of the Domestic Violence and Matrimonial Proceedings Act 1976.~~

Address all communications to the Chief Clerk, County Court,
quoting the number of the matter mentioned above.
The Court Office is open from 10 am - 4 pm, Monday to Friday.

Form 411: Order 46, Rule 28(3)   Power of Arrest attached to Injunction, DV&MP Act 1976

MCR 26703/1/8093730 650 2/80 TL

SPECIMEN

Draft transfer for registered land

Transfer of Whole to Joint Proprietors[(1)]

HM Land Registry
Land Registration Acts, 1925 to 1986

Form 19(JP)
(Rules 98 or 115 Land Registration Rules, 1925)

Stamp pursuant to section 28 of the Finance Act 1931 to be impressed here.

When the transfer attracts Inland Revenue Duty, the stamps should be impressed here before lodging the transfer for registration.

(1) For a transfer to a sole proprietor use printed form 19.

County and District (or London Borough) BLANKSHIRE (BROXMORE)

Title number(s) BLK 2088

Property Red Tiles Cabot Road Broxmore

Date 25 March 1992 In consideration of *thirty four thousand*

(2) Delete the words in italics if not required.

pounds (£ 34,000 —) *receipt of which is acknowledged* [(2)]

(3) In BLOCK LETTERS enter the full name(s), postal address(es) (including postcode) and occupation(s) of the proprietor(s) of the land.

I/We [(3)] JAMES ALEXANDER BLACK and GILLIAN SUSAN BLACK both of RED TILES, CABOT ROAD, BROXMORE, BLANKSHIRE 2BR 9LA

(4) If desired or otherwise as the case may be (see rules 76 and 77).

as beneficial owner(s)[(4)] transfer to

(5) In BLOCK LETTERS enter the full name(s), postal address(es) (including postcode) and occupation(s) of the transferees for entry in the register.

(5)

JOHN WILLIAM BERRY and JANE BERRY both of 2 Humberstone Court Broxmore Blankshire

(6) Enter any special clause here.

the land comprised in the title(s) above referred to [(6)(7)]

(7) A transfer for charitable purposes should follow form 36 in the schedule to the Land Registration Rules 1925 (see rules 121 and 122).

(continued overleaf)

SPECIMEN

1026

Draft transfer for registered land (continued)

(8) Delete the inappropriate alternative.

The transferees declare that the survivor of them(8) ~~can~~ cannot give a valid receipt for capital money arising on a disposition of the land.

(9) If a certificate of value for the purposes of the Stamp Act 1891 and amending Acts is not required delete this paragraph.

(9) ~~It is hereby certified that the transaction hereby effected does not form part of a larger transaction or series of transactions in respect of which the amount or value or aggregate amount or value of the consideration exceeds £~~ ....

(10) This transfer must be executed by the transferees as well as the transferor(s).

(10)Signed as a deed by
James Alexander Black   J A Black.

in the presence of
Name of Witness   J Smith   Signature   J. Smith
Address 3 The Cottages Broxmore
Occupation School Teacher

(10)Signed as a deed by
Gillian Susan Black   GS-Black

in the presence of
Name of Witness J Smith   Signature J. Smith
Address as above
Occupation

(10)Signed as a deed by
John William Berry   J W Berry

in the presence of
Name of Witness T Price   Signature T Price
Address 3 Humberstone Court Broxmore
Occupation Probation officer

(10)Signed as a deed by
Jane Berry   J Berry

in the presence of
Name of Witness T Price   Signature T Price
Address as above
Occupation

SPECIMEN

Land registry certificate

Land registry certificate (continued)

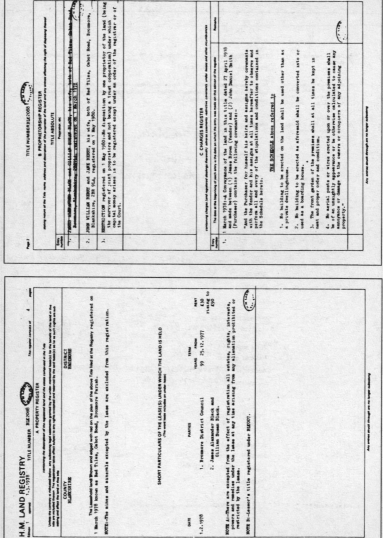

SPECIMEN

SPECIMEN

Land registry certificate (continued)

Land registry certificate (continued)

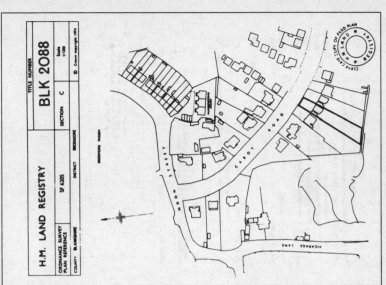

TITLE NUMBER BLK2088 Page 3

C CHARGES REGISTER

containing charges, incumbrances etc. adversely affecting the land and registered dealings therewith

Entry Number	The date at the beginning of each entry is the date on which the entry was made on that edition of the register	Remarks

2. ~~1 March 1970-CHARGE dated 30 December 1957 registered on 1 March 1970 to secure the moneys including the further advances therein mentioned.~~

3. PROPRIETOR—THE WEYMOOR BUILDING SOCIETY of Society House, The Avenue, Weyford, Blankshire, 1WK 2AB, registered on 1 March 1970.

4. 1 May 1980—CHARGE dated 25 March 1980 registered on 1 May 1980 to secure the monies therein mentioned.

5. PROPRIETOR—REPUTABLE BUILDING SOCIETY (Account No.12670) of Plunch Lane, High Street, Weyford, Blankshire, 1WK 6CB registered on 1 May 1980.

6. 1 December 1980—CHARGE dated 30 November 1980 registered on 1 December 1980 to secure the moneys including the further advances therein mentioned.

7. PROPRIETOR—SAFEWAY BANK LIMITED (Co.Regn. No.4761) of 17 Church Street, Weyford, Blankshire, 1WK 5AB, registered on 1 December 1980.

Particulars of claim (continued)

PARTICULARS OF SPECIAL DAMAGE

1966 Mini Clubman Saloon, damaged beyond repair. Value - £850.00

Accessories and contents of Mini Clubman;

(i)	Toolbox and tools	£68.00
(ii)	5 cassettes smashed in crash @ £6.99 each	£34.95
(iii)	Petrol can with gallon of petrol	£10.70
(iv)	2 large sponge dice lost in wreckage	£5.25

Fares and travel expenses	£11.23
Loss of earnings	£53.92

Total £1034.05

AND THE PLAINTIFF CLAIMS:

(1) Under paragraph 4 above £1034.05

(2) Interest pursuant to Section 69 of the County Courts Act 1984.

(3) costs

The plaintiff abandons that part of his claim which exceeds £1,000.It is certified that the value of this claim does not exceed £5000.

Dated the   day of   1992

Signed.................

Edward Price-Jones, plaintiff
whose address for service is 17
Council Houses, Canal lane, West
Acre Norfolk.

To the District Judge and
to the above named Defendant.

SPECIMEN

Particulars of claim

IN THE CASTLE ACRE COUNTY COURT   Case No: 9203422

B E T W E E N   EDWARD PRICE-JONES   plaintiff

                       AND

                       SUSAN TRACEY FYFIELD   defendant

PARTICULARS OF CLAIM

1. On 10th February 1992 the Plaintiff was driving his car along the Littlepoe road in Mudford, heading out of the town, when he was in collision with a car driven by the Defendant.

2. The said collision was caused by the negligence of the Defendant

PARTICULARS OF NEGLIGENCE

(1) Overtaking two cars when it was not safe to do so into the path of Plaintiff's car and colliding with the Plaintiff;

(2) Driving too fast;

(3) Failing to give any proper warning of her approach;

(4) Failing to keep any or any proper look out or to observe or heed the presence or approach of the Plaintiff;

(5) Failing to apply her brakes in time or at all or so to steer slow down control or otherwise manage her vehicle as to avoid the said collision;

(6) Failing to observe or obey traffic signs;

(7) Failing to take sufficient or any account of the road conditions.

3. The Plaintiff will in addition to the matters pleaded in paragraphs 1 to 2 inclusive rely upon the fact that on 15th April 1992 the Defendant was convicted bye the Mudford Magistrates' Court of the offence of having driven without due care and attentionon 10th February 1992. She was fined £240 and had 5 penalty points imposed. The facts upon which the conviction was based were the facts as alleged in paragraphs 1 to 2 herein which caused the injuries loss and damages to the Plaintiff. The said conviction is relevant to the issue of negligence.

4. By reason of the matters aforesaid the Plaintiff has suffered loss and damage.

SPECIMEN

Particulars of claim

IN THE CASTLE ACRE COUNTY COURT   Case No: 920342

BETWEEN

EDWARD PRICE-JONES

plaintiff

AND

SUSAN TRACEY FYFIELD

defendant

DEFENCE

1. The Defendant admits that on 10th February 1992 a collision occurred between the Plaintiff along the Littlepot Road out of Mudford, between the Plaintiff's Mini Clubman saloon and the Defendant's Ford Cortina.

2. The Defendant denies that this collision was caused by her negligence as alleged in paragraph 2 of the Particulars of Claim or at all.

3. The Defendant admits that on 15th April 1992 she was convicted of the offence of driving without due care and attention. She denies that this has any relevance to the Plaintiff's claim.

4. The collision was caused solely by the negligence of the Plaintiff.

PARTICULARS OF NEGLIGENCE

The Plaintiff was negligent in that he:

(a) Drove too fast;
(b) Failed to keep a proper lookout;
(c) Drove on the wrong side of the road;
(d) Drove on to and across the white line on the road;
(e) Ran in to the front of the Defendant's Ford Cortina;
(f) Failed to maintain the engine of his car in such condition so that it did not emit clouds of smoke, thereby making it impossible for the defendant to see the approach of the the plaintiff in his vehicle;
(g) Failed to slow down, stop, swerve, or take such other action as was necessary to avoid the collision.

5. If, which is denied, there was any negligence on the part of the Defendant, the said collision was nevertheless caused or substantially contributed to by the Plaintiff. The defendant repeats the allegations set out in paragraph 4 above.

SPECIMEN

Particulars of claim (continued)

6. The Defendant does not admit that the Plaintiff suffered loss and damage as alleged in the Particulars of Claim. She puts the plaintiff to full proof of the alleged losses.

7. Save as aforesaid the Defendant denies each and every allegation in the Statement of Claim as if the same were here set forth and traversed seriatim.

Signed.................

Served the   day of   1992 by Toft & Tweed, solicitors, of Manour House, Church Road, Little Snoring, Norfolk, BW44 1PG solicitors for the Defendant.

To:
The Court and to
the Plaintiff

SPECIMEN

List of Documents

IN THE CASTLE ACRE COUNTY COURT   Case No: 9203422

BETWEEN   EDWARD PRICE-JONES   plaintiff

AND

SUSAN TRACEY FYFIELD   defendant

PLAINTIFF'S LIST OF DOCUMENTS
Order 14 rule 1(5)

The following is a list of the documents which contain information about matters in dispute in this case which are or have been in the Plaintiff's possession.

SCHEDULE 1. Part 1

The Plaintiff has in his possession the documents numbered and listed here.
The Plaintiff does not object to the Defendant inspecting them.

No.	DATE	DOCUMENT
1.	15/02/92	Copy letter plaintiff to defendant
2.	17/02/92	Letter defendant to plaintiff
3.	22/02/92	Copy letter plaintiff to defendant
4.	27/02/92	Picture postcard defendant to plaintiff
5.	01/04/92	Copy letter plaintiff to defendant
6.	07/04/92	Letter defendant's solicitor to plaintiff.
7.	08/04/92	Estimate: Shady Carsales
8.	various	Bundle of wage slips
9.	various	bundle of receipts.

SCHEDULE 1. Part 2

The Plaintiff has in his possession the documents numbered and listed here but he objects to the Defendant inspecting them:

Bundle of letters passing between the plaintiff and his solicitors, and other documents which have been brought into being for the purposes of this litigation.

The Plaintiff objects to the Defendant inspecting these documents because: they are by their very nature privileged.

SCHEDULE 2

The Plaintiff has had the documents numbered and listed below, but they are no longer in his possession:

SPECIMEN

List of Documents (continued)

The originals of those documents listed in Schedule 1 part 1 which are indicated as being copy documents.

The documents were in the possession of the Plaintiff on the date(s) of the documents but they are (unless otherwise stated) in the possession of those to whom they are addressed.

All the documents which are or have been in the possession of the Plaintiff and which contain information about the matters in dispute in this case are listed in schedules 1 and 2.

Dated   1992

signed...............

Edward Price-Jones, plaintiff whose address for service is 17 Council Houses, Canal lane, West Acre Norfolk.

TO:
The Court
The Defendant

SPECIMEN

Affidavit

Affidavit (continued)

IN THE CASTLE ACRE COUNTY COURT

PLT:
E PRICE-JONES:
First:
1992:

BETWEEN

EDWARD PRICE-JONES

Case No: 9203422

plaintiff

AND

SUSAN TRACEY FYFIELD

defendant

AFFIDAVIT

I Edward Price-Jones, of 17 Council Houses, Canal lane, West Acre Norfolk make oath and say as follows:

1. I am the plaintiff in this action

2. Except where otherwise stated the facts as stated are from my own personal knowledge.

3. I make this affidavit in support of my application for summary judgment against the defendant in this case.

4. The proceedings were issued on 5 May 1992. The defence was served on 17 May 1992. Liability is denied.

5. Notwithstanding the filing of what purports to be a defence, I believe that the defendant has no defence to my claim, nor is there any question of my having been contributorily negligent.

6. I confirm that to the best of my knowledge and belief the facts as set out in the particulars of claim are true in every respect.

7. In support of my submission I produce ('marked EPJ 1') a copy of the police report. I draw the court's attention to the statements of independent witnesses D S Poole and W Y Rixon which confirm that at the time the defendant was not only overtaking into my path but also looking at her front seat passenger.

8. Notwithstanding what is alleged in the defence I believe that the defendant's conviction on a charge of driving without due care and attention is conclusive evidence of her negligence.

Appendix 2: (8)

Barr/Wong

9. In the circumstances I invite the court to enter judgment against the defendant in the sum of £1000 plus interest.

Sworn by the said Edward)

Price-Jones at)

Mudford, Norfolk this)

day of 1992)

Before me

A Commissioner for oaths.

This affidavit is filed on behalf of the Plaintiff

SPECIMEN

SPECIMEN

3 Legal Jargon: An A–Z Guide

abate. To reduce or make less (e.g. general *legacies* are abated – reduced proportionately – when the deceased's estate is insufficient to pay all the general legacies in full; a nuisance is abated when it is reduced).

abstract of title. A summary of the legal title to *unregistered land*. The abstract shows the history and validity of the title; cf. an epitome of title, which lists all the documents going back to the *root of title*.

accord and satisfaction. When a creditor accepts an agreement suggested by the debtor, which satisfies the debt and so prevents the creditor from suing the debtor.

acknowledgement of service. When defendants are served with a *writ* they should enter a written acknowledgement of service with the court. If they do not do so within fourteen days, the plaintiff may be able to obtain *judgement in default* against them.

action. Civil proceedings in a court of law.

act of God. 'An extraordinary circumstance which could not be foreseen, and which could not be guarded against' (Pandorf 1886). Insurance policies do not usually cover acts of God.

actus reus. The guilty act; cf. *mens rea*.

administrator, administratrix. The personal representative appointed by the court to administer the estate of someone who has died intestate (i.e. without a will) or who left a will which did not appoint executors.

ad valorem. According to the value: e.g. stamp duty on sale of land is charged according to the price paid.

affidavit. A written statement to be used as evidence in court proceedings. The deponent swears (or affirms) as to its truth before a commissioner of oaths, a solicitor or a court official, who then witnesses the deponent's signature.

amicus curiae. A friend of the court. A barrister appointed in certain cases to assist the court who can bring matters that have been overlooked to the court's attention.

ancient lights. Windows which have had an uninterrupted access of light for at least twenty years. Buildings cannot be erected which interfere with this right of light.

annul. When court proceedings, or their outcome, are declared no longer to have effect.

antenuptial. Before marriage.

Anton Piller order. A search warrant allowing the papers of a defendant in a civil (*not* criminal) case to be seized and his or her premises searched. Usually applies when the court thinks the defendant might destroy incriminating evidence.

arraign. To bring an accused person to the bar of the court so that the indictment can be read to him or her.

arrestable offence. A criminal offence carrying a maximum penalty of five years' or more imprisonment. All arrestable offences allow the offender to be arrested without a warrant.

assault. Strictly speaking, merely attempting to strike another person is an assault. If touching takes place, then it is *battery*. In practice, the word assault is always taken to include the battery.

attestation. The signature of a witness to the signing of a document by another person.

attorney. Since the Judicature Act 1875, attorneys have been officially called solicitors.

Attorney-General. The chief law officer of the Crown and head of the barristers' profession.

automatism. An involuntary act done by a person who is not aware of what he or she is doing or who is unable to control his or her muscles.

autrefois. A person cannot be tried for the same offence twice.

bailiff. A person employed by the sheriff to serve and enforce court documents and processes.

bailment. When goods are left by one person (the 'bailor') with another (the 'bailee') to hold in accordance with instructions: e.g. leaving luggage at railway luggage offices.

bank holidays. In England and Wales, these are laid down in the Banking and Financial Dealings Act 1971 as Easter Monday, the first and last Mondays in May, the last Monday in August, 26 December and, if either 25 or 26 December is a Sunday, then also 27 December.

bankruptcy. When a court takes over a debtor's assets on behalf of his or her creditors. See Chapter 40.

battery. Using force on another person, whether or not harm results.

bench. The term used to describe the magistrates and judges in a court.

beneficiary. A person who is entitled to property which is held for him or her by trustees. Also, someone who receives a gift under a will.

bequeath. To leave *personal* (cf. *real*) *property* under a will. The gift is called a *legacy*.

bona vacantia. Goods that do not have an owner. Generally, they go to the finder except in cases of shipwreck and treasure trove, when they go to the Crown.

brewster sessions. Annual meeting of licensing justices to consider applications (and renewals) for licences to sell alcoholic liquor.

bridle way. A public right of way to pass on horseback.

burden of proof. The obligation of proving the case.

by-law. Rules laid down by a local authority or other body in accordance with powers given to them by an act of Parliament. These local rules have the full force of law.

capital punishment. Death by hanging is now restricted to high treason and piracy with violence.

case stated. When a case is submitted by a court to a higher court for its opinion, the lower court will summarize the facts of the case and the relevant points of law. Most commonly arises when a magistrates' court decision is appealed to the Divisional Court of the Queen's Bench Division.

caveat emptor. Let the buyer beware.

certiorari. An order of the High Court to review and quash the decision of the lower court which was based on an irregular procedure.

champerty. Financing another's legal action in return for a share of the profits. Such a contract is unenforceable, but is not a criminal offence.

charge on land. A *mortgage*.

charity. A body that has legally charitable objectives. Only bodies which are for the relief of poverty, the advancement of education, the advancement of religion, or for other purposes beneficial to the community, can qualify as charities.

chattels. All property other than *freehold* real estate. Chattels can be 'chattels real' (leaseholds) or 'chattels personal' (all other property – also called pure personalty).

c.i.f. Cost, insurance, freight. The cost of the goods includes these items.

civil law. The law administered by the civil courts (i.e. non-criminal law).

Class F. A spouse whose name is not on the title deeds of the matrimonial home can register a Class F charge which warns all purchasers that she claims the right to live in the home, even if it is sold by the other spouse. See Chapter 5.

codification. The bringing together into one act of Parliament of all the law on one topic without altering the law.

commorientes. When people die together at the same time, their deaths are presumed to have occurred in order of seniority by age.

complaint. The initial step in beginning civil proceedings in the magistrates' court.

condonation. When one spouse forgives the other's matrimonial misconduct. It is no longer a bar to divorce.

consideration. If a person promises to do something for another (e.g. pay money) that promise can be enforced only if the other person gave, or promised, something of value in return; that is said to be the consideration for the promise. Thus every contract requires consideration. The only exception is when the promise is in a *deed*.

conversion. A tort which arises when someone's title to his or her chattels is denied or if a bailee negligently allows his or her bailor's goods to be damaged.

conveyance. A written document transferring ownership of *land* from one person to another.

corporeal hereditaments. Visible, tangible property (e.g. house, car, books).

costs. The expenses relating to legal services. See Chapter 66.

counterclaim. When defendants are sued they can include in their defence any claim that they may have against the plaintiff, even if it arises from a different matter.

coverture. Legal status of a married woman.

crime. Defined in Halsbury's *Law of England* as an unlawful act or default which is an offence against the public and which renders the person guilty of the act liable to legal punishment.

curtesy. An ancient right whereby a widower had a life estate in the land of his late wife. Very rare nowadays.

curtilage. The garden, field, yard etc. surrounding a house and which belongs to the house.

custom. An unwritten law dating back to time immemorial.

damage feasant. Damage by animals of A on the land of B. If B seizes the animals (distress damage feasant) he or she cannot sue for damages.

declaratory judgement. When the court makes a declaration as to the law, or rights between parties, without making an order to enforce those rights.

deed. A written document that has been signed, sealed and delivered by its maker. The signature is witnessed. These days, makers only sign for there is rarely any need for them formally to *seal* or deliver the deed.

defendant. A person who is sued or prosecuted, or who has any court proceedings brought against him or her.

demise. The grant of a lease in land.

deposition. A statement made on oath by a witness.

detinue. An action formerly brought to recover chattels wrongly detained, but abolished by the Torts (Interference with Goods) Act 1977.

devise. A gift of *land* in a will (if not land, it is a bequest).

Director of Public Prosecutions. The DPP is a solicitor or barrister of at least ten years' standing who works under the Lord Chancellor. Only the DPP can prosecute for certain serious crimes.

discovery of documents. In many civil actions the parties disclose all their relevant documents to each other, even if the disclosed documents injure their case.

distrain. To levy *distress.*

distress. Seizing a personal chattel from a debtor or wrongdoer in satisfaction of the debt, etc.

dock brief. A prisoner being tried on indictment (i.e. in the crown court) can request any robed barrister in court to represent him or her for a nominal fee. The practice has become rare since the introduction of legal aid.

domicile. Where a person has their permanent home.

dominant tenement. Land which has the benefit of rights over another piece of land: e.g. if plot A has a right of light over plot B, plot A is the dominant tenement and plot B is the *servient tenement.*

duty solicitor. Many magistrates' courts have rotas of solicitors who attend the court and give advice and help to unrepresented defendants.

easement. The right which an owner of land (called the *dominant tenement*) has over the land of another person, called the *servient tenement* (e.g. right of way, light, support).

enactment. An act of Parliament, or part of an act.

encumbrance. A liability affecting property (e.g. a lease, *mortgage, restrictive covenant*).

engross. When a draft document has been approved by everyone concerned, it is then retyped in its final form. That is the engrossment.

equity. Body of doctrines and maxims which developed alongside the common law, and which aimed to mould the rigid and inflexible common-law principles into a more just and equitable legal system.

equity of redemption. The right of a mortgagor (i.e. borrower) to redeem his or her *mortgage* after the date stated in his or her mortgage deed.

estate. An interest in *land* (e.g. a lease).

estoppel. A rule which prevents a person denying the truth of a statement or the existence of facts which they have led another to believe; e.g. if X spends money on Y's property because Y says he will give it to X, then Y may not be able to change his mind and refuse to give the property to X.

execution. Enforcing a court's judgement by compelling the defendant to comply with it; e.g. a bailiff who seizes goods by *distress* is executing the judgement.

executor (executrix). A personal representative appointed by will.

ex parte. An application to the court by one party to the proceedings, without the other party being present.

expert witness. An expert witness can give his or her opinion on a subject. This is an exception to the general rule that witnesses must not tell the court their opinions: e.g. a witness cannot say, 'I thought he was driving dangerously.'

extinguishment. When a right or obligation ends: e.g. a debt is repaid and so the right to sue for recovery of the debt is extinguished.

fatal accident. When a man is killed by the negligence of another, his or her dependants can sue for their financial loss arising from his death. Only the spouse, parent, grandparent, child, grandchild, nephew, niece or cousin can sue; a common-law spouse cannot sue (Fatal Accidents Act 1976).

fee simple. The absolute ownership of land. Basically the same as a freehold.

fee tail. An interest in land which descends to the direct issue (i.e. children) of the owner and which he or she cannot give to anyone else.

feme covert. A married woman.

feme sole. An unmarried woman (i.e. spinster, widow, divorced woman).

fieri facias. A court order to sheriffs requiring them to seize a debtor's goods to pay off a creditor's judgement.

foreclosure. When a mortgagee (e.g. a building society) forecloses on a *mortgage*, the mortgagor (the borrower) forfeits his or her *equity of redemption*. The court therefore allows the mortgagee to take possession of the property, sell it and deduct the amount it is owed from the proceeds of sale. Any balance goes to the mortgagor.

freehold. cf. *leasehold*, under which property is held for a specified period of time.

frustration. A contract is frustrated if it becomes impossible to perform because of a reason that is beyond the control of the parties (e.g. war). The contract is cancelled.

garnishee order. When a creditor commences proceedings against someone who owes his or her debtor money, so as to intercept the repayment before it reaches the debtor; e.g. A is owed money by B, but B is owed money by C; A can obtain a garnishee order against C.

good faith. Honestly.

goodwill. 'The whole advantage, wherever it may be, of the reputation and connection of the firm' (Trego 1896).

ground rent. The rent paid by a person with a long lease (commonly ninety-nine years) to the freeholder.

guarantor. A person who guarantees another's debts; also called a *surety*.

habeas corpus. (Latin for 'that you have the body'.) A court order which requires that a named individual be produced before the court; applied for when a person is illegally detained.

half-blood. The relationship between people who have one common ancestor: e.g. between A and B who have the same father, but different mothers.

heirloom. 'Any piece of household stuff which, by custom of some countries, having belonged to a house for certain descents, goes with the house after the death of the owner, unto the heir and not to the executors.'

high seas. The seas more than 5 kilometres from the coast.

holding charge. A minor charge used as a device for holding a suspect while a more serious offence is investigated.

holograph. A document written in the maker's own handwriting: e.g. a holograph will.

hostile witness. A court can declare a witness to be hostile if it believes that he or she is hostile to the party calling him or her and that he or she is unwilling to tell the truth. This then allows the witness to be cross-examined by the party who called him or her. (Parties cannot usually cross-examine their own witnesses.)

ignorance of the law is no excuse. 'Every man must be taken to be cognizant of the law, otherwise there is no knowing of the extent to which the excuse of ignorance might be carried. It would be urged in almost every case' (Bailey, 1800).

illegal. An act is illegal when it involves breaking the criminal law; cf. an *unlawful* act.

immovables. *Land* and the property attached to it.

in camera. When evidence is not heard in open court – for instance, because it relates to a person's sexual capacity or to official secrets.

indictable offence. An offence which could be tried on indictment in the crown court.

indictment. The written accusation, prepared by the Crown, charging a crown-court defendant. It is read out at the beginning of the trial.

infant. A person under eighteen. Also called a minor.

information. Strictly speaking, an information is any proceeding brought by the Crown other than by *indictment*. In practice, the word is now mainly used to describe a statement placed before a magistrate which informs him or her of the commission of an offence for which a summons or warrant must be issued by the magistrate. This is called 'laying an information'.

injunction. A court order requiring someone to do, or to refrain from doing, something.

interim. In the meantime. An 'interim order' in an action is made prior to the full hearing of the case, when a 'final order' will be made. The hearing of the application for an interim order will be an *interlocutory* proceeding.

interlocutory. An interim stage in the course of the action (e.g. interlocutory injunction). 'Interlocutory proceedings' usually describe the events in a civil case between its commencement (by issuing a *writ* or summons) and its ending (by judgement being given).

interpleader summons. When a person holds property to which they have no claim, but two or more people claim it from him or her, he or she can issue an interpleader summons asking the court to decide who has the best claim to the property.

interrogatories. In the course of a civil action a party can ask the court for leave to put written questions to the other party. Their purpose is to narrow down the differences between the parties by asking the other party to make admissions.

intervener. A person who intervenes in an action to which he or she is not a party. Generally applies to a woman accused of adultery in another's divorce and who wishes to intervene to deny that allegation.

inter vivos. Made between people who are alive (e.g. a gift *inter vivos*); cf. a testamentary gift.

intestate. Dying without leaving a will. See page 226.

invitation to treat. An offer to receive an offer: e.g. a shopkeeper's display of goods in a window is an invitation to treat – he or she is offering the customer an opportunity to offer to buy those goods, whereupon he or she might accept that offer. See page 535.

issue. Offspring (i.e. children, grandchildren etc.).

jactitation of marriage. If A wrongly claims to be married to B, then B can ask the court to confirm that they are not married.

jointly and severally. If A and B are jointly and severally liable to C, then C has three possible courses of action: he can sue A or B, or A and B.

joint tenancy. When two or more people hold property as joint tenants, they own it between them, and if one dies the other(s) take his or her share: e.g. A, B and C own a house; if C dies his share passes to A and B, who now have half each, instead of one-third each. The alternative to having a joint tenancy is to have a *tenancy in common*.

joint tortfeasors. Two or more people who are responsible for a tort. For example, A negligently drives his car into B. But A was acting in the course of employment for C, her employer, who therefore has a *vicarious liability* for A's negligence. Thus, as far as B is concerned, A and C are joint tortfeasors. They are *jointly* and *severally* liable.

judgement debtor. A debtor who has had a court judgement for the debt made against him or her, but who has not yet paid off the debt.

judgement in default. A plaintiff can enter judgement in default against a defendant who fails to carry out a procedural step in time: e.g. fails to file a defence to the claim.

judicial review. Application for judicial review is made to the Divisional Court when a lower court or tribunal has behaved incorrectly. The court can make an order of *certiorari, mandamus or prohibition.*

judicial separation. Similar to divorce in that it makes both husband and wife single persons again for all legal purposes. However, unlike a divorce, it does not allow either party to remarry.

jurat. The sentence at the end of an affidavit or statutory declaration which shows when, where and before whom it was made.

jurisdiction. Our courts have jurisdiction over England, Wales, Berwick on Tweed, territorial waters and English boats on the *high seas*.

kin. Blood relatives.

knock for knock. Agreement between insurance companies to pay claims made by their own insured and so avoid the expense of claiming from each other. See Chapter 51.

laches. Unreasonable delay in pursuing a legal right. See *limitation*.

land. 'Land in the legal signification comprehendeth any ground, soil or earth whatsoever, as meadows, pastures, woods, moors, waters, marshes, furzes and heath ... It legally includeth also all castles, houses and other buildings' (Coke).

Land Charges Register. A register of all adverse rights and interests affecting *unregistered land* (e.g. *mortgages, restrictive covenants, easements, Class F* etc.). Unless the right or interest is registered it will not bind an innocent purchaser of the property.

laying an information. Starting magistrates' court criminal proceedings. See *information*.

leading question. One which suggests the answer or which allows only a 'yes' or 'no' answer: e.g. 'Were you scared?' Allowed only in cross-examination.

leasehold. An estate in land that is less than a *freehold*. Generally used to describe an interest for a fixed term (e.g. for ninety-nine years).

legacy. A gift of *personal property* by will (cf. *devise*).

legal separation. The same as *judicial separation*.

legitimation. Legitimization of a bastard by the subsequent marriage of the parents.

lessee. Person who takes a lease (i.e. the tenant).

lessor. Person who grants a lease (i.e. the landlord).

lien. A creditor has a lien over property of the debtor until the debt is paid off: e.g. if a solicitor holds title deeds to a house for a client who has not paid the solicitor's bill, the solicitor need not release the title deeds until the bill has been paid.

limitation. Court proceedings must be begun within the limitation period. There are different periods for different types of claims. See page 892.

liquidated sum. A specific sum, or a sum that can be worked out as a matter of arithmetic; cf. *unliquidated damages*, when the amount is not easily ascertainable.

liquidator. Person who winds up a company.

London Gazette. Government journal for publication of official notices (e.g. proclamations; winding up; receivership orders).

long vacation. Generally, the whole of August. The Supreme Court transacts only urgent business during this time.

McNaghten Rules. Three rules for use when deciding whether an accused person can plead insanity as a defence.

maintenance pending suit. In divorce, nullity or separation proceedings the court can order maintenance to be paid before the full hearing of the petition.

mandamus. A command from the Divisional Court of the High Court that a lower court does something: e.g. hears a claim which it denied having jurisdiction to hear.

Mareva injunction. A court order freezing assets so they cannot be taken out of the country (if the court thinks the defendant might try to thwart a claim by moving all his or her money abroad).

master. A practice master deals with routine *interlocutory* proceedings in a High Court action.

mens rea. The 'criminal intention' to commit a crime. The mens rea and the *actus reus* together make the crime.

mesne profits. Damages payable by trespassers who have stayed in possession after their right to occupy the land has ended: e.g. a tenant who stays on after the end of his tenancy. Generally, the mesne profits will equal the rent for the premises.

messuage. A dwelling-house with its *curtilage*.

minor interest. An interest in *registered land* (e.g. *mortgage*) which bind purchasers only if it is registered on the title register.

misdemeanour. Criminal offences used to be either misdemeanours or (more serious) felonies. The classification was abolished in 1967.

misfeasance. The improper or negligent carrying out of a legal act (e.g. a company director who misapplies the company's money).

moiety. One half.

mortgage. A loan of money on the security of a property. The lender is the mortgagee and the borrower is the mortgagor.

naturalization. Whereby an alien becomes a citizen and subject of his or her adopted country.

negotiable instrument. A transferable security (e.g. cheque, promissory note, bill of exchange).

nemo dat quod non habet. No one can give what does not belong to him. So a thief cannot pass ownership of property to a person who buys it from him: it still belongs to the person from whom it was stolen.

next friend. Person through whom either an *infant* or a mental health patient acts in a legal action. See page 154.

nolle prosequi. The plaintiff discontinues his action. More usually in a criminal case when the *Attorney-General* stays a prosecution; he has power to do this in any indictable prosecution.

non-cohabitation order. Magistrates' court order releasing a spouse from the obligation to live with the other spouse.

non-contentious business. Non-court legal work (e.g. conveyancing, probate). See page 939.

nuncupative will. An oral will. Valid only if made while on active service.

obiter dictum. A statement of opinion by a judge which is not relevant to the case being tried. It is not of such authority as if it had been relevant to the case being tried. (See *ratio decidendi*.)

official referee. Layperson appointed by the High Court to try complex matters in which he or she is a specialist (e.g. accountancy disputes).

official solicitor. Acts in High Court cases as a *next friend* for those who have no one to assist them.

Old Bailey. The Central Criminal Court, one of the crown courts.

option. A right to buy something.

originating summons. Similar to a *writ* in that it commences proceedings in the High Court. For instance, when an *infant* is injured and his *next friend* wants the court to approve a settlement.

parol. An informally made contract. Previously used to describe any contract not under *seal* but now generally taken to mean an oral contract.

passing off. A tort whereby A passes off his goods or business as being that of B (e.g. by using a similar name or label). B can apply for an *injunction* and damages.

peppercorn rent. A nominal rent which it is not intended that the landlord will collect (e.g. a red rose on Midsummer Day). But it preserves the landlord's legal title.

per incuriam. A mistaken decision by a court; other courts need not follow it.

periodic tenancy. A tenancy which is not for a fixed term. The tenant pays rent periodically (e.g. weekly, monthly) and the tenancy continues until notice is given by either party. See Chapter 17.

personal property. All property except *land*. Also called personalty.

plaintiff. Person who sues (i.e. brings a civil action).

plc. A public limited company. Most used to have 'Ltd' after their names, but changed this to 'plc' when UK company law was brought into line with EC law in 1981.

pleadings. Formal written documents in a civil action. The plaintiff submits a statement of claim, the defendant a defence.

polygamy. Legally having more than one spouse.

portion. Parental gift to establish a child in life.

possessory title. Title acquired by a squatter through adverse possession.

pre-emption. A right of first refusal if a property is sold.

premium. In a tenancy, the premium is the price paid other than in rent: e.g. a flat is sold on a ninety-nine-year lease at an annual rent of £50, for £15,000 – the £15,000 is the premium.

prescription. Method of acquiring rights over another's land by usage over a period of time.

presumption of death. 'If a person has not been heard of for seven years, there is a presumption of law that he is dead' (Lal Chand, 1925).

pre-trial review. Preliminary meeting of parties in county-court action to consider administrative matters and what agreement can be reached prior to the trial.

privacy. There is no *tort* of interfering with another's privacy, although the European Convention on Human Rights states that 'everyone has the right to respect for his private and family life, his home and his correspondence'.

profit a prendre. The right to take something off someone else's *land* (e.g. collect firewood).

prohibition. An order of a Divisional Court of the High Court preventing an inferior court from doing something (e.g. hearing a case that is outside its jurisdiction).

public policy. Acts which are against public policy are illegal (e.g. gambling debts cannot be sued for; nor can a prostitute sue for her payment).

purchaser. Generally taken to mean one who buys property, but, strictly speaking, it covers any person who acquires the *fee simple in land* other than by descent (for instance, a person who receives the land as an *inter vivos* gift).

putative father. The man who is alleged to be the father of an illegitimate child.

quantum meruit. As much as he or she has earned.

Queen's Proctor. A solicitor representing the Crown who can intervene in divorce cases (for instance, if the divorce was obtained on the basis of false evidence) before the decree is made absolute.

rack rent. 'A rent that represents the full annual value of the holding' (Newman 1975).

ratio decidendi. The reason for a judicial decision. A statement of legal principle in a ratio decidendi is more authoritative than if in an *obiter dictum*.

real property. Freehold estates in *land*; it is often used to describe any interest in land.

recognizance. Sum of money that will be forfeited by an accused person who fails to answer to his or her bail.

re-examination. Examination of a witness by the party calling him or her after their cross-examination by the other party.

registered land. Land that is registered under the Land Registration Act 1925. See page 251.

relator. A private individual on whose suggestion the *Attorney-General* brings an action for the public good – a relator action.

remainder. When a person has an interest in land that will come into their possession when someone else's interest ends, they have an interest in remainder: e.g. A gives land to B for life, the remainder to C. (See *reversion*.)

rentcharge. A rental payment on freehold land. Largely abolished in 1977 except when used to enforce covenants between freeholders.

replevin. Recovering goods seized by the sheriff or bailiff, after paying off the *judgement debt*.

requisition. An inquiry by a purchaser of *land* concerning the vendor's title to that land.

res ipsa loquitur. The matter speaks for itself. Normally a plaintiff must prove his or her case, but in accident claims in which the circumstances raise a prima facie indication of negligence, the defendant has to prove he or she was not negligent. The circumstances indicate negligence – it speaks for itself.

restitutio in integrum. Restoring the status quo.

restrictive covenant. A covenant that allows one landowner to control the use of another's land. See page 363.

retrospective legislation. An act that applies to a period before the act was passed.

reversion. If an owner of land disposes of it for a period, after which it will revert back to him or her, he or she is said to hold the reversion: e.g. a landlord grants a lease for twenty years; he will acquire the freehold in twenty years' time. See also *remainder*.

right of re-entry. Right of landlord to take possession if tenant breaks the terms of the tenancy.

riparian. Connected with the bank of a river or stream.

root of title. Title deed which forms the basis of the vendor's title to the *land*. Must be at least fifteen years old.

salvage. The right of a person who saves a ship or its cargo from shipwreck to receive compensation. Usually assessed by the court.

seal. Used to be the impression of a piece of wax on to a document. Now a small red sticky label is used instead, although the absence of the seal will not invalidate the document, since 'to constitute a sealing neither wax nor wafer nor a piece of paper, not even an impression is necessary' (Sandilands, (1871)).

section 6(2) committal. Short form of committal by magistrates.

servient tenement. See *dominant tenement*.

settlement. Tying *land* up for the future by leaving it to trustees to hold for successive limited owners.

sine die. Indefinitely.

small claim. Colloquial phrase generally referring to consumer claims for no more than £1,000 in the county court. (Above that figure, the loser usually has to pay the winner's legal costs; see page 946.)

solus agreement. When a retailer agrees to buy all their goods from one supplier. Common in the petrol-supply business.

special damage. Financial loss that can be proved (e.g. wage loss).

specialty contract. A contract under seal.

specific performance. When a party to a contract is ordered to carry out their part of the bargain (e.g. to sell a house). Ordered only if damages (money) would be an inadequate remedy.

stakeholder. One who holds money as an impartial observer. He or she will part with it only if both parties agree or if ordered by the court.

stare decisis. To stand by decided matters. Alternative name for the doctrine of precedent.

statute. An act of Parliament.

statute-barred. When there has been so much delay before commencing proceedings that the *limitation* period has expired.

statutory instrument. Subordinate legislation made by the Queen in Council or a minister, in exercise of a power granted by *statute*.

stay of proceedings. When a court action is stopped by the court.

subpoena. A court order that a person attends court, either to give evidence (subpoena ad testificandum) or to produce documents (subpoena ducas tecum).

substituted service. When a document cannot be served on the defendant or their solicitor, the court may allow substituted service by, for example, its being sent to the last known address, or advertised in newspapers.

summary judgement. If the defendant does not show an arguable defence to the claim, the plaintiff can apply for summary judgement. Also known as 'Order 14' (after the Rule of the Supreme Court that lays down the procedure).

surety. A *guarantor*.

taxation of costs. Examination and approval by the court of legal fees. See page 943.

tenancy in common. When two or more people hold land as tenants in common, they each have equal shares in it. If one dies his share does not pass to the other (cf. *joint tenancy*). For example, A, B and C own a house. If C dies, his share will pass under his will to his family etc. A and B will still own one-third each of the house; the other third will be owned by the person who inherited C's share. Joint owners are presumed to be joint tenants, not tenants in common.

term of years. A lease for a fixed period of duration.

testate. Dying having left a will.

testator. The person who makes a will.

third-party proceedings. When a party to an action sues someone else. For example, A sues B for damages after B drove his car into A. But B's negligent driving was partly caused by C, a pedestrian, who was jay-walking. B starts third-party proceedings against C, and if the court orders B to pay damages to A, it can also order C to pay damages to B.

tort. A civil wrong (other than breach of contract) giving rise to the right to bring an action in the civil courts (e.g. nuisance, negligence, trespass, defamation).

Treasury counsel. Barristers who receive briefs from the *Director of Public Prosecutions* for *Old Bailey* prosecutions. They are nominated by the Lord Chancellor.

uberrimae fidei. Of the utmost good faith. See Chapter 39.

ultra vires. Outside the powers (e.g. of a company).

unenforceable. A contract or other right that cannot be enforced because of a technical defect (e.g. *statute-barred*).

unlawful. An act is unlawful when it involves a breach of the law and so allows civil proceedings to be brought. It does not involve a breach of the criminal law (cf. *illegal*).

unliquidated damages. Damages which cannot be arithmetically calculated in advance and are dependent upon the opinion (and generosity) of the court (e.g. for the loss of a limb). (See *liquidated sum*.)

unregistered land. *Land* that is not *registered land*.

unsound mind. As defined in the Mental Health Act 1983. See Chapter 58.

vendor and purchaser summons. Procedure whereby parties to a contract for the sale of *land* who are in dispute can apply relatively speedily to a judge in chambers for a decision.

vexatious litigant. A person who cannot bring any action without the permission of the court, because he or she has previously brought vexatious or frivolous proceedings.

vicarious liability. When one person is responsible for the actions of another because of their relationship: e.g. an employer is liable for the actions of his or her employee. The plaintiff can sue either or both of them.

void. Of no legal effect. If a marriage is void it is as though it had never taken place (cf. *voidable*).

voidable. Capable of being set aside. A voidable marriage will end when it is annulled (i.e. avoided) but it will be recognized as having existed until that time (cf. *void*).

volenti non fit injuria. A person cannot sue over an injury to which he or she has consented. 'Knowledge of the risk of injury is not enough. Nor is a willingness to take the risk of injury. Nothing will suffice short of an agreement to waive any claim for negligence' (Nettleship, 1971).

volunteer. A person who is given, or who inherits, property without giving any *consideration*.

wager. A bet. A betting or gambling debt is *unenforceable* as being contrary to *public policy*.

waste. Causing lasting damage to land (e.g. by a tenant).

with costs. If judgement is entered 'with costs', it means that the winner's *costs* will be paid by the loser. See Chapter 66.

writ. Document for commencing many High Court actions. It commands the defendant to file an *acknowledgement of service*.

Index of Cases

Index of Cases

Cases from other Jurisdictions

Key: ECHR – European Court of Human Rights
ECJ – European Court of Justice

Index of Legislative Material

General Index

abduction of child, 163
abortion, 120
absolute discharge, 774
abstracting water, 388
Accident Legal Advice Service, 955
accidents at home: building contractors, negligence
of, 395; insurance for, 396; landlord, liability of,
395; liability for, 393–4; local authority, liability
of, 395; professional advisers, liability of, 395;
visitors, to, 394
accidents at work: competent workmates, duty to
employ, 440–41; employer, duties of, 440; employer, suing, 443; procedure on, 444; reporting,
444; safe equipment and plant, provision of 441–
2; safe system of working, 442–3
Acts of Parliament, 865–7
administration of estates: grant, no need for, 218;
intestacy, 226–9; legal fees, 219–20; money nominated before death, 226; personal representatives,
216–17; probate, see probate; small estates, 225–
6; step-by-step guide to, 221–6
administration order, 601; judgement, enforcing,
1005
adoption: procedure, 127–8; registration of, 112–13;
step-parent, by, 159
adultery: co-respondent, position of, 43; living together after, 42; meaning, 41; proving, 41–2
adverse possession, 368
advice by way of representation: application for,
963–4; generally, 956; introduction of, 963; merits
test, 964; withdrawal of, 964
advice centres, 924
affiliation proceedings, 116–17
affray, 833
age: consent, of, 126; criminal responsibility, of,
176–7; driving, for, 173–4; marriage, for, 25–6;
minimum, table of, 132–3
airports, examination and detention at, 738–9
airspace, 373–4
alcohol, children and, 173
Alternative Dispute Resolution, 885

American Express, 585
animals: damage caused by, liability for, 389–93;
dangerous, 389–90; dogs, see dogs; importing,
391; keeping, requirements, 391; licences, 391;
noisy, 381, 393; straying, 390
arbitration, 562–3, 885
arrest: charge, and, 743, 745; police questioning,
727–8; rights on, 727; warrant of, 726; warrant,
without, 726–7; wrongful, 731
Association of British Travel Agents, 563–4
assured shorthold tenancy: divorce, transfer on, 313;
excessive rent, reduction of, 312; fixed term,
expiry of, 309–11; meaning, 308; requirements,
308–9; tenant, death of, 312–13
assured tenancy: divorce, transfer on, 313; dwelling-
house, of, 297; excluded tenancies, 298–9; individual, tenant being, 297; meaning, 294; obtaining
possession, 305; possession, grounds for, 301–5;
principal home, of, 298; rent increases, 305–7;
resident landlords, 299; security of tenure, 300;
tenancy, meaning, 294–7; tenant, death of, 312–
13; unlawful eviction and harassment, protection
from, 324
attachment of earnings, 80, 1003; bankruptcy, effect
of, 599
attendance centre order, 772

bail: asking magistrate for, 747–8; committal, after,
760; grant of, 749–50; police, 747; refusal of, 748–
9; sureties, 749–50; warrant backed for, 747
bailiffs, 1002
bank account: joint, 66–7; marriage, effect of, 30
Banking Ombudsman, 587–8
bankruptcy, 902; discharge from, 598; effect of,
598–600; judgement, enforcing, 1004–5; laws, 595;
making oneself bankrupt, 596, 598; making
person bankrupt, 595–6; petition, 595; statutory
demand, 596; steps to, 597
barristers: becoming, 930–32; cab rank rule, 926;
complaints against, 929–30; conduct of work, 926;
court, in, 927; dealings with, 927; disciplinary

General Index

income tax: amount due, working out, 650; cohabitees, position of, 14; husband and wife, separate taxation of, 66; mortgage interest relief, 246–7

indecency, 841–2

industrial action: dismissal for taking part in, 476–7; occupations, 527; secondary, 518; sit-ins, 527; strike ballot, need for, 518; striking, effect of, 517–20

industrial tribunals: application to, 481–3; costs, 488–9; employer's response to claim, 483; employment law disputes in, 481; hearing, 487–8; orders of, 490; pre-hearing assessment, 487; preparing for hearing, 485–7; rules, 481; three-month limitation period, 482; witnesses, 486–7

information, sources of, 1009–19

inheritance, marriage, effect of, 31

inheritance tax, cohabitees, position of, 15

injunction, 902

insolvency, 600–601; administration, 601

insulting words/behaviour, 833

insurance: business premises, for, 643–4; claims, 591; contract, as, 590; disclosure requirements, 590; home, 396; motor, 673–9; policy, wording, 591; terms, 592; void policies, 591

Insurance Ombudsman Bureau, 589

International Court of Justice, 883

intestacy: entitlement, rules for, 226–9; partial, 229

judgement, enforcing: administration order, making, 1005; attachment of earnings, 1003; bankruptcy, 1004–5; charging order, 1000–1001; garnishee orders, 1004; methods of, 999–1005; oral examination, 1000; warrant of execution, 1002

judges, 860; appointment, 934; hierarchy of, 933; retirement, 935; social background, 934–5; suing, 935–6

judicial separation, 38

jury: civil cases, in, 890; compensation to, 766; disqualified people, 765; eligibility to serve on, 764; excused people, 765; importance of service, 766–7; ineligible people, 764–5; mentally disordered persons, exclusion of, 819; service, being called for, 765–6; verdict, 763–4

juvenile court, procedure in, 182–4; trial in, 181–2

land: ownership of, 242–3; rights over, 243–6

law centres, 924

Law Society, role of, 904–5, 908

learner drivers, duty of care, 715

lease, assignment of, 640–42

leasehold reform: basic requirements, 286–8; cost of, 288; guide to, 287

legal advice, sources of, 924

legal aid: abroad, 985; administration of, 956; advice by way of representation, 956, 963–4; civil, *see* civil legal aid; cost of 955; criminal, 957, 982–4; criminal offences, for, 750–51; divorce, for, 53–4; duty solicitor scheme, 957, 985; emergency, 972; European Court of Human Rights, for, 874; green-form scheme, *see* green-form scheme; introduction of, 956; juvenile court, in, 188

legal executives, 922

legal forms, 1021–34

legal jargon, 1035–52

Legal Services Ombudsman, 917, 930

libel, 835

licensed conveyancers, 922

listed buildings: grants for, 354; planning permission, 362

livestock, straying, 390

living together, *see* cohabitation

Loan Guarantee Scheme, 629

local authority: buildings, inspection of, 395; children, powers and duties to, 163–70; home improvement grants, 353–4; homeless, obligations to, 850–51; rented accommodation, enforcement of repair and maintenance, 342–51

logos, 633–4

magistrates' court: acquittal in, 756; advantages of trial in, 751–2; appeals, 756; civil court, as, 878; committal proceedings, 758–60; compensation in, 798; criminal court, as, 876–7; pleading guilty by post, 756–7; procedure, 752–6; proceedings, starting, 1005–6; sentencing powers, 767

Magna Carta, 857

mail order, 559–60

Mail Order Protection Scheme, 560

maintenance: amount, changing, 79–80; application for, 77–9; attachment of earnings, 80; breach of order for, 84; calculation of, 72; children, for, 75–6, 124; claim by DSS, 86–7; clean breaks, 74–5; cohabitees, claim by, 16; conduct, relevance of, 73; county court, application in, 82; divorce court, application in, 83; DSS, signing order over to, 81–2; ending, 80; enforcement of, 80–81; income support instead of, 84; marriage, liability on, 31; non-marital children, for, 115–17; one-third rule, 69, 71–2; out-of-court agreement for, 85–6; remarriage, effect of, 76; short marriages, 73–4; small incomes, where, 73; tax position, 87–90; whether worth applying for, 84–5; wife earning more, where, 73

marital secrets, 33

market overt, sale of goods in, 542–3

marriage: annulment, 62–3; bank account, changing name on, 30; breakdown, *see* marriage breakdown; Church of England, in, 27–8; civil, 28;

cohabit, duty to, 31; cohabitation, differences, 17–19; common-law, abolition, 5; contracts, 33–4; contractual obligations, 32–3; custom and repute, by, 5; debts, liability for, 67; domicile, effect on, 29; financial effects, 30–31; formalities, 27–8; gifts between spouses, 65–6; home, choice of, 31; joint bank accounts, 66–7; legal effects of, 28–34; legal requirements, 23–6; marital confidences, 33; minimum age for, 25–6; minor, of, consent to, 25–6; name, changing, 28–9; nationality, no change of, 29; new passport on, 29–30; parties of opposite sex, between, 26; polygamous, 26–7; prohibited degrees, 26–7; rape within, 32; return of gifts on cancellation, 22–3; sex, agreement to have, 32; single people, between, 24–5; special licences, 28; taxation on, 64–6; void, 62; voidable, 62–3; voluntary, to be, 24; will, revocation of, 30, 203; woman, legal consequences for, 28–30

marriage breakdown: annulment, 62–3; divorce, *see* divorce; family assets, division of, 68–71; family home, *see* family home; maintenance on, *see* maintenance; procedures on, 35; separation, 36–8; short-term protection on, 36

maternity: ante-natal care, time off for, 433; leave, 435–8; pregnancy, dismissal for, 474–6; rights, draft letter to employers, 438–9; statutory pay, 433–5

McKenzie men, 991

medical suspension pay, 418

medical treatment for child, 124, 126

mental health: law on, 814; disorders, types of, 814

Mental Health Review Tribunal, 820–21

mental hospital: compulsory admission to, 814–16; criminal court admissions, 816; detention in, 816–17; in-patients, civil liberties, 818–20; treatment in, 817–18

mental patient, actions involving, 892

misrepresentation, 546–7

mitigation, 767

moral rights, 667

mortgage interest relief: cohabitees, for, 14; conditions for, 246–7

mortgages: application for, 259–61; arrears, 249–50; brokers, 578–9; costs of, 248; fees, 278–9

MOT certificate, where required, 672

Motor Agents Association, code of practice, 564–5, 682–5

motor insurance: car-sharing, for, 678–9; excesses, 678; failure to have, 677–8; invalid, 675–7; invalidated, effect of, 677; no-claims bonus, 678; third-party, 673; using vehicle without, 673–5

Motor Insurers Bureau, 678, 718, 885

motoring offences: attitude to, 686; careless driving,

698–9; categories of, 686–7; charges, checking, 687; defending, 688–9; disqualification for, 694–7; drunk-driving, 703–6; endorsement, 690; failing to report accident, 702–3; failing to stop and give particulars after accident, 701–2; fixed penalties, 707; more than one, convictions for, 691–2; parking, 700–701; penalties, 689–90; penalty chart, 707–10; penalty points, 691–5; proceedings, beginning, 687–9; reckless driving, 697–8; special reasons, rule on, 693; speeding, 699–700; taking vehicle without consent, 700; warning of prosecution, 687–8

motorists as consumers, 682–5

names, changing: children, of, 21, 161–2; marriage, on, 28–9; procedure, 21; surname, 20

National House Building Council Buildmark guarantee, 258–9

nationality: child, of, 130; marriage, effect of, 29

natural justice, rules of, 861–2

navigation rights, 387

negligence: child, of, 134; definition, 549–50; development of law, 864; liability for, 534; motorists, of, 714–19

neighbours: noise by, 378–82; nuisance by, 376–8; right to light, 365, 374–6; rights of, 366; troublesome, remedies for, 367

noise: abatement, 380; by-laws, 381; long-usage defence, 379; nuisance claim for, 378–9; planes, from, 382; remedies for, 380–81; vehicles, from, 381–2

notary public, 919

NSPCC records, secrecy of, 129

nuisance: building works, from 383–4; enjoyment of property, interference with, 378; existence of, 377–8; legal sense, in, 376–7; noise, 378–82; smells, 382–3; trees, from, 384–6

obscenity: children, in relation to, 841; defence of merit, 841; drugs and violence, 841; test of, 840–41

occupiers' liability, 393–4

Office of Fair Trading, 570

official secrets, 844–5

ombudsmen, 886

out of court settlement, 888

parental responsibility: court orders, 114; introduction of, 121; meaning, 121–2, 147; people having, 122; practice, in, 123; sharing, agreement on, 113–14

parking offences, 700–701

Parliament, 858

partnership: accounts, 610; actions involving, 891;

association property, 338; improvement distinguished, 341–2; landlord not carrying out, remedies on, 342–51; law on, 340; renewal area, 351; repair notice, 350; service charges, 351–2; tenant not allowing, 340–41

renting from private landlord: assured shorthold tenancies, *see* assured shorthold tenancy; assured tenancies, *see* assured tenancy; eviction, 290–91; harassment of tenant, 293; Housing Act tenancies, 294–313; protected tenancies, 313–18; questions arising, 290; Rent Act tenancies, 313–21; Rent Act tenant, death of, 318; rent, increase or decrease in, 293; repossession of property, 291–3; statutory protection, 294; tenancies outside Rent Acts, 320–21; unlawful eviction and harassment, protection from, 321–6

repair notice, 350

rescission, 903

residence: divorce, requirements for, 51; order, 148

restitution orders, 798

restraint of trade, 453–5, 605–6

restrictive covenants, 363–4

Restrictive Practices Court, 880

right to light, 365, 374–6

rights of way: private footpaths, 368–9; public, 369–70; use of, 370

riot, 834

road accidents: blame, apportioning, 713–19; checklist, 712; compensation, claiming, 719–21; details to be recorded, 711; division of liability for, 716; driver not traced after, 718; failing to report, 702–3; failing to stop and give particulars after, 701–2; Highway Code, breaking, 715–16; learners, duty of care, 715; mechanical defects, due to, 716; negligence basis of compensation, 718; negligence, due to, 714–19; negotiation of claim, 721; on-the-spot settlements, 721; reporting, 713; responsibility for, 711; seat belts, failure to wear, 717

road fund licence, 672

Rylands v. Fletcher, rule in, 387

safe equipment and plant, provision at work, 441–2

sale of goods: description, corresponding with, 544; doorstep selling, 560; exclusion clauses, 547–9; faulty, redress for, 551–4; fitness for purpose, 545–6; guarantees, 552; implied terms, 541; merchantable quality, 545–6; misrepresentation, 546–7; negligence, 549–50; post, by, 559–60; prices, *see* prices; private sales, 546; product liability, 550–51; product safety, 566–7; sample, correspondence with, 544; seller's right to sell, 543–4; trade descriptions, 567–70; unusual purpose, goods required for, 545

samples, right of police to take, 734–5

schools: accidents at, 171; attendance, 138; charges, 143; choice of, 136–7; classes, size of, 144; corporal punishment in, 140; exclusion from, 139; expulsion, 139; leaving, 141; records, 143; rules, 139; special, 137–8; starting, 141; suspension, 139–40; types of, 135–6; uniforms, 142–3

search warrants, 737

seat belts, 174, 681–2; failure to wear in accident, 717

secrecy offences, 844–5

security for costs, 899

self-employed: husband or wife, employing, 613; national insurance contributions, 613, 650–51; rights of, 399; tests of, 411–14

sentencing: absolute discharge, 774; aims of, 767; attendance centre order, 772; available sentences, 780; binding over, 775; combination order, 771; community service order, 771; conditional discharge, 774; curfew order, 771; deferred sentence, 774; early release, 769; enforcement, 773–4; financial penalties, 772–4; first-time imprisonment, 768; life, 770; maximum penalties, 776–9; non-custodial, 770; prison, to, 767; probation orders, 770–71; spent, 787; supervision order, 772; suspended sentence, 768–9; young offenders, 184–7, 775

separation: formal deed, 37; informal agreement, 36–7; judicial, 38; legal, methods of, 36; magistrates' court order, 38

separation of powers, 861

sequestration, 902

services, supply of: delivery, time for, 558; deposits, 558; estimates and quotes, obtaining, 556–9; implied terms, 555; reasonable care and skill, exercising, 555–6; reasonable price for, 557; reasonable time, within, 556

sexual intercourse: age of consent, 126; marriage, within, 32

shoplifting, 746

shopper's charge cards, 585

sick pay: right to, 417; statutory, 418–19

slander, 835

smells, nuisance from, 382–3

social security benefits: marriage, effect of, 30; strike, during, 519–20

societies, actions involving, 892

sole trader: accounts, 610; bankruptcy, risk of, 607; business, control of, 606; business names, 632; death and retirement, 611–12; firm's money, using, 610; formation, costs of, 609; loss, making, 650; money, raising, 608–9; pensions, 611; self-employment, 613; setting up as, 614; taxation, 610–11, 646–52; VAT registration, 612

solicitors: Accident Legal Advice Service, 955; advertising, 910; agreed fees, 951; articles, 920, 922;

READ MORE IN PENGUIN

In every corner of the world, on every subject under the sun, Penguin represents quality and variety – the very best in publishing today.

For complete information about books available from Penguin – including Puffins, Penguin Classics and Arkana – and how to order them, write to us at the appropriate address below. Please note that for copyright reasons the selection of books varies from country to country.

In the United Kingdom: Please write to *Dept. EP, Penguin Books Ltd, Bath Road, Harmondsworth, West Drayton, Middlesex UB7 ODA*

In the United States: Please write to *Consumer Sales, Penguin Putnam Inc., P.O. Box 999, Dept. 17109, Bergenfield, New Jersey 07621-0120.* VISA and MasterCard holders call 1-800-253-6476 to order Penguin titles

In Canada: Please write to *Penguin Books Canada Ltd, 10 Alcorn Avenue, Suite 300, Toronto, Ontario M4V 3B2*

In Australia: Please write to *Penguin Books Australia Ltd, P.O. Box 257, Ringwood, Victoria 3134*

In New Zealand: Please write to *Penguin Books (NZ) Ltd, Private Bag 102902, North Shore Mail Centre, Auckland 10*

In India: Please write to *Penguin Books India Pvt Ltd, 210 Chiranjiv Tower, 43 Nehru Place, New Delhi 110 019*

In the Netherlands: Please write to *Penguin Books Netherlands bv, Postbus 3507, NL-1001 AH Amsterdam*

In Germany: Please write to *Penguin Books Deutschland GmbH, Metzlerstrasse 26, 60594 Frankfurt am Main*

In Spain: Please write to *Penguin Books S. A., Bravo Murillo 19, 1° B, 28015 Madrid*

In Italy: Please write to *Penguin Italia s.r.l., Via Benedetto Croce 2, 20094 Corsico, Milano*

In France: Please write to *Penguin France, Le Carré Wilson, 62 rue Benjamin Baillaud, 31500 Toulouse*

In Japan: Please write to *Penguin Books Japan Ltd, Kaneko Building, 2-3-25 Koraku, Bunkyo-Ku, Tokyo 112*

In South Africa: Please write to *Penguin Books South Africa (Pty) Ltd, Private Bag X14, Parkview, 2122 Johannesburg*

READ MORE IN PENGUIN

REFERENCE

Medicines: A Guide for Everybody Peter Parish

Now in its seventh edition and completely revised and updated, this bestselling guide is written in ordinary language for the ordinary reader yet will prove indispensable to anyone involved in health care – nurses, pharmacists, opticians, social workers and doctors.

Media Law Geoffrey Robertson QC and Andrew Nichol

Crisp and authoritative surveys explain the up-to-date position on defamation, obscenity, official secrecy, copyright and confidentiality, contempt of court, the protection of privacy and much more.

The Penguin Careers Guide
Anna Alston and Anne Daniel; Consultant Editor: Ruth Miller

As the concept of a 'job for life' wanes, this guide encourages you to think broadly about occupational areas as well as describing day-to-day work and detailing the latest developments and qualifications such as NVQs. Special features include possibilities for working part-time and job-sharing, returning to work after a break and an assessment of the current position of women.

The Penguin Dictionary of Troublesome Words Bill Bryson

Why should you avoid discussing the *weather conditions*? Can a married woman be celibate? Why is it eccentric to talk about the aroma of a cowshed? A straightforward guide to the pitfalls and hotly disputed issues in standard written English.

The Penguin Dictionary of Musical Performers Arthur Jacobs

In this invaluable companion volume to *The Penguin Dictionary of Music* Arthur Jacobs has brought together the names of over 2,500 performers. Music is written by composers, yet it is the interpreters who bring it to life; in this comprehensive book they are at last given their due.